STUDY GUIDE
for use with
McConnell, Brue, and Flynn
E C O N O M I C S

Eighteenth Edition

WILLIAM B. WALSTAD

PROFESSOR OF ECONOMICS

UNIVERSITY OF NEBRASKA–LINCOLN

McGraw-Hill Irwin

Boston Burr Ridge, IL Dubuque, IA New York
San Francisco St. Louis Bangkok Bogotá Caracas Kuala Lumpur
Lisbon London Madrid Mexico City Milan Montreal New Delhi
Santiago Seoul Singapore Sydney Taipei Toronto

Study Guide for use with
Economics, Eighteenth Edition
Campbell R. McConnell, Stanley L. Brue, Sean M. Flynn, and William B. Walstad

Published by McGraw-Hill/Irwin, a business unit of The McGraw-Hill Companies, Inc., 1221 Avenue of the Americas, New York, NY 10020. Copyright © 2009 by The McGraw-Hill Companies, Inc. All rights reserved.

2 3 4 5 6 7 8 9 0 WDQ/WDQ 0

ISBN 978-0-07-336880-1
MHID 0-07-336880-6

www.mhhe.com

About the Author

William B. Walstad is a professor of economics at the University of Nebraska-Lincoln, where he directs the National Center for Research in Economic Education and has been honored with a Distinguished Teaching Award. Professor Walstad also has been recognized with the Henry H. Villard Research Award for his published research in economic education by the National Association of Economic Educators and National Council on Economic Education. He is an associate editor of the *Journal of Economic Education* and was the previous chair of the Committee on Economic Education of the American Economic Association. He is a co-editor and contributor to *Teaching Undergraduate Economics: A Handbook for Instructors* (McGraw-Hill). He serves as the principal investigator for a National Science Foundation project for economics faculty members on interactive teaching and learning. Professor Walstad received his Ph.D. degree from the University of Minnesota.

_To_
Tammie, Laura, Kristin, Eileen, Clara, and Martha

Contents

How to Use the Study Guide to Learn Economics

This *Study Guide* should help you read and understand the McConnell, Brue, and Flynn textbook, *Economics*, 18th edition. If used properly, a study guide can be a great aid to you for what is probably your first course in economics.

No one pretends that the study of economics is easy, but it can be made easier with this *Study Guide*. Of course, it will not do your work for you, and its use is no substitute for reading the text. You must first be willing to read the text and work at learning if you wish to understand economics.

Many students, however, do read their text and work hard on their economics course and still fail to learn the subject. This problem occurs because economics is a new subject for these students. They want to learn economics, but do not know how to do it because they have no previous experience with the subject. Here is where the *Study Guide* can help students. Let's first see what the *Study Guide* contains and then how to use it.

■ WHAT THE *STUDY GUIDE* IS

This *Study Guide* contains 38 chapters to support your learning of each of the 38 textbook chapters in *Economics*. There also are two more Study Guide chapters and one supplement that fully support the two **Bonus Web Chapters** and one **Web Supplement** for *Economics*. In addition, the *Study Guide* has a **glossary**. This *Study Guide* should give you a complete set of resources to advance your learning of principles of economics.

Each *Study Guide* chapter has 11 sections to give you complete coverage of the textbook material in each chapter. The first five sections help you to **understand** the economics content in each chapter.

1. An *introduction* explains what is in the chapter of the text and how it is related to material in earlier and later chapters. It points out topics to which you should give special attention and reemphasizes difficult or important principles and facts.

2. A *checklist* tells you the things you should be able to do when you have finished the chapter.

3. A *chapter outline* shows how the chapter is organized and summarizes briefly the essential points made in the chapter, including the Last Word.

4. Selected *hints and tips* for each chapter help you identify key points and make connections with any previous discussion of a topic.

5. A list of the *important terms* points out what you must be able to define to understand the material in the chapter. Each term is defined in the glossary at the end of the *Study Guide*.

The next six sections of the *Study Guide* allow you to **self-test** your understanding of the chapter material.

6. *Fill-in questions* (short-answer and list questions) help you learn and remember the important generalizations and facts in the chapter.

7. *True-false questions* test your understanding of the material in the chapter.

8. *Multiple-choice questions* also give you a chance to check your knowledge of the chapter content and prepare for this type of course examination.

9. *Problems* help you learn and understand economic concepts by requiring different skills—drawing a graph, completing a table, or finding relationships—to solve the problems.

10. *Short answer* and *essay questions* can be used as a self-test, to identify important questions in the chapter and to prepare for examinations.

11. *Answers* to fill-in questions, true-false questions, multiple-choice questions, and problems are found at the end of each chapter. References to the specific pages in the textbook for each true-false, multiple-choice, and short answer or essay questions are also provided.

■ HOW TO STUDY AND LEARN WITH THE HELP OF THE *STUDY GUIDE*

1. *Read and outline.* For best results, quickly read the introduction, outline, list of terms, and checklist in the *Study Guide* before you read the chapter in *Economics*. Then read the chapter in the text slowly, keeping one eye on the *Study Guide* outline and the list of terms. Highlight the chapter as you read it by identifying the *major and minor* points and by placing *Study Guide* outline numbers or letters (such as I or A or 1 or a) in the margins. When you have completed the chapter, you will have the chapter highlighted, and the *Study Guide* outline will serve as a handy set of notes on the chapter.

2. *Review and reread.* After you have read the chapter in the text once, return to the introduction, outline, and list of terms in the *Study Guide*. Reread the introduction and outline. Does everything there make sense? If not, go back to the text and reread the topics that you do not remember well or that still confuse you. Look at the outline. Try to recall each of the minor topics that were contained in the text under each of the major points in the outline. When you come to the list of terms, go over them one by one. *Define or explain each to yourself and then look for the definition of the term either in the text chapter or in the glossary.* Compare your own definition or explanation with that in the *text or glossary*. The quick way to find the definition of a term in the text is to look in the text index for the page(s) in which that term or concept is mentioned. Make any necessary correction or change in your own definition or explanation.

3. *Test and check answers.* When you have done the above reading and review, you will have a good idea of what is in the text chapter. Now complete the self-test sections of the *Study Guide* to check your understanding.

In doing the self-test, start with the *fill-in, true-false, multiple-choice,* and *problems* sections. Tackle each of these four sections one at a time, using the following procedures: (1) answer as many self-test items as you can without looking in the text or in the answer section of the *Study Guide*; (2) check the text for whatever help you need in answering the items; and (3) consult the answer section of the *Study Guide* for the correct answers and reread any section of the text for which you missed items.

The self-test items in these four sections are not equally difficult. Some will be easy to answer and others will be harder. Do not expect to get them all correct the first time. Some are designed to pinpoint material of importance that you will probably miss the first time you read the text and answering them will get you to read the text again with more insight and understanding.

The *short answer and essay questions* cover the major points in the chapter. For some of the easier questions, all you may do is mentally outline your answer. For the more difficult questions, you may want to write out a brief outline of the answer or a full answer. Do not avoid the difficult questions just because they are more work. Answering these questions is often the most valuable work you can do toward acquiring an understanding of economic relationships and principles.

Although no answers are given in the *Study Guide* to the short answer and essay questions, the answer section does list text page references for each question. You are *strongly* encouraged to read those text pages for an explanation of the question or for better insight into the question content.

4. *Double check.* Before you turn to the next chapter in the text and *Study Guide*, return to the checklist. If you cannot honestly check off each item in the list, you have not learned what the authors of the text and of this Study Guide hoped you would learn.

■ BONUS WEB CHAPTERS FOR *ECONOMICS*

The *Study Guide* fully supports the two Web-based chapters in *Economics*. These chapters are: (1) Technology, R&D, and Efficiency (Chapter 11W); (2) Economics of Developing Countries (Chapter 39W. There also is a Web supplement on Previous International Exchange-Rate Systems (Supplement 38S). They are located at *www.mcconnell18e.com*. The *Study Guide* includes full content and self-test materials for these two chapters and one supplement.

■ GLOSSARY

All of the important terms and concepts in *Essentials of Economics* are defined and described in the glossary. It is included in the *Study Guide* for easy reference when you see a term or concept you do not know. It will also aid your work on self-test items in the *Study Guide*.

■ SOME FINAL WORDS

Perhaps the method of using the *Study Guide* outlined above seems like a lot of work. It is! Study and learning requires work on your part. This fact is one you must accept if you are to learn economics.

After you have used the *Study Guide* to study one or two chapters, you will find that some sections are more valuable to you than others. Let your own experience determine how you will use it. But do not discontinue use of the *Study Guide* after one or two chapters merely because you are not sure whether it is helping you. ***Stick with it.***

■ ACKNOWLEDGMENTS

Special thanks are due to Sharon Nemeth for her hard work in preparing the print and electronic versions of this *Study Guide*. I am also indebted to Stan Brue, Campbell McConnell, and Sean Flynn for their on-going support during the development of this *Study Guide*. While I am most grateful for all these contributions, I alone am responsible for an errors or omissions. You are welcome to send me comments or suggestions.

William B. Walstad

CHAPTER 1

Limits, Alternatives, and Choices

Chapter 1 introduces you to economics—the social science that studies how individuals, institutions, and society make the optimal best choices under conditions of scarcity. The first section of the chapter describes the three key features of the **economic perspective**. This perspective first recognizes that all choices involve costs and that these costs must be involved in an economic decision. The economic perspective also incorporates the view that to achieve a goal, people make decisions that reflect their purposeful self-interest. The third feature considers that people compare marginal benefits against marginal costs when making decisions and will choose the situation where the marginal benefit is greater than the marginal cost. You will develop a better understanding of these features as you read about the economic issues in this book.

Economics relies heavily on the **scientific method** to develop theories and principles to explain the likely effects from human events and behavior. It involves gathering data, testing hypotheses, and developing theories and principles. In essence, economic theories and principles (and related terms such as laws and models) are generalizations about how the economic world works.

Economists develop economic theories and principles at two levels. **Microeconomics** targets specific units in the economy. Studies at this level research such questions as how prices and output are determined for particular products and how consumers will react to price changes. **Macroeconomics** focuses on the whole economy, or large segments of it. Studies at this level investigate such issues as how to increase economic growth, control inflation, or maintain full employment. Studies at either level have elements of **positive economics**, which investigates facts or cause-and-effect relationships, or **normative economics**, which incorporates subjective views of what ought to be or what policies should be used to address an economic issue.

Several sections of the text are devoted to a discussion of the **economizing problem** from individual or society perspectives. This problem arises from a fundamental conflict between economic wants and economics resources: (1) individuals and society have *unlimited* economic wants; (2) the economic means or resources to satisfy those wants are *limited*. This economic problem forces individuals and societies to make a choice. And anytime a choice is made there is an opportunity cost—the next best alternative that was not chosen.

The economizing problem for individuals is illustrated with a microeconomic model that uses a **budget line.** It shows graphically the meaning of many concepts defined

in the chapter: scarcity, choice, trade-offs, opportunity cost, and optimal allocation. The economizing problem for society is illustrated with a macroeconomics model that uses a **production possibilities curve.** It also shows graphically the economic concepts just listed, and in addition it can be used to describe macroeconomic conditions related to unemployment, economic growth, and trade. The production possibilities model can also be applied to many real economic situations, such as the economics of war, as you will learn from the text.

■ CHECKLIST

When you have studied this chapter you should be able to

☐ Write a formal definition of economics.
☐ Describe the three key features of the economic perspective.
☐ Give applications of the economic perspective.
☐ Identify the elements of the scientific method.
☐ Define hypothesis, theory, principle, law, and model as they relate to economics.
☐ State how economic principles are generalizations and abstractions.
☐ Explain the "other-things-equal" assumption (*ceteris paribus*) and its use in economics.
☐ Distinguish between microeconomics and macroeconomics.
☐ Give examples of positive and normative economics.
☐ Explain the economizing problem for an individual (from a microeconomic perspective).
☐ Describe the concept of a budget line for the individual.
☐ Explain how to measure the slope of a budget line and determine the location of the budget line.
☐ Use the budget line to illustrate trade-offs and opportunity costs.
☐ Describe the economizing problem for society.
☐ Define the four types of economic resources for society.
☐ State the four assumptions made when a production possibilities table or curve is constructed.
☐ Construct a production possibilities curve when given the data.
☐ Define opportunity cost and utilize a production possibilities curve to explain the concept.
☐ Show how the law of increasing opportunity costs is reflected in the shape of the production possibilities curve.
☐ Explain the economic rationale for the law of increasing opportunity costs.

☐ Use marginal analysis to define optimal allocation.

☐ Explain how optimal allocation determines the optimal point on a production possibilities curve.

☐ Use a production possibilities curve to illustrate unemployment.

☐ Use the production possibilities curve to illustrate economic growth.

☐ Explain how international trade affects a nation's production possibilities curve.

☐ Give other applications of the production possibilities model.

☐ Identify the five pitfalls to sound economic reasoning (Last Word).

■ **CHAPTER OUTLINE**

1. *Economics* studies how individuals, institutions, and society make the optimal or best choices under conditions of *scarcity*, for which economic wants are *unlimited* and the means or resources to satisfy those wants are *limited*.

2. The *economic perspective* has three interrelated features.

a. It recognizes that scarcity requires choice, and that making a choice has an *opportunity cost*—giving up the next best alternative to the choice that was made.

b. It views people as purposeful decision makers who make choices based on their self-interests. People seek to increase their satisfaction, or *utility,* from consuming a good or service. They are purposeful because they weigh the costs and benefits in deciding how best to increase that utility.

c. It uses *marginal analysis* to assess how the marginal costs of a decision compare with the marginal benefits.

3. Economics relies on the *scientific method* for analysis.

a. Several terms are used in economic analysis that are related to this method.

(1) A *hypothesis* is a proposition that is tested and used to develop an economic *theory*.

(2) A highly tested and reliable economic theory is called an *economic principle* or *law*. Theories, principles, and laws are meaningful statements about economic behavior or the economy that can be used to predict the likely outcome of an action or event.

(3) An economic *model* is created when several economic laws or principles are used to explain or describe reality.

b. There are several other aspects of economic principles.

(1) Each principle or theory is a generalization that shows a tendency or average effect.

(2) The *other-things-equal assumption* (*ceteris paribus*) is used to limit the influence of other factors when making a generalization.

(3) Many economic models can be illustrated graphically and are simplified representations of economic reality.

4. Economic analysis is conducted at two levels, and for each level there can be elements of positive or normative economics.

a. *Microeconomics* studies the economic behavior of individuals, particular markets, firms, or industries.

b. *Macroeconomics* looks at the entire economy or its major *aggregates* or sectors, such as households, businesses, or government.

c. *Positive economics* focuses on facts and is concerned with what is, or the scientific analysis of economic behavior.

d. *Normative economics* suggests what ought to be and answers policy questions based on value judgments. Most disagreements among economists involve normative economics.

5. Individuals face an *economizing problem* because economic wants are greater than the economic means to satisfy those wants. It can be illustrated with a microeconomic model with several features.

a. Individuals have limited income to spend.

b. Individuals have virtually unlimited wants for more goods and services, and higher-quality goods and services.

c. The economizing problem for the individual can be illustrated with a budget line and two products (for instance, DVDs and books). The *budget line* shows graphically the combinations of the two products a consumer can purchase with his or her money income.

(1) All combinations of the two products on or inside the budget line are *attainable* by the consumer; all combinations beyond the budget line are *unattainable*.

(2) To obtain more DVDs the consumer has to give up some books, so there is a *trade-off*; if to get a second DVD the consumer must give up two books, then the *opportunity* cost of the additional DVD is two books.

(3) Limited income forces individuals to evaluate the marginal cost and marginal benefit of a choice to maximize their satisfaction.

(4) Changes in money income shift the budget line: an increase in income shifts the line to the right; a decrease in income shifts the line to the left.

6. Society also faces an economizing problem due to scarcity.

a. *Economic resources* are scarce natural, human, or manufactured inputs used to produce goods and services.

b. Economic resources are sometimes called *factors of production* and are classified into four categories:

(1) *land,* or natural resources.

(2) *labor,* or the contributed time and abilities of people who are producing goods and services.

(3) *capital* (or capital goods), or the machines, tools, and equipment used to make other goods and services; economists refer to the purchase of such capital goods as *investment.*

(4) *entrepreneurial ability,* or the special human talents of individuals who combine the other factors of production.

7. A macroeconomic model of production possibilities illustrates the economizing problem for society. The four assumptions usually made when such a production possibilities model is used are: (1) there is full employment of available resources; (2) the quantity and quality of resources are fixed; (3) the state of technology does not change; and, (4) there are two types of goods being produced (**consumer goods** and **capital goods**).

a. The **production possibilities table** indicates the alternative combinations of goods an economy is capable of producing when it has achieved full employment and optimal allocation. The table illustrates the fundamental choice every economy must make: what quantity of each product it must sacrifice to obtain more of another.

b. The data in the production possibilities table can be plotted on a graph to obtain a **production possibilities curve.** Each point on the curve shows some maximum output of the two goods.

c. The opportunity cost of producing an additional unit of one good is the amount of the other good that is sacrificed. The **law of increasing opportunity costs** states that the opportunity cost of producing one more unit of a good (the marginal opportunity cost) increases as more of the good is produced.

(1) The production possibilities curve is bowed out from the origin because of the law of increasing opportunity costs.

(2) The reason the opportunity cost of producing an additional unit of a good increases as more of it is produced is because resources are not completely adaptable to alternative uses.

d. Optimal allocation means that resources are devoted to the best mix of goods to maximize satisfaction in society. This optimal mix is determined by assessing marginal costs and benefits.

(1) The marginal-cost curve for a good increases because of the law of increasing opportunity costs; the marginal-benefit curve decreases because the consumption of a good yields less and less satisfaction.

(2) When the marginal benefit is greater than the marginal cost, there is an incentive to produce more of the good, but when the marginal cost is greater than the marginal benefit there is an incentive to produce less of the good.

(3) Optimal or efficient allocation is achieved when the marginal cost of a product equals the marginal benefit of a product.

8. Different outcomes will occur when assumptions underlying the production possibilities model are relaxed.

a. Unemployment. When the economy is operating at a point inside the production possibilities curve it means that resources are not fully employed.

b. **Economic growth.** The production possibilities curve shifts outward from economic growth because resources are no longer fixed and technology improves.

(1) Expansion in the quantity and quality of resources contributes to economic growth and shifts the production possibilities curve outward.

(2) Advancement in technology contributes to economic growth and also shifts the production possibilities curve outward.

(3) The combination of capital goods and consumer goods an economy chooses to produce in the present can determine the position of the production possibilities curve in the future. Greater production of capital goods relative to consumer goods in the present shifts the production possibilities curve farther outward in the future because that economy is devoting more of its resources to investment than consumption.

c. Trade. When there is international specialization and trade, a nation can obtain more goods and services than is indicated by the production possibilities curve for a domestic economy. The effect on production possibilities is similar to an increase in economic growth.

9. (Last Word). Sound reasoning about economic issues requires the avoidance of five pitfalls.

a. *Bias* is a preconceived belief or opinion that is not warranted by the facts.

b. *Loaded terminology* is the use of terms in a way that appeals to emotion and leads to a nonobjective analysis of the issues.

c. The *fallacy of composition* is the assumption that what is true of the part is necessarily true of the whole.

d. The *post hoc fallacy* ("after this, therefore because of this") is the mistaken belief that when one event precedes another, the first event is the cause of the second.

e. *Confusing correlation with causation* means that two factors may be related, but that does not mean that one factor caused the other.

■ **HINTS AND TIPS**

1. The **economic perspective** presented in the first section of the chapter has three features related to decision making: scarcity and the necessity of choice, purposeful self-interest in decision making, and marginal analysis of the costs and benefits of decisions. Although these features may seem strange to you at first, they are central to the economic thinking used to examine decisions and problems throughout the book.

2. The chapter introduces two pairs of terms: **microeconomics** and **macroeconomics;** and, **positive economics** and **normative economics.** Make sure you understand what each pair means and how they are related to each other.

3. The **budget line** shows the consumer what it is possible to purchase in the two-good world, given an income. Make sure that you understand what a budget line is. To test your understanding, practice with different income levels and prices. For example, assume you had an income of $100 to spend for two goods (A and B). Good A costs $10 and Good B costs $5. Draw a budget line to show the possible combinations of A and B that you could purchase.

4. The **production possibilities curve** is a simple and useful economic model for an economy. Practice your understanding of it by using it to explain the following economic concepts: scarcity, choice, opportunity cost, the law of increasing opportunity costs, full employment, optimal allocation, unemployment, and economic growth.

5. Opportunity cost is always measured in terms of a forgone alternative. From a production possibilities table, you can easily calculate how many units of one product you forgo when you get another unit of a product.

■ **IMPORTANT TERMS**

Note: See the Glossary in the back of the book for definitions of terms.

economics	budget line
economic perspective	economic resources
opportunity cost	land
utility	labor
marginal analysis	capital
scientific method	investment
economic principle	entrepreneurial ability
other-things-equal assumption (ceteris paribus)	factors of production
	consumer goods
	capital goods
microeconomics	production possibilities curve
macroeconomics	
aggregate	law of increasing opportunity costs
positive economics	
normative economics	economic growth
economizing problem	

SELF-TEST

■ **FILL-IN QUESTIONS**

1. The economic perspective recognizes that (resources, scarcity) _____ require(s) choice and that choice has an opportunity (benefit, cost) _____. "There is no such thing as a free lunch" in economics because scarce resources have (unlimited, alternative) _____ uses.

2. The economic perspective also assumes that people make choices based on their self-interest and that they are (random, purposeful) _____. It also is based on comparisons of the (extreme, marginal) _____ costs and benefits of an economic decision.

3. Economics relies on the (model, scientific) _____ method. Statements about economic behavior that enable the prediction of the likely effects of certain actions are economic (facts, theories) _____. The most well-tested of these that have strong predictive accuracy, are called economic (hypotheses, principles) _____, or sometimes they are called (laws, actions) _____. Simplified representations of economic behavior or how an economy works are called (policies, models) _____.

4. Economic principles are often expressed as tendencies or what is typical, and are (fallacies, generalizations) _____ about people's economic behavior. When studying a relationship between two economic variables, economists assume that other variables or factors (do,

do not) _____ change, or in other words they are using the (utility, other-things-equal) _____ assumption.

5. The study of output in a particular industry or of a particular product is the subject of (microeconomics, macroeconomics) _____, and the study of the total output of the economy or the general level of prices is the subject of _____.

6. The collection of specific units that are being added and treated as if they were one unit is an (assumption, aggregate) _____.

7. Two different types of statements can be made about economic topics. A (positive, normative) _____ statement explains what is, by offering a scientific proposition about economic behavior that is based on economic theory and facts, but a _____ statement includes a value judgment about an economic policy or the economy that suggests what ought to be. Many of the reported disagreements among economists usually involve (positive, normative) _____ statements.

8. The economizing problem arises because individuals' and society's economic wants for more goods and services or higher-quality goods and services are (limited, unlimited) _____ and the economic means or resources to satisfy those wants are _____.

9. A schedule or curve that shows the various combinations of two products a consumer can (buy, sell) _____ with a money income is called (a budget, marginal cost) _____ line.

10. All combinations of goods inside a budget line are (attainable, unattainable) _____, and all combinations of goods outside the budget line are _____.

11. When a consumer's income increases, the budget line shifts to the (left, right) _____, while a decrease in income shifts the budget line to the _____.

12. The four types of economic resources are

a. _____

b. _____

c. _____

d. _____

13. When a production possibilities table or curve is constructed, four assumptions are made:

a. _____

b. _____

c. _____

d. _____

14. Goods that satisfy economic wants directly are (consumer, capital goods) _____, and goods that do so indirectly by helping produce other goods are _____ goods. Assume an economy can produce two basic types of goods, consumer and capital goods. If the economy wants to produce more consumer goods, then the capital goods the economy must give up are the opportunity (benefit, cost) _____ of producing those additional consumer goods.

15. The law of increasing opportunity costs explains why the production possibilities curve is (convex, concave) _____ from the origin. The economic rationale for the law is that economic resources (are, are not) _____ completely adaptable to alternative uses.

16. Optimal allocation of resources to production occurs when the marginal costs of the productive output are (greater than, less than, equal to) _____ the marginal benefits.

17. Following is a production possibilities curve for capital goods and consumer goods.

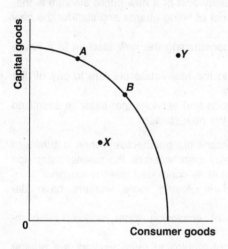

a. If the economy moves from point **A** to point **B**, it will produce (more, fewer) _____ capital goods and (more, fewer) _____ consumer goods.
b. If the economy is producing at point **X**, some resources in the economy are either (not available, unemployed) _____ or (underemployed, overemployed) _____.
c. If the economy moves from point **X** to point **B** (more, fewer) _____ capital goods and (more, fewer) _____ consumer goods will be produced.
d. If the economy is to produce at point **Y**, there must be (unemployment, economic growth) _____.

18. Economic growth will shift a nation's production possibilities curve (inward, outward) _____, and it

occurs because of a resource supply (decrease, increase) _____ or because of a technological (decline, advance) _____.

19. An economy can produce goods for the present such as (consumer, capital) _____ goods and goods for the future such as _____ goods. If an economy produces more goods for the future, then this is likely to lead to a (greater, smaller) _____ shift outward in the production possibilities curve over time compared to the case where the economy produces more goods for the present.

20. International specialization and trade enable a nation to obtain (more, less) _____ of output than is possible with the output limits imposed by domestic production possibilities. The gains in output for an economy from greater international specialization and trade are similar to those that occur because of resource (increases, decreases) _____ or a technological (decline, advance) _____.

■ **TRUE–FALSE QUESTIONS**

Circle T if the statement is true, F if it is false.

1. Economics is the social science that studies how individuals, institutions, and society make choices under conditions of scarcity. **T F**

2. From the economic perspective, "there is no such thing as a free lunch." **T F**

3. The economic perspective views individuals or institutions as making purposeful choices based on the marginal analysis of the costs and benefits of decisions. **T F**

4. The scientific method involves the observation of real world data, the formulation of hypotheses based on the data, and the testing of those hypotheses to develop theories. **T F**

5. A well-tested or widely accepted economic theory is often called an economic principle or law. **T F**

6. The other-things-equal assumption (*ceteris paribus*) is made to simplify the economic analysis. **T F**

7. Microeconomic analysis is concerned with the performance of the economy as a whole or its major aggregates. **T F**

8. Macroeconomic analysis is concerned with the economic activity of specific firms or industries. **T F**

9. The statement that "the legal minimum wage should be raised to give working people a decent income" is an example of a normative statement. **T F**

10. A person is using positive economics when the person makes value judgments about how the economy should work. **T F**

11. The conflict between the scarce economic wants of individuals or societies and limited economic means and resources of individuals or societies gives rise to the economizing problem. **T F**

12. The budget line shows all combinations of two products that the consumer can purchase, given money income and the prices of the products. **T F**

13. A consumer is unable to purchase any of the combinations of two products which lie below (or to the left) of the consumer's budget line. **T F**

14. An increase in the money income of a consumer shifts the budget line to the right. **T F**

15. The factors of production are land, labor, capital, and entrepreneurial ability. **T F**

16. From the economist's perspective, investment refers to money income. **T F**

17. Given full employment and optimal allocation, it is not possible for an economy capable of producing just two goods to increase its production of both at any one point in time. **T F**

18. The opportunity cost of producing more consumer goods is the other goods and services the economy is unable to produce because it has decided to produce these additional consumer goods. **T F**

19. The opportunity cost of producing a good tends to increase as more of it is produced because resources less suitable to its production must be employed. **T F**

20. Drawing a production possibilities curve bowed out from the origin is a graphical way of showing the law of increasing opportunity costs. **T F**

21. The economic rationale for the law of increasing opportunity costs is that economic resources are fully adaptable to alternative uses. **T F**

22. Optimal allocation is determined by assessing the marginal costs and benefits of the output from the allocation of resources to production. **T F**

23. Economic growth means an increase in the production of goods and services and is shown by a movement of the production possibilities curve outward and to the right. **T F**

24. The more capital goods an economy produces today, the greater will be the total output of all goods it can produce in the future, other things being equal. **T F**

25. International specialization and trade permit an economy to overcome the limits imposed by domestic production possibilities and have the same effect on the economy as having more and better resources. **T F**

■ **MULTIPLE-CHOICE QUESTIONS**

Circle the letter that corresponds to the best answer.

1. What statement would best complete a short definition of economics? "Economics studies
(a) how businesses produce goods and services"
(b) the equitable distribution of society's income and wealth"
(c) the printing and circulation of money throughout the economy"
(d) how individuals, institutions, and society make optimal choices under conditions of scarcity"

2. The idea in economics that "there is no such thing as a free lunch" means that
(a) the marginal benefit of such a lunch is greater than its marginal cost
(b) businesses cannot increase their market share by offering free lunches
(c) scarce resources have alternative uses or opportunity costs
(d) consumers are irrational when they ask for a free lunch

3. The opportunity cost of a new public stadium is the
(a) money cost of hiring guards and staff for the new stadium
(b) cost of constructing the new stadium in a future year
(c) change in the real estate tax rate to pay off the new stadium
(d) other goods and services that must be sacrificed to construct the new stadium

4. From the economic perspective, when a business decides to employ more workers, the business decision maker has most likely concluded that the marginal
(a) costs of employing more workers have decreased
(b) benefits of employing more workers have increased
(c) benefits of employing more workers are greater than the marginal costs
(d) costs of employing more workers are not opportunity costs for the business because more workers are needed to increase production

5. The combination of economic theories or principles into a simplified representation of reality is referred to as an economic:
(a) fact
(b) model
(c) assumption
(d) hypothesis

6. Which would be studied in microeconomics?
(a) the output of the entire U.S. economy
(b) the general level of prices in the U.S. economy
(c) the output and price of wheat in the United States
(d) the total number of workers employed in the United States

7. When we look at the whole economy or its major aggregates, our analysis would be at the level of
(a) microeconomics
(b) macroeconomics
(c) positive economics
(d) normative economics

8. Which is a normative economic statement?
(a) The consumer price index rose 1.2 percent last month.
(b) The unemployment rate of 6.8 percent is too high.
(c) The average rate of interest on loans is 4.6 percent.
(d) The economy grew at an annual rate of 3.6 percent.

9. Sandra states that "there is a high correlation between consumption and income." Arthur replies that the correlation occurs because "people consume too much of their income and don't save enough."
(a) Both Sandra's and Arthur's statements are positive.
(b) Both Sandra's and Arthur's statements are normative.
(c) Sandra's statement is positive and Arthur's statement is normative.
(d) Sandra's statement is normative and Arthur's statement is positive.

10. Assume that a consumer can buy only two goods, *A* and *B,* and has an income of $100. The price of *A* is $10 and the price of *B* is $20. The maximum amount of *A* the consumer is able to purchase is
(a) 5
(b) 10
(c) 20
(d) 30

11. Assume that a consumer can buy only two goods, *A* and *B,* and has an income of $100. The price of *A* is $10 and the price of B is $20. What is the slope of the budget line if *A* is measured horizontally and *B* is measured vertically?
(a) −0.5
(b) −1.0
(c) −2.0
(d) −4.0

12. Tools, machinery, or equipment used to produce other goods would be examples of
(a) public goods
(b) capital goods
(c) social goods
(d) consumer goods

13. An "innovator" is defined as an entrepreneur who
(a) makes basic policy decisions in a business firm
(b) combines factors of production to produce a good or service
(c) invents a new product or process for producing a product
(d) introduces new products on the market or employs a new method to produce a product

14. When a production possibilities schedule is written (or a production possibilities curve is drawn) in this chapter,

four assumptions are made. Which is one of those assumptions?
(a) The state of technology changes.
(b) More than two products are produced.
(c) The economy has full employment of available resources.
(d) The quantities of all resources available to the economy are variable, not fixed.

Answer Questions 15, 16, and 17 on the basis of the data given in the following production possibilities table.

	Production possibilities (alternatives)					
	A	B	C	D	E	F
Capital goods	100	95	85	70	50	0
Consumer goods	0	100	180	240	280	300

15. If the economy is producing at production alternative **D**, the opportunity cost of 40 more units of consumer goods is
(a) 5 units of capital goods
(b) 10 units of capital goods
(c) 15 units of capital goods
(d) 20 units of capital goods

16. In the table above, the law of increasing opportunity costs is suggested by the fact that
(a) capital goods are relatively more scarce than consumer goods
(b) greater and greater quantities of consumer goods must be given up to get more capital goods
(c) smaller and smaller quantities of consumer goods must be given up to get more capital goods
(d) the production possibilities curve will eventually shift outward as the economy expands

17. The present choice of alternative **B** compared with alternative **D** would tend to promote
(a) increased consumption in the present
(b) decreased consumption in the future
(c) a greater increase in economic growth in the future
(d) a smaller increase in economic growth in the future

18. What is the economic rationale for the law of increasing opportunity costs?
(a) Optimal allocation and full employment of resources have not been achieved.
(b) Economic resources are not completely adaptable to alternative uses.
(c) Economic growth is being limited by the pace of technological advancement.
(d) An economy's present choice of output is determined by fixed technology and fixed resources.

19. The underallocation of resources by society to the production of a product means that the
(a) marginal benefit is greater than the marginal cost
(b) marginal benefit is less than the marginal cost
(c) opportunity cost of production is rising
(d) consumption of the product is falling

Answer Questions 20, 21, and 22 based on the following graph for an economy.

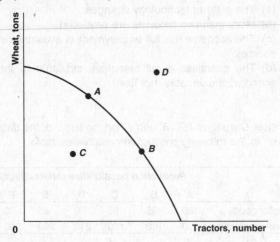

20. Unemployment and productive inefficiency would best be represented in the graph by point:

(a) *A*
(b) *B*
(c) *C*
(d) *D*

21. The choice of point *B* over point *A* as the optimal product mix for society would be based on

(a) the state of technology
(b) full employment of resources
(c) the law of increasing opportunity costs
(d) a comparison of marginal costs and benefits

22. Economic growth could be represented by

(a) a movement from point *A* to point *B*
(b) a movement from point *B* to point *A*
(c) a shift in the production possibilities curve out to point *C*
(d) a shift in the production possibilities curve out to point *D*

23. If there is an increase in the resources available within the economy,

(a) the economy will be capable of producing fewer goods
(b) the economy will be capable of producing more goods
(c) the standard of living in the economy will decline
(d) the state of technology will deteriorate

24. Which situation would most likely shift the production possibilities curve for a nation in an outward direction?

(a) deterioration in product quality
(b) reductions in the supply of resources
(c) increases in technological advance
(d) rising levels of unemployment

25. You observe that more education is associated with more income and conclude that more income leads to more education. This would be an example of

(a) the post hoc fallacy
(b) the fallacy of composition

(c) confusing correlation and causation
(d) using the other-things-equal assumption

■ **PROBLEMS**

1. Use the appropriate number to match the terms with the phrases below.

1. **economics**   4. **normative economics**
2. **microeconomics**   5. **macroeconomics**
3. **positive economics** 6. **marginal analysis**

a. The attempt to establish scientific statements about economic behavior; a concern with "what is" rather than "what ought to be." _____

b. Part of economics that involves value judgments about what the economy should be like or the way the economic world should be. _____

c. Social science that studies how individuals, institutions, and society make optimal choices under conditions of scarcity. _____

d. Part of economics concerned with the economic behavior of individual units such as households, firms, and industries (particular markets). _____

e. The comparison of additional benefits and additional costs. _____

f. Part of economics concerned with the whole economy or its major sectors. _____

2. News report: "The worldwide demand for wheat from the United States increased and caused the price of wheat in the United States to rise." This is a *specific* instance of a more *general* economic principle. Of which economic *generalization* is this a particular example?

_____

_____

3. Following is a list of economic statements. Indicate in the space to the right of each statement whether it is positive (**P**) or normative (**N**). Then, in the last four lines below, write two of your own examples of positive economic statements and two examples of normative economic statements.

a. New York City should control the rental price of apartments. _____

b. Consumer prices rose at an annual rate of 4% last year. _____

c. Most people who are unemployed are just too lazy to work. _____

d. Generally, if you lower the price of a product, people will buy more of that product. _____

e. The profits of oil companies are too large and ought to be used to conduct research on alternative energy sources. _____

f. Government should do more to help the poor.

_____

g. _____ P

h. _____ P

i. _____ N

j. _____ N

4. Following is a list of resources. Indicate in the space to the right of each whether the resource is land (**LD**), labor (**LR**), capital (**C**), entrepreneurial ability (**EA**), or some combinations of these resources.

    a. Fishing grounds in the North Atlantic _____

    b. A computer in a retail store _____

    c. Oil shale deposits in Canada _____

    d. An irrigation ditch in Nebraska _____

    e. Bill Gates in his work in starting Microsoft _____

    f. The oxygen breathed by human beings _____

    g. A McDonald's restaurant in Rochester, Minnesota _____

    h. The shelves of a grocery store _____

    i. A machine in an auto plant _____

    j. A person who creates a new website and uses it to start a successful business _____

    k. A carpenter working for a construction company that is building a house _____

5. Following is a production possibilities table for two products, corn and cars. The table is constructed using the usual assumptions. Corn is measured in units of 100,000 bushels and cars in units of 100,000.

Combination	Corn	Cars
A	0	7
B	7	6
C	13	5
D	18	4
E	22	3
F	25	2
G	27	1
H	28	0

    a. Follow the general rules for making graphs (see the appendix to Chapter 1); plot the data from the table on the graph below to obtain a production possibilities curve. Place corn on the vertical axis and cars on the horizontal axis.

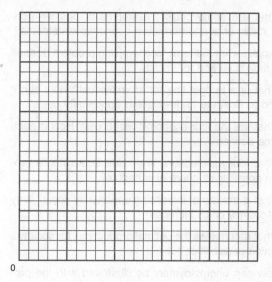

0

    b. Fill in the following table showing the opportunity cost per unit of producing the 1st through the 7th car unit in terms of corn units.

Cars	Cost of production
1st	_____
2nd	_____
3rd	_____
4th	_____
5th	_____
6th	_____
7th	_____

    c. What is the *marginal* opportunity cost of the 3rd car unit in terms of units of corn? _____

    d. What is the *total* opportunity cost of producing 6 car units in terms of units of corn? _____

■ **SHORT ANSWER AND ESSAY QUESTIONS**

1. What are the three interrelated features of the economic perspective?

2. What is the economic meaning of the statement "there is no such thing as a free lunch"?

3. What are the differences and similarities among the terms *hypothesis, theory, principle, law,* and *model*?

4. Why do economists use the "other things equal" assumption?

5. Why are economic principles necessarily generalized and abstract?

6. Explain the difference between microeconomics and macroeconomics.

7. What are some current examples of positive economic statements and normative economic statements?

8. Explain what the term "economizing problem" means for an individual and for society.

9. What is a budget line for an individual? How can it be used to illustrate trade-offs and opportunity costs?

10. What are the four economic resources? How is each resource defined?

11. What four assumptions are made in drawing a production possibilities curve or schedule?

12. What is the law of increasing opportunity costs? Why do opportunity costs increase?

13. What determines the optimal product mix for society's production possibilities?

14. How can unemployment be illustrated with the production possibilities curve?

15. What will be the effect of increasing resource supplies on production possibilities?

16. Describe how technological advances will affect the production possibilities curve.

17. Explain the trade-off between goods for the present and goods for the future and the effect of this trade-off on economic growth.

18. What qualification does international specialization and trade make for the interpretation of production possibilities?

19. Explain how the production possibilities curve can be used to explain the economics of war.

20. Explain each of the five pitfalls to sound economic reasoning.

ANSWERS

Chapter 1 Limits, Alternatives, and Choices

FILL-IN QUESTIONS

1. scarcity, cost, alternative
2. purposeful, marginal
3. scientific, theories, principles, laws, models
4. generalizations, do not, other-things-equal (or *ceteris paribus*)
5. microeconomics, macroeconomics
6. aggregate
7. positive, normative, normative
8. unlimited, limited
9. buy, a budget
10. attainable, unattainable
11. right, left
12. *a.* land or natural resources; *b.* labor; *c.* capital; *d.* entrepreneurial ability

13. *a.* there is full employment and optimal allocation; *b.* the available supplies of the factors of production are fixed; *c.* technology does not change during the course of the analysis; *d.* the economy produces only two products (any order for *a–d*)
14. consumer, capital, cost
15. concave, are not
16. equal to
17. *a.* fewer, more; *b.* unemployed, underemployed; *c.* more, more; *d.* economic growth
18. outward, increase, advance
19. consumer, capital, greater
20. more, increases, advance

TRUE–FALSE QUESTIONS

1. T, p. 4	**10.** F, p. 7	**19.** T, p. 13
2. T, p. 4	**11.** T, pp. 7, 10	**20.** T, pp. 12–13
3. T, pp. 4–5	**12.** T, pp. 8–9	**21.** F, p. 13
4. T, pp. 5–6	**13.** F, p. 9	**22.** T, p. 13
5. T, p. 6	**14.** T, p. 10	**23.** T, p. 15
6. T, p. 6	**15.** T, pp. 10–11	**24.** T, pp. 17–18
7. F, p. 6	**16.** F, p. 10	**25.** T, p. 18
8. F, pp. 6–7	**17.** T, pp. 11, 13	
9. T, p. 7	**18.** T, pp. 12–13	

MULTIPLE-CHOICE QUESTIONS

1. d, p. 4	**10.** b, p. 8	**19.** a, pp. 13–14
2. c, p. 4	**11.** a, pp. 8–9	**20.** c, pp. 14-15
3. d, p. 4	**12.** b, p. 10	**21.** d, pp. 13–14
4. c, p. 5	**13.** d, pp. 10–11	**22.** d, pp. 15–16
5. b, pp. 5–6	**14.** c, p. 11	**23.** b, p. 15
6. c, p. 6	**15.** d, p. 11	**24.** c, pp. 15–16
7. b, p. 6–7	**16.** b, pp. 11–12	**25.** c, pp. 16–17
8. b, p. 7	**17.** c, p. 15	
9. c, p. 7	**18.** b, p. 13	

PROBLEMS

1. *a.* 3; *b.* 4; *c.* 1; *d.* 2; *e.* 6; *f.* 5
2. An increase in the demand for an economic good will cause the price of that good to rise.
3. *a.* N; *b.* P; *c.* N; *d.* P; *e.* N; *f.* N
4. *a.* LD; *b.* C; *c.* LD; *d.* C; *e.* EA; *f.* LD; *g.* C; *h.* C; *i.* C; *j.* EA; *k.* LR
5. *b.* 1, 2, 3, 4, 5, 6, 7 units of corn; *c.* 3; *d.* 21

SHORT ANSWER AND ESSAY QUESTIONS

1. pp. 4–5	**8.** pp. 7,10	**15.** pp. 15–16
2. p. 4	**9.** pp. 8–10	**16.** p. 16
3. pp. 5–6	**10.** pp. 10–11	**17.** pp. 17–18
4. p. 6	**11.** p. 11	**18.** p. 18
5. p. 6	**12.** pp. 12–13	**19.** p. 14
6. pp. 6–7	**13.** p. 13	**20.** pp. 16–17
7. p. 7	**14.** pp. 14–15	

Graphs and Their Meaning

This appendix introduces graphing in economics. Graphs help illustrate and simplify the economic theories and models presented throughout this book. The old saying that "a picture is worth 1000 words" applies to economics; graphs are the way that economists "picture" relationships between economic variables.

You must master the basics of graphing if these "pictures" are to be of any help to you. This appendix explains how to achieve that mastery. It shows you how to construct a graph from a table with data of two variables, such as income and consumption.

Economists usually, but not always, place the **independent variable** (income) on the horizontal axis and the **dependent variable** (consumption) on the vertical axis of the graph. Once the data points are plotted and a line drawn to connect the plotted points, you can determine whether there is a **direct** or an **inverse relationship** between the variables. Identifying direct and inverse relationships between variables is an essential skill used repeatedly in this book.

Information from data in graphs and tables can be written in an equation. This work involves determining the **slope** and **intercept** from a straight line in a graph or data in a table. Using values for the slope and intercept, you can write a **linear equation** that will enable you to calculate what the dependent variable would be for a given level of the independent variable.

Some graphs used in the book are *nonlinear*. With **nonlinear curves,** the slope of the line is no longer constant throughout but varies as one moves along the curve. This slope can be estimated at a point by determining the slope of a straight line that is drawn tangent to the curve at that point. Similar calculations can be made for other points to see how the slope changes along the curve.

■ **APPENDIX CHECKLIST**

When you have studied this appendix you should be able to

☐ Explain why economists use graphs.
☐ Construct a graph of two variables using the numerical data from a table.
☐ Make a table with two variables from data on a graph.
☐ Distinguish between a direct and an inverse relationship when given data on two variables.
☐ Identify dependent and independent variables in economic examples and graphs.

☐ Describe how economists use the other-things-equal assumption (*ceteris paribus*) in graphing two variables.
☐ Calculate the slope of a straight line between two points when given the tabular data, and indicate whether the slope is positive or negative.
☐ Describe how slopes are affected by the choice of the units of measurement for either variable.
☐ Explain how slopes are related to marginal analysis.
☐ Graph infinite or zero slopes and explain their meaning.
☐ Determine the vertical intercept for a straight line in a graph with two variables.
☐ Write a linear equation using the slope of a line and the vertical intercept; when given a value for the independent variable, determine a value for the dependent variable.
☐ Estimate the slope of a nonlinear curve at a point using a line that is tangent to the curve at that point.

■ **APPENDIX OUTLINE**

1. Graphs illustrate the relationship between variables and give economists and students another way, in addition to verbal explanation, of understanding economic phenomena. Graphs are aids in describing economic theories and models.

2. The construction of a simple graph involves plotting the numerical data of two variables from a table.

   a. Each graph has a **horizontal axis** and a **vertical axis** that can be labeled for each variable and then scaled for the range of the data point that will be measured on the axis.

   b. Data points are plotted on the graph by drawing straight lines from the scaled points on the two axes to the place on the graph where the straight lines intersect.

   c. A line or curve can then be drawn to connect the points plotted on the graph. If the graph is a straight line, it is *linear*. (It is acceptable and typical to call these straight lines "curves.")

3. A graph provides information about relationships between variables.

   a. An upward-sloping line to the right on a graph indicates that there is a positive or ***direct relationship*** between two variables: an increase in one is associated with an increase in the other; a decrease in one is associated with a decrease in the other.

   b. A downward-sloping line to the right means that there is a negative or ***inverse relationship*** between the two variables: an increase in one is associated with a decrease in the other; a decrease in one is associated with an increase in the other.

4. Economists are often concerned with determining cause and effect in economic events.

    a. A *dependent variable* changes (increases or decreases) because of a change in another variable.

    b. An *independent variable* produces or "causes" the change in the dependent variable.

    c. In a graph, mathematicians place an independent variable on the horizontal axis and a dependent variable on the vertical axis; economists are more arbitrary in the placement of the dependent or independent variable on an axis.

5. Economic graphs are simplifications of economic relationships. When graphs are plotted, usually an implicit assumption is made that all other factors are being held constant. This "other-things-equal" or *ceteris paribus* assumption is used to simplify the analysis so the study can focus on the two variables of interest.

6. The *slope of a straight line* in a two-variable graph is the ratio of the vertical change to the horizontal change between two points.

    a. A *positive* slope indicates that the relationship between the two variables is *direct*.

    b. A *negative* slope indicates that there is an *inverse* relationship between the two variables.

    c. Slopes are affected by the *measurement units* for either variable.

    d. Slopes measure *marginal* changes.

    e. Slopes can be *infinite* (line parallel to vertical axis) or zero (line parallel to horizontal axis).

7. The *vertical intercept* of a straight line in a two-variable graph is the point where the line intersects the vertical axis of the graph.

8. The slope and intercept of a straight line can be expressed in the form of a *linear equation,* which is written as $y = a + bx$. Once the values for the intercept (a) and the slope (b) are calculated, then given any value of the independent variable (x), the value of the dependent variable (y) can be determined.

9. The slope of a straight line is constant, but the slope of a nonlinear curve changes throughout. To estimate the slope of a *nonlinear curve* at a point, the slope of a line *tangent* to the curve at that point is calculated.

■ HINTS AND TIPS

1. This appendix will help you understand the graphs and problems presented throughout the book. Do not skip reading the appendix or working on the self-test questions and problems in this *Study Guide*. The time you invest now will pay off in improved understanding in later chapters. Graphing is a basic skill for economic analysis.

2. Positive and negative relationships in graphs often confuse students. To overcome this confusion, draw a two-variable graph with a positive slope and another two-variable graph with a negative slope. In each graph, show what happens to the value of one variable when there is a change in the value of the other variable.

3. A straight line in a two-variable graph can be expressed in an equation. Make sure you know how to interpret each part of the linear equation.

■ IMPORTANT TERMS

vertical axis	independent variable
horizontal axis	slope of a straight line
direct (positive) relationship	vertical intercept
inverse (negative) relationship	linear equation
dependent variable	nonlinear curve

SELF-TEST

■ FILL-IN QUESTIONS

1. The relationship between two economic variables can be visualized with the aid of a two-dimensional (graph, matrix) _____, which has (a horizontal, an inverse) _____ axis and a (vertical, direct) _____ axis.

2. Customarily, the (dependent, independent) _____ variable is placed on the horizontal axis and the _____ is placed on the vertical axis. The _____ variable is said to change because of a change in the _____ variable.

3. The vertical and horizontal (scales, ranges) _____ of the graph are calibrated to reflect the _____ of values in the table of data points on which the graph is based.

4. The graph of a straight line that slopes downward to the right indicates that there is (a direct, an inverse) _____ relationship between the two variables. A graph of a straight line that slopes upward to the right tells us that the relationship is (direct, inverse) _____. When the value of one variable increases and the value of the other variable increases, then the relationship is _____; when the value of one increases, while the other decreases, the relationship is _____.

5. When interpreting an economic graph, the "cause" or the "source" is the (dependent, independent) _____ variable and the "effect" or "outcome" is the _____ variable.

6. Other variables, beyond the two in a two-dimensional graph, that might affect the economic relationship are assumed to be (changing, held constant) _____. This assumption is also referred to as the other-things-equal assumption or as (*post hoc*, *ceteris paribus*) _____.

7. The slope of a straight line between two points is defined as the ratio of the (vertical, horizontal) _____ change to the _____ change.

8. When two variables move in the same direction, the slope will be (negative, positive) _____; when the variables move in opposite directions, the slope will be _____.

9. The slope of a line will be affected by the (units of measurement, vertical intercept) _____.

10. The concept of a slope is important to economists because it reflects the influence of a (marginal, total) _____ change in one variable on another variable.

11. A graph of a line with an infinite slope is (horizontal, vertical) _____, while a graph of a line with a zero slope is _____.

12. The point at which the slope of the line meets the vertical axis is called the vertical (tangent, intercept) _____.

13. We can express the graph of a straight line with a linear equation that can be written as $y = a + bx$.

    a. *a* is the (slope, intercept) _____ and *b* is the _____

    b. *y* is the (dependent, independent) _____ variable and *x* is the _____ variable.

    c. If *a* were 2, *b* were 4, and *x* were 5, then *y* would be _____. If the value of x changed to 7, then *y* would be _____. If the value of *x* changed to 3, then *y* would be _____.

14. The slope of a (straight line, nonlinear curve) _____ is constant throughout; the slope of a _____ varies from point to point.

15. An estimate of the slope of a nonlinear curve at a certain point can be made by calculating the slope of a straight line that is (tangent, perpendicular) _____ to the point on the curve.

■ **TRUE–FALSE QUESTIONS**

Circle T if the statement is true, F if it is false.

  1. Economists design graphs to confuse people. **T F**

2. If the straight line on a two-variable graph slopes downward to the right, then there is a positive relationship between the two variables. **T F**

3. A variable that changes as a consequence of a change in another variable is considered a dependent variable. **T F**

4. Economists always put the independent variable on the horizontal axis and the dependent variable on the vertical axis of a two-variable graph. **T F**

5. *Ceteris paribus* means that other variables are changing at the same time. **T F**

6. In the ratio for the calculation of the slope of a straight line, the vertical change is in the numerator and the horizontal change is in the denominator. **T F**

7. If the slope of the linear relationship between consumption and income was .90, then it tells us that for every $1 increase in income there will be a $.90 increase in consumption. **T F**

8. The slope of a straight line in a two-variable graph will *not* be affected by the choice of the units for either variable. **T F**

9. The slopes of lines measure marginal changes. **T F**

10. Assume in a graph that price is on the vertical axis and quantity is on the horizontal axis. The absence of a relationship between price and quantity would be a straight line parallel to the horizontal axis. **T F**

11. A line with an infinite slope in a two-variable graph is parallel to the horizontal axis. **T F**

12. In a two-variable graph, income is graphed on the vertical axis and the quantity of snow is graphed on the horizontal axis. If income was independent of the quantity of snow, then this independence would be represented by a line parallel to the horizontal axis. **T F**

13. If a linear equation is $y = 10 + 5x$, the vertical intercept is 5. **T F**

14. When a line is tangent to a nonlinear curve, then it intersects the curve at a particular point. **T F**

15. If the slope of a straight line on a two-variable (*x*, *y*) graph were .5 and the vertical intercept were 5, then a value of 10 for *x* would mean that *y* is also 10. **T F**

16. A slope of –4 for a straight line in a two-variable graph indicates that there is an inverse relationship between the two variables. **T F**

17. If *x* is an independent variable and *y* is a dependent variable, then a change in *y* results in a change in *x*. **T F**

18. An upward slope for a straight line that is tangent to a nonlinear curve indicates that the slope of the nonlinear curve at that point is positive. **T F**

19. If one pair of *x, y* points was (13, 10) and the other pair was (8, 20), then the slope of the straight line between the two sets of points in the two-variable graph, with **x** on the horizontal axis and **y** on the vertical axis, would be 2. **T F**

20. When the value of **x** is 2, a value of 10 for **y** would be calculated from a linear equation of **y** = −2 + 6**x**. **T F**

■ **MULTIPLE-CHOICE QUESTIONS**

Circle the letter that corresponds to the best answer.

1. If an increase in one variable is associated with a decrease in another variable, then we can conclude that the variables are
   (a) nonlinear
   (b) directly related
   (c) inversely related
   (d) positively related

2. The ratio of the vertical change to the horizontal change between two points of a straight line is the
   (a) slope
   (b) vertical intercept
   (c) horizontal intercept
   (d) point of tangency

3. There are two sets of **x, y** points on a straight line in a two-variable graph, with **y** on the vertical axis and **x** on the horizontal axis. If one set of points was (0, 5) and the other set (5, 20), the linear equation for the line would be
   (a) **y** = 5**x**
   (b) **y** = 5 + 3**x**
   (c) **y** = 5 + 15**x**
   (d) **y** = 5 + .33**x**

4. In a two-variable graph of data on the price and quantity of a product, economists place
   (a) price on the horizontal axis because it is the independent variable and quantity on the vertical axis because it is the dependent variable
   (b) price on the vertical axis because it is the dependent variable and quantity on the horizontal axis because it is the independent variable
   (c) price on the vertical axis even though it is the independent variable and quantity on the horizontal axis even though it is the dependent variable
   (d) price on the horizontal axis even though it is the dependent variable and quantity on the vertical axis even though it is the independent variable

5. In a two-dimensional graph of the relationship between two economic variables, an assumption is usually made that
   (a) both variables are linear
   (b) both variables are nonlinear
   (c) other variables are held constant
   (d) other variables are permitted to change

6. If the slope of a straight line is zero, then the straight line is
   (a) vertical
   (b) horizontal

(c) upward sloping
(d) downward sloping

Questions 7, 8, 9, and 10 are based on the following four data sets. In each set, the independent variable is in the left column and the dependent variable is in the right column.

(1)		(2)		(3)		(4)	
A	**B**	**C**	**D**	**E**	**F**	**G**	**H**
0	1	0	12	4	5	0	4
3	2	5	8	6	10	1	3
6	3	10	4	8	15	2	2
9	4	15	0	10	20	3	1

7. There is an inverse relationship between the independent and dependent variables in data sets
   (a) 1 and 4
   (b) 2 and 3
   (c) 1 and 3
   (d) 2 and 4

8. The vertical intercept is 4 in data set
   (a) 1
   (b) 2
   (c) 3
   (d) 4

9. The linear equation for data set 1 is
   (a) **B** = 3**A**
   (b) **B** = 1 + 3**A**
   (c) **B** = 1 + .33**A**
   (d) **A** = 1 + .33**B**

10. The linear equation for data set 2 is
    (a) **C** = 12 − 1.25**D**
    (b) **D** = 12 + 1.25**C**
    (c) **D** = 12 − .80**C**
    (d) **C** = 12 − .80**D**

Answer Questions 11, 12, 13, and 14 on the basis of the following diagram.

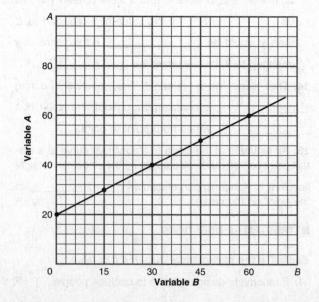

11. The variables **A** and **B** are
  (a) positively related
  (b) negatively related
  (c) indirectly related
  (d) nonlinear

12. The slope of the line is
  (a) .33
  (b) .67
  (c) 1.50
  (d) 3.00

13. The vertical intercept is
  (a) 80
  (b) 60
  (c) 40
  (d) 20

14. The linear equation for the slope of the line is
  (a) $A = 20 + .33B$
  (b) $B = 20 + .33A$
  (c) $A = 20 + .67B$
  (d) $B = 20 + .67A$

Answer Questions 15, 16, and 17 on the basis of the following diagram.

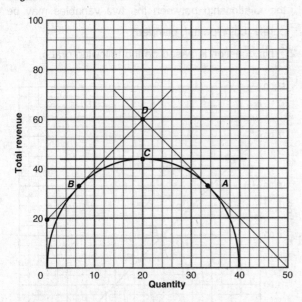

15. The slope of the line tangent to the curve at point **A** is
  (a) 2
  (b) −2
  (c) −1.5
  (d) −0.5

16. The slope of the line tangent to the curve at point **B** is
  (a) −2
  (b) 2
  (c) 3
  (d) 0.5

17. The slope of the line tangent to the curve at point **C** is
  (a) −1
  (b) 1
  (c) 0
  (d) undefined

18. Assume that the relationship between concert ticket prices and attendance is expressed in the equation $P = 25 - 1.25Q$, where **P** equals ticket price and **Q** equals concert attendance in thousands of people. On the basis of this equation, it can be said that
  (a) more people will attend the concert when the price is high compared to when the price is low
  (b) if 12,000 people attended the concert, then the ticket price was $10
  (c) if 18,000 people attend the concert, then entry into the concert was free
  (d) an increase in ticket price by $5 reduces concert attendance by 1000 people

19. If you know that the equation relating consumption (**C**) to income (**Y**) is $C = \$7,500 + .2Y$, then
  (a) consumption is inversely related to income
  (b) consumption is the independent variable and income is the dependent variable
  (c) if income is $15,000, then consumption is $10,500
  (d) if consumption is $30,000, then income is $10,000

20. If the dependent variable changes by 22 units when the independent variable changes by 12 units, then the slope of the line is
  (a) 0.56
  (b) 1.83
  (c) 2.00
  (d) 3.27

■ **PROBLEMS**

  1. Following are three tables for making graphs. On the graphs, plot the economic relationships contained in each table. Be sure to label each axis of the graph and indicate the unit measurement and scale used on each axis.
  a. Use the table at the top of the next page to graph national income on the horizontal axis and consumption expenditures on the vertical axis in the graph below; connect the seven points and label the curve "Consumption." The relationship between income and consumption is (a direct, an inverse) _____ one and the consumption curve is (an up-, a down-) _____ sloping curve.

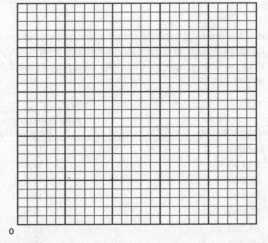

National income, billions of dollars	Consumption expenditures, billions of dollars
$ 600	$ 600
700	640
800	780
900	870
1000	960
1100	1050
1200	1140

b. Use the next table to graph investment expenditures on the horizontal axis and the rate of interest on the vertical axis on the graph below; connect the seven points and label the curve "Investment." The relationship between the rate of interest and investment expenditures is (a direct, an inverse) _____ one and the investment curve is (an up-, a down-) _____ sloping curve.

Rate of interest, %	Investment expenditures, billions of dollars
8	$220
7	280
6	330
5	370
4	400
3	420
2	430

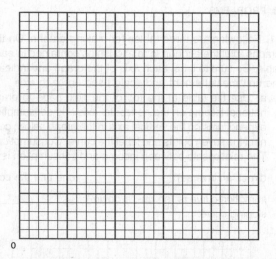

c. Use the next table to graph average income on the horizontal axis and milk consumption on the vertical axis on the graph in the next column; connect the seven points.

Average income	Annual per capita milk consumption in gallons
$62,000	11.5
63,000	11.6
64,000	11.7
65,000	11.8
66,000	11.9
67,000	12.0
68,000	12.1

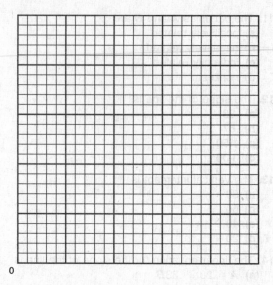

Based on the data, the average income and milk consumption (are, are not) _____ *correlated.*

The higher average income (is, is not) _____ the *cause* of the greater consumption of milk because the relationship between the two variables may be purely (coincidental, planned) _____.

2. This question is based on the following graph.

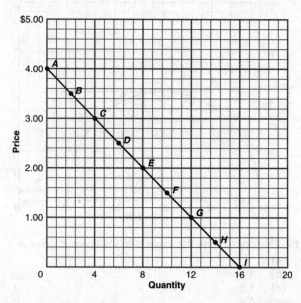

a. Construct a table for points **A–I** from the data shown in the graph.

b. According to economists, price is the (independent, dependent) _____ variable and quantity is the _____ variable.

c. Write a linear equation that summarizes the data.

3. The following three sets of data each show the relationship between an independent variable and a dependent variable. For each set, the independent variable is in the left column and the dependent variable is in the right column.

(1)		(2)		(3)	
A	**B**	**C**	**D**	**E**	**F**
0	10	0	100	0	20
10	30	10	75	50	40
20	50	20	50	100	60
30	70	30	25	150	80
40	90	40	0	200	100

a. Write an equation that summarizes the data for each of the sets (1), (2), and (3).

b. State whether each data set shows a positive or an inverse relationship between the two variables.

c. Plot data sets 1 and 2 on the following graph. Use the same horizontal scale for both sets of independent variables and the same vertical scale for both sets of dependent variables.

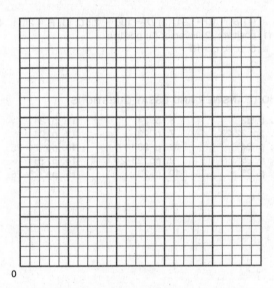

0

4. This problem is based on the following graph.

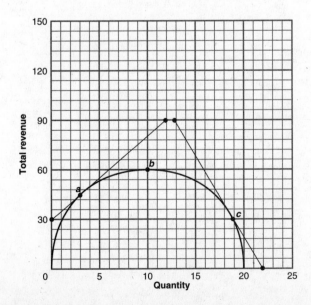

a. The slope of the straight line through point **a** is?

b. The slope of the straight line through point **b** is?

c. The slope of the straight line through point **c** is?

■ SHORT ANSWER AND ESSAY QUESTIONS

1. Why do economists use graphs in their work?

2. Give two examples of a graph that illustrates the relationship between two economic variables.

3. What does the slope tell you about a straight line? How would you interpret a slope of 4? A slope of −2? A slope of .5? A slope of −.25?

4. If the vertical intercept increases in value but the slope of a straight line stays the same, what happens to the graph of the line? If the vertical intercept decreases in value, what will happen to the line?

5. How do you interpret a vertical line on a two-variable graph? How do you interpret a horizontal line?

6. When you know that the price and quantity of a product are inversely related, what does this tell you about the slope of a line where price is on the vertical axis and quantity is on the horizontal axis? What do you know about the slope when the two variables are positively related?

7. Which variable is the dependent and which is the independent in the following economic statement: "A decrease in business taxes had a positive effect on investment spending."

8. How do you tell the difference between a dependent and independent variable when examining economic relationships?

9. Why is an assumption made that all other variables are held constant when we construct a two-variable graph of the price and quantity of a product?

10. How do mathematicians and economists differ at times in how they construct two-dimensional graphs? Give an example.

11. How is the slope of a straight line in a two-variable graph affected by the choice of the units for either variable? Explain and give an example.

12. What is the relationship between the slopes of lines and marginal analysis?

13. Describe a case in which a straight line in a two-variable graph would have an infinite slope and a case in which the slope of a line would be zero.

14. If you know that the equation relating consumption (**C**) to income (**Y**) is $C = 10,000 + 5Y$, then what would consumption be when income is $5000? Construct an income-consumption table for five different levels of income.

15. How do the slopes of a straight line and a nonlinear curve differ? How do you estimate the slope of a nonlinear curve?

ANSWERS

Appendix to Chapter 1 Graphs and Their Meaning

FILL-IN QUESTIONS

1. graph, a horizontal, vertical
2. independent, dependent, dependent, independent
3. scales, ranges
4. an inverse, direct, direct, inverse
5. independent, dependent
6. held constant, *ceteris paribus*
7. vertical, horizontal
8. positive, negative
9. units of measurement
10. marginal
11. vertical, horizontal
12. intercept
13. *a.* intercept, slope; *b.* dependent, independent; *c.* 22, 30, 14
14. straight line, nonlinear curve
15. tangent

TRUE–FALSE QUESTIONS

1. F, p. 22	**8.** F, p. 24	**15.** T, p. 25
2. F, p. 23	**9.** T, p. 24	**16.** T, p. 24
3. T, p. 23	**10.** T, pp. 24–25	**17.** F, p. 23
4. F, p. 23	**11.** F, pp. 24–25	**18.** T, pp. 25–26
5. F, pp. 23–24	**12.** T, pp. 24–25	**19.** F, p. 25
6. T, p. 24	**13.** F, p. 25	**20.** T, p. 25
7. T, p. 24	**14.** F, pp. 25–26	

MULTIPLE-CHOICE QUESTIONS

1. c, p. 23	**8.** d, p. 25	**15.** b, pp. 25–26
2. a, p. 24	**9.** c, p. 25	**16.** b, pp. 25–26
3. b, p. 25	**10.** c, p. 25	**17.** c, pp. 25–26
4. c, p. 23	**11.** a, p. 23	**18.** b, p. 25
5. c, pp. 23–24	**12.** b, p. 24	**19.** c, p. 25
6. b, pp. 24–25	**13.** d, p. 25	**20.** b, p. 24
7. d, p. 23	**14.** c, p. 25	

PROBLEMS

1. *a.* a direct, an up-; *b.* an inverse, a down-; *c.* are, is not, coincidental
2. *a.* table below; *b.* independent, dependent; *c.* $P = 4.00 - .25Q$

Point	Price	Quantity
A	$4.00	0
B	3.50	2
C	3.00	4
D	2.50	6
E	2.00	8
F	1.50	10
G	1.00	12
H	.50	14
I	.00	16

3. *a.* (1) $B = 10 + 2A$; (2) $D = 100 - 2.5C$; (3) $F = 20 + .4E$; *b.* (1) positive; (2) inverse; (3) positive
4. *a.* 5; *b.* 0; *c.* −10

SHORT ANSWER AND ESSAY QUESTIONS

1. p. 22	**6.** p. 24	**11.** p. 24
2. pp. 22-23	**7.** p. 23	**12.** p. 24
3. p. 24	**8.** p. 23	**13.** pp. 24–25
4. p. 25	**9.** pp. 23–24	**14.** p. 25
5. p. 25	**10.** p. 23	**15.** pp. 25–26

CHAPTER 2

The Market System and the Circular Flow

Every economy needs to develop an **economic system** to respond to the economizing problem of limited resources and unlimited wants. The two basic types of systems are the **command system** and the **market system.** In the command system, there is extensive public ownership of resources and the use of central planning for most economic decision making in the economy. In the market system there is extensive private ownership of resources and the use of markets and prices to coordinate and direct economic activity.

A major purpose of Chapter 2 is to explain the major characteristics of the market system because it is the one used in most nations. The first part of this section describes the **ideological** and **institutional** characteristics of the market system. In this system, most of the resources are owned as private property by citizens, who are free to use them as they wish in their own self-interest. Prices and markets express the self-interests of resource owners, consumers, and business firms. Competition regulates self-interest—to prevent the self-interest of any person or any group from working to the disadvantage of the economy and to make self-interests work for the benefit of the entire economy. Government plays an active, but limited, role in a market economy.

Three other characteristics are also found in a market economy. They are the employment of large amounts of **capital goods,** the development of **specialization,** and the **use of money.** Economies use capital goods and engage in specialization because this is a more efficient use of their resources; it results in larger total output and the greater satisfaction of wants. When workers, business firms, and regions within an economy specialize, they become dependent on each other for the goods and services they do not produce for themselves and they must engage in trade. Trade is made more convenient by using money as a medium of exchange.

The chapter also explains in detail how the market system works. There are **Five Fundamental Questions** that any economic system must answer in its attempt to use its scarce resources to satisfy its material wants. The five questions or problems are: (1) What goods and services will be produced? (2) How will the goods and services be produced? (3) Who will get the goods and services? (4) How will the system accommodate change? (5) How will the system promote progress?

The explanation of how the market system finds answers to the Five Fundamental Questions is only an approximation—a simplified explanation—of the methods actually employed by the U.S. economy and other market economies. Yet this explanation contains enough realism to be truthful and is general enough to be understandable. If the aims of this chapter are accomplished, you can begin to understand the market system and methods our economy uses to solve the economizing problem presented in Chapter 1.

Although central planning served as a powerful form of economic decision making in command systems such as the Soviet Union and China (before its market reform), it had two serious problems. The first problem was one of **coordination,** which resulted in production bottlenecks and managers and bureaucrats missing production targets. Central planning also created an **incentive problem** because it sent out incorrect and inadequate signals for directing the efficient allocation of an economy's resources and gave workers little reason to work hard. The lack of incentives killed entrepreneurship and stifled innovation and technological advance.

The chapter ends with a description of the **circular flow model** (or **diagram**). In a market economy, there is a resource market and product market that connect households and businesses. There is also a flow of money and flows of goods and services and resources that indicate that households and businesses have dual roles as buyers and sellers depending on whether they are operating in the product market or resource market.

■ **CHECKLIST**

When you have studied this chapter you should be able to

☐ Compare and contrast the command system with the market system.
☐ Identify the nine important characteristics of the market system.
☐ Describe the role of private property rights in the market system.
☐ Distinguish between freedom of enterprise and freedom of choice.
☐ Explain why self-interest is a driving force of the market system.
☐ Identify two features of competition in the market system.
☐ Explain the roles of markets and prices in the market system.
☐ Describe how the market system relies on technology and capital.
☐ Discuss how two types of specialization improve efficiency in the market system.

☐ Describe the advantages of money over barter for the exchange of goods and services in the market system.

☐ Describe the size and role of government in the market system.

☐ List the Five Fundamental Questions to answer about the operation of a market economy.

☐ Explain how a market system determines what goods and services will be produced and the role of consumer sovereignty and dollar votes.

☐ Explain how goods and services will be produced in a market system.

☐ Find the least costly combination of resources needed for production when given the technological data and the prices of the resources.

☐ Explain how a market system determines who will get the goods and services it produces.

☐ Describe the guiding function of prices to accommodate change in the market system.

☐ Explain how the market system promotes progress by fostering technological advances and capital accumulation.

☐ State how the "invisible hand" in the market system tends to promote public or social interests.

☐ List three virtues of the market system.

☐ Compare how a command economy coordinates economic activity with how a market economy coordinates economic activity.

☐ Explain the problems with incentives in a command economy.

☐ Draw the circular flow model, correctly labeling the two markets and the real and money flows between the two markets.

☐ Describe the role private property plays in helping a market economy find the most productive combination of resources (Last Word).

■ CHAPTER OUTLINE

1. An *economic system* is a set of institutions and a coordinating mechanism to respond to the economizing problem for an economy.

   a. The *command system* (also called *socialism* or *communism*) is based primarily on extensive public ownership of resources and the use of central planning for most economic decision making. There used to be many examples of command economies (Soviet Union), but today there are few (North Korea, Cuba). Most former socialistic nations have been or are being transformed into capitalistic and market-oriented economies.

   b. The *market system* (*capitalism*) has extensive private ownership of resources and uses markets and prices to coordinate and direct economic activity. In pure (*laissez-faire*) capitalism there is a limited government role in the economy. In a capitalist economy such as the United States, government plays a large role, but the two characteristics of the market system—private property and markets—dominate.

2. The market system has the following nine characteristics:

   a. Private individuals and organizations own and control their property resources by means of the institution of *private property.*

   b. These individuals and organizations possess both the *freedom of enterprise* and the *freedom of choice*

   c. These economic units are motivated largely by *self-interest.*

   d. *Competition* is based on the independent actions of buyers and sellers. They have the freedom to enter or leave markets. This competition spreads economic power and limits its potential abuse.

   e. A *market* is a place, institution, or process where buyers and sellers interact with each other. Markets and prices are used to communicate and coordinate the decisions of buyers and sellers.

   f. The market system employs complicated and advanced methods of production, new technology, and large amounts of capital equipment to produce goods and services efficiently.

   g. It is a highly specialized economy. Human and geographic *specialization* increase the productive efficiency of the economy. Human specialization is also called *division of labor.* It increases productivity because it allows people to split up work into separate tasks and lets people do the task which they are best at doing. Geographic specialization lets nations produce what they do best and then trade with other nations for what else they want.

   h. It uses *money* exclusively to facilitate trade and specialization. Money functions as a *medium of exchange* that is more efficient to use than *barter* for trading goods.

   i. Government has an active but limited role.

3. The system of prices and markets and households' and business firms' choices furnish the market economy with answers to **Five Fundamental Questions.**

   a. *What goods and services will be produced?* In a market economy, there is *consumer sovereignty* because consumers are in command and express their wishes for the goods and services through *dollar votes.* The demands of consumers for products and the desires of business firms to maximize their profits determine what and how much of each product is produced and its price.

   b. *How will the goods and services be produced?* The desires of business firms to maximize profits by keeping their costs of production as low as possible guide them to use the most efficient techniques of production and determine their demands for various resources; competition forces them to use the most efficient techniques and ensures that only the most efficient will be able to stay in business.

   c. *Who will get the goods and services?* With resource prices determined, the money income of each household is determined; and with product prices determined, the quantity of goods and services these money incomes will buy is determined.

   d. *How will the system accommodate change?* The market system is able to accommodate itself to changes in consumer tastes, technology, and resource supplies. The desires of business firms for maximum profits and competition lead the economy to make the appropriate adjustments in the way it uses its resources.

e. *How will the system promote progress?* Competition and the desire to increase profits promote better techniques of production and capital accumulation.

(1) The market system encourages technological advance because it can help increase revenue or decrease costs for businesses, thus increasing profits. The use of new technology spreads rapidly because firms must stay innovative or fail. There can also be *creative destruction* where new technology creates market positions of firms adopting the new technology and destroys the market position of firms using the old technology.

(2) Business owners will take their profit income and use it to make more capital goods that improve production and increase profits.

4. Competition in the economy compels firms seeking to promote their own interests to promote (as though led by an *"invisible hand"*) the best interests of society as a whole.

    a. Competition results in an allocation of resources appropriate to consumer wants, production by the most efficient means, and the lowest possible prices.

    b. Three noteworthy merits of the market system are

    (1) The *efficient* use of resources

    (2) The *incentive* the system provides for productive activity

    (3) The personal *freedom* allowed participants as consumers, producers, workers, or investors.

5. The demise of command systems occurred largely because of two basic problems with a centrally planned economy.

    a. The *coordination problem* involved the difficulty of coordinating the economy's many interdependent segments and avoiding the chain reaction that would result from a bottleneck in any one of the segments. This coordination problem became even more difficult as the economy grew larger and more complex, and more economic decisions had to be made in the production process. There were also inadequate measures of economic performance to determine the degree of success or failure of enterprises or to give clear signals to the economy.

    b. The *incentive problem* arose because in a command economy incentives are ineffective for encouraging economic initiatives and work and for directing the most efficient use of productive resources. In a market economy, profits and losses signal what firms should produce, how they should produce, and how productive resources should be allocated to best meet the wants of a nation. Central planning in the two economies also lacked entrepreneurship and stifled innovation, both of which are important forces for achieving long-term economic growth. Individual workers lacked much motivation to work hard because pay was limited and there were either few consumer goods to buy or they were of low quality.

6. The *circular flow model* or *diagram* is a device used to clarify the relationships between households and business firms in a market economy. In the *resource market,* households sell and firms buy resources, and in the *product market,* the firms sell and households buy products. Households use the incomes they obtain from selling resources to purchase the goods and services produced by the firms, and in the economy there is a real flow of resources and products and a money flow of incomes and expenditures.

7. (Last Word). There are tens of billions of ways that resources could be arranged in a market economy, but most combinations would be useless. The reason that a market economy produces the few combinations from the total possible that are productive and serve human goals is because of private property. With it, people have an incentive to make the best use of their resources and find the most rewarding combination.

■ HINTS AND TIPS

1. This chapter describes nine characteristics and institutions of a market system. After reading the section, check your understanding by listing the nine points and writing a short explanation of each one.

2. The section on the *Five Fundamental Questions* is both the most important and the most difficult part of the chapter. Detailed answers to the five questions are given in this section of the chapter. If you examine each one individually and in the order in which it is presented, you will more easily understand how the market system works. (Actually, the market system finds the answers simultaneously, but make your learning easier for now by considering them one by one.)

3. Be sure to understand the *importance* and *role* of each of the following in the operation of the market system: (1) the guiding function of prices, (2) the profit motive of business firms, (3) the entry into and exodus of firms from industries, (4) the meaning of competition, and (5) consumer sovereignty.

■ IMPORTANT TERMS

economic system	medium of exchange
command system	barter
market system	money
private property	consumer sovereignty
freedom of enterprise	dollar votes
freedom of choice	creative destruction
self-interest	"invisible hand"
competition	circular flow diagram
market	resource market
specialization	product market
division of labor	

SELF-TEST

■ FILL-IN QUESTIONS

  1. The institutional arrangements and coordinating mechanisms used to respond to the economic problem are called

(*laissez-faire*, an economic system) _____.

2. In a command economy, property resources are primarily (publicly, privately) _____ owned. The coordinating device(s) in this economic system (is central planning, are markets and prices) _____.

3. In capitalism, property resources are primarily (publicly, privately) _____ owned. The means used to direct and coordinate economic activity (is central planning, are markets and prices) _____.

4. The ownership of property resources by private individuals and organizations is the institution of private (resources, property) _____. The freedom of private businesses to obtain resources and use them to produce goods and services is the freedom of (choice, enterprise) _____, while the freedom to dispose of property or money as a person sees fit is the freedom of _____.

5. Self-interest means that each economic unit attempts to do what is best for itself, but this might lead to an abuse of power in a market economy if it were not directed and constrained by (government, competition) _____. Self-interest and selfishness (are, are not) _____ the same thing in a market economy.

6. Broadly defined, competition is present if two conditions prevail; these two conditions are

a. _____

_____

b. _____

_____

7. In a capitalist economy, individual buyers communicate their demands and individual sellers communicate their supplies in the system of (markets, prices) _____, and the outcomes from economic decisions are a set of product and resource _____ that are determined by demand and supply.

8. In market economies, money functions chiefly as a medium of (commerce, exchange) _____. Barter between two individuals will take place only if there is a coincidence of (resources, wants) _____.

9. In a market system, government is active, but is assigned (a limited, an extensive) _____ role.

10. List the Five Fundamental Questions every economy must answer.

a. _____

b. _____

c. _____

d. _____

e. _____

11. Consumers vote with their dollars for the production of a good or service when they (sell, buy) _____ it, and because of this, consumers are said to be (dependent, sovereign) _____ in a market economy. The buying decisions of consumers (restrain, expand) _____ the possible choices of firms over what they produce so they make what is profitable.

12. Firms are interested in obtaining the largest economic profits possible, so they try to produce a product in the (most, least) _____ costly way. The most efficient production techniques depend on the available (income, technology) _____ and the (prices, quotas) _____ of needed resources.

13. The market system determines how the total output of the economy will be distributed among its households by determining the (incomes, expenditures) _____ of each household and by determining the (prices, quality) _____ for each good and service produced.

14. In market economies, change is almost continuous in consumer (preferences, resources) _____, in the supplies of _____, and in technology. To make the appropriate adjustments to these changes, a market economy allows price to perform its (monopoly, guiding) _____ function.

15. The market system fosters technological change. The incentive for a firm to be the first to use a new and improved technique of production or to produce a new and better product is a greater economic (profit, loss) _____, and the incentive for other firms to follow its lead is the avoidance of a _____.

16. Technological advance will require additional (capital, consumer) _____ goods, so the entrepreneur uses profit obtained from the sale of _____ goods to acquire (capital, consumer) _____ goods.

17. A market system promotes (unity, disunity) _____ between private and public interests. Firms and resource suppliers seem to be guided by (a visible, an invisible) _____ hand to allocate the economy's resources efficiently. The two *economic* arguments for a market system are that it promotes (public, efficient) _____ use of resources and that it uses (incentives, government) _____ for directing economic activity. The major *noneconomic* argument for the market system is that it allows for personal (wealth, freedom) _____.

18. Coordination and decision making in a market economy are (centralized, decentralized) _____, but in a command economy they are _____. The market system tends to produce a reasonably (efficient, inefficient) _____ allocation of resources, but in command economies it is _____ and results in production bottlenecks. As a command economy grows over time, the coordination problem becomes (more, less) _____ complex and indicators of economic performance are (adequate, inadequate) _____ for determining the success or failure of economic activities.

19. Another problem with the command economies is that economic incentives are (effective, ineffective) _____ for encouraging work or for giving signals to planners for efficient allocation of resources in the economy. Command economies do not have (production targets, entrepreneurship) _____ that is (are) important for technological advance, and because there was no business competition innovation (fostered, lagged) _____.

20. In the circular flow model,
  a. Households are buyers and businesses are sellers in (product, resource) _____ markets, and businesses are buyers and households are sellers in _____ markets.
  b. The flow of economic resources and finished goods and services is the (money, real) _____ flow, and the flow of income and expenditures is the _____ flow.

■ **TRUE–FALSE QUESTIONS**

Circle T if the statement is true, F if it is false.

1. A command economy is characterized by the private ownership of resources and the use of markets and prices to coordinate and direct economic activity.   **T F**

2. In a market system, the government owns most of the property resources (land and capital).   **T F**

3. Pure capitalism is also called *laissez-faire* capitalism.   **T F**

4. Property rights encourage investment, innovation, exchange, maintenance of property, and economic growth.   **T F**

5. The freedom of business firms to produce a particular consumer good is always limited by the desires of consumers for that good.   **T F**

6. The pursuit of economic self-interest is the same thing as selfishness.   **T F**

7. When a market is competitive, the individual sellers of a product are unable to reduce the supply of the product and control its prices.   **T F**

8. The market system is an organizing mechanism and also a communication network.   **T F**

9. Increasing the amount of specialization in an economy generally leads to the more efficient use of its resources.   **T F**

10. One way human specialization can be achieved is through a division of labor in productive activity.   **T F**

11. Money is a device for facilitating the exchange of goods and services.   **T F**

12. "Coincidence of wants" means that two persons want to acquire the same good or service.   **T F**

13. Shells may serve as money if sellers are generally willing to accept them as money.   **T F**

14. One of the Five Fundamental Questions is who will control the output.   **T F**

15. Industries in which economic profits are earned by the firms in the industry will attract the entry of new firms.   **T F**

16. The consumers are sovereign in a market economy and register their economic wants with "dollar votes."   **T F**

17. Economic efficiency requires that a given output of a good or service be produced in the least costly way.   **T F**

18. If the market price of resource A decreases, firms will tend to employ smaller quantities of resource A.   **T F**

19. The incentive that the market system provides to induce technological improvement is the opportunity for economic profits.   **T F**

20. Creative destruction is the hypothesis that the creation of new products and production methods simultaneously destroys the market power of existing monopolies and businesses.   **T F**

21. The tendency for individuals pursuing their own self-interests to bring about results that are in the best interest of society as a whole is often called the "invisible hand."   **T F**

22. A basic economic argument for the market system is that it promotes an efficient use of resources.   **T F**

23. A command economy is significantly affected by missed production targets.   **T F**

24. Profit is the key indicator of success and failure in a command economy.   **T F**

25. In the circular flow model, there is a *real flow* of economic resources and finished goods and services and a *money flow* of income and consumption expenditures.   **T F**

■ MULTIPLE-CHOICE QUESTIONS

Circle the letter that corresponds to the best answer.

1. The private ownership of property resources and use of markets and prices to direct and coordinate economic activity is characteristic of
(a) socialism
(b) communism
(c) a market economy
(d) a command economy

2. Which is one of the main characteristics of the market system?
(a) central economic planning
(b) limits on freedom of choice
(c) the right to own private property
(d) an expanded role for government in the economy

3. In the market system, freedom of enterprise means that
(a) government is free to direct the actions of businesses
(b) businesses are free to produce products that consumers want
(c) consumers are free to buy goods and services that they want
(d) resources are distributed freely to businesses that want them

4. The maximization of profit tends to be the driving force in the economic decision making of
(a) workers
(b) consumers
(c) legislators
(d) entrepreneurs

5. How do consumers typically express self-interest?
(a) by minimizing their economic losses
(b) by maximizing their economic profits
(c) by seeking the lowest price for a product
(d) by seeking jobs with the highest wages and benefits

6. Which is a characteristic of competition as economists see it?
(a) a few sellers of all products
(b) the widespread diffusion of economic power
(c) a small number of buyers in product markets
(d) the relatively difficult entry into and exit from industries by producers

7. To decide how to use its scarce resources to satisfy economic wants, a market economy primarily relies on
(a) prices
(b) planning
(c) monopoly power
(d) production targets

8. The market system is a method of
(a) making economic decisions by central planning
(b) communicating and coordinating economic decisions
(c) promoting specialization, but not division of labor
(d) allocating money, but not economic profits or losses

9. When workers specialize in various tasks to produce a commodity, the situation is referred to as
(a) division of labor
(b) freedom of choice
(c) capital accumulation
(d) a coincidence of wants

10. In what way does human specialization contribute to an economy's output?
(a) It is a process of creative destruction.
(b) It serves as consumer sovereignty.
(c) It acts like an "invisible hand."
(d) It fosters learning by doing.

11. Which is a prerequisite of specialization?
(a) market restraints on freedom
(b) having a convenient means of exchanging goods
(c) letting government create a plan for the economy
(d) deciding who will get the goods and services in an economy

12. In the market system, the role of government is best described as
(a) limited
(b) extensive
(c) significant
(d) nonexistent

13. Which would necessarily result, sooner or later, from a decrease in consumer demand for a product?
(a) a decrease in the profits of firms in the industry
(b) an increase in the output of the industry
(c) an increase in the supply of the product
(d) an increase in the prices of resources employed by the firms in the industry

14. The demand for resources is
(a) increased when the price of resources falls
(b) most influenced by the size of government in a capitalist economy
(c) derived from the demand for the products made with the resources
(d) decreased when the product that the resources produce becomes popular

Answer Questions 15, 16, and 17 on the basis of the following information.

Suppose 50 units of product X can be produced by employing just labor and capital according to the four techniques (A, B, C, and D) shown below. Assume the prices of labor and capital are $5 and $4, respectively.

	A	B	C	D
Labor	1	2	3	4
Capital	5	3	2	1

15. Which technique is economically most efficient in producing product X?
(a) A
(b) B
(c) C
(d) D

16. If the price of product X is $1, the firm will realize
(a) an economic profit of $28
(b) an economic profit of $27
(c) an economic profit of $26
(d) an economic profit of $25

17. Now assume that the price of labor falls to $3 and the price of capital rises to $5. Which technique is economically most efficient in producing product X?
(a) A
(b) B
(c) C
(d) D

18. Which is the primary factor determining the share of the total output of the economy received by a household?
(a) the tastes of the household
(b) the medium of exchange used by the household
(c) the prices at which the household sells its resources
(d) ethical considerations in the operation of a market economy

19. If an increase in the demand for a product and a rise in its price cause an increase in the quantity supplied, price is successfully performing its
(a) guiding function
(b) circular flow role
(c) division-of-labor role
(d) medium-of-exchange function

20. In the market system, if one firm introduces a new and better method of production that enhances the firm's economic profits, other firms will be forced to adopt the new method to
(a) increase circular flow
(b) follow rules for capital accumulation
(c) avoid economic losses or bankruptcy
(d) specialize and divide the labor in an efficient way

21. The advent of personal computers and word processing software that eliminated the market for electric typewriters would be an example of
(a) specialization
(b) derived demand
(c) the "invisible hand"
(d) creative destruction

22. The chief economic virtue of the competitive market system is that it
(a) allows extensive personal freedom
(b) promotes the efficient use of resources
(c) provides an equitable distribution of income
(d) eliminates the need for decision making

23. In the system of central planning, the outputs of some industries became the inputs for other industries, but a failure of one industry to meet its production target would cause
(a) widespread unemployment
(b) inflation in wholesale and retail prices
(c) profit declines and potential bankruptcy of firms
(d) a chain reaction of production problems and bottlenecks

24. The two kinds of markets found in the circular flow model are
(a) real and money markets
(b) real and socialist markets
(c) money and command markets
(d) product and resource markets

25. In the circular flow model, businesses
(a) buy products and resources
(b) sell products and resources
(c) buy products and sell resources
(d) sell products and buy resources

■ PROBLEMS

1. Use the appropriate number to match the terms with the phrases below.

1. invisible hand   4. consumer sovereignty
2. coincidence of wants   5. creative destruction
3. division of labor   6. specialization

a. Using the resources of an individual, a firm, a region, or a nation to produce one (or a few) goods and services. _____
b. The tendency of firms and resource suppliers seeking to further their own self-interest while also promoting the interests of society in a market economy. _____
c. The situation where new products and production methods eliminate the market position of firms doing business using existing products or older production methods. _____
d. Splitting the work required to produce a product into a number of different tasks that are performed by different workers. _____
e. A situation in which the product the first trader wants to sell is the same as the product the second trader wants to buy, and the product the second trader wants to sell is the same as the product the first trader wants to buy. _____
f. Determination by consumers of the types and quantities of goods and services that will be produced in a market economy. _____

2. Assume that a firm can produce product A, product B, *or* product C with the resources it currently employs. These resources cost the firm a total of $50 per week. Assume, for the purposes of the problem, that the firm's employment of resources cannot be changed. Their market prices, and the quantities of A, B, and C these resources will produce per week are given in the table below. Compute the firm's profit when it produces A, B, or C, and enter these profits in the table.

Product	Market Price	Output	Economic Profit
A	$7.00	8	$_____
B	4.50	10	_____
C	.25	240	_____

a. Which product will the firm produce? _____

b. If the price of A rose to $8, the firm would

_____

(Hint: You will have to recompute the firm's profit from the production of A.)

c. If the firm were producing A and selling it at a price of $8, what would tend to happen to the number of firms producing A?

_____

3. Suppose that a firm can produce 100 units of product X by combining labor, land, capital, and entrepreneurial ability using three different methods. If it can hire labor at $2 per unit, land at $3 per unit, capital at $5 per unit, and entrepreneurship at $10 per unit, and if the amounts of the resources required by the three methods of producing 100 units of product X are as indicated in the table, answer the following questions.

Resource	Method 1	Method 2	Method 3
Labor	8	13	10
Land	4	3	3
Capital	4	2	4
Entrepreneurship	1	1	1

a. Which method is the least expensive way of producing 100 units of X? _____

b. If X sells for 70 cents per unit, what is the economic profit of the firm? $ _____

c. If the price of labor should rise from $2 to $3 per unit and if the price of X is 70 cents,

(1) the firm's use of

labor would change from _____ to _____

land would change from _____ to _____

capital would change from _____ to _____

entrepreneurship would not change

(2) The firm's economic profit would change from

$_____ to $_____

4. In the circular flow diagram below, the upper pair of flows (*a* and *b*) represents the resource market and the lower pair (*c* and *d*) the product market.

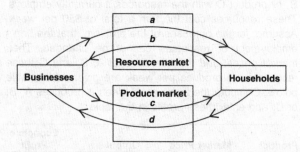

Supply labels or explanations for each of the four flows:

a. _____

b. _____

c. _____

d. _____

■ SHORT ANSWER AND ESSAY QUESTIONS

1. The command system and the market system differ in two important ways. Compare and contrast the two economic systems.

2. Explain the major characteristics—institutions and assumptions—embodied in a market system.

3. What do each of the following seek if they pursue their own self-interest: consumers, resource owners, and business firms?

4. Explain what economists mean by competition. For a market to be competitive, why is it important that there be buyers and sellers and easy entry and exit?

5. How does an economy benefit from specialization and the division of labor?

6. Give an example of how specialization can benefit two separate and diversely endowed geographic regions.

7. What is money? What important function does it perform? Explain how money performs this function and how it overcomes the disadvantages associated with barter.

8. In what way do the desires of entrepreneurs to obtain economic profits and avoid losses make consumer sovereignty effective?

9. Why is the ability of firms to enter industries that are prosperous important to the effective functioning of competition?

10. Explain in detail how an increase in the consumer demand for a product will result in more of the product being produced and more resources being allocated to its production.

11. Describe the production factor for businesses that determines what combinations of resources and technologies will be used to produce goods and services.

12. Who will get the output from a market economy? Explain.

13. How can the market system adapt to change? How is it done?

14. How do prices communicate information and guide and direct production in a market economy?

15. Explain how the market system provides a strong incentive for technological advance and creative destruction.

16. Who "votes" for the production of capital goods, why do they "vote" for capital goods production, and where do they obtain the dollars needed to cast these "votes"?

17. "An invisible hand operates to identify private and public interests." What are private interests and what is the public interest? What is it that leads the economy to operate as if it were directed by an invisible hand?

18. Describe three virtues of the market system.

19. Explain the two major economic problems with command economies and why market economies avoid such problems.

20. In the circular flow model, what are the two markets? What roles do households play and what roles do businesses play in each market?

ANSWERS

Chapter 2 The Market System and the Circular Flow

FILL-IN QUESTIONS

1. an economic system
2. publicly, is central planning
3. privately, are markets and prices
4. property, enterprise, choice
5. competition, are not
6. *a.* independently acting buyers and sellers operating in markets; *b.* freedom of buyers and sellers to enter or leave these markets
7. markets, prices
8. exchange, wants
9. a limited
10. *a.* What goods and services will be produced? *b.* How will the goods and services be produced? *c.* Who will get the goods and services? *d.* How will the system accommodate change? *e.* How will the system promote progress?
11. buy, sovereign, restrain
12. least, technology, prices
13. incomes, prices
14. preferences, resources, guiding
15. profit, loss
16. capital, consumer, capital
17. unity, an invisible, efficient, incentives, freedom
18. decentralized, centralized, efficient, inefficient, more inadequate
19. ineffective, entrepreneurship, lagged
20. *a.* product, resource; *b.* real, money

TRUE–FALSE QUESTIONS

1. F, p. 30	**10.** T, p. 33	**19.** T, p. 37
2. F, p. 30	**11.** T, pp. 33–34	**20.** T, p. 37
3. T, p. 30	**12.** F, p. 33	**21.** T, p. 38
4. T, pp. 30–31	**13.** T, p. 33	**22.** T, p. 38
5. T, p. 31	**14.** F, p. 34	**23.** T, pp. 38–39
6. F, pp. 31–32	**15.** T, pp. 34–35	**24.** F, pp. 38–39
7. T, p. 32	**16.** T, p. 35	**25.** T, pp. 39–40, 42
8. T, p. 32	**17.** T, pp. 35–36	
9. T, p. 33	**18.** F, p. 36	

MULTIPLE-CHOICE QUESTIONS

1. c, pp. 30–32	**10.** d, p. 33	**19.** a, pp. 36–37
2. c, pp. 30–31	**11.** b, p. 33	**20.** c, p. 37
3. b, p. 31	**12.** a, p. 34	**21.** d, p. 37
4. d, pp. 31–32	**13.** a, pp. 34–35	**22.** b, p. 38
5. c, pp. 31–32	**14.** c, pp. 35–36	**23.** d, p. 38
6. b, p. 32	**15.** b, pp. 35–36	**24.** d, pp. 39–40, 42
7. a, p. 32	**16.** a, pp. 35–36	**25.** d, pp. 39–40, 42
8. b, p. 32	**17.** d, pp. 35–36	
9. a, p. 33	**18.** c, p. 36	

PROBLEMS

1. *a.* 6; *b.* 1; *c.* 5; *d.* 3; *e.* 2; *f.* 4
2. $6, –$5, $10; *a.* C; *b.* produce A and have an economic profit of $14; *c.* it would increase
3. *a.* method 2; *b.* 15; *c.* (1) 13, 8; 3, 4; 2, 4; (2) 15, 4
4. *a.* money income payments (wages, rent, interest, and profit); *b.* services or resources (land, labor, capital, and entrepreneurial ability); *c.* goods and services; d. expenditures for goods and services

SHORT ANSWER AND ESSAY QUESTIONS

1. p. 30	**8.** pp. 34–35	**15.** p. 37
2. pp. 30–34	**9.** pp. 34–35	**16.** p. 37
3. pp. 31–32	**10.** pp. 34–35	**17.** p. 38
4. p. 32	**11.** pp. 35–36	**18.** p. 38
5. p. 33	**12.** p. 36	**19.** pp. 38–39
6. p. 33	**13.** pp. 36–37	**20.** pp. 39–40, 42
7. pp. 33–34	**14.** p. 37	

CHAPTER 3

Demand, Supply, and Market Equilibrium

Chapter 3 introduces you to the most fundamental tools of economic analysis: demand and supply. Demand and supply are simply "boxes" or categories into which all the forces and factors that affect the price and the quantity of a good bought and sold in a competitive market are placed. Demand and supply determine price and quantity exchanged. It is necessary to understand *why* and *how* they do this.

Many students never learn to *define* demand and supply. They never learn (1) what an increase or decrease in demand or supply means, (2) the important distinctions between "demand" and "quantity demanded" and between "supply" and "quantity supplied," and (3) the equally important distinctions between a change in demand and a change in quantity demanded, and between a change in supply and a change in quantity supplied.

Having learned these, however, it is no great trick to comprehend the so-called laws of demand and supply. The equilibrium price—that is, the price that will tend to prevail in the market as long as demand and supply do not change—is simply the price at which **quantity demanded** and **quantity supplied** are equal. The quantity bought and sold in the market (the equilibrium quantity) is the quantity demanded and supplied at the equilibrium price. If you can determine the equilibrium price and quantity under one set of demand and supply conditions, you can determine them under any other set.

This chapter includes a brief examination of the factors that determine demand and supply and the ways in which changes in these determinants will affect and cause changes in demand and supply. A graphic method is used in this analysis to illustrate demand and supply, equilibrium price and quantity, changes in demand and supply, and the resulting changes in equilibrium price and quantity. The **demand curve** and the **supply curve** are graphic representations of the same data contained in the schedules of demand and supply.

The application section at the end of the chapter explains government-set prices. When the government sets a legal price in a competitive market, it creates a **price ceiling** or **price floor.** This prevents supply and demand from determining the equilibrium price and quantity of a product that will be provided by a competitive market. As you will learn, the economic consequence of a price ceiling is that it will result in a persistent shortage of the product. An example of a price ceiling would be price controls on apartment rents. A price floor will result in a persistent surplus of a product, and the example given is price supports for an agricultural product.

You will use demand and supply over and over. It will turn out to be as important to you in economics as jet propulsion is to the pilot of an airplane: You can't get off the ground without it.

■ **CHECKLIST**

When you have studied this chapter you should be able to

☐ Explain the economic meaning of markets.
☐ Define demand and state the law of demand.
☐ Give three explanations for the inverse relationship between price and quantity demanded.
☐ Graph the demand curve when you are given a demand schedule.
☐ Explain the difference between individual demand and market demand.
☐ List the five major determinants of demand and explain how each one shifts the demand curve.
☐ Explain how changes in income affect the demand for normal goods and inferior goods.
☐ Explain how changes in the prices of a substitute good or a complementary good affect the demand for a product.
☐ Distinguish between change in demand and change in the quantity demanded.
☐ Define supply and state the law of supply.
☐ Graph the supply curve when given a supply schedule.
☐ Explain the difference between individual supply and market supply.
☐ List the major determinants of supply and explain how each shifts the supply curve.
☐ Distinguish between changes in supply and changes in the quantity supplied.
☐ Describe how the equilibrium price and quantity are determined in a competitive market.
☐ Define surplus and shortage.
☐ Determine, when you are given the demand for and the supply of a good, the equilibrium price and the equilibrium quantity.
☐ Explain the meaning of the rationing function of prices.
☐ Distinguish between productive efficiency and allocative efficiency.
☐ Predict the effects of changes in demand on equilibrium price and quantity.
☐ Predict the effects of changes in supply on equilibrium price and quantity.
☐ Predict the effects of changes in both demand and supply on equilibrium price and quantity.

☐ Explain the economic effects of a government-set price ceiling on product price and quantity in a competitive market.

☐ Describe the economic consequences of a government-set price floor on product price and quantity.

■ **CHAPTER OUTLINE**

1. A market is any institution or mechanism that brings together buyers ("demanders") and sellers ("suppliers") of a particular good or service. This chapter assumes that markets are highly competitive.

2. Demand is a schedule of prices and the quantities that buyers would purchase at each of these prices during a selected period of time.

    a. The **law of demand** states that there is an inverse or negative relationship between price and quantity demanded. Other things equal, as price increases, buyers will purchase fewer quantities, and as price decreases they will purchase more quantities. There are three explanations for the law of demand:

    (1) **Diminishing marginal utility:** After a point, consumers get less satisfaction or benefit from consuming more and more units.

    (2) **Income effect.** A higher price for a good decreases the purchasing power of consumers' incomes so they can't buy as much of the good.

    (3) **Substitution effect.** A higher price for a good encourages consumers to search for cheaper substitutes and thus buy less of it.

    b. The **demand curve** has a downward slope and is a graphic representation of the law of demand.

    c. Market demand for a good is a sum of all the demands of all consumers of that good at each price. Although price has the most important influence on quantity demanded, other factors can influence demand. The factors, called **determinants of demand** are consumer tastes (preferences), the number of buyers in the market, consumers' income, the prices of related goods, and consumer expectations.

    d. An increase or decrease in the entire demand schedule and the demand curve (a change in demand) results from a change in one or more of the determinants of demand. For a particular good,

    (1) an increase in *consumer tastes or preferences* increases its demand;

    (2) an increase in *the number of buyers* increases its demand;

    (3) *consumers' income* increases its demand if it is a **normal good** (one where income and demand are positively related), but an increase in consumers' income decreases its demand if it is an **inferior good** (one where income and demand are negatively related);

    (4) an increase in *the price of a related good* will increase its demand if the related good is a **substitute good** (one that can be used in place of another) but an increase in the price of a related good will decrease its demand if the related good is a **complementary good** (one that is used with another good).

    (5) an increase in *consumer expectations* of a future price increase or a future rise in income increases its current demand.

    e. A **change in demand** means that the entire demand curve or schedule has changed because of a change in one of the above determinants of demand, but a **change in the quantity demanded** means that there has been a movement along an existing demand curve or schedule because of a change in price.

3. Supply is a schedule of prices and the quantities that sellers will sell at each of these prices during some period of time.

    a. The **law of supply** shows a positive relationship between price and quantity supplied. Other things equal, as the price of the good increases more quantities will be offered for sale, and that as the price of the good decreases, fewer quantities will be offered for sale.

    b. The **supply curve** is a graphic representation of supply and the law of supply; it has an upward slope indicating the positive relationship between price and quantity supplied.

    c. The market supply of a good is the sum of the supplies of all sellers or producers of the good at each price.

    d. Although price has the most important influence on the quantity supplied, other factors can also influence supply. The factors, called **determinants of supply,** are changes in (1) resource prices; (2) technology; (3) taxes and subsidies; (4) prices of other good; (5) price expectation; and (6) the number of sellers in a market.

    e. A **change in supply** is an increase or decrease in the entire supply schedule and the supply curve. It is the result of a change in one or more of the determinants of supply that affect the cost of production. For a particular product,

    (1) a decrease in *resource prices* increases its supply;

    (2) an improvement in technology increases its supply;

    (3) a decrease in *taxes* or an increase in *subsidies* increases its supply;

    (4) a decrease in *the price of another good* that could be produced leads to an increase in its supply;

    (5) an increase in *producer expectations* of higher prices for the good may increase or decrease its supply.

    (6) an increase in the number of sellers or suppliers is likely to increase its supply.

    f. A **change in supply** means that the entire supply curve or schedule has changed because of a change in one of the above determinants of supply, but a **change in the quantity supplied** means that there has been a movement along an existing supply curve or schedule because of a change in price.

4. The **equilibrium price** (or *market-clearing price*) of a product is that price at which quantity demanded and quantity supplied are equal. The quantity exchanged in the market (the **equilibrium quantity**) is equal to the quantity demanded and supplied at the equilibrium price.

    a. If the price of a product is above the market equilibrium price, there will be a **surplus** or *excess supply*. In this case, the quantity demanded is less than the quantity supplied at that price.

b. If the price of a product is below the market equilibrium price, there will be a **shortage** or *excess demand*. In this case, the quantity demanded is greater than the quantity supplied at that price.

c. The rationing function of prices is the elimination of surpluses and shortages of a product.

d. Competitive markets produce **productive efficiency,** in which the goods and services society desires are being produced in the least costly way. They also create **allocative efficiency,** in which resources are devoted to the production of goods and services society most highly values.

e. Changes in supply and demand result in changes in the equilibrium price and quantity. The simplest cases are ones where demand changes and supply remains constant, or where supply changes and demand remains constant. More complex cases involve simultaneous changes in supply and demand.

(1) *Demand changes.* An increase in demand, with supply remaining the same, will increase the equilibrium price and quantity; a decrease in demand with supply remaining the same will decrease the equilibrium price and quantity.

(2) *Supply changes.* An increase in supply, with demand staying the same, will decrease the equilibrium price and increase the equilibrium quantity; a decrease in supply, with demand staying the same, will increase the equilibrium price and decrease the equilibrium quantity.

(3) *Complex cases.* These four cases involve changes in demand *and* supply: both increase; both decrease; one increases and one decreases; and, one decreases and one increases. For the possible effects on the equilibrium price and quantity in the four complex cases, see #4 in "Hints and Tips" section.

5. Supply and demand analysis has many important applications to government-set prices.

a. A **price ceiling** set by government prevents price from performing its rationing function in a market system. It creates a shortage (quantity demanded is greater than the quantity supplied) at the government-set price.

(1) Another rationing method must be found, so government often steps in and establishes one. But all rationing systems have problems because they exclude someone.

(2) A government-set price creates an illegal *black market* for those who want to buy and sell above the government-set price.

(3) One example of a legal price ceiling that creates a shortage would be rent control established in some cities to restrain the rental price of apartments.

b. A **price floor** is a minimum price set by government for the sale of a product or resource. It creates a surplus (quantity supplied is greater than the quantity demanded) at the fixed price. The surplus may induce the government to increase demand or decrease supply to eliminate the surplus. The use of price floors has often been applied to agricultural products such as wheat.

6. (Last Word). The supply and demand analysis can be used to understand the shortage of organ transplants. The demand curve for such organs is downsloping and the supply is fixed (vertical) and left of the zero price on the demand curve. Transplanted organs have a zero price. At that price the quantity demanded is much greater than the quantity supplied creating a shortage that is rationed with a waiting list. A competitive market for organs would increase the price of organs and then make more available for transplant (make the supply curve up-sloping), but there are moral and cost objections to this change.

■ HINTS AND TIPS

1. This chapter is the most important one in the book. Make sure you spend extra time on it and master the material. If you do, your long-term payoff will be a much easier understanding of the applications in later chapters.

2. One mistake students often make is to confuse **change in demand** with **change in quantity demanded.** A change in demand causes the entire demand curve to *shift*, whereas a change in quantity demanded is simply a *movement* along an existing demand curve.

3. It is strongly recommended that you draw supply and demand graphs as you work on supply and demand problems so you can see a picture of what happens when demand shifts, supply shifts, or both demand and supply shift.

4. Make a chart and related graphs that show the eight possible outcomes from changes in demand and supply. Figure 3.7 in the text illustrates the *four single shift* outcomes:

1. **D increase: P ↑, Q ↑**   3. **S increase: P ↓, Q ↑**
2. **D decrease: P ↓, Q ↓**   4. **S decrease: P ↑, Q ↓**

Four shift combinations are described in Table 3.3 of the text. Make a figure to illustrate each combination.

1. **S ↑, D ↓: P ↓, Q ?**   3. **S ↑, D ↑: P ?, Q ↑**
2. **S ↓, D ↑: P ↑, Q ?**   4. **S ↓, D ↓: P ?, Q ↓**

5. Make sure you understand the "other-things-equal" assumption described the Consider This box on salsa and coffee beans (p. 59). It will help you understand why the law of demand is not violated even if the price and quantity of a product increase over time.

6. Practice always helps in understanding graphs. Without looking at the textbook, draw a supply and demand graph with a **price ceiling** below the equilibrium price and show the resulting shortage in the market for a product. Then, draw a supply and demand graph with a **price floor** above the equilibrium price and show the resulting surplus. Explain to yourself what the graphs show. Check your graphs and your explanations by referring to textbook Figures 3.8 and 3.9 and the related explanations.

IMPORTANT TERMS

demand	law of demand
demand schedule	diminishing marginal utility

income effect

substitution effect

demand curve

determinants of demand

normal goods

inferior goods

substitute good

complementary good

change in demand

change in quantity
  demanded

supply

supply schedule

law of supply

supply curve

determinants of supply

change in supply

change in quantity supplied

equilibrium price

equilibrium quantity

surplus

shortage

productive efficiency

allocative efficiency

price ceiling

price floor

SELF-TEST

FILL-IN QUESTIONS

1. A market is the institution or mechanism that brings together buyers or (demanders, suppliers) _____ and sellers or _____ of a particular good or service.

2. The relationship between price and quantity in the demand schedule is (a direct, an inverse) _____ relationship; in the supply schedule the relationship is _____ one.

3. The added satisfaction or pleasure a consumer obtains from additional units of a product decreases as the consumer's consumption of the product increases. This phenomenon is called diminishing marginal (equilibrium, utility) _____.

4. A consumer tends to buy more of a product as its price falls because

  a. The purchasing power of the consumer is increased and the consumer tends to buy more of this product (and of other products); this is called the (income, substitution) _____ effect;

  b. The product becomes less expensive relative to similar products and the consumer tends to buy more of the original product and less of the similar products, which is called the _____ effect.

5. When demand or supply is graphed, price is placed on the (horizontal, vertical) _____ axis and quantity on the _____ axis.

6. The change from an individual to a market demand schedule involves (adding, multiplying) _____ the quantities demanded by each consumer at the various possible (incomes, prices) _____.

7. When the price of one product and the demand for another product are directly related, the two products are called (substitutes, complements) _____;

however, when the price of one product and the demand for another product are inversely related, the two products are called _____.

8. When a consumer demand schedule or curve is drawn up, it is assumed that five factors that determine demand are fixed and constant. These five determinants of consumer demand are

  a. _____

  b. _____

  c. _____

  d. _____

  e. _____

9. A decrease in demand means that consumers will buy (larger, smaller) _____ quantities at every price, or will pay (more, less) _____ for the same quantities.

10. A change in income or in the price of another product will result in a change in the (demand for, quantity demanded of) _____ the given product, while a change in the price of the given product will result in a change in the _____ the given product.

11. An increase in supply means that producers will make and be willing to sell (larger, smaller) _____ quantities at every price, or will accept (more, less) _____ for the same quantities.

12. A change in resource prices or the prices of other goods that could be produced will result in a change in the (supply, quantity supplied) _____ of the given product, but a change in the price of the given product will result in a change in the _____.

13. The fundamental factors that determine the supply of any commodity in the product market are

  a. _____

  b. _____

  c. _____

  d. _____

  e. _____

  f. _____

14. The equilibrium price of a product is the price at which quantity demanded is (greater than, equal to) _____ quantity supplied, and there (is, is not) _____ a surplus or a shortage at that price.

15. If quantity demanded is greater than quantity supplied, price is (above, below) _____ the equilibrium price; and the (shortage, surplus) _____ will cause the price to (rise, fall) _____. If quantity demanded is less than the quantity supplied, price is (above, below) _____ the equilibrium price, and the (shortage, surplus) _____ will cause the price to (rise, fall) _____.

16. In the spaces next to **a–h**, indicate the effect [*increase* (+), *decrease* (−), or *indeterminate* (?)] on equilibrium price (**P**) and equilibrium quantity (**Q**) of each of these changes in demand and/or supply.

	P	**Q**
a. Increase in demand, supply constant	____	____
b. Increase in supply, demand constant	____	____
c. Decrease in demand, supply constant	____	____
d. Decrease in supply, demand constant	____	____
e. Increase in demand, increase in supply	____	____
f. Increase in demand, decrease in supply	____	____
g. Decrease in demand, decrease in supply	____	____
h. Decrease in demand, increase in supply	____	____

17. If supply and demand establish a price for a good so that there is no shortage or surplus of the product, then price is successfully performing its (utility, rationing) _____ function. The price that is set is a market- (changing, clearing) _____ price.

18. A competitive market produces two types of efficiency: goods and services will be produced in the least costly way, so there will be (allocative, productive) _____ efficiency; and, resources are devoted to the production of the mix of goods and services society most wants, or there is _____ efficiency.

19. A price ceiling is the (minimum, maximum) _____ legal price a seller may charge for a product or service, whereas a price floor is the _____ legal price set by government.

20. If a price ceiling is below the market equilibrium price, a (surplus, shortage) _____ will arise in a competitive market, and if a price floor is above the market equilibrium price, a (surplus, shortage) _____ will arise in a competitive market.

■ **TRUE–FALSE QUESTIONS**

Circle T if the statement is true, F if it is false.

1. A market is any arrangement that brings together the buyers and sellers of a particular good or service. **T   F**

2. Demand is the amount of a good or service that a buyer will purchase at a particular price. **T   F**

3. The law of demand states that as price increases, other things being equal, the quantity of the product demanded increases. **T   F**

4. The law of diminishing marginal utility is one explanation of why there is an inverse relationship between price and quantity demanded. **T   F**

5. The substitution effect suggests that, at a lower price, you have the incentive to substitute the more expensive product for similar products which are relatively less expensive. **T   F**

6. There is no difference between individual demand schedules and the market demand schedule for a product. **T   F**

7. In graphing supply and demand schedules, supply is put on the horizontal axis and demand on the vertical axis. **T   F**

8. If price falls, there will be an increase in demand. **T   F**

9. If consumer tastes or preferences for a product decrease, the demand for the product will tend to decrease. **T   F**

10. An increase in income will tend to increase the demand for a product. **T   F**

11. When two products are substitute goods, the price of one and the demand for the other will tend to move in the same direction. **T   F**

12. If two goods are complementary, an increase in the price of one will tend to increase the demand for the other. **T   F**

13. A change in the quantity demanded means that there has been a change in demand. **T   F**

14. Supply is a schedule that shows the amounts of a product a producer can make in a limited time period. **T   F**

15. An increase in resource prices will tend to decrease supply. **T   F**

16. A government subsidy for the production of a product will tend to decrease supply. **T   F**

17. An increase in the prices of other goods that could be made by producers will tend to decrease the supply of the current good that the producer is making. **T   F**

18. A change in supply means that there is a movement along an existing supply curve. **T   F**

19. A surplus indicates that the quantity demanded is less than the quantity supplied at that price. **T   F**

20. If the market price of a product is below its equilibrium price, the market price will tend to rise because demand will decrease and supply will increase. **T   F**

21. The rationing function of prices is the elimination of shortages and surpluses. **T   F**

22. Allocative efficiency means that goods and services are being produced by society in the least costly way. **T   F**

23. If the supply of a product increases and demand decreases, the equilibrium price and quantity will increase.

T   F

24. If the demand for a product increases and the supply of the product decreases, the equilibrium price will increase and equilibrium quantity will be indeterminate.

T   F

25. A price ceiling set by government below the competitive market price of a product will result in a surplus.

T   F

■ **MULTIPLE-CHOICE QUESTIONS**

Circle the letter that corresponds to the best answer.

1. A schedule that shows the various amounts of a product consumers are willing and able to purchase at each price in a series of possible prices during a specified period of time is called
(a) supply
(b) demand
(c) quantity supplied
(d) quantity demanded

2. The reason for the law of demand can best be explained in terms of
(a) supply
(b) complementary goods
(c) the rationing function of prices
(d) diminishing marginal utility

3. Assume that the price of video game players falls. What will most likely happen to the equilibrium price and quantity of video games, assuming this market is competitive?
(a) Price will increase; quantity will decrease.
(b) Price will decrease; quantity will increase.
(c) Price will decrease; quantity will decrease.
(d) Price will increase; quantity will increase.

4. Given the following individuals' demand schedules for product X, and assuming these are the only three consumers of X, which set of prices and output levels below will be on the market demand curve for this product?

Price X	Consumer 1 Q_{dx}	Consumer 2 Q_{dx}	Consumer 3 Q_{dx}
$5	1	2	0
4	2	4	0
3	3	6	1
2	4	8	2
1	5	10	3

(a) ($5, 2); ($1, 10)
(b) ($5, 3); ($1, 18)
(c) ($4, 6); ($2, 12)
(d) ($4, 0); ($1, 3)

5. Which change will decrease the demand for a product?
(a) a favorable change in consumer tastes
(b) an increase in the price of a substitute good

(c) a decrease in the price of a complementary good
(d) a decrease in the number of buyers

6. The income of a consumer decreases and the consumer's demand for a particular good increases. It can be concluded that the good is
(a) normal
(b) inferior
(c) a substitute
(d) a complement

7. Which of the following could cause a decrease in consumer demand for product X?
(a) a decrease in consumer income
(b) an increase in the prices of goods that are good substitutes for product X
(c) an increase in the price that consumers expect will prevail for product X in the future
(d) a decrease in the supply of product X

8. If two goods are substitutes for each other, an increase in the price of one will necessarily
(a) decrease the demand for the other
(b) increase the demand for the other
(c) decrease the quantity demanded of the other
(d) increase the quantity demanded of the other

9. If two products, A and B, are complements, then
(a) an increase in the price of A will decrease the demand for B
(b) an increase in the price of A will increase the demand for B
(c) an increase in the price of A will have no significant effect on the price of B
(d) a decrease in the price of A will decrease the demand for B

10. If two products, X and Y, are independent goods, then
(a) an increase in the price of X will significantly increase the demand for Y
(b) an increase in the price of Y will significantly increase the demand for X
(c) an increase in the price of Y will have no significant effect on the demand for X
(d) a decrease in the price of X will significantly increase the demand for Y

11. The law of supply states that, other things being constant, as price increases
(a) supply increases
(b) supply decreases
(c) quantity supplied increases
(d) quantity supplied decreases

12. If the supply curve moves from S_1 to S_2 on the graph in the next column, there has been
(a) an increase in supply
(b) a decrease in supply

(c) an increase in quantity supplied
(d) a decrease in quantity supplied

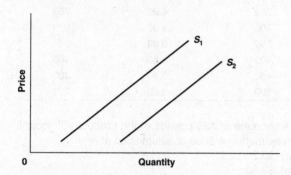

13. A decrease in the supply of a product would most likely be caused by
(a) an increase in business taxes
(b) an increase in consumer incomes
(c) a decrease in resource costs for production
(d) a decrease in the price of a complementary good

14. If the quantity supplied of a product is greater than the quantity demanded for a product, then
(a) there is a shortage of the product
(b) there is a surplus of the product
(c) the product is a normal good
(d) the product is an inferior good

15. If the price of a product is below the equilibrium price, the result will be
(a) a surplus of the good
(b) a shortage of the good
(c) a decrease in the supply of the good
(d) an increase in the demand for the good

16. Which would be the best example of allocative efficiency? When society devoted resources to the production of
(a) slide rules instead of handheld calculators
(b) horse-drawn carriages instead of automobiles
(c) computers with word processors instead of typewriters
(d) long-playing records instead of compact discs

Answer Questions 17, 18, and 19 on the basis of the data in the following table. Consider the following supply and demand schedules for bushels of corn.

Price	Quantity demanded	Quantity Supplied
$20	395	200
22	375	250
24	350	290
26	320	320
28	280	345
30	235	365

17. The equilibrium price in this market is
(a) $22
(b) $24

(c) $26
(d) $28

18. An increase in the cost of labor lowers the quantity supplied by 65 bushels at each price. The new equilibrium price would be
(a) $22
(b) $24
(c) $26
(d) $28

19. If the quantity demanded at each price increases by 130 bushels, then the new equilibrium quantity will be
(a) 290
(b) 320
(c) 345
(d) 365

20. A decrease in supply and a decrease in demand will
(a) increase price and decrease the quantity exchanged
(b) decrease price and increase the quantity exchanged
(c) increase price and affect the quantity exchanged in an indeterminate way
(d) affect price in an indeterminate way and decrease the quantity exchanged

21. An increase in demand and a decrease in supply will
(a) increase price and increase the quantity exchanged
(b) decrease price and decrease the quantity exchanged
(c) increase price and the effect upon quantity exchanged will be indeterminate
(d) decrease price and the effect upon quantity exchanged will be indeterminate

22. An increase in supply and an increase in demand will
(a) increase price and increase the quantity exchanged
(b) decrease price and increase the quantity exchanged
(c) affect price in an indeterminate way and decrease the quantity exchanged
(d) affect price in an indeterminate way and increase the quantity exchanged

23. A cold spell in Florida devastates the orange crop. As a result, California oranges command a higher price. Which of the following statements best explains the situation?
(a) The supply of Florida oranges decreases, causing the supply of California oranges to increase and their price to increase.
(b) The supply of Florida oranges decreases, causing their price to increase and the demand for California oranges to increase.
(c) The supply of Florida oranges decreases, causing the supply of California oranges to decrease and their price to increase.
(d) The demand for Florida oranges decreases, causing a greater demand for California oranges and an increase in their price.

Answer Questions 24, 25, 26, and 27 based on the following graph showing the market supply and demand for a product.

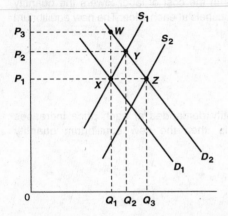

24. Assume that the market is initially in equilibrium where D_1 and S_1 intersect. If there is an increase in the number of buyers, then the new equilibrium would most likely be at point

(a) *W*
(b) *X*
(c) *Y*
(d) *Z*

25. Assume that the equilibrium price and quantity in the market are P_2 and Q_2. Which factor would cause the equilibrium price and quantity to shift to P_1 and Q_3?

(a) an increase in product price
(b) an increase in demand
(c) an increase in supply
(d) a decrease in quantity

26. What would cause a shift in the equilibrium price and quantity from point *Z* to point *X*?

(a) a decrease in production costs and more favorable consumer tastes for the product
(b) an increase in the number of suppliers and an increase in consumer incomes
(c) an increase in production costs and a decrease in consumer incomes
(d) an improvement in production technology and a decrease in the price of a substitute good

27. Assume that the market is initially in equilibrium where D_1 and S_1 intersect. If consumer incomes increased and the technology for making the product improved, then new equilibrium would most likely be at

(a) P_1 and Q_1
(b) P_2 and Q_2
(c) P_1 and Q_3
(d) P_3 and Q_1

28. The demand curve and its inverse relationship between price and quantity demanded is based on the assumption of

(a) other things equal
(b) complementary goods
(c) increasing marginal utility
(d) changing consumer expectations

Questions 29 and 30 relate to the following table that shows a hypothetical supply and demand schedule for a product.

Quantity demanded (pounds)	Price (per pound)	Quantity supplied (pounds)
200	$4.40	800
250	4.20	700
300	4.00	600
350	3.80	500
400	3.60	400
450	3.40	300
500	3.20	200

29. A shortage of 150 pounds of the product will occur if a government-set price is established at

(a) $3.20
(b) $3.40
(c) $3.80
(d) $4.00

30. If a price floor set by the government is established at $4.20, there will be a

(a) surplus of 300 pounds
(b) shortage of 300 pounds
(c) surplus of 450 pounds
(d) shortage of 450 pounds

■ **PROBLEMS**

1. Using the demand schedule below, plot the demand curve on the graph below the schedule. Label the axes and indicate for each axis the units being used to measure price and quantity.

Price	Quantity demanded 1000 bushels of soybeans
$7.20	10
7.00	15
6.80	20
6.60	25
6.40	30
6.20	35

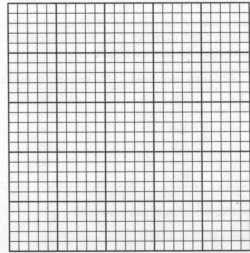

a. Plot the following supply schedule on the same graph.

Price	Quantity demanded 1000 bushels of soybeans
$7.20	40
7.00	35
6.80	30
6.60	25
6.40	20
6.20	15

b. The equilibrium price of soybeans will be $____.
c. How many thousand bushels of soybeans will be exchanged at this price? _____
d. Indicate clearly on the graph the equilibrium price and quantity by drawing lines from the intersection of the supply and demand curves to the price and quantity axes.
e. If the Federal government supported a price of $7.00 per bushel there would be a (shortage, surplus) _____ of _____ bushels of soybeans.

2. The demand schedules of three individuals (Ellie, Sam, and Lynn) for loaves of bread are shown in the following table. Assuming there are only three buyers of bread, determine and graph the total or market demand schedule for bread.

Price	Quantity demanded, loaves of bread			
	Ellie	Sam	Lynn	Total
$1.50	1	4	0	____
1.40	3	5	1	____
1.30	6	6	5	____
1.20	10	7	10	____
1.10	15	8	16	____

3. Following is a demand schedule for bushels of apples. In columns 3 and 4 insert any new figures for quantity that represent in column 3 an increase in demand and in column 4 a decrease in demand.

(1) Price	(2) Quantity demanded	(3) Demand increases	(4) Demand decreases
$6.00	400	____	____
5.90	500	____	____
5.80	600	____	____
5.70	700	____	____
5.60	800	____	____
5.50	900	____	____

4. Assume that O'Rourke has, when his income is $100 per week, the demand schedule for good A shown in columns 1 and 2 of the following table and the demand schedule for good B shown in columns 4 and 5. Assume that the prices of A and B are $.80 and $5, respectively.

Demand for A (per week)			Demand for B (per week)		
(1) Price	(2) Quantity demanded	(3) Quantity demanded	(4) Price	(5) Quantity demanded	(6) Quantity demanded
$.90	10	0	$5.00	4	7
.85	20	10	4.50	5	8
.80	30	20	4.00	6	9
.75	40	30	3.50	7	10
.70	50	40	3.00	8	11
.65	60	50	2.50	9	12
.60	70	60	2.00	10	13

a. How much A will O'Rourke buy? _____
How much B?_____
b. Suppose that as a consequence of a $10 increase in O'Rourke's weekly income, the quantities demanded of A become those shown in column 3 and the quantities demanded of B become those shown in column 6.

(1) How much A will he now buy? _____
How much B? _____

(2) Good A is (normal, inferior) _____.
(3) Good B is _____.

5. The market demand for good X is shown in columns 1 and 2 of the following table. Assume the price of X to be $2 and constant.

(1) Price	(2) Quantity demanded	(3) Quantity demanded	(4) Quantity demanded
$2.40	1600	1500	1700
2.30	1650	1550	1750
2.20	1750	1650	1850
2.10	1900	1800	2000
2.00	2100	2000	2200
1.90	2350	2250	2450
1.80	2650	2550	2750

a. If as the price of good Y rises from $1.25 to $1.35, the quantities demanded of good X become those shown in column 3, it can be concluded that X and Y are (substitute, complementary) _____ goods.

b. If as the price of good Y rises from $1.25 to $1.35, the quantities of good X become those shown in column 4, it can be concluded that X and Y are _____ goods.

6. The existing demand and supply schedules are given in columns 1, 2, and 3 of the following table.

Demand and Supply Schedules			New Demand and Supply Schedules		
(1) Price	(2) Quantity demanded	(3) Quantity supplied	(4) Price	(5) Quantity demanded	(6) Quantity supplied
$5.00	10	50	$5.00	____	____
4.00	20	40	4.00	____	____
3.00	30	30	3.00	____	____
2.00	40	20	2.00	____	____
1.00	50	10	1.00	____	____

a. Now the demand *increases* by 10 units at each price and supply *decreases* by 10 units. Enter the new amounts for quantity demanded and quantity supplied in columns 5 and 6.

b. What was the old equilibrium price? _____

What will be the new equilibrium price? _____

c. What was the old equilibrium quantity? _____

What will be the new equilibrium quantity? _____

7. In a local market for hamburger on a given date, each of 300 identical sellers of hamburger has the following supply schedule.

(1) Price	(2) Quantity supplied—one seller, lbs	(3) Quantity supplied—all sellers, lbs
$2.05	150	_____
2.00	110	_____
1.95	75	_____
1.90	45	_____
1.85	20	_____
1.80	0	_____

a. In column 3 construct the market supply schedule for hamburger.

b. Following is the market demand schedule for hamburger on the same date and in the same local market as that given above.

Price	Quantity demanded, lbs
$2.05	28,000
2.00	31,000
1.95	36,000
1.90	42,000
1.85	49,000
1.80	57,000

If the federal government sets a price on hamburger of $1.90 a pound, the result would be a (shortage, surplus)

_____ of _____ pounds of hamburger in this market.

8. Each of the following events would tend to increase or decrease either the demand for or the supply of electronic games and, as a result, will increase or decrease the price of these games. In the first blank indicate the effect on demand or supply (increase, decrease); in the second blank, indicate the effect on price (increase, decrease). Assume that the market for electronic games is a competitive one.

a. It becomes known by consumers that there is going to be a major sale on these games one month from now.

_____ ; _____

b. The workers in the electronic games industry receive a $3 an hour wage increase. _____ ;

_____

c. It is announced by a respected research institute that children who play electronic games also improve their grades in school. _____ ;

_____

d. Because of an increase in productivity, the amount of labor necessary to produce a game decreases.

_____ ; _____

e. The consumers who play these games believe that a shortage of the games is developing in the economy.

_____ ; _____

f. The federal government imposes a $5 tax per game on the manufacturers of the electronic games.

_____ ; _____

■ SHORT ANSWER AND ESSAY QUESTIONS

1. Define demand and the law of demand.

2. Use the diminishing marginal utility concept to explain why the quantity demanded of a product will tend to rise when the price of the product falls.

3. In past decades, the price of coffee in the United States rose significantly as a result of bad weather in coffee-producing regions. Use the income effect and the substitution effect concepts to explain why the quantity of coffee demanded in the United States significantly decreased.

4. What is the difference between individual demand and market demand? What is the relationship between these two types of demand?

5. Explain the difference between an increase in demand and an increase in the quantity demanded.

6. What are the factors that cause a change in demand? Use supply and demand graphs to illustrate what happens to price and quantity when demand increases.

7. How are inferior and normal (or superior) goods defined? What is the relationship between these goods and changes in income?

8. Why does the effect of a change in the price of related goods depend on whether a good is a substitute or complement? What are substitutes and complements?

9. A newspaper reports that "blue jeans have become even more popular and are now the standard clothing that people wear for both play and work." How will this change affect the demand for blue jeans? What will happen to the price and quantity of blue jeans sold in the market? Explain and use a supply and demand graph to illustrate your answer.

10. Compare and contrast the supply schedule with the demand schedule.

11. Supply does not remain constant for long because the factors that determine supply change. What are these factors? How do changes in them affect supply?

12. Explain the difference between an increase in supply and an increase in the quantity supplied.

13. Describe and illustrate with a supply and demand graph the effect of an increase in supply on price and quantity. Do the same for a decrease in supply.

14. The U.S. Congress passes a law that raises the excise tax on gasoline by $1 per gallon. What effect will this change have on the demand and supply of gasoline? What will happen to gasoline prices and quantity? Explain and use a supply and demand graph to illustrate your answer.

15. Given the demand for and the supply of a commodity, what price will be the equilibrium price of this commodity? Explain why this price will tend to prevail in the market and why higher (lower) prices, if they do exist temporarily, will tend to fall (rise).

16. What is the relationship between the price of a product and a shortage of the product? What is the relationship between the price of a product and a surplus of the product?

17. Explain why competition implies both productive efficiency and allocative efficiency.

18. Analyze the following quotation and explain the fallacies contained in it: "An increase in demand will cause price to rise; with a rise in price, supply will increase and the increase in supply will push price down. Therefore, an increase in demand results in little change in price because supply will increase also."

19. What are the consequences of a price ceiling for a product if it is set below the equilibrium price? Illustrate your answer with a graph.

20. What are the economic problems with price floors? How have they been used by government?

ANSWERS

Chapter 3 Demand, Supply, and Market Equilibrium

FILL-IN QUESTIONS

1. demanders, suppliers
2. an inverse, a direct
3. utility
4. *a.* income; *b.* substitution
5. vertical, horizontal
6. adding, prices
7. substitutes, complements
8. *a.* the tastes or preferences of consumers; *b.* the number of consumers in the market; *c.* the money income of consumers; *d.* the prices of related goods; *e.* consumer expectations with respect to future prices and income (any order for *a–e*)
9. smaller, less
10. demand for, quantity demanded of
11. larger, less
12. supply, quantity supplied
13. *a.* the technology of production; *b.* resource prices; *c.* taxes and subsidies; *d.* prices of other goods; *e.* producer expectations of price; *f.* the number of sellers in the market (any order for *a–f*)
14. equal to, is not
15. below, shortage, rise, above, surplus, fall

16. *a.* +, +; *b.* −, +; *c.* −, −; *d.* +, −; *e.* ?, +; *f.* +, ?; *g.* ?, −; *h.* −, ?
17. rationing, clearing
18. productive, allocative
19. maximum, minimum
20. shortage, surplus

TRUE–FALSE QUESTIONS

1. T, p. 46	**10.** T, pp. 49–50	**19.** T, pp. 54–55
2. F, p. 46	**11.** T, p. 50	**20.** F, pp. 55–56
3. F, p. 47	**12.** F, p. 50	**21.** T, p. 56
4. T, p. 47	**13.** F, p. 51	**22.** F, pp. 56–57
5. F, p. 47	**14.** F, p. 51	**23.** F, pp. 57–58
6. F, pp. 47–48	**15.** T, pp. 52–53	**24.** T, pp. 57–58
7. F, pp. 46–47	**16.** F, p. 53	**25.** F, p. 59
8. F, pp. 48–49	**17.** T, p. 53	
9. T, p. 49	**18.** F, pp. 52–54	

MULTIPLE-CHOICE QUESTIONS

1. b, p. 46	**11.** c, p. 51	**21.** c, pp. 57–58
2. d, p. 47	**12.** a, pp. 51–53	**22.** d, pp. 57–58
3. d, pp. 54–56	**13.** a, pp. 52–53	**23.** b, pp. 57–58
4. b, p. 48	**14.** b, pp. 54–55	**24.** c, pp. 57–58
5. d, pp. 49–50	**15.** b, pp. 54–55	**25.** c, pp. 57–58
6. b, pp. 49–50	**16.** c, pp. 56–57	**26.** c, pp. 57–58
7. a, pp. 49–50	**17.** c, pp. 54–55	**27.** c, pp. 57–58
8. b, p. 50	**18.** d, pp. 52–55	**28.** a, p. 46
9. a, p. 50	**19.** d, pp. 54–55	**29.** b, p. 59
10. c, p. 50	**20.** d, pp. 57–58	**30.** c, pp. 61–62

PROBLEMS

1. *a.* graph; *b.* 6.60; *c.* 25,000; *d.* graph; *e.* surplus, 20,000
2. Total: 5, 9, 17, 27, 39
3. Each quantity in column 3 is greater than in column 2, and each quantity in column 4 is less than in column 2.
4. *a.* 30, 4; *b.* (1) 20, 7; (2) inferior; (3) normal (superior)
5. *a.* complementary; *b.* substitute
6. *a.* column 5 (quantity demanded): 20, 30, 40, 50, 60; column 6 (quantity supplied): 40, 30, 20, 10, 0; *b.* $3.00, $4.00; *c.* 30, 30
7. *a.* 45,000; 33,000; 22,500; 13,500; 6,000; 0; *b.* shortage, 28,500
8. *a.* decrease demand, decrease price; *b.* decrease supply, increase price; *c.* increase demand, increase price; *d.* increase supply, decrease price; *e.* increase demand, increase price; *f.* decrease supply, increase price

SHORT ANSWER AND ESSAY QUESTIONS

1. pp. 46–47	**8.** p. 50	**15.** pp. 54–55
2. p. 47	**9.** pp. 48–49	**16.** pp. 54–56
3. p. 47	**10.** pp. 46–47, 51	**17.** pp. 56–57
4. p. 48	**11.** pp. 52–54	**18.** pp. 57–58
5. p. 51	**12.** pp. 52–54	**19.** pp. 59–61
6. p. 50	**13.** pp. 57–58	**20.** pp. 61–62
7. pp. 49–50	**14.** pp. 57–58	

Additional Examples of Supply and Demand

The first section of the appendix gives more examples of the effects of **changes in supply and demand** on price and quantity. You first will read about simple changes in which either the demand curve changes or the supply curve changes, but not both. These simple changes result in predictable effects on the price and quantity of a product, such as lettuce or corn. Then you are given examples of complex changes, using pink salmon, gasoline, and sushi. In these cases, there is a simultaneous shift in supply and demand. Here the effect of changes in supply and demand on price and quantity will be less certain and will depend on the direction and extent of the changes.

The appendix then extends your understanding of what happens in markets if **pre-set prices** are above or below the equilibrium price. You have already learned that when the government intervenes in a competitive market and sets the price below equilibrium (a price ceiling), it creates a shortage of a product. Similarly, when government sets a price above the equilibrium price (a price floor), it will result in a surplus. As you will learn, shortages and surpluses can also occur in competitive markets when sellers set the price in advance of sales and that pre-set price turns out to be below or above the equilibrium or actual price. The examples given in the text are ticket prices for sporting events that are priced too low or too high by the sellers, resulting in shortages and surpluses.

Supply and demand analysis is one of the most important means for improving your understanding of the economic world. If you master its use, it will help you explain many events and outcomes in everyday life. This appendix helps you achieve that mastery and understanding.

■ **APPENDIX CHECKLIST**

When you have studied this appendix you should be able to

☐ Explain and graph the effect of a decrease in the supply of a product (lettuce) on its equilibrium price and quantity.
☐ Describe and graph the effect of an increase in the demand for a product (corn) on its equilibrium price and quantity.
☐ Discuss and graph the effects of an increase in the supply of and a decrease in demand for a product (pink salmon) on its equilibrium price and quantity.

☐ Predict and graph the effects of a decrease in the supply of and an increase in the demand for a product (gasoline) on its equilibrium price and quantity.
☐ Explain and graph the effects of an equal increase in the supply of and demand for a product (sushi) on its equilibrium price and quantity.
☐ Discuss and graph how a seller price for a service (Olympic figure skating finals) that is set below the equilibrium price will result in a shortage.
☐ Describe and graph how a seller price for a service (Olympic curling preliminaries) that is set above the equilibrium price will result in a surplus.

■ **APPENDIX OUTLINE**

1. **Changes in supply and demand** result in changes in the equilibrium price and quantity. The simplest cases are ones where demand changes and supply remains constant, or where supply changes and demand remains constant. More complex cases involve simultaneous changes in supply and demand.

  a. *Supply increase.* In a competitive market for lettuce, if a severe freeze destroys a portion of the lettuce crop, then the supply of lettuce will decrease. The decrease in the supply of lettuce, with demand remaining the same, will increase the equilibrium price and decrease the equilibrium quantity.

  b. *Demand increase.* In a competitive market for corn, an increase in the demand for ethanol will increase the demand for corn because corn is used to make ethanol. This increase in the demand for corn, with supply remaining the same, will increase the equilibrium price and quantity of corn.

  c. *Supply increase and demand decrease.* Over the years, improved fishing techniques and technology contributed to an increase in the supply of pink salmon. Also, an increase in consumer incomes and a lowering of the price of substitute fish contributed to reducing the demand for pink salmon. As a result the price of pink salmon fell. The equilibrium quantity could have increased, decreased, or stayed the same. In this case, the increase in supply was greater than the decrease in demand, so the equilibrium quantity increased.

  d. *Demand increase and supply decrease.* An increase in the price of oil, a resource used to produce gasoline, resulted in a decrease in the supply of gasoline. At the same time, rising incomes and a stronger economy created a greater demand for gasoline. This decrease in supply and increase in demand increased the equilibrium price. The equilibrium quantity could have increased, decreased, or stayed the same. In this case, the decrease in supply was less than the increase in demand, so the equilibrium quantity increased.

e. *Demand increase and supply increase.* An increase in the taste for sushi among U.S. consumers resulted in an increase in the demand for this product. At the same time, there was an increase in the number of sushi bars and other food outlets that provide sushi, thus increasing its supply. This increase in both demand and supply increased the equilibrium quantity of sushi. The equilibrium price could have increased, decreased, or stayed the same. In this case, the increase in demand was the same as the increase in supply, so the equilibrium price remained the same.

2. ***Pre-set prices*** that the seller establishes below or above the equilibrium price can produce shortages and surpluses. If a price is set below the equilibrium price by a seller, then at that pre-set price the quantity demanded is greater than the quantity supplied, resulting in a ***shortage.*** If a price is set above the equilibrium price by a seller, then at that pre-set price the quantity demanded is less than the quantity supplied, resulting in a ***surplus.***

a. The shortage is typical of the market for tickets to more popular sporting events such as Olympic figure skating finals. The shortage of tickets at the pre-set price creates a secondary market (*black market*) for tickets in which buyers bid for tickets held by the initial purchaser. The ticket scalping drives up the price of tickets.

b. The surplus is typical of the market for tickets to less popular sporting events such as Olympic curling preliminaries at which there are many empty seats.

■ **HINTS AND TIPS**

1. This appendix offers applications and extensions of Chapter 3 in the textbook, so check your understanding of the corresponding text and appendix sections: (a) Review the Chapter 3 section on "Changes in Supply, Demand, and Equilibrium" (pp. 57–59) before reading the Web appendix section on "Changes in Supply and Demand"; and (b) review the text Chapter 3 section on "Application: Government-Set Prices" (pp. 59–62) before reading the appendix section on "Pre-Set Prices."

2. Correct terminology is important for mastering supply and demand analysis. You must remember the distinction between a change in demand and a change in quantity demanded or a change in supply and a change in quantity supplied. Consider the case of a single shift in demand with supply staying the same. As the demand curve increases along the existing supply curve, it increases the quantity supplied, but it does not increase supply (which would be a shift in the entire supply curve).

SELF-TEST

■ **FILL-IN QUESTIONS**

1. A decrease in the supply of lettuce will result in an equilibrium price that (increases, decreases) _____ and an equilibrium quantity that _____ .

2. An increase in the demand for corn will result in an equilibrium price that (increases, decreases) _____ and an equilibrium quantity that _____ .

3. An increase in the price of corn resulted in an increase in the (demand for, supply of) _____ farmland in the corn belt and a decrease in the _____ corn-fed beef.

4. An increase in the supply of pink salmon that is greater than the decrease in the demand for pink salmon will result in an equilibrium price that (increases, decreases, stays the same) _____ and an equilibrium quantity that _____ .

5. An increase in the demand for gasoline that is greater than the decrease in the supply of gasoline will result in an equilibrium price that (increases, decreases, stays the same) _____ and an equilibrium quantity that _____ .

6. A large increase in the price of gasoline is most likely to (increase, decrease) _____ the demand for low-gas-mileage SUVs and trucks and _____ the demand for high-gas-mileage hybrid cars.

7. An increase in the demand for sushi that is equal to the increase in the supply of sushi will result in an equilibrium price that (increases, decreases, stays the same) _____ and an equilibrium quantity that _____ .

8. If government sets a legal price for a product, a shortage would arise from a price (ceiling, floor) _____ and a surplus would arise from a price _____ .

9. If a pre-set price is set by the seller below the equilibrium price it will create a (surplus, shortage) _____ , but if a pre-set price is set by the seller above the equilibrium price it will create a _____ .

10. A market for tickets to popular sporting events in which buyers bid for tickets held by initial purchasers is referred to as a (primary, secondary) _____ market. In these markets, ticket (destruction, scalping) _____ occurs.

■ TRUE–FALSE QUESTIONS

Circle T if the statement is true, F if it is false.

1. An increase in the supply of lettuce decreases its equilibrium price and increases its equilibrium quantity.
T F

2. A decrease in the demand for tomatoes increases the equilibrium price and decreases the equilibrium quantity.
T F

3. When demand for corn increases, there is an increase in the quantity supplied as the equilibrium price rises, but no increase in supply.
T F

4. In the market for pink salmon, the reason that the equilibrium quantity increased was that the increase in supply was greater than the decrease in demand.
T F

5. In a market for beef, the equilibrium quantity will increase when the increase in supply is greater than the increase in demand.
T F

6. In the market for sushi, an equal increase in supply and demand will increase the equilibrium price, but have no effect on the equilibrium quantity.
T F

7. In a market for flat-screen TVs, an increase in supply that is greater than the increase in demand will result in a lower equilibrium price.
T F

8. If a seller pre-sets a price that turns out to be below the actual equilibrium price, a shortage will develop in the market.
T F

9. Ticket scalping often occurs in markets where there is a surplus of tickets.
T F

10. If a sporting event is not sold out, this indicates that the ticket prices for the event were pre-set above the actual equilibrium price.
T F

■ MULTIPLE-CHOICE QUESTIONS

Circle the letter that corresponds to the best answer.

1. Bad weather in coffee-producing regions of the world devastated the coffee crop. As a result, coffee prices increased worldwide. Which of the following statements best explains the situation?
  (a) The demand for coffee increased.
  (b) The supply of coffee decreased.
  (c) The demand for coffee increased and the supply of coffee increased.
  (d) The demand for coffee decreased and the supply of coffee decreased.

2. Assume that the supply of tomatoes in a competitive market increases. What will most likely happen to the equilibrium price and quantity of tomatoes?
  (a) Price will increase; quantity will decrease
  (b) Price will decrease; quantity will increase
  (c) Price will decrease; quantity will decrease
  (d) Price will increase; quantity will increase

3. Assume that the demand for security services increases in a competitive market. What will most likely happen to the equilibrium price and quantity of security services?
  (a) price will increase; quantity will decrease
  (b) price will decrease; quantity will increase
  (c) price will decrease; quantity will decrease
  (d) price will increase; quantity will increase

4. A decrease in the demand for beef is more than offset by an increase in its supply. As a result the equilibrium price will
  (a) increase and the equilibrium quantity will decrease
  (b) increase and the equilibrium quantity will increase
  (c) decrease and the equilibrium quantity will decrease
  (d) decrease and the equilibrium quantity will increase

5. A decrease in the supply of oil is more than offset by an increase in its demand. As a result, the equilibrium price will
  (a) increase and the equilibrium quantity will decrease
  (b) increase and the equilibrium quantity will increase
  (c) decrease and the equilibrium quantity will decrease
  (d) decrease and the equilibrium quantity will increase

6. An increase in the demand for lumber that is less than the increase in the supply of lumber will
  (a) increase the equilibrium price and quantity of lumber
  (b) decrease the equilibrium price and quantity of lumber
  (c) increase the equilibrium price and decrease the equilibrium quantity of lumber
  (d) decrease the equilibrium price and increase the equilibrium quantity of lumber

7. What will happen to the equilibrium quantity and price of a product in a competitive market when there is an equal increase in demand and supply?
  (a) equilibrium quantity and price will both increase
  (b) equilibrium quantity and price will both decrease
  (c) equilibrium quantity will increase and equilibrium price will stay the same
  (d) equilibrium quantity will stay the same and equilibrium price will increase

8. What will happen to the equilibrium quantity and price of a product in a competitive market when the decrease in demand exactly offsets the increase in supply?
  (a) equilibrium quantity will increase and equilibrium price will decrease
  (b) equilibrium quantity will decrease and equilibrium price will increase
  (c) equilibrium quantity will increase and equilibrium price will stay the same
  (d) equilibrium quantity will stay the same and equilibrium price will decrease

9. Which of the following is a correct statement?
  (a) price ceilings increase supply
  (b) price ceilings create shortages
  (c) price floors create shortages
  (d) price floors increase demand

10. If a seller sets a price for a product that turns out to be below the equilibrium price, then there will be a
(a) shortage of the product
(b) surplus of the product
(c) price floor for a product
(d) a zero price for the product

11. A surplus means that
(a) demand for a product is greater than the supply
(b) supply of the product is greater than the demand
(c) quantity demanded is less than the quantity supplied at that price
(d) quantity demanded is greater than the quantity supplied at that price

Answer Questions 12, 13, and 14 based on the following graph showing the market supply and demand for a product.

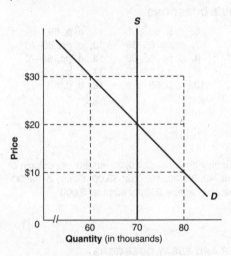

12. Given this market, if a seller pre-sets the price at $10, then this action results in a
(a) surplus of 10,000 units
(b) surplus of 80,000 units
(c) shortage of 10,000 units
(d) shortage of 80,000 units

13. Given this market, if a seller pre-sets the price at $30, then this action results in a
(a) surplus of 10,000 units
(b) surplus of 60,000 units
(c) surplus of 70,000 units
(d) shortage of 10,000 units

14. What price will eliminate a surplus or shortage in this market
(a) $0
(b) $10
(c) $20
(d) $30

15. A market for tickets in which buyers bid for tickets held by initial purchasers rather than the original seller is a
(a) primary market
(b) secondary market
(c) pre-set market
(d) surplus market

■ **PROBLEMS**

1. The existing demand and supply schedules are given in columns 1, 2, and 3 of the following table.

Demand and Supply Schedules			New Demand and Supply Schedules		
(1) Price	(2) Quantity demanded	(3) Quantity supplied	(4) Price	(5) Quantity demanded	(6) Quantity supplied
$5.00	10	50	$5.00	___	___
4.00	20	40	4.00	___	___
3.00	30	30	3.00	___	___
2.00	40	20	2.00	___	___
1.00	50	10	1.00	___	___

Now the demand *increases* by 10 units at each price and supply *decreases* by 10 units. Enter the new amounts for quantity demanded and quantity supplied in columns 5 and 6.

a. What was the old equilibrium price? _____

What will be the new equilibrium price? _____

b. What was the old equilibrium quantity? _____

What will be the new equilibrium quantity? _____

2. The demand and supply schedules for a certain product are those given in the following table. Answer the related questions.

Quantity demanded	Price	Quantity supplied
12,000	$10	18,000
13,000	9	17,000
14,000	8	16,000
15,000	7	15,000
16,000	6	14,000
17,000	5	13,000
18,000	4	12,000

The equilibrium price of the product is $ _____

and the equilibrium quantity is _____.
a. If a seller established a pre-set price of $5 on this product, there would be a (shortage, surplus)

_____ of _____ units.
b. If a seller established a pre-set price of $8, there

would be a (shortage, surplus) _____ of

_____ units.

■ **SHORT ANSWER AND ESSAY QUESTIONS**

1. Explain, using a supply and demand graph, how a freeze in a vegetable crop will affect the equilibrium price and quantity.

2. In a competitive market, if the supply of a product decreases and demand remains the same, what happens to the quantity demanded?

3. When there are single shifts in the supply or demand curve, you can predict the effects on both equilibrium price and quantity. When there are simultaneous shifts in demand and supply you can make only one prediction of the effects with any certainty. Why?

4. You observe that the equilibrium price has decreased and the equilibrium quantity has increased. What supply and demand conditions would best explain this outcome?

5. If increase in the demand for gasoline outweighs the decrease in the supply of gasoline, what is the most likely effect on the equilibrium price and quantity? Explain and show your answer with a graph.

6. You observe that the equilibrium quantity has increased but the equilibrium price has stayed the same. What supply and demand conditions would best explain this outcome?

7. What are price ceilings and price floors?

8. What are the consequences if a seller sets a price below the actual equilibrium price?

9. Why do secondary markets arise? Give examples of such markets.

10. Explain, using a supply and demand graph, the situation that arises when there are many unsold tickets to a sporting event. Why does this occur?

ANSWERS

Appendix to Chapter 3 Additional Examples of Supply and Demand

FILL-IN QUESTIONS

1. increases, decreases
2. increases, increases
3. demand for, supply of
4. decreases, increases
5. increases, increases
6. decrease, increase
7. stays the same, increases
8. ceiling, floor
9. shortage, surplus
10. secondary, scalping

TRUE–FALSE QUESTIONS

1. T, p. 66	5. F, p. 67	9. F, p. 69
2. F, p. 66	6. F, pp. 68–69	10. T, pp. 69–70
3. T, pp. 66–67	7. T, pp. 68–69	
4. T, p. 67	8. T, p. 69	

MULTIPLE-CHOICE QUESTIONS

1. b, p. 66	6. d, p. 68	11. c, p. 69
2. b, p. 66	7. c, pp. 68–69	12. c, pp. 69–70
3. d, pp. 66–67	8. d, pp. 68–69	13. a, pp. 69–70
4. d, p. 67	9. b, pp. 69–70	14. c, pp. 69–70
5. b, p. 68	10. a, p. 69	15. b, p. 69

PROBLEMS

1. column 5 (quantity demanded): 20, 30, 40, 50, 60; column 6 (quantity supplied): 40, 30, 20, 10, 0; *a.* $3.00, $4.00; *b.* 30, 30
2. $7, 15,000; *a.* shortage, 4,000; *b.* surplus, 2,000

SHORT ANSWER AND ESSAY QUESTIONS

1. p. 66	5. p. 68	9. p. 69
2. pp. 66–67	6. pp. 68–69	10. pp. 69–70
3. pp. 67–68	7. pp. 69–70	
4. pp. 67–68	8. p. 69	

CHAPTER 4

The U.S. Economy: Private and Public Sectors

The U.S. economy is divided into a private sector and a public sector. The first half of Chapter 4 discusses the private sector—the characteristics of millions of households and business firms. The second half of Chapter 4 describes the public sector—the functions and financing of the Federal, state, and local governments. Learning about these two sectors will give you the basic facts and framework you need for understanding the U.S. economy.

Chapter 4 begins with an examination of the **households** of the economy. Two different distributions of household income are examined. The way in which the total personal income received by all U.S. households is divided among the five types of earned income is called the *functional distribution of income*. The way in which the total personal income received by all households is distributed among the various income classes is called the *personal distribution of income*. Households dispose of the income they receive by spending money on *personal consumption expenditures*, paying *personal taxes*, or allocating funds to *personal saving*.

Businesses in the United States are also a focus of the chapter. It is apparent that what most characterizes U.S. businesses is the differences among firms in size and legal form, as well as in the products they produce. You should note the distinctions between a *sole proprietorship*, a *partnership*, and a *corporation*. You will also learn about the principal–agent problem with corporations that can arise from the separation of ownership (the principals) and management (the agents).

Chapter 4 also introduces you to the five basic functions performed by **government** in the U.S. economy. The chapter does not attempt to list all the specific ways in which government affects the behavior of the economy. Instead, it provides a general classification and description of the five functions that government performs.

The chapter also returns to the **circular flow model** first presented in Chapter 2. The model has now been modified to include government along with business and household sectors. This addition changes the real and monetary flows in the model.

The facts of **government finance** in the United States are presented in the final sections of Chapter 4. The organization of the discussion is relatively simple. First, the trends for taxes collected and expenditures made by all levels of government—Federal, state, and local—are examined. Second, an explanation is given for the major items on which the Federal government spends its income, the principal taxes it levies to obtain its income, and the relative importance of these taxes. Third, the chapter closes with a look at the major expenditures and taxes of the state and local governments.

■ **CHECKLIST**

When you have studied this chapter you should be able to

☐ Define and distinguish between a functional and a personal distribution of income.
☐ State the five sources of personal income in the functional distribution.
☐ List the three uses for which households dispose of their personal incomes and state the relative size of each.
☐ Distinguish among durable goods, nondurable goods, and services in personal consumption expenditures.
☐ Give definitions for a plant, a firm, and an industry.
☐ List the three legal forms of business enterprise.
☐ Describe the advantages of corporations in finance, risk and liability, and longevity.
☐ Explain the principal–agent problem as it applies to corporations.
☐ List the five economic functions of government in the United States.
☐ Give examples of how government provides the legal framework for the economy.
☐ Define monopoly and explain why government wishes to prevent monopoly and to maintain competition in the economy.
☐ Explain why government redistributes income and list the three principal policies it uses for this purpose.
☐ Define negative externality and positive externality.
☐ Explain why a competitive market fails to allocate resources efficiently when there are external costs and benefits.
☐ List two actions government can take to reduce external costs.
☐ List three actions government can take to encourage external benefits.
☐ Give definitions of a public good and a quasi-public good.
☐ Explain how the government reallocates resources from the production of private goods to the production of public or quasi-public goods.
☐ Describe the two macroeconomic stabilization policies of government and the two main economic problems they are designed to address.
☐ Explain the qualifications to government's role in the economy.

☐ Draw the circular flow model that includes businesses, households, and government.

☐ Explain the difference between government purchases and transfer payments and the effect of each on the composition of national output.

☐ Identify the four largest categories of Federal expenditures.

☐ List the three main sources of Federal tax revenues.

☐ Define and explain the differences between marginal and average tax rates.

☐ Identify the major expenditures by state and local governments.

☐ Describe how state and local governments raise tax revenue.

☐ Explain the problems facing the Social Security program and what solutions have been proposed (Last Word).

■ **CHAPTER OUTLINE**

1. Households play a dual role in the economy. They supply the economy with resources, and they purchase the greatest share of the goods and services produced by the economy. They obtain their personal incomes in exchange for the resources they furnish the economy and from the transfer payments they receive from government.

a. The *functional distribution of income* indicates the way in which total personal income is divided among the five sources of earned income in 2007: wages and salaries (71%); proprietors' income (9%); corporate profits (14%); interest (5%); and rents (1%).

b. The *personal distribution of income* indicates the way in which total personal income is divided among households in different income classes. The 2006 data show an unequal distribution of income by five household classes (20% of household in each). The percentage of total personal income by class is: lowest (3.4%); second (8.6%); middle (14.5%); fourth (22.9%), and highest (50.5%).

2. Households use their incomes to pay taxes, accumulate savings, and purchase consumer goods.

a. *Personal taxes* constitute a deduction from a household's personal income; what remains after taxes can be either saved or spent. Taxes account for 13% of household income.

b. *Saving* is what a household does not spend of its after-tax income. It was 1 percent in 2007.

c. *Personal consumption expenditures* account for most of the disposition of household income (86% in 2007). This category is spent on *durable goods* (11%)—products with lives of three or more years, *nondurable goods* (29%)—products with lives of less than three years, and *services* (60%)—work or a product supplied by others for a consumer.

3. The businesses of the U.S. economy consist of three major types of entities. A *plant* is a physical structure that produces a product. A *business firm* is an organization that owns and operates plants. (Multiplant firms may be horizontally or vertically integrated, or they may be conglomerates.) An *industry* is a group of firms producing the same or similar goods or services.

4. There are three principal *legal forms* of business firms. The *sole proprietorship* is a business owned and operated by a single person. The *partnership* is a business owned and operated by two or more persons. The *corporation* is a legal entity that operates as a business. The dominant form of business is the corporation. Although they represent only 20 percent of U.S. business firms, they account for 84 percent of total sales or output value.

a. Corporations have several advantages. They can raise substantial financial capital through the sale of *stocks* (equity financing), which represents a share of ownership in the corporation. They can also obtain funds through the sale of corporate *bonds* (debt financing), which is similar to a loan to a corporation from the bond buyer and over time the corporation pays the bond buyer interest on the amount of the bond. Corporations also provide *limited liability* for their owners (the stockholders) because they are only liable for losses that would equal the value of their stock holdings and the stockholders cannot be sued as individuals. Corporations, as legal entities, have unlimited life independent of their current owners and managers, and thus they can make long-term plans for continued growth.

b. Large corporations are a major feature of the U.S. economy, but their size creates a *principal–agent problem.* This problem arises from the separation of corporate ownership (by stockholders) and control (by corporate executives). This problem can sometimes be overcome by aligning the interests of executives with those of stockholders through stock payment plans.

5. Government performs five economic functions.

a. The first of these functions is to provide the *legal framework and services* that contribute to the effective operation of the market economy.

b. The second function of government is *to maintain competition* by controlling *monopoly* through regulation and antitrust laws. (A monopoly is the domination of an industry by a single seller.

c. Government performs its third function when it *redistributes income* to reduce income inequality. The policies and programs it uses to achieve this objective are transfer payments, market interventions (changing market prices), and taxation.

d. When government *reallocates resources* it performs its fourth function; in doing so it addresses externality problems or provides public goods.

(1) It reallocates resources to take into account negative or positive externalities or spillovers from market outcomes.

(a) *Negative externalities* are production or consumption costs paid for by a third party without compensation. For example, when a corporation pollutes the environment while making a product and neither the corporation nor the consumer of the product pays for the cost of that pollution, then the pollution cost is an external cost that is borne by third parties, who are the other members of society adversely affected by the pollution.

(b) Negative externalities can be discouraged either with legislation (prohibiting practices which create external costs), or by imposing taxes (and thus raising the cost of production). Some negative externalities get resolved through private bargaining if the externalities are not widespread and the negotiating costs can be kept low.

(c) *Positive externalities* are outcomes that benefit third parties without these parties paying for the benefits. Health immunizations and education are examples of services that have external benefits to others who do not pay for the services.

(d) External benefits can be encouraged by subsidizing consumers or producers (or by having government provide the goods when the external benefits are large).

(2) Government provides *public goods.* These goods have the characteristics of *nonrivalry* (benefits are not reduced by consumption by others) and *nonexcludability* (people cannot be excluded from the benefits). Examples of such public goods would be national defense or street lighting. The inability to exclude people from a public good once they exist creates a *free-rider problem,* in which people can receive the benefit of the public good without contributing to its cost.

(3) Government also provides *quasi-public goods* that have large external benefits. Although these goods (such as education) can be provided by the private market, because people can be excluded from obtaining them if they do not pay they will be underproduced or underconsumed if left to the private market alone. Government will provide access to these goods at a reduced cost to encourage their production or consumption and increase the external benefits.

(4) Government levies taxes and uses tax revenues to reallocate income and resources from private uses to public ones (for providing public and quasi-public goods).

e. The fifth function of government is to promote macroeconomic stabilization of the economy by controlling inflation and reducing unemployment. It does so through the prudent use of *fiscal policy* (government spending and taxation) and *monetary policy* (interest rates set by the nation's central bank).

f. The economic role of government is conducted in the context of politics. This process can lead to imperfect and inefficient outcomes.

6. A *circular flow model* that was first introduced in Chapter 2 showed business firms and households in the private sector of the economy. In Chapter 4 the public sector is now added. It shows that government purchases public goods from private businesses, collects taxes from and makes transfer payments to these firms, purchases labor services from households, collects taxes from and makes transfer payments to these households, and can alter the distribution of income, reallocate resources, and change the level of economic activity by affecting the real and monetary flows in the diagram.

7. *Government finance* is important in the economy. Total government spending consists of *government purchases* of goods and services and *transfer payments* (payments made to people for which no contribution is made by the people in return for them). The two types of spending have different effects on the economy. Government purchases are *exhaustive* because they directly use the economy's resources, while transfers are *nonexhaustive.* Total government spending is equal to three-tenths (31.5%) of domestic output.

8. The expenditures and tax revenues for the Federal government are of several types.

a. *Federal Expenditures*: most spending goes for pensions and income security (34%), national defense (21%), health care (24%), and interest on the public debt (9%).

b. *Federal Tax Revenues*: the major sources are *personal income taxes* (45%), *payroll taxes* (34%), and *corporate income taxes* (14%).

(1) The Federal personal income tax is progressive, which means it is one whose average rate rises as income increase.

(2) The *average tax rate* is the total tax paid divided by total taxable income.

(3) The *marginal tax rate* is the rate paid on additional income.

9. State and local governments have different sources of revenue and spend their funds on different types of public goods.

a. *State governments* depend largely on *sales and excise taxes* (47%), and also personal income taxes (35%); they spend their revenues on education (36%), public welfare (28%), health care (7%), highways (7%), and public safety (4%).

b. *Local governments* rely heavily on *property taxes* (72%) and to some extent on sales and excise taxes (16%); they spend much of the revenue on education (44%), welfare and health care (12%), public safety (11%), housing, parks, sewerage (8%), and streets and highways (4%).

10. (Last Word). The Social Security program is financed by payments into the system from current workers, and these payments are made to current Social Security retirees. The program will experience financial problems in the future because the number of workers paying into the system is declining and the number of retirees receiving benefits is rising. Several options have been proposed to shore up the finances such as cutting program benefits, extending the retirement age, raising taxes, and setting up individual retirement accounts.

■ HINTS AND TIPS

1. This chapter is a long one, so do not try to learn everything at once. Break the chapter into its three natural parts and work on each one separately. The first part describes features of the private sector. The second part explains the functions of government. The third part looks at government finance.

2. There are many descriptive statistics about the private and public sectors. Avoid memorizing these statistics. Instead, look for the trends and generalizations that these statistics illustrate about the private or public sector. For example, the discussion of government finance describes recent trends in government expenditures and taxes and indicates the relative importance of taxes and expenditures at each level of government.

■ **IMPORTANT TERMS**

functional distribution of income	monopoly
personal distribution of income	externality
	negative externalities
durable goods	positive externalities
nondurable goods	public goods
services	free-rider problem
plant	quasi-public goods
firm	government purchases
industry	transfer payments
sole proprietorship	personal income tax
partnership	marginal tax rate
corporation	average tax rate
stock	payroll taxes
bond	corporate income tax
limited liability	sales and excise taxes
principal–agent problem	property taxes

SELF-TEST

■ **FILL-IN QUESTIONS**

1. There are approximately 114 million (businesses, households) _____ in the United States. They play a dual role in the economy because they (sell, buy) _____ their resources and _____ most of the total output of the economy.

2. Data on the functional distribution of household income shows that the largest single source in the United States is (rents, wages and salaries) _____ and the smallest is _____.

3. Data on the personal distribution of household income in the United States show that about 3 percent of household income is received by the (poorest, richest) _____ 20 percent of households, and about 50 percent of household income is received by the _____ 20 percent of households.

4. The total income of households is disposed of in three ways: personal _____, personal _____, and personal _____.

5. If a product has an expected life of three years or more it is a (durable, nondurable) _____ good, whereas if it has an expected life of less than three years it is a _____ good.

6. There are millions of business (firms, industries) _____ in the United States. The legal form of the great majority of them is the (sole proprietorship, partnership, corporation) _____, but the legal form that produces about 84 percent of the sales of the U.S. economy is the _____.

7. Shares of ownership of corporations are called (stocks, bonds) _____, and promises by corporations to repay a loan, usually at a fixed rate of interest are _____. The liabilities of corporations are (limited, unlimited) _____, and the lifespan for a corporation is _____.

8. The separation of ownership and control in a corporation may create a (free-rider, principal–agent) _____ problem. In this case, stockholders would be the (riders, principals, agents) _____ and managers would be the _____.

9. List the five economic functions of government.

a. _____

b. _____

c. _____

d. _____

e. _____

10. To control monopoly, the U.S. government has created commissions to (tax, regulate) _____ natural monopolies, and in cases at the local level, government has become an (agent, owner) _____. Government has also enacted (trust, antitrust) _____ laws to maintain competition.

11. The market system, because it is an impersonal mechanism, results in an (equal, unequal) _____ distribution of income. To redistribute income from the upper- to the lower-income groups, the government has provided (transfer, tax) _____ payments, engaged in (military, market) _____ intervention, and used the (income, sales) _____ tax to raise much of its revenues.

12. Government frequently reallocates resources when it finds instances of (market, public) _____ failure. The two major cases of such failure occur when the competitive market system either

a. _____; or

b. _____

13. There is an externality whenever some of the costs of producing a product accrue to people other than the (seller, buyer) _____ or some of the benefits from consuming a product accrue to people other than the _____. Competitive markets bring about an efficient allocation of resources only if there are no (private, external) _____ costs or benefits in the consumption and production of a good or service.

  a. What two things can government do to make the market reflect external costs?

  (1) _____

  (2) _____

  b. What three things can government do to make the market reflect external benefits?

  (1) _____

  (2) _____

  (3) _____

14. One characteristic of a public good is (rivalry, non-rivalry) _____ and the other characteristic of a public good is (excludability, nonexcludability) _____. A private firm will not find it profitable to produce a public good because there is a (free-rider, principal–agent) _____ problem.

15. To reallocate resources from the production of private goods to the production of public and quasi-public goods, government reduces the demand for private goods by (taxing, subsidizing) _____ consumers and then uses the (profits, tax revenue) _____ to buy public or quasi-public goods.

16. To stabilize the economy with less than full employment, government may increase total spending by (increasing, decreasing) _____ its expenditures for public goods and services, or by (increasing, decreasing) _____ taxes. When there are inflationary pressures, the nation's central bank may decrease total spending by (raising, lowering) _____ interest rates and when there is high unemployment, it may increase total spending by _____ interest rates.

17. An examination of government finance reveals that since 1960 government *purchases* of goods and services as a percentage of domestic output have (increased, decreased) _____, and government *transfer payments* as a percentage of domestic output have (increased, decreased) _____. Government purchases of goods and services are (exhaustive, nonexhaustive) _____ because they absorb resources, and government transfer payments are (exhaustive, nonexhaustive) _____ because they do not absorb resources or create output.

18. The most important source of revenue for the Federal government is the (personal income, payroll) _____ tax; next in importance is the _____ tax. The largest category of Federal expenditures is for (national defense, pensions and income security) _____.

19. Federal income tax rates are progressive, which means that people with (lower, higher) _____ incomes pay a larger percentage of that income as taxes than do persons with _____ incomes. The tax rate paid on an additional unit of income is the (average, marginal) _____ tax rate, while the total tax paid divided by the total taxable income is the _____ tax rate.

20. Many state governments rely primarily on the (property, sales) _____ tax and many local governments rely primarily on the _____ tax. The largest category of spending for both state and local governments is (education, public safety) _____.

■ **TRUE–FALSE QUESTIONS**

Circle T if the statement is true, F if it is false.

1. The personal distribution of income describes the manner in which society's total personal income is divided among wages and salaries, corporate profits, proprietors' income, interest, and rents. **T F**

2. Dissaving means that personal consumption expenditures exceed after-tax income. **T F**

3. A durable good is defined as a good that has an expected life of three years or more. **T F**

4. A plant is defined as a group of firms under a single management. **T F**

5. An industry is a group of firms that produce the same or nearly the same products. **T F**

6. Limited liability refers to the fact that all members of a partnership are liable for the debts incurred by one another. **T F**

7. The corporate form of organization is the least used by firms in the United States. **T F**

8. Whether a business firm should incorporate or not depends chiefly on the amount of money capital it must have to finance the enterprise. **T F**

9. Bonds are shares of ownership in a corporation. **T F**

10. When the interests of the principals are the same as those of agents, there is a free-rider problem. **T F**

11. When the Federal government provides for a monetary system, it is doing so primarily to maintain competition.　**T F**

12. Transfer payments are one means government uses to redistribute income.　**T F**

13. If demand and supply reflected all the benefits and costs of producing a product, there would be efficient resource use.　**T F**

14. When there are external costs, more resources are allocated to the production of the product and more is produced than is efficient.　**T F**

15. One way for government to correct for external costs from a product is to increase its demand.　**T F**

16. When there are external benefits from a product, there will be an overallocation of resources for its production.　**T F**

17. One way for government to correct external benefits from a product is to subsidize consumers of the product.　**T F**

18. Nonexcludability means government provides public goods so as to exclude private businesses from providing them.　**T F**

19. Obtaining the benefits of private goods requires that they be purchased; obtaining benefits from public goods requires only that they be produced.　**T F**

20. Government provides homeland defense services because these services have public benefits and because private producers of such services experience the free-rider problem.　**T F**

21. When the Federal government takes actions to control unemployment or inflation it is performing the allocative function of government.　**T F**

22. Government purchases of goods and services are called nonexhaustive expenditures and government transfer payments are called exhaustive expenditures.　**T F**

23. When a government levies taxes and uses the tax revenue to make transfer payments, it shifts resources from the production of private goods to the production of public goods.　**T F**

24. The chief source of revenue for the Federal government is the corporate income tax.　**T F**

25. Property taxes are the largest percentage of the total revenues of local governments.　**T F**

■ MULTIPLE-CHOICE QUESTIONS

Circle the letter that corresponds to the best answer.

1. The functional distribution for the United States shows that the largest part of the nation's earned income is
- **(a)** wages and salaries
- **(b)** proprietors' income
- **(c)** corporate profits
- **(d)** interest and rents

2. The part of after-tax income which is not consumed is defined as
- **(a)** saving
- **(b)** capital investment
- **(c)** wages and salaries
- **(d)** nondurable goods expenditure

3. If personal consumption expenditures were 80% of income and personal taxes were 8% of income, then personal savings would be
- **(a)** 8% of income
- **(b)** 10% of income
- **(c)** 12% of income
- **(d)** 88% of income

4. Consumer products that have expected lives of three years or more are
- **(a)** durable goods
- **(b)** nondurable goods
- **(c)** quasi-public goods
- **(d)** services

5. A firm owns and operates a farm growing wheat, a flour-milling plant, and a plant that bakes and sells bakery products. This firm would best be described as
- **(a)** a horizontally integrated firm
- **(b)** a vertically integrated firm
- **(c)** a conglomerate
- **(d)** a monopoly

6. Limited liability is associated with
- **(a)** sole proprietorships
- **(b)** partnerships
- **(c)** free-riders
- **(d)** corporations

7. Which form of business can most effectively raise money capital?
- **(a)** corporation
- **(b)** partnership
- **(c)** proprietorship
- **(d)** households

8. The separation of ownership and control in a corporation may create
- **(a)** a principal–agent problem
- **(b)** a free-rider problem
- **(c)** a monopoly
- **(d)** limited liability

9. One major means that government uses to deal with a monopoly is to
- **(a)** increase the demand for its product
- **(b)** decrease the supply of its product
- **(c)** stabilize incomes
- **(d)** regulate the firm

10. Government redistributes income through
- **(a)** limited liability
- **(b)** conglomerates
- **(c)** transfer payments
- **(d)** sole proprietorships

11. To redistribute income from high-income to low-income households, government might

(a) increase transfer payments to high-income and decrease transfer payments to low-income households

(b) increase the taxes paid by high-income households and increase the transfer payments to low-income households

(c) increase the taxes paid by low-income households and decrease the taxes paid by high-income households

(d) decrease the taxes paid by high-income households and decrease the transfer payments to low-income households

12. Which is the best example of a good or service providing the economy with an external cost?

(a) a textbook

(b) an automobile

(c) a business suit

(d) an audit of a business firm's books

13. Which economic situation would result in overallocation of resources to the production of a good?

(a) a good with external benefits

(b) a good with external costs

(c) a good with free-rider problem

(d) a good with an inflation problem

14. How does government correct for external benefits?

(a) by taxing consumers

(b) by taxing producers

(c) by subsidizing producers

(d) by separating ownership from control

15. Which is characteristic of public goods?

(a) nonrivalry

(b) excludability

(c) limited liability

(d) external costs

16. There is a free-rider problem when people

(a) are willing to pay for what they want

(b) are not willing to pay for what they want

(c) benefit from a good without paying for its cost

(d) want to buy more than is available for purchase in the market

17. Quasi-public goods are goods and services

(a) that are indivisible

(b) that have large external costs

(c) that have large external benefits

(d) that would not be produced by private producers through the market system

18. In the circular flow model, government provides goods and services and receives net taxes from

(a) colleges and universities

(b) businesses and households

(c) resource and product markets

(d) foreign nations and corporations

19. Which accounts for the largest percentage of all Federal expenditures?

(a) health care

(b) national defense

(c) interest on the public debt

(d) pensions and income security

20. Which is the largest source of the tax revenues of the Federal government?

(a) payroll taxes

(b) property taxes

(c) sales and excise taxes

(d) personal income taxes

21. A progressive tax is one where people with

(a) lower incomes pay the same percentage of their income in taxes as people do with higher incomes

(b) lower incomes pay a larger percentage of their income in taxes as people do with higher incomes

(c) higher incomes pay a smaller percentage of their income in taxes than people do with higher incomes

(d) higher incomes pay a larger percentage of their income in taxes than people do with lower incomes

Questions 22 and 23 are based on the tax table given below. [Note: Total tax is for the highest income in that tax bracket.]

Taxable income	Total tax
$ 0	$ 0
30,000	5,000
70,000	15,000
150,000	42,000

22. The marginal tax rate at the $70,000 level of taxable income is

(a) 16.6%

(b) 21.4%

(c) 25.0%

(d) 28.0%

23. The average tax rate at the $150,000 level of taxable income is

(a) 21.4%

(b) 28.0%

(c) 31.5%

(d) 33.8%

24. Which pair represents the chief source of income and the most important type of expenditure of *state* governments?

(a) personal income tax and expenditures for hospitals

(b) personal income tax and expenditures for highways

(c) sales and excise taxes and expenditures for education

(d) sales and excise taxes and expenditures for public safety

25. Which pair represents the chief source of income and the most important type of expenditure of local governments?

(a) property tax and expenditures for highways

(b) property tax and expenditures for education

(c) sales and excise taxes and expenditures for public welfare

(d) sales and excise taxes and expenditures for police, fire, safety, and general government

■ PROBLEMS

1. The following table shows the functional distribution of total income in the United States in a recent year.

	Billions of dollars
Wages and salaries	$ 7,874
Proprietors' income	1,043
Corporate profits	1,595
Interest	603
Rents	65
Total income	$11,180

Of the total income about _____% were wages and salaries, and about _____% were corporate profits.

2. Following is a list of various government activities. Indicate in the space to the right of each into which of the five classes of government functions the activity falls. If it falls under more than one of the functions, indicate this.

a. Maintaining an army _____

b. Providing for a system of unemployment compensation _____

c. Establishment of the Federal Reserve Banks

_____

d. Providing medical care for government employees

_____

e. Establishment of an Antitrust Division in the Department of Justice _____

f. Making it a crime to sell stocks and bonds under false pretenses _____

g. Providing low-cost lunches to school children

_____

h. Taxation of beer and wine _____

i. Regulation of organized stock, bond, and commodity markets _____

j. Setting tax rates higher for larger incomes than for smaller ones _____

3. The following circular flow diagram includes business firms, households, and the government (the public sector). Also shown are the product and resource markets.

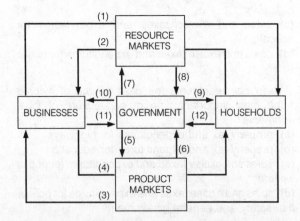

a. Supply a label or an explanation for each of the 12 flows in the model:

(1) _____

(2) _____

(3) _____

(4) _____

(5) _____

(6) _____

(7) _____

(8) _____

(9) _____

(10) _____

(11) _____

(12) _____

b. If government wished to
(1) expand output and employment in the economy, it would increase expenditure flows _____ or _____, decrease net tax flows _____ or _____, or do both;
(2) increase the production of public goods and decrease the production of private goods in the economy, it would increase flows _____ and _____ or _____;
(3) redistribute income from high-income to low-income households, it would (increase, decrease) _____ the net taxes (taxes minus transfers) paid by the former and _____ the net taxes paid by the latter in flow _____.

4. In the following table are several levels of taxable income and hypothetical marginal tax rates for each $1000 increase in income.

Taxable income	Marginal tax rate,%	Tax	Average tax rate,%
$1500		$300	20
2500	22	520	20.8
3500	25	____	____
4500	29	____	____
5500	34	____	____
6500	40	____	____

a. At the four income levels compute the tax and the average tax rate
b. As the marginal tax rate
(1) increases the average tax rate (increases, decreases, remains constant) _____.
(2) decreases the average tax rate _____.
c. This tax is (progressive, regressive) _____ because the average tax rate increases as income (decreases, increases) _____.

■ SHORT ANSWER AND ESSAY QUESTIONS

1. Explain the difference between a functional and a personal distribution of income. List the five major categories for functional income and their relative sizes. Describe the difference between the poorest and richest categories in the personal distribution of income.

2. In what ways do households dispose of their income? How is it possible for a family's personal consumption expenditures to exceed its after-tax income?

3. What is the difference between a plant and a firm? Between a firm and an industry?

4. Define the three legal forms of business organization.

5. Explain the advantages of corporations in terms of financing, liability, and longevity.

6. Explain what "separation of ownership and control" of the modern corporation means. What problem does this separation create for stockholders and managers?

7. How does government provide a legal framework and services for the effective operation of the economy?

8. What does the government do to maintain competition?

9. Why does the market system provide some people with lower incomes than it provides others?

10. What is meant by an externality in general and by an external cost and an external benefit in particular?

11. How does the existence of positive and negative externalities affect the allocation of resources and the prices of products?

12. What methods does government use to reallocate resources to take account of negative and positive externalities?

13. Distinguish between a private and a public good. Include in your answer an explanation of rivalry, excludability, and the free-rider problem.

14. What basic method does government in the United States use to reallocate resources away from the production of private goods and toward the production of public and quasi-public goods?

15. What is the macroeconomic stabilization function of government? What are the two policies that the government or the nation's central bank uses to address problems with unemployment or inflation?

16. How does politics affect the five economic functions of government in practice?

17. In a circular flow diagram that includes not only business firms and households but also government (or the public sector), what are the four flows of money into or out of the government sector of the economy? Using this diagram, explain how government redistributes income, reallocates resources from the private to the public sector, and stabilizes the economy.

18. Government expenditures fall into two broad classes: expenditures for goods and services and transfer payments. Explain the difference between these, and give examples of expenditures that fall into each of the two classes.

19. Explain precisely the difference between the marginal tax rate and the average tax rate.

20. Explain in detail the differences that exist among Federal, state, and local governments in the taxes on which they primarily rely for their revenues and the major purposes for which they use these revenues.

ANSWERS

Chapter 4 The U.S. Economy: Private and Public Sectors

FILL-IN QUESTIONS

1. households, sell, buy
2. wages and salaries, rents
3. poorest, richest
4. consumption, saving, taxes (any order)
5. durable, nondurable
6. firms, sole proprietorship, corporation
7. stocks, bonds, unlimited, unlimited
8. principal–agent, principals, agents
9. *a.* provide legal foundation; *b.* maintain competition; *c.* redistribute income; *d.* reallocate resources; *e.* stabilize the economy (any order for *a–e*)
10. regulate, owner, antitrust
11. unequal, transfer, market, income
12. market; *a.* produces the "wrong" amounts of certain goods and services; *b.* fails to allocate any resources to the production of certain goods and services whose production is economically justified
13. seller, buyer, external; *a.* (1) enact legislation, (2) pass special taxes; *b.* (1) subsidize consumers, (2) subsidize suppliers, (3) government financing or production of the product
14. nonrivalry, nonexcludability, free-rider
15. taxing, tax revenue
16. increasing, decreasing, raising, lowering
17. decreased, increased, exhaustive, nonexhaustive
18. personal income, payroll, pensions and income security
19. higher, lower, marginal, average
20. sales, property, education

TRUE–FALSE QUESTIONS

1. F, pp. 73–74	**10.** F, pp. 77–78	**19.** T, p. 80
2. T, p. 74	**11.** F, p. 78	**20.** T, pp. 80–81
3. T, pp. 74–75	**12.** T, pp. 77–79	**21.** F, pp. 81–82
4. F, p. 75	**13.** T, p. 79	**22.** F, p. 83
5. T, p. 75	**14.** T, p. 79	**23.** F, p. 83
6. F, p. 76	**15.** F, pp. 79–80	**24.** F, pp. 85–87
7. F, p. 76	**16.** F, p. 80	**25.** T, p. 88
8. T, p. 76	**17.** T, p. 80	
9. F, p. 76	**18.** F, p. 80	

MULTIPLE-CHOICE QUESTIONS

1. a, p. 73	**10.** c, pp. 78–79	**19.** d, pp. 84–85
2. a, p. 74	**11.** b, pp. 78–79	**20.** d, p. 85
3. c, p. 74	**12.** b, p. 79	**21.** d, p. 85
4. a, pp. 74–75	**13.** b, p. 79	**22.** c, p. 85
5. b, p. 75	**14.** c, pp. 79–80	**23.** b, p. 85
6. d, p. 76	**15.** a, p. 80	**24.** c, pp. 87–88
7. a, p. 76	**16.** c, p. 80	**25.** b, p. 88
8. a, pp. 77–78	**17.** c, p. 81	
9. d, p. 78	**18.** b, pp. 82–83	

PROBLEMS

1. 70, 14

2. *a.* reallocates resources; *b.* redistributes income; *c.* provides a legal foundation and stabilizes the economy; *d.* reallocates resources; *e.* maintains competition; *f.* provides a legal foundation and maintains competition; *g.* redistributes income; *h.* reallocates resources; *i.* provides a legal foundation; *j.* redistributes income

3. *a.* (1) businesses pay costs for resources that become money income for households; (2) households provide resources to businesses; (3) household expenditures become receipts for businesses; (4) businesses provide goods and services to households; (5) government spends money in product market; (6) government receives goods and services from product market; (7) government spends money in resource market; (8) government receives resources from resource market; (9) government provides goods and services to households; (10) government provides goods and services to businesses; (11) businesses pay net taxes to government; (12) households pay net taxes to government; *b.* (1) 5, 7 (either order), 11, 12 (either order); (2) 9, 10, 11 (any order); (3) increase, decrease, 12

4. *a.* tax: $770, 1,060, 1,400, 1,800; average tax rate: 22%, 23.6%, 25.5%, 27.7%; *b.* (1) increases, (2) decreases; *c.* progressive, increases

SHORT ANSWER AND ESSAY QUESTIONS

1. pp. 73–74	**8.** p. 78	**15.** pp. 81–82
2. pp. 74–75	**9.** pp. 78–79	**16.** p. 82
3. p. 75	**10.** pp. 79–80	**17.** pp. 82–83
4. pp. 75–76	**11.** pp. 79–80	**18.** pp. 83–84
5. pp. 76–77	**12.** pp. 79–80	**19.** pp. 85–86
6. pp. 77–78	**13.** pp. 80–81	**20.** pp. 85–88
7. p. 78	**14.** p. 81	

CHAPTER 5

The United States in the Global Economy

The United States is linked to the global economy in many ways. As you will learn in the first section of Chapter 5, there are four types of **economic flows** among nations: trade; resource; information and technology; and financial.

The second section explains **why international trade is important** to the United States. In *relative* terms, other nations have exports and imports that are a larger percentage of their GDPs because they often have a small domestic market and a limited resource base. By contrast, the exports and imports of the United States account for a smaller percentage of its GDP because it has a larger domestic market and a more abundant resource base. In *absolute* terms, however, the United States is the world's largest trading nation. Most of the trade is with Canada, Mexico, the European Union, Japan, China, and OPEC countries. This volume of trade has grown over the years with expansion of the global economy and the emergence of new trading nations.

In the third section, you learn about the principle of **comparative advantage,** which is the basis for all trade between individuals, regions, and nations. A nation, for example, will specialize in the production of a product for which it has a lower domestic opportunity cost and trade to obtain those products for which its domestic opportunity cost is higher. Thus, specialization and trade increase productivity within a nation and increase a nation's output and standard of living.

Trading in a global economy requires a **foreign exchange market** in which national currencies are exchanged, as you discover in the fourth section. When the U.S. dollar price of another currency has increased, the value of the U.S. dollar has *depreciated* relative to the other currency. Conversely, when the U.S. dollar price of another currency has decreased, the value of the U.S. dollar has *appreciated* in value relative to the other currency.

Government can affect international trade in many ways, as you learn in the fifth section. Governments can impose protective tariffs, import quotas, and nontariff barriers, or they can foster exports through subsidies. The reasons for the interventions are difficult to explain given the strong economic rationale for free trade based on the principle of comparative advantage. Nevertheless, public misunderstanding of the gains from trade, or political considerations designed to protect domestic industries, often lead to government policies that create trade barriers and distort the free flow of products between nations, thus increasing costs for society.

The sixth section discusses **multilateral agreements** among nations and the creation of **free-trade zones** that

have been designed to reduce trade barriers and increase world trade. In the United States, the process of gradual tariff reduction began with the Reciprocal Trade Agreements Act of 1934. Since 1947, worldwide multilateral negotiations to reduce trade barriers have been conducted through the General Agreement on Tariffs and Trade (GATT). The Uruguay Round of GATT negotiations established the World Trade Organization (WTO) as GATT's successor. Trade negotiations under the WTO continue in the Doha Round that began in 2001.

The other major development has been the formation of free-trade zones. The European Union (EU), which was originally started in 1958 as the Common Market, is now a trading bloc of 27 European nations. A major accomplishment of the EU, in addition to the reduction of trade barriers among member nations, was the establishment of a common currency (the **euro**) that is used by 15 nations. The United States, Canada, and Mexico also established a free-trade zone in 1993 through the North American Free Trade Agreement (NAFTA).

As you will learn in the next-to-last section of the chapter, international trade can impose adverse effects on domestic workers and industries. One measure passed by the U.S. Congress to help workers displaced by international trade is the Trade Assistance Act. Although the offshoring of domestic jobs creates difficulties for some workers, there also can be benefits from it for the economy and domestic businesses and workers.

The final section of the chapter briefly explores the issue of the effects of **increased competition in the global economy.** Global competition has certainly changed production practices and employment in U.S. industry. Many U.S. firms have adapted to the changes by increasing productivity to reduce costs, improving product quality, and expanding export markets. Although some firms have failed and domestic jobs have been lost, the benefits of free trade to the economy in the form of lower prices, greater economic efficiency, and a wider variety of products far outweigh any losses.

■ **CHECKLIST**

When you have studied this chapter you should be able to

☐ Identify the four main categories of economic flows linking nations.

☐ Explain the importance of international trade to the U.S. economy in terms of volume, dependence, trade patterns, and financial linkages.

☐ Describe several factors that have facilitated the rapid growth of international trade since World War II.

☐ Identify the key participating nations in international trade.

☐ Explain the basic principle of comparative advantage based on an individual example.

☐ Compute the comparative costs of production from production possibilities data when you are given an example with cost data for two countries.

☐ Determine which of two countries has a comparative advantage in an example.

☐ Indicate the range in which the terms of trade will be found in an example.

☐ Show the gains from specialization and trade in an example.

☐ Define the main characteristics of the foreign exchange market.

☐ Distinguish between the appreciation and depreciation of a currency.

☐ Identify four means by which governments interfere with free trade.

☐ Discuss two reasons why governments intervene in international trade.

☐ Give estimates of the cost to society from trade restrictions.

☐ List the major features of the Reciprocal Trade Agreements Act.

☐ State the three principles of the General Agreement on Tariffs and Trade (GATT).

☐ Identify the major provisions of the Uruguay round of GATT.

☐ Describe the World Trade Organization (WTO).

☐ Describe the history of and results from the European Union (EU).

☐ Explain what the euro is and the results from using it.

☐ Describe the North American Free Trade Agreement (NAFTA).

☐ Describe the Trade Adjustment Assistance Act of 2002.

☐ Evaluate reasons for and outcomes from offshoring.

☐ Discuss the effects of global competition on U.S. firms, workers, and consumers.

☐ Evaluate the overall effectiveness of fair-trade approaches to economic development (Last Word).

■ CHAPTER OUTLINE

1. Four main categories of *economic flows* link nations: goods and services flows, capital and labor flows, information and technology flows, and financial flows.

2. Trade is important and thus warrants special attention.
   a. Although the relative importance of international trade to the United States is less than it is for other nations, it is still vital.
   (1) Exports and imports are about 12–17% of GDP, and the United States is the largest trading nation in the world.
   (2) The U.S. economy depends on international trade for vital raw materials and a variety of finished products.

(3) There are some patterns in U.S. trade: The United States has a trade deficit because its exports exceed its imports. About half of U.S. export and import trade is with industrially advanced nations, with Canada being the largest trade partner; overall imports exceed exports, but the trade deficits are greatest with China, Japan, and OPEC countries.

(4) International trade must be financed, and, in the case of the United States, large trade deficits have required the selling of business ownership (securities) to companies in other nations.

   b. Factors facilitating trade since World War II include improvements in transportation and communications technology, and a general decline in tariffs.

   c. There are many participants in international trade. The United States, the nations of the European Union, Japan, and China are the major players in international trade.

3. Specialization and international trade are advantageous because they increase the productivity of a nation's resources, increase total output, and increase incomes.

4. *Comparative advantage* explains the gains from trade and is directly related to opportunity cost. In essence, a nation has a comparative advantage in the production of a good when it can produce the good at a lower domestic opportunity cost than can a trading partner. A nation will specialize in the production of a product for which it is the low (opportunity) cost producer and trade for the other goods it wants.

   a. Suppose the world is composed of only two nations (the United States and Mexico), each of which is capable of producing two different goods (avocados and soybeans). The production possibilities table for each nation assumes a constant opportunity cost, so a constant amount of one good must be given up to get more of another good. With different domestic opportunity cost ratios, each nation will have a comparative (cost) advantage in the production of one of the two goods.

   b. The ratio at which one product is traded for another—the *terms of trade*—lies between the opportunity cost ratios of the two nations.

   c. Each nation gains from this trade because specialization permits a greater total output from the same resources and a better allocation of the world's resources.

5. The *foreign exchange market* is where national currencies, such as the European euro, Japanese yen, and U.S. dollar, are traded for each other. The equilibrium prices for national currencies are called *exchange rates* and represent how much of each nation's currency can be exchanged for another nation's currency.

   a. In the dollar–yen market, the dollar price of a yen would be on the vertical axis and the quantity of yen would be on the horizontal axis. The intersection of the up-sloping supply of yen curve and downsloping demand for yen curve would determine the dollar price of a yen.

   b. If U.S. demand for Japanese goods increased, then more yen will be needed to pay for the goods, and so the demand for yen would increase. This change increases the dollar price of yen, which means there has been a *depreciation* of the U.S. dollar relative to the yen. Conversely, if Japanese demand for U.S. goods increased, then more dollars would be needed to pay for the goods, and the supply of yen would increase. This change will decrease the dollar price of yen, which means there has been an *appreciation* of the U.S. dollar relative to the yen.

6. Governments often restrict trade in several ways and that has consequences.

a. There are four ways by which governments restrict trade:

(1) placing *protective tariffs* (excise taxes or duties) on imported goods to protect domestic producers;

(2) setting *import quotas* to limit the quantity or value of goods that can be imported;

(3) imposing *nontariff barriers* such as burdensome and costly licensing or regulatory requirements;

(4) using *export subsidies* that are government payments to domestic producers of imported goods.

b. Governments intervene in trade for two basic reasons:

(1) The gains from trade are misunderstood. Exports are thought to be good because they increase domestic employment and imports are thought to be bad because they reduce domestic employment. The gains from trade come from increased output resulting from specialization and exchange that require importing and exporting.

(2) Trade may be good for a nation as a whole, but certain groups or industries can be adversely affected by imports and thus they seek political protection through trade restrictions.

c. Trade restrictions impose substantial costs. Domestic consumers pay higher prices for products for which trade restrictions are imposed and so do domestic firms that use such products or other imported commodities in their production.

7. International trade policies have changed over the years with the development of multilateral agreements and free-trade zones. They are used to counter the destructive aspects of trade wars that arise when nations imposed high tariffs. A classic example is the *Smoot-Hawley Tariff Act* of 1930 that caused other nations to impose equally high tariffs, caused a trade war, and reduced worldwide trade.

a. U.S. trade policy has been significantly affected by the *Reciprocal Trade Agreements Act* of 1934. Until 1934, the United States steadily increased tariff rates to protect private interest groups, but since the passage of the 1934 act, tariff rates have been substantially reduced. This act gave the president the authority to negotiate with foreign nations and included most-favored-nation status (now renamed *normal-trade-relation [NTR] status*).

b. The *General Agreement on Tariffs and Trade* *(GATT)* began in 1947. GATT provided equal treatment of all member nations and sought to reduce tariffs and eliminate import quotas by multilateral negotiations.

The Uruguay Round of GATT negotiations started in 1986 and was completed in 1993. The major provisions, which were phased in through 2005, reduced tariffs on products, cut restrictive rules applying to services, phased out quotas on textiles and apparel, and decreased subsidies for agriculture.

c. The *World Trade Organization (WTO)* was the successor to GATT. It oversees trade agreements and provides a forum for trade negotiations, the latest of which is the *Doha Round* that was launched in 2001 in Doha, Qatar. The WTO works to expand trade and reduce protectionism, but the outcomes can be controversial.

d. The *European Union (EU)* is an example of a regional free-trade zone or *trade bloc* among 27 European nations.

(1) The EU abolished tariffs among member nations and developed common policies on various economic issues, such as the tariffs on goods to and from nonmember nations. The EU has produced freer trade and increased economies of scale for production in its member nations, but such a trading bloc creates trade frictions with nonmember nations like the United States.

(2) Some 15 of the EU nations share a common currency—the *euro.* The chief advantages of such a currency is that it reduces transactions costs for exchanging goods and services in Euro Zone nations and allows consumers and businesses to comparison shop.

e. In 1993, the *North American Free Trade Agreement (NAFTA)* created a free-trade zone or trade bloc covering the United States, Mexico, and Canada. Critics of this agreement feared job losses and the potential for abuse by other nations using Mexico as a base for production, but the dire outcomes have not occurred. There has been increased trade among Canada, Mexico, and the United States because of the agreement.

8. Although increased trade and trade liberalization raise total output and income, they also create controversies and calls for assistance.

a. The *Trade Adjustment Assistance Act* of 2002 provides support to qualified workers displaced by imports or plant relocations from international trade. It gives cash assistance, education and training benefits, subsidies for health care, and wage subsidies (for those aged 50 or older). Critics contend that such dislocations are part of a market economy and workers in the international sector should not get special subsidies for their job losses.

b. Offshoring shifts work done in the United States to workers and locations in other nations. While it has long been used in manufacturing, improvement in communication and technology make it possible to do it in services. Offshoring, imports, and plant closings account for only about 3 percent of U.S. job losses, but these losses from international trade are often offset by gains in productivity and growth of other jobs.

9. Increased international trade has resulted in more global competition. Most U.S. firms have been able to meet the competitive challenge by lowering production costs, improving products, or using new technology. Some firms and industries have had difficulty remaining competitive and continue to lose market share and employment. Overall, increased trade has produced substantial benefits for U.S. consumers (lower prices and more products) and enabled the nation to make more efficient use of its scarce resources.

10. (Last Word). Fair-trade policies advocated by consumer organizations in the high-income nations seek to pay producers in low-income nations a higher-than-market price for certain products (such as coffee or cocoa). In return, the producers agree to pay their workers a higher-than-market wage. Such policies may help workers and producers in particular industries, but overall they are ineffective as a means for economic development because they simply shift and distort product and labor demand.

■ HINTS AND TIPS

1. When the production possibilities schedules for two nations that trade two products have constant cost ratios, you can reduce the schedules to a 2 × 2 table. Put the two products in the two columns and the two nations in the two rows of the matrix. In each cell of the matrix put the *maximum* of each product that can be produced by that row's nation. Then for each nation, divide the maximum of one product into the maximum amount of the other product to get the domestic opportunity cost of one product in terms of the other.

This point can be illustrated with an example from problem 2 in this study guide chapter. Lilliput can produce a *maximum* of 40 pounds of apples or 20 pounds of bananas. Brobdingnag can produce a *maximum* of 75 pounds of apples or 25 pounds of bananas. The 2 × 2 matrix would look like this:

	Apples	Bananas
Lilliput	40	20
Brobdingnag	75	25

For Lilliput, the domestic opportunity cost of producing 1 pound of apples is .5 pound of bananas. In Brobdingnag, the domestic opportunity cost of producing 1 pound of apples is .33 pound of bananas. Brobdingnag is the lower (opportunity) cost producer of apples and will specialize in the production of that product. Lilliput is the lower (opportunity) cost producer of bananas, because producing 1 pound of bananas requires giving up 2 pounds of apples, whereas in Brobdingnag producing 1 pound of bananas requires giving up 3 pounds of apples.

2. Foreign exchange rates often confuse students because they can be expressed in two ways: the U.S. dollar price of a unit of foreign currency ($1.56 for 1 British pound), or the amount of foreign currency that can be purchased by one U.S. dollar ($1 can purchase .64 British pound). If you know the exchange rate in one way, you

can easily calculate it the other way. Using the information from the first way, dividing $1.56 into 1 British pound gives you the British pound price for 1 U.S. dollar (1/1.56 = .64 of a British pound). Using information from the second way, dividing .64 of a British pound into 1 U.S. dollar gives you the dollar price of a British pound (1/.64 = 1.56). Both ways may be used, although one way may be used more often than the other. Rates for British pounds or Canadian dollars are usually expressed the first way, in terms of U.S. dollars. Rates for the Swiss franc, Japanese yen, or European euro are expressed the second way, per U.S. dollar.

■ IMPORTANT TERMS

comparative advantage	normal-trade-relation status
terms of trade	General Agreement on Tariffs and Trade (GATT)
foreign exchange market	World Trade Organization (WTO)
exchange rates	
depreciation	Doha Round
appreciation	European Union (EU)
protective tariffs	trade bloc
import quotas	euro
nontariff barriers	North American Free Trade Agreement (NAFTA)
export subsidies	
Smoot-Hawley Tariff Act	Trade Adjustment Assistance Act
Reciprocal Trade Agreements Act	offshoring

SELF-TEST

■ FILL-IN QUESTIONS

1. List the four major economic flows among nations.

a. _____

b. _____

c. _____

d. _____

2. The importance of international trade varies by nation. Nations in which exports account for a relatively high percentage of GDP tend to have a (limited, diversified) _____ resource base and domestic market, whereas nations in which exports account for a lower percentage of GDP tend to have a _____ resource base and domestic market. An example of a higher exporting nation would be the (United States, Netherlands) _____, and a lower exporting nation would be the _____.

3. In relative terms, the imports and exports of the United States amounted to about (12–17, 31–36) _____ %

of the economy's GDP in 2007. In absolute terms, the United States is the world's (smallest, largest) _____ trading nation. The largest trading partner for the United States is (Canada, Japan) _____. The United States has a large trade deficit with (Mexico, China) _____.

4. Factors that have helped increase the growth of world trade since World War II include improvement in _____ and _____ technology and a general decline in _____.

5. Specialization and trade (increase, decrease) _____ the productivity of a nation's resources and _____ total output more than would be the case without it.

6. When one nation has a lower opportunity cost of producing a product relative to another nation it has a (nontariff barrier, comparative advantage) _____. The amount of one product that must be given up to obtain 1 unit of another product is the (foreign exchange, opportunity cost) _____.

7. When the dollar price of foreign currency increases, there has been a(n) (appreciation, depreciation) _____ in value of the dollar. When the dollar price of foreign currency decreases, there has been a(n) _____ in the value of the dollar. For example, if the dollar price of a euro decreases from $1.00 = 1 euro to $0.90 = 1 euro, then it means that there has been a(n) (appreciation, depreciation) _____ in the value of the dollar; but if the dollar price of a euro increases from $0.95 = 1 euro to $1.05 = 1 euro, then it means that there has been a(n) _____ in the value of the dollar.

8. In the market for Japanese yen, an increase in the (demand for, supply of) _____ yen will decrease the dollar price of yen, while an increase in the _____ yen will increase the dollar price of yen. If the dollar price of the yen increases, then Japanese goods imported into the United States will be (more, less) _____ expensive.

9. The major government policies that restrict trade include
  a. excise taxes or duties on imported goods that are called _____,
  b. limits on the quantities or total value of specific items that may be imported, referred to as _____,
  c. licensing requirements, unreasonable standards, and hurdles and delays in customs procedures related to a product, which are _____,
  d. government payments to domestic producers of export goods, known as _____.

10. Governments may intervene in trade between nations because they mistakenly think of (exports, imports) _____ as helpful and _____ as harmful for a national economy. In fact, there are important gains from trade in the form of the extra output obtained from abroad. Trade makes it possible to obtain (exports, imports) _____ at a lower cost than would be the case if they were produced using domestic resources, and the earnings from _____ help a nation pay for these lower cost (exports, imports) _____.

11. Another reason governments interfere with free trade is (private, political) _____ considerations. Groups and industries seek protection from foreign competition through (GATT, tariffs) _____ and import (quotas, subsidies) _____, or other kinds of trade restrictions. The costs of trade protectionism are (clear to, hidden from) _____ consumers in the protected product so there is little opposition to demands for protectionism.

12. Tariffs and quotas (benefit, cost) _____ domestic firms in the protected industries, but _____ domestic consumers in the form of (lower, higher) _____ prices than would be the case if there were free trade. They also (benefit, cost) _____ domestic firms that use the protected goods as inputs in their production processes.

13. Until 1934, the trend of tariff rates in the United States was (upward, downward) _____. The trend has been (upward, downward) _____ since the 1934 passage of the (Smoot-Hawley Tariff, Reciprocal Trade Agreements) _____ Act. This act empowered the President to lower (tariffs, quotas) _____ by up to 50% in return for a reduction in foreign restrictions on U.S. goods. It incorporated most-favored-nation status into U.S. trade agreements for the first time. This status is now so common that it has been renamed (free-trade zone, normal-trade-relations) _____ status.

14. The three cardinal principles established in the General Agreement on Tariffs and Trade (GATT) of 1947 were
  a. _____
  b. _____
  c. _____

15. GATT negotiations were conducted as (circles, rounds) "_____" that last many years. One of the major provisions of the eighth round (the Uruguay Round) was to create a successor to GATT that is called the (Reciprocal, World) _____ Trade Organization. The current ninth round of negotiations is the (Abba,

Doha) _____ Round and it continues to focus on (increasing, reducing) _____ tariffs and quotas and _____ agricultural subsidies.

16. An example of a free-trade zone or trade bloc is the (Western, European) _____ Union.

> **a.** The specific aims of the EU were the abolition of (capital and labor, tariffs and quotas) _____, the establishment of (common, different) _____ tariffs on goods imported from outside the EU, the (restricted, free) _____ movement of capital and labor within the EU, and common policies on other matters.
>
> **b.** The EU created (small, large) _____ markets and stimulated production that has allowed industries to achieve (higher, lower) _____ costs. The economic effects of the EU on nonmember nations such as the United States are mixed because economic growth in the EU causes U.S. exports to the EU to (decrease, increase) _____ while the tariff barriers cause U.S. exports to _____.
>
> **c.** The common currency of many of the member nations of the EU is called the (peso, euro) _____.

17. The North American Free Trade Agreement (NAFTA) formed a trade (barrier, bloc) _____ among the United States, Canada, and Mexico. This agreement will eliminate (terms of trade, tariffs) _____ among the nations. Critics in the United States said that it would (increase, decrease) _____ jobs, but the evidence shows a(n) _____ in jobs and total output since its passage.

18. The Trade Adjustment Assistance Act of 2002 is designed to help some of the (workers, businesses) _____ hurt by shifts in international trade patterns. Critics contend that such job losses are a (small, large) _____ fraction of the total each year and that such a program is another type of special (tariff, subsidy) _____ that benefits one type worker over another.

19. The shifting of work previously done by U.S. workers to workers located in other nations is (dumping, offshoring) _____. It reflects a (growth, decline) in the specialization and international trade of services. It may (decrease, increase) _____ some jobs moved to other nations, but also _____ jobs and productivity in the United States.

20. Many U.S. firms can (monopolize, compete) _____ and be successful in the global economy; however, some firms that benefited from past trade protection may find it difficult to adjust to global (control, competition) _____ and may go out of business.

■ TRUE–FALSE QUESTIONS

Circle T if the statement is true, F if it is false.

1. The United States exports and imports goods and services with a dollar value greater than any other nation in the world. **T F**

2. The United States is dependent on trade for certain commodities that cannot be obtained in domestic markets. **T F**

3. Canada is the most important trading partner for the United States in terms of the volume of exports and imports. **T F**

4. If a person, firm, or region has a comparative advantage in the production of a particular commodity, it should specialize in the production of that commodity. **T F**

5. If one nation has a comparative advantage in the production of a commodity over another nation, then it has a higher opportunity cost of production relative to the other nation. **T F**

6. The economic effects of specialization and trade between nations are similar to increasing the quantity of resources or to achieving technological progress. **T F**

7. The interaction of the demand for, and supply of, Japanese yen will establish the dollar price of Japanese yen. **T F**

8. An increase in incomes in the United States would tend to cause the dollar price of the Japanese yen to fall. **T F**

9. When the dollar price of another nation's currency increases, there has been an appreciation in the value of the dollar. **T F**

10. When the dollar depreciates relative to the value of the currencies of the trading partners of the United States, then goods imported into the United States will tend to become more expensive. **T F**

11. Export subsidies are government payments to reduce the price of a product to buyers from other nations. **T F**

12. Nontariff barriers include excise taxes or duties placed on imported goods. **T F**

13. Through world trade, an economy can reach a point beyond its domestic production possibilities curve. **T F**

14. One reason that trade restrictions get public support is that the alleged benefits of the restrictions are often immediate and clear-cut, but the adverse effects are often obscure and dispersed over the economy. **T F**

15. Tariffs and quotas benefit domestic firms in the protected industries and also help domestic consumers by lowering the prices for those products. **T F**

16. The Smoot-Hawley Tariff Act of 1930 reduced tariffs in the United States to the lowest level ever in an attempt to pull the nation out of the Great Depression. **T F**

17. If the United States concludes a tariff agreement that lowers the tariff rates on goods imported from another nation, the lower tariff rates are then applied to those goods when they are imported from nations with normal-trade-relation (NTR) status. **T F**

18. The World Trade Organization (WTO) is the world's major advocate for trade protectionism. **T F**

19. The members of the European Union (EU) have experienced freer trade since it was formed. **T F**

20. The economic integration of nations creates larger markets for firms within the nations that integrate and makes it possible for these firms and their customers to benefit from the economies of large-scale (mass) production. **T F**

21. The formation of the European Union (EU) may make it more difficult for U.S. firms to compete for European customers with firms located within the Union. **T F**

22. The 1993 North American Free Trade Agreement (NAFTA) includes all Central American nations. **T F**

23. The Trade Adjustment Assistance Act of 2002 provided compensation to U.S. workers who were displaced by shifts in international trade patterns. **T F**

24. Although offshoring decreases some U.S. jobs, it also lowers production costs, expands sales, and may create other U.S. jobs. **T F**

25. Major U.S. firms are unable to compete in global markets without significant protection from foreign competition. **T F**

MULTIPLE-CHOICE QUESTIONS

Circle the letter that corresponds to the best answer.

1. Which is a major economic flow that links the U.S. economy with the economies of other nations?
(a) tariff flow
(b) seasonal flow
(c) financial flow
(d) government flow

2. Which of the following is true?
(a) Exports as a percentage of GDP are greatest in the United States.
(b) The United States is almost totally dependent on other nations for aircraft, machine tools, and coal.
(c) About half of the exports and imports trade of the United States is with industrially advanced nations.
(d) The United States has a trade surplus with Japan.

3. A trade deficit occurs when
(a) exports exceed imports
(b) imports exceed exports
(c) tariff costs exceed tariff benefits
(d) tariff benefits exceed tariff costs

4. What is one way the United States finances its trade deficit?
(a) by lending to foreigners
(b) by selling real assets to foreigners
(c) by purchasing real assets from foreigners
(d) by passing protective tariffs on foreign products

5. Which factor has greatly facilitated international trade since World War II?
(a) greater import quotas
(b) expanded export subsidies
(c) increased nontariff barriers
(d) improved communications

6. Which industrializing nation would be considered one of the new participants in international trade since 1990?
(a) Canada
(b) Germany
(c) Japan
(d) China

7. Why do nations specialize and engage in trade?
(a) to increase output and income
(b) to improve communications
(c) to protect corporations
(d) to control other nations

Answer Questions 8, 9, 10, and 11 on the basis of the data given for two regions, Slobovia and Utopia, which have the following production possibilities tables.

SLOBOVIA PRODUCTION POSSIBILITIES TABLE

Product	Production alternatives					
	A	B	C	D	E	F
Cams	1500	1200	900	600	300	0
Widgets	0	100	200	300	400	500

UTOPIA PRODUCTION POSSIBILITIES TABLE

Product	Production alternatives				
	A	B	C	D	E
Cams	4000	3000	2000	1000	0
Widgets	0	200	400	600	800

8. In Slobovia, the comparative cost of
(a) 1 cam is 3 widgets
(b) 1 widget is .33 of a cam
(c) 1 cam is .33 of a widget
(d) 3 widgets is 1 cam

9. Which of the following statements is *not* true?
(a) Slobovia should specialize in the production of widgets.
(b) Slobovia has a comparative advantage in the production of widgets.
(c) Utopia should specialize in the production of widgets.
(d) Utopia has a comparative advantage in the production of cams.

10. The terms of trade will be
(a) greater than 7 cams for 1 widget
(b) between 7 cams for 1 widget and 5 cams for 1 widget
(c) between 5 cams for 1 widget and 3 cams for 1 widget
(d) less than 3 cams for 1 widget

11. Assume that if Slobovia did not specialize it would produce alternative C and that if Utopia did not specialize it would select alternative B. The gains from specialization are
(a) 100 cams and 100 widgets
(b) 200 cams and 200 widgets
(c) 400 cams and 500 widgets
(d) 500 cams and 400 widgets

12. If the dollar–yen exchange rate is $1 for 110 yen, then a Sony VCR priced at 27,500 yen would cost a U.S. consumer
(a) $200
(b) $250
(c) $275
(d) $300

13. If the equilibrium exchange rate changes so that the dollar price of Japanese yen increases
(a) the dollar has appreciated in value
(b) the dollar has depreciated in value
(c) U.S. citizens will be able to buy more Japanese goods
(d) Japanese citizens will be able to buy fewer U.S. goods

14. A decrease in the United States demand for Japanese goods will
(a) increase the demand for Japanese yen and increase the dollar price of yen
(b) increase the demand for Japanese yen but decrease the dollar price of yen
(c) decrease the demand for Japanese yen and decrease the dollar price of yen
(d) decrease the demand for Japanese yen but increase the dollar price of yen

15. If the exchange rate for one U.S. dollar changes from 1.0 euro to 1.1 euros, then there has been
(a) an appreciation in the value of the euro
(b) a depreciation in the value of the dollar
(c) a depreciation in the value of the euro
(d) an increase in the price of the euro

16. Which of the following is designed to restrict trade?
(a) GATT
(b) NAFTA
(c) import quotas
(d) normal-trade-relations status

17. Why do governments often intervene to restrict international trade?
(a) to expand a nation's production possibilities
(b) to improve the position of global businesses
(c) to protect domestic industries from foreign competition
(d) to increase revenue from tariff duties and excise taxes

18. Tariffs and quotas in a nation benefit domestic
(a) consumers and foreign producers of the protected product
(b) consumers and producers of the protected product
(c) producers of the protected product, but harm domestic consumers of the product
(d) producers and foreign producers of the product

19. Which one of the following specifically empowered the president of the United States to reduce tariff rates up to 50% if other nations would reduce their tariffs on American goods?
(a) the Smoot-Hawley Tariff Act of 1930
(b) the Reciprocal Trade Agreements Act of 1934
(c) the General Agreement on Tariffs and Trade of 1947
(d) North American Free Trade Agreement of 1993

20. Which of the following is characteristic of the General Agreement on Tariffs and Trade? Nations signing the agreement were committed to
(a) the expansion of import quotas
(b) the establishment of a world customs union
(c) the reciprocal increase in tariffs by negotiation
(d) the nondiscriminatory treatment of all member nations

21. One important outcome from the Uruguay Round of GATT was
(a) an increase in tariff barriers on services
(b) establishment of the World Trade Organization
(c) removal of voluntary export restraints in manufacturing
(d) abolishment of patent, copyright, and trademark protection

22. One of the potential problems with the European Union is that
(a) an unregulated free flow of labor and capital may reduce productivity
(b) economies of large-scale production may increase consumer prices
(c) tariffs may reduce trade with nonmember nations
(d) governments may have difficulty covering the shortfall from the elimination of duties and taxes

23. An example of the formation of a trade bloc would be the
(a) Smoot-Hawley Tariff Act
(b) North American Free Trade Agreement
(c) Reciprocal Trade Agreements Act
(d) General Agreement on Tariffs and Trade

24. The Trade Adjustment Assistance Act
(a) increased funding for the World Trade Organization
(b) provided more foreign aid to nations that trade with the United States
(c) extended normal-trade-relations status to more less-developed countries
(d) gave cash assistance to U.S. workers displaced by imports or plant relocations abroad

25. The increase in global competition has resulted in
  (a) greater inefficiency among U.S. producers
  (b) lower quality in the production of goods
  (c) the inability of most U.S. firms to compete
  (d) lower prices for many consumer goods and services

■ **PROBLEMS**

1. The following problem will help you understand the principle of comparative advantage and the benefits of specialization. A tailor named Hart has the production possibilities table for trousers and jackets as given. He chooses production alternative D.

HART'S PRODUCTION POSSIBILITIES TABLE

Product	Production alternatives					
	A	**B**	**C**	**D**	**E**	**F**
Trousers	75	60	45	30	15	0
Jackets	0	10	20	30	40	50

Another tailor, Schaffner, has the following production possibilities table and produces production alternative E.

SCHAFFNER'S PRODUCTION POSSIBILITIES TABLE

Product	Production alternatives						
	A	**B**	**C**	**D**	**E**	**F**	**G**
Trousers	60	50	40	30	20	10	0
Jackets	0	5	10	15	20	25	30

a. To Hart,

(1) the cost of one pair of trousers is _____ jackets

(2) the cost of one jacket is _____ pairs of trousers
b. To Schaffner,

(1) the cost of one pair of trousers is _____ jackets

(2) the cost of one jacket is _____ pairs of trousers
c. If Hart and Schaffner were to form a partnership to make suits,

(1) _____ should specialize in the making of trousers because he can make a pair of trousers at the cost of

_____ of a jacket while it costs his partner _____ of a jacket to make a pair of trousers.

(2) _____ should specialize in the making of jackets because he can make a jacket at the cost of _____

pairs of trousers while it costs his partner _____ pairs of trousers to make a jacket.
d. Without specialization, Hart and Schaffner were able to make 50 pairs of trousers and 50 jackets. If each specializes completely in the item in the production in which he has a comparative advantage, their

combined production will be _____ pairs of trousers

and _____ jackets. Thus the gain from specialization

is _____.

e. When Hart and Schaffner come to divide the income of the partnership between them, the manufacture of a pair of trousers should be treated as the equivalent of from _____ to _____ jackets (or a jacket should be treated as the equivalent of from _____ to _____ pairs of trousers).

2. The countries of Lilliput and Brobdingnag have the production possibilities tables for apples and bananas shown below.
  Note that the costs of producing apples and bananas are constant in both countries.

LILLIPUT PRODUCTION POSSIBILITIES TABLE

Product	Production alternatives					
	A	**B**	**C**	**D**	**E**	**F**
Apples	40	32	24	16	8	0
Bananas	0	4	8	12	16	20

BROBDINGNAG PRODUCTION POSSIBILITIES TABLE

Product	Production alternatives					
	A	**B**	**C**	**D**	**E**	**F**
Apples	75	60	45	30	15	0
Bananas	0	5	10	15	20	25

a. In Lilliput the cost of producing

(1) 8 apples is _____ bananas

(2) 1 apple is _____ bananas
b. In Brobdingnag the cost of producing

(1) 15 apples is _____ bananas

(2) 1 apple is _____ bananas
c. In Lilliput the cost of producing

(1) 4 bananas is _____ apples

(2) 1 banana is _____ apples
d. In Brobdingnag the cost of producing

(1) 5 bananas is _____ apples

(2) 1 banana is _____ apples
e. The cost of producing 1 apple is lower in the coun-

try of _____ and the cost of producing 1

banana is lower in the country of _____.

f. Lilliput has a comparative advantage in the pro-

duction of _____ and Brobdingnag has a comparative advantage in the production of

_____.

g. The information in this problem is not sufficient to determine the exact terms of trade, but the terms of

trade will be greater than _____ apples for

1 banana and less than _____ apples for 1 banana. Put another way, the terms of trade will be

between _____ bananas for 1 apple and

_____ bananas for 1 apple.

h. If neither nation could specialize, each would produce production alternative C. The combined production of apples in the two countries would be

_____ apples and the combined production of bananas would be _____ bananas.

(1) If each nation specializes in producing the fruit for which it has a comparative advantage, their combined production will be _____ apples and _____ bananas.

(2) Their gain from specialization will be _____ apples and _____ bananas.

3. Use the following table that shows 10 different currencies and how much of each currency can be purchased with a U.S. dollar.

Country	Currency	Currency per U.S. $ Year 1	Year 2	A or D
Brazil	Real	0.85	0.91	_____
Britain	Pound	0.65	0.59	_____
Canada	Dollar	1.41	1.51	_____
Switzerland	Franc	1.33	1.19	_____
Germany	Euro	1.58	1.69	_____
India	Rupee	31.39	34.55	_____
Japan	Yen	100.15	110.23	_____
Mexico	Peso	4.65	5.09	_____
Norway	Krone	6.88	6.49	_____
Thailand	Bhat	25.12	23.22	_____

a. In the far right column of the table, indicate whether the U.S. dollar has appreciated (**A**) or depreciated (**D**) from year 1 to year 2.

b. In year 1, a U.S. dollar would purchase _____ Swiss francs, but in year 2, it would purchase _____ Swiss francs. The U.S. dollar has (appreciated, depreciated) _____ against the Swiss franc from year 1 to year 2.

c. In year 1, a U.S. dollar would purchase _____ Japanese yen, but in year 2, it would purchase _____ Japanese yen. The U.S. dollar has (appreciated, depreciated) _____ against the Japanese yen from year 1 to year 2.

4. This problem asks you to calculate prices based on exchange rates. Use the data in the table for Problem 3 to answer the following items.

a. Using the exchange rates shown for year 1, what would be the U.S. dollar cost for the following products?

(1) Japanese television costing 30,000 yen.

$_____

(2) Swiss scarf costing 200 francs. $_____
(3) Thai artwork costing 3,768 bhats. $_____
(4) German auto costing 79,000 euros. $_____
(5) Mexican silver bracelet costing 1,376 pesos.

$_____

b. Using the exchange rates shown for year 2, what would be the U.S. dollar cost of the following products?

(1) Japanese television costing 30,000 yen.

$_____

(2) Swiss scarf costing 200 francs. $_____
(3) Thai artwork costing 3,768 bhats. $_____
(4) German auto costing 79,000 euros. $_____
(5) Mexican silver bracelet costing 1,376 pesos.

$_____

c. Indicate whether the U.S. dollar cost of each product in 4b has increased (+) or decreased (−) from year 1 to year 2 _____

d. What is the relationship between your answers in 4c to the ones you gave for the corresponding nations in 3a?

(1) When the U.S. dollar *appreciates* in value against a foreign currency, the U.S. dollar cost of a product from that nation will (increase, decrease) _____.

(2) When the U.S. dollar *depreciates* in value against a foreign currency, the U.S. dollar cost of a product from that nation will (increase, decrease) _____.

■ **SHORT ANSWER AND ESSAY QUESTIONS**

1. Describe the four major economic flows that link the United States to other nations.

2. What are the principal exports and imports of the U.S. economy? What commodities used in the economy come almost entirely from abroad, and what American industries sell large percentages of their outputs abroad?

3. What is meant by comparative cost and comparative advantage? Explain how comparative advantage determines the terms of trade between nations.

4. What is the gain for a nation that results from specialization in the production of products for which there is a comparative advantage?

5. Describe the characteristics of a foreign exchange market and of exchange rates. Why is an exchange rate an unusual price?

6. Why might an appreciation of the value of the U.S. dollar relative to the Japanese yen depress the U.S. economy and stimulate the Japanese economy? Why might a government intervene in the foreign exchange market and try to increase or decrease the value of its currency?

7. What are the major trade impediments and subsidies? How do they restrict international trade?

8. Why do governments intervene in international trade and develop restrictive trade policies?

9. What is the cost to society from trade protectionism? Who benefits and who is hurt by trade protectionism?

10. What was the Smoot-Hawley Tariff Act of 1930? What international trade problems are illustrated by this act?

11. Explain the basic provisions of the Reciprocal Trade Agreements Act of 1934.

12. What were the cardinal principles contained in the General Agreement on Tariffs and Trade (GATT)? What were the basic provisions and important results of the Uruguay Round of GATT negotiations?

13. Describe the purpose of the World Trade Organization (WTO). Why is it controversial?

14. What is the European Union? What has it achieved?

15. Discuss the potential effects of the European Union on the trade of the United States.

16. What is the euro and what have been its likely economic effects?

17. What is the North American Free Trade Agreement (NAFTA)? What do critics and defenders say about the agreement?

18. Discuss the purpose of the Trade Adjustment Assistance Act of 2002 and its advantages and disadvantages.

19. Explain the reasons U.S. businesses have turned to offshoring and evaluate the costs and benefits of such actions.

20. Evaluate the effects of increased global competition on U.S. firms, workers, and consumers.

ANSWERS

Chapter 5 The United States in the Global Economy

FILL-IN QUESTIONS

1. *a.* goods and services flows (trade flows); *b.* capital and labor flows (resource flows); *c.* information and technology flows; *d.* financial flows (any order for *a–d*)
2. limited, diversified, Netherlands, United States
3. 12–17, largest, Canada, China
4. transportation, communications (any order), tariffs
5. increase, increase
6. comparative advantage, opportunity cost
7. depreciation, appreciation, appreciation, depreciation
8. supply of, demand for, more
9. *a.* protective tariffs; *b.* import quotas; *c.* nontariff barriers; *d.* export subsidies
10. exports, imports, imports, exports, imports
11. political, tariffs, quotas, hidden from
12. benefit, cost, higher, cost
13. upward, downward, Reciprocal Trade Agreements, tariffs, normal-trade-relations
14. *a.* equal, nondiscriminatory treatment of all member nations; *b.* reduction of tariffs by multilateral negotiations; *c.* elimination of import quotas
15. rounds, World, Doha, reducing, reducing

16. European; *a.* tariffs and quotas, common, free; *b.* large, lower, increase, decrease; *c.* euro
17. bloc, tariffs, decrease, increase
18. workers, small, subsidy
19. offshoring, growth, decrease, increase
20. compete, competition

TRUE–FALSE QUESTIONS

1. T, p. 93
2. T, p. 93
3. T, pp. 94–95
4. T, pp. 96–98
5. F, pp. 96–98
6. T, pp. 98–99
7. T, pp. 99–100
8. F, p. 100
9. F, p. 100
10. T, p. 100
11. T, p. 101
12. F, p. 101
13. T, p. 99
14. T, pp. 101–102
15. F, p. 102
16. F, p. 102
17. T, pp. 102–103
18. F, pp. 103–104
19. T, p. 104
20. T, p. 104
21. T, p. 104
22. F, p. 105
23. T, pp. 105–106
24. T, pp. 106–107
25. F, p. 108

MULTIPLE-CHOICE QUESTIONS

1. c, p. 92
2. c, pp. 93–95
3. b, p. 94
4. b, p. 95
5. d, p. 95
6. d, p. 96
7. a, p. 96
8. c, pp. 96–98
9. c, pp. 96–98
10. c, p. 98
11. a, pp. 98–99
12. b, pp. 99–100
13. b, p. 100
14. c, p. 100
15. c, p. 100
16. c, p. 101
17. c, pp. 101–102
18. c, p. 102
19. b, pp. 102–103
20. d, p. 103
21. b, p. 103
22. c, p. 104
23. b, p. 105
24. d, pp. 105–106
25. d, p. 108

PROBLEMS

1. *a.* (1) .67, (2) 1.5; *b.* (1) .5, (2) 2; *c.* (1) Schaffner, .5, .67; (2) Hart, 1.5, 2; *d.* 60, 50, 10 pairs of trousers; *e.* .5, .67, 1.5, 2
2. *a.* (1) 4, (2) .5; *b.* (1) 5, (2) .33; *c.* (1) 8, (2) 2; *d.* (1) 15, (2) 3; *e.* Brobdingnag, Lilliput; *f.* bananas, apples; *g.* 2, 3, .33, .5; *h.* 69, 18, (1) 75, 20, (2) 6, 2
3. *a.* A, D, A, D, A, A, A, A, D, D; *b.* 1.33, 1.19, depreciated; *c.* 100.15, 110.23, appreciated
4. *a.* (1) 299.55 (2) 150.38 (3) 150 (4) 50,000 (5) 295.91; *b.* (1) 272.16 (2) 168.07 (3) 162.27 (4) 46,745.56 (5) 270.33; *c.* (1) − (2) + (3) + (4) − (5) −; *d.* (1) decrease (2) increase

SHORT ANSWER AND ESSAY QUESTIONS

1. p. 92
2. pp. 92–95
3. pp. 96–98
4. pp. 98–99
5. p. 99
6. pp. 99–100
7. p. 101
8. pp. 101–102
9. p. 102
10. p. 102
11. pp. 102–103
12. p. 103
13. pp. 103–104
14. p. 104
15. p. 104
16. pp. 104–105
17. p. 105
18. pp. 105–106
19. pp. 106–107
20. p. 108

CHAPTER 6

Elasticity, Consumer Surplus, and Producer Surplus

Chapter 6 is basically a continuation of Chapter 3. In the earlier part of the book, you needed only an elementary knowledge of supply and demand. Now the economic principles, problems, and policies to be studied require a more detailed discussion of supply and demand.

The concept of **price elasticity of demand,** to which the major portion of Chapter 6 is devoted, is of great importance for studying the material found in the remainder of the text. You must understand (1) what price elasticity measures; (2) how the price-elasticity formula is applied to measure the price elasticity of demand; (3) the difference between price elastic, price inelastic, and unit elasticity; (4) how total revenue varies by the type of price elasticity of demand; (5) the meaning of perfect price elasticity and of perfect price inelasticity of demand; (6) the four major determinants of price elasticity of demand; and (7) the practical application of the concept to many economic issues.

When you have become thoroughly acquainted with the concept of price elasticity of demand, you will find that you have very little trouble understanding the **price elasticity of supply.** The transition requires no more than the substitution of the words "quantity supplied" for the words "quantity demanded." You should concentrate your attention on the meaning of price elasticity of supply and how it is affected by time. Several examples are provided to show how it affects the prices of many products.

The chapter also introduces you to two other elasticity concepts. The **cross elasticity of demand** measures the sensitivity of a change in the quantity demanded for one product due to a change in the price of another product. This concept is especially important in identifying substitute, complementary, or independent goods. The **income elasticity of demand** assesses the change in the quantity demanded of a product resulting from a change in consumer incomes. It is useful for categorizing goods as superior, normal, or inferior.

Supply and demand analysis is used to enhance your understanding of **economic efficiency** in the fourth section of the chapter. This extension requires an explanation of the concepts of **consumer surplus** and **producer surplus.** Consumer surplus is the difference between the maximum price consumers are willing to pay for a product and the actual price. Producer surplus is the difference between the minimum price producers are willing to accept for a product and the actual price. The chapter also revisits the concept of **allocative efficiency** and explains that it is achieved when the combination of consumer and producer surplus is at a maximum.

■ CHECKLIST

When you have studied this chapter you should be able to

☐ Define price elasticity of demand and compute its coefficient when given the demand data.

☐ State the midpoint formula for price elasticity of demand and explain how it refines the original formula for price elasticity.

☐ State two reasons why the formula for price elasticity of demand uses percentages rather than absolute amounts in measuring consumer responsiveness.

☐ Explain the meaning of elastic, inelastic, and unit elasticity as they relate to demand.

☐ Define and illustrate graphically the concepts of perfectly elastic demand and perfectly inelastic demand.

☐ Apply the total-revenue test to determine whether demand is elastic, inelastic, or unit elastic.

☐ Describe the relationship between price elasticity of demand and the price range for most demand curves.

☐ Explain why the slope of the demand curve is not a sound basis for judging price elasticity.

☐ Illustrate graphically the relationship between price elasticity of demand and total revenue.

☐ List the four major determinants of the price elasticity of demand, and explain how each determinant affects price elasticity.

☐ Describe several applications of the concept of price elasticity of demand.

☐ Define the price elasticity of supply and compute its coefficient when given the relevant data.

☐ Explain the effect of time (short run and long run) on price elasticity of supply.

☐ Describe several applications of price elasticity of supply.

☐ Define cross elasticity of demand and compute its coefficient when given relevant data.

☐ Use the cross elasticity of demand to categorize substitute goods, complementary goods, and independent goods.

☐ Give applications of cross elasticity of demand.

☐ Define income elasticity of demand and compute its coefficient when given relevant data.

☐ Use the income elasticity of demand to categorize goods as normal or inferior.

☐ Provide some insights using the concept of income elasticity.

☐ Define consumer surplus and give a graphical example.

☐ Define producer surplus and give a graphical example.

☐ Use consumer surplus and producer surplus to explain how allocative efficiency is achieved in a competitive market.

☐ List the three conditions for achieving allocative efficiency at a quantity level in a competitive market.

☐ Use a supply and demand graph to illustrate efficiency losses when the quantity is greater or less than its equilibrium in a competitive market.

☐ Use the concept of elasticity of demand to explain why different consumers pay different prices (Last Word).

■ CHAPTER OUTLINE

1. *Price elasticity of demand* is a measure of the responsiveness or sensitivity of quantity demanded to changes in the price of a product. When quantity demanded is relatively responsive to a price change, demand is said to be *elastic*. When quantity demanded is relatively unresponsive to a price change, demand is said to be *inelastic*.

a. The exact degree of elasticity can be measured by using a formula to compute the elasticity coefficient.

(1) The changes in quantity demanded and in price are comparisons of consumer responsiveness to price changes of different products.

(2) A ***midpoint formula*** calculates price elasticity across a price and quantity range to overcome the problem of selecting the reference points for price and quantity. In this formula, the average of the two quantities and the average of the two prices are used as reference points.

(3) Because price and quantity demanded are inversely related, the price elasticity of demand coefficient is a negative number, but economists ignore the minus sign in front of the coefficient and focus their attention on its absolute value.

b. The coefficient of price elasticity has several interpretations.

(1) ***Elastic demand*** occurs when the percentage change in quantity demanded is greater than the percentage change in price. The elasticity coefficient is greater than 1.

(2) ***Inelastic demand*** occurs when the percentage change in quantity demanded is less than the percentage change in price. The elasticity coefficient is less than 1.

(3) ***Unit elasticity*** occurs when the percentage change in quantity demanded is equal to the percentage change in price. The elasticity coefficient is equal to 1.

(4) ***Perfectly inelastic demand*** means that a change in price results in no change in quantity demanded of a product, whereas ***perfectly elastic demand*** means that a small change in price causes buyers to purchase all they desire of a product.

c. ***Total revenue (TR)*** changes when price changes. The ***total-revenue test*** shows that when demand is:

(1) *elastic,* a decrease in price will increase total revenue and an increase in price will decrease total revenue.

(2) *inelastic,* a decrease in price will decrease total revenue and an increase in price will increase total revenue.

(3) *unit elastic,* an increase or decrease in price will not affect total revenue.

d. Note several points about the graph of a linear demand curve and price elasticity of demand.

(1) It is not the same at all prices. Demand is typically elastic at higher prices and inelastic at lower prices.

(2) It cannot be judged from the slope of the demand curve.

e. The relationship between price elasticity of demand and total revenue can be shown by graphing the demand curve and the total-revenue curve, one above the other. In this case, the horizontal axis for each graph uses the same quantity scale. The vertical axis for demand represents price. The vertical axis for the total-revenue graph measures total revenue.

(1) When demand is price elastic, as price declines and quantity increases along the demand curve, total revenue increases in the total-revenue graph.

(2) Conversely, when demand is price inelastic, as price declines and quantity increases along the demand curve, total revenue decreases.

(3) When demand is unit elastic, as price and quantity change along the demand curve, total revenue remains the same.

f. The price elasticity of demand for a product depends on four determinants.

(1) The number of good substitutes for the product. The more substitute goods that are available for a product, the greater the price elasticity of demand for the product.

(2) Its relative importance in the consumer's budget. The higher the price of product relative to consumers' incomes, the greater the price elasticity of demand.

(3) Whether it is a necessity or a luxury. Luxuries typically have a greater price elasticity of demand than necessities.

(4) The period of time under consideration. The longer the time period, the greater the elasticity of demand for a product.

g. Price elasticity of demand has practical applications to public policy and business decisions. The concept is relevant to bumper crops in agriculture, excise taxes, and the decriminalization of illegal drugs.

2. *Price elasticity of supply* is a measure of the sensitivity of quantity supplied to changes in the price of a product. Both the general formula and the midpoint formula for price elasticity of supply are similar to those for the price elasticity of demand, but "quantity supplied" replaces "quantity demanded." This means that the price elasticity of supply is the percentage change in quantity supplied of a product divided by its percentage change in the price of the product. There is a midpoint formula that is an average of quantities and prices and is used for calculating the elasticity of supply across quantity or price ranges. The price elasticity of supply depends primarily on the amount of time sellers have to adjust to a price change. The easier and faster suppliers can respond to changes in price, the greater the price elasticity of supply.

a. In the *market period,* there is too little time for producers to change output in response to a change in price. As a consequence supply is perfectly inelastic. Graphically, this means that the supply curve is vertical at that market level of output.

b. In the *short run,* producers have less flexibility to change output in response to a change in price because they have fixed inputs that they cannot change. They have only a limited control over the range in which they can vary their output. As a consequence, supply is *price inelastic* in the short run.

c. In the *long run,* producers can make adjustments to all inputs to vary production. As a consequence, supply is *price elastic* in the long run. There is no total-revenue test for price elasticity of supply because price and total revenue move in the same direction regardless of the degree of price elasticity of supply.

d. Price elasticity of supply has many practical applications for explaining price volatility. The concept is relevant to the pricing of antiques and gold, for which the supply is perfectly inelastic.

3. Two other elasticity concepts are important.

a. The *cross elasticity of demand* measures the degree to which the quantity demanded of one product is affected by a change in the price of another product. Cross elasticities of demand are:
(1) positive for goods that are substitutes;
(2) negative for goods that are complements; and
(3) zero or near zero for goods that are unrelated or independent.

b. The *income elasticity of demand* measures the effect of a change in income on the quantity demanded of a product. Income elasticities of demand are:
(1) positive for normal or superior goods, which means that more of them are demanded as income rises; and
(2) negative for inferior goods, which means that less of them are demanded as income rises.

4. In market transactions, consumers can obtain a beneficial surplus and so can producers.

a. *Consumer surplus* is the difference between the maximum price consumers are willing to pay for a product and the actual (equilibrium) price paid. Graphically, it is the triangular area bounded by the portion of the vertical axis between the equilibrium price and the demand curve intersection, the portion of the demand curve above the equilibrium price, and the horizontal line at the equilibrium price from the vertical axis to the demand curve. Price and consumer surplus are inversely (negatively) related: Higher prices reduce it and lower prices increase it.

b. *Producer surplus* is the difference between the minimum price producers are willing to accept for a product and the actual (equilibrium) price received. Graphically, it is the triangular area bounded by the portion of the vertical axis between the equilibrium price and the supply curve intersection, the portion of the supply curve below the equilibrium price, and the horizontal line at the equilibrium price from the vertical axis to the supply curve. Price and producer surplus are directly (positively) related: Higher prices increase it and lower prices decrease it.

c. The equilibrium quantity shown by the intersection of demand and supply curves reflects *economic efficiency.*
(1) **Productive efficiency** is achieved because production costs are minimized at each quantity level of output.
(2) **Allocative efficiency** is achieved at the equilibrium quantity of output because three conditions are satisfied: Marginal benefit equals marginal cost; maximum willingness to pay equals minimum acceptable price; and the combination of the consumer and producer surplus is at a maximum.

d. If quantity is less than or greater than the equilibrium quantity or most efficient level, there are **efficiency losses** (or **deadweight losses**) to buyers and sellers. The efficiency losses reduce the maximum possible size of the combined consumer and producer surplus.

5. (Last Word). There are many examples of dual or multiple pricing of products. The main reason for the differences is differences in the price elasticity of demand among groups. Business travelers have a more inelastic demand for travel than leisure travelers and thus can be charged more for an airline ticket. Prices for children are often lower than prices for adults for the same service (for example, movie tickets or restaurant meals) because children have more elastic demand for the service. Low-income groups have a more elastic demand for higher education than high-income groups, so high-income groups are charged the full tuition price and lower-income groups get more financial aid to offset the tuition price.

■ HINTS AND TIPS

1. This chapter is an extension of the material presented in Chapter 3. Be sure you thoroughly read and study Chapter 3 again before you read and do the self-test exercises for this chapter.

2. You should **not judge** the price elasticity of demand based on the slope of the demand curve unless it is horizontal (*perfectly elastic*) or vertical (*perfectly inelastic*). Remember that elasticity varies from elastic to inelastic along a downsloping, linear demand curve. The price elasticity equals 1 at the midpoint of a downsloping linear demand curve.

3. Master the **total-revenue test** for assessing the price elasticity of demand (review Table 6.2). For many problems, the total-revenue test is easier to use than the midpoint formula for identifying the type of elasticity (elastic, inelastic, unit), and the test has many practical applications.

4. Do not just memorize the elasticity formulas in this chapter. Instead, work on understanding what they mean and how they are used for economic decisions. The elasticity formulas simply measure the *responsiveness* of a percentage change in *quantity* to a percentage change in some other characteristic (price or income). The elasticity formulas each have a similar structure: A percentage change in some type of *quantity* (demanded, supplied) is divided by a percentage change in the other variable. The price elasticity of demand measures the responsiveness of a percentage change in *quantity demanded* for a product to a percentage change in its *price*. The cross elasticity of demand measures the percentage change in the *quantity demanded of product X* to a percentage change in the *price of product Y*. The income elasticity of demand is the percentage change in *quantity demanded* for a product to a percentage change in *income*. The price elasticity of supply is the percentage change in the *quantity supplied* of a product to a percentage change in its price.

5. The term "surplus" in this chapter should not be confused with its previous use related to pre-set prices and price floors. What the consumer surplus refers to is the extra utility or satisfaction that consumers get when they do not have to pay the price they were willing to pay and pay the lower equilibrium price. The producer surplus arises when producers receive an equilibrium price that is above the minimum price that they consider acceptable to selling the product.

IMPORTANT TERMS

price elasticity of demand	market period
midpoint formula	short run
elastic demand	long run
inelastic demand	cross elasticity of demand
unit elasticity	income elasticity of demand
perfectly inelastic demand	consumer surplus
perfectly elastic demand	producer surplus
total revenue	efficiency losses
total-revenue test	(or deadweight losses)
price elasticity of supply	

SELF-TEST

FILL-IN QUESTIONS

1. If a relatively large change in price results in a relatively small change in quantity demanded, demand is (elastic, inelastic) _____. If a relatively small change in price results in a relatively large change in quantity demanded, demand is (elastic, inelastic) _____.

2. The midpoint formula for the price elasticity of demand uses the (total, average) _____ of the two quantities as a reference point in calculating the percentage change in quantity and the (total, average) _____ of the two prices as a reference point in calculating the percentage change in price.

3. The price elasticity formula is based on (absolute amounts, percentages) _____ because it avoids the problems caused by the arbitrary choice of units and permits meaningful comparisons of consumer (responsiveness, incomes) _____ to changes in the prices of different products.

4. If a change in price causes no change in quantity demanded, demand is perfectly (elastic, inelastic) _____ and the demand curve is (horizontal, vertical) _____. If an extremely small change in price causes an extremely large change in quantity demanded, demand is perfectly (elastic, inelastic) _____ and the demand curve is (horizontal, vertical) _____.

5. Two characteristics of the price elasticity of a linear demand curve are that elasticity (is constant, varies) _____ over the different price ranges, and that the slope is (a sound, an unsound) _____ basis for judging its elasticity.

6. Assume the price of a product declines.
   a. When demand is inelastic; the loss of revenue due to the lower price is (less, greater) _____ than the gain in revenue due to the greater quantity demanded.
   b. When demand is elastic; the loss of revenue due to the lower price is (less, greater) _____ than the gain in revenue due to the greater quantity demanded.
   c. When demand is unit elastic; the loss of revenue due to the lower price (exceeds, is equal to) _____ the gain in revenue due to the greater quantity demanded.

7. Complete the following summary table.

If demand is	The elasticity coefficient is	If price rises, total revenue will	If price falls, total revenue will
Elastic	_____	_____	_____
Inelastic	_____	_____	_____
Unit elastic	_____	_____	_____

8. What are the four most important determinants of the price elasticity of demand?
   a. _____
   b. _____

c. _____

d. _____

9. The demand for most farm products is highly (elastic, inelastic) _____ which means that large crop yields will most likely (increase, decrease) _____ the total revenue of farmers. Governments often tax products such as liquor, gasoline, and cigarettes because the price elasticity of the demand is (elastic, inelastic) _____. A higher tax on such products will (increase, decrease) _____ tax revenue.

10. The price elasticity of supply measures the percentage change in (price, quantity supplied) _____ divided by the percentage change in _____. The most important factor affecting the price elasticity of supply is (revenue, time) _____. It is easier to shift resources to alternative uses when there is (more, less) _____ time.

11. In the immediate market period, the price elasticity of supply will be perfectly (elastic, inelastic) _____ and the supply curve will be (horizontal, vertical) _____. Typically, in the short run the price elasticity of supply is (more, less) _____ elastic but in the long run the price elasticity of supply is _____ elastic.

12. There is a total-revenue test for the elasticity of (demand, supply) _____. There is no total-revenue test for the elasticity of (demand, supply) _____ because regardless of the degree of elasticity, price and total revenue are (directly, indirectly) _____ related.

13. The measure of the sensitivity of the consumption of one product given a change in the price of another product is the (cross, income) _____ elasticity of demand, while the measure of the responsiveness of consumer purchases to changes in income is the _____ elasticity of demand.

14. When the cross elasticity of demand is positive, two products are (complements, substitutes, independent) _____, but when the cross elasticity of demand is negative, they are _____; a zero cross elasticity suggests that two products are _____.

15. If consumers increase purchases of a product as consumer incomes increase, then a good is classified as (inferior, normal or superior) _____, but if consumers decrease purchases of a product as consumer incomes increase, then a good is classified as _____.

16. A consumer surplus is the difference between the actual price and the (minimum, maximum) _____ price a consumer is (or consumers are) willing to pay for a product. In most markets, consumers individually or collectively gain more total utility or satisfaction when the actual or equilibrium price they have to pay for a product is (less, more) _____ than what they would have been willing to pay to obtain the product. Consumer surplus and price are (positively, negatively) _____ related. This means that higher prices (increase, decrease) _____ consumer surplus and lower prices _____ it.

17. A producer surplus is the difference between the actual or equilibrium price and the (minimum, maximum) _____ acceptable price a producer is (or producers are) willing to accept in exchange for a product. In most markets, sellers individually or collectively benefit when they sell their product at an actual or equilibrium price that is (less, more) _____ than what they would have been willing to receive in exchange for the product. Producer surplus and price are (positively, negatively) _____ related. This means that higher prices (increase, decrease) _____ producer surplus and lower prices _____ it.

18. When competition forces producers to use the best techniques and combinations of resources to make a product, then (allocative, productive) _____ efficiency is being achieved. When the correct or optimal quantity of output of a product is being produced relative to the other goods and services, then _____ efficiency is being achieved.

19. Allocative efficiency occurs at quantity levels where marginal benefit is (greater than, less than, equal to) _____ marginal cost, maximum willingness to pay by consumers is _____ the minimum acceptable price for producers, and the combined consumer and producer surplus is at a (minimum, maximum) _____.

20. When there is overproduction of a product, there are efficiency (gains, losses) _____ and when there is underproduction there are efficiency _____. In both cases, the combined consumer and producer surplus is (greater than, less than) _____ the maximum that would occur at the efficient quantity of output.

■ TRUE–FALSE QUESTIONS

Circle T if the statement is true, F if it is false.

1. If the percentage change in price is greater than the percentage change in quantity demanded, the price elasticity coefficient is greater than 1.　**T　F**

2. If the quantity demanded for a product increases from 100 to 150 units when the price decreases from $14 to $10, using the midpoint formula, the price elasticity of demand for this product in this price range is 1.2.　**T　F**

3. A product with a price elasticity of demand equal to 1.5 is described as price inelastic.　**T　F**

4. If the price of a product increases from $5 to $6 and the quantity demanded decreases from 45 to 25, then according to the total-revenue test, the product is price inelastic in this price range.　**T　F**

5. Total revenue will not change when price changes if the price elasticity of demand is unitary.　**T　F**

6. When the absolute value of the price elasticity coefficient is greater than 1 and the price of the product decreases, then the total revenue will increase.　**T　F**

7. The flatness or steepness of a demand curve is based on absolute changes in price and quantity, while elasticity is based on relative or percentage changes in price and quantity.　**T　F**

8. Demand tends to be inelastic at higher prices and elastic at lower prices.　**T　F**

9. Price elasticity of demand and the slope of the demand curve are two different things.　**T　F**

10. In general, the larger the number of substitute goods that are available, the less the price elasticity of demand.　**T　F**

11. Other things equal, the higher the price of a good relative to consumers' incomes, the greater the price elasticity of demand.　**T　F**

12. Other things equal, the higher the price of a good relative to the longer the time period the purchase is considered, the greater the price elasticity of demand.　**T　F**

13. The more that a good is considered to be a "luxury" rather than a "necessity," the less is the price elasticity of demand.　**T　F**

14. The demand for most agricultural products is price inelastic. Consequently, an increase in supply will reduce the total income of producers of agricultural products.　**T　F**

15. A state government seeking to increase its excise-tax revenues is more likely to increase the tax rate on restaurant meals than on gasoline.　**T　F**

16. The degree of price elasticity of supply depends on how easily and quickly producers can shift resources between alternative uses.　**T　F**

17. If an increase in product price results in no change in the quantity supplied, supply is perfectly elastic.　**T　F**

18. The market period is a time so short that producers cannot respond to a change in demand and price.　**T　F**

19. The price elasticity of supply will tend to be more elastic in the long run.　**T　F**

20. There is a total revenue test for the elasticity of supply.　**T　F**

21. For a complementary good, the coefficient of the cross elasticity of demand is positive.　**T　F**

22. Cross elasticity of demand is measured by the percentage change in quantity demanded over the percentage change in income.　**T　F**

23. A negative cross elasticity of demand for two goods indicates that they are complements.　**T　F**

24. Inferior goods have a positive income elasticity of demand.　**T　F**

25. Consumer surplus is the difference between the minimum and maximum price a consumer is willing to pay for a good.　**T　F**

26. Consumer surplus is a utility surplus that reflects a gain in total utility or satisfaction.　**T　F**

27. Consumer surplus and price are directly or positively related.　**T　F**

28. Producer surplus is the difference between the actual price a producer receives for a product and the minimum price the producer would have been willing to accept for the product.　**T　F**

29. The higher the actual price, the less the amount of producer surplus.　**T　F**

30. Efficiency losses are increases in the combined consumer and producer surplus.　**T　F**

■ MULTIPLE-CHOICE QUESTIONS

Circle the letter that corresponds to the best answer.

1. If, when the price of a product rises from $1.50 to $2, the quantity demanded of the product decreases from 1000 to 900, the price elasticity of demand coefficient, using the midpoint formula, is
  (a) 3.00
  (b) 2.71
  (c) 0.37
  (d) 0.33

2. If a 1% fall in the price of a product causes the quantity demanded of the product to increase by 2%, demand is
  (a) inelastic
  (b) elastic
  (c) unit elastic
  (d) perfectly elastic

3. In the following diagram, D_1 is a
  (a) perfectly elastic demand curve
  (b) perfectly inelastic demand curve
  (c) unit elastic demand curve
  (d) a long-run demand curve

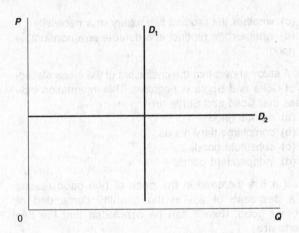

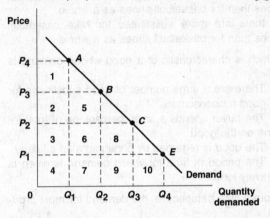

Questions 9, 10, and 11 are based on the following graph.

4. Compared to the lower-right portion, the upper-left portion of most demand curves tends to be
(a) more inelastic
(b) more elastic
(c) unit elastic
(d) perfectly inelastic

5. In which range of the demand schedule is demand price inelastic?

Price	Quantity demanded
$11	50
9	100
7	200
5	300
3	400

(a) $11–$9
(b) $9–$7
(c) $7–$5
(d) $5–$3

6. If a business increased the price of its product from $7 to $8 when the price elasticity of demand was inelastic, then
(a) total revenues decreased
(b) total revenues increased
(c) total revenues remain unchanged
(d) total revenues were perfectly inelastic

7. You are the sales manager for a pizza company and have been informed that the price elasticity of demand for your most popular pizza is greater than 1. To increase total revenues, you should
(a) increase the price of the pizza
(b) decrease the price of the pizza
(c) hold pizza prices constant
(d) decrease demand for your pizza

8. Assume Amanda Herman finds that her total spending on compact discs remains the same after the price of compact discs falls, other things equal. Which of the following is true about Amanda's demand for compact discs with this price change?
(a) It is unit price elastic.
(b) It is perfectly price elastic.
(c) It is perfectly price inelastic.
(d) It increased in response to the price change.

9. If price is P_3, then total revenue is measured by the area
(a) $0P_3CQ_3$
(b) $0P_3BQ_2$
(c) $0P_3BQ_3$
(d) $0P_3CQ_2$

10. If price falls from P_2 to P_1, then in this price range demand is
(a) relatively inelastic because the loss in total revenue (areas 3 + 6 + 8) is greater than the gain in total revenue (area 10)
(b) relatively elastic because the loss in total revenue (areas 3 + 6 + 8) is greater than the gain in total revenue (area 10)
(c) relatively inelastic because the loss in total revenue (area 10) is less than the gain in total revenue (areas 3 + 6 + 8)
(d) relatively inelastic because the loss in total revenue (areas 4 + 7 + 9 + 10) is greater than the gain in total revenue (areas 3 + 6 + 8)

11. As price falls from P_4 to P_3, you know that demand is
(a) elastic because total revenue decreased from $0P_4AQ_1$ to $0P_3BQ_2$
(b) inelastic because total revenue decreased from $0P_3BQ_2$ to $0P_4AQ_1$
(c) elastic because total revenue increased from $0P_4AQ_1$ to $0P_3BQ_2$
(d) inelastic because total revenue decreased from $0P_4AQ_1$ to $0P_3BQ_2$

12. Which is characteristic of a product whose demand is elastic?
(a) The price elasticity coefficient is less than 1.
(b) Total revenue decreases if price decreases.
(c) Buyers are relatively insensitive to price changes.
(d) The percentage change in quantity is greater than the percentage change in price.

13. The demand for Nike basketball shoes is more price elastic than the demand for basketball shoes as a whole. This is best explained by the fact that
(a) Nike basketball shoes are a luxury good, not a necessity
(b) Nike basketball shoes are the best made and widely advertised

(c) there are more complements for Nike basketball shoes than for basketball shoes as a whole

(d) there are more substitutes for Nike basketball shoes than for basketball shoes as a whole

14. Which is characteristic of a good whose demand is inelastic?

(a) There are a large number of good substitutes for the good for consumers.

(b) The buyer spends a small percentage of total income on the good.

(c) The good is regarded by consumers as a luxury.

(d) The period of time for which demand is given is relatively long.

15. From a time perspective, the demand for most products is

(a) less elastic in the short run and unit elastic in the long run

(b) less elastic in the long run and unit elastic in the short run

(c) more elastic in the short run than in the long run

(d) more elastic in the long run than in the short run

16. If a 5% fall in the price of a commodity causes quantity supplied to decrease by 8%, supply is

(a) inelastic

(b) unit elastic

(c) elastic

(d) perfectly inelastic

17. In the following diagram, what is the price elasticity of supply between points **A** and **C** (using the midpoint formula)?

(a) 1.33

(b) 1.67

(c) 1.85

(d) 2.46

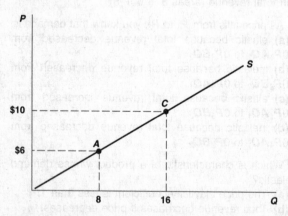

18. If supply is inelastic and demand decreases, the total revenue of sellers will

(a) increase

(b) decrease

(c) decrease only if demand is elastic

(d) increase only if demand is inelastic

19. The chief determinant of the price elasticity of supply of a product is

(a) the number of good substitutes the product has

(b) the length of time sellers have to adjust to a change in price

(c) whether the product is a luxury or a necessity

(d) whether the product is a durable or a nondurable good

20. A study shows that the coefficient of the cross elasticity of Coke and Sprite is negative. This information indicates that Coke and Sprite are

(a) normal goods

(b) complementary goods

(c) substitute goods

(d) independent goods

21. If a 5% increase in the price of one good results in a decrease of 2% in the quantity demanded of another good, then it can be concluded that the two goods are

(a) complements

(b) substitutes

(c) independent

(d) normal

22. Most goods can be classified as *normal* goods rather than inferior goods. The definition of a normal good means that

(a) the percentage change in consumer income is greater than the percentage change in price of the normal good

(b) the percentage change in quantity demanded of the normal good is greater than the percentage change in consumer income

(c) as consumer income increases, consumer purchases of a normal good increase

(d) the income elasticity of demand is negative

23. Based on the information in the table, which product would be an inferior good?

Product	% change in income	% change in quantity demanded
A	−10	+10
B	+10	+10
C	+5	−5
D	−5	−5

(a) Product A

(b) Product B

(c) Product C

(d) Product D

24. For which product is the income elasticity of demand most likely to be negative?

(a) automobiles

(b) bus tickets

(c) computers

(d) tennis rackets

25. Katie is willing to pay $50 for a product and Tom is willing to pay $40. The actual price that they have to pay is $30. What is the amount of the consumer surplus for Katie and Tom combined?

(a) $30

(b) $40

(c) $50

(d) $60

26. Given the demand curve, the consumer surplus is
   (a) increased by higher prices and decreased by lower prices
   (b) decreased by higher prices and increased by lower prices
   (c) increased by higher prices but not affected by lower prices
   (d) decreased by lower prices, but not affected by higher prices

27. The difference between the actual price that a producer receives (or producers receive) and the minimum acceptable price is producer
   (a) cost
   (b) wealth
   (c) surplus
   (d) investment

28. The minimum acceptable price for a product that Juan is willing to receive is $20. It is $15 for Carlos. The actual price they receive is $25. What is the amount of the producer surplus for Juan and Carlos combined?
   (a) $10
   (b) $15
   (c) $20
   (d) $25

29. When the combined consumer and producer surplus is at a maximum for a product,
   (a) the quantity supplied is greater than the quantity demanded
   (b) the market finds alternative ways to ration the product
   (c) the market is allocatively efficient
   (d) the product is a nonpriced good

30. When the output is greater than the optimal level of output for a product there are efficiency
   (a) gains from the underproduction of the product
   (b) losses from the underproduction of the product
   (c) gains from the overproduction of the product
   (d) losses from the overproduction of the product

■ **PROBLEMS**

1. Complete the following table, using the demand data given, by computing total revenue at each of the seven prices and the six price elasticity coefficients between each of the seven prices, and indicate whether demand is elastic, inelastic, or unit elastic between each of the seven prices.

Price	Quantity demanded	Total revenue	Elasticity coefficient	Character of demand
$1.00	300	_____		
.90	400	_____	_____	_____
.80	500	_____	_____	_____
.70	600	_____	_____	_____
.60	700	_____	_____	_____
.50	800	_____	_____	_____
.40	900	_____	_____	_____

2. Use the data from the table for this problem. On the *first* of the two following graphs, plot the demand curve (price and quantity demanded) and indicate the elastic, inelastic, and unit elastic portions of the demand curve. On the *second* graph, plot the total revenue on the vertical axis and the quantity demanded on the horizontal axis. (*Note:* The scale for quantity demanded that you plot on the horizontal axis of each graph should be the same.)

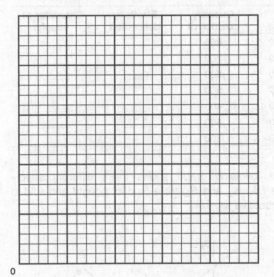

0

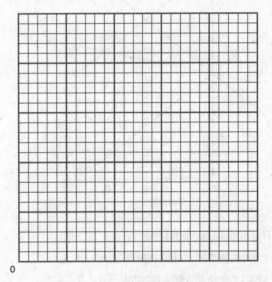

0

a. As price decreases from $1.00 to $0.70, demand is (elastic, inelastic, unit elastic) _____ and total revenue (increases, decreases, remains the same) _____.

b. As price decreases from $0.70 to $0.60, demand is (elastic, inelastic, unit elastic) _____ and total revenue (increases, decreases, remains the same) _____.

c. As price decreases from $0.60 to $0.40, demand is (elastic, inelastic, unit elastic) _____ and total revenue (increases, decreases, remains the same) _____.

3. Using the supply data in the following schedule, complete the table by computing the six price elasticity of supply coefficients between each of the seven prices, and indicate whether supply is elastic, inelastic, or unit elastic.

Price	Quantity coefficient	Elasticity demanded	Character of supply
$1.00	800		
.90	700		
.80	600	_____	_____
.70	500	_____	_____
.60	400	_____	_____
.50	300	_____	_____
.40	200	_____	_____

4. The following graph shows three different supply curves (S_1, S_2, and S_3) for a product bought and sold in a competitive market.

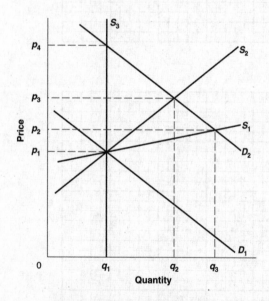

a. The supply curve for the

(1) market period is the one labeled _____.

(2) short run is the one labeled _____.

(3) long run is the one labeled _____.

b. No matter what the period of time under consideration, if the demand for the product were D_1, the equilibrium price of the product would be _____

and the equilibrium quantity would be _____.

(1) If demand were to increase to D_2 in the market period the equilibrium price would increase to _____

and the equilibrium quantity would be _____.

(2) In the short run the price of the product would increase to _____ and the quantity would increase to _____.

(3) In the long run the price of the product would be _____ and the quantity would be _____.

c. The longer the period of time allowed to sellers to adjust their outputs the (more, less) _____ elastic is the supply of the product.

d. The more elastic the supply of a product, the (greater, less) _____ the effect on equilibrium price and the _____ the effect on equilibrium quantity of an increase in demand.

5. For the following three cases, use a midpoint formula to calculate the coefficient for the cross elasticity of demand and identify the relationship between the two goods (complement, substitute, or independent).

a. The quantity demanded for good A increases from 300 to 400 as the price of good B increases from $1 to $2.

Coefficient: _____ Relationship: _____

b. The quantity demanded for good J decreases from 2000 to 1500 as the price of good K increases from $10 to $15.

Coefficient: _____ Relationship: _____

c. The quantity demanded for good X increases from 100 to 101 units as the price of good Y increases from $8 to $15.

Coefficient: _____ Relationship: _____

6. Use the information in the following table to identify the income characteristic of each product A–E using the following labels: **N** = normal (or superior), **I** = inferior.

Product	% change in income	% change in quantity demanded	Income type (N or I)
A	10	10	_____
B	1	15	_____
C	5	−12	_____
D	5	−2	_____
E	10	1	_____

7. Given the following information, calculate the consumer surplus for each individual A to F.

(1) Person	(2) Maximum price willing to pay	(3) Actual price (equilibrium price)	(4) Consumer surplus
A	$25	$12	_____
B	23	12	_____
C	18	12	_____
D	16	12	_____
E	13	12	_____
F	12	12	_____

8. Given the following information, calculate the producer surplus for each producer A to F.

(1) Producers	(2) Minimum Acceptable Price	(3) Actual price (equilibrium price)	(4) Producer surplus
A	$4	$12	_____
B	5	12	_____
C	7	12	_____
D	9	12	_____
E	10	12	_____
F	12	12	_____

9. Answer this question based on the following graph showing the market supply and demand for a product. Assume that the output level is Q_1.

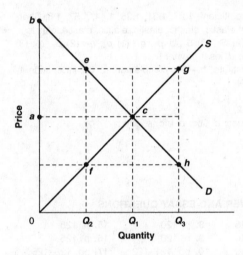

a. The area of consumer surplus would be shown by the area _____.
b. The area of producer surplus would be shown by the area _____.
c. The area that maximizes the combined consumer and producer surplus is _____.
d. If the output level is now Q_2, then there are efficiency losses shown by area _____.
e. If the output level is now Q_3, then there are efficiency losses shown by area _____.

■ **SHORT ANSWER AND ESSAY QUESTIONS**

1. Define and explain the price elasticity of demand in terms of the relationship between the relative (percentage) change in quantity demanded and the relative (percentage) change in price. Use the elasticity coefficient in your explanation.

2. What is meant by perfectly elastic demand? By perfectly inelastic demand? What does the demand curve look like when demand is perfectly elastic and when it is perfectly inelastic?

3. Demand seldom has the same elasticity at all prices. What is the relationship between the price of most products and the price elasticity of demand for them?

4. What is the relationship—if there is one—between the price elasticity of demand and the slope of the demand curve?

5. When the price of a product declines, the quantity demanded of it increases. When demand is elastic, total revenue is greater at the lower price, but when demand is inelastic, total revenue is smaller. Explain why total revenue will sometimes increase and why it will sometimes decrease.

6. Explain the effect of the number of substitutes on the price elasticity of demand.

7. Why does the price elasticity of demand differ based on the price of a good as a proportion of household income? Give examples.

8. Is the quantity demanded for necessities more or less responsive to a change in price? Explain using examples.

9. What role does time play in affecting the elasticity of demand?

10. How do opponents of the decriminalization of illegal drugs use elasticity to make their arguments?

11. Explain what determines the price elasticity of supply of an economic good or service.

12. Why is there no total revenue test for the elasticity of supply?

13. Discuss the supply and demand conditions for antiques. Why are antique prices so high?

14. Use the concepts of the elasticity of supply to explain the volatility of gold prices.

15. How can goods be classified as complementary, substitute, or independent? On what basis is this judgment made?

16. Give definitions of a normal good and an inferior good. Illustrate each definition with an example.

17. What are two examples of insights that income elasticity of demand coefficients provide about the economy?

18. How is the consumer surplus related to utility or satisfaction? Explain, using a supply and demand graph.

19. Define, using a supply and demand graph, the meaning of producer surplus.

20. Use consumer and producer surplus to describe efficiency losses in a competitive market. Provide a supply and demand graph to show such losses.

ANSWERS

Chapter 6 Elasticity, Consumer Surplus, and Producer Surplus

FILL-IN QUESTIONS

1. inelastic, elastic
2. average, average
3. percentages, responsiveness
4. inelastic, vertical, elastic, horizontal
5. varies, an unsound
6. *a.* greater; *b.* less; *c.* is equal to
7. Elastic: greater than 1, decrease, increase; Inelastic: less than 1, increase, decrease; Unit elastic: equal to 1, remain constant, remain constant
8. *a.* The number of good substitute products; *b.* The relative importance of the product in the total budget of the buyer; *c.* Whether the good is a necessity or a luxury; *d.* The period of time in which demand is being considered (any order *a–d*)
9. inelastic, decrease, inelastic, increase
10. quantity supplied, price, time, more
11. inelastic, vertical, less, more
12. demand, supply, directly
13. cross, income
14. substitutes, complements, independent
15. normal or superior, inferior
16. maximum, less, negatively, decrease, increase
17. minimum, more, positively, increase, decrease
18. productive, allocative
19. equal to, equal to, maximum
20. losses, losses, less than

TRUE-FALSE QUESTIONS

1. F, p.114	**11.** T, p. 120	**22.** F, pp. 124–125
2. T, p. 114	**12.** T, p. 120	**23.** T, p. 125
3. F, p. 115	**13.** F, p. 120	**24.** F, p. 125
4. F, pp. 116–118	**14.** T, p. 121	**25.** F, pp. 126–127
5. F, p. 118	**15.** F, p. 121	**26.** T, pp. 126–127
6. T, pp. 116–118, 120	**16.** T, p. 122	**27.** F, pp. 126–127
7. F, pp. 118–119	**17.** F, p. 122	**28.** T, pp. 127–128
8. T, pp. 120–121	**18.** T, pp. 122–123	**29.** F, pp. 127–128
9. T, pp. 120–122	**19.** T, pp. 123–124	**30.** F, p. 129
10. F, p. 120	**20.** F, p. 124	
	21. F, pp. 124–125	

MULTIPLE-CHOICE QUESTIONS

1. c, p. 114	**11.** c, pp. 116–118	**21.** a, p. 125
2. b, p. 115	**12.** d, pp. 117–118	**22.** c, p. 125
3. b, pp. 115–116	**13.** d, p. 120	**23.** a, p. 125
4. b, pp. 118–119	**14.** b, p. 120	**24.** b, p. 125
5. d, pp. 118–119	**15.** d, p. 120	**25.** a, pp. 126–127
6. b, pp. 119–120	**16.** c, p. 122	**26.** b, pp. 126–127
7. b, pp. 119–120	**17.** a, p. 122	**27.** c, pp. 127–128
8. a, pp. 116–118	**18.** b, p. 122	**28.** b, pp. 127–128
9. b, p. 117	**19.** b, pp. 122–123	**29.** c, pp. 128–129
10. a, pp. 116–118	**20.** b, p. 125	**30.** d, p. 129

PROBLEMS

1. Total revenue: $300, 360, 400, 420, 420, 400, 360; Elasticity coefficient: 2.71, 1.89, 1.36, 1, 0.73, 0.53; Character of demand: elastic, elastic, elastic, unit elastic, inelastic, inelastic
2. *a.* elastic, increases; *b.* unit elastic, remains the same; *c.* inelastic, decreases
3. Elasticity coefficient: 1.27, 1.31, 1.36, 1.44, 1.57, 1.8; Character of supply: elastic, elastic, elastic, elastic, elastic, elastic
4. *a.* (1) S_3; (2) S_2; (3) S_1; *b.* p_1, q_1, (1) p_4, q_1; (2) p_3, q_2; (3) p_2, q_3; *c.* more; *d.* less, greater
5. *a.* .43, substitute; *b.* –.71, complement; *c.* .02, independent
6. N, N, I, I, N
7. 13, 11, 6, 4, 1, 0
8. 8, 7, 5, 3, 2, 0
9. *a.* abc; *b.* 0ac; *c.* 0bc; *d.* efc; *e.* ghc

SHORT ANSWER AND ESSAY QUESTIONS

1. pp. 114–115	**8.** p. 120	**15.** p. 125
2. pp. 115–116	**9.** p. 120	**16.** p. 125
3. pp. 118–119	**10.** pp. 121–122	**17.** pp. 125–126
4. pp. 118–119	**11.** p. 122	**18.** pp. 126–127
5. pp. 116–118	**12.** p. 124	**19.** pp. 127–128
6. p. 120	**13.** p. 124	**20.** p. 129
7. p. 120	**14.** p. 124	

CHAPTER 7

Consumer Behavior

Previous chapters explained that consumers typically buy more of a product as its price decreases and less of a product as its price increases. Chapter 7 looks behind this law of demand to explain why consumers behave this way.

The chapter first explains the **law of diminishing marginal utility** and uses it to explain why the demand curve slopes downward. This explanation is based on the concept of marginal utility. In this view, the additional satisfaction (or marginal utility) that a consumer obtains from the consumption of each additional unit of a product will tend to decline; therefore a consumer will have an incentive to purchase additional units of a product only if its price falls. (Another explanation of the law of demand that is more complete, but more complex, is based on indifference curves and is presented in the appendix to this chapter.)

Most of this chapter presents the **marginal-utility** view of consumer behavior. This explanation requires that you first understand the concepts and assumptions on which this theory of consumer behavior rests, and second, do some rigorous reasoning using these concepts and assumptions. It is an exercise in logic, but be sure that you follow the reasoning. To help you, the text provides several numerical examples for you to follow.

No one believes that consumers actually perform these mental gymnastics before they spend their incomes or make purchases. But we study the marginal-utility approach to consumer behavior because the consumers behave as if they made their purchases on the basis of very fine calculations. Thus, this approach explains what we do in fact observe and makes it possible for us to predict with a good deal of precision how consumers will react to changes in their incomes and the prices of products.

The final section of the chapter describes how the theory of consumer behavior can be used to explain many economic events in the real world. The five applications discussed are the takeover by iPods of the market for recorded music, the water–diamond paradox, the value of time in consumption, the reasons for increased consumer purchases of medical care, and the economic effects of cash and noncash gifts. Be sure you understand how consumer theory is used to explain these five phenomena.

■ CHECKLIST

When you have studied this chapter you should be able to

☐ Describe the law of diminishing marginal utility.
☐ Define utility, marginal utility and total utility.

☐ Explain the relationship of the law of diminishing marginal utility to demand.
☐ List four dimensions of the typical consumer's situation.
☐ State the utility-maximizing rule.
☐ Use the utility-maximizing rule to determine how consumers would spend their fixed incomes when given the utility and price data.
☐ Explain how a consumer decides between an optimal solution and an inferior solution to a utility-maximization problem.
☐ Give an algebraic restatement of the utility-maximizing rule based on an example using two products, A and B.
☐ Derive a consumer's demand schedule for a product from utility, income, and price data.
☐ Explain how the income and substitution effects are involved in utility maximization and the deriving of the demand curve for a product.
☐ Give examples of how consumer theory can be used to explain such economic situations as the: popularity of iPods; diamond–water paradox; value of time in consumption; consumer purchases of medical care; and, trade-offs between cash and noncash gifts.
☐ Use insights from behavioral economics to explain decisions about consuming M&M's, preparing for final exams, and saving for retirement (Last Word).

■ CHAPTER OUTLINE

1. The *law of diminishing marginal utility* can be used to explain why the demand curve slopes downward.

   a. *Utility* is subjective and difficult to quantify. For the purposes of this chapter it will be assumed that utility is the satisfaction or pleasure a person gets from consuming a product. It will be measured in hypothetical units called *utils.*

   b. *Total utility* is the total amount of satisfaction that a consumer obtains from consuming a product. *Marginal utility* is the extra satisfaction that a consumer obtains from consuming an additional or extra unit of a product. The principle that the marginal utility of a product falls as a consumer uses (consumes) additional units of a product is the law of diminishing marginal utility. There is a relationship between total and marginal utility. As shown in text Figure 7.1, total utility increases, but at a decreasing rate until it reaches a maximum and then declines. Marginal utility decreases as total utility increases. When total utility reaches a maximum, marginal utility is zero. When total utility declines, marginal utility is negative.

c. The law of diminishing marginal utility explains why the demand curve for a product slopes downward. As more and more of a product is consumed, each additional unit consumed provides less satisfaction. The consumer will only buy more of a product if the price falls.

2. The law of diminishing marginal utility is also the basis of the **theory of consumer behavior** that explains how consumers will spend their incomes for particular goods and services.

a. In the simple case, it is assumed that the typical consumer engages in *rational behavior,* knows marginal-utility schedules for the various goods available (has preferences), has a limited money income to spend (a *budget constraint*), and must pay a price to acquire each of the goods that yields utility.

b. Given these assumptions, the consumer maximizes the total utility obtained when the marginal utility of the last dollar spent on each product is the same for all products (the *utility-maximizing rule*). When the consumer follows this rule, he or she has achieved *consumer equilibrium* and has no incentive to change expenditures.

c. A numerical example is used to illustrate the rule using two products, A and B, and assuming that all money income is spent on one of the two products. In making the decision, the rational consumer must compare the extra or marginal utility from each product with its added cost (as measured by its price). Thus, marginal utility is compared on a per dollar basis.

d. The allocation rule states that consumers will maximize their satisfaction when they allocate their money income so that the last dollar spent on each product yields the same marginal utility. In the two-product case, this can be stated algebraically as

$$\frac{\text{Marginal utility of A}}{\text{Price of A}} = \frac{\text{Marginal utility of B}}{\text{Price of B}}$$

Total utility is a maximum when the marginal utility of the last unit of a product purchased divided by its price is the same for all products.

3. The utility-maximizing rule can be applied to determine the amount of the product the consumer will purchase at different prices with income, tastes, and the prices of other products remaining constant.

a. The numerical example that is used is based on one price for a product. If the price of the product falls, it is possible to use the utility-maximizing rule to determine how much more of the product the consumer will purchase. Based on this exercise it is possible to show the inverse relationship between price and quantity demanded as shown by a demand curve.

b. Utility maximization can also be understood in terms of the *income* and *substitution effects* to explain the law of demand. As the price of a product drops, a consumer increases the amounts purchased to restore equilibrium following the utility-maximizing rule. The change can be viewed as the consumer substituting more of the now less expensive product for another product and having more real income to spend.

4. Five of the many **applications** and **extensions** of consumer theory for the real world are discussed in this chapter.

a. iPods have gained popularity among consumers relative to portable CD players because many consumers have concluded that iPods have a higher ratio of marginal utility to price than the ratio for portable CD players.

b. Diamonds are high in price, but of limited usefulness, while water is low in price, but essential for life. This diamond–water paradox is explained by distinguishing between marginal and total utility. Water is low in price because it is generally in plentiful supply and thus has low marginal utility. Diamonds are high in price because they are relatively scarce and thus have high marginal utility. Water, however, is considered more useful than diamonds because it has much greater total utility.

c. The facts that consumption takes time and time is a scarce resource can be included in the marginal-utility theory. The full price of any consumer good or service is equal to its market price plus the value of time taken to consume it (i.e., the income the consumer could have earned had he or she used that time for work).

d. Expenditures on medical care have increased because of its financing through insurance. Under this system, the consumer does not pay the full price of medical care services and thus has an incentive to consume more than would be the case if the consumer paid the full price.

e. Cash gifts tend to be more efficient for consumers because they are more likely to match consumer preferences and increase the total utility compared to noncash gifts that restrict consumer choice.

5. (Last Word). Studies in behavioral economics offer further insights about consumer choices than what is provided by the standard theory of consumer behavior. Experiments with M&M's indicate that diminishing marginal utility sets in more slowly when there is more product variety. Consumers also show time inconsistency in their decision making. For example, students attach less value to postponing a final exam by one day at the beginning of semester than they do at the end of the semester. And saving for retirement is more highly valued near retirement than early in a career. To counter this time inconsistency problem with retirement savings, legislation has been passed to encourage employers to enroll workers automatically in a retirement plan when they start working for a business.

■ **HINTS AND TIPS**

1. Utility is simply an abstraction useful for explaining consumer behavior. Do not become overly concerned with the precise measurement of utility or satisfaction. What you should focus on is the relative comparison of the additional satisfaction (marginal utility) from a dollar spent on one good to the additional satisfaction obtained from a dollar spent on another good. The choice of producing more additional utility satisfaction from one good than the other will maximize consumer satisfaction. Thus, you just need to know which good won the contest, not the final score (how much additional utility was added).

2. Master the difference between marginal utility and total utility. Once you think you understand the difference, use the concepts to explain to someone the diamond–water paradox at the end of the chapter.

3. The utility-maximization model provides insights about the income and substitution effects that occur with a change in price. For most products, a price decrease gives consumers more income to spend on that product and other products, so the quantity demanded for that product increases. The three steps in the logic for a typical product A are (1) $P_A\downarrow$, (2) income$\uparrow$, and (3) $Q_{dA}\uparrow$. A price decrease also makes product A more attractive to buy relative to its substitutes, so the demand for these substitutes decreases and the quantity demanded for product A increases. Again, there are three steps in the logic: (1) $P_A\downarrow$, (2) demand for substitutes$\downarrow$, and (3) $Q_{dA}\uparrow$. In both cases, the end result is the same: $Q_{dA}\uparrow$. Practice your understanding by showing the logic for an increase in the price of product A.

■ IMPORTANT TERMS

law of diminishing
   marginal utility

utility

total utility

marginal utility

rational behavior

budget constraint

utility-maximizing rule

consumer equilibrium

income effect

substitution effect

SELF-TEST

■ FILL-IN QUESTIONS

1. The reason that demand curves slope downward can be explained by the law of (comparative advantage, diminishing marginal utility) _____.

2. The overall satisfaction a consumer gets from consuming a good or service is (marginal, total) _____ utility, but the extra or additional satisfaction that a consumer gets from a good or service is (marginal, total) _____ utility.

3. Utility is (an objective, a subjective) _____ concept and (is, is not) _____ the same thing as usefulness.

4. The law of diminishing marginal utility states that marginal utility will (increase, decrease) _____ as a consumer increases the quantity consumed of a product.

5. A graph of total utility and marginal utility shows that when total utility is increasing, marginal utility is (positive, negative) _____ , and when total utility is at a maximum, marginal utility is at (a maximum, zero, a minimum) _____.

6. The marginal-utility theory of consumer behavior assumes that the consumer is (wealthy, rational) _____ and has certain (preferences, discounts) _____ for various goods.

7. A consumer cannot buy every good and service desired because income is (subsidized, limited) _____ and goods and services are (unlimited, scarce) _____ in relation to the demand for them; thus they have (prices, quantities) _____ attached to them.

8. When the consumer is maximizing the utility the consumer's income will obtain, the ratio of the marginal utility of the (first, last) _____ unit purchased of a product to its price is (the same, greater than) _____ for all the products bought.

9. If the marginal utility of the last dollar spent on one product is greater than the marginal utility of the last dollar spent on another product, the consumer should (increase, decrease) _____ purchases of the first and _____ purchases of the second product.

10. Assume there are only two products, X and Y, that a consumer can purchase with a fixed income. The consumer is maximizing utility algebraically when:

a. _____   b. _____

c. _____ = d. _____

11. In deriving a consumer's demand for a particular product, the two factors (other than the preferences or tastes of the consumer) that are held constant are

a. _____

b. _____

12. The utility-maximizing rule and the demand curve are logically (consistent, inconsistent) _____. Because marginal utility declines, a lower price is needed to get the consumer to buy (less, more) _____ of a particular product.

13. A fall in the price of a product tends to (increase, decrease) _____ a consumer's real income, and a rise in its price tends to _____ real income. This is called the (substitution, income) _____ effect.

14. When the price of a product increases, the product becomes relatively (more, less) _____ expensive than it was and the prices of other products become relatively (higher, lower) _____ than they were; the consumer will therefore buy (less, more) _____ of the product in question and _____ of the other products. This is called the (substitution, income) _____ effect.

15. When consumer preferences changed from portable CD players to iPods, and the prices of iPods (increased, decreased) _____ significantly, this led to (increased, decreased) _____ purchases of iPods.

16. Water is low in price because its (total, marginal) _____ utility is low, while diamonds are high in price because their _____ utility is high.

Water, however, is more useful than diamonds because the (total, marginal) _____ utility of water is much greater than the _____ utility of diamonds.

17. The theory of consumer behavior has been generalized to account for (supply, time) _____. This is a valuable economic resource because it is (limited, unlimited) _____. Its value is (greater than, equal to) _____ the income that can be earned with it. The full price to the consumer of any product is, therefore, the market (time, price) _____ plus the value of the consumption _____.

18. With health insurance coverage, the price consumers pay for health care services is less than the "true" value or opportunity (benefit, cost) _____. The lower price to consumers encourages them to consume (more, less) _____ health care services.

19. A comparison of food consumption at an all-you-can-eat buffet with a pay-per-item cafeteria would show that people tend to eat (less, more) _____ at the buffet because the marginal utility of an extra food item is (positive, zero) _____ while its price is _____.

20. Noncash gifts are (less, more) _____ preferred than cash gifts because they yield (less, more) _____ total utility to consumers.

■ **TRUE–FALSE QUESTIONS**

Circle T if the statement is true, F if it is false.

1. Utility is the benefit or satisfaction a person receives from consuming a good or service. **T F**

2. Utility and usefulness are not synonymous. **T F**

3. Marginal utility is the change in total utility from consuming one more unit of a product. **T F**

4. Because utility cannot actually be measured, the marginal-utility theory cannot really explain how consumers will behave. **T F**

5. The law of diminishing marginal utility indicates that gains in satisfaction become smaller as successive units of a specific product are consumed. **T F**

6. A consumer's demand curve for a product is downsloping because total utility decreases as more of the product is consumed. **T F**

7. If total utility is increasing, then marginal utility is positive and may be either increasing or decreasing. **T F**

8. The theory of consumer behavior assumes that consumers act rationally to get the most from their money. **T F**

9. All consumers are subject to budget constraints. **T F**

10. To find a consumer's demand for a product, the price of the product is varied while tastes, income, and the prices of other products remain unchanged. **T F**

11. The theory of consumer behavior assumes that consumers attempt to maximize marginal utility. **T F**

12. If the marginal utility per dollar spent on product A is greater than the marginal utility per dollar spent on product B, then to maximize utility, the consumer should purchase less of A and more of B. **T F**

13. When consumers are maximizing total utility, the marginal utilities of the last unit of every product they buy are identical. **T F**

14. The marginal utility of product X is 15 and its price is $5, while the marginal utility of product Y is 10 and its price is $2. The utility-maximizing rule suggests that there should be *less* consumption of product Y. **T F**

15. In most cases, a change in incomes will cause a change in the portfolio of goods and services purchased by consumers. **T F**

16. An increase in the real income of a consumer will result from an increase in the price of a product the consumer is buying. **T F**

17. The income and substitution effects will induce the consumer to buy less of normal good Z when the price of Z increases. **T F**

18. A fall in the price of iPods will decrease the demand for iTunes. **T F**

19. The diamond–water paradox is explained by the fact that the total utility derived from water is low while the total utility derived from diamonds is high. **T F**

20. If a consumer can earn $10 an hour and it takes 2 hours to consume a product, the value of the time required for the consumption of the product is $5. **T F**

21. Paying $300 to fly from one city to another may be cheaper than paying $50 for a bus trip between the two cities when the economic value of time is taken into account. **T F**

22. A decrease in the productivity of labor will tend over time to increase the value of time. **T F**

23. One reason for the increased use of health care services is that consumers pay only part of the full price of the services. **T F**

24. People tend to eat more at an "all-you-can-eat buffet" because the "price" of additional items is zero but the marginal utility for these items is likely to be positive. **T F**

25. Noncash gifts add more to total utility than cash gifts. **T F**

■ **MULTIPLE-CHOICE QUESTIONS**

Circle the letter that corresponds to the best answer.

1. Utility as defined in this chapter refers to the
(a) usefulness of a purchased product
(b) value of the money a consumer spends on a good

(c) satisfaction or pleasure from consuming a good

(d) extra income a consumer gets from buying a good at a lower price

2. Which best expresses the law of diminishing marginal utility?

(a) The more a person consumes of a product, the smaller becomes the utility that he receives from its consumption.

(b) The more a person consumes of a product, the smaller becomes the additional utility that she receives as a result of consuming an additional unit of the product.

(c) The less a person consumes of a product, the smaller becomes the utility that she receives from its consumption.

(d) The less a person consumes of a product, the smaller becomes the additional utility that he receives as a result of consuming an additional unit of the product.

3. Summing the marginal utilities of each unit consumed will determine total

(a) cost

(b) revenue

(c) utility

(d) consumption

The following table shows a hypothetical total utility schedule for a consumer of chocolate candy bars. Use the table to answer Questions 4, 5, and 6.

Number consumed	Total utility
0	0
1	9
2	19
3	27
4	35
5	42
6	42
7	40

4. This consumer begins to experience diminishing marginal utility when he consumes the

(a) first candy bar

(b) second candy bar

(c) third candy bar

(d) fourth candy bar

5. Marginal utility becomes negative with the consumption of the

(a) fourth candy bar

(b) fifth candy bar

(c) sixth candy bar

(d) seventh candy bar

6. Based on the data, you can conclude that the

(a) marginal utility of the fourth unit is 6

(b) marginal utility of the second unit is 27

(c) total utility of 5 units is 42

(d) total utility of 3 units is 55

7. After eating eight chocolate chip cookies, you are offered a ninth cookie. You turn down the cookie. Your refusal indicates that the

(a) marginal utility for chocolate chip cookies is negative

(b) total utility for chocolate chip cookies is negative

(c) marginal utility is positive for the eighth and negative for the ninth cookie

(d) total utility was zero because you ate one cookie and refused the other

8. Which is a dimension or assumption of the marginal-utility theory of consumer behavior?

(a) The consumer has a small income.

(b) The consumer is rational.

(c) Goods and services are free.

(d) Goods and services yield continually increasing amounts of marginal utility as the consumer buys more of them.

9. A consumer is making purchases of products A and B such that the marginal utility of product A is 20 and the marginal utility of product B is 30. The price of product A is $10 and the price of product B is $20. The utility-maximizing rule suggests that this consumer should

(a) increase consumption of product B and decrease consumption of product A

(b) increase consumption of product B and increase consumption of product A

(c) increase consumption of product A and decrease consumption of product B

(d) make no change in consumption of A or B

10. Suppose that the prices of A and B are $3 and $2, respectively, that the consumer is spending her entire income and buying 4 units of A and 6 units of B, and that the marginal utility of both the fourth unit of A and the sixth unit of B is 6. It can be concluded that the consumer should buy

(a) more of both A and B

(b) more of A and less of B

(c) less of A and more of B

(d) less of both A and B

11. Robert Woods is maximizing his satisfaction consuming two goods, X and Y. If the marginal utility of X is half that of Y, what is the price of X if the price of Y is $1.00?

(a) $0.50

(b) $1.00

(c) $1.50

(d) $2.00

Answer Questions 12, 13, and 14 based on the following table showing the marginal-utility schedules for goods X and Y for a hypothetical consumer. The price of good X is $1 and the price of good Y is $2. The income of the consumer is $9.

Good X		Good Y	
Quantity	MU	Quantity	MU
1	8	1	10
2	7	2	8
3	6	3	6
4	5	4	4
5	4	5	3
6	3	6	2
7	2	7	1

12. To maximize utility, the consumer will buy
- **(a)** 7X and 1Y
- **(b)** 5X and 2Y
- **(c)** 3X and 3Y
- **(d)** 1X and 4Y

13. When the consumer purchases the utility-maximizing combination of goods X and Y, total utility will be
- **(a)** 36
- **(b)** 45
- **(c)** 48
- **(d)** 52

14. Suppose that the consumer's income increased from $9 to $12. What would be the utility-maximizing combination of goods X and Y?
- **(a)** 5X and 2Y
- **(b)** 6X and 3Y
- **(c)** 2X and 5Y
- **(d)** 4X and 4Y

15. A decrease in the price of product Z will
- **(a)** increase the marginal utility per dollar spent on Z
- **(b)** decrease the marginal utility per dollar spent on Z
- **(c)** decrease the total utility per dollar spent on Z
- **(d)** cause no change in the marginal utility per dollar spent on Z

Answer Questions 16, 17, 18, and 19 on the basis of the following total utility data for products A and B. Assume that the prices of A and B are $6 and $8, respectively, and that consumer income is $36.

Units of A	Total utility	Units of B	Total utility
1	18	1	32
2	30	2	56
3	38	3	72
4	42	4	80
5	44	5	84

16. What is the level of total utility for the consumer in equilibrium?
- **(a)** 86
- **(b)** 102
- **(c)** 108
- **(d)** 120

17. How many units of the two products will the consumer buy?
- **(a)** 1 of A and 4 of B
- **(b)** 2 of A and 2 of B
- **(c)** 2 of A and 3 of B
- **(d)** 3 of A and 4 of B

18. If the price of A decreases to $4, then the utility-maximizing combination of the two products is
- **(a)** 2 of A and 2 of B
- **(b)** 2 of A and 3 of B
- **(c)** 3 of A and 3 of B
- **(d)** 4 of A and 4 of B

19. Which of the following represents the demand curve for A?

(a)		(b)		(c)		(d)	
P	Q_d	P	Q_d	P	Q_d	P	Q_d
$6	1	$6	2	$6	2	$6	2
4	4	4	5	4	3	4	4

20. Kristin Hansen buys only two goods, food and clothing. Both are normal goods for Kristin. Suppose the price of food decreases. Kristin's consumption of clothing will
- **(a)** decrease due to the income effect
- **(b)** increase due to the income effect
- **(c)** increase due to the substitution effect
- **(d)** not change due to the substitution effect

21. The reason the substitution effect works to encourage a consumer to buy more of a product when its price decreases is because
- **(a)** the real income of the consumer has been increased
- **(b)** the real income of the consumer has been decreased
- **(c)** the product is now relatively less expensive than it was
- **(d)** other products are now relatively less expensive than they were

22. The price of water is substantially less than the price of diamonds because
- **(a)** the marginal utility of a diamond is significantly less than the marginal utility of a gallon of water
- **(b)** the marginal utility of a diamond is significantly greater than the marginal utility of a gallon of water
- **(c)** the total utility of diamonds is greater than the total utility of water
- **(d)** diamonds have a low marginal utility

23. The full price of a product to a consumer is
- **(a)** its market price
- **(b)** its market price plus the value of its consumption time
- **(c)** its market price less the value of its consumption time
- **(d)** the value of its consumption time less its market price

24. A consumer has two basic choices: rent a movie for $4.00 and spend 2 hours of time watching it or spend $15 for dinner at a restaurant that takes 1 hour of time. If the marginal utilities of the movie and the dinner are the same, and the consumer values time at $15 an hour, the rational consumer will most likely
- **(a)** rent more movies and buy fewer restaurant dinners
- **(b)** buy more restaurant dinners and rent fewer movies
- **(c)** buy fewer restaurant dinners and rent fewer movies
- **(d)** make no change in the consumption of both

25. Compared to cash gifts, noncash gifts are preferred
- **(a)** more because they decrease total utility
- **(b)** more because they increase total utility
- **(c)** less because they increase total utility
- **(d)** less because they decrease total utility

■ **PROBLEMS**

1. Assume that Harriet Palmer finds only three goods, A, B, and C, for sale and that the amounts of utility that their consumption will yield her are as shown in the table below. Compute the marginal utilities for successive units of A, B, and C and enter them in the appropriate columns.

	Good A			Good B			Good C	
Quantity	Total utility	Marginal utility	Quantity	Total utility	Marginal utility	Quantity	Total utility	Marginal utility
1	21	___	1	7	___	1	23	___
2	41	___	2	13	___	2	40	___
3	59	___	3	18	___	3	52	___
4	74	___	4	22	___	4	60	___
5	85	___	5	25	___	5	65	___
6	91	___	6	27	___	6	68	___
7	91	___	7	28.2	___	7	70	___

2. Using the marginal-utility data for goods A, B, and C that you obtained in Problem 1, assume that the prices of A, B, and C are $5, $1, and $4, respectively and that Palmer has an income of $37 to spend.

   a. Complete the table below by computing the *marginal utility per dollar* for successive units of A, B, and C.

	Good A		Good B		Good C
Quantity	Marginal utility per dollar	Quantity	Marginal utility per dollar	Quantity	Marginal utility per dollar
1	___	1	___	1	___
2	___	2	___	2	___
3	___	3	___	3	___
4	___	4	___	4	___
5	___	5	___	5	___
6	___	6	___	6	___
7	___	7	___	7	___

   b. Palmer would *not* buy 4 units of A, 1 unit of B, and 4 units of C because _____.

   c. Palmer would *not* buy 6 units of A, 7 units of B, and 4 units of C because _____.

   d. When Palmer is maximizing her utility, she will buy _____ units of A, _____ units of B, _____ units of C; her total utility will be _____, and the marginal utility of the last dollar spent on each good will be

   _____.

   e. If Palmer's income increased by $1, she would spend it on good _____, assuming she can buy fractions of a unit of a good, because _____.

3. Sam Thompson has an income of $36 to spend each week. The only two goods he is interested in purchasing are H and J. The marginal-utility schedules for these two goods are shown in the table at the bottom of the page.

   The price of J does not change from week to week and is $4. The marginal utility per dollar from J is also shown in the table. But the price of H varies from one week to the next. The marginal utilities per dollar from H when the prices of H are $6, $4, $3, $2, and $1.50 are shown in the table.

	Good H						Good J	
Quantity	MU	MU/$6	MU/$4	MU/$3	MU/$2	MU/$1.50	MU	MU/$4
1	45	7.5	11.25	15	22.5	30	40	10
2	30	5	7.5	20	15	20	36	9
3	20	3.33	5	6.67	10	13.33	32	8
4	15	2.5	3.75	5	7.5	10	28	7
5	12	2	3	4	6	8	24	6
6	10	1.67	2.5	3.33	5	6.67	20	5
7	9	1.5	2.25	3	4.5	6	16	4
8	7.5	1.25	1.88	2.5	3.75	5	12	3

a. Complete the table below to show how much of H Thompson will buy each week at each of the five possible prices of H.

Price of H	Quantity of H demanded
$6.00	____
4.00	____
3.00	____
2.00	____
1.50	____

b. What is the table you completed in part **a** called?

_____

4. Assume that a consumer can purchase only two goods: R (recreation) and M (material goods). The market price of R is $2 and the market price of M is $1. The consumer spends all her income in such a way that the marginal utility of the last unit of R she buys is 12 and the marginal utility of the last unit of M she buys is 6.

a. If we ignore the time it takes to consume R and M, is the consumer maximizing the total utility she obtains

from the two goods? _____

b. Suppose it takes 4 hours to consume each unit of R, 1 hour to consume each unit of M, and the consumer can earn $2 an hour when she works.

(1) The full price of a unit of R is $_____.

(2) The full price of a unit of M is $_____.

c. If we take into account the full price of each of the commodities, is the consumer maximizing her total utility?

_____ How do you know this? _____

d. If the consumer is not maximizing her utility, should she increase her consumption of R or of M? _____

Why should she do this? _____

e. Will she use more or less of her time for consuming

R? _____

■ **SHORT ANSWER AND ESSAY QUESTIONS**

1. Define the law of diminishing marginal utility and give an example of it in practice.

2. Why is utility a "subjective concept"?

3. How does the subjective nature of utility limit the practical usefulness of the marginal-utility theory of consumer behavior?

4. Define total utility and marginal utility. What is the relationship between total utility and marginal utility?

5. What is the law of diminishing marginal utility?

6. What essential assumptions are made about consumers and the nature of goods and services in developing the marginal-utility theory of consumer behavior?

7. What is meant by "budget constraint"?

8. When is the consumer in equilibrium and maximizing total utility? Explain why any deviation from this equilibrium will decrease the consumer's total utility.

9. Why must the amounts of extra utility derived from differently priced goods mean that marginal utility must be put on a per-dollar-spent basis? Give an example.

10. How can saving be incorporated into the utility-maximizing analysis?

11. Give and explain an algebraic restatement of the utility-maximizing rule.

12. Using the marginal-utility theory of consumer behavior, explain how an individual's demand schedule for a particular consumer good can be obtained.

13. Why does the demand schedule that is based on the marginal-utility theory almost invariably result in an inverse or negative relationship between price and quantity demanded?

14. What insights does the utility-maximization model provide about the income and substitution effects from a price decline?

15. What aspects of the theory of consumer behavior explain why consumers started buying iPods in larger numbers instead of portable CD players in the past decade?

16. Why does water have a lower price than diamonds despite the fact that water is more useful than diamonds?

17. Explain how a consumer might determine the value of his or her time. How does the value of time affect the full price the consumer pays for a good or service?

18. What does taking time into account explain that the traditional approach to consumer behavior does not explain?

19. How does the way that we pay for goods and services affect the quantity purchased? Explain by using medical care as an example.

20. Why are noncash gifts less preferred than cash gifts?

ANSWERS

Chapter 7 Consumer Behavior

FILL-IN QUESTIONS

1. diminishing marginal utility
2. total, marginal
3. a subjective, is not
4. decrease
5. positive, zero
6. rational, preferences
7. limited, scarce, prices
8. last, the same
9. increase, decrease
10. *a.* MU of product *X*; *b.* price of *X*; *c.* MU of product *Y*; *d.* price of *Y*
11. *a.* the income of the consumer; *b.* the prices of other products

12. consistent, more
13. increase, decrease, income
14. more, lower, less, more, substitution
15. decreased, increased
16. marginal, marginal, total, total
17. time, limited, equal to, price, time
18. cost, more
19. more, positive, zero
20. less, less

TRUE–FALSE QUESTIONS

1. T, p. 135	**10.** T, pp. 137–138	**19.** F, pp. 142–143
2. T, p. 135	**11.** F, pp. 137–138	**20.** F, pp. 143–144
3. T, pp. 135–137	**12.** F, p. 138	**21.** T, pp. 143–144
4. F, pp. 135–137	**13.** F, pp. 138–139	**22.** F, pp. 143–144
5. T, p. 135	**14.** F, pp. 138–139	**23.** T, p. 144
6. F, p. 137	**15.** T, pp. 140–141	**24.** T, p. 144
7. T, pp. 135–137	**16.** F, pp. 140–141	**25.** F, p. 144
8. T, pp. 137–138	**17.** T, pp. 140–141	
9. T, pp. 137–138	**18.** F, pp. 140–141	

MULTIPLE-CHOICE QUESTIONS

1. c, p. 135	**10.** c, pp. 138–139	**19.** c, p. 140
2. b, p. 135	**11.** a, pp. 138–139	**20.** b, pp. 140–141
3. c, pp. 135–137	**12.** b, pp. 139–140	**21.** c, pp. 140–141
4. c, pp. 135–137	**13.** c, pp. 139–140	**22.** b, pp. 142–143
5. d, pp. 135–137	**14.** b, pp. 139–140	**23.** b, pp. 143–144
6. c, pp. 315–137	**15.** a, pp. 139–140	**24.** b, pp. 143–144
7. c, pp. 135–137	**16.** b, pp. 135–137	**25.** d, p. 144
8. b, pp. 137–138	**17.** c, pp. 136–137	
9. c, pp. 138–139	**18.** c, pp. 135–137	

PROBLEMS

1. marginal utility of good A: 21, 20, 18, 15, 11, 6, 0; marginal utility of good B: 7, 6, 5, 4, 3, 2, 1.2; marginal utility of good C: 23, 17, 12, 8, 5, 3, 2

2. *a.* marginal utility per dollar of good A: 4.2, 4, 3.6, 3, 2.2, 1.2, 0; marginal utility per dollar of good B: 7, 6, 5, 4, 3, 2, 1.2; marginal utility of good C: 5.75, 4.25, 3, 2, 1.25, .75, .5; *b.* the marginal utility per dollar spent on good B (7) is greater than the marginal utility per dollar spent on good A (3), and the latter is greater than the marginal utility per dollar spent on good C (2); *c.* she would be spending more than her $37 income; *d.* 4, 5, 3, 151, 3; *e.* A, she would obtain the greatest marginal utility for her dollar (2.2)

3. *a.* 2, 3, 4, 6, 8; *b.* the demand schedule (for good H)

4. *a.* yes; *b.* (1) 10, (2) 3; *c.* no, the marginal utility to price ratios are not the same for the two goods; *d.* of M, because its MU/P ratio is greater; *e.* less

SHORT ANSWER AND ESSAY QUESTIONS

1. p. 135	**8.** pp. 138–139	**15.** pp. 141–142
2. p. 135	**9.** p. 138	**16.** pp. 142–143
3. p. 135	**10.** pp. 138–139	**17.** pp. 143–144
4. pp. 135–137	**11.** pp. 139–140	**18.** pp. 143–144
5. p. 135	**12.** p. 140	**19.** p. 144
6. pp. 137–138	**13.** p. 140	**20.** p. 144
7. p. 137	**14.** pp. 140–141	

Indifference Curve Analysis

This brief appendix contains another explanation of or approach to the theory of consumer behavior. It is based on *ordinal utility* (the rank-ordering of consumer preferences) rather than *cardinal utility* (the precise measurement of utility). For this explanation you are introduced first to the **budget line** and then to the **indifference curve.** These two geometrical concepts are then combined to explain when a consumer is purchasing the combination of two products that maximizes the satisfaction obtainable with his or her income. The last step is to vary the price of one of the products to find the consumer's demand (schedule or curve) for the product.

■ **CHECKLIST**

When you have studied this appendix you should be able to

☐ Distinguish between cardinal utility and ordinal utility.
☐ Describe the concept of a budget line and its characteristics.
☐ Explain how to measure the slope of a budget line and determine the location of the budget line.
☐ Describe the concept of an indifference curve.
☐ State two characteristics of indifference curves.
☐ Explain the meaning of an indifference map.
☐ Given an indifference map, determine which indifference curves bring more or less total utility to consumers.
☐ Use indifference curves to identify which combination of two products maximizes the total utility of consumers.
☐ Derive a consumer's demand for a product using indifference curve analysis.
☐ Compare and contrast the marginal-utility and the indifference curve analyses of consumer behavior.

■ **APPENDIX OUTLINE**

1. Indifference curve analysis is based on ordinal utility in which consumer preferences are rank-ordered, but not measured. By contrast, the utility-maximization analysis and rule present in Chapter 7 is based on cardinal utility, or the precise measurement of utility or satisfaction.

2. A **budget line** shows graphically the different combinations of two products a consumer can purchase with a particular money income. A budget line has a negative slope.

a. An increase in the money income of the consumer will shift the budget line to the right without affecting its slope. A decrease in money income will shift the budget line to the left.
b. An increase in the prices of both products shifts the budget line to the left. A decrease in the prices of both products shifts the budget line to the right. An increase (decrease) in the price of the product, the quantity of which is measured horizontally (the price of the other product remaining constant), pivots the budget line around a fixed point on the vertical axis in a clockwise (counterclockwise) direction.

3. An **indifference curve** shows graphically the different combinations of two products that bring a consumer the same total utility.
a. An indifference curve is downsloping. If the utility is to remain the same when the quantity of one product increases, the quantity of the other product must decrease.
b. An indifference curve is also convex to the origin. The more a consumer has of one product, the smaller the quantity of a second product he or she is willing to give up to obtain an additional unit of the first product. The slope of an indifference curve is the **marginal rate of substitution** (MRS), the rate at which the consumer will substitute one product for another to remain equally satisfied.

4. The consumer has an indifference curve for every level of total utility or satisfaction. The nearer a curve is to the origin in this **indifference map,** the smaller is the utility of the combinations on that curve. The further a curve is from the origin, the larger is the utility of the combinations on that curve.

5. The consumer is in an **equilibrium position** and purchasing the combination of two products that brings the maximum utility to her or him, when the budget line is tangent to the highest attainable indifference curve.

6. In the marginal-utility approach to consumer behavior, it is assumed that utility is cardinal and it is measurable. In the indifference-curve approach, utility is ordinal and rank-ordered. It need only be assumed that a consumer can say whether a combination of products has more utility than, less utility than, or the same amount of utility as another combination.

7. The demand (schedule or curve) for one of the products is derived by varying the price of that product and

shifting the budget line, holding the price of the other product and the consumer's income constant, and finding the quantity of the product the consumer will purchase at each price when in equilibrium.

■ HINTS AND TIPS

1. This appendix simplifies the analysis by limiting consumer choice to just two goods. The **budget line** shows the consumer what it is possible to purchase in the two-good world, given an income. Make sure that you understand what a budget line is. To test your understanding, practice with different income levels and prices. For example, assume you had an income of $100 to spend for two goods (A and B). Good A costs $10 and Good B costs $5. Draw a budget line to show the possible combinations of A and B that you could purchase.

2. **Indifference curves** and the marginal rate of substitution are perhaps the most difficult concepts to understand in this appendix. Remember that the points on the curve show the possible combinations of two goods for which the consumer is *indifferent*, and thus does not care what combination is chosen. The **marginal rate of substitution** is the rate at which the consumer gives up units of one good for units of another along the indifference curve. This rate will change (diminish) as the consumer moves down an indifference curve because the consumer is less willing to *substitute* one good for the other.

■ IMPORTANT TERMS

budget line
indifference curve
marginal rate of
   substitution (MRS)

indifference map
equilibrium position

SELF-TEST

■ FILL-IN QUESTIONS

1. A schedule or curve that shows the various combinations of two products a consumer can buy with a specific (income, feature) _____ is called (a budget, an indifference) _____ line.

2. Given two products X and Y, and a graph with the quantities of X measured horizontally and the quantities of Y measured vertically, the budget line has a slope equal to the ratio of the _____ to the _____.

3. When a consumer's income increases, the budget line shifts to the (left, right) _____, while a decrease in income shifts the budget line to the _____.

4. Given two products, A and B, and a budget line graph with the quantities of A measured horizontally and

the quantities of B measured vertically, an increase in the price of A will fan the budget line (outward, inward) _____, and a decrease in the price of A will fan the budget line _____ around a fixed point on the (A, B) _____ axis.

5. (A demand, An indifference) _____ curve shows the various combinations of two products that give a consumer the same total satisfaction or total (cost, utility) _____.

6. An indifference curve slopes (upward, downward) _____ and is (concave, convex) _____ to the origin.

7. The slope of the indifference curve at each point measures the (marginal, total) _____ rate of substitution of the combination represented by that point.

8. The more a consumer has of the first product than the second product, the (greater, smaller) _____ is the quantity of the first product the consumer will give up to obtain an additional unit of the second product. As a result, the marginal rate of substitution (MRS) of the first for the second product (increases, decreases) _____ as a consumer moves from left to right (downward) along an indifference curve.

9. A set of indifference curves reflects different levels of (marginal, total) _____ utility and is called an indifference (plan, map) _____.

10. The farther from the origin an indifference curve lies, the (greater, smaller) _____ the total utility obtained from the combinations of products on that curve.

11. A consumer obtains the greatest attainable total utility or satisfaction when he or she purchases that combination of two products at which his or her budget line is (tangent to, greater than) _____ an indifference curve. At this point the consumer's marginal rate of substitution is equal to the (slope, axis) _____ of the budget line.

12. Were a consumer to purchase a combination of two products that lie on her budget line and at which her budget line is steeper than the indifference curve intersecting that point, she could increase her satisfaction by trading (down, up) _____ her budget line.

13. The marginal-utility approach to consumer behavior requires that we assume utility is (cardinal, ordinal) _____, or numerically measurable; the indifference-curve approach assumes the utility is _____, and that preferences are ranked.

14. When quantities of product X are measured along the horizontal axis, a decrease in the price of X

    a. fans the budget line (inward, outward) _____ and to the (right, left) _____;

    b. puts the consumer, when in equilibrium, on a (higher, lower) _____ indifference curve; and

    c. normally induces the consumer to purchase (more, less) _____ of product X.

15. Using indifference curves and different budget lines to determine how much of a particular product an individual consumer will purchase at different prices makes it possible to derive that consumer's (supply, demand)

_____ curve or schedule for that product.

■ **TRUE–FALSE QUESTIONS**

Circle T if the statement is true, F if it is false.

1. The budget line shows all combinations of two products that the consumer can purchase, given money income and the prices of the products. **T F**

2. The slope of the budget line when quantities of Alpha are measured horizontally and quantities of Beta are measured vertically is equal to the price of Beta divided by the price of Alpha. **T F**

3. A consumer is unable to purchase any of the combinations of two products which lie below (or to the left) of the consumer's budget line. **T F**

4. An increase in the money income of a consumer shifts the budget line to the right. **T F**

5. If a consumer moves from one combination (or point) on an indifference curve to another combination (or point) on the same curve, the total utility obtained by the consumer does not change. **T F**

6. An indifference curve is concave to the origin. **T F**

7. The marginal rate of substitution shows the rate, at the margin, at which the consumer is prepared to substitute one good for the other so as to remain equally satisfied. **T F**

8. The closer to the origin an indifference curve lies, the smaller the total utility a consumer obtains from the combinations of products on that indifference curve. **T F**

9. On an indifference map, the further from the origin, the lower the level of utility associated with each indifference curve. **T F**

10. There can be an intersection of consumer indifference curves. **T F**

11. A consumer maximizes total utility when she or he purchases the combination of the two products at which her or his budget line crosses an indifference curve. **T F**

12. On an indifference map, the consumer's equilibrium position will be where the slope of the highest attainable indifference curve equals the slope of the budget line. **T F**

13. It is assumed in the marginal-utility approach to consumer behavior that utility is cardinal, or numerically measurable. **T F**

14. In both the marginal-utility and indifference curve approaches to consumer behavior, it is assumed that a consumer is able to say whether the total utility obtained from combination A is greater than, equal to, or less than the total utility obtained from combination B. **T F**

15. A decrease in the price of a product normally enables a consumer to reach a higher indifference curve. **T F**

■ **MULTIPLE-CHOICE QUESTIONS**

Circle the letter that corresponds to the best answer.

1. Suppose a consumer has an income of $8, the price of *R* is $1, and the price of *S* is $0.50. Which of the following combinations is on the consumer's budget line?
    (a) 8*R* and 1*S*
    (b) 7*R* and 1*S*
    (c) 6*R* and 6*S*
    (d) 5*R* and 6*S*

2. If a consumer has an income of $100, the price of *U* is $10, and the price of *V* is $20, the maximum quantity of *U* the consumer is able to purchase is
    (a) 5
    (b) 10
    (c) 20
    (d) 30

3. When the income of a consumer is $20, the price of *T* is $5, the price of *Z* is $2, and the quantity of *T* is measured horizontally, the slope of the budget line is
    (a) 0.4
    (b) 2.5
    (c) 4
    (d) 10

4. Assume that everything else remains the same, but there is a decrease in a consumer's money income. The most likely effect is
    (a) an inward shift in the indifference curves because the consumer can now satisfy fewer wants
    (b) an inward shift in the budget line because the consumer can now purchase less of both products
    (c) an increase in the marginal rate of substitution
    (d) no change in the equilibrium of the consumer

5. An indifference curve is a curve that shows the different combinations of two products that
    (a) give a consumer equal marginal utilities
    (b) give a consumer equal total utilities
    (c) cost a consumer equal amounts
    (d) have the same prices

6. In the following schedule for an indifference curve, how much of *G* is the consumer willing to give up to obtain the third unit of *H*?
    (a) 3
    (b) 4
    (c) 5
    (d) 6

Quantity of *G*	Quantity of *H*
18	1
12	2
7	3
3	4
0	5

7. The slope of the indifference curve measures the
  (a) slope of the budget line
  (b) total utility of a good
  (c) space on an indifference map
  (d) marginal rate of substitution

8. The marginal rate of substitution
  (a) may rise or fall, depending on the slope of the budget line
  (b) rises as you move downward along an indifference curve
  (c) falls as you move downward along an indifference curve
  (d) remains the same along a budget line

9. Which of the following is characteristic of indifference curves?
  (a) They are concave to the origin.
  (b) They are convex to the origin.
  (c) Curves closer to the origin have the highest level of total utility.
  (d) Curves closer to the origin have the highest level of marginal utility.

10. To derive the demand curve of a product, the price of the product is varied. For the indifference curve analysis, the
  (a) budget line is held constant
  (b) money income of the consumer changes
  (c) tastes and preferences of the consumer are held constant
  (d) prices of other products the consumer might purchase change

Questions 11, 12, 13, and 14 are based on the diagram below.

11. The budget line is best represented by line
  (a) *AB*   **(b)** *AD*
  (c) *FG*   **(d)** *DG*

12. Which combination of goods *I* and *J* will the consumer purchase?
  (a) *A*   **(b)** *B*
  (c) *C*   **(d)** *E*

13. Suppose the price of good *I* increases. The budget line will shift
  (a) inward around a point on the *J* axis
  (b) outward around a point on the *J* axis
  (c) inward around a point on the *I* axis
  (d) outward around a point on the *I* axis

14. If the consumer chooses the combination of goods *I* and *J* represented by point *E,* then the consumer could
  (a) obtain more goods with the available money income
  (b) not obtain more goods with the available money income
  (c) shift the budget line outward so that it is tangent with point *C*
  (d) shift the budget line inward so that it is tangent with point *E*

15. In indifference curve analysis, the consumer will be in equilibrium at the point where the
  (a) indifference curve is concave to the origin
  (b) budget line crosses the vertical axis
  (c) two indifference curves intersect and are tangent to the budget line
  (d) budget line is tangent to an indifference curve

16. If a consumer is initially in equilibrium, a decrease in money income will
  (a) move the consumer to a new equilibrium on a lower indifference curve
  (b) move the consumer to a new equilibrium on a higher indifference curve
  (c) make the slope of the consumer's indifference curves steeper
  (d) have no effect on the equilibrium position

Questions 17, 18, 19, and 20 are based on the following graph.

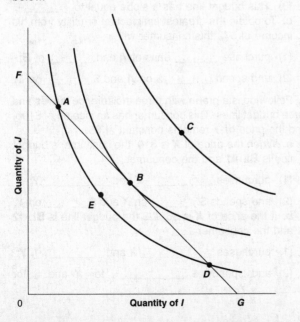

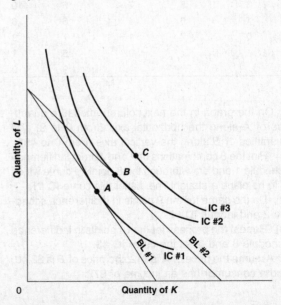

17. If the budget line shifts from **BL #1** to **BL #2**, it is because the price of
 (a) *K* increased
 (b) *K* decreased
 (c) *L* increased
 (d) *L* decreased

18. If the budget line shifts from **BL #2** to **BL #1**, it is because the price of
 (a) *K* increased
 (b) *K* decreased
 (c) *L* increased
 (d) *L* decreased

19. When the budget line shifts from **BL #2** to **BL #1**, the consumer will buy
 (a) more of *K* and *L*
 (b) less of *K* and *L*
 (c) more of *K* and less of *L*
 (d) less of *K* and more of *L*

20. Point *C* on indifference curve **IC #3** can be an attainable combination of products *K* and *L*, if
 (a) the price of *K* increases
 (b) the price of *L* increases
 (c) money income increases
 (d) money income decreases

■ **PROBLEMS**

1. Following are the schedules for three indifference curves.

Indifference schedule 1		Indifference schedule 2		Indifference schedule 3	
A	B	A	B	A	B
1	28	0	36	0	45
2	21	1	28	1	36
3	15	2	21	2	28
4	10	3	15	3	21
5	6	4	11	4	15
6	3	5	7	5	10
7	1	6	4	6	6
	0	7	1	7	3
			0	8	1
				9	0

 a. On the graph in the next column, measure quantities of *A* along the horizontal axis (from 0 to 9) and quantities of *B* along the vertical axis (from 0 to 45).
 (1) Plot the 8 combinations of *A* and *B* from indifference schedule 1 and draw through the 8 points a curve which is in no place a straight line. Label this curve **IC #1**.
 (2) Do the same for the 9 points in indifference schedule 2 and label it **IC #2**.
 (3) Repeat the process for the 10 points in indifference schedule 3 and label the curve **IC #3**.
 b. Assume the price of *A* is $12, the price of *B* is $2.40, and a consumer has an income of $72.

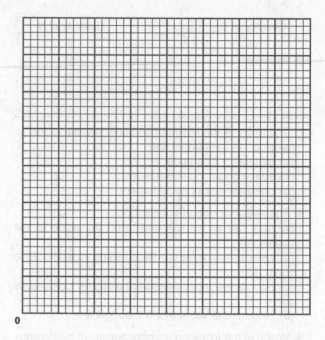

 (1) Complete the following table to show the quantities of *A* and *B* this consumer is able to purchase.

A	B
0	
1	
2	
3	
4	
5	
6	

 (2) Plot this budget line on the graph you completed in part **a.**

 (3) This budget line has a slope equal to _____.
 c. To obtain the greatest satisfaction or utility from his income of $72 this consumer will

 (1) purchase _____ units of *A* and _____ of *B*;

 (2) and spend _____ $ on *A* and $ _____ on *B*.

2. Following is a graph with three indifference curves and three budget lines. This consumer has an income of $100, and the price of *Y* remains constant at $5.
 a. When the price of *X* is $10, the consumer's budget line is **BL #1** and the consumer

 (1) purchases _____ *X* and _____ *Y*;

 (2) and spends $ _____ on *X* and $ _____ on *Y*.
 b. If the price of *X* is $6, 2/3 the budget line is **BL #2** and the consumer

 (1) purchases _____ *X* and _____ *Y*;

 (2) and spends $ _____ for *X* and $ for _____ *Y*.

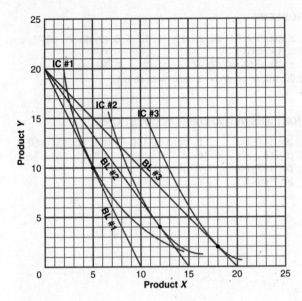

1. Why is the slope of the budget line negative?

2. How will each of the following events affect the budget line?
(a) a decrease in the money income of the consumer
(b) an increase in the prices of both products
(c) a decrease in the price of one of the products

3. Explain why the budget line can be called "objective" and an indifference curve "subjective."

4. What is the relationship between an indifference curve and total utility? Between an indifference map and total utility?

5. Why is the slope of an indifference curve negative and convex to the origin?

6. You are given two products, alpha and beta. Why will the utility-maximizing combination of the two products be the one lying on the highest attainable indifference curve?

7. Suppose a consumer purchases a combination of two products that is on her budget line but the budget line is not tangent to an indifference curve at that point. Of which product should the consumer buy more, and of which should she buy less? Why?

8. What is the important difference between the marginal-utility theory and the indifference-curve theory of consumer demand in terms of how utility is considered or measured?

9. Explain how the indifference map of a consumer and the budget line are utilized to derive the consumer's demand for one of the products. In deriving demand, what is varied and what is held constant?

10. How does a change in the price of one product shift the budget line and determine a new equilibrium point? Explain and illustrate with a graph.

c. And when the price of **X** is $5, the consumer has budget line **BL #3** and

(1) buys _____ **X** and _____ **Y**; and

(2) spends $_____ on **X** and $ _____on **Y**.
d. On the following graph, plot the quantities of **X** demanded at the three prices.

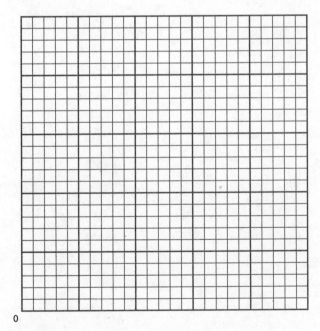

e. Between $10 and $5 this consumer's demand for

X is (elastic, inelastic) _____, and for him products **X** and **Y** are (substitutes, complements)

_____.

ANSWERS

Appendix to Chapter 7 Indifference Curve Analysis

FILL-IN QUESTIONS

1. income, a budget
2. price of X, price of Y
3. right, left
4. inward, outward, B
5. An indifference, utility
6. downward, convex
7. marginal
8. greater, decreases
9. total, map
10. greater
11. tangent, slope
12. up
13. cardinal, ordinal
14. *a.* outward, right; *b.* higher; *c.* more
15. demand

TRUE–FALSE QUESTIONS

1. T, pp. 147–148
2. F, pp. 147–148
3. F, pp. 147–148
4. T, p. 148
5. T, p. 148

6. F, pp. 148–149
7. T, p. 149
8. T, pp. 149–150
9. F, pp. 149–150
10. F, p. 149

11. F, p. 150
12. T, p. 150
13. T, p. 150
14. T, p. 150
15. T, pp. 150–151

MULTIPLE-CHOICE QUESTIONS

1. d, pp. 147–148
2. b, pp. 147–148
3. b, pp. 147–148
4. b, p. 148
5. b, p. 148
6. c, p. 148
7. d, pp. 148–149

8. c, pp. 148–149
9. b, p. 149
10. c, pp. 148–149
11. c, pp. 149–150
12. b, pp. 149–150
13. a, p. 150
14. a, pp. 149–150

15. d, p. 150
16. a, pp. 148, 150
17. b, pp. 151–152
18. a, pp. 151–152
19. b, pp. 151–152
20. c, pp. 148, 150

PROBLEMS

1. *a.* graph; *b.* (1) 30, 25, 20, 15, 10, 5, 0, (2) graph, (3) –5; *c.* (1) 3, 15, (2) 36, 36

2. *a.* (1) 5, 10, (2) 50, 50; *b.* (1) 12, 4, (2) 80, 20; *c.* (1) 18, 2, (2) 90, 10; *d.* graph; *e.* elastic, substitutes

SHORT ANSWER AND ESSAY QUESTIONS

1. pp. 147–148
2. p. 148
3. pp. 147–148
4. pp. 148–150

5. pp. 148–149
6. p. 150
7. p. 150
8. pp. 150–151

9. pp. 151–152
10. pp. 151–152

CHAPTER 8

The Costs of Production

Previous chapters discussed consumer behavior and product demand. This chapter switches to producer behavior and business firms. It explains how a firm's **costs of production** change as the firm's output changes, in the short run and in the long run.

This chapter begins with a definition of cost and profit. You should be somewhat familiar with these terms because they were first introduced in Chapters 1 and 2. The explanation is now more detailed. Several definitions of cost and profit are given in the chapter, so you must know the distinctions if you are to understand the true meaning of **economic cost** and **economic profit.**

The second and third sections of the chapter focus on **short-run** variable relationships and production costs for the firm. You are first introduced to the important **law of diminishing returns,** which defines the relationship between the quantity of resources used by the firm and the output the firm produces in the short run. The chapter discussion then shifts to costs because resource prices are associated with the fixed and variable resources the typical firm uses to produce its output. The three basic types of short-run costs—total, average, and marginal—vary for the firm as the quantity of resources and output changes. The chapter describes the relationship among the various cost curves and how they are shaped by the law of diminishing returns.

The fourth section of the chapter looks at production costs in the **long run.** All resources, and also production costs, are variable in the long run. You will learn that the long-run cost curve for the typical firm is based on the short-run cost curves for firms of different sizes. In the long run, firms can experience **economies of scale** and **diseconomies of scale** that will shape the long-run cost curve for the firm. The chapter concludes with several practical applications of the concept of scale economies.

It is important that you master this material on the costs of production because it sets the foundation for understanding the price and output decisions of a firm operating under different market structures that you will be reading about in the next three chapters.

■ CHECKLIST

When you have studied this chapter you should be able to

☐ Define economic cost in terms of opportunity cost.
☐ Distinguish between an explicit cost and an implicit cost.
☐ Explain the difference between normal profit and economic profit.

☐ Distinguish between the short run and the long run in production.
☐ Define total product, marginal product, and average product.
☐ State the law of diminishing returns and explain its rationale.
☐ Compute marginal product and average product to illustrate the law of diminishing returns when you are given the necessary data.
☐ Describe the relationship between marginal product and average product.
☐ Define fixed costs, variable costs, and total cost.
☐ Define average fixed cost, average variable cost, and average total cost.
☐ Explain how average product is related to average variable cost.
☐ Define marginal cost.
☐ Explain how marginal product is related to marginal cost.
☐ Compute and graph average fixed cost, average variable cost, average total cost, and marginal cost when given total-cost data.
☐ Describe the relation of marginal cost to average variable cost and average total cost.
☐ Explain why short-run cost curves shift.
☐ Illustrate the difference between short-run average total cost curves for a firm at different outputs and its long-run average total cost curve.
☐ Describe various possible long-run average total cost curves.
☐ Define and list reasons for the economies and diseconomies of scale.
☐ Explain the concept of minimum efficient scale and its relation to industry structure.
☐ Give examples of short-run costs, economies of scale, and minimum efficient scale in the real world.
☐ Explain why sunk costs are irrelevant in decision-making (Last Word).

■ CHAPTER OUTLINE

1. Resources are scarce and are used to produce many different products. The **economic cost** of using resources to produce a product is an opportunity cost: the value or worth of the resources in its best alternative use.

   a. Economic costs can be explicit or implicit. **Explicit costs** are the monetary payments that a firm makes to obtain resources from nonowners of the firm. *Implicit costs* are the monetary payments that would have been paid for self-owned or self-employed resources if they had been used in their next best alternative outside the firm.

    b. *Normal profit* is an implicit cost and is the minimum payment that entrepreneurs must receive for performing the entrepreneurial functions for the firm.

    c. *Economic,* or pure, *profit* is the revenue a firm receives in excess of all its explicit and implicit economic (opportunity) costs. (The firm's accounting profit is its revenue less only its explicit costs.)

    d. A distinction is made between the *short run* and the *long run.* The firm's economic costs vary as the firm's output changes. These costs depend on whether the firm is able to make short-run or long-run changes in its resource use. In the short run, the firm's plant is a fixed resource, but in the long run it is a variable resource. So, in the short run the firm cannot change the size of its plant and can vary its output only by changing the quantities of the variable resources it employs.

2. There are **short-run** relationships between inputs and outputs in the production process.

    a. Several product terms need to be defined to show these relationships. *Total product (TP)* is the total quantity of output produced. *Marginal product (MP)* is the change made in total product from a change in a variable resource input. *Average product (AP),* or productivity, is the total product per unit of resource input.

    b. The *law of diminishing returns* determines the manner in which the costs of the firm change as it changes its output in the short run. As more units of a variable resource are added to a fixed resource, beyond some point the marginal product from each additional unit of a variable resource will decline.

    (1) There are three phases reflected in a graph of the total product and marginal product curves: increasing, decreasing, and negative marginal returns.

    (2) When total product is increasing at an increasing rate, marginal product is rising; when total product is increasing at a decreasing rate, marginal product is falling; and when total product declines, marginal product is negative.

    (3) When marginal product is greater than average product, average product rises, and when marginal product is less than average product, average product falls.

3. When input, output, and price information is available, it is possible to calculate **short-run production costs.**

    a. The *total cost* is the sum of the firm's fixed costs and variable costs. As output increases,

    (1) *fixed costs* do not change;

    (2) at first, the *variable costs* increase at a decreasing rate, and then increase at an increasing rate;

    (3) and at first total costs increase at a decreasing rate and then increase at an increasing rate.

    b. **Average costs** consist of *average fixed costs (AFC), average variable costs (AVC),* and *average total costs (ATC).* They are equal, respectively, to the firm's fixed, variable, and total costs divided by its output. As output increases

    (1) average fixed cost decreases

    (2) at first, average variable cost decreases and then increases

    (3) and at first, average total cost also decreases and then increases

    c. *Marginal cost (MC)* is the extra cost incurred in producing one additional unit of output.

    (1) Because the marginal product of the variable resource increases and then decreases (as more of the variable resource is employed to increase output), marginal cost decreases and then increases as output increases.

    (2) At the output at which average variable cost is a minimum, average variable cost and marginal cost are equal, and at the output at which average total cost is a minimum, average total cost and marginal cost are equal.

    (3) On a graph, marginal cost will always intersect average variable cost at its minimum point and marginal cost will always intersect average total cost at its minimum point. These intersections will always have marginal cost approaching average variable cost and average total cost from below.

    d. Changes in either resource prices or technology will cause the cost curves to shift.

4. In the long run, all the resources employed by the firm are variable resources. **Long-run production costs** are all variable costs.

    a. As the firm expands its output by increasing the size of its plant, average total cost tends to fall at first because of the *economies of scale,* but as this expansion continues, sooner or later, average total cost begins to rise because of the *diseconomies of scale.*

    b. The long-run average total cost curve shows the least average total cost at which any output can be produced after the firm has had time to make all changes in its plant size. Graphically, it is made up of all the points of tangency of the unlimited number of short-run average total cost curves.

    c. The economies and diseconomies of scale encountered in the production of different goods are important factors influencing the structure and competitiveness of various industries.

    (1) *Economies of scale* (a decline in long-run average total costs) arise because of labor specialization, managerial specialization, efficient capital, and other factors such as spreading the start-up, advertising, or development costs over an increasing level of output.

    (2) *Diseconomies of scale* arise primarily from the problems of efficiently managing and coordinating the firm's operations as it becomes a large-scale producer.

    (3) *Constant returns to scale* are the range of output where long-run average total cost does not change.

    d. Economies and diseconomies of scale can determine the structure in an industry. *Minimum efficient scale (MES)* is the smallest level of output at which a firm can minimize long-run average costs. This concept explains why relatively large and small firms could co-exist in an industry and be viable when there is an extended range of constant returns to scale.

(1) In some industries the long-run average cost curve will decline over a range of output. Given consumer demand, efficient production will be achieved only with a small number of large firms.

(2) If economies of scale extend beyond the market size, the conditions for a **natural monopoly** are produced, which is a rare situation where unit costs are minimized by having a single firm produce a product.

(3) If there are few economies of scale, then there is minimum efficient size at a low level of output and there are many firms in an industry.

5. There are several applications and illustrations of short-run costs, economies of scale, and minimum efficient cost.

a. A rise in the cost of corn raises short-run cost curves (AVC, MC, ATC) for businesses that use corn as a product input.

b. Economies of scale can be seen in successful start-up firms such as Intel, Microsoft, or Starbucks. Economies of scale are also exhibited in the Verson stamping machine that makes millions of auto parts per year.

c. A small price can be charged for a newspaper because the fixed costs are spread across a large amount of output, thus achieving economies of scale.

d. Economies of scale are extensive in aircraft production, but modest in concrete mixing, which achieves minimum efficient scale at a low level of output. As a consequence, there are few aircraft factories and many concrete mixing companies.

6. (Last Word). Sunk costs are irrelevant to economic decision making because they are already incurred and cannot be recovered. Sunk costs are the result of making a past decision, not a current decision. A current decision is made on the basis of evaluating marginal costs and marginal benefits. If the marginal costs are less than the marginal benefits, the action will be taken.

■ HINTS AND TIPS

1. Many **cost** terms are described in this chapter. Make yourself a glossary so that you can distinguish among them. You need to know what each one means if you are to master the material in the chapter. If you try to learn them in the order in which you encounter them, you will have little difficulty because the later terms build on the earlier ones.

2. Make sure you know the difference between **marginal** and **average** relationships in this chapter. Marginal product (MP) shows the *change* in total output associated with each additional input. Average product (AP) is simply the output per unit of resource input. Marginal cost (MC) shows the change in total cost associated with producing another unit of output. Average cost shows the per-unit cost of producing a level of output.

3. Practice drawing the different sets of **cost curves** used in this chapter: (1) short-run total cost curves, (2) short-run average and marginal cost curves, and (3) long-run cost curves. Also, explain to yourself the relationship between the curves in each set that you draw.

4. In addition to learning *how* the costs of the firm vary as its output varies, be sure to understand *why* the costs vary the way they do. In this connection note that the behavior of short-run costs is the result of the law of diminishing returns and that the behavior of long-run costs is the consequence of economies and diseconomies of scale.

■ IMPORTANT TERMS

economic (opportunity) cost

explicit costs

implicit costs

normal profit

economic profit

short run

long run

total product (TP)

marginal product (MP)

average product (AP)

law of diminishing returns

fixed costs

variable costs

total cost (TC)

average fixed cost (AFC)

average variable cost (AVC)

average total cost (ATC)

marginal cost (MC)

economies of scale

diseconomies of scale

constant returns to scale

minimum efficient scale (MES)

natural monopoly

SELF-TEST

■ FILL-IN QUESTIONS

1. The value or worth of any resource in its best alternative use is called the (out-of-pocket, opportunity) _____ cost of that resource.

2. The economic cost of producing a product is the amount of money or income the firm must pay or provide to (government, resource suppliers) _____ to attract land, labor, and capital goods away from alternative uses in the economy. The monetary payments, or out-of-pocket payments, are (explicit, implicit) _____ costs, and the costs of self-owned or self-employed resources are _____ costs.

3. Normal profit is a cost because it is the payment that the firm must make to obtain the services of the (workers, entrepreneurs) _____. Accounting profit is equal to the firm's total revenue less its (explicit, implicit) _____ costs. Economic profit is not a cost and is equal to the firm's total (costs, revenues) _____ less its economic _____.

4. In the short run the firm can change its output by changing the quantity of the (fixed, variable) _____ resources it employs, but it cannot change the quantity of the _____ resources. This means that the firm's plant capacity is fixed in the (short, long) _____ run and variable in the _____ run.

5. The law of diminishing returns is that as successive units of a (fixed, variable) _____ resource are added to a _____ resource, beyond some point the (total, marginal) _____ product of the former resource will decrease. The law assumes that all units of input are of (equal, unequal) _____ quality.

6. If the total product increases at an increasing rate, the marginal product is (rising, falling) _____. If it increases at a decreasing rate, the marginal product is (positive, negative, zero) _____, but (rising, falling) _____.

7. If total product is at a maximum, the marginal product is (positive, negative, zero) _____, but if it decreases, the marginal product is _____.

8. If the marginal product of any input exceeds its average product, the average product is (rising, falling) _____, but if it is less than its average product, the average product is _____. If the marginal product is equal to its average product, the average product is at a (minimum, maximum) _____.

9. Those costs that in total do not vary with changes in output are (fixed, variable) _____ costs, but those costs that in total change with the level of output are _____ costs. The sum of fixed and variable costs at each level of output is (marginal, total) _____ cost.

10. The law of diminishing returns explains why a firm's average variable, average total, and marginal cost may at first tend to (increase, decrease) _____ but ultimately _____ as the output of the firm increases.

11. Marginal cost is the increase in (average, total) _____ variable cost or _____ cost that occurs when the firm increases its output by one unit.

12. If marginal cost is less than average variable cost, average variable cost will be (rising, falling, constant) _____ but if average variable cost is less than marginal cost, average variable cost will be _____.

13. Assume that labor is the only variable input in the short run and that the wage rate paid to labor is constant.

a. When the marginal product of labor is rising, the marginal cost of producing a product is (rising, falling) _____.

b. When the average variable cost of producing a product is falling, the average product of labor is (rising, falling) _____.

c. At the output at which marginal cost is at a minimum, the marginal product of labor is at a (minimum, maximum) _____.

d. At the output at which the average product of labor is at a maximum, the average variable cost of producing the product is at a (minimum, maximum) _____.

e. At the output at which the average variable cost is at a minimum, average variable cost and (marginal, total) _____ cost are equal and average product and _____ product are equal.

14. Changes in either resource prices or technology will cause cost curves to (shift, remain unchanged) _____. If average fixed costs increase, then the average fixed costs curve will (shift up, shift down, remain unchanged) _____ and the average total cost curve will _____, but the average variable cost curve will _____ and the marginal cost curve will (shift up, shift down, remain unchanged) _____.

15. If average variable costs increase, then the average variable cost curve will (shift up, shift down, remain unchanged) _____ and the average total cost curve will _____, and the marginal cost curve will (shift up, shift down, remain unchanged) _____, but the average fixed cost curve would _____.

16. The short-run costs of a firm are fixed and variable costs, but in the long run all costs are (fixed, variable) _____. The long-run average total cost of producing a product is equal to the lowest of the short-run costs of producing that product after the firm has had all the time it requires to make the appropriate adjustments in the size of its (workforce, plant) _____.

17. List the three important sources of economies of scale:

a. _____

b. _____

c. _____

18. When the firm experiences diseconomies of scale, it has (higher, lower) _____ average total costs as output increases. Where diseconomies of scale are operative, an increase in all inputs will cause a (greater, less) _____-than-proportionate increase in output. The factor that gives rise to large diseconomies of scale is managerial (specialization, difficulties) _____.

19. The smallest level of output at which a firm can minimize long-run average costs is (maximum, minimum) _____ efficient scale. Relatively large and small firms could coexist in an industry and be equally viable when there is an extended range of (increasing, decreasing, constant) _____ returns to scale.

20. In some industries, the long-run average cost curve will (increase, decrease) _____ over a long range of output and efficient production will be achieved with only a few (small, large) _____ firms. The conditions for a natural monopoly are created when (economies, diseconomies) _____ of scale extend beyond the market's size so that unit costs are minimized by having a single firm produce a product.

■ **TRUE–FALSE QUESTIONS**

Circle T if the statement is true, F if it is false.

1. The economic costs of a firm are the payments it must make to resource owners to attract their resources from alternative employments. **T F**

2. Economic or pure profit is an explicit cost, while normal profit is an implicit cost. **T F**

3. In the short run the size (or capacity) of a firm's plant is fixed. **T F**

4. The resources employed by a firm are all variable in the long run and all fixed in the short run. **T F**

5. The law of diminishing returns states that as successive amounts of a variable resource are added to a fixed resource, beyond some point total output will diminish. **T F**

6. An assumption of the law of diminishing returns is that all units of variable inputs are of equal quality. **T F**

7. When total product is increasing at a decreasing rate, marginal product is positive and increasing. **T F**

8. When average product is falling, marginal product is greater than average product. **T F**

9. When marginal product is negative, total production (or output) is decreasing. **T F**

10. The larger the output of a firm, the smaller the fixed cost of the firm. **T F**

11. The law of diminishing returns explains why increases in variable costs associated with each 1-unit increase

in output become greater and greater after a certain point. **T F**

12. Fixed costs can be controlled or altered in the short run. **T F**

13. Total cost is the sum of fixed and variable costs at each level of output. **T F**

14. Marginal cost is the change in fixed cost divided by the change in output. **T F**

15. The marginal cost curve intersects the average total cost (ATC) curve at the ATC curve's minimum point. **T F**

16. If the fixed cost of a firm increases from one year to the next (because the premium it must pay for the insurance on the buildings it owns has been increased) while its variable cost schedule remains unchanged, its marginal cost schedule will also remain unchanged. **T F**

17. Marginal cost is equal to average variable cost at the output at which average variable cost is at a minimum. **T F**

18. When the marginal product of a variable resource increases, the marginal cost of producing the product will decrease, and when marginal product decreases, marginal cost will increase. **T F**

19. If the price of a variable input should increase, the average variable cost, average total cost, and marginal cost curves would all shift upward, but the position of the average fixed cost curve would remain unchanged. **T F**

20. One explanation why the long-run average total cost curve of a firm rises after some level of output has been reached is the law of diminishing returns. **T F**

21. If a firm increases all its inputs by 20% and its output increases by 30%, the firm is experiencing economies of scale. **T F**

22. The primary cause of diseconomies of scale is increased specialization of labor. **T F**

23. If a firm has constant returns to scale in the long run, the *total* cost of producing its product does not change when it expands or contracts its output. **T F**

24. Minimum efficient scale occurs at the largest level of output at which a firm can minimize long-run average costs. **T F**

25. The fundamental reason that newspapers have such low prices is the low production costs from economies of scale. **T F**

■ **MULTIPLE-CHOICE QUESTIONS**

Circle the letter that corresponds to the best answer.

1. Suppose that a firm produces 100,000 units a year and sells them all for $5 each. The explicit costs of

production are $350,000 and the implicit costs of production are $100,000. The firm has an accounting profit of
   (a) $200,000 and an economic profit of $25,000
   (b) $150,000 and an economic profit of $50,000
   (c) $125,000 and an economic profit of $75,000
   (d) $100,000 and an economic profit of $50,000

2. Economic profit for a firm is defined as the total revenue of the firm minus its
   (a) accounting profit
   (b) normal profit
   (c) implicit costs
   (d) economic cost

3. Which would best describe the short run for a firm as defined by economists?
   (a) The plant capacity for a firm is variable.
   (b) The plant capacity for a firm is fixed.
   (c) There are diseconomies of scale.
   (d) There are economies of scale.

4. Which is most likely to be a long-run adjustment for a firm that manufactures golf carts on an assembly line basis?
   (a) an increase in the amount of steel the firm buys
   (b) a reduction in the number of shifts of workers from three to two
   (c) a change in the production managers of the assembly line
   (d) a change from the production of golf carts to motorcycles

5. The change in total product divided by the change in resource input defines
   (a) total cost
   (b) average cost
   (c) average product
   (d) marginal product

Use the following table to answer Questions 6 and 7. Assume that the only variable resource used to produce output is labor.

Amount of labor	Amount of output
1	3
2	8
3	12
4	15
5	17
6	18

6. The marginal product of the fourth unit of labor is
   (a) 2 units of output
   (b) 3 units of output
   (c) 4 units of output
   (d) 15 units of output

7. When the firm hires four units of labor the average product of labor is
   (a) 3 units of output
   (b) 3.75 units of output
   (c) 4.25 units of output
   (d) 15 units of output

8. Because the marginal product of a variable resource initially increases and later decreases as a firm increases its output,
   (a) average variable cost decreases at first and then increases
   (b) average fixed cost declines as the output of the firm expands
   (c) variable cost at first increases by increasing amounts and then increases by decreasing amounts
   (d) marginal cost at first increases and then decreases

9. Because the marginal product of a resource at first increases and then decreases as the output of the firm increases,
   (a) average fixed cost declines as the output of the firm increases
   (b) average variable cost at first increases and then decreases
   (c) variable cost at first increases by increasing amounts and then increases by decreasing amounts
   (d) total cost at first increases by decreasing amounts and then increases by increasing amounts

For Questions 10, 11, and 12, use the data given in the following table. The fixed cost of the firm is $500, and the firm's total variable cost is indicated in the table.

Output	Total variable cost
1	$ 200
2	360
3	500
4	700
5	1000
6	1800

10. The average variable cost of the firm when 4 units of output are produced is
   (a) $175
   (b) $200
   (c) $300
   (d) $700

11. The average total cost of the firm when 4 units of output are being produced is
   (a) $175
   (b) $200
   (c) $300
   (d) $700

12. The marginal cost of the sixth unit of output is
   (a) $200
   (b) $300
   (c) $700
   (d) $800

13. Marginal cost and average variable cost are equal at the output at which
   (a) marginal cost is a minimum
   (b) marginal product is a maximum
   (c) average product is a maximum
   (d) average variable cost is a maximum

14. Average variable cost may be either increasing or decreasing when
(a) marginal cost is decreasing
(b) marginal product is increasing
(c) average fixed cost is decreasing
(d) average total cost is increasing

15. Why does the short-run marginal cost curve eventually increase for the typical firm?
(a) diseconomies of scale
(b) minimum efficient scale
(c) the law of diminishing returns
(d) economic profit eventually decreases

16. If the price of labor or some other variable resource increased, the
(a) AVC curve would shift downward
(b) AFC curve would shift upward
(c) AFC curve would shift downward
(d) MC curve would shift upward

Questions 17, 18, 19, and 20 are based on the following figure.

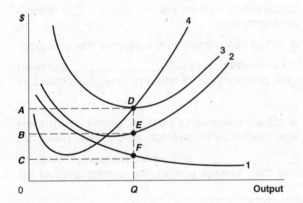

17. In the figure, curves **1, 3,** and **4,** respectively, represent
(a) average variable cost, marginal cost, and average total cost
(b) average total cost, average variable cost, and marginal cost
(c) average fixed cost, average total cost, and marginal cost
(d) marginal cost, average total cost, and average variable cost

18. At output level **Q,** the average fixed cost is measured by the vertical distance represented by
(a) **DE**
(b) **DF**
(c) **DQ**
(d) **EF**

19. As output increases beyond the level represented by **Q,**
(a) marginal product is rising
(b) marginal product is falling

(c) total fixed costs are rising
(d) total costs are falling

20. If the firm is producing at output level **Q,** then the total variable costs of production are represented by area
(a) 0**QFC**
(b) 0**QEB**
(c) 0**QDC**
(d) **CFEB**

21. At an output of 10,000 units per year, a firm's total variable costs are $50,000 and its average fixed costs are $2. The total costs per year for the firm are
(a) $50,000
(b) $60,000
(c) $70,000
(d) $80,000

22. A firm has total fixed costs of $4,000 a year. The average variable cost is $3.00 for 2000 units of output. At this level of output, its average total costs are
(a) $2.50
(b) $3.00
(c) $4.50
(d) $5.00

23. If you know that total fixed cost is $100, total variable cost is $300, and total product is 4 units, then
(a) marginal cost is $50
(b) average fixed cost is $45
(c) average total cost is $125
(d) average variable cost is $75

24. If the short-run average variable costs of production for a firm are falling, then this indicates that
(a) average variable costs are above average fixed costs
(b) marginal costs are below average variable costs
(c) average fixed costs are constant
(d) total costs are falling

Answer Questions 25 and 26 using the following table. Three short-run cost schedules are given for three plants of different sizes that a firm might build in the long run.

Plant 1		Plant 2		Plant 3	
Output	ATC	Output	ATC	Output	ATC
10	$10	10	$15	10	$20
20	9	20	10	20	15
30	8	30	7	30	10
40	9	40	10	40	8
50	10	50	14	50	9

25. What is the long-run average cost of producing 40 units of output?
(a) $7
(b) $8
(c) $9
(d) $10

26. At what output is long-run average cost at a minimum?
(a) 20
(b) 30
(c) 40
(d) 50

27. If the long-run average total cost curve for a firm is downsloping, then it indicates that there
(a) is a minimum efficient scale
(b) are constant returns to scale
(c) are diseconomies of scale
(d) are economies of scale

28. Which factor contributes to economies of scale?
(a) less efficient use of capital goods
(b) less division of labor and specialization
(c) greater specialization in management of a firm
(d) greater difficulty controlling the operations of a firm

29. A firm is encountering constant returns to scale when it increases all of its inputs by 20% and its output increases by
(a) 10%
(b) 15%
(c) 20%
(d) 25%

30. If economies of scale are limited and diseconomies appear quickly in an industry, then minimum efficient scale occurs at a
(a) high level of output, and there will be a few firms
(b) high level of output, and there will be many firms
(c) low level of output, and there will be few firms
(d) low level of output, and there will be many firms

■ **PROBLEMS**

1. On the following graph, sketch the way in which the average product and the marginal product of a resource change as the firm increases its employment of that resource.

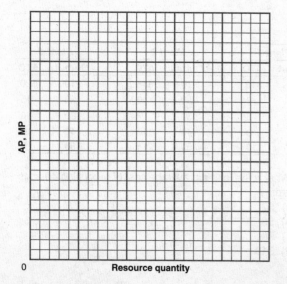

2. The table shows the total production of a firm as the quantity of labor employed increases. The quantities of all other resources employed remain constant.

  a. Compute the marginal products of the first through the eighth units of labor and enter them in the table.

Units of labor	Total production	Marginal product of labor	Average product of labor
0	0		0
1	80	____	____
2	200	____	____
3	330	____	____
4	400	____	____
5	450	____	____
6	480	____	____
7	490	____	____
8	480	____	____

  b. Now compute the average products of the various quantities of labor and enter them in the table.

  c. There are increasing returns to labor from the first through the _____ units of labor and decreasing returns from the _____ through the eighth units.

  d. When total production is increasing, marginal product is (positive, negative) _____ and when total production is decreasing, marginal product is _____.

  e. When marginal product is greater than average product, then average product will (rise, fall) _____, and when marginal product is less than average product, the average product will _____.

3. On the graph below sketch the manner in which fixed cost, variable cost, and total cost change as the output the firm produces in the short run changes.

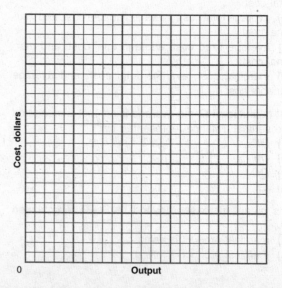

Quantity of labor employed	Total output	Marginal product of labor	Average product of labor	Total cost	Marginal cost	Average variable cost
0	0	—	—	$____	—	—
1	5	5	5	____	$____	$____
2	11	6	5.50	____	____	____
3	18	7	6	____	____	____
4	24	6	6	____	____	____
5	29	5	5.80	____	____	____
6	33	4	5.50	____	____	____
7	36	3	5.14	____	____	____
8	38	2	4.75	____	____	____
9	39	1	4.33	____	____	____
10	39	0	3.90	____	____	____

4. Assume that a firm has a plant of fixed size and that it can vary its output only by varying the amount of labor it employs. The table at the top of the page shows the relationships among the amount of labor employed, the output of the firm, the marginal product of labor, and the average product of labor.

a. Assume each unit of labor costs the firm $10. Compute the total cost of labor for each quantity of labor the firm might employ, and enter these figures in the table.

b. Now determine the marginal cost of the firm's product as the firm increases its output. Divide the increase in total labor cost by the *increase* in total output to find the marginal cost. Enter these figures in the table.

c. When the marginal product of labor
(1) increases, the marginal cost of the firm's product

(increases, decreases) _____.
(2) decreases, the marginal cost of the firm's product

_____.

d. If labor is the only variable input, the total labor cost and total variable cost are equal. Find the average variable cost of the firm's product (by dividing the total labor cost by total output) and enter these figures in the table.

e. When the average product of labor
(1) increases, the average variable cost (increases,

decreases) _____.
(2) decreases, the average variable cost _____.

5. The law of diminishing returns causes a firm's average variable, average total, and marginal cost to decrease at first and then to increase as the output of the firm increases.

Sketch these three cost curves on the following graph in such a way that their proper relationship to each other is shown.

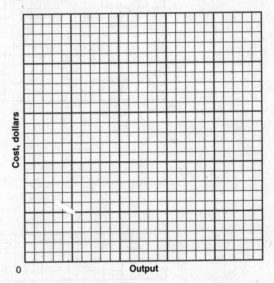

6. The table that follows is a schedule of a firm's fixed cost and variable cost.

a. Complete the table by computing total cost, average fixed cost, average total cost, and marginal cost.

b. On the graph at the top of the next page, plot and label fixed cost, variable cost, and total cost.

c. On the graph at the bottom of the next page, plot average fixed cost, average variable cost, average total cost, and marginal cost. Label the four curves.

Output	Total fixed cost	Total variable cost	Total cost	Average fixed cost	Average variable cost	Average total cost	Marginal cost
0	$200	$ 0	$____				
1	200	50	____	$____	$50.00	$____	$____
2	200	90	____	____	45.00	____	____
3	200	120	____	____	40.00	____	____
4	200	160	____	____	40.00	____	____
5	200	220	____	____	44.00	____	____
6	200	300	____	____	50.00	____	____
7	200	400	____	____	57.14	____	____
8	200	520	____	____	65.00	____	____
9	200	670	____	____	74.44	____	____
10	200	900	____	____	90.00	____	____

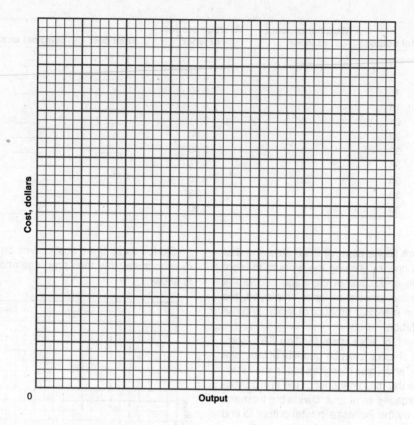

Cost, dollars

0   Output

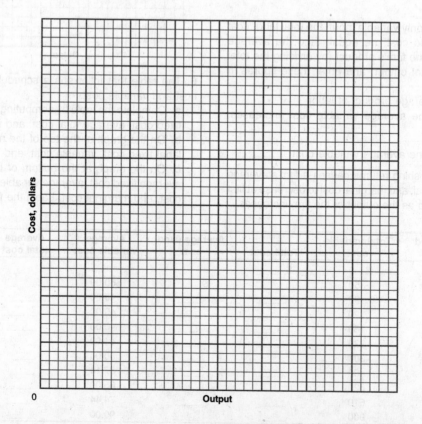

Cost, dollars

0   Output

7. Following are the short-run average cost curves of producing a product with three different sizes of plants, Plant 1, Plant 2, and Plant 3. Draw the firm's long-run average cost on this graph.

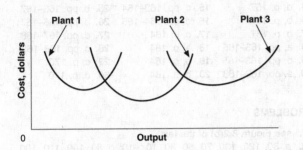

8. Following are the short-run average total cost schedules for three plants of different sizes that a firm might build to produce its product. Assume that these are the only possible sizes of plants that the firm might build.

Plant size A		Plant size B		Plant size C	
Output	ATC	Output	ATC	Output	ATC
10	$ 7	10	$17	10	$53
20	6	20	13	20	44
30	5	30	9	30	35
40	4	40	6	40	27
50	5	50	4	50	20
60	7	60	3	60	14
70	10	70	4	70	11
80	14	80	5	80	8
90	19	90	7	90	6
100	25	100	10	100	5
110	32	110	16	110	7
120	40	120	25	120	10

a. Complete the long-run average cost schedule for the firm in the following table.

Output	Average cost	Output	Average cost
10	$_____	70	$_____
20	_____	80	_____
30	_____	90	_____
40	_____	100	_____
50	_____	110	_____
60	_____	120	_____

b. For outputs between

(1) _____ and _____, the firm should build Plant A.

(2) _____ and _____, the firm should build Plant B.

(3) _____ and _____, the firm should build Plant C.

■ SHORT ANSWER AND ESSAY QUESTIONS

1. Explain the meaning of the opportunity cost of producing a product and the difference between an explicit cost and an implicit cost. How would you determine the implicit money cost of a resource?

2. What is the difference between normal profit and economic profit? Why is the former an economic cost? How do you define accounting profit?

3. What type of adjustments can a firm make in the long run that it cannot make in the short run? What adjustments can it make in the short run? How long is the short run?

4. Why is the distinction between the short run and the long run important?

5. State precisely the law of diminishing returns. Exactly what is it that diminishes, and why does it diminish?

6. Distinguish between a fixed cost and a variable cost.

7. Why are short-run total costs partly fixed and partly variable costs, and why are long-run costs entirely variable?

8. Why do short-run variable costs increase at first by decreasing amounts and later increase by increasing amounts?

9. How does the behavior of short-run variable costs influence the behavior of short-run total costs?

10. Describe the way in which short-run average fixed cost, average variable cost, average total cost, and marginal cost vary as the output of the firm increases.

11. What are the connections between marginal product and marginal cost, and between average product and average variable cost? How will marginal cost behave as marginal product decreases and increases? How will average variable cost change as average product rises and falls?

12. What are the precise relationships between marginal cost and minimum average variable cost, and between marginal cost and minimum average total cost? Why are these relationships necessarily true?

13. What happens to the average total cost, average variable cost, average fixed cost, and marginal cost curves when the price of a variable input increases or decreases? Describe what other factor can cause short-run cost curves to shift.

14. What does the long-run average cost curve of a firm show? What relationship is there between long-run average cost and the short-run average total cost schedules of the different-sized plants which a firm might build?

15. Why is the long-run average cost curve of a firm U-shaped?

16. What is meant by economies of scale and by diseconomies of scale?

17. What are factors that contribute to economies of scale?

18. What causes diseconomies of scale?

19. What is minimum efficient scale? How can this concept, combined with economies and diseconomies of scale, be used to describe the number and size of firms in an industry?

20. Describe real examples of short-run costs, economies of scale, and minimum efficient scale.

ANSWERS

Chapter 8 The Costs of Production

FILL-IN QUESTIONS

1. opportunity
2. resource suppliers, explicit, implicit
3. entrepreneurs, explicit, revenues, costs
4. variable, fixed, short, long
5. variable, fixed, marginal, equal
6. rising, positive, falling
7. zero, negative
8. rising, falling, maximum
9. fixed, variable, total
10. decrease, increase
11. total, total
12. falling, rising
13. *a.* falling; *b.* rising; *c.* maximum; *d.* minimum; *e.* marginal, marginal
14. shift, shift up, shift up, remain unchanged, remain unchanged
15. shift up, shift up, shift up, remain unchanged
16. variable, plant
17. *a.* labor specialization; *b.* managerial specialization; *c.* more efficient use
18. higher, less, difficulties
19. minimum, constant
20. decrease, large, economies

TRUE–FALSE QUESTIONS

1. T, p. 155	**10.** F, p. 159	**19.** T, p. 165
2. F, pp. 155–156	**11.** T, p. 161	**20.** F, pp. 166–167
3. T, p. 156	**12.** F, p. 159	**21.** T, pp. 168–169
4. F, p. 156	**13.** T, p. 161	**22.** F, p. 169
5. F, pp. 157–158	**14.** F, p. 163	**23.** F, p. 170
6. T, pp. 157–158	**15.** T, pp. 164–165	**24.** F, p. 170
7. F, pp. 159–160	**16.** T, p. 163	**25.** T, p. 171
8. F, pp. 159–160	**17.** T, pp. 164–165	
9. T, pp. 159–160	**18.** T, pp. 163–164	

MULTIPLE-CHOICE QUESTIONS

1. b, p. 155	**11.** c, p. 163	**21.** c, pp. 162–163
2. d, p. 156	**12.** d, p. 163	**22.** d, pp. 162–163
3. b, p. 156	**13.** c, pp. 163–165	**23.** d, pp. 162–163
4. d, p. 156	**14.** c, pp. 163–165	**24.** b, pp. 163–165
5. d, p. 157	**15.** c, pp. 163–164	**25.** b, pp. 166–167
6. b, p. 157	**16.** d, pp. 164–165	**26.** b, pp. 166–167
7. b, p. 157	**17.** c, p. 164	**27.** d, pp. 167–168
8. a, pp. 163–165	**18.** a, p. 164	**28.** c, pp. 168–169
9. d, pp. 163–165	**19.** b, p. 164	**29.** c, p. 170
10. a, pp. 162–163	**20.** b, p. 164	**30.** d, p. 170

PROBLEMS

1. see Figure 8.2(b) of the text
2. *a.* 80, 120, 130, 70, 50, 30, 10, –10; *b.* 80, 100, 110, 100, 90, 80, 70, 60; *c.* third, fourth; *d.* positive, negative; *e.* rise, fall
3. see Figure 8.3 of the text
4. *a.* \$0, 10, 20, 30, 40, 50, 60, 70, 80, 90, 100; *b.* \$2.00, 1.67, 1.43, 1.67, 2.00, 2.50, 3.33, 5.00, 1.00, NA; *c.* (1) decreases, (2) increases; *d.* 2.00, 1.82, 1.67, 1.67, 1.72, 1.82, 1.94, 2.11, 2.31, 2.56; *e.* (1) decreases, (2) increases
5. see Figure 8.5 of the text
6. *a.* see table below; *b.* graph; *c.* graph

Total cost	Average fixed cost	Average total cost	Marginal cost
\$ 200	—	—	—
250	\$200.00	\$250.00	\$ 50
290	100.00	145.00	40
320	66.67	106.67	30
360	50.00	90.00	40
420	40.00	84.00	60
500	33.33	83.33	80
600	28.57	85.71	100
720	25.00	90.00	120
870	22.22	96.67	150
1100	20.00	110.00	230

7. see Figures 8.7 and 8.8 of the text
8. *a.* \$7.00, 6.00, 5.00, 4.00, 4.00, 3.00, 4.00, 5.00, 6.00, 5.00, 7.00, 10.00; *b.* (1) 10, 40, (2) 50, 80, (3) 90, 120

SHORT ANSWER AND ESSAY QUESTIONS

1. p. 155	**8.** p. 161	**15.** pp. 167–168
2. pp. 155–156	**9.** pp. 161–162	**16.** pp. 167–169
3. p. 156	**10.** pp. 162–165	**17.** pp. 168–169
4. p. 156	**11.** pp. 163–165	**18.** p. 169
5. pp. 157–158	**12.** pp. 163–165	**19.** p. 170
6. pp. 159–161	**13.** p. 165	**20.** pp. 170–171
7. pp. 161–162	**14.** pp. 166–167	

CHAPTER 9

Pure Competition

Chapter 9 is the first of three chapters that bring together the previous discussion of demand and production costs. These chapters examine demand and production costs under four different market structures: pure competition, monopoly, oligopoly, and monopolistic competition. This chapter focuses exclusively on the pure competition market structure, which is characterized by (1) a large number of firms, (2) the selling of a standardized product, (3) firms that are price takers rather than price makers, and (4) ease of entry into and exit from the industry.

The main section of the chapter describes profit maximization for the purely competitive firm in the **short run.** Although two approaches to profit maximization are presented, the one given the greatest emphasis is the **marginal revenue—marginal cost** approach. You will learn the rule that a firm maximizes profit or minimizes losses by producing the output level at which marginal revenue equals marginal cost. Finding this equality provides the answers to the three central questions each firm has to answer: (1) Should we produce? (2) If so, how much output? (3) What profit (or loss) will be realized?

Answers to these questions also give insights about the **short-run supply curve** for the individual firm. The firm will find it profitable to produce at any output level where marginal revenue is greater than marginal costs. The firm will also produce in the short run, but it will experience losses if marginal revenue is less than marginal costs and greater than the minimum of average total cost. You will be shown how to construct the short-run supply curve for the purely competitive firm, given price and output data. The market supply curve for the industry is the sum of all supply curves for individual firms.

This chapter also discusses what happens to competitive firms in the **long run** as equilibrium conditions change. Over time, new firms will enter an industry that is making economic profits and existing firms will exit an industry that is experiencing economic losses, and changing price and output in the industry. Here you will learn that the shape of the **long-run supply curve** is directly affected by whether the industry is one characterized by constant costs, increasing costs, or decreasing costs as output increases.

In the long run, pure competition produces almost ideal conditions for **economic efficiency.** These ideal conditions and their qualifications are discussed in detail near the end of the chapter. Pure competition results in products produced in the least costly way, and thus it is *productively efficient.* Pure competition also allocates resources to firms so that they produce the products most wanted by society, and therefore it is *allocatively efficient.*

You will find out that these two efficiency conditions can be expressed in the triple equality: Price (and marginal revenue) = marginal cost = minimum of average total cost.

You must understand the purely competitive model because it is the efficiency standard or norm for evaluating different market structures. You will be using it often for comparison with the pure monopoly model in Chapter 10 and with the models for monopolistic competition and oligopoly in Chapter 11.

■ CHECKLIST

When you have studied this chapter you should be able to

☐ List the five characteristics of each of the four basic market models.

☐ Give examples of industries related to the four basic market models.

☐ Describe the major features of pure competition.

☐ Explain why a purely competitive firm is a price taker.

☐ Describe the demand curve for a purely competitive firm.

☐ Explain the relationship between marginal revenue and price in pure competition.

☐ Compute average, total, and marginal revenues when given a demand schedule faced by a purely competitive firm.

☐ Use the total-revenue and total-cost approaches to determine the output that a purely competitive firm will produce in the short run in the profit-maximizing case.

☐ Use the marginal-revenue and marginal-cost approach to determine the output that a purely competitive firm will produce in the short run in the profit-maximizing, loss-minimizing, and shutdown cases.

☐ State characteristics of the MR = MC rule.

☐ Find the firm's short-run supply curve when you are given the firm's short-run cost schedules.

☐ Explain the links among the law of diminishing returns, production costs, and product supply in the short run.

☐ Graph a shift in the firm's short-run supply curve and cite factors that cause the curve to increase or decrease.

☐ Find the industry's short-run supply curve (or schedule) when you are given the typical firm's short-run cost schedules.

☐ Determine, under short-run conditions, the price at which the product will sell, the output of the industry, and the output of the individual firm.

☐ Describe the basic goal for long-run adjustments in pure competition.

☐ Determine, under long-run conditions, the price at which the product will sell, the output of the firm, and the output of the industry.

☐ Explain the role played by the entry and exit of firms in a purely competitive industry in achieving equilibrium in the long run.

☐ Describe the characteristics and rationale for the long-run supply curve in a constant-cost industry, in an increasing-cost industry, and in a decreasing-cost industry.

☐ Distinguish between productive and allocative efficiency.

☐ Explain the significance of MR (= *P*) = MC = minimum ATC.

☐ Describe how allocative efficiency is related to maximum consumer and producer surplus.

☐ Discuss how pure competition makes dynamic adjustments.

☐ Describe how the "invisible hand" works in competitive markets.

☐ Explain how a fall in the price of drugs increases the consumer surplus and society experiences efficiency gains (Last Word).

■ **CHAPTER OUTLINE**

1. The price a firm charges for the good or service it produces and its output of that product depend not only on the demand for and the cost of producing it, but on the characteristics of the market (industry) in which it sells the product. The **four market models** are *pure competition, pure monopoly, monopolistic competition,* and *oligopoly.* These models are defined by the number of firms, whether the product is standardized or differentiated, the firm's control over price, the conditions for entry into the industry, and degree of nonprice competition (see Table 9.1 in text). Compared with **pure competition,** the other three market models are considered different forms of *imperfect competition.*

2. This chapter examines **pure competition,** in which a very large number of independent firms, no one of which is able to influence market price by itself, sell a standardized product in a market where firms are free to enter and to leave in the long run. Although pure competition is rare in practice, it is the standard against which the *efficiency* of the economy and other market models can be compared.

3. Demand as seen by the purely competitive firm is unique because a firm selling its product cannot influence the price at which the product sells, and therefore is a *price taker.*

   a. The demand for its product is perfectly elastic.

   b. There are three types of revenue. *Average revenue* is the amount of revenue per unit. *Total revenue* is calculated as the price times the quantity a firm can sell. *Marginal revenue* is the change in total revenue from selling one more unit. Average revenue (or price) and marginal revenue are equal and constant at the fixed (equilibrium) market price ($AR = P = MR$). Total revenue increases at a constant rate as the firm increases its output.

   c. The demand (average revenue) and marginal revenue curves faced by the firm are horizontal and identical at the market price. The total revenue curve has a constant positive slope.

4. The purely competitive firm operating in the **short run** is a price taker that can maximize profits (or minimize losses) only by changing its level of output. Two approaches can be used to determine the optimal level of output for the firm.

   a. The **total revenue–total cost** approach to profit maximization sets the level of output at that quantity where the difference between total revenue minus total cost is greatest. An output at which total revenue covers total costs (including a normal profit) is a *break-even point.*

   b. The **marginal revenue–marginal cost** approach to profit maximization basically sets the level of output at the quantity where marginal revenue (or price) equals marginal cost. There are three possible cases to consider when using this approach.

   (1) The firm uses the *MR = MC rule* to evaluate profit maximization. The firm will produce that level of output where the marginal revenue from each additional unit produced is equal to the marginal cost of each additional unit to produce. The rule is an accurate guide to profit maximization for the four basic types of firms. For the purely competitive firm, however, the rule can be restated as $P = $ MC.

   (2) The firm will **maximize profits** when MR = MC at an output level where price is greater than average total cost.

   (3) The firm will **minimize losses** when MR = MC at an output level where price is greater than the minimum average variable cost (but less than average total cost).

   (4) The firm will **shut down** when MR = MC at an output level where price is less than average variable cost.

5. There is a close relationship between marginal cost and the *short-run supply curve* for the purely competitive firm and industry.

   a. The short-run supply curve for the purely competitive firm is the portion of the marginal-cost curve that lies above average variable cost.

   b. There are links among the law of diminishing returns, production costs, and product supply. The law of diminishing returns suggests that marginal costs will increase as output expands. The firm must receive more revenue (get higher prices for its products) if it is to expand output.

   c. Changes in variable inputs will change the marginal cost or supply curve for the purely competitive firm. For example, an improvement in technology that increases productivity will decrease the marginal cost curve (shift it downward).

   d. The **short-run supply curve of the industry** (which is the sum of the supply curves of the individual firms) and the total demand for the product determine the short-run equilibrium price and equilibrium output of the industry. Firms in the industry may be either prosperous or unprosperous in the short run.

6. In the **long run,** the price of a product produced under conditions of pure competition will equal the minimum average total cost (**P = minimum ATC**). The firms in the industry will neither earn economic profits nor suffer economic losses.

a. If economic profits are being received in the industry in the short run, firms will enter the industry in the long run (attracted by the profits), increase total supply, and thereby force price down to the minimum average total cost, leaving only a normal profit.

b. If losses are being suffered in the industry in the short run, firms will leave the industry in the long run (seeking to avoid losses), reduce total supply, and thereby force price up to the minimum average total cost, leaving only a normal profit.

c. If an industry is a **constant-cost industry,** the entry of new firms will not affect the average-total-cost schedules or curves of firms in the industry.

(1) An increase in demand will result in no increase in the long-run equilibrium price, and the industry will be able to supply larger outputs at a constant price.

(2) Graphically, the **long-run supply curve** in a constant-cost industry is horizontal at the minimum of the average total cost curve, indicating that firms make only normal profits, but not economic profits.

d. If an industry is an **increasing-cost industry,** the entry of new firms will raise the average-total-cost schedules or curves of firms in the industry.

(1) An increase in demand will result in an increase in the long-run equilibrium price, and the industry will be able to supply larger outputs only at higher prices.

(2) Graphically, the long-run supply curve in an increasing-cost industry is upsloping at the minimum of the average-total-cost curve, indicating that firms make only normal profits but not economic profits.

e. If an industry is a **decreasing-cost industry,** the entry of new firms will lower the average total cost schedules or curves of firms in the industry.

(1) An increase in demand will result in a decrease in the long-run equilibrium price, and the industry will be able to supply larger outputs only at lower prices.

(2) Graphically, the long-run supply curve in a decreasing-cost industry is downsloping at the minimum of the average total cost curve, indicating that firms make only normal profits, but not economic profits.

7. In the long run, **competition** and **efficiency** compel the purely competitive firm to produce that output at a price at which marginal revenue, average cost, and marginal cost are equal and average cost is a minimum. An economy in which all industries are purely competitive makes efficient use of its resources.

a. There is **productive efficiency** when the average total cost of producing goods is at a minimum; buyers benefit most from this efficiency when they are charged a price just equal to minimum average total cost (**P = minimum ATC**).

b. There is **allocative efficiency** when goods are produced in such quantities that the total satisfaction obtained from the economy's resources is at a maximum, or when the price of each good is equal to its marginal cost (**P = MC**).

(1) When price is greater than marginal cost, there is an *underallocation* of resources to the production of a product.

(2) When price is less than marginal cost, there is an *overallocation* of resources to the production of a product.

(3) When price is equal to marginal cost, there is efficient allocation of resources to the production of a product.

(4) Pure competition maximizes the **consumer surplus** (the difference between the maximum prices that consumers are willing to pay for a product and the market price of that product). It also maximizes the **producer surplus** (the difference between the minimum prices that producers are willing to accept for a product and the market price of the product).

(5) The purely competitive economy makes dynamic adjustments to changes in demand or supply that restore equilibrium and efficiency.

(6) The "invisible hand" is at work in a competitive market system by organizing the private interests of producers that will help achieve society's interest in the efficient use of scarce resources.

8. (Last Word). The competitive model predicts that when there are new entrants into a previously monopolized market, prices will fall, output will increase, and efficiency will improve. Such is the case in the drug market when a drug patent expires and the drug can be produced as a generic. Generic drugs are cheaper for consumers. The decline in price for these drugs compared with the patented versions boosts output and increases the consumer surplus.

■ **HINTS AND TIPS**

1. The purely competitive model is extremely important for you to master even if examples of it in the real world are rare. The model is the standard against which the other market models—pure monopoly, monopolistic competition, and oligopoly—will be compared for effects on economic efficiency. Spend extra time learning the material in this chapter so you can make model comparisons in later chapters.

2. Make sure that you understand why a purely competitive firm is a **price "taker"** and not a price "maker." The purely competitive firm has no influence over the price of its product and can only make decisions about the level of output.

3. Construct a table for explaining how the purely competitive firm maximizes profits or minimizes losses in the short run. Ask yourself the three questions in the table: (1) Should the firm produce? (2) What quantity should be produced to maximize profits? (3) Will production result in economic profit? Answer the questions using a marginal revenue–marginal cost approach. Check your answers against those presented in the text.

4. The average purely competitive firm in long-run equilibrium will not make economic profits. Find out why by following the graphical analysis in Figures 9.8 and 9.9.

5. The triple equality of MR (= *P*) = MC = minimum ATC is the most important equation in the chapter because it allows you to judge the allocative and productive efficiency of a purely competitive economy. Check your understanding of this triple equality by explaining what happens to productive efficiency when *P* > minimum ATC, or to allocative efficiency when *P* < MC or *P* > MC.

■ IMPORTANT TERMS

pure competition	break-even point
pure monopoly	MR = MC rule
monopolistic competition	short-run supply curve
oligopoly	long-run supply curve
imperfect competition	constant-cost industry
price taker	increasing-cost industry
average revenue	decreasing-cost industry
total revenue	productive efficiency
marginal revenue	allocative efficiency

SELF-TEST

■ FILL-IN QUESTIONS

1. The four market models examined in this and the next two chapters are

a. _____

b. _____

c. _____

d. _____

2. The four market models differ in terms of the (age, number) _____ of firms in the industry, whether the product is (a consumer good, standardized) _____ or (a producer good, differentiated) _____, and how easy or difficult it is for new firms to (enter, leave) _____ the industry.

3. What are the four specific conditions that characterize pure competition?

a. _____

b. _____

c. _____

d. _____

4. The individual firm in a purely competitive industry is a price (maker, taker) _____ and finds that the demand for its product is perfectly (elastic, inelastic) _____.

5. The firm's demand schedule is also a (cost, revenue) _____ schedule. The price per unit to the seller is (marginal, total, average) _____ revenue; price multiplied by the quantity the firm can sell is _____ revenue; and the extra revenue that results from selling one more unit of output is _____ revenue.

6. In pure competition, product price (rises, falls, is constant) _____ as an individual firm's output increases. Marginal revenue is (less than, greater than, equal to) _____ product price.

7. Economic profit is total revenue (plus, minus) _____ total cost. If the firm is making only a normal profit, total revenue is (greater than, equal to) _____ total cost. In the latter case, this output level is called the (profit, break-even) _____ point by economists.

8. If a purely competitive firm produces any output at all, it will produce that output at which its profit is at a (maximum, minimum) _____ or its loss is at a _____. Or, said another way, the output at which marginal cost is (equal to, greater than) _____ marginal revenue.

9. A firm will be willing to produce at an economic loss in the short run if the price which it receives is greater than its average (fixed, variable, total) _____ cost.

10. In the short run, the individual firm's supply curve in pure competition is that portion of the firm's (total, marginal) _____ cost curve which lies (above, below) _____ the average variable cost curve.

11. The short-run market supply curve is the (average, sum) _____ of the (short-run, long-run) _____ supply curves of all firms in the industry.

12. In the short run in a purely competitive industry, the equilibrium price is the price at which quantity demanded is equal to (average cost, quantity supplied) _____, and the equilibrium quantity is the quantity demanded and _____ at the equilibrium price.

13. In a purely competitive industry, in the short run the number of firms in the industry and the sizes of their plants are (fixed, variable) _____, but in the long run they are _____.

14. When a purely competitive industry is in long-run equilibrium, the price that the firm is paid for its product is equal to (total, average) _____ revenue, and to long-run _____ cost. In this case, the long-run average cost is at a (maximum, minimum) _____.

15. An industry will be in long-run equilibrium when firms are earning (normal, economic) _____ profits, but firms tend to enter an industry if the firms in the industry are earning _____ profits. Firms will tend to leave an industry when they are realizing economic (profits, losses) _____.

16. If the entry of new firms into an industry tends to raise the costs of all firms in the industry, the industry is said to be (a constant-, an increasing-, a decreasing-) _____ cost industry. Its long-run supply curve is (horizontal, downsloping, upsloping) _____.

17. If the entry of new firms into an industry tends to lower costs of all firms in the industry, the industry is said to be (a constant-, an increasing-, a decreasing-) _____ cost industry. Its long-run supply curve is (horizontal, downsloping, upsloping) _____.

18. The purely competitive economy achieves productive efficiency in the long run because price and (total, average) _____ cost are equal and the latter is at a (maximum, minimum) _____.

19. In the long run the purely competitive economy is allocatively efficient because price and (total, marginal) _____ cost are equal.

20. One of the attributes of purely competitive markets is their ability to restore (monopoly, efficiency) _____ when disrupted by changes in the economy. The "invisible hand" also operates in a competitive market system because it (maximizes, minimizes) _____ the profits of individual producers and at the same time the system creates a pattern of resource allocation that _____ consumer satisfaction.

■ **TRUE–FALSE QUESTIONS**

Circle T if the statement is true, F if it is false.

1. The structures of the markets in which business firms sell their products in the U.S. economy are very similar. **T F**

2. There are significant obstacles to entry in a purely competitive industry. **T F**

3. Only in a purely competitive industry do individual firms have no control over the price of their product. **T F**

4. Imperfectly competitive markets are defined as all markets except those that are purely competitive. **T F**

5. One reason for studying the pure competition model is that most industries are purely competitive. **T F**

6. The purely competitive firm views an average revenue schedule as identical to its marginal revenue schedule. **T F**

7. The demand curves for firms in a purely competitive industry are perfectly inelastic. **T F**

8. Under purely competitive conditions, the product price charged by the firm increases as output increases. **T F**

9. The purely competitive firm can maximize its economic profit (or minimize its loss) only by adjusting its output. **T F**

10. Economic profit is the difference between total revenue and average revenue. **T F**

11. The break-even point means that the firm is realizing normal profits, but not economic profits. **T F**

12. A purely competitive firm that wishes to produce and not close down will maximize profits or minimize losses at that output at which marginal costs and marginal revenue are equal. **T F**

13. Assuming that the purely competitive firm chooses to produce and not close down, to maximize profits or minimize losses it should produce at that point where price equals average cost. **T F**

14. If a purely competitive firm is producing output less than its profit-maximizing output, marginal revenue is greater than marginal cost. **T F**

15. If, at the profit-maximizing level of output for the purely competitive firm, price exceeds the minimum average variable cost but is less than average total cost, the firm will make a profit. **T F**

16. A purely competitive firm will produce in the short run the output at which marginal cost and marginal revenue are equal provided that the price of the product is greater than its average variable cost of production. **T F**

17. The short-run supply curve of a purely competitive firm tends to slope upward from left to right because of the law of diminishing returns. **T F**

18. If a purely competitive firm is in short-run equilibrium and its marginal cost is greater than its average total cost, firms will leave the industry in the long run. **T F**

19. When firms in a purely competitive industry are earning profits that are less than normal, the supply of the product will tend to decrease in the long run. **T F**

20. The long-run supply curve for a competitive, increasing-cost industry is upsloping. **T F**

21. Pure competition, if it could be achieved in all industries in the economy, would result in the most efficient allocation of resources. **T F**

22. Under conditions of pure competition, firms are forced to employ the most efficient production methods available to survive. **T F**

23. The marginal costs of producing a product are society's measure of the marginal worth of alternative products. **T F**

24. In a purely competitive market, product price measures the marginal benefit, or additional satisfaction, that society obtains from producing additional units of the product.   **T F**

25. Pure competition minimizes the consumer and producer surplus.   **T F**

■ **MULTIPLE-CHOICE QUESTIONS**

Circle the letter that corresponds to the best answer.

1. For which market model are there a very large number of firms?
  (a) monopolistic competition
  (b) oligopoly
  (c) pure monopoly
  (d) pure competition

2. In which market model is the individual seller of a product a price taker?
  (a) pure competition
  (b) pure monopoly
  (c) monopolistic competition
  (d) oligopoly

3. Which industry comes *closest* to being purely competitive?
  (a) wheat
  (b) shoes
  (c) electricity
  (d) automobile

4. In a purely competitive industry,
  (a) each existing firm will engage in various forms of nonprice competition
  (b) new firms are free to enter and existing firms are able to leave the industry very easily
  (c) individual firms have a price policy
  (d) each firm produces a differentiated (nonstandardized) product

5. The demand schedule or curve confronted by the individual purely competitive firm is
  (a) perfectly inelastic
  (b) inelastic but not perfectly inelastic
  (c) perfectly elastic
  (d) elastic but not perfectly elastic

6. Total revenue for producing 10 units of output is $6. Total revenue for producing 11 units of output is $8. Given this information, the
  (a) average revenue for producing 11 units is $2.
  (b) average revenue for producing 11 units is $8.
  (c) marginal revenue for producing the 11th unit is $2.
  (d) marginal revenue for producing the 11th unit is $8.

7. In pure competition, product price is
  (a) greater than marginal revenue
  (b) equal to marginal revenue
  (c) equal to total revenue
  (d) greater than total revenue

8. Suppose that when 2000 units of output are produced, the marginal cost of the 2001st unit is $5. This amount is equal to the minimum of average total cost, and marginal cost is rising. If the optimal level of output in the short run is 2500 units, then at that level,
  (a) marginal cost is greater than $5 and marginal cost is less than average total cost
  (b) marginal cost is greater than $5 and marginal cost is greater than average total cost
  (c) marginal cost is less than $5 and marginal cost is greater than average total cost
  (d) marginal cost is equal to $5 and marginal cost is equal to average total cost

9. The Zebra, Inc., is selling in a purely competitive market. Its output is 250 units, which sell for $2 each. At this level of output, marginal cost is $2 and average variable cost is $2.25. The firm should
  (a) produce zero units of output
  (b) decrease output to 200 units
  (c) continue to produce 250 units
  (d) increase output to maximize profits

Questions 10, 11, 12, and 13 are based on the following graph.

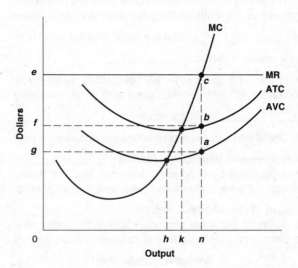

10. If the firm is producing at output level 0*n*, the rectangular area *fecb* is
  (a) total variable cost
  (b) total fixed costs
  (c) total revenue
  (d) total economic profit

11. At the profit-maximizing output, average fixed cost is
  (a) *ab*
  (b) *ac*
  (c) *na*
  (d) *nb*

12. At the profit-maximizing output, the total variable costs are equal to the area
  (a) 0*fbn*
  (b) 0*ecn*
  (c) 0*gan*
  (d) *gfba*

13. The demand curve for this firm is equal to
(a) **MR,** and the supply curve is the portion of the **MC** curve where output is greater than level *n*
(b) **MR,** and the supply curve is the portion of the **MC** curve where output is greater than level *k*
(c) **MR,** and the supply curve is the portion of the **MC** curve where output is greater than level *h*
(d) **MR,** and the supply curve is the portion of the **ATC** curve where output is greater than level *k*

Answer Questions 14, 15, 16, 17, and 18 on the basis of the following cost data for a firm that is selling in a purely competitive market.

Output	AFC	AVC	ATC	MC
1	$300	$100	$400	$100
2	150	75	225	50
3	100	70	170	60
4	75	73	148	80
5	60	80	140	110
6	50	90	140	140
7	43	103	146	180
8	38	119	156	230
9	33	138	171	290
10	30	160	190	360

14. If the market price for the firm's product is $140, the competitive firm will produce
(a) 5 units at an economic loss of $150
(b) 6 units and break even
(c) 7 units and break even
(d) 8 units at an economic profit of $74

15. If the market price for the firm's product is $290, the competitive firm will produce
(a) 7 units at an economic profit of $238
(b) 8 units at an economic profit of $592
(c) 9 units at an economic profit of $1071
(d) 10 units at an economic profit of $1700

16. If the product price is $179, the *per-unit* economic profit at the profit-maximizing output is
(a) $15
(b) $23
(c) $33
(d) $39

17. The total fixed costs are
(a) $100
(b) $200
(c) $300
(d) $400

Assume there are 100 identical firms in this industry and total or market demand is as shown.

Price	Quantity demanded
$360	600
290	700
230	800
180	900
140	1000
110	1100
80	1200

18. The equilibrium price will be
(a) $140
(b) $180
(c) $230
(d) $290

19. The individual firm's short-run supply curve is that part of its marginal cost curve lying above its
(a) average total cost curve
(b) average variable cost curve
(c) average fixed cost curve
(d) average revenue curve

20. Which statement is true of a purely competitive industry in short-run equilibrium?
(a) Price is equal to average total cost.
(b) Total quantity demanded is equal to total quantity supplied.
(c) Profits in the industry are equal to zero.
(d) Output is equal to the output at which average total cost is a minimum.

21. Assume that the market for wheat is purely competitive. Currently, firms growing wheat are experiencing economic losses. In the long run, we can expect this market's
(a) supply curve to increase
(b) demand curve to increase
(c) supply curve to decrease
(d) demand curve to decrease

22. The long-run supply curve under pure competition will be
(a) downsloping in an increasing-cost industry and upsloping in a decreasing-cost industry
(b) horizontal in a constant-cost industry and upsloping in a decreasing-cost industry
(c) horizontal in a constant-cost industry and upsloping in an increasing-cost industry
(d) upsloping in an increasing-cost industry and vertical in a constant-cost industry

23. The long-run supply curve in a constant-cost industry will be
(a) perfectly elastic
(b) perfectly inelastic
(c) unit elastic
(d) income elastic

24. In a decreasing-cost industry, the long-run
(a) demand curve would be perfectly inelastic
(b) demand curve would be perfectly elastic
(c) supply curve would be upsloping
(d) supply curve would be downsloping

25. Increasing-cost industries find that their costs rise as a consequence of an increased demand for the product because of
(a) the diseconomies of scale
(b) diminishing returns
(c) higher resource prices
(d) a decreased supply of the product

26. When a purely competitive industry is in long-run equilibrium, which statement is true?
(a) Firms in the industry are earning normal profits.
(b) Price and long-run average total cost are not equal to each other.

(c) Marginal cost is at its minimum level.
(d) Marginal cost is equal to total revenue.

27. Which triple identity results in the most efficient use of resources?
(a) $P = MC$ = minimum ATC
(b) $P = AR = MR$
(c) $P = MR$ = minimum MC
(d) $TR = MC = MR$

28. An economy is producing the goods most wanted by society when, for each and every good, its
(a) price and average cost are equal
(b) price and marginal cost are equal
(c) marginal revenue and marginal cost are equal
(d) price and marginal revenue are equal

29. If there is an increase in demand for a product in a purely competitive industry, it results in an industry
(a) contraction that will end when the price of the product is greater than its marginal cost
(b) contraction that will end when the price of the product is equal to its marginal cost
(c) expansion that will end when the price of the product is greater than its marginal cost
(d) expansion that will end when the price of the product is equal to its marginal cost

30. The idea of the "invisible hand" operating in the competitive market system means that
(a) there is a unity of private and social interests that promotes efficiency
(b) the industries in this system are described as decreasing-cost industries
(c) there is an overallocation of resources to the production of goods and services
(d) productive efficiency is more important than allocative efficiency

■ PROBLEMS

1. Using the following set of terms, complete the following table by inserting the appropriate letter or letters in the blanks.

a. one   h. considerable
b. few   i. very easy
c. many   j. blocked
d. a very large number   k. fairly easy
e. standardized   l. fairly difficult
f. differentiated   m. none
g. some   n. unique

Market characteristics	Market model			
	Pure competition	Monopolistic competition	Oligopoly	Pure monopoly
Number of firms	___	___	___	___
Type of product	___	___	___	___
Control over price	___	___	___	___
Conditions of entry	___	___	___	___
Nonprice competition	___	___	___	___

2. Following is the demand schedule facing the individual firm.

Price	Quantity demanded	Average revenue	Total revenue	Marginal revenue
$10	0	$___	$___	—
10	1	___	___	$___
10	2	___	___	___
10	3	___	___	___
10	4	___	___	___
10	5	___	___	___
10	6	___	___	___

a. Complete the table by computing average revenue, total revenue, and marginal revenue.
b. Is this firm operating in a market that is purely competitive? _____ How can you tell? _____
_____

c. The coefficient of the price elasticity of demand is the same between every pair of quantities demanded.
What is it? _____
d. What relationship exists between average revenue and marginal revenue? _____
_____

e. On the graph at the top of next page, plot the demand schedule, average revenue, total revenue, and marginal revenue; label each curve.
f. The demand, average revenue, and marginal revenue curves are all _____ lines at a price
of $_____ across all quantities.
g. The total revenue curve is an upsloping line with a
_____ slope because marginal revenue is
_____.

3. Assume that a purely competitive firm has the following schedule of costs.

Output	TFC	TVC	TC
0	$300	$ 0	$ 300
1	300	100	400
2	300	150	450
3	300	210	510
4	300	290	590
5	300	400	700
6	300	540	840
7	300	720	1020
8	300	950	1250
9	300	1240	1540
10	300	1600	1900

a. Complete the following table to show the total revenue and total profit of the firm at each level of output the firm might produce. Assume the market price is $200.

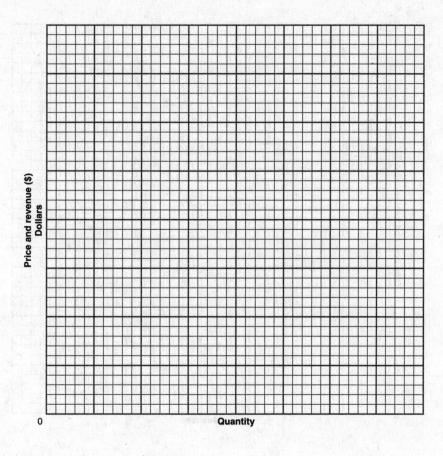

Price and revenue ($)
Dollars

0   Quantity

	Market price = $200	
Output	Revenue	Profit
0	$_____	$_____
1	_____	_____
2	_____	_____
3	_____	_____
4	_____	_____
5	_____	_____
6	_____	_____
7	_____	_____
8	_____	_____
9	_____	_____
10	_____	_____

b. At a price of $200, the firm would produce an output of _____ units and earn a profit of $_____.

c. Plot the cost data for total variable cost and total cost on the graph at the top of the next page. Then plot the total revenue when the price is $200. For this price, indicate the level of output and the economic profit or loss on the graph.

4. Now assume that the same purely competitive firm has the following schedule of average and marginal costs:

Output	AFC	AVC	ATC	MC
1	$300	$100	$400	$100
2	150	75	225	50
3	100	70	170	60
4	75	73	148	80
5	60	80	140	110
6	50	90	140	140
7	43	103	146	180
8	38	119	156	230
9	33	138	171	290
10	30	160	190	360

a. At a price of $55, the firm would produce _____ units of output. At a price of $120, the firm would produce _____ units of output. At a price of $200, the firm would produce _____ units of output. At the $200 price compare your answers to those you gave in Problem 3.

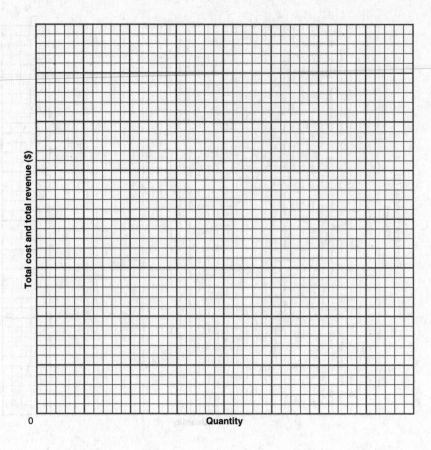

Total cost and total revenue ($)

0   Quantity

b. The *per-unit* economic profit (or loss) is calculated by subtracting _____ at a particular level of output from the product price. This *per-unit* economic profit is then multiplied by the number of units of _____ to determine the economic profit for the competitive firm.

(1) At the product price of $200, the average total costs are $_____, so *per-unit* economic profit is $_____. Multiplying this amount by the number of units of output results in an economic profit of $_____.

(2) At the product price of $120, the average total costs are $ _____, so *per-unit* economic losses are $_____. Multiplying this amount by the number of units of output results in an economic loss of $_____.

c. Plot the data for average and marginal cost in the larger graph on the next page. Then plot each marginal revenue when the price is $55, $120, and $200. For each price, indicate the level of output and the economic profit or loss on the graph.

5. Use the average and marginal cost data in Problem 4 in your work on Problem 5.

a. In the following table, complete the supply schedule for the competitive firm and state what the economic profit will be at each price.

Price	Quantity supplied	Profit
$360	_____	$_____
290	_____	_____
230	_____	_____
180	_____	_____
140	_____	_____
110	_____	_____
80	_____	_____
60	_____	_____

b. If there are 100 firms in the industry and all have the same cost schedule,
(1) complete the market supply schedule in the following table.

Quantity demanded	Price	Quantity supplied
400	$360	_____
500	290	_____
600	230	_____
700	180	_____
800	140	_____
900	110	_____
1000	80	_____

(2) Using the demand schedule given in (1):
(a) What will the market price of the product be?

$_____

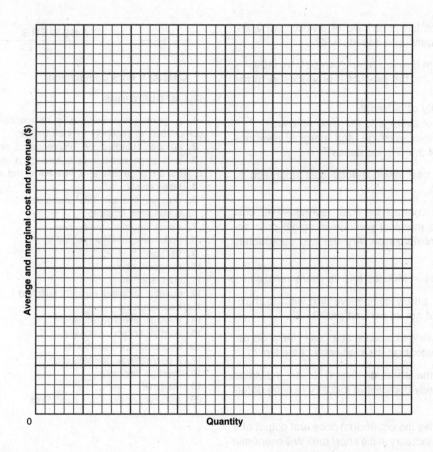

Quantity

(b) What quantity will the individual firm produce?
_____

(c) How large will the firm's profit be? $_____
(d) Will firms tend to enter or leave the industry in the
long run? _____ Why? _____
_____

6. If the average total costs assumed for the individual
firm in Problem 4 were long-run average total costs and
if the industry were a constant-cost industry,
    a. what would be the market price of the product in
the long run? $ _____
    b. what output would each firm produce when the in-
dustry was in long-run equilibrium? _____
    c. approximately how many firms would there be in
the industry in the long run, given the present demand
for the product as shown in the table in Problem 5b?
_____
    d. if the following table were the market demand sched-
ule for the product, how many firms would there be in
the long run in the industry? _____

Price	Quantity demanded
$360	500
290	600
230	700
180	800
140	900
110	1000
80	1100

7. On the following graph, draw a long-run supply curve of
    a. a constant-cost industry
    b. an increasing-cost industry

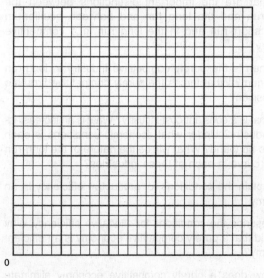

0

■ **SHORT ANSWER AND ESSAY QUESTIONS**

1. What are the four market models (or situations) that
economists employ, and what are the major characteristics of each type of market?

2. Describe in detail four characteristics of pure
competition.

3. If pure competition is so rare in practice, why are students of economics asked to study it?

4. Explain how the firm in a purely competitive industry sees the demand for the product it produces in terms of the
    a. price elasticity of demand
    b. relationship of average to marginal revenue
    c. behavior of total, average, and marginal revenues as the output of the firm increases

5. Describe the total revenue–total cost approach to profit maximization.

6. Compare and contrast the total revenue–total cost approach with the marginal revenue–marginal cost approach to profit maximization. Are the two approaches consistent?

7. Explain the MR = MC rule and its characteristics.

8. Why does the purely competitive firm want to maximize total profit but not its per-unit profit?

9. Why is a firm willing to produce at a loss in the short run if the loss is no greater than the fixed costs of the firm?

10. Explain how the short-run supply of an individual firm and of the purely competitive industry is each determined.

11. What determines the equilibrium price and output of a purely competitive industry in the short run? Will economic profits in the industry be positive or negative?

12. Why do the MC = MR rule and MC = P rule mean the same thing under conditions of pure competition?

13. What are the important distinctions between the short run and the long run and between equilibrium in the short run and in the long run in a competitive industry?

14. When is the purely competitive industry in long-run equilibrium? What forces the purely competitive firm into this position?

15. What is a constant-cost industry? What is an increasing-cost industry? Under what economic conditions is each likely to be found? What will be the nature of the long-run supply curve in each of these industries?

16. Explain the conditions for productive efficiency in an economy.

17. Describe the conditions for allocative efficiency. Why is it said that a purely competitive economy is an efficient economy?

18. How does a purely competitive economy eliminate an overallocation for resources for the production of a product and correct for an underallocation?

19. Explain how dynamic adjustments are made in pure competition as a result of changes in demand for a product or the supply of a resource.

20. Explain how pure competition maximizes the consumer and producer surplus.

ANSWERS

Chapter 9 Pure Competition

FILL-IN QUESTIONS

1. *a.* pure competition; *b.* pure monopoly; *c.* monopolistic competition; *d.* oligopoly (any order *a–d*)
2. number, standardized, differentiated, enter
3. *a.* a large number of sellers; *b.* a standardized product; *c.* firms are price takers; *d.* free entry and exit of firms
4. taker, elastic
5. revenue, average, total, marginal
6. is constant, equal to
7. minus, equal to, break-even
8. maximum, minimum, equal to
9. variable
10. marginal, above
11. sum, short-run
12. quantity supplied, quantity supplied
13. fixed, variable
14. average, average, minimum
15. normal, economic, losses
16. an increasing-, upsloping
17. a decreasing-, downsloping
18. average, minimum
19. marginal
20. efficiency, maximizes, maximizes

TRUE–FALSE QUESTIONS

1. F, p. 177
2. F, p. 177
3. T, pp. 177–178
4. T, p. 177
5. F, p. 177
6. T, pp. 178–179
7. F, p. 178
8. F, pp. 178–179
9. T, pp. 179–181
10. F, p. 180
11. T, pp. 180–181
12. T, pp. 181–182
13. F, pp. 181–182
14. T, pp. 181–182, 184
15. F, pp. 181–184
16. T, pp. 181–184
17. T, pp. 186–187
18. F, pp. 186–188
19. T, pp. 190–191
20. T, pp. 192–193
21. T, pp. 193–194
22. T, p. 195
23. T, p. 195
24. T, p. 195
25. F, pp. 195, 197

MULTIPLE-CHOICE QUESTIONS

1. d, p. 177
2. a, pp. 177–178
3. a, p. 178
4. b, pp. 177–178
5. c, p. 178
6. c, pp. 178–179
7. b, pp. 178–179
8. b, pp. 181–182
9. a, pp. 182–185
10. d, pp. 182–185
11. a, pp. 182–185
12. c, pp. 182–185
13. c, pp. 182–185
14. b, pp. 182–185
15. c, pp. 180–184
16. d, pp. 182–183
17. c, pp. 186–187
18. c, pp. 188–189
19. b, pp. 187–188
20. b, pp. 188–189
21. c, pp. 191–192
22. c, pp. 192–193
23. a, p. 192
24. d, p. 193
25. c, pp. 192–193
26. a, pp. 190–194
27. a, p. 195
28. b, pp. 195–196
29. d, p. 195
30. a, p. 197

PROBLEMS

1. Number of firms: d, a, c, b; Type of product: e, n, f, e, or f; Control over price: m, h, g, g; Conditions of entry: i, j, k, l; Nonprice competition: m, g, h, g, or h

2. *a.* Average revenue: all are $10.00; Total revenue: $0, 10.00, 20.00, 30.00, 40.00, 50.00, 60.00; Marginal revenue: all are $10.00; *b.* yes, because price (average revenue) is constant and equal to marginal revenue; *c.* infinity; *d.* they are equal; *e.* see Figure 9.1 of the text for an example; *f.* horizontal, $10; *g.* constant, constant

3. *a.* see following table; *b.* 7, 380; *c.* see Figure 9.2 of the text for an example

| | Market price = $200 | |
Output	Revenue	Profit
0	$ 0	$ −300
1	200	−200
2	400	−50
3	600	90
4	800	210
5	1000	300
6	1200	360
7	1400	380
8	1600	350
9	1800	260
10	2000	100

4. *a.* 0, 5, 7 (last answer is the same as 3b); *b.* average total cost, output; (1) $146, ($200 − $146 = $54), ($54 × 7 = $378), (2) $140, ($120 − $140 = −$20), (−$20 × 5 = −$100); *c.* see Figure 9.3 of the text for an example

5. *a.* see following table; *b.* (1) Quantity supplied: 1000, 900, 800, 700, 600, 500, 400, (2) (a) 180, (b) 7, (c) 238, (d) enter, profits in the industry will attract them into the industry

Price	Quantity supplied	Profit
$360	10	$ 1700
290	9	1071
230	8	592
180	7	238
140	6	0
110	5	−150
80	4	−272
60	0	−300

6. *a.* 140; *b.* 6; *c.* 133 = 800 [the total quantity demanded at $140 divided by 6 (the output of each firm)]; *d.* 150 = 900 divided by 6

7. *a.* The curve is a horizontal line (see Figure 9.10 in the text); *b.* the curve slopes upward (see Figure 9.11 in the text)

SHORT ANSWER AND ESSAY QUESTIONS

1. p. 177
2. pp. 177–178
3. p. 177
4. pp. 178–179
5. pp. 179–181
6. pp. 179–182
7. p. 182
8. pp. 182–183
9. pp. 183–185
10. pp. 186–188
11. pp. 188–189
12. p. 182
13. pp. 188–189
14. pp. 190–192
15. pp. 192–193
16. p. 195
17. p. 195
18. p. 195
19. p. 197
20. pp. 195–197

CHAPTER 10

Pure Monopoly

This chapter looks at the other end of the spectrum and examines pure monopoly, a market structure in which there is a **single seller.** Like pure competition, pure monopoly is rarely found in the U.S. economy, but it is still important. Many government-owned or government-regulated public utilities (electricity, water, natural gas, or cable television) are close to being pure monopolies, and other business firms are near monopolies because they have a large share of a market. Monopolies play a key role in the allocation of resources and the production of goods and services in the economy.

It is possible for a single seller or pure monopolist to dominate an industry if firms are prevented in some way from entering the industry. Factors that restrict firms from entering an industry are referred to as **barriers to entry.** The second section of this chapter is devoted to a description of the more important types of these barriers, such as economies of scale, patents and licenses, control of essential resources, and strategies for product pricing.

The chapter answers certain questions about the pure monopolist, such as what output will the firm produce, what price it will charge, and the amount of profit for the firm. In answering these questions and in comparing pure competition and pure monopoly, note the following:

1. Both the competitive and monopoly firm try to maximize profits by producing the output at which marginal cost and marginal revenue are equal (**MR = MC**).

2. The individual firm in a perfectly competitive industry sees a perfectly price elastic demand for its product at the going market price because it is but one of many firms in the industry, but the monopolist sees a market demand schedule that is less than perfectly price elastic because the **monopolist is the industry.** The purely competitive firm has *only* an output policy and is a price taker, but the monopolist is able to determine the price at which it will sell its product and is a price maker.

3. When demand is perfectly price elastic, price is equal to marginal revenue and is constant, but when demand is less than perfectly price elastic, marginal revenue is less than price and both decrease as the output of the firm increases.

4. Because entry is blocked in the long run, firms cannot enter a monopolistic industry to compete away profits as they can under conditions of pure competition.

This chapter has three other goals that deserve your study time and careful attention. One goal is to evaluate **economic efficiency** under pure monopoly. Here the purely competitive industry that you read about in Chapter 9 serves as the standard for comparison. You will learn that unlike the purely competitive industry, pure monopoly does not result in allocative efficiency. Although the inefficiencies of monopoly are offset or reduced by economies of scale and technological progress, they are reinforced by the presence of X-inefficiency and rent-seeking behavior.

The second goal is to discuss the possible pricing strategies of the pure monopolist. The monopolist may be able to set multiple prices for the same product even when the price differences are not justified by cost differences, a situation called **price discrimination.** This type of pricing power works only under certain conditions, and when it is effective it results in higher profits for the monopolist and also greater output.

The pricing power and inefficiency of the pure monopoly have made it a target for **regulation.** Therefore, the last section of the chapter explains the economic choices a regulatory agency faces when it must determine the maximum price that a public utility will be allowed to charge for its product. Here you will learn about the **socially optimum price** and the **fair-return price** and their effects on efficiency and profits. You will also discover the difficult economic dilemma regulatory officials face as they decide what prices they should permit a monopolist to charge.

■ **CHECKLIST**

When you have studied this chapter you should be able to

☐ Define pure monopoly based on five characteristics.
☐ Give several examples of monopoly and explain its importance.
☐ List and explain four potential barriers that would prevent or deter the entry of new firms into an industry.
☐ Define a natural monopoly using an average total-cost curve.
☐ Compare the demand curve for the pure monopolist with that of the purely competitive firm.
☐ Compute marginal revenue when you are given the demand for the monopolist's product.
☐ Explain the relationship between the price a monopolist charges and the marginal revenue from the sale of an additional unit of the product.

☐ Explain why the monopolist is a price maker.

☐ Use elasticity to explain the region of the demand curve where the monopolist produces.

☐ State the rule that explains what output the monopolist will produce and the price that will be charged.

☐ Determine the profit-maximizing output and price for the pure monopolist when you are given the demand and cost data.

☐ Explain why there is no supply curve for the pure monopolist.

☐ Counter two popular misconceptions about the price charged and the profit target in pure monopoly.

☐ Explain why monopolists can experience losses.

☐ Compare the economic effects of pure monopoly in terms of price, output, efficiency, and income distribution with a purely competitive industry producing the same product.

☐ Discuss the cost complications caused by economies of scale, X-inefficiency, rent-seeking behavior, and technological advance for pure monopoly and a purely competitive industry.

☐ Describe three general policy options for dealing with the economic inefficiency of monopoly.

☐ Define and give examples of price discrimination.

☐ List three conditions that are necessary for price discrimination.

☐ Explain the economic consequences of price discrimination.

☐ Use graphical analysis to identify the socially optimal price and the fair-return price for the regulated monopoly.

☐ Explain the dilemma of regulation based on a graphical analysis of a regulated monopoly.

☐ Discuss the market forces that made De Beers change its monopoly behavior and end its attempts to control the diamond market (Last Word).

■ **CHAPTER OUTLINE**

1. *Pure monopoly* is a market structure in which a single firm sells a product for which there are no close substitutes. These characteristics make the monopoly firm a **price maker** rather than a price taker, as was the case for the purely competitive firm. Entry into the industry is blocked, and there can be nonprice competition through advertising to influence the demand for the product.

   a. Examples of monopolies typically include regulated public utilities such as firms providing electricity, natural gas, local telephone service, and cable television, but they can also be unregulated, such as the De Beers diamond syndicate.

   b. The study of monopoly is useful for understanding the economic effects of other market structures—oligopoly and monopolistic competition—where there is some degree of monopoly power.

2. Pure monopoly can exist in the long run only if potential competitors find there are *barriers* that prevent their entry into the industry. There are four major **barriers to entry** that can prevent or severely restrict entry into an industry.

   a. **Economies of scale** can reduce production costs in the long run so that one producer can supply a range of output at a minimum total cost. If other producers try to enter the industry, extensive financing would be required and they may not be able to produce output at a lower cost than the monopolist. The conditions for a **natural monopoly** arise in the extreme case in which the market demand curve cuts the long-run ATC curve where they are still declining. One firm can supply the market demand at a minimum cost.

   b. Government creates legal restrictions through issuing patents and licenses. **Patents** give the inventor the exclusive right to use or allow others to use the invention. **Licenses** give a firm the exclusive right to provide a good or service.

   c. The ownership or control of essential resources can effectively block entry into an industry.

   d. Pricing and other strategic practices, such as price cuts, advertising campaigns, and producing excess capacity, can deter entry into an industry by making entry very costly for a firm.

3. The **demand curve** of the pure monopolist is downsloping because the monopolist is the industry. By contrast, the purely competitive firm has a horizontal (perfectly price elastic) demand curve because it is only one of many small firms in an industry. There are several implications of the downsloping shape of the monopolist's demand curve.

   a. The monopolist can increase sales only by lowering product price; thus price will exceed marginal revenue (**P > MR**) for every unit of output but the first.

   b. The monopolist will have a pricing policy, and is a *price maker;* the purely competitive firm has no price policy and is a price taker.

   c. The monopolist will avoid setting price in the inelastic segment of its demand curve because total revenue will be decreasing and marginal revenue will be negative; price will be set in the *elastic* portion of the demand curve.

4. The **output** and **price determination** of the profit-maximizing pure monopolist entails several considerations.

   a. Monopoly power in the sale of a product does not necessarily affect the prices that the monopolist pays for resources or the costs of production; an assumption is made in this chapter that the monopolist hires resources in a competitive market and uses the same technology as competitive firms.

   b. The monopolist produces that output at which marginal cost and marginal revenue are equal (**MR = MC**) and charges a price at which this profit-maximizing output can be sold.

   c. The monopolist has **no supply curve** because there is no unique relationship between price and quantity supplied; price and quantity supplied will change when demand and marginal revenue change. By contrast, a purely competitive firm has a supply curve that is the portion of the marginal cost curve above average variable cost, and there is a unique relationship between price and quantity supplied.

d. Two popular misconceptions about monopolists are that they charge as high a price as possible and that they seek maximum profit per unit of output.

e. The monopolist is **not guaranteed a profit** and can experience losses because of weak demand for a product or high costs of production.

5. Pure monopoly has significant **economic effects** on the economy when compared to outcomes that would be produced in a purely competitive market.

a. The pure monopolist charges a *higher price* and *produces less output* than would be produced by a purely competitive industry. Pure monopoly is **not productively efficient** because price is greater than the minimum of average cost. It is **not allocatively efficient** because price is greater than marginal cost.

b. Monopoly contributes to income inequality in the economy by transferring income from consumers to stockholders who own the monopoly.

c. A pure monopolist in an industry may produce output at a lower or higher average cost than would be the case for a purely competitive industry producing the same product. The costs of production may differ between the two industries for four reasons.

(1) **Economies of scale** in the production of the product allow the pure monopolist to produce it at a lower long-run average cost than a large number of small pure competitors. In the extreme, a firm may be a **natural monopoly** that can supply the market demand at the lowest average cost. There can also be other factors such as *simultaneous consumption* (a product's ability to satisfy a large number of consumers at the same time) and *network effects* (increases in the value of the product for users as the number of users increase) that create extensive economies of scale for firms, especially those firms involved in information technology.

(2) If a pure monopolist is more susceptible to *X-inefficiency* (having an output level that is higher than the lowest possible cost of producing it) than firms in a purely competitive industry, then long-run average costs at every level of output for the monopolist are higher than those purely competitive firms.

(3) *Rent-seeking* expenditures in the form of legal fees, lobbying, and public-relations expenses to obtain or maintain a position as a monopoly add nothing to output, but do increase monopoly costs.

(4) Monopoly is not likely to contribute to technological advance because there is little incentive for the monopolist to produce a more advanced product. The threat of potential competition, however, may stimulate research and more technological advance, but the purpose of this effort is often to restrict or block entry into the industry.

d. Monopoly causes problems for an economy because of higher prices and restricted output. Monopoly, however, is relatively rare. Technological advance and the development of substitute products can also undermine a monopoly. The policy options for dealing with the economic inefficiency of monopoly include the use of antitrust laws and the breakup of firms, the regulation of price, output, and profits of the monopolist, and simply ignoring the monopoly because its position cannot be sustained.

6. To increase profits a pure monopolist may engage in *price discrimination* by charging different prices to different buyers of the same product (when the price differences do not represent differences in the costs of producing the product).

a. To discriminate, the seller must have some monopoly power, be capable of separating buyers into groups with different price elasticities of demand, and be able to prevent the resale of the product from one group to another group.

b. Price discrimination is common in the U.S. economy. Airlines charge different fares to different passengers for the same flight. Movie theaters vary prices for the same product based on time of day or age. Discount coupons allow firms to charge different prices to different customers for the purchase of the same product.

c. Graphical analysis can be used to show price discrimination to different groups of buyers. The monopolist maximizes its total profit by dividing the market in the segmented groups based on the differences in elasticity of demand. It then produces and sells that output in each market where MR = MC. It charges a higher price to customers with a less elastic demand and a lower price to customers with a more elastic demand.

7. Monopolies are often **regulated** by government to reduce the misallocation of resources and control prices.

a. A price ceiling determined by the intersection of the marginal cost and demand schedules is the *socially optimal price* and improves the allocation of resources.

b. This ceiling may force the firm to produce at a loss, and therefore government may set the ceiling at a level determined by the intersection of the average cost and demand schedules to allow the monopolist a *fair-return price.*

c. The dilemma of regulation is that the socially optimum price may cause losses for the monopolist, and a fair-return price may result in a less efficient allocation of resources. Also, fair-return price regulation can be complex to conduct in the real world.

8. (Last Word). The price and output decisions of the original De Beers firm fit the monopoly model. It controlled a large supply of diamonds and was able to sell a limited quantity to yield price that was in excess of production costs, and thus obtain monopoly profits. Several factors undercut the monopoly power of De Beers. New discoveries increased supply and previous agreements to sell diamonds exclusively to De Beers were terminated. The firm could no longer control price by manipulating supply and placed more emphasis on increasing demand to maintain price.

■ HINTS AND TIPS

1. Make sure you understand **how pure monopoly differs from pure competition.** Here are key distinctions: (a) The monopolist's demand curve is downsloping, not horizontal as in pure competition; (b) the monopolist's marginal revenue is less than price (or average revenue) for each level of output except the first, whereas in pure competition marginal revenue equals price; (c) the monopoly firm is a price maker, not a price taker as in pure competition; (d) *the firm is the industry* in monopoly, but not in pure competition; (e) there is the potential for long-run economic profits in pure monopoly, but purely competitive firms will only break even in the long run; and (f) there is no supply curve for a pure monopoly, but there is one for the purely competitive firm.

2. A key similarity between a profit-maximizing pure monopolist and a purely competitive firm is that both types of firms will produce up to that output level at which marginal revenue equals marginal cost (**MR = MC**).

3. Figure 10.3 helps explain why the profit-maximizing monopolist will always want to select some price and quantity combination in the **elastic** and not in the **inelastic** portion of the demand curve. In the inelastic portion, total revenue declines and marginal revenue is negative.

4. Drawing the marginal revenue curve for a monopolist with a linear demand curve is easy if you remember that the marginal revenue curve will always be a straight line that intersects the quantity axis at half of the level of output as the demand curve. (See Figure 10.3.)

5. Spend extra time studying Figure 10.8 and reading the related discussion. It will help you see how **price discrimination** results in more profits, a greater output, and a higher price for some consumers and lower prices for other consumers.

■ IMPORTANT TERMS

pure monopoly	rent-seeking behavior
barriers to entry	price discrimination
simultaneous consumption	socially optimal price
network effects	fair-return price
X-inefficiency	

SELF-TEST

■ FILL-IN QUESTIONS

1. Pure monopoly is an industry in which a single firm is the sole producer of a product for which there are no close (substitutes, complements) _____ and into which entry in the long run is effectively (open, blocked) _____.

2. The closest example of pure monopoly would be government-regulated (nonprofit organizations, public utilities) _____ that provide water, electricity, or natural gas. There are also "near monopolies," such as private businesses that might account for (40, 80) _____% of a particular market, or businesses in a geographic region that are the (multiple, sole) _____ suppliers of a good or service.

3. If there are substantial economies of scale in the production of a product, a small-scale firm will find it difficult to enter into and survive in an industry because its average costs will be (greater, less) _____ than those of established firms, and a firm will find it (easy, difficult) _____ to start out on a large scale because it will be nearly impossible to acquire the needed financing.

4. Legal barriers to entry by government include granting an inventor the exclusive right to produce a product for 20 years, or a (license, patent) _____, and limiting entry into an industry or occupation through its issuing of a _____.

5. Other barriers to entry include the ownership of essential (markets, resources) _____ and strategic changes in product (price, regulation) _____.

6. The demand schedule confronting the pure monopolist is (perfectly elastic, downsloping) _____. This means that marginal revenue is (greater, less) _____ than average revenue (or price) and that both marginal revenue and average revenue (increase, decrease) _____ as output increases.

7. When demand is price elastic, a decrease in price will (increase, decrease) _____ total revenue, but when demand is price inelastic, a decrease in price will _____ total revenue. The demand curve for the purely competitive firm is (horizontal, downsloping) _____, but it is _____ for the monopolist. The profit-maximizing monopolist will want to set price in the price (elastic, inelastic) _____ portion of its demand curve.

8. The supply curve for a purely competitive firm is the portion of the (average variable cost, marginal cost) _____ curve that lies above the _____ curve. The supply curve for the monopolist (is the same, does not exist) _____.

9. When the economic profit of a monopolist is at a maximum, (marginal, average) _____ revenue equals _____ cost and price is (greater, less) _____ than marginal cost.

10. Two common misconceptions about pure monopoly are that it charges the (lowest, highest) _____ price possible and seeks the maximum (normal, per-unit) _____ profit.

11. The pure monopolist (is, is not) _____ guaranteed an economic profit; in fact, the pure monopolist can experience economic losses in the (short run, long run) _____ because of (strong, weak) _____ demand for the monopoly product.

12. The monopolist will typically charge a (lower, higher) _____ price and produce (less, more) _____ output and is (less, more) _____ efficient than if the product was produced in a purely competitive industry.

  a. The monopolist is inefficient *productively* because the average (variable, total) _____ cost of producing a product is not at a (maximum, minimum) _____.

  b. It is inefficient *allocatively* because (marginal revenue, price) _____ is not equal to (marginal, total) _____ cost.

  c. Monopolies seem to result in a greater inequality in the distribution of income because the owners of monopolies are largely in the (upper, lower) _____ income groups.

13. Resources can be said to be more efficiently allocated by pure competition than by pure monopoly only if the purely competitive firms and the monopoly have the same (costs, revenues) _____, and they will not be the same if the monopolist

  a. by virtue of being a large firm enjoys (economies, diseconomies) _____ of scale not available to a pure competitor;

  b. is more susceptible to X-(efficiency, inefficiency) _____ than pure competitors;

  c. may need to make (liability, rent-seeking) _____ expenditures to obtain or maintain monopoly privileges granted by government; and,

  d. reduces costs through adopting (higher prices, new technology) _____.

14. The incidence of pure monopoly is relatively (rare, common) _____ because eventually new developments in technology (strengthen, weaken) _____ monopoly power or (substitute, complementary) _____ products are developed.

15. Three general policy options to reduce the economic (losses, inefficiency) _____ of a monopoly are to file charges against it through (liability, antitrust) _____ laws, have government regulate it if it is a (conglomerate, natural monopoly) _____, or ignore it if it is unsustainable.

16. Price discrimination occurs whenever a product is sold at different (markets, prices) _____, and these differences are not equal to the differences in the (revenue from, cost of) _____ producing the product.

17. Price discrimination is possible when the following three conditions exist:

  a. _____

  b. _____

  c. _____

18. One economic consequence of a monopolist's use of price discrimination is (an increase, a decrease) _____ in profits.

19. If the monopolist were regulated and a socially optimal price for the product were sought, the price would be set equal to (marginal, average total) _____ cost. Such a legal price would achieve (productive, allocative) _____ efficiency but might result in losses for the monopolist.

20. If a regulated monopolist is allowed to earn a fair return, the ceiling price for the product would be set equal to (marginal, average total) _____ cost. Such a legal price falls short of (allocative, productive) _____ efficiency.

■ **TRUE–FALSE QUESTIONS**

Circle T if the statement is true, F if it is false.

1. The pure monopolist produces a product for which there are no close substitutes.　　**T　F**

2. The weaker the barriers to entry into an industry, the more competition there will be in the industry, other things equal.　　**T　F**

3. In pure monopoly, there are strong barriers to entry.　　**T　F**

4. A monopolist may create an entry barrier by price cutting or substantially increasing the advertising of its product.　　**T　F**

5. The monopolist can increase the sales of its product if it charges a lower price.　　**T　F**

6. As a monopolist increases its output, it finds that its total revenue at first decreases, and that after some output level is reached, its total revenue begins to increase.　　**T　F**

7. A purely competitive firm is a price taker but a monopolist is a price maker.　　**T　F**

8. A monopolist will avoid setting a price in the *inelastic* segment of the demand curve and prefer to set the price in the e*lastic* segment. **T F**

9. The monopolist determines the profit-maximizing output by producing that output at which marginal cost and marginal revenue are equal and sets the product price equal to marginal cost and marginal revenue at that output. **T F**

10. The supply curve for a monopolist is the upsloping portion of the marginal cost curve that lies above the average variable cost. **T F**

11. A monopolist will charge the highest price it can get. **T F**

12. A monopolist seeks maximum total profits, not maximum unit profits. **T F**

13. Pure monopoly guarantees economic profits. **T F**

14. Resources are misallocated by monopoly because price is not equal to marginal cost. **T F**

15. One of the economic effects of monopoly is less income inequality. **T F**

16. When there are substantial economies of scale in the production of a product, the monopolist may charge a price that is lower than the price that would prevail if the product were produced by a purely competitive industry. **T F**

17. The purely competitive firm is more likely to be affected by X-inefficiency than a monopolist. **T F**

18. Rent-seeking expenditures that monopolists make to obtain or maintain monopoly privilege have no effect on the firm's costs. **T F**

19. The general view of economists is that a pure monopoly is efficient because it has strong incentives to be technologically progressive. **T F**

20. One general policy option for a monopoly that creates substantial economic inefficiency and is long lasting is to directly regulate its prices and operation. **T F**

21. Price discrimination occurs when a given product is sold at more than one price and these price differences are not justified by cost differences. **T F**

22. A discriminating monopolist who can segment its market based on elasticity of demand will charge a higher price to the customers with a less elastic demand and a lower price to customers with a more elastic demand. **T F**

23. The regulated utility is likely to make an economic profit when price is set to achieve the most efficient allocation of resources (*P = MC*). **T F**

24. A fair-return price for a regulated utility would have price set to equal average total cost. **T F**

25. The dilemma of monopoly regulation is that the production by a monopolist of an output that causes no

misallocation of resources may force the monopolist to suffer an economic loss. **T F**

■ **MULTIPLE-CHOICE QUESTIONS**

Circle the letter that corresponds to the best answer.

1. Which would be defining characteristics of pure monopoly?
(a) The firm does no advertising and it sells a standardized product.
(b) No close substitutes for the product exist and there is one seller.
(c) The firm can easily enter into or exit from the industry and profits are guaranteed.
(d) The firm holds a patent and is technologically progressive.

2. A barrier to entry that significantly contributes to the establishment of a monopoly would be
(a) economies of scale
(b) price-taking behavior
(c) technological progress
(d) X-inefficiency

3. The demand curve for the pure monopolist is
(a) perfectly price elastic
(b) perfectly price inelastic
(c) downsloping
(d) upsloping

4. Which is true with respect to the demand data confronting a monopolist?
(a) Marginal revenue is greater than average revenue.
(b) Marginal revenue decreases as average revenue decreases.
(c) Demand is perfectly price elastic.
(d) Average revenue (or price) increases as the output of the firm increases.

5. When the monopolist is maximizing total profits or minimizing losses,
(a) total revenue is greater than total cost
(b) average revenue is greater than average total cost
(c) average revenue is greater than marginal cost
(d) average total cost is less than marginal cost

6. At which combination of price and marginal revenue is the price elasticity of demand less than 1?
(a) Price equals $102, marginal revenue equals $42.
(b) Price equals $92, marginal revenue equals $22.
(c) Price equals $82, marginal revenue equals $2.
(d) Price equals $72, marginal revenue equals −$18.

7. The region of demand in which the monopolist will choose a price-output combination will be the
(a) elastic one because total revenue will increase as price declines and output increases
(b) inelastic one because total revenue will increase as price declines and output increases
(c) elastic one because total revenue will decrease as price declines and output increases
(d) inelastic one because total revenue will decrease as price declines and output increases

8. At present output a monopolist determines that its marginal cost is $18 and its marginal revenue is $21. The monopolist will maximize profits or minimize losses by

(a) increasing price while keeping output constant
(b) decreasing price and increasing output
(c) decreasing both price and output
(d) increasing both price and output

Answer Questions 9, 10, and 11 based on the demand and cost data for a pure monopolist given in the following table.

Quantity demanded	Price	Total cost
0	$700	$ 300
1	650	400
2	600	450
3	550	510
4	500	590
5	450	700
6	400	840
7	350	1020
8	300	1250
9	250	1540
10	200	1900

9. The profit-maximizing output and price for this monopolist would be

(a) 5 units and $450
(b) 6 units and $400
(c) 7 units and $350
(d) 8 units and $300

10. The profit-maximizing price for this monopolist would be

(a) $300 price
(b) $350 price
(c) $400 price
(d) $450 price

11. At the profit-maximizing price and output, the amount of profit for the monopolist would be

(a) $1410
(b) $1430
(c) $1550
(d) $1560

12. The supply curve for a pure monopolist

(a) is the portion of the marginal cost curve that lies above the average variable cost curve
(b) is perfectly price elastic at the market price
(c) is upsloping
(d) does not exist

13. The analysis of monopoly indicates that the monopolist

(a) will charge the highest price it can get
(b) will seek to maximize total profits
(c) is guaranteed an economic profit
(d) is only interested in normal profit

14. When compared with the purely competitive industry with identical costs of production, a monopolist will charge a

(a) higher price and produce more output
(b) lower price and produce more output

(c) lower price and produce less output
(d) higher price and produce less output

15. At an equilibrium level of output, a monopolist is *not* productively efficient because

(a) the average total cost of producing the product is not at a minimum
(b) the marginal cost of producing the last unit is equal to its price
(c) it is earning a profit
(d) average revenue is less than the cost of producing an extra unit of output

16. A product's ability to satisfy a large number of consumers at the same time is called

(a) network effects
(b) X-inefficiency
(c) economies of scale
(d) simultaneous consumption

17. Which will tend to increase the inefficiencies of the monopoly producer?

(a) price-taking behavior
(b) rent-seeking behavior
(c) economies of scale
(d) technological progress

18. Which is one of the conditions that must be met before a seller finds that price discrimination is workable?

(a) The demand for the product is perfectly elastic.
(b) The seller must be able to segment the market.
(c) The buyer must be able to resell the product.
(d) The product must be a service.

19. A monopolist can segment two groups of buyers of its product based on elasticity of demand. Assume that ATC remains constant. The monopolist will maximize profit by charging

(a) the highest price to all customers
(b) the lowest price to all customers
(c) a higher price to customers with an elastic demand and a lower price to customers with an inelastic demand
(d) a lower price to customers with an elastic demand and a higher price to customers with an inelastic demand

Answer Questions 20, 21, and 22 based on the demand and cost data for a pure monopolist given in the following table.

Output	Price	Total cost
0	$1000	$ 500
1	600	520
2	500	580
3	400	700
4	300	1000
5	200	1500

20. The profit-maximizing output and price for this monopolist would be

(a) 1 and $100
(b) 2 and $200

(c) 3 and $400
(d) 4 and $300

21. At the profit-maximizing price and output, the amount of profit for the monopolist would be
  (a) $200
  (b) $340
  (c) $420
  (d) $500

22. If the monopolist were forced to produce the socially optimal output by the imposition of a ceiling price, the ceiling price would have to be
  (a) $200
  (b) $300
  (c) $400
  (d) $500

23. A monopolist who is limited by the imposition of a ceiling price to a fair return sells the product at a price equal to
  (a) average total cost
  (b) average variable cost
  (c) marginal cost
  (d) average fixed cost

Questions 24 and 25 are based on the following graph.

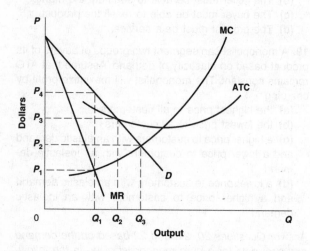

24. The price and output combination for the unregulated profit-maximizing monopoly compared with the socially optimal price and output combination for the regulated monopoly would be, respectively,
  (a) P_4 and Q_1 versus P_3 and Q_2
  (b) P_4 and Q_1 versus P_2 and Q_3
  (c) P_3 and Q_2 versus P_4 and Q_1
  (d) P_2 and Q_3 versus P_3 and Q_2

25. The dilemma of regulation that compares the fair-return price and output with the socially optimal price and output would be, respectively,

  (a) P_4 and Q_1 versus P_3 and Q_2
  (b) P_4 and Q_1 versus P_2 and Q_3
  (c) P_3 and Q_2 versus P_4 and Q_1
  (d) P_2 and Q_3 versus P_3 and Q_2

■ **PROBLEMS**

1. The demand schedule for the product produced by a monopolist is given in the following table.

Quantity demanded	Price	Total revenue	Marginal revenue	Price elasticity
0	$700	$____		
1	650	____	$____	____
2	600	____	____	____
3	550	____	____	____
4	500	____	____	____
5	450	____	____	____
6	400	____	____	____
7	350	____	____	____
8	300	____	____	____
9	250	____	____	____
10	200	____	____	____
11	150	____	____	____
12	100	____	____	____
13	50	____	____	____
14	0	____	____	____

a. Complete the table by computing total revenue, marginal revenue, and the price elasticity of demand (use midpoints formula).
b. The relationships in the table indicate that
(1) total revenue rises from $0 to a maximum of $_____ as price falls from $700 to $_____, and as price falls to $0, total revenue falls from its maximum to $_____;
(2) the relationship between price and total revenue suggests that demand is price (elastic, inelastic) _____ when quantity demanded is between 0 and 7 units of output, but that demand is price (elastic, inelastic) _____ when quantity demanded is between 8 units and 14 units;
(3) when demand is price elastic and total revenue rises from $0 to a maximum, marginal revenue is (negative, positive) _____, but when demand is price inelastic and total revenue falls from its maximum, marginal revenue is _____.
c. Use the data in the previous table and the graph on the next page to plot and graph the demand curve and the marginal revenue curve for the monopolist. Indicate the portion of the demand curve that is price elastic and the portion that is price inelastic.

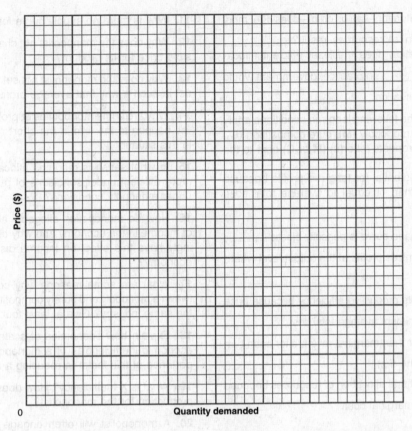

Price ($)

0   Quantity demanded

2. The following table shows demand and cost data for a pure monopolist.

Quantity demanded	Price	Total revenue	Marginal revenue	Total cost	Marginal cost
0	$17	$_____		$10	
1	16		$_____	18	$_____
2	15			23	
3	14	_____	_____	25	_____
4	13	_____	_____	27	_____
5	12	_____	_____	28	_____
6	11	_____	_____	32	_____
7	10	_____	_____	40	_____
8	9	_____	_____	50	_____
9	8	_____	_____	64	_____
10	7	_____	_____	80	_____

a. Complete the table by filling in the columns for total revenue, marginal revenue, and marginal cost.
b. Answer the next three questions using the data you calculated in the table.
(1) What output will the monopolist produce?

_____

(2) What price will the monopolist charge?

_____

(3) What total profit will the monopolist receive at the profit-maximizing level of output? _____

3. In the following table are cost and demand data for a pure monopolist.

Quantity demanded	Price	Marginal revenue	Average cost	Marginal cost
0	$17.50			
1	16.00	$16.00	$24.00	$24.00
2	14.50	13.00	15.00	6.00
3	13.00	10.00	11.67	5.00
4	11.50	7.00	10.50	7.00
5	10.00	4.00	10.00	8.00
6	8.50	1.00	9.75	8.50
7	7.00	−2.00	9.64	9.00
8	5.50	−5.00	9.34	9.25
9	4.00	−8.00	9.36	9.50

a. An unregulated monopolist would produce _____ units of this product, sell it at a price of $ _____, and receive a total profit of $_____.
b. If this monopolist were regulated and the maximum price it could charge were set equal to marginal cost, it would produce _____ units of a product, sell it at a price of $ _____, and receive a total profit of $ _____. Such regulation would either _____ the firm or require that the regulating government _____ the firm.
c. If the monopolist were regulated and allowed to charge a fair-return price, it would produce _____ units of product, charge a price of $ _____, and receive a profit of $_____.

d. From which situation—*a, b,* or *d*—does the most efficient allocation of resources result? _____ From which situation does the least efficient allocation result? _____ In practice, government would probably select situation _____.

4. Identify whether the following long-run conditions apply to a firm under pure monopoly (**M**), pure competition (**C**), or both. Put the appropriate letter(s) (**M** or **C**) next to the condition.

    a. There is the potential for long-run profits because price is greater than or equal to average total cost.

    _____

    b. The firm's demand curve is perfectly elastic. _____

    c. The firm maximizes profits at the output level where MC = MR. _____

    d. The firm exhibits productive efficiency because price is equal to the minimum average total cost. _____

    e. Price is greater than marginal revenue for each output level except the first. _____

    f. There is an optimal allocation of resources because price is equal to marginal cost. _____

■ SHORT ANSWER AND ESSAY QUESTIONS

1. What is pure monopoly? Define its characteristics.

2. Give examples of monopoly. How might a professional sports team be considered a monopoly when there are other such teams in the nation?

3. Why are the economies of scale a barrier to entry?

4. Why are most natural monopolies also public utilities? What does government hope to achieve by granting exclusive franchises to and regulating such natural monopolies?

5. How do patents and licenses create barriers to entry? Cite examples.

6. How can the monopolist use changes in price and other strategic actions to maintain a monopoly position?

7. Compare the pure monopolist and the individual pure competitor with respect to: (a) the demand schedule; (b) the marginal revenue schedule; (c) the relationship between marginal revenue and average revenue; (d) price policy, and (e) the ability to administer (or set) price.

8. Explain why marginal revenue is always less than average revenue (price) when demand is less than perfectly elastic.

9. Suppose a pure monopolist discovered it was producing and selling an output at which the demand for its product was inelastic. Explain why a decrease in its output would increase its economic profits.

10. How does the profit-maximizing monopolist determine what output to produce? What price will it charge?

11. Why is there no supply curve for a monopoly?

12. Why does the monopolist not charge the highest possible price for its product?

13. Why does the monopolist not set the price for its product in such a way that average profit is a maximum?

14. Why are some monopolies unprofitable? Explain what will happen to the firm in the short run and the long run in this situation.

15. In what sense is resource allocation and production more efficient under conditions of pure competition than under monopoly conditions?

16. How do monopolies allegedly affect the distribution of income in the economy and why do monopolies seemingly have this effect on income distribution in the U.S. economy?

17. What are some reasons why costs might differ between a monopoly and purely competitive firms operating in the same industry? Give at least four possible reasons.

18. Explain how economies of scale offset some of the economic inefficiencies of a monopoly. Evaluate the importance of this factor in reducing a monopolist's cost.

19. What is X-inefficiency? How does it affect the cost of production for the monopolist?

20. A monopolist will often engage in rent-seeking behavior. Explain what this means and how it changes a monopolist's cost.

21. Evaluate this statement from an economic perspective: "A pure monopoly has great incentive to discover and use new technology."

22. What is meant by price discrimination? Define it. What conditions must be met before it is workable?

23. Explain how a monopolist who can segment its market based on elasticity determines the price to charge for each unit of the product sold (or to charge each group of buyers).

24. How does price discrimination affect the profits and the output of the monopolist? How does it affect consumers?

25. Explain what public-utility regulatory agencies attempt to do to eliminate the misallocation of resources that results from monopoly. Describe the dilemma of regulation for these agencies and explain why a fair-return policy only reduces but does not eliminate misallocation.

ANSWERS

Chapter 10 Pure Monopoly

FILL-IN QUESTIONS

1. substitutes, blocked
2. public utilities, 80, sole
3. greater, difficult
4. patent, license
5. resources, price

6. downsloping, less, decrease
7. increase, decrease, horizontal, downsloping, elastic
8. marginal cost, average variable cost, does not exist
9. marginal, marginal, greater
10. highest, per-unit
11. is not, short run, weak
12. higher, less, less; *a.* total, minimum; *b.* price, marginal; *c.* upper
13. costs; *a.* economies; *b.* inefficiency; *c.* rent-seeking; *d.* new technology
14. rare, weaken, substitute
15. inefficiency, antitrust, natural monopoly
16. prices, cost of
17. *a.* the seller has some monopoly power; *b.* the seller is able to separate buyers into groups that have different elasticities of demand for the product; *c.* the original buyers cannot resell the product
18. an increase
19. marginal, allocative
20. average total, allocative

TRUE–FALSE QUESTIONS

1. T, p.202	10. F, pp. 208–209	19. F, p. 213
2. T, p. 202	11. F, p. 209	20. T, pp. 213–214
3. T, p. 202	12. T, p. 209	21. T, p. 214
4. T, pp. 203–204	13. F, pp. 209–210	22. T, pp. 214–215
5. T, pp. 204–205	14. T, pp. 210–211	23. F, pp. 216–217
6. F, pp. 205–206	15. F, p. 211	24. T, pp. 217, 219
7. T, pp. 206–207	16. T, pp. 211–212	25. T, p. 219
8. T, p. 207	17. F, pp. 212–213	
9. F, pp. 207–208	18. F, p. 213	

MULTIPLE-CHOICE QUESTIONS

1. b, p. 202	10. c, pp. 207–208	19. d, pp. 215–216
2. a, pp. 202–203	11. d, pp. 207–208	20. c, pp. 210–211
3. c, pp. 204–205	12. d, pp. 208–209	21. d, pp. 210–211
4. b, pp. 205–206	13. b, p. 209	22. b, p. 217
5. c, pp. 205–206	14. d, pp. 210–211	23. a, pp. 217, 219
6. d, pp. 205–206	15. a, pp. 210–211	24. b, pp. 209–210, 217
7. a, p. 207	16. d, p. 212	25. d, pp. 217, 219
8. b, pp. 207–208	17. b, p. 213	
9. b, pp. 207–208	18. b, pp. 214–215	

PROBLEMS

1. *a.* Total revenue: $0, 650, 1200, 1650, 2000, 2250, 2400, 2450, 2400, 2250, 2000, 1650, 1200, 650, 0; Marginal revenue: $650, 550, 450, 350, 250, 150, 50, −50, −150, −250, −350, −450, −550, −650; Price elasticity: 27, 8.33, 4.60, 3.00, 2.11, 1.55, 1.15, .87, .65, .47, .33, .22, .12, .04; *b.* (1) $2450, $350, 0, (2) elastic, inelastic, (3) positive, negative; *c.* see Figure 10.3a in the text as an example

2. *a.* Total revenue: $0, 16, 30, 42, 52, 60, 66, 70, 72, 72, 70; Marginal revenue: $16, 14, 12, 10, 8, 6, 4, 2, 0, −2; Marginal cost: $8, 5, 2, 2, 1, 4, 8, 10, 14, 16; *b.* (1) 6, (2) $11, (3) $34 (TR of $66 minus TC of $32)

3. *a.* 4, 11.50, 4.00; *b.* 6, 8.50, −7.50, bankrupt, subsidize; *c.* 5, 10.00, zero; *d.* b or c, a, d

4. *a.* M; *b.* C; *c.* C, M; *d.* C; *e.* M; *f.* C

SHORT ANSWER AND ESSAY QUESTIONS

1. p. 202	10. pp. 207–208	19. pp. 212–213
2. p. 202	11. pp. 208–209	20. p. 213
3. p. 203	12. p. 209	21. p. 213
4. p. 204	13. p. 209	22. pp. 214–215
5. pp. 203–204	14. pp. 209–210	23. p. 214
6. p. 204	15. pp. 210–211	24. pp. 215–216
7. pp. 204–207	16. p. 211	25. pp. 216–217, 219
8. pp. 205–206	17. pp. 211–213	
9. p. 207	18. pp. 211–212	

CHAPTER 11
Monopolistic Competition and Oligopoly

This chapter examines two market structures, monopolistic competition and oligopoly, that fall between the extremes of pure competition and pure monopoly. Both structures are important because they offer descriptions of firms and industries typically found in the U.S. economy.

Monopolistically competitive firms are prevalent because most retail establishments, such as clothing stores and restaurants, fall into the monopolistically competitive category. In such industries, there are a relatively large number of firms, so no one has a large market share, they sell differentiated products, and each has limited pricing power.

Economists use **four-firm concentration ratios** and the **Herfindahl index** to measure the degree of firm dominance of an industry and to determine whether an industry is monopolistically competitive or oligopolistic.

The first part of the chapter focuses on the **demand curve** for the monopolistically competitive firm. This demand curve differs from those found in pure competition and pure monopoly. As the individual firm changes the character of its product, or changes product promotion, both the costs of the firm and the demand for its product will change.

The **price–output** analysis of the monopolistic competitor is relatively simple. In the short run, this analysis is identical with the analysis of the price–output decision of a pure monopolist. Only in the long run does the competitive element make itself apparent: The entry of firms forces the price a firm charges to fall. This price, however, is not equal either to minimum average cost or to marginal cost; consequently, monopolistic competition can be said to be less efficient than pure competition.

This chapter also discusses **product variety** under monopolistic competition. A part of the competitive effort of individual firms is devoted to product differentiation, product development, and advertising. Each firm has three things to manipulate—price, product, and advertising—in maximizing profits. Although monopolistic competition has been characterized as inefficient, some of the positive benefits of product variety may offset some of the inefficiencies of this market structure.

The concept of **oligopoly** is fairly easy to grasp: a few firms that are mutually interdependent dominate the market for a product. The underlying causes of oligopoly are economies of scales and barriers to entry. More difficult to grasp is oligopoly behavior. **Game theory** helps explain what is meant by mutual interdependence and why it exists in an oligopoly. It also explains why specific conclusions cannot be drawn about the price and output decisions of individual firms. Oligopolists are loath to engage in price competition because of **mutual interdependence,** and frequently resort to **collusion**

to set prices and sometimes use nonprice competition to determine market share. Collusion, however, does not give firms complete protection from competition because there are incentives to cheat on collusive agreements.

There is no standard model of oligopoly because of the diversity of markets and the uncertainty caused by mutual interdependence among firms. **Three oligopoly models,** however, cover the range of most market situations. The **kinked-demand curve** explains why, in the absence of collusion, oligopolists will not raise or lower their prices even when their costs change. This model does not explain what price oligopolists will set; it only explains why prices will be relatively inflexible.

The second model examines how oligopolists resort to **collusion** to set price. The collusion can be **overt,** as in a cartel agreement, or the collusion can be **covert,** as in a secret agreement. The OPEC oil cartel is a classic example of covert collusion. Obstacles, such as cheating on price, make collusive agreements difficult to establish and maintain.

The third model of oligopoly is **price leadership.** In some industries a dominant firm serves as the price leader for other firms. There is no overt collusion, only unwritten, informal (tacit) understandings about price and competition among firms. This model explains why there are infrequent price changes, why the lead firm makes price and output announcements for other firms to follow, and why low pricing is used to prevent new entry. Such covert collusion, however, can be undermined by price wars.

The next-to-last section of the chapter looks at **advertising** in oligopoly. Product development and advertising are often the means of competition in oligopoly. Drawing conclusions about the effects of advertising, however, is difficult. Reasonable arguments can be made that advertising is both beneficial and costly for consumers and about whether advertising helps or hurts economic efficiency.

Compared with pure competition, oligopoly does not result in allocative or productive efficiency. Nevertheless, the qualifications noted at the end of the chapter may offset some of oligopoly's shortcomings.

■ CHECKLIST

When you have studied this chapter you should be able to

□ Describe monopolistic competition in terms of the number of sellers, type of product, entry and exit conditions, and advertising.

☐ Cite three consequences from having relatively large numbers of sellers in monopolistic competition.

☐ Describe five aspects of differentiated products in monopolistic competition.

☐ Describe the entry and exit conditions in monopolistic competition.

☐ State the role of advertising and nonprice competition in monopolistic competition.

☐ Define four-firm concentration ratio and use it to describe whether industries are monopolistically competitive or oligopolistic.

☐ Define the Herfindahl index and use it to assess influence of dominant firms in different types of industries.

☐ Compare the firm's demand curve under monopolistic competition with firms' demand curves in pure competition and pure monopoly.

☐ Determine the output of and the price charged by a monopolistic competitor in the short run when given cost and demand data.

☐ Explain why the price charged by a monopolistic competitor will in the long run tend to equal average cost and result in only a normal profit.

☐ Cite two real-world complications that may affect the outcome for monopolistically competitive firms in the long run.

☐ Show graphically how the typical firm in monopolistic competition achieves neither productive nor allocative efficiency and how excess capacity occurs.

☐ Discuss the effects of product variety in monopolistic competition.

☐ Explain why monopolistic competition is more complex in practice.

☐ Define oligopoly in terms of the number of producers, type of product, control over price, and interdependence.

☐ Explain how entry barriers and mergers contribute to the existence of oligopolies.

☐ Use game theory to explain three characteristics of oligopoly behavior.

☐ Cite two reasons why there is no standard model of oligopoly.

☐ Use the kinked-demand theory to explain the tendency for prices to be inflexible in a noncollusive model oligopoly.

☐ Describe the price and output conditions for a cartel or collusive pricing model of oligopoly.

☐ Give real examples of overt and covert collusion.

☐ State six obstacles to collusion.

☐ Describe the price leadership model of oligopoly and its outcomes.

☐ Explain why advertising is often heavily used in oligopoly.

☐ Cite the potential positive and negative effects of advertising.

☐ Compare economic efficiency in oligopoly to other market structures.

☐ Describe the major demand and supply factors over the years that turned the beer industry into an oligopoly (Last Word).

■ **CHAPTER OUTLINE**

1. Monopolistic competition has several defining characteristics.

a. The *relatively large number of sellers* means that each has a small market share, there is no collusion, and firms take actions that are independent of each other.

b. Monopolistic competition exhibits **product differentiation.** This differentiation occurs through: differences in attributes or features of products; services to customers; location and accessibility; brand names and packaging; and some control over price.

c. *Entry* into the industry or *exit* is relatively easy.

d. There is **nonprice competition** in the form of product differentiation and advertising.

e. Monopolistically competitive firms are common, and examples include asphalt paving, quick printing, saw mills, retail bakeries, clothing stores, restaurants, and grocery stores (see Table 11.1). (An explanation of how all industries are classified based on market type or market power is provided in section **5.g.** of this chapter outline.)

2. Given the products produced in a monopolistically competitive industry and the amounts of promotional activity, it is possible to analyze the **price and output decisions** of a firm.

a. The **demand curve** confronting each firm will be highly but not perfectly price elastic because each firm has many competitors who produce close but not perfect substitutes for the product it produces.

(1) Comparing the demand curve for the monopolistic competitor to other market structures suggests that it is not perfectly elastic, as is the case with the pure competitor, but it is also more elastic than the demand curve of the pure monopolist.

(2) The degree of elasticity, however, for each monopolistic competitor will depend on the number of rivals and the extent of product differentiation.

b. In the **short run** the individual firm will produce the output at which marginal cost and marginal revenue are equal and charge the price at which the output can be sold; either economic profits or losses may result in the short run.

c. In the **long run** the entry and exodus of firms will tend to change the demand for the product of the individual firm in such a way that economic profits are eliminated and there are only normal profits. (Price and average costs are made equal to each other.)

3. Monopolistic competition among firms producing a given product and engaged in a given amount of promotional activity results in **less economic efficiency and more excess capacity** than does pure competition.

a. The average cost of each firm is equal in the long run to its price. The industry **does not achieve allocative efficiency** because output is smaller than the output at which marginal cost and price are equal. The industry **does not achieve productive efficiency** because the output is less than the output at which average cost is a minimum.

b. *Excess capacity* results because firms produce less output than at the minimum of average total cost. In monopolistic competition, many firms operate below optimal capacity.

4. Each monopolistically competitive firm attempts to differentiate its product and advertise it to increase the firm's profit. These activities give rise to **nonprice competition** among firms.

   a. The benefit of product variety is that firms offer consumers a wide range of types, style, brands, and quality variants of a product. Products can also be improved. The expanded range of consumer choice from product differentiation and improvement may offset some of the economic inefficiency (excess capacity problem) of monopolistic competition.

   b. Monopolistic competition is more complex than the simple model presented in the chapter because the firm must constantly juggle three factors—price, product characteristics, and advertising—in seeking to maximize profits.

5. *Oligopoly* is frequently encountered in the U.S. economy.

   a. It is composed of a few firms that dominate an industry.

   b. It can be a *homogeneous oligopoly* that produces standardized industrial products such as steel, or a *differentiated oligopoly* that produces different types of consumer products such as automobiles.

   c. Firms have control over price, and thus are price makers. Oligopolistic firms engage in *strategic behavior,* which means they take into account the actions of other firms in making their decisions. *Mutual interdependence* exists because firms must consider the reaction of rivals to any change in price, output, product characteristic, or advertising.

   d. Barriers to entry, such as economies of scale or ownership, control over raw materials, patents, and pricing strategies, can explain the existence of oligopoly.

   e. Some industries have become oligopolistic not from internal growth but from external factors such as mergers.

   f. Most large industries are oligopolistic. They include ones such as primary copper, electric light bulbs, petrochemicals, motor vehicles, tires, and breakfast cereals (see Table 11.2).

   g. The degree of concentration or market power in an industry is measured in several ways. A *four-firm concentration ratio* gives the percentage of an industry's total sales provided by the four largest firms. If the ratio is very small, the industry is competitive. If the ratio is less than 40 percent, but not very small, the industry is considered monopolistically competitive. If the ratio is 40 percent or greater, the industry is classified as oligopolistic. There are, however, shortcomings with concentration ratios:

   (1) The ratio may understate concentration if markets are more local than national because the ratio is based on national data.

   (2) The ratio may overstate concentration because definitions of industries can be somewhat arbitrary and there may be substantial *interindustry competition.*

   (3) The ratio may overstate concentration if there is *import competition* because the ratio does not account for world trade.

   (4) The ratio may understate concentration if there is a dominant firm or firms among the firms in an industry. The *Herfindahl index* addresses the dominant firm problem because it accounts for the market share of each firm. It is the sum of the squared percentage market shares of all firms in the industry. This formula gives a greater weight in the index to larger firms in an industry.

6. Insight into the pricing behavior of oligopolists can be gained by thinking of the oligopoly as a game of strategy. This *game-theory model* leads to three conclusions.

   a. Firms in an oligopolistic industry are mutually interdependent and must consider the actions of rivals when they make price decisions.

   b. Oligopoly often leads to overt or covert collusion among the firms to fix prices or to coordinate pricing because competition among oligopolists results in low prices and profits; collusion helps maintain higher prices and profits.

   c. Collusion creates incentives to cheat among oligopolists by lowering prices or increasing production to obtain more profit.

7. Economic analysis of oligopoly is difficult because of the diversity among the firms and complications resulting from mutual interdependence. Nevertheless, two important characteristics of oligopoly are inflexible prices and simultaneous price changes by firms. An analysis of three oligopoly models helps explain the pricing practices of oligopolists.

   a. In the *kinked-demand model* there is no collusion. Each firm believes that if it lowers its price its rivals will lower their prices, but if it raises its price its rivals *will not* increase their prices. Therefore the firm is reluctant to change its price for fear of reducing its profits. The model has two shortcomings: it does not explain how the going price gets set; prices are not as rigid as the model implies.

   b. Mutual interdependence indicates there is *collusion* among oligopoly firms to maintain or increase profits.

   (1) Firms that collude tend to set their prices and joint output at the same level a pure monopolist would set them.

   (2) Collusion may be overt, as in a *cartel* agreement. The OPEC cartel is an example of effective overt collusion.

   (3) Collusion may be covert whereby agreements or unwritten, informal (tacit) understandings between firms set price or market share. Examples of such collusion have included bid rigging on milk prices for schools or fixing worldwide prices for a livestock feed additive.

   (4) At least six obstacles make it difficult for firms to collude or maintain collusive arrangements: difference in demand and cost among firms, the number of firms in the arrangement, incentives to cheat, changing economic conditions, potential for entry by other firms, and legal restrictions and penalties.

   c. *Price leadership* is a form of covert collusion in which one firm initiates price changes and the other firms in the industry follow the lead. Three price leadership tactics have been observed.

   (1) Price adjustments tend to be made infrequently, only when cost and demand conditions change to a significant degree.

(2) The price leader announces the price change in various ways, through speeches, announcements, or other such activities.

(3) The price set may not maximize short-run profits for the industry, especially if the industry wants to prevent entry by other firms.

(4) Price leadership can break down and result in a *price war.* Eventually the wars end, and a price leader re-emerges.

8. Oligopolistic firms often avoid price competition but engage in **product development and advertising** for two reasons: Price cuts are easily duplicated, but nonprice competition is more unique; and firms have more financial resources for advertising and product development.

a. The potential positive effects of advertising include providing low-cost information to consumers that reduces search time and monopoly power, thus enhancing economic efficiency.

b. The potential negative effects of advertising include manipulating consumers to pay higher prices, serving as a barrier to entry into an industry, and offsetting campaigns that raise product costs and prices.

9. The **efficiency of oligopoly** is difficult to evaluate.

a. Many economists think that oligopoly price and output characteristics are similar to those of monopoly. Oligopoly firms set output where price exceeds marginal cost and the minimum of average total cost. Oligopoly is allocatively inefficient ($P > $ MC) and productively inefficient ($P > $ minimum ATC).

b. This view must be qualified because of increased foreign competition to oligopolistic firms, the use of limit pricing that sets prices at less than the profit-maximizing price, and the technological advances arising from this market structure.

10. (Last Word). In 1947, there were over 400 independent brewers in the United States, but today the two major brewers account for 76 percent of the market. One reason for this change is that demand changed. Preferences shifted from stronger-flavored beers to lighter, dryer products. Consumption also shifted from taverns to homes, which results in different packaging. On the supply side, technology changed to produce significant economies of scale that now are barriers to entry. Mergers have occurred, but they are not the fundamental cause of increased concentration. Advertising and product differentiation have also been important in the growth of some firms.

■ HINTS AND TIPS

1. Review the four basic market models in Table 9.1 so that you see how monopolistic competition and oligopoly compare with the other market models on five characteristics.

2. The same MC = MR rule for maximizing profits or minimizing losses for the firm from previous chapters is now used to determine output and price in monopolistic competition and in certain oligopoly models. If you understood how the rule applied under pure competition and pure monopoly, you should have no trouble applying it here.

3. Make sure you know how to interpret Figure 11.1 because it is an important graph. It illustrates why a representative firm in monopolistic competition just breaks even in the long run, and earns just a normal rather than an economic profit. It also shows how economic inefficiency in monopolistic competition produces excess capacity.

4. Where is the kink in the kinked-demand model? To find out, practice drawing the model. Then use Figure 11.4 to check your answer. Explain to yourself what each line means in the graph.

5. Price and output determinations under collusive oligopoly or a cartel are essentially the same as those for pure monopoly.

■ IMPORTANT TERMS

monopolistic competition	strategic behavior
product differentiation	mutual interdependence
nonprice competition	interindustry competition
four-firm concentration ratio	import competition
Herfindahl index	game theory
excess capacity	collusion
oligopoly	kinked-demand curve
homogeneous oligopoly	price war
differentiated oligopoly	cartel
	price leadership

SELF-TEST

■ FILL-IN QUESTIONS

1. In a monopolistically competitive market, there are a relatively (large, small) _____ number of producers who sell (standardized, differentiated) _____ products. Entry into such a market is relatively (difficult, easy) _____. The number of firms means that each one has a (large, small) _____ market share, the firms (do, do not) _____ collude, and they operate in (an independent, a dependent) _____ manner.

2. Identify the different aspects of production differentiation in monopolistic competition:

a. _____

b. _____

c. _____

d. _____

e. _____

3. In the *short run* for a monopolistically competitive firm,

a. the demand curve will be (more, less) _____

elastic than that facing a monopolist and _____ elastic than that facing a pure competitor;

b. the elasticity of this demand curve will depend on

(1) _____ and

(2) _____; and

c. it will produce the output level where marginal cost is (less than, equal to, greater than) _____ marginal revenue.

4. In the *long run* for a monopolistically competitive industry,

a. the *entry* of new firms will (increase, decrease) _____ the demand for the product produced by each firm in the industry and _____ the elasticity of that demand.

b. the price charged by the individual firm will tend to equal (average, marginal) _____ cost, its economic profits will tend to be (positive, zero) _____, and its average cost will be (greater, less) _____ than the minimum average cost of producing and promoting the product.

5. Although representative firms in monopolistic competition tend to earn (economic, normal) _____ profits in the long run, there can be complications that may result in firms earning _____ profits in the long run. Some firms may achieve a degree of product differentiation that (can, cannot) _____ be duplicated by other firms. There may be (collusion, barriers to entry) _____ that prevent penetration of the market by other firms.

6. In monopolistic competition, price is (less than, equal to, greater than) _____ marginal cost, and so the market structure (does, does not) _____ yield allocative efficiency. Also, average total cost is (less than, equal to, greater than) _____ the minimum of average total cost, and so the market structure (does, does not) _____ result in (allocative, productive) _____ efficiency.

7. In the long run, the monopolistic competitor tries to earn economic profits by using (price, nonprice) _____ competition in the form of product differentiation and advertising. This results in a trade-off between a choice of more consumer goods and services and (more, less) _____ economic efficiency.

8. The more complex model of monopolistic competition suggests that in seeking to maximize profits, each firm juggles the factors of (losses, price) _____, changes in (collusion, product _____, and decisions about

(controls, advertising) _____ until the firm feels no further change in the variables will result in greater profit.

9. The percentage of the total industry sales accounted for by the top four firms in an industry is known as a four-firm (Herfindahl index, concentration ratio) _____, whereas summing the squared percentage market shares of each firm in the industry is the way to calculate the _____.

10. In an oligopoly (many, a few) _____ large firms produce either a differentiated or a (heterogeneous, homogeneous) _____ product, and entry into such an industry is (easy, difficult) _____. The oligopolistic firm is a price (maker, taker) _____ and there is mutual (independence, interdependence) _____ among firms in an industry. The existence of oligopoly can be explained by (exit, entry) _____ barriers and by (markets, mergers) _____.

11. The basics of the pricing behavior of oligopolists can be understood from a (game, advertising) _____ theory perspective. Oligopoly consists of a few firms that are mutually (funded, interdependent) _____. This means that when setting the price of its product, each producer (does, does not) _____ consider the reaction of its rivals. The monopolist (does, does not) _____ face this problem because it has no rivals, and the pure competitor, or monopolistic competitor, _____ face the problem because it has many rivals.

12. It is difficult to use formal economic analysis to explain the prices and outputs of oligopolists because oligopoly encompasses (diverse, similar) _____ market situation(s), and when firms are mutually interdependent, each firm is (certain, uncertain) _____ about how its rivals will react when it changes the price of its product. Despite the analytical problems, oligopoly prices tend to be (flexible, inflexible) _____ and oligopolists tend to change their prices (independently, together) _____.

13. The noncolluding oligopolist has a kinked-demand curve that

a. is highly (elastic, inelastic) _____ at prices above the current or going price and tends to be only slightly _____ or (elastic, inelastic) _____ below that price.

b. is drawn on the assumption that if the oligopolist raises its price its rivals (will, will not) _____ raise their prices or if it lowers its price its rivals _____ lower their prices.

c. has an associated marginal (cost, revenue) _____ curve with a gap, such that small changes in the marginal _____ curve do not change the price the oligopolist will charge.

14. A situation in which firms in an industry reach an agreement to fix prices, divide up the market, or otherwise restrict competition among themselves is called (concentration, collusion) _____. In this case, the prices they set and their combined output tend to be the same as that found with pure (competition, monopoly) _____.

15. A formal written agreement among sellers in which the price and the total output of the product and each seller's share of the market are specified is a (cartel, duopoly) _____. It is a form of (covert, overt) _____ collusion, whereas tacit understandings among firms to divide up a market would be _____ collusion.

16. Six obstacles to collusion among oligopolists are

a. _____

b. _____

c. _____

d. _____

e. _____

f. _____

17. When one firm in an oligopoly is almost always the first to change its price and the other firms change their prices after the first firm has changed its price, the oligopoly model is called the (price war, price leadership) _____ model. The tactics of this model include (infrequent, frequent) _____ price changes, announcements of such price changes, and (limit, no limit) _____ pricing. One event that can undermine this practice is (price leadership, price wars) _____.

18. There tends to be very little (price, nonprice) _____ competition among oligopolists and a great deal of _____ competition such as product development and advertising used to determine each firm's share of the market.

a. The positive view of advertising contends that it is (efficient, inefficient) _____ because it provides important information that (increases, reduces) _____ search costs, and information about competing goods _____ monopoly power.

b. The negative view of advertising suggests that it is (inefficient, efficient) _____ because the advertising campaigns are (offsetting, reinforcing) _____, the creation of brand loyalty serves as

a barrier to (entry, exit) _____, and consumers are persuaded to pay (lower, higher) _____ prices than they would have paid otherwise.

19. Although it is difficult to evaluate the economic efficiency of oligopoly, when comparisons are made to pure competition, the conclusion drawn is that oligopoly (is, is not) _____ allocatively efficient and (is, is not) _____ productively efficient. The price and output behavior of the oligopolist is more likely to be similar to that found under (competition, monopoly) _____.

20. The view that oligopoly is inefficient in the short run needs to be qualified because of the effects of (decreased, increased) _____ foreign competition that make pricing more competitive, policies to restrict entry into an industry that keep consumer prices (high, low) _____, and profits that are used to fund (more, less) _____ research and development that produces improved products.

■ **TRUE–FALSE QUESTIONS**

Circle T if the statement is true, F if it is false.

1. Monopolistic competitors have no control over the price of their products.   **T   F**

2. The firm's reputation for servicing or exchanging its product is a form of product differentiation under monopolistic competition.   **T   F**

3. Entry is relatively easy in pure competition, but there are significant barriers to entry in monopolistic competition.   **T   F**

4. The smaller the number of firms in an industry and the greater the extent of product differentiation, the greater will be the elasticity of the individual seller's demand curve.   **T   F**

5. The demand curve of the monopolistic competitor is likely to be less elastic than the demand curve of the pure monopolist.   **T   F**

6. In the short run, firms that are monopolistically competitive may earn economic profits or incur losses. **T   F**

7. The long-run equilibrium position in monopolistic competition would be where price is equal to marginal cost.   **T   F**

8. Representative firms in a monopolistically competitive market earn economic profits in the long run.   **T   F**

9. One reason why monopolistic competition is economically inefficient is that the average cost of producing the product is greater than the minimum average cost at which the product could be produced.   **T   F**

10. The more product variety offered to consumers by a monopolistically competitive industry, the less excess capacity there will be in that industry.   **T   F**

11. Successful product improvement by one firm has little or no effect on other firms under monopolistic competition. **T F**

12. The products produced by the firms in an oligopolistic industry may be either homogeneous or differentiated. **T F**

13. Oligopolistic industries contain a few large firms that act independently of one another. **T F**

14. Concentration ratios include adjustments for interindustry competition in measuring concentration in an industry. **T F**

15. The Herfindahl index is the sum of the market shares of all firms in the industry. **T F**

16. Game theory analysis of oligopolist behavior suggests that oligopolists will not find any benefit in collusion. **T F**

17. One shortcoming of kinked-demand analysis is that it does not explain how the going oligopoly price was established in the first place. **T F**

18. Collusion occurs when firms in an industry reach an overt or covert agreement to fix prices, divide or share the market, and in some way restrict competition among the firms. **T F**

19. A cartel is usually a written agreement among firms which sets the price of the product and determines each firm's share of the market. **T F**

20. Secret price concessions and other forms of cheating will strengthen collusion. **T F**

21. The practice of price leadership is almost always based on a formal written or oral agreement. **T F**

22. Limit pricing is the leadership tactic of limiting price increases to a certain percentage of the basic price of a product. **T F**

23. Those contending that advertising contributes to monopoly power argue that the advertising by established firms creates barriers to the entry of new firms into an industry. **T F**

24. Oligopolies are allocatively and productively efficient when compared with the standard set in pure competition. **T F**

25. Increased competition from foreign firms in oligopolistic industries has stimulated more competitive pricing in those industries. **T F**

■ **MULTIPLE-CHOICE QUESTIONS**

Circle the letter that corresponds to the best answer.

1. Which would be most characteristic of monopolistic competition?
   (a) collusion among firms
   (b) firms selling a homogeneous product
   (c) a relatively large number of firms
   (d) difficult entry into and exit from the industry

2. The concern that monopolistically competitive firms express about product attributes, services to customers, or brand names are aspects of
   (a) allocative efficiency in the industry
   (b) collusion in the industry
   (c) product differentiation
   (d) concentration ratios

3. The demand curve a monopolistically competitive firm faces is
   (a) perfectly elastic
   (b) perfectly inelastic
   (c) highly, but not perfectly inelastic
   (d) highly, but not perfectly elastic

4. In the short run, a typical monopolistically competitive firm will earn
   (a) only a normal profit
   (b) only an economic profit
   (c) only an economic or normal profit
   (d) an economic or normal profit or suffer an economic loss

5. A monopolistically competitive firm is producing at an output level in the short run where average total cost is $3.50, price is $3.00, marginal revenue is $1.50, and marginal cost is $1.50. This firm is operating
   (a) with an economic loss in the short run
   (b) with an economic profit in the short run
   (c) at the break-even level of output in the short run
   (d) at an inefficient level of output in the short run

6. If firms enter a monopolistically competitive industry, we would expect the typical firm's demand curve to
   (a) increase and the firm's price to increase
   (b) decrease and the firm's price to decrease
   (c) remain the same but the firm's price to increase
   (d) remain the same and the firm's price to remain the same

Answer Questions 7, 8, 9, and 10 on the basis of the following diagram for a monopolistically competitive firm in short-run equilibrium.

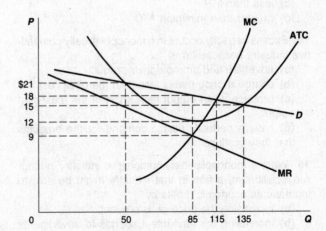

7. The firm's profit-maximizing price will be
- **(a)** $9
- **(b)** $12
- **(c)** $15
- **(d)** $18

8. The equilibrium output for this firm will be
- **(a)** 50
- **(b)** 85
- **(c)** 115
- **(d)** 135

9. This firm will earn an economic profit of
- **(a)** $510
- **(b)** $765
- **(c)** $1021
- **(d)** $1170

10. If firms enter this industry in the long run,
- **(a)** demand will decrease
- **(b)** demand will increase
- **(c)** the marginal revenue curve will shift upward
- **(d)** economic profits will increase

11. Given a representative firm in a typical monopolistically competitive industry, in the long run
- **(a)** the firm will produce that output at which marginal cost and price are equal
- **(b)** the elasticity of demand for the firm's product will be less than it was in the short run
- **(c)** the number of competitors the firm faces will be greater than it was in the short run
- **(d)** the economic profits being earned by the firm will tend to equal zero

12. *Productive* efficiency is not achieved in monopolistic competition because production occurs where
- **(a)** MR is greater than MC
- **(b)** MR is less than MC
- **(c)** ATC is greater than minimum ATC
- **(d)** ATC is less than MR and greater than MC

13. The *underallocation* of resources in monopolistic competition means that at the profit-maximizing level of output, price is
- **(a)** greater than MC
- **(b)** less than MC
- **(c)** less than MR
- **(d)** greater than minimum ATC

14. Excess capacity occurs in a monopolistically competitive industry because firms
- **(a)** advertise and promote their product
- **(b)** charge a price that is less than marginal cost
- **(c)** produce at an output level short of the least-cost output
- **(d)** have a perfectly elastic demand for the products that they produce

15. Were a monopolistically competitive industry in long-run equilibrium, a firm in that industry might be able to increase its economic profits by
- **(a)** increasing the price of its product
- **(b)** increasing the amounts it spends to advertise its product

(c) decreasing the price of its product
(d) decreasing the output of its product

16. Which would be most characteristic of oligopoly?
- **(a)** easy entry into the industry
- **(b)** a few large producers
- **(c)** product standardization
- **(d)** no control over price

17. Mutual interdependence means that
- **(a)** each firm produces a product similar but not identical to the products produced by its rivals
- **(b)** each firm produces a product identical to the products produced by its rivals
- **(c)** each firm must consider the reactions of its rivals when it determines its price policy
- **(d)** each firm faces a perfectly elastic demand for its product

18. One major problem with concentration ratios is that they fail to take into account
- **(a)** the national market for products
- **(b)** competition from imported products
- **(c)** excess capacity in production
- **(d)** mutual interdependence

19. Industry A is composed of four large firms that hold market shares of 40, 30, 20, and 10. The Herfindahl index for this industry is
- **(a)** 100
- **(b)** 1000
- **(c)** 3000
- **(d)** 4500

Questions 20, 21, and 22 are based on the following payoff matrix for a duopoly in which the numbers indicate the profit in thousands of dollars for a high-price or a low-price strategy.

		Firm A Strategy	
		High-price	Low-price
Firm B Strategy	High-price	A = $425 B = $425	A = $525 B = $275
	Low-price	A = $275 B = $525	A = $300 B = $300

20. If both firms collude to maximize joint profits, the total profits for the two firms will be
- **(a)** $400,000
- **(b)** $800,000
- **(c)** $850,000
- **(d)** $950,000

21. Assume that Firm B adopts a low-price strategy while Firm A maintains a high-price strategy. Compared to the results from a high-price strategy for both firms, Firm B will now
- **(a)** lose $150,000 in profit and Firm A will gain $150,000 in profit
- **(b)** gain $100,000 in profit and Firm A will lose $150,000 in profit

(c) gain $150,000 in profit and Firm A will lose $100,000 in profit

(d) gain $525,000 in profit and Firm A will lose $275,000 in profit

22. If both firms operate independently and do not collude, the most likely profit is
(a) $300,000 for Firm A and $300,000 for Firm B
(b) $525,000 for Firm A and $275,000 for Firm B
(c) $275,000 for Firm A and $525,000 for Firm B
(d) $425,000 for Firm A and $425,000 for Firm B

23. If an individual oligopolist's demand curve is kinked, it is necessarily
(a) perfectly elastic at the going price
(b) less elastic above the going price than below it
(c) more elastic above the going price than below it
(d) of unitary elasticity at the going price

Use the following diagram to answer Question 24.

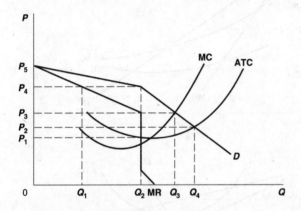

24. The profit-maximizing price and output for this oligopolistic firm is
(a) P_5 and Q_2
(b) P_4 and Q_2
(c) P_3 and Q_3
(d) P_2 and Q_4

25. What is the situation called whenever firms in an industry reach an agreement to fix prices, divide up the market, or otherwise restrict competition?
(a) interindustry competition
(b) incentive to cheat
(c) price leadership
(d) collusion

26. When oligopolists collude the results are generally
(a) greater output and higher price
(b) greater output and lower price
(c) smaller output and lower price
(d) smaller output and higher price

27. To be successful, collusion requires that oligopolists be able to
(a) keep prices and profits as low as possible
(b) block or restrict the entry of new producers
(c) reduce legal obstacles that protect market power
(d) keep the domestic economy from experiencing high inflation

28. Which is a typical tactic that has been used by the price leader in the price leadership model of oligopoly?
(a) limit pricing
(b) frequent price changes
(c) starting a price war with competitors
(d) giving no announcement of a price change

29. Market shares in oligopoly are typically determined on the basis of
(a) product development and advertising
(b) covert collusion and cartels
(c) tacit understandings
(d) joint profit maximization

30. Many economists think that relative to pure competition, oligopoly is
(a) allocatively efficient, but not productively efficient
(b) productively efficient, but not allocatively efficient
(c) both allocatively and productively efficient
(d) neither allocatively nor productively efficient

■ **PROBLEMS**

1. Assume that the short-run cost and demand data given in the following table confront a monopolistic competitor selling a given product and engaged in a given amount of product promotion.

Output	Total cost	Marginal cost	Quantity demanded	Price	Marginal revenue
0	$ 50		0	$120	
1	80	$_____	1	110	$_____
2	90	_____	2	100	_____
3	110	_____	3	90	_____
4	140	_____	4	80	_____
5	180	_____	5	70	_____
6	230	_____	6	60	_____
7	290	_____	7	50	_____
8	360	_____	8	40	_____
9	440	_____	9	30	_____
10	530	_____	10	20	_____

a. Compute the marginal cost and marginal revenue of each unit of output and enter these figures in the table.

b. In the short run the firm will (1) produce _____ units of output, (2) sell its output at a price of $_____, and (3) have a total economic profit of $_____.

c. In the long run, (1) the demand for the firm's product will _____, (2) until the price of the product equals _____, and (3) the total economic profits of the firm are _____.

2. Match the following descriptions to the six graphs on the next page. Indicate on each graph the area of economic profit or loss or state if the firm is just making normal profits.

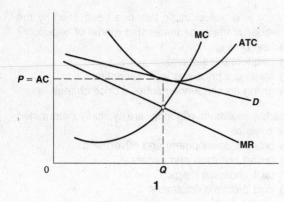

1

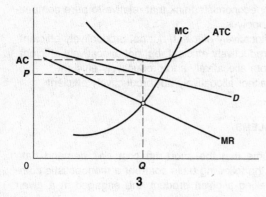

3

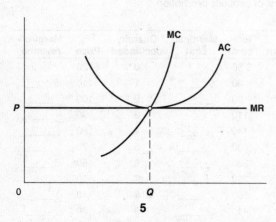

5

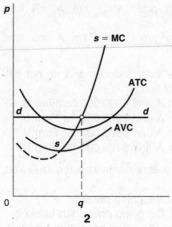

2

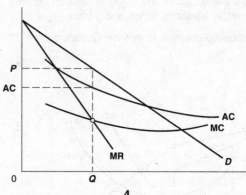

4

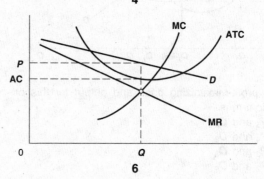

6

a. a purely competitive firm earning economic profits in the short run   Graph _____

b. a purely competitive firm in long-run equilibrium   Graph _____

c. a natural monopoly   Graph _____

d. a monopolistically competitive firm earning economic profits in the short run   Graph _____

e. a monopolistically competitive firm experiencing economic losses in the short run   Graph _____

f. a monopolistically competitive firm in long-run equilibrium   Graph _____

3. Consider the following payoff matrix in which the numbers indicate the profit in millions of dollars for a duopoly based on either a high-price or a low-price strategy.

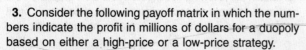

		Firm X Strategy	
		High-price	Low-price
Firm Y Strategy	**High-price**	X = $200 Y = $200	X = $250 Y = $ 50
	Low-price	X = $ 50 Y = $250	X = $ 50 Y = $ 50

a. Situation 1: Each firm chooses a high-price strategy.

Result: Each firm will earn $_____ million in profit for a total of $_____ million for the two firms.

b. Situation 2: Firm X chooses a low-price strategy while Firm Y maintains a high-price strategy. **Result:** Firm X will earn $_____ million and Firm Y will earn $_____ million. Compared to Situation 1, Firm X has an incentive to cut prices because it will earn $_____ million more in profit and Firm Y will earn $_____ million less in profit. Together, the firms will earn $_____ million in profit, which is $_____ million less than in Situation 1.

c. *Situation 3:* Firm Y chooses a low-price strategy while Firm X maintains a high-price strategy. ***Result:*** Compared to Situation 1, Firm Y has an incentive to cut prices because it will earn $_____ million and Firm X will earn $_____. Compared to Situation 1, Firm Y will earn $_____ million more in profit and Firm X will earn $_____ million less in profit. Together, the firms will earn $_____ million in profit, which is $_____ less than in Situation 1.

d. *Situation 4:* Each firm chooses a low-price strategy. ***Result:*** Each firm will earn $_____ million in profit for a total of $_____ million for the two firms. This total is $_____ less than in Situation 1.

e. *Conclusions:*

(1) The two firms have a strong incentive to collude and adopt the high-price strategy because there is the potential for $_____ million more in profit for the two firms than with a low-price strategy (Situation 4), or the potential for $_____ million more for the two firms than with a mixed-price strategy (Situations 2 or 3).

(2) There is also a strong incentive for each firm to cheat on the agreement and adopt a low-price strategy when the other firm maintains a high-price strategy because this situation will produce $_____ million more in profit for the cheating firm compared to its honoring a collusive agreement for a high-price strategy.

4. The kinked-demand schedule which an oligopolist believes confronts the firm is presented in the following table.

Price	Quantity demanded	Total revenue	Marginal revenue per unit
$2.90	100	$_____	
2.80	200	_____	$_____
2.70	300	_____	_____
2.60	400	_____	_____
2.50	500	_____	_____
2.40	525	_____	_____
2.30	550	_____	_____
2.20	575	_____	_____
2.10	600	_____	_____

a. Compute the oligopolist's total revenue at each of the nine prices and enter these figures in the table.

b. Also compute marginal revenue *for each unit* between the nine prices and enter these figures in the table.

c. What is the current, or going, price for the oligopolist's product? $_____ How much is it selling? _____

d. On the graph below plot the oligopolist's demand curve and marginal revenue curve. Connect the demand points and the marginal revenue points with as straight a line as possible. (Be sure to plot the marginal revenue figures at the average of the two quantities involved, that is, at 150, 250, 350, 450, 512.5, 537.5, 562.5, and 587.5.)

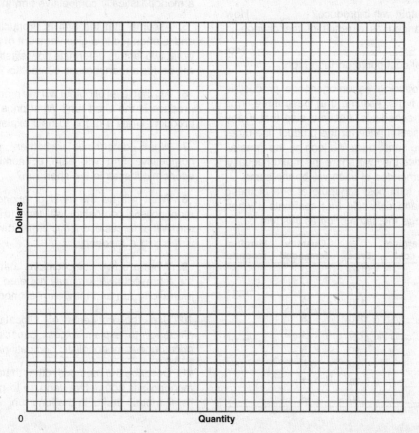

Dollars

0   Quantity

e. Assume that the marginal cost schedule of the oligopolist is given in columns 1 and 2 of the following table. Plot the marginal cost curve on the graph on which demand and marginal revenue were plotted.

(1) Output	(2) MC	(3) MC′	(4) MC″
150	$1.40	$1.90	$.40
250	1.30	1.80	.30
350	1.40	1.90	.40
450	1.50	2.00	.50
512.5	1.60	2.10	.60
537.5	1.70	2.20	.70
562.5	1.80	2.30	.80
587.5	1.90	2.40	.90

(1) Given demand and marginal cost, what price should the oligopolist charge to maximize profits? $_____ How many units of product will it sell at this price? _____

(2) If the marginal cost schedule changed from that shown in columns 1 and 2 to that shown in columns 1 and 3, what price should it charge? $_____ What level of output will it produce? _____ How have profits changed as a result of the change in costs? _____ Plot the new marginal cost curve on the graph.

(3) If the marginal-cost curve schedule changed from that shown in columns 1 and 2 to that shown in columns 1 and 4, what price should it charge? $_____ What level of output will it produce? _____ How have profits changed as a result of the change in costs? _____ Plot the new marginal cost curve on the graph.

5. An oligopoly producing a homogeneous product is composed of three firms. Assume that these three firms have identical cost schedules. Assume also that if any one of these firms sets a price for the product, the other two firms charge the same price. As long as the firms all charge the same price they will share the market equally, and the quantity demanded of each will be the same.

Following is the total cost schedule of one of these firms and the demand schedule that confronts it when the other firms charge the same price as this firm.

Output	Total cost	Marginal cost	Price	Quantity demanded	Marginal revenue
0	$ 0		$140	0	
1	30	$_____	130	1	$_____
2	50	_____	120	2	_____
3	80	_____	110	3	_____
4	120	_____	100	4	_____
5	170	_____	90	5	_____
6	230	_____	80	6	_____
7	300	_____	70	7	_____
8	380	_____	60	8	_____

a. Complete the marginal cost and marginal revenue schedules facing the firm.

b. What price would this firm set if it wished to maximize its profits? $_____

c. How much would

(1) it sell at this price? _____

(2) its profits be at this price? $_____

d. What would be the industry's

(1) total output at this price? _____

(2) joint profits at this price? $_____

e. Is there any other price this firm can set, assuming that the other two firms charge the same price, that would result in a greater joint profit for them? _____

f. If these three firms colluded in order to maximize their joint profit, what price would they charge? $_____

■ SHORT ANSWER AND ESSAY QUESTIONS

1. What are the three characteristics of monopolistic competition?

2. What is meant by product differentiation? By what methods can products be differentiated?

3. How does product differentiation affect the kind of competition and the degree of monopoly in monopolistic competition?

4. Describe the elasticity of the demand curve faced by a monopolistically competitive firm in the short run.

5. Assume that the firm is producing a given product and is engaged in a given amount of promotional activity. What two factors determine how elastic the demand curve will be for a monopolistic competitor?

6. At what level of output will the monopolistic competitor produce in the short run? What price will it charge for its product? Draw a graph to help explain your answer.

7. What determines whether a monopolistically competitive firm will earn economic profits or suffer economic losses in the short run?

8. What will be the level of economic profit that the monopolistic competitor will tend to receive in the long run? What forces economic profits toward this level? Why is this just a *tendency*?

9. What are two complications that would explain why the representative firm may not earn only a normal profit in the long run and may earn economic profits?

10. Use the concepts of allocative and productive efficiency to explain excess capacity and the level of prices under monopolistic competition.

11. Describe the methods, other than price cutting, that a monopolistic competitor can use to protect and increase its economic profits in the long run.

12. Explain how product variety and improvement may offset the economic inefficiency associated with monopolistic competition.

13. What are the essential characteristics of an oligopoly? How does oligopoly differ from pure competition, pure monopoly, and monopolistic competition?

14. Explain how the concentration ratio in a particular industry is computed. What is the relationship between this ratio and fewness? What are the shortcomings of the concentration ratio as a measure of the extent of competition in an industry?

15. What is the Herfindahl index? How can it be used to correct problems with concentration ratios?

16. How can game theory be used to explain strategic behavior under oligopoly? What do mutual interdependence and collusion mean with respect to oligopoly?

17. Why is it difficult to use one standard model to explain the prices charged by and the outputs of oligopolists?

18. How can the kinked-demand curve be used to explain why oligopoly prices are relatively inflexible?

19. Suppose a few firms produce a homogeneous product, have identical cost curves, and charge the same price (act as a cartel). Compare the results in terms of price, combined output, and joint profits with those from a pure monopoly producing the same market output.

20. Why do oligopolists find it advantageous to collude? What are the obstacles to collusion?

21. What is the price leadership model, and what leadership tactics do oligopolistic firms use?

22. Why do oligopolists engage in little price competition and in extensive product development and advertising?

23. How is it possible for consumers to get a lower price on a product with advertising than they would in its absence?

24. Explain how the advertising efforts of firms may be offsetting and lead to higher prices for consumers.

25. Evaluate the economic efficiency of the oligopoly market structure. What qualifications should be noted for the evaluation?

ANSWERS

Chapter 11 Monopolistic Competition and Oligopoly

FILL-IN QUESTIONS

1. large, differentiated, easy, small, do not, an independent
2. *a.* product attributes; *b.* services; *c.* location; *d.* brand names and packaging; *e.* some control over price
3. *a.* more, less; *b.* (1) number of rivals the firm has, (2) the degree of product differentiation; *c.* equal to
4. *a.* decrease, increase; *b.* average, zero, greater
5. normal, economic, cannot, barriers to entry
6. greater than, does not, greater than, does not, productive
7. nonprice, more
8. price, product, advertising

9. concentration ratio, Herfindahl index
10. a few, homogeneous, difficult, maker, interdependence, entry, mergers
11. game, interdependent, does, does not, does not
12. diverse, uncertain, inflexible, together
13. *a.* elastic, elastic, inelastic; *b.* will not, will; *c.* revenue, cost
14. collusion, monopoly
15. cartel, overt, covert
16. *a.* demand and cost differences; *b.* a large number of firms; *c.* cheating (secret price cutting); *d.* a recession; *e.* potential entry; *f.* legal obstacles (antitrust laws) (any order for *a–f*)
17. price leadership, infrequent, limit, price wars
18. price, nonprice; *a.* efficient, reduces, reduces; *b.* inefficient, offsetting, entry, higher
19. is not, is not, monopoly
20. increased, low, more

TRUE–FALSE QUESTIONS

1. F, pp. 223–224
2. T, p. 223
3. F, p. 224
4. F, pp. 225–226
5. F, pp. 225–226
6. T, pp. 225–227
7. F, pp. 226–227
8. F, p. 227
9. T, pp. 227–228
10. F, pp. 228–229
11. F, p. 229
12. T, p. 230
13. F, p. 229
14. F, p. 231
15. F, pp. 231–232
16. F, pp. 232–233
17. T, pp. 234–236
18. T, pp. 232–233
19. T, pp. 237–238
20. F, pp. 238–239
21. F, p. 239
22. F, p. 239
23. T, pp. 240–241
24. F, p. 241
25. T, p. 241

MULTIPLE-CHOICE QUESTIONS

1. c, p. 223
2. c, pp. 223–224
3. d, pp. 225–226
4. d, pp. 225–226
5. a, pp. 225–226
6. b, p. 227
7. d, pp. 225–226
8. b, pp. 225–226
9. a, pp. 225–226
10. a, pp. 226–227
11. d, pp. 225–226
12. c, pp. 227–228
13. a, pp. 227–228
14. c, p. 228
15. b, pp. 228–229
16. b, p. 229
17. c, p. 230
18. b, p. 231
19. c, p. 231
20. c, p. 232
21. b, p. 232
22. a, pp. 232
23. c, pp. 234–236
24. b, pp. 234–236
25. d, pp. 232–233
26. d, pp. 236–237
27. b, p. 239
28. a, p. 239
29. a, pp. 240–241
30. d, p. 241

PROBLEMS

1. *a.* Marginal cost: $30, 10, 20, 30, 40, 50, 60, 70, 80, 90,; Marginal revenue: $110, 90, 70, 50, 30, 10, −10, −30, −50, −70; *b.* (1) 4, (2) $80, (3) $180; *c.* (1) decrease, (2) average cost, (3) equal to zero
2. *a.* 2; *b.* 5; *c.* 4; *d.* 6; *e.* 3; *f.* 1
3. *a.* 200, 400; *b.* 250, 50, 50, 150, 300, 100; *c.* 250, 50, 50, 150, 300, 100; *d.* 50, 100, 300; *e.* (1) 300, 100, (2) 50
4. *a.* Total revenue: 290, 560, 810, 1,040, 1,250, 1,265, 1,265, 1,265, 1,260; *b.* Marginal revenue: 2.70, 2.50, 2.30, 2.10, 0.40, 0.20, 0, −0.20; *c.* 2.50, 500; *d.* graph; *e.* (1) 2.50, 500, (2) 2.50, 500, they have decreased, (3) 2.50, 500, they have increased
5. *a.* Marginal cost: $30, 20, 30, 40, 50, 60, 70, 80; Marginal revenue: $130, 110, 90, 70, 50, 30, 10, −10; *b.* $90; *c.* (1) 5, (2) $280; *d.* (1) 15, (2) $840; *e.* no; *f.* $90

SHORT ANSWER AND ESSAY QUESTIONS

Additional Game Theory Applications

This appendix provides some additional applications of oligopoly based on game theory and behavior. The first section of the appendix discusses strategies and equilibrium for games that occur just one time between two rivals. Here you will learn about the **Nash equilibrium,** which is an outcome from which neither rival wants to deviate because each firm sees its strategy as optimal given the strategy of its rival. The second section introduces the ideas of a **credible threat** and an **empty threat** and evaluates how each will affect Nash equilibrium. The third section turns to **repeated games,** which are games played more than once, and explains how strategies are influenced by the thought that there will be reciprocity from a rival, or less direct or intense competition. The final section turns to the topic of **sequential games,** in which the outcome depends on **first-mover advantage** and the ability to preclude entry by rivals.

■ CHECKLIST

When you have studied this appendix you should be able to

☐ Describe a one-time game and simultaneous game.

☐ Define positive-sum game, zero-sum game, and negative-sum game.

☐ Give an example of a dominant strategy in a game.

☐ Define the Nash equilibrium for a one-time game.

☐ Explain how a credible threat affects the Nash equilibrium.

☐ Explain how an empty threat affects the Nash equilibrium.

☐ Describe a repeated game and the effect of a reciprocity strategy on game outcomes.

☐ Supply an example of a sequential game.

☐ Explain how first-mover advantages in a sequential game affect decisions by rivals and entry into markets.

■ APPENDIX OUTLINE

1. In a **one-time game,** two firms (rivals) select their optimal strategies in a single time period without considering subsequent time periods. If both firms make their strategies at the same time, it is also a **simultaneous game.**

a. If the net outcome from such one-time and simultaneous games is positive, it is a **positive-sum game.** If the net outcome is negative, it a **negative-sum game.** If the net outcome is zero, it is a **zero-sum game.**

b. If one option in a game is better for a firm than any alternative option in a game regardless of the choice made by another firm, the better option is a **dominant strategy.** Not all games have a dominant strategy, however.

c. The dominant strategy for each firm determines the game's **Nash equilibrium.** It is the outcome from which neither firm wants to deviate because it is optimal given the strategic choice made by the other firm.

2. If there is a **credible threat** in a single-period and simultaneous game, then it can cause the firms to abandon the Nash equilibrium. The credible threat can occur if one firm is believed to have the power to dictate the decision of another firm and thus the firms collude. It is, however, difficult to enforce such a threat and if it is not credible, it is an **empty threat.** In this case, the Nash equilibrium will hold.

3. A **repeated game** is not a one-time event, but occurs more often or somewhat regularly. In this situation, the optimal strategy for a firm may be to limit competition with the other firm, if the other firm reciprocates by limiting its competition. Thus reciprocity strategies, and whether they will be used, are important for determining outcomes in repeated games.

4. A sequential game is one in which the final outcome may depend on which firm makes the first move because the first-mover may be able to establish the Nash equilibrium. A real-world example would be a large store such as Wal-Mart that, by making a first-mover decision to enter a market, prevents other large firms from also entering the same market because it would not be profitable.

■ HINTS AND TIPS

1. This appendix extends your understanding of game theory and strategic behavior described in Chapter 11. Before you start the appendix, make sure you master how the profit-payoff matrix works for two-firm oligopolies as in the example shown in Figure 11.3. A similar matrix is used illustrate each two-firm game discussed in this appendix.

2. There is nothing complicated about the content of this appendix, but it does introduce subtle distinctions in the definitions and conditions for games that you will need to learn as shown in the following list of important terms.

■ IMPORTANT TERMS

Nash equilibrium	one-time games
credible threat	simultaneous games
empty threat	positive-sum games
repeated games	zero-sum games
sequential games	negative-sum games
first-mover advantage	dominant strategy

SELF-TEST

■ FILL-IN QUESTIONS

1. If firms select their optimal strategies in a single time period, it is a (one-time, repeated) _____ game, but if firms select their optimal strategies based on a situation that is recurring, it is a _____ game.

2. Outcomes from games can be used to categorize games: if there is an "I win and you lose" outcome, it is a (positive, zero, negative) _____-sum game; if there is a "win-win" outcome, it is a _____ -sum game; and, if there is a "lose-lose" outcome, it is a _____-sum game.

3. A strategic choice for a firm that is better than any other option is a (subordinate, dominant) _____ strategy.

4. In a two-firm game, the dominant strategy for each firm determines the (Crowe, Nash) _____ equilibrium.

5. At such an equilibrium, both firms consider their current strategy as optimal and (do, do not) _____ want to deviate from it; so such an equilibrium is (stable, unstable) _____.

6. If a firm is capable or likely to use coercion to force a desired decision on a rival firm, the threat is (credible, empty) _____, but if the firm cannot use coercion to force a desired decision, the threat is _____.

7. If a threat is credible, firms will (deviate, not deviate) _____ from the Nash equilibrium and seek greater profits, but if a threat is empty, threatening firms will _____ from the Nash equilibrium and be unable to seek greater profits.

8. In a repeated game, if one firm avoids taking advantage of another firm because the firm knows the other firm will take advantage of it in a subsequent game, then there is likely to be a (monopolistic, reciprocity) _____ strategy enacted by the firms that can (harm, improve) _____ the outcomes from such games.

9. If one firm moves first and commits to a strategy and the other firm must then respond, it is a (repeated, sequential) _____ game.

10. In a sequential game involving two large, but similar retailers, the first-move retailer may have the opportunity to (establish, destroy) _____ a Nash equilibrium and it may make it (profitable, unprofitable) _____ for the other retailer to enter the market.

■ TRUE–FALSE QUESTIONS

Circle T if the statement is true, F if it is false.

1. Games can either be one-time games or repeated games. **T F**

2. Negative-sum games feature an "I win and you lose" outcome. **T F**

3. Decisions in games may be made simultaneously, but not sequentially. **T F**

4. When two firms are playing a strategic game, a firm has a dominant strategy if one option leads to a better result than all other options no matter what the other firm does. **T F**

5. The Nash equilibrium is an outcome from which neither firm wants to deviate because both firms see their current strategy is optimal given the selected strategy of the other firm. **T F**

6. A Nash equilibrium is unstable and changing. **T F**

7. An empty threat in a two-firm game will change outcomes and the Nash equilibrium. **T F**

8. Reciprocity means that one firm avoids taking advantage of the other firm because it knows that the other firm can take advantage of it in subsequent games. **T F**

9. Reciprocity makes outcomes worse for firms participating in repeated games. **T F**

10. If there is a first-mover advantage for two rival firms seeking to enter a market, it may be possible for the first-mover firm to preempt entry by the other firm. **T F**

■ MULTIPLE-CHOICE QUESTIONS

Circle the letter that corresponds to the best answer.

1. If one firm's gain equals another firm's loss it is a
(a) negative-sum game
(b) zero-sum game
(c) repeated game
(d) sequential game

*Questions 2, 3, and 4 are based on the following payoff matrix for a single-period, two-firm game for firms **Rig** and **Dig**. The numbers in the matrix indicate the profit in millions of dollars for a national or regional strategy. The profit outcome cells are **A, B, C,** and **D**.*

		Rig Strategy	
		National	Regional
Dig Strategy	National	(A) Rig = $24 / Dig = $24	(B) Rig = $12 / Dig = $42
	Regional	(C) Rig = $42 / Dig = $12	(D) Rig = $36 / Dig = $36

2. Which strategies are the dominant ones for Rig and Dig?
(a) national for Rig and regional for Dig
(b) regional for Rig and national for Dig
(c) national for Rig and national for Dig
(d) regional for Rig and regional for Dig

3. The Nash equilibrium will be represented by which cell showing the set of profit outcomes for the two firms?
(a) A
(b) B
(c) C
(d) D

4. If Dig can make a credible threat that determines the strategy for Rig, then which combinations of strategies will be selected?
(a) national for Rig and regional for Dig
(b) regional for Rig and national for Dig
(c) national for Rig and national for Dig
(d) regional for Rig and regional for Dig

5. If Dig makes a threat, but it is an empty threat that is not believable for Rig, then which cell shows the set of profit outcomes for the two firms?
(a) A
(b) B
(c) C
(d) D

6. In a repeated game among two firms, if the optimal strategy for one firm is to cooperate with the other firm and restrain competition in the expectation that the other firm will do the same, then the firm is using a

(a) dominant strategy
(b) reciprocity strategy
(c) credible threat strategy
(d) empty threat strategy

7. If one firm make the first move and then the other firm responds, it would be a
(a) zero-sum game
(b) negative-sum game
(c) simultaneous game
(d) sequential game

*Questions 8, 9, and 10 are based on the following payoff matrix for a single-period, two-firm game for the two major aircraft makers, **Fly** and **Sky**. The numbers in the matrix indicate the profit in billions of dollars if a firm builds or does not build a new aircraft to compete with the other firm. The profit outcome cells are **A, B, C,** and **D**.*

		Fly Strategy	
		Build	Don't build
Sky Strategy	Build	(A) Fly = −$12 / Sky = −$12	(B) Fly = $ 0 / Sky = $15
	Don't build	(C) Fly = $15 / Sky = $ 0	(D) Fly = $ 0 / Sky = $ 0

8. What will be the total amount of profit or losses for both firms if both firms decide simultaneously to build a new aircraft?
(a) $0
(b) $15 billion
(c) −$12 million
(d) −$24 million

9. Which pair of cells contains the possible Nash equilibrium?
(a) A and B
(b) B and C
(c) C and D
(d) A and D

10. If Sky makes the first move and builds an aircraft then
(a) Sky will earn $15 billion and Fly will earn $0
(b) Sky will lose $12 billion and Fly will lose $12 billion
(c) Sky will earn $15 billion and Fly will earn $15 billion
(d) Neither firm will make a profit, but neither firm will suffer a loss

■ PROBLEMS

For problems 1 to 4 use the following payoff matrix for two retail firms, **Top** and **Pop,** in a single-period, one-time game. The numbers in each cell (**A, B, C,** or **D**) indicate the profit in millions of dollars based on whether they adopt a high-price or a low-price strategy.

		Top Strategy	
		High-price	**Low-price**
Pop Strategy	**High-price**	(A) Top = $30 / Pop = $30	(B) Top = $15 / Pop = $60
	Low-price	(C) Top = $60 / Pop = $15	(D) Top = $45 / Pop = $45

1. Determine the dominant strategy for Pop.

a. If Top adopts a high-price strategy, then Pop will be better off if it chooses a high-price strategy because it can earn $ _____ million. By contrast, if Pop had used a low-price strategy in this case, it only would earn $ _____ million in profit.

b. If Top adopts a low-price strategy, then Pop will be better off if it chooses a high-price strategy because it can earn $ _____ million. By contrast, if Pop used a low-price strategy in this case, it only would earn $ _____ million in profit.

c. Regardless of whether Top adopts a high-price or low-price strategy, Pop will be better off it if adopts a high-price strategy because it can earn either $ _____ million or $ _____ million. A high-price strategy is the dominant strategy for Pop.

2. Determine the dominant strategy for Pop.

a. If Pop adopts a high-price strategy, then Top will be better off if it chooses a high-price strategy because it can earn $ _____ million. By contrast, if Top used a low-price strategy in this case, it only would earn $ _____ million in profit.

b. If Pop adopts a low-price strategy, then Top will still be better off if it chooses a high-price strategy because it can earn $_____ million. By contrast, if Top used a low-price strategy in this case, it only would earn $ _____ million in profit.

c. Regardless of whether Pop adopts a high-price or low-price strategy, Top will be better off it if adopts a high-price strategy because it can earn either $ _____ million or $ _____ million. A high-price strategy is the dominant strategy for Top.

3. Identify the Nash equilibrium.

a. Each firm will adopt a _____-price strategy because such a strategy is dominant over all other choices for each firm. The Nash equilibrium will be in cell _____.

b. At the Nash equilibrium each firm will earn $ _____ million.

4. Identify the effects of credible and empty threats.

a. If Pop chooses a low-price strategy and makes a credible threat to get Top to adopt a low-price strategy, then both firms will abandon the Nash equilibrium at cell _____ and move to cell _____ in the profit-payoff matrix. Pop will earn a profit of $ _____ million.

b. If Pop chooses a low-price strategy and makes a threat to get Top to adopt a low-price strategy, but Pop cannot enforce that threat or it is not believable, then the Nash equilibrium will be at cell _____.

The profit for each form will be $ _____.

5. Determine outcomes from repeated games and reciprocity.

Use the following payoff matrix for two shoe firms, **Skip** and **Jump**, who are involved in a two-period game. The numbers in each cell (**A**, **B**, **C**, or **D**) indicate the profit in millions of dollars based on whether they adopt more advertising or less advertising for the introduction of a new shoe. Assume that in period 1, Jump introduces a new shoe, Clog, and it adopts an advertising strategy of placing more ads to sell the new shoe.

Period 1: Jump introduces a new shoe, Clog

		Skip Strategy	
		More-ads	**Fewer-ads**
Jump Strategy	**More-ads**	(A) Skip = $20 / Jump = $20	(B) Skip = $16 / Jump = $32
	Fewer-ads	(C) Skip = $32 / Jump = $16	(D) Skip = $24 / Jump = $24

a. If, in response, Skip counters by placing more ads, the amount of profit for each firm will be $ _____ million. The profit outcomes for both firms will be at cell _____.

b. But if, in response, Skip adopts a fewer-ads strategy in hopes that Jump will do the same when Skip launches its new shoe, then Skip will earn $ _____ million in profit. The profit outcomes for both firms will be at cell _____.

Now assume that in period 2 Skip launches its new shoe, Fleet, and adopts a more-ads strategy.

Period 2: Skip introduces a new shoe, Fleet

		Skip Strategy	
		More-ads	**Fewer-ads**
Jump Strategy	**More-ads**	(A) Skip = $22 / Jump = $22	(B) Skip = $20 / Jump = $28
	Fewer-ads	(C) Skip = $30 / Jump = $20	(D) Skip = $28 / Jump = $26

c. If, in response, Jump counters by placing more ads, the amount of profit earned by each firm will be $_____$ million. The profit outcomes for both firms will be at cell _____.

d. But if, in response, Jump cooperates and adopts a reciprocity strategy of fewer ads, Jump will earn $ _____ million. The profit outcomes for both firms will be at cell _____.

e. By cooperating and showing reciprocity to each other, the firms will earn more total profit. In period 1, Jump will earn $ _____ million and in period 2 Jump will earn $ _____ million, for a total of $ _____ million. In period 1, Skip will earn $ _____ million and in period 2 Skip will earn $_____ million for a total of $_____ million.

f. Had there been no cooperation or reciprocity, each firm would have earned $_____ million in the first period and $ _____ million in the second period, for a total of $ _____ million.

■ SHORT ANSWER AND ESSAY QUESTIONS

1. What are the differences between positive-sum, negative-sum, and zero-sum games?

2. How can decisions in games be either simultaneous or sequential? Give examples of each type.

3. Explain what is meant by a dominant strategy in a one-period game involving two rival firms.

4. Define the Nash equilibrium. Is it stable or unstable?

5. How does the use of credible threats or empty threats from firms affect outcomes and the Nash equilibrium in one-period games?

6. Give examples of real-world companies for which repeated games apply.

7. What strategies might two dominant firms use in repeated games to increase profits over what might be achieved with competitive strategies?

8. Explain how the first mover might have an advantage in a sequential game. Does such an advantage always produce a positive outcome?

9. Why might there be two outcomes that could create the Nash equilibrium in sequential games with first-mover advantages?

10. Supply some real-world examples of firms that have used first-mover advantages to saturate markets or preempt entry by rivals.

ANSWERS

Appendix to Chapter 11: Additional Game Theory Applications

FILL-IN QUESTIONS

1. one-time, repeated
2. zero, positive, negative
3. dominant
4. Nash
5. do not, stable
6. credible, empty
7. deviate, not deviate
8. reciprocity, improve
9. sequential
10. establish, unprofitable

TRUE–FALSE QUESTIONS

1. T, pp. 246–247	**6.** F, p. 246
2. F, p. 246	**7.** F, p. 247
3. F, pp. 246, 248	**8.** T, p. 247
4. T, p. 246	**9.** F, p. 248
5. T, p. 246	**10.** T, pp. 248–249

MULTIPLE-CHOICE QUESTIONS

1. b, p. 246	**6.** b, p. 247
2. c, p. 246	**7.** d, p. 248
3. a, p. 246	**8.** d, pp. 248–249
4. d, pp. 246–247	**9.** b, pp. 248–249
5. a, p. 247	**10.** a, pp. 248–249

PROBLEMS

1. *a.* 30, 15; *b.* 60, 45; *c.* 30, 60
2. *a.* 30, 15; *b.* 60, 45; *c.* 30, 60
3. *a.* high, A; *b.* 30
4. *a.* A, D, 45; *b.* A, 30
5. *a.* 20, A; *b.* 16, B; *c.* 22, A; *d.* 20, C; *e.* 32, 20, 52, 16, 46, 46; f. 20, 22, 42

SHORT ANSWER AND ESSAY QUESTIONS

1. p. 247	**6.** p. 247
2. pp. 247, 249	**7.** p. 248
3. p. 247	**8.** pp. 248-249
4. p. 247	**9.** p. 249
5. pp. 247-248	**10.** p. 249

Technology, R&D, and Efficiency

Note: The bonus Web chapter is available at: **www.mcconnell18e.com.**

A market economy is not static but subject to change over time. One dynamic force affecting an economy and industries is **technological advance.** This advance occurs over a very long time and allows firms to introduce new products and adopt new methods of production.

The chapter begins by discussing the three-step process that constitutes technological advance: **invention, innovation,** and **diffusion.** Here the text describes many real-world examples of how technological change has affected firms and industries. You will also find out that research and development (R&D) expenditures by firms and government play an integral role in directly supporting this technological advance. The traditional view of economists was that technological advance was something external to the economy, but most contemporary economists think that technological advance is integral to capitalism and arises from intense rivalry among firms.

Entrepreneurs and other innovators play a major role in encouraging innovation and technological change. Entrepreneurs typically form small companies—**start-ups**—to create and introduce new products and production techniques. In this activity entrepreneurs assume personal financial risk, but if they are successful, they can be highly rewarded in the marketplace. There also are innovators within existing firms who can use R&D work to develop new products. University and government research also can contribute output that can be useful for fostering technological advance.

A major section of this chapter analyzes how the firm determines the **optimal amount of R&D spending.** The decision is made by equating marginal benefit with marginal cost. The marginal cost is measured by the interest-rate cost of funds that the firm borrows or obtains from other sources to finance its R&D expenditures. The expected rate of return from the last dollar spent on R&D is the measure of marginal benefit. You should remember that the outcomes from R&D spending are only expected, not guaranteed for the firm.

Technological changes can increase a firm's profit in two ways. Recall that profit is simply the difference between total revenue and total cost. **Product innovation** can increase revenues because people buy more products from the innovative firm. These increased revenues will increase profits, assuming that costs stay the same. **Process innovation** also can increase profits by reducing costs. This type of innovation leads to better methods

for producing a product and decreases the average total cost for the firm.

One problem with technological advance is that it encourages **imitation.** Successful innovative firms often are emulated by others. This imitation problem can be especially threatening to innovative, smaller firms because the dominant firms in the industry can challenge them. A firm, however, has some advantages in taking the lead in innovation because there are protections and rewards. Legal protections include patents, copyrights, and trademarks; other advantages are early brand-name recognition or the potential for a profitable buyout.

You spent the past three chapters learning about the differences in the four market structures. Now you may be wondering whether one market structure is better suited than another for encouraging technological progress. The answer is clearly mixed because each structure has its strengths and shortcomings. The **inverted-U theory of R&D** gives you an even better framework for figuring out the optimal industry structure for R&D.

The chapter ends by returning to the issue of **economic efficiency,** a topic discussed throughout the text. Technological advance has a double benefit because it enhances both productive efficiency and allocative efficiency. Productive efficiency increases from process innovation that reduces production costs. Allocative efficiency increases because product innovation gives consumers more choice and gives society a more desired mix of products. The efficiency results are not automatic, and the outcome may depend on whether innovation strengthens or weakens monopoly power.

■ CHECKLIST

When you have studied this chapter you should be able to

☐ Define technological advance.
☐ Describe each of the three steps in technological advance.
☐ Explain the role of research and development (R&D) in technological advance.
☐ Contrast the traditional with the modern view of technological advance.
☐ Distinguish between entrepreneurs and other innovators and between start-ups and innovation in existing firms.
☐ Explain how innovators are rewarded for anticipating the future.

☐ Describe the role that universities and government play in fostering technological advance.

☐ Identify five means for financing R&D that are available to firms.

☐ Describe and give a rationale for the interest-rate cost-of-funds curve and the expected-rate-of-return curve.

☐ Show graphically with an example how the optimal level of R&D expenditures is determined.

☐ State three important points from the analysis of optimal R&D expenditures.

☐ Explain how product innovation can increase profits by increasing revenues.

☐ Describe how process innovation can increase profits by reducing costs.

☐ Explain the imitation problem for firms.

☐ Identify six protections for or advantages to being the first to develop a new product or process.

☐ Evaluate which of the four market structures is best suited to technological advance.

☐ Explain the inverted-U theory of R&D and its implications for technological progress.

☐ Describe how technological advance enhances both productive and allocative efficiency.

☐ Explain how innovation may lead to creative destruction and describe the criticisms of this view.

☐ Describe how technological advance is reflected in the development of the modern computer and emergence of the Internet (Last Word).

■ **CHAPTER OUTLINE**

1. *Technological advance* involves the development of new and improved products and new and improved ways of producing and distributing the products. The technological change occurs in the *very long run.* It is a three-step process of invention, innovation, and diffusion.

a. *Invention* is the most basic part of technological advance and involves the discovery of a product or process. Governments encourage invention by granting the inventor a *patent,* which is an exclusive right to sell a product for a period of time.

b. *Innovation* is the first successful commercial use of a new product or method or the creation of a new form of business. There are two major types: *product innovation,* which involves new and improved products or services, and *process innovation,* which involves new and improved production or distribution methods. Innovation is an important factor in competition because it can enable a firm to leapfrog competitors by making their products or methods obsolete.

c. *Diffusion* is the spread of an innovation through imitation or copying. New and existing firms copy or imitate successful innovation of other firms to profit from new opportunities or to protect their profits.

d. In business, research and development (R&D) includes work and expenditures directed toward invention, innovation, and diffusion. Government also supports R&D through defense expenditures and the funding of other activities.

e. The traditional view of technological advance was that it was external to the economy. It was viewed as a random force to which the economy adjusted and it depended on the advance of science. The modern view is that it is internal to capitalism. Intense rivalry among individuals and firms motivates them to seek and exploit new or expand existing opportunities for profit. Entrepreneurs and other innovators are the drivers of technological advance.

2. The **entrepreneur** is an initiator, innovator, and risk bearer. Other innovators are key people involved in the pursuit of innovation but who do not bear personal financial risk.

a. Entrepreneurs often form small new companies called *start-ups,* which are firms that create and introduce a new product or production technique.

b. Innovators are found within existing corporations. R&D work in major corporations has resulted in technological improvements, often by splitting off units to form innovative firms.

c. Innovators attempt to anticipate future needs. Product innovation and development are creative activities with both nonmonetary and monetary rewards. More resources for further innovation by entrepreneurs often come from past successes. Successful businesses that meet consumer wants are given the opportunity to produce goods and services for the market.

d. New scientific knowledge is important to technological advance. Entrepreneurs study the scientific results from university and government laboratories to find those with commercial applicability.

3. The *optimal amount of R&D* expenditures for the firm depends on the marginal benefit and marginal cost of R&D activity. To earn the greatest profit, the firm will expand an activity until its marginal benefit equals its marginal cost.

a. Several sources are available for financing firms' R&D activities: bank loans, bonds, retained earnings, *venture capital,* or personal savings. A firm's marginal cost of these funds is an interest rate i.

b. A firm's marginal benefit of R&D is its expected profit (or return) from the last dollar spent on R&D.

c. The *optimal amount of R&D* in marginal-cost and marginal-benefit analysis is the point where the *interest-rate cost-of-funds* (marginal-cost) *curve* and the *expected-rate-of-return* (marginal-benefit) *curve* intersect. This analysis leads to three important points. First, R&D expenditures can be justified only if the expected return equals or exceeds the cost of financing R&D. Second, the firm expects positive outcomes from R&D, but the results are not guaranteed. Third, firms adjust R&D spending when expected rates of return change on various projects.

4. A firm's profit can be increased through **innovation** in two ways.

a. The firm can increase revenues through *product innovation.* From a utility perspective, consumers will purchase a new product only if it increases total utility from their limited incomes. The purchases of the product by consumers increase the firm's revenues.

Note three other points.

(1) Consumer acceptance of a new product depends on both its marginal utility and price.

(2) Many new products are not successful, so the firm fails to realize the expected return in these instances.

(3) Most product innovations are small or incremental improvements to existing products, not major changes.

b. *Process innovation,* the introduction of better ways to make products, is another way to increase profit and obtain a positive return on R&D expenditures. It results in a shift upward in the firm's total product curve and a shift downward in the firm's average total cost curve, which increases the firm's profit.

5. The *imitation problem* is that the rivals of a firm may copy or emulate the firm's product or process and thus decrease the profit from the innovator's R&D effort. When a dominant firm quickly imitates the successful new product of smaller competitors with the goal of becoming the second firm to adopt the innovation, it is using a *fast-second strategy.*

a. Taking the lead in innovation offers the firm several protections and potential advantages from being first to produce a product.

(1) Patents limit imitation and protect profits over time.

(2) Copyrights and trademarks reduce direct copying and increase the incentives for product innovation.

(3) Brand names may provide a major marketing asset.

(4) Trade secrets and learning by doing give firms advantages.

(5) The time lags between innovation and diffusion give innovators time to make substantial economic profits.

(6) There is the potential purchase of the innovating firm by a larger firm at a high price.

6. Certain market structures may foster **technological advance.**

a. Each **market structure** has strengths and limitations.

(1) *Pure competition:* Strong competition gives firms the reason to innovate, but the expected rate of return on R&D may be low or negative for a pure competitor.

(2) *Monopolistic competition:* These firms have a strong profit incentive to develop and differentiate products, but they have limited ability to obtain inexpensive R&D financing. It is also difficult for these firms to extract large profits because the barriers to entry are relatively low.

(3) *Oligopoly:* Although the size of these firms makes them capable of promoting technological progress, there is little reason for them to introduce costly new technology and new products when they earn large economic profits without doing it.

(4) *Pure monopoly:* This type of firm has little incentive to engage in R&D because its high profit is protected by high barriers to entry.

b. *Inverted-U theory of R&D* suggests that R&D effort is weak in industries with very low concentration (pure competition) and very high concentration (pure monopoly). The optimal industry structure for R&D is one in which expected returns on R&D spending are high and funds are readily available and inexpensive to finance. This generally occurs in industries with a few firms that are absolutely and relatively large, but the concentration ratio is not so high as to limit strong competition by smaller firms.

c. General support for the inverted-U theory of R&D comes from industry studies. The optimal market structure for technological advance appears to be an industry with a mix of large oligopolistic firms (a 40–60% concentration ratio) and several highly innovative smaller firms. The technical characteristics of an industry, however, may be a more important factor influencing R&D than its market structure.

7. Technological advance enhances **economic efficiency.**

a. *Process innovation* improves productive efficiency by increasing the productivity of inputs and reducing average total costs.

b. *Product innovation* enhances allocative efficiency by giving society a more preferred mixture of goods and services.

(1) The efficiency gain from innovation, however, can be reduced if patents and the advantages of being first lead to monopoly power.

(2) Monopoly power can be reduced or destroyed by innovation because it provides competition where there was none.

c. Innovation may foster **creative destruction,** whereby the creation of new products and production methods simultaneously destroys the monopoly positions of firms protecting existing products and methods. This view is expressed by Joseph Schumpeter, and there are many examples of it in business history. Another view suggests that creative destruction is not inevitable or automatic. In general, innovation improves economic efficiency, but in some cases it can increase monopoly power.

8. (Last Word). The history of the development of the modern computer and the Internet are examples of technological advance. This Last Word chronicles the developments and changes from 1945–2007.

■ **HINTS AND TIPS**

1. The section of the chapter on a firm's **optimal amount of R&D** uses marginal-cost and marginal-benefit analysis similar to what you saw in previous chapters. In this case, the interest rate or expected return is graphed on the vertical axis and the amount of R&D spending on the horizontal axis. The only difference from previous MB-MC graphs is that the marginal cost in this example is assumed to be constant at the given interest rate. *It is graphed as a horizontal line.* The expected-rate-of-return curve is downward sloping because there are fewer opportunities for R&D expenditures with higher expected rates of return than at lower expected rates of return.

2. The explanation for how new products gain acceptance by consumers is based on the marginal utility theory that you learned about in Chapter 7. Be sure to review the text discussion of Table 7.1 before reading about the example in Table 11W.1.

3. When new processes are developed, they can increase a firm's total product curve and decrease a firm's average total cost curve. Review the section in Chapter 8, "Shifting the Cost Curves," to understand these points.

■ IMPORTANT TERMS

technological advance	venture capital
very long run	interest-rate cost-of-funds curve
invention	
patent	expected-rate-of-return curve
innovation	optimal amount of R&D
product innovation	imitation problem
process innovation	fast-second strategy
diffusion	inverted-U theory of R&D
start-ups	creative destruction

SELF-TEST

■ FILL-IN QUESTIONS

1. Technological advance is a three-step process of

a. _____

b. _____

c. _____

2. The first discovery of a product or process is (innovation, invention) _____, whereas the first commercial introduction of a new product or process is _____; patent protection is available for (invention, innovation) _____ but not _____. The spread of an innovation through imitation or copying is (trademarking, diffusion) _____.

3. The development of new or improved products is (process, product) _____ innovation; the development of new or improved production or distribution methods is _____ innovation.

4. The traditional view of technological advance was that it was (internal, external) _____ to the economy, but the modern view is that technological advance is _____. In the modern view, technological advance arises from (scientific progress, rivalry among firms) _____, but the traditional view holds that it arises from _____ that is largely

(internal, external) _____ to the market system.

5. The individual who is an initiator, innovator, and risk bearer who combines resources in unique ways to produce new goods and services is called an (entrepreneur, intrapreneur) _____, but an individual who promotes entrepreneurship within existing corporations is called an _____. Entrepreneurs tend to form (large, small) _____ companies called start-ups, and if they are successful they will receive _____ monetary rewards.

6. Past successes often give entrepreneurs access to (more, less) _____ resources for further innovation because the market economy (punishes, rewards) _____ those businesses that meet consumer wants.

7. To earn the greatest profit from R&D spending, the firm should expand the activity until its marginal benefit is (greater than, less than, equal to) _____ its marginal cost, but a firm should cut back its R&D if its marginal benefit is _____ its marginal cost.

8. Five ways a firm can obtain funding to finance R&D spending are

a. _____

b. _____

c. _____

d. _____

e. _____

9. Product innovation will tend to increase a firm's profit by increasing the (costs, revenues) _____ of the firm; process innovation will tend to increase a firm's profit by reducing the (costs, revenues) _____ of the firm.

10. Consumer acceptance of a new product depends on its marginal utility (and, or) _____ its price. The expected return that motivates product innovation (is, is not) _____ always realized. Most product innovations are (major, minor) _____ improvements to existing products.

11. Process innovation results in a shift (downward, upward) _____ in the firm's total product curve and a shift _____ in the firm's average-total-cost curve, which in turn (increases, decreases) _____ the firm's profit.

12. The imitation problem occurs when rivals of a firm copy or emulate the firm's product or process and thus (increase, decrease) _____ the innovator's profit from the R&D effort. When a dominant firm quickly imitates the successful new product of smaller competitors with the goal of becoming the second firm to adopt the innovation, it is using a (second-best, fast-second) _____ strategy.

13. An example of legal protection for taking the lead in innovation would be (copyrights, trade secrets) _____, but a nonlegal advantage might come from (patents, learning by doing) _____.

14. In regard to R&D, purely competitive firms tend to be (less, more) _____ complacent than monopolists, but the expected rate of return for a pure competitor may be (high, low) _____, and they (may, may not) _____ be able to finance R&D.

15. Monopolistically competitive firms have a (weak, strong) _____ profit incentive to develop and differentiate products, but they have (extensive, limited) _____ ability to obtain inexpensive R&D financing, and it is (difficult, easy) _____ for these firms to extract large profits because the barriers to entry are relatively (high, low) _____.

16. The size of oligopolistic firms makes them (capable, incapable) _____ of promoting technological advance, but there is (much, little) _____ reason for them to introduce costly new technology and new products when they earn (small, large) _____ economic profit without doing it.

17. Pure monopoly has a (strong, weak) _____ incentive to engage in R&D because its high profit is protected by (low, high) _____ barriers to entry. This type of firm views R&D spending as (an offensive, a defensive) _____ move to protect the monopoly from new products that would undercut its monopoly position.

18. Inverted-U theory suggests that R&D effort is at best (strong, weak) _____ in industries with very low and very high concentrations. The optimal industry structure for R&D is one in which expected returns on R&D spending are (low, high) _____ and funds are readily available and inexpensive to finance R&D. This generally occurs in industries with (many, a few) _____ firms that are absolutely and relatively large, but the concentration ratio is not so high as to limit strong competition by smaller firms.

19. Technological advance increases the productivity of inputs, and by reducing average total costs it enhances (allocative, productive) _____ efficiency; when it gives society a more preferred mixture of goods and services it enhances _____ efficiency. The efficiency gain from innovation can be (increased,

decreased) _____ if patents and the advantages of being first lead to monopoly power, but it can be _____ if innovation provides competition where there was none.

20. Innovation may foster creative destruction, where the (destruction, creation) _____ of new products and production methods simultaneously leads to the _____ of the monopoly positions of firms committed to existing products and methods. Another view, however, suggests that creative destruction (is, is not) _____ automatic. In general, innovation improves economic efficiency, but in some cases it can increase monopoly power.

■ **TRUE–FALSE QUESTIONS**

Circle T if the statement is true, F if it is false.

1. Technological advance consists of new and improved goods and services and new and improved production or distribution processes.　　　　　　**T F**

2. In economists' models, technological advance occurs in the short run, not the long run.　　　　**T F**

3. Invention is the first successful commercial introduction of a new product.　　　　　　　**T F**

4. Firms channel a majority of their R&D expenditures to innovation and imitation rather than to basic scientific research.　　　　　　　　　　**T F**

5. Historically, most economists viewed technological advance as a predictable and internal force to which the economy adjusted.　　　　　　　**T F**

6. The modern view of economists is that capitalism is the driving force of technological advance and such advance occurs in response to profit incentives within the economy.　　　　　　　　　　**T F**

7. The entrepreneur is an innovator but not a risk bearer.　　　　　　　　　　　**T F**

8. Start-ups are small companies focused on creating and introducing a new product or using a new production or distribution technique.　　　　　　**T F**

9. The only innovators are entrepreneurs.　　**T F**

10. The market entrusts the production of goods and services to businesses that have consistently succeeded in fulfilling consumer wants.　　　　　**T F**

11. Research and development rarely occur outside the labs of major corporations.　　　　　**T F**

12. When entrepreneurs use personal savings to finance the R&D for a new venture, the marginal cost of financing is zero.　　　　　　　　　　**T F**

13. The optimal amount of R&D spending for the firm occurs where its expected return is greater than its interest-rate cost-of-funds to finance it.　　　　　**T F**

14. Most firms are guaranteed a profitable outcome when making an R&D expenditure because the decisions are carefully evaluated.　　**T　F**

15. A new product succeeds when it provides consumers with higher marginal utility per dollar spent than do existing products.　　**T　F**

16. Most product innovations consist of major changes to existing products and are not incremental improvements.　　**T　F**

17. Process innovation increases the firm's total product, lowers its average total cost, and increases its profit.　　**T　F**

18. Imitation poses no problems for innovators because there are patent and trademark protections for their innovations.　　**T　F**

19. A fast-second strategy involves letting the dominant firm set the price of the product and then smaller firms quickly undercutting that price.　　**T　F**

20. Pure competition is the best market structure for encouraging R&D and innovation.　　**T　F**

21. One major shortcoming of monopolistic competition in promoting technological progress is its limited ability to secure inexpensive financing for R&D.　　**T　F**

22. The inverted-U theory of R&D suggests that R&D effort is strongest in very low-concentration industries and weakest in very high-concentration industries.　　**T　F**

23. The technical and scientific characteristics of an industry may be more important than its structure in determining R&D spending and innovation.　　**T　F**

24. Technological advance enhances productive efficiency but not allocative efficiency.　　**T　F**

25. Creative destruction is the process the inventor goes through in developing new products and innovations.　　**T　F**

■ **MULTIPLE-CHOICE QUESTIONS**

Circle the letter that corresponds to the best answer.

1. The period in which technology can change and in which firms can introduce entirely new products is the
   (a) short run
   (b) very short run
   (c) long run
   (d) very long run

2. Technological progress is a three-step process of
   (a) creation, pricing, and marketing
   (b) invention, innovation, and diffusion
   (c) manufacturing, venturing, and promotion
   (d) start-ups, imitation, and creative destruction

3. The first discovery of a product or process through the use of imagination, ingenious thinking, and experimentation and the first proof that it will work is
   (a) process innovation
   (b) product innovation
   (c) creative destruction
   (d) invention

4. An exclusive right to sell any new and useful process, machine, or product for a set number of years is called a
   (a) trademark
   (b) copyright
   (c) patent
   (d) brand

5. Innovation is a major factor in competition because it can
   (a) be patented to protect the investment of the developers
   (b) enable firms to make competitors' products obsolete
   (c) guarantee the monopoly position of innovative firms
   (d) reduce research and development costs for firms

6. What idea is best illustrated by the example of McDonald's successfully introducing the fast-food hamburger and then that idea being adopted by other firms such as Burger King and Wendy's?
   (a) start-ups
   (b) diffusion
   (c) invention
   (d) fast-second strategy

7. About what percentage of GDP in the United States is spent on research and development?
   (a) 2.6%
   (b) 7.6%
   (c) 10.6%
   (d) 21.2%

8. The modern view of technological advance is that it is
   (a) rooted in the independent advancement of science
   (b) best stimulated through government R&D spending
   (c) a result of intense rivalry among individuals and firms
   (d) a random outside force to which the economy adjusts

9. The major difference between entrepreneurs and other innovators is
   (a) innovators work in teams, but entrepreneurs do not
   (b) innovators manage start-ups, but entrepreneurs do not
   (c) entrepreneurs bear personal financial risk, but innovators do not
   (d) entrepreneurs invent new products and processes, but innovators do not

10. Past successes in developing products often mean that entrepreneurs and innovative firms
   (a) have access to more private resources for further innovation
   (b) have access to less private resources for further innovation
   (c) have access to more public support for further innovation
   (d) experience no change in the availability of private or public resources for further innovation

Questions 11, 12, and 13 are based on the following table showing the expected rate of return, R&D spending, and interest-rate cost of funds for a hypothetical firm.

Expected rate of return (%)	R&D (millions of $)	Interest-rate cost of funds (%)
15	20	9
13	40	9
11	60	9
9	80	9
7	100	9

11. In a supply and demand graph, the interest-rate cost-of-funds curve would be a(n)
(a) vertical line at 9%
(b) horizontal line at 9%
(c) upward sloping line over the 15 to 7% range
(d) downward sloping line over the 15 to 7% range

12. The optimal amount of R&D would be
(a) $40 million
(b) $60 million
(c) $80 million
(d) $100 million

13. If the interest-rate cost-of-funds curve rose to 13%, the optimal amount of R&D spending would be
(a) $40 million
(b) $60 million
(c) $80 million
(d) $100 million

14. Product innovation tends to increase the profits of firms primarily by
(a) decreasing the firm's average costs
(b) increasing the firm's total revenue
(c) decreasing marginal utility per dollar spent
(d) increasing the success of R&D spending

15. Consumers will buy a new product only if
(a) it has a lower marginal utility per dollar spent than another product
(b) there is a substantial budget for promotion and marketing
(c) it can be sold at a lower price than that for a competing product
(d) it increases the total utility they obtain from their limited income

16. Process innovation produces a(n)
(a) downward shift in the total-product curve and an upward shift in the average-cost curve
(b) upward shift in the total-product curve and a downward shift in the average-cost curve
(c) upward shift in both the total-product and average-cost curves
(d) downward shift in both the total-product and average-cost curves

17. Some dominant firms in an industry use a fast-second strategy that involves
(a) developing two products to compete with rivals
(b) cutting the development time for the introduction of a new product
(c) moving quickly to buy the second largest firm in the industry to gain larger market share
(d) letting smaller firms initiate new products and then quickly imitating the success

18. One legal protection for taking the lead in innovation is
(a) venture capital
(b) trademarks
(c) trade secrets
(d) mergers

19. One major advantage of being the first to develop a product is the
(a) use of the fast-second strategy
(b) increase in retained earnings
(c) lower interest-rate costs of funds
(d) potential for profitable buyouts

20. Which firm has a strong incentive for product development and differentiation?
(a) a monopolistically competitive firm
(b) a purely competitive firm
(c) an oligopolistic firm
(d) a pure monopoly

21. In which market structure is there the least incentive to engage in R&D?
(a) a monopolistically competitive firm
(b) a purely competitive firm
(c) an oligopolistic firm
(d) a pure monopoly

22. The inverted-U theory of R&D suggests that R&D effort is at best weak in
(a) low-concentration industries only
(b) high-concentration industries only
(c) low- and high-concentration industries
(d) low- to middle-concentration industries

23. The optimal market structure for technological advance seems to be an industry in which there
(a) are many purely competitive firms
(b) are monopolists closely regulated by government
(c) is a mix of large oligopolistic firms with several small and highly innovative firms
(d) is a mix of monopolistically competitive firms and a few large monopolists in industries with high capital costs

24. Technological advance as embodied in process innovation typically
(a) decreases allocative efficiency
(b) increases allocative efficiency
(c) decreases productive efficiency
(d) increases productive efficiency

25. Why did Joseph Schumpeter view capitalism as a process of "creative destruction"?
(a) Innovation would lead to monopoly power and thus destroy the economy.
(b) The creation of new products and production methods would destroy the market for existing products.

(c) Invention would create new products, but diffusion would destroy many potentially good ideas.

(d) Firms are being creative with learning by doing, but this spirit is destroyed by the inability of firms to finance R&D expenditures.

■ **PROBLEMS**

1. Match the terms with the phrases using the appropriate number.

1. invention   **2.** innovation   **3.** diffusion

a. Imitation of the DaimlerChrysler Corporation's Jeep Grand Cherokee with sport utility vehicles developed by other auto companies _____

b. The first working model of the microchip _____

c. Computers and word processing software that eliminated the need for typewriters _____

d. Adoption of Alamo's offer of unlimited mileage by other major car rental companies _____

e. The creation of the first electric light bulb _____

f. Development of iPhones by Apple _____

2. Use the following table that shows the rate of return and R&D spending for a hypothetical firm.

Expected rate of return (%)	R&D (millions of $)
24	3
20	6
16	8
12	12
9	15
6	18
3	21

a. Assume the interest-rate cost of funds is 12%. The optimal amount of R&D expenditures will be $_____ million. At this amount, the marginal cost of R&D spending is _____% and the marginal benefit (the expected rate of return) is _____%.

b. Graph the expected-rate-of-return and the interest-rate cost-of-fund curves of R&D spending in the graph at the top of the next column. Be sure to label the axes.

c. Now assume that the interest-rate cost of funds falls to 6%. The optimal amount of spending will be $_____ million. For this amount of R&D spending, the marginal cost of R&D spending is _____% and the marginal benefit (expected rate of return) is _____%.

d. Show on the graph how the interest-rate cost-of-funds curve changed in the answer that you gave for **b.**

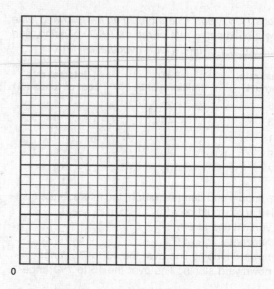

0

3. Following are two average-total-cost schedules for a firm. The first schedule (ATC$_1$) shows the cost of producing the product at five levels of output before a new innovation. The second schedule (ATC$_2$) shows the average total cost at the five output levels after the innovation.

Output	Before ATC$_1$	After ATC$_2$
10	$30	$27
20	25	18
30	18	14
40	22	19
50	28	26

a. Plot the average-cost curves for the schedules on the following graph.

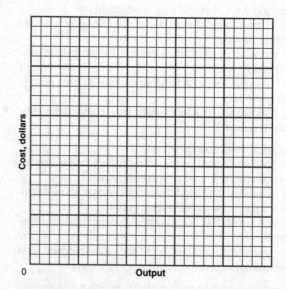

Cost, dollars

0   Output

b. What was the reduction in average total cost at each of the five levels of output as a result of the innovation? 10 _____, 20 _____,

30 _____, 40 _____, 50 _____.

c. If the product price is $20 per unit and the firm was producing at 30 units of output, the profit for the firm before the innovation was $_____. At this level of output, the profit after the innovation was $_____.

■ **SHORT ANSWER AND ESSAY QUESTIONS**

1. Give a definition of technological advance. According to economists, what role does time play in the definition?

2. Explain and give examples of invention. What does government do to protect it?

3. How does innovation differ from invention and diffusion? How does innovation affect competition among firms?

4. Compare and contrast the modern view of technological advance with the traditional view.

5. In what ways do entrepreneurs differ from other innovators? In what types of business does each tend to work? How have the characteristics of entrepreneurs changed over time?

6. What does it mean that "innovators try to anticipate the future"? What are the economic consequences of this effort?

7. Why do entrepreneurs and other innovators actively study the scientific output of universities and government laboratories?

8. What are the many different sources of funding to finance firms' R&D expenditures? If an entrepreneur uses personal funds, is there a cost for financing?

9. Explain how the firm decides on the optimal amount of research and development. Use a marginal-cost and marginal-benefit graph in your explanation.

10. Why might many R&D expenditures be affordable but not worthwhile? Are outcomes from R&D guaranteed?

11. Describe how a firm's revenues and profits are increased through product innovation. Why does consumer acceptance of a new product depend on both its marginal utility and price?

12. Explain how process innovation reduces cost and increases profits. Illustrate the point graphically using a total-product and average-cost curve graph.

13. Describe the fast-second strategy and give an example of it.

14. What is the imitation problem resulting from technological advance?

15. Describe the legal protections and potential advantages of taking the lead in innovation.

16. Compare and contrast the suitability of different market structures for fostering technological advance.

17. Explain the basic conclusions from inverted-U theory of R&D. What will be the optimal market structure for technological progress?

18. How does technological advance enhance economic efficiency? Distinguish between its effects on productive efficiency and allocative efficiency.

19. How might innovation create or reduce monopoly power? Why might both effects be possible?

20. Explain the idea of creative destruction as championed by Joseph Schumpeter. What are the objections to that idea?

ANSWERS

Chapter 11 Web Technology, R&D, and Efficiency

FILL-IN QUESTIONS

1. *a.* invention; *b.* innovation; *c.* diffusion
2. invention, innovation, invention, innovation, diffusion
3. product, process
4. external, internal, rivalry among firms, scientific progress, external
5. entrepreneur, intrapreneur, small, large
6. more, rewards
7. equal to, less than
8. *a.* bank loans; *b.* bonds; *c.* retained earnings; *d.* venture capital; *e.* personal savings (any order *a–e*)
9. revenues, costs
10. and, is not, minor
11. upward, downward, increases
12. decrease, fast-second
13. copyrights, learning by doing
14. less, low, may not
15. strong, limited, difficult, low
16. capable, little, large
17. weak, high, a defensive
18. weak, high, a few
19. productive, allocative, decreased, increased
20. creation, destruction, is not

Note: Page numbers for True–False, Multiple Choice, and Short Answer and Essay Questions refer to Bonus Web Chapter 11.

TRUE–FALSE QUESTIONS

1. T, pp. 1–2	**10.** T, p. 5	**19.** F, p. 10
2. F, p. 2	**11.** F, p. 5	**20.** F, p. 13
3. F, p. 2	**12.** F, p. 6	**21.** T, p. 13
4. T, p. 3	**13.** F, pp. 7–8	**22.** F, p. 14
5. F, pp. 3–4	**14.** F, p. 8	**23.** T, pp. 14–15
6. T, pp. 3–4	**15.** T, p. 9	**24.** F, p. 15
7. F, p. 4	**16.** F, p. 9	**25.** F, p. 15
8. T, p. 4	**17.** T, pp. 9–10	
9. F, p. 4	**18.** F, p. 10	

MULTIPLE-CHOICE QUESTIONS

1. d, p. 2	**10.** a, pp. 4–5	**19.** d, pp. 11–12
2. b, pp. 2–3	**11.** b, p. 6	**20.** a, p. 13
3. d, p. 2	**12.** c, pp. 7–8	**21.** d, p. 14
4. c, p. 2	**13.** a, pp. 7–8	**22.** c, p. 14
5. b, p. 2	**14.** b, pp. 8–9	**23.** c, pp. 14–15
6. b, pp. 2–3	**15.** d, pp. 8–9	**24.** d, p. 15
7. a, p. 3	**16.** b, pp. 9–10	**25.** b, p. 15
8. c, pp. 3–4	**17.** d, p. 10	
9. c, p. 4	**18.** b, p. 11	

PROBLEMS

1. *a.* 3; *b.* 1; *c.* 2; *d.* 3; *e.* 1; *f.* 2

2. *a.* 12, 12, 12; *b.* similar to Figure 11 W.4 in the text; *c.* 18, 6, 6; *d. horizontal* interest-rate-cost-of-funds curve will drop from 12 to 6%

3. *a.* Put output on the horizontal axis, and put average cost on the vertical axis. Plot the set of points. Connect the set with lines; *b.* 3, 7, 4, 3, 2; *c.* Before: TR is $600 (30 × $20), TC is $540 (30 × $18), profit is $60; After: TR is $600, TC is $420 (30 × $14), profit is $180

SHORT ANSWER AND ESSAY QUESTIONS

1. pp. 1–2	**8.** pp. 5–6	**15.** pp. 10–12
2. p. 2	**9.** pp. 7–8	**16.** pp. 13–14
3. pp. 2–3	**10.** p. 8	**17.** p. 14
4. pp. 3–4	**11.** pp. 8–9	**18.** p. 15
5. p. 4	**12.** pp. 9–10	**19.** p. 15
6. pp. 4–5	**13.** p. 10	**20.** pp. 15–17
7. p. 5	**14.** p. 10	

CHAPTER 12

The Demand for Resources

This chapter is the first of three that examine the market for economic resources such as labor, capital, land, and natural resources. In resource markets the demanders are the employers of the resources and the suppliers are the owners of the resources. As you already know, the demand for and the supply of a resource will determine the resource price and the quantities in a competitive market.

Chapter 12 focuses on the demand or employer side of the resource market. It offers a general explanation of what determines demand for any resource. Chapters 13 and 14 discuss the characteristics of the market for particular resources—labor, capital, land, or entrepreneurial ability—and present the supply side of the resource market.

The **resource market is important** for several reasons, as you will learn in the first section of the chapter. Resource prices determine what resource owners (or households) receive in exchange for supplying their resources, and thus they determine the incomes of households. Prices allocate resources to their most efficient uses and encourage the least costly methods of production in our economy. Many public policy issues also involve resource pricing, such as setting a minimum wage.

The next section of the chapter focuses on the **marginal productivity theory of resource demand.** When a firm wishes to maximize its profits, it produces that output at which marginal revenue and marginal cost are equal. But how much of each resource does the firm hire if it wishes to maximize its profits? You will learn that the firm hires that amount of each resource up to the point that the marginal revenue product and the marginal resource cost of that resource are equal (MRP = MRC).

There is another similarity between the output and the resource markets for the firm. Recall that the competitive firm's supply curve is a portion of its marginal-cost curve. The purely competitive firm's demand curve for a resource is a portion of its marginal-revenue-product curve. Just as cost is the important determinant of supply, the revenue derived from the use of a resource is the important factor determining the demand for that resource in a competitive market for resources.

The next major section of the chapter presents the **determinants of resource demand.** Three major ones are discussed—changes in product demand, productivity, and the prices of other resources. The last one is the most complicated because you must consider whether the other resources are substitutes or complements and also the underlying factors affecting them.

This chapter has a section on the **elasticity of resource demand,** which is no different from the elasticity concept you learned about in Chapter 6. In this case, it is the relation of the percentage change in quantity demanded of the resource to a percentage change in the price of the resource. As you will discover, three factors that affect elasticity are the availability of other substitute resources, the elasticity of product demand, and the ratio of resource cost to total cost.

Most of the chapter examines the situation in which there is only one variable resource. The next-to-last section of the chapter, however, offers a general perspective on the **combination of resources** the firm will choose to use when multiple inputs are used and all inputs are variable. Two rules are presented. The least-cost rule states that the firm will minimize costs when the last dollar spent on each resource results in the same marginal product. The profit-maximizing rule means that in a competitive market the firm will maximize its profits when each resource is used so that its marginal product is equal to its price. The second rule is equally important because a firm that employs the quantity of resources that maximizes its profits also produces the output that maximizes its profits and is thus producing at the least cost.

The marginal productivity theory of resource demand is not without criticism, as you will learn in the last section of the chapter. If resource prices reflect marginal productivity, then this relationship can produce income inequality in society. In addition, market imperfection may skew the distribution of income.

■ **CHECKLIST**

When you have studied this chapter you should be able to

☐ Present four reasons for studying resource pricing.
☐ Explain why the demand for an economic resource is a derived demand.
☐ Define the marginal revenue product and relate it to the productivity and price of a resource.
☐ Determine the marginal-revenue-product schedule of a resource for a product sold in a purely competitive market, when given the data.
☐ Define the marginal resource cost.
☐ State the rule used by a profit-maximizing firm to determine how much of a resource it will employ.

☐ Apply the MRP = MRC rule to determine the quantity of a resource a firm will hire, when you are given the necessary data.

☐ Explain why the marginal-revenue-product schedule of a resource is the firm's demand for the resource.

☐ Find the marginal-revenue-product schedule of a resource for a product sold in an imperfectly competitive market, when given the data.

☐ Derive the market demand for a resource.

☐ List the three factors which would change a firm's demand for a resource.

☐ Predict the effect on resource demand of an increase or decrease in one of its three determinants.

☐ Give trends on the occupations with the fastest growth in jobs both in percentage terms and in absolute numbers.

☐ State three determinants of the price elasticity of resource demand.

☐ Describe how a change in each determinant would change the price elasticity of demand for a resource.

☐ State the rule used by a firm for determining the least-cost combination of resources.

☐ Use the least-cost rule to find the least-cost combination of resources for production, when given data.

☐ State the rule used by a profit-maximizing firm to determine the quantity of each of several resources to employ.

☐ Apply the profit-maximizing rule to determine the quantity of each resource a firm will hire, when given the data.

☐ Explain the marginal productivity theory of income distribution.

☐ Give two criticisms of the marginal productivity theory of income distribution.

☐ Explain using the least-cost rule why ATMs have replaced tellers (Last Word).

■ **CHAPTER OUTLINE**

1. The study of what determines the prices of resources *is important* because resource prices influence the size of individual incomes and the resulting distribution of income. They allocate scarce resources and affect the way in which firms combine resources in production. Resource pricing also raises policy and ethical issues about income distribution.

2. The marginal productivity theory of resource demand assumes that the firm is a "price taker" or "wage taker" in the resource market.

   a. The demand for a single resource is a *derived demand* that depends on the demand for the goods and services it can produce.

   b. Because resource demand is a derived demand, it depends on two factors: the marginal productivity of the resource and the market price of the good or service it is used to produce.

   (1) *Marginal revenue product (MRP)* is the change in total revenue divided by a one-unit change in resource quantity.

   (2) It combines two factors—the *marginal product* (the additional output from each additional unit of

resource) of a resource and the market price of the product it produces—into a single useful tool.

   c. *Marginal resource cost (MRC)* is the change in total resource cost divided by a one-unit change in resource quantity. A firm will hire resources until the marginal revenue product of the resource is equal to its marginal resource cost (*MRP = MRC*).

   d. The firm's marginal-revenue-product schedule for a resource is that firm's demand schedule for the resource.

   e. If a firm sells its output in an **imperfectly competitive product market,** the more the firm sells, the lower the price of the product becomes. This causes the firm's marginal-revenue-product (resource demand) schedule to be less elastic than it would be if the firm sold its output in a purely competitive market.

   f. The market (or total) demand for a resource is the horizontal summation of the demand schedules of all firms using the resource.

3. The **determinants of resource demand** are changes in the demand for the product produced, changes in the productivity of the resource, and changes in the prices of other resources.

   a. A change in the demand for a product produced by a resource will change the demand of a firm for labor in the same direction.

   b. A change in the productivity of a resource will change the demand of a firm for the resource in the same direction.

   c. A change in the price of a

   (1) *substitute resource* will change the demand for a resource in the same direction if the *substitution effect* outweighs the *output effect* and in the opposite direction if the output effect outweighs the substitution effect

   (2) *complementary resource* will change the demand for a resource in the opposite direction

   d. Changes in the demand for labor have significant effects on employment growth in occupations, both in percentage and absolute terms. Projections (2006–2016) are reported for the fastest growing occupations (e.g., network systems and data communication analysts; home health aides) and the most rapidly declining occupations (e.g., photographic processing machine operators; file clerks).

4. The price *elasticity of resource demand* measures the sensitivity of resource quantity to changes in resource prices.

   a. Three factors affect the price elasticity of resource demand:

   (1) the ease of substitution of other resources: the greater the substitutability of other resources, the more elastic the resource demand

   (2) the elasticity of the demand for the product that the resource produces: the more elastic the product demand, the more elastic the resource demand

   (3) the ratio of labor cost to total cost: the greater the ratio of labor cost to total cost, the greater the price elasticity of demand for labor.

5. Firms often employ more than one resource in producing a product.

a. The firm employing resources in purely competitive markets is hiring resources in the *least-cost combination of resources* when the ratio of the marginal product of a resource to its price is the same for all the resources the firm hires.

b. The firm is hiring resources in the *profit-maximizing combination of resources* if it hires resources in a purely competitive market when the marginal revenue product of each resource is equal to the price of that resource.

c. A numerical example illustrates the least-cost and profit-maximizing rules for a firm that employs resources in purely competitive markets.

6. The *marginal productivity theory of income distribution* seems to result in an equitable distribution of income because each unit of a resource receives a payment equal to its marginal contribution to the firm's revenue. The theory has at least two serious faults.

a. The distribution of income will be unequal because resources are unequally distributed among individuals in the economy.

b. The income of those who supply resources will not be based on their marginal productivities if there is monopsony or monopoly in the resource markets of the economy.

7. (Last Word). ATMs have eliminated many human teller positions over the past few decades as explained by the resource theory presented in this chapter. The least-cost combination of resources rule implies that firms will change inputs in response to technological change or changes in input prices. If the marginal product of an ATM divided by its price is greater than the marginal product of a human teller divided by its price, then more ATMs will be used in the banking sector.

■ HINTS AND TIPS

1. The list of important terms for Chapter 12 is relatively short, but included in the list are two very important concepts—**marginal revenue product** and **marginal resource cost**—which you must grasp if you are to understand how much of a resource a firm will hire. These two concepts are similar to, but not identical with, the marginal-revenue and marginal-cost concepts used in the study of product markets and in the explanation of the quantity of output a firm will produce.

2. Marginal revenue and marginal cost are, respectively, the change in the firm's total revenue and the change in the firm's total cost when it produces and sells an additional unit of *output*. Marginal revenue product and marginal resource cost are, respectively, the change in the firm's total revenue and the change in the firm's total cost when it hires an additional unit of *input*. Note that the two new concepts deal with changes in revenue and costs as a consequence of hiring more of a *resource*.

3. The marginal revenue product (MRP) of a resource is simply the marginal product of the resource (MP) times the price of the product that the resource produces (P), or MRP = MP $\times$ P. Under pure competition, MP changes, but P is constant as more resources are added to production. Under imperfect competition, both MP and P change as more resources are added, and thus each variable (MP and P) affects MRP. Compare the data in Tables 12.1 and 12.2 in the textbook to see this difference.

4. Make sure you understand the rule **MRP = MRC**. A firm will hire one more unit of a resource only so long as the resource adds more to the firm's revenues than it does to its costs. If MRP > MRC, the firm will hire more resources. If MRP < MRC, the firm will cut back on resource use.

5. It can be difficult to figure out what outcome will result from a change in the price of a substitute resource (capital) on the demand for another resource (labor). It is easy to understand why the demand for labor might decrease if the price of capital decreases because cheaper capital would be substituted for labor. It is harder to explain why the opposite might be true. That insight requires an understanding of both the **substitution effect** and the **output effect**. Find out how one effect may offset the other.

6. The **profit-maximizing rule** for a combination of resources may seem difficult, but it is relatively simple. Just remember that the price of any resource must be equal to its marginal revenue product, and thus *the ratio must always equal 1.*

■ IMPORTANT TERMS

derived demand	elasticity of resource demand
marginal product	
marginal revenue product (MRP)	least-cost combination of resources
marginal resource cost (MRC)	profit-maximizing combination of resources
MRP = MRC rule	marginal productivity theory of income distribution
substitution effect	
output effect	

SELF-TEST

■ FILL-IN QUESTIONS

1. Resource prices allocate (revenues, resources) _____ and are one factor that determines household (incomes, costs) _____ and business _____.

2. The demand for a resource is a (constant, derived) _____ demand that depends on the (productivity, cost) of the resource and the (cost, price) _____ of the product made from the resource.

3. A firm will find it profitable to hire units of a resource up to the quantity at which the marginal revenue (cost, product) _____ equals the marginal resource _____.

4. If the firm hires the resource in a purely competitive market, the marginal resource (cost, product) _____ will be (greater than, less than, equal to) _____ the price of the resource.

5. A firm's demand schedule for a resource is the firm's marginal revenue (cost, product) _____ schedule for that resource because both indicate the quantities of the resource the firm will employ at various resource (costs, prices) _____.

6. A producer in an imperfectly competitive market finds that the more of a resource it employs, the (higher, lower) _____ becomes the price at which it can sell its product. As a consequence, the (supply, demand) _____ schedule for the resource is (more, less) _____ elastic than it would be if the output were sold in a purely competitive market.

7. Adding the quantity demanded for the resource at each and every price for each firm using the resource gives the market (supply, demand) _____ curve for the resource.

8. The demand for a resource will change if the (demand, supply) _____ of the product the resource produces changes, if the (productivity, price) _____ of the resource changes, or if the (price, elasticity) _____ of other resources change.

9. If the demand for a product increases, then the demand for the resource that produces that product will (increase, decrease) _____. Conversely, if the demand for a product decreases, then the demand for the resource that produces that product will _____.

10. When the productivity of a resource falls, the demand for the resource (rises, falls) _____, but when the productivity of a resource rises, the demand for the resource _____.

11. The output of the firm being constant, a decrease in the price of resource A will induce the firm to hire (more, less) _____ of resource A and _____ of other resources; this is called the (substitution, output) _____ effect. But if the decrease in the price of A results in lower total costs and an increase in output, the firm may hire (more, less) _____ of both resources; this is called the (substitution, output) _____ effect.

12. A decrease in the price of a complementary resource will cause the demand for labor to (increase, decrease) _____, but an increase in the price of a complementary resource will cause the demand for labor to _____.

13. The three determinants of the price elasticity of demand for a resource are the ease with which other resources can be (substitutes, complements) _____ for it, the price elasticity of (supply, demand) _____ for the product the resource produces, and the ratio of resource (demand, cost) _____ to total (demand, cost) _____.

14. If the marginal product of labor declines slowly when added to a fixed stock of capital, the demand curve for labor (MRP) will decline (rapidly, slowly) _____ and will tend to be highly (elastic, inelastic) _____.

15. The greater the substitutability of other resources for a resource, the (greater, less) _____ will be the elasticity of demand for a resource.

16. Suppose a firm employs resources in purely competitive markets. If the firm wishes to produce any given amount of its output in the least costly way, the ratio of the marginal (cost, product) _____ of each resource to its (demand, price) _____ must be the same for all resources.

17. A firm that hires resources in purely competitive markets is employing the combination of resources that will result in maximum profits for the firm when the marginal (revenue product, resource cost) _____ of every resource is equal to its (demand, price) _____.

18. If the marginal revenue product of a resource is equal to the price of that resource, the marginal revenue product divided by its price is equal to (1, infinity) _____.

19. In the marginal productivity theory, the distribution of income is an equitable one because each unit of each resource is paid an amount equal to its (total, marginal) _____ contribution to the firm's (revenues, costs) _____.

20. The marginal productivity theory rests on the assumption of (competitive, imperfect) _____ markets. In the real world, there are many labor markets with imperfections because of employer pricing or monopoly power, so wage rates and other resource prices (do, do not) _____ perfectly measure contributions to domestic output.

■ **TRUE–FALSE QUESTIONS**

Circle T if the statement is true, F if it is false.

1. In the resource markets of the economy, resources are demanded by business firms and supplied by households.   **T F**

2. The prices of resources are an important factor in the determination of resource allocation.   **T F**

3. The demand for a resource is a derived demand based on the demand for the product it produces. **T F**

4. A resource that is highly productive will always be in great demand. **T F**

5. A firm's demand schedule for a resource is the firm's marginal-revenue-product schedule for the resource. **T F**

6. It will be profitable for a firm to hire additional units of labor resources up to the point where the marginal revenue product of labor is equal to its marginal resource cost. **T F**

7. A firm with one worker can produce 30 units of a product that sells for $4 a unit, but the same firm with two workers can produce 70 units of that product. The marginal revenue product of the second worker is $400. **T F**

8. The competitive firm's marginal revenue product of labor will fall as output expands because marginal product diminishes and product price falls. **T F**

9. A producer's demand schedule for a resource will be more elastic if the firm sells its product in a purely competitive market than it would be if it sold the product in an imperfectly competitive market. **T F**

10. The market demand for a particular resource is the sum of the individual demands of all firms that employ that resource. **T F**

11. An increase in the price of a resource will cause the demand for the resource to decrease. **T F**

12. The demand curve for labor will increase when the demand for (and price of) the product produced by that labor increases. **T F**

13. There is an inverse relationship between the productivity of labor and the demand for labor. **T F**

14. The demand for a resource will be increased with improvements in its quality. **T F**

15. When two resources are substitutes for each other, both the substitution effect and the output effect of a decrease in the price of one of these resources operate to increase the quantity of the other resource employed by the firm. **T F**

16. The output effect of an increase in the price of a resource increases the quantity demanded of that resource. **T F**

17. If two resources are complementary, an increase in the price of one will reduce the demand for the other. **T F**

18. Price declines for computer equipment have had stronger output effects than substitution effects, increasing the demand for computer software engineers and specialists. **T F**

19. The greater the substitutability of other resources, the less will be the elasticity of demand for a particular resource. **T F**

20. The greater the elasticity of product demand, the greater the elasticity of resource demand. **T F**

21. The demand for labor will be less elastic when labor is a smaller proportion of the total cost of producing a product. **T F**

Use the following information as the basis for answering Questions 22 and 23. The marginal revenue product and price of resource A are $12 and a constant $2, respectively, and the marginal revenue product and price of resource B are $25 and a constant $5, respectively. The firm sells its product at a constant price of $1.

22. The firm should decrease the amount of A and increase the amount of B it employs if it wishes to decrease its total cost without affecting its total output. **T F**

23. If the firm wishes to maximize its profits, it should increase its employment of both A and B until their marginal revenue products fall to $2 and $5, respectively. **T F**

24. The marginal productivity theory of income distribution results in an equitable distribution if resource markets are competitive. **T F**

25. The marginal productivity theory rests on the assumption of imperfectly competitive markets. **T F**

■ MULTIPLE-CHOICE QUESTIONS

Circle the letter that corresponds to the best answer.

1. The prices paid for resources affect
(a) the money incomes of households in the economy
(b) the allocation of resources among different firms and industries in the economy
(c) the quantities of different resources employed to produce a particular product
(d) all of the above

2. In a competitive resource market, the firm employing a resource such as labor is a
(a) price maker
(b) cost maker
(c) wage taker
(d) revenue taker

3. The demand for a resource is *derived* from the
(a) demand for the products it helps produce
(b) price of the resource
(c) supply of the resource
(d) income of the firm selling the resource

4. The law of diminishing returns explains why
(a) the MRP of an input in a purely competitive market decreases as a firm increases the quantity of an employed resource
(b) the MRC of an input in a purely competitive market decreases as a firm increases the quantity of an employed resource
(c) resource demand is a derived demand
(d) there are substitution and output effects for resources

Answer Questions 5, 6, and 7 on the basis of the information in the following table for a purely competitive market.

Number of workers	Total product	Product price ($)
0	0	4
1	16	4
2	26	4
3	34	4
4	40	4
5	44	4

5. At a wage rate of $15, the firm will choose to employ
(a) 2 workers
(b) 3 workers
(c) 4 workers
(d) 5 workers

6. At a wage rate of $30, the firm will choose to employ
(a) 2 workers
(b) 3 workers
(c) 4 workers
(d) 5 workers

7. If the product price increases to a constant $8, then at a wage rate of $30, the firm will choose to employ
(a) 2 workers
(b) 3 workers
(c) 4 workers
(d) 5 workers

Use the following total-product and marginal-product schedules for a resource to answer Questions 8, 9, 10, and 11. Assume that the quantities of other resources the firm employs remain constant.

Units of resource	Total product	Marginal product
0	0	—
1	8	8
2	14	6
3	18	4
4	21	3
5	23	2

8. If the product the firm produces sells for a constant $3 per unit, the marginal revenue product of the fourth unit of the resource is
(a) $3
(b) $6
(c) $9
(d) $12

9. If the firm's product sells for a constant $3 per unit and the price of the resource is a constant $15, the firm will employ how many units of the resource?
(a) 2
(b) 3
(c) 4
(d) 5

10. If the firm can sell 14 units of output at a price of $1 per unit and 18 units of output at a price of $0.90 per

unit, the marginal revenue product of the third unit of the resource would be
(a) $4
(b) $3.60
(c) $2.20
(d) $0.40

11. If the firm can sell 8 units at a price of $1.50, 14 units at a price of $1.00, 18 units at a price of $0.90, 21 units at a price of $0.70, and 23 units at a price of $0.50, then the firm is
(a) maximizing profits at a product price of $0.50
(b) minimizing its costs at a product price of $1.00
(c) selling in an imperfectly competitive market
(d) selling in a purely competitive market

12. As a firm that sells its product in an imperfectly competitive market increases the quantity of a resource it employs, the marginal revenue product of that resource falls because
(a) the price paid by the firm for the resource falls
(b) the marginal product of the resource falls
(c) the price at which the firm sells its product falls
(d) both the marginal product and the price at which the firm sells its product fall

13. Which would increase a firm's demand for a particular resource?
(a) an increase in the prices of complementary resources used by the firm
(b) a decrease in the demand for the firm's product
(c) an increase in the productivity of the resource
(d) an increase in the price of the particular resource

14. The substitution effect indicates that a firm will use
(a) more of an input whose relative price has decreased
(b) more of an input whose relative price has increased
(c) less of an input whose relative price has decreased
(d) less of an input whose relative price has remained constant

15. Suppose resource A and resource B are substitutes and the price of A increases. If the output effect is greater than the substitution effect,
(a) the quantity of A employed by the firm will increase and the quantity of B employed will decrease
(b) the quantities of both A and B employed by the firm will decrease
(c) the quantities of both A and B employed by the firm will increase
(d) the quantity of A employed will decrease and the quantity of B employed will increase

16. Two resource inputs, capital and labor, are complementary and used in fixed proportions. A decrease in the price of capital will
(a) increase the demand for labor
(b) decrease the demand for labor
(c) decrease the quantity demanded for labor
(d) have no effect because the relationship is fixed

17. Which would result in an increase in the elasticity of demand for a particular resource?
(a) an increase in the demand for the resource
(b) a decrease in the elasticity of demand for the product that the resource helps to produce
(c) an increase in the percentage of the firm's total costs accounted for by the resource
(d) a decrease in the ease of resource substitutability for the particular resource

18. The demand for labor would most likely become more inelastic as a result of
(a) an increase in the elasticity of the demand for the product that the labor produces
(b) an increase in the time for employers to make technological changes or purchase new equipment
(c) a decrease in the proportion of labor costs to total costs
(d) a decrease in the demand for the product

19. A firm is allocating its expenditures for resources in a way that will result in the least total cost of producing any given output when the
(a) amount the firm spends on each resource is the same
(b) marginal revenue product of each resource is the same
(c) marginal product of each resource is the same
(d) marginal product per dollar spent on the last unit of each resource is the same

20. A business is employing inputs such that the marginal product of labor is 20 and the marginal product of capital is 45. The price of labor is $10 and the price of capital is $15. If the business wants to minimize costs while keeping output constant, then it should
(a) use more labor and less capital
(b) use less labor and less capital
(c) use less labor and more capital
(d) make no change in resource use

21. Assume that a computer disk manufacturer is employing resources so that the MRP of the last unit hired for resource X is $240 and the MRP of the last unit hired for resource Y is $150. The price of resource X is $80 and the price of resource Y is $50. To maximize profit the firm should
(a) hire more of resource X and less of resource Y
(b) hire less of resource X and more of resource Y
(c) hire less of both resource X and resource Y
(d) hire more of both resource X and resource Y

22. Which does not suggest that a firm that hires resources in a purely competitive market is maximizing its profits?
(a) The marginal revenue product of every resource is equal to 1.
(b) The marginal revenue product of every resource is equal to its price.
(c) The ratio of the marginal revenue product of every resource to its price is equal to 1.
(d) The ratio of the price of every resource to its marginal revenue product is equal to 1.

23. Assume that a purely competitive firm uses two resources—labor (**L**) and capital (**C**)—to produce a product. In which situation would the firm be maximizing profit?

	MRP$_L$	MRP$_C$	P$_L$	P$_C$
(a)	10	20	30	40
(b)	10	20	10	20
(c)	15	15	10	10
(d)	30	40	10	5

24. In the marginal productivity theory of income distribution, when all markets are purely competitive, each unit of each resource receives a money payment equal to
(a) its marginal product
(b) its marginal revenue product
(c) the needs of the resource owner
(d) the payments received by each of the units of the other resources in the economy

25. A major criticism of the marginal productivity theory of income distribution is that
(a) the demand for labor resources is price elastic
(b) labor markets are often subject to imperfect competition
(c) the theory suggests that there will be equality in incomes
(d) purely competitive firms are only interested in profit maximization

■ **PROBLEMS**

1. The table below shows the total production a firm will be able to obtain if it employs varying amounts of resource **A** while the amounts of the other resources the firm employs remain constant.

Quantity of resource A employed	Total product	Marginal product of A	Total revenue	Marginal revenue product of A
0	0		$_____	
1	12	_____	_____	$_____
2	22	_____	_____	_____
3	30	_____	_____	_____
4	36	_____	_____	_____
5	40	_____	_____	_____
6	42	_____	_____	_____
7	43	_____	_____	_____

a. Compute the marginal product of each of the seven units of resource **A** and enter these figures in the table.
b. Assume the product the firm produces sells in the market for $1.50 per unit. Compute the total revenue of the firm at each of the eight levels of output and the marginal revenue product of each of the seven units of resource **A.** Enter these figures in the table below.
c. On the basis of your computations, complete the firm's demand schedule for resource **A** by indicating in the following table how many units of resource **A** the firm would employ at the given prices.

Price of A	Quantity of A demanded
$21.00	_____
18.00	_____
15.00	_____
12.00	_____
9.00	_____
6.00	_____
3.00	_____
1.50	_____

2. In the table below are the marginal product data for resource **B.** Assume that the quantities of other resources employed by the firm remain constant.

a. Compute the total product (output) of the firm for each of the seven quantities of resource **B** employed and enter these figures in the table.
b. Assume that the firm sells its output in an imperfectly competitive market and that the prices at which it can sell its product are those given in the table. Compute and enter in the table:

(1) the total revenue for each of the seven quantities of **B** employed.
(2) the marginal revenue product of each of the seven units of resource **B.**
c. How many units of **B** would the firm employ if the market price of **B** were

(1) $25? _____
(2) $20? _____
(3) $15? _____
(4) $9? _____
(5) $5? _____
(6) $1? _____

3. Use the following total-product schedule as a resource to answer questions **a, b,** and **c.** Assume that the quantities of other resources the firm employs remain constant.

Units of resource	Total product
0	0
1	15
2	28
3	38
4	43
5	46

a. If the firm's product sells for a constant $2 per unit, what is the marginal revenue product of the second unit of the resource? _____
b. If the firm's product sells for a constant $2 and the price of the resource is $10, how many units of the resource will the firm employ? _____
c. If the firm can sell 15 units of output at a price of $2.00 and 28 units of output at a price of $1.50, what is the marginal revenue product of the second unit of the resource? _____

4. In the space to the right of each of the following changes, indicate whether the change would tend to increase (+) or decrease (−) a firm's demand for a particular resource.
a. An increase in the demand for the firm's product _____
b. A decrease in the price of the firm's output _____
c. An increase in the productivity of the resource _____
d. An increase in the price of a substitute resource when the output effect is greater than the substitution effect _____
e. A decrease in the price of a complementary resource _____
f. A decrease in the price of a substitute resource when the substitution effect is greater than the output effect _____

Quantity of resource B employed	Marginal product of B	Total product	Product price	Total revenue	Marginal revenue product of B
0	—	0		$0.00	—
1	22	_____	$1.00	_____	_____
2	21	_____	.90	_____	_____
3	19	_____	.80	_____	_____
4	16	_____	.70	_____	_____
5	12	_____	.60	_____	_____
6	7	_____	.50	_____	_____
7	1	_____	.40	_____	_____

Quantity of resource C employed	Marginal product of C	Marginal revenue product of C	Quantity of Resource D employed	Marginal product of D	Marginal revenue product of D
1	10	$5.00	1	21	$10.50
2	8	4.00	2	18	9.00
3	6	3.00	3	15	7.50
4	5	2.50	4	12	6.00
5	4	2.00	5	9	4.50
6	3	1.50	6	6	3.00
7	2	1.00	7	3	1.50

5. The above table shows the marginal-product and marginal-revenue-product schedules for resource **C** and resource **D**. Both resources are variable and are employed in purely competitive markets. The price of **C** is $2 and the price of **D** is $3. (Assume that the productivity of each resource is independent of the quantity of the other.)

a. The least-cost combination of **C** and **D** that would enable the firm to produce

(1) units of its product is _____ **C** and _____ **D**.

(2) 99 units of its product is _____ **C** and _____ **D**.

b. The profit-maximizing combination of **C** and **D** is

_____ **C** and _____ **D**.

c. When the firm employs the profit-maximizing combination of **C** and **D**, it is also employing **C** and **D** in

the least-cost combination because _____

equals _____.

d. Examination of the figures in the table reveals that

the firm sells its product in a _____ com-

petitive market at a price of $_____.

e. Employing the profit-maximizing combination of **C** and **D**, the firm's

(1) total output is _____.

(2) total revenue is $_____.

(3) total cost is $_____.

(4) total profit is $_____.

■ **SHORT ANSWER AND ESSAY QUESTIONS**

1. Give four reasons why it is important to study resource pricing.

2. How does the demand for a product differ from the demand for a resource? Explain why the demand for a resource is a derived demand.

3. What two factors determine the strength of the demand for a resource?

4. Explain why firms that wish to maximize their profits follow the MRP = MRC rule.

5. What effects do marginal product and marginal price have on a firm's resource demand curve under pure competition and under imperfect competition?

6. Why is the demand schedule for a resource less elastic when the firm sells its product in an imperfectly competitive market than when it sells it in a purely competitive market?

7. How do you derive the market demand for a resource?

8. Identify and describe three factors that will cause the demand for a resource to increase or decrease. Give examples of how each factor influences changes in demand.

9. What is the difference between the substitution effect and the output effect?

10. If the price of capital falls, what will happen to the demand for labor if capital and labor are substitutes in production? Describe what happens when the substitution effect outweighs the output effect and when the output effect outweighs the substitution effect. What can you conclude?

11. Why does a change in the price of a complementary resource cause the demand for labor to change in the opposite direction?

12. Describe trends in occupational employment data. Give examples of jobs with the greatest projected growth and decline.

13. What are the three factors that determine the elasticity of demand for a resource?

14. Use an example to explain what happens to elasticity when substitutability for a resource is greater rather than lesser.

15. How can the ratio of labor cost to the total cost influence how producers react to changes in the price of labor?

16. Assume that a firm employs resources in purely competitive markets. How does the firm know that it is spending money on resources in such a way that it can produce a given output for the least total cost?

17. Why is minimizing cost not sufficient for maximizing profit for a firm?

18. When is a firm that employs resources in purely competitive markets using these resources in amounts that will maximize the profits of the firm?

19. What is the marginal productivity theory of income distribution? What ethical proposition must be accepted if this distribution is to be fair and equitable?

20. What are the two major shortcomings of the marginal productivity theory of income distribution?

ANSWERS

Chapter 12 The Demand for Resources

FILL-IN QUESTIONS

1. resources, incomes, costs
2. derived, productivity, price
3. product, cost
4. cost, equal to
5. product, prices
6. lower, demand, less
7. demand
8. demand, productivity, price
9. increase, decrease
10. falls, rises
11. more, less, substitution, more, output
12. increase, decrease
13. substitutes, demand, cost, cost
14. slowly, elastic
15. greater
16. product, price
17. revenue product, price
18. 1
19. marginal, revenues
20. competitive, do not

TRUE–FALSE QUESTIONS

1. T, p. 252	14. T, pp. 257–258
2. T, p. 253	15. F, p. 258
3. T, p. 253	16. F, p. 258
4. F, pp. 253–254	17. T, pp. 258–259
5. T, p. 254	18. T, pp. 258–259
6. T, p. 254	19. F, pp. 260–261
7. F, p. 254	20. T, pp. 260–261
8. F, p. 254	21. T, pp. 260–261
9. T, pp. 254–256	22. F, pp. 263–264
10. T, pp. 256–257	23. T, pp. 262–263
11. F, p. 257	24. F, pp. 264–265
12. T, p. 257	25. F, pp. 264–265
13. F, pp. 257–258	

MULTIPLE-CHOICE QUESTIONS

1. d, p. 253	14. a, p. 258
2. c, p. 253	15. b, p. 258
3. a, p. 253	16. a, pp. 258–259
4. a, pp. 253–254	17. c, pp. 260–261
5. d, pp. 254–255	18. c, pp. 260–261
6. b, pp. 254–255	19. d, p. 262
7. d, pp. 254–255	20. c, pp. 263–264
8. c, pp. 254–255	21. d, p. 264
9. a, pp. 254–255	22. a, p. 264
10. c, pp. 254–255	23. b, pp. 263–264
11. c, pp. 254–255	24. b, pp. 264–265
12. d, pp. 255–256	25. b, pp. 264–265
13. c, pp. 257–258	

PROBLEMS

1. *a.* Marginal product of A: 12, 10, 8, 6, 4, 2, 1; *b.* Total revenue: 0, 18.00, 33.00, 45.00, 54.00, 60.00, 63.00, 64.50; Marginal revenue product of A: 18.00, 15.00, 12.00, 9.00, 6.00, 3.00, 1.50; *c.* 0, 1, 2, 3, 4, 5, 6, 7

2. *a.* Total product: 22, 43, 62, 78, 90, 97, 98; *b.* (1) Total revenue: 22.00, 38.70, 49.60, 54.60, 54.00, 48.50, 39.20, (2) Marginal revenue product of B: 22.00, 16.70, 10.90, 5.00, −0.60, −5.50, −9.30; *c.* (1) 0, (2) 1, (3) 2, (4) 3, (5) 4, (6) 4

3. *a.* $26. The second worker increases TP by 13 units (13 × $2 = $26); *b.* 4 units. The marginal product of the fourth resource is 5 units of output (5 × $2 = $10). Thus MRP = $10 and MRC = $10 when the fourth resource is employed; *c.* $12. The total revenue from 1 unit is $30.00 (15 × $2.00). The total revenue with 2 units is $42 (28 × $1.50). The difference is the MR of the second unit.

4. *a.* +; *b.* −; *c.* +; *d.* −; *e.* +; *f.* −

5. *a.* (1) 1, 3, (2) 3, 5; *b.* 5, 6; *c.* the marginal product of **C** divided by its price, the marginal product of **D** divided by its price; *d.* purely, $.50; *e.* (1) 114, (2) $57, (3) $28, (4) $29

SHORT ANSWER AND ESSAY QUESTIONS

1. p. 253	11. pp. 258–259
2. p. 253	12. pp. 259–260
3. pp. 253–254	13. pp. 260–261
4. p. 254	14. p. 261
5. pp. 254–256	15. p. 261
6. pp. 255–256	16. p. 262
7. pp. 256–257	17. p. 262
8. pp. 257–259	18. pp. 262–264
9. p. 258	19. pp. 264–265
10. p. 258	20. pp. 264–265

CHAPTER 13

Wage Determination

The preceding chapter explained the demand for any resource in a competitive resource market. Chapter 13 uses demand and supply analysis to describe what determines the quantity of a particular resource—**labor**—and the price paid for it—**wages**—in different markets.

The chapter begins by defining terms and briefly discussing the general level of wages in the United States and other advanced economies. You will learn about the role that productivity plays in explaining the long-run growth of real wages and the increased demand for labor over time.

In a product market, the degree of competition significantly influences how prices are determined and what output is produced. In a labor resource market, the degree of competition directly affects the determination of **wage rates** and the level of employment. The main purpose of the chapter is to explain how wage rates and the quantity of labor are determined in labor markets varying in competitiveness.

Six labor markets are discussed in the chapter: (1) the **purely competitive** market, in which the number of employers is large and labor is nonunionized; (2) the **monopsony** market, in which a single employer hires labor under competitive (nonunion) conditions; (3) a market in which a union controls the supply of labor, the number of employers is large, and the union attempts to increase the total demand for labor; (4) a similar market in which the union attempts to reduce the total supply of labor; (5) another similar market in which the union attempts to obtain a wage rate that is above the competitive-equilibrium level by threatening to strike; and (6) the **bilateral monopoly** market, in which a single employer faces a labor supply controlled by a single union.

What is important for you to learn is how the characteristics of each labor market affect wage rates and employment. In the purely competitive or monopsony labor market, there is no union. The determination of the wage rate and employment will be quite definite, although different for each market. In the next four types of labor markets, **unions** control the supply of labor, and thus the outcomes for wage rates and employment will be less definite. If the demand for labor is competitive, the wage rate and the amount of employment will depend on how successful the union is in increasing the demand for labor, restricting the supply of labor, or setting a wage rate that employers will accept. If there is both a union and one employer (a bilateral monopoly), wages and employment will fall within certain limits, but exactly where will depend on the bargaining power of the union or the employer.

Three other issues are discussed in the last three sections of the chapter. First, for many years the Federal government has set a legal **minimum wage** for labor. The chapter uses supply and demand analysis to make the case for and against the minimum wage and then discusses its real-world effects. Second, wage rates are not homogeneous and differ across workers and occupations. The chapter presents important reasons why these **wage differentials** exist. Third, there is a **principal–agent problem** in most types of employment that may lead to shirking on the job. Different pay schemes have been devised to tie workers' pay to performance in an effort to overcome this problem. Each of these issues should be of direct interest to you and deepen your understanding about how labor markets work.

■ CHECKLIST

When you have studied this chapter you should be able to

☐ Define wages (or the wage rate).

☐ Distinguish between nominal and real wages.

☐ List five reasons for high productivity in the United States and other advanced economies.

☐ Describe the long-run relationship between real wages and productivity in the United States.

☐ Evaluate the importance of the two factors contributing to the long-run trend of growth in U.S. real wages.

☐ Define the three characteristics of a purely competitive labor market.

☐ Use demand and supply graphs to explain wage rates and the equilibrium level of employment in a purely competitive labor market.

☐ Define the three characteristics of a labor market monopsony and compare it with a purely competitive labor market.

☐ Explain why the marginal resource cost exceeds the wage rate in monopsony.

☐ Use demand and supply graphs to explain wage rates and the equilibrium level of employment in the monopsony model.

☐ Give examples of monopsony power.

☐ List three types of union models.

☐ Identify two strategies of labor unions to increase the demand for labor and their effects on wage rates and employment.

☐ Explain and illustrate graphically the effects of actions taken by craft unions to decrease the supply of labor on wages and the employment of workers.

☐ Explain and illustrate graphically how the organization of workers by an industrial union in a previously competitive labor market would affect the wage rate and the employment level.

☐ Describe the effect of unions on wage increases and union employment.

☐ Use a graph to explain why the equilibrium wage rate and employment level are indeterminate when a labor market is a bilateral monopoly and to predict the range for the wage rate.

☐ Present the case for and the case against a legally established minimum wage.

☐ Use supply and demand analysis to explain wage differentials.

☐ Connect wage differentials to marginal revenue productivity.

☐ Give two reasons why noncompeting groups of workers earn different wages.

☐ Explain why some wage differentials are due to compensatory differences in the nonmonetary aspects of jobs.

☐ Cite four types of labor market imperfections that contribute to wage differentials.

☐ Describe the principal–agent problem in worker pay and performance.

☐ Describe four pay schemes employers use to prevent shirking or to tie worker pay to performance.

☐ Explain the negative side effects of pay-for-performance schemes.

☐ Evaluate from an economic perspective the issue of whether chief executive officers (CEOs) of corporations are overpaid (Last Word).

■ **CHAPTER OUTLINE**

1. A *wage* (or the *wage rate*) is the price paid per unit of time for any type of labor. Earnings are equal to the wage multiplied by the amount of time worked. Wages can be measured either in nominal or real terms. A *real wage* is adjusted for the effects of inflation. It reflects the quantity of goods and services a worker can purchase with a *nominal wage.*

2. The **general level of real wages** in the United States and other advanced economies is high because the demand for labor has been large relative to the supply of labor.

   a. The demand for labor in the United States and advanced economies has been strong because labor is highly productive for several reasons: substantial quantities of capital goods and natural resources; technological advancement; improvements in labor quality; and other intangible factors (management techniques, business environment, and size of the domestic market).

   b. The real hourly wage rate and output per hour of labor are closely and directly related to each other, and real income per worker can increase only at the same rate as output per worker (productivity).

   c. The long-run trend shows that real wages have increased because increases in the demand for labor

over time have been greater than increases in the supply of labor in the United States.

3. In a *purely competitive labor market* many firms compete in hiring a specific type of labor and there are many qualified workers with identical skills who independently supply this labor. Both firms and workers are "wage takers" who do not influence the price of labor.

   a. The market *demand curve* for labor is a horizontal summation of the demand curves for individual firms.

   b. The market *supply curve* slopes upward, indicating that a higher wage will entice more workers to supply their labor.

   c. The *wage rate* for labor in this market is determined by the interaction of the market demand for and the supply of that labor. For the individual firm, the supply of labor is perfectly elastic at this wage rate (so the marginal labor cost is equal to the wage rate). The firm will hire the amount of labor at which its marginal revenue product of labor is equal to its marginal labor cost.

4. In a *monopsony* market for labor, there is only one buyer of a particular kind of labor, the labor is relatively immobile, and the hiring firm is a "wage maker" (the wage rate a firm pays varies with the number of workers it employs).

   a. The supply curve is upsloping and indicates that the firm (the single buyer of labor) must pay higher wages to attract more workers.

   b. A monopsonistic firm's marginal labor costs are greater than the wage rates it must pay to obtain various amounts of labor because once it offers a higher wage to one worker, it must offer the same wage to all workers.

   c. The firm hires the amount of labor at which marginal labor cost and the marginal revenue product of labor are equal. Both the wage rate and the level of employment are less than they would be under purely competitive conditions in labor markets.

   (1) Note that if the firm employs resources in imperfectly competitive markets, it is hiring resources in the least-cost combination when the ratio of the marginal product of a resource to its marginal resource cost is the same for all resources.

   (2) it is hiring resources in the most profitable combination when the marginal revenue product of each resource is equal to its marginal resource cost.

   d. Monopsony power can be found in such situations as small cities where there are one or two firms that hire most of the workers of a particular type in a region or in professional sports franchises that have exclusive rights to obtain the service of professional athletes.

5. In labor markets in which **labor unions** represent workers, the unions attempt to raise wages in three ways.

   a. The union can increase *the demand for labor* by increasing the demand for the products the union workers produce through political lobbying. They also can increase demand by increasing the prices of resources that are substitutes for the labor provided by the members of the union or by reducing the price of a complementary resource.

b. With *exclusive unionism*, a **craft union** will seek to increase wages by reducing the supply of labor. *Occupational licensing* is another means of restricting the supply of a particular type of labor.

c. With *inclusive unionism* an industrial union will try to increase wages by forcing employers to pay wages in excess of the equilibrium rate that would prevail in a purely competitive labor market.

d. Labor unions are aware that their actions to increase wage rates may also increase the unemployment of their members, which tends to limit the demands for higher wages.

6. A *bilateral monopoly* is a labor market with a monopsony (single buyer of labor) and an inclusive union (single seller of labor).

a. In this situation, the wage rate depends, within certain limits, on the relative bargaining power of the union and of the employer.

b. This model may be desirable because the monopoly power on the buy side is offset by the monopoly power on the sell side. The resulting wage rate may be close to levels found in purely competitive markets.

7. The *minimum wage* is a price floor that has been used to set a minimum price for unskilled labor.

a. Critics argue that it increases wage rates and reduces the employment of workers. It is a poor policy for reducing household poverty because the benefits largely go to teenagers who do not need the assistance.

b. Defenders think that in a monopsonistic market, it can increase the wage rate and employment. A minimum wage also may increase productivity, thus increasing the demand for labor and reducing labor turnover.

c. The evidence is mixed. In theory, a higher wage should reduce employment, but in practice the negative effects on employment may be minor or nil. The minimum wage, however, is not a strong antipoverty policy, despite its popular appeal in this respect.

8. *Wage differentials* are found across many occupations. They are often explained by the forces of demand and supply.

a. The strength of the demand for workers in an occupation, given the supply of workers, is due largely to the productivity of workers and the revenues they generate for the firm (or *marginal revenue productivity*).

b. One major reason for wage differentials is that workers are not homogeneous and can be thought of as falling into many *noncompeting groups.* The wages for each group differ because of

(1) differences in the abilities or skills possessed by workers, the number of workers in each group, and the demand for those abilities or skills in the labor market

(2) the stock of knowledge and skills people have, called *human capital.* Investment in human capital by workers through education and training can lead to higher future wages.

c. A second reason for wage differentials is that jobs vary in difficulty and attractiveness, so there are *compensating differences.* Higher wages may be necessary to compensate for less desirable nonmonetary aspects of some jobs.

d. A third reason for wage differentials is market imperfections. These arise from a lack of job information, geographic immobilities, union or government restraints, and discrimination.

9. Wage payments in labor markets are often more complex in practice and are often designed to make a connection between **worker pay and performance.**

a. A principal–agent problem arises when the interests of agents (workers) diverge from the interests of the principals (firms). For example, shirking on the job can occur if workers give less than the desired level of performance for pay received.

b. Firms can try to reduce shirking by monitoring worker activity, but this monitoring is costly; therefore, *incentive pay plans* are adopted by firms to tie worker compensation more closely to performance. Among the various incentive schemes are

(1) piece rate payments, commissions, royalties, bonuses, and profit sharing plans

(2) efficiency wages that pay workers above-market wages to get greater effort.

c. Sometimes the "solutions" to principal–agent problems lead to negative results. Commissions may cause employees to pad bills; changes in work rules may demoralize workers.

10. (Last Word). The basic argument for why CEOs are highly paid is related to market conditions. On the supply side, there is a restrictive supply of corporate talent to provide leadership and direction. On the demand side, there is a high demand for individuals who have the qualities necessary to make the major managerial decisions and lead corporations. These market conditions of limited supply and high demand explain the high salaries. In addition, becoming a CEO has the elements of a game or tournament. The fact that there is a prize for winning will encourage intense competition and increase productivity. Critics of CEO payment think corporate boards that set CEO pay are too controlled by the CEO and these board members overvalue CEO work.

■ **HINTS AND TIPS**

1. The reason why the market supply curve for labor rises in competitive markets is based on an economic concept from Chapter 2 that you may want to review. To obtain more workers, firms must increase wages to cover the **opportunity cost** of workers' time spent on other alternatives (other employment, household work, or leisure).

2. In monopsony, the marginal resource cost exceeds the wage rate (and the marginal-resource-cost curve lies above the supply curve of labor). The relationship is difficult to understand, so you should pay careful attention to the discussion of Table 13.2 and Figure 13.4.

3. To illustrate the differences in the three union models presented in this chapter, draw supply and demand graphs of each model.

4. The chapter presents the positive economic explanations for the differences in wages between occupations. Remember that whether these wage differentials are "fair" is a normative question. (See Chapter 1 for the positive and normative distinction.)

■ IMPORTANT TERMS

wage rate	bilateral monopoly
nominal wages	minimum wage
real wages	wage differentials
purely competitive labor market	marginal revenue productivity
monopsony	noncompeting groups
exclusive unionism	human capital
occupational licensing	compensating differences
inclusive unionism	incentive pay plan

SELF-TEST

■ FILL-IN QUESTIONS

1. The price paid for labor per unit of time is the (piece, wage) _____ rate. The earnings of labor are equal to the _____ rate (divided, multiplied) _____ by the amount of time worked. The amount of money received per hour or day by a worker is the (nominal, real) _____ wage, while the purchasing power of that money is the _____ wage.

2. The general level of wages is high in the United States and other advanced economies because the demand for labor in these economies is (weak, strong) _____ relative to the supply of labor. United States labor tends to be highly productive, among other reasons, because it has access to relatively large amounts of (consumer, capital) _____ goods, plentiful (financial, natural) _____ resources, a high-quality (service sector, labor force) _____, and superior (wages, technology) _____. There is a close (short-run, long-run) _____ relationship between output per labor hour and real hourly wages in the United States.

3. In a purely competitive labor market,
a. the supply curve slopes upward from left to right because it is necessary for employers to pay (higher, lower) _____ wages to attract workers from alternative employment. The market supply curve rises because it is an (average cost, opportunity cost) _____ curve.

b. the demand is the sum of the marginal (revenue product, resource cost) _____ schedules of all firms hiring this type of labor.

c. the wage rate will equal the rate at which the total quantity of labor demanded is (less than, equal to, greater than) _____ the total quantity of labor supplied.

4. Insofar as an individual firm hiring labor in a purely competitive market is concerned, the supply of labor is perfectly (elastic, inelastic) _____ because the individual firm is unable to affect the wage rate it must pay. The firm will hire that quantity of labor at which the wage rate, or marginal labor cost, is (less than, equal to, greater than) _____ the marginal revenue product.

5. A monopsonist employing labor in a market that is competitive on the supply side will hire that amount of labor at which the marginal revenue product is (less than, equal to, greater than) _____ marginal labor cost. In such a market, the marginal labor cost is (less, greater) _____ than the wage rate, so the employer will pay a wage rate that is _____ than both the marginal revenue product of labor and the marginal labor cost.

6. A monopsonist facing a competitive supply of labor
a. is employing the combination of resources that enables it to produce any given output in the least costly way when the marginal product of every resource (divided, multiplied) _____ by its marginal resource cost is the same for all resources.

b. is employing the combination of resources that maximizes its profits when the marginal revenue product of every resource is (equal to, greater than) _____ its marginal resource cost or when the marginal revenue product of each resource (divided, multiplied) _____ by its marginal resource cost is equal to (infinity, 1) _____.

7. When compared with a competitive labor market, a market dominated by a monopsonist results in (higher, lower) _____ wage rates and in (more, less) _____ employment.

8. The basic objective of labor unions is to increase wages, and they attempt to accomplish this goal either by increasing the (demand for, supply of) _____ labor, restricting the _____ labor, or imposing (a below, an above) _____-equilibrium wage rate on employers.

9. Labor unions can increase the demand for the services of their members by increasing the (demand for, supply of) _____ the products they produce, by (increasing, decreasing) _____ the prices of resources that are substitutes for the services supplied by their members, and by (increasing, decreasing) _____ the price of a complementary resource used to produce a product.

10. Restricting the supply of labor to increase wages is the general policy of (exclusive, inclusive) _____ unionism, and imposing above-equilibrium wage rates is the strategy used in _____ unionism. An example of exclusive unionism is (an industrial, a craft) _____ union, while an example of inclusive unionism would be _____ union.

11. If unions are successful in increasing wages, employment in the industry will (increase, decrease) _____, but this effect on members may lead unions to _____ their wage demands. Unions, however, will not worry too much about the effect on employment from the higher wage rates if the economy is growing or if the demand for labor is relatively (elastic, inelastic) _____.

12. In a labor market that is a bilateral monopoly, the monopsonist will try to pay a wage (less, greater) _____ than the marginal revenue product of labor; the union will ask for some wage _____ than the competitive and monopsonist equilibrium wage. Within these limits, the (wage rate, elasticity) _____ of labor will depend on the relative bargaining strength of the union and the monopsonist.

13. Critics of the minimum wage contend that in purely competitive labor markets, the effect of imposing such a wage is to (increase, decrease) _____ the wage rate and to _____ employment. Defenders of the minimum wage argue that such labor markets are monopsonistic, so the effect is to (increase, decrease) _____ the wage rate and to _____ employment. The evidence suggests that the employment and antipoverty effects from increasing the minimum wage are (positive, uncertain) _____.

14. Actual wage rates received by different workers tend to differ because workers (are, are not) _____ homogeneous, jobs (vary, do not vary) _____ in attractiveness, and labor markets may be (perfect, imperfect) _____.

15. The total labor force is composed of a number of (competing, noncompeting) _____ groups of workers. Wages differ among these groups as a consequence of differences in (ability, wealth) _____ and because of different investments in (the stock market, human capital) _____.

16. Within each of these noncompeting groups, some workers receive higher wages than others to compensate these workers for the less desirable (monetary, nonmonetary) _____ aspects of a job. These wage differentials are called (monopsony, compensating) _____ differences.

17. Workers performing identical jobs often receive different wages due to market imperfections such as lack of information about (investment, job) _____ opportunities, geographic (mobility, immobility) _____, union or government (subsidies, restraints) _____, and (taxes, discrimination) _____.

18. Firms, or parties, who hire others to achieve their objectives may be regarded as (agents, principals) _____, while workers, or parties, who are hired to advance firms' interests can be regarded as the firms' _____. The objective of a firm is to maximize (wages, profits) _____ and workers are hired to help a firm achieve that objective in return for _____, but when the interests of a firm and the workers diverge, a principal–agent problem is created.

19. An example of this type of problem is a situation in which workers provide less than the agreed amount of work effort on the job, which is called (licensure, shirking) _____. To prevent this situation, firms can closely monitor job (pay, performance) _____, but this is costly; therefore, many firms offer different incentive _____ plans.

20. Examples of such pay-for-performance schemes include (efficiency, piece) _____ rate payments, commissions and royalties, bonuses and profit sharing, and _____ wages, which means that workers are paid above equilibrium wages to encourage greater work effort. Such plans must be designed with care because of possible (positive, negative) _____ side effects.

■ **TRUE–FALSE QUESTIONS**

Circle T if the statement is true, F if it is false.

1. If you received a 5% increase in your nominal wage and the price level increased by 3%, then your real wage has increased by 8%. **T F**

2. The general level of wages is high in the United States and other advanced economies because the supply of labor is large relative to the demand for it. **T F**

3. One reason for the high productivity of labor in the United States and other advanced economies is access to large amounts of capital equipment. **T F**

4. Real hourly compensation per worker can increase only at about the same rate as output per worker. **T F**

5. In a purely competitive labor market, there are few qualified workers who supply labor and few firms who employ labor. **T F**

6. If an individual firm employs labor in a purely competitive market, it finds that its marginal labor cost is equal to the wage rate in that market.   **T   F**

7. Given a purely competitive employer's demand for labor, a lower wage will result in more workers being hired.   **T   F**

8. Both monopsonists and firms hiring labor in purely competitive markets hire labor up to the quantity at which the marginal revenue product of labor and marginal labor cost are equal.   **T   F**

9. Political lobbying for special projects or legislation is used by unions to increase the demand for labor.   **T   F**

10. One strategy unions use to bolster the demand for union workers is to lobby against a higher minimum wage for nonunion workers.   **T   F**

11. Restricting the supply of labor is a means of increasing wage rates more commonly used by craft unions than by industrial unions.   **T   F**

12. Occupational licensing is a means of increasing the supply of specific kinds of labor.   **T   F**

13. Unions that seek to organize all available or potential workers in an industry are called craft unions.   **T   F**

14. The imposition of an above-equilibrium wage rate will cause employment to fall off more when the demand for labor is inelastic than it will when the demand is elastic.   **T   F**

15. Union members are paid wage rates that on the average are greater by about 15% than the wage rates paid to nonunion members.   **T   F**

16. The actions of both exclusive and inclusive unions that raise the wage rates paid to them by competitive employers of labor also cause, other things remaining constant, an increase in the employment of their members.   **T   F**

17. In a bilateral monopoly, the negotiated wage will be below the competitive equilibrium wage in that labor market.   **T   F**

18. If a labor market is purely competitive, the imposition of an effective minimum wage will increase the wage rate paid and decrease employment in that market.   **T   F**

19. If an effective minimum wage is imposed on a monopsonist, the wage rate paid by the firm will increase and the number of workers employed by it may also increase.   **T   F**

20. The strength of labor demand differs greatly among occupations due to differences in how much each occupation contributes to its employer's revenue.   **T   F**

21. Actual wage rates received in different labor markets tend to differ because the demands for particular types of labor relative to their supplies differ.   **T   F**

22. Wage differentials that are used to compensate workers for unpleasant aspects of a job are called efficiency wages.   **T   F**

23. Market imperfections that impede workers from moving from lower- to higher-paying jobs help explain wage differentials.   **T   F**

24. Shirking is an example of a principal–agent problem.   **T   F**

25. There are examples of solutions that have been implemented to solve principal–agent problems that produce negative results.   **T   F**

■ MULTIPLE-CHOICE QUESTIONS

Circle the letter that corresponds to the best answer.

1. Real wages would decline if the
(a) prices of goods and services rose more rapidly than nominal-wage rates
(b) prices of goods and services rose less rapidly than nominal-wage rates
(c) prices of goods and services and wage rates both rose
(d) prices of goods and services and wage rates both fell

2. The basic explanation for high real wages in the United States and other industrially advanced economies is that the
(a) price levels in these nations have increased at a faster rate than nominal wages
(b) governments in these nations have imposed effective minimum wage laws to improve the conditions of labor
(c) demand for labor in these nations is quite large relative to the supply of labor
(d) supply of labor in these nations is quite large relative to the demand for labor

3. A characteristic of a purely competitive labor market would be
(a) firms hiring different types of labor
(b) workers supplying labor under a union contract
(c) wage taker behavior by the firms
(d) price maker behavior by the firms

4. The supply curve for labor in a purely competitive market is upward sloping because the
(a) opportunity costs for workers rise
(b) marginal resource cost is constant
(c) wage rate paid to workers falls
(d) marginal revenue product rises

5. The individual firm that hires labor under purely competitive conditions faces a supply curve for labor that
(a) is perfectly inelastic
(b) is of unitary elasticity
(c) is perfectly elastic
(d) slopes upward from left to right

6. Which is a characteristic of a monopsonist?
(a) The type of labor is relatively mobile.
(b) The supply curve is the marginal resource cost curve.

(c) There are many buyers of a particular kind of labor.
(d) The wage rate it must pay workers varies directly with the number of workers it employs.

7. A monopsonist pays a wage rate that is
(a) greater than the marginal revenue product of labor
(b) equal to the marginal revenue product of labor
(c) equal to the firm's marginal labor cost
(d) less than the marginal revenue product of labor

8. If a firm employs resources in imperfectly competitive markets, to maximize its profits the marginal revenue product of each resource must equal
(a) its marginal product
(b) its marginal resource cost
(c) its price
(d) 1

9. Compared with a purely competitive labor market, a monopsonistic market will result in
(a) higher wage rates and a higher level of employment
(b) higher wage rates and a lower level of employment
(c) lower wage rates and a higher level of employment
(d) lower wage rates and a lower level of employment

10. The monopsonistic labor market for nurses that would be found in a smaller city with two hospitals would lead to
(a) lower starting salaries
(b) higher starting salaries
(c) more employment opportunities
(d) greater demand for nursing services

11. Higher wage rates and a higher level of employment for workers are the usual consequences of
(a) inclusive or craft unionism
(b) exclusive or industrial unionism
(c) an above-equilibrium wage rate
(d) an increase in the productivity of labor

12. Which would increase the demand for a particular type of labor?
(a) a decrease in the wages of that type of labor
(b) an increase in the prices of those resources that are substitutes for that type of labor
(c) an increase in the prices of the resources that are complements to that type of labor
(d) a decrease in the demand for the products produced by that type of labor

13. Occupational licensing laws have the economic effect of
(a) increasing the demand for labor
(b) decreasing the supply of labor
(c) strengthening the bargaining position of an industrial union
(d) weakening the bargaining position of a craft union

14. Industrial unions typically attempt to increase wage rates by
(a) imposing an above-equilibrium wage rate on employers
(b) increasing the demand for labor

(c) decreasing the supply of labor
(d) forming a bilateral monopoly

Answer Questions 15, 16, and 17 using the data in the following table.

Wage rate	Quantity of labor supplied	Marginal labor cost	Marginal revenue product of labor
$10	0	—	—
11	100	$11	$17
12	200	13	16
13	300	15	15
14	400	17	14
15	500	19	13
16	600	21	12

15. If the firm employing labor were a monopsonist, the wage rate and the quantity of labor employed would be, respectively,
(a) $14 and 300
(b) $13 and 400
(c) $14 and 400
(d) $13 and 300

16. But if the market for this labor were purely competitive, the wage rate and the quantity of labor employed would be, respectively,
(a) $14 and 300
(b) $13 and 400
(c) $14 and 400
(d) $13 and 300

17. If the firm employing labor were a monopsonist and the workers were represented by an industrial union, the wage rate would be
(a) between $13 and $14
(b) between $13 and $15
(c) between $14 and $15
(d) below $13 or above $15

*Answer Questions 18, 19, 20, and 21 on the basis of the following labor market diagram, where **D** is the demand curve for labor, **S** is the supply curve for labor, and **MRC** is the marginal resource (labor) cost.*

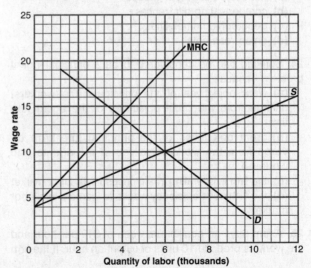

18. If this were a purely competitive labor market, the number of workers hired and the wage rate in equilibrium would be
  (a) 4000 and $14
  (b) 4000 and $8
  (c) 6000 and $10
  (d) 8000 and $12

19. If this were a monopsonistic labor market, the number of workers hired and the wage rate in equilibrium would be
  (a) 4000 and $14
  (b) 4000 and $8
  (c) 6000 and $10
  (d) 8000 and $12

20. Suppose an inclusive union seeks to maximize the employment of workers with the monopsonist. If successful, the number of workers employed and the wage rate would be
  (a) 4000 and $14
  (b) 6000 and $12
  (c) 6000 and $10
  (d) 8000 and $12

21. If the market were characterized as a bilateral monopoly, the number of workers hired and the wage rate in equilibrium would be
  (a) 6000 and $10
  (b) 4000 and $14
  (c) 4000 and $8
  (d) indeterminate

22. The major reason that major league baseball players receive an average salary of over $1 million a year and teachers receive an average salary of about $40,000 a year can best be explained in terms of
  (a) noncompeting labor groups
  (b) compensating differences
  (c) lack of job information
  (d) discrimination

23. The fact that unskilled construction workers typically receive higher wages than bank clerks is best explained in terms of
  (a) noncompeting labor groups
  (b) compensating differences
  (c) geographic immobilities
  (d) union restraints

24. Shirking can be considered to be a principal–agent problem because
  (a) work objectives of the principals (the workers) diverge from the profit objectives of the agent (the firm)
  (b) profit objectives of the principal (the firm) diverge from the work objectives of the agents (the workers)
  (c) the firm is operating in a monopsonistic labor market
  (d) the firm pays efficiency wages to workers in a labor market

25. A firm pays an equilibrium wage of $10 per hour and the workers produce 10 units of output an hour. If the firm adopts an efficiency wage and it is successful, then the wage rate for these workers will
  (a) rise and output will fall
  (b) fall and output will rise
  (c) rise and output will rise
  (d) fall and output will fall

■ **PROBLEMS**

1. Suppose a single firm has for a particular type of labor the marginal-revenue-product schedule given in the following table.

Number of units of labor	MRP of labor
1	$15
2	14
3	13
4	12
5	11
6	10
7	9
8	8

a. Assume there are 100 firms with the same marginal-revenue-product schedules for this particular type of labor. Compute the total or market demand for this labor by completing column 1 in the following table.

(1) Quantity of labor demanded	(2) Wage rate	(3) Quantity of labor supplied
_____	$15	850
_____	14	800
_____	13	750
_____	12	700
_____	11	650
_____	10	600
_____	9	550
_____	8	500

b. Using the supply schedule for labor given in columns 2 and 3,

(1) what will be the equilibrium wage rate? $_____
(2) what will be the total amount of labor hired in the market? _____

c. The individual firm will

(1) have a marginal labor cost of $_____.

(2) employ _____ units of labor.

(3) pay a wage of $_____.

d. On the following graph, plot the market demand and supply curves for labor and indicate the equilibrium wage rate and the total quantity of labor employed.

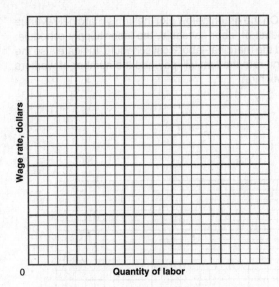

0   **Quantity of labor**

(Wage rate, dollars)

(1) Number of labor units	(2) MRP of labor	(3) Wage rate	(4) Total labor cost	(5) Marginal labor cost
0		$ 2	$____	
1	$36	4	____	$____
2	32	6	____	____
3	28	8	____	____
4	24	10	____	____
5	20	12	____	____
6	16	14	____	____
7	12	16	____	____
8	8	18	____	____

a. Compute the firm's total labor costs at each level of employment and the marginal labor cost of each unit of labor, and enter these figures in columns 4 and 5.

b. The firm will

1. hire _____ units of labor.

2. pay a wage of $_____.

3. have a marginal revenue product for labor of

$_____ for the last unit of labor employed.

c. Plot the marginal revenue product of labor, the supply curve for labor, and the marginal-labor-cost curve on the following graph and indicate the quantity of labor the firm will employ and the wage it will pay.

e. On the following graph, plot the individual firm's demand curve for labor, the supply curve for labor, and the marginal-labor-cost curve which confronts the individual firm, and indicate the quantity of labor the firm will hire and the wage it will pay.

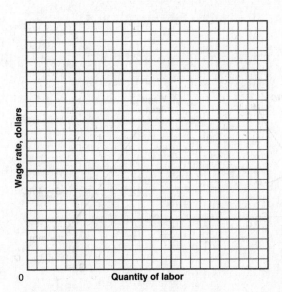

0   **Quantity of labor**

(Wage rate, dollars)

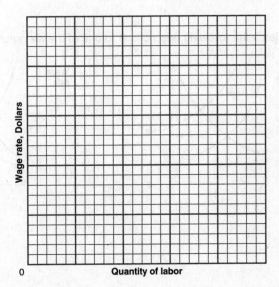

0   **Quantity of labor**

(Wage rate, Dollars)

d. If this firm's labor market were competitive, there would be at least _____ units hired at a wage of at least $_____.

f. The imposition of a $12 minimum wage rate would change the total amount of labor hired in this market to

_____.

2. In the following table, assume a monopsonist has the marginal-revenue-product schedule for a particular type of labor given in columns 1 and 2 and that the supply schedule for labor is that given in columns 1 and 3.

3. Assume that the employees of the monopsonist in Problem 2 organize a strong industrial union. The union demands a wage rate of $16 for its members, and the monopsonist decides to pay this wage because a strike would be too costly.

a. In the following table, compute the supply schedule for labor that now confronts the monopsonist by completing column 2.

(1) Number of labor units	(2) Wage rate	(3) Total labor cost	(4) Marginal labor cost
0	$____	$____	
1	____	____	$____
2	____	____	____
3	____	____	____
4	____	____	____
5	____	____	____
6	____	____	____
7	____	____	____
8	____	____	____

b. Compute the total labor cost and the marginal labor cost at each level of employment and enter these figures in columns 3 and 4.

c. The firm will hire_____ units of labor, pay a wage of $_____, and pay total wages of $_____.

d. As a result of unionization, the wage rate has _____, the level of employment has_____, and the earnings of labor have_____.

e. On the graph below plot the firm's marginal revenue product of labor schedule, the labor supply schedule, and the marginal-labor-cost schedule. Indicate also the wage rate the firm will pay and the number of workers it will hire.

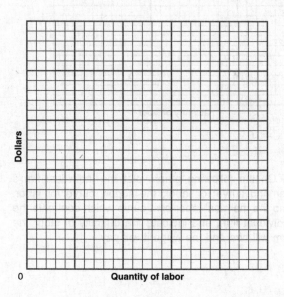

4. Match the following descriptions to one of the six graphs.

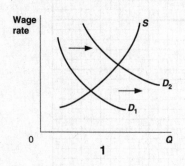

1

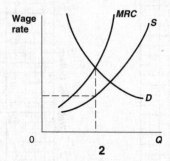

2

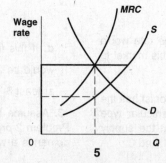

3

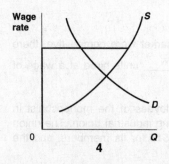

4

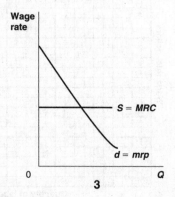

5

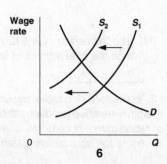

6

a. A bilateral monopoly   Graph _____

b. The supply and demand for labor for a purely competitive firm   Graph _____

c. The labor strategy used by a craft union to raise wages   Graph _____

d. A monopsonistic labor market   Graph _____

e. The strategy used by an industrial union to raise wages above a competitive level   Graph _____

f. A strategy used by a union to get people to buy union-made products   Graph _____

■ **SHORT ANSWER AND ESSAY QUESTIONS**

1. What is meant by the term *wages?* What is the difference between real wages and nominal wages?

2. How does the level of wages in the United States compare with that in other nations?

3. Explain why the productivity of the U.S. labor force has increased to its present high level.

4. Why has the level of real wages continued to increase even though the supply of labor has continually increased?

5. In the competitive model, what determines the market demand for labor and the wage rate? What kind of supply situation do all firms as a group confront? What kind of supply situation does the individual firm confront? Why?

6. In the monopsony model, what determines employment and the wage rate? What kind of supply situation does the monopsonist face? Why? How do the wage rate paid and the level of employment compare with what would result if the market were competitive?

7. In what sense is a worker who is hired by a monopsonist "exploited" and one who is employed in a competitive labor market "justly" rewarded? Why do monopsonists wish to restrict employment?

8. When supply is less than perfectly elastic, marginal labor cost is greater than the wage rate. Why?

9. What political methods do labor unions use to try to increase the wages their members receive? Give examples.

10. When labor unions attempt to restrict the supply of labor to increase wage rates, what devices do they use to do this for the economy as a whole, and what means do they use to restrict the supply of a given type of worker?

11. How do industrial unions attempt to increase wage rates, and what effect does this method of increasing wages have on employment in the industry affected?

12. Both exclusive and inclusive unions are able to raise the wage rates their members receive. Why might unions limit or temper their demands for higher wages? What two factors determine the extent to which they will or will not reduce their demands for higher wages?

13. Have U.S. unions been successful in raising the wages of their members? Evaluate the evidence on wages and employment effects.

14. What is bilateral monopoly? What determines wage rates in a labor market of this type?

15. Using supply and demand graphs, describe the effect of minimum wage laws on wage rates and employment in (a) purely competitive labor markets and (b) monopsony labor markets.

16. Offer an evaluation of the employment and antipoverty effects of the minimum wage based on past and current evidence.

17. What is meant by the term "noncompeting" groups in a labor market? What two factors tend to explain wage differentials in noncompeting groups?

18. How are wages used to equalize differences in the characteristics of jobs? Give examples.

19. Describe four types of imperfections in labor markets. Discuss how these imperfections contribute to wage differentials.

20. Explain what is meant by the principal–agent problem, and relate it to shirking. What are the different pay incentive plans that correct for shirking on the job? How does profit sharing reduce shirking? What is the reason for efficiency wages?

ANSWERS

Chapter 13 Wage Determination

FILL-IN QUESTIONS

1. wage, wage, multiplied, nominal, real
2. strong, capital, natural, labor force, technology, long-run
3. *a.* higher, opportunity cost; *b.* revenue product; *c.* equal to
4. elastic, equal to
5. equal to, greater, less
6. *a.* divided; *b.* equal to, divided, 1
7. lower, less
8. demand for, supply of, an above
9. demand for, increasing, decreasing
10. exclusive, inclusive, a craft, an industrial
11. decrease, decrease, inelastic
12. less, greater, wage rate
13. increase, decrease, increase, increase, uncertain
14. are not, vary, imperfect
15. noncompeting, ability, human capital
16. nonmonetary, compensating
17. job, immobility, restraints, discrimination
18. principals, agents, profits, wages
19. shirking, performance, pay
20. piece, efficiency, negative

TRUE–FALSE QUESTIONS

1. F, p. 270	**6.** T, pp. 272–274
2. F, p. 270	**7.** T, pp. 272–274
3. T, pp. 270–271	**8.** T, pp. 274–276
4. T, pp. 271–272	**9.** T, pp. 276–277
5. F, p. 272	**10.** F, pp. 276–277

11. T, p. 277	**19.** T, pp. 279–280
12. F, p. 277	**20.** T, pp. 281–282
13. F, pp. 277–278	**21.** T, p. 283
14. F, pp. 277–278	**22.** F, p. 285
15. T, p. 278	**23.** T, pp. 283–284
16. F, pp. 277–278	**24.** T, pp. 284–285
17. F, pp. 278–279	**25.** T, pp. 285, 287
18. T, pp. 279–280	

MULTIPLE-CHOICE QUESTIONS

1. a, p. 270	**14.** a, pp. 277–278
2. c, p. 270	**15.** d, pp. 274–276
3. c, p. 272	**16.** c, pp. 272–274
4. a, p. 272	**17.** b, pp. 277–278
5. c, pp. 272–274	**18.** c, pp. 272–274
6. d, p. 274	**19.** b, pp. 274–276
7. d, pp. 275–276	**20.** c, p. 277
8. b, pp. 275–276	**21.** d, pp. 278–279
9. d, pp. 274–276	**22.** a, pp. 282–283
10. a, p. 276	**23.** b, p. 283
11. d, pp. 271, 276–278	**24.** b, pp. 284–285
12. b, pp. 276–277	**25.** c, p. 285
13. b, p. 277	

PROBLEMS

1. *a.* Quantity of labor demanded: 100, 200, 300, 400, 500, 600, 700, 800; *b.* (1) 10.00, (2) 600; *c.* (1) 10.00, (2) 6, (3) 10.00; *d.* graph; *e.* graph; *f.* 400

2. *a.* Total labor cost: 0, 4.00, 12.00, 24.00, 40.00, 60.00, 84.00, 112.00, 144.00, Marginal labor cost: 4.00, 8.00, 12.00, 16.00, 20.00, 24.00, 28.00, 32.00; *b.* (1) 5, (2) 12.00, (3) 20.00; *c.* graph; *d.* 6, 14.00

3. *a.* Wage rate: 16.00, 16.00, 16.00, 16.00, 16.00, 16.00, 16.00, 16.00, 16.00; *b.* Total labor cost: 0, 16.00, 32.00, 48.00, 64.00, 80.00, 96.00, 112.00, 128.00; Marginal labor cost: 16.00, 16.00, 16.00, 16.00, 16.00, 16.00, 16.00, 16.00; *c.* (1) 6, (2) 16.00, (3) 96.00; *d.* increased, increased, increased; *e.* graph (similar to Figure 13.8)

4. *a.* 5; *b.* 3; *c.* 6; *d.* 2; *e.* 4; *f.* 1

SHORT ANSWER AND ESSAY QUESTIONS

1. p. 270	**11.** pp. 277–278
2. p. 270	**12.** pp. 277–278
3. pp. 270–271	**13.** p. 278
4. pp. 271–272	**14.** pp. 278–279
5. pp. 272–274	**15.** pp. 279–280
6. pp. 274–276	**16.** pp. 279–280
7. pp. 274–276	**17.** pp. 282–283
8. pp. 274–275	**18.** p. 283
9. pp. 276–277	**19.** pp. 283–284
10. p. 277	**20.** pp. 284–285

Labor Unions and Their Impacts

This appendix provides some additional information about American **labor unions,** collective bargaining, and union impacts. The labor union is an important economic institution in the U.S. economy. About 15.7 million workers covering about 12.1 percent of the labor force belong to unions. Unions typically focus on specific economic objectives such as improving pay, hours, and working conditions. Union members are more likely to work in government or to be employed in transportation, construction, manufacturing, and mining industries. In spite of its importance, unionism has been on the decline since the mid-1950s.

In Chapter 13 you learned how unions directly and indirectly seek to influence wage rates. The impact of the union on its own membership, on employers, and on the economy is more than just a matter of wages; it involves a contract between a union and an employer. This appendix discusses **collective bargaining** to give you some insights about the union goals and other issues over which employers and employees bargain. Another important idea discussed is that labor-management relations involve more than the periodic signing of a contract, they also involve the day-to-day relations between the union and the employer and the new issues not settled in the contract but which must be resolved under the general provisions of the contract.

The appendix elaborates on **the economic effects of unions** on the economy. Unions improve their members' wage rates relative to the wage rates for nonunionized workers. The effects of unions on output and efficiency, however, are more negative for three reasons that you will learn about in the chapter, although there is one factor that in the long-run may offset some of these negative effects.

■ CHECKLIST

When you have studied this appendix you should be able to

☐ Identify the number and percentage of union members and the major union organizations.
☐ Describe the characteristics of workers belonging to unions.
☐ State how unions have declined since the mid-1950s.
☐ Present two reasons to explain unionism's decline.
☐ Explain the four basic areas covered by work agreements in collective bargaining.

☐ Describe the bargaining process and major labor relations law.
☐ Draw conclusions about the effects of unions on the wages of workers.
☐ Identify three negative effects unions might have on output and efficiency.
☐ Use a supply and demand model to show how a union might lead to a misallocation of labor resources and reduced output.
☐ Explain the potentially positive effect that unions might have on output and efficiency in the long run because of lower rate of worker turnover.

■ APPENDIX OUTLINE

1. About 15.7 million workers in the United States belong to *unions*, and they account for only about 12.1 percent of wage and salary workers. Over half (8 million) of these workers are members of unions affiliated with the *American Federation of Labor and Congress of Industrial Organizations* (AFL-CIO). About 6 million workers are members of a loose federation of seven unions called *Change to Win* that include Service Workers and Teamsters. The rest of the union members belong to *independent unions* that are not affiliated with the other major organizations.

Occupation and industry are important factors that explain who belongs to unions. The *unionization rate* is high in government, and in the transportation, construction, manufacturing, and mining industries. Men, African-Americans, and those living in urban areas are more likely to be union members.

2. Union membership has declined since the mid-1950s, when about 25 percent of the workforce was unionized. Two complementary hypotheses explain the decline. One reason for the decline is that changes in the structure of the economy and the labor force have limited the expansion of union membership. A second reason for the decline is that the opposition of management to unions increased because union firms were thought to be less profitable than nonunion firms. The policies management used against unions decreased union membership.

3. *Collective bargaining* between labor and management results in work agreements that take many different forms, but usually cover four basic areas: union status and managerial prerogatives; wages and hours; seniority and job protection; and grievance procedures.

a. Union status can be of several types. In a **closed shop**, a worker must be a member of the union before being hired or must become one. In a **union shop**, employers can hire nonunion members but they must become one within a certain period. An **agency shop** requires that nonunion members pay union dues or make a donation to charity similar to the amount of the dues. Twenty-two states prohibit union or agency shops through **right-to-work laws**. In an **open shop**, an employer can hire either union or nonunion members and nonunion members do not have to pay dues. Contracts also typically contain clauses that give management prerogatives over certain work and business practices.

b. Wages (and fringe benefits) and hours of work are the main focus of collective bargaining agreements. Such wage and hour negotiations are influenced by what other workers are being paid, the profitability of the firm, cost of living concerns, and increase in labor productivity.

c. Unions typically are concerned about giving preference for promotion based on the seniority of workers. Unions also may seek job protection for their workers by limiting businesses' discretion to shift work abroad, change production locations, or use nonunion labor,

d. Grievance procedures are specified in labor contracts to help resolve disputes with management over changes in work assignment and other matters affecting workers.

4. The bargaining process on a new contract typically occurs in the 60-day period before the end of the existing contract. After the deadline, a union can **strike**, or there can be a **lockout** by the firm. Most contract agreements are compromises; strikes, lockouts, and violence are rare. The **National Labor Relations Act** specifies legal and illegal practices in collective bargaining, and the **National Labor Relations Board** is authorized to investigate unfair labor practices.

5. Labor unions have economic effects. The most direct effect is that unions typically increase the wages of their members relative to the wages of nonunion members (the wage advantage averages 15 percent). Whether unions increase output and efficiency is more complicated, but the overall effect appears negative.

a. Decreased output and efficiency result from feather-bedding and establishing work rules that increase the cost of production.

b. Unions reduce output when they conduct strikes and work stoppages.

c. There are efficiency losses from the misallocation of labor to union and nonunion jobs because of the union wage advantage.

d. One long-run factor that may offset some of these negative effects of unions on output and efficiency is that unions may reduce the turnover or quit rate of workers. Unions offer a collective **voice mechanism** to help correct work problems before workers think they have to express their **exit mechanism** by quitting a job. Reducing the turnover rate may help businesses benefit from their investment in worker training and the experience of workers.

■ **HINTS AND TIPS**

1. This appendix deals with unionism, which can provoke emotional reactions. Make sure you remember the distinction between *positive* and *normative* economics made in Chapter 1. The purpose of the appendix is to analyze and explain the economics of unions (*what is*), and not the ideal world (*what ought to be*).

2. In the graph in Figure 2 on page 293 of the text, the wage rate is plotted on the vertical axis and the quantity of labor is on the horizontal axis. The graph shows how unionization of a labor market affects the wage rate, employment, and domestic output. Problem 2 in this appendix will help you master this material.

■ **IMPORTANT TERMS**

American Federation of Labor-Congress of Industrial Organizations (AFL-CIO)	**open shop**
	strike
	lockout
Change to Win	**National Labor Relations Act (NLRA)**
unionization rate	
independent unions	**National Labor Relations Board (NLRB)**
collective bargaining	
closed shop	**voice mechanism**
union shop	**exit mechanism**
agency shop	
right-to-work laws	

SELF-TEST

■ **FILL-IN QUESTIONS**

1. About (15.7, 32.4) _____ million workers belong to labor unions in the United States. This number represents about (12.1, 28.9) _____% of wage and salary workers.

2. The unionization rate is relatively (low, high) _____ among workers in government, transportation, construction, and manufacturing, and it is _____ among protective service workers, machine operators, and craft workers. Men are (more, less) _____ likely to be union members than women; African-Americans are _____ likely to be union members than whites; and those in urban areas are _____ likely to be union members than those workers in other locations.

3. Since the mid-1950s, union membership as a percentage of the labor force has (increased, decreased) _____ and, since 1980, the number of unionized workers has _____.

4. Two reasons can be used to explain the changes in the size of union membership. The (structural-change, managerial-opposition) _____ reason suggests that conditions unfavorable to the expansion of unions have occurred in the economy and labor; the _____ reason suggests that union growth has been deterred by the policies of firms to limit or dissuade workers from joining unions.

5. A typical work agreement between a union and an employer covers the following four basic areas:

    a. _____

    b. _____

    c. _____

    d. _____

6. Collective bargaining typically begins about (20, 60) _____ days before a labor contract is set to expire. If the contract demands from workers are not met satisfactorily by the employer, a labor union may authorize a (lockout, strike) _____ that results in a work stoppage, but employers can put pressure on workers to settle the contract by engaging in a _____ that prevents workers from returning to work.

7. Federal labor laws sets the framework for bargaining, strikes, and lockout through the National Labor Relations (Act, Board) _____ and the organization that is responsible for investigating charges of unfair labor practices is the National Labor Relations _____.

8. Unionization of workers in the U.S. economy has (increased, decreased) _____ the wage rates of union members relative to the wage rates of nonunion workers, with the wage premium being about (15, 25) _____ percent.

9. Unions have a negative effect on output and efficiency in the economy to the extent that they engage in (collective bargaining, featherbedding) _____ and impose burdensome (exit mechanisms, work rules) _____ on their employers, or impose (above, below) _____-equilibrium wage rates on employers that lead to misallocation of labor resources.

10. In the long-run, unions can have a positive effect on output and efficiency in the economy because unions can (increase, decrease) _____ labor turnover.

■ TRUE–FALSE QUESTIONS

Circle T if the statement is true, F if it is false.

1. Most union members in the U.S. belong to independent unions not affiliated with the AFL-CIO. **T F**

2. The rate of unionization is relatively high in transportation, construction, and manufacturing industries. **T F**

3. Union membership as a percentage of the labor force has been rising since the 1950s. **T F**

4. The structural changes in the economy that shift workers from manufacturing employment to service employment is one main reason for the decline in union membership. **T F**

5. Collective bargaining between labor and management means no more than deciding on the wage rates employees will receive during the life of the contract. **T F**

6. Bargaining, strikes, and lockouts occur within a framework of Federal labor laws such as the National Labor Relations Act. **T F**

7. The wages of union members exceed the wages of nonunion members on the average by more than 40%. **T F**

8. Strikes in the U.S. economy result in little lost work time and reductions in total output. **T F**

9. The loss of output in the U.S. economy resulting from increases in wage rates imposed by unions on employers is relatively large. **T F**

10. Over time, labor unions reduce worker turnover, which offsets some of the negative effects of union on output and efficiency. **T F**

■ MULTIPLE-CHOICE QUESTIONS

Circle the letter that corresponds to the best answer.

1. About what percent of employed wage and salary workers in the United States belong to unions?
    (a) 7.5%
    (b) 12.1%
    (c) 21.3%
    (d) 35.4%

2. The rate of unionization is highest in
    (a) services
    (b) retail trade
    (c) government
    (d) manufacturing

3. If workers at the time they are hired have a choice of joining the union and paying dues or of not joining the union and paying no dues, there exists
    (a) a union shop
    (b) an open shop
    (c) a nonunion shop
    (d) a closed shop

4. A major responsibility of the National Labor Relations Board is to
    (a) enforce right-to-work laws
    (b) keep unions from becoming politically active
    (c) investigate unfair labor practices under labor law
    (d) maintain labor peace between the AFL and CIO

5. Unionization has tended to
(a) increase the wages of union workers and decrease the wages of some nonunion workers
(b) increase the wages of some nonunion workers and decrease wages of union workers
(c) increase the wages of both union and nonunion workers
(d) increase the average level of real wages in the economy

6. The higher wages imposed on employers in a unionized labor market tend to result in
(a) lower wage rates in nonunionized labor markets and a decline in domestic output
(b) lower wage rates in nonunionized labor markets and an expansion in domestic output
(c) higher wage rates in nonunionized labor markets and a decline in domestic output
(d) higher wage rates in nonunionized labor markets and an expansion in domestic output

7. Which tends to decrease or have a have a negative effect on output and efficiency in the economy?
(a) the seniority system
(b) reduced labor turnover
(c) featherbedding and union-imposed work rules
(d) the shock effect of higher union-imposed wage rates

8. The reallocation of a unit of labor from employment where its MRP is $50,000 to employment where its MRP is $40,000 will
(a) increase the output of the economy by $10,000
(b) increase the output of the economy by $90,000
(c) decrease the output of the economy by $10,000
(d) decrease the output of the economy by $90,000

9. Which tends to increase or have a positive effect on output and efficiency in the economy?
(a) strikes
(b) reduced labor turnover
(c) featherbedding and union-imposed work rules
(d) a decrease in the training programs for workers

10. Unions tend to reduce labor turnover by providing workers with all but one of the following. Which one?
(a) an exit mechanism
(b) a voice mechanism
(c) a collective voice
(d) a wage advantage

■ **PROBLEMS**

1. Match the union term with the phrase using the appropriate number.

1. lockout   5. open shop
2. union shop   6. agency shop
3. closed shop   7. National Labor Relations
                       Act
4. right-to-work laws 8. collective bargaining

a. Employer can hire union or nonunion workers. _____

b. Acts by states to make compulsory union membership, or the union shop, illegal. _____
c. A worker must be a member of the union before he or she is eligible for employment in the firm. _____
d. First passed as the Wagner Act of 1935 and sets forth the dos and don'ts of union and management-labor practices. _____
e. Requires a worker to pay union dues or donate an equivalent amount to charity. _____
f. A firm forbids its workers from returning to work until a new contract is signed. _____
g. Permits the employer to hire nonunion workers, but provides that these workers must join the union within a specified period or relinquish their jobs. _____
h. The negotiations of labor contracts. _____

2. Suppose there are two identical labor markets in the economy. The supply of workers and the demand for workers in each of these markets are shown in the following table.

Quantity of labor demanded	Wage rate (MRP of labor)	Quantity of labor supplied
1	$100	7
2	90	6
3	80	5
4	70	4
5	60	3
6	50	2
7	40	1

a. In each of the two labor markets the equilibrium wage rate in a competitive labor market would be $_____ and employment would be _____ workers.
b. Now suppose that in the first of these labor markets workers form a union and the union imposes an above-equilibrium wage rate of $90 on employers.
(1) Employment in the unionized labor market will (rise, fall) _____ to _____ workers; and
(2) the output produced by workers employed by the firms in the unionized labor market will (expand, contract) _____ by $_____.
c. If the workers displaced by the unionization of the first labor market all enter and find employment in the second labor market which remains nonunionized and competitive,
(1) the wage rate in the second labor market will (rise, fall) _____ to $_____.
(2) the output produced by the workers employed by firms in the second labor market will (expand, contract) _____ by $_____.
d. While the total employment of labor in the two labor markets has remained constant, the total output produced by the employers in the two labor markets has (expanded, contracted) _____ by $_____.

■ SHORT ANSWER AND ESSAY QUESTIONS

1. Describe the current status of unions in the United States and the major union organization.

2. Who belongs to unions? Answer in terms of the types of industries and occupations and the personal characteristics of workers.

3. What evidence is there that the labor movement in the United States has declined? What are two possible causes of this decline?

4. What are the four basic areas usually covered in collective-bargaining agreements between management and labor?

5. What four arguments does labor (management) use in demanding (resisting) higher wages?

6. Describe the bargaining process in labor negotiations. What are the two aspects of Federal labor laws that set the framework for this negotiation?

7. How large is the union wage advantage in the United States? How has the unionization of many labor markets affected the average level of real wages in the U.S. economy?

8. Explain how featherbedding and work rules by unions imposes a negative effect on output and efficiency in the economy.

9. What effect does the unionization of a particular labor market have on the wage rate in that market, wage rates in other labor markets, and the total output of the economy?

10. Explain how unions reduce labor turnover and improve the skills of younger workers.

ANSWERS

Appendix to Chapter 13 Labor Unions and Their Impacts

FILL-IN QUESTIONS

1. 15.7, 12.1
2. high, high, more, more, more
3. decreased, decreased
4. structural-change, managerial-opposition
5. *a.* the degree of recognition and status accorded the union and the prerogatives of management; *b.* wages and hours; *c.* seniority and job opportunities; *d.* a procedure for settling grievances (any order for *a–d*)
6. 60, strike, lockout
7. Act, Board
8. increased, 15
9. featherbedding, work rules, above
10. decrease

TRUE–FALSE QUESTIONS

1. F, p. 290
2. T, p. 290
3. F, pp. 290–291
4. T, pp. 290–291
5. F, pp. 291–292
6. T, p. 292
7. F, p. 292
8. T, pp. 292–293
9. F, pp. 293–294
10. T, p. 294

MULTIPLE-CHOICE QUESTIONS

1. b, p. 290
2. c, p. 290
3. b, p. 291
4. c, p. 292
5. a, p. 292
6. a, p. 292
7. c, p. 292
8. c, pp. 293–294
9. b, p. 294
10. a, p. 294

PROBLEMS

1. *a.* 5; *b.* 4; *c.* 3; *d.* 7; *e.* 6; *f.* 1; *g.* 2; *h.* 8
2. *a.* 70, 4; *b.* (1) fall, 2, (2) contract, 150; *c.* (1) fall, 50, (2) expand, 110; *d.* contracted, 40

SHORT ANSWER AND ESSAY QUESTIONS

1. p. 290
2. p. 290
3. pp. 290–291
4. pp. 291–292
5. pp. 291–292
6. p. 292
7. pp. 292–293
8. p. 292
9. pp. 292–294
10. p. 294

CHAPTER 14

Rent, Interest, and Profit

Chapter 14 concludes the study of the **prices of resources** by examining rent, interest, and profits. There is nothing difficult about this chapter. By now you should understand that the marginal revenue product of a resource determines the demand for that resource. This understanding can be applied to the demand for land and capital. It will be on the supply side of the land market that you will encounter whatever difficulties there are. The **supply of land** is unique because **it is perfectly inelastic:** Changes in rent do not change the quantity of land that will be supplied. Given the quantity of land available, **demand is the sole determinant of economic rent.** Of course land varies in productivity and can be used for different purposes, but these are merely the factors that explain why the rent on all lands is not the same.

Capital, as the economist defines it, means capital goods. Is the rate of interest, then, the price paid for the use of capital goods? No, not quite. Capital is not one kind of good; it is many different kinds. To be able to talk about the price paid for the use of capital goods, there must be a simple way of adding up different kinds of capital goods. The simple way is to measure the quantity of capital goods in terms of money. **Interest** is the price paid for the use of money (or of financial capital) that in turn is used to purchase **capital goods** such as factories, technology, or machines. (Of course the concept of interest applies to purchases of consumer goods too, but the basic demand and supply model for interest presented in the chapter focuses on capital goods.)

The **demand for and supply of loanable funds** in the economy determines the **interest rate.** In a simplified model, businesses are the primary demanders of loanable funds because they want to use this financial capital to buy capital goods (e.g., equipment, machinery, factories). As with the demand for any good or service, the greater the price of using loanable funds (the interest rate), the smaller the amount of loanable funds that firms will be able and willing to borrow. A business will most likely borrow funds and make an investment in capital goods if the expected rate of return on the investment is greater than the interest rate. Therefore, the lower the interest rate, the greater the opportunities for profitable investments and the greater the amount of loanable funds demanded.

On the supply side, households are the typical suppliers of loanable funds. At a higher rate of interest, households are willing to supply more loanable funds than at lower interest rates because of the weighing of present consumption to future consumption. Most consumers prefer present consumption, but they would be willing to forgo this current use of funds and make them available for loan if there is compensation in the form of interest payments. Thus, the greater the interest rate, the more saving by households, which in turn creates a greater supply of loanable funds.

The intersection of the demand curve and the supply curve for loanable funds determines the equilibrium rate of interest, or the price of loanable funds, and the equilibrium quantity. This relationship is illustrated in Figure 14.2. The demand and supply curves of loanable funds can also shift due to a variety of factors. For example, there could be an increase in the rates of return on investments, which would increase the demand for loanable funds at each and every interest rate; changes in the tax laws could make savings more attractive and this change would increase the supply of loanable funds. Note too that while in the simplified model businesses are the demanders and households the suppliers of loanable funds, in reality these sectors can operate on both sides of the market.

It should be noted that there is a **time-value of money** that is reflected in the rate of interest. Interest is the price that borrowers need to pay lenders for transferring purchasing power from the present to the future. With interest and compounding, a given amount of money today will be equivalent to a larger amount of money in the future. Or conversely, a future amount of money will be equivalent to a smaller amount of money today. Several simple formulas are presented in the chapter to calculate the **present value** and **future value** of money based on different rates of interest.

When it comes to **economic profit,** supply and demand analysis fails the economist. Profits are not merely a wage for a particular type of labor; rather, they are rewards for taking risks and the gains of the monopolist. Such things as "the quantity of risks taken" or "the quantity of effort required to establish a monopoly" simply cannot be measured; consequently, it is impossible to talk about the demand for or the supply of them. Nevertheless, profits are important in the economy. They are largely rewards for doing things that have to be done if the economy is to allocate resources efficiently and to progress and develop; they are the lure or the bait that makes entrepreneurs willing to take the risks that result in efficiency and progress.

The final section of Chapter 14 explains what part of the income paid to American resource suppliers goes to workers and what part goes to capitalists—those who provide the economy with land, capital goods, and entrepreneurial ability. You may be surprised to learn that the lion's share—about 80%—of the income paid to American

191

resource suppliers goes to workers today and went to workers at the beginning of the century, and that only about 20% of it goes to the capitalists today or went to them in 1900.

■ **CHECKLIST**

When you have studied this chapter you should be able to

☐ Define economic rent.
☐ Explain why supply of land does not affect economic rent.
☐ Illustrate how changes in demand determine economic rent.
☐ Explain why land rent is a surplus payment.
☐ Give the rationale for a single tax on land proposed by Henry George.
☐ State four criticisms of the single tax on land.
☐ Illustrate graphically how productivity differences affect land rent.
☐ Contrast society's and a firm's perspectives on the alternative uses of land and economic rent.
☐ Define interest and state two aspects of it.
☐ Describe the loanable funds theory of interest using supply and demand analysis.
☐ Show how the equilibrium rate of interest is established in the loanable funds market using supply and demand analysis.
☐ Explain why the supply of loanable funds curve has a positive slope.
☐ Explain why the demand for loanable funds curve has a negative slope.
☐ List factors that change the supply or demand for loanable funds.
☐ Distinguish between a change in demand or supply and a change in quantity demanded or supplied as applied to the loanable funds market.
☐ Identify the different sides that participants (households, businesses, or government) take in the demand or supply of loanable funds.
☐ Describe the time-value of money and calculate the present value or future value of an amount of money when given different interest rates.
☐ List five reasons why interest rates differ.
☐ Define the pure rate of interest and state how it is measured.
☐ Explain how the interest rate affects investment spending, total output, the allocation of capital, and research and development (R&D) spending.
☐ Distinguish between nominal and real interest rates.
☐ Use graphical analysis to explain the three effects of usury laws.
☐ Distinguish between economic and normal profit.
☐ Describe the return to the entrepreneurial ability in terms of economic and normal profit.
☐ List three sources of economic profit.
☐ Explain the relationship between insurable and uninsurable risks and economic profit.
☐ Describe how innovation affects economic profit.
☐ Discuss the influence of monopoly on economic profit.

☐ Identify two functions of profits for the economy.
☐ Describe the shares of income paid to American resource suppliers going to labor and capital.
☐ Identify the different factors that affect the calculation of interest rates and the price of credit (Last Word).

■ **CHAPTER OUTLINE**

1. *Economic rent* is the price paid for the use of land or natural resources whose supply is perfectly inelastic.

a. The **supply of land is perfectly inelastic** because it is virtually fixed in the quantity available. Supply has no influence in determining economic rent.

b. The demand for land is the active determinant of economic rent. As demand increases or decreases, economic rent will increase or decrease given the perfectly inelastic supply of land.

c. Economic rent serves no **incentive function** given the fixed supply of land. It is not necessary to increase economic rent to bring forth more quantity, as is the case with other natural resources. Economists, therefore, consider economic rent a surplus payment.

d. Socialists have argued that land rent is unearned income and that land should be nationalized.

(1) Henry George, in his 1879 book, *Progress and Poverty*, called for a **single tax** on land as the sole source of government tax revenue. He based his argument on the grounds of equity and efficiency. Such a tax would not alter the supply of land because economic rent serves no incentive function.

(2) Critics of the single tax cite its inadequacy for meeting government needs, the difficulty of identifying the portion of rent in incomes, the conflicting interpretations of unearned income, and adverse equity effects arising from changes in land ownership.

e. Economic rents on different types of land vary because different plots of land vary in productivity or might have location advantages.

f. From society's perspective, economic rent is a surplus payment, but from a firm's perspective, economic rent is a cost. A firm must pay economic rent to bid the land it wants to use for its production away from alternative uses of the land.

2. Interest is the price paid for the use of money. Interest is stated as a percentage. Money is *not* an economic resource because it is not productive. People borrow money at an interest rate and use it to buy capital goods. These capital goods are economic resources that can be used to produce other goods and services.

a. The *loanable funds theory of interest* describes how the interest rate is determined by the demand for and supply of loanable funds. The intersection of the demand for and supply of loanable funds determines the equilibrium interest rate and the quantity of funds loaned.

(1) The **supply of loanable funds** is generally provided by households through savings. There is a positive relationship between the interest rate and the

quantity of loanable funds supplied. The supply curve, however, may be relatively inelastic and thus not very responsive to changes in the interest rate.

(2) The **demand for loanable funds** typically comes from businesses for investment in capital goods. There is an inverse relationship between the interest rate and the quantity of loanable funds demanded. Lower interest rates provide more profitable investment opportunities; higher interest rates reduce investments.

b. There are some extensions to the simplified model of the loanable funds market.

(1) Financial institutions serve as intermediaries in the supply and demand market for loanable funds.

(2) The supply of funds can change because of changes in factors that affect the thriftiness of households.

(3) The demand for funds can change because of changes in the rate of return on potential investments.

(4) Households and businesses can operate on both sides of the market—as both demanders and suppliers of loanable funds. Government also participates on both sides of the loanable fund market.

c. The *time-value of money* is the concept that a specific amount of money is more valuable for an individual or business the sooner it is obtained.

(1) If an amount of money is placed in an interest-bearing account, the amount will become larger in the future because of **compound interest** that accumulates over time. This compound interest is composed of interest paid both on the initial amount of money deposited (the principal) and interest is paid on interest earnings from the principal.

(2) The *future value* of money is the value of money in the future given a current value today. Because of compound interest, the higher the interest rate, the larger is the future value for a specific amount today. By contrast, the *present value* of money is the value of money today for a specific amount that will be received in the future. With present value, the higher the interest rate, the smaller will be the present value of money today for a specific amount that is to be received in the future.

d. There is a range of interest rates, although it is convenient to speak as if there were one interest rate. These rates differ because of difference in four factors: risk, maturity, loan size, and taxability.

e. When economists talk about "the interest rate," they are referring to the *pure rate of interest* which is best measured by the interest paid on long-term and riskless securities, such as 20-year bonds of the U.S. government.

f. The interest rate plays several roles in the economy.

(1) It affects the total output because of the inverse relationship between the interest rate and investment spending; government often tries to influence the interest rate to achieve its policy goals.

(2) It allocates financial and real capital among competing firms and determines the level and composition of the total output of capital goods.

(3) It changes the level and composition of spending on research and development.

(4) These effects are based on changes in the *real interest rate,* which is the rate expressed in inflation-adjusted dollars, not the *nominal interest rate,* which is the rate expressed in current dollars.

g. *Usury laws* specify a maximum interest rate for loans. They were passed to limit borrowing costs, but they can have other effects. First, they may cause a shortage of credit, which is then given only to the most worthy borrowers. Second, borrowers gain from paying less for credit and borrowers lose from receiving less interest income. Third, it creates inefficiency in the economy because funds get directed to less-productive investments.

3. *Economic profit* is what remains of the firm's revenue after all its *explicit* and *implicit* opportunity costs have been deducted.

a. Economic profit is a payment for entrepreneurial ability. *Normal profit* is the payment necessary to keep the entrepreneur in current work and is thus a cost. Economic profit is the residual payment to the entrepreneur from total revenues after all other costs have been subtracted.

b. Economic profit comes from three basic sources that reflect the dynamic nature of real-world capitalism:

(1) rewards for assuming *uninsurable risk* that arises from changes in economic conditions, the structure of the economy, and government policy.

(2) a return for assuming the uncertainties in innovation; and

(3) surpluses that firms obtain from monopoly power.

c. The expectation of economic profit serves several functions in the economy. Profits encourage businesses to innovate, and this innovation contributes to economic growth. Profits (and losses) guide businesses to produce products and to use resources in the way desired by society.

4. Income paid to American resource suppliers is distributed among wages, rent, interest, and profit. Using a broad definition, the share of this income going to labor is about 80%. The share going to capitalists from rent, interest, and profit is about 20%. These percentages have remained relatively stable since 1900.

5. (Last Word). To determine the interest rate paid for the use of credit, compare the interest rate paid to the amount borrowed. The calculation of the interest rate, however, is not that simple. The calculation can be affected by the payback period, the amount of a discount, the number of installments, the number of days in a year used in the calculation, and whether the interest is compounded. Several types of legislation have tried to clarify the explanations of how the interest rate is calculated.

■ **HINTS AND TIPS**

1. Although this chapter focuses on three resource payments (rent, interest, and profit), the discussion is much simpler and easier to understand than it was for the one resource payment (wages) in the previous chapter. It will help if you think of this chapter as three mini-chapters.

2. Use a supply and demand graph for land to explain to yourself why **land rent is surplus payment.** Draw a vertical (perfectly inelastic) supply curve and a downsloping demand curve. Identify the price and quantity combination where the two curves intersect. Then draw a new demand curve showing an increase in demand. What happens to price? (It increases.) What happens to quantity? (No change.) Changes in land rent perform no incentive function for the economy because they bring forth no more supply of land. Land rents are unnecessary (surplus) payments for the economy.

3. The **loanable funds theory of interest** will be easy to understand if you think of it as an application of supply and demand analysis. You need to remember, however, who are the suppliers and who are the demanders of loanable funds. In this simplified model, the *suppliers* of loanable funds are *households* who have a different quantity of savings to make available for loans at different interest rates; the higher the interest rate, the greater the quantity of loanable funds supplied. The *demanders* of loanable funds are *businesses* that want to borrow a quantity of money at each interest rate; the higher the interest rate, the smaller the quantity of loanable funds demanded for investment purposes.

4. Remember that it is the **expectation of profit,** not the certainty of it, that drives the entrepreneur. The generation of profit involves risk taking by the entrepreneur. You should distinguish, however, between **insurable risks** and those that are not insurable. A major source of profit for the entrepreneur comes from the **uninsurable risks** that the entrepreneur is willing to assume in an uncertain world.

■ **IMPORTANT TERMS**

economic rent	real interest rate
incentive function	usury laws
single-tax movement	explicit costs
loanable funds theory of interest	implicit costs
time-value of money	economic or pure profit
future value	normal profit
present value	static economy
pure rate of interest	insurable risks
nominal interest rate	uninsurable risks

SELF-TEST

FILL-IN QUESTIONS

1. Economic rent is the price paid for the use of (labor, land)_____ and (capital, natural) _____ resources which are completely (fixed, variable) _____ in supply.

2. The active determinant of economic rent is (demand, supply) _____ and the passive determinant is _____.

3. Economic rent does not bring forth more supply and serves no (profit, incentive) _____ function. Economists consider economic rent a (tax, surplus) _____ payment that is not necessary to ensure that land is available to the economy.

4. Socialists argue that land rents are (earned, unearned) _____ incomes. Henry George called for a single (price, tax) _____ on land to transfer economic rent to government because it would not affect the amount of land. One criticism of George's proposal is that it would not generate enough (revenue, profit) _____.

5. Rents on different pieces of land are not the same because land differs in (price, productivity) _____. From a business firm's perspective, land rent is a (surplus payment, cost) _____ because land (is a free good, has alternative uses) _____, but from society's perspective, land rent is _____.

6. The price paid for the use of money is (profit, interest) _____. It is typically stated as a (price, percentage) _____ of the amount borrowed. Money (is, is not) _____ an economic resource because money _____ productive.

7. Money or financial capital is obtained in the (mutual, loanable) _____ funds market. At the equilibrium rate of interest, the quantity demanded for loanable funds is (greater than, equal to, less than) _____ the quantity supplied of loanable funds.

8. The quantity supplied of loanable funds is (inversely, directly) _____ related to the interest rate while the quantity demanded for loanable funds is _____ related to the interest rate.

9. With a higher interest rate, there are (greater, fewer) _____ opportunities for profitable investment and hence a (larger, smaller) _____ quantity demanded for loanable funds.

10. An increase in the thriftiness of households will result in (an increase, a decrease) _____ in the (supply, demand) _____ of loanable funds. Anything that increases the rate of return on potential investments will (increase, decrease) _____ the (supply, demand) _____ of loanable funds.

11. The concept that a specific amount of money is more valuable for an individual or business the sooner it is obtained is the (pure rate of interest, time-value of money) _____. Interest that is composed of interest paid both on the initial amount of money deposited (the principal) and interest is paid on interest earnings from the principal is (usury, compound) _____ interest. The higher the interest rate, the (larger, smaller) _____ is the future value for a specific amount today, but with a higher interest rate, the _____ will be the present value of money today for a specific amount that is to be received in the future.

12. State four reasons why there is a range of interest rates:

a. _____

b. _____

c. _____

d. _____

13. Economists often talk of the (loan, pure) _____ rate of interest. It is approximated by the interest paid on (short-term, long-term) _____ U.S. government bonds.

14. A higher equilibrium interest rate often (increases, decreases) _____ business borrowing for investment and thus _____ total spending in the economy, whereas a lower equilibrium interest rate (increases, decreases) _____ business borrowing and thus _____ total spending in the economy.

15. The rate of interest expressed in purchasing power, or inflation-adjusted dollars, is the (real, nominal) _____ interest rate, while the rate of interest expressed in dollars of current value is the _____ interest rate.

16. Laws that state the maximum interest rate at which loans can be made are called (antitrust, usury) _____ laws. These laws cause (market, non-market) _____ rationing of credit that favors creditworthy (lenders, borrowers) _____ and leads to (less, more) _____ economic efficiency in the allocation of credit.

17. The difference between total revenue and total cost is (economic, normal) _____ profit. The minimum payment for the entrepreneur to keep him or her in the current line of business is (economic, normal) _____ profit. The excess of total revenue above total cost is (economic, normal) _____ profit.

18. Economic profit is a reward for either assuming (insurable, uninsurable) _____ risk or for dealing with the uncertainty of (taxation, innovation) _____.

19. Economic profit over time can also arise from (pure competition, monopoly) _____ and this source of profit is typically based on (increased, decreased) _____ output, _____ prices above competitive levels, and (increased, decreased) _____ economic efficiency.

20. Defining labor income broadly to include both wages and salaries and proprietors' income, labor's share of the total income paid to American resource suppliers is about (20%, 50%, 80%) _____, while capitalists' share of income is about _____. The share of income going to capitalists has (increased, decreased, remained stable) _____ since 1900.

■ **TRUE–FALSE QUESTIONS**

Circle T if the statement is true, F if it is false.

1. Rent is the price paid for use of capital resources.
T F

2. The determination of economic rent for land and other natural resources is based on a demand curve that is perfectly inelastic. **T F**

3. Rent is a surplus payment because it does not perform an incentive function. **T F**

4. Rent is unique because it is not determined by demand and supply. **T F**

5. For individual producers, rental payments are surplus payments, but for society they are a cost. **T F**

6. Money is an economic resource and the interest rate is the price paid for this resource. **T F**

7. The quantity of loanable funds demanded is inversely related to the interest rate. **T F**

8. The quantity of loanable funds supplied is directly related to the interest rate. **T F**

9. An increase in the demand for loanable funds would tend to increase the interest rate. **T F**

10. An increase in the rate of return on investments would most likely increase the supply of loanable funds. **T F**

11. The time-value of money is the concept that one U.S. dollar can be converted into more than one U.S. dollar of future value through compound interest. **T F**

12. The higher the rate of interest, the greater will be the future value of a specific amount of money today. **T F**

13. Other things equal, long-term loans usually command lower rates of interest than do short-term loans. **T F**

14. The pure rate of interest is best approximated by the interest paid on long-term bonds with very low risk, such as 20-year U.S. Treasury bonds.   **T   F**

15. A higher equilibrium interest rate discourages business borrowing for investment, reducing investment and total spending.   **T   F**

16. The interest rate rations the supply of loanable funds to investment projects whose rate of return will be less than the interest rate.   **T   F**

17. If the nominal rate of interest is 6% and the inflation rate is 3%, the real rate of interest is 9%.   **T   F**

18. Usury laws result in a shortage of loanable funds and nonmarket rationing in credit markets.   **T   F**

19. Lenders or banks are the main beneficiaries of usury laws.   **T   F**

20. If the economists' definition of profit were used, total profit in the economy would be greater than would be the case if the accountants' definition were used.   **T   F**

21. A normal profit is the minimum payment the entrepreneur must receive to induce him or her to provide entrepreneurial ability for the production of a certain good.   **T   F**

22. It is the static competitive economy that gives rise to economic profit.   **T   F**

23. Insurable risk is one of the sources of economic profit.   **T   F**

24. Economic profit arising from monopoly is more economically desirable than economic profit arising from uncertainty.   **T   F**

25. Economic profit influences both the level of economic output and the allocation of resources among alternative uses.   **T   F**

■ **MULTIPLE-CHOICE QUESTIONS**

Circle the letter that corresponds to the best answer.

1. The price paid for a natural resource that is completely fixed in supply is
   (a) profit
   (b) interest
   (c) rent
   (d) a risk payment

2. In total, the supply of land is
   (a) perfectly inelastic
   (b) of unitary elasticity
   (c) perfectly elastic
   (d) elastic but not perfectly elastic

3. The economic rent from land will increase, *ceteris paribus*, whenever the
   (a) price of land decreases
   (b) demand for land increases
   (c) demand for land decreases
   (d) supply curve for land increases

4. A major criticism of the single tax on land is that it would
   (a) bring in more tax revenues than is necessary to finance all current government spending
   (b) not distinguish between payments for the use of land and those for improvements to land
   (c) take into account the history of ownership of the land in determining the tax
   (d) not tax "unearned" income

5. Which is true?
   (a) The greater the demand for land, the greater the supply of land.
   (b) A windfall profits tax on the increases in the profits of petroleum producers was proposed by Henry George.
   (c) Individual users of land have to pay a rent to its owner because that land has alternative uses.
   (d) The less productive a particular piece of land is, the greater will be the rent its owner is able to earn from it.

6. When the supply curve for a plot of land lies entirely to the right of the demand curve,
   (a) landowners will receive an economic rent
   (b) landowners will not receive an economic rent
   (c) the interest rate on loans for land will increase
   (d) the interest rate on loans for land will decrease

7. Which of the following do economists consider a productive economic resource?
   (a) money
   (b) capital goods
   (c) interest
   (d) profit

8. The upsloping supply of loanable funds is best explained by the idea that most people prefer
   (a) current consumption to future consumption
   (b) future consumption to present consumption
   (c) saving over consumption
   (d) investment over saving

9. Why is the demand for loanable funds downsloping?
   (a) At lower interest rates, fewer investment projects will be profitable to businesses, and hence a small quantity of loanable funds will be demanded.
   (b) At lower interest rates, more investment projects will be profitable to businesses, and hence a small quantity of loanable funds will be demanded.
   (c) At higher interest rates, more investment projects will be profitable to businesses, and hence a large quantity of loanable funds will be demanded.
   (d) At higher interest rates, fewer investment projects will be profitable to businesses, and hence a small quantity of loanable funds will be demanded.

10. In the competitive market for loanable funds, when the quantity of funds demanded exceeds the quantity supplied, then the
   (a) interest rate will decrease
   (b) interest rate will increase
   (c) demand curve will increase
   (d) supply curve will decrease

11. A decrease in the productivity of capital goods will, *ceteris paribus*,
 (a) increase the supply of loanable funds
 (b) decrease the supply of loanable funds
 (c) increase the demand for loanable funds
 (d) decrease the demand for loanable funds

12. If a person invests $1,000 in an account that pays 5% interest at the end of each year, then after two years what will be the total amount in the account?
 (a) $1,050.00
 (b) $1,075.25
 (c) $1,100.00
 (d) $1,102.50

13. Which would tend to result in a lower interest rate for a loan?
 (a) the greater the risk involved
 (b) the shorter the length of the loan
 (c) the smaller the amount of the loan
 (d) the greater the monopoly power of the lender

14. What is the most likely reason why a lender would prefer a high-quality municipal bond that pays a 6% rate of interest rather than a high-quality corporate bond paying 8%?
 (a) The municipal bond is tax-exempt.
 (b) The municipal bond is a long-term investment.
 (c) The corporate bond is safer than the municipal bond.
 (d) The municipal bond is easier to purchase than a corporate bond.

15. The pure rate of interest is best approximated by the interest paid on
 (a) consumer credit cards
 (b) tax-exempt municipal bonds
 (c) 90-day Treasury bills
 (d) 20-year Treasury bonds

16. If the annual rate of interest were 18% and the rate of return a firm expects to earn annually by building a new plant were 20%, the firm would
 (a) not build the new plant
 (b) build the new plant
 (c) have to toss a coin to decide whether to build the new plant
 (d) not be able to determine from these figures whether to build the plant

Questions 17 and 18 refer to the following data.

Expected rate of return	Amount of capital goods investment (in billions)
19%	$220
17	250
15	300
13	360
11	430
9	500

17. If the interest rate is 13%,
 (a) $300 billion of investment will be undertaken
 (b) $360 billion of investment will be undertaken
 (c) $430 billion of investment will be undertaken
 (d) $500 billion of investment will be undertaken

18. An increase in the interest rate from 15% to 17% would
 (a) increase investment by $40 billion
 (b) increase investment by $50 billion
 (c) decrease investment by $50 billion
 (d) decrease investment by $40 billion

19. Which is the definition of a usury law? It is a law that specifies the
 (a) alternative uses of surplus government land
 (b) tax rate on interest paid for state and municipal bonds
 (c) maximum interest rate at which loans can be made
 (d) interest paid on long-term, virtually riskless bonds of the U.S. government

20. Which would be a likely economic effect of a usury law?
 (a) There would be an increase in economic efficiency.
 (b) There would be a decrease in the rationing of credit.
 (c) Creditworthy borrowers would lose and lenders would gain.
 (d) Creditworthy borrowers would gain and lenders would lose.

21. Which is the minimum return or payment necessary to retain the entrepreneur in some specific line of production?
 (a) normal profit
 (b) explicit cost
 (c) real interest rate
 (d) pure rate of interest

22. Which is an economic cost?
 (a) uninsurable risk
 (b) normal profit
 (c) economic profit
 (d) monopoly profit

23. One basic reason why there is economic profit is that
 (a) risks are insurable
 (b) economies are static
 (c) there is innovation
 (d) there are purely competitive markets

24. Monopoly profit is typically based on
 (a) uncertainty and innovation
 (b) insurable and uninsurable risk
 (c) productivity and economic efficiency
 (d) reduced output and above-competitive prices

25. Since 1900, the share of income paid to American resource suppliers
 (a) has increased for capitalists, but decreased for labor
 (b) has decreased for capitalists, but increased for labor
 (c) has increased for capitalists and for labor
 (d) has remained relatively constant for capitalists and labor

■ PROBLEMS

1. Assume that the quantity of a certain type of land available is 300,000 acres and the demand for this land is that given in the following table.

Pure land rent, per acre	Land demanded, acres
$350	100,000
300	200,000
250	300,000
200	400,000
150	500,000
100	600,000
50	700,000

a. The pure rent on this land will be $ _____.

b. The total quantity of land rented will be _____ acres.

c. On the following graph, plot the supply and demand curves for this land and indicate the pure rent for land and the quantity of land rented.

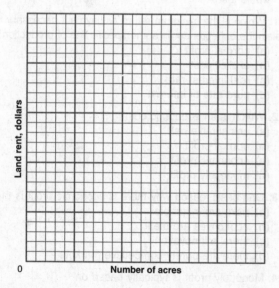

d. If landowners were taxed at a rate of $250 per acre for their land, the pure rent on this land after taxes would be $ _____ but the number of acres rented would be _____.

2. The following schedule shows interest rates (column 1), the associated quantity demanded of loanable funds (column 2), and the quantity supplied of loanable funds (column 4) in billions of dollars at those interest rates.

Interest rate (1)	Quantity demanded		Quantity supplied	
	(2)	(3)	(4)	(5)
12	50	____	260	____
10	100	____	240	____
8	150	____	220	____
6	200	____	200	____
4	250	____	180	____
2	300	____	160	____

a. Plot the demand and supply schedule on the graph on the next page. (The interest rate is measured along the vertical axis and the quantity demanded or supplied is measured on the horizontal axis.)

(1) The equilibrium interest rate is _____ %. The quantity demanded is $ _____ billion and the quantity supplied is $ _____ billion.

(2) At an interest rate of 10%, the quantity demanded of loanable funds is $_____ billion and the quantity supplied of loanable funds is $ _____ billion. There is an excess of loanable funds of $ _____ billion.

(3) At an interest rate of 4%, the quantity demanded of loanable funds is $ _____ billion and the quantity supplied of loanable funds is $ _____ billion. There is a shortage of loanable funds of $ _____ billion.

b. If technology improves and the demand for loanable funds increases by $70 billion at each interest rate, then the new equilibrium interest rate will be _____ % and the equilibrium quantity of loanable funds will be $ _____ billion. Fill in the new demand schedule in column 3 of the table, and plot this new demand curve on the graph.

c. Then, because of changes in the tax laws, households become thriftier by $140 at each interest rate. The new equilibrium interest rate will be _____ % and the new equilibrium quantity of loanable funds will be $ _____ billion. Fill in the new supply schedule in column 5 of the table, and plot this new supply curve on the graph.

3. Firms make investment decisions based on the rate of return and the interest rate.

a. In each of the following simple cases, calculate the rate of return on an investment.

(1) You invest in a new machine that costs $2000 but which is expected to increase total revenues by $2075 in 1 year._____%

(2) You invest in a new piece of equipment that costs $150,000 but which is expected to increase total revenues in 1 year by $160,000. _____%

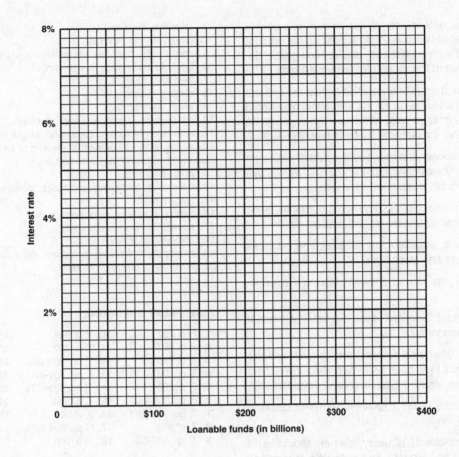

Interest rate (y-axis: 2%, 4%, 6%, 8%)

Loanable funds (in billions) (x-axis: 0, $100, $200, $300, $400)

(3) You invest in a new plant that costs $3 million and which is expected to increase total revenues in 1 year by $3.5 million. _____ %

b. Given each of the following interest rates, in which cases (1, 2, and 3) in **3a** would you make an investment?

(1) An interest rate of 5% _____

(2) An interest rate of 8% _____

(3) An interest rate of 15% _____

4. In the table below, enter the value at year's end of $100 compounded at 4 percent interest that is paid at the end of each year.

Years of compounding	Value at year's end
1	$ _____
2	_____
3	_____
4	_____

5. The following table shows estimated wages and salaries, proprietors' income, corporate profits, interest, rent, and the total income paid to American resource suppliers in a recent year.

Wages and salaries	$5642 billion
Proprietors' income	717 billion
Corporate profits	967 billion
Interest	571 billion
Rent	139 billion
Total income	$8036 billion

a. Wages and salaries were _____ % of the total income.

b. Labor's share of the total income was _____ % and capital's share was _____ %.

■ **SHORT ANSWER AND ESSAY QUESTIONS**

1. Explain what determines the economic rent paid for the use of land. What is unique about the supply of land?

2. What economic difficulties would be encountered if the government adopted Henry George's single tax proposal as a means of confiscating this surplus? What do the critics think of the concept of a single tax on land?

3. Even though land rent is an economic surplus payment, it is also an economic cost for the individual use of land. Why and how can it be both an economic surplus payment and an economic cost?

4. Explain what determines (a) the amount of loanable funds that households are willing to supply, (b) the amount that businesses wish to demand, and (c) how these desires are resolved in the market for loanable funds.

5. How might a change in productivity affect the interest rate? How might a change in the tax laws affect household savings and the interest rate? What are the implications if the supply curve for loanable funds is highly inelastic?

6. What is the connection between the rate of return on a capital goods investment and the interest rate? Give examples of possible investment situations.

7. Explain the concept of the time-value of money using compound interest, future value, and present value.

8. Why are there actually many different interest rates in the economy at any given time?

9. What is the pure rate of interest? How is it approximated?

10. What important functions does the rate of interest perform in the economy?

11. What is the difference between the nominal and the real interest rates? How does each one affect investment spending or decisions about research and development?

12. What are usury laws? Explain in terms of demand and supply analysis.

13. What are the effects of usury laws on allocation of credit, borrowers and lenders, and economic efficiency?

14. What is economic profit? In what way is economic profit a return to entrepreneurial ability?

15. Why would there be no economic profit in a purely competitive and static economy?

16. Why is the distinction between insurable and uninsurable risk important from an economic profit perspective? What are three sources that contribute to uninsurable risk?

17. How does economic profit arise from innovation?

18. "The risks that an entrepreneur assumes arise because of uncertainties that are external to the firm and because of uncertainties that are developed by the initiative of the firm itself." Explain.

19. Explain why profit arising from monopoly is not economically desirable, while profit arising from uncertainty is economically desirable.

20. What part of the income paid to American resource suppliers is labor's share, and what part is capitalists' share? Have the shares changed much since 1900?

ANSWERS

Chapter 14 Rent, Interest, and Profit

FILL-IN QUESTIONS

1. land, natural, fixed
2. demand, supply

3. incentive, surplus
4. unearned, tax, revenue
5. productivity, cost, has alternative uses, surplus payment
6. interest, percentage, is not, is not
7. loanable, equal to
8. directly, inversely
9. fewer, smaller
10. an increase, supply, increase, demand
11. time-value of money, compound, larger, smaller
12. *a.* risk; *b.* length of loan; *c.* amount of loan; *d.* tax status of loan (or investment) (any order for *a–d*)
13. pure, long-term
14. decreases, decreases, increases, increases
15. real, nominal
16. usury, nonmarket, borrowers, less
17. economic, normal, economic
18. uninsurable, innovation
19. monopoly, decreased, increased, decreased
20. 80%, 20%, remained stable

TRUE–FALSE QUESTIONS

1. F, p. 297	10. F, p. 301	19. F, p. 305
2. F, p. 297	11. T, p. 302	20. F, p. 306
3. T, p. 298	12. T, pp. 302–303	21. T, p. 306
4. F, pp. 297–298	13. F, pp. 303–304	22. F, p. 306
5. F, p. 298	14. T, pp. 303–304	23. F, pp. 306–307
6. F, pp. 299–300	15. T, p. 304	24. F, p. 307
7. T, pp. 300–301	16. F, p. 304	25. T, pp. 307–308
8. T, p. 300	17. F, pp. 304–305	
9. T, pp. 300–301	18. T, p. 305	

MULTIPLE-CHOICE QUESTIONS

1. c, p. 297	10. b, pp. 300–301	19. c, p. 305
2. a, p. 297	11. d, p. 301	20. d, p. 305
3. b, pp. 297–298	12. d, p. 302	21. a, p. 306
4. b, pp. 298–299	13. b, pp. 303–304	22. b, p. 306
5. c, p. 299	14. a, pp. 303–304	23. c, pp. 306–307
6. b, pp. 297, 299	15. d, p. 304	24. d, p. 307
7. b, p. 300	16. b, p. 304	25. d, p. 309
8. a, p. 300	17. b, p. 304	
9. d, pp. 300–301	18. c, p. 304	

PROBLEMS

1. *a.* 250; *b.* 300,000; *c.* graph; *d.* 0, 300,000
2. *a.* (1) 6, 200, 200, (2) 100, 240, 140, (3) 250, 180, 70; *b.* 8, 220; 120, 170, 220, 270, 320, 370; *c.* 4, 320; 400, 380, 360, 340, 320, 300
3. *a.* (1) 3.75; (2) 6.67; (3) 16.67; *b.* (1) 2, 3; (2) 3; (3) 3
4. 104.00, 108.16, 112.49, 116.99.
5. *a.* 70; *b.* 79, 21

SHORT ANSWER AND ESSAY QUESTIONS

1. p. 297	8. pp. 303–304	15. p. 306
2. pp. 298–299	9. p. 304	16. pp. 306–307
3. p. 299	10. pp. 304–305	17. p. 307
4. pp. 300–301	11. pp. 304–305	18. pp. 306–307
5. pp. 301	12. p. 305	19. p. 307
6. p. 301	13. p. 305	20. p. 309
7. pp. 302–303	14. p. 306	

CHAPTER 15

Natural Resource and Energy Economics

This chapter discusses many issues related to natural resource and energy economics. The material is important because it provides an understanding of why dire predictions for the economy related to energy or resource use turn out to be false. It also shows how resources can be efficiently managed to increase economic output and how such resources can be conserved and sustained over time.

The first major section of the chapter investigates two dire predictions. The first one is that **population growth** will overwhelm the economy and thus lead to declining living standards. The second one is that the economy will run out of **supplies of resources** for sustaining economic growth. Neither prediction has turned out to be true for many reasons as you will learn from the chapter. As nations have grown and living standards have improved, nations have experienced a decline in birthrates such that they are lower than the replacement rate necessary to keep the population from falling over time. Also, the economy is not likely to run out of resource supplies because total demand for resources is starting to decline and the supply of resources to meet the demand is ample and increasing.

The second section of the chapter looks at **energy economics.** Here you will learn that energy demand has leveled off in recent years in developed countries such as the United States. One reason for this change is that there has been a huge increase in energy efficiency. This efficiency keeps improving because of new developments in technology that help make better use of energy inputs. As a consequence, the U.S. economy has been able to increase real output per capita by slightly more than one-third from 1988–2007 while at the same time energy inputs per capita have remained relatively constant.

Another dire prediction addressed in this section of the chapter is that the economy is running out of energy. This prediction is another false one because it fails to take into account the effects of increasing energy prices on the viability of alternative energy sources. In a dynamic economy, as one energy resource becomes scarcer and higher-priced, it creates incentives to find and use other energy resources that will substitute for that energy resource. As energy prices rise, they will provide incentives for greater energy production.

The third and remaining sections of the chapter discuss **natural resource economics** and how to manage natural resources for efficient and sustainable use in the economy. One important tool that is used to make resource decisions is the calculation of present value. The ability of policy makers to compare the present value of current or future uses in the calculation of the net benefits of resources helps them decide how much of a resource to consume today or conserve for the future. This approach provides economic incentives for efficient management and conservation of resources.

There are two basic types of natural resources. **Non-renewable resources** such as oil, coal, metal ores, or natural gas must be pumped out or mined from the ground before they can be used. The determination of how much to pump or mine in the present or the future again involves the calculation of present value. A simple model is used to show that under the right incentive structure, profit-maximizing firms will extract nonrenewable resources in an efficient manner over time to maximize the net benefits and the profit stream. If, however, there are weak or uncertain property rights, there is a market failure and it leads to more extraction in the present and less conservation. Two applications are used to illustrate this final point: the mining of conflict diamonds and the preservation of elephants.

The second type of resources is **renewable resources** such as forests, wildlife, and fisheries. In this case, too, clear and enforceable property rights are important for the optimal and efficient harvesting of such resources, and for the conservation and sustainable use of such resources over time. If property rights are not clear or enforceable, then firms have more of a profit incentive to harvest today and less of an incentive to conserve such resources for the future.

The property rights problem is especially complex when considering the conservation and sustainability of fisheries. For this issue, economists have recommended the limits on the total catch of fish and the use of tradable catch quotas for individual fishers so their fishing is conducted in the least-costly way and the fish population remains large enough to reproduce and grow.

■ CHECKLIST

When you have studied this chapter you should be able to

☐ Explain Malthus's theory about population and economic growth.
☐ Discuss the trends in living standards and birthrates over time.
☐ Describe the predictions for future population growth.
☐ Identify the two major factors affecting the demand for resources.

☐ Explain the trends in the long-run supply of commodity resources.

☐ Describe the trends in resource consumption per person since the 1950s.

☐ Compare the expected demand for resources to the expected supply of resources.

☐ Discuss why there is cause for optimism about the availability of supply of resources in the future.

☐ Define energy economics.

☐ Explain why the demand for energy resources has not outstripped the supply.

☐ Use electrical power generation as an example to illustrate why energy use has become more efficient.

☐ Define natural resource economics.

☐ Distinguish between renewable and nonrenewable natural resources.

☐ Use present value to evaluate decisions about the optimal use of a limited supply of a nonrenewable resource.

☐ Define user cost of exaction and extraction costs.

☐ Use a graph of user cost and extraction cost to show how a firm will decide how much of a resource to extract in the present or the future.

☐ Use a graph of user cost and extraction cost to show how an increase in expected future profits leads to less extraction.

☐ Explain how market failures lead to excessive present use of a resource.

☐ Discuss the situation of conflict diamonds and elephant preservation.

☐ Explain why property rights are important for conservation of forests.

☐ Discuss the optimal harvesting of forests.

☐ Describe optimal management of fisheries.

☐ Evaluate alternative government policies to limit catch sizes for fish.

☐ Explain the economic incentives of a policy of TAC and ITQs.

☐ Explain the relationship between environmental quality and economic growth based on GDP per capita (Last Word).

■ **CHAPTER OUTLINE**

1. Living standards for the average American today are at least 12 times higher than they were in 1800. The population is larger today and resource use per person is higher. The increasing demand for and concerns about a limited supply of resources have raised questions about whether these high living standards can be sustained.

   a. There are many aspects of **population growth** that have changed over time.

   (1) Thomas Malthus in his "An Essay on the Principle of Population" argued that human living standards could only temporarily rise above subsistence levels. In his view, higher living standards would bring forth more population and the increased population would eventually reduce living standards. The opposite, however, has occurred. Higher living standards have resulted in birthrates that are lower than the *replacement rate*

that is necessary to keep a population from declining over time. The majority of the world's population now resides in nations where the *total fertility rate* is less than that needed to keep a nation's population stable over time.

(2) *Demographers,* the scientists who study human population, find that the world population growth is slowing and turning negative in many nations. Many demographers think that the world's population will only rise to fewer than 9 billion people in the next 50 years and then decline rapidly. This possible demographic shift means that there will be a substantial decrease in the demand for resources.

(3) The world's population increased rapidly from 1800 to the present because of the rapid fall in the death rate due to better medical care and modernization. As living standards begin to rise and the death rate to fall, people still are slow to realize that they need few children to ensure that some of the children will survive to adulthood.

(4) The overall world population is increasing because countries such as India and Indonesia are still in the transition phase where death rates have fallen, but birthrates are still high. In other nations with rising standards of living and modernization birthrates are falling below the replacement rate. This change is likely to produce a decline in world population during this century.

(5) Demographers have been surprised by the rapid decline in the fertility rate below the replacement rate in many nations and attribute the change to changing attitudes towards religion, greater labor market opportunities for women outside the household, and the increasing cost of raising children. It appears that the view of children has changed from one of their being an economic asset for families, as was the case in countries with an agricultural economy, to one of their being an economic liability, costly to raise to adulthood, as is the case in nations that have modernized.

   b. Resource consumption per person has also changed over time.

(1) Many individuals and groups have made dire predictions about the decline in living standards and explosive population growth that will outstrip the capacity of the economy to supply resources, but the predictions have been wrong. The reasons are twofold. The population growth rate has fallen substantially as living standards have risen around the world. Also, the supply of productive resources has been increasing faster than the demand for resources, thus driving down the price of resources.

(2) The real cost (inflation adjusted) of buying resource commodities in 2007 was about 70 percent lower than it was in the initial 1845–1850 period. The long-run decline in the prices of these commodities indicates that the supply of such resources has grown faster than the demand for them that arises because of the population increase and rising consumption per person.

(3) The demand trends are likely to continue into the future. There is likely to be a decline in population this century and resource consumption per person is likely

to remain relatively constant or decline. The demand trends and the long-run decline in resource commodity prices indicate that resource supplies have been able to meet growth and exceed demand.

(4) The decline in resource consumption per person can be seen in data from the United States on total and per capita water use, trash generation, and energy use. In fact, annual per capita energy use in the United States peaked in 1979 at 360 million **British thermal units** (BTU). (A BTU is the amount of energy required to raise the temperature of 1 pound of water by 1 degree Fahrenheit.)

(5) Resource demand is likely to increase significantly during the next few decades as more countries modernize and begin to consume more energy and other resources per capita. The increasing demand in developing countries will be offset somewhat by the declining demand in richer nations as population growth and resource use per capita decline in these nations. Improvements in technology should also contribute to more efficient resource use.

(6) There will continue to be imbalances in resource availability and demand in certain regions that can cause conflicts and challenges. Water is very scarce in the Middle East and other arid and desert regions of the world. Oil is more plentiful in the Middle East and highly sought in Europe and the United States.

2. Energy economics studies how people deal with the fact there are relatively unlimited wants for energy and relatively limited energy resources. This scarcity problem involves changes in demand and supply and applies to all types of energy resources or sources such as oil, coal, natural gas, nuclear power, hydroelectric power, and renewables.

a. In recent years, the demand for energy has leveled off in the United States and developing countries. One reason for this development is that the economy has become increasingly efficient at using energy to produce goods and services. For example, as energy input per capita has remained relatively constant, real GDP per capita rose by 37% from 1988 to 2007.

b. The increase in energy efficiency has been part of a long-term trend. From 1950 to 2006, real GDP increased by about 2.25 times per million BTUs of energy consumed. One factor contributing to this more efficient use of energy has been the availability of better technology over the period.

c. One of the interesting aspects of energy efficiency is that it involves using a mix of energy inputs, some of which are more expensive than others. Electrical power generation provides an illustration of this point. An electric plant faces varying demands for power during the day and night. To meet these varying demands, electric companies will build a large plant that requires a high fixed cost to build, but produces energy at a low price when it is fully operational and meets most of peak consumer demand. To supplement its energy production for peak demand periods, instead of building another large plant, it will build a smaller plant that has a lower fixed cost to build, but produces energy at a higher cost.

d. One concern people have about energy is whether the economy is running out of the energy, particularly oil. Economists view this situation rather as one where the economy is running out of *cheap* energy. As is known from basic economics, as the price of oil rises, alternative sources of energy become economically viable. And as technology reduces the cost of producing such alternatives, their prices will fall, bringing forth more energy production. However, there are other concerns about the types of alternative energy sources developed and the degree to which they impose negative externalities on the environment.

3. Natural resource economics focuses on maximizing the net benefits from policies or actions taken to extract or harvest a natural resource.

a. The term **net benefits** refers to the difference between the total dollar value of all the benefits of a project and the total dollar value of all the costs. The decision can be a complex one because some of these costs and benefits are incurred in the present and others are incurred in the future.

b. The type of natural resource makes a large difference in the application of this net benefits rule. **Renewable natural resources** include such items as forests, wildlife, rivers, lakes, oceans, the atmosphere, and solar energy. These resources are capable of growing back or renewing themselves, and thus can provide benefits in perpetuity if managed well. **Nonrenewable natural resources** include such items as oil, coal, natural gas, and metal ores that are found in relatively fixed supply.

c. The challenge of natural resource economics is to design incentive structures that maximize the net benefits, and also conserve resources in the present so they are available in the future.

4. Natural resource economists use **present value** to evaluate future possibilities.

a. For example, assume it costs $50 a barrel to pump oil today, but it costs $60 a barrel to pump it in five years. If there is a 5 percent interest rate, it makes more sense to pump oil today because $60 received five years in the future would be worth only $47.01 today [$60/(1 + .05)^5 = $47.01] (see Chapter 14 for more discussion of present value).

b. Present value calculations enable decision makers to compare the net benefits of using a natural resource today with conserving the natural resource for future use. As a result of such net benefit decisions, natural resources will be used more efficiently in the economy either in the present or in the future.

5. Nonrenewable resources include oil, coal, and other resources that must be pumped or mined from the ground. A company has the goal of maximizing profits, but this involves maximizing the stream of profits over the extraction period. Every bit of a nonrenewable natural resource that is extracted and sold today has a **user cost** in the form of its not being extracted and sold in the future. Current extraction and use means lower future extraction and use.

a. The decision between present and future extraction can be illustrated with a graph that shows a firm's cost of extraction for mining a resource. The graph shows cost or dollars on the vertical axis and the first-year quantity extracted on the horizontal axis. The *extraction cost (EC)* line will be upward sloping because it typically costs more to extract more of the resource in the first year. Where the EC line crosses the horizontal market price line determines the quantity (Q_0) extraction of the resource.

b. But the EC line does not account for all the costs. For each unit extracted today there is a user cost, which is the present value of the profits that the firm would earn if the extraction and sale of each ton of coal were delayed until the second year. When this user cost (UC) is added to the *extraction costs (EC)*, it creates a total cost (TC) line that is parallel to the EC line but shifted upward by the amount of the user cost. This TC line crosses the market price line at a lower quantity (Q_1). This result means that a small quantity will be extracted than would be the case if only EC is considered.

c. The general point is that the firm will produce a quantity of the resource the first year so long as the first-year profit is greater than the present value of the second-year profit. A firm will not mine all of its resource the first year, but seek to maximize the stream of profits over time.

d. If future profits are expected to increase, then the user cost will increase and thus shift the TC line upward. The higher TC line means that the firm will extract less of the resource today and more of the resource in the future than was the previous case. Thus, given the right institutional structure and incentives, profit-maximizing firms will extract resources efficiently over time to obtain the most net benefits.

e. Firms are willing to reduce current extraction if they have the ability to profit from future extraction and sale of their products. Market failures, however, can lead to excessive present use of resources. If property rights are uncertain, then a firm has less incentive to conserve a resource for future extraction and will increase extraction today. Weak or uncertain property rights reduce the user cost to zero and give more incentive to extract today.

f. Two cases where resources will be extracted too quickly if there is no way to profit from conservation are the following.

(1) *Conflict diamonds* are diamonds that are mined in war zones. This mining is very wasteful precisely because of the uncertainty over the control of the mine, as the war can change which army controls the mine. The incentive in this case is thus more current extraction, which will result in more difficult and expensive extraction in the future when the war ends and the nation needs the revenue.

(2) *Elephant preservation* is also affected by property rights. In those cases where villages have been given financial incentives to protect the elephant herd because they receive a share of the tourist dollars, herds grow. In those cases in which the state controls the resource, and property rights are not enforced, there is illegal poaching and elephant herds decline.

6. Profit incentives and property rights affect the extraction or harvesting of renewable resources influencing whether they are preserved and provide a steady stream of profits over time. Property rights need to be structured properly and enforced so there is a strong profit incentive to manage the resource on a sustainable basis and not extract or harvest too much of the resource today.

a. Forests in different countries are managed differently and this explains why forests in some countries are increasing and in other countries there is widespread deforestation. In countries where the forests are increasing, there are clear property rights and they are enforced, so there are good profit incentives to harvest woods on a sustainable basis over time. In countries experiencing deforestation, the property rights are uncertain or not enforced, so there is a strong profit incentive to harvest more trees today because the possibility of future harvesting or profitability is uncertain.

b. Optimal harvesting of trees in a forest involves understanding the growth rate of trees in those cases in which property rights are clear and enforceable. For example, trees may grow at a slow rate during their first 50 years, then growth at a fast rate from 50 to 100 years, and then grow at a slow or zero rate thereafter. A lumber company will have a strong profit incentive to harvest young trees some time during the fast growth period because it will produce the most wood in the least amount of time. Of course the market demand condition and the cost of harvesting will affect the precise year for optimal harvesting that produces the greatest net benefits for the company.

c. A *fishery* is defined as a stock of fish or marine animals that is considered to be a distinct group such as Pacific tuna or Alaskan crab. Oceans are common property resources without ownership. The only property rights come after a fisher catches the fish. In this case, there are strong incentives for the fisher to overfish the ocean to catch more fish before another fisher does so. This overfishing of a fishery can lead to *fishery collapse* when a fish population becomes so depleted that it can no longer reproduce at a sustainable rate. Data from 2003 show that only 3% of the world's fisheries are underexploited, but 76% are fully exploited, overexploited, depleted, or recovering from depletion.

d. Governments have adopted policies to reduce the number of fish caught each year so that fisheries can be prevented from collapsing. Some policies, such as limiting the number of days of fishing or the number of fishing boats, have not worked because the fishers would use bigger boats that would allow them to catch the same number of fish as before but in a fewer number of days and with fewer boats.

(1) One policy that seems to work is to use a *total allowable catch* (TAC) system in which biologists specify the TAC for a fishery. The chief advantage of this system is that it limits the actual amount of the catch so that the uncaught fish will still be able to *sustain* the population. One problem with the TAC is that fishing costs rise because fishers buy bigger boats to catch as many fish as possible before the TAC limit is reached.

(2) Economists like the TAC system, but prefer it to be used with *individual transferable quotas (ITQs)* that also limit the individual catch size by a fisher to a specified quantity. This policy provides disincentives to use bigger boats under a TAC system alone because each fisher has a specified catch limit, and thus it reduces fishing costs. The ITQs issued will also add up to the TAC limit so the fish population can be sustained. It also encourages fishing to be done at the least cost because ITQs are tradable quotas. An ITQ held by a fisher who is less efficient at fishing can be traded to one who is more efficient at fishing. The overall result is that there will be efficiency gains for society and fishing will be less costly.

7. (Last Word). The evidence indicates that economic growth and rising living standards are good for the environment because as nations become wealthier, they tend to spend more on environmental protection and adopt better economic policies to correct environmental problems. A graph with an environmental performance index on the vertical axis and GDP per capita on the horizontal axis shows that nations with a low level of GDP per capita have a low EPI score and nations with a high GDP per capita have a high EPI score. The results indicate that economic growth can promote a healthier environment.

■ HINTS AND TIPS

1. This chapter builds on ideas and concepts presented in previous chapters. Make sure you review the concept of present value presented in Chapter 14.

2. It might be easy to get lost in the tables and graphs presented in this chapter and miss the general point. All of the tables and graphs in this chapter are simply used to illustrate trends or general points described in the text. Make sure you find and highlight those general points in the text.

3. One of the great advantages of understanding the material in this chapter is that it is useful for showing that dire predictions about economic catastrophes are wrong. These predictions include population growth undermining living standards, energy resources being exhausted, or demise of renewable resources. The economic analysis in this chapter shows that the economy and ecosystems are more robust than realized, especially when there are clear and enforceable property rights and good economic incentives for proper resource use.

■ IMPORTANT TERMS

replacement rate	extraction costs
total fertility rate	conflict diamonds
demographers	fishery
British thermal unit (BTU)	fishery collapse
net benefits	sustainable fishing
renewable natural resources	total allowable catch (TAC)
nonrenewable natural resources	individual transferable quota (ITQ)
user cost	

SELF-TEST

■ FILL-IN QUESTIONS

1. Per capita living standards in the United States are at least (2, 12) _____ times higher than they were in 1800. This increase in living standards has required using much (larger, smaller) _____ amounts of resources to produce more goods and services.

2. The increase in resource use is the result of two factors: There has been a large (increase, decrease) _____ in resource use per person and there are now (more, less) _____ people consuming resources than in previous periods.

3. Thomas Malthus predicted that higher living standards would tend to lead to (higher, lower) _____ birthrates, but the opposite has occurred because higher living standards have led to _____ birthrates.

4. The majority of the world's population now lives in countries where the total fertility rate is (greater, less) _____ than the replacement rate of (2.1, 3.3) _____ births per woman per lifetime that is necessary to keep a country's population stable over time.

5. The world population growth is slowing and in many countries is it is turning (positive, negative) _____. As a result the demand for resources in the future will be (higher, lower) _____ than would be case if population levels continued to increase.

6. Many demographers expect the world's population will reach a maximum of (9, 18) _____ billion people in the next 50 years before beginning to (rise, decline) _____.

7. The expected (rise, decline) _____ in population levels and the fact that per capita resource use has leveled off or (risen, fallen) _____ suggests that the total demand for resources is likely to reach a peak in the relatively near future before (rising, falling) _____ over time.

8. The confidence that resource supplies will be likely to grow faster than resource demands in the future is based on the fact that since 1850 the real (inflation-adjusted) prices of resources have fallen by about (20, 70) _____ percent. This fall in price happened at the same time that total resource use was (increasing, decreasing) _____.

9. In the future, resource supplies should grow (slower, faster) _____ than resource demands because the population is growing _____ and resource use per capita has leveled off or turned negative.

10. Living standards can continue to rise without consuming more energy due to (more, less) _____ efficient technologies for producing energy. Real GDP per capita in the United States increased by slightly more than (one-third, two-thirds) _____ from 1988 to 2007 while annual per capita energy consumption (increased, decreased, remained constant) _____.

11. Differences in (variable, fixed) _____ costs in energy production mean that a wide variety of energy sources are used in the economy even if some sources are (more, less) _____ costly than others.

12. For example, coal-fired electric generating plants that generate large amounts of electricity use a (low-cost, high-cost) _____ energy source, but these plants are _____ to build; other plants that produce small amounts of electricity use _____ fuel sources, but are _____ to build. An investment's proper current price is equal to the sum of the (present, future) _____ values of each of the investment's expected _____ payments.

13. The United States (is, is not) _____ running out of energy such as oil because there are other energy sources that become viable to produce and sell as the price of energy (falls, rises) _____.

14. Natural resources such as forests and wildlife are (nonrenewable, renewable) _____ whereas natural resources such as oil or coal are _____.

15. Renewable and nonrenewable natural resources tend to be overused in the (present, future) _____ unless there are arrangements created that provide resource users with a way to benefit from conservation. Governments can ensure that there are net benefits from conservation by strictly defining and enforcing (civil, property) _____ rights so that resource owners know that if they conserve a resource, they will be able to use it in the (future, present) _____.

16. The optimal level of extraction of a nonrenewable resource over time is based on calculation of a total cost, which is the combination of the cost of not being able to extract it in the future, which is called the (user, extraction) _____ cost, plus the cost of producing the resource, which is called the _____ cost.

17. In a mining situation, if only extraction costs were considered as the total cost, there would be (more, less) _____ of the resource extracted in the present and _____ will be extracted in the future, but if total costs include both the user cost and extraction costs, then _____ will be extracted in the present and _____ will be extracted in the future.

18. It is difficult to encourage conservation in the open ocean because it is difficult to define or enforce (civil, property) _____ rights. This situation means that there is a rush by each fisher to catch as much as possible in the (least, most) _____ amount of time. These actions cause (over-, under-) _____ fishing and the fish population to (expand, collapse) _____.

19. Closer to shore nations can define property rights within the waters they control and set (limits, prices) _____ on the fish caught.

20. A policy that specifies the complete amount that all fishers can catch of a fishery is the (total allowable catch, individual transferable quota) _____ whereas the policy that specifies that amount each fisher can catch is the _____.

■ **TRUE–FALSE QUESTIONS**

Circle T if the statement is true, F if it is false.

1. The average American enjoys a standard of living at least 12 times higher than that of the average American living in 1800. **T F**

2. Higher living standards are associated with lower birthrates. **T F**

3. The replacement rate is the average number of children that a woman is expected to have during her lifetime. **T F**

4. Total fertility rates in many nations are well below the 2.1 rate necessary to keep the population stable over time. **T F**

5. Demographers expect the world's population to reach a peak of about 9 billion people or fewer around the middle of this century before beginning to decline. **T F**

6. The long-run evidence indicates that the available supply of productive resources to be made into goods and services has been increasing faster than the demand for those resources for at least 150 years. **T F**

7. The long-run fall of commodity prices implies that commodity supplies have grown slower than the demand for them. **T F**

8. Resource consumption per person has either leveled off or declined in the past decade. **T F**

9. A BTU is a measure of trash generation and refers to a biodegradable trash unit.　　**T F**

10. If per capita consumption continues to stay the same or decrease while the population declines, total resource demand will decline.　　**T F**

11. Resource demand is likely to increase substantially for the next few decades as large parts of the world modernize and begin to consume as much per capita as the citizens of rich countries do today.　　**T F**

12. Since energy is only one input into a production process, often the best energy source to use is sometimes rather expensive, but still the best choice when other costs are taken into account.　　**T F**

13. In developed countries, per capita energy use has increased significantly in recent years.　　**T F**

14. Better technology means that more output can be produced with the same amount of energy input, so rising living standards in the future will not necessarily depend on using more energy.　　**T F**

15. It is highly likely that the United States will run out of energy when the cost of a barrel of oil reaches $250.　　**T F**

16. Net benefits are the total dollar value of all benefits minus the total dollar value of all costs.　　**T F**

17. Aquifers are considered to be a nonrenewable resource.　　**T F**

18. Present value calculation provides a financial incentive to make sure that resources will be conserved for future use whenever doing so will generate higher net benefits than using them in the present.　　**T F**

19. A mining company's goal of maximizing profits means choosing a strategy that maximizes the stream of profits over the time of extraction.　　**T F**

20. Extraction cost means that a resource that is extracted and sold today will come at a cost of its not being extracted and sold in the future.　　**T F**

21. Under the right institutional structure, profit-maximizing firms will extract resources efficiently over time so that each unit of resource will tend to be extracted when the gains from doing so are greatest.　　**T F**

22. Resources will tend to be extracted too slowly if there is no way to benefit from conservation.　　**T F**

23. In the case of forests, if property rights are ill-defined or not enforced, resource owners have more incentive to cut trees today and less incentive to conserve trees for future use.　　**T F**

24. A fishery collapse occurs when a fishery's population is sent into a rapid decline because the fish are being raised and released into the water at too fast a rate.　　**T F**

25. Where governments can define property rights for fishing, the best system for limiting fishing involves combining total allowable catch (TAC) with individual transferable quota (ITQ) limits for individual fishers.　　**T F**

■ **MULTIPLE-CHOICE QUESTIONS**

Circle the letter that corresponds to the best answer.

1. Which is a factor that explains why resource use has increased?
(a) fewer people are alive today
(b) living standards have decreased
(c) the cost of resources has increased
(d) consumption per person has increased

2. What is the total fertility rate that is needed to keep the population constant over time?
(a) 1.5 births
(b) 2.1 births
(c) 3.0 births
(d) 3.6 births

3. One major reason why the world's population increased so rapidly from 1800 to the present is because
(a) the total fertility rate was less than the death rate
(b) the total fertility rate was less than the replacement rate
(c) higher living standards contributed to a large increase in the number of births over time
(d) higher living standards improved health care and resulted in a lower death rate

4. One major reason predictions that population growth would outstrip the economy's capacity to support a population turned out to be false is that
(a) the supply of resources increased faster than the demand for them
(b) the demand for resources increased faster than the supply of them
(c) the population growth rate slowed and so did living standards around the world
(d) governments around the world set strict quotas on the total fertility rates

5. Compared with the 1845–1850 period, the real cost of buying commodities today is about
(a) 20 percent higher
(b) 20 percent lower
(c) 70 percent higher
(d) 70 percent lower

6. Which would be a factor that would make the prospects hopeful for overcoming the demand for resources in the future?
(a) Total fertility rates are increasing in many nations.
(b) Total death rates are increasing in many nations.
(c) Resource consumption per person has leveled off in wealthier nations.
(d) Resource consumption per person has leveled off in developing nations such as China and India.

7. Recent trends in water use, energy consumption, and trash generation indicate that the total demand for resources is likely to
(a) increase substantially over time
(b) decrease and then increase substantially over time
(c) trough in the near future before rising as populations grow
(d) peak in the near future before falling as populations decline

8. About what percentage of energy was generated by coal-fired plants in 2006?
(a) 39 percent
(b) 49 percent
(c) 79 percent
(d) 99 percent

9. The main reason the nation will not run out of energy is that
(a) the demand for energy has risen substantially
(b) the demand for energy has fallen substantially
(c) the government can control the price of energy and keep it low
(d) rising energy prices bring forth more supply from alternative sources

10. A forestry company wants to spend $1000 per acre today to plant seedlings that will grow into $125,000 in 100 years. The present value of $125,000 in 100 years at an interest rate of 5 percent is $950.56. The present value results indicate that the company should
(a) not make the investment because the future is too uncertain
(b) make the investment because an acre is worth $125,000 today
(c) make the invest because the benefits are greater then the costs
(d) not make the investment because the costs are greater than the benefits

Answer Questions 11, 12, 13, 14, and 15 based on the following graph for a firm that mines coal over a two-year period. P is the market price.

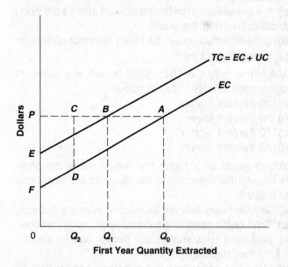

First Year Quantity Extracted

11. User cost is measured by the difference between
(a) A–B
(b) E–F
(c) P–B
(d) P–F

12. If only extraction cost is considered, then during the first year the firm will extract
(a) 0
(b) Q_0
(c) Q_1
(d) Q_2

13. If the firm considers both extraction costs and user costs, then during the first year the firm will extract
(a) 0
(b) Q_0
(c) Q_1
(d) Q_2

14. The profit that a firm can extract at Q_2 the first year is equal to
(a) C–D
(b) E–F
(c) P–E
(d) P–F

15. Assume that the firm is producing at Q_1. If user costs increased in the first year because of an increase in expected future profits, this increase will shift the TC line
(a) down and reduce the quantity extracted to less than Q_1
(b) down and increase the quantity extracted to more than Q_1
(c) up and reduce the quantity extracted to less than Q_1
(d) up and increase the quantity extracted to more than Q_1

16. Conflict diamonds are diamonds that are mined
(a) under production conditions that use old technology rather than new technology
(b) under war conditions where there is little incentive to conserve them
(c) where the government specifies that the diamonds cannot be sold outside the nation
(d) where the diamond producer is fighting a takeover offer from another company

17. Which offers the best economic explanation as to why elephant populations have declined in many parts of Africa?
(a) The prices of ivory tusks and elephant hides have declined.
(b) Governments spend too much money on defining and enforcing property rights.
(c) There is less interest in hunting elephants for sport or photographing them.
(d) There are few economic incentives to provide benefits from preserving elephants.

18. If the property rights to renewable resources are clear and enforced, resource owners will have
(a) strong incentives to preserve the resources and will harvest them slowly over time
(b) weak incentives to preserve the resources and will harvest them quickly over time
(c) strong incentives to turn to government for a subsidy to preserve the resources
(d) weak incentives to profit from the resources by harvesting them either in the present or the future

19. Forestry companies have an incentive
(a) to harvest the trees early in the growth cycle because of the expense of growing for so many years
(b) to harvest the trees only after they have fully matured because more profit can be made at that point

(c) not to harvest the trees early in the growth cycle, but cut them down before they are fully mature

(d) not to harvest the trees in middle age, but cut them down either early in the growth cycle or after they have fully matured

20. A stock of fish or other marine animal that can be thought of as a logically distinct group is a
(a) catch
(b) quota
(c) fishery
(d) school

21. In the case of Maine red hake, the annual catch fell from 190.3 million metric tons in 1986 to less than 1 ton per year for most of the 1990s. This situation would be an example of
(a) fishery collapse
(b) replacement rate
(c) total fertility rate
(d) total allowable catch

22. Approximately what percentage of the world's fisheries are underexploited?
(a) 0%
(b) 3%
(c) 9%
(d) 18%

23. If a fisher is given the right to catch a specified amount of fish during a period of time and the fisher can trade this right, this would be called
(a) total allowable catch
(b) fish market allocation
(c) exchangeable fishery tariff
(d) individual transferable quota

Answer Questions 24 and 25 based on the following information. The market price of tuna is $10 per ton. It costs fisher Sven $9 a ton to catch tuna and it costs fisher Tammy $6 a ton to catch tuna. Both Sven and Tammy have ITQs to catch 1000 tons of tuna.

24. If Sven agrees to sell his ITQ to Tammy for $2 a ton, then Sven is
(a) better off because he gets $2000 from selling the ITQ and he can earn $1000 in profit from fishing
(b) better off because he gets $2000 from selling the ITQ rather than $1000 if he fished on his own
(c) worse off because he gets paid $2000 for selling the ITQ, but Tammy makes $2000 more in profit from buying his ITQ
(d) worse off because he will get $2000 by selling the ITQ but could have made $9000 in profit

25. If Sven agrees to sell his ITQ to Tammy, then there is a
(a) net cost to society because fishing costs for Sven's 1000 tons are increased by $3000
(b) net cost to society because fishing costs for Sven's 1000 tons are increased by $6000
(c) net benefit to society because fishing costs for Sven's 1000 tons are reduced by $3000
(d) net benefit to society because fishing costs for Sven's 1000 tons are reduced by $9000

■ **PROBLEMS**

1. Assume that a mining company can mine a ton of ore so that it can make a certain profit per ton by selling it in five years or selling it today. The table below shows the value in five years and the present value today and assumes a 5 percent interest rate.

Value in 5 years	Value today
$50	$39.18
60	47.01
70	54.85
80	62.68
90	70.52

a. Given a choice between selling a ton of ore to get $40 profit per barrel today or $60 profit per ton in five years, the mining company will sell the ton of ore for $_____.

b. Given a choice between selling a ton of ore to get $50 profit per ton today or $60 profit per ton in five years, the mining company will sell the ton of ore for $_____.

c. Given a choice between selling a ton of ore to get $50 profit per ton today or $70 profit per ton in five years, the mining company will sell the ton of ore for $_____.

d. Given a choice between selling a ton of ore to get $60 profit per ton today or $70 profit per ton in five years, the mining will sell the ton of ore for $_____.

e. Given a choice between selling a ton of ore to get $70 profit per ton today or $90 profit per ton in five years, the mining company will sell the ton of ore for $_____.

2. Fisher Harvey can catch tuna for $10 per ton and fisher Jose can catch tuna for $7 per ton. Both Harvey and Jose each have an individual transferable quota to catch 1000 tons of tuna. The market price of tuna is $12 per ton.

a. If both Harvey and Jose catch fish that year, the profit for Harvey will be $ and the profit for Jose will be $_____.

b. If next year, Harvey trades his quota for the year to Jose, how much should Harvey be paid for the quota to make more than he can by fishing? At least $_____.

c. Harvey decides to trade his ITQ for the year to Jose. What will be the reduction in fishing cost to society now that only Jose is doing the fishing? $_____.

d. If the market price for tuna should rise to $13 a ton, and Harvey still wants to sell his ITQ for the year to Jose, how much should Harvey be paid for the quota to be better off? At least $_____.

e. If the market price for tuna should rise to $15 a ton and Harvey sells his ITQ for the year to Jose, what will be the reduction in fishing costs to society now that only Jose is doing the fishing? $_____.

■ **SHORT ANSWER AND ESSAY QUESTIONS**

1. Describe the changes in population and living standards since 1800. What implications do these changes mean for human beings?

2. Explain how Thomas Malthus viewed population growth and contrast it with what has happened since.

3. Define total fertility rate and replacement rate and use the terms to describe the population prospects for many developed countries.

4. State the predictions about population growth offered by demographers and explain the bases on which they are made.

5. What are likely factors that have contributed to declining birthrates in developing nations?

6. Discuss whether governments are able to increase birthrates in their nations.

7. What has happened to the supply of productive resources relative to the demand for them since the 1850s? What factors account for this development?

8. Will the supply of resources be able to meet the demand for resources in the future? What evidence can you cite to make the case that the supply will meet or exceed the demand?

9. Describe the trends in total and per capita water use, energy consumption, and trash generation in the United States from 1950 to 2000. What do they indicate about resource use?

10. What is energy economics and what does it have to say about energy demand and efficiency?

11. Use the case of electrical power generation to explain why the energy resource inputs that are used are sometimes low-cost and other times high-cost.

12. Make the case that the United States is not running out of oil or energy.

13. What are net benefits, nonrenewable resources, and renewable resources?

14. Explain how present value calculations are used to evaluate future possibilities in the case of renewable resources such as a forest.

15. What is the trade-off in the extraction of nonrenewable resources? How can this trade-off be analyzed in an economic framework?

16. Explain the difference between user cost and extraction costs. How does the addition of user cost to extraction costs affect the quantity extracted in the present compared with the future? What will happen to the quantity extracted in the present compared with profitability increase in the future? Illustrate the change with a graph.

17. Explain how market failures and the lack of property rights affect resource use. Give applications using conflict diamonds and elephant preservation.

18. Explain what is needed for optimal harvesting of a forest. How do changes in economic incentives and structures affect present and future decisions?

19. Define fisheries and describe their optimal management. Why do fishery collapses occur?

20. Discuss the use of policies for total allowable catch (TAC) and individual transferable quotas (ITQs) for making fishing more efficient and sustainable.

ANSWERS

Chapter 15 Natural Resource and Energy Economics

FILL-IN QUESTIONS

1. 12, larger
2. increase, more
3. higher, lower
4. less, 2.1
5. negative, lower
6. 9, decline
7. decline, fallen, falling
8. 70, increasing
9. slower, slower
10. more, one-third, remained constant
11. fixed, more
12. low-cost, high-cost, high-cost, low-cost, present, future
13. is not, rises
14. renewable, nonrenewable
15. present, property, future
16. user, extraction
17. more, less, less, more
18. property, least, over-, collapse
19. limits
20. total allowable catch, individual transferable quota

TRUE–FALSE QUESTIONS

1. T, p. 313	**14.** T, p. 318
2. T, p. 313	**15.** F, pp. 319–320
3. F, p. 313	**16.** T, p. 321
4. T, pp. 313–314	**17.** F, p. 321
5. T, pp. 313–314	**18.** T, pp. 321–322
6. T, pp. 314–315	**19.** T, pp. 322–324
7. F, p. 315	**20.** F, pp. 322–323
8. T, p. 315	**21.** T, pp. 322–324
9. F, p. 316	**22.** F, p. 324
10. T, p. 316	**23.** T, p. 326
11. T, p. 317	**24.** F, pp. 327–328
12. T, pp. 317–318	**25.** T, pp. 328–329
13. F, p. 318	

MULTIPLE-CHOICE QUESTIONS

1. d, p. 313	**14.** a, pp. 323–324
2. b, p. 313	**15.** c, pp. 323–324
3. d, pp. 313–314	**16.** b, p. 325
4. a, p. 315	**17.** d, p. 325
5. d, p. 315	**18.** a, pp. 324–325
6. c, p. 315	**19.** c, pp. 326–327
7. d, pp. 315–317	**20.** c, p. 327
8. b, p. 319	**21.** a, pp. 327–328
9. d, pp. 319–320	**22.** b, p. 328
10. d, pp. 321–322	**23.** d, p. 329
11. b, pp. 323–324	**24.** b, p. 329
12. b, pp. 323–324	**25.** c, p. 329
13. c, pp. 323–324	

PROBLEMS

1. *a.* 60; *b.* 50; *c.* 70; *d.* 70; *e.* 90
2. *a.* 2000, 5000; *b.* 2000; *c.* 2000; *d.* 3000; *e.* 3000

SHORT ANSWER AND ESSAY QUESTIONS

1. pp. 313–314	**8.** pp. 315–317	**15.** pp. 322–324
2. p. 313	**9.** pp. 315–317	**16.** pp. 322–324
3. pp. 313–314	**10.** pp. 317–319	**17.** pp. 324–325
4. pp. 313–314	**11.** pp. 318–319	**18.** pp. 326–327
5. pp. 313–314	**12.** pp. 319–320	**19.** pp. 327–328
6. p. 314	**13.** p. 321	**20.** pp. 328–329
7. pp. 314–315	**14.** pp. 321–322	

Public Goods, Externalities, and Information Asymmetries

This chapter is the first of two on the economic role of government, a topic that was first introduced in Chapter 4. The focus is **market failure** that occurs in our economy. This failure often results in government interventions to provide public goods and services, to address externality problems such as pollution or climate change, and to improve the quality and amount of information for buyers and sellers in the private markets.

The chapter first reviews the characteristics of a **public good.** Recall from Chapter 4 that a private good is characterized by rivalry and excludability, but a public good is not. What is new in Chapter 16 is that you are shown how the demand curve and schedule for a public good are constructed and how the optimal allocation of a public good is determined. The demand and supply curves for a public good are related to the collective marginal benefit and cost of providing the good.

Governments sometimes use **cost-benefit analysis** to determine if they should undertake some specific action or project. This analysis requires the government to estimate the marginal costs and the marginal benefits of the project, and it can be used to decide when such projects should be expanded, contracted, or eliminated.

The second topic of the chapter is **externalities,** situations in market transactions that create negative externalities or positive externalities for parties not involved in the transactions. You learned in Chapter 4 that government can reduce negative externalities to society and increase positive externalities. This general point is now modified by the **Coase theorem,** which shows that government intervention is not always required because in many cases individual bargaining can settle externality disputes. If this solution is not possible, government action with direct controls or taxes may be used.

Pollution is a prime example of a negative externality. Over the years, the government has developed antipollution policies, but the market-based ones merit your attention in your study of economics. You will discover that the government can create a **market for externality rights,** and that there is a rule for the **optimal reduction of an externality.** All of this analysis has direct application to the problem of climate change and what to do about it as it relates to the economy.

Another type of market failure you will encounter in the last major section of this chapter is **asymmetric information.** You have probably never thought about the role of information in the functioning of markets, but you will discover how important information is to both buyers and sellers. For example, buyers need some assurance about the measurement standards or quality of products that they purchase, be it gasoline or medical care. The government may intervene in some markets to ensure that this information is made available to buyers.

Inadequate information in markets creates problems for sellers, too. In certain markets, such as insurance, sellers experience a **moral hazard problem** because buyers change their behavior and become less careful, and the change in behavior makes the insurance more costly to sellers. There is also an **adverse selection problem** in the insurance market because those buyers most likely to benefit (higher-risk buyers) are more likely to purchase the insurance; therefore this group imposes higher costs on sellers than if the riskers were more widely spread among the population. Actions of sellers to screen buyers would mean that fewer people will be covered by insurance and create situations that may lead to the provision of social insurance by government. Government may provide better information about workplace safety or enforce safety standards to address these information problems.

You should not finish this chapter with the sole thought that all market failures require government intervention and direct control. Some problems do require a specific government action, but other problems may be handled more efficiently or in a more optimal way through individual negotiations, lawsuits, or the use of market incentives. What is important for you to understand is the range of solutions to externality and information problems.

■ CHECKLIST

When you have studied this chapter you should be able to

☐ Compare the characteristics of a public good with a private good.

☐ Calculate the demand for a public good when given tabular data.

☐ Explain how marginal benefit is reflected in the demand for a public good.

☐ Describe the relationship between marginal cost and the supply of a public good.

☐ Identify on a graph where there is an overallocation, an underallocation, and an optimal allocation of a public good.

☐ Use cost–benefit analysis to determine the extent to which government should apply resources to a project or program when you are given the cost and benefit data.

☐ Define and give examples of positive and negative externalities.

☐ Use supply and demand graphs to illustrate how negative externalities and positive externalities affect the allocation of resources.

☐ State the conditions that are necessary for individual bargaining with the Coase theorem and give an example.

☐ Explain how liability rules and lawsuits are used to resolve externality problems.

☐ Discuss two means government uses to achieve allocative efficiency when there are negative externalities.

☐ Identify the four major provisions of the Clean Air Act of 1990 as examples of direct control by government to reduce negative externalities.

☐ Describe three government options to correct for the underallocation of resources when positive externalities are large and diffuse.

☐ Define the "tragedy of the commons."

☐ Determine the price a government agency should charge in a market for externality rights (e.g., cap-and-trade program for air pollution), when given the data for analysis.

☐ Compare the advantages of a market for externality rights with the policy of direct government controls.

☐ Explain how pollution rights are traded under the Clean Air and Clean Water Acts and in the policies of the EPA.

☐ Explain and illustrate with a graph a rule for determining society's optimal reduction of a negative externality.

☐ Discuss the economics issues involved in climate change policies and the use of a carbon tax and cap-and-trade programs.

☐ Define the terms "information failure" and "asymmetric information."

☐ Explain how inadequate information about sellers can cause market failure and give two examples of government response.

☐ Define the terms "moral hazard" and "adverse selection."

☐ Describe how inadequate information about buyers can create a moral hazard problem, an adverse selection problem, and a workplace problem, and give examples of how government can respond.

☐ Cite examples of how information failures are overcome without government intervention.

☐ Explain how the Lojack creates a positive externality.

■ **CHAPTER OUTLINE**

1. Two characteristics of a **private good** are *rivalry* and *excludability*. Rivalry means that consumption of the product by a buyer eliminates the possibility of consumption of that product by another person. Excludability refers to the ability of the seller to exclude a person from consuming the product if the person does not pay for it. A **public good,** such as national defense, is characterized by non-rivalry and nonexcludability. *Nonrivalry* means that once a public good is consumed by one person, it is still available for consumption by another person. *Nonexcludability* means that those individuals who do not pay for the public good can still obtain the benefits from the public good. These two characteristics create a **free-rider problem** where once a producer provides a public good everyone including nonpayers can receive the benefits.

a. The **demand for a public good** is determined by summing the prices that people are willing to pay collectively for the last unit of the public good at each possible quantity demanded, whereas the demand for a private good is determined by summing the quantities demanded at each possible price. The demand curve for a public good is downsloping because of the law of diminishing marginal utility.

b. The **supply curve of a public good** is upsloping because of the law of diminishing returns; additional units supplied reflect increasing marginal costs.

c. The **optimal allocation** of a public good is determined by the intersection of the supply and demand curves.

(1) If the marginal benefit exceeds the marginal cost, there is an underallocation of a public good.

(2) If the marginal cost exceeds the marginal benefit there will be an overallocation.

(3) Only when the marginal benefits equal the marginal costs is there an optimal allocation of public goods.

d. Government uses **cost-benefit analysis** to decide if it should use resources for a project and to determine the total quantity of resources it should devote to a project. The **marginal cost = marginal benefit rule** is used to make the decision. Additional resources should be devoted to a project only so long as the marginal benefits to society from the project exceed society's marginal costs. In this case, the total benefits minus the total costs are at a maximum.

2. Market failure can arise from **externalities,** or spillovers, whereby a third party bears a portion of the cost associated with the production or consumption of a good or service.

a. **Negative externalities** result in an *overallocation* of resources to the production of a product. All the costs associated with the product are not reflected in the supply curve. The producer's supply curve lies to the right of the full-cost supply curve.

b. **Positive externalities** result in an *underallocation* of resources to the production of a product. All the benefits from the product are not reflected in the demand curve. The demand curve lies to the left of the full-benefits demand curve.

c. Individual bargaining can be used to correct negative externalities or to encourage positive externalities. The **Coase theorem** suggests that private negotiations rather than government intervention should be the course of action if there is clear ownership of the property, the number of people involved is small, and the cost of bargaining is minimal. When these conditions do not hold, however, it may be necessary for government intervention.

d. The legal system can be used to resolve disputes arising from externalities. This system defines *property rights* and specifies *liability rules* that can be used for *lawsuits* on externality issues. This method has limitations because of the expense, the length of time to resolve the disputes, and the uncertainty of the outcomes.

e. When there is the potential for severe harm to common resources, such as air or water, and when the situation involves a large number of people, two types of government intervention may be necessary.

(1) **Direct controls** use legislation to ban or limit the activities that produce a negative externality. These actions reduce the supply of the products that create the negative externalities to levels that are allocatively efficient.

(2) **Specific taxes** are also applied to productive activity that creates negative externalities. These taxes increase the cost of production, and thus decrease the supply to levels that are allocatively efficient.

f. With positive externalities other government actions may be necessary to correct for the underallocation of resources.

(1) The government can give subsidies to buyers to encourage the purchase or consumption of a good or service.

(2) The government can give subsidies to producers to reduce the cost of production and increase output of a good or service.

(3) When positive externalities are extremely large, government may decide to provide the good or service.

g. There are market-based approaches to externality problems.

(1) The *tragedy of the commons* refers to situations where common resources such as air, water, or oceans are subject to pollution problems because no individual or organization has a monetary incentive to maintain the quality or purity of the resource.

(2) One solution to the problem has been to create a *market for externality rights* (or cap-and-trade program) to internalize the negative externality in a market.

(3) For example, in a cap-and-trade program, the government (a pollution-control agency) might set a limit for the amount of pollution permitted in a region (a cap). This limit means that the supply curve is perfectly inelastic (vertical) at some level of pollution. The demand curve would reflect the willingness of polluters to pay for the right to pollute at different prices. The price for pollution rights would be determined by the intersection of the demand and supply curves. Given a fixed supply curve, an increase in demand because of economic growth in the region would increase the price of pollution rights that could be traded in the market.

(4) This market solution has advantages over direct government controls. It is more efficient and thus reduces society's costs. It puts a price on pollution and thus creates a monetary incentive for businesses to not pollute or to reduce their level of pollution.

(5) Real examples of this cap-and-trade approach are found in provisions in the Clean Air Act of 1990 and policies of the Environmental Protection Agency (EPA).

h. In most cases, the *optimal reduction of an externality* is not zero from society's perspective.

(1) It occurs where the marginal cost to society from the externality and the marginal benefit of reducing it are equal (MB = MC).

(2) Over time, shifts in the marginal-cost and marginal-benefit curves change the optimal level of externality reduction.

i. A *climate-change problem* from increased carbon dioxide and other greenhouse gases may be permanently altering climate patterns and will have economic effects on different regions. In designing government policies, economists stress the use of markets to provide price and profit incentives to reduce pollution and increase energy alternatives that are less harmful to the environment. They also advocate evaluating the costs and benefits of alternative policies such as the use of carbon tax or a cap-and-trade program to reduce carbon emissions.

3. Economic inefficiency from information failures can occur in markets. These information failures arise from *asymmetric information*—unequal knowledge that is held by parties to a market transaction.

a. When information involving sellers is incomplete, inaccurate, or very costly, there will be market failures. For example, in the market for gasoline, consumers need accurate information about the amount and quality of gasoline they purchase from sellers. In the market for medical services, it is important that consumers have some assurances about the credentials of physicians. Government can respond to these information failures by such actions as establishing measurement standards and by testing and licensing.

b. Inadequate information involving buyers creates market failures.

(1) A market may produce less than the optimal amount of goods and services from society's perspective because of a *moral hazard problem,* which results when buyers alter their behavior and increase the costs of sellers. For example, the provision of insurance may cause the insured to be less cautious.

(2) An *adverse selection problem* occurs in many markets. In the case of insurance, the buyers most likely to need or benefit from insurance are the ones most likely to purchase it. These higher-risk buyers impose higher costs on sellers. Sellers then screen out the higher-risk buyers, but this action reduces the population covered by insurance in the private market. In some cases, government may establish a social insurance system that is designed to cover a much broader group of the population than would be covered by the private insurers, such as with Social Security.

(3) Market failures occur in resource markets when there is inadequate information for workers about the health hazards or safety of a workplace. Government can act to correct these problems by publishing health and safety information or by forcing businesses to provide more information. The typical approach to this problem has been the enforcement of standards for health and safety on the job.

c. Government does not always need to intervene in the private market to address information problems. Businesses can adopt policies to correct these problems, and some firms or other organizations can specialize in providing important market information for buyers or sellers.

4. (Last Word). The Lojack is a device planted in a car or truck that emits radio transmissions to indicate the location of the vehicle and is used to find a vehicle when it is stolen. There is a direct benefit to the owners because vehicles with a Lojack are recovered at a 90 percent rate versus 60 percent for those vehicle owners without one. Most of the benefit, however, comes to society in the form of a positive externality from the increased arrests of auto thieves that in turn reduce vehicle crime for everyone. Two economists estimate the positive externality from the device to be 15 times greater than the cost of the device.

■ **HINTS AND TIPS**

1. Review Chapter 4's discussion of public goods and externalities.

2. Make sure you understand the difference between the demand for public and private goods. The **demand for a private good** is determined by adding the quantities demanded at each possible price. The **demand for a public good** is determined by adding the prices people collectively are willing to pay for the last unit of the public good at each possible quantity demanded.

3. Table 16.3 is important because it summarizes the private actions and government policies taken to correct for negative or positive externalities. The government can influence the allocation of resources in a private market by taking actions that increase or decrease demand or supply.

4. Problems occur because information in a market is sometimes asymmetric, which means that there is **unequal** information for sellers or buyers about product price, quality, or other product conditions. Use the examples in the text to help you distinguish between the different types of information problems created by sellers or buyers.

■ **IMPORTANT TERMS**

cost-benefit analysis	optimal reduction of an externality
marginal cost = marginal benefit rule	
	climate-change problem
externalities	asymmetric information
Coase theorem	moral hazard problem
tragedy of the commons	adverse selection problem
market for externality rights	

SELF-TEST

■ **FILL-IN QUESTIONS**

1. Rivalry means that when one person buys and consumes a product, it (is, is not) _____ available for purchase and consumption by another person. Excludability means that the seller (can, cannot) _____ keep people who do not pay for the product from obtaining its benefits. Rivalry and excludability apply to (private, public) _____ goods, but these characteristics do not apply to _____ goods.

2. With a private good, to compute the market demand you add together the (prices people are willing to pay, quantities demanded) _____ at each possible (price, quantity demanded) _____. With a public good, to compute the collective demand you add together the (prices people are willing to pay, quantities demanded) _____ for the last unit of the public good at each possible (price, quantity demanded) _____.

3. The demand curve for a public good slopes downward because of the law of diminishing marginal (returns, utility) _____; the supply curve for a public good is upsloping because of the law of diminishing _____. The demand curve for a public good is, in essence, a marginal-(benefit, cost) _____ curve; the supply curve for a public good reflects rising marginal _____. The optimal quantity of a public good will be shown by the intersection of the collective demand and supply curves, which means that marginal (benefit, cost) _____ of the last unit equals that unit's marginal _____.

4. In applying cost–benefit analysis, government should use more resources in the production of public goods if the marginal (cost, benefit) _____ from the additional public goods exceeds the marginal _____ that results from having fewer private goods. This rule will determine which plan from a cost–benefit analysis will result in the (maximum, minimum) _____ net benefit to society.

5. One objective of government is to correct for market failures called spillovers or (internalities, externalities) _____. If there is a cost to an individual or group that is a third party to the market transaction, it is a (positive, negative) _____ externality. If there is a benefit to an individual or group that is a third party to a market transaction, it is a (positive, negative) _____ externality.

6. When there are negative externalities in competitive markets, the result is an (over, under) _____ allocation of resources to the production of the good or service. When there are positive externalities, the result is an (over, under) _____ allocation of resources to the production of the good or service.

7. The (liability, Coase) _____ theorem suggests that when there are negative or positive externalities in situations in which the ownership of property is (undefined, defined) _____, the number of people involved is (large, small) _____, and the costs of bargaining are (major, minor) _____, then government intervention (is, is not) _____ required.

8. The legal system is also important for settling externality disputes between individuals because laws define (political, property) _____ rights and specify (business, liability) _____ rules that can be used for lawsuits. This method, however, has limitations because of its cost, the length of time, and the (certainty, uncertainty) _____ of the results.

9. Government may use direct controls to reduce (positive, negative) _____ externalities by passing legislation that restricts business activity. When direct controls are used, the government is trying to (increase, decrease) _____ the supply curve.

10. The government may correct for the underallocation of resources where (negative, positive) _____ externalities are large and diffuse. This objective can be achieved by (taxing, subsidizing) _____ buyers or producers and through government (provision, consumption) _____ of a good or service.

11. From a demand and supply perspective, the taxes imposed on businesses by government to reduce a negative externality will (increase, decrease) _____ the supply curve from a product and a subsidy given to businesses to expand positive externalities will _____ the supply curve of the product.

12. When no private individual or institution has a monetary incentive to maintain the purity or quality of resources such as air, water, oceans, or lands, it creates an externality problem that is sometime called the tragedy of the (firm, commons) _____. A policy approach to negative externality problems is to create a (market, government) _____ for externality rights.

13. Consider how such a market for pollution rights or cap-and-trade program would work.
  a. If the regional government agency sets a limit (a cap) on the amount of air pollution, the supply curve for the air pollution rights would be perfectly (elastic, inelastic) _____.
  b. The demand curve for air pollution rights would be (up, down) _____ sloping and intersect the supply curve to determine the (quantity, price) _____ for the right to pollute the air.
  c. If the demand for air pollution rights increased over time, then the price or right to pollute would (rise, fall, stay the same) _____ and this right could be traded, but the quantity supplied would _____.

14. Reducing negative externalities comes at a "price" to society, and therefore society must decide how much of a decrease it wants to (buy, sell) "_____." Further abatement of a negative externality increases economic efficiency if the marginal cost is (greater than, equal to, less than) _____ the marginal benefit, but it is economically inefficient if the marginal benefit is _____ the marginal cost. The optimal reduction of a negative externality occurs where the society's marginal benefit is (greater than, equal to, less than) _____ society's marginal cost.

15. One of the most controversial and continuing problems with air pollution abatement is the issue of (asymmetric information, climate change) _____. Over the past few decades, there has been a noticeable (increase, decrease) _____ in the temperature of the earth's surface. Economists stress that in designing policies to address this problem, the benefits of reducing greenhouse-gas emissions problems should be (greater than, less than) _____ the costs. They also note that economic adjustment to climate change will occur naturally because of changes in prices and profits in the (environment, market) _____.

16. Markets can produce failures because of (symmetric, asymmetric) _____ information. When information involving sellers is (complete, incomplete) _____ or obtaining such information is (costless, costly) _____, the market will (under, over) _____ allocate resources to the production of that good or service.

17. To correct such problems in the gasoline market, the government establishes quality (prices, standards) _____. In the medical market, the government protects consumers by (taxing, licensing) _____ physicians.

18. Inadequate information involving buyers can lead to two problems. First, if a market situation arises whereby buyers alter their behavior and increase the cost to sellers, (an adverse selection, a moral hazard) _____ problem is created. Second, if buyers withhold information from sellers that would impose a large cost on sellers, _____ problem is created. The moral hazard problem occurs (at the same time, after) _____ a person makes a purchase, but the adverse selection problem occurs _____ the buyer makes a purchase.

19. Another example of information failure occurs in labor markets in which there is incomplete or inadequate information about (productivity, safety) _____. The government will intervene in these situations to enforce (quotas, standards) _____ or provide (health care, information) _____ related to workplace hazards.

20. Private businesses overcome some information problems about the product reliability or quality through (prices, warranties) _____ for products or the (penalizing, franchising) _____ of businesses that make them more uniform. Some businesses and organizations also collect and publish product information that is useful for (sellers, buyers) _____. Despite these actions, there may still be a need for government actions to correct (wage, information) _____ problems and to promote an efficient allocation of society's scarce resources.

■ **TRUE–FALSE QUESTIONS**

Circle T if the statement is true, F if it is false.

1. Excludability applies to public goods but not to private goods.   **T F**

2. When determining the collective demand for a public good, you add the prices people are willing to pay for the last unit of the public good at each possible quantity demanded.   **T F**

3. When the marginal benefit of a public good exceeds the marginal cost, there will be an overallocation of resources to that public good use.   **T F**

4. The optimal allocation of a public good is determined by the rule that marginal cost (MC) equals marginal revenue (MR).   **T F**

5. "Reducing government spending" means the same as "economy in government."   **T F**

6. An externality is a cost or benefit accruing to an individual or group—a third party—which is external to the market transaction.   **T F**

7. In a competitive product market and in the absence of negative externalities, the supply curve or schedule reflects the costs of producing the product.   **T F**

8. If demand and supply reflected all the benefits and costs of a product, the equilibrium output of a competitive market would be identical with its optimal output.   **T F**

9. There is an underallocation of resources to the production of a commodity when negative externalities are present.   **T F**

10. The inclusion of the positive externalities would increase the demand for a product.   **T F**

11. When negative externalities are involved in the production of a product, more resources are allocated to the production of that product and more of the product is produced than is optimal or most efficient.   **T F**

12. The Coase theorem suggests that government intervention is required whenever there are negative or positive externalities.   **T F**

13. Lawsuits and liability rules create externality problems instead of helping resolve them.   **T F**

14. Taxes that are imposed on businesses that create an externality will lower the marginal cost of production and increase supply.   **T F**

15. Subsidizing the firms producing goods that provide positive externalities will usually result in a better allocation of resources.   **T F**

16. The tragedy of the commons refers to the situation where no private individual or institution has a monetary incentive to maintain the purity or quality of common resources such as air, water, oceans, or lands, and as a result the resources are polluted.   **T F**

17. One solution to the negative externalities caused by pollution is to create a market for pollution rights in which the social costs of pollution are turned into private costs.   **T F**

18. In a market for pollution rights, if a government agency sets a fixed level for pollution or a cap, the supply curve of pollution rights will be perfectly elastic.   **T F**

19. The Clean Air Act established a limited tradable market for pollution rights.   **T F**

20. If a society has marginal costs of $10 for pollution abatement and the marginal benefit of pollution abatement is $8, to achieve an optimal amount of the pollution the society should increase the amount of pollution abatement.   **T F**

21. The economic effects of climate change will be uniform across regions of the world.   **T F**

22. Asymmetric information is a market failure that occurs when parties to a market transaction possess unequal knowledge.   **T F**

23. The inspection of meat products by the Federal government for quality is justified on the grounds that it reduces the costs of obtaining information in the market for meat.   **T F**

24. If the provision of government health insurance encourages people to take more health risks, it has created a moral hazard.   **T F**

25. Adverse selection problems primarily result when the government begins enforcing standards for safety in the workplace.   **T F**

■ **MULTIPLE-CHOICE QUESTIONS**

Circle the letter that corresponds to the best answer.

1. How do public goods differ from private goods? Public goods are characterized by
  (a) rivalry and excludability
  (b) rivalry and nonexcludability
  (c) nonrivalry and excludability
  (d) nonrivalry and nonexcludability

Answer Questions 2, 3, 4, and 5 on the basis of the following information for a public good. P_1 and P_2 represent the prices individuals 1 and 2, the only two people in the *society, are willing to pay for the last unit of a public good. P_c represents the price (or collective willingness to pay) for a public good, and Q_s represents the quantity supplied of the public good at those prices.*

Q_d	P_1	P_2	P_c	Q_s
1	$4	$5	$9	5
2	3	4	7	4
3	2	3	5	3
4	1	2	3	2
5	0	1	1	1

2. What amount is this society willing to pay for the first unit of the public good?
(a) $10
(b) $9
(c) $8
(d) $7

3. What amount is this society willing to pay for the third unit of the public good?
(a) $5
(b) $6
(c) $7
(d) $8

4. Given the supply curve Q_s, the optimal price and quantity of the public good in this society will be
(a) $9 and 5 units
(b) $5 and 3 units
(c) $5 and 4 units
(d) $3 and 2 units

5. If this good were a private good instead of a public good, the total quantity demanded at the $4 price would be
(a) 3 units
(b) 4 units
(c) 5 units
(d) 6 units

Answer Questions 6, 7, and 8 for a public good on the basis of the following graph.

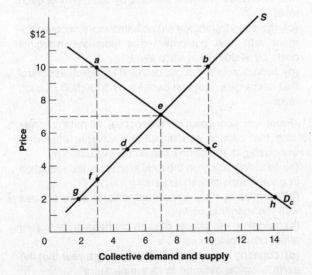

Collective demand and supply

6. Where the marginal benefits equal the collective marginal costs is represented by point
(a) *b*
(b) *c*
(c) *d*
(d) *e*

7. Which line segment would indicate the amount by which the marginal benefit of this public good is less than the marginal cost?
(a) *ab*
(b) *bc*
(c) *fa*
(d) *gh*

8. If 3 units of this public good are produced, the marginal
(a) cost of $10 is greater than the marginal benefit of $3
(b) cost of $10 is greater than the marginal benefit of $5
(c) benefit of $10 is greater than the marginal cost of $5
(d) benefit of $10 is greater than the marginal cost of $3

9. Assume that a government is considering a new antipollution program and may choose to include in this program any number of four different projects. The marginal cost and the marginal benefits of each of the four projects are given in the table below. What total amount should this government spend on the antipollution program?
(a) $2 million
(b) $5 million
(c) $17 million
(d) $37 million

Project	Marginal cost	Marginal benefit
#1	$ 2 million	$ 5 million
#2	5 million	7 million
#3	10 million	9 million
#4	20 million	15 million

10. When the production and consumption of a product entail negative externalities, a competitive product market results in a(n)
(a) underallocation of resources to the product
(b) overallocation of resources to the product
(c) optimal allocation of resources to the product
(d) higher price for the product

11. A positive externality in the production of some product will result in
(a) overproduction
(b) underproduction
(c) the optimal level of production if consumers are price takers
(d) the optimal level of production if consumers are utility maximizers

12. One condition for the Coase theorem to hold is that there be
(a) clear ownership of the property rights
(b) a large number of people involved in the dispute

(c) active government intervention to solve the externality problem

(d) a sizable cost for bargaining to settle the dispute between the private parties

Use the following graph which shows the supply and demand for a product to answer Questions 13, 14, and 15.

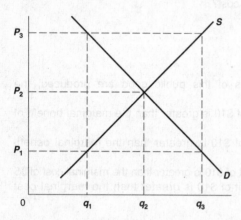

13. If there are neither negative nor positive externalities, the output that results in the optimal allocation of resources to the production of this product is

(a) q_1
(b) q_2
(c) q_3
(d) 0

14. If the market for a product was in equilibrium at output level q_2 but the optimal level of output for society was at q_1, the government could correct for this

(a) negative externality with a subsidy to consumers
(b) negative externality with a subsidy to producers
(c) positive externality with a subsidy to producers
(d) negative externality with a tax on producers

15. If the market for a product was in equilibrium at output level q_2 but the optimal level of output for society was at q_3, the government could correct for this

(a) overallocation of resources by direct controls on consumers
(b) underallocation of resources through taxes on producers
(c) overallocation of resources through a market for externality rights
(d) underallocation of resources through subsidies to producers

16. If government were to sell pollution rights, an increase in the demand for pollution rights would

(a) increase both the quantity of pollutants discharged and the market price of pollution rights
(b) increase the quantity discharged and have no effect on the market price
(c) have no effect on the quantity discharged and increase the market price
(d) have no effect on either the quantity discharged or the market price

17. The Clean Air Act of 1990

(a) permits the trading of pollution rights within firms and between firms in an area
(b) sets stricter limits on the dumping of garbage in landfills
(c) funds research on applications of asymmetric information and transaction cost
(d) forces companies to clean up toxic waste dumps

Use the following table to answer Questions 18, 19, and 20. The data in the table show the marginal costs and marginal benefits to a city for five different levels of pollution abatement.

Quantity of pollution abatement	Marginal cost	Marginal benefit
500 tons	$500,000	$100,000
400 tons	300,000	150,000
300 tons	200,000	200,000
200 tons	100,000	300,000
100 tons	50,000	400,000

18. If the city seeks an optimal reduction of the externality, it will select how many tons of pollution abatement?

(a) 100
(b) 300
(c) 400
(d) 500

19. If the marginal benefit of pollution abatement increased by $150,000 at each level because of the community's desire to attract more firms, the optimal level of pollution abatement in tons would be

(a) 200
(b) 300
(c) 400
(d) 500

20. What would cause the optimal level of pollution abatement to be 200 tons?

(a) technological improvement in production that decreases marginal costs by $150,000 at each level
(b) an increase in the health risk from this pollution that increases marginal benefits by $200,000 at each level
(c) the need to replace old pollution monitoring equipment with new equipment that increases marginal costs by $200,000 at each level
(d) reduction in the public demand for pollution control that decreases marginal benefits by $100,000 at each level

21. From an economist's perspective, climate change policies that reduce or mitigate the adverse effects of greenhouse-gas emissions should be evaluated by

(a) focusing solely on the total amount of the reduction in greenhouse-gas emissions
(b) comparing the marginal benefits of such policies with the marginal costs
(c) targeting the effects of such changes on how they affect other resources
(d) counting the number of days during a year that the earth is below average in its temperature

22. Inadequate information about sellers and their product can cause market failure in the form of
(a) an increase in the number of market sellers
(b) an increase in the number of market buyers
(c) an overallocation of resources to the product
(d) an underallocation of resources to the product

23. A situation in which one party to a contract alters his or her behavior after signing the contract in ways that can be costly to the other party would be
(a) an adverse selection problem
(b) a moral hazard problem
(c) a tragedy of the commons
(d) a positive externality

24. If Congress adopted an increase in government insurance on bank deposits, this action would create a moral hazard problem because it may
(a) lead to careful screening of depositors and the source of their funds
(b) restrict the amount of deposits made by bank customers
(c) encourage bank officers to make riskier loans
(d) reduce bank investments in real estate

25. Assume that individuals who are most likely to benefit substantially from an insurance policy decide to buy one and the insurance company does not know this information. This situation would be an example of
(a) a free-rider problem
(b) a principal–agent problem
(c) a moral hazard problem
(d) an adverse selection problem

■ **PROBLEMS**

1. Data on two individuals' preferences for a public good are reflected in the following table. P_1 and P_2 represent the prices individuals 1 and 2, the only two people in the society, are willing to pay for the last unit of the public good.

Quantity	P_1	P_2
1	$6	$6
2	5	5
3	4	4
4	3	3
5	2	2
6	1	1

a. Complete the table below showing the collective demand for the public good in this society.

Q_d	Price	Q_s
1	_____	7
2	_____	6
3	_____	6
4	_____	4
5	_____	3
6	_____	2

b. Given the supply schedule for this public good as shown by the Q_s column, the optimal quantity of this public good is _____ units and the optimal price is $_____.

c. When 3 units of this public good are produced, the perceived marginal benefit is $_____ and the marginal cost is $_____; there will be an (overallocation, underallocation) _____ of resources to this public good.

d. When 6 units of this public good are produced, the perceived marginal benefit is $_____ and the marginal cost is $_____; there is an (underallocation, overallocation) _____ of resources to this public good.

2. Imagine that a state government is considering constructing a new highway to link its two largest cities. Its estimate of the total costs and the total benefits of building 2-, 4-, 6-, and 8-lane highways between the two cities are shown in the table below. (All figures are in millions of dollars.)

Project	Total cost	Marginal cost	Total benefit	Marginal benefit
No highway	$ 0		$ 0	
2-lane highway	500	$_____	650	$_____
4-lane highway	680	_____	750	_____
6-lane highway	760	_____	800	_____
8-lane highway	860		825	_____

a. Compute the marginal cost and the marginal benefit of the 2-, 4-, 6-, and 8-lane highways.
b. Will it benefit the state to allocate resources to construct a highway? _____
c. If the state builds a highway,
(1) it should be a _____-lane highway.
(2) the total cost will be $_____ million.
(3) the total benefit will be $_____ million.
(4) the *net* benefit will be $_____ million.

3. The following graph shows the demand and supply curves for a product bought and sold in a competitive market. Assume that there are no positive or negative externalities.

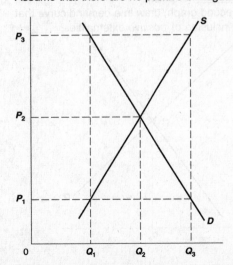

a. Were this market to produce an output of Q_1, there would be an (optimal, under, over) _____ allocation of resources to the production of this product.

b. Were this market to produce Q_3, there would be an _____ allocation of resources to this product.

c. The equilibrium output is _____, and at this output there is an _____ allocation of resources.

4. The two following graphs show product demand and supply curves that do *not* reflect either the negative externalities of producing the product or the positive externalities obtained from its consumption.

a. On the first graph, draw in another curve that reflects the inclusion of *negative* externalities.

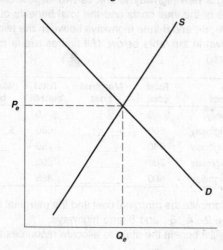

(1) Government might force the (demand for, supply of) _____ the product to reflect the negative externalities of producing it by (taxing, subsidizing) _____ the producers.

(2) The inclusion of negative externalities in the total cost of producing the product (increases, decreases) _____ the output of the product and _____ its price.

b. On the second graph, draw in a demand curve that reflects the inclusion of *positive* externalities.

(1) Indicate on the graph the output that is optimal when positive externalities are included.

(2) To bring about the production of this optimal output, government might (tax, subsidize) _____ the consumers of this product, which would (increase, decrease) _____ the demand of the product.

(3) This optimal output is (greater than, less than, equal to) _____ Q_e; and the price of the product is (above, below, equal to) _____ P_e.

5. Assume the atmosphere of a large metropolitan area is able to reabsorb 1500 tons of pollutants per year. The following schedule shows the price polluters would be willing to pay for the right to dispose of 1 ton of pollutants per year and the total quantity of pollutants they would wish to dispose of at each price.

Price (per ton of pollutant rights)	Total quantity of pollutant rights demanded (tons)
$ 0	4000
1000	3500
2000	3000
3000	2500
4000	2000
5000	1500
6000	1000
7000	500

a. If there were no emission fee, polluters would put _____ tons of pollutants in the air each year, and this quantity of pollutants would exceed the ability of nature to reabsorb them by _____ tons.

b. To reduce pollution to the capacity of the atmosphere to recycle pollutants, an emission fee of $_____ per ton should be set.

c. Were this emission fee set, the total emission fees set would be $_____.

d. Were the quantity of pollution rights demanded at each price to increase by 500 tons, the emission fee could be increased by $_____ and total emission fees collected would increase by $_____.

■ **SHORT ANSWER AND ESSAY QUESTIONS**

1. What are the basic characteristics of public goods?

2. How do public goods differ from private goods?

3. Contrast how you construct the demand curve for a public good with the procedure for constructing the demand curve for a private good using individual demand schedules.

4. Explain the relationship between the marginal cost and benefit of a public good when there is an underallocation, an overallocation, and an optimal allocation of resources for the provision of the public good.

5. Describe benefit–cost analysis, and state the rules used to make decisions from marginal and total perspectives.

6. Is "economy in government" the same as "reduced government spending"? Explain the distinction.

7. What are externalities? Give examples of positive externalities and negative externalities.

8. Under what conditions might it be worthwhile for the government to intervene or not to intervene to settle an externality problem?

9. Should the government intervene in an externality dispute between two property owners over the use of one party's land? Should government intervene in the case of acid rain?

10. How do lawsuits and liability rules resolve externality problems? How would these actions be justified?

11. What actions can government take to correct for negative externalities in a market?

12. What is the tragedy of the commons? Give examples of it.

13. How do you create a market for externality rights or a cap-and-trade program in the case of pollution? What are some advantages and limitations of this approach to the pollution problem?

14. Describe some real world examples of the creation of markets for pollution rights.

15. What rule can society use to determine the optimal level of pollution abatement? What is the problem with this approach?

16. Discuss the economic issues involved in climate change and the use of a carbon tax or cap-and-trade program to reduce or mitigate the adverse effects from greenhouse gases.

17. Describe how inadequate information about sellers creates market problems for buyers. Give examples.

18. Explain what is meant by a "moral hazard problem" and describe how it affects sellers. Give some examples of the application of this problem.

19. How can the market for insurance result in an adverse selection problem? What actions might government take to correct this information problem?

20. In what way does workplace safety become an information problem? How might this problem be resolved by government or businesses?

ANSWERS

Chapter 16 Public Goods, Externalities, and Information Asymmetries

FILL-IN QUESTIONS

1. is not, can, private, public
2. quantities demanded, price, prices, quantity demanded
3. utility, returns, benefit, cost, benefit, cost (*either order for last two*)
4. benefit, cost, maximum
5. externalities, negative, positive
6. over, under
7. Coase, defined, small, minor, is not
8. property, liability, uncertainty
9. negative, decrease
10. positive, subsidizing, provision
11. decrease, increase
12. commons, market
13. *a.* inelastic; *b.* down, price; *c.* rise, stay the same
14. buy, less than, less than, equal to
15. climate change, increase, greater than, market
16. asymmetric, incomplete, costly, under
17. standards, licensing
18. a moral hazard, an adverse selection, after, at the same time
19. safety, standards, information
20. warranties, franchising, buyers, information

TRUE–FALSE QUESTIONS

1. F, p. 336	14. F, pp. 342–343
2. T, pp. 337–338	15. T, p. 343
3. F, pp. 338–339	16. T, pp. 343–344
4. F, pp. 338–339	17. T, p. 344
5. F, pp. 339–340	18. F, p. 344
6. T, p. 340	19. T, p. 345
7. T, p. 340	20. F, pp. 345–346
8. T, p. 340	21. F, p. 347
9. F, p. 340	22. T, pp. 348–349
10. T, p. 340	23. T, pp. 349–350
11. T, p. 340	24. T, p. 350
12. F, p. 341	25. F, pp. 350–351
13. F, pp. 341–342	

MULTIPLE-CHOICE QUESTIONS

1. d, p. 336	14. d, pp. 342–343
2. b, pp. 337–338	15. d, p. 343
3. a, pp. 337–338	16. c, p. 344
4. b, pp. 337–338	17. a, p. 345
5. a, pp. 337–338	18. b, pp. 345–346
6. d, pp. 338–340	19. c, pp. 346–347
7. b, pp. 338–340	20. c, pp. 346–347
8. d, pp. 338–340	21. b, pp. 347–348
9. b, p. 339	22. d, pp. 349–350
10. b, p. 340	23. b, pp. 350–351
11. b, p. 340	24. c, p. 350
12. a, p. 341	25. d, pp. 350–351
13. b, pp. 340–341	

PROBLEMS

1. *a.* $12, 10, 8, 6, 4, 2; *b.* 4, 6; *c.* 8, 4, underallocation; *d.* 2, 10, overallocation

2. *a.* Marginal cost: $500, $180, $80, $100; Marginal benefit: $650, $100, $50, $25; *b.* yes; *c.* (1) 2, (2) $500, (3) $650, (4) $150

3. *a.* under; *b.* over; *c.* Q_2, optimal

4. *a.* (1) supply of, taxing, (2) decreases, increases; *b.* (1) graph; (2) subsidize, increase, (3) greater than, above

5. *a.* 4000, 2500; *b.* 5000; *c.* 7,500,000; *d.* 1000, 1,500,000

SHORT ANSWER AND ESSAY QUESTIONS

1. p. 336
2. p. 336
3. pp. 337–338
4. pp. 338–340
5. pp. 338–340
6. pp. 339–340
7. pp. 340–341
8. pp. 342–343
9. pp. 342–343
10. pp. 341–342
11. pp. 342–343
12. pp. 343–344
13. p. 344
14. p. 345
15. pp. 345–346
16. pp. 347–348
17. pp. 348–350
18. p. 350
19. pp. 350–351
20. p. 351

Public Choice Theory and the Economics of Taxation

Although both Chapters 16 and 17 analyze the role of government in the economy, they look at government from opposite perspectives. Chapter 16 discussed market failure issues and what actions government takes to correct these market problems. Chapter 17 now examines government failure, or why government makes inefficient use of the scarce resources. For this explanation, you will first be introduced to **public choice theory,** or the economic analysis of public decision making. Later in the chapter you will learn more about the **economics of taxation,** which includes such topics as tax principles and the economic effects of specific taxes.

Many public decisions are made by **majority voting,** but this decision-making procedure may distort the true preferences of society. In the first section of the chapter you will find out how majority voting may lead to inefficient outcomes in the provision of public goods. In some choices, the benefits of a public good are greater than the costs, but the majority votes against having it. In other choices, the benefits outweigh the costs, but the provision of the public good is supported by the majority vote. Although actions by interest groups and the use of logrolling may tend to reduce inefficiencies created by majority rule, the final result depends on the circumstances of the decision.

Also note that there is a **paradox of voting** from majority voting. Depending on how a vote or election is arranged, it is possible for majority rule to produce choices that are inconsistent with the ranking of preferences among voters. You should spend time working through the example in the textbook so you understand how opposing outcomes can result from majority rule. You should also learn why the median voters strongly influence the result of a vote or an election when there is majority rule. In fact, the **median-voter model** is very useful for explaining why the middle position on issues is often adopted in public decisions.

The second section of Chapter 17 discusses other reasons for inefficiencies by government. Here you will learn that (1) the **special-interest effect** and **rent seeking** impair public decisions; (2) politicians often have a strong incentive to adopt an economic policy that has clear benefits to voters, but hidden or uncertain costs; (3) public choice is more limited and less flexible than private choice because it entails voting for or accepting a "bundle" of programs, some good and some bad; and (4) bureaucratic inefficiencies in the public sector arise from the lack of the economic incentives and competitive pressures found in the private sector.

Chapter 17 then shifts from public choice theory to taxation. In this third section of the chapter you will learn the economic principles used in levying taxes. You also will learn about the **regressive, progressive,** and **proportional** classifications for taxes and how most U.S. taxes fit into this classification scheme.

The **tax incidence** and **efficiency loss of a tax** are described in the fourth section of the chapter. Incidence means "who ends up paying the tax." As you will discover, the elasticities of demand and of supply determine how much of the tax will be paid by buyers and how much of it will be paid by sellers. No matter who pays the tax, however, there is an efficiency loss to society from the tax, the size of which is also affected by the elasticities of demand and of supply. With this knowledge, you are now ready to study the probable incidence of five taxes—personal income, corporate income, sales, excise, and property—that are used to raise most of the tax revenue for government in the United States.

■ **CHECKLIST**

When you have studied this chapter you should be able to

☐ Explain the purpose of public choice theory and the topics it covers.
☐ Illustrate how majority voting procedures can produce inefficient outcomes when the vote is "yes" or the vote is "no."
☐ Describe how interest groups and political logrolling affect the efficiency of outcomes from voting.
☐ Give an example of the paradox of voting.
☐ Describe the median-voter model, its applicability to the real world, and two implications of the model.
☐ Explain the meaning of the phrase "government failure" and cite examples.
☐ Give an example of a special-interest effect and an example of rent-seeking behavior.
☐ Describe the economic problem that arises when a political decision involves clear benefits and hidden costs.
☐ Compare the type of choices consumers make in the private market with the type of limited and bundled choices citizens as voters make.
☐ Contrast the incentives for economic efficiency in private business with those found in public agencies and bureaucracies.
☐ Discuss how government and markets are imperfect in allocating resources.

☐ Distinguish between the ability-to-pay principle of taxation and the benefits-received principle of taxation.
☐ Determine whether a tax is regressive, progressive, or proportional when given the data.
☐ Describe the progressivity or regressivity of the five major taxes used in the United States.
☐ Illustrate the incidence of an excise tax with a supply and demand graph.
☐ Explain how demand and supply elasticities affect tax incidence.
☐ Describe the efficiency loss of a tax with a supply and demand graph.
☐ Explain the effects of demand or supply elasticities on the efficiency loss of a tax.
☐ Evaluate the probable incidence of the personal income, corporate income, sales and excise, and property taxes.
☐ Describe the progressivity of the U.S. tax structure overall and at the Federal, state, and local levels.
☐ Cite examples of government actions that illustrate pork-barrel politics, limited and bundled choices, earmarks, or bureaucratic inefficiencies (Last Word).

■ **CHAPTER OUTLINE**

1. Most decisions about government activity are made collectively through **majority voting,** but the procedure is not without problems.

a. Voting outcomes may be economically *inefficient* in cases where voters reject a public good whose total benefits exceed total costs or fail to reject a public good whose total costs are greater than the total benefits. These inefficiencies can be resolved sometimes by
(1) the formation of special interest groups that work to overcome inefficient outcomes, (2) the use of *logrolling,* in which votes are traded to secure a favorable and efficient decision. However, logrolling can also lead to inefficient decisions.

b. The *paradox of voting* suggests that the public may not be able to make consistent choices that reflect its preferences.

c. Based on the *median-voter model,* it is suggested that the person or groups holding the middle position on an issue will likely determine the outcome from a majority rule election. Public decisions tend to reflect the median view.

2. *Public choice theory* suggests that there is *government failure* because the process it uses to make decisions is inherently weak and results in an economically inefficient allocation of resources.

a. The weakness of the decision-making process in the public sector and the resulting inefficient allocation of resources is often the result of pressures exerted on Congress and the bureaucracy by special interests and other groups.
(1) There can be a *special-interest effect* in which a small number of people obtain a government program or policy giving them large gains at the expense of a large number of people who individually suffer small losses. This effect is also present in *pork-barrel politics* where a government program will mostly benefit one constituency. An example of pork-barrel politics are *earmarks,* which are specific authorizations for government expenditures to benefit a group or organization in legislator's district.
(2) *Rent-seeking* behavior is reflected in appeals to government for special benefits or treatment at the taxpayers' or someone else's expense. Government can dispense such rents through laws, rules, hiring, and purchases.

b. Those seeking election to public office frequently favor programs whose benefits are clear and immediate and whose costs are uncertain and deferred, even when the benefits are less than the costs. Conversely, they frequently oppose programs whose costs are clear and immediate and whose benefits are uncertain and deferred, even when the benefits are greater than the costs.

c. There are limited and bundled choices in political decisions. When citizens must vote for candidates who represent different but complete programs, the voters are unable to select those parts of a program which they favor and reject the other parts of the program.

d. It is argued that the public sector (unlike the private sector) is inefficient because those employed there are offered no incentive to be efficient; there is no way to measure efficiency in the public sector; and government bureaucrats can join with the special-interest groups to block budget cuts or lobby for increased funding.

e. Just as the private or market sector of the economy does not allocate resources perfectly, the public sector does not perform its functions perfectly; the imperfections of both sectors make it difficult to determine which sector will be more efficient in providing a good or service.

3. The financing of public goods and services through taxation also raises an important question about how the **tax burden** is allocated among people.

a. The *benefits-received principle* and the *ability-to-pay principle* are widely used to determine how the tax bill should be apportioned among the economy's citizens.
(1) The benefits-received principle suggests that those people who benefit most from public goods should pay for them.
(2) The ability-to-pay principle states that taxes for the support of public goods should be tied to the incomes and wealth of people or their ability to pay.

b. Taxes can be classified as progressive, regressive, or proportional according to the way in which the average tax rate changes as incomes change.
(1) The average tax rate increases as income increases with a *progressive tax,* it decreases as income increases with a *regressive tax*, and it remains the same as income increases with a *proportional tax.*
(2) In the United States, the personal income tax tends to be mildly progressive. The corporate income tax is proportional (unless the tax in the long run is partially passed to workers through less capital accumulation

in lower wages, in which case it is partially regressive). The payroll, sales, and property taxes are regressive.

4. *Tax incidence* and the *efficiency loss of a tax* are also important in discussion of the economics of taxation.

   a. The price elasticities of demand and supply determine the incidence of a sales or excise tax.

   (1) The imposition of such a tax on a product decreases the supply of the product and increases its price. The amount of the price increase is the portion of the tax paid by the buyer; the seller pays the rest.

   (2) The price elasticities of demand and supply for a product affect the portions paid by buyers and sellers: (a) the more *elastic* the demand, the greater the portion paid by the seller; (b) the more *inelastic* the demand, the smaller the portion paid by the seller; (c) the more *elastic* the supply, the greater the portion paid by the buyer; and (d) the more *inelastic* the supply, the smaller the portion paid by the buyer.

   b. There is an efficiency loss of a tax. This loss occurs because there is a reduction in output, despite the fact that the marginal benefits of that output are greater than the marginal cost. Thus, the consumption and production of the taxed product have been reduced below the optimal level by the tax.

   (1) The degree of the efficiency loss of a sales or an excise tax depends on the elasticities of supply and demand. Other things equal, the *greater* the elasticity of supply and demand, the *greater* the efficiency loss of a sales or an excise tax; consequently, the total tax burden to society may not be equal even though two taxes produce equal tax revenue.

   (2) Other tax goals, however, may be more important than minimizing efficiency losses from taxes. These goals may include redistributing income or reducing negative externalities.

   c. A tax levied on one person or group of persons may be shifted partially or completely to another person or group; and to the extent that a tax can be shifted or passed on through lower prices paid or higher prices received, its incidence is passed on to others. Table 17.2 in the text summarizes the probable shifting and incidence of the personal income tax, payroll tax, corporate income tax, general sales tax, specific excise taxes, and property taxes.

   d. Estimates of the progressivity of the tax system depend on the assumed incidence of various taxes and transfer payments made by governments to reduce income inequality in the United States. Overall, the U.S. tax structure is progressive. The progressivity of the Federal income tax offsets the regressivity of payroll and excise taxes or regressive effects from state or local taxes.

5. (Last Word). There are many examples of government actions that illustrate pork-barrel politics, limited and bundled choices, or bureaucratic inefficiency. For example, Congressional spending bills often contain *earmarks* that authorize funding for home-state projects with a narrow purpose and little national benefit.

■ **HINTS AND TIPS**

1. The first part of the chapter presents **public choice theory,** but this theory has many practical applications to politics. As you read about the reasons for inefficient voting outcomes, the influence of special-interest groups, political logrolling, the median-voter model, rent-seeking behavior, limited and bundled choices, and government failures, see if you can apply the ideas to current public issues at the local, state, or Federal level. Also ask your instructor for current examples of the ideas from public choice theory.

2. Remember that what happens to the **average tax rate** as income increases determines whether a tax is progressive, regressive, or proportional. The average tax rate increases for progressive taxes, decreases for regressive taxes, and remains the same for proportional taxes as income increases.

3. This chapter applies supply, demand, and elasticity concepts to taxation issues. Chapter 6 is worth checking to review your understanding of elasticity. Figure 17.5 and the related discussion in the text are crucially important for understanding the efficiency loss from a tax.

■ **IMPORTANT TERMS**

public choice theory	benefits-received principle
logrolling	ability-to-pay principle
paradox of voting	progressive tax
median-voter model	regressive tax
government failure	proportional tax
special-interest effect	tax incidence
earmarks	efficiency loss of a tax
rent seeking	

SELF-TEST

■ **FILL-IN QUESTIONS**

1. Many collective decisions are made on the basis of (minority, majority) _____ voting. One problem with this voting system is that it results in (efficient, inefficient) _____ voting outcomes because it fails to incorporate the strength of (individual, majority) _____ preferences. Voters may defeat a proposal even though the total costs are (less than, greater than) _____ the total benefits, or they might accept a proposal even though the total costs are _____ the total benefits.

2. The voting problem might be resolved or reversed through the influence of (interest, social) _____ groups or through political (primaries, logrolling) _____.

3. Another problem with this voting system occurs in a situation in which the public may not be able to rank its preferences with consistency; this is called the (fallacy, paradox) _____ of voting.

4. There are also insights into majority voting based on the (motor-voter, median-voter) _____ model, whereby the person holding the (lower, middle, upper) _____ position is likely to determine the outcome of an election.

5. When governments use resources to attempt to solve problems and the employment of these resources (does, does not) _____ result in solutions to these problems, there has been (market, government) _____ failure. This means that there are shortcomings in government that promote economic (efficiency, inefficiency) _____.

6. One reason for this type of failure is that there can be a special-interest effect whereby a (large, small) _____ number of people benefit from a government program at the expense of a _____ number of persons who individually suffer (large, small) _____ losses. An example of such a special-interest effect would be (logrolling, earmarks) _____ that provide(s) public expenditures for narrow, home-state projects without careful evaluation or competitive bidding.

7. Inefficiencies can also be caused by an appeal to government for special benefits at taxpayers' or someone else's expense that is called (revealed preferences, rent-seeking behavior) _____.

8. Another reason for the failure is that the benefits from a government program or project are often (clear, hidden) _____ to citizens or groups, but the costs are frequently _____ when legislation is passed or programs are funded.

9. There can also be inefficiencies in government because voters or elected representatives have to accept political choices that are (limited, unlimited) _____ and (bundled, unbundled) _____, which means government legislation forces voters or elected representatives to take bad programs with the good programs.

10. The incentives for economic efficiency tend to be stronger in the (private, public) _____ sector because there is a profit incentive in the _____ sector but not a similar incentive in the (private, public) _____ sector. As a result, there tends to be

(more, less) _____ government bureaucracy and _____ efficient use of scarce resources.

11. Although the public sector can experience (market, government) _____ failure, the private sector can also experience _____ failure, and thus both government and markets can be considered (perfect, imperfect) _____ economic institutions.

12. The tax philosophy that asserts that households and businesses should purchase public goods and services in about the same way as private goods and services are bought is the (ability-to-pay, benefits-received) _____ principle of taxation, but the tax philosophy that the tax burden should be based on a person's wealth or income is the _____ principle of taxation.

13. If the average tax rate remains constant as income increases, the tax is (regressive, progressive, proportional) _____. If the average tax rate decreases as income increases, the tax is _____. If the average tax rate increases as income increases, the tax is (regressive, progressive, proportional) _____.

14. In the United States, the Federal personal income tax is (regressive, progressive, proportional) _____, but sales taxes, property taxes, and payroll taxes are _____. If corporate shareholders bear the burden of the corporate income tax, then it is (regressive, progressive, proportional) _____, but in the long run, if part of the tax reduces wage rates or capital formation, then the tax is _____.

15. The person or group who ends up paying a tax is called the tax (avoidance, incidence) _____. When an excise tax is placed on a product, the supply curve will (increase, decrease) _____, or shift to the (right, left) _____. The amount the product price rises as a result of the tax is the portion of the tax burden borne by (buyers, sellers) _____, and the difference between the original price and the after-tax price is the portion of the tax burden borne by _____.

16. The incidence of an excise tax primarily depends on the (price, income) _____ elasticity of demand and of supply. The buyer's portion of the tax is larger the (more, less) _____ elastic the demand and the _____ elastic the supply. The seller's portion of the tax is larger the (more, less) _____ elastic the demand and the _____ elastic the supply.

17. When an excise tax reduces the consumption and production of the taxed product below the level of economic efficiency, there is an efficiency (gain, loss) _____ of the tax. Other things equal, the greater the elasticity of supply and demand, the (greater, less) _____ the efficiency (gain, loss) _____ of the tax.

18. The incidence of the personal income tax is on (individuals, businesses) _____. In the short run, the incidence of the corporate income tax falls on (businesses, workers) _____ but in the long run, it also can fall on _____ because such taxes may reduce capital accumulation or lower wage rates.

19. The incidence of the sales tax is generally shifted to the (sellers, buyers) _____ of the product, and with excise taxes, if the demand for a product is inelastic, the tax incidence will be shifted to the _____. In the case of the property tax, the incidence of the tax for owner-occupied housing is borne by (owners, government) _____ and with renter-occupied housing it is borne by (owners, renters) _____. In the case of business property, the tax incidence is shifted to (businesses, consumers) _____.

20. The Federal tax system is generally (progressive, regressive, proportional) _____, state and local tax systems are generally _____, and overall the U.S. tax system is slightly _____, but these conditions depend on the incidence of the taxes. The tax system has a relatively (large, small) _____ effect on the distribution of income in the United States, but income inequality is (increased, decreased) _____ by transfer payments made by governments.

■ **TRUE–FALSE QUESTIONS**

Circle T if the statement is true, F if it is false.

1. Majority voting may deliver outcomes that are economically inefficient because it fails to take into account the strength of preferences of the individual voter. **T F**

2. Logrolling will always diminish economic efficiency in government. **T F**

3. The paradox of voting is that majority voting will result in consistent choices that reflect the preferences of the public. **T F**

4. The proposition that the person holding the middle position on an issue will likely determine the outcome of an election is suggested by the median-voter model. **T F**

5. There is a failure in the public sector whenever a governmental program or activity has been expanded to the level at which the marginal social cost exceeds the marginal social benefit. **T F**

6. Those concerned with public choice theory argue that the special-interest effect tends to reduce government failures because the pressures exerted on government by one special-interest group are offset by the pressures brought to bear by other special-interest groups. **T F**

7. The appeal to government for special benefits at taxpayers' or someone else's expense is called rent seeking. **T F**

8. When the costs of programs are hidden and the benefits are clear, vote-seeking politicians tend to reject economically justifiable programs. **T F**

9. The limited choice of citizens refers to the inability of individual voters to select the precise bundle of social goods and services that will best satisfy the citizen's wants when he or she must vote for a candidate and the candidate's entire program. **T F**

10. Critics of government contend that there is a tendency for government bureaucracy to justify continued employment by finding new problems to solve. **T F**

11. When comparing government with markets, government is imperfect, whereas markets are perfect in efficiently allocating resources. **T F**

12. The chief difficulty in applying the benefits-received principle of taxation is determining who receives the benefit of many of the goods and services that government supplies. **T F**

13. The state and Federal taxes on gasoline are good examples of taxes levied on the benefits-received principle. **T F**

14. The ability-to-pay principle of taxation states that those with greater incomes should be taxed less, absolutely and relatively, than those with lesser incomes. **T F**

15. A tax is progressive when the average tax rate decreases as income increases. **T F**

16. A general sales tax is considered a proportional tax with respect to income. **T F**

17. A payroll (Social Security) tax is regressive. **T F**

18. When an excise tax is placed on a product bought and sold in a competitive market, the portion of the tax borne by the seller equals the amount of the tax less the rise in the price of product due to the tax. **T F**

19. The more elastic the demand for a good, the greater the portion of an excise tax on the good borne by the seller. **T F**

20. The efficiency loss of an excise tax is the gain in net benefits for the producers from the increase in the price of the product. **T F**

21. The degrees of efficiency loss from an excise tax vary from market to market and depend on the elasticities of supply and demand.   **T   F**

22. The evidence on the incidence of the corporate income tax is that this tax is borne by company stockholders or owners in the short run.   **T   F**

23. The probable incidence of the tax on rented apartment properties is on the landlord, not on the tenant.   **T   F**

24. The Federal income tax system is progressive. **T   F**

25. The state and local tax structures are largely regressive.   **T   F**

■ **MULTIPLE-CHOICE QUESTIONS**

Circle the letter that corresponds to the best answer.

1. Deficiencies in the processes used to make collective decisions of government and economic inefficiencies caused by government are the primary focus of
  (a) public goods theory
  (b) public choice theory
  (c) the study of tax incidence
  (d) the study of tax shifting

2. The trading of votes to secure favorable outcomes on decisions that otherwise would be adverse is referred to as
  (a) logrolling, and it increases economic efficiency
  (b) logrolling, and it may increase or decrease economic efficiency
  (c) rent-seeking behavior, and it decreases economic efficiency
  (d) rent-seeking behavior, and it may increase or decrease economic efficiency

Answer Questions 3, 4, 5, and 6 on the basis of the following table, which shows the rankings of the public goods by three voters: A, B, and C.

Public good	Voter A	Voter B	Voter C
Dam	1	2	3
School	3	1	2
Road	2	3	1

3. In a choice between a dam and the school
  (a) a majority of voters favor the dam
  (b) a majority of voters favor the school
  (c) a majority of voters favor both the dam and the school
  (d) there is no majority of votes for either the dam or the school

4. In a choice between a road and a dam
  (a) a majority of voters favor the dam
  (b) a majority of voters favor the road
  (c) a majority of voters favor both the dam and the road
  (d) there is no majority of votes for either the road or the dam

5. In a choice between a school and a road
  (a) a majority of voters favor the road
  (b) a majority of voters favor the school
  (c) a majority of voters favor both the road and the school
  (d) there is no majority of votes for either the road or the school

6. What do the rankings in the table indicate about choices made under majority rule? Majority voting in this case
  (a) reflects irrational preferences
  (b) produces inconsistent choices
  (c) produces consistent choices in spite of irrational preferences
  (d) results in economically efficient outcomes because they have been influenced by special interests

7. The idea that the person holding the middle position will in a sense determine the outcome of an election is suggested by the
  (a) rent-seeking behavior
  (b) paradox of voting
  (c) median-voter model
  (d) special-interest effect

8. Actions that groups take to seek government legislation that puts tariffs on foreign products to limit foreign competition or that gives tax breaks to specific corporations would best be an example of
  (a) how the median-voter model works
  (b) how political choices are bundled
  (c) rent-seeking behavior
  (d) the paradox of voting

9. It is difficult to determine whether provision for a particular good or service should be assigned to the private or public sector of the economy because the
  (a) institutions in both sectors function efficiently
  (b) markets function efficiently and the agencies of government perform imperfectly
  (c) markets are faulty and government agencies function with much greater efficiency
  (d) institutions in both sectors are imperfect

10. Which is true of the ability-to-pay principle as applied in the United States?
  (a) It is less widely applied than the benefits-received principle.
  (b) Tax incidence is generally taken as the measure of the ability to pay.
  (c) Gasoline taxes are based on this principle.
  (d) As an individual's income increases, taxes paid increase both absolutely and relatively.

11. Taxing people according to the principle of ability to pay would be most characteristic of
  (a) a payroll tax
  (b) a value-added tax
  (c) a general sales tax
  (d) a progressive income tax

12. With a regressive tax, as income
  (a) increases, the tax rate remains the same
  (b) decreases, the tax rate decreases

(c) increases, the tax rate increases
(d) increases, the tax rate decreases

13. Which tends to be a progressive tax in the United States?
(a) income tax
(b) property tax
(c) sales tax
(d) payroll tax

14. In a competitive market, the portion of an excise tax borne by a buyer is equal to the
(a) amount the price of the product rises as a result of the tax
(b) amount of the tax
(c) amount of the tax less the amount the price of the product rises as a result of the tax
(d) amount of the tax plus the amount the price of the product rises as a result of the tax

15. Which statement is correct?
(a) The more elastic the supply, the greater the portion of an excise tax borne by the seller.
(b) The more elastic the demand, the greater the portion of an excise tax borne by the seller.
(c) The more inelastic the supply, the greater the portion of an excise tax borne by the buyer.
(d) The more inelastic the demand, the greater the portion of an excise tax borne by the seller.

Answer Questions 16, 17, 18, and 19 based on the following graph of an excise tax imposed by government.

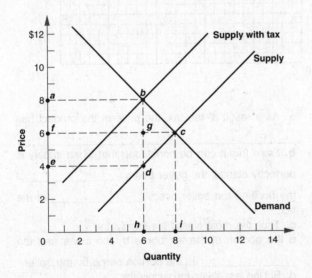

16. What is the amount of the excise tax paid by the seller in terms of price per unit sold?
(a) $1
(b) $2
(c) $3
(d) $4

17. The amount of the excise tax paid by consumers is
(a) $2
(b) $6

(c) $12
(d) $16

18. The tax revenue for government is represented by area
(a) *abde*
(b) *abgf*
(c) *fgde*
(d) *abcde*

19. The efficiency loss of the tax is represented by area
(a) *bgc*
(b) *bdc*
(c) *abcf*
(d) *hbci*

20. The efficiency loss of an excise tax is
(a) greater, the greater the elasticity of supply and demand
(b) greater, the less the elasticity of supply and demand
(c) less, the greater the elasticity of supply and demand
(d) not affected by the elasticity of supply and demand

21. If government imposes a tax on wine to shift the market supply to reduce the amount of resources allocated to wine, then the primary purpose of this tax is to
(a) redistribute income
(b) improve tax progressivity
(c) reduce negative externalities
(d) minimize efficiency losses

22. The probable incidence of a sales tax is borne by
(a) government units that collect the tax
(b) businesses that make the product
(c) businesses that sell the product
(d) consumers who buy the product

23. Which tax is the most difficult to shift to others?
(a) personal income tax
(b) corporate income tax
(c) specific excise taxes
(d) business property taxes

24. Which of the following is most likely to pay the incidence of a property tax on a business property that sells a consumer product?
(a) consumers of the product
(b) the business that produces the product
(c) government that taxes the property
(d) resource suppliers to the business

25. The Federal tax system is
(a) proportional, while state and local tax structures are largely progressive
(b) progressive, while state and local tax structures are largely regressive
(c) regressive, while state and local tax structures are largely proportional
(d) proportional, while state and local tax structures are largely regressive

■ PROBLEMS

1. The following table shows the demand and supply schedules for copra in the New Hebrides Islands.

Quantity demanded (pounds)	price (per pounds)	Before-tax Quantity supplied (pounds)	After-tax Quantity supplied (pounds)
150	$4.60	900	_____
200	4.40	800	_____
250	4.20	700	_____
300	4.00	600	_____
350	3.80	500	_____
400	3.60	400	_____
450	3.40	300	_____
500	3.20	200	_____
550	3.00	100	_____

a. Before a tax is imposed on copra, its equilibrium price is $_____.

b. The government of New Hebrides now imposes an excise tax of $.60 per pound on copra. Complete the after-tax supply schedule in the right-hand column of the table.

c. After the imposition of the tax, the equilibrium price of copra is $_____.

d. Of the $.60 tax, the amount borne by

(1) the buyer is $_____ or _____%.

(2) the seller is $_____ or _____%.

2. On the following graph, draw a perfectly elastic demand curve and a normal upsloping supply curve for a product. Now impose an excise tax on the product, and draw the new supply curve that would result.

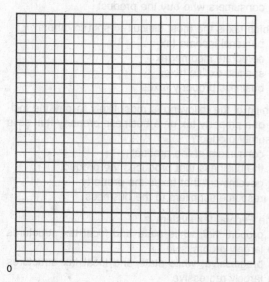

a. As a consequence of the tax, the price of the product has _____.

b. It can be concluded that when demand is perfectly elastic, the buyer bears _____ of the tax and the seller bears _____ of the tax.

c. Thus the *more* elastic the demand, the _____ is the portion of the tax borne by the buyer and the _____ is the portion borne by the seller.

d. But the *less* elastic the demand, the _____ is the portion borne by the buyer and the _____ is the portion borne by the seller.

3. In the graph below, draw a perfectly elastic supply curve and a normal downsloping demand curve. Impose an excise tax on the product, and draw the new supply curve.

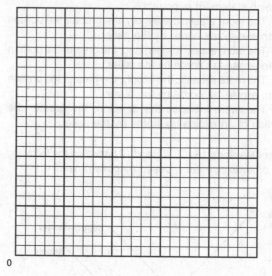

a. As a result of the tax, the price of the product has _____.

b. From this it can be concluded that when supply is perfectly elastic, the buyer bears _____ of the tax and the seller bears _____ of the tax.

c. Thus the *more* elastic the supply, the _____ is the portion of the tax borne by the buyer and the _____ is the portion borne by the seller.

d. But the *less* elastic the supply, the _____ is the portion borne by the buyer and the _____ is the portion borne by the seller.

4. The table at the top of the next page shows five levels of taxable income and the amount that would be paid at each of the five levels under three tax laws: *A, B,* and *C.* Compute for each of the three tax laws the average rate of taxation at each of the four remaining income levels. Indicate whether the tax is regressive, proportional, progressive, or some combination thereof.

Income	Tax A			Tax B			Tax C		
	Tax paid	Av. tax rate		Tax paid	Av. tax rate		Tax paid	Av. tax rate	
$ 1500	$ 45.00	3%		$ 30.00	2%		$ 135.00	9%	
3000	90.00	___		90.00	___		240.00	___	
5000	150.00	___		150.00	___		350.00	___	
7500	225.00	___		187.50	___		450.00	___	
10,000	300.00	___		200.00	___		500.00	___	
Type of tax:	___			___			___		

5. Assume a state government levies a 4% sales tax on all consumption expenditures. Consumption expenditures at six income levels are shown in the following table.

Income	Consumption expenditures	Sales tax paid	Average tax rate,%
$ 5000	$5000	$200	4.0
6000	5800	232	3.9
7000	6600	___	___
8000	7400	___	___
9000	8200	___	___
10,000	9000	___	___

a. Compute the sales tax paid at the next four incomes.
b. Compute the average tax rate at these incomes.
c. Using income as the tax base, the sales tax is a _____ tax.

■ **SHORT ANSWER AND ESSAY QUESTIONS**

1. Why has there been dissatisfaction with government decisions and the economic efficiency in government?

2. What is the relationship between majority voting and the efficiency of outcomes from an election? How do special interest groups or the use of logrolling influence the efficiency of outcomes?

3. Why is there a paradox with majority voting? Do the outcomes from majority voting suggest that voters are irrational in their preferences?

4. Describe how median voters influence the election results and debates over public issues. What are two important implications of the median-voter model?

5. Explain what is meant by "government failure." Is it related to market failure and externalities?

6. Public choice theory suggests that there are a number of reasons for government failures. What are the reasons? Explain how each would tend to result in the inefficient allocation of the economy's resources.

7. It is generally agreed that "national defense must lie in the public sector while wheat production can best be accomplished in the private sector." Why is there no agreement on where many other goods or services should be produced?

8. What are the two basic philosophies for apportioning the tax burden in the United States? Explain each one.

9. What are the difficulties encountered in putting the two basic tax philosophies into practice?

10. Explain the difference among progressive, regressive, and proportional taxes. Which types of taxes fall into each of these categories?

11. Explain the effect the imposition of an excise tax has on the supply of a product that is bought and sold in a competitive market.

12. Illustrate with a supply and demand graph what part of an excise tax is passed on to the buyer and what part is borne by the seller. What determines the division of the tax between the buyer and the seller?

13. What is the relationship between the price elasticity of demand for a commodity and the portion of an excise tax on a commodity borne by the buyer and the seller?

14. What is the relationship between the price elasticity of supply and the incidence of an excise tax?

15. How does an excise tax produce an efficiency loss for society? Explain and illustrate with a supply and demand graph.

16. How is the efficiency loss from an excise tax affected by the elasticity of supply or demand? All else equal, shouldn't the total tax burden be equal for two taxes that produce equal revenues?

17. Describe the probable incidence of the personal income tax, the sales tax, and the excise tax.

18. Who bears the burden of the corporate income tax in the short run and in the long run?

19. Explain whether businesses or consumers are likely to bear the incidence of a corporate income tax or a business property tax.

20. What general conclusion can be drawn about the progressivity or regressivity of the Federal tax system, taxation by state and local governments, and the overall U.S. tax system?

ANSWERS

Chapter 17 Public Choice Theory and the Economics of Taxation

FILL-IN QUESTIONS

1. majority, inefficient, individual, less than, greater than
2. interest, logrolling
3. paradox
4. median-voter, middle
5. does not, government, inefficiency
6. small, large, small, earmarks
7. rent-seeking behavior
8. clear, hidden
9. limited, bundled
10. private, private, public, more, less
11. government, market, imperfect
12. benefits-received, ability-to-pay
13. proportional, regressive, progressive
14. progressive, regressive, proportional, regressive
15. incidence, decrease, left, buyers, sellers
16. price, less, more, more, less
17. loss, greater, loss
18. individuals, businesses, workers
19. buyers, buyers, owners, renters, consumers
20. progressive, regressive, progressive, small, decreased

TRUE–FALSE QUESTIONS

1. T, pp. 357–358
2. F, p. 358
3. F, pp. 358–359
4. T, pp. 359–360
5. T, p. 360
6. F, pp. 360–361
7. T, p. 361
8. F, p. 361
9. T, pp. 361–362
10. T, p. 362
11. F, pp. 362–363
12. T, p. 363
13. T, p. 363
14. F, pp. 363–364
15. F, p. 364
16. F, p. 364
17. T, pp. 364–365
18. T, pp. 365–366
19. T, pp. 364–367
20. F, p. 367
21. T, pp. 367–368
22. T, p. 368
23. F, pp. 369–370
24. T, p. 371
25. T, p. 371

MULTIPLE-CHOICE QUESTIONS

1. b, pp. 356–357
2. b, p. 358
3. b, pp. 358–359
4. a, pp. 358–359
5. a, pp. 358–359
6. b, p. 359
7. c, pp. 359–360
8. c, pp. 360–361
9. d, pp. 362–363
10. d, pp. 363–364
11. d, pp. 363–364
12. d, p. 364
13. a, p. 364
14. a, pp. 365–366
15. b, pp. 365–367
16. b, pp. 365–367
17. c, pp. 365–367
18. a, pp. 365–367
19. b, p. 367
20. a, pp. 367–368
21. c, p. 368
22. d, pp. 368–369
23. a, p. 368
24. a, pp. 369–370
25. b, p. 371

PROBLEMS

1. *a.* $3.60; *b.* (reading down) 600, 500, 400, 300, 200, 100; *c.* $4.00; *d.* (1) $.40, 67, (2) $.20, 33
2. *a.* not changed; *b.* none, all; *c.* smaller, larger; *d.* larger, smaller
3. *a.* increased by the amount of the tax; *b.* all, none; *c.* larger, smaller; *d.* smaller, larger
4. Tax A: 3, 3, 3, 3, proportional; Tax B: 3, 3, 2.5, 2, combination; Tax C: 8, 7, 6, 5, regressive
5. *a.* $264, 296, 328, 360; *b.* 3.8, 3.7, 3.64, 3.6; *c.* regressive

SHORT ANSWER AND ESSAY QUESTIONS

1. pp. 357–358
2. pp. 357–358
3. pp. 358–359
4. pp. 359–360
5. pp. 360–363
6. p. 360–363
7. p. 362
8. pp. 363–364
9. pp. 363–364
10. pp. 364–365
11. pp. 365–366
12. pp. 365–366
13. pp. 366–367
14. pp. 366–367
15. pp. 367–368
16. pp. 367–368
17. pp. 368–370
18. p. 368
19. pp. 368–370
20. p. 371

Antitrust Policy and Regulation

Chapter 18 examines issues related to antitrust policy and the regulation of markets and society. These issues are important for you to study because they affect prices, economic efficiency, and economic welfare.

Over the years the Federal government has taken action to curb or limit the growth of monopolies in the United States through the passage of **antitrust laws** and the establishment of regulatory agencies. The Sherman Act of 1890 was the first major antitrust law. It was followed by other antitrust legislation and the creation of regulatory agencies and commissions.

The chapter discusses major antitrust issues and evaluates the effectiveness of **antitrust policy.** Several issues of interpretation address whether businesses should be judged for antitrust violations on the basis of monopoly behavior or structure and what should be the definition of the market. You will learn about the two conflicting perspectives on the enforcement of antitrust laws—activist and laissez-faire. The effectiveness of antitrust policy is also evaluated in the chapter based on such factors as the degree of the monopoly control, mergers, price fixing, price discrimination, and tying contracts.

Industrial regulation focuses on the control of natural monopolies so that they produce economic outcomes that benefit society. It is based on the public interest theory of regulation. This regulation by agencies and commissions has several problems of which you should be aware. One problem is that some of the regulated industries may not be natural monopolies at all and would be competitive industries if they were left unregulated. From this problem comes the legal cartel theory of regulation: Many industries want to be regulated so that competition among the firms will be reduced and the profits will increase.

Beginning in the 1970s, many industries in the United States underwent **deregulation.** These included the airline, trucking, banking, railroad, natural gas, television broadcasting, and telecommunications industries. The results generally show that this deregulation was beneficial for consumers and the efficiency of the economy. A more recent experience with deregulation occurred in the market for electricity. The outcomes from this experiment in deregulation have been less certain because of pricing problems in California.

Beginning in the early 1960s, new agencies and commissions began to engage in **social regulation** that differed from the regulation of the prices, services, and output provided by specific industries. This regulation focused on production conditions, product attributes, and production effects on society. This regulation increases product prices and indirectly reduces worker productivity, but supporters argue that the social benefits over time will exceed the costs. Critics contend that it is costly, often poorly conceived, and has negative secondary effects. The debate over the optimal level of social regulation is not easily resolved because the costs and benefits are difficult to measure. You should spend time understanding both sides of the issue.

■ CHECKLIST

When you have studied this chapter you should be able to

☐ State the purpose of antitrust policy.

☐ Discuss the historical background and rationale for antitrust laws and regulatory agencies.

☐ Describe the purpose and major provisions of the Sherman Act, Clayton Act, Federal Trade Commission Act, Wheeler-Lea Act, and Celler-Kefauver Act.

☐ Contrast the monopoly behavior view of the antitrust laws with the monopoly structure view using two landmark Supreme Court decisions.

☐ Explain the importance of market definition in the interpretation of antitrust laws.

☐ Compare and contrast the active antitrust perspective with the laissez-faire perspective.

☐ Describe the application of antitrust laws to monopoly.

☐ Distinguish among a horizontal, vertical, and conglomerate merger.

☐ Explain the concept of the Herfindahl index and its application to merger guidelines.

☐ Describe antitrust policy toward price fixing and price discrimination.

☐ Discuss the antitrust issue in tying contracts.

☐ Define a natural monopoly and cite two ways government controls natural monopolies.

☐ Explain the public interest theory of regulation.

☐ Describe two problems with industrial regulation by government agencies and commissions.

☐ Explain the legal cartel theory of regulation.

☐ Discuss the outcomes from deregulation of selected U.S. industries since the 1970s.

☐ State three distinguishing features of social regulation.

☐ Make a case for social regulation in terms of benefits and costs.

☐ Present a case against social regulation in terms of benefits and costs.

☐ Offer two economic reminders about social regulation.

☐ Explain the charges, findings, and rulings in the Microsoft antitrust case (Last Word).

■ CHAPTER OUTLINE

1. The basic purposes of **antitrust policy** are to restrict monopoly power, promote competition, and achieve allocative efficiency.

  a. Following the Civil War, the expansion of the U.S. economy brought with it the creation of trusts (or monopolies) in many industries. The economic problem with monopolies is that they produce less output and charge higher prices than would be the case if their industries were more competitive. To control them, government has passed antitrust laws and created regulatory agencies.

  b. The **Sherman Act** of 1890 was the first antitrust legislation. It made restraint of trade and monopolization criminal offenses.

  c. The **Clayton Act** of 1914 outlawed price discrimination not based on cost, **tying contracts,** mergers that lessened competition, and **interlocking directorates.**

  d. The **Federal Trade Commission Act** of 1914 established the **Federal Trade Commission** to investigate unfair practices that might lead to the development of monopoly power. It can issue **cease-and-desist orders** for cases involving unfair competition. In 1938 this act was amended by the **Wheeler-Lea Act** to prohibit deceptive practices (including false and misleading advertising and misrepresentation of products).

  e. The **Celler-Kefauver Act** of 1950 plugged a loophole in the Clayton Act and prohibited mergers that might lead to a substantial reduction in competition.

2. The effectiveness of antitrust laws in preventing monopoly and maintaining competition has depended on judicial interpretation of the laws and enforcement of these laws by Federal agencies.

  a. Two issues arise in the judicial interpretation of the antitrust laws.

  (1) Should a firm be judged on the basis of its monopoly structure or behavior? In the **Standard Oil case** of 1911, the U.S Supreme Court found the company guilty of monopolizing the petroleum industry. The **U.S. Steel case** of 1920, which also came before the Supreme Court, applied the **rule of reason** and said that a firm should be judged on the basis of its *behavior*. The **Alcoa case** of 1945 judged a firm on the basis of its *structure* (large control of a market). The courts and most economists now use the rule of reason that bases antitrust action on market behavior, not structure.

  (2) Should a broad or narrow definition of the market in which firms sell their products be used to judge monopoly power? In the 1956 **DuPont cellophane case,** the court ruled that DuPont did not monopolize the industry because there were other types of packaging materials that could be used.

  b. There are differences in political philosophies about whether antitrust enforcement should be more or less strictly enforced. The active antitrust perspective calls for enforcement of antitrust laws to stop illegal business activity, prevent anticompetitive mergers, and counter monopoly practices. The laissez-faire perspective contends that enforcement is largely unnecessary because market forces will control monopoly behavior and undermine monopoly positions.

  c. A question can be raised about whether the antitrust laws have been effective regarding monopoly, mergers, price fixing, price discrimination, and tying contracts.

  (1) For existing market structures, enforcement of antitrust laws has been lenient in general if the expansion of market share by a monopolistic firm is reasonable. The Sherman Act, however, has still been invoked in several high profile cases in which anticompetitive practices were alleged (2000 **Microsoft case**). The European Union also generally has been more aggressive in prosecuting monopolies.

  (2) For **horizontal, vertical,** or **conglomerate mergers,** the application of the laws usually varies by the type of merger and the particulars of a case. Merger guidelines are based on the Herfindahl index (the sum of the squared values of market shares within an industry), but other factors such as economies of scale, degree of foreign competition, and ease of entry, are considered.

  (3) Prohibitions against price fixing are strictly enforced. These activities are viewed as **per se violations,** so even the attempt, and not the actual outcome, will bring legal action and penalties.

  (4) Price discrimination is rarely challenged on antitrust grounds because in most cases it benefits consumers, but the practice can be challenged if the purpose is to reduce competition or block entry into a business.

  (5) The laws against tying contracts that require a buyer to purchase other products or take certain actions as a condition of a sale have been strictly enforced.

  (6) Overall, antitrust laws have not been very effective in breaking up monopolies or in preventing the growth of large oligopolies that have developed legally and because of market conditions. The laws have been effective against abusive or predatory monopolies. They have also been effective in blocking anticompetitive mergers, preventing price fixing, and restricting the use of tying contracts.

3. Industrial regulation occurs in some industries for economic reasons.

  a. A **natural monopoly** exists if a single producer can provide a good or service for the entire market at a lower average cost (because of economies of scale) than several producers, making competition uneconomical. To achieve better economic outcomes from this situation, government may opt for public ownership of the business or public (industrial) regulation. The latter option is based on the **public interest theory of regulation** that calls for controlling the economic decisions of the monopoly producers to achieve lower costs and greater output benefits for the public.

  b. The effectiveness of the regulation of business firms by regulatory agencies has been criticized for two main reasons.

  (1) Regulation increases costs and leads to an inefficient allocation of resources and higher prices.

  (2) Regulated monopolies get perpetuated over time and would be more competitive firms if they were not regulated. Regulatory agencies contribute to

the problem by protecting these industries, and these actions hurt the public and consumers.

c. The *legal cartel theory of regulation* holds that potentially competitive industries often want and support the regulation of their industries to increase their profits by limiting competition among firms. The government regulatory agency in essence creates a government-sponsored cartel in an industry.

4. Since the 1970s there has been **deregulation** of many industries in the United States: airline, trucking, banking, railroad, natural gas, electricity, television broadcasting, and communications. The overall consensus among economists is that deregulation has produced large net benefits because it has resulted in lower prices, lower costs of production, and increased output. It has also allowed for greater technological advances in many industries. There is less certainty about the positive outcomes from deregulation in electricity markets because of pricing problems in California and illegal manipulations of electricity supplies by some business firms.

5. *Social regulation* has developed since the 1960s and resulted in the creation of additional regulatory agencies that focus on production conditions, product qualities, and production effects on society.

a. Social regulation differs in three ways from industrial regulation: broader coverage of industries; more intrusion into the day-to-day production process; and rapid expansion into many areas.

b. Discussions about social regulation involve deciding whether there is an optimal level of such regulation. The costs and benefits are difficult to measure, so ideology often influences the debate over the proper amount of this regulation.

c. Supporters of social regulation contend it is needed to fight serious problems such as job and auto safety, environment pollution, product defects, and discrimination. Although such regulation is costly, the social benefits would exceed the costs over time, if they could be easily measured. Defenders point to many specific benefits resulting from such regulation.

d. Critics argue that this social regulation is inefficient because the regulations are poorly drawn and targeted. The rules and regulations are also often made based on limited and inadequate information. In addition, there are unintended secondary effects from the regulation that boost product costs. Regulatory agencies tend to attract "overzealous" workers who dislike the market system and advocate government intervention as the only solution.

e. Two reminders are needed in the debate over social regulation.

(1) Supporters need to remember that there is no "free lunch," and that social regulation increases product prices, may slow product innovation, and may lessen competition.

(2) Defenders need to remember that the market system has flaws that sometimes need to be addressed by government through social regulation and that by doing so, government creates continuing support of the operation of the market system.

6. (Last Word). In 1998, Microsoft was charged with violating Section 2 of the Sherman Act by using business practices that maintained its Windows software monopoly. Microsoft denied the charges and argued that technological advances made any monopoly highly transitory. The ruling from the Federal district court divided the company into two firms, one for software applications and the other for the Windows operating system. The breakup ruling was overturned on appeals, but it still affirmed that Microsoft used illegal business practices to maintain its monopoly. Microsoft was prevented from using these anticompetitive practices in the future. A behavior remedy for antitrust violations was used rather than a structural (breakup) remedy in this case.

■ **HINTS AND TIPS**

1. The first section of the chapter discusses several Federal antitrust laws. After looking at this section, many students ask, "Am I expected to know these laws?" Yes, you should have an understanding of these laws. A related question asked is, "Why should I know them?" To examine a current economic issue, you need to know how the problem arose, what actions have been taken over time to solve it, and what the outcomes are. Many of these major antitrust laws are enforced to some degree today and may affect a business for which you may work.

2. The *Herfindahl index* was first introduced in Chapter 11. Reread that material if you cannot remember what the index is. In Chapter 18 you will learn how the index is used for merger guidelines.

3. This chapter discusses controversies about many topics—antitrust policy, industrial regulation, deregulation, and social regulation. To help understand these controversies, make a table showing the pro and con positions for each issue. See Problem 4 for an example.

■ **IMPORTANT TERMS**

antitrust policy	U.S. Steel case
industrial regulation	rule of reason
social regulation	Alcoa case
Sherman Act	DuPont cellophane case
Clayton Act	
tying contracts	Microsoft case
interlocking directorate	horizontal merger
	vertical merger
Federal Trade Commission Act	conglomerate merger
	per se violations
cease-and-desist order	natural monopoly
	public interest theory of regulation
Wheeler-Lea Act	
Celler-Kefauver Act	legal cartel theory of regulation
Standard Oil case	

SELF-TEST

■ FILL-IN QUESTIONS

1. Laws and government actions designed to prevent monopoly and promote competition are referred to as (industrial regulation, antitrust policy) _____. Action taken to control a firm's prices within selected industries is referred to as (social, industrial) _____ regulation whereas establishing the conditions under which goods are produced, monitoring the physical characteristics of products, and reducing the negative effects of production fall under the category of _____ regulation.

2. The two techniques of Federal control that have been adopted as substitutes for, or to maintain competition, in markets are

a. _____

b. _____

3. Antitrust legislation in 1890 that made it illegal to monopolize or restrain trade between the states or between nations was the (Clayton, Sherman) _____ Act. Legislation passed in 1914 that prohibited such practices as price discrimination, acquisition of the stock of corporations to reduce competition, tying contracts, and interlocking directorates was the (Clayton, Sherman) _____ Act.

4. The 1914 act that had set up an agency to investigate unfair competitive practices, hold public hearings on such complaints, and issue cease-and-desist orders was the (Clayton, Federal Trade Commission) _____ Act.

5. The 1938 antitrust act that had the effect of prohibiting false and misleading advertising was the (Celler-Kefauver, Wheeler-Lea) _____ Act, while the act that plugged a loophole in the Clayton Act by banning the acquisition of assets of one firm by another when it would lessen competition was the _____ Act.

6. When the judicial courts used the rule of reason to evaluate industrial concentration by U.S. Steel in 1920, they were judging the firm on the basis of its market (behavior, structure) _____, but when the courts made a decision to break up Alcoa in 1945, they were judging the firm on the basis of its market _____. Since 1945, the courts have returned to evaluating a firm on the basis of its market (behavior, structure) _____.

7. One major issue of interpretation in antitrust law is the definition of a market. The firm's market share will appear small if the courts define a market (narrowly, broadly) _____, but the firm's market share will appear large if the courts define a market share _____. In 1956, the courts ruled that although DuPont sold nearly all the cellophane produced in the United States, it (did, did not) _____ dominate the market for flexible packaging materials.

8. The active antitrust perspective is that antitrust laws need to be (strictly, loosely) _____ enforced to promote (monopoly, competition) _____ in business. The laissez-faire perspective contends that enforcement is largely (necessary, unnecessary) _____ because monopoly power and control can be countered by (government, markets) _____.

9. A merger between two competitors selling similar products in the same market is a (vertical, horizontal, conglomerate) _____ merger; a _____ merger occurs among firms at different stages in the production process of the same industry; a _____ merger results when a firm in one industry is purchased by a firm in an unrelated industry.

10. The (Sherman, Herfindahl) _____ index is used as a guideline for mergers. An industry of only four firms, each with a 25 percent market share, has an index score of (2500, 10,000) _____ but if the industry was a pure monopoly with only one firm its index score would be _____.

11. If a firm attempted to fix prices, even if the attempt were not effective, it would be an example of a (tying contract, per se violation) _____ under antitrust laws; if a producer will only sell a desired product on condition that the buyer acquire other products, this is an example of a _____ under antitrust laws. In both cases, the laws are (loosely, strictly) _____ enforced.

12. Most economists conclude that, overall, U.S. antitrust policy (has, has not) _____ been effective in achieving its goal of promoting competition and efficiency and that the application of antitrust laws _____ been effective against predatory and abusive monopoly.

13. A natural monopoly exists when a single firm is able to supply the entire market at a (higher, lower) _____ average cost than a number of competing firms. In the United States, many of these natural monopolies are controlled by (business cartels, regulatory commissions) _____.

14. The two major criticisms of regulation of industries by a government agency or commission are

a. The regulated firms have no incentive to lower their costs because the commission will then require them to (raise, lower) _____ their prices, and because the prices they are allowed to charge are based on the value of their capital equipment, firms tend to make uneconomical substitutions of (labor, capital) _____ for _____.

b. Regulation has been applied to industries that (are, are not) _____ natural monopolies, which in the absence of regulation would be more competitive.

15. The public interest theory of regulation assumes that the objective of regulating an industry is to (encourage, discourage) _____ the abuses of monopoly power. An alternative theory assumes firms wish to be regulated because it enables them to form, and the regulatory commission helps them to create, a profitable and legal (conglomerate, cartel) _____.

16. The available evidence indicates that deregulation of many industries that began in the 1970s generally resulted in (decreased, increased) _____ prices because _____ competition among firms led to _____ costs and _____ output.

17. The Food and Drug Administration would be an example of a Federal regulatory commission engaged in (social, industrial) _____ regulation and the Federal Communications Commission would be an example of an agency engaged in _____ regulation.

18. Compared with industrial regulation, social regulation applies to (more, fewer) _____ firms, affects day-to-day production to a (greater, lesser) _____ extent, and has expanded more (rapidly, slowly) _____.

19. It should be remembered by supporters of social regulation that there is "no free lunch" because it can (increase, decrease) _____ product prices and _____ worker productivity, and it also may _____ the rate of innovation.

20. It should be remembered by critics of social regulation that it can be (anti-, pro-) _____ capitalist because when such social problems in the market are addressed, the public support for the market system is (increased, decreased) _____.

■ **TRUE–FALSE QUESTIONS**

Circle T if the statement is true, F if it is false.

1. The basic purposes of antitrust policy are to prevent monopolization, promote competition, and achieve allocative efficiency. **T F**

2. The issue of antitrust arose from the emergence of trusts and monopolies in the U.S. economy in the two decades before the U.S. Civil War. **T F**

3. The economic problem with monopolists is that they charge a lower price and produce more output than if their industries were competitive. **T F**

4. The Clayton Act declares that price discrimination, tying contracts, stock acquisitions between corporations, and interlocking directorates are illegal when their effect is to reduce competition. **T F**

5. The Federal Trade Commission is in charge of stimulating more international trade between domestic and foreign producers. **T F**

6. The Celler-Kefauver Act of 1950 prohibits one firm from acquiring the assets of another firm when the result is to lessen competition. **T F**

7. In 1920 the courts applied the rule of reason to the U.S. Steel Corporation and decided that the corporation possessed monopoly power and had unreasonably restrained trade. **T F**

8. Those who believe an industry should be judged on the basis of its structure contend that any industry with a monopolistic structure must behave like a monopolist. **T F**

9. The courts broadly defined the market for cellophane in the DuPont cellophane case of 1956. **T F**

10. There is only one perspective on the enforcement of antitrust laws, and it calls for strict enforcement of all laws. **T F**

11. A horizontal merger is a merger between firms at different stages of the production process. **T F**

12. The Herfindahl index is the sum of the squared values of the market shares within an industry. **T F**

13. To gain a conviction under *per se violations*, the party making the charge must show that the conspiracy to fix prices actually succeeded or caused damage. **T F**

14. There is substantial evidence that antitrust policy has *not* been effective in identifying and prosecuting price fixing by businesses. **T F**

15. Industrial regulation pertains to regulation of the conditions under which products are made, the impact of products on society, and the physical qualities of the products. **T F**

16. Public ownership rather than public regulation has been the primary means used in the United States to ensure that the behavior of natural monopolists is socially acceptable. **T F**

17. The rationale underlying the public interest theory of regulation of natural monopolies is to allow the consumers of their goods or services to benefit from the economies of scale. **T F**

18. Regulated firms, because the prices they are allowed to charge enable them to earn a "fair" return over their costs, have a strong incentive to reduce their costs. **T F**

19. From the perspective of the legal cartel theory of regulation, some industries want to be regulated by government. **T F**

20. Deregulation of industries since the 1970s has resulted in large gains in economic efficiency for the U.S. economy. **T F**

21. The marginal costs and benefits of social regulation are easy to measure for determining the optimal level of such regulation. **T F**

22. Those who favor social regulation believe that the expenditures on it are needed to obtain a hospitable, sustainable, and just society. **T F**

23. Critics of social regulation argue that its marginal costs exceed its marginal benefits. **T F**

24. The likely effect of social regulation is that it lowers product prices, raises worker productivity, and increases product innovation. **T F**

25. Social regulation can contribute to public support for a market system by addressing production and consumption problems arising from the system. **T F**

■ MULTIPLE-CHOICE QUESTIONS

Circle the letter that corresponds to the best answer.

1. Which term describes the laws and government actions designed to prevent monopoly and promote competition?
   (a) industrial regulation
   (b) social regulation
   (c) legal cartel policy
   (d) antitrust policy

2. Which law stated that contracts and conspiracies in restraint of trade, monopolies, attempts to monopolize, and conspiracies to monopolize are illegal?
   (a) Sherman Act
   (b) Clayton Act
   (c) Federal Trade Commission Act
   (d) Wheeler-Lea Act

3. Which act specifically outlawed tying contracts and interlocking directorates?
   (a) Sherman Act
   (b) Clayton Act
   (c) Federal Trade Commission Act
   (d) Wheeler-Lea Act

4. Which act has given the Federal Trade Commission the task of preventing false and misleading advertising and the misrepresentation of products?
   (a) Sherman Act
   (b) Clayton Act
   (c) Federal Trade Commission Act
   (d) Wheeler-Lea Act

5. Which act banned the acquisition of a firm's assets by a competing firm when the acquisition would tend to reduce competition?
   (a) Celler-Kefauver Act
   (b) Wheeler-Lea Act
   (c) Clayton Act
   (d) Federal Trade Commission Act

6. The argument that an industry that is highly concentrated will behave like a monopolist and the Alcoa court case of 1945 would both provide support for the case that the application of antitrust laws should be based on industry
   (a) behavior
   (b) structure
   (c) efficiency
   (d) rule of reason

7. If the market is defined broadly to include a wide range of somewhat similar products, then
   (a) firms in the industry will be able to behave as monopolists
   (b) firms in the industry will follow the rule of reason
   (c) a firm's market share will appear large
   (d) a firm's market share will appear small

8. Which perspective holds that the enforcement of antitrust laws is largely unnecessary, especially as related to monopoly, because market forces will counter monopoly?
   (a) concentration perspective
   (b) active antitrust perspective
   (c) relevant market perspective
   (d) laissez-faire perspective

9. The merger of a firm in one industry with a firm in an unrelated industry is called a
   (a) horizontal merger
   (b) vertical merger
   (c) secondary merger
   (d) conglomerate merger

10. Which is most likely to be the focus of antitrust law scrutiny and enforcement?
   (a) a publicly regulated utility
   (b) a conglomerate merger
   (c) a vertical merger
   (d) a horizontal merger

11. An industry has four firms, each with a market share of 25%. There is no foreign competition, entry into the industry is difficult, and no firm is on the verge of bankruptcy. If two of the firms in the industry sought to merge, this action would most likely be opposed by the government because the new Herfindahl index for the industry would be
   (a) 2000 and the merger would increase the index by 1000
   (b) 2500 and the merger would increase the index by 1000
   (c) 3750 and the merger would increase the index by 1250
   (d) 5000 and the merger would increase the index by 1250

12. When the government or another party making a charge can show that there was a conspiracy to fix prices, even if the conspiracy did not succeed, this would be an example of
   (a) a tying contract
   (b) a per se violation
   (c) the rule of reason
   (d) the legal cartel theory

13. Antitrust laws have been most effective in
(a) breaking up monopolies
(b) prosecuting price fixing in business
(c) expanding industrial concentration
(d) blocking entry of foreign competition in domestic markets

14. If a movie distributor forced theaters to "buy" projection rights to a full package of films as a condition of showing a blockbuster movie, then this would be an example of
(a) price fixing
(b) a tying contract
(c) a per se violation
(d) an interlocking directorate

15. An example of a government organization involved primarily in industrial regulation would be the
(a) Federal Communications Commission
(b) Food and Drug Administration
(c) Occupational Safety and Health Administration
(d) Environmental Protection Agency

16. Legislation designed to regulate natural monopolies would be based on which theory of regulation?
(a) cartel
(b) public interest
(c) rule of reason
(d) public ownership

17. Those who oppose the regulation of industry by regulatory agencies contend that
(a) many of the regulated industries are natural monopolies
(b) the regulatory agencies may favor industry because they are often staffed by former industry executives
(c) regulation contributes to an increase in the number of mergers in industries
(d) regulation helps moderate costs and improves efficiency in the production of a good or service produced by the regulated industry

18. The legal cartel theory of regulation
(a) would allow the forces of demand and supply to determine the rates (prices) of the good or service
(b) would attempt to protect the public from abuses of monopoly power
(c) assumes that the regulated industry wishes to be regulated
(d) assumes that both the demand for and supply of the good or service produced by the regulated industry are perfectly inelastic

19. Deregulation of previously regulated industries in the United States has resulted in
(a) higher prices, higher costs, and decreased output
(b) higher prices and costs, but increased output
(c) lower prices and costs, but decreased output
(d) lower prices, lower costs, and increased output

20. Which is a concern of social regulation?
(a) the prices charged for goods
(b) the service provided to the public
(c) the conditions under which goods are manufactured
(d) the impact on business profits from the production of goods

21. A major difference between industrial regulation and social regulation is that social regulation
(a) covers fewer industries across the economy
(b) has expanded slowly and waned in recent years
(c) is targeted at the prices charged, the costs of production, and amount of profit
(d) focuses on product design, employment conditions, and the production process

22. Which government organization is primarily engaged in social regulation?
(a) the Federal Trade Commission
(b) the Interstate Commerce Commission
(c) the Environmental Protection Agency
(d) the Federal Energy Regulatory Commission

23. Supporters of social regulation contend that
(a) there is a pressing need to reduce the number of mergers in U.S. business
(b) the presence of natural monopoly requires strong regulatory action by government
(c) the social benefits will exceed the social costs
(d) there are no social costs associated with it

24. A criticism of social regulation by its opponents is that it
(a) is a strong procapitalist force
(b) will decrease the rate of innovation in the economy
(c) will increase the amount of price fixing among businesses
(d) will require too long a time to achieve its objectives

25. The captions for two reminders for proponents and opponents of social regulation are
(a) "there is no free lunch" and "less government is not always better than more"
(b) "the rule of reason will prevail" and "restraint of trade will not be tolerated by government"
(c) "the public interest will win over the powerful" and the "legal cartel will be broken by government"
(d) "demand the lowest price" and "protect the greatest number"

■ **PROBLEMS**

1. Following is a list of Federal laws. Next is a series of provisions found in Federal laws. Match each law with the appropriate provision by placing the appropriate capital letter after each provision.

A. Sherman Act   **D.** Wheeler-Lea Act
B. Clayton Act   **E.** Celler-Kefauver Act
C. Federal Trade
  Commission Act

a. Established a commission to investigate and prevent unfair methods of competition _____
b. Made monopoly and restraint of trade illegal and criminal _____
c. Prohibited the acquisition of the assets of a firm by another firm when such an acquisition would lessen competition _____

d. Had the effect of prohibiting false and misleading advertising and the misrepresentation of products _____

e. Clarified the Sherman Act and outlawed specific techniques or devices used to create monopolies and restrain trade _____

2. Indicate with the letter **L** for leniently and the letter **S** for strictly how the antitrust laws tend to be applied to each of the following.

a. Vertical mergers in which each of the merging firms sells a small portion of the total output of its industry _____

b. Price fixing by a firm in an industry _____

c. Conglomerate mergers _____

d. Existing market structures in which no firm sells 60% or more of the total output of its industry _____

e. Horizontal mergers in which the merged firms would sell a large portion of the total output of their industry and no firm is on the verge of bankruptcy _____

f. Action by firms in an industry to divide up sales _____

g. Horizontal mergers where one of the firms is on the verge of bankruptcy _____

3. The following table contains data on five different industries and the market shares for each firm in the industry. Assume that there is no foreign competition, entry into the industry is difficult, and that no firm in each industry is on the verge of bankruptcy.

	Market share of firms in industry						
Industry	**1**	**2**	**3**	**4**	**5**	**6**	**Herfindahl index**
A	35	25	15	11	10	4	_____
B	30	25	25	20	—	—	_____
C	20	20	20	15	15	10	_____
D	60	25	15	—	—	—	_____
E	22	21	20	18	12	7	_____

a. In the last column, calculate the Herfindahl index.

b. The industry with the most concentration is Industry _____, and the industry with the least monopoly power is Industry _____.

c. If the *sixth* firm in Industry A sought to merge with the *fifth* firm in that industry, then the government (would, would not) _____ be likely to challenge the merger. The Herfindahl index for this industry is _____, which is higher than the merger guideline of _____ points used by the government, but the merger increases the index by only _____ points.

d. If the *fourth* firm in Industry B sought to merge with the *third* firm in that industry, then the government

(would, would not) _____ be likely to challenge the merger. The Herfindahl index for this industry is _____, which is higher than the merger guideline of the government, and the merger increases the index by _____ points.

e. A *conglomerate* merger between the *fourth* firm in Industry C and the *fourth* firm in Industry E (would, would not) _____ likely be challenged by the government. The Herfindahl index would (increase, remain the same) _____ with this merger.

f. If a *vertical* merger between the *first* firm in Industry B with the *first* firm in Industry D lessened competition in each industry, then the merger (would, would not) _____ likely be challenged by the government, but the merger _____ likely be challenged if it did not lessen competition in each industry.

4. Social regulation has had its critics and defenders. In the blank spaces in the following table, indicate the effect that critics and defenders thought social regulation would have on each characteristic. Mark an **I** for increase and **D** for decrease. If the text states nothing about this effect, mark an **N**.

	Critics	**Defenders**
a. Prices	_____	_____
b. Output	_____	_____
c. Competition	_____	_____
d. Product innovation	_____	_____
e. Net benefits to society	_____	_____

■ **SHORT ANSWER AND ESSAY QUESTIONS**

1. Explain the basic differences between antitrust policy, industrial regulation, and social regulation.

2. What are the historical background to and the main provisions of the Sherman Act?

3. The Clayton Act and the Federal Trade Commission Act amended or elaborated on the provisions of the Sherman Act, and both aimed at preventing rather than punishing monopoly. What were the chief provisions of each act, and how did they attempt to prevent monopoly? In what two ways is the FTC Act important?

4. What loophole in the Clayton Act did the Celler-Kefauver Act plug in 1950, and how did it alter the coverage of the antitrust laws with respect to mergers?

5. Contrast the two different approaches to court interpretation of antitrust laws that are illustrated by the decisions of the courts in the U.S. Steel and Alcoa cases.

6. Why is defining the market an important issue in the application of the antitrust laws? How did the courts define the market in the case brought against DuPont for monopolizing the market for cellophane?

7. Discuss two perspectives on strict enforcement of antitrust laws.

8. How have the antitrust laws been applied in the past and in recent years to monopoly in the United States and by the European Union? Give examples.

9. Explain the difference between horizontal, vertical, and conglomerate mergers. Give an example of each type.

10. What is the Herfindahl index and how is it used as a guideline for mergers?

11. What are per se violations? Give examples of recent price-fixing investigations and court cases.

12. What is a natural monopoly? What two alternative ways can a natural monopoly be used to ensure that it behaves in a socially acceptable fashion?

13. Explain how public interest regulation can lead to increased costs and economic inefficiency as it is practiced by U.S. commissions and agencies.

14. Discuss the issue involved in regulation that perpetuates a natural monopoly after the conditions for it have evaporated. Give examples.

15. What is the legal cartel theory of regulation? Contrast it with the public interest theory of regulation.

16. Why were a number of industries in the U.S. economy deregulated beginning in the 1970s? What have been the economic effects of deregulation?

17. How does social regulation differ from industrial (or public) regulation? Describe three major differences.

18. Can the optimal level of social regulation be determined? Explain.

19. What are the major arguments for social regulation?

20. What are the major criticisms of social regulation?

ANSWERS

Chapter 18 Antitrust Policy and Regulation

FILL-IN QUESTIONS

1. antitrust policy, industrial, social
2. *a.* establishing regulatory agencies; *b.* passing antitrust laws (either order for *a* and *b*)
3. Sherman, Clayton
4. Federal Trade Commission
5. Wheeler-Lea, Celler-Kefauver
6. behavior, structure, behavior
7. broadly, narrowly, did not
8. strictly, competition, unnecessary, markets
9. horizontal, vertical, conglomerate
10. Herfindahl, 2500, 10,000
11. per se violation, tying contract, strictly
12. has, has
13. lower, regulatory commissions

14. *a.* lower, capital, labor; *b.* are not
15. discourage, cartel
16. decreased, increased, decreased, increased
17. social, industrial
18. more, greater, rapidly
19. increase, decrease, decrease
20. pro-, increased

TRUE–FALSE QUESTIONS

1. T, p. 376	**14.** F, p. 381
2. F, p. 376	**15.** F, pp. 382–383
3. F, p. 376	**16.** F, p. 382
4. T, p. 377	**17.** T, p. 383
5. F, p. 377	**18.** F, p. 383
6. T, p. 377	**19.** T, pp. 383–384
7. F, p. 378	**20.** T, p. 384
8. T, p. 378	**21.** F, pp. 385–386
9. T, p. 378	**22.** T, pp. 386–387
10. F, p. 379	**23.** T, pp. 387–388
11. F, p. 380	**24.** F, p. 388
12. T, pp. 380–381	**25.** T, p. 388
13. F, p. 381	

MULTIPLE-CHOICE QUESTIONS

1. d, p. 375	**14.** b, pp. 381–382
2. a, pp. 376–377	**15.** a, p. 382
3. b, p. 377	**16.** b, p. 383
4. d, p. 377	**17.** b, p. 383
5. a, p. 377	**18.** c, pp. 383–384
6. b, p. 378	**19.** d, p. 384
7. d, p. 378	**20.** c, p. 385
8. d, p. 379	**21.** d, p. 385
9. d, p. 380	**22.** c, p. 385
10. d, p. 380	**23.** c, pp. 386–387
11. c, pp. 380–381	**24.** b, pp. 387–388
12. b, p. 381	**25.** a, p. 388
13. b, p. 381	

PROBLEMS

1. *a.* C; *b.* A; *c.* E; *d.* D; *e.* B
2. *a.* L; *b.* S; *c.* L; *d.* L; *e.* S; *f.* S; *g.* L
3. *a.* 2312, 2550, 1750, 4450, 1842; *b.* D, C; *c.* would not, 2312, 1800, 80; *d.* would, 2550, 1000; *e.* would not, remain the same; *f.* would, would not
4. *a.* I, N; *b.* D, N; *c.* D, N; *d.* D, N; *e.* D, I

SHORT ANSWER AND ESSAY QUESTIONS

1. p. 375	**8.** pp. 379–380	**15.** pp. 383–384
2. pp. 376–377	**9.** p. 380	**16.** p. 384
3. p. 377	**10.** pp. 381–382	**17.** p. 385
4. p. 377	**11.** p. 381	**18.** pp. 385–386
5. pp. 377–378	**12.** pp. 382–383	**19.** pp. 386–387
6. p. 378	**13.** p. 383	**20.** pp. 387–388
7. p. 379	**14.** p. 383	

Agriculture: Economics and Policy

Agriculture is a large and vital part of the U.S. and world economies, and so it merits the special attention it receives in Chapter 19. As you will learn, the economics of farm policies of the Federal government are of concern not only to those directly engaged in farming, but also to U.S. consumers and businesses that purchase farm products and to U.S. taxpayers who subsidize farm incomes. Agriculture is also important in the world economy because each nation must find a way to feed its population, and domestic farm policies designed to enhance farm incomes often lead to distortions in world trade and economic inefficiency in world agricultural production.

The chapter begins by examining a short-run problem of **price and income instability** and the long-run problem of the **declining output** of U.S. agriculture as a percentage of GDP. The short-run price and income instability results from farm prices and incomes having fluctuated sharply from year to year. Agriculture is a declining industry in the long run, and as a consequence, farm incomes have fallen over time. To understand the causes of each economic condition, you will have to use the concept of inelastic demand and your knowledge of how demand and supply determine price in a competitive market. The effort you have put into the study of these tools in previous chapters will now pay a dividend: an understanding of the causes of a real-world situation and the policies designed to address it.

The agricultural policies of the Federal government have been directed at enhancing and stabilizing farm incomes by supporting farm prices. In connection with the support of farm prices, you are introduced to the **parity concept.** Once you understand parity and recognize that the parity price in the past has been above what the competitive price would have been, you will come to some important conclusions. Consumers paid higher prices for and consumed smaller quantities of the various farm products, and at the prices supported by the Federal government, there were surpluses of these products. The Federal government bought these surpluses to keep the price above the competitive market price. The purchases of the surpluses were financed by U.S. taxpayers. To eliminate these surpluses, government looked for ways to increase the demand for or to decrease the supply of these commodities. Programs to increase demand and decrease supply were put into effect, but they failed to eliminate the annual surpluses.

Over the years, farm policies have not worked well and the price-support system has been criticized for several reasons. First, the policies confuse the symptoms of the agricultural economic condition (low farm prices and incomes) with its causes (resource allocation). Second, the costly farm subsidies are also misguided because they tend to benefit the high-income instead of the low-income farmer. Third, some policies of the Federal government contradict or offset other policies to help farmers.

The politics of farm policy can also be studied from the public choice perspective first presented in Chapter 17. In this chapter you will learn how the special interest effect and rent-seeking behavior related to farm policies result in costly programs that have been supported by political leaders and subsidized by the Federal government for so many years. Nevertheless, the political backing for farm price supports is declining because of a reduction in the farm population. There is also international pressure to reduce farm price supports in all nations to eliminate distortions in world trade and improve worldwide economic efficiency.

The chapter concludes with a discussion of the recent reform of agricultural policy in the United States. The **Freedom to Farm Act** of 1996 was an attempt to eliminate price supports and acreage allotments for many major agricultural products. In return, U.S. farmers were to receive income payments through 2002 to help them make the transition to working in a more competitive market. The deterioration in economic conditions before the end of the act led to emergency aid payments to farmers to stabilize crop prices and incomes for farmers. As you will learn, the features of that legislation have now been extended and expanded with the passage of the *Food, Conservation and Energy Act of 2008.* It provides direct payments, countercyclical payments, and marketing loans to help farmers. The subsidies and new legislation again demonstrate that U.S. agriculture retains strong special-interest and political support.

■ CHECKLIST

When you have studied this chapter you should be able to

☐ Give several reasons why it is important to study the economics of U.S. agriculture.

☐ Distinguish between farm commodities and food products.

☐ List three causes of the short-run price and income instability in agriculture.

☐ Explain why the demand for agricultural products is price inelastic.

☐ Cite a reason for the fluctuations in agricultural output.
☐ Discuss the fluctuations in domestic demand for agricultural products.
☐ Describe the instability of foreign demand for agricultural products.
☐ Identify the two major factors contributing to the long-run declining output in U.S. agriculture.
☐ Describe how technological change affects the long-run supply of agricultural products.
☐ Give two reasons why increases in demand lag increases in supply over time in U.S. agriculture.
☐ Use a supply and demand graph to illustrate the long-run declining output in U.S. agriculture.
☐ Explain the consequences of the long-run declining output in agriculture for industry structure, crop prices, and income.
☐ Compare farm-household income with nonfarm household income.
☐ List the six features of the "farm program."
☐ Give cost estimates of the size of U.S. farm subsidies in recent years.
☐ Present several arguments in support of farm subsidies.
☐ Define the parity ratio and explain its significance to agricultural policy.
☐ Use a supply and demand graph to identify the economic effects of price supports for agricultural products on output, farm income, consumer and taxpayer expenditures, economic efficiency, the environment, and international trade.
☐ Give examples of how the Federal government restricts supply and bolsters demand for farm products.
☐ Explain criticisms of the parity concepts.
☐ Present three criticisms of the price-support system in agriculture.
☐ Use insights from public choice theory to discuss the politics of agricultural legislation and expenditures by the Federal government for farm programs.
☐ Give two reasons, one domestic and one international, to explain the change in the politics of farm subsidies.
☐ Describe the major features of the Freedom to Farm Act of 1996.
☐ Explain the elements of the Food, Conservation and Energy Act of 2008 and how it affects crop prices, farm incomes, and subsidies in agriculture.
☐ Discuss the domestic and global effects of the U.S. sugar program (Last Word).

■ **CHAPTER OUTLINE**

1. The economic analysis of U.S. agriculture is important for several reasons: It is one of the nation's largest industries and is a real-world example of the purely competitive model; it illustrates the economic effects of government intervention in markets; it illustrates the special-interest effect and rent-seeking behavior; and it reflects changes in global markets.

2. The agricultural industry is very diverse because it covers many types of farm and ranch operations. Agriculture also includes farm products or **farm commodities** such as wheat, corn, soybeans, cattle, and rice, and also **food products** that are sold in stores. The major focus of the chapter is on farm commodities (or farm products) because they tend to be sold in highly competitive markets. Some of these farm commodities are also subject to extensive government subsidies to maintain the prices for farm products or bolster farm incomes. Agriculture also has short-run and long-run problems. In the short run, there is price and income instability and in the long run there has been declining output as a percentage of GDP.

a. The reasons for the short-run price and income instability are several:

(1) The demand for farm products is inelastic, which means that the percentage change in quantity demanded is less than the percentage change in price.

(2) Weather or growing conditions cause fluctuations in the output of agricultural products; and

(3) Demand fluctuates in both domestic and foreign markets.

b. The causes of agriculture's long-run decline as an industry stem from two basic factors:

(1) The supply of agricultural products increased significantly over most of this century because of technological advances in agriculture.

(2) The demand for agricultural products failed to match the large increase in supply even though there were large increases in income (and population) because the demand for agricultural products is *income* inelastic (that is, increases in income lead to less than proportionate increases in expenditures on farm products).

The consequences of the two factors are that there has been considerable consolidation in the number of farms and the emergence of **agribusiness,** or large corporate farms, in some types of farming.

c. Farm-household income used to be well below nonfarm household incomes, but that is no longer the case because of out-migration from farming, consolidation, rising farm productivity, and government subsidies. Many farmers also supplement their farm incomes with nonfarm income from jobs in towns. Some households also operate profitable commercial farms.

3. Since the 1930s, farmers have been able to obtain various forms of public aid, but the primary purposes of the Federal **government subsidies** have been to enhance and stabilize farm prices and incomes.

a. Several arguments are used to justify these expenditures, such as the poor incomes of farmers, the importance of the family farm, the hazards of farming, and market power problems.

b. The cornerstone of the Federal policy to raise farm prices is the **parity concept** which would give the farmer year after year the same real income per unit of output. It is measured by the **parity ratio** which is the ratio of the prices received by farmers divided by the prices paid by farmers.

c. Historically, farm policy provided **price supports** at some percentage of the parity price. But because the supported price was almost always above the market price, government had to support the price by purchasing and accumulating surpluses of agricultural products; while farmers gained from this policy, there were losses for consumers and society, and problems were created in the environment and international sectors.

d. To reduce the annual and accumulated surpluses, government attempted to

(1) reduce the output (or supply) of farm products by *acreage allotments* and soil bank programs and

(2) expand the demand for farm products by finding new uses for farm products, expanding domestic demand, and increasing the foreign demand for agricultural commodities.

4. Agricultural policies designed to stabilize farm incomes and prices have not worked well. The policies have been subject to **criticisms and political debate.**

a. Economists have criticized the **parity concept** for its lack of economic logic. There is no reason why the prices received by farmers should be about equal to the prices paid by farmers over time. Prices for commodities produced by farmers and prices for products purchased change because of changes in supply and demand in different markets.

b. There are three basic **criticisms of price-support programs.**

(1) Price-support programs have confused the *symptoms* of the agricultural economic condition (a low amount of farm products and low farm incomes) with its *causes* (resource allocation) and have encouraged people to stay in agriculture.

(2) The major benefits from price-support programs are *misguided* because low-income farmers often receive small government subsidies while high-income farmers often receive large government subsidies; price supports also affect land values and become a subsidy for owners of farmland who rent their land and do not farm.

(3) The various farm programs of the Federal government have often *offset* or contradicted each other. Price-support programs have tried to stabilize prices, while other programs have increased supply, thus putting downward pressure on prices.

c. The **politics of farm policy** explain why costly and extensive subsidies have persisted in the United States.

(1) Four insights from public choice theory serve to explain this development: rent-seeking behavior by farm groups, the special-interest effect that impairs public decision making, political logrolling to turn negative outcomes into positive outcomes, and the clear benefits and hidden costs of farm programs.

(2) Changing politics also explains why there has been a reduction in the political support for agricultural subsidies.

(a) There has been a decline in the farm population and its political power.

(b) The United States also is committed to reducing agricultural subsidies worldwide because they distort world trade. This U.S. support for freer trade makes it harder to support domestic farm subsidies.

5. Since the mid-1990s there have been several attempts to reform farm policy to make the farm sector more market-oriented and less dependent on government subsidies, but they have met with mixed success.

a. The *Freedom to Farm Act* of 1996 tried to change 60 years of U.S. farm policy. The law ended price supports and acreage allotments for eight agricultural commodities. In return for accepting more risk, income payments were made to farmers through the year 2002 to help them make the transition to operating in a more competitive market. The change was expected to increase agricultural output, crop diversity, and risk management by farmers. The decline in several farm commodity prices in recent years created pressure to change the Freedom to Farm Act. The U.S. government responded to the problem by increasing subsidies to farmers with emergency aid, but it was only a temporary solution.

b. The *Food, Conservation and Energy Act of 2008* is the current law and it contains three types of subsidies for farm commodities. It continues the policy of giving farmers freedom to plant and provides constant *direct payments* to farmers that are based on past crop production levels. It provides *countercyclical payments (CCPs)* that cover any gap if the market price of a commodity falls below the target price. It offers *marketing loans* on a per-unit-of-output basis from a government lender with limits on the amount of loan repayment should crop prices fall below a certain level. The 2008 legislation makes it clear that the special-interest lobby for agriculture is still strong and that agriculture will continue to receive large government subsidies in spite of the market and output distortions that result from the large subsidies.

6. (Last Word). Price supports and import quotas have doubled U.S. sugar prices relative to world market prices. The estimated cost to consumers is between $1.5 and $1.9 billion per year. Import quotas have been imposed to keep low-priced foreign sugar out of the U.S. market so that price supports can be maintained. In 1975, 30 percent of U.S. sugar was imported, but today only about 20 percent is imported. This import policy has had significant effects on less developed nations and the world market for sugar. The decline in potential sugar revenue has hurt developing countries. The sugar that could have been sold in the U.S. is dumped on world markets, where the world price is then further depressed. Overall, both domestically and worldwide, the sugar program has distorted resources allocation and world trade.

■ **HINTS AND TIPS**

1. This chapter applies several economic ideas—supply and demand, elasticity, price controls, and public choice theory—that you learned about in previous chapters. If your understanding of these ideas is weak, review supply and demand in Chapter 3, elasticity and price controls in Chapter 6, and public choice theory in Chapter 17.

2. Make sure you understand the distinction between the short-run and long-run economic conditions in U.S. agriculture. There is a short-run price and income instability that involves the year-to-year changes in the prices of farm products and farm incomes. The changes in supply and demand over time have made agriculture a declining industry in the U.S. economy over the long run.

3. Figure 19.6 and the related discussion are very important to your study. The figure illustrates the economic effects that agricultural price supports have on different groups and the overall economy.

■ **IMPORTANT TERMS**

farm commodities	Freedom to Farm Act
food products	Food, Conservation and
agribusiness	Energy Act of 2008
parity concept	direct payments
parity ratio	countercyclical payments (CCP)
price supports	marketing loan program
acreage allotments	

SELF-TEST

■ **FILL-IN QUESTIONS**

1. It is important to study the economics of U.S. agriculture for many reasons; it is one of the (largest, smallest) _____ industries in the nation; it provides a real-world example of pure (monopoly, competition) _____; it demonstrates the intended and unintended effects of (consumer, government) _____ policies that interfere with forces of supply and demand; it reflects the (decreased, increased) _____ globalization of agricultural markets; and it illustrates aspects of (public, private) _____ choice theory.

2. The basic cause of the short-run price and income instability in agriculture is the (elastic, inelastic) _____ demand for farm products. This demand occurs because farm products have few good (complements, substitutes) _____ and because of rapidly diminishing marginal (product, utility) _____.

3. The elasticity of demand for farm products contributes to unstable farm prices and incomes because relatively (large, small) _____ changes in the output of farm products result in relatively _____ changes in prices and incomes and because relatively _____ changes in domestic or foreign demand result in relatively _____ changes in prices and incomes.

4. From a long-run perspective, the (demand for, supply of) _____ agricultural products increased rapidly over the past 60 years because of technological progress, but the _____ agricultural products did not increase as fast, in large part because food demand is income (elastic, inelastic) _____ and because the rate of population increase has not matched the increase in production.

5. Four arguments used to justify expenditures for farm subsidies are: the (inelastic, low) _____ income of farmers, the (cost, value) _____ of the family farm as a U.S. institution; the (rent-seeking, hazards) _____ of farming from many natural disasters, and the fact that the farmers sell their output in (purely, imperfectly) _____ competitive markets and purchase their inputs in _____ competitive markets.

6. If farmers were to receive a parity price for a product, year after year a given output would enable them to acquire a (fixed, increased) _____ amount of goods and services.

7. If the government supports farm prices at an above-equilibrium level, the results will be (shortages, surpluses) _____ that the government must (buy, sell) _____ to maintain prices at their support level.

8. With price-support programs, farmers (benefit, are hurt) _____ and consumers _____. The incomes of farmers (increase, decrease) _____, while the price consumers pay for products _____ and the quantities of the agricultural product that they purchase _____.

9. Society also is hurt by farm price-support programs because they encourage economic (efficiency, inefficiency) _____, an (over, under) _____ allocation of resources to agriculture, and a (small, large) _____ government bureaucracy for agriculture.

10. Agricultural price supports have (increased, decreased) _____ domestic agricultural production and _____ the use of inputs such as pesticides and fertilizers, resulting in (positive, negative) _____ effects on the environment.

11. The above-equilibrium price supports make U.S. agricultural markets (more, less) _____ attractive to foreign producers who try to sell _____ of their agricultural products in the United States. This activity is likely to (increase, decrease) _____ trade barriers, and _____ the efficiency of U.S. agriculture. The trade barriers will have a (negative, positive) _____ effect on developing nations, which are often dependent on worldwide agricultural markets.

12. To bring the equilibrium level of prices in the market up to their support level, government has attempted to (increase, decrease) _____ the demand for and to _____ the supply of farm products.

13. To decrease supply, the Federal government has used (acreage-allotment, rent-seeking) _____ programs. To increase demand, the Federal government has encouraged (new, old) _____ uses for agricultural products and sought to increase domestic and foreign (supply, demand) _____ for agricultural products through the domestic food stamps program or the foreign Food for Peace program.

14. The policies of government to support agricultural prices and income (have, have not) _____ worked well over the past 60 years because they have confused the symptoms of the farm economic condition, which are (high, low) _____ prices and incomes, with its root cause, which is (efficient, inefficient) _____ allocation of resources.

15. There are two other criticisms. Many of the benefits from farm price supports go to (high, low) _____ -income farmers instead of _____ -income farmers. The effects of price-support programs of the Federal government are (reinforced, offset) _____ by other government programs.

16. Despite these criticisms, farm policies have received strong support in Congress over the years; the result of this can be explained by insights from (monopoly, public choice) _____ theory. When farm groups lobby for Federal programs that transfer income to them, they are exhibiting (parity, rent-seeking) _____ behavior. There is also a special-interest effect because the costs to individual taxpayers are (large, small) _____ but the benefits to farmers are _____ from farm programs.

17. In addition, when agricultural groups or farm-state politicians trade votes to turn negative into positive outcomes, they are using political (allotments, logrolling) _____. Another public choice problem with farm subsidies is that the benefits of farm programs are (clear, hidden) _____, while much of the costs are _____ in the form of higher consumer prices for agricultural products.

18. There are also world (aid, trade) _____ considerations from agricultural subsidies. The effects of supports for the prices of agricultural products in the United States and European Union (EU) have been to

(increase, decrease) _____ domestic production in these nations, _____ export subsidies for farm products in these nations, and _____ world prices for agricultural products, thus distorting worldwide trade in agricultural products.

19. Calls for reforms of farm policy in the United States led in 1996 to the Freedom to (Trade, Farm) _____ Act that sought to (expand, eliminate) _____ price supports for eight farm crops in return for giving farmers freedom to (plant, export) _____ crops. To make the transition from price-supported agriculture to market-oriented agriculture, farmers received transition (licenses, payments) _____, but the fall in several crop prices later in the decade led to emergency measures to (increase, decrease) _____ farm subsidies.

20. The Food, Conservation and Energy Act of 2008 continues the policy of freedom to (export, plant) _____, and provides income support for farmers in the form of direct (insurance, payments) _____. In addition, there are price-support subsidies in the form of countercyclical (insurance, payments) _____ and marketing (campaigns, loans) _____. As a result of the act, the government's subsidy for agriculture has (increased, decreased) _____, which in turn contributes to _____ crop production and low crop price. This resulting condition then leads to demands for (more, less) _____ farm subsidies.

■ **TRUE–FALSE QUESTIONS**

Circle T if the statement is true, F if it is false.

1. Agriculture experiences year-to-year fluctuations in farm prices and farm incomes. **T F**

2. The demand for farm products is price elastic. **T F**

3. The quantities of agricultural commodities produced tend to be fairly *insensitive* to changes in agricultural prices because a large percentage of farmers' total costs are variable. **T F**

4. The foreign demand for farm products is relatively stable. **T F**

5. Appreciation of the dollar will tend to increase the demand for farm products. **T F**

6. The supply of agricultural products has tended to increase more rapidly than the demand for these products in the United States. **T F**

7. Most of the recent technological advances in agriculture have been initiated by farmers. **T F**

8. The demand for farm products is income elastic.　T　F

9. One reason for the lagging demand for U.S. farm products is a slow rate of population growth in the United States.　**T　F**

10. The consequences over time of supply and demand conditions in agriculture are that minimum efficient scale has increased.　**T　F**

11. The size of the farm population in the United States has declined in both relative and absolute terms since about 1960.　**T　F**

12. The major aim of agricultural policy in the United States for the past 75 years or so was to support agricultural prices and incomes.　**T　F**

13. If the prices paid by farmers were 500% higher than in the base year and the price received by farmers were 400% higher than in the base year, the parity ratio would be 125%.　**T　F**

14. Application of the parity concept to farm prices causes farm prices to decline and results in agricultural surpluses.　**T　F**

15. When government supports farm prices at above-equilibrium levels, it can reduce the annual surpluses of agricultural commodities either by increasing the supply or by decreasing the demand for them.　**T　F**

16. The acreage allotment program was designed to decrease the supply of farm products.　**T　F**

17. Restricting the number of acres that farmers use to grow agricultural products has been only a partially successful method of reducing surpluses because farmers tend to cultivate their land more intensively when the acreage is reduced.　**T　F**

18. Public policy has been effective in alleviating the resource allocation problem in U.S. agriculture, not just the symptoms.　**T　F**

19. The price-income support programs for agriculture have given the most benefit to those farmers with the least need for the government assistance.　**T　F**

20. A political action committee organized by a group of sugar beet farmers to lobby Congress for subsidies for sugar beets is an example of political logrolling.　**T　F**

21. The reason that farmers, who are a small proportion of the population, can impose a large cost to taxpayers in the form of agricultural subsidies is because the cost imposed on each individual taxpayer is small and not given much attention by each taxpayer.　**T　F**

22. One hidden cost of agricultural price-support programs is the higher prices that consumers pay for the product.　**T　F**

23. The decline in farm population and in the related political representation in rural areas is one reason why political support for farm subsidies has increased.　**T　F**

24. Domestic farm subsidies distort world trade and contribute to the inefficiencies in the international allocation of agricultural resources.　**T　F**

25. Although the Food, Conservation and Energy Act of 2008 helped reduce the risk for farmers and raised farm incomes, it continues the Federal government policy of subsidizing agricultural production.　**T　F**

■ MULTIPLE-CHOICE QUESTIONS

Circle the letter that corresponds to the best answer.

1. The inelasticity of demand for agricultural products can be explained by
  (a) parity ratio
  (b) economies of scale
  (c) rent-seeking behavior
  (d) diminishing marginal utility

2. The inelastic demand for agricultural products means that a relatively small increase in output will result in a relatively
  (a) small increase in farm prices and incomes
  (b) large decrease in farm prices and incomes
  (c) small decrease in farm prices and a relatively large increase in farm incomes
  (d) large increase in farm prices and a relatively small decrease in farm incomes

3. The reason that large declines in farm prices do not significantly reduce farm production in the short run is that farmers'
  (a) fixed costs are high relative to their variable costs
  (b) variable costs are high relative to their fixed costs
  (c) prices received are greater than prices paid for agricultural products
  (d) prices paid are greater than prices received for agricultural products

4. One reason for the year-to-year instability of agricultural product prices is
  (a) stable production of domestic agricultural products
  (b) stable production of foreign agricultural products
  (c) fluctuations in incomes received for agricultural products
  (d) fluctuations in the foreign demand for agricultural products

5. If, over time, the increases in the supply of an agricultural product are much greater than the increases in demand for it, the supply and demand model would suggest that the product price
  (a) and quantity will both increase
  (b) and quantity will both decrease
  (c) will increase, but the quantity will decrease
  (d) will decrease, but the quantity will increase

6. Which is a significant reason why increases in demand for agricultural products have been small relative to increases in supply?
  (a) Increases in the population of the United States have been greater than increases in the productivity of agriculture.
  (b) Increases in the population of the United States have been greater than decreases in the productivity of agriculture.

(c) Increases in the incomes of U.S. consumers result in less than proportionate increases in their spending on agricultural products.

(d) Increases in the incomes of U.S. consumers result in more than proportionate increases in their spending on agricultural products.

7. Given an inelastic demand for farm products, a more rapid increase in the

(a) demand for such products relative to the supply creates a persistent downward pressure on farm incomes

(b) supply for such products relative to the demand creates a persistent upward pressure on farm incomes

(c) supply for such products relative to the demand creates a persistent downward pressure on farm incomes

(d) demand for such products relative to the supply creates a persistent downward pressure on agricultural product prices

8. The consequences of the long-run supply and demand conditions in agriculture are that minimum efficient scale has

(a) increased and crop prices have decreased

(b) increased and crop prices have increased

(c) decreased and crop prices have increased

(d) decreased and crop prices have decreased

9. The migration out of farming over the years, consolidation in farming, greater farm productivity, and government subsidies have caused farm-household incomes to

(a) decrease relative to nonfarm household incomes

(b) increase relative to nonfarm household incomes

(c) stay about the same as nonfarm household incomes

(d) be more stable than nonfarm household incomes

10. Which is a major rationale for public aid for agriculture in the United States?

(a) Farmers are more affected by competition from foreign producers than other parts of the economy.

(b) Farmers sell their products in highly competitive markets and buy resources in highly imperfect markets.

(c) Technological progress in farming has greatly increased the demand for farm products.

(d) The demand for farm products is income elastic.

11. Farm parity means that over time,

(a) the real income of the farmer remains constant

(b) a given output will furnish the farmer with a constant amount of real income

(c) the purchasing power of the farmer's nominal income remains constant

(d) the nominal income of the farmer will buy a constant amount of goods and services

12. If the index of prices paid by farmers were 1000 and the prices received by farmers were 600, then the parity ratio would be

(a) 2.1 (or 210%)

(b) 1.7 (or 170%)

(c) 0.6 (or 60%)

(d) 0.4 (or 40%)

13. The necessary consequence of the government's support of agricultural prices at an above-equilibrium level is

(a) a surplus of agricultural products

(b) increased consumption of agricultural products

(c) reduced production of agricultural products

(d) the destruction of agricultural products

14. Another consequence of having government support farm prices at an above-equilibrium level is that consumers pay higher prices for farm products, and

(a) consume more of these products and pay higher taxes

(b) consume less of these products and pay higher taxes

(c) consume more of these products and pay lower taxes

(d) consume less of these products and pay lower taxes

Use the graph below to answer Questions 15, 16, and 17. D is the demand for and S is the supply of a certain product.

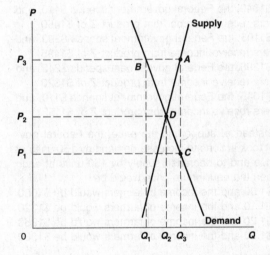

15. If the Federal government supported the price of this product at P_3, the total amount it would have to spend to purchase the surplus of the product would be

(a) $0Q_3AP_3$

(b) Q_1Q_3AB

(c) P_1CAP_3

(d) $0Q_1BP_3$

16. With a support price of P_3, the total income of producers of the product will be

(a) $0Q_3AP_3$

(b) $0Q_1BP_3$

(c) $0Q_3CP_1$

(d) $0Q_2DP_2$

17. With a support price of P_3, the amount spent by consumers will be

(a) $0Q_3AP_3$

(b) $0Q_1BP_3$

(c) $0Q_2DP_2$

(d) Q_1Q_3AB

Answer Questions 18, 19, and 20 on the basis of the demand and supply schedules for agricultural product Z as shown below.

Pounds of Z demanded	Price	Pounds of Z supplied
850	$1.30	1150
900	1.20	1100
950	1.10	1050
1000	1.00	1000
1050	.90	950
1100	.80	900
1150	.70	850

18. If the Federal government supports the price of **Z** at $1.30 a pound, then at this price, there is
(a) a surplus of 200 pounds of **Z**
(b) a surplus of 300 pounds of **Z**
(c) a surplus of 400 pounds of **Z**
(d) a shortage of 400 pounds of **Z**

19. With a Federal price support of $1.30 a pound, consumers spend
(a) $1040, the Federal government spends $410, and farmers receive income from product **Z** of $1450
(b) $1105, the Federal government spends $390, and farmers receive income from product **Z** of $1495
(c) $1296, the Federal government spends $240, and farmers receive income from product **Z** of $1320
(d) $1045, the Federal government spends $110, and farmers receive income from product **Z** of $1155

20. If, instead of supporting the price, the Federal government took actions to increase demand by 150 units at each price and to decrease supply by 150 units at each price, then the equilibrium price would be
(a) $1.00 and the income of farmers would be $1000
(b) $1.10 and the income of farmers would be $1320
(c) $1.20 and the income of farmers would be $1260
(d) $1.30 and the income of farmers would be $1300

21. To help eliminate the agricultural surpluses created by farm subsidies, the Federal government has tried to
(a) increase supply and demand
(b) decrease supply and demand
(c) increase supply and decrease demand
(d) decrease supply and increase demand

22. Which is a major criticism of agricultural price supports?
(a) Restricting agricultural output increases farm prices but reduces farm incomes when demand is inelastic.
(b) The principal beneficiaries of these supports have been farmers with low incomes who would be better off in another type of work.
(c) They fail to treat the underlying problem of the misallocation of resources between agriculture and the rest of the economy.
(d) They duplicate other economic policies that are designed to increase the prices for agricultural products.

23. When farmers and farm organizations lobby Congress for a larger appropriation for agricultural price and income programs, according to public choice theory this action would be an example of
(a) confusing symptoms with causes
(b) misguided subsidies
(c) rent-seeking behavior
(d) political logrolling

24. Which has been a consequence of protective trade barriers for agricultural products established by the European Union (EU)?
(a) higher prices for U.S. agricultural products
(b) restriction of exports of EU agricultural products
(c) lower worldwide prices for agricultural products
(d) more sales of U.S. agricultural products to the EU

25. A consistent feature in both the Freedom to Farm Act of 1996 and the Food, Conservation and Energy Act of 2008 was
(a) decreasing crop price-support subsidies for farmers
(b) giving farmers the freedom to plant various agriculture crops
(c) bolstering of the domestic and foreign demand for U.S. agricultural products
(d) improving of the parity ratio so that the prices farmers paid for their inputs were similar to the prices they received for their output

■ **PROBLEMS**

1. The following table is a demand schedule for agricultural product **X**.

(1) Price	(2) Bushels of X demanded	(3) Bushels of X demanded
$2.00	600	580
1.80	620	600
1.60	640	620
1.40	660	640
1.20	680	660
1.00	700	680
.80	720	700
.60	740	720

a. Based on columns 1 and 2, is demand elastic or inelastic in the price range given? _____

b. Based on columns 1 and 2, if the amount of **X** produced should increase from 600 to 700 bushels, the income of producers of **X** would _____

from $ _____ to $ _____ ; an

increase of _____ % in the amount of **X**

produced would cause income to _____ by

_____ %.

c. If the amount of **X** produced were 700 bushels and the demand for **X** decreased from that shown in columns 1 and 2 to that shown in columns 1 and 3, the

price of X would _____ from $_____

to $_____; the income of farmers would _____

_____ from $_____ to $_____.

d. Assume that the government supports a price of $1.80, that the demand for **X** is that shown in columns 1 and 2, and that farmers grow 720 bushels of **X**.

(1) At the supported price there will be a surplus of _____ bushels of X.

(2) If the government buys this surplus at the support price the cost to the taxpayers of purchasing the surplus is $ _____.

(3) The total income of the farmers producing product **X** when they receive the support price of $1.80 per bushel for their entire crop of 720 bushels is $_____.

(4) Had farmers sold the crop of 720 bushels at the free-market price, the price of **X** would be only $_____ per bushel, and the total income of these farmers would be $ _____.

(5) The gain to farmers producing **X** from the price-support program is therefore $_____.

(6) In addition to the cost to taxpayers of purchasing the surplus, consumers pay a price that is $_____ greater than the free-market price and receive a quantity of **X** that is _____ bushels less than they would have received in a free market.

2. The following table gives the index of prices farmers paid in three different years. The price farmers received in year 1, the base year, for a certain agricultural product was $3.50 per bushel.

Year	Index of prices paid	Parity price	Price received	Parity ratio
1	100	$3.50	$3.50	100%
2	120	_____	3.78	_____%
3	200	_____	5.25	_____%

a. Compute the parity price of the product in years 2 and 3 and enter them in the table.

b. The prices received for the product in each year are also shown in the table. Complete the table by computing the parity *ratio* in years 2 and 3. (*Hint:* It is *not* necessary to construct an index of prices received in order to compute the parity ratio. This ratio can be computed by dividing the price received by the parity price.)

3. The demand schedule for agricultural product **Y** is given in columns 1 and 2 of the following table.

(1) Price	(2) Bales of Y demanded	(3) Bales of Y demanded
$5.00	40,000	41,000
4.75	40,200	41,200
4.50	40,400	41,400
4.25	40,600	41,600
4.00	40,800	41,800
3.75	41,000	42,000
3.50	41,200	42,200

a. If farmers were persuaded by the government to reduce the size of their crop from 41,000 to 40,000 bales, the income of farmers would _____ from $_____ to $_____.

b. If the crop remained constant at 41,000 bales and the demand for **Y** increased to that shown in columns 1 and 3, the income of farmers would _____ from $_____ to $_____.

4. Suppose the demand for sow jowls during a certain period of time was that shown in the table below and the Federal government wished to support the price of sow jowls at $.70 a pound.

Price (per pound)	Quantity demanded (pounds)
$1.00	1000
.90	1020
.80	1040
.70	1060
.60	1080
.50	1100
.40	1120

a. If the output of sow jowls were 1100 pounds during that period of time, the market price of sow jowls would be $_____ and the Federal government would (buy, sell) _____ (how many?) _____ pounds of sow jowls.

b. But if the output were 1000 pounds during that period of time, the market price of sow jowls would be $_____ and the Federal government would not have to intervene.

■ **SHORT ANSWER AND ESSAY QUESTIONS**

1. Why are the economics of agriculture and agricultural policy important topics for study?

2. What are the causes of the short-run price and income instability in U.S. agriculture?

3. Why does the demand for agricultural products tend to be inelastic? What are the implications for agriculture?

4. What have been the specific causes of the large increases in the supply of agricultural products over time?

5. Why has the demand for agricultural products failed to increase at the same rate as the supply of these products?

6. What have been the consequences of long-run supply and demand conditions in agriculture?

7. What is meant by "the farm program"? What particular aspect of the farm program has traditionally received the major attention of farmers and their representatives in Congress?

8. Why do agricultural interests claim that farmers have a special right to aid from the Federal government?

9. Explain the concept of parity and the parity ratio.

10. Why is the result of government-supported prices invariably a surplus of farm commodities?

11. What are the effects of farm price-support programs on farmers, consumers, and resource allocation in the economy?

12. Identify and describe three ways that society at large loses from farm price-support programs.

13. Explain how U.S. farm policy may cause environmental problems.

14. Discuss the effects of farm price-support programs on international trade and developing nations.

15. What programs has the government used to try to restrict farm production? Why have these programs been relatively unsuccessful in limiting agricultural production?

16. How has the Federal government tried to increase the demand for farm products?

17. Explain the three major criticisms of agricultural price supports.

18. How can public choice theory explain the persistence of Federal government support for farm subsidies for so many decades? Discuss the application of rent-seeking behavior, the special-interest effect, political logrolling, and hidden costs to subsidies for agriculture.

19. What domestic and international factors are contributing to the reduction in political support for agricultural subsidies?

20. What are the key features of the Freedom to Farm Act of 1996 and the Food, Conservation and Energy Act of 2008? In what ways are the two acts similar and how are they different in terms of government intervention in agriculture, the provision of agricultural price supports, and income payments to farmers?

ANSWERS

Chapter 19 Agriculture: Economics and Policy

FILL-IN QUESTIONS

1. largest, competition, government, increased, public
2. inelastic, substitutes, utility
3. small, large, small, large
4. supply of, demand for, inelastic
5. low, value, hazards, purely, imperfectly
6. fixed
7. surpluses, buy
8. benefit, are hurt, increase, increase, decrease
9. inefficiency, over, large
10. increased, increased, negative
11. more, more, increase, decrease, negative
12. increase, decrease
13. acreage-allotment, new, demand
14. have not, low, inefficient
15. high, low, offset
16. public choice, rent-seeking, small, large
17. logrolling, clear, hidden
18. trade, increase, increase, decrease
19. Farm, eliminate, plant, payments, increase
20. plant, payments, payments, loans, increased, increased, more

TRUE–FALSE QUESTIONS

1. T, p. 392		14. F, p. 399	
2. F, p. 392		15. F, p. 399	
3. F, pp. 393–394		16. T, p. 401	
4. F, p. 394		17. T, p. 401	
5. F, p. 394		18. F, pp. 402–403	
6. T, pp. 395–396		19. T, p. 402	
7. F, p. 395		20. F, p. 403	
8. F, pp. 395–396		21. T, p. 403	
9. T, pp. 395–396		22. T, p. 403	
10. T, pp. 396–397		23. F, p. 403	
11. T, p. 397		24. T, pp. 403–405	
12. T, p. 398		25. T, p. 406	
13. F, p. 399			

MULTIPLE-CHOICE QUESTIONS

1. d, p. 392		14. b, p. 399	
2. b, pp. 392–393		15. b, p. 399	
3. a, pp. 393–394		16. a, p. 399	
4. d, p. 394		17. b, p. 399	
5. d, pp. 394–396		18. b, p. 399	
6. c, pp. 395–396		19. b, p. 399	
7. c, pp. 396–397		20. d, p. 399	
8. a, pp. 396–397		21. d, p. 401	
9. b, pp. 397–398		22. c, pp. 402–403	
10. b, p. 398		23. c, p. 403	
11. b, p. 399		24. c, pp. 403–405	
12. c, p. 399		25. b, pp. 405–406	
13. a, p. 399			

PROBLEMS

1. *a.* inelastic; *b.* decrease, 1200.00, 700.00, 16.67, decrease, 41.67; *c.* fall, 1.00, 0.80, fall, 700.00, 560.00; *d.* (1) 100, (2) 180, (3) 1296, (4) 0.80, 576, (5) 720, (6) 1.00, 100
2. *a.* 4.20, 7.00; *b.* 90, 75
3. *a.* increase, 153,750.00, 200,000.00; *b.* increase, 153,750.00, 205,000.00
4. *a.* .50, buy, 40; *b.* 1.00

SHORT ANSWER AND ESSAY QUESTIONS

1. p. 391	8. p. 398	15. p. 401
2. pp. 392–394	9. p. 399	16. p. 401
3. p. 392	10. p. 399	17. pp. 402–403
4. pp. 392–393	11. pp. 399–400	18. p. 403
5. pp. 393–394	12. p. 400	19. pp. 403–405
6. pp. 394–397	13. p. 400	20. pp. 405–406
7. p. 398	14. p. 400	

Income Inequality, Poverty, and Discrimination

Chapter 20 examines three current problems in the economy of the United States. The chapter begins with a look at the facts of **income inequality.** You will discover that there is substantial income inequality in the United States and learn how it is measured with the Lorenz curve and Gini ratio. You should also note that the degree of income inequality for individuals and households will be less over time because of income mobility and because government taxes and transfer payments also will reduce the amount of income inequality.

The chapter discusses the multiple factors that contribute to income inequality. The seven causes that are described should indicate to you that there is no simple explanation as to why some people have more income than others. It is not the result of some grand conspiracy; it can be attributed to ability differences, education and training, discrimination, preferences for jobs and risk, wealth, market power, and luck or misfortune.

Over time there have been changes in the relative distribution of income that indicate income inequality in the United States is increasing. In this section of the chapter, you will learn about the probable reasons for growing income inequality that include shifts in the demand for skilled labor, changes in the demographics of the workforce, and other factors.

A case can be made for both income equality and income inequality. Few people, however, would advocate that there should be an absolutely equal distribution of income. The question to be decided is not one of inequality or equality but of how much or how little inequality there should be. A major insight from the chapter is that there is a fundamental **trade-off between equality and efficiency** in the economy. If the society wants more equality, it will have to give up some economic efficiency in the form of less output and employment.

The reason for the focus on income distribution is ultimately the concern about **poverty.** In the later sections of the chapter you will learn about the extent of the poverty problem, who poverty affects, and the actions government has taken to alleviate it. Recall from Chapter 4 that one economic function of government is to redistribute income. Poverty and other income distribution problems are addressed through the Federal government's income-maintenance system. This system consists of **social insurance programs,** such as Social Security, and **public assistance programs,** or welfare. You will discover how these programs are designed to meet the needs of different groups, either those who are poor or those who require more stability in their incomes.

Discrimination has always been present in labor markets in the form of wage, employment, occupational, or human capital discrimination. This discrimination causes significant costs for individuals who earn lower wages or have fewer work opportunities than would otherwise be the case. There are also costs to society because valuable labor resources are being inefficiently used.

The economic analysis of labor market discrimination gives you several insights into this significant problem. The taste-for-discrimination model explains the hiring practices of prejudiced employers and the effects on the wages and employment of nonpreferred groups. You will also learn how statistical discrimination, which bases decisions on average characteristics, may disadvantage individuals. The crowding model of occupational discrimination described in the chapter also explains how occupational segregation affects pay and output in an economy.

■ CHECKLIST

When you have studied this chapter you should be able to

☐ Describe income inequality in the United States based on the percentage of households in income categories.

☐ Describe income inequality in the United States based on the percentage of personal income received by households in income quintiles.

☐ Explain the Lorenz curve by defining each axis, the diagonal line, and the meaning of the curve.

☐ Use a Lorenz curve to describe the degree of income inequality in the United States.

☐ Use a Gini ratio to measure income inequality.

☐ Explain the effects of time on income mobility and the distribution of U.S. income.

☐ Discuss the effects of government redistribution on income equality in the United States and illustrate the effects using a Lorenz curve.

☐ Explain the seven causes of income inequality in the United States (ability; education and training; discrimination; preferences and risks; unequal distribution of wealth; market power; and, luck, connections, misfortune).

☐ Identify three probable causes of growing income inequality in the United States over the past three decades.

☐ Present a case for income equality based on the maximization of total utility.

☐ Make the case for income inequality based on incentives and efficiency.

☐ Explain the trade-off between equality and efficiency

in the debate over how much income inequality there should be.

☐ Give a definition of poverty based on U.S. government standards.

☐ Describe the incidence of poverty among different demographic groups in the United States.

☐ Describe the trends in the poverty rate in the United States since 1959.

☐ Explain issues or problems with the measurement of poverty.

☐ Identify the two basic kinds of programs in the U.S. system for income maintenance.

☐ Describe the characteristics of major social insurance programs (Social Security, Medicare, and unemployment compensation).

☐ Explain the purposes of the major public assistance programs (SSI, TANF, food stamps, Medicaid, and EITC).

☐ Define discrimination and give examples of it.

☐ Use a wage equation to explain the taste-for-discrimination model in labor markets.

☐ Use a supply and demand graph to illustrate the taste-for-discrimination model in labor markets.

☐ Explain and give an example of statistical discrimination.

☐ Use the crowding model of occupational discrimination to explain differences in wages among groups and efficiency effects.

☐ Describe the costs of discrimination for society as well as for individuals.

☐ Explain the changes in the amount and distribution of wealth among families from 1995 to 2004 (Last Word).

■ **CHAPTER OUTLINE**

1. There is considerable *income inequality* in the United States.

a. One way to show this inequality is with a table showing the personal distribution of income by households. In 2006, 25.2% of all households had annual before-tax incomes of less than $25,000, but 19.1% had annual incomes of $100,000 or more.

b. A table of the personal distribution of income by households in quintiles is a second way to show the inequality. In 2006, the 20% of households with the lowest incomes accounted for 3.4% of personal income while the 20% of households with the highest incomes accounted for 50.5% of personal income.

c. The degree of income inequality can be shown with a *Lorenz curve.* The percentage of households is plotted on the horizontal axis and the percentage of income is plotted on the vertical axis. The diagonal line between the two axes represents a perfectly equal distribution of income. A Lorenz curve that is bowed to the right from the diagonal shows income inequality. If the actual income distribution were perfectly equal, the Lorenz curve and the diagonal would coincide. The visual measurement of income inequality described by the Lorenz curve can be converted to a *Gini ratio,*

which is the area between the Lorenz curve and the diagonal divided by the total area below the diagonal. As the income inequality increases, the ratio will increase.

d. Income data shows that there is considerably *less* income inequality over a longer time period than a single year. In fact, there is significant *income mobility* for individuals and households over time. The longer the time period considered for individuals and households, the more equal the distribution of income.

e. Government redistribution has had a significant effect on income distribution. The distribution of income can be examined after taxes and transfer payments. When this adjustment is made, the distribution of income is more equal. *Noncash transfers,* which provide specific goods or services, account for most of the reduction in income inequality, and they include Medicare, Medicaid, housing subsidies, subsidized school lunches, and food stamps. The effect of the government transfers is to shift the Lorenz curve toward more equality.

2. The market system is impersonal and does not necessarily result in a fair distribution of income. At least seven factors explain **why income inequality exists:**

a. Abilities and skills differ greatly among people, which influences the work they can do and their pay.

b. There are differences in education and training that affect wages and salaries.

c. Discrimination in education, hiring, training, and promotion will affect incomes.

d. People have different preferences for certain types of jobs, for their willingness to accept risk on the job, and also for the amount of leisure that will be earned through their work.

e. Wealth can provide a source of income in the form of rents, interest, and dividends, and since there are inequalities in the distribution of wealth, it will contribute to income inequalities.

f. Some individuals have a degree of market power in either resource or product markets that create higher incomes.

g. Other factors, such as luck, personal connections, and misfortunes can play a role in contributing to income inequality.

3. Income inequality in the United States has changed over time.

a. From 1970 through 2006, the distribution of income became more unequal. In 2006 the lowest 20 percent of households received 3.4% of total before-tax income compared with 4.1% in 1970. The highest 20 percent of households received 50.5% of total before-tax income in 2006 compared with 43.3% in 1970.

b. Among the factors that explain the growing income inequality in the United States over the past three decades are:

(1) increases in the demand for highly skilled workers compared with the demand for less-skilled workers;

(2) changes in labor demographics from the influx of less-skilled baby boomers into the labor force, the

increase in dual incomes among high-wage households, and more single-parent households earning less income; and

(3) decreases in wages for less-skilled workers and less job security because of more international trade competition, the influx of less-skilled immigrants into the labor force, and a decline in unionism.

4. An important question to answer for an economy is not whether there will be income inequality, but what is an acceptable amount of inequality.

a. Those who **argue for equality** contend that it leads to the maximum satisfaction of consumer wants (utility) in the economy.

b. Those who **argue for inequality** contend that equality would reduce the incentives to work, save, invest, and take risks, and that these incentives are needed if the economy is to be efficient to produce as large an output (and income) as it is possible for it to produce from its available resources.

c. In the United States there is an *equality–efficiency trade-off.* A more nearly equal distribution of income results in less economic efficiency (a smaller output and income) and greater economic efficiency (a larger output and income) leads to a more unequal distribution of income. The debate over the right amount of inequality depends on how much output society is willing to sacrifice to reduce income inequality.

5. Aside from inequality in the distribution of income, there is a great concern today with the problem of poverty in the United States.

a. Using the generally accepted definition, the *poverty rate,* which is the percentage of the U.S. population living in poverty, was 12.3% in 2006.

b. The poor are found among many groups and in all parts of the nation. Compared with the poverty rate for the population as a whole (12.3%), there are higher poverty rates among female-headed households (30.5%), African-Americans (24.3%), Hispanics (20.6%), foreign-born who are not citizens (19%), children under 18 years of age (17.4%), and women (13.6%).

c. The poverty rate has varied over time, as shown in Figure 20.5 of the text. It fell significantly from 1959–1969 and was in the 11–13% range in the 1970s. The rate rose around periods of recession in the economy (early 1980s and early 1990s), and fluctuated in the 11–13% range in other periods.

d. There are issues with the measurement of poverty. Some contend that it is understated because the official income thresholds are set low and do not cover the high cost of living in urban areas. Others contend that the poverty definition understates the standard of living for many who are classified as poor because the poverty rate is an income and not a consumption measure.

6. The **income-maintenance system** of the United States is intended to reduce poverty and includes both social insurance and public assistance (welfare) programs. These are *entitlement programs* because all eligible persons are granted or entitled to the benefits of the programs.

a. The principal *social insurance programs* are *Social Security* and *Medicare.* They are financed by payroll taxes levied on employers and employees. The unemployment insurance programs that provide *unemployment compensation,* maintained by the states and financed by taxes on employers, are also social insurance programs in the United States.

b. The *public assistance programs* include *Supplemental Security Income (SSI), Temporary Assistance for Needy Families (TANF),* the *food-stamp program,* and *Medicaid.* The *earned-income tax credit* (EITC) is for low-income working households, with or without children. Other public assistance programs provide noncash transfers for education, job training, and housing assistance.

7. *Discrimination* involves giving people different and inferior treatment in employment or living situations (such as hiring, education, training, promotion, wages, working conditions, or housing) based on some unrelated factor or characteristic (such as race, ethnicity, gender, or religion). Discrimination reflects a personal bias or prejudice against a particular group.

8. The economic analysis of discrimination provides some insights even though the issue is complex and multifaceted.

a. The *taste-for-discrimination model* explains prejudice using demand theory. The model assumes that a prejudiced employer is willing to pay a "price" to avoid interactions with a nonpreferred group.

(1) The *discrimination coefficient* measures in monetary units the cost of the employer's prejudice. An employer will hire nonpreferred workers only if their wage rates are below those of the preferred workers by an amount at least equal to the discrimination coefficient.

(2) In the supply and demand model for nonpreferred workers, an increase in the prejudice of employers will decrease the demand for this labor, the number of workers, and their wage rate. A decrease in the prejudice of employers will increase the demand for this labor, the number employed, and the wage rate.

(3) The taste-for-discrimination model suggests that in the very long run, competition will reduce discrimination, but critics question this conclusion, given the insufficient progress in reducing discrimination over time in the United States.

b. *Statistical discrimination* involves judging people based on the average characteristics of the group to which they belong instead of productivity or personal characteristics. In labor markets, employers may stereotype workers by applying the average characteristics of the group in work assessments of individual members of that group. The practice may be profitable and on average it may produce correct decisions, but it fails to take into account the individual skills and capabilities and limits opportunities for workers.

c. The practice of *occupational segregation* suggests that women and minorities are crowded into a small number of occupations. In this crowding model, the supply of these workers is large relative to the demand for them, and thus their wage rates and incomes are lower in these crowded occupations. Eliminating occupational segregation would raise wage rates and incomes for these workers and also increase the economy's output.

d. Discrimination imposes a cost to society as well as to individuals. The cost to individuals comes in the form of lower wages, fewer job opportunities, inferior treatment, and poorer working or living conditions. The costs to society come in the form of reduced total output and income for the economy. These costs arise because discrimination creates artificial barriers to competition.

9. (Last Word). The Federal Reserve's Survey of Consumer Finances shows that median and average family wealth, adjusted for the effects of inflation, rose considerably from 1995 to 2004. The distribution of this wealth is highly unequal and there has been a general trend to greater income inequality of wealth since 1995.

■ HINTS AND TIPS

1. The distribution of income, poverty, and discrimination raise issues of **normative economics.** For example, some people may say that "no person should be allowed to make that much money" when a high salary is reported in the media for a sports star or business executive. This chapter focuses on the **positive economics** related to the three topics. It explains and analyzes why incomes differ, why there is poverty, and why discrimination is costly for individuals and society.

2. The **Lorenz curve** looks more complicated than it really is. The curve shows how the cumulative percentage of income is distributed across the percentage of households. The easiest way to learn about the curve is to use income and household data to construct one. Problem 1 in this chapter will help you with that objective.

■ IMPORTANT TERMS

income inequality	Supplemental Security Income (SSI)
Lorenz curve	
Gini ratio	Temporary Assistance for Needy Families (TANF)
income mobility	
noncash transfers	food-stamp program
equality-efficiency trade-off	Medicaid
poverty rate	earned income tax credit (EITC)
entitlement programs	discrimination
social insurance programs	taste for discrimination model
Social Security	
Medicare	discrimination coefficient
poverty	statistical discrimination
unemployment compensation	occupational segregation
public assistance programs	

■ SELF-TEST

■ FILL-IN QUESTIONS

1. The data on the distribution of personal income by households suggest that there is considerable income (equality, inequality) _____ in the United States. The data show that households with annual incomes of less than $10,000 are about (7.5, 19.1) _____ % of all households, and households with $100,000 or more in income are about _____ % of all households.

2. Income inequality can be portrayed graphically by drawing a (Phillips, Lorenz) _____ curve.

   a. When such a curve is plotted, the cumulative percentage of (income, households) _____ is measured along the horizontal axis, and the cumulative percentage of _____ is measured along the vertical axis.

   b. The curve that would show a completely (perfectly) equal distribution of income is a diagonal line that would run from the (lower, upper) _____ left to the _____ right corner of the graph.

   c. The extent or degree of income inequality is measured by the area that lies between the line of complete equality and the (horizontal axis, Lorenz curve) _____.

   d. The Gini ratio measures the area between the line of equality and the Lorenz curve (multiplied, divided) _____ by the total area below the line of equality.

3. One major limitation with census data on the distribution of income in the United States is that the income-accounting period is too (short, long) _____. There appears to be significant income (mobility, loss) _____ over time. Also, the longer the time period considered, the (more, less) _____ equal is the distribution of income.

4. The tax system and the transfer programs in the U.S. economy significantly (reduce, expand) _____ the degree of inequality in the distribution of income. The distribution of household income is substantially less equal (before, after) _____ taxes and transfers are taken into account and substantially more equal _____ taxes and transfers are taken into account.

5. As described in the text, the important factors that explain income inequality are: differences in _____; education and _____; labor market _____; differences in job preferences and _____; the unequal distribution of _____; market _____; and, _____, connections, and misfortune.

6. Since 1970, the distribution of income by quintiles has become (more, less) _____ unequal. The data show that since 1970 the lowest 20 percent of households are receiving a (greater, lesser) _____ percentage of total income and the highest 20 percent of households are receiving a _____ percentage of total income.

7. The causes of the growing inequality of incomes are (more, less) _____ demand for highly skilled workers, entrance into the labor force of _____ -experienced baby boomers, and _____ households headed by single-wage earners. Other factors include (more, less) _____ international competition that has reduced the average wage of low-skilled workers, _____ immigration that has increased the number of low-income households, and _____ unionism.

8. Those who argue for the equal distribution of income contend that it results in the maximization of total (income, utility) _____ in the economy, while those who argue for the unequal distribution of income believe it results in a greater total _____.

9. The fundamental trade-off is between equality and (welfare, efficiency) _____. This means that less income equality leads to a (greater, smaller) _____ total output, and a larger total output requires (more, less) _____ income inequality.

10. The economic problem for a society that wants more equality is how to (minimize, maximize) _____ the adverse effects on economic efficiency.

11. Using the official definition of poverty for 2006, the poor included any household of four with an income of less than ($20,000; $26,800) _____ and any individual with an income of less than ($9800; $20,000) _____ a year. In 2006, (12.3, 28.2) _____ % of the population, or about (36.5, 54.1) _____ million people were poor.

12. Poverty tends to be concentrated among the (children, elderly) _____, among (whites, African-Americans) _____, and in households headed by (men, women) _____.

13. The measurement of poverty rates is not without criticisms. Some contend that the high cost of living in major metropolitan areas means that poverty rates are (over, under) _____-reported by official statistics. Others contend that poverty rates would be lower in the United States if statistics were based on (income, consumption) _____ and the standard of living.

14. One part of the income-maintenance system in the United States consists of social insurance programs such as (Social Security, AFDC) _____, (Medicare, Medicaid) _____, and (employment, unemployment) _____ compensation.

15. The other part of the income-maintenance system consists of public assistance or welfare programs such as (Social Security, SSI) _____, (Medicare, Medicaid) _____, and the food stamp program. Also included in public assistance programs are state-administered ones that provide cash assistance for households with children or (EITC, TANF) _____, and a tax credit program for low-income working households, or _____. Other public assistance programs offer help in the form of (cash, noncash) _____ transfers, such as rent subsidies for housing and education assistance such as Head Start.

16. In the taste-for-discrimination model, the discrimination coefficient *d* measures the (utility, disutility) _____ that prejudiced employers experience when they must interact with those they are biased against. This coefficient is measured in monetary units and becomes part of the (benefit, cost) _____ of hiring nonpreferred workers. The prejudiced employer will hire nonpreferred workers only if their wage rate is (above, below) _____ that of the preferred workers by at least the amount of the discrimination coefficient.

17. An increase in the prejudice of employers against nonpreferred workers will (increase, decrease) _____ their wage rate and the number employed; a decrease in the prejudice of employers against nonpreferred workers will (increase, decrease) _____ their wage rate and the number employed.

18. When employers base employment decisions about individuals on the average characteristics of groups of workers, this is (reverse, statistical) _____ discrimination. The decisions that firms make based on this type of discrimination may be (irrational, rational) _____ and profitable, on average, but hurt individuals to whom the averages (do, do not) _____ apply.

19. The occupational discrimination that pushes women and African-Americans into a small number of occupations in which the supply of labor is large relative to the demand for it is explained by the (managerial-opposition, crowding) _____ model. Because supply is large relative to demand, wages and incomes in these occupations are (high, low) _____. The reduction or elimination of this occupational discrimination would result in a (more, less) _____ efficient allocation of the labor resources of the economy and (an expansion, a contraction) _____ in the domestic output.

20. Discrimination (increases, decreases) _____ the wages of workers in the discriminated group and _____ the wages of workers in the preferred group; it _____ economic efficiency and _____ total output in the economy.

■ TRUE–FALSE QUESTIONS

Circle T if the statement is true, F if it is false.

1. If you knew the average income in the United States, you would know a great deal about income inequality in the United States.　　**T　F**

2. The data on the distribution of personal income by households in the United States indicates that there is considerable income inequality.　　**T　F**

3. In a Lorenz curve, the percentage of households in each income class is measured along the horizontal axis and the percentage of total income received by those households is measured on the vertical axis.　　**T　F**

4. Income mobility is the movement of individuals or households from one income quintile to another over time.　　**T　F**

5. Income is less equally distributed over a longer time period than a shorter time period.　　**T　F**

6. The distribution of income in the United States *after* taxes and transfers are taken into account is more equal than it is *before* taxes and transfers are taken into account.　　**T　F**

7. Differences in preferences for market work relative to nonmarket activities are one reason for income differences in the United States.　　**T　F**

8. The ownership of wealth is fairly equally distributed across households in the United States.　　**T　F**

9. Neither luck nor misfortune is a factor contributing to income inequality in the United States.　　**T　F**

10. From 1970 to 2006, there was an increase in income inequality in the United States.　　**T　F**

11. A significant contributor to the growing income inequality of the past three decades was the greater demand for highly skilled and highly educated workers.　　**T　F**

12. Growing income inequality means that the "rich are getting richer" in terms of absolute income.　　**T　F**

13. The basic argument for an equal distribution of income is that income equality is necessary if consumer satisfaction (utility) is to be maximized.　　**T　F**

14. Those who favor equality in the distribution of income contend that it will lead to stronger incentives to work, save, and invest and thus to a greater national income and output.　　**T　F**

15. In the trade-off between equality and economic efficiency, an increase in equality will lead to an increase in efficiency.　　**T　F**

16. Using the government definition of poverty, 12.3% of the population was poor in 2006.　　**T　F**

17. The incidence of poverty is very high among female-headed households.　　**T　F**

18. Social Security, Medicare, and unemployment compensation are public assistance or welfare programs.　　**T　F**

19. Social insurance programs provide benefits for those who are unable to earn income because of permanent handicaps or who have no or very low income and also have dependent children.　　**T　F**

20. The Temporary Assistance for Needy Families (TANF) has among its provisions work requirements for those receiving welfare and a specified limit on the number of years for receiving welfare benefits.　　**T　F**

21. In the taste-for-discrimination model, employer preference for discrimination is measured in dollars by discrimination coefficient *d*. These employers will hire non-preferred workers only if their wages are at least *d* dollars below the wages of preferred workers.　　**T　F**

22. In the taste-for-discrimination model, a decline in the prejudice of employers will decrease the demand for black workers and lower the black wage rate and the ratio of black to white wages.　　**T　F**

23. Statistical discrimination occurs when employers base employment decisions about individuals on the average characteristics of groups of workers.　　**T　F**

24. The crowding model of occupational segregation shows how white males earn higher earnings at the expense of women and minorities, who are restricted to a limited number of occupations.　　**T　F**

25. Discrimination redistributes income and reduces the economy's output.　　**T　F**

■ MULTIPLE-CHOICE QUESTIONS

Circle the letter that corresponds to the best answer.

1. Recent data on the personal distribution of income in the United States indicate that
  (a) average incomes are falling
  (b) average incomes are constant
  (c) there is considerable income equality
  (d) there is considerable income inequality

Use the graph at the top of the next column to answer Questions 2, 3, and 4. The graph shows four different Lorenz curves (1, 2, 3, and 4).

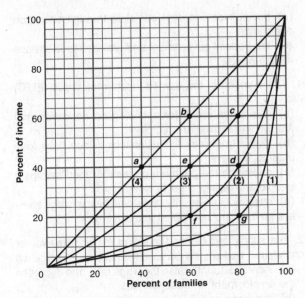

2. The greatest increase in income equality would occur with a shift in a Lorenz curve from
- **(a)** 1 to 2
- **(b)** 1 to 4
- **(c)** 4 to 1
- **(d)** 3 to 1

3. The movement from point **b** to point **f** in the graph would indicate that
- **(a)** 60% of households now receive 40% of income instead of 60% of income
- **(b)** 60% of income goes to 20% of households instead of 60% of households
- **(c)** 20% of income goes to 20% of households instead of 60% of households
- **(d)** 60% of households now receive 20% of income instead of 60% of income

4. Which change would indicate that there has been an increase in income inequality and an increase in the Gini ratio? A movement from point
- **(a)** **b** to **a**
- **(b)** **g** to **d**
- **(c)** **g** to **f**
- **(d)** **e** to **d**

5. Suppose that Laura earns $5000 in year 1 and $50,000 in year 2, while Kristin earns $50,000 in year 1 and only $5000 in year 2. Is there income inequality for the two individuals?
- **(a)** Both the annual and the 2-year data indicate equality.
- **(b)** Both the annual and the 2-year data indicate inequality.
- **(c)** The annual data indicate inequality, but the 2-year data indicate equality.
- **(d)** The annual data indicate equality, but the 2-year data indicate inequality.

6. The empirical data indicate that the tax system and the transfer programs of the government
- **(a)** significantly reduce the degree of inequality in the distribution of income
- **(b)** produce only a slight reduction in the degree of inequality in the distribution of income
- **(c)** significantly increase the degree of inequality in the distribution of income
- **(d)** produce only a slight increase in the degree of inequality in the distribution of income

7. Most of the contribution to government redistribution of income comes from
- **(a)** taxes
- **(b)** transfers
- **(c)** income mobility
- **(d)** unemployment insurance

8. Which is one cause of unequal income distribution in the United States?
- **(a)** an equitable distribution of wealth and property
- **(b)** differences in education and training
- **(c)** the high levels of noncash transfers
- **(d)** the low benefit-reduction rate

9. The fact that some individuals are willing to take riskier jobs or assume more risk in their businesses is one major reason why there are differences in
- **(a)** social insurance programs
- **(b)** entitlement programs
- **(c)** welfare
- **(d)** income

10. Inequality in the distribution of wealth contributes to
- **(a)** the same percentage of income received by the highest and lowest percentages of households
- **(b)** a smaller percentage of income received by the highest 20 percent of households
- **(c)** a greater percentage of income received by the highest 20 percent of households
- **(d)** a greater percentage of income received by the lowest 20 percent of households

11. Which would be evidence of a decrease in income inequality over time in the United States?
- **(a)** A decrease in the percentage of total personal income received by the lowest quintile
- **(b)** An increase in the percentage of total personal income received by the highest quintile
- **(c)** An increase in the percentage of total personal income received by the four lowest quintiles
- **(d)** A decrease in the percentage of total personal income received by the four lowest quintiles

12. A factor contributing to the increase in income inequality since 1970 has been
- **(a)** less international competition from imports
- **(b)** less demand for highly skilled workers in the labor force
- **(c)** more marriages among men and women with high income potential
- **(d)** more power by unions to obtain wage increases for union workers

13. Suppose Ms. Anne obtains 5 units of utility from the last dollar of income received by her, and Mr. Charles obtains 8 units of utility from the last dollar of his income.

Assume both Ms. Anne and Mr. Charles have the same capacity to derive utility from income. Those who favor an equal distribution of income would

(a) advocate redistributing income from Charles to Anne

(b) advocate redistributing income from Anne to Charles

(c) be content with this distribution of income between Anne and Charles

(d) argue that any redistribution of income between them would increase total utility

14. The case for income inequality is primarily made on the basis that income inequality

(a) is reduced by the transfer payment programs for the poor

(b) is necessary to maintain incentives to work and produce output

(c) depends on luck and chance, which cannot be corrected by government action

(d) is created by education and training programs that distort the distribution of income

15. The debate over income redistribution focuses on the trade-off between equality and

(a) efficiency

(b) unemployment

(c) inflation

(d) economic freedom

16. What was the poverty rate for the U.S. population in 2006?

(a) 6.2%

(b) 9.1%

(c) 12.3%

(d) 21.5%

17. In 2006, which group had the *smallest* percentage in poverty?

(a) Hispanics

(b) households headed by women

(c) children under 18 years of age

(d) persons 65 years and older

18. An example of a social insurance program would be

(a) Medicare

(b) Medicaid

(c) food stamps

(d) Head Start

19. Which is designed to provide a nationwide minimum income for the aged, the blind, and the disabled?

(a) SSI

(b) FFS

(c) AFDC

(d) Social Security

20. The Temporary Assistance for Needy Families (TANF) program is administered by

(a) states and puts a lifetime limit of five years on receiving welfare payments

(b) religious institutions and places people in temporary jobs

(c) businesses and develops skills through education assistance

(d) the Federal government and provides food stamps for the needy

21. The purpose of the earned income tax credit (EITC) is to

(a) give a tax credit for spending on education and job training for welfare recipients

(b) give a tax break to businesses if they have low-income workers

(c) substitute the payment of cash for food stamps if people are willing to go to work

(d) offset Social Security taxes paid by low-wage earners so they are not "taxed into poverty"

22. In a supply and demand model of the labor market for nonpreferred workers, an increase in employer prejudice will

(a) increase supply, raise the wage rate, and decrease the employment of these workers

(b) decrease supply, lower the wage rate, and decrease employment of these workers

(c) decrease demand, lower the wage rate, and decrease the employment of these workers

(d) increase demand, raise the wage rate, and increase the employment of these workers

23. Suppose the market wage rate for a preferred worker is $12 and the monetary value of disutility the employer attaches to hiring a nonpreferred worker is $3. The employer will be indifferent between either type of worker when the wage rate for nonpreferred workers is

(a) $15

(b) $12

(c) $9

(d) $3

24. When people are judged on the basis of the average characteristics of the group to which they belong rather than on their own personal characteristics or productivity, this is

(a) human-capital discrimination

(b) occupational discrimination

(c) employment discrimination

(d) statistical discrimination

25. The crowding of women and minorities into certain occupations results in

(a) higher wages and more efficient allocation of labor resources

(b) lower wages and less efficient allocation of labor resources

(c) lower wages, but more efficient allocation of labor resources

(d) lower wages, but no effect on the efficient allocation of labor resources

■ PROBLEMS

1. The distribution of personal income among households in a hypothetical economy is shown in the at the top of the next page.

(1) Personal income class	(2) Percentage of all households in this class	(3) Percentage of total income received by this class	(4) Percentage of all households in this and all lower classes	(5) Percentage of total income received by this and all lower classes
Under $10,000	18	4	_____	_____
$10,000–$14,999	12	6	_____	_____
$15,000–$24,999	14	12	_____	_____
$25,000–$34,999	17	14	_____	_____
$35,000–$49,999	19	15	_____	_____
$50,000–$74,999	11	20	_____	_____
$75,000 and over	9	29	_____	_____

a. Complete the table by computing the
(1) percentage of all households in each income class and all lower classes; enter these figures in column 4.
(2) percentage of total income received by each income class and all lower classes; enter these figures in column 5.
b. From the distribution of income data in columns 4 and 5, it can be seen that
(1) households with less than $15,000 a year income constitute the lowest _____ % of all households and receive _____ % of the total income.
(2) households with incomes of $50,000 a year or more constitute the highest _____ % of all households and receive _____ % of the total income.
c. Use the figures you entered in columns 4 and 5 to draw a Lorenz curve on the graph on the next page. (Plot the seven points and the zero-zero point and connect them with a smooth curve.) Be sure to label the axes.
(1) Draw a diagonal line that would indicate complete equality in the distribution of income.
(2) Shade the area of the graph that shows the degree of income inequality.

2. Match the terms with the correct phrases below using the appropriate number.
  1. entitlement programs
  2. noncash transfers
  3. public assistance programs
  4. social insurance programs
  a. Government programs such as social insurance, food stamps, Medicare, and Medicaid that guarantee particular levels of transfer payments to all who fit the programs' criteria. _____
  b. Government programs that pay benefits to those who are unable to earn income (because of permanent handicaps or because they have very low incomes and dependent children). _____
  c. Government transfer payments in the form of goods and services rather than money. _____
  d. Government programs that replace earnings lost when people retire or are temporarily unemployed. _____

3. Suppose there are only three labor markets in the economy and each market is perfectly competitive. The following table contains the demand (or marginal-revenue-product) schedule for labor in each of these three markets.

Wage rate (marginal revenue product of labor per hour)	Quantity of labor (millions per hour)
$11	4
10	5
9	6
8	7
7	8
6	9
5	10
4	11
3	12

a. Assume there are 24 million homogeneous workers in the economy and that 12 million of these workers are male and 12 million are female.
(1) If the 12 million female workers can be employed only in the labor market Z, for them all to find employment the hourly wage rate must be $ _____.
(2) If of the 12 million male workers 6 million are employed in labor market X and 6 million are employed in labor market Y, the hourly wage rate in labor markets X and Y will be $ _____.
b. Imagine now that the impediment to the employment of females in labor markets X and Y is removed and that as a result (and because the demand and marginal revenue product of labor is the same in all three markets) 8 million workers find employment in each labor market.
(1) In labor market Z (in which only females had previously been employed)

(a) the hourly wage rate will rise to $ _____.
(b) the *decrease* in national output that results from the decrease in employment from 12 million to 8 million workers is equal to the loss of the marginal revenue products of the workers no longer employed, and it totals $ _____.

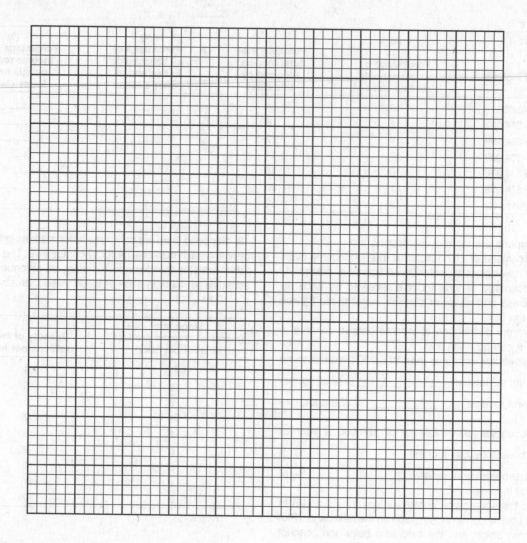

(2) In labor market X and in labor market Y (in each of which only males had previously been employed)

(a) the hourly wage rate will fall to $ _____.

(b) the *increase* in national output that results from the increase in employment from 6 million to 8 million workers is equal to the marginal revenue products of the additional workers employed; the gain in each of these markets is $ million, and the total gain in the two markets is $ _____.

(c) the *net* gain to society from the reallocation of female workers is $ million. _____

■ SHORT ANSWER AND ESSAY QUESTIONS

1. How much income inequality is there in the U.S. economy? Cite figures to support your conclusion.

2. What is measured along each of the two axes when a Lorenz curve is drawn?

(a) If the distribution of income were completely equal, what would the Lorenz curve look like?

(b) If one household received all of the income of the economy, what would the Lorenz curve look like?

(c) After the Lorenz curve for an economy has been drawn, how is the degree of income inequality in that economy measured?

(d) What is the difference between the Lorenz curve and the Gini ratio?

3. Explain how time affects the distribution of income and interpretations of income trends.

4. What effect do taxes and transfers have on the distribution of income in the United States? How much of this change in the distribution of income is the result of the transfer payments made by government?

5. What seven factors contribute to income inequality in the United States?

6. What has been the trend in income distribution in the United States since 1970?

7. What are three probable explanations for the increase in income inequality in the United States since 1970?

8. State the case for equal distribution of income.

9. Explain the advantage to the nation from an unequal distribution of income.

10. What is the fundamental trade-off involving income inequality? Explain the slicing the pizza pie analogy.

11. What is poverty? What is the minimum income level below which the Federal government defines a person or household as "in poverty"? How many people and what percentage of the U.S. population are "in poverty" using this definition?

12. What characteristics—other than the small amounts of money they have to spend—do the greatest concentrations of the poor households of the nation *tend* to have?

13. What have been the trends in the poverty rate from 1960 to 2000? What were the trends since 2000?

14. What are some of the problems with measuring poverty that would cause it to be understated or overstated?

15. List and briefly describe three social insurance programs of the income-maintenance system of the United States.

16. Explain the major public assistance programs of the income-maintenance system of the United States. How do they cover welfare needs?

17. How can discrimination be viewed as resulting from a preference or taste for which the prejudiced employer is willing to pay? What will determine whether the prejudiced employer hires nonpreferred workers in this model?

18. How do changes in employer prejudice affect wage rates for nonpreferred workers and the ratio of wages between preferred and nonpreferred workers?

19. Explain the concept of statistical discrimination and give an example of it. How can it lead to discrimination even in the absence of prejudice?

20. Describe the economic effects of occupational segregation on the wages of women and minorities. How does this type of segregation affect the domestic output of the economy?

ANSWERS

Chapter 20 Income Inequality, Poverty, and Discrimination

FILL-IN QUESTIONS

1. inequality, 7.5, 19.1
2. Lorenz; *a.* households, income; *b.* lower, upper; *c.* Lorenz curve; *d.* divided
3. short, mobility, more
4. reduce, before, after
5. ability, training, discrimination, risks, wealth, power, luck
6. more, lesser, greater
7. more, less, more, more, more, less
8. utility, income
9. efficiency, greater, more
10. minimize
11. $20,000, $9800, 12.3, 36.5
12. children, African-Americans, women
13. under, consumption
14. Social Security, Medicare, unemployment
15. SSI, Medicaid, TANF, EITC, noncash
16. disutility, cost, below
17. decrease, increase
18. statistical, rational, do not
19. crowding, low, more, an expansion
20. decreases, increases, decreases, decreases

TRUE–FALSE QUESTIONS

1. F, p. 410	**14.** F, pp. 417–418
2. T, pp. 410–411	**15.** F, p. 418
3. T, pp. 410–411	**16.** T, pp. 418–419
4. T, p. 411	**17.** T, p. 419
5. F, pp. 411–412	**18.** F, pp. 420–422
6. T, pp. 412–413	**19.** F, pp. 420–422
7. T, p. 413	**20.** T, p. 422
8. F, pp. 413–414	**21.** T, pp. 423–424
9. F, p. 414	**22.** F, p. 424
10. T, p. 415	**23.** T, p. 425
11. T, p. 415	**24.** T, pp. 425–426
12. F, p. 416	**25.** T, p. 428
13. T, pp. 416–417	

MULTIPLE-CHOICE QUESTIONS

1. d, pp. 410–411	**14.** b, pp. 417–418
2. b, pp. 410–411	**15.** a, p. 418
3. d, pp. 410–411	**16.** c, pp. 418–419
4. d, pp. 410–411	**17.** d, p. 419
5. c, pp. 411–412	**18.** a, pp. 420–422
6. a, pp. 412–413	**19.** a, p. 422
7. b, pp. 412–413	**20.** a, p. 422
8. b, pp. 413–414	**21.** d, p. 422
9. d, p. 413	**22.** c, pp. 423–424
10. c, pp. 413–414	**23.** c, pp. 423–424
11. c, p. 415	**24.** d, p. 425
12. c, p. 415	**25.** b, p. 428
13. b, pp. 416–417	

PROBLEMS

1. a. (1) column 4: 18, 30, 44, 61, 80, 91, 100, (2) column 5: 4, 10, 22, 36, 51, 71, 100; b. (1) 30, 10, (2) 20, 49; c. graph
2. a. 1; b. 3; c. 2; d. 4
3. a. (1) 3, (2) 9; b. (1) (a) 7, (b) 18, (2) (a) 7, (b) 15, 30, (c) 12

SHORT ANSWER AND ESSAY QUESTIONS

1. pp. 410–411	**12.** p. 419
2. pp. 410–411	**13.** pp. 419–420
3. pp. 411–412	**14.** p. 420
4. pp. 412–413	**15.** pp. 420–422
5. pp. 413–414	**16.** pp. 422–423
6. p. 415	**17.** pp. 423–424
7. pp. 415–416	**18.** p. 424
8. pp. 416–417	**19.** p. 425
9. pp. 417–418	**20.** pp. 425–426, 428
10. p. 418	
11. pp. 418–419	

CHAPTER 21

Health Care

Health care has been a topic of major national debate. One reason is that health care costs have risen. Another reason is that fewer people in the United States are being covered by the health care system or many have only limited access to health care. The first four sections of the chapter discuss the rising costs and limited access problems of the U.S. health care system. The economics you learned in previous chapters will now be put to good use in analyzing these twin problems of health care.

The explanations for the first problem—the rapid **rise in cost**—rely on your prior knowledge of supply and demand. Before you can appreciate the demand and supply factors that influence health care costs, however, you need to recognize the peculiar features of the market for health care that make it different from the other markets with which you are familiar. Society is reluctant to ration health care based solely on price or income, as is the case with most products. The market is also subject to asymmetric information between the buyer (patient) and seller (health care provider), with the seller making most of the decisions about the amount of services to be consumed and the prices to be paid. Medical care generates positive externalities that may lead to underproduction in the private market and require some government intervention to achieve efficient allocation of resources. The system of third-party payments reduces the price to buyers and distorts the traditional price signals of the marketplace.

With this background in mind, you are ready to read about the **demand for health care.** The demand factors have significantly increased the cost of health care. Health care is relatively price insensitive, so increases in price result in little reduction in the quantity consumed. The demand for health care has increased as per capita incomes have increased because health care is a normal good. Adding to the demand pressures are an aging population, unhealthy lifestyles, and the practices of physicians that are influenced by medical ethics and a fee-for-service payment system. The medical insurance system also contributes to increased demand by reducing the costs to the consumer, as does the Federal government with its tax subsidy of employer-financed health insurance.

Supply has not increased at the same rate as demand in health care. Although the supply of physicians has increased, it has had little effect on reducing health care costs. Health care is also an area of slow productivity growth because of the personal attention required for services. Also, the development and use of new medical technology have increased cost pressures in health care rather than reduced them.

The **reforms** for the health care system that you will read about in the last section of the chapter focus on achieving universal coverage and cost containment. A number of schemes have been proposed to increase coverage. These include play-or-pay insurance programs for businesses, tax credits and vouchers, and a national health insurance system. Suggestions for cost containment call for increased uses of incentives, such as increased deductibles and copayments for medical services, the adoption of more managed care such as is found in health maintenance organizations, and tighter controls over Medicare payments based on specific classifications of treatments. The reform section concludes with a brief discussion of recent health care legislation.

■ CHECKLIST

When you have studied this chapter you should be able to

☐ Describe the major characteristics of the health care industry.
☐ State the twin problems with the health care system.
☐ Cite data on health care spending in absolute and relative terms.
☐ Discuss the quality of medical care in the United States.
☐ Explain three economic implications of rising health care spending.
☐ Describe three effects on the labor market from rising health care spending.
☐ Discuss whether rising spending on health care is a good development for the U.S. economy.
☐ State reasons why people have limited access to health care and often do not have medical insurance.
☐ List four peculiarities of the market for health care.
☐ Discuss the four demand factors that have increased health care costs over time.
☐ Explain how health insurance affects health care spending by creating a moral hazard problem and tax subsidies.
☐ Use supply and demand analysis to explain the rapid rise in health care expenditures.
☐ Identify the supply factors affecting the costs of health care.
☐ Evaluate the relative importance of the demand and supply factors affecting health care.
☐ Discuss proposals to reform the health care system so that there can be universal access.

☐ Cite arguments for and against national health insurance.

☐ Explain how incentives can be used to help contain health care costs.

☐ Describe three recent changes or issues in health care reforms.

☐ Explain the purposes and features of the mandatory health insurance legislation enacted in Massachusetts (Last Word).

■ CHAPTER OUTLINE

1. The **health care industry** in the United States covers a broad range of services provided by doctors, hospitals, dentists, nursing homes, and medical laboratories. It employs about 14 million people, about 790,000 of whom are practicing physicians. There are about 5750 hospitals. Americans make more than 1 billion visits to physicians each year.

2. Two major problems face the health care system. The **costs** of health care are high and rapidly rising. Some U.S. citizens do not have **access** to health care or adequate coverage by the system.

3. **Health care costs** are rising for many reasons.
   a. Costs have risen in absolute and relative terms.
   (1) Total health care spending pays for many items such as hospitals, doctors, dentists, prescription drugs, nursing homes, and program administration and is obtained from many sources, such as private health insurance, Medicare, Medicaid, *copayments* and *deductibles,* and other sources, as shown in text Figure 21.1.
   (2) Expenditures were about 16% of domestic output in 2006.
   (3) The health care expenditures as a percentage of GDP are highest in the United States compared with other industrial nations.
   b. There is general agreement that medical care in the United States is probably the best in the world, which is a consequence of its high expenditures for health care. That does not mean, however, that the United States is the healthiest nation. In fact, it ranks low internationally on many health indicators.
   c. Rising health care expenditures and costs have negative economic effects that include
   (1) reduced access and coverage for workers and others;
   (2) labor market problems such as slower wage growth, more use of part-time or temporary workers, and outsourcing (and offshoring);
   (3) an increase in personal bankruptcies; and,
   (4) more demands on government budgets at all levels.
   d. The question of whether there is too much spending on health care is difficult to evaluate. Some economists argue that the greater spending contributes to society's GDP and well-being. Other economists argue that the basic problem is that there is an *overallocation* of resources to health care and *less* economic efficiency in the use of the nation's resources.

4. A major problem with health care is **limited access.** A large percentage of the population (about 15% in 2006) has no medical coverage. Those medically uninsured are generally the poor, although some young adults with good health choose not to buy insurance. Low-income workers and those employed in smaller businesses are less likely to be covered, or have limited coverage, because of the higher costs of health care for smaller firms.

5. There are many reasons for the **rapid rise in health care costs.**
   a. The market for health care is different from other markets. Medical care has ethical and equity considerations not found in most other markets. Health care suppliers have more information than do buyers, so there is asymmetric information in the market. Medical care spending and treatment often create positive externalities. The third-party payment system for insurance reduces incentives to control health care spending and leads to overconsumption.
   b. Several demand factors have increased health care costs over time.
   (1) Health care is a normal good with an income elasticity of about +1.0, so that spending on it will rise in proportion to per capita income. Health care is also price *inelastic,* which means that total health care spending will increase even as the price of health care rises.
   (2) The aging population of the United States increases the demand for health care.
   (3) Unhealthy lifestyles because of alcohol, tobacco, or drug abuse increase the demand for and spending on health care.
   (4) Doctors can add to costs because there is asymmetric information—the provider knows more than the buyer—and thus there is supplier-induced demand.
   (a) Doctors have no strong incentive to reduce costs for the buyer and perhaps an economic interest in increasing them because they are paid as a *fee for service.*
   (b) **Defensive medicine,** which involves the use of extra testing, may be used to prevent possible lawsuits, but it increases costs.
   (c) Medical ethics require the best (and often the most expensive) procedures.
   c. Although health insurance plays a positive role in giving people protection against health risks, it contributes to increased costs and demand for health care.
   (1) It creates a *moral hazard problem* by encouraging some people to be less careful about their health and gives some people incentives to overconsume health care than would be the case without insurance.
   (2) Health insurance financed by employers is exempt from both Federal income and payroll taxation. This *tax subsidy* increases the demand for health care.
   (3) From a supply and demand perspective, health insurance reduces the price to the buyer below the no-insurance equilibrium price. This lower price induces more health care consumption and creates an efficiency loss for society.

d. Supply factors affect health care costs.

(1) The increase in the supply of physicians has not kept up with the increase in demand for health care, thus increasing physician costs. One reason is that the rising cost of education and training for physicians limits the number completing medical programs.

(2) The productivity growth in health care has been slow relative to other sectors of the economy.

(3) Most new medical technology has increased costs, despite the fact that some technological advances in medicine have decreased costs.

e. Only a relatively minor portion of the increase in health care costs can be attributed to increasing incomes, the aging of the population, or defensive medicine. The most likely explanations for the rise in health care costs are the use of advanced medical technology, medical ethics that require best treatment, and a third-party system of insurance payments with little incentive to control costs.

6. Reforms for the health care system call for increased access to health care and cost containment.

a. There are three basic proposals for increasing universal access.

(1) *"Play-or-pay"* schemes would require all employers either to fund a basic health insurance program (play) or finance health care through a special payroll tax (pay).

(2) Tax credits and vouchers are another option designed to make health insurance more affordable for the poor.

(3) A *national health insurance (NHI)* program would provide universal coverage at no cost or at a low cost and would be financed out of tax revenues. The basic arguments for NHI are its simplicity, its allowing patients their choice of physician, the reduction in administrative costs, the improvement in labor market mobility, and increased government bargaining power to contain costs. Arguments against NHI are the ineffectiveness of price controls, increased waiting for doctors and tests, the inefficiency of the Federal government, and income redistribution problems.

b. To contain health care costs, alternatives that use incentives have been adopted.

(1) Insurance companies have increased deductibles and copayments to give consumers more incentives to reduce health costs.

(2) Managed care organizations are being more widely used to control health care costs and are of two types. *Preferred provider organizations (PPOs)* offer discounts to insurance companies and consumers who use them. *Health maintenance organizations (HMOs)* are prepaid health plans that closely monitor health care costs because they operate with fixed budgets.

(3) The *diagnosis-related-group (DRG) system* is used to classify treatments and fix fees to reduce the costs of Medicare payments, although the DRG systems may also reduce the quality of care.

c. Three recent laws or proposals for reforms to the health care system have been designed to increase coverage or contain costs.

(1) Prescription drug coverage was added to Medicare in 2003 and took effect in 2006. It is referred to as *Medicare Part D.* The change was demanded because of the rising cost and importance of prescription drugs to health care treatments. Typically the enrollees pay a premium, an annual deductible, and a certain percentage of prescription drug cost that vary by the cost amount.

(2) *Heath savings accounts (HSAs)* also were established as part of the 2003 Medicare reform. Individuals make tax-deductible contributions into their HSAs and they can use them to pay for qualified medical expenses. This program is thought to promote the use of personal savings for health care expenditures and add more incentives to reduce costs because bills would be paid directly by the account holder and not a third party.

(3) There have been congressional efforts to limit the size of medical malpractice awards to contain health care costs. Thirty-three states have caps on "pain and suffering" provisions of malpractice awards.

7. (Last Word). In 2006 Massachusetts enacted a mandatory health insurance law for its residents requiring them to provide proof of medical insurance or face penalties. The law is intended to reduce the cost of "free riders" who do not have health care coverage but who use the medical facilities essentially for free. It encourages employers to offer health insurance to employees and provides subsidized health insurance for low-income groups. Critics contend that the program will increase demand for health care and increase, not reduce, health care costs. The program is experimental and whether it will become a model for a universal health insurance program is unknown.

■ **HINTS AND TIPS**

1. This chapter contains many health care terms (e.g., preferred provider organization) with which you may not be familiar. Make sure you review the meaning of each important term before reading the text chapter and taking the self-test in this chapter.

2. The two economic ideas that are the most difficult to comprehend are asymmetric information and moral hazard. The buyer and seller information problems were discussed extensively in Chapter 16. To remember the meaning of these ideas, associate them with examples from the text or ones that you construct.

3. This chapter uses the concepts of income elasticity and price elasticity of demand to explain the demand for health care. Reread the text discussion of these concepts in Chapter 6 if you cannot recall how these elasticities are defined.

4. The graphical presentation of a market with and without health insurance (Figure 21.3) is a relatively straightforward application of supply and demand. The one difficult concept is efficiency loss. This concept was discussed in Chapters 6 and 17; you will now see it applied to health care.

■ IMPORTANT TERMS

deductibles

copayments

fee for service

defensive medicine

tax subsidy

"play or pay"

national health
  insurance (NHI)

preferred provider
  organizations
  (PPOs)

health maintenance
  organizations
  (HMOs)

diagnosis-related-
  group (DRG) system

Medicare Part D

health savings
  accounts (HSAs)

SELF-TEST

■ FILL-IN QUESTIONS

1. The health care industry in the United States employs about (2, 14) _____ million people, about (330, 790) _____ thousand of whom are physicians. There are about (2250, 5750) _____ hospitals.

2. The twin problems facing the health care system are high and rapidly growing (benefits, costs) _____ and the fact that many U.S. citizens (do, do not) _____ have access to health care or adequate coverage by the system.

3. In 1960, health care spending was about (5, 16) _____% of domestic output, but in 2006 it was _____% of domestic output. Compared to other industrialized nations, the United States has the (lowest, highest) _____ level of per capita health care expenditures.

4. The economic effects of rising health care costs are (more, less) _____ access to health care and _____ coverage for workers. There are labor market problems, such as (more, less) _____ wage growth, _____ labor mobility, and (more, less) _____ use of temporary or part-time workers. Health care costs also create _____ demands on the budgets of governments at the Federal, state, and local levels.

5. The basic problem with growing health care expenditures is that there is an (underallocation, overallocation) _____ of resources to health care. The large expenditures for health care mean that at the margin, health care is worth (more, less) _____ than

alternative products that could have been produced with the resources.

6. The uninsured represent about (16, 30) _____% of the population. They are concentrated among the poor, many of whom work at (low-wage, high-wage) _____ jobs, (do, do not) _____ qualify for Medicaid, and may work for (small, large) _____ businesses. Others who are uninsured include (older, younger) _____ adults in excellent health and people with (minor, major) _____ health problems.

7. The market for health care is different from other markets because of (technology, ethical–equity) _____ considerations, (symmetric, asymmetric) _____ information, (positive, negative) _____ externalities, and (first-party, third-party) _____ payments.

8. Health care is (an inferior, a normal, a superior) _____ good with an income elasticity of about (0, 1) _____. In this case, a 10% increase in incomes will result in a (1, 10) _____% increase in health care expenditures.

9. Health care is price (inelastic, elastic) _____, with a coefficient estimated to be (0.2, 1.5) _____. The price elasticity of demand for health care means that a 10% increase in price would decrease health care spending by (2, 15) _____%.

10. Other factors increasing the demand for health care include a(n) (older, younger) _____ population and lifestyles that are often (entertaining, unhealthy) _____.

11. The demand for health care is affected by the problem of asymmetric information in the practice of medicine, which means that the (demander, supplier) _____ will decide the types and amount of health care to be consumed. Physicians (have, do not have) _____ an incentive to reduce costs for the buyer and perhaps an economic interest in increasing them because they are paid on a (play-or-pay, fee-for-service) _____ basis.

12. Increased demand and costs can arise from the practice of (offensive, defensive) _____ medicine to limit the possibility of a lawsuit or from medical (insurance, ethics) _____ that require the use of the best medical techniques by doctors.

13. Health insurance increases demand because it creates a moral (dilemma, hazard) _____ problem. It makes people (more, less) _____ careful about their health and gives people incentives to (underconsume, overconsume) _____ health care more than they otherwise would without health insurance.

14. Health insurance financed by employers is (taxed, tax-exempt) _____ at the Federal level. This (tax, tax subsidy) _____ (increases, decreases) _____ the demand for health care.

15. In a supply and demand analysis, health insurance (raises, lowers) _____ the price to the buyer below the no-insurance equilibrium price. This (higher, lower) _____ price induces (less, more) _____ health care consumption and creates an efficiency (benefit, loss) _____ for society.

16. The supply factors that affect health care costs include the (high, low) _____ cost of physician services, (fast, slow) _____ growth in productivity in health care, and the use of (new, old) _____ medical technology.

17. Increasing access to health care could be achieved by a (fee-for-service, play-or-pay) _____ requirement for all employers either to fund a basic health insurance program or pay a special payroll tax to finance health care for workers. Another option would be the use of tax (levies, credits) _____ and vouchers to make health insurance more affordable for the poor.

18. A program that would provide universal coverage at no cost or at a low cost and would be financed out of tax revenues is (managed care, national health insurance) _____.

   a. Some of its advantages are that it is a simple and (direct, indirect) _____ way to provide universal coverage, it allows patients to choose their own (insurance, physician) _____, it (increases, decreases) _____ administrative costs, it _____ labor market mobility, and (increases, decreases) _____ government bargaining power with medical care providers.

   b. One argument against it is the ineffectiveness of price (ceilings, floors) _____ on physician services. It may also (increase, decrease) _____ waiting for doctors and tests, _____ the inefficiency of the Federal government, and (increase, decrease) _____ redistribution of income.

19. Actions have been taken to contain health care costs. Insurance companies have (increased, decreased) _____ deductibles and copayments to provide incentives for consumers to reduce expenditures, and there has been _____ use of preferred provider organizations (PPOs) to get consumers to use lower-cost health care providers. Businesses and other organizations have formed health maintenance organizations (HMOs) that have prepaid health plans and use a (fee-for-service, managed care) _____ approach to control health costs. Medical treatments have been classified according to a diagnosis-related-group (DRG) system and the government has (fixed, variable) _____ fee payments for each treatment.

20. In recent years, the U.S. Congress has passed laws and considered several types of health care legislation. The cost of prescription drug coverage has been added to (Social Security, Medicare) _____, individuals with high-deductible private insurance can place tax-free dollars into (health maintenance organizations, health savings accounts) _____, and there has been action taken by 33 states to place financial limits on "pain and suffering" portions of awards for medical (research, malpractice) _____.

■ **TRUE–FALSE QUESTIONS**

Circle T if the statement is true, F if it is false.

  1. The twin problems of health care are the rapidly rising cost of health care and the general decline in the quality of health care. **T F**

  2. Medicaid is the nationwide Federal health care program available to Social Security beneficiaries and the disabled. **T F**

  3. Per capita expenditures on health care are high in the United States but even higher in Japan and United Kingdom. **T F**

  4. Rising health care costs reduce workers' access to health care. **T F**

  5. Increasing health care expenditures cause problems for the budgets of Federal, state, and local governments. **T F**

  6. Aggregate consumption of health care is so great that at the margin it is worth more than the alternative goods and services these resources could otherwise have produced. **T F**

  7. About 60% of the population of the United States had no health insurance for the entire year. **T F**

  8. Minimum-wage workers have health insurance because their insurance premiums are covered by the Federal government. **T F**

9. There is asymmetric information in the market for health care because the supplier (doctor) acts as the agent for the buyer (patient) and tells the buyer what health care services should be consumed.   **T   F**

10. The market for health care is characterized by negative externalities.   **T   F**

11. Third-party payments are a factor in the health care market because about three-fourths of all health care expenses are paid through public or private insurance. **T   F**

12. The demand for health care is price elastic.   **T   F**

13. There is a strong incentive to underconsume health care because consumers have little information about the costs of medical treatments and doctors are paid on a fee-for-service basis.   **T   F**

14. "Defensive medicine" refers to the medical practice of physicians using preventive medicine to reduce illness and disease in patients.   **T   F**

15. Health care insurance is a means by which one pays a relatively small known cost for protection against an uncertain and much larger cost in the future.   **T   F**

16. A moral hazard problem arises from health insurance because those covered tend to take fewer health risks and consume less health care than would be the case without insurance.   **T   F**

17. The demand for health care is increased by a Federal tax policy that exempts employer-financed health insurance from taxation.   **T   F**

18. There is overwhelming evidence that the American Medical Association has purposely kept admissions to medical school artificially low to restrict the supply of doctors.   **T   F**

19. Productivity growth has been slow in the health care industry.   **T   F**

20. The development and use of new technology in health care has been a major factor in increasing the costs of health care.   **T   F**

21. The basic intent of reform proposals calling for tax credits and vouchers to pay for health insurance is to reduce or contain costs.   **T   F**

22. Proposals for national health insurance would provide a basic package of health care for each citizen at no direct charge or at a low-cost rate and would be financed out of tax revenues rather than health insurance premiums.   **T   F**

23. A problem with a government-imposed ceiling on the prices for physician services is that physicians can protect their incomes from fixed prices by altering the quantity and quality of care they give a patient.   **T   F**

24. The diagnostic-related-group (DRG) system is a health maintenance organization that specializes in the diagnoses of illnesses to reduce costs.   **T   F**

25. The growth of managed care organizations has transformed the medical industry into one dominated by large insurance and health care firms.   **T   F**

■ **MULTIPLE-CHOICE QUESTIONS**

Circle the letter that corresponds to the best answer.

1. The two major problems facing the health care system of the United States are
(a) the formation of health alliances and preferred provider organizations
(b) a decline in innovation and the rate of technological changes
(c) increasing supply and decreasing demand for health care
(d) access to health care and rapidly increasing costs

2. The health care industry employs about how many physicians?
(a) 51,300
(b) 150,700
(c) 790,000
(d) 1,984,000

3. What was total spending for health care as a percentage of GDP in 1960 and in 2006?

	1960	2006
(a)	1	4
(b)	2	6
(c)	5	16
(d)	9	18

4. The contradiction about health care in the United States is that the country's
(a) medical care is the best in the world, but the nation ranks low on many health indicators
(b) expenditures for health care are modest, but its medical care is the best in the world
(c) expenditures for health care are the highest in the world, but its quality of medical care is the worst of all industrial nations
(d) advances in medicine have fallen at a time when its need for better medicine has risen

5. Which is a labor market effect from rapidly rising health care costs?
(a) A decrease in the number of health care workers
(b) An increase in the rate of growth of real wages
(c) An increase in the use of part-time workers
(d) A decrease in the skill of the labor force

6. Which person is most likely to be uninsured or ineligible for health insurance?
(a) A college professor working at a state university
(b) A full-time worker at a big manufacturing plant
(c) An accountant employed by a large corporation
(d) A dishwasher working for minimum wage at a restaurant

7. Which would be considered a peculiarity of the market for health care?
(a) Third-party payments
(b) Employer mandates
(c) Tax credits and vouchers
(d) Fee-for-service payments

8. The demand for health care is
(a) price elastic
(b) price inelastic

(c) income elastic

(d) income inelastic

9. From an income perspective, health care is considered

(a) an inferior good

(b) a normal good

(c) a superior good

(d) a supply-induced good

10. Which is a demand factor in the market for health care?

(a) Asymmetric information

(b) Advances in new medical technology

(c) Slow productivity growth in the health care industry

(d) The number of physicians graduating from medical school

11. Asymmetric information causes problems in the health care market because

(a) the buyer, not the supplier, of health care services, makes most of the decisions about the amount and type of health care to be provided

(b) the supplier, not the buyer, of the health care services, makes most of the decisions about the amount and type of health care to be provided

(c) government has less information than the health care providers and can inflate fees

(d) insurance companies, not the health care consumer, control deductibles and copayment policies

12. Most experts attribute a major portion of the relative rise in health care spending to

(a) rising incomes

(b) an aging population

(c) advances in medical technology

(d) an increase in the number of physicians

13. Unhealthy lifestyles may be encouraged by medical insurance because people figure that health insurance will cover illnesses or accidents. This attitude is characteristic of

(a) asymmetric information

(b) the play-or-pay problem

(c) a moral hazard problem

(d) a reduced access problem

Answer Questions 14, 15, 16, and 17 based on the following demand and supply graph of the market for health care.

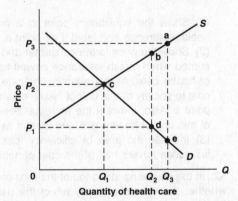

Quantity of health care

14. If there were no health insurance, the equilibrium price and quantity of health care would be

(a) P_1 and Q_2

(b) P_2 and Q_1

(c) P_2 and Q_2

(d) P_3 and Q_3

15. Assume that health insurance pays half the cost of health care. For the consumer, the price and quantity of health care consumed would be

(a) P_1 and Q_2

(b) P_2 and Q_2

(c) P_2 and Q_1

(d) P_3 and Q_3

16. With health insurance paying half the cost of health care, there is allocative

(a) efficiency because at Q_1 the marginal cost to society equals the marginal benefit

(b) efficiency because at Q_2 the marginal cost to society is less than the marginal benefit by the difference between points **b** and **d**

(c) inefficiency because at Q_2 the marginal cost to society exceeds the marginal benefit by the difference between points **b** and **d**

(d) inefficiency because at Q_3 the marginal cost to society exceeds the marginal benefit by the difference between points **a** and **e**

17. The efficiency loss caused by the availability of health insurance is shown by area

(a) $Q_1 ca Q_3$

(b) $Q_1 cb Q_2$

(c) *cae*

(d) *cbd*

18. Which is a supply factor in the health care market?

(a) Medical technology

(b) An aging population

(c) Defensive medicine

(d) Growing incomes

19. The play-or-pay proposal for health care reform is intended to

(a) increase access to health care through the use of tax credits and vouchers as part of a national health insurance system

(b) expand health care coverage by requiring all employers to offer a health insurance program for workers or pay a special payroll tax for health care

(c) make states become bigger players in health care reform by having the Federal government match state expenditures for health care and Medicaid

(d) reduce consumption of health care by increasing deductibles and copayments for health insurance

20. Which is primarily designed to increase access to health care rather than contain costs?

(a) National health insurance

(b) Diagnosis-related-group system

(c) Health maintenance organizations

(d) Preferred provider organizations

21. A substantive criticism of national health insurance is that

(a) the Federal government provision of tax credits and vouchers for health care would be inefficient

(b) it would establish a diagnosis-related-group system for the payment of health provider services that is unnecessary and inefficient

(c) it would increase deductibles and copayments that are borne by individuals, making health care more costly

(d) the Federal government does not have a good record of containing the costs of health care programs

22. Insurance companies often have policies that require the insured to pay the fixed portion (e.g., $500) of each year's health costs and a fixed percentage (e.g., 20%) of all additional costs. The expenditures by the insured are
(a) credits and vouchers
(b) deductibles and copayments
(c) fee-for-service payments
(d) diagnosis-related-group expenditures

23. An organization that requires hospitals and physicians to provide discounted prices for their services as a condition for inclusion in the insurance plan is a
(a) health maintenance organization
(b) preferred provider organization
(c) fee-for-service organization
(d) health alliance

24. With Medicare Part D, individuals would pay small monthly premiums for subsidized private insurance coverage for
(a) dental care
(b) cosmetic surgery
(c) prescription drugs
(d) medical aids such a wheelchairs

25. With health savings accounts (HSAs), individuals
(a) make tax-deductible contributions to the accounts and then use the funds to pay for health care expenditures
(b) contract with health maintenance organizations and use the accounts to get medical services at the lowest possible rate
(c) obtain discounted prices for health care services that are provided by the diagnosis-related-group system
(d) deposit money in a bank and receive a certificate of deposit that is indexed to the inflation rate for health care

■ **PROBLEMS**

1. Following is a table showing a supply and demand schedule for health care. In the left column is the price of health care. The middle column shows the quantity demanded (Q_d) for health care. The right column shows the quantity supplied (Q_s) of health care.

Price ($)	Q_d	Q_s
3000	100	500
2500	200	400
2000	300	300
1500	400	200
1000	500	100

a. Assume that there is no health insurance in this market. At a price of $2000, the quantity demanded will be _____ units of health care and the quantity supplied will be _____ units. There will be (a surplus, a shortage, equilibrium) _____ in this market for health care at _____ units.
b. Now assume that health insurance cuts the price of health care in half for the consumer. The new price to the consumer will be $_____ and the quantity consumed will be _____ units. At this level of quantity, the marginal cost to society of a unit of health care is $_____ while the marginal benefit is _____.
c. Draw a supply and demand graph in the following graph based on the data in the preceding table. Make sure to label the axes and identify prices and quantities.

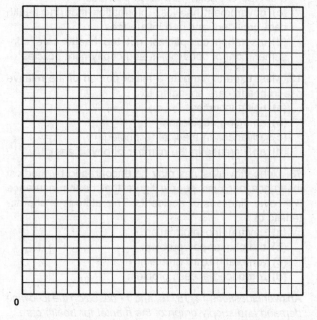

(1) Show the equilibrium point in a market without health insurance and label it as point *a*.
(2) Show the price to the consumer and quantity consumed when health insurance covers half of the cost of health care. At this quantity, indicate the marginal cost to society of this unit of health care and label it at point *b*. Also, indicate the marginal benefit to society of this unit of health care and label it as point *c*.
(3) Indicate the area of efficiency loss when health insurance covers half of the cost of health care.

2. In the situations at the top of the next column indicate whether the events primarily affect the demand (**D**) for health care or the supply (**S**) of health care. Also, indicate whether it would increase (**+**) or decrease (**−**) the demand for or supply of health care.

D or S + or −

a. An aging population ___ ___
b. More use of defensive medicine ___ ___
c. Healthier lifestyles ___ ___
d. Less health insurance coverage ___ ___
e. Increased productivity in health care ___ ___
f. Newer and more costly medical technology ___ ___
g. A sharp reduction in the number of physicians ___ ___
h. A tax subsidy to consumers to cover health care ___ ___
i. Rising per capita incomes ___ ___
j. More use of a fee-for-service payment system ___ ___

3. Match the terms with the correct phrases using the appropriate number.

1. copayments
2. play-or-pay
3. diagnosis-related-group system
4. preferred provider organization
5. health maintenance organization
6. deductibles

a. A unit set up by insurance companies that requires hospitals and physicians to provide discounted prices for their services as a condition for being included in the insurance plan _____

b. The percentage of cost that an insured individual pays while the insurer pays the remainder _____

c. A health care organization that contracts with employers, insurance companies, and other groups to provide health care for their workers or others who are insured _____

d. The dollar sum of costs that an insured individual must pay before the insurer begins to pay _____

e. An arrangement that gives the hospital a fixed payment for treating each patient with the payments based on hundreds of detailed health categories for patient conditions and needs _____

f. A way to expand health coverage by requiring employers to either provide insurance for their workers or be assessed a special payroll tax to finance insurance for uncovered workers _____

■ SHORT ANSWER AND ESSAY QUESTIONS

1. Define and describe the major features of the health care industry.

2. Explain the relationship between the cost of and access to health care.

3. What are the dimensions of the cost increases in health care in absolute and relative terms?

4. How do health care expenditures in the United States compare with those in other industrialized nations?

5. What are the economic implications of rising health care costs?

6. Why is the aggregate consumption of health care in the United States a basic problem?

7. Who are the uninsured in the United States? What are the characteristics of the uninsured?

8. What are four peculiarities of the market for health care?

9. How do income and price elasticity affect the demand for health care?

10. In what ways do an aging population and unhealthy lifestyles influence and shape the demand for health care?

11. Why is there asymmetric information in health care? How does it affect consumption and the cost of health care?

12. What role does health insurance play in affecting health care costs? Explain the advantages and disadvantages of health insurance.

13. Why might physicians' high incomes have nothing to do with supply restrictions?

14. How have changes in medical technology affected health care costs?

15. What is the relative importance of demand and supply factors in affecting the rise in health care costs?

16. How would play-or-pay or tax credit and voucher reforms be used to achieve universal access to health care?

17. Discuss the arguments for and against national health insurance.

18. What actions have insurance companies and the Federal government taken to reduce or contain health care costs?

19. The Medicare Prescription Drug, Improvement, and Modernization Act of 2003 established Medicare Part D, which took effect in 2006. Describe the features of the coverage and the advantages and disadvantages of the coverage.

20. Explain how health savings accounts work and what economic incentives health savings accounts provide for containing health care costs.

ANSWERS

Chapter 21 Health Care

FILL-IN QUESTIONS

1. 14, 790, 5750
2. costs, do not
3. 5, 16, highest
4. less, less, less, less, more, more
5. overallocation, less

6. 16, low-wage, do not, small, younger, major
7. ethical–equity, asymmetric, positive, third-party
8. a normal, 1, 10
9. inelastic, 0.2, 2
10. older, unhealthy
11. supplier, do not have, fee-for-service
12. defensive, ethics
13. hazard, less, overconsume
14. tax-exempt, tax subsidy, increases
15. lowers, lower, more, loss
16. high, slow, new
17. play-or-pay, credits
18. national health insurance; *a.* direct, physician, decreases, increases, increases; *b.* ceilings, increase, increase, increase
19. increased, increased, managed care, fixed
20. Medicare, health savings accounts, malpractice

TRUE–FALSE QUESTIONS

1. F, p. 432	**10.** F, p. 436	**19.** T, pp. 440–441
2. F, pp. 432–433	**11.** T, pp. 436–437	**20.** T, p. 441
3. F, pp. 433–434	**12.** F, p. 437	**21.** F, p. 442
4. T, p. 434	**13.** F, pp. 437–438	**22.** T, pp. 442–443
5. T, p. 435	**14.** F, p. 438	**23.** T, p. 443
6. F, p. 435	**15.** T, p. 438	**24.** F, p. 444
7. F, p. 435	**16.** F, pp. 438–439	**25.** T, p. 444
8. F, pp. 435–436	**17.** T, p. 439	
9. T, p. 436	**18.** F, p. 440	

MULTIPLE-CHOICE QUESTIONS

1. d, p. 432	**10.** a, p. 436	**19.** b, p. 442
2. c, p. 432	**11.** b, p. 436	**20.** a, pp. 442–443
3. c, p. 433	**12.** c, p. 441	**21.** d, p. 443
4. a, pp. 433–434	**13.** c, pp. 438–439	**22.** b, p. 444
5. c, p. 434	**14.** b, pp. 439–440	**23.** b, p. 444
6. d, p. 434	**15.** a, pp. 439–440	**24.** c, pp. 444–445
7. a, pp. 436–437	**16.** c, pp. 439–440	**25.** a, p. 445
8. b, p. 437	**17.** d, pp. 439–440	
9. b, p. 437	**18.** a, p. 441	

PROBLEMS

1. *a.* 300, 300, equilibrium, 300; *b.* 1000, 500, 3000, 1000; *c.* (1) the intersection of price of $2000 and quantity of 300, (2) point *b* is the intersection of $3000 and quantity of 500 units, and point *c* is the intersection of $1000 and quantity of 500 units, (3) the area of efficiency loss is the area in the triangle outlined by points *a*, *b*, and *c*

2. *a.* D, +; *b.* D, +; *c.* D, –; *d.* D, –; *e.* S, +; *f.* S, –; *g.* S, –; *h.* D, +; *i.* D, +; *j.* D, +

3. *a.* 4; *b.* 1; *c.* 5; *d.* 6; *e.* 3; *f.* 2

SHORT ANSWER AND ESSAY QUESTIONS

1. p. 432	**8.** pp. 436–437	**15.** pp. 441–442
2. pp. 432–436	**9.** p. 437	**16.** p. 442
3. pp. 432–433	**10.** p. 437	**17.** pp. 442–443
4. pp. 433–434	**11.** pp. 437–438	**18.** pp. 443–444
5. pp. 434–435	**12.** pp. 438–439	**19.** pp. 444–445
6. p. 435	**13.** p. 440	**20.** p. 445
7. pp. 435–436	**14.** p. 441	

CHAPTER 22

Immigration

Immigration is a topic often misunderstood and subject to heated controversy. The unique feature of this chapter is that it uses the power of economic information and analysis to offer significant insights and findings that should improve your understanding of this complex and controversial issue.

Simply stated, immigration involves the movement of labor resources from one nation to another. The chapter begins with a brief description of **economic immigrants** who typically move to the United States for some desired economic gain. These immigrants are of two types. They consist of **legal immigrants** who have permission to permanently reside in the United States or who have permission to work and live in the nation for a temporary period of time. They also include **illegal immigrants** who enter the country without the legal permission of the U.S. government.

The second section of the chapter explains the **economic reasons for immigration** into the United States from a cost and benefit perspective. A prime reason people make the move is to expand their opportunities to gain the benefits of a greater income. Moving costs, however, also influence the immigration decision because immigration can be considered an investment decision. Other factors also come into the cost-benefit decision such as the distance of the move, the age of the worker, and language skills.

The third section focuses on the **economics of immigration** in general. It uses a labor demand model to analyze what happens to wage rates, efficiency, output, and income. The conclusions drawn about immigration using the supply and demand analysis are definite, but as you discover at the end of the section, the real world is more complicated, so any conclusions will be modified by various factors such as the cost of migration, remittances, backflows, resource complementarities, capital investment, and unemployment.

The fourth section extends the economic analysis and applies it to **illegal immigration.** A supply and demand model for low-wage labor is used to illustrate the economic effects of illegal immigration on employment, wage rates, the prices of goods and services, and on government. The analysis reveals that illegal immigration can have both negative and positive effects depending on the economic conditions and circumstances.

Immigration is one of those controversial issues that are the subject of ongoing debate in the United States. Although the issue can be viewed from a political, social, legal, or cultural dimension, this chapter shows how the basic economics you have learned throughout your textbook can be used to gain new understanding of this issue.

■ CHECKLIST

When you have studied this chapter you should be able to

☐ Explain how immigrants are classified as legal immigrants and illegal immigrants.

☐ Describe trends in the level of legal immigration since 1980.

☐ Identify the major categories of admission for legal immigration.

☐ List the major countries of origin for legal immigrants.

☐ Supply estimates of the number of illegal immigrants (average number per year in recent years and the total number overall).

☐ List three reasons why legal or illegal immigrants decide to migrate.

☐ Discuss the role of earning opportunities in migration decisions.

☐ Explain how immigration can be viewed as an investment decision.

☐ Discuss how distance and age, or other factors, affect the cost–benefit evaluation of the migration decision.

☐ Describe the personal gains from economic immigration.

☐ Use a supply and demand model to explain the economic effects of worker migration from Mexico to the United States in terms of wage rates, efficiency, output, and income shares.

☐ Explain how five factors complicate or modify the economic effects of migration on the two economies.

☐ Discuss the fiscal effects of the economics of migration between the two economies.

☐ Describe the research findings on the economic effects of immigration.

☐ Use a supply and demand model to explain the economic effects of illegal immigration on employment and wages.

☐ Explain how illegal immigration affects the prices of goods and services produced by illegal immigration.

☐ Discuss the fiscal impact of illegal immigration on state and local governments and other concerns.

☐ Offer a description of optimal immigration from an economic perspective.

☐ Describe some key elements in the history of immigration reform and recent attempts to offer a comprehensive reform (Last Word).

■ **CHAPTER OUTLINE**

1. The United States is a nation shaped and influenced by *economic immigrants,* who are motivated to move to the United States for economic gain. The number of immigrants consists of two types. First, there are legal immigrants who have been granted the right to live and work in the United States, some of which are *permanent legal residents* (holding "green cards") and others who are *temporary legal immigrants* with permission to reside in the United States for a specific period. Second, there are illegal immigrants who have entered the country without legal permission or overstayed a temporary visa.

a. The number of *legal immigrants* to the United States was about 500,000 from 1980 to 1988. From 1989 to 1992, it spiked to over 1.75 million because of an amnesty program, and then ranged from 750,000 to 1.25 million. From 2000 to 2007 it averaged 1 million a year; in 2007 it was 1.05 million. Legal immigrants are admitted for many reasons such as family sponsorship (65.5%), employment-based preferences (15.4%), refugee status (12.9%), diversity (4.0%), and other reasons (3.4%). Some are admitted through the *H1-B provision* of the immigration law that allows a limited number of high-skilled workers to be admitted to work in specialty occupations for six years. Among the top nations for legal immigrants are Mexico, China, the Philippines, India, Colombia, Haiti, Cuba, Vietnam, Dominican Republic, and El Salvador.

b. The number of *illegal immigrants* has averaged about 350,000 per year in recent years with most people coming from Mexico, the Caribbean, and Central America. About 12 million illegal immigrants reside continuously in the United States.

2. The three main **reasons that people immigrate** into the United States are to take advantage of better economic opportunities, to escape political or religious persecution, and to reunite with family members or friends.

a. The main economic attraction of the United States for immigrants is the **opportunity for a higher-paying job.** Such jobs enable workers to get a better financial return on their stock of *human capital,* or the knowledge, know-how, and skills a person possesses. Typically, a large difference in wages increases the incentive to migrate from low-wage nations to high-wage nations or "magnet" countries such as Australia, Switzerland, the United States, and some Western European nations.

b. The decision to immigrate is a **cost–benefit** calculation and entails giving up current income or consumption for future benefit. There are explicit costs such as paying for application fees and moving expenses for legal immigrants (or paying for an expediter, or "coyote" for illegal immigrants). There are implicit or opportunity costs related to lost income while moving, and personal costs of leaving a family or culture. In making the decision, the immigrant evaluates whether the expected benefits of higher earnings and career possibilities are greater than the explicit and implicit costs of moving.

c. Nonwage factors can affect the cost–benefit analysis of the immigration decision.

(1) In most cases, the greater the **distance** required for migration, the less the likelihood that it will occur because more uncertainty and risk associated are with the move. These distance costs can be reduced if migrants follow *beaten paths,* or migration routes taken by family or friends who previously made the move. Previous immigrants can reduce the costs for prospective immigrants by providing vital information and connections.

(2) Age too is a factor affecting the migration decision, with immigrants more likely to be younger than older. Younger workers can expect to accumulate more earnings benefits from the move because of their longer life spans. In addition, younger workers have lower opportunity costs, more flexibility, and fewer family responsibilities than older workers.

(3) Other factors can affect the migration decision too such as English-language skills, lower tax rates, more entrepreneurial opportunities, or interest in the future welfare of children.

3. The **economic effects of immigration** involve personal gain, but also influence wage rates, efficiency, output, and income shares.

a. The large inflows of legal and illegal immigrants to the United States are evidence that there is personal gain in the form of higher real wages from securing a job and working in the United States.

(1) Nevertheless, the move may not produce the expected gains for some immigrants, so there can be major *backflows,* or return migration to the home country.

(2) Although immigrants, on average, improve their standard of living, they may not achieve pay parity with native-born workers if there is a lack of work *skill transferability,* especially for those workers with poor English-language skills.

(3) *Self-selection* may be a factor that helps to overcome some of the lack of skill transferability because only those immigrants who are strongly motivated to succeed make the move. The potential may be greatest for those immigrants who bring a high skill level (e.g., engineers or scientists).

b. The impact of immigration on wage rates, efficiency, and output can be shown in a two-nation model, with one low-wage nation (Mexico) and one high-wage nation (the United States). The movement of workers from Mexico raises the average wages of workers in Mexico and lowers the average wage rates in the United States. Domestic output in Mexico will decline and domestic output in the United States will expand, but the net effect from an overall perspective is an increase in output and economic efficiency. The elimination of barriers to the international flow of labor can provide overall *efficiency gains from migration* because the same number of workers will produce more output.

c. Immigration has three effects on output or income shares.

(1) Output in the United States will increase, but output will decrease in Mexico. This outcome helps explain why the United States has high annual quotas for immigration. Some poorer nations, however, may discourage emigration of their highly educated workers because such outflows of skilled labor create a **brain drain** in a nation.

(2) The wage income falls for native-born U.S. workers and rises for native-born Mexican workers who stay in Mexico. Total wage income (for native-born plus immigrant workers) in a nation may increase or decrease depending on the elasticity of labor demand. For example, if labor demand is elastic, a wage decrease will increase total wage income.

(3) The incomes of businesses in the United States will increase, but the incomes of businesses will decrease in Mexico because the United States gains "cheap" labor and Mexico loses "cheap" labor.

d. The conclusions from the model must be adjusted to take into account *complexity and modifications.*

(1) There is a cost to migration for workers that will reduce the world gain in output which wage differences between the two nations will not equalize.

(2) **Remittances** reduce the gains from immigration for the United States. If immigrant workers send some of their increased wage income to relatives in Mexico, then some income gain for the U.S. economy is lost to Mexico. Such remittances help explain why Mexico favors liberal U.S. immigration laws. In addition, the return of immigrant workers from the United States to Mexico creates an output and income loss for the United States. Such backflows alter output and income gains and losses.

(3) Whether workers in a domestic U.S. industry see their incomes fall because of the immigration of labor from Mexico depends on whether the workers in an industry are **complementary resources** or **substitute resources.** If such workers are complementary resources, then the lower wage rates caused by immigration may increase the demand for all labor because of an output effect and thus create more employment and income.

(4) The model assumes that the stock of capital is constant, but immigration can change investment in capital goods. In the long run an increase in business income in the United States from immigration may increase the rate of return on capital and stimulate more capital investment. The additional capital may increase labor productivity, lower production costs, and lower prices, and thus increase the demand for labor and increase wages. Conversely, the inflow of immigrants from Mexico into low-wage and labor-intensive occupations such agricultural harvesting in the United States may stifle capital investment in such industries.

(5) The model assumes full employment in both nations. If there is unemployment or underemployment in Mexico, it can increase domestic output in Mexico when the surplus workers move to the United States. And such immigrant workers may be less motivated and capable than the native-born Mexican workers who stay in Mexico. Such a **negative self-selection** may be a reason Mexico opposes strict border enforcement. Native-born workers in the United States may prefer strong border enforcement if such negative self-selection means that the immigrant workers wind up being unemployed in the United States and require more government support that eventually decreases the after-tax income of U.S. domestic workers.

e. Immigration can affect government tax revenues and spending. If immigrants take advantage of welfare benefits in the United States, it imposes an additional cost on the nation. Prior to the 1970s immigrants were less likely to receive public assistance than domestic residents, but between the 1970s and 1998 immigrants used the welfare system more than domestic residents because more of the immigrants were low-skill workers. Welfare reform in 1996 reduced this public assistance at the Federal level because the eligibility requirements for immigrants were changed to add a five-year waiting period. State and local governments, however, have to bear the burden of increased spending for public schools, health care, and other government services used by low-income immigrants.

f. The research findings indicate that immigration increases output and incomes in the United States and that the nation benefits from the human capital obtained from highly skilled immigrant workers. The effect of immigration on the wages of native-born U.S. workers is less certain, and estimates range from minus 3% to plus 2%. Immigration appears to reduce the wages of native-born U.S. workers with low education, and also perhaps reduces the wages of highly trained native-born U.S. workers.

4. The **debate over illegal immigration** has heated up because more low-skilled jobs are being filled by illegal immigrants. Their entry into the domestic labor markets for low-skilled workers is viewed as lowering wage rates and placing greater demands on public goods and services. A labor supply and demand model is used to evaluate these concerns.

a. The effects of illegal workers in a market for low-wage labor can be shown in a demand and supply graph that has a demand curve for labor and *two* supply curves. One supply curve is for domestic workers only and it is left of the total supply curve for all workers (domestic plus illegal). In equilibrium, the wage rate for all workers (domestic and illegal) will be lower than the wage rate for domestic workers alone. The model shows that the lower wage rate for all workers does reduce the employment of some of the domestic workers. Such domestic workers require a **compensating wage differential** to attract them to this otherwise undesirable work. The substitution of illegal workers for domestic workers, however, is not one-for-one, and it is less than the total amount of employment created by having both illegal and domestic workers in the labor force.

b. The model shows that the entry of illegal workers into low-wage markets for labor reduces wage rates in that market. The overall effect of immigration on average wages is either slightly negative or slightly positive. If illegal workers are complementary resources for domestic workers, the lower wage rate caused by the entry of illegal workers into a labor market can increase the demand for domestic workers in a complementary labor market. If, however, illegal workers are a substitute for domestic workers, the wage rates for domestic workers will decline. From a national or overall perspective, illegal workers do not affect the average wage rate for all workers because it is dependent on worker productivity, not illegal immigration.

c. The entry of illegal workers into particular industries puts downward pressure on the prices of goods and services produced by those industries. The lower prices for goods and services produced by these illegal workers can help increase the standard of living for all Americans.

d. Illegal immigration places a sizable burden on state and local governments with high concentrations of illegal immigrants because they use school, health care, and other public goods. Such immigrants pay for some of these public costs through sales taxes, gasoline taxes, and the property taxes built into rent. The state and local fiscal burdens for each low-skill immigrant household are estimated to be as high as $9,000 per year and for all such households in total about $50 billion annually. There is a lesser burden on the Federal government than on state and local governments because illegal immigrants do not receive much Federal assistance, but they do pay payroll taxes and income taxes.

e. There are other concerns about illegal immigration. It can undermine respect and support for laws and increase crime rates. It is unfair to legal immigrants who follow proper rules and procedures to enter the nation. There also are risks to national security from weak enforcement of borders.

5. Economic analysis can improve the discussion over immigration because the analysis suggests that immigration can make a positive or negative contribution to a nation, depending on such factors as the number of immigrants, the nation's capacity to absorb them into the economy, their level of education and skills, and their work ethic. Immigration is not an all-or-nothing decision. Economic analysis shows that a nation should expand its immigration until the marginal benefit equals the marginal cost. Also, some immigrants create more benefits than other immigrants, so not all immigrants should be thought of as the same.

6. (Last Word). Immigration quotas have been a mainstay of immigration law and reform since the 1920s although the preferences in the quotas and the legal limits have changed over time. In more recent years, the major concern with immigration has been with illegal immigration. In 2006, there were an estimated 12 million illegal immigrants residing in the United States. An attempt was made in 2007 in the U.S. Senate to address the illegal immigration issue with many proposed reforms, such as improved monitoring of the U.S. border, increased fines for employers hiring illegal immigrants, amnesty for illegal immigrants, and a guest-worker program. The reform legislation failed to pass and the debate over what to do continues.

■ HINTS AND TIPS

1. This chapter deals with the issue of immigration, which can provoke emotional reactions. Make sure you remember the distinction between *positive* and *normative* economics made in Chapter 1. The purpose of the chapter is to analyze and explain the economics of immigration (*what is*), and not the ideal world (*what ought to be*).

2. The graph in Figure 22.3 presents a simple model of immigration between two nations that shows only the demand curve for each nation and how the change in the equilibrium wage in each nation changes the quantity of labor. The wage rate is plotted on the vertical axis and the quantity of labor is on the horizontal axis. The graph shows how immigration affects the wage rate, employment, and domestic output. Problem 1 in this chapter will help you master this material.

■ IMPORTANT TERMS

economic immigrants	brain drain
legal immigrants	remittances
unauthorized (illegal) immigrants	complementary resources
H1-B provision	substitute resources
human capital	negative self-selection
beaten paths	
backflows	compensating wage differential
skill transferability	
self-selection	
efficiency gains from migration	

SELF-TEST

■ FILL-IN QUESTIONS

1. U.S. immigration consists of two basic types: those immigrants who have government permission to reside and work in the United States and are referred to as (legal, illegal) _____ immigrants, and those immigrants who are not authorized to reside or work in the United States, and are referred to as _____ immigrants.

2. In 2006, the number of legal immigrants to the United States was about (1.27, 9.54) _____ million. Almost two-thirds of legal U.S. immigrants get their legal status through ties to (employment, family) _____. The leading nation for legal immigration is (Russia, Mexico) _____.

3. The net annual flow of illegal immigrants is about (350, 950) _____ thousand. The number of illegal immigrants who reside continuously in the United States is about (2, 12) _____ million, and of this group, about half are from (China, Mexico) _____.

4. List three main reasons why people immigrate into the United States:

a. _____

b. _____

c. _____

5. Other things equal, if there are larger wage differences between nations, then incentives (increase, decrease) _____ for migrating to the nations providing higher-wage opportunities. An example of a "magnet country" that attracts a lot of immigrants would be (Vietnam, Australia) _____.

6. Immigration can be viewed as a(n) (consumption, investment) _____ decision. A person will migrate if he or she estimates that the stream of future earnings in a new nation is (less than, greater than) _____ the explicit and implicit costs of moving.

7. Other things equal, the greater the distance a person has to travel to migrate to another country the (more, less) _____ likely the person is to migrate; also, workers who migrate are _____ likely to be younger in age.

8. In general, the constant flow of immigrants to the United States indicates that the economic benefits to immigrants are (greater, less) _____ than the costs, but some immigrants may return to their home nation if they conclude that the benefits are _____ than the costs. Such return migration is referred to as (self-selection, backflows) _____.

9. The simple model of immigration shows that the movement of workers from a poor nation (Mexico) to a rich nation (United States) (increases, decreases) _____ wage rates in Mexico and _____ wage rates in the United States.

10. Movement of labor from Mexico to the United States (increases, decreases) _____ the real output of goods and services in the United States and _____ the real output of goods and services in Mexico, but from a combined or overall perspective, the total output _____ indicating that there are efficiency (gains, losses) _____ from migration.

11. The outflow of highly educated workers from one nation to another nation is commonly called a (self-selection, brain drain) _____, and this may be one reason why some nations that provide subsidized education for citizens (support, oppose) _____ such outflows.

12. Although an inflow of workers from Mexico to the United States will decrease wage rates in the United States, if the demand for labor in the United States is

elastic it will (increase, decrease) _____ total wage income, but if the demand for labor is inelastic, it will _____ total wage income.

13. Unrestricted immigration of workers into the United States from Mexico will (increase, decrease) _____ business incomes in the United States and _____ business incomes in Mexico because the United States is (losing, gaining) _____ "cheap" labor and Mexico is _____ "cheap" labor.

14. The simplified model of immigration of workers into the United States from Mexico assumes that migration is costless. If there are costs to migration, then wage rates will remain somewhat (higher, lower) _____ in the United States, but the wage-rate difference between the two nations (will, will not) _____ encourage more migration of workers from Mexico to close the gap because the cost of migration is (greater, less) _____ than the expected benefit.

15. When Mexican workers who have immigrated to the United States send some of their wage income back to Mexico, they are making (remittances, backflows) _____, which can reduce the net gain from migration; and if some of these Mexican workers gain labor market skills in the United States and then return home, these _____ can reduce the net gains from migration.

16. If immigrant workers and domestic-born workers are complementary resources, then the lower wage rate resulting from large-scale immigration (increases, decreases) _____ production costs and creates an output effect that _____ the demand for labor.

17. The simple model of immigration assumes (full, partial) _____ employment, but in many cases Mexican workers are either unemployed or underemployed, and if these unemployed or underemployed Mexican workers immigrate into the United States, they (raise, lower) _____ the net gain from migration for Mexico. The movement of such workers may reflect (negative, positive) _____ self-selection if these workers who move are less capable or less motivated.

18. The introduction of illegal workers in the domestic U.S. labor market, (increases, decreases) _____ the total supply of workers and _____ the wage rate from what it would be without illegal workers, and _____ the number of domestic workers employed. The deportation of illegal workers (will, will not) _____ increase the wage rate for domestic workers, but the employment of domestic workers _____ increase on a one-for-one basis because the quantity supplied of domestic workers is less than the total demand for workers.

19. The entry of illegal workers into certain low-wage occupations will (increase, decrease) _____ the wage rate, but the overall effect of illegal immigration on average wage rates can be slightly positive if illegal workers are a (substitute, complementary) _____ resource for some domestic workers, or slightly negative if the illegal workers are a _____ for some domestic workers.

20. If illegal workers provide important help for producing goods and services in the U.S. economy, then prices of those goods and services will be (higher, lower) _____ than they otherwise would be without those illegal workers, and the standard of living for Americans will be _____.

■ **TRUE–FALSE QUESTIONS**

Circle T if the statement is true, F if it is false.

1. More than 10 million immigrants enter the United States each year, about half of whom are legal and the other half illegal.   **T   F**

2. The largest bulk of legal U.S. immigrants obtain their legal status via family ties to American residents.   **T   F**

3. The top country of origin for illegal immigrants is Cuba.   **T   F**

4. The main driver of economic immigration is the opportunity to improve the immigrant's earnings and standard of living.   **T   F**

5. Other things equal, larger wage differences between nations weaken the incentive to migrate and therefore increase the flow of immigrants toward the country providing the greater wage opportunities.   **T   F**

6. Immigration can be viewed as an investment decision because the prospective immigrant weighs all the costs of moving against the expected benefits.   **T   F**

7. Immigrants often reduce their costs of long moves by following beaten paths, which are routes taken previously by family, relatives, and friends.   **T   F**

8. From an economic perspective, a person who estimates that the stream of future earnings exceeds the explicit and implicit cost of moving is likely to migrate.   **T   F**

9. Younger workers are much less likely to migrate than older workers.   **T   F**

10. Immigrants who lack English language skills do not, in general, fare as well in the U.S. workforce as immigrants who have those skills when they arrive in the United States.   **T   F**

11. The sizable and continuous flow of immigrants to the United States shows that, overall, the economic benefits of immigration into the United States are greater than the costs for those who make the move.   **T   F**

12. Return migration or backflows seldom occur when people immigrate into the United States from other nations.   **T   F**

13. The lack of skill transferability means that although migrants may increase their wages through immigration into the United States, they may not earn as much as similarly employed domestic workers.   **T   F**

14. Economic immigration is characterized by self-selection, which means that migrants who choose to move may be more motivated and able to overcome the lack of skill transferability.   **T   F**

15. The simple demand and supply model of immigration suggests that the movement of workers from a low-wage nation to a high-wage nation decreases domestic output in the high-wage nation and increases domestic output in the low-wage nation.   **T   F**

16. An increase in the mobility of labor because of the elimination of barriers to the international flows of labor tends to increase the world's output of goods and services.   **T   F**

17. Brain drain in immigration refers to the fact that the rate of immigration is higher among illegal than legal workers.   **T   F**

18. If the demand for labor is elastic in the United States, then a decrease in wages from immigration will increase total wage income.   **T   F**

19. Mexican workers who have migrated to the United States and send remittances to their families in Mexico increase the gain to domestic output in the United States and reduce it in Mexico.   **T   F**

20. If immigrant workers and domestic-born workers are complementary resources, then the lower wage rate that results from large-scale immigration will create an output effect that increases the demand for labor among these domestic-born workers.   **T   F**

21. When unemployed or underemployed laborers from a poor nation migrate to a rich nation, the poor nation suffers a loss in domestic output because it loses workers.   **T   F**

22. The immigration of workers into the United States reduces domestic output and income in the U.S. economy.   **T   F**

23. In a market for low-wage labor in the United States, an increase in illegal workers increases the supply of labor in such markets and reduces the wage rate.   **T   F**

24. If illegal workers provide a substantial amount of low-wage labor in a particular industry, then the prices of goods and services in that industry will be higher.   **T   F**

25. Illegal immigration tends to impose a higher net fiscal burden on state and local governments.   **T   F**

■ **MULTIPLE-CHOICE QUESTIONS**

Circle the letter that corresponds to the best answer.

1. Immigrants who have permission to reside and work in the United States are:
(a) aliens
(b) legal immigrants
(c) illegal immigrants
(d) undocumented workers

2. The H1-B provision of the immigration law allows:
(a) high-skilled workers in specialty occupations to enter and work continuously in the United States for six years
(b) low-skilled workers in the agricultural industry to enter and work on a temporary basis during harvest season
(c) "green card" holders to stay in the United States on an indefinite basis
(d) the immediate deportation of those individuals who enter the United States illegally

3. Which one of the following is the major category for legal immigration?
(a) Diversity
(b) Refugee status
(c) Family sponsorship
(d) Employment-based preferences

4. What is the approximate number of legal and illegal immigrants who entered the United States *per year* in a recent year (2006)?
(a) 350 thousand legal and 105 thousand illegal
(b) 556 thousand legal and 221 thousand illegal
(c) 1.27 million legal and 350 thousand illegal
(d) 8.45 million legal and 3.47 million illegal

5. Which nation accounts for most of the legal immigrants admitted to the United States each year and also is the source of the largest number of illegal immigrants?
(a) China
(b) India
(c) Cuba
(d) Mexico

6. By moving from a low-wage nation to a high-wage nation, immigrants can increase the value of their
(a) backflows
(b) remittances
(c) brain drains
(d) human capital

7. Which nation would be considered a "magnet country" that attracts a lot of immigrants?
(a) Japan
(b) Sweden
(c) Australia
(d) South Korea

8. Other things equal, which person is more likely to migrate to the United States to work?
(a) A younger worker, who lives in a nation near the United States
(b) An older worker, who lives in a nation near the United States
(c) A younger worker, who lives in a nation far from the United States
(d) An older worker, who lives in a nation far from the United States

9. If there is full employment in both nations and unimpeded immigration, the effect of the migration of workers from a low-wage nation to a high-wage nation is to increase the
(a) average wage rate in the high-wage nation
(b) domestic output in the high-wage nation
(c) business incomes in the low-wage nation
(d) domestic output in the low-wage nation

10. In general, the elimination of barriers to the international flow of labor tends to
(a) lower the wage rates for high-skilled labor
(b) raise the wage rates for high-skilled labor
(c) create worldwide efficiency gains from migration
(d) eliminate worldwide efficiency gains from migration

Answer questions 11, 12, 13, and 14 on the basis of the following graph that shows a simple model of unimpeded immigration from Mexico to the United States as described in your textbook.

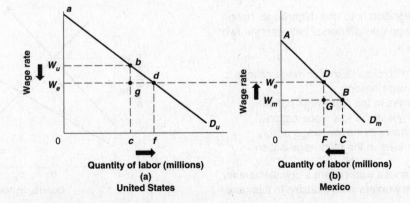

Quantity of labor (millions)
(a)
United States

Quantity of labor (millions)
(b)
Mexico

11. Before immigration is allowed from Mexico to the United States, what will be the wage rate and quantity of labor employed in each nation?
  (a) U.S.: W_u and c Mexico: W_m and C
  (b) U.S.: W_e and f Mexico: W_m and C
  (c) U.S.: W_u and c Mexico: W_e and F
  (d) U.S.: W_e and f Mexico: W_e and F

12. After immigration is allowed from Mexico to the United States, what will be the wage rate and quantity of labor employed in each nation?
  (a) U.S.: W_u and c Mexico: W_m and C
  (b) U.S.: W_e and f Mexico: W_m and C
  (c) U.S.: W_u and c Mexico: W_e and F
  (d) U.S.: W_e and f Mexico: W_e and F

13. With unimpeded immigration, what will happen to domestic output in the United States and in Mexico?
  (a) increase in the U.S. from $0abc$ to $0adf$ and increase in Mexico from $0ADF$ to $0ABC$
  (b) increase in the U.S. from $0abc$ to $0adf$ and decrease in Mexico from $0ABC$ to $0ADF$
  (c) decrease in the U.S. from $0adf$ to $0abc$ and decrease in Mexico from $0ABC$ to $0ADF$
  (d) decrease in the U.S. from $0adf$ to $0abc$ and increase in Mexico from $0ADF$ to $0ABC$

14. With unimpeded immigration, what will happen to business income in the United States and in Mexico?
  (a) decrease in the U.S. from W_ead to W_uab to and decrease in Mexico from W_mAB to W_eAD
  (b) increase in the U.S. from W_uab to W_ead and increase in Mexico from W_eAD to W_mAB
  (c) increase in the U.S. from W_uab to W_ead and decrease in Mexico from W_mAB to W_eAD
  (d) decrease in the U.S. from W_ead to W_uab and increase in Mexico from W_eAD to W_mAB

15. If the cost of migration from a low-wage nation to a high-wage nation is high, it
  (a) increases immigration into the high-wage nation and keeps some of the wage-rate difference between the two nations
  (b) increases immigration into the high-wage nation and closes the wage-rate difference between the two nations
  (c) reduces immigration into the high-wage nation and keeps some of the wage-rate difference between the two nations
  (d) reduces immigration into the high-wage nation and closes the wage-rate difference between the two nations

16. Remittances from immigrants in high-wage nations to their families in low-wage nations
  (a) increase incomes in the high-wage nation
  (b) increase incomes in the low-wage nation
  (c) increase backflows in the low-wage nation
  (d) increase backflows in the high-wage nation

17. Assume that American workers are a complementary resource to immigrant workers in an industry. In this case,

an increase in the number of immigrant workers in this industry will
  (a) lower production costs and increase the demand for all labor in the industry
  (b) raise production costs and increase the demand for all labor in the industry
  (c) lower production costs and decrease the demand for all labor in the industry
  (d) raise production costs and decrease the demand for all labor in the industry

18. In the long run, some of the adverse wage effects of immigration on native-born workers may be mitigated by
  (a) negative self-selection by unemployed workers
  (b) compensating wage differentials for immigrants
  (c) greater incentives for investment in capital goods to boost productivity
  (d) more expenditures by state and local governments to cover the cost of immigration

19. Which would increase the gains realized in a low-wage nation from the migration of its workers to a high-wage nation?
  (a) An increase in the explicit and implicit costs of migration
  (b) A decline in the remittances of migrants to their low-wage nation
  (c) An increase in the migration of unemployed workers from the low-wage nation to the high-wage nation
  (d) A reduction in the welfare benefits in the high-wage nation for immigrants who come from a low-wage nation

20. The research evidence indicates that the overall effect of immigration on the average American wage ranges from
  (a) zero to plus 10 percent
  (b) minus 3 percent to plus 2 percent
  (c) plus 8 percent to plus 12 percent
  (d) minus 8 percent to minus 12 percent

Answer questions 21, 22, and 23 on the basis of the following graph which shows the market for unskilled labor in agriculture. The demand for labor is shown by the demand curve D. The supply of domestic-born workers is shown by supply curve S_d. The total supply of domestic-born and illegal workers is shown by supply curve S_t.

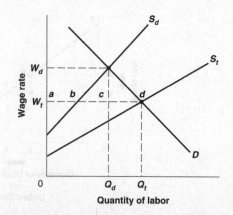

21. If there are only domestic-born workers in this market, the equilibrium wage rate and quantity of workers employed will be:

(a) W_d and Q_d

(b) W_t and Q_t

(c) W_d and Q_t

(d) W_t and Q_d

22. At a low wage of W_t what will be the quantity of domestic-born workers who will be employed and what will be the quantity of illegal workers who will be employed?

(a) bd domestic-born workers and ac illegal workers

(b) cd domestic-born worker and ab illegal workers

(c) ab domestic-born workers and bd illegal workers

(d) ac domestic-born workers and cd illegal workers

23. If illegal immigrants were originally able to work in this market, but then were excluded, the employment of domestic-born workers would increase by:

(a) ac and the total employment of all workers would increase by cd

(b) bc and the total employment of all workers would decrease by cd

(c) ab and the total employment of all workers would increase by bc

(d) ac and the total employment of all workers would decrease by cd

24. Which of the following statements is generally valid about illegal immigration?

(a) It imposes a high net fiscal burden on state and local governments.

(b) It raises the prices for products in those industries where illegal workers are concentrated.

(c) It reduces the standard of living of all Americans and their families.

(d) It increases the employment of domestic-born workers on a one-to-one basis for the number of illegal workers who are deported.

25. From a strictly economic perspective, nations seeking to maximize net benefits from immigration should

(a) expand immigration because it benefits society with a greater supply of products and increased demand for them

(b) contract immigration because the benefits are minor and it reduces the wage rates of domestic workers

(c) expand immigration until its marginal benefits equal its marginal costs

(d) contract immigration until the extra welfare cost for taxpayers is zero

■ **PROBLEMS**

1. The two tables at the top of next column show the demands for labor and the levels of domestic output that can be produced at each level of employment in two countries, **A** and **B**.

Country A		
Wage rate	Quantity of labor demanded	Real output
$20	95	$1900
18	100	1990
16	105	2070
14	110	2140
12	115	2200
10	120	2250
8	125	2290

Country B		
Wage rate	Quantity of labor demanded	Real output
$20	10	$200
18	15	290
16	20	370
14	25	440
12	30	500
10	35	550
8	40	590

a. If there were full employment in both countries and if

(1) the labor force in Country **A** were 110, the wage rate in Country **A** would be $_____.

(2) the labor force in Country **B** were 40, the wage rate in Country **B** would be $_____.

b. With these labor forces and wage rates

(1) total wages paid in **A** would be $_____ and the incomes of businesses (capitalists) in **A** would be $_____. (*Hint:* Subtract total wages paid from the real output.)

(2) total wages paid in **B** would be $_____ and business incomes in **B** would be $_____.

c. Assume the difference between the wage rates in the two countries induces 5 workers to migrate from **B** to **A**. So long as both countries maintain full employment,

(1) the wage rate in **A** would (rise, fall) _____ to $_____,

(2) and the wage rate in **B** would _____ to $_____.

d. The movement of workers from **B** to **A** would

(1) (increase, decrease) _____ the output of **A** by $_____,

(2) (increase, decrease) _____ the output of **B** by $_____, and

(3) (increase, decrease) _____ their combined (and the world's) output by $_____.

e. This movement of workers from **B** to **A** also (increased, decreased) _____ business incomes in **A** by $_____ and (increased, decreased) business incomes in **B** by $ _____.

2. Consider the following wage and quantity of labor data for a low-wage market. The demand column shows the quantity of labor demanded at each wage rate. The domestic supply column shows the number of domestic-born workers willing to work at each wage rate. The total supply column shows the total number of workers (domestic-born plus illegal immigrants) who are willing to work at each wage rate.

Wage rate	Demand	Domestic supply	Total supply
$14	200	400	1100
13	300	300	900
12	400	200	700
11	500	100	500
10	600	0	300

a. What will be the equilibrium wage rate if there is no illegal immigration? _____ What is the quantity of domestic-born workers employed at this wage rate? _____

b. What will be the equilibrium wage rate if there is illegal immigration in this low-wage industry? _____ What is the quantity of total workers (domestic-born and illegal) employed at this wage rate? _____

c. At the equilibrium wage rate for total workers, how many workers will be domestic-born? _____ How many will be illegal workers? _____

d. How many more domestic-born workers will be employed if the wage rate for total workers rises to the wage rate for domestic-born workers only? _____ What is this compensating wage differential? _____

e. Do illegal workers reduce the employment of domestic-born workers by an amount equal to the employment of illegal workers? (Yes or No) _____ With illegal immigration, there are _____ illegal workers employed. If they are prevented from working, the employment of domestic-born workers at the total supply wage rate would only be _____ workers, and thus there would be another _____ illegal workers not replaced by domestic workers at this total supply wage rate.

■ **SHORT ANSWER AND ESSAY QUESTIONS**

1. Describe the numbers and trends in legal immigration in recent years. From where do most illegal immigrants come to the United States and for what reason do they get admitted?

2. Describe the estimated number of illegal immigrants who come annually, and also those who reside continuously, in the United States.

3. Use the concept of human capital to explain how earnings opportunities affect the decision to migrate.

4. How do moving costs affect the decision to migrate? What are these costs?

5. Discuss how distance, age, and other factors influence the decision to migrate.

6. How does the lack of skill transferability affect the wages earned by immigrants? What role does self-selection play in overcoming the wage differential?

7. Explain the effects of the migration of labor from a low-wage nation to a high-wage nation. Give your answer in terms of the effects on the wage rate, domestic output, and business incomes in the two nations.

8. Why might some high-wage nations encourage a relatively high level of immigration through its quotas? Why might some low-wage nations want to restrict the emigration of highly educated workers?

9. How does the cost of migration create rather than eliminate a wage gap between the equilibrium wages for workers in a high-wage nation and workers in a low-wage nation in similar industries?

10. What are remittances? What effect do they have on the gains and losses from the migration of labor from a low-wage nation to a high-wage nation?

11. Explain the economic effect on the demand for domestic labor when immigrant labor is a complementary resource rather than a substitute resource.

12. How might capital investment be affected by the use of immigrant labor? Describe a positive and negative scenario.

13. What effects will unemployment or underemployment in a low-wage nation have on the gains from the migration of workers to a high-wage nation?

14. Discuss the effects of immigrants on tax revenues and government spending in the United States? Which unit of government bears the largest net fiscal burden?

15. Offer a brief summary of the research findings about immigration on wages.

16. Describe the employment effects of illegal immigration for domestic-born workers in a low-wage industry in the United States. Do illegal workers fill most jobs that domestic-born workers do not want? Is the substitution one-for-one?

17. Why does illegal immigration have very little effect on the average level of wages in the United States?

18. What are the price effects from illegal immigration? In what way does illegal immigration affect the standard of living?

19. Describe the fiscal impact of illegal immigration and other concerns with it.

20. Explain from an economic perspective how a nation finds an optimal level of immigration.

ANSWERS

Chapter 22 Immigration

FILL-IN QUESTIONS

1. legal, illegal
2. 1.27, family, Mexico
3. 350, 12, Mexico
4. *a.* take advantage of employment opportunities; *b.* escape political or religious persecution; *c.* reunite with family or loved ones
5. increase, Australia
6. investment, greater than
7. less, more
8. greater, less, backflows
9. increases, decreases
10. increases, decreases, increases, gains
11. brain drain, oppose
12. increase, decrease,
13. increase, decrease, gaining, losing
14. higher, will not, greater
15. remittances, backflows
16. decreases, increases
17. full, raise, negative
18. increases, decreases, decreases, will, will not
19. decrease, complementary, substitute
20. lower, higher

TRUE–FALSE QUESTIONS

1. F, pp. 450–451
2. T, p. 451
3. F, p. 451
4. T, p. 451
5. F, p. 452
6. T, p. 452
7. T, p. 453
8. T, p. 452
9. F, p. 453
10. T, p. 453
11. T, p. 453
12. F, p. 454
13. T, p. 454
14. T, p. 454
15. F, p. 455
16. T, p. 455
17. F, p. 456
18. T, p. 456
19. F, p. 456
20. T, p. 457
21. F, pp. 457–458
22. F, p. 458
23. T, p. 459
24. F, p. 459
25. T, p. 462

MULTIPLE-CHOICE QUESTIONS

1. b, p. 450
2. a, p. 450
3. c, pp. 450–451
4. c, p. 451
5. d, p.451
6. d, pp. 451–452
7. c, p. 452
8. a, pp. 452–453
9. b, p. 455
10. c, p. 455
11. a, p. 455
12. d, p. 455
13. b, p. 455
14. c, p. 456
15. c, p. 456
16. b, p. 457
17. a, p. 457
18. c, p. 457
19. c, p. 457
20. b, p. 458
21. a, p. 459
22. c, p. 459
23. b, p. 459
24. a, p. 460
25. c, p. 462

PROBLEMS

1. *a.* (1) 14, (2) 8; *b.* (1) 1540, 600, (2) 320, 270; *c.* (1) fall, 12, (2) rise, 10; *d.* (1) increase, 60, (2) decrease, 40, (3) increase, 20; *e.* increased, 220, decreased, 70
2. *a.* $13, 300; *b.* $11, 500; *c.* 100, 400; *d.* 100 $2; *e.* no, 400, 200, 200

SHORT ANSWER AND ESSAY QUESTIONS

1. pp. 450–451
2. p. 451
3. pp. 451–452
4. p. 451
5. pp. 452–453
6. p. 454
7. pp. 454–456
8. p. 455
9. p. 456
10. pp. 456–457
11. p. 457
12. p. 457
13. pp. 457–458
14. p. 458
15. p. 458
16. pp. 459–460
17. p. 460
18. p. 460
19. p. 460
20. p. 462

Introduction to Macroeconomics

The purpose of this chapter is to introduce you to **macroeconomics,** which studies the entire economy or its major aspects such as consumption and investment. Macroeconomics is concerned with both short-run fluctuations that create conditions giving rise to an up-and-down **business cycle** and also long-run trends for economic growth that bring rising living standards.

The monitoring of the macro economy requires measures of performance. Three such measures are briefly described in this chapter; more will be explained about them in later chapters. Real gross domestic product or **real GDP** provides an overall indicator of output or production in the economy. **Unemployment** measures the degree to which labor resources are being fully used in the economy. **Inflation** tracks the overall increase in the level of prices in the economy. Each measure is important for tracking the short-run and long-run health of the economy and for creating macroeconomic models to address important policy questions.

Since the late 1770s we have witnessed the miracle of **modern economic growth.** Before that time economic output per person had remained relatively constant, but since that time economic output per person has risen substantially and along with it the standard of living in those nations that have experienced such growth. In fact, much of the difference between rich and poor nations today can be attributed to their historical participation in this modern economic growth, as you will learn in a later chapter in this section of the textbook. To achieve such economic growth requires savings and investment and a banking and financial system to allocate resources to economic investment in newly created capital goods.

The **expectations** that people hold are important for macroeconomics because they influence economic behavior. When business firms expect economic conditions to be bad, they are less likely to invest in new plant and equipment and not taking these actions can reduce future economic growth. And when expectations go unmet, they can be experienced as **economic shocks** to the economy that can change economic decisions. Although there are both demand shocks and supply shocks in a macro economy, the focus of the attention in the chapter is on *demand* shocks because they result in the short-run fluctuations that can significantly change output and employment.

To understand what happens when there is a demand shock to the economy the chapter makes a distinction between situations in which there are flexible prices and those in which there are inflexible prices (or "sticky

prices"). If prices are perfectly flexible in an economy, then a change or shock from demand results in a change in the overall level of prices. If, however, prices are inflexible or sticky as they often are in the short run, then a change in demand results in a change in output and employment in the economy. As you will learn from this introductory chapter, the macroeconomic models that will be presented in more detail in later chapters can be categorized based on whether prices are considered to be flexible or inflexible and whether there is a short-run or long-run time horizon.

■ **CHECKLIST**

When you have studied this chapter you should be able to

☐ Explain what macroeconomics studies are.
☐ Define real gross domestic product or real GDP.
☐ Distinguish between real GDP and nominal GDP.
☐ Explain why unemployment is a loss to the economy.
☐ Describe the problem that inflation presents to the economy.
☐ Give examples of the types of policy questions that are investigated with the use of macroeconomic models.
☐ Compare economic growth in ancient and preindustrial times with modern economic growth.
☐ Explain how participating or not participating in modern economic growth accounts for differences in the standards of living of nations.
☐ Offer some comparisons of GDP per person across rich and poor nations.
☐ Define savings and investment.
☐ Distinguish between economic investment and financial investment.
☐ Explain why savings and investment are so important for economic growth.
☐ Discuss the role of banks and other financial institutions as related to savings and investment in the economy.
☐ Explain why macroeconomics must take into account expectations and shocks.
☐ Distinguish between demand shocks and supply shocks.
☐ Discuss why demand shocks present a major problem for the macro economy.
☐ Illustrate graphically what happens for a firm when there is a demand shock and prices are flexible.
☐ Illustrate graphically what happens for a firm when there is a demand shocks and prices are inflexible or sticky.

□ Explain how firms use inventories to adjust to demand shocks.

□ Describe the effects of demand shocks on output, employment, and inventories in an economy when prices are inflexible.

□ Cite economic evidence on the stickiness of prices.

□ Present two reasons for why prices are often inflexible in the short run.

□ Categorize macroeconomic models on the basis of price flexibility and time perspective.

□ Explain the possible relationship between the use of computerized inventory tracking systems and recessions (Last Word).

■ **CHAPTER OUTLINE**

1. This chapter is an introduction to **macroeconomics,** which studies the behavior of the whole economy, or its major aggregates such as consumption and investment. It focuses on two topics: long-run economic growth and short-run changes in output and employment (the **business cycle**). The long-term growth trend leads to higher output and standards of living for an economy, but along the way there can be short-run variability that produces a decline in output (**recession**). The purpose of the chapter is to give an overview of the major performance measures for the economy and then preview the short-run and long-run macro models that will be described in more detail in later chapters.

2. Several performance measures are used for tracking the macro economy and to develop policies to address short-run or long-run conditions or problems.

   a. Real gross domestic product, or **real GDP,** is a measure of the value of final goods and services produced by the domestic economy during a time period, typically a year. The term real refers to the fact that in comparing the value of GDP (prices times quantities) from one year to the next, prices are held constant so only quantities of goods and services produced by the economy (or real output) changes. Output also can be measured by **nominal GDP.** There is a problem with this measure for measuring output changes because both prices and quantities change from one year to the next.

   b. Unemployment is a condition that arises when a person who is willing to work seeks a job but does not find one. High rates of unemployment mean that an economy is not fully employing its labor resources, which reduces potential production and leads to other social problems.

   c. Inflation is an increase in the general level of prices. Prices for individual products can rise or fall, but if there is a rise in prices overall, then an economy is experiencing inflation. Inflation erodes the purchasing power of incomes and reduces the value of savings.

   d. Policymakers seek to maximize economic growth and at the same time minimize the adverse effects of unemployment and inflation. To do so, they construct

macroeconomic models to assess the short-run and long-run performance of the economy. Such models can be useful for addressing important macroeconomic questions such as what can be done by government policies to control information or foster long-run economic growth.

3. In ancient times and in the preindustrial periods of human history, the characteristic of economic growth was that output would increase, but so would the population. As a consequence, output per person remained fairly constant and living standards stayed about the same. With the Industrial Revolution of the late 1700s, however, economies experienced **modern economic growth** in which output per person and standards of living increased. Such growth explains the large differences in living standards today among nations. Richer nations have a longer history of modern economic growth than poorer nations.

   a. Economic growth depends on devoting some current output to increase future output. This process involves the use of savings (when current spending is less than current income) and investment (when resources are devoted to the production of future output). The amount of economic investment is limited by the amount of savings available for such investment.

   (1) There often is confusion about the term investment. **Economic investment** refers to the purchase of newly created capital goods such as new tools, new machinery, or new buildings that are bought with the purpose of expanding a business.

   (2) **Financial investment** refers to the purchase of an asset such as a stock, bond, or real estate that is made for the purpose of financial gain. Financial investment simply transfers ownership of an asset from one party to another.

   b. The primary source of savings is households and the primary economic investors are businesses. Savings get transferred to economic investors through banks and other financial institutions such as insurance companies and mutual funds. For these reasons, the condition of the banking and financial sector is important for economic growth and macroeconomic policy.

4. Uncertainty, expectations, and shocks all affect macroeconomic behavior.

   a. The future is uncertain so the consumer and business participants in the economy have to act from **expectations** of what will happen. Their expectations about the future will shape their economic decisions.

   (1) When expectations differ significantly from reality, that is, the unexpected happens, then the participants in the economy experience **economic shocks. Demand shocks** occur with unexpected changes in the demand for products. **Supply shocks** occur with unexpected changes in the supply of products. Such shocks can be positive or negative depending on whether the surprising changes are beneficial or costly for a person or group. In the view of many economists, most short-run fluctuations in the economy come from demand shocks, so demand shocks will be given the primary focus in this chapter and subsequent chapters.

b. For an individual firm, if the price for the product is flexible, a change in the demand for the product will result in a change in price to achieve equilibrium at the set quantity of output (vertical supply curve). Such a change in demand would not change the output for a firm, but only the price of a product. Similarly, for the entire economy, if prices of products are completely flexible, then output would remain the same both in the short run or the long run and only the level of prices for products would change.

c. Demand shocks, however, present a major macroeconomic problem for the economy because the prices of most products are inflexible or slow to change in the short run ("sticky").

(1) For an individual firm, when a price is inflexible, then the response to a demand shock is a change in output and employment. Similarly, for the entire economy, if most prices are fixed or "sticky," a demand shock will cause short-term fluctuations in output and employment. For example, if the demand for most products falls, firms will cut production, causing output and economic growth to decrease and unemployment to increase.

(2) Firms attempt to address the problem of fluctuating demand by maintaining an **inventory,** which is a store of output that has been produced but not sold. When demand is low, the inventory stock would rise as unsold products are added. When demand is high, the inventory would fall as previously produced products are sold from the inventory stock. But such a practice of using inventories to meet unexpected changes in demand only helps for a short period of time. If inventories become large and remain so for a long period of time, they are costly to maintain and end up hurting business profits. As a result, firms will cut production and employment to reduce the inventory buildup. These changes in turn will reduce GDP and increase unemployment.

d. The economic data indicate that there are many **inflexible prices** or **"sticky prices"** for goods and services in the economy. In fact, for many final goods and services there is a 4.3-month time lag before prices change. There are several reasons for sticky prices. First, consumers prefer stable and predictable prices, so there is pressure on businesses to keep prices stable and not upset consumers. Second, businesses may not want to cut prices because that may result in a price war with competing firms.

5. Macroeconomic models can be categorized based on price stickiness. In the very short run, prices are almost totally inflexible, so that any change in demand will result in a change in output and employment. As time passes, however, prices become more flexible and a change in demand produces little change in output or employment. The price flexibility/inflexibility distinction is important for categorizing macroeconomic models. Short-run macroeconomic models assume that prices are inflexible or sticky, and thus demand shocks change output and employment. Long-run macroeconomic models assume that prices are flexible, and thus demand shocks only have an effect on prices and not on output or employment.

■ **HINTS AND TIPS**

1. This chapter is an introduction to what will be presented in later chapters. It is best first to read for a conceptual understanding of what is to come in the later chapters, so do not get bogged down in the mere definitions of terms. A key idea is that *the flexibility of prices determines the degree to which demand shocks influence output and employment in an economy.* The distinction between flexible and inflexible prices is useful for categorizing the macroeconomic models and for understanding economic growth as discussed in later chapters.

2. One important definitional distinction the chapter makes is between *economic* investment and *financial* investment. Economic investment involves the purchase of *newly created* capital goods to be used for production of goods or services by a business. Financial investment typically means purchasing ownership of a paper asset such as a stock or bond, or in other cases a used asset, such as an antique car, in the expectation that the price will appreciate and there will be financial gain when the asset is sold.

■ **IMPORTANT TERMS**

the business cycle	financial investment
recession	economic investment
real GDP (Gross Domestic Product)	expectations
nominal GDP	shocks
unemployment	demand shocks
inflation	supply shocks
modern economic growth	inventory
savings	inflexible prices ("sticky prices")
investment	flexible prices

SELF-TEST

■ **FILL-IN QUESTIONS**

1. Macroeconomics studies the business cycle or (short-run, long-run) _____ fluctuations in output and employment and _____ economic growth that leads to higher standards of living over time.

2. To tell if an economy is growing from one year to the next year, economists compare (nominal, real) _____ GDP from one year to the next because it shows if there is a change in output rather than prices.

3. An increase in the overall level of prices is called (sticky prices, inflation) _____. The condition where a person is willing to work but cannot get a job is (recession, unemployment) _____.

4. The basic difference between modern economic growth and economic growth in ancient or preindustrial times is that with modern economic growth output per person (increases, stays about the same) _____ whereas with growth in ancient or preindustrial times, output per person _____.

5. Richer nations have experienced modern economic growth for (shorter, longer) _____ time periods than have poorer nations and as a consequence their standards of living are significantly (lower, higher) _____.

6. When current consumption is less than current output, it creates (investment, savings) _____, and when economic resources are devoted to increasing future output, such activity is considered to be _____.

7. The purchase of newly created capital goods for the purpose of expanding or growing a business would be considered by economists to be an example of (financial, economic) _____ investment whereas the purchase of an asset such as a share of stock in a corporation in the expectation that its price would appreciate would be an example of _____ investment.

8. The amount of economic investment is ultimately limited by the amount of (savings, inventory) _____, and for there to be more investment then _____ must increase. Such an increase, however, means that there will be a(n) (increase, decrease) _____ in current consumption.

9. The principal source of savings is (businesses, households) _____ and the main economic investors are _____. The transfer of savings to investors is done primarily through (government, banks) _____ and other financial institutions.

10. Expectations are important in macroeconomics because people will save and invest more if they hold (positive, negative) _____ expectations about the future, but they will save and invest less if they hold _____ expectations about the future.

11. Uncertainty about the future means that expectations may not be met, which creates a(n) (investment, shock) _____, and there can be a demand _____ or a supply _____.

12. A situation where demand turns out to be higher than expected would be a (positive, negative) _____ demand shock, but a situation in which demand turns out to be lower than expected would be a _____ demand shock.

13. Many economists think that most short-run fluctuations are the result of (supply, demand) _____ shocks,

although it is also possible for there to be _____ shocks; but the textbook will focus primarily on _____ shocks.

14. In the short run, real world prices are often (flexible, inflexible) _____, but in the long run, prices are more _____. When prices are inflexible, they are referred to as being ("sticky", "stuck") _____.

15. In the short run, the only way for the economy to adjust to demand shocks when prices are inflexible or sticky is through changes in (prices, output) _____ and employment, but in the long run, the adjustments are made through changes in _____.

16. A store of output that has been produced but not sold is a(n) (financial investment, inventory) _____ and they help businesses adjust to short-run changes in demand.

17. If demand for a product increases, then business firms can respond by (increasing, decreasing) _____ their inventories of the product, and if the demand for the product decreases, then business firms can respond by _____ their inventories of the product.

18. If prices are fixed and there is a negative demand shock, it will cause sales to (increase, decrease) _____ and inventories to _____, and if they become too high, then firms will have to _____ output and _____ employment.

19. One reason that prices are sticky is that consumers prefer (stable, fluctuating) _____ prices, and businesses do not want to annoy consumers. Another reason is that cutting prices may result in a price (shock, war) _____ with competing firms that will be counterproductive for business.

20. In short-run macroeconomic models, prices tend to be (inflexible, flexible) _____ and output and employment change with changes in demand, but in macroeconomic models with a longer time horizon, prices tend to be _____ and output and employment remain relatively constant.

■ **TRUE–FALSE QUESTIONS**

Circle T if the statement is true, F if it is false.

1. Macroeconomics studies long-run economic growth and short-run economic fluctuations.   **T F**

2. Real GDP totals the dollar value of all goods and services within the borders of a given country using their current prices during the year they were produced.   **T F**

3. Unemployment is a waste of resources because the economy gives up the goods and services that unemployed workers could have produced if they had been working. **T F**

4. If a household's income does not rise as fast as the prices of goods and services that it consumes, its standard of living will rise. **T F**

5. An example of a macroeconomic policy question would be "Can governments promote long-run economic growth?" **T F**

6. Modern economic growth means that output rises at about the same rate as the population. **T F**

7. The vast differences in living standards between rich and poor nations today are largely the result of only some nations having experienced modern economic growth. **T F**

8. To raise living standards over time, an economy must devote at least some fraction of its current output to increasing future output. **T F**

9. An example of economic investment, as economists use the term, would be the purchase of a corporate stock or bond. **T F**

10. The only way that an economy can pay for more investment to achieve higher consumption in the future is to increase savings in the present. **T F**

11. Banks and other financial institutions collect the savings of households after paying interest, dividends or capital gains and then lend those funds to businesses. **T F**

12. Expectations about the future are important because if people expect a good future, households will increase their savings and businesses will reduce their investments. **T F**

13. Economies are exposed to both demand shock and supply shocks. **T F**

14. A positive demand shock refers to a situation where demand turns out to be lower than expected. **T F**

15. Economists believe that most short-run fluctuations in the economy are the result of demand shocks. **T F**

16. In the short run, the prices of most goods and services change very quickly. **T F**

17. Fluctuations in the business cycle arise because the actual demand for goods and services is either higher or lower than what people expected. **T F**

18. If prices are flexible for an economy, an increase in demand will result in a significant change in output and employment. **T F**

19. An inventory is a store of output that has been produced and sold. **T F**

20. Given fixed prices, a negative demand shock for businesses will reduce sales, increase inventories, and eventually reduce output and employment. **T F**

21. The prices for most goods and services that people consume are sticky in the short run. **T F**

22. One reason that prices are sticky is that business firms try to please consumers by giving them predictable and stable prices for planning. **T F**

23. Another reason prices are sticky is that business firms want to engage in a price war with rival firms to gain market share. **T F**

24. Only in the short run are prices totally inflexible. **T F**

25. A macroeconomic model that allows for flexible prices would be more useful for understanding how the economy behaves over time. **T F**

■ **MULTIPLE-CHOICE QUESTIONS**

Circle the letter that corresponds to the best answer.

1. Short-run fluctuations in output and employment are often referred to as
   (a) recession
   (b) inflation
   (c) the business cycle
   (d) modern economic growth

2. Economic growth in an economy is best measured from one year to the next by comparing the change in
   (a) the rate of inflation
   (b) the rate of unemployment
   (c) nominal GDP
   (d) real GDP

3. Unemployment is undesirable because it
   (a) increases inflation
   (b) wastes labor resources
   (c) contributes to sticky prices
   (d) raises interest rates in the economy

4. A major problem with inflation is that it
   (a) lowers housing prices
   (b) increases the rate of savings
   (c) reduces purchasing power
   (d) decreases government spending

5. Which one of the following is a question that a macroeconomic model would help to clarify?
   (a) Can governments promote long-run economic growth?
   (b) Is the purchase of General Electric stock a worthwhile financial investment?
   (c) Should the sales tax in a city be raised from 7 percent to 9 percent?
   (d) Does a large rise in the price of gasoline significantly reduce consumer spending on gasoline?

6. What was the average percentage increase in the output of the United States from 1995 to 2007?
   (a) 1.1 percent
   (b) 2.7 percent
   (c) 3.6 percent
   (d) 4.1 percent

7. Before the Industrial Revolution began in England in the late 1700s, standards of living showed
- **(a)** significant growth
- **(b)** significant decline
- **(c)** virtually no growth
- **(d)** wide swings from growth to decline

8. Modern economic growth is characterized as a situation in which
- **(a)** inflation is almost zero
- **(b)** output per person is rising
- **(c)** unemployment is minimal
- **(d)** the prices of products are flexible

9. An annual growth rate of 2 percent implies that the standard of living in an economy will double in
- **(a)** 10 years
- **(b)** 20 years
- **(c)** 35 years
- **(d)** 70 years

10. What accounts for the vast differences in the living standards today between rich and poor countries?
- **(a)** purchasing power parity
- **(b)** rising rates of inflation
- **(c)** increases in nominal GDP
- **(d)** modern economic growth

11. About how many times greater, on average, are the material standards of living of citizens in the richest nations compared with the material living standards of citizens in the poorest nations?
- **(a)** 5 times
- **(b)** 10 times
- **(c)** 50 times
- **(d)** 100 times

12. When current spending is less than current income, it generates
- **(a)** savings
- **(b)** investment
- **(c)** demand shocks
- **(d)** supply shocks

13. Which of the following *purchases* would be an example of an economic investment by a business?
- **(a)** shares of stock in another business
- **(b)** a used factory from another business
- **(c)** new computers to improve data analysis
- **(d)** a certificate of deposit with a high interest rate

14. The reason that economic investment is important is that it
- **(a)** enables higher levels of consumption in the future
- **(b)** enables higher levels of consumption in the present
- **(c)** increases the rate of savings in the present
- **(d)** decreases the rate of savings in the future

15. A well-functioning banking and financial system helps to promote economic growth and stability by
- **(a)** paying high interest rates on deposits
- **(b)** offering dividends on corporate stocks
- **(c)** directing savings to the most productive investments
- **(d)** increasing current consumption and future consumption

16. If people and businesses hold positive attitudes about the future they are more likely to
- **(a)** save less and invest less
- **(b)** save more and invest more
- **(c)** save more and invest less
- **(d)** save less and invest more

17. Macroeconomic behavior is most significantly influenced by
- **(a)** purchasing power parity
- **(b)** expectations about the future
- **(c)** the price of agricultural land
- **(d)** employment in the construction industry

18. Economic forecasters had expected consumer spending to increase by 5 percent this year, but instead it increases by 0.5 percent. This situation would be an example of a
- **(a)** positive supply shock
- **(b)** negative supply shock
- **(c)** positive demand shock
- **(d)** negative demand shock

19. The primary reason that economists think most short-run fluctuations in the economy are the result of demand shocks is that the prices of many goods and services are
- **(a)** flexible in the short run
- **(b)** inflexible in the short run
- **(c)** flexible in the long run
- **(d)** inflexible in the long run

20. Alpha Dog Foods is a business firm which produces 10,000 units of dog food a week, which is the optimal output for the firm. If prices for this product are flexible and Alpha Dog Foods experiences an unexpected decrease in demand, it is most likely to
- **(a)** increase the product price
- **(b)** decrease the product price
- **(c)** increase the production of the product
- **(d)** decrease the production of the product

21. Swirlpool typically sells 5,000 energy-efficient dishwashers at the fixed price of $1,000 a month, which is a price it has used for a long time. If there is an unexpected decrease in the demand for this product, then Swirlpool is most likely to
- **(a)** increase the product price
- **(b)** decrease the product price
- **(c)** increase production of the product
- **(d)** decrease production of the product

22. If demand falls for many goods and services across the entire economy for an extended period of time and prices are sticky, most firms that produce those goods and services will be forced to
- **(a)** increase production and increase employment
- **(b)** decrease production and decrease employment
- **(c)** decrease production, but increase employment
- **(d)** increase production, but decrease employment

23. Reliable economic reports indicate that consumers are spending more on goods and services this year. This trend is highly likely to continue for the next few years

because of a growing economy. If prices for these goods and services are sticky, then the businesses producing these goods and services are most likely to
  (a) lower prices and hire more workers
  (b) raise prices and hire more workers
  (c) increase output and hire more workers
  (d) decrease output and hire fewer workers

24. Which of the following good or service is most inflexible, or sticky, in price?
  (a) milk
  (b) gasoline
  (c) newspapers
  (d) airline tickets

25. Macroeconomic models of the economy over the long term are more likely to assume that the economy has
  (a) stuck prices
  (b) sticky prices
  (c) flexible prices
  (d) inflexible prices

■ **PROBLEMS**

1. Assume that in Year 1 an economy produces 100 units of output that sell for $50 a unit, on average. In Year 2, the economy produces the same 100 units of output, but sells them for $55 a unit, on average.

  a. What is nominal GDP in Year 1? _____.

  What is nominal GDP in Year 2? _____.
  Nominal GDP increased from Year 1 to Year 2 because

  (prices, output) _____ increased.
  b. Use Year 1 prices to calculate real GDP in Year 1 and

  Year 2. What is real GDP in Year 1? _____.

  What is real GDP in Year 2? _____. Real GDP did not increase from Year 1 to Year 2 because

  (prices, output) _____ did not change.

2. The following is a demand and supply model for a business firm producing a product. Assume that 100 units of output is the optimal and most profitable level of production for the firm. Assume that the price for the product is flexible.

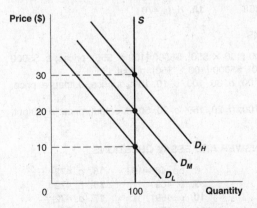

  a. At the medium level of demand (D_M), the equilibrium
  price will be $_____ and the equilibrium
  quantity will be _____ units.

  b. If there is a demand shock that unexpectedly lifts demand higher (D_H), the equilibrium price will be

  $_____ and the equilibrium quantity will

  be _____ units.
  c. If there is a demand shock that unexpectedly lowers demand (D_L), the equilibrium price will be

  $_____ and the equilibrium quantity will

  be _____ units.
  d. Generalizing for the individual firm, if there are demand shocks, they get accommodated by a change in

  (price, output) _____, but not a change in

  _____.

  e. And applying this logic to the economy as a whole, if prices are flexible in the economy and there are demand shocks, the economy would adjust through a

  change in (price, output) _____, but not a

  change in _____.

3. The following is a different demand and supply model for the same business firm producing a product as in Problem 2. Assume that 100 units of output is the optimal and most profitable level of production for the firm. Now assume that the price for the product is inflexible.

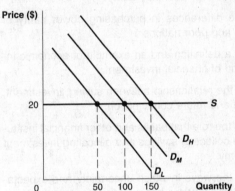

  a. At the medium level of demand (D_M), the equilibrium

  price will be $_____ and the equilibrium

  quantity will be _____ units.
  b. If there is a demand shock that unexpectedly lifts demand higher (D_H), the equilibrium price will be

  $_____ and the equilibrium quantity will

  be _____ units.
  c. If there is a demand shock that unexpectedly lowers demand (D_L), the equilibrium price will be

  $_____ and the equilibrium quantity will be

  _____ units.
  d. Generalizing for the individual firm, if there are demand shocks, they get accommodated by a change in

  (price, output) _____, but not a change in

  _____.

  e. And applying this logic to the economy as a whole, if prices are inflexible in the economy and there are demand shocks, the economy would adjust through a change in (price, output) _____, but not a change in _____.

■ SHORT ANSWER AND ESSAY QUESTIONS

1. Explain how business cycles can be thought of as short-term fluctuations or variability in the rate of economic growth.

2. Describe the basic difference between real GDP and nominal GDP. Which concept is more useful for measuring change in the economy over time? Why?

3. What is the opportunity cost of unemployment for the economy?

4. How does inflation affect people's standard of living and savings?

5. What types of policy questions can macroeconomic models help answer? Give two examples.

6. Compare and contrast the characteristics of economic growth in ancient or preindustrial times with modern economic growth today.

7. What accounts for differences in living standards between rich and poor countries today?

8. Describe differences in purchasing power parity of rich nations and poor nations.

9. Provide a definition and an example of economic investment and of financial investment.

10. Explain the relationship between saving, investment, and present and future consumption.

11. Discuss the role that banks and other financial institutions play in collecting savings and allocating investment in an economy.

12. Explain the ways in which uncertainty and expectations influence economic behavior in macroeconomics.

13. How are shocks related to expectations? Give an example of a positive and a negative demand shock.

14. Discuss the relationship between demand shocks and business cycle fluctuations.

15. How does an economy adjust to a demand shock when prices are flexible?

16. How does an economy adjust to a demand shock when prices are sticky?

17. Explain what happens to inventories when prices are sticky and there is a demand shock.

18. Describe and give examples of the stickiness of prices based on the average number of months between price changes for selected goods and services.

19. Describe two reasons why businesses hesitate to change prices.

20. How can price stickiness be used to categorize macroeconomic models?

ANSWERS

Chapter 23 Introduction to Macroeconomics

FILL-IN QUESTIONS

1. short-run, long-run
2. real
3. inflation, unemployment
4. increases, stays about the same
5. longer, higher
6. savings, investment
7. economic, financial
8. savings, savings, decrease
9. households, businesses, banks
10. positive, negative
11. shock, shock, shock
12. positive, negative
13. demand, supply, demand
14. inflexible, flexible, sticky
15. output, prices
16. inventory
17. decreasing, increasing
18. decrease, increase, decrease, decease
19. stable, war
20. inflexible, flexible

TRUE–FALSE QUESTIONS

1. T, p. 466	10. T, p. 469	19. F, p. 472
2. F, p. 467	11. T, p. 470	20. T, pp. 472–473
3. T, p. 467	12. F, p. 470	21. T, p. 473
4. F, p. 467	13. T, p. 470	22. T, p. 474
5. T, p. 467	14. F, p. 470	23. F, p. 474
6. F, p. 468	15. T, p. 470	24. T, p. 475
7. T, p. 468	16. F, p. 470	25. T, p. 475
8. T, p. 469	17. T, p. 472	
9. F, p. 469	18. F, p. 472	

MULTIPLE-CHOICE QUESTIONS

1. c, p. 467	10. d, p. 468	19. b, p. 470
2. d, p. 467	11. c, p. 468	20. b, p. 471
3. b, p. 467	12. a, p. 469	21. d, p. 472
4. c, p. 467	13. c, p. 469	22. b, p. 473
5. a, p. 467	14. a, pp. 469–470	23. c, p. 473
6. b, p. 468	15. c, p. 470	24. c, p. 473
7. c, p. 468	16. b, p. 470	25. c, p. 475
8. b, p. 468	17. b, p. 470	
9. c, p. 468	18. d, p. 470	

PROBLEMS

1. *a.* $5000 (100 × $50), $5500 (100 × $55), prices; *b.* $5000 (100 × $50), $5000 (100 × $50), output

2. *a.* 20, 100; *b.* 30, 100; *c.* 10, 100; *d.* price, output; *e.* price, output

3. *a.* 20, 100; *b.* 20, 150; *c.* 20, 50; *d.* output, price; *e.* output, price

SHORT ANSWER AND ESSAY QUESTIONS

1. p. 466	8. pp. 468–469	15. p. 472
2. p. 467	9. p. 469	16. p. 472
3. p. 467	10. p. 469	17. p. 472
4. p. 467	11. p. 470	18. p. 473
5. p. 467	12. p. 470	19. p. 474
6. p. 468	13. p. 470	20. p. 475
7. p. 468	14. p. 471	

Measuring Domestic Output and National Income

The subject of Chapter 24 is **national income accounting.** The first measure that you will learn about in the chapter is the **gross domestic product** (GDP). The GDP is an important economic statistic because it provides the best estimate of the total market value of all final goods and services produced by our economy in one year. You will also discover why GDP is a monetary measure that counts only the value of final goods and services and excludes nonproductive transactions such as secondhand sales.

National income accounting involves estimating output, or income, for the nation's society as a whole, rather than for an individual business firm or family. Note that the terms **output** and **income** are interchangeable because the nation's domestic output and its income are identical. The value of the nation's output equals the total expenditures for this output, and these expenditures become the income of those who have produced this output. Consequently, there are two equally acceptable methods—expenditures or income—for determining GDP.

From an **expenditure** perspective, GDP is composed of four expenditure categories: personal consumption expenditures **(C)**, gross private domestic investment **(I$_g$)**, government purchases **(G)**, and net exports **(X$_n$)**. These expenditures become income for people or the government when they are paid out in the form of employee compensation, rents, interest, proprietors' income, corporate profits, and taxes on production and imports. GDP can be calculated from national income by making adjustments to account for net foreign factor income, a statistical discrepancy, and depreciation. In national income accounting, the amount spent to purchase this year's total output is equal to money income derived from production of this year's output.

This chapter also explains the relationship of GDP to other **national income** accounts. These accounts include *net domestic product* (NDP), *national income* (NI) as derived from NDP, *personal income* (PI), and *disposable income* (DI). The relationship between GDP, NDP, NI, PI, and DI is shown in Table 24.4 of the text. The circular flow using the expenditures and income approaches to GDP are illustrated in Figure 24.3 of the text.

The next to the last section of the chapter shows you how to calculate **real GDP** from **nominal GDP.** This adjustment is important because nominal GDP is measured in monetary units, so if accurate comparisons are to be made for GDP over time, these monetary measures must be adjusted to take account of changes in the price level. A simple example is presented to show how a GDP price index is constructed. The index is then used to adjust *nominal GDP* to obtain *real GDP* and make correct GDP comparisons from one year to the next. The text also provides data for the U. S. economy so you can see why the calculation of real GDP is necessary and how it is used.

The last section of the chapter looks at the **shortcomings of GDP** as a measure of total output and economic well-being. You will learn about economic factors that are excluded from GDP measurement—nonmarket or illegal transactions, changes in leisure and product quality, differences in the composition and distribution of output, and the environmental effects of GDP production—and how their exclusion can lead to an under- or overstatement of economic well-being. Although national income accounts are not perfect measures of all economic conditions, they are still reasonably accurate and useful indicators of the performance of the national economy.

■ CHECKLIST

When you have studied this chapter you should be able to

☐ Identify three ways national income accounting can be used for economic decision making.

☐ Give a definition of the gross domestic product (GDP).

☐ Explain why GDP is a monetary measure.

☐ Describe how GDP measures value added and avoids multiple counting.

☐ Give examples of two types of nonproduction transactions that are excluded from GDP.

☐ Describe the relationship between the expenditures and income approaches to GDP accounting.

☐ List the three types of expenditures included in personal consumption expenditures (C).

☐ Identify three items included in gross private domestic investment (I$_g$).

☐ Explain how positive or negative changes in inventories affect investment.

☐ Distinguish between gross and net investment.

☐ Discuss how differences in the amount of net investment affect the production capacity of the economy.

☐ List the two components included in government purchases (G).

☐ Describe the meaning and calculation of net exports (X$_n$).

☐ Compute GDP using the expenditures approach when given national income accounting data.

☐ Identify the six income items that make up U. S. national income.

☐ List three things that can happen to corporate profits.

☐ Explain why taxes on production and imports are included as part of national income.

☐ Describe the effect of net foreign factor income on national income accounts.

☐ Define consumption of fixed capital and discuss how it affects national income accounts.

☐ Compute GDP using the income approach when given national income accounting data.

☐ Define net domestic product (NDP).

☐ Show how to derive U. S. national income (NI) from net domestic product (NDP).

☐ Define personal income (PI) in national income accounts.

☐ Explain how to obtain disposable income (DI) from personal income (PI).

☐ Use Figure 24.3 in the text to describe the circular flow model for GDP.

☐ Distinguish between nominal and real GDP.

☐ Construct a price index when given price and quantity data.

☐ Obtain a price index when given data on nominal and real GDP.

☐ Discuss some real-world factors that affect the GDP price index.

☐ List seven shortcomings of GDP as a measure of total output and economic well-being.

☐ Identify some of the sources of data the Bureau of Economic Analysis uses to estimate consumption, investment, government purchases, and net exports (Last Word).

■ CHAPTER OUTLINE

1. **National income accounting** consists of concepts that enable those who use them to measure the economy's output, to compare it with past outputs, to explain its size and the reasons for changes in its size, and to formulate policies designed to increase it.

2. The market value of all final goods and services produced in the domestic economy during the year is measured by the **gross domestic product (GDP).**

   a. GDP is a *monetary measure* that is calculated in dollar terms rather than in terms of physical units of output.

   b. GDP includes in its calculation only the value of **final goods** (consumption goods, capital goods, and services purchased by final users and that will not be resold or processed further during the *current* year).

   (1) GDP excludes the value of **intermediate goods** (ones that are purchased for resale or further processing) because including both final goods and intermediate goods would result in **multiple counting** of the goods and overstate GDP.

   (2) Another way to avoid multiple counting is to measure and add only the **value added** at each stage of the production process. Value added is the market

value of a firm's output minus the value of the inputs the firm bought from others to produce the output.

   c. Nonproduction transactions are not included in GDP.

   (1) Purely financial transactions such as public transfer payments, private transfer payments, and stock market transactions are simply exchanges of money or paper assets and do not create output.

   (2) Sales of secondhand or used goods are excluded because they were counted in past production and do not contribute to current production.

   d. Measurement of GDP can be accomplished by either the expenditures approach or the income approach, but the same result is obtained by the two methods.

3. Computation of the GDP by the **expenditures approach** requires the summation of the total amounts of the four types of spending for final goods and services.

   a. **Personal consumption expenditures (C)** are the expenditures of households for *durable goods* and *nondurable goods* and for *services*.

   b. **Gross private domestic investment (I_g)** is the sum of the spending by business firms for machinery, equipment, and tools; spending by firms and households for new construction (buildings); and the changes in the inventories of business firms.

   (1) An increase in inventories in a given year increases investment that year because it is part of the output of the economy that was produced but not sold that year; a decrease in inventories in a given year decreases investment that year because it was included as part of the output from a prior year.

   (2) Investment does not include expenditures for stocks or bonds (a transfer of paper assets) or for used or secondhand capital goods (because they were counted as part of investment in the year they were new capital goods).

   (3) Gross investment exceeds net investment by the value of the capital goods worn out during the year. An economy in which net investment is positive is one with an expanding production capacity.

   c. **Government purchases (G)** are the expenditures made by all levels of governments (Federal, state, and local) for final goods from businesses, and for the direct purchases of resources, including labor.

   (1) The government purchases are made to provide public goods and services, and for spending on publicly owned capital (public goods with a long lifetime such as highways or schools).

   (2) It should be noted that transfer payments made by the government to individuals, such as Social Security payments, are not included in government purchases because they simply transfer income to individuals and do not generate production.

   d. **Net exports (X_n)** in an economy is calculated as the difference between exports (X) and imports (M). It is equal to the expenditures made by foreigners for goods and services produced in the economy minus the expenditures made by the consumers, governments, and investors of the economy for goods and services produced in foreign nations.

   e. In equation form, $C + I_g + G + X_n = GDP$.

4. Computation of GDP by the ***income approach*** requires adding the income derived from the production and sales of final goods and services. The six income items are:

 a. *Compensation of employees* (the sum of wages and salaries *and* wage and salary supplements, such as social insurance and private pension or health funds for workers).

 b. *Rents* (the income received by property owners). This rent is a net measure of the difference between gross rent and property depreciation.

 c. *Interest* (only the interest payments made by financial institutions or business firms are included; interest payments made by government are excluded).

 d. *Proprietors' income* (the profits or net income of sole proprietors or unincorporated business firms).

 e. *Corporate profits* (the earnings of corporations). They are allocated in the following three ways: as corporate income taxes, dividends paid to stockholders, and undistributed corporate profits retained by corporations.

 f. ***Taxes on production and imports*** are added because they are initially income for households that later gets paid to government in the form of taxes. This category includes general sales taxes, excise taxes, business property taxes, license fees, and custom duties.

 g. The sum of all of the above six categories equal national income (employee compensation, rents, interest, proprietor's income, corporate profits, and taxes on production and imports). To obtain GDP from national income, three adjustments must be made.

 (1) Net foreign factor income is subtracted from national income because it reflects income earned from production outside the United States. Net foreign factor income is income earned by American-owned resources abroad minus income earned by foreign-owned resources in the United States.

 (2) A statistical discrepancy is added to national income to make the income approach match the expenditures approach.

 (3) The ***consumption of fixed capital*** is added to national income to get to GDP because it is a cost of production that does not add to anyone's income. It covers depreciation of private capital goods and publicly owned capital goods such as roads or bridges.

5. Four other national accounts are important in evaluating the performance of the economy. Each has a distinct definition and can be computed by making additions to or deductions from another measure.

 a. ***Net domestic product (NDP)*** is the annual output of final goods and services over and above the privately and publicly owned capital goods worn out during the year. It is equal to the GDP minus depreciation (consumption of fixed capital).

 b. ***National income (NI)*** is the total income *earned* by U. S. owners of land and capital and by the U. S. suppliers of labor and entrepreneurial ability during the year *plus* taxes on production and imports. It equals NDP *minus* a statistical discrepancy and plus net foreign factor income.

 c. ***Personal income (PI)*** is the total income *received*—whether it is earned or unearned—by the households of the economy before the payment of personal taxes. It is found by taking national income and *adding* transfer payments, and then *subtracting* taxes on production and imports, Social Security contributions, corporate income taxes, and undistributed corporate profits.

 d. ***Disposable income (DI)*** is the total income available to households after the payment of personal taxes. It is calculated by taking personal income and then *subtracting* personal taxes. It is also equal to personal consumption expenditures plus personal saving.

 e. The relationships among the five income–output measures are summarized in Table 24.4.

 f. Figure 24.3 is a more realistic and complex circular flow diagram that shows the flows of expenditures and incomes among the households, business firms, and governments in the economy.

6. ***Nominal GDP*** is the total output of final goods and services produced by an economy in 1 year multiplied by the market prices when they were produced. Prices, however, change each year. To compare total output over time, nominal GDP is converted to ***real GDP*** to account for these price changes.

 a. There are two methods for deriving *real GDP* from *nominal GDP.* The first method involves computing a ***price index.***

 (1) This price index is a ratio of the price of a market basket in a given year to the price of the same market basket in a base year, with the ratio multiplied by 100. If the market basket of goods in the base year was $10 and the market basket of the same goods in the next year was $15, then the price index would be 150 [$15/10 × 100].

 (2) To obtain real GDP, divide nominal GDP by the price index expressed in hundredths. If nominal GDP was $14,000 billion and the price index was 120, then real GDP would be $11,666.6 billion [$14,000 billion/1.20].

 b. In the second method, nominal GDP is broken down into prices and quantities for each year. Real GDP is found by using base-year prices and multiplying them by each year's physical quantities. The GDP price index for a particular year is the ratio of nominal GDP to real GDP for that year. If nominal GDP was $14,000 billion and real GDP was $11,666.6 billion, then the GDP index would be 1.20 [$14,000 billon/$11,666.6 billion].

 c. In the real world, complex methods are used to calculate the GDP price index. The price index is useful for calculating real GDP. The price index number for a reference period is arbitrarily set at 100.

 (1) For years when the price index is below 100, dividing nominal GDP by the price index (in hundredths) inflates nominal GDP to obtain real GDP.

 (2) For years when the price index is greater than 100, dividing nominal GDP by the price index (in hundredths) deflates nominal GDP to obtain real GDP.

7. GDP has shortcomings as a measure of total output and economic well-being.

 a. It excludes the value of nonmarket final goods and services that are not bought and sold in the markets, such as the unpaid work done by people on their houses.

b. It excludes the amount of increased leisure enjoyed by the participants in the economy.

c. It does not fully account for the value of improvements in the quality of products that occur over the years.

d. It does not measure the market value of the final goods and services produced in the underground sector of the economy because that income and activity is not reported.

e. It does not record the pollution or environmental costs of producing final goods and services.

f. It does not measure changes in the composition and the distribution of the domestic output.

g. It does not measure noneconomic sources of well-being such as a reduction in crime, drug or alcohol abuse, or better relationships among people and nations.

8. (Last Word). The Bureau of Economic Analysis (BEA) is a unit of the Department of Commerce that is responsible for compiling the National Income and Product Accounts. It obtains data from multiple sources to estimate consumption, investment, government purchases, and net exports for the calculation of GDP.

■ **HINTS AND TIPS**

1. Read through the chapter several times. A careful reading will enable you to avoid the necessity of memorizing. Begin by making sure you know precisely what GDP means and what is included in and excluded from its measurement.

2. Accounting is essentially an adding-up process. This chapter explains in detail and lists the items that must be added to obtain GDP by the *expenditures approach* or *income approach*. It is up to you to learn what to add on the expenditure side and what to add on the income side. Figure 24.1 is an important accounting reference for this task.

3. Changes in the price level have a significant effect on the measurement of GDP. Practice converting nominal GDP to real GDP using a price index. Problems 4 and 5 in this *Study Guide* should help you understand nominal and real GDP and the conversion process.

4. GDP is a good measure of the market value of the output of final goods and services that are produced in an economy in 1 year; however, the measure is not perfect, so you should be aware of its limitations, which are noted at the end of the chapter.

■ **IMPORTANT TERMS**

national income accounting

gross domestic product (GDP)

intermediate goods

final goods

multiple counting

value added

expenditures approach

income approach

personal consumption expenditures (C)

gross private domestic investment (I_g)

net private domestic investment

government purchases (G)

net exports (X_n)

taxes on production and imports

national income (NI)

consumption of fixed capital (depreciation)

net domestic product (NDP)

personal income (PI)

disposable income (DI)

nominal GDP

real GDP

price index

SELF-TEST

■ **FILL-IN QUESTIONS**

1. National income accounting is valuable because it provides a means of keeping track of the level of (unemployment, production) _____ in the economy and the course it has followed over the long run and the information needed to make public (policies, payments) _____ that will improve the performance of the economy.

2. Gross domestic product (GDP) measures the total (market, nonmarket) _____ value of all (intermediate, final) _____ goods and services produced in a country (in 1 year, over 2 years) _____

3. GDP for a nation includes goods and services produced (within, outside) _____ its geographic boundaries. This condition means that the production of cars at a Toyota plant located in the United States would be (included, excluded) _____ in the calculation of U. S. GDP.

4. GDP is a (monetary, nonmonetary) _____ measure that permits comparison of the (relative, absolute) _____ worth of goods and services.

5. In measuring GDP, only (intermediate, final) _____ goods and services are included; if _____ goods and services were included, the accountant would be (over-, under-) _____ stating GDP, or (single, multiple) _____ counting.

6. GDP accounting excludes (production, nonproduction) _____ transactions. These include (financial, nonfinancial) _____ transactions such as public or private transfer payments or the sale of securities, and (first-, second-) _____ hand sales.

7. Personal consumption expenditures are the expenditures of households for goods such as automobiles, which are (durable, nondurable) _____, and goods such as food, which are _____, plus expenditures for (housing, services) _____.

8. Gross private domestic investment basically includes the final purchases of (capital, consumer) _____ goods by businesses, all (construction of new, sales of existing) _____ buildings and houses, and changes in (services, inventories) _____.

9. The difference between gross and net private domestic investment is equal to (depreciation, net exports) _____. If gross private domestic investment is greater than depreciation, net private domestic investment is (positive, negative) _____ and the production capacity of the economy is (declining, expanding) _____.

10. An economy's *net* exports equal its exports (minus, plus) _____ its imports. If exports are less than imports, net exports are (positive, negative) _____, but if exports are greater than imports, net exports are _____.

11. Using the expenditure approach, the GDP equation equals ($NDP + NI + PI$, $C + I_g + G + X_n$) _____.

12. The compensation of employees in the system of national income accounting consists of actual wages and salaries (plus, minus) _____ wage and salary supplements. Salary supplements are the payments employers make to Social Security or (public, private) _____ insurance programs and to _____ pension, health, and welfare funds.

13. Corporate profits are disposed of in three ways: corporate income (taxes, interest) _____, (depreciation, dividends) _____, and undistributed corporate (taxes, profits) _____.

14. Three adjustments are made to national income to obtain (GDP, DI) _____. Net foreign factor income is (added, subtracted) _____, a statistical discrepancy is _____, and the consumption of fixed capital is _____.

15. Gross domestic product overstates the economy's production because it fails to make allowance for (multiple counting, depreciation) _____ or the need to replace (consumer, capital) _____ goods. When the adjustment is made, the calculations produce (net domestic product, national income) _____.

16. National income is equal to net domestic product (plus, minus) _____ net foreign factor income _____ a statistical discrepancy. Personal income equals national income (plus, minus) _____ transfer payments _____ the sum of taxes on production and imports, Social Security contributions, corporate income taxes, and undistributed corporate profits. Disposable income equals personal income (plus, minus) _____ personal taxes.

17. A GDP that reflects the prices prevailing when the output is produced is called unadjusted, or (nominal, real) _____ GDP, but a GDP figure that is deflated or inflated for price level changes is called adjusted or _____ GDP.

18. To calculate a price index in a given year, the combined price of a market basket of goods and services in that year is (divided, multiplied) _____ by the combined price of the market basket in the base year. The result is then _____ by 100.

19. Real GDP is calculated by dividing (the price index, nominal GDP) _____ by _____. The price index expressed in hundredths is calculated by dividing (real, nominal) _____ GDP by _____ GDP.

20. For several reasons, GDP has shortcomings as a measure of total output or economic well-being.

   a. It does not include the (market, nonmarket) _____ transactions that result in the production of goods and services or the amount of (work, leisure) _____ of participants in the economy.

   b. It fails to record improvements in the (quantity, quality) _____ of the products produced, or the changes in the (level, composition) _____, and distribution of the economy's total output.

   c. It does not take into account the undesirable effects of GDP production on the (government, environment) _____ or the goods and services produced in the (market, underground) _____ economy.

■ **TRUE–FALSE QUESTIONS**

Circle T if the statement is true, F if it is false.

1. National income accounting allows us to assess the performance of the economy and make policies to improve that performance.   **T   F**

2. Gross domestic product measures at their market values the total output of all goods and services produced in the economy during a year.   **T   F**

3. GDP is a count of the physical quantity of output and is not a monetary measure. **T F**

4. Final goods are consumption goods, capital goods, and services that are purchased by their end users rather than being ones used for further processing or manufacturing. **T F**

5. GDP includes the sale of intermediate goods and excludes the sale of final goods. **T F**

6. The total value added to a product and the value of the final product are equal. **T F**

7. Social Security payments and other public transfer payments are counted as part of GDP. **T F**

8. The sale of stocks and bonds is excluded from GDP. **T F**

9. In computing gross domestic product, private transfer payments are excluded because they do not represent payments for currently produced goods and services. **T F**

10. The two approaches to the measurement of the gross domestic product yield identical results because one approach measures the total amount spent on the products produced by business firms during a year while the second approach measures the total income of business firms during the year. **T F**

11. Personal consumption expenditures only include expenditures for durable and nondurable goods. **T F**

12. The expenditure made by a household to have a new home built is a personal consumption expenditure. **T F**

13. In national income accounting, any increase in the inventories of business firms is included in gross private domestic investment. **T F**

14. If gross private domestic investment is greater than depreciation during a given year, the economy's production capacity has declined during that year. **T F**

15. Government purchases include spending by all units of government on the finished products of business, but exclude all direct purchases of resources such as labor. **T F**

16. The net exports of an economy equal its exports of goods and services less its imports of goods and services. **T F**

17. The income approach to GDP includes compensation of employees, rents, interest income, proprietors' income, corporate profits, and taxes on production and imports. **T F**

18. Taxes on production and imports are the difference between gross private domestic investment and net private domestic investment. **T F**

19. Net foreign factor income is the difference between the earnings of foreign-owned resources in the United States and the earnings from U. S.-supplied resources abroad. **T F**

20. A GDP that has been deflated or inflated to reflect changes in the price level is called real GDP. **T F**

21. To adjust nominal GDP for a given year to obtain real GDP, it is necessary to multiply nominal GDP by the price index (expressed in hundredths) for that year. **T F**

22. If nominal GDP for an economy is $11,000 billion and the price index is 110, then real GDP is $10,000 billion. **T F**

23. GDP is a precise measure of the economic well-being of society. **T F**

24. The productive services of a homemaker are included in GDP. **T F**

25. The external costs from pollution and other activities associated with the production of the GDP are deducted from total output. **T F**

■ MULTIPLE-CHOICE QUESTIONS

Circle the letter that corresponds to the best answer.

1. Which is a primary use for national income accounting?
  (a) It provides a basis for assessing the performance of the economy.
  (b) It measures economic efficiency in specific industries.
  (c) It estimates expenditures on nonproduction transactions.
  (d) It analyzes the cost of pollution to the economy.

2. Gross domestic product (GDP) is defined as
  (a) personal consumption expenditures and gross private domestic investment
  (b) the sum of wage and salary compensation of employees, corporate profits, and interest income
  (c) the market value of final goods and services produced within a country in 1 year
  (d) the market value of all final and intermediate goods and services produced by the economy in 1 year

3. GDP provides an indication of society's valuation of the relative worth of goods and services because it
  (a) provides an estimate of the value of secondhand sales
  (b) gives increased weight to security transactions
  (c) is an estimate of income received
  (d) is a monetary measure

4. To include the value of the parts used in producing the automobiles turned out during a year in gross domestic product for that year would be an example of
  (a) including a nonmarket transaction
  (b) including a nonproduction transaction
  (c) including a noninvestment transaction
  (d) multiple counting

5. Which of the following is a public transfer payment?
  (a) the Social Security benefits sent to a retired worker
  (b) the sale of shares of stock in Microsoft Corporation

(c) the sale of a used (secondhand) toy house at a garage sale

(d) the birthday gift of a check for $50 sent by a grandmother to her grandchild

6. The sale in year 2 of an automobile produced in year 1 would not be included in the gross domestic product for year 2; doing so would involve

(a) including a nonmarket transaction

(b) including a nonproduction transaction

(c) including a noninvestment transaction

(d) public transfer payments

7. The service a babysitter performs when she stays at home with her baby brother while her parents are out and for which she receives no payment is not included in the gross domestic product because

(a) this is a nonmarket transaction

(b) this is a nonproduction transaction

(c) this is a noninvestment transaction

(d) multiple counting would be involved

8. According to national income accounting, money income derived from the production of this year's output is equal to

(a) corporate profits and the consumption of fixed capital

(b) the amount spent to purchase this year's total output

(c) the sum of interest income and the compensation of employees

(d) gross private domestic investment less the consumption of fixed capital

9. Which would be considered an investment according to economists?

(a) the purchase of newly issued shares of stock in Microsoft

(b) the construction of a new computer chip factory by Intel

(c) the resale of stock originally issued by the General Electric corporation

(d) the sale of a retail department store building by Sears to JCPenney

10. A refrigerator was produced by its manufacturer in year 1, sold to a retailer in year 1, and sold by the retailer to a final consumer in year 2. The refrigerator was

(a) counted as consumption in year 1

(b) counted as savings in year 1

(c) counted as investment in year 1

(d) not included in the gross domestic product of year 1

11. The annual charge that estimates the amount of private capital equipment used up in each year's production is called

(a) investment

(b) depreciation

(c) value added

(d) multiple counting

12. If gross private domestic investment is greater than depreciation, the economy will most likely be

(a) static

(b) declining

(c) expanding

(d) inflationary

13. GDP in an economy is $3452 billion. Consumer expenditures are $2343 billion, government purchases are $865 billion, and gross investment is $379 billion. Net exports are

(a) + $93 billion

(b) + $123 billion

(c) − $45 billion

(d) − $135 billion

14. What can happen to the allocation of corporate profits?

(a) It is paid to proprietors as income.

(b) It is paid to stockholders as dividends.

(c) It is paid to the government as interest income.

(d) It is retained by the corporation as rents.

15. The allowance for the private and publicly owned capital that has been used up or consumed in producing the year's GDP is

(a) net domestic product

(b) consumption of fixed capital

(c) undistributed corporate profits

(d) taxes on production and imports

Questions 16 through 22 use the national income accounting data given in the following table.

	Billions of dollars
Net private domestic investment	$ 32
Personal taxes	39
Transfer payments	19
Taxes on production and imports	8
Corporate income taxes	11
Personal consumption expenditures	217
Consumption of fixed capital	7
U.S. exports	15
Dividends	15
Government purchases	51
Net foreign factor income	0
Undistributed corporate profits	10
Social Security contributions	4
U.S. imports	17
Statistical discrepancy	0

16. Gross private domestic investment is equal to

(a) $32 billion

(b) $39 billion

(c) $45 billion

(d) $56 billion

17. Net exports are equal to

(a) − $2 billion

(b) $2 billion

(c) − $32 billion

(d) $32 billion

18. The gross domestic product is equal to

(a) $298 billion

(b) $302 billion

(c) $317 billion

(d) $305 billion

19. The net domestic product is equal to
(a) $298 billion
(b) $302 billion
(c) $317 billion
(d) $321 billion

20. National income is equal to
(a) $245 billion
(b) $278 billion
(c) $290 billion
(d) $310 billion

21. Personal income is equal to
(a) $266 billion
(b) $284 billion
(c) $290 billion
(d) $315 billion

22. Disposable income is equal to
(a) $245 billion
(b) $284 billion
(c) $305 billion
(d) $321 billion

23. If both nominal gross domestic product and the level of prices are rising, it is evident that
(a) real GDP is constant
(b) real GDP is declining
(c) real GDP is rising but not so rapidly as prices
(d) no conclusion can be drawn concerning the real GDP of the economy on the basis of this information

24. Suppose nominal GDP rose from $500 billion to $600 billion while the GDP price index increased from 125 to 150. Real GDP
(a) was constant
(b) increased
(c) decreased
(d) cannot be calculated from these figures

25. In an economy, the total expenditure for a market basket of goods in year 1 (the base year) was $4000 billion. In year 2, the total expenditure for the same market basket of goods was $4500 billion. What was the GDP price index for the economy in year 2?
(a) .88
(b) 1.13
(c) 188
(d) 113

26. Nominal GDP is less than real GDP in an economy in year 1. In year 2, nominal GDP is equal to real GDP. In year 3, nominal GDP is slightly greater than real GDP. In year 4, nominal GDP is significantly greater than real GDP. Which year is most likely to be the base year that is being used to calculate the price index for this economy?
(a) 1
(b) 2
(c) 3
(d) 4

27. Nominal GDP was $3774 billion in year 1 and the GDP deflator was 108 and nominal GDP was $3989 in year 2 and the GDP deflator that year was 112. What was real GDP in years 1 and 2, respectively?

(a) $3494 billion and $3562 billion
(b) $3339 billion and $3695 billion
(c) $3595 billion and $3725 billion
(d) $3643 billion and $3854 billion

28. A price index one year was 145, and the next year it was 167. What is the approximate percentage change in the price level from one year to the next as measured by that index?
(a) 12%
(b) 13%
(c) 14%
(d) 15%

29. GDP accounting includes
(a) the goods and services produced in the underground economy
(b) expenditures for equipment to reduce the pollution of the environment
(c) the value of the leisure enjoyed by citizens
(d) the goods and services produced but not bought and sold in the markets of the economy

30. Which is a major reason why GDP is *not* an accurate index of society's economic well-being?
(a) It includes changes in the value of leisure.
(b) It excludes many improvements in product quality.
(c) It includes transactions from the underground economy.
(d) It excludes transactions from the buying and selling of stocks.

■ PROBLEMS

1. Following are national income accounting figures for the United States.

	Billions of dollars
Exports	$ 367
Dividends	60
Consumption of fixed capital	307
Corporate profits	203
Compensation of employees	1722
Government purchases	577
Rents	33
Taxes on production and imports	255
Gross private domestic investment	437
Corporate income taxes	88
Transfer payments	320
Interest	201
Proprietors' income	132
Personal consumption expenditures	1810
Imports	338
Social Security contributions	148
Undistributed corporate profits	55
Personal taxes	372
Net foreign factor income	0
Statistical discrepancy	0

a. In the following table, use any of these figures to prepare an income statement for the economy similar to the one found in Table 24.3 of the text.

Receipts: Expenditures approach		Allocations: Income approach	
Item	Amount	Item	Amount
_____	$_____	_____	$_____
_____	$_____	_____	$_____
_____	$_____	_____	$_____
_____	$_____	_____	$_____
			$_____
		National income	$_____
		_____	$_____
		_____	$_____
		_____	$_____
Gross domestict product	$_____	Gross domestic product	$_____

b. Use the other national accounts to find

(1) Net domestic product is $_____

(2) National income is $_____

(3) Personal income is $_____

(4) Disposable income is $_____

2. A farmer owns a plot of ground and sells the right to pump crude oil from his land to a crude oil producer. The crude oil producer agrees to pay the farmer $50 a barrel for every barrel pumped from the farmer's land.

a. During one year 10,000 barrels are pumped.

(1) The farmer receives a payment of $_____ from the crude oil producer.

(2) The value added by the farmer is $_____.

b. The crude oil producer sells the 10000 barrels pumped to a petroleum refiner at a price of $110 a barrel.

(1) The crude oil producer receives a payment of $_____ from the refiner.

(2) The value added by the crude oil producer is $_____.

c. The refiner employs a pipeline company to transport the crude oil from the farmer's land to the refinery and pays the pipeline company a fee of $5 a barrel for the oil transported.

(1) The pipeline company receives a payment of $_____ from the refiner.

(2) The value added by the pipeline company is $_____.

d. From the 10,000 barrels of crude oil, the refiner produces 400,000 gallons of gasoline which is sold to distributors and gasoline service stations at an average price of $3.50 per gallon.

(1) The total payment received by the refiner from its customers is $_____.

(2) The value added by the refiner is $_____.

e. The distributors and service stations sell the 400,000 gallons of gasoline to consumers at an average price of $3.75 a gallon.

(1) The total payment received by distributors and service stations is $_____.

(2) The value added by them is $_____.

f. The total of the value added by the farmer, crude oil producer, pipeline company, refiner, and distributors and service stations is $_____, and the market value of the gasoline sold to customers (the final good) is $_____.

3. Following is a list of items which may or may not be included in the five income-output measures of the national income accounts **(GDP, NDP, NI, PI, DI)**. Indicate in the space to the right of each which of the income-output measures includes this item; it is possible for the item to be included in none, one, two, three, four, or all of the measures. If the item is included in none of the measures, indicate why it is not included.

a. Interest on the national debt _____

b. The sale of a used computer _____

c. The production of shoes that are not sold by the manufacturer _____

d. The income of a dealer in illegal drugs _____

e. The purchase of a share of common stock on the New York Stock Exchange _____

f. The interest paid on the bonds of the General Motors Corporation _____

g. The labor performed by a homemaker _____

h. The labor performed by a paid babysitter _____

i. The monthly check received by a college student from her parents _____

j. The purchase of a new tractor by a farmer _____

k. The labor performed by an assembly line worker in repapering his own kitchen _____

l. The services of a lawyer _____

m. The purchase of shoes from the manufacturer by a shoe retailer _____

n. The monthly check received from the Social Security Administration by a college student whose parents have died _____

o. The rent a homeowner would receive if she did not live in her own home _____

4. At the top of the next column is hypothetical data for a market basket of goods in year 1 and year 2 for an economy.

a. Compute the expenditures for year 1.

MARKET BASKET FOR YEAR 1 (BASE YEAR)

Products	Quantity	Price	Expenditures
Toys	3	$10	$_____
Pencils	5	2	$_____
Books	7	5	$_____
Total			$_____

b. Compute the expenditures for year 2.

MARKET BASKET FOR YEAR 2

Products	Quantity	Price	Expenditures
Toys	3	$11	$_____
Pencils	5	3	$_____
Books	7	6	$_____
Total			$_____

c. In the space below, show how you computed the GDP price index for year 2.

5. The following table shows nominal GDP figures for 3 years and the price indices for each of the 3 years. (The GDP figures are in billions.)

Year	Nominal GDP	Price Index	Real GDP
1929	$104	121	$_____
1933	56	91	$_____
1939	91	100	$_____

a. Use the price indices to compute the real GDP in each year. (You may round your answers to the nearest billion dollars.) Write answers in the table.
b. Which of the 3 years appears to be the base year?

_____

c. Between
(1) 1929 and 1933 the economy experienced (inflation, deflation) _____.

(2) 1933 and 1939 it experienced _____.
d. The nominal GDP figure

(1) for 1929 was (deflated, inflated, neither)_____.

(2) for 1933 was _____.

(3) for 1939 was _____.
e. The price level

(1) fell by _____% from 1929 to 1933.

(2) rose by _____% from 1933 to 1939.

■ SHORT ANSWER AND ESSAY QUESTIONS

1. Of what use is national income accounting to economists and policymakers?

2. What is the definition of GDP? How are the values of output produced at a U.S.-owned factory in the United States and a foreign-owned factory in the United States treated in GDP accounting?

3. Why is GDP a monetary measure?

4. How does GDP accounting avoid multiple counting and exaggeration of the value of GDP?

5. Why does GDP accounting exclude nonproduction transactions?

6. What are the two principal types of nonproduction transactions? List examples of each type.

7. What are the two sides to GDP accounting? What are the meaning and relationship between the two sides?

8. What would be included in personal consumption expenditures by households?

9. How is gross private domestic investment defined?

10. Is residential construction counted as investment or consumption? Explain.

11. Why is a change in inventories an investment?

12. How do you define an expanding production capacity using the concepts of gross private domestic investment and depreciation?

13. What do government purchases include and what do they exclude?

14. How are imports and exports handled in GDP accounting?

15. What are six income components of GDP that add up to national income? Define and explain the characteristics of each component.

16. What are the three adjustments made to the national income to get it to equal GDP? Define and explain the characteristics of each one.

17. Explain how to calculate net domestic product (NDP), national income (NI), personal income (PI), and disposable income (DI).

18. What is the difference between real and nominal GDP? Describe two methods economists use to determine real GDP. Illustrate each method with an example.

19. Describe the real world relationship between nominal and real GDP in the United States. Explain why nominal GDP may be greater or less than real GDP depending on the year or period selected.

20. Why might GDP not be considered an accurate measure of total output and the economic well-being of society? Identify seven shortcomings of GDP.

ANSWERS

Chapter 24 Measuring Domestic Output and National Income

FILL-IN QUESTIONS

1. production, policies
2. market, final, in 1 year
3. within, included
4. monetary, relative
5. final, intermediate, over, multiple

6. nonproduction, financial, second
7. durable, nondurable, services
8. capital, construction of new, inventories
9. depreciation, positive, expanding
10. minus, negative, positive
11. $C + I_g + G + X_n$
12. plus, public, private
13. taxes, dividends, profits
14. GDP, subtracted, added, added
15. depreciation, capital, net domestic product
16. plus, minus, plus, minus, minus
17. nominal, real
18. divided, multiplied
19. nominal GDP, the price index, nominal, real
20. *a.* nonmarket, leisure; *b.* quality, composition; *c.* environment, underground

TRUE–FALSE QUESTIONS

1. T, p. 480	**10.** F, p. 482	**19.** T, pp. 486–487
2. F, p. 480	**11.** F, p. 482	**20.** T, p. 490
3. F, p. 480	**12.** F, pp. 482–483	**21.** F, pp. 491–492
4. T, p. 480	**13.** T, pp. 482–483	**22.** T, pp. 491–492
5. F, p. 480	**14.** F, p. 483	**23.** F, p. 495
6. T, pp. 480–481	**15.** F, pp. 483–484	**24.** F, p. 493
7. F, p. 481	**16.** T, pp. 484–485	**25.** F, p. 495
8. T, p. 481	**17.** T, pp. 485–486	
9. T, p. 481	**18.** F, p. 486	

MULTIPLE-CHOICE QUESTIONS

1. a, p. 480	**11.** b, p. 483	**21.** b, pp. 485, 488
2. c, p. 480	**12.** c, p. 483	**22.** a, pp. 485–486
3. d, p. 480	**13.** d, p. 485	**23.** d, p. 490
4. d, pp. 480–481	**14.** b, p. 486	**24.** a, p. 491
5. a, p. 481	**15.** b, p. 487	**25.** d, p. 491
6. b, p. 481	**16.** b, pp. 483, 485	**26.** b, p. 491
7. a, pp. 481, 483, 493	**17.** a, pp. 484–485	**27.** a, p. 492
8. b, p. 482	**18.** d, p. 485	**28.** d, pp. 491–492
9. b, pp. 482–483	**19.** a, pp. 485, 487	**29.** b, p. 495
10. c, p. 483	**20.** c, pp. 485, 487–488	**30.** b, p. 493

PROBLEMS

1. *a.* See the following table; *b.* (1) 2546, (2) 2291, (3) 2320, (4) 1948

Receipts: Expenditures approach		Allocations: Income approach	
Item	**Amount**	**Item**	**Amount**
Personal consumption expenditures	$1810	Compensation of employees	$1722
Gross private domestic investment	437	Rents	33
		Interest	201
		Proprietors' income	132
		Corporate profits	203
Government purchases	577	Taxes on production and imports	203
			255
Net exports	29	National income	$2546
		Net foreign factor Income	0
		Consumption of fixed capital	307
Gross domestic product	$2853	Gross domestic product	$2853

2. *a.* 500,000, (2) 500,000; *b.* (1) 1,100,000, (2) 600,000; *c.* (1) 50,000, (2) 50,000; *d.* (1) 1,400,000, (2) 250,000; *e.* (1) 1,500,000, (2) 100,000; *f.* 1,500,000, 1,500,000

3. *a.* personal income and disposable income, a public transfer payment; *b.* none, a secondhand sale; *c.* all, represents investment (additions to inventories); *d.* none, illegal production and incomes are not included if not reported; *e.* none, a purely financial transaction; *f.* all; *g.* none, a nonmarket transaction; *h.* all if reported as income, none if not reported; *i.* none, a private transfer payment; *j.* all; *k.* none, a nonmarket transaction; *l.* all; *m.* all, represents additions to the inventory of the retailer; *n.* personal income and disposable income, a public transfer payment; *o.* all, estimate of rental value of owner-occupied homes is included in rents as if it were income and in personal consumption expenditures as if it were payment for a service

4. *a.* 30, 10, 35, 75; *b.* 33, 15, 42, 90; *c.* ($90/$75) 100 = 120

5. *a.* 86, 62, 91; *b.* 1939; *c.* (1) deflation, (2) inflation; *d.* (1) deflated, (2) inflated, (3) neither; *e.* (1) 24.8 (2) 9.9

SHORT ANSWER AND ESSAY QUESTIONS

1. p. 480	**8.** p. 482	**15.** pp. 485–486
2. p. 480	**9.** pp. 482–483	**16.** pp. 486–487
3. p. 480	**10.** p. 483	**17.** pp. 487–488
4. pp. 480–481	**11.** p. 483	**18.** pp. 490–492
5. p. 481	**12.** p. 483	**19.** p. 492
6. pp. 481–482	**13.** pp. 483–484	**20.** pp. 493, 495
7. p. 482	**14.** pp. 484–485	

CHAPTER 25

Economic Growth

The economic health of a nation relies on economic growth because it reduces the burden of scarcity. Small differences in real growth rates result in large differences in the standards of living in nations. The first short section of the chapter describes how economists measure economic growth, explains why economic growth is important, and presents some basic facts about the U.S. growth rates.

What is especially fascinating about this topic is that continuous and sustained increases in economic growth and the resulting significant improvements in living standards within a lifetime are a relatively new development from a historical perspective. As described in the second section of the chapter, the era of **modern economic growth** began with the invention of the steam engine in 1776 and the industrial revolution that followed it. Not all nations, however, experienced such modern growth at the same time or period, which explains why some nations have a higher standard of living than other nations. As you will learn, it is possible for the poorer nations to catch up with the richer nations if they can sustain a higher level of growth.

The third section of the chapter describes the institutional structures that also promote and sustain modern economic growth in the richer, **leader countries.** These structures involve establishing strong property rights, protecting patents and copyrights, maintaining efficient financial institutions, providing widespread education, advocating free trade among nations, and using a system of markets and prices to allocate scarce resources. The poorer, **follower countries** are often missing one or more of these institutional features.

A major purpose of the chapter is to explain the factors that contribute to this economic growth. The fourth section presents the six main ingredients of economic growth. The four **supply factors** increase the output potential of the economy. Whether the economy actually produces its full potential—that is, whether the economy has both full employment and full production—depends upon two other factors: the level of aggregate demand (the **demand factor**) and the efficiency with which the economy allocates resources (the **efficiency factor**).

The fifth section of the chapter places the factors contributing to economic growth in graphical perspective with the use of the production possibilities model that was originally presented in Chapter 1. It is now used to discuss how the two major supply factors—labor input and labor productivity—shift the production possibilities curve outward.

Growth accounting is discussed in the sixth section of the chapter. Economic growth in the United States depends on the increase in the size of its labor force and on the increase in labor productivity. This latter element has been especially important in recent years and is attributed to five factors: technological advances, the expansion of the stock of capital goods, the improved education and training of its labor force, economies of scale, and the reallocation of resources.

The seventh section of the chapter evaluates the **recent productivity acceleration.** A major development in recent years was the almost doubling of the rate of labor productivity from 1995–2007 compared with that in the 1973–1995 period. This change heralded to some observers that the United States had achieved recent productivity acceleration that is characterized by advances in technology, more entrepreneurship, increasing returns from resource inputs, and greater global competition. Whether this higher rate of growth is a permanent trend remains to be seen because the trend may simply be a short-run rather than a long-run change.

The eighth and last section of the chapter raises an important question: Is more economic growth **desirable and sustainable?** This controversy has two sides. The antigrowth view is based on the environmental problems it creates, its effects on human values, and doubts about whether growth can be sustained. The defense of growth is based in part on its contribution to higher standards of living, improvements in worker safety and the environment, and history of sustainability.

■ CHECKLIST

When you have studied this chapter you should be able to

☐ Define economic growth in two different ways.
☐ Explain why economic growth is an important goal.
☐ Use the rule of 70 to show how different growth rates affect real domestic output over time.
☐ Describe the growth record of the U.S. economy since 1950.
☐ Explain how modern economic growth changed work, living standards, and societies.
☐ Discuss reasons for the uneven distribution of economic growth in modern times.
☐ Describe the differences in economic growth for leader countries and follower countries.
☐ Explain how substantial differences in living standards can be caused by differences in labor supply.

☐ List and describe six institutional structures that promote economic growth.

☐ Identify four supply factors that are ingredients of economic growth.

☐ Explain the demand factor as an ingredient of economic growth.

☐ Describe the efficiency factor as an ingredient of economic growth.

☐ Show graphically how economic growth shifts the production possibilities curve.

☐ Explain the rationale for an equation for real GDP that is based on labor inputs and labor productivity.

☐ Compare the relative importance of the two major means of increasing the real GDP in the United States.

☐ Describe the main sources of growth in the productivity of labor in the United Sates and state their relative importance.

☐ Describe the growth of labor productivity in the United States since 1973.

☐ Explain the relationship between productivity growth and the standard of living and state why it is important.

☐ Discuss how the microchip and information technology have contributed to the recent productivity acceleration.

☐ Describe the sources of increasing returns and economies of scale within the recent productivity acceleration.

☐ Explain how productivity acceleration increases global competition.

☐ Discuss the implications from productivity acceleration for economic growth.

☐ Offer a skeptical perspective on the permanency of the productivity acceleration.

☐ Present several arguments against more economic growth.

☐ Make a case for more economic growth.

☐ Explain the factors that have contributed to China's high rate of economic growth over the past 25 years and the challenges for that economy (Last Word).

■ **CHAPTER OUTLINE**

1. *Economic growth* can be defined in two ways: as an increase in real GDP over some time period; or as an increase in **real GDP per capita** over some time period. This second definition takes into account the size of the population. With either definition economic growth is calculated as a percentage rate of growth per year.

   a. Economic growth is important because it lessens the burden of scarcity; it provides the means of satisfying economic wants more fully and fulfilling new wants.

   b. One or two percentage point differences in the rate of growth result in substantial differences in annual increases in the economy's output. The approximate number of years required to double GDP can be calculated by the **rule of 70** which involves dividing 70 by the annual percentage rate of growth.

   c. In the United States, the rate of growth in real GDP has been about 3.5% annually since 1950. The growth rate for real per capita GDP in the United States has been about 2.3% annually since 1950.

(1) The growth record, however, may be understated because it does not take into account improvements in product quality or increases in leisure time. The effects of growth on the environment or quality of life could be negative *or* positive.

(2) U.S. growth rates vary quarterly and annually depending on a variety of factors; sustained growth is both a historically new occurrence and also one that is not shared equally by all countries.

2. *Modern economic growth* can be described as an improvement in living standards that is continual and sustained over time. The result is a substantial improvement in the standard of living in less than a human lifetime. Such modern economic growth began in England around 1776 with the invention and use of the steam engine, the mass production of goods, and expanded trade among nations. Subsequent developments include the use of electric or other sources of power, more technological development, and new products and services. This modern economic growth contributed to the transformation of the culture, society, and politics of nations.

   a. There has been an uneven distribution of this modern economic growth among nations, and such a distribution accounts for the large differences in per capita GDP among nations. The United States and nations of western Europe experienced modern economic growth many years earlier than did other nations, and as a result have standards of living that are much higher than most other nations.

   b. It is possible for poorer countries with a lower per capita income (*follower countries*) to catch up with richer nations that have a higher per capita income (*leader countries*). Leader countries must invent and implement new technology to grow their economies, but such a process means the growth rates in leader nations will be slow. Follower countries can have a faster growth rate because they simply adopt the existing technologies and apply them to the country, thereby skipping the lengthy process of technological development of the leader countries.

(1) Small differences in growth rates can lead to the eventual convergence and similarity in real GDP per capita of leader countries and follower countries over time (see Table 25.2).

(2) The real GDP per capita of the United States is higher than other leader countries (e. g., France) because of differences in labor supply: a larger fraction of the U. S. population is employed and U.S. employees work more hours per week.

3. Institutional structures are important for starting and sustaining modern economic growth because they increase saving and investment, develop new technologies, and promote more efficient allocation of resources. Such institutional structures include strong support for property rights, the use of patents and copyrights, efficient financial institutions, widespread education and literacy, free trade, and a competitive market system. There are other factors that also contribute, such as a stable political system and positive social or cultural attitudes toward work and risk taking.

4. The **ingredients of growth** depend on supply, demand, and efficiency factors.

a. The *supply factor* includes the quantity and quality of resources (natural, human, and capital) and technology.

b. The *demand factor* influences the level of aggregate demand in the economy that is important for sustaining full employment of resources.

c. The *efficiency factor* affects the efficient use of resources to obtain maximum production of goods and services (productive efficiency) and to allocate them to their highest and best use by society (allocative efficiency).

5. A familiar **economic model** can be used for the analysis of economic growth.

a. In the **production possibilities model,** economic growth shifts the production possibilities curve outward because of improvement in supply factors. Whether the economy operates on the frontier of the curve or inside the curve depends on the demand factor and efficiency factors.

b. Discussions of growth, however, focus primarily on supply factors. From this perspective, economic growth is obtained by increasing the *labor inputs* and by increasing the labor productivity. This relationship can be expressed in equation terms: real GDP = worker-hours × labor productivity.

(1) The hours of work are determined by the size of the working-age population and the *labor-force participation rate* (the percentage of the working age population in the labor force).

(2) *Labor productivity* (real output per work hour) is determined by many factors such as technological advance, the quantity of capital goods, the quality of labor, and the efficiency in the use of inputs.

6. Several factors are important in *growth accounting.*

a. The two main factors are increases in quantity of labor (hours of work) and increases in labor productivity. In recent years the most important factor has been increased labor productivity, so it is worthwhile identifying the main *five factors* to help increase labor productivity.

b. Technological advance is combining given amounts of resources in new and innovative ways that result in a larger output. It involves the use of new managerial methods and business organizations that improve production. Technological advance is also embodied in new capital investment that adds to the productive capacity of the economy. It accounted for about 40% of the recent increase in productivity growth.

c. The **quantity of capital** has expanded with the increase in saving and investment spending in capital goods. This private investment has increased the quantity of each worker's tools, equipment, and machinery. There is also public investment in *infrastructure* in the United States. The increase in the quantity of capital goods explains about 30% of productivity growth.

d. Increased investment in *human capital* (the training and education of workers) has expanded the productivity of workers, and has accounted for about 15% of productivity growth.

e. Two other factors, taken together, account for about 15% of productivity growth.

(1) *Economies of scale* means that there are reductions in the per-unit cost for firms as output expands. These economies occur as the market for products expands and firms have the opportunity to increase output to meet this greater demand.

(2) **Improved allocation of resources** occurs when workers are shifted from lower-productivity employment to higher-productivity employment in an economy. Included in this category would be reductions in discrimination in labor markets and reduced barriers to trade, both of which increase the efficient use of labor resources.

7. Increases in **productivity growth,** even small ones, can have a substantial effect on average real hourly wages and the standard of living in an economy. From 1973–1995, labor productivity grew by an average of 1.4% annually, but from 1995–2007 it grew by 2.7% annually. Productivity has accelerated since 1995. The recent productivity acceleration means there can be a faster rate of economic growth and improvement in standards of living.

a. The reasons for the productivity acceleration are based on several factors.

(1) There has been a dramatic rise in entrepreneurship and innovation based on the microchip and *information technology.*

(2) The new *start-up firms* often experience *increasing returns*, which means a firm's output increases by a larger percentage than the increase in its resource inputs. These increasing returns have been achieved by more specialized inputs, the spreading of development costs, simultaneous consumption, *network effects,* and *learning by doing.*

(3) The new technology and improvements in communication have increased global competition, thus lowering production costs, restraining price increases, and stimulating innovation to remain competitive.

b. The recent productivity acceleration means there can be a faster rate of economic growth and improvement in standards of living. This development does not mean that the business cycle is dead, but rather that the trend line for productivity growth and economic growth has become steeper.

c. Questions remain about whether there is a new trend of higher productivity rates or just a short upturn in the business cycle. Skeptics wonder whether the increase in productivity growth can be sustained over a longer period of time or whether the economy will return to its long-term trend in productivity.

d. The conclusion is that the prospects for productivity growth to continue are good because of the wider use of information technology, yet in the past few years productivity growth has slowed, which raises questions about whether the acceleration is a long-run trend and sustainable.

8. There is an ongoing debate about whether economic growth is **desirable and sustainable.**

a. The antigrowth view sees several problems: Growth pollutes the environment; may produce more goods and services, but does not create a better life; and may not be sustainable at the current rate of resource depletion.

b. The defense of economic growth is based on several considerations: Growth produces a higher standard of living and reduces the burden of scarcity; the technology it creates improves people's lives and can reduce pollution; and it is sustainable because market incentives encourage the use of substitute resources.

9. (Last Word). China has experienced annual rates of economic growth of almost 9% over the past 25 years. Real income per capita has also increased by about 8 percent annually since 1980. The increased output and rising incomes have fueled increases in saving and investment that in turn contribute to an increase in the stock of capital goods and technological advance. This economic growth is not without economic problems such as trade disputes, rising inflation, the unemployment of rural workers, and government inefficiencies.

■ **HINTS AND TIPS**

1. Chapter 25 contains very little economics that should be new to you. Chapter 1 introduced you to the production possibilities model that is now discussed in more detail. Chapter 23 introduced you to GDP and modern economic growth.

2. Table 25.3 is important if you want to understand the factors that influence economic growth in the United States. The figures in the table indicate the relative importance of each major factor in different periods. In recent years, almost all of U.S. economic growth arose from increases in labor productivity. Five factors affecting the growth of labor productivity include technological advance, quantity of capital, education and training, economies of scale, and resource allocation.

3. The last two sections of the chapter focus on major economic issues about which there is some debate. You will want to evaluate the evidence for and against the idea that there is a lasting increase in productivity growth. You will want to understand the advantages and disadvantages of economic growth.

■ **IMPORTANT TERMS**

economic growth

modern economic growth

follower countries

leader countries

supply factor

demand factor

efficiency factor

labor productivity

labor-force
   participation rate

growth accounting

infrastructure

human capital

economies of scale

information technology

start-up firms

increasing returns

network effects

learning by doing

■ **SELF-TEST**

■ **FILL-IN QUESTIONS**

1. Economic growth is best measured either by an increase in (nominal, real) _____ GDP over a time period or by an increase in _____ GDP per capita over a time period. A rise in real GDP per capita (increases, decreases) _____ the standard of living and _____ the burden of scarcity in the economy.

2. Assume an economy has a real GDP of $3600 billion. If the growth rate is 5%, real GDP will increase by ($360, $180) _____ billion next year; but if the rate of growth is only 3%, the annual increase in real GDP will be ($54, $108) _____ billion. A two percentage point difference in the growth rate results in a ($72, $254) _____ billion difference in the annual increase in real GDP.

3. Since 1950, real GDP in the United States increased at an annual rate of about (2.3, 3.5) _____% and real GDP per capita increased at an annual rate of about _____%.

4. Modern economic growth is uneven across countries because leader countries have experienced such growth for a (shorter, longer) _____ time period and follower countries have experienced such growth for _____ time period. It is possible for a follower country to catch up with the standard of living of a leader country if the economic growth rates for the follower country is significantly (smaller, larger) _____ than the growth rate for the leader country, and the difference is sustained over time.

5. Among the institutional structures that contribute to modern economic growth in leader countries are established property (lines, rights) _____, protection for copyrights and (movies, patents) _____, the efficient channeling of savings and investment (financial, government) _____ institutions, widespread programs for (immigration, education) _____, specialization in production by nations that comes from (free, restricted) _____ trade, and the use of the competitive market system.

6. The four supply factors in economic growth are

a. _____

b. _____

c. _____

d. _____

7. To realize its growing production potential, a nation must fully employ its expanding supplies of resources, which is the (efficiency, demand) _____ factor in economic growth, and it must also achieve productive and allocative _____, the other factor contributing to economic growth.

8. In the production possibilities model, economic growth increases primarily because of (demand, supply) _____ factors that shift the production possibilities curve to the (left, right) _____; but if there is less than full employment and production, the economy (may, may not) _____ realize its potential.

9. Real GDP of any economy in any year is equal to the quantity of labor employed (divided, multiplied) _____ by the productivity of labor. The quantity of labor is measured by the number of (businesses, hours of labor) _____. Productivity is equal to real GDP per (capita, worker-hour) _____.

10. The quantity of labor employed in the economy in any year depends on the size of the (unemployed, employed) _____ labor force and the length of the average workweek. The size element depends on the size of the working-age population and the labor-force (unemployment, participation) _____ rate.

11. The recent record of economic growth in the United States shows that the increase in the quantity of labor is (more, less) _____ important than increases in labor productivity in accounting for economic growth.

12. Factors contributing to labor productivity include

    a. technological _____

    b. increases in the quantity of _____ and in the quantity available per _____

    c. the improved _____ and _____ of workers

    d. economies of _____

    e. the improved _____ of resources.

13. An increase in the quantity of the capital stock of a nation is the result of saving and (consumption, investment) _____. A key determinant of labor productivity is the amount of capital goods available per (consumer, worker) _____.

14. Infrastructure, such as highways and bridges, is a form of (private, public) _____ investment that complements _____ capital goods.

15. The knowledge and skills that make a productive worker are a form of (physical, human) _____

capital. This type of capital is often obtained through (consumption, education) _____.

16. Reductions in per-unit costs that result from the increase in the size of markets and firms are called (improved resource allocation, economies of scale) _____, but the movement of a worker from a job with lower productivity to one with higher productivity would be an example of _____.

17. An increase in labor productivity will (increase, decrease) _____ real output, real income, and real wages. Assuming an economy has an increase in labor productivity of 1.5%, it will take (28, 47) _____ years for its standard of living to double, but an increase in labor productivity of 2.5% annually will increase its standard of living in _____ years.

18. The characteristics of the recent productivity acceleration are (advances, declines) _____ in information technology, business firms that experience returns to scale that are (decreasing, increasing) _____, and global competition that is _____.

19. Skeptics contend that the increase in the rate of productivity growth may be a (short-run, long-run) _____ trend that is not sustainable over a _____ period.

20. Critics of economic growth contend that it (cleans up, pollutes) _____ the environment, it (does, does not) _____ solve problems such as poverty and homelessness, and (is, is not) _____ sustainable. Defenders of economic growth say that it creates (less, greater) _____ material abundance, results in a (higher, lower) _____ standard of living, and an efficient and sustainable allocation of resources based on price (discounts, incentives) _____.

■ TRUE–FALSE QUESTIONS

Circle T if the statement is true, F if it is false.

1. Economic growth is measured as either an increase in real GDP or an increase in real GDP per capita.   **T F**

2. Real GDP is the best measure of economic growth for comparing standards of living among nations.   **T F**

3. Suppose two economies both have GDPs of $500 billion. If the GDPs grow at annual rates of 3% in the first economy and 5% in the second economy, the difference in their amounts of growth in one year is $10 billion.   **T F**

4. Since 1950, the U. S. data show that the average annual rate of growth was greater for real GDP per capita than for real GDP. **T   F**

5. Growth rate estimates generally attempt to take into account changes in the quality of goods produced and changes in the amount of leisure members of the economy enjoy. **T   F**

6. Before the advent of modern economic growth starting in England in the later 1700s, living standards showed no sustained increases over time. **T   F**

7. Poorer follower countries can never catch up with and or surpass the living standards of rich leader countries. **T   F**

8. An institutional structure that promotes economic growth is a competitive market system. **T   F**

9. Changes in the physical and technical agents of production are supply factors for economic growth that enable an economy to expand its potential GDP. **T   F**

10. The demand factor in economic growth refers to the ability of the economy to expand its production as the demand for products grows. **T   F**

11. An increase in the quantity and quality of natural resources is an efficiency factor for economic growth. **T   F**

12. A shift outward in the production possibilities curve is the direct result of improvements in supply factors for economic growth. **T   F**

13. The real GDP of an economy in any year is equal to its input of labor divided by the productivity of labor. **T   F**

14. The hours of labor input depend on the size of the employed labor force and the length of the average workweek. **T   F**

15. Increased labor productivity has been more important than increased labor inputs in the growth of the U.S. economy since 1995. **T   F**

16. The largest factor increasing labor productivity in the U.S. economy has been technological advance. **T   F**

17. One determinant of labor productivity is the quantity of capital goods available to workers. **T   F**

18. Public investment in the form of new infrastructure often complements private capital investment. **T   F**

19. Education and training contribute to a worker's stock of human capital. **T   F**

20. Economies of scale are reductions in per-unit cost that result in a decrease in the size of markets and firms. **T   F**

21. If the rate of growth in labor productivity averages 2.5% a year, it will take about 50 years for the standard of living to double. **T   F**

22. Productivity growth is the basic source of improvements in real wage rates and the standard of living. **T   F**

23. More specialized inputs and network effects are two sources of increasing returns and economies of scale in the recent productivity acceleration. **T   F**

24. Critics of economic growth say that it adds to environmental problems, increases human stress, and exhausts natural resources. **T   F**

25. Defenders of economic growth say it is sustainable in the short run, but not in the long run. **T   F**

■ **MULTIPLE-CHOICE QUESTIONS**

Circle the letter that corresponds to the best answer.

1. Which of the following is the best measure of economic growth?
  (a) the supply factor
  (b) the demand factor
  (c) real GDP per capita
  (d) nominal GDP per capita

2. If the real output of an economy were to increase from $2000 billion to $2100 billion in 1 year, the rate of growth of real output during that year would be
  (a) 1%
  (b) 5%
  (c) 10%
  (d) 50%

3. Which is a benefit of real economic growth to a society?
  (a) The society is less able to satisfy new wants.
  (b) Everyone enjoys a greater nominal income.
  (c) The burden of scarcity increases.
  (d) The standard of living increases.

4. Which concept would be associated with sustained and ongoing increases in living standards that can cause dramatic increases in the standard of living within less than a single human lifetime?
  (a) increasing returns
  (b) economies of scale
  (c) growth accounting
  (d) modern economic growth

5. Which one of the following is true?
  (a) Poor follower countries can catch up and even surpass the living standards of rich leader countries.
  (b) As a result of modern economic growth, there are no sustained increases in growth over time.
  (c) Differences in labor supply make a minimal contribution to differences in living standards.
  (d) There is a relatively even distribution of economic growth across nations.

6. Which is an institutional structure that most promotes economic growth?
  (a) enforcing property rights
  (b) moving to a command economy
  (c) eliminating patents and copyrights
  (d) placing restrictions on international trade

7. A supply factor in economic growth would be
  (a) an increase in the efficient use of resources
  (b) a decline in the rate of resource depletion

(c) an improvement in the quality of labor

(d) an increase in consumption spending

8. Which is a demand factor in economic growth?

(a) an increase in the purchasing power of the economy

(b) an increase in the economy's stock of capital goods

(c) more natural resources

(d) technological progress

Use the following graph to answer Questions 9 and 10.

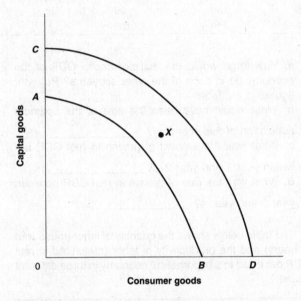

9. If the production possibilities curve of an economy shifts from **AB** to **CD,** it is most likely the result of what factor affecting economic growth?

(a) a supply factor

(b) a demand factor

(c) an efficiency factor

(d) an allocation factor

10. If the production possibilities curve for an economy is at **CD** but the economy is operating at point **X,** the reasons are most likely

(a) supply and environmental factors

(b) demand and efficiency factors

(c) labor inputs and labor productivity

(d) technological progress

11. Total output or real GDP in any year is equal to

(a) labor inputs divided by resource outputs

(b) labor productivity multiplied by real output

(c) worker-hours multiplied by labor productivity

(d) worker-hours divided by labor productivity

12. Assume that an economy has 1000 workers, each working 2000 hours per year. If the average real output per worker-hour is $9, then total output or real GDP will be

(a) $2 million

(b) $9 million

(c) $18 million

(d) $24 million

13. What is the other major factor that, when combined with the growth of labor productivity, accounts for long-term economic growth in the United States?

(a) an increase in government spending

(b) an increase in the quantity of labor

(c) a decrease in the interest rate

(d) a decrease in personal taxes

14. The factor accounting for the largest increase in the productivity of labor in the United States has been

(a) economies of scale

(b) technological advance

(c) the quantity of capital

(d) the education and training of workers

15. How does a nation typically acquire more capital goods?

(a) by reducing the workweek and increasing leisure

(b) by saving income and using it for capital investment

(c) by increasing government regulation on the capital stock

(d) by reducing the amount of capital goods available per worker

16. An example of U. S. public investment in infrastructure would be

(a) an airline company

(b) a natural gas pipeline

(c) an auto and truck plant

(d) an interstate highway

17. Economists call the knowledge and skills that make a productive worker

(a) the labor-force participation rate

(b) learning by doing

(c) human capital

(d) infrastructure

18. What economic concept would be most closely associated with a situation where a large manufacturer of food products uses extensive assembly lines with computerization and robotics that serve to reduce per-unit costs of production?

(a) economies of scale

(b) sustainability of growth

(c) network effects

(d) simultaneous consumption

19. The decline of discrimination in education and labor markets increased the overall rate of labor productivity in the economy by giving groups freedom to move from jobs with lower productivity to ones with higher productivity. This development would be an example of a(n)

(a) fall in the labor-force participation rate

(b) rise in the natural rate of unemployment

(c) technological advance

(d) improvement in resource allocation

20. If the annual growth in a nation's productivity is 2% rather than 1%, then the nation's standard of living will double in

(a) 25 years

(b) 35 years

(c) 50 years

(d) 70 years

21. The recent productivity acceleration is described as having
(a) more tax revenues and more government spending
(b) a faster rate of inflation and fewer specialized inputs
(c) more experienced workers, but fewer available jobs for them
(d) a faster rate of productivity growth and faster economic growth

22. Increasing returns would be a situation where a firm
(a) triples its workforce and other inputs, and its output doubles
(b) doubles its workforce and other inputs, and its output triples
(c) doubles its workforce and other inputs, and its output doubles
(d) quadruples its workforce and other inputs, and its output triples

23. Which would be a source of increasing returns and economies of scale within the recent productivity acceleration?
(a) social environment
(b) noninflationary growth
(c) simultaneous consumption
(d) less specialized inputs

24. A skeptic of the permanency of the increase in productivity growth would argue that it
(a) is based on learning by doing instead of infrastructure
(b) raises tax revenues collected by government
(c) lowers the natural rate of unemployment
(d) is based on a short-run trend

25. Defenders of rapid economic growth say that it
(a) produces an equitable distribution of income
(b) creates common property resources
(c) leads to higher living standards
(d) spreads costs of development

■ **PROBLEMS**

1. Given the hypothetical data in the table below, calculate the annual rates of growth in real GDP and real per capita GDP over the period given. The numbers for real GDP are in billions.

Year	Real GDP	Annual growth in%	Real GDP per capita	Annual growth in%
1	$2,416		$11,785	
2	2,472	_____	11,950	_____
3	2,563	_____	12,213	_____
4	2,632	_____	12,421	_____
5	2,724	_____	12,719	_____
6	2,850	_____	12,948	_____

2. Suppose the real GDP and the population of an economy in seven different years were those shown in the following table.

Year	Population, million	Real GDP, billions of dollars	Per capita real GDP
1	30	$ 9	$300
2	60	24	_____
3	90	45	_____
4	120	66	_____
5	150	90	_____
6	180	99	_____
7	210	105	_____

a. How large would the real per capita GDP of the economy be in each of the other six years? Put your figures in the table.
b. What would have been the size of the optimum population of this economy? _____
c. What was the *amount* of growth in real GDP between year 1 and year 2? $ _____
d. What was the rate of growth in real GDP between year 3 and year 4? _____%

3. The table below shows the quantity of labor (measured in hours) and the productivity of labor (measured in real GDP per hour) in a hypothetical economy in three different years.

Year	Quantity of labor	Productivity of labor	Real GDP
1	1000	$100	$_____
2	1000	105	_____
3	1100	105	_____

a. Compute the economy's real GDP in each of the three years and enter them in the table.
b. Between years 1 and 2, the quantity of labor remained constant, but
(1) the productivity of labor increased by _____%, and
(2) as a consequence, real GDP increased by _____%.
c. Between years 2 and 3, the productivity of labor remained constant, but
(1) the quantity of labor increased by _____%, and
(2) as a consequence, real GDP increased by _____%.
d. Between years 1 and 3
(1) real GDP increased by _____%, and
(2) this rate of increase is approximately equal to the sum of the rates of increase in the (quantity, productivity) _____ and the _____ of labor.

4. In the table below, indicate how may years it will take to double the standard of living (Years) in an economy given different annual rates of growth in labor productivity.

Productivity	Years
1.0%	_____
1.4%	_____
1.8%	_____
2.2%	_____
2.6%	_____
3.0%	_____

What can you conclude about the importance of small changes in the growth rate of productivity on the standard of living?

■ **SHORT ANSWER AND ESSAY QUESTIONS**

1. What two ways are used to measure economic growth? Why does the size of the population matter when considering growth rates?

2. Why is economic growth a widely held and desired economic goal? Explain the reasons.

3. Describe the growth rate for the United States since 1950. What three qualifications should be made about the rate?

4. Explain how modern economic growth occurred and how it has affected nations and societies.

5. Why is there an uneven distribution of economic growth?

6. Explain how it is possible for the standards of living in poorer nations to catch up with the standards of living in richer nations. What role does technology play in the catch-up process?

7. Why is the GDP per capita in the United States so much higher than that of other rich leader nations?

8. Describe six institutional structures that promote economic growth in a nation. What other factors also influence a nation's capacity for economic growth?

9. What are the six basic ingredients of economic growth? What are the essential differences between the supply, demand, and efficiency factors?

10. How does economic growth affect production possibilities? What demand and efficiency assumptions are necessary to achieve maximum productive potential?

11. What is the relationship between the real GDP produced in any year and the quantity of labor employed and labor productivity? What factor appears to be more important for growth?

12. What is technological advance, and why are technological advance and capital formation closely related processes?

13. What is the relationship between investment and the stock of capital? What is the connection between increases in the capital stock and the rate of economic growth?

14. What increases the "quality" or human capital of labor? How is this quality usually measured? What are some of the problems with this path to improving the quality of the labor force?

15. Explain how economies of scale and resource allocation contribute to labor productivity.

16. Explain the relationship between productivity growth and real output, real income, and real wages.

17. Discuss how the microchip and information technology contributed to the recent productivity acceleration.

18. Describe at least four sources of increasing returns and economies of scale within the recent productivity acceleration.

19. Identify and explain implications from the recent productivity acceleration for economic growth. Is the recent productivity acceleration a permanent trend?

20. What arguments are made for and against economic growth in the United States?

ANSWERS

Chapter 25 Economic Growth

FILL-IN QUESTIONS

1. real, real, increases, decreases
2. $180, $108, $72
3. 3.5, 2.3
4. longer, shorter, larger
5. rights, patents, financial, education, free
6. *a.* quantity and quality of natural resources; *b.* quantity and quality of human resources; *c.* the supply or stock of capital goods; *d.* technology (any order for *a–d*)
7. demand, efficiency
8. supply, right, may not
9. multiplied, hours of labor, worker-hour
10. employed, participation
11. less
12. *a.* advance; *b.* capital, worker; *c.* education, training (either order); *d.* scale; *e.* allocation
13. investment, worker
14. public, private
15. human, education
16. economies of scale, improved resource allocation
17. increase, 47, 28
18. advances, increasing, increasing
19. short-run, long-run
20. pollutes, does not, is not, greater, higher, incentives

TRUE–FALSE QUESTIONS

1. T, p. 499	**10.** F, p. 506	**19.** T, p. 509
2. F, p. 499	**11.** F, p. 506	**20.** F, pp. 510–511
3. T, p. 499	**12.** T, p. 506	**21.** F, p. 512
4. F, p. 500	**13.** F, p. 507	**22.** T, p. 512
5. F, p. 500	**14.** T, p. 507	**23.** T, p. 512
6. T, p. 504	**15.** T, p. 508	**24.** T, p. 515
7. F, p. 502	**16.** T, p. 508	**25.** F, p. 515
8. T, p. 505	**17.** T, p. 509	
9. T, pp. 505–506	**18.** T, p. 509	

MULTIPLE-CHOICE QUESTIONS

1. c, p. 499	**10.** b, p. 506	**19.** d, p. 511
2. b, p. 499	**11.** c, p. 507	**20.** b, p. 512
3. d, p.499	**12.** c, p. 507	**21.** d, p. 512
4. d, p. 501	**13.** b, p. 507	**22.** b, p. 512
5. a, p. 502	**14.** b, p. 508	**23.** c, p. 513
6. a, p. 504	**15.** b, p. 509	**24.** d, p. 514
7. c, p. 506	**16.** d, p. 509	**25.** c, p. 515
8. a, p. 506	**17.** c, p. 509	
9. a, p. 506	**18.** a, p. 510	

PROBLEMS

1. *real GDP*: years 1–2 (2.3%); years 2–3 (3.7%); years 3–4 (2.7%); years 4–5 (3.5%); years 5–6 (4.6%); *real GDP per capita*: years 1–2 (1.4%); years 2–3 (2.2%); years 3–4 (1.7%); years 4–5 (2.4%); years 5–6 (1.8%)

2. *a.* 400, 500, 550, 600, 550, 500; *b.* 150 million; *c.* $15 billion; *d.* 46.7%

3. *a.* 100,000, 105,000, 115,500; *b.* (1) 5, (2) 5; *c.* (1) 10, (2) 10; *d.* (1) 15.5, (2) quantity, productivity

4. 70, 50, 39, 31, 27, 23. Small changes make a large difference in the number of years it takes for the standard of living to double in an economy, especially at very low rates of growth in productivity.

SHORT ANSWER AND ESSAY QUESTIONS

1. p. 499	**8.** p. 505	**15.** pp. 510–511
2. p. 499	**9.** pp. 505–506	**16.** pp. 511–512
3. p. 500	**10.** p. 507	**17.** p. 512
4. p. 501	**11.** p. 508	**18.** pp. 512–513
5. pp. 501–502	**12.** p. 509	**19.** pp. 513–514
6. p. 502	**13.** p. 509	**20.** p. 515
7. pp. 503–504	**14.** pp. 509–510	

CHAPTER 26

Business Cycles, Unemployment, and Inflation

This chapter begins with an explanation of **business cycles:** the ups and downs in real output of the economy that occur over the years. What may not be immediately evident to you, but will become clear as you read this chapter, is that these alternating periods of prosperity and hard times have taken place over a long period in which the trends in real output, employment, and the standard of living have been upward. During this long history booms and busts have occurred quite irregularly; their duration and intensity have been so varied that it is better to think of them as economic instability rather than regular business cycles.

Two principal problems result from the instability of the economy. The first problem is described in the second section of the chapter. Here you will find an examination of the **unemployment** that accompanies a downturn in the level of economic activity in the economy. You will first learn how economists measure the unemployment rate in the economy and the problems they encounter. You will also discover that there are three different kinds of unemployment and that full employment means that less than 100% of the labor force is employed. You will also find out how unemployment imposes an economic cost on the economy and that this cost is unequally distributed among different groups in our society.

The second major problem that results from economic instability is **inflation.** It is examined in the third section of the chapter, and also in the following two sections. Inflation is an increase in the general (or average) level of prices in an economy. It does not have a unique cause: it may result from increases in demand, from increases in costs, or from both sources.

Regardless of its cause, inflation may impose a real hardship on different groups in our society as you will learn in the fourth section of the chapter. **Inflation arbitrarily redistributes real income and wealth** in the economy. Unanticipated inflation hurts those on fixed incomes, those who save money, and those who lend money. If inflation is anticipated, some of its burden can be reduced, but that depends on whether a group can protect their income with cost-of-living or interest rate adjustments.

Finally, inflation has redistribution effects on the real output of the economy as described in the last section of the chapter. **Cost-push inflation and demand-pull inflation** have different effects on output and employment that vary with the severity of the inflation. In the extreme, an economy can experience very high rates of inflation—**hyperinflation**—that can result in its breakdown.

Understanding the business cycle and the twin problems of unemployment and inflation are important because it prepares you for later chapters and the explanations of how the macroeconomy works.

■ **CHECKLIST**

When you have finished this chapter you should be able to

☐ Explain what is meant by the business cycle.
☐ Describe the four phases of a generalized business cycle.
☐ Explain the relationship between business cycles and economic shocks to the economy.
☐ Describe the immediate cause of the cyclical changes in the levels of real output and employment.
☐ Identify differences in the way cyclical fluctuations affect industries producing capital and consumer durable goods, and how they affect industries producing consumer nondurable goods and services.
☐ Describe how the Bureau of Labor Statistics (BLS) measures the rate of unemployment, and list the two criticisms of their survey data.
☐ Distinguish among frictional, structural, and cyclical types of unemployment, and explain the causes of these three kinds of unemployment.
☐ Define full employment and the full-employment unemployment rate (or the natural rate of unemployment).
☐ Use actual and potential GDP to define a GDP gap.
☐ State Okun's law on the economic cost of unemployment.
☐ Discuss the unequal burdens of unemployment.
☐ Describe the noneconomic costs of unemployment.
☐ Offer international comparisons of unemployment.
☐ Define the meaning of inflation.
☐ Calculate the rate of inflation using the Consumer Price Index.
☐ Make international comparisons of inflation rates.
☐ Define demand-pull inflation.
☐ Define cost-push inflation and per-unit production costs.
☐ Describe the complexities involved in distinguishing between demand-pull and cost-push inflation.
☐ Distinguish between real and nominal income.
☐ Calculate real income using data on nominal income and the price level.
☐ Explain how fixed-income receivers, savers, and creditors are hurt by unanticipated inflation.

☐ Explain how flexible-income receivers or debtors are not harmed and may be helped by unanticipated inflation.

☐ Discuss why the redistributive effects of inflation are less severe when it is anticipated.

☐ Explain the difference between the real and the nominal interest rates.

☐ Make three final points about the redistribution effects of inflation.

☐ Describe the effect of cost-push inflation on real output.

☐ Compare and contrast the views of economists about the effects of mild demand-pull inflation on real output.

☐ Describe hyperinflation and its effects on prices and real output.

☐ Explain the relationship, or lack of it, between stock market and the macroeconomy (Last Word).

■ **CHAPTER OUTLINE**

1. Although the long-term trend for the U.S. economy is one of economic growth and expansion, the growth pattern has been interrupted by periods of economic instability, or *business cycles.*

a. The business cycle means alternating periods of prosperity and recession even if the long-term trends show economic growth.

(1) The typical cyclical pattern, however, is peak, recession, trough, and expansion, to another peak. *Peak* is the maximum level of real output at the start of the cycle. It is followed by a *recession,* which is a period of decline in real output that lasts six months or longer. When real output is no longer declining, it has hit its *trough.* This low point is followed by *expansion* or recovery in which the economy experiences an increase in real output.

(2) These recurrent periods of ups and downs in real output (and associated income and employment) are irregular in their duration and intensity.

b. Economists think that changes in the levels of output and employment are largely the result of unexpected changes in the level of total spending in the economy. These economic shocks require difficult adjustments to be made by households and businesses in the economy, but such adjustments are not easily or quickly made because prices tend to be sticky. For example, if total spending unexpectedly falls and prices are relatively fixed, business firms will not be able to sell all their output and have to cut back on production. As a consequence, GDP falls, income falls, unemployment rises, and the economy moves into recession.

c. The business cycle affects almost the entire economy, but it does not affect all parts in the same way and to the same degree: The production of capital and consumer durable goods fluctuates more than the production of consumer nondurable goods and services during the cycle, because the purchase of capital and consumer durable goods can be postponed.

2. One of the twin problems arising from the economic instability of the business cycle is **unemployment.**

a. The *unemployment rate* is calculated by dividing the number of persons in the *labor force* who are unemployed by the total number of persons in the labor force. Unemployment data have been criticized for at least two reasons:

(1) Part-time workers are considered fully employed.

(2) *Discouraged workers* who have left the labor force are not counted as unemployed.

b. Full employment does not mean that all workers in the labor force are employed and there is no unemployment; some unemployment is normal. There are at least three types of unemployment.

(1) *Frictional unemployment* is due to workers with marketable skills searching for new jobs or waiting to take new jobs. This type of unemployment is short-term, inevitable, and also generally desirable because it allows people to find more optimal employment.

(2) *Structural unemployment* is due to the changes in technology and in the types of goods and services consumers wish to buy. These changes affect the total demand for labor in particular industries or regions. Such unemployed workers have few desired marketable skills so they often need retraining, more education, or have to move if they are to be employed.

(3) *Cyclical unemployment* arises from a decline in total spending in the economy that pushes an economy into an economic downturn or recession. With the onset of recession, businesses cut production, real GDP falls, and unemployment eventually rises.

c. "Full employment" is less than 100% because some frictional and structural unemployment are unavoidable. The *full-employment unemployment rate* or the *natural rate of unemployment (NRU)* is the sum of frictional and structural unemployment and is achieved when cyclical unemployment is zero (the real output of the economy is equal to its *potential output*). NRU is the unemployment rate that is consistent with full employment. It is not, however, automatically achieved and changes over time. Currently it is about 4 to 5% of the labor force.

d. Unemployment has an economic cost.

(1) The *GDP gap* is a measure of that cost. It is the difference between actual and potential GDP. When the difference is negative, it means that the economy is underperforming relative to its potential.

(2) *Okun's law* predicts that for every 1% the actual unemployment rate exceeds the natural rate of unemployment, there is a negative GDP gap of about 2%.

(3) This cost of unemployment is unequally distributed among different groups of workers in the labor force. Workers in lower-skilled occupations have higher unemployment than workers in higher-skilled occupations. Teenagers have higher unemployment rates than do adults. The unemployment rate for African Americans and Hispanics is higher than it is for whites. Less educated workers have higher unemployment rates than more educated workers.

e. Unemployment also has noneconomic costs in the form of social, psychological, and health problems for individuals and families. High unemployment rates in nations also can contribute to political unrest and violence.

f. Unemployment rates differ across nations because of differences in phases of the business cycle and natural rates of unemployment.

3. Over its history, the U.S. economy has experienced not only periods of unemployment but periods of **inflation.**

a. Inflation is an increase in the general level of prices in the economy. During any period, the prices of products can rise, fall, or stay the same. Inflation occurs when there is an overall rise in the prices of products.

b. The primary measure of inflation in the United States is the **Consumer Price Index (CPI).**

(1) The index is calculated by comparing the prices of a "market basket" of consumer goods in a particular year to the prices for that same market basket in a base period, and then multiplying it by 100 to get a percentage change.

(2) The rate of inflation from one year to the next is equal to the percentage change in the CPI between the current year and the preceding year. The CPI was 210.00 in 2007 and 201.8 in 2006. The rate of inflation was 4.1%. The calculation is $[(210.0 - 201.8)/201.8] \times 100 = 4.1\%$.

(3) **The rule of 70** can be used to calculate the number of years it will take for the price level to double at any given rate of inflation. For example, if the rate of inflation is 3 percent a year, it will take about 23 years for the price level to double $[70/3 = 23]$.

c. The United States has experienced both inflation and deflation, but the past half-century has been a period of inflation. Other industrial nations have also experienced inflation.

d. There are at least two types of inflation. They may operate separately or simultaneously to raise the price level.

(1) **Demand-pull inflation** is the result of excess total spending in the economy, or "too much spending chasing too few goods." With this inflation, increasing demand is pulling up the price level.

(2) **Cost-push inflation** is the result of factors that raise **per-unit production costs.** This average cost is found by dividing the total cost of the resource inputs by the amount of output produced. As these costs rise, profits get squeezed and firms cut back on production. The rising costs push the price level higher, and output also declines. The major source of this inflation has been supply shocks from an increase in the prices of resource inputs.

e. It is difficult to distinguish between demand-pull and cost-push inflation in the real world. Demand-pull inflation can continue as long as there is excess spending. Cost-push inflation is self-limiting because as the price level rises, it reduces output and employment, and these recession effects constrain additional price increases.

4. Inflation arbitrarily redistributes real income and wealth. It benefits some groups and hurts other groups in the economy.

a. Whether someone benefits or is hurt by inflation is measured by what happens to real income. Inflation injures those whose real income falls and benefits those whose real income rises.

(1) **Real income** is determined by dividing **nominal income** by the price level expressed in hundredths.

(2) The percentage change in real income can be approximated by subtracting the percentage change in the price level from the percentage change in nominal income.

(3) The redistribution effects of inflation depend on whether it is anticipated or unanticipated.

b. **Unanticipated inflation** hurts *fixed-income receivers, savers,* and *creditors* because it lowers the real value of their assets.

c. Unanticipated inflation may not affect or may help *flexible-income receivers.* For example, some union workers get automatic **cost-of-living adjustments (COLAs)** in their pay when the CPI rises. It helps *debtors* because it lowers the real value of debts to be repaid.

d. When there is **anticipated inflation** people can adjust their nominal incomes to reflect the expected rise in the price level, and the redistribution of income and wealth is lessened. To reduce the effects of inflation on a **nominal interest rate,** an inflation premium (the expected rate of inflation) is added to the **real interest rate.**

e. There are three other redistribution issues associated with inflation. There can be a decline in the price level, or **deflation,** and if unanticipated, it has the reverse effects that inflation has on various groups. Inflation can have mixed effects (positive or negative), depending on the composition of a household's assets. The effects of inflation are arbitrary and not directed at any one group or type.

5. Inflation also has an effect on real output that varies by the type of inflation and its severity.

a. Cost-push inflation reduces real output, employment, and income.

b. Views of mild demand-pull inflation vary. It may reduce real output, or it may be a necessary by-product of economic growth.

c. *Hyperinflation*—extremely high rates of inflation—can lead to a breakdown of the economy by redistributing income and reducing real output and employment.

6. (Last Word). Do changes in the stock market affect the economy? The evidence indicates that changes in stock prices have only a weak effect on consumption and investment and the macroeconomy. Stock market bubbles where there is a large increase in stock prices that then decline rapidly can adversely affect the macroeconomy. Stock prices are a relatively good indicator of future business conditions because they are related to business profits.

■ HINTS AND TIPS

1. Some students get confused by the seemingly contradictory term **full-employment unemployment rate** and related unemployment concepts. Full employment does not mean that everyone who wants to work has a job; it means that the economy is achieving its potential output and has a natural rate of unemployment. Remember that there are three types of unemployment: frictional, structural, and cyclical. There will always be some unemployment arising from frictional reasons (e.g., people searching for jobs) or structural reasons (e.g., changes in industry demand), and these two types of unemployment are "natural" for an economy. When there is cyclical unemployment because of a downturn in the business cycle, the economy is not producing its potential output. Thus, full-employment unemployment rate means that there are no cyclical reasons causing unemployment, only frictional or structural reasons.

2. To verify your understanding of how to calculate the unemployment rate, GDP gap, or inflation rate, do Problems 1, 2, and 3 in this *Study Guide* chapter.

3. Inflation is a rise in the *general* level of prices, not just a rise in the prices of a few products. An increase in product price is caused by supply or demand factors. You now know why the prices for many products rise in an economy. The macroeconomic reasons given in Chapter 26 for the increase in the general level of prices are different from the microeconomic reasons for a price increase that you learned about in Chapter 3.

■ IMPORTANT TERMS

business cycle	Okun's law
peak	inflation
recession	Consumer Price Index (CPI)
trough	
expansion	demand-pull inflation
labor force	cost-push inflation
unemployment rate	per-unit production costs
discouraged workers	nominal income
frictional unemployment	real income
structural unemployment	anticipated inflation
cyclical unemployment	unanticipated inflation
full-employment rate of unemployment	cost-of-living adjustments (COLAs)
natural rate of unemployment (NRU)	real interest rate
	nominal interest rate
potential output	deflation
GDP gap	hyperinflation

SELF-TEST

■ FILL-IN QUESTIONS

1. The business cycle is a term that encompasses the recurrent ups, or (decreases, increases) _____, and downs, or _____, in the level of business activity in the economy. The order of the four phases of a typical business cycle are peak, (expansion, trough, recession) _____, _____, and _____.

2. Business cycle fluctuations arise because of economic (shocks, deflation) _____ that the economy has difficulty adjusting to quickly or easily because in the short run, prices are (flexible, sticky) _____. Such economic shocks cause unexpected changes in the level of total (money, spending) _____.

3. Expansion and contraction of the economy affect to a greater extent the production and employment in the consumer (durables, nondurables) _____ and (capital, consumer) _____ goods industries than they do (durable, nondurable) _____ goods and service industries.

4. The unemployment rate is found by dividing the number of (employed, unemployed) _____ persons by the (population, labor force) _____ and (multiplying, dividing) _____ by 100.

5. In calculating the unemployment rate, the U.S. Bureau of Labor Statistics treats part-time workers as (unemployed, employed, not in the labor force) _____ and discouraged workers who are not actively seeking work as _____. Critics of the official BLS calculation contend that such designations mean that unemployment is (overstated, understated) _____.

6. When workers are searching for new jobs or waiting to start new jobs, this type of unemployment is called (structural, frictional, cyclical) _____, but when workers are laid off because of changes in the consumer demand and technology in industries or regions, this unemployment is called _____; when workers are unemployed because of insufficient total spending in the economy, this type of unemployment is called _____.

7. The full-employment unemployment rate is called the (Okun, natural) _____ rate of unemployment. It is equal to the total of (frictional and structural, cyclical and frictional) _____ unemployment in the economy. It is realized when the (frictional, cyclical) _____ unemployment in the economy is equal to zero and when the actual output of the economy is (less than, equal to) _____ its potential output.

8. The GDP gap is equal to the actual GDP (minus, plus) _____ the potential GDP. For every percentage point the unemployment rate rises above the natural rate, there will be a GDP gap of (2, 5) _____%.

9. The burdens of unemployment are borne more heavily by (black, white) _____, (adult, teenage) _____, and (white-collar, blue-collar) workers, and the percentage of the labor force unemployed for 15 or more weeks is much (higher, lower) _____ than the overall unemployment rate.

10. Inflation means (an increase, a decrease) _____ in the general level of (unemployment, prices) _____ in the economy.

11. To calculate the rate of inflation from year 1 to year 2, subtract the price index for year 1 from year 2, then (multiply, divide) _____ the result by the price index for year 1, and _____ by 100.

12. To find the approximate number of years it takes the price level to double, (multiply, divide) _____ 70 by the percentage annual increase in the rate of inflation. This approximation is called (Okun's law, rule of 70) _____.

13. The basic cause of demand-pull inflation is (an increase, a decrease) _____ in total spending beyond the economy's capacity to produce. This type of inflation is characterized as "too (little, much) _____ spending chasing too (few, many) _____ goods."

14. Cost-push inflation is explained in terms of factors that raise per-unit (inflation, production) _____ costs. When these costs rise, they (increase, decrease) _____ profits and _____ the amount of output firms are willing to supply, which causes the price level for the economy as a whole to _____.

15. The amount of goods and services one's nominal income can buy is called (variable, real) _____ income. If one's nominal income rises by 10% and the price level by 7%, the percentage of increase in (variable, real) _____ income would be (1, 2, 3) _____. If nominal income was $60,000 and the price index, expressed in hundredths, was 1.06, then (variable, real) _____ income would be ($56,604, $63,600) _____.

16. Unanticipated inflation hurts those whose nominal incomes are relatively (fixed, flexible) _____, penalizes (savers, borrowers) _____, and hurts (creditors, debtors) _____.

17. The redistributive effects of inflation are less severe when it is (anticipated, unanticipated) _____. Clauses in labor contracts that call for automatic adjustments of workers' incomes from the effects of inflation are called (unemployment benefits, cost-of-living) _____ adjustments.

18. The percentage increase in purchasing power that the lender receives from the borrower is the (real, nominal) _____ rate of interest; the percentage increase in money that the lender receives is the _____ rate of interest. If the nominal rate of interest is 8% and the real interest rate is 5%, then the inflation premium is (8, 5, 3) _____%.

19. Cost-push inflation (increases, decreases) _____ real output. The output effects of demand-pull inflation are (more, less) _____ certain. Some economists argue that mild demand-pull inflation (increases, decreases) _____ real output while others argue that it _____ real output.

20. An extraordinary rapid rise in the general price level is (deflation, hyperinflation) _____. Economists generally agree that there may be an economic collapse, and often political chaos, from _____.

■ TRUE–FALSE QUESTIONS

Circle T if the statement is true, F if it is false.

1. The business cycle is best defined as alternating periods of increases and decreases in the rate of inflation in the economy. **T F**

2. Business cycles tend to be of roughly equal duration and intensity. **T F**

3. Fluctuations in real output in the economy are caused by economic shocks, and because prices are sticky, it is difficult for the economy to quickly adjust to such shocks. **T F**

4. During a recession, industries that produce capital goods and consumer durables typically suffer smaller output and employment declines than do industries providing service and nondurable consumer goods. **T F**

5. The unemployment rate is equal to the number of people in the labor force divided by the number of people who are unemployed. **T F**

6. Discouraged workers, those people who are able to work but quit looking for work because they cannot find a job, are counted as unemployed by the U.S. Bureau of Labor Statistics. **T F**

7. Frictional unemployment is not only inevitable but also partly desirable so that people can voluntarily move to better jobs. **T F**

8. The essential difference between frictionally and structurally unemployed workers is that the former *do not have* and the latter *do have* marketable skills. **T F**

9. Most frictionally unemployed workers stay in the unemployment pool for a long time. **T F**

10. Cyclical unemployment is caused by a decline in total spending. **T F**

11. If unemployment in the economy is at its natural rate, the actual and potential outputs of the economy are equal. **T F**

12. An economy cannot produce an actual real GDP that exceeds its potential real GDP. **T F**

13. The economy's GDP gap is measured by subtracting its potential GDP from its actual GDP. **T F**

14. The economic cost of cyclical unemployment is the goods and services that are not produced. **T F**

15. Unemployment imposes equal burdens on different groups in the economy. **T F**

16. Inflation is defined as an increase in the total output of an economy. **T F**

17. From one year to the next, the Consumer Price Index rose from 154.5 to 160.5. The rate of inflation was therefore 6.6%. **T F**

18. If the price level increases by 10% each year, the price level will double every 10 years. **T F**

19. The essence of demand-pull inflation is "too much spending chasing too few goods." **T F**

20. Cost-push inflation explains rising prices in terms of factors that increase per-unit production cost. **T F**

21. A person's real income is the amount of goods and services that the person's nominal (or money) income will enable him or her to purchase. **T F**

22. Whether inflation is anticipated or unanticipated, the effects of inflation on the distribution of income are the same. **T F**

23. Borrowers are hurt by unanticipated inflation. **T F**

24. Cost-push inflation reduces real output. **T F**

25. Hyperinflation is caused by reckless expansion of the money supply and causes severe declines in real output. **T F**

■ **MULTIPLE-CHOICE QUESTIONS**

1. Which is one of the four phases of a business cycle?
(a) inflation
(b) recession
(c) unemployment
(d) hyperinflation

2. Most economists believe that the immediate determinant of the levels of domestic output and employment is
(a) the price level
(b) the level of total spending
(c) the size of the civilian labor force
(d) the nation's stock of capital goods

3. Production and employment would be *least* affected by a severe recession in which type of industry?
(a) nondurable consumer goods
(b) durable consumer goods
(c) capital goods
(d) labor goods

4. The unemployment rate in an economy is 8%. The total population of the economy is 250 million, and the size of the civilian labor force is 150 million. The number of employed workers in this economy is
(a) 12 million
(b) 20 million
(c) 138 million
(d) 140 million

5. The labor force includes those who are
(a) less than 16 years of age
(b) in mental institutions
(c) not seeking work
(d) employed

6. The unemployment data collected by the Bureau of Labor Statistics have been criticized because
(a) part-time workers are not counted in the number of workers employed
(b) discouraged workers are not considered a part of the labor force
(c) it covers frictional unemployment, but not cyclical unemployment, which inflates unemployment figures
(d) the underground economy may understate unemployment

7. A worker who loses a job at a petroleum refinery because consumers and business firms switch from the use of oil to the burning of coal is an example of
(a) frictional unemployment
(b) structural unemployment
(c) cyclical unemployment
(d) disguised unemployment

8. A worker who has quit one job and is taking 2 weeks off before reporting to a new job is an example of
(a) frictional unemployment
(b) structural unemployment
(c) cyclical unemployment
(d) disguised unemployment

9. Insufficient total spending in the economy results in
(a) frictional unemployment
(b) structural unemployment
(c) cyclical unemployment
(d) disguised unemployment

10. The full-employment unemployment rate in the economy has been achieved when
(a) frictional unemployment is zero
(b) structural unemployment is zero
(c) cyclical unemployment is zero
(d) the natural rate of unemployment is zero

11. Which has helped decrease the natural rate of unemployment in the United States since 1980?
(a) a smaller proportion of young workers in the labor force
(b) the increased size of benefits for the unemployed
(c) less competition in product and labor markets
(d) more workers covered by unemployment programs

12. Okun's law predicts that when the actual unemployment rate exceeds the natural rate of unemployment by two percentage points, there will be a negative GDP gap of about
(a) 2% of the potential GDP
(b) 3% of the potential GDP

(c) 4% of the potential GDP

(d) 5% of the potential GDP

13. If the negative GDP gap were equal to 6% of the potential GDP, the actual unemployment rate would exceed the natural rate of unemployment by

(a) two percentage points

(b) three percentage points

(c) four percentage points

(d) five percentage points

14. The burden of unemployment is *least* felt by

(a) white-collar workers

(b) African-Americans

(c) teenagers

(d) males

15. If the Consumer Price Index was 110 in one year and 117 in the next year, then the rate of inflation from one year to the next was

(a) 3.5%

(b) 4.7%

(c) 6.4%

(d) 7.1%

16. The price of a good has doubled in about 14 years. The approximate annual percentage rate of increase in the price level over this period has been

(a) 2%

(b) 3%

(c) 4%

(d) 5%

17. Which contributes to cost-push inflation?

(a) an increase in employment and output

(b) an increase in per-unit production costs

(c) a decrease in resource prices

(d) an increase in unemployment

18. Only two resources, capital and labor, are used in an economy to produce an output of 300 million units. If the total cost of capital resources is $150 million and the total cost of labor resources is $50 million, then the per-unit production costs in this economy are

(a) $0.67 million

(b) $1.50 million

(c) $2.00 million

(d) $3.00 million

19. If a person's nominal income increases by 8% while the price level increases by 10%, the person's real income

(a) increases by 2%

(b) increases by 18%

(c) decreases by 18%

(d) decreases by 2%

20. If the average level of nominal income in a nation is $21,000 and the price level index is 154, the average real income would be about

(a) $12,546

(b) $13,636

(c) $15,299

(d) $17,823

21. Who would be hurt by *unanticipated* inflation?

(a) those living on incomes with cost-of-living adjustments

(b) those who find prices rising less rapidly than their nominal incomes

(c) those who lent money at a fixed interest rate

(d) those who became debtors when prices were lower

22. With no inflation, a bank would be willing to lend a business firm $10 million at an annual interest rate of 8%. But if the rate of inflation was anticipated to be 6%, the bank would charge the firm an annual interest rate of

(a) 2%

(b) 6%

(c) 8%

(d) 14%

23. Cost-push inflation

(a) lowers interest rates

(b) lowers the price level

(c) deceases real output

(d) increases real output

24. What do economists think about the effects of mild demand-pull inflation on real output?

(a) They are positive because businesses must change prices.

(b) They are negative because economic growth depends on total spending.

(c) They are mixed, and could be positive or negative.

(d) They are zero and it indicates that there are no effects.

25. If an economy has experienced an inflation rate of over 1000% per year for several years, this economic condition would best be described as

(a) a cost-of-living adjustment

(b) cost-push inflation

(c) hyperinflation

(d) GDP gap

■ PROBLEMS

1. The following table gives statistics on the labor force and total employment during year 1 and year 5. Make the computations necessary to complete the table. (Numbers of persons are in thousands.)

	Year 1	Year 5
Labor force	84,889	95,453
Employed	80,796	87,524
Unemployed	_____	_____
Unemployment rate	_____	_____

a. How is it possible that *both* employment and unemployment increased? _____

b. In relative terms, if unemployment increases, employment will decrease. Why? _____

c. Would you say that year 5 was a year of full employment? _____

d. Why is the task of maintaining full employment over the years more than just a problem of finding jobs for those who happen to be unemployed at any given time? _____

_____

2. Suppose that in year 1 an economy is at full employment, has a potential and actual real GDP of $3000 billion, and has an unemployment rate of 5.5%.

a. Compute the GDP gap in year 1 and enter it in the table below.

Year	Actual GDP	Potential GDP	GDP gap
1	$3000.0	$3000	$_____
2	3724.0	3800	_____
3	3712.5	4125	_____

b. The actual and potential real GDPs in years 2 and 3 are also shown in the table. Compute and enter into the table the GDP gaps in these 2 years.

c. In year 2, the actual real GDP is _____% of the potential real GDP. (Hint: Divide the actual real GDP by the potential real GDP and multiply by 100.)

(1) The actual real GDP is _____% less than the potential real GDP.
(2) Using Okun's law, the unemployment rate will rise from 5.5% in year 1 and be _____% in year 2.

d. In year 3 the actual real GDP is _____% of the potential real GDP.

(1) The actual real GDP is _____% less than the potential real GDP.
(2) The unemployment rate, according to Okun's law, will be _____%.

3. The following table shows the price index in the economy at the end of four different years.

Year	Price index	Rate of inflation
1	100.00	
2	112.00	_____%
3	123.20	_____
4	129.36	_____

a. Compute and enter in the table the rates of inflation in years 2, 3, and 4.

b. Employing the rule of 70, how many years would it take for the price level to double at each of these three inflation rates? _____

c. If nominal income increased by 15% from year 1 to year 2, what was the approximate percentage change in real income? _____

d. If nominal income increased by 7% from year 2 to year 3, what was the approximate percentage change in real income? _____

e. If nominal income was $25,000 in year 2, what was real income that year? _____

f. If nominal income was $25,000 in year 3, what was real income that year? _____

g. If the nominal interest rate was 14% to borrow money from year 1 to year 2, what was the approximate real rate of interest over that period? _____

h. If the nominal interest rate was 8% to borrow money from year 3 to year 4, what was the approximate real rate of interest over that period? _____

4. Indicate the most likely effect—beneficial **(B)**, detrimental **(D)**, or indeterminate **(I)**—of unanticipated inflation on each of these persons:

a. A retired business executive who now lives each month by spending a part of the amount that was saved and deposited in a fixed-rate savings account for a long term. _____

b. A retired private-school teacher who lives on the dividends received from shares of stock owned. _____

c. A farmer who borrowed $500,000 from a bank at a fixed rate; the loan must be repaid in the next 10 years. _____

d. A retired couple whose sole source of income is the pension they receive from a former employer.

e. A widow whose income consists entirely of interest received from the corporate bonds she owns.

f. A public school teacher. _____

g. A member of a union who works for a firm that produces computers. _____

■ **SHORT ANSWER AND ESSAY QUESTIONS**

1. Define the business cycle. Describe the four phases of a business cycle.

2. In the opinion of most economists, what is the cause of the fluctuations in the levels of output in the economy?

3. Compare the manner in which the business cycle affects output and employment in the industries producing capital and durable goods with the way it affects industries producing nondurable goods and services. What causes these differences?

4. How is the unemployment rate measured in the United States?

5. What two criticisms have been made of the method the Bureau of Labor Statistics uses to determine the unemployment rate?

6. Distinguish among frictional, structural, and cyclical unemployment.

7. Do frictionally unemployed workers remain unemployed for a long period of time? Explain your answer.

8. When is there full employment in the U.S. economy? (Answer in terms of the unemployment rate, the actual and potential output of the economy, and the markets for labor.)

9. What is the natural rate of unemployment? Will the economy always operate at the natural rate? Why is the natural rate subject to revision?

10. What is the economic cost of unemployment, and how is this cost measured? What is the quantitative relationship (called Okun's law) between the unemployment rate and the cost of unemployment?

11. What groups in the economy tend to bear the burdens of unemployment?

12. How does the unemployment rate in the United States compare with the rates for other industrialized nations in recent years?

13. What is inflation, and how is the rate of inflation measured?

14. What has been the experience of the United States with inflation since the 1960s? How does the inflation rate in the United States compare with those of other industrialized nations in recent years?

15. Compare and contrast demand-pull and cost-push types of inflation.

16. What groups benefit from and what groups are hurt by inflation?

17. What is the difference between the effects of unanticipated inflation and the effects of anticipated inflation on the redistribution of real incomes in the economy?

18. What are the effects of cost-push inflation on real output?

19. What are the effects of demand-pull inflation on real output? Are economists in agreement about these effects? Discuss.

20. Why does hyperinflation have such a devastating impact on real output and employment? Explain what happens during hyperinflation.

ANSWERS

Chapter 26 Business Cycles, Unemployment, and Inflation

FILL-IN QUESTIONS

1. increases, decreases, recession, trough, expansion
2. shocks, sticky, spending
3. durables, capital, nondurable
4. unemployed, labor force, multiplying
5. employed, not in the labor force, understated
6. frictional, structural, cyclical
7. natural, frictional and structural, cyclical, equal to
8. minus, 2
9. black, teenage, blue-collar, lower
10. an increase, prices
11. divide, multiply
12. divide, rule of 70
13. an increase, much, few
14. production, decrease, decrease, increase

15. real, real, 3, real, $56,604
16. fixed, savers, creditors
17. anticipated, cost-of-living
18. real, nominal, 3
19. increases, less, increases, decreases
20. hyperinflation, hyperinflation

TRUE–FALSE QUESTIONS

1. F, p. 521	**10.** T, p. 525	**19.** T, pp. 530–531
2. F, p. 521	**11.** T, p. 525	**20.** T, p. 531
3. T, p. 522	**12.** F, pp. 525–526	**21.** T, p. 532
4. F, pp. 522–523	**13.** T, pp. 525–526	**22.** F, pp. 532–533
5. F, p. 523	**14.** T, p. 526	**23.** F, p. 533
6. F, p. 524	**15.** F, pp. 526–527	**24.** T, p. 535
7. T, p. 524	**16.** F, p. 529	**25.** T, pp. 535, 537
8. F, pp. 524–525	**17.** F, p. 529	
9. F, p. 524	**18.** F, pp. 529–530	

MULTIPLE-CHOICE QUESTIONS

1. b, p. 521	**10.** c, p. 525	**19.** d, p. 532
2. b, p. 522	**11.** a, p. 525	**20.** b, p. 533
3. a, pp. 522–523	**12.** c, p. 526	**21.** c, pp. 534
4. c, p. 523	**13.** b, p. 526	**22.** d, p. 534
5. d, p. 523	**14.** a, p. 526, 528	**23.** c, p. 535
6. b, p. 524	**15.** c, p. 529	**24.** c, p. 535
7. b, p. 524	**16.** d, pp. 529–530	**25.** c, pp. 535, 537
8. a, p. 524	**17.** b, p. 531	
9. c, p. 525	**18.** a, p. 531	

PROBLEMS

1. year 1: 4,093, 4.8; year 5: 7,929, 8.3; *a.* the labor force increased more than employment increased; *b.* because unemployment and employment in relative terms are percentages of the labor force and *always* add to 100%, and if one increases the other must decrease; *c.* no economist would argue that the full-employment unemployment rate is as high as 8.3% and year 5 was not a year of full employment; *d.* the number of people looking for work expands

2. *a.* 0; *b.* 76, 412.5; *c.* 98, (1) 2, (2) 6.5; *d.* 90, (1) 10, (2) 10.5

3. *a.* 12, 10, 5; *b.* 5.8, 7, 14; *c.* 3; *d.* –3; *e.* $22,321; *f.* $20,292; *g.* 2; *h.* 3

4. *a.* D; *b.* I; *c.* B; *d.* D; *e.* D; *f.* I; *g.* I

SHORT ANSWER AND ESSAY QUESTIONS

1. p. 521	**8.** p. 525	**15.** pp. 530–531
2. p. 522	**9.** p. 525	**16.** pp. 532–533
3. pp. 522–523	**10.** pp. 525–526	**17.** pp. 532–534
4. p. 523	**11.** pp. 526, 528	**18.** p. 535
5. p. 524	**12.** p. 528	**19.** p. 535
6. pp. 524–525	**13.** p. 529	**20.** pp. 535, 537
7. p. 524	**14.** p. 530	

Basic Macroeconomic Relationships

This chapter introduces you to three basic relationships in the economy: income and consumption, the interest rate and investment, and changes in spending and changes in output. The relationships between these economic "aggregates" are essential building blocks for understanding the macro models that will be presented in the next two chapters.

The first section of Chapter 27 describes the relationship between the largest aggregate in the economy—**consumption.** An explanation of consumption, however, also entails a study of saving because saving is simply the part of disposable income that is not consumed. This section develops the consumption and saving schedules and describes their main characteristics. Other key concepts are also presented: average propensities to consume (APC) and save (APS), marginal propensities to consume (MPC) and save (MPS), and the nonincome determinants of consumption and saving.

Investment is the subject of the next section of the chapter. The purchase of capital goods depends on the rate of return that business firms expect to earn from an investment and on the real rate of interest they have to pay for the use of money. Because firms are anxious to make profitable investments and to avoid unprofitable ones, they undertake all investments that have an expected rate of return greater than (or equal to) the real rate of interest and do not undertake an investment when the expected rate of return is less than the real interest rate. This relationship between the real interest rate and the level of investment spending is an inverse one: the lower the interest rate, the greater the investment spending. It is illustrated by a downsloping **investment demand curve.** As you will learn, this curve can be shifted by six factors that can change the expected rate of return on investment. You will also learn that investment, unlike consumption, is quite volatile and is the most unstable component of total spending in the economy.

The third section of the chapter introduces you to the concept of the **multiplier.** It shows how an initial change in spending for consumption or investment changes real GDP by an amount that is larger than the initial stimulus. You also will learn about the rationale for the multiplier and how to interpret it. The multiplier can be derived from the marginal propensity to consume and the marginal propensity to save. You will have learned about these marginal propensities at the beginning of the chapter and now they are put to further use as you end the chapter.

■ CHECKLIST

When you have studied this chapter you should be able to

☐ Explain how consumption and saving are related to disposable income.

☐ Draw a graph to illustrate the relationships among consumption, saving, and disposable income.

☐ Construct a hypothetical consumption schedule.

☐ Construct a hypothetical saving schedule, and identify the level of break-even income.

☐ Compute the four propensities (APC, APS, MPC, and MPS) when given the necessary data.

☐ State the relationship between the APC and the APS as income increases.

☐ Demonstrate that the MPC is the slope of the consumption schedule and the MPS is the slope of the saving schedule.

☐ Explain each of the four nonincome determinants of consumption and saving.

☐ Use a graph with real GDP on the horizontal axis to show shifts in consumption and saving schedules.

☐ Explain the difference between a change in the amount consumed (or saved) and a change in the consumption (or saving) schedule.

☐ Describe how a change in taxes shifts consumption and saving schedules.

☐ Explain how the expected rate of return affects investment decisions.

☐ Describe the influence of the real interest rate on an investment decision.

☐ Draw a graph of an investment demand curve for the business sector and explain what it shows.

☐ Explain how each of the six noninterest determinants of investment will shift the investment demand curve.

☐ Give four reasons why investment spending tends to be unstable.

☐ Define the multiplier effect in words, with a ratio, and using an equation.

☐ Make three clarifying points about the multiplier.

☐ Cite two facts on which the rationale for the multiplier is based.

☐ Discuss the relationship between the multiplier and the marginal propensities.

☐ Find the value of the multiplier when you are given the necessary data.

☐ Explain the significance of the multiplier.

□ Discuss the reasons for the difference between the textbook example for the multiplier and the actual multiplier for the U.S. economy.

□ Give a humorous example of the multiplier effect (Last Word).

■ CHAPTER OUTLINE

1. There is a positive or direct relationship between consumption and disposable income (after-tax income) because as disposable income increases so does consumption. Saving is disposable income not spent for consumer goods. Disposable income is the most important determinant of both consumption and saving. The relationship among disposable income, consumption, and saving can be shown by a graph with consumption on the vertical axis and disposable income on the horizontal axis. The **45-degree line** on the graph would show where consumption would equal disposable income. If consumption is less than disposable income, the difference is saving.

a. The **consumption schedule** shows the amounts that households plan to spend for consumer goods at various levels of income, given a price level. **Break-even income** is where consumption is equal to disposable income.

b. The **saving schedule** indicates the amounts households plan to save at different income levels, given a price level.

c. The average propensity to consume (APC) and the average propensity to save (APS) and the marginal propensity to consume (MPC) and the marginal propensity to save (MPS) can be computed from the consumption and saving schedules.

(1) The **average propensity to consume (APC)** and the **average propensity to save (APS)** are, respectively, the percentages of income spent for consumption and saved, and they sum to 1.

(2) The **marginal propensity to consume (MPC)** and the **marginal propensity to save (MPS)** are, respectively, the percentages of additional income spent for consumption and saved, and sum to 1.

(3) The MPC is the slope of the consumption schedule, and the MPS is the slope of the saving schedule when the two schedules are graphed.

d. In addition to income, there are several other important nonincome determinants of consumption and saving. Changes in *these nonincome determinants* will cause the consumption and saving schedules to change. An increase in spending will shift the consumption schedule upward and a decrease in spending will shift it downward. Similarly, an increase in saving will shift the saving schedule upward and a decrease in saving will shift it downward.

(1) The amount of wealth affects the amount that households spend and save. Wealth is the difference between the values of a household's assets and its liabilities. If household wealth increases, people will spend more because they think they have more assets from which to support current consumption possibilities (the **wealth effect**), and they will save less.

(2) The level of household *borrowing* influences consumption. Increased borrowing will increase current consumption possibilities, which shift the consumption schedule upward. But borrowing reduces wealth by increasing debt, which in turn reduces future consumption possibilities because the borrowed money must be repaid.

(3) *Expectations* about the future affect spending and saving decisions. If prices are expected to rise in the future, people will spend more today and save less.

(4) *Real interest rates* change spending and saving decisions. When real interest rates fall, households tend to consume more, borrow more, and save less.

e. Several other considerations need to be noted:

(1) Macroeconomists are more concerned with the effects of changes in consumption and saving on *real GDP*, so it replaces disposable income on the horizontal axis of the consumption or saving schedules.

(2) A change in the amount consumed (or saved) is a movement along the consumption (or saving) schedule, but a change in the consumption (or saving) due to a change in one of the nonincome determinants is a shift in the entire consumption (or saving) schedule.

(3) Changes in wealth, borrowing, expectations, and real interest rates shift consumption and saving schedules in opposite directions. For example, an increase in wealth will increase consumption and will decrease saving as people consume more out of current income. If households borrow they can expand current consumption, but that will decrease current saving. Expectations of rising future prices will increase current consumption and decrease current saving. A fall in real interest rates increases current consumption and provides less incentive for current saving.

(4) Changes in taxes shift the consumption and saving schedules in the same direction. An increase in taxes will reduce both consumption and saving; a decrease in taxes will increase both consumption and saving.

(5) Both consumption and saving schedules tend to be stable over time unless changed by major tax increases or decreases. The stability arises from long-term planning and because some nonincome determinants cause shifts that offset each other.

2. The investment decision is a marginal benefit and marginal cost decision that depends on the expected rate of return (r) from the purchase of additional capital goods and the real rate of interest (i) that must be paid for borrowed funds.

a. The **expected rate of return** is directly related to the net profits (revenues less operating costs) that are expected to result from an investment. It is the marginal benefit of investment for a business.

b. The *real rate of interest* is the price paid for the use of money. It is the marginal cost of investment for a business. When the expected real rate of return is greater (less) than the real rate of interest, a business will (will not) invest because the investment will be profitable (unprofitable).

c. For this reason, the lower (higher) the real rate of interest, the greater (smaller) will be the level of investment spending in the economy; the **investment**

demand curve shows this inverse relationship between the real rate of interest and the level of spending for capital goods. The amount of investment by the business sector is determined at the point where the marginal benefit of investment (*r*) equals the marginal cost (*i*).

d. There are at least six noninterest determinants of investment demand, and a change in any of these determinants will shift the investment demand curve.

(1) If the *acquisition, maintenance, and operating costs* for capital goods change, then this change in costs will change investment demand. Rising costs decrease investment demand and declining costs increase it.

(2) Changes in *business taxes* are like a change in costs so they have a similar effect on investment demand as the previous item.

(3) *An increase in technological progress* will stimulate investment and increase investment demand.

(4) *The stock of existing capital goods* will influence investment decisions. If the economy is overstocked, there will be a decrease in investment demand, and if the economy is understocked, there will be an increase in investment demand.

(5) *Planned changes in inventories* affect investment demand. If there is a planned increase in inventories, then investment demand will increase; a planned decrease in inventories will decrease investment demand.

(6) *Expectations* of the future are important. If expectations are positive because of more expected sales or profits, there is likely to be an increase in investment demand. Negative expectations will have an opposite effect on investment demand.

e. Unlike consumption and saving, investment is inherently unstable. Four factors explain this instability.

(1) *Capital goods are durable*, so when they get replaced may depend on the optimism or pessimism of business owners. If owners are more optimistic about the future they will likely spend more to obtain new capital goods.

(2) *Innovation is not regular*, which means that technological progress is highly variable and contributes to instability in investment spending decisions.

(3) *Profit expectations* influence the investment spending of businesses, but profits are highly variable.

(4) *Other expectations* concerning such factors as exchange rates, the state of the economy, and the stock market can create positive or negative expectations that change investment spending.

3. There is a direct relationship between a change in spending and a change in real GDP, assuming that prices are sticky. An initial change in spending, however, results in a change in real GDP that is greater than the initial change in spending. This outcome is called the *multiplier effect*. The **multiplier** is the ratio of the change in the real GDP to the initial change in spending. The initial change in spending typically comes from investment spending, but changes in consumption, net exports, or government spending can also have multiplier effects.

a. The multiplier effect occurs because a change in the dollars spent by one person alters the income of another person in the same direction, and because any change in the income of one person will change the person's consumption and saving in the same direction by a fraction of the change in income. For example, assuming a marginal propensity to consume (MPC) of .75, a change in investment spending of $5.00 will cause a change in consumption of $3.75. The change in consumption ($3.75) will become someone else's income in the second round. The process will continue through successive rounds, but the amount of income in each round will diminish by 25 percent because that is the amount saved from each change in income. After all rounds are completed, the initial change of $5 in investment spending produces a total of $20 change because the multiplier was 4 (see Table 27.3 in the text).

b. There is a formula for calculating the multiplier. The multiplier is directly related to the marginal propensity to consume (MPC) and inversely related to the marginal propensity to save (MPS). The multiplier is equal to [1/(1 − MPC)]. It is also equal to [1/MPS]. The significance of the multiplier is that relatively small changes in the spending plans of business firms or households bring about large changes in the equilibrium real GDP.

c. The simple multiplier that has been described differs from the actual multiplier for the economy. In the simple case the only factor that reduced income in successive rounds was the fraction that went to savings. For the domestic economy, there are other leakages from consumption besides saving, such as spending on imports, payment of taxes, or inflation. These factors reduce the value of the multiplier. For the U.S. economy the multiplier is estimated to be about 2.

4. (Last Word). Art Buchwald once wrote a humorous story about the multiplier that illustrates the spiral effect on consumer spending from a reduction in income. A car salesman reserved a new car for a regular customer, but the customer can't buy the car because he is getting a divorce. The car salesman then tells his painter he can't afford to have his house painted. The house painter then decides to return a new television he bought from the store. And so the story continues from one person to another.

■ **HINTS AND TIPS**

1. An important graph in the chapter is the **consumption schedule** (see the Key Graph on page 544 of the text). Know how to interpret it. There are two lines on the graph. The 45-degree reference line shows all points where disposable income equals consumption (there is no saving). The consumption schedule line shows the total amount of disposable income spent on consumption at each and every income level. Where the two lines *intersect*, all disposable income is spent (consumed). At all income levels to the right of the intersection, the consumption line lies below the 45-degree line, and not all disposable income is spent (there is saving). To the left of the intersection, the consumption line lies above the 45-degree line and consumption exceeds disposable income (there is dissaving).

2. Always remember that **marginal propensities** sum to 1 (MPC + MPS = 1). The same is true for average propensities (APC + APS = 1). Thus, if you know the value of one marginal propensity (e.g., MPC), you can always figure out the other (e.g., 1 − MPC = MPS).

3. The **multiplier** effect is a key concept in this chapter and in the ones that follow, so make sure you understand how it works.

    a. The multiplier is simply the ratio of the change in real GDP to the *initial* changes in spending. Multiplying the *initial* change in spending by the *multiplier* gives you the amount of change in real GDP.

    b. The multiplier effect works in both positive and negative directions. An *initial* decrease in spending will result in a larger decrease in real GDP, or an *initial* increase in spending will create a larger increase in real GDP.

    c. The multiplier is directly related to the marginal propensities. The multiplier equals 1/MPS. The multiplier also equals 1/(1 − MPC).

    d. The main reason for the multiplier effect is that the *initial* change in income (spending) induces additional rounds of income (spending) that add progressively less in each round as some of the income (spending) gets saved because of the marginal propensity to save (see Table 27.3 of the text).

■ **IMPORTANT TERMS**

45° (degree) line	marginal propensity to save (MPS)
consumption schedule	wealth effect
saving schedule	expected rate of return
break-even income	
average propensity to consume (APC)	investment demand curve
average propensity to save (APS)	multiplier
marginal propensity to consume (MPC)	

___

SELF-TEST

___

■ **FILL-IN QUESTIONS**

1. The consumption schedule shows the various amounts that households plan to (save, consume) _____ at various levels of disposable income, while the saving schedule shows the various amounts that households plan to _____.

2. Both consumption and saving are (directly, indirectly) _____ related to the level of disposable income. At lower levels of disposable income, households tend to spend a (smaller, larger) _____ proportion of this income and save a _____ proportion,

but at higher levels of disposable income, they tend to spend a (smaller, larger) _____ proportion of this income and save a _____ proportion. At the break-even income, consumption is (greater than, less than, equal to) _____ disposable income.

3. As disposable income falls, the average propensity to consume (APC) will (rise, fall) _____ and the average propensity to save (APS) will _____.

4. The sum of APC and APS is equal to (0, 1) _____. If the APC is .90, then the APS is (.10, 1) _____.

5. The marginal propensity to consume (MPC) is the change in (consumption, income) _____ divided by the change in _____.

6. The marginal propensity to save (MPS) is the change in (saving, income) _____ divided by the change in _____.

7. The sum of MPC and MPS is equal to (0, 1) _____. If the MPC is .75, then the MPS is (0, .25) _____.

8. The MPC is the numerical value of the slope of the (consumption, saving) _____ schedule, and the MPS is the numerical value of the slope of the _____ schedule.

9. The most important determinants of consumption spending, other than the level of income, are

    a. _____

    b. _____

    c. _____

    d. _____

10. An increase in the consumption schedule means that the consumption schedule shifts (upward, downward) _____ and a decrease in the consumption schedule means that it will shift _____, and these shifts occur because of a change in one of the nonincome determinants. An increase in the amount consumed occurs because of an increase in (income, stability) _____.

11. The investment spending decision depends on the expected rate of (interest, return) _____ and the real rate of _____.

12. The expected rate of return is the marginal (cost, benefit) _____ of investment and the real rate of return is the marginal _____ of investment.

13. If the expected rate of return on an investment is greater than the real rate of interest for the use of money, a business firm will (increase, decrease) _____ its investment spending, but if the expected rate of return is less than the real rate of interest, the firm will _____ its investment spending.

14. The relationship between the real rate of interest and the total amount of investment in the economy is (direct, inverse) _____ and is shown in the investment (supply, demand) _____ curve. This curve shows that if the real rate of interest rises, the quantity of investment will (increase, decrease) _____, but if the real rate of interest falls, the quantity of investment will _____.

15. Six noninterest determinants of investment demand are

a. _____

b. _____

c. _____

d. _____

e. _____

f. _____

16. The demand for new capital goods tends to be unstable because of the (durability, nondurability) _____ of capital goods, the (regularity, irregularity) _____ of innovation, the (stability, variability) _____ of current and expected profits, and the _____ of expectations.

17. The multiplier is the change in real GDP (multiplied, divided) _____ by an initial change in spending. When the initial change in spending is _____ by the multiplier, the result equals the change in real GDP.

18. The multiplier means that an increase in initial spending may create a multiple (increase, decrease) _____ in real GDP, and also that a decrease in initial spending may create a multiple _____ in real GDP.

19. The multiplier has a value equal to 1 divided by the marginal propensity to (consume, save) _____, which is the same thing as 1 divided by the quantity of 1 minus the marginal propensity to _____.

20. The higher the value of the marginal propensity to consume, the (larger, smaller) _____ the value of the multiplier, but the larger the value of the marginal propensity to save, the _____ the value of the multiplier.

Circle T if the statement is true, F if it is false.

1. Consumption equals disposable income plus saving. **T F**

2. The most significant determinant of the level of consumer spending is disposable income. **T F**

3. Historical data suggest that the level of consumption expenditures is directly related to the level of disposable income. **T F**

4. Consumption rises and saving falls when disposable income increases. **T F**

5. Empirical data suggest that households tend to spend a similar proportion of a small disposable income as they do of a larger disposable income. **T F**

6. The break-even income is the income level at which business begins to make a profit. **T F**

7. The average propensity to save is equal to the level of saving divided by the level of consumption. **T F**

8. The marginal propensity to consume is the change in consumption divided by the change in income. **T F**

9. The slope of the saving schedule is equal to the average propensity to save. **T F**

10. An increase in wealth will increase the consumption schedule (shift the consumption curve upward). **T F**

11. An increase in the taxes paid by consumers will decrease both the amount they spend for consumption and the amount they save. **T F**

12. Both the consumption schedule and the saving schedule tend to be relatively stable over time. **T F**

13. The real interest rate is the nominal interest rate minus the rate of inflation. **T F**

14. A business firm will purchase additional capital goods if the real rate of interest it must pay exceeds the expected rate of return from the investment. **T F**

15. An increase in the stock of capital goods on hand will decrease the investment demand. **T F**

16. An increase in planned inventories will decrease the investment demand. **T F**

17. Investment tends to be relatively stable over time. **T F**

18. The irregularity of innovations and the variability of business profits contribute to the instability of investment expenditures. **T F**

19. The multiplier is equal to the change in real GDP multiplied by the initial change in spending. **T F**

20. The initial change in spending for the multiplier is usually associated with investment spending because of investment's volatility. **T F**

21. The multiplier effect works only in a positive direction in changing GDP. **T F**

22. The multiplier is based on the idea that any change in income will cause both consumption and saving to vary in the same direction as a change in income and by a fraction of that change in income. **T F**

23. The higher the marginal propensity to consume, the larger the size of the multiplier. **T F**

24. When it is computed as 1/MPS, the multiplier reflects only the leakage of income into saving. **T F**

25. The value of the actual multiplier for the economy will usually be greater than the value of a textbook multiplier because the actual multiplier is based only on the marginal propensity to save. **T F**

■ **MULTIPLE-CHOICE QUESTIONS**

Circle the letter that corresponds to the best answer.

1. Saving equals
  (a) investment plus consumption
  (b) investment minus consumption
  (c) disposable income minus consumption
  (d) disposable income plus consumption

2. As disposable income decreases, *ceteris paribus*,
  (a) both consumption and saving increase
  (b) consumption increases and saving decreases
  (c) consumption decreases and saving increases
  (d) both consumption and saving decrease

3. Households tend to spend a larger portion of
  (a) a small disposable income than a large disposable income
  (b) a large disposable income than a small disposable income
  (c) their disposable income on saving when the rate of return is high
  (d) their saving than their disposable income when the rate of return is low

4. If consumption spending increases from $358 to $367 billion when disposable income increases from $412 to $427 billion, it can be concluded that the marginal propensity to consume is
  (a) 0.4
  (b) 0.6
  (c) 0.8
  (d) 0.9

5. If disposable income is $375 billion when the average propensity to consume is 0.8, it can be concluded that
  (a) the marginal propensity to consume is also 0.8
  (b) the marginal propensity to save is 0.2
  (c) consumption is $325 billion
  (d) saving is $75 billion

6. As the disposable income of the economy increases
  (a) both the APC and the APS rise
  (b) the APC rises and the APS falls
  (c) the APC falls and the APS rises
  (d) both the APC and the APS fall

7. The slope of the consumption schedule or line for a given economy is the

  (a) marginal propensity to consume
  (b) average propensity to consume
  (c) marginal propensity to save
  (d) average propensity to save

Answer Questions 8 and 9 on the basis of the following graph.

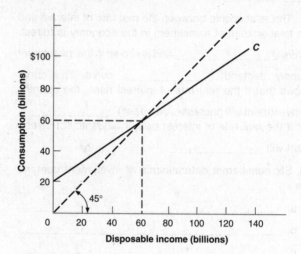

8. This graph indicates that
  (a) consumption decreases after the $60 billion level of disposable income
  (b) the marginal propensity to consume decreases after the $60 billion level of disposable income
  (c) consumption decreases as a percentage of disposable income as disposable income increases
  (d) consumption increases as disposable income decreases

9. If the relevant saving schedule were constructed, one would find that
  (a) the marginal propensity to save is negative up to the $60 billion level of disposable income
  (b) the marginal propensity to save increases after the $60 billion level of disposable income
  (c) saving is zero at the $60 billion level of disposable income
  (d) saving is $20 billion at the $0 level of disposable income

Answer Questions 10, 11, and 12 on the basis of the following disposable income (DI) and consumption (C) schedules for a private, closed economy. All figures are in billions of dollars.

DI	C
$ 0	$ 4
40	40
80	76
120	112
160	148
200	184

10. If plotted on a graph, the slope of the consumption schedule would be
  (a) 0.6

(b) 0.7
(c) 0.8
(d) 0.9

11. At the $160 billion level of disposable income, the average propensity to save is
(a) 0.015
(b) 0.075
(c) 0.335
(d) 0.925

12. If consumption increases by $5 billion at each level of disposable income, then the marginal propensity to consume will
(a) change, but the average propensity to consume will not change
(b) change, and the average propensity to consume will change
(c) not change, but the average propensity to consume will change
(d) not change, and the average propensity to consume will not change

13. If the slope of a linear saving schedule decreases, then it can be concluded that the
(a) MPS has decreased
(b) MPC has decreased
(c) income has decreased
(d) income has increased

14. An increase in wealth shifts the consumption schedule
(a) downward and the saving schedule upward
(b) upward and the saving schedule downward
(c) downward and the saving schedule downward
(d) upward and the saving schedule upward

15. Expectations of a recession are likely to lead households to
(a) increase consumption and saving
(b) decrease consumption and saving
(c) decrease consumption and increase saving
(d) increase consumption and decrease saving

16. Higher real interest rates are likely to
(a) increase consumption and saving
(b) decrease consumption and saving
(c) decrease consumption and increase saving
(d) increase consumption and decrease saving

17. An increase in taxes shifts the consumption schedule
(a) downward and the saving schedule upward
(b) upward and the saving schedule downward
(c) downward and the saving schedule downward
(d) upward and the saving schedule upward

18. Which relationship is an inverse one?
(a) consumption and disposable income
(b) investment spending and the rate of interest
(c) saving and disposable income
(d) investment spending and GDP

19. A decrease in investment demand would be a consequence of a decline in
(a) the rate of interest
(b) the level of wages paid
(c) business taxes
(d) expected future sales

20. Which would increase investment demand?
(a) an increase in business taxes
(b) an increase in planned inventories
(c) a decrease in the rate of technological change
(d) an increase in the cost of acquiring capital goods

21. Which best explains the variability of investment?
(a) the predictable useful life of capital goods
(b) constancy or regularities in business innovations
(c) instabilities in the level of profits
(d) business pessimism about the future

22. If there was a change in investment spending of $10 and the marginal propensity to save was .25, then real GDP would increase by
(a) $10
(b) $20
(c) $25
(d) $40

23. If the value of the marginal propensity to consume is 0.6 and real GDP falls by $25, this was caused by a decrease in initial spending of
(a) $10.00
(b) $15.00
(c) $16.67
(d) $20.00

24. If the marginal propensity to consume is 0.67 and initial spending increases by $25, real GDP will
(a) increase by $75
(b) decrease by $75
(c) increase by $25
(d) decrease by $25

25. If in an economy a $150 billion increase in investment spending creates $150 billion of new income in the first round of the multiplier process and $105 billion in the second round, the multiplier and the marginal propensity to consume will be, respectively,
(a) 5.00 and 0.80
(b) 4.00 and 0.75
(c) 3.33 and 0.70
(d) 2.50 and 0.40

PROBLEMS

1. The following table is a consumption schedule. Assume taxes and transfer payments are zero and that all saving is personal saving.

(GDP = DI)	C	S	APC	APS
1500	$1540	$____	1.027	−.027
1600	1620	____	1.013	−.013
1700	1700	____	____	____
1800	1780	____	.989	.011
1900	1860	____	.979	.021
2000	1940	____	____	____
2100	2020	____	.962	.038
2200	2100	____	____	____

a. Compute saving at each of the eight levels of disposable income and the missing average propensities to consume and to save.

b. The break-even level of disposable income is

$_____.

c. As disposable income rises, the marginal propensity to consume remains constant. Between each two GDPs the MPC can be found by dividing

$_____ by $_____, and is

equal to _____.

d. The marginal propensity to save also remains constant when the GDP rises. Between each two

GDPs the MPS is equal to $_____ divided

by $_____, or to _____.

e. Plot the consumption schedule, the saving schedule, and the 45-degree line on the graph below.

(1) The numerical value of the slope of the consump-

tion schedule is _____, and the term that

is used to describe it is the _____.

(2) If the relevant saving schedule were constructed, the numerical value of the slope of the saving schedule

would be _____, and the term that is used

to describe it would be the _____.

2. Indicate in the space to the right of each of the following events whether the event will tend to increase (+) or decrease (−) the saving schedule.

a. Development of consumer expectations that prices

will be higher in the future _____

b. Gradual shrinkage in the quantity of real assets

owned by consumers _____

c. Increase in household borrowing _____

d. Growing belief that disposable income will be lower

in the future _____

e. Expectations that there will be a current shortage

of consumer goods _____

f. Rise in the actual level of disposable income

_____

g. An increase in household wealth _____

h. Development of a belief by consumers that the Federal government can and will prevent recessions

in the future _____

3. The following schedule has eight different expected rates of return, and the dollar amounts of the investment projects expected to have each of these return rates.

Expected rate of return	Investment projects (billions)
18%	$ 0
16	10
14	20
12	30
10	40
8	50
6	60
4	70

a. If the real rate of interest in the economy were 18%,

business firms would plan to spend $_____

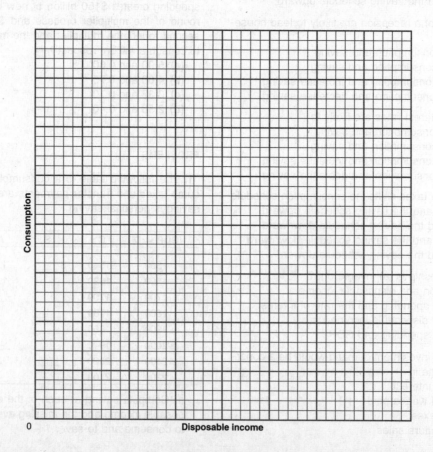

Consumption

0   Disposable income

billion for investment, but if the real interest rate were 16%, they would plan to spend $_____ for investment.

b. Should the real interest rate be 14%, and they would still wish to make the investments they were willing to make at real interest rates of 18% and 16%, they would plan to spend an additional $_____ billion for investment, and their total investment would be $_____ billion.

c. If the real rate of interest were 12%, they would make all the investments they had planned to make at higher real interest rates plus an additional $_____ billion, and their total investment spending would be $_____ billion.

d. Complete the following table by computing the amount of planned investment at the four remaining real interest rates.

Real rate of interest	Amount of investment (billions)
18%	$ 0
16	10
14	20
12	60
10	____
8	____
6	____
4	____

e. Graph the schedule you completed on the graph below. Plot the real rate of interest on the vertical axis and the amount of investment planned at each real rate of interest on the horizontal axis.

f. Both the graph and the table show that the relationship between the real rate of interest and the amount of investment spending in the economy is _____. This means that when the real rate of interest
(1) increases, investment will (increase, decrease) _____.

(2) decreases, investment will _____.
g. It also means that should we wish to
(1) increase investment, we would need to _____ the real rate of interest.
(2) decrease investment, we would have to _____ the real rate of interest.

h. This graph (or table) is the _____ curve.

4. Indicate in the spaces to the right of the following events whether the event would tend to increase (+) or decrease (−) investment spending.

a. Rising stock market prices _____
b. Development of expectations by business executives that business taxes will be higher in the future _____
c. Step-up in the rates at which new products and new production processes are being introduced _____
d. Business beliefs that wage rates may be lower in the future and labor and capital are complementary resources _____
e. An expectation of a recession _____
f. A belief that business is "too good" and the economy is due for a period of "slow" consumer demand _____
g. Rising costs in the construction industry _____
h. A rapid increase in the size of the economy's population _____
i. A recent period of a high level of investment spending, which has resulted in productive capacity in excess of the current demand for goods and services _____

5. Assume the marginal propensity to consume is 0.8 and the change in investment is $10. Complete the following table modeled after Table 27.3 in the textbook.

	Change in income	Change in consumption	Change in saving
Increase in gross investment of $10	$ + 10	$____	$____
Second round	____	____	____
Third round	____	____	____
Fourth round	____	____	____
Fifth round	____	____	____
All other rounds	16.38	13.10	3.28
Totals	____	____	____

SHORT ANSWER AND ESSAY QUESTIONS

1. What is the most important determinant of consumer spending and personal saving? What is the relationship between consumer spending and personal saving?

0

2. Use a graph to illustrate the historical relationship between consumption and disposable income in the U.S. economy. Explain why the slope of the consumption line will be less than the 45-degree reference line.

3. Describe the relationship between consumption and disposable income, called the consumption schedule. Draw a graph of this schedule.

4. Describe the relationship between saving and disposable income, called the saving schedule. Draw a graph of this schedule.

5. Define the two average propensities and the two marginal propensities.

6. Explain briefly how the average propensity to consume and the average propensity to save vary as disposable income varies. Why do APC and APS behave this way? What happens to consumption and saving as disposable income varies?

7. Why do the sum of the APC and the APS and the sum of the MPC and the MPS always equal exactly 1?

8. What is the relationship between MPC and MPS and the slopes of the consumption schedule and saving schedule?

9. Explain briefly and explicitly *how* changes in the four nonincome determinants will affect the consumption schedule and the saving schedule and *why* such changes will affect consumption and saving in the way you have indicated.

10. Why does taxation shift both the consumption and saving schedules in the same direction?

11. What is the difference between a change in the amount consumed and a change in the consumption schedule? Explain your answer using a graph.

12. Are consumption and saving schedules relatively stable? Explain.

13. Discuss the marginal cost and marginal benefit of an investment decision. How are the marginal cost and the marginal benefit of investment measured?

14. Draw an investment demand curve. Use it to explain why investment spending tends to rise when the real rate of interest falls, and vice versa.

15. Identify and explain how six noninterest determinants of investment spending can increase or decrease the amount of investment. Illustrate the changes with a graph.

16. Why does the level of investment spending tend to be highly unstable? State four reasons.

17. What is the multiplier effect? Give an equation and example to show how it works.

18. State the rationale for the multiplier effect.

19. How is the multiplier effect related to the marginal propensities? Explain in words and equations.

20. How large is the actual multiplier effect? Explain the reasons for the difference between the textbook example of the multiplier and actual multiplier for the economy.

ANSWERS

Chapter 27 Basic Macroeconomic Relationships

FILL-IN QUESTIONS

1. consume, save
2. directly, larger, smaller, smaller, larger, equal to
3. rise, fall
4. 1, .10
5. consumption, income
6. saving, income
7. 1, .25
8. consumption, saving
9. *a.* wealth; *b.* borrowing; *c.* expectations; *d.* real interest rate; (any order for *a–d*)
10. upward, downward, income
11. return, interest
12. benefit, cost
13. increase, decrease
14. inverse, demand, decrease, increase
15. *a.* the cost of acquiring, maintaining, and operating capital goods; *b.* business taxes; *c.* technological change; *d.* the stock of capital goods on hand; *e.* planned changes in inventories; *f.* expectations
16. durability, irregularity, variability, variability
17. divided, multiplied
18. increase, decrease
19. save, consume
20. larger, smaller

TRUE–FALSE QUESTIONS

1. F, p. 542	**10.** T, p. 546	**19.** F, p. 554
2. T, p. 542	**11.** T, p. 548	**20.** T, p. 554
3. T, p. 542	**12.** T, p. 548	**21.** F, pp. 554–555
4. F, pp. 543–544	**13.** T, p. 549	**22.** T, pp. 554–555
5. F, pp. 543–544	**14.** F, pp. 549–551	**23.** T, p. 556
6. F, pp. 543–545	**15.** T, p. 552	**24.** T, p. 556
7. F, p. 545	**16.** F, p. 552	**25.** F, pp. 556, 558
8. T, p. 545	**17.** F, pp. 552–553	
9. F, p. 546	**18.** T, p. 553	

MULTIPLE-CHOICE QUESTIONS

1. c, p. 542	**10.** d, p. 546	**19.** d, p. 552
2. d, pp. 542–543	**11.** b, p. 545	**20.** b, p. 552
3. a, pp. 542–543	**12.** c, p. 545	**21.** c, pp. 553–554
4. b, p. 545	**13.** a, p. 546	**22.** d, pp. 554–556
5. d, p. 545	**14.** b, p. 546	**23.** a, pp. 554–556
6. c, p. 545	**15.** c, p. 547	**24.** a, pp. 554–556
7. a, p. 546	**16.** c, p. 47	**25.** c, pp. 554–556
8. c, pp. 542–543	**17.** c, p. 548	
9. c, pp. 542–543	**18.** b, pp. 549–550	

PROBLEMS

1. *a.* S: −40, −20, 0, 20, 40, 60, 80, 100; APC: 1.000, 0.970, 0.955; APS: 0.000, 0.030, 0.045; *b.* 1700; *c.* 80, 100, .8; *d.* 20, 100, .20; *e.* (1) .8, MPC, (2) .2, MPS

2. *a.*−; *b.* +; *c.* −; *d.* +; *e.* −; *f.* none; *g.* −; *h.* −

3. *a.* 0, 10; *b.* 20, 30; *c.* 30, 60; *d.* 100, 150, 210, 280; *f.* inverse, (1) decrease, (2) increase; *g.* (1) lower, (2) raise; *h.* investment-demand

4. *a.* +; *b.* −; *c.* +; *d.* +; *e.* −; *f.* −; *g.* −; *h.* +; *i.* −

5. Change in income: 8.00, 6.40, 5.12, 4.10, 50; Change in consumption: 8.00, 6.40, 5.12, 4.10, 3.28, 40.00; Change in saving: 2.00, 1.60, 1.28, 1.02, 0.82, 10.00

SHORT ANSWER AND ESSAY QUESTIONS

CHAPTER 28

The Aggregate Expenditures Model

This chapter develops the first macroeconomic model of the economy presented in the textbook—the **aggregate expenditures model.** You will find out what determines the demand for real domestic output (real GDP) and how an economy achieves an equilibrium level of output. The chapter begins with some history and simplifying assumptions for the model. As you will learn, one of the main assumptions is that the prices are fixed.

The chapter then explains how the investment decisions of individual firms can be used to construct an **investment schedule.** The investment schedule is then combined with the consumption schedule to form an aggregate expenditures schedule that shows the various amounts that will be spent in a private closed economy at each possible output or income level. These aggregate expenditures in tabular or graphical form can be used to find **equilibrium GDP** for this economy. It will be important for you to understand how equilibrium GDP is determined and why this level of output will be produced when you are given information about consumption and investment schedules.

Two other features of this simplified aggregate expenditures model are worth noting. Saving and *actual* investment are always equal because they are defined in exactly the same way: the output of the economy minus its consumption. **Saving and planned investment,** however, are equal only when real GDP is at its equilibrium level. When real GDP is *not* at its equilibrium level, saving and planned investment are *not* equal and there are **unplanned changes in inventories.** Equilibrium real GDP is achieved when saving and *planned* investment are equal and there are no unplanned changes in inventories.

From Chapter 28 you will also learn **what causes real GDP to rise and fall** based on changes or additions to aggregate expenditures. The first change that will be discussed is the effect of a change in investment spending on equilibrium real GDP in a closed private economy. The initial change in investment will increase equilibrium real GDP by more than the initial investment stimulus because of the multiplier effect.

The methods used to find the equilibrium real GDP in an open economy (one that exports and imports) is the same one as for a closed economy. The economy will tend to produce a real GDP that is equal to aggregate expenditures. The only difference is that now the aggregate expenditures include not only consumption and investment but also the **net exports** (exports minus imports). An increase in net exports, like an increase in investment, will increase the equilibrium real GDP. A change in net exports also has a multiplier effect on real GDP just like a change in investment.

The section "Adding the Public Sector" introduces **government taxing and spending** into the analysis of equilibrium real GDP. Government purchases of goods and services add to aggregate expenditures, and taxation reduces the disposable income of consumers, thereby reducing both the amount of consumption and the amount of saving that will take place at any level of real GDP. You will need to know the level of real GDP that will be produced and why.

It is important to be aware that the equilibrium real GDP is not necessarily the real GDP at which full employment is achieved. Aggregate expenditures may be greater or less than the full-employment real GDP. If they are greater, there is an **inflationary expenditure gap.** If they are less, there exists a **recessionary expenditure gap.** The chapter explains how to measure the size of each expenditure gap: the amount by which the aggregate expenditures schedule must change to bring the economy to its full-employment real GDP. Several historical examples are given to help you see the application of recessionary and inflationary expenditure gaps.

The aggregate expenditures model is a valuable tool for explaining such economic events as recession, inflation, and economic growth.

■ CHECKLIST

When you have studied this chapter you should be able to

☐ Describe the history, assumptions, and simplifications underpinning the aggregate expenditures model.

☐ Construct an investment schedule showing the relationship between planned investment and GDP.

☐ Combine the consumption and investment schedule to form an aggregate expenditures schedule to explain the equilibrium levels of output, income, and employment in a private closed economy.

☐ Explain why the economy will tend to produce its equilibrium GDP rather than some smaller or larger level of real GDP.

☐ Illustrate graphically equilibrium in an aggregate expenditure model with consumption and investment components.

☐ Explain the relationship between saving and planned investment at equilibrium GDP.

☐ State the conditions for changes in inventories at equilibrium GDP.

☐ Discuss why equilibrium real GDP changes when the aggregate expenditure schedule shifts upward due to an increase in investment spending.

☐ Use the concept of net exports to define aggregate expenditures in an open economy.

☐ Describe the net export schedule and its relationship to real GDP.

☐ Explain what the equilibrium real GDP in an open economy will be when net exports are positive and when net exports are negative.

☐ Find the equilibrium real GDP in an open economy when given the tabular or graphical data.

☐ Give three examples of how circumstances or policies abroad can affect domestic GDP.

☐ List three simplifying assumptions used to add the public sector to the aggregate expenditures model.

☐ Find the equilibrium real GDP in an economy in which the government purchases goods and services when given the tabular or graphical data.

☐ Determine the effect on the equilibrium real GDP when lump-sum taxes are included in the aggregate expenditures model.

☐ Describe the conditions for leakages and injections and unplanned changes in inventories at the equilibrium level of GDP.

☐ Distinguish between the equilibrium real GDP and the full-employment real GDP.

☐ Explain the meaning of a recessionary gap and calculate one when you are provided with the relevant data.

☐ Present Keynes's solution to a recessionary expenditure gap.

☐ Define inflationary expenditure gap and calculate one when you are provided with the relevant data.

☐ Apply the concepts of recessionary and inflationary expenditure gaps to two historical events in the United States.

☐ Describe Say's law and Keynes's critique of it (Last Word).

■ **CHAPTER OUTLINE**

1. The development of the *aggregate expenditures model* occurred during the Great Depression when there were high unemployment and underutilized capital. Prices in such an economy were fixed or stuck (an extreme version of the sticky price model already discussed in Chapter 23) because the oversupply of productive resources kept prices low. As a result, business had to make output and employment decisions based on unplanned changes in inventories arising from economic shocks.

 a. The aggregate expenditures model with its constant price assumption is valuable for analysis of our modern economy because in many cases prices are sticky or stuck in the short run. The model can be useful for understanding how economic shocks affect output and employment when prices are fixed or sticky.

 b. Two simplifications are made to begin the model construction. First, it is assumed that the economy is private

and closed, which means there is no international trade or government spending (or taxes). Second it is assumed that output or income measures are equal (real GDP = disposable income, DI). These simplifications are relaxed later in the chapter.

2. The investment decisions of businesses in an economy can be aggregated to form an *investment schedule* that shows the amounts business firms collectively intend to invest (their *planned investment*) at each possible level of GDP. An assumption is made that investment is independent of disposable income or real GDP.

3. In the aggregate expenditures model, the *equilibrium GDP* is the real GDP at which

 a. aggregate expenditures (consumption plus planned investment) equal real GDP, or $C + I_g = GDP$;

 b. in graphical terms, the aggregate expenditures schedule crosses the 45-degree line. The slope of this curve is equal to the marginal propensity to consume.

4. There are two other features of equilibrium GDP.

 a. The investment schedule indicates what investors plan to do. Actual investment consists of both planned and unplanned investment (unplanned changes in inventories). At above equilibrium levels of GDP, saving is greater than planned investment, and there will be unintended or unplanned investment through increases in inventories. At below equilibrium levels of GDP, planned investment is greater than saving, and there will be unintended or unplanned disinvestment through a decrease in inventories.

 b. Equilibrium is achieved when planned investment equals saving and there are no *unplanned changes in inventories.*

5. Changes in investment (or consumption) will cause the equilibrium real GDP to change in the same direction by an amount greater than the initial change in investment (or consumption). The reason for this greater change is due to the **multiplier effect.**

6. In an **open economy** there are *net exports* (X_n), which are defined as exports (X) minus imports (M).

 a. The equilibrium real GDP in an open economy means real GDP is equal to consumption plus investment plus net exports.

 b. The net export schedule will be positive or negative. The schedule is positive when exports are greater than imports; it is negative when imports are greater than exports.

 c. Any increase in X_n will increase the equilibrium real GDP with a multiplier effect. A decrease in X_n will do just the opposite.

 d. In an open economy model, circumstances and policies abroad can affect the real GDP in the United States.

 (1) If there is an increase in real output and incomes in other nations that trade with the United States, then the United States can sell more goods abroad, which increases net exports, and thus increases real GDP. A decline in the real output or incomes of other trading nations has the opposite effects.

(2) High tariffs or strict quotas can have an adverse effect on net exports and thus reduce real GDP. Lower tariffs or eliminating quotas has the opposite effects.

(3) A depreciation in the value of the U.S. dollar will increase the purchasing power of foreign currency and this change will increase U.S. exports. The result is an increase in net exports and real GDP. An appreciation in the value of the U.S. dollar has the opposite effects.

7. Changes in **government spending and tax rates** can affect equilibrium real GDP. This simplified analysis assumes that government purchases do not affect investment or consumption, that taxes are purely personal taxes, and that a fixed amount of tax revenue is collected regardless of the level of GDP (a *lump-sum tax*).

a. Government purchases of goods and services add to the aggregate expenditures schedule and increase equilibrium real GDP; an increase in these purchases has a multiplier effect on equilibrium real GDP.

b. Taxes decrease consumption and the aggregate expenditures schedule by the amount of the tax times the **MPC.** They decrease saving by the amount of the tax times the **MPS.** An increase in taxes has a negative multiplier effect on the equilibrium real GDP.

(1) When government both taxes and purchases goods and services, the equilibrium GDP is the real GDP at which aggregate expenditures (*consumption + investment + net exports + government purchases of goods and services*) equals real GDP.

(2) From a *leakages* and *injections* perspective, the equilibrium GDP is the real GDP at which leakages (*saving + imports + taxes*) equals injections (*investment + exports + government purchases*).

(3) At equilibrium real GDP, there are no unplanned changes in inventories.

8. The **equilibrium level of real GDP** may turn out to be an equilibrium that is at less than full employment, at full employment, or at full employment with inflation.

a. If the equilibrium real GDP is less than the real GDP consistent with full-employment real GDP, there exists a *recessionary expenditure gap.* Aggregate expenditures are less than what is needed to achieve full-employment real GDP. The size of the recessionary expenditure gap equals the amount by which the aggregate expenditures schedule must increase (shift upward) to increase real GDP to its full-employment level.

(1) Keynes's solution to close a recessionary expenditure gap and achieve full-employment GDP was either to increase government spending or decrease taxes. An increase in government expenditures or a cut in taxes would work through the multiplier to lift aggregate expenditures. One caution about the price assumption, however, is worth noting. As an economy moves to its full-employment or potential GDP, prices should not be assumed to be stuck or sticky, and thus will rise because there is no longer a large supply of unemployed resources to restrain price increases. Such a flexible-prices condition will be analyzed in the aggregate demand–aggregate supply model of the next chapter.

b. If aggregate expenditures are *greater* than those consistent with full-employment real GDP, then there is an *inflationary expenditure gap.* This expenditure gap results from excess spending and will increase the price level, creating demand-pull inflation. The size of the inflationary expenditure gap equals the amount by which the aggregate expenditures schedule must decrease (shift downward) if the economy is to achieve full-employment real GDP.

c. The U.S. recession of 2001 is an example of a recessionary expenditure gap as investment spending declined, thus reducing aggregate expenditures. Aggregate expenditures were insufficient to achieve a full-employment level of GDP.

d. The economy can achieve full-employment output with large negative net exports as it did in 2007. Although economic theory suggests that the large negative net exports should reduce equilibrium real GDP below its potential, this result did not occur in the U.S. economy because it was offset by additional consumption, investment, and government spending during that period.

9. (Last Word). Classical economists held the view that when there were deviations from full employment in the economy, it would eventually adjust and achieve equilibrium. This view was based on Say's law which says that supply creates its own demand. It implies that the production of goods will create the income needed to purchase the produced goods. The events of the Great Depression led to doubts about this law and it was challenged by John Maynard Keynes in his 1936 book, *General Theory of Employment, Interest, and Money.* Keynes showed that supply may not create its own demand because not all income need be spent in the period it was earned, thus creating conditions for high levels of unemployment and economic decline.

■ HINTS AND TIPS

1. Do not confuse the **investment demand curve** for the business sector with the **investment schedule** for an economy. The former shows the inverse relationship between the real interest rate and the amount of total investment by the business sector, whereas the latter shows the collective investment intentions of business firms at each possible level of disposable income or real GDP.

2. The distinction between **actual investment, planned investment,** and **unplanned investment** is important for determining the equilibrium level of real GDP. Actual investment includes both planned and unplanned investment. At any level of real GDP, saving and actual investment will always be equal by definition, but saving and planned investment may not equal real GDP because there may be unplanned investment (unplanned changes in inventories). Only at the equilibrium level of real GDP will saving and planned investment be equal (there is no unplanned investment).

3. There is an important difference between **equilibrium** and **full-employment real GDP** in the aggregate expenditures model. Equilibrium means no tendency for the economy to change its output (or employment) level. Thus, an economy can experience a low level of output and high unemployment and still be at equilibrium. The *recessionary expenditure gap* shows how much aggregate expenditures need to increase, so that when this increase is multiplied by the multiplier, it will shift the economy to a higher equilibrium and to the full-employment level of real GDP. Remember that you multiply the needed increase in aggregate expenditures (the recessionary expenditure gap) by the multiplier to calculate the change in real GDP that moves the economy from below to full-employment equilibrium.

■ IMPORTANT TERMS

planned investment

investment schedule

aggregate
   expenditures
   schedule

equilibrium GDP

leakage

injection

unplanned changes in
   inventories

net exports

lump-sum tax

recessionary
   expenditure gap

inflationary
   expenditure gap

SELF-TEST

■ FILL-IN QUESTIONS

1. In the aggregate expenditures model, when total spending falls, then total output and employment (increase, decrease) _____, and when total spending rises, then total output and employment _____.

2. Some simplifying assumptions used in the first part of the chapter are that the economy is (an open, a closed) _____ economy, the economy is (private, public) _____, that real GDP equals disposable (consumption, income) _____, and that an increase in aggregate expenditures will (increase, decrease) _____ real output and employment, but not raise the price level.

3. A schedule showing the amounts business firms collectively intend to invest at each possible level of GDP is the (consumption, investment) _____ schedule. For this schedule, it is assumed that planned (saving, investment) _____ is independent of the level of current disposable income or real output.

4. Assuming a private and closed economy, the equilibrium level of real GDP is determined where aggregate expenditures are (greater than, less than, equal to) _____ real domestic output, consumption plus investment is _____ real domestic output, and the aggregate expenditures schedule or curve intersects the (90-degree, 45-degree) _____ line.

5. A leakage is (an addition to, a withdrawal from) _____ the income expenditure stream, whereas an injection is _____ the income expenditure stream. In this chapter, an example of a leakage is (investment, saving) _____, and an example of an injection is _____.

6. If aggregate expenditures are greater than the real domestic output, saving is (greater than, less than) _____ planned investment, there are unplanned (increases, decreases) _____ in inventories, and real GDP will (rise, fall) _____.

7. If aggregate expenditures are less than the real domestic output, saving is (greater than, less than) _____ planned investment, there are unplanned (increases, decreases) _____ in inventories, and real GDP will (rise, fall) _____.

8. If aggregate expenditures are equal to the real domestic output, saving is (greater than, less than, equal to) _____ planned investment, unplanned changes in inventories are (negative, positive, zero) _____, and real GDP will neither rise nor fall.

9. An upshift in the aggregate expenditures schedule will (increase, decrease) _____ the equilibrium GDP. The upshift in the aggregate expenditures schedule can result from (an increase, a decrease) _____ in the consumption schedule or _____ in the investment schedule.

10. When investment spending increases, the equilibrium real GDP (increases, decreases) _____, and when investment spending decreases, the equilibrium real GDP _____. The changes in the equilibrium real GDP are (greater, less) _____ than the initial changes in investment spending because of the (lump-sum tax, multiplier) _____.

11. In an open economy, a nation's net exports are equal to its exports (plus, minus) _____ its imports. In the open economy, aggregate expenditures are equal to consumption (plus, minus) _____ investment (plus, minus) _____ net exports.

12. What would be the effect, an increase (+) or a decrease (−), of each of the following on an open economy's equilibrium real GDP?

a. an increase in imports _____

b. an increase in exports _____

c. a decrease in imports _____

d. a decrease in exports _____

e. an increasing level of national income among trading partners _____

f. an increase in trade barriers imposed by trading partners _____

g. a depreciation in the value of the economy's currency

_____

13. Increases in public spending will (decrease, increase) _____ the aggregate expenditures schedule and equilibrium real GDP, but decreases in public spending will _____ the aggregate expenditures schedule and equilibrium real GDP.

14. A tax yielding the same amount of tax revenue at each evel of GDP is a (lump-sum, constant) _____ tax.

15. Taxes tend to reduce consumption at each level of real GDP by an amount equal to the taxes multiplied by the marginal propensity to (consume, save) _____; saving will decrease by an amount equal to the taxes multiplied by the marginal propensity to _____.

16. In an economy in which government both taxes and purchases goods and services, the equilibrium level of real GDP is the real GDP at which aggregate (output, expenditures) _____ equal(s) real domestic _____, and at which real GDP is equal to consumption (plus, minus) _____ investment (plus, minus) _____ net exports (plus, minus) _____ purchases of goods and services by government.

17. When the public sector is added to the model, the equation for the leakages and injections shows (consumption, investment) _____ plus (imports, exports)_____, plus purchases of goods and services by government equals (consumption, saving) _____ plus (exports, imports) _____ plus taxes.

18. A recessionary expenditure gap exists when equilibrium real GDP is (greater, less) _____ than the full-employment real GDP. To bring real GDP to the full-employment level, the aggregate expenditures schedule must (increase, decrease) _____ by an amount equal to the difference between the equilibrium

and the full-employment real GDP (multiplied, divided) _____ by the multiplier.

19. Keynes believed that prices during the Great Depression were (flexible, fixed) _____ because large amounts of productive resources in the economy were unemployed. In such conditions, he thought the government could increase real GDP to achieve full-employment without a rise in the price level by (increasing, decreasing) _____ government spending or _____ taxes.

20. The amount by which aggregate spending at the full-employment GDP exceeds the full-employment level of real GDP is (a recessionary, an inflationary) _____ expenditure gap. To eliminate this expenditure gap, the aggregate expenditures schedule must (increase, decrease) _____.

■ **TRUE–FALSE QUESTIONS**

Circle T if the statement is true, F if it is false.

1. The basic premise of the aggregate expenditures model is that the amount of goods and services produced and the level of employment depend directly on the level of total spending. **T F**

2. In the aggregate expenditures model of the economy, the price level is assumed to be fixed or stuck. **T F**

3. The investment schedule is a schedule of planned investment rather than a schedule of actual investment.
T F

4. The equilibrium level of GDP is that GDP level corresponding to the intersection of the aggregate expenditures schedule with the 45-degree line. **T F**

5. At levels of GDP below equilibrium, the economy wants to spend at higher levels than the levels of GDP the economy is producing. **T F**

6. At levels of GDP below equilibrium, aggregate expenditures are less than GDP, which causes inventories to rise and production to fall. **T F**

7. Saving is an injection into and investment is a leakage from the income expenditures stream. **T F**

8. Saving and actual investment are always equal. **T F**

9. Saving at any level of real GDP equals planned investment plus unplanned changes in inventories. **T F**

10. The equilibrium level of GDP will change in response to changes in the investment schedule or the consumption schedule. **T F**

11. If there is a decrease in the investment schedule, there will be an upshift in the aggregate expenditures schedule. **T F**

12. Through the multiplier effect, an initial change in investment spending can cause a magnified change in domestic output and income. **T F**

13. The net exports of an economy equal the sum of its exports and imports of goods and services. **T F**

14. An increase in the volume of a nation's exports, other things being equal, will expand the nation's real GDP. **T F**

15. An increase in the imports of a nation will increase the exports of other nations. **T F**

16. A falling level of real output and income among U.S. trading partners enables the United States to sell more goods abroad. **T F**

17. An appreciation of the dollar will increase net exports. **T F**

18. If the MPS were 0.3 and taxes were levied by the government so that consumers paid $20 in taxes at each level of real GDP, consumption expenditures at each level of real GDP would be $14 less. **T F**

19. Equal changes in government spending and taxes do not have equivalent effects on real GDP. **T F**

20. At equilibrium, the sum of leakages equals the sum of injections. **T F**

21. The equilibrium real GDP is the real GDP at which there is full employment in the economy. **T F**

22. The existence of a recessionary expenditure gap in the economy is characterized by the full employment of labor. **T F**

23. Keynes's solution to the recessionary expenditure gap of the Great Depression was to increase government spending and cut taxes. **T F**

24. The closer an economy is to its full-employment level of output, the less likely it is that any increase in aggregate expenditures will lead to inflation rather than an increase in real GDP. **T F**

25. An inflationary expenditure gap is the amount by which the economy's aggregate expenditures schedule must shift downward to eliminate demand-pull inflation and still achieve the full-employment GDP. **T F**

■ **MULTIPLE-CHOICE QUESTIONS**

Circle the letter that corresponds to the best answer.

1. The premise of the model in this chapter is that the amount of goods and services produced, and therefore the level of employment, depends
  (a) directly on the rate of interest
  (b) directly on the level of total expenditures
  (c) inversely on the level of disposable income
  (d) inversely on the quantity of resources available

2. If the economy is private, closed to international trade, and government neither taxes nor spends, then real GDP equals
  (a) saving
  (b) consumption

  (c) disposable income
  (d) investment spending

Question 3 is based on the following consumption schedule.

Real GDP	C
$200	$200
240	228
280	256
320	284
360	312
400	340
440	368
480	396

3. If the investment schedule is $60 at each level of output, the equilibrium level of real GDP will be
  (a) $320
  (b) $360
  (c) $400
  (d) $440

4. If real GDP is $275 billion, consumption is $250 billion, and investment is $30 billion, real GDP
  (a) will tend to decrease
  (b) will tend to increase
  (c) will tend to remain constant
  (d) equals aggregate expenditures

5. On a graph, the equilibrium real GDP is found at the intersection of the 45-degree line and the
  (a) saving curve
  (b) consumption curve
  (c) investment demand curve
  (d) aggregate expenditures curve

6. Which is an injection of spending into the income expenditures stream?
  (a) investment
  (b) imports
  (c) saving
  (d) taxes

7. When the economy's real GDP exceeds its equilibrium real GDP,
  (a) leakages equal injections
  (b) planned investment exceeds saving
  (c) there is unplanned investment in the economy
  (d) aggregate expenditures exceed the real domestic output

8. If saving is greater than planned investment
  (a) saving will tend to increase
  (b) businesses will be motivated to increase their investments
  (c) real GDP will be greater than planned investment plus consumption
  (d) aggregate expenditures will be greater than the real domestic output

9. At the equilibrium level of GDP,
  (a) actual investment is zero
  (b) unplanned changes in inventories are zero

(c) saving is greater than planned investment

(d) saving is less than planned investment

Answer Questions 10 and 11 on the basis of the following table for a private, closed economy. All figures are in billions of dollars.

Real rate of return	Investment	Consumption	GDP
10%	$ 0	$200	$200
8	50	250	300
6	100	300	400
4	150	350	500
2	200	400	600
0	250	450	700

10. If the real rate of interest is 4%, then the equilibrium level of GDP will be

(a) $300 billion

(b) $400 billion

(c) $500 billion

(d) $600 billion

11. An *increase* in the real interest rate by 4% will

(a) increase the equilibrium level of GDP by $200 billion

(b) decrease the equilibrium level of GDP by $200 billion

(c) decrease the equilibrium level of GDP by $100 billion

(d) increase the equilibrium level of GDP by $100 billion

12. Compared with a closed economy, aggregate expenditures and GDP will

(a) increase when net exports are positive

(b) decrease when net exports are positive

(c) increase when net exports are negative

(d) decrease when net exports are zero

Use the data in the following table to answer Questions 13 and 14.

Real GDP	$C + I_g$	Net exports
900	$ 913	$3
920	929	3
940	945	3
960	961	3
980	977	3
1000	993	3
1020	1009	3

13. The equilibrium real GDP in this open economy is

(a) $960

(b) $980

(c) $1000

(d) $1020

14. If net exports are increased by $4 billion at each level of GDP, the equilibrium real GDP would be

(a) $960

(b) $980

(c) $1000

(d) $1020

15. An increase in the real GDP of an economy will, other things remaining constant,

(a) increase its imports and the real GDPs in other economies

(b) decrease its imports and the real GDPs in other economies

(c) increase its imports and decrease the real GDPs in other economies

(d) decrease its imports and increase the real GDPs in other economies

16. Other things remaining constant, which would increase an economy's real GDP and employment?

(a) an increase in the exchange rate for foreign currencies

(b) the imposition of tariffs on goods imported from abroad

(c) an appreciation of the dollar relative to foreign currencies

(d) an increase in the level of national income among the trading partners for this economy

17. The economy is operating at the full-employment level of output. A depreciation of the dollar will most likely result in

(a) a decrease in exports

(b) an increase in imports

(c) a decrease in real GDP

(d) an increase in the price level

Answer Questions 18 and 19 on the basis of the following diagram.

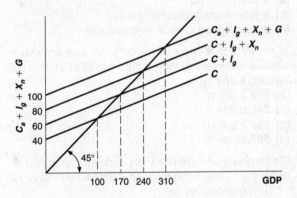

18. If this were an open economy without a government sector, the level of GDP would be

(a) $100

(b) $170

(c) $240

(d) $310

19. In this graph it is assumed that investment, net exports, and government expenditures

(a) vary directly with GDP

(b) vary inversely with GDP

(c) are independent of GDP

(d) are all negative

Questions 20 and 21 are based on the following consumption schedule.

Real GDP	C
$300	$290
310	298
320	306
330	314
340	322
350	330
360	338

20. If taxes were zero, government purchases of goods and services $10, planned investment $6, and net exports zero, equilibrium real GDP would be

(a) $310
(b) $320
(c) $330
(d) $340

21. If taxes were $5, government purchases of goods and services $10, planned investment $6, and net exports zero, equilibrium real GDP would be

(a) $300
(b) $310
(c) $320
(d) $330

22. The amount by which an economy's aggregate expenditures must shift upward to achieve full-employment GDP is

(a) an injection
(b) a lump-sum tax
(c) a recessionary expenditure gap
(d) an unplanned change in inventories

23. If the MPC in an economy is 0.75, government could eliminate a recessionary expenditure gap of $50 billion by decreasing taxes by

(a) $33.3 billion
(b) $50 billion
(c) $66.7 billion
(d) $80 billion

24. To eliminate an inflationary expenditure gap of $50 in an economy in which the marginal propensity to save is 0.1, it will be necessary to

(a) decrease the aggregate expenditures schedule by $50
(b) decrease the aggregate expenditures schedule by $5
(c) increase the aggregate expenditures schedule by $50
(d) increase the aggregate expenditures schedule by $5

25. A major limitation of the aggregate expenditures model is that it

(a) gives more weight to cost-push than demand-pull inflation
(b) makes a false distinction between planned and unplanned investment

(c) assumes that prices are stuck or inflexible even as the economy moves near potential GDP
(d) explains recessionary expenditure gaps but not inflationary expenditure gaps

■ **PROBLEMS**

1. Following are two schedules showing several GDPs and the level of investment spending (*I*) at each GDP. (All figures are in billions of dollars.)

Schedule number 1		Schedule number 2	
GDP	I	GDP	I
$1850	$90	$1850	$75
1900	90	1900	80
1950	90	1950	85
2000	90	2000	90
2050	90	2050	95
2100	90	2100	100
2150	95	2150	105

a. Each schedule is an _____ schedule.
b When such a schedule is drawn up, it is assumed that the real rate of interest is _____.
c. In schedule
(1) number 1, GDP and *I* are (unrelated, directly related) _____.
(2) number 2, GDP and *I* are _____.
d. Should the real rate of interest rise, investment spending at each GDP would (increase, decrease) _____ and the curve relating GDP and investment spending would shift (upward, downward) _____.

2. The following table shows consumption and saving at various levels of real GDP. Assume the price level is constant, the economy is closed to international trade, and there is no government, no business savings, no depreciation, and no net foreign factor income earned in the United States.

Real GDP	C	S	I_g	$C + I_g$	UI
$1300	$1290	$10	$22	1312	−12
1310	1298	12	22	1320	−10
1320	1306	14	___	___	___
1330	1314	16	___	___	___
1340	1322	18	___	___	___
1350	1330	20	___	___	___
1360	1338	22	___	___	___
1370	1346	24	___	___	___
1380	1354	26	___	___	___
1390	1362	28	22	1384	+6
1400	1370	30	22	1392	+8

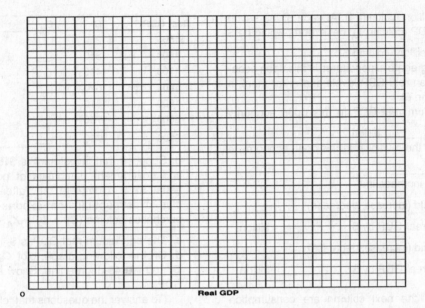

Real GDP

a. The next table is an investment demand schedule that shows the amounts investors plan to invest at different rates of interest. Assume the rate of interest is 6%. In the previous table, complete the gross investment, the consumption-plus-investment, and unplanned investment (**UI**) columns, showing unplanned increase in inventories with a + and unplanned decrease in inventories with a −.

Interest rate	I_g
$10%	$ 0
9	7
8	13
7	18
6	22
5	25

b. The equilibrium real GDP will be $ _____.

c. The value of the marginal propensity to consume in this problem is _____, and the value of the marginal propensity to save is _____.

d. The value of the simple multiplier is _____.

e. If the rate of interest should fall from 6% to 5%, investment would (increase, decrease) _____ by $;_____; and the equilibrium real GDP would, as a result, (increase, decrease) _____ by $_____.

f. Suppose the rate of interest were to rise from 6% to 7%. Investment would (increase, decrease) _____ by $, _____ and the equilibrium real GDP would _____ by $_____.

g. Assuming the rate of interest is 6%, on the graph at the top of this page, plot **C**, **C** + **I**$_g$, and the 45-degree line, and indicate the equilibrium real GDP.

3. The second column of the schedule below shows what aggregate expenditures (consumption plus investment) would be at various levels of real domestic product in a closed economy.

a. Were this economy to become an open economy, the volume of exports would be a constant $90 billion (column 3), and the volume of imports would be a

(1) Possible levels of, real GDP (billions)	(2) Aggregate expenditures closed economy (billions)	(3) Exports (billions)	(4) Imports (billions)	(5) Net exports (billions)	(6) Aggregate expenditures, open economy (billions)
$ 750	$ 776	$90	$86	$_____	$_____
800	816	90	86	_____	_____
850	856	90	86	_____	_____
900	896	90	86	_____	_____
950	936	90	86	_____	_____
1000	976	90	86	_____	_____
1050	1016	90	86	_____	_____

constant $86 billion (column 4). At each of the seven levels of real GDP (column 1), net exports would be $ _____ billion (column 5).

b. Compute aggregate expenditures in this open economy at the seven real GDP levels and enter them in the table (column 6).

c. The equilibrium real GDP in this open economy would be_____ billion.

d. The value of the multiplier in this open economy is equal to _____.

e. A $10 billion increase in

(1) exports would (increase, decrease) _____ the equilibrium real GDP by $ _____ billion.

(2) imports would (increase, decrease) _____ the equilibrium real GDP by $ _____ billion.

4. At the top of the next column are consumption schedules.

  a. Assume government levies a lump-sum tax of $100. Also assume that imports are $5. Because the marginal propensity to consume in this problem is _____, the imposition of this tax will reduce consumption at all levels of real GDP by $ _____. Complete the C_a column to show consumption at each real GDP after this tax has been levied.

Real GDP	C	C_a	$C + I_g + X_n + G$
$1500	$1250	$___	$___
1600	1340	___	___
1700	1430	___	___
1800	1520	___	___
1900	1610	___	___
2000	1700	___	___
2100	1790	___	___

b. Suppose that investment is $150, exports are $5, and government purchases of goods and services equal $200. Complete the (after-tax) consumption-plus-investment-plus-net-exports-plus-government-purchases column ($C_a + I_g + X_n + G$).

c. The equilibrium real GDP is $ _____.

d. On the following graph, plot C_a, $C_a + I_g + X_n + G$, and the 45-degree line. Show the equilibrium real GDP.

(To answer the questions that follow, it is *not* necessary to recompute C_a, or $C_a + I_g + X_n + G$. They can be answered by using the multipliers.)

e. If taxes remained at $100 and government purchases rose by $10, the equilibrium real GDP would (rise, fall) _____ by $_____.

f. If government purchases remained at $200 and the lump-sum tax increased by $10, the equilibrium real GDP would _____ by $_____.

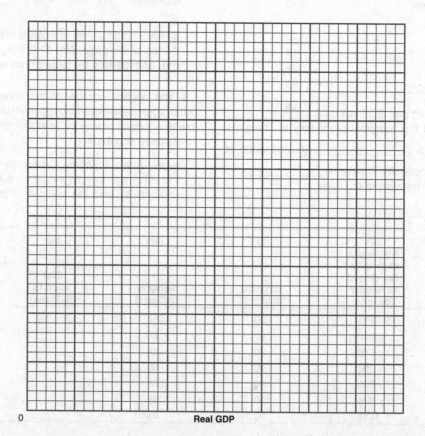

0   **Real GDP**

g. The combined effect of a $10 increase in government purchases *and* a $10 increase in taxes is (raise, lower) _____ to real GDP by $_____.

5. Here is a consumption schedule for a closed economy. Assume that the level of real GDP at which full employment without inflation is achieved is $590.

Real GDP	C
$550	$520
560	526
570	532
580	538
590	544
600	550
610	556
620	562
630	568

a. The value of the multiplier is _____.
b. If planned investment is $58, the equilibrium nominal GDP is $ _____ and exceeds full-employment real GDP by $_____. There is a(n) _____ expenditure gap of $_____.
c. If planned investment is $38, the equilibrium real GDP is $ _____ and is less than full-employment real GDP by $ _____. There is a(n) _____ expenditure gap of $ _____.

■ **SHORT ANSWER AND ESSAY QUESTIONS**

1. What does it mean that an economy is private and closed?

2. What assumptions are made in this chapter about production capacity, unemployment, and the price level?

3. What is the difference between an investment demand curve and an investment schedule?

4. Why is the equilibrium level of real GDP that level of real GDP at which domestic output equals aggregate expenditures? What will cause real GDP to rise if it is below this level, and what will cause it to fall if it is above this level?

5. Explain what is meant by a leakage and by an injection. Which leakage and which injection are considered in this chapter? Why is the equilibrium real GDP the real GDP at which the leakages equal the injections?

6. Why is it important to distinguish between planned and actual investment in explaining how a private, closed economy achieves its equilibrium level of real GDP?

7. Why does the equilibrium level of real GDP change?

8. How do exports and imports get included in the aggregate expenditures model?

9. What happens to the aggregate expenditures schedule when net exports increase or decrease?

10. Give some examples of international economic linkages affecting the domestic level of GDP.

11. Explain the simplifying assumptions used to include the public sector in the aggregate expenditures model.

12. Describe how government expenditures affect equilibrium GDP.

13. What effect will taxes have on the consumption schedule?

14. Explain why, with government taxing and spending, the equilibrium real GDP is the real GDP at which real GDP equals consumption plus investment plus net exports plus government purchases of goods and services.

15. Use leakages and injections to explain how changes in the different components of aggregate expenditures cause GDP to move to its equilibrium level.

16. Explain what is meant by a recessionary expenditure gap.

17. What was Keynes's solution to a recessionary gap? Explain one major limitation caution with the use the aggregate expenditures model.

18. What is an inflationary expenditure gap? Could an economy actually achieve and maintain an equilibrium real GDP that is substantially above the full-employment level of output? Explain.

19. What economic conditions contributed to the recessionary expenditure gap in the U.S. economy in 2001?

20. Why did the large negative net exports in 2007 not cause a decline in the U.S. economy below its potential and substantial unemployment?

ANSWERS

Chapter 28 The Aggregate Expenditures Model

FILL-IN QUESTIONS

1. decrease, increase
2. a closed, private, income, increase
3. investment, investment
4. equal to, equal to, 45-degree
5. a withdrawal from, an addition to, saving, investment
6. less than, decreases, rise
7. greater than, increases, fall
8. equal to, zero
9. increase, an increase, an increase
10. increases, decreases, greater, multiplier
11. minus, plus, plus
12. a. −; b. +; c. +; d. −; e. +; f. −; g. +
13. increase, decrease
14. lump-sum
15. consume, save
16. expenditures, output, plus, plus, plus
17. investment, exports, saving, imports
18. less, increase, divided
19. fixed, increasing, decreasing
20. an inflationary, decrease

TRUE–FALSE QUESTIONS

1. T, p. 561
2. T, p. 562
3. T, p. 562
4. T, pp. 564–565
5. T, p. 564
6. F, p. 564
7. F, p. 566
8. T, pp. 566–567
9. T, pp. 566–567
10. T, p. 567
11. F, p. 567
12. T, p. 567
13. F, p. 568

14. T, pp. 569–570
15. T, p. 570
16. F, p. 570
17. F, p. 571
18. T, pp. 572–573
19. T, pp. 573–574
20. T, p. 574
21. F, p. 574
22. F, p. 575
23. T, p. 575
24. F, pp. 575–576
25. T, pp. 576–577

MULTIPLE-CHOICE QUESTIONS

1. b, p. 561
2. c, p. 562
3. c, pp. 562–563
4. b, pp. 564–565
5. d, p. 565
6. a, p. 566
7. c, pp. 566–567
8. c, pp. 566–567
9. b, pp. 566–567
10. c, pp. 562–564
11. b, pp. 562–564
12. a, p. 570
13. b, pp. 569–570

14. c, pp. 569–570
15. a, pp. 569–570
16. d, pp. 570–571
17. d, p. 571
18. c, pp. 563–564
19. c, pp. 571–572
20. c, p. 575
21. b, p. 575
22. c, p. 575
23. c, p. 575
24. a, pp. 576–577
25. c, pp. 575–576

PROBLEMS

1. *a.* investment; *b.* constant (given); *c.* (1) unrelated, (2) directly related; *d.* decrease, downward

2. *a.* I_g: 22, 22, 22, 22, 22, 22, 22; **$C + I_g$**: 1,328, 1,336, 1,344, 1,352, 1,360, 1,368, 1,376; **UI**: −8, −6, −4, −2, 0, +2, +4; *b.* 1,360; *c.* 0.8, 0.2; *d.* 5; *e.* increase, 3, increase, 15; *f.* decrease, 4, decrease, 20 *g.* graph similar to Figure 11.2 in text.

3. *a.* $4 (and put $4 in each of the seven net exports values in the table); *b.* $780, 820, 860, 900, 940, 980, 1,020; *c.* $900; *d.* 5; *e.* (1) increase, $50, (2) decrease, $50

4. *a.* 0.9, 90, C_a: 1,160, 1,250, 1,340, 1,430, 1,520, 1,610, 1,700; *b.* **$C_a + I_g + X_n + G$**: 1510, 1600, 1690, 1780, 1870, 1960, 2050; *c.* 1600; *d.* plot graph; *e.* rise, 100; *f.* fall, *90; g.* raise, *10*

5. *a.* 2.5; *b.* 620, 30, inflationary, 12; *c.* 570, 20, recessionary, 8

SHORT ANSWER AND ESSAY QUESTIONS

1. p. 562
2. p. 562
3. pp. 562–563
4. pp. 563–564
5. pp. 566–567
6. pp. 566–567
7. p. 567

8. pp. 568–570
9. pp. 568–570
10. pp. 570–571
11. p. 571
12. pp. 571–572
13. pp. 572–573
14. pp. 572–573

15. p. 574
16. p. 575
17. p. 575
18. pp. 576–577
19. p. 577
20. pp. 577–578.

CHAPTER 29

Aggregate Demand and Aggregate Supply

Chapter 29 introduces another macro model of the economy, one based on aggregate demand and aggregate supply. This model can be used to explain real domestic output and the level of prices at any point in time and to understand what causes output and the price level to change.

The **aggregate demand (AD) curve** is downsloping because of the real balances, interest rate, and foreign purchases effects resulting from changes in the price level. With a downsloping aggregate demand curve, changes in the price level have an inverse effect on the level of spending by domestic consumers, businesses, government, and foreign buyers, and thus on real domestic output, assuming *other things equal*. This change would be equivalent to a movement along an existing aggregate demand curve: A lower price level increases the quantity of real domestic output demanded, and a higher price level decreases the quantity of real domestic output demanded.

The aggregate demand curve can increase or decrease because of a change in one of the nonprice level **determinants of aggregate demand.** The determinants include changes affecting consumer, investment, government, and net export spending. You will learn that underlying each demand determinant are various factors that cause the determinant to change. The size of the change involves two components. For example, if one of these spending determinants increases, then aggregate demand will increase. The change in aggregate demand involves an increase in initial spending plus a multiplier effect that results in a greater change in aggregate demand than the initial change.

The **aggregate supply (AS) curve** shows the relationship between the output of producers and the price level, but it varies based on the time horizon and variability of input and output prices. In the immediate short run, the aggregate supply curve is horizontal at one price level because input prices and output prices are inflexible or fixed. In the short run, however, the upsloping shape of the aggregate supply curve reflects what happens to per-unit production costs as real domestic output increases or decreases. In the long run, the aggregate supply curve is vertical because input and output prices are fully flexible, so a change in the price level does not change resource utilization at the full-employment level of output.

You should remember that an assumption has also been made that other things are equal when one moves along an aggregate supply curve. When other things change, the short-run aggregate supply curve can shift.

The **determinants of aggregate supply** include changes in input prices, changes in productivity, and changes in the legal and institutional environment for production. As with aggregate demand, you will learn that there are underlying factors that cause these supply determinants to change.

The intersection of the aggregate demand and aggregate supply curves determines **equilibrium real output** and the **equilibrium price level.** Assuming that the determinants of aggregate demand and aggregate supply do not change, there are pressures that will tend to keep the economy at equilibrium. If a determinant changes, then aggregate demand, aggregate supply, or both, can shift.

When aggregate demand increases, this will lead to changes in equilibrium real output and the price level. If the economy is operating at full employment, the increase in AD may not have its full multiplier effect on the real GDP of the economy, and it will result in **demand-pull inflation.** There can also be a decrease in aggregate demand, but it may reduce output and not the price level. In this case, there can be downward price inflexibility for several reasons, as you will learn in the chapter.

Aggregate supply may increase or decrease. An increase in aggregate supply gives a double bonus for the economy because the price level falls, and output and employment increase. Conversely, a decrease in aggregate supply doubly harms the economy because the price level increases, and output and employment fall, and thus the economy experiences **cost-push inflation.**

The aggregate demand–aggregate supply model is an important framework for determining the equilibrium level of real domestic output and prices in an economy. The model will be used extensively throughout our remaining macroeconomics discussion to analyze how different parts of the economy function.

■ CHECKLIST

When you have studied this chapter you should be able to

☐ Define aggregate demand.

☐ Describe the characteristics of the aggregate demand curve.

☐ Use the real-balances, interest-rate, and foreign purchases effects to explain why the aggregate demand curve slopes downward.

☐ Use a graph to distinguish between a movement along a fixed aggregate demand curve and a shift in aggregate demand.

☐ Give an example of the effect of the multiplier on an increase in aggregate demand.

☐ Explain the four factors that can change the consumer spending determinant of aggregate demand.

☐ Explain the two factors that can change the investment spending determinant of aggregate demand.

☐ Explain what changes the government spending determinant of aggregate demand.

☐ Explain the two factors that can cause changes in the net export spending determinant of aggregate demand.

☐ Discuss how the four major spending determinants of aggregate demand (and their underlying factors) can increase or decrease aggregate demand.

☐ Define aggregate supply in the immediate short run, the short run, and the long run.

☐ Explain why the aggregate supply curve in the immediate short run is horizontal.

☐ Explain why the aggregate supply curve in the short run is upsloping.

☐ Explain why the aggregate supply curve in the long run is vertical.

☐ Identify the three major spending determinants of aggregate supply.

☐ Describe two factors that change the input prices determinant of aggregate supply.

☐ Explain what changes the productivity determinant of aggregate supply.

☐ Identify two factors that change the legal-institutional environment determinant of aggregate supply.

☐ Explain how the three major determinants of aggregate supply (and their underlying factors) can increase or decrease aggregate supply.

☐ Explain why in equilibrium the economy will produce a particular combination of real output and the price level rather than another combination.

☐ Show the effects of an increase in aggregate demand on the real output and the price level and relate the changes to demand-pull inflation.

☐ Illustrate the effects of a decrease in aggregate demand on real output and the price level in the economy and relate the changes to recession and unemployment.

☐ Explain the meaning of the terms deflation and disinflation.

☐ Give five reasons for downward inflexibility of changes in the price level when aggregate demand decreases.

☐ Explain the effects of a decrease in aggregate supply on real output and the price level and relate the changes to cost-push inflation.

☐ Describe the effects of an increase in aggregate supply on real output and the price level.

☐ Explain how increases in productivity reduce inflationary pressures using an aggregate demand—aggregate supply graph.

☐ Explain why increases in oil prices have lost their strong effect on core inflation and the U.S. economy (Last Word).

■ **CHAPTER OUTLINE**

1. This chapter introduces the *aggregate demand–aggregate supply model* (AD–AS model). It explains why real domestic output *and* the price level fluctuate in the economy. The chapter begins by explaining the meaning and characteristics of aggregate demand.

a. *Aggregate demand* is a curve that shows the total quantity of goods and services (real output) that will be purchased (demanded) at different price levels. With aggregate demand there is an inverse or negative relationship between the amount of real output demanded and the price level, so the curve slopes downward.

b. Three reasons account for the inverse relationship between real output and the price level, and the downward slope of the aggregate demand curve.

(1) *Real-balances effect:* An increase in the price level decreases the purchasing power of financial assets with a fixed money value, and because those who own such assets are now poorer, they spend less for goods and services. A decrease in the price level has the opposite effects.

(2) *Interest-rate effect:* With the supply of money fixed, an increase in the price level increases the demand for money, increases interest rates, and as a result reduces those expenditures (by consumers and business firms) that are sensitive to increased interest rates. A decrease in the price level has the opposite effects.

(3) *Foreign purchases effect:* An increase in the price level (relative to foreign price levels) will reduce U.S. exports because U.S. products are now more expensive for foreigners and expand U.S. imports because foreign products are less expensive for U.S. consumers. As a consequence, net exports will decrease, which means there will be a decrease in the quantity of goods and services demanded in the U.S. economy as the price level rises. A decrease in the price level (relative to foreign price levels) will have opposite effects.

2. Spending by domestic consumers, businesses, government, and foreign buyers that is independent of changes in the price level are *determinants of aggregate demand.* The amount of changes in aggregate demand involves two components: the amount of the initial change in one of the determinants and a multiplier effect that multiplies the initial change. These determinants are also called aggregate demand shifts because a change in one of them, other things equal, will shift the entire aggregate demand curve. Figure 29.2 shows the shifts. What follows is a description of each of the four major determinants and underlying factors.

a. Consumer spending can increase or decrease AD. If the price level is constant, and consumers decide to spend more, then AD will increase; if consumers decide to spend less then AD will decrease. Four factors increase or decrease consumer spending.

(1) *Consumer wealth:* If the real value of financial assets such as stocks, bond, or real estate increases (minus any liabilities for these assets), then consumers will feel wealthier, spend more, and AD increases. If the real value of financial assets falls, consumers will spend less and AD will decrease.

(2) *Household borrowing:* If consumers borrow more money, they can increase their consumption spending,

thus increasing AD. Conversely, if consumers cut back on their borrowing for consumption spending, AD decreases. Also, if consumers increase their savings rate to pay off their debt, AD decreases.

(3) *Consumer expectations:* If consumers become more optimistic about the future, they will likely spend more and AD will increase. If consumers expect the future to be worse, they will decrease their spending and AD will decrease.

(4) *Personal taxes:* Cuts in personal taxes increase disposable income and the capacity for consumer spending, thus increasing AD. A rise in personal taxes decreases disposable income, consumer spending, and AD.

b. Investment spending can increase or decrease AD. If the price level is constant, and businesses decide to spend more on investment, then AD will increase. If businesses decide to spend less on investment, then AD will decrease. Three factors increase or decrease investment spending.

(1) *Real interest rates:* A decrease in real interest rates will increase the quantity of investment spending, thus increasing AD. An increase in real interest rates will decrease the quantity of investment spending, thus decreasing AD.

(2) *Expected returns:* If businesses expect higher returns on investments in the future, they will likely increase their investment spending today, so AD will increase. If businesses expect lower returns on investments in the future, they will decrease their investment spending today, and AD will decrease. These expected returns are influenced by expectations about future business conditions, the state of technology, the degree of excess capacity (the amount of unused capital goods), and business taxes.

(a) More positive future expectations, more technological progress, less excess capacity, and lower taxes will increase investment spending and thus increase AD.

(b) Less positive future expectations, less technological progress, more excess capacity, and higher taxes will decrease investment spending and thus decrease AD.

c. Government spending has a direct effect on AD, assuming that tax collections and interest rates do not change as a result of the spending. More government spending tends to increase AD and less government spending will decrease AD.

d. Net export spending can increase or decrease AD. If the price level is constant and net exports (exports minus imports) should increase, then AD will increase. If net exports are negative, then AD will decrease. Two factors explain the increase or decrease in net export spending.

(1) *National income abroad:* An increase in the national income of other nations will increase the demand for all goods and services, including U.S. exports. If U.S. exports increase relative to U.S. imports, then net exports will increase, and so will AD. A decline in national incomes abroad will tend to reduce U.S. net exports and thus reduce AD.

(2) *Exchange rates:* A depreciation in the value of the U.S. dollar means that U.S. imports should decline because domestic purchasers cannot buy as many imports as they used to buy. U.S. exports should increase because foreigners have more purchasing power to buy U.S. products. These events increase net exports, and thus increase AD. An appreciation in the value of the dollar will decrease net exports, and thus decrease AD.

3. Aggregate supply is a curve that shows the total quantity of goods and services that will be produced (supplied) at different price levels. The shape of the aggregate supply curve will differ depending on the time horizon and how quickly input prices and output prices can change.

a. In the **immediate short run, the aggregate supply curve** is horizontal because both input prices and output prices remain fixed. The horizontal shape implies that the total amount of output supplied in the economy depends directly on the amount of spending at the fixed price level.

b. In the **short run,** the aggregate supply curve is upsloping because input prices are fixed or highly inflexible and output prices are flexible, and thus changes in the price level increase or decrease the real profits of firms. The curve is relatively flat below the full-employment level of output because there is excess capacity and unemployed resources so per-unit production costs stay relatively constant as output expands, but beyond the full-employment level of output, per-unit production costs rise rapidly as output increases because resources are fully employed and efficiency falls.

c. In the **long run,** the aggregate supply curve is vertical at the full-employment level of output for the economy because both input prices and output prices are flexible. Any change in output prices is matched by a change in input prices, so there is no profit incentive for firms to produce more than is possible at full-employment output.

4. The **determinants of aggregate supply** that shift the curve include changes in the prices of inputs for production, changes in productivity, and changes in the legal and institutional environment in the economy, as outlined in Figure 29.5.

a. A change in **input prices** for resources used for production will change aggregate supply in the short run. Lower input prices increase AS and higher input prices decrease AS. These input prices are for both domestic and imported resources.

(1) *Domestic resource prices* include the prices for labor, capital, and natural resources used for production. If any of these input prices decrease, then AS will increase because the per-unit cost of production will decrease. When the prices of these domestic factors of production increase, then AS will decrease.

(2) The *prices of imported resources* are the cost of paying for resources imported from other nations. If the value of the dollar appreciates, then it will cost less to pay for imported resources used for production. As a result, per-unit production costs will decrease, and AS will increase. Conversely, if the value of the dollar depreciates, then it will cost more to import resources, so AS will decrease.

b. As *productivity* improves, per-unit production costs will fall and AS will increase. This outcome occurs because productivity (output divided by input) is the denominator for the formula for per-unit production costs (total input cost divided by productivity). As productivity declines, per-unit production costs will increase, so AS will decrease.

c. Changes in the **legal and institutional environment** for business can affect per-unit production costs and thus AS.

(1) A decrease in *business taxes* is like a reduction in the per-unit cost of production, so it will increase AS. The same effect occurs when there is an increase in *business subsidies*. The raising of taxes or lowering of subsidies for business will increase per-unit production costs and decrease AS.

(2) A decrease in the amount of *government regulation* is similar to a decrease in the per-unit cost of production, so it will increase AS. An increase in government regulation will raise costs, and thus will decrease AS.

5. The **equilibrium real output** and the **equilibrium price level** are at the intersection of the aggregate demand and the aggregate supply curves. If the price level were below equilibrium, then producers would supply less real output than was demanded by purchasers. Competition among buyers would bid up the price level and producers would increase their output, until an equilibrium price level and quantity was reached. If the price level were above equilibrium, then producers would supply more real output than was demanded by purchasers. Competition among sellers would lower the price level and producers would reduce their output, until an equilibrium price level and quantity was reached. The aggregate demand and aggregate supply curves can also *shift to change equilibrium.*

a. An **increase in aggregate demand** would result in an increase in both real domestic output and the price level. An increase in the price level beyond the full-employment level of output is associated with *demand-pull inflation*. A classic example occurred during the late 1960s because of a sizable increase in government spending for domestic programs and the war in Vietnam.

b. A **decrease in aggregate demand** reduces real output and increases cyclical unemployment, but it may not decrease the price level. In 2001, there was a significant decline in investment spending that reduced aggregate demand and led to a fall in real output and a rise in cyclical unemployment. The rate of inflation fell (there was disinflation), but there was no decline in the price level (deflation). The reason the economy experiences a "GDP gap with no deflation" is that the *price level is inflexible downward*. The price level is largely influenced by labor costs, which account for most of the input prices for the production of many goods and services. There are at least five interrelated reasons for this downward inflexibility of the price level.

(1) There is the fear of starting a *price war* in which firms compete with each other on lowering prices regardless of the cost of production. Price wars hurt business profits, and they make firms reluctant to cut prices for fear of starting one.

(2) Firms are reluctant to change input prices if there are costs related to changing the prices or announcing the change. Such **menu costs** increase the waiting time before businesses make any price changes.

(3) If wages are determined largely by *long-term contracts*, it means that wages cannot be changed in the short run.

(4) *Morale, effort, and productivity* may be affected by changes in wage rates. If current wages are **efficiency wages** that maximize worker effort and morale, employers may be reluctant to lower wages because such changes reduce work effort and productivity.

(5) The *minimum wage* puts a legal floor on the wages for the least skilled workers in the economy.

c. A **decrease in aggregate supply** means there will be a decrease in real domestic output (economic growth) and employment along with a rise in the price level, or *cost-push inflation*. This situation occurred in the mid-1970s when the price of oil substantially increased and significantly increased the cost of production for many goods and services and reduced productivity.

d. An **increase in aggregate supply** arising from an increase in productivity has the beneficial effects of improving real domestic output and employment while maintaining a stable price level. Between 1996 and 2000, the economy experienced strong economic growth, full employment and very low inflation. These outcomes occurred because of an increase in aggregate demand in combination with an increase in aggregate supply from an increase in productivity due to technological change.

6. (Last Word). In the mid-1970s, sizable increases in the price of oil increased production costs and reduced productivity, thus decreasing aggregate supply. These changes led to cost-push inflation, higher unemployment, and a decline in real output. More recent increases in oil prices during 2000 and again in 2005 did not have the adverse effects on the U.S. economy as was the case in the past. Although there were many reasons for this switch, perhaps most important was that oil was not as significant a resource for production in the U.S. economy as it had been in the past. The U.S. economy was about 33 percent less sensitive to fluctuations in oil prices than in the early 1980s.

■ **HINTS AND TIPS**

1. Aggregate demand and supply are the tools used to explain what determines the economy's real output and price level. These tools, however, are **different from the demand and supply** used in Chapter 3 to explain what determines the output and price of a *particular* product. Instead of thinking about the quantity of a *particular* good or service demanded or supplied, it is necessary to think about the total or *aggregate* quantity of all final goods and services demanded (purchased) and supplied (produced). You will have no difficulty with the way demand

and supply are used in this chapter once you switch from thinking about a *particular* good or service and its price to the *aggregate* of all final goods and services and their average price.

2. Make a chart showing each of the **determinants** of aggregate demand (see Figure 29.2) and aggregate supply (Figure 29.5). In the chart, state the direction of the change in each determinant, and then state the likely resulting change in AD or AS. For example, if consumer wealth *increases*, then AD *increases*. Or, if imported prices for resources *increase*, then AS *decreases*. This simple chart can help you quickly see in one quick glance all the possible changes in determinants and their likely effects on AD or AS. Problem 2 in this *Study Guide* will give you an application for this chart.

3. Make sure you know the difference between a **movement** along an existing aggregate demand or supply curve and a **shift** in (increase or decrease in) an aggregate demand or supply curve. Figures 29.7 and 29.9 illustrate the distinction.

4. Unlike the aggregate demand curve, the shape of the aggregate supply curve actually varies based on time horizon and how quickly input prices and output prices change. In the immediate short run, input prices and output prices are fixed, so AS is horizontal at a particular price level (Figure 29.3). In the short run, input prices are fixed, but output prices can change, so the AS is upsloping around the full-employment level of output (Figure 29.4). In the long run, input and output prices are flexible, but the economy can only produce at the full-employment level of output, so AS is vertical (Figure 29.5).

■ IMPORTANT TERMS

aggregate demand–
    aggregate supply
    (AD–AS) model

aggregate demand (AD)

real-balances effect

interest-rate effect

foreign purchases effect

determinants of
    aggregate demand

aggregate supply (AS)

immediate-short-run
    aggregate supply curve

short-run aggregate
    supply curve

long-run aggregate
    supply curve

determinants of
    aggregate supply

productivity

equilibrium price level

equilibrium real output

efficiency wages

menu costs

SELF-TEST

■ FILL-IN QUESTIONS

1. Aggregate demand and aggregate supply together determine the equilibrium real domestic (price, output) _____ and the equilibrium _____ level.

2. The aggregate demand curve shows the quantity of goods and services that will be (supplied, demanded) _____ or purchased at various price levels. For aggregate demand, the relationship between real output and the price level is (positive, negative) _____.

3. The aggregate demand curve slopes (upward, downward) _____ because of the (real-balances, consumption) _____ effect, the (profit, interest) _____-rate effect, and the (domestic, foreign) _____ purchases effect.

4. For the aggregate demand curve, an increase in the price level (increases, decreases) _____ the quantity of real domestic output demanded, whereas a decrease in the price level _____ the quantity of real domestic output demanded, assuming other things equal.

5. For the aggregate demand curve, when the price level changes, there is a (movement along, change in) _____ the curve. When the entire aggregate demand curve shifts, there is a change in (the quantity of real output demanded, aggregate demand) _____.

6. List the four factors that may change consumer spending, and thus shift aggregate demand:

a. _____

b. _____

c. _____

d. _____

7. List two major factors that may change investment spending, and thus shift aggregate demand:

a. _____

b. _____

8. If government spending increases, then aggregate demand is likely to (increase, decrease) _____, but if government spending decreases, it is likely to _____.

9. If there is an increase in national income abroad, then net exports spending is most likely to (increase, decrease) _____ and if there is a depreciation of the value of the U.S. dollar, then net exports are likely to _____. When net exports increase, aggregate demand will (increase, decrease) _____.

10. The aggregate supply curve shows the quantity of goods and services that will be (demanded, supplied) _____ or produced at various price levels. The shape of the immediate-short-run aggregate supply curve is (vertical, horizontal, upsloping) _____, while the shape of the short-run aggregate supply curve is _____, and the shape of the long-run aggregate supply curve is _____.

11. For the short-run aggregate supply curve, as the price level increases, real domestic output (increases, decreases) _____, and as the price level decreases, real domestic output _____. The relationship between the price level and real domestic output supplied is (positive, negative) _____.

12. Aggregate supply shifts may result from:
   a. a change in input prices caused by a change in

   (1)_____

   (2)_____

   b. a change in (consumption, productivity) _____
   c. a change in the legal and institutional environment caused by a change in

   (1)_____

   (2)_____

13. The equilibrium real domestic output and price level are found at the (zero values, intersection) _____ of the aggregate demand and the aggregate supply curves. At this price level, the aggregate quantity of goods and services demanded is (greater than, less than, equal to) _____ the aggregate quantity of goods and services supplied. And at this real domestic output, the prices producers are willing to (pay, accept) _____ are equal to the prices buyers are willing to _____.

14. If the price level were below equilibrium, the quantity of real domestic output supplied would be (greater than, less than) _____ the quantity of real domestic output demanded. As a result competition among buyers eliminates the (surplus, shortage) _____ and bids up the price level.

15. If the price level were above equilibrium, the quantity of real domestic output supplied would be (greater than, less than) _____ the quantity of real domestic output demanded. As a result competition among producers eliminates the (surplus, shortage) _____ and lowers the price level.

16. An increase in aggregate demand will (increase, decrease) _____ real domestic output and will _____ the price level. If the economy is initially operating at its full-employment level of output, and aggregate demand increases, it will produce (demand-pull, cost-push) _____ inflation.

17. If aggregate demand decreases, then real domestic output will (increase, decrease) _____. Such

a change often produces economic conditions called (inflation, recession) _____ and unemployment (rises, falls) _____.

18. When aggregate demand decreases, the price level is often inflexible (upward, downward) _____. This inflexibility occurs because of wage (contracts, flexibility) _____, workers are paid (efficiency, inefficiency) _____ wages, there is a (maximum, minimum) _____ wage, businesses experience menu (benefits, costs) _____, and there is fear of (price, wage) _____ wars.

19. A decrease in aggregate supply will (increase, decrease) _____ real output and _____ the price level. Such a change in aggregate supply contributes to (demand-pull, cost-push) _____ inflation.

20. An increase in aggregate supply will (increase, decrease) _____ real domestic output and _____ the price level. If aggregate demand increased, the price level would (increase, decrease) _____, but a simultaneous increase in aggregate supply (reinforces, offsets) _____ this change and helps keep the price level stable.

■ **TRUE–FALSE QUESTIONS**

Circle T if the statement is true, F if it is false.

1. Aggregate demand reflects a positive relationship between the price level and the amount of real output demanded.   **T F**

2. The explanation as to why the aggregate demand curve slopes downward is the same as the explanation as to why the demand curve for a single product slopes downward.   **T F**

3. A fall in the price level increases the real value of financial assets with fixed money values and, as a result, increases spending by the holders of these assets.   **T F**

4. Given a fixed supply of money, a rise in the price level increases the demand for money in the economy and drives interest rates downward.   **T F**

5. A rise in the price level of an economy (relative to foreign price levels) tends to increase that economy's exports and to reduce its imports of goods and services.   **T F**

6. A movement along a fixed aggregate demand curve is the same as a shift in aggregate demand.   **T F**

7. Changes in aggregate demand involve a change in initial spending from one of the determinants and a multiplier effect on spending.   **T F**

8. A change in aggregate demand is caused by a change in the price level, *other things equal.* **T F**

9. The real-balances effect is one of the determinants of aggregate demand. **T F**

10. A large decline in household borrowing will increase consumption spending and aggregate demand. **T F**

11. A fall in excess capacity, or unused existing capital goods, will retard the demand for new capital goods and therefore reduce aggregate demand. **T F**

12. Appreciation of the dollar relative to foreign currencies will tend to increase net exports and aggregate demand. **T F**

13. The immediate short-run aggregate supply curve is horizontal and the short-run aggregate supply curve is upsloping. **T F**

14. The aggregate supply curve is vertical in the long run at the full-employment level of output. **T F**

15. When the determinants of short-run aggregate supply change, they alter the per-unit production cost at each price level and thereby aggregate supply. **T F**

16. Productivity is a measure of real output per unit of input. **T F**

17. Per-unit production cost is determined by dividing total input cost by units of output. **T F**

18. At the equilibrium price level, the real domestic output purchased is equal to the real domestic output produced. **T F**

19. An increase in aggregate demand will increase both the price level and the real domestic output. **T F**

20. An increase in aggregate demand is associated with cost-push inflation. **T F**

21. The greater the increase in the price level that results from an increase in aggregate demand, the greater will be the increase in the equilibrium real GDP. **T F**

22. A significant decrease in aggregate demand can result in recession and cyclical unemployment. **T F**

23. Fear of price wars tends to make the price level more flexible rather than less flexible. **T F**

24. A decrease in aggregate supply decreases the equilibrium real domestic output and increases the price level, resulting in cost-push inflation. **T F**

25. An increase in aggregate supply driven by productivity increases can offset the inflationary pressures from an increase in aggregate demand. **T F**

■ **MULTIPLE-CHOICE QUESTIONS**

Circle the letter that corresponds to the best answer.

1. The aggregate demand curve is the relationship between the

(a) price level and what producers will supply
(b) price level and the real domestic output purchased
(c) price level and the real domestic output produced
(d) real domestic output purchased and the real domestic output produced

2. When the price level rises,
(a) the demand for money and interest rates rises
(b) spending that is sensitive to interest-rate changes increases
(c) holders of financial assets with fixed money values increase their spending
(d) holders of financial assets with fixed money values have more purchasing power

3. One explanation for the downward slope of the aggregate demand curve is that a change in the price level results in
(a) a multiplier effect
(b) an income effect
(c) a substitution effect
(d) a foreign purchases effect

4. A sharp decline in the real value of stock prices, which is independent of a change in the price level, would best be an example of
(a) the interest-rate effect
(b) the foreign purchases effect
(c) a change in household borrowing
(d) a change in real value of consumer wealth

5. The aggregate demand curve will be increased by
(a) a decrease in the price level
(b) an increase in the price level
(c) a depreciation in the value of the U.S. dollar
(d) an increase in the excess capacity of factories

6. The aggregate supply curve is the relationship between the
(a) price level and the real domestic output purchased
(b) price level and the real domestic output produced
(c) price level that producers are willing to accept and the price level purchasers are willing to pay
(d) real domestic output purchased and the real domestic output produced

7. The short-run aggregate supply curve assumes that
(a) nominal wages respond to changes in the price level
(b) nominal wages do not respond to changes in the price level
(c) the economy is operating at full-employment output
(d) the economy is operating at less than full-employment output

8. In the long run, the aggregate supply curve is
(a) upsloping
(b) downsloping
(c) vertical
(d) horizontal

9. If the prices of imported resources increase, then this event would most likely
(a) decrease aggregate supply
(b) increase aggregate supply
(c) increase aggregate demand
(d) decrease aggregate demand

Suppose that real domestic output in an economy is 50 units, the quantity of inputs is 10, and the price of each input is $2. Answer Questions 10, 11, 12, and 13 on the basis of this information.

10. The level of productivity in this economy is
(a) 5
(b) 4
(c) 3
(d) 2

11. The per-unit cost of production is
(a) $0.40
(b) $0.50
(c) $2.50
(d) $3.50

12. If productivity increased such that 60 units are now produced with the quantity of inputs still equal to 10, then per-unit production costs would
(a) remain unchanged and aggregate supply would remain unchanged
(b) increase and aggregate supply would decrease
(c) decrease and aggregate supply would increase
(d) decrease and aggregate supply would decrease

13. All else equal, if the price of each input increased from $2 to $4, productivity would
(a) decrease from $4 to $2 and aggregate supply would decrease
(b) decrease from $5 to $3 and aggregate supply would decrease
(c) decrease from $4 to $2 and aggregate supply would increase
(d) remain unchanged and aggregate supply would decrease

14. If Congress passed much stricter laws to control the air pollution from businesses, this action would tend to
(a) increase per-unit production costs and shift the aggregate supply curve to the right
(b) increase per-unit production costs and shift the aggregate supply curve to the left
(c) increase per-unit production costs and shift the aggregate demand curve to the left
(d) decrease per-unit production costs and shift the aggregate supply curve to the left

15. An increase in business taxes will tend to
(a) decrease aggregate demand but not change aggregate supply
(b) decrease aggregate supply but not change aggregate demand
(c) decrease aggregate demand and decrease aggregate supply
(d) decrease aggregate supply and increase aggregate demand

16. If at a particular price level, real domestic output from producers is less than real domestic output desired by buyers, there will be a
(a) surplus and the price level will rise
(b) surplus and the price level will fall
(c) shortage and the price level will rise
(d) shortage and the price level will fall

Answer Questions 17, 18, and 19 on the basis of the following aggregate demand–aggregate supply schedule for a hypothetical economy.

Real domestic output demanded (in billions)	Price level	Real domestic output supplied (in billions)
$1500	175	$4500
$2000	150	$4000
$2500	125	$3500
$3000	100	$3000
$3500	75	$2500
$4000	50	$2000

17. The equilibrium price level and quantity of real domestic output will be
(a) 100 and $2500
(b) 100 and $3000
(c) 125 and $3500
(d) 150 and $4000

18. If the quantity of real domestic output demanded increased by $2000 at each price level, the new equilibrium price level and quantity of real domestic output would be
(a) 175 and $4000
(b) 150 and $4000
(c) 125 and $3500
(d) 100 and $3000

19. Using the original data from the table, if the quantity of real domestic output demanded *increased* by $1500 and the quantity of real domestic output supplied *increased* by $500 at each price level, the new equilibrium price level and quantity of real domestic output would be
(a) 175 and $4000
(b) 150 and $4500
(c) 125 and $4000
(d) 100 and $3500

20. An increase in aggregate demand will increase
(a) the price level and have no effect on real domestic output
(b) the real domestic output and have no effect on the price level
(c) the price level and decrease the real domestic output
(d) both real output and the price level

21. In the aggregate demand–aggregate supply model, an increase in the price level will
(a) increase the real value of wealth
(b) increase the strength of the multiplier
(c) decrease the strength of the multiplier
(d) have no effect on the strength of the multiplier

22. Aggregate demand decreases and real output falls but the price level remains the same. Which factor most likely contributes to downward price inflexibility?
(a) an increase in aggregate supply
(b) the foreign purchases effect
(c) lower interest rates
(d) efficiency wages

23. Fear of price wars, menu costs, and wage contracts are associated with
(a) a price level that is inflexible upward
(b) a price level that is inflexible downward
(c) a domestic output that cannot be increased
(d) a domestic output that cannot be decreased

24. If there were cost-push inflation,
(a) both the real domestic output and the price level would decrease
(b) the real domestic output would increase and rises in the price level would become smaller
(c) the real domestic output would decrease and the price level would rise
(d) both the real domestic output and rises in the price level would become greater

25. An increase in aggregate supply will
(a) increase the price level and real domestic output
(b) decrease the price level and real domestic output
(c) decrease the price level and increase the real domestic output
(d) decrease the price level and have no effect on real domestic output

■ **PROBLEMS**

1. Following is an aggregate supply schedule.

Price level	Real domestic output supplied
250	2100
225	2000
200	1900
175	1700
150	1400
125	1000
100	900

a. Plot this aggregate supply schedule on the graph below.
b. The following table has three aggregate demand schedules.

Price level	Real domestic output demanded		
(1)	(2)	(3)	(4)
250	1400	1900	500
225	1500	2000	600
200	1600	2100	700
175	1700	2200	800
150	1800	2300	900
125	1900	2400	1000
100	2000	2500	1100

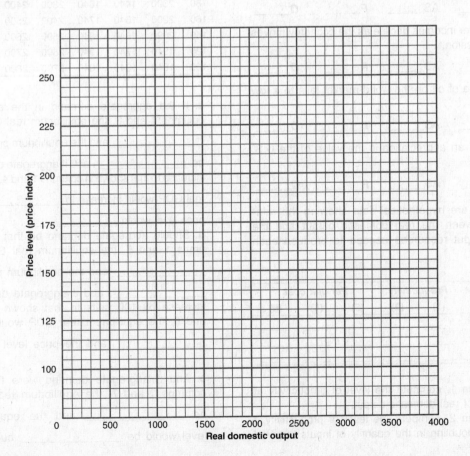

(1) On the graph, plot the aggregate demand curve shown in columns 1 and 2; label this curve **AD₁**. At this level of aggregate demand, the equilibrium

real domestic output is _____ and the

equilibrium price level is _____.
(2) On the same graph, plot the aggregate demand curve shown in columns 1 and 3; label this curve **AD₂**. The equilibrium real domestic output

is _____ and the equilibrium price level is

_____.

(3) On the same graph, plot the aggregate demand curve shown in columns 1 and 4; label it **AD₃**. The

equilibrium real domestic output is _____

and the equilibrium price level is _____.

2. In the following list, what will most likely happen as a result of each event to (1) aggregate demand (AD); (2) aggregate supply (AS); (3) the equilibrium price level (**P**); and (4) equilibrium real domestic output (**Q**)? Assume that all other things remain constant when the event occurs and that the aggregate supply curve is a short-run one. Use the following symbols to indicate the expected effects: **I** = increase, **D** = decrease, **S** = remains the same, and **U** = uncertain.

a. A decrease in labor productivity.

AD_____   AS_____   **P**_____   **Q**_____

b. A fall in the interest rate for business loans.

AD_____   AS_____   **P**_____   **Q**_____

c. Consumer incomes decline as the economy moves into a recession.

AD_____   AS_____   **P**_____   **Q**_____

d. The price of oil on the world market falls to a low level.

AD_____   AS_____   **P**_____   **Q**_____

e. There is an appreciation in the value of the U.S. dollar.

AD_____   AS_____   **P**_____   **Q**_____

3. Following are hypothetical data showing the relationships between the real domestic output and the quantity of input resources needed to produce each level of output.

Output	Input	Productivity		Per unit cost		
		(1)	(2)	(3)	(4)	(5)
2500	500	____	____	____	____	____
2000	400	____	____	____	____	____
1500	300	____	____	____	____	____

a. In column 1, compute the level of productivity at each level of real domestic output.
b. In column 2, compute the level of productivity if there is a doubling in the quantity of inputs required

to produce each level of output.
c. In column 3, compute the per-unit production cost at each level of output if each unit of input costs $15, given the level of productivity in column 1.
d. In column 4, compute the new per-unit production cost at each level of output if each unit of input costs $15, given that there has been a doubling in the required quantity of inputs to produce each level of output as shown in column 2. If this situation occurs, will aggregate supply (decrease, increase, stay the

same)? _____.
e. In column 5, compute the new per-unit production cost at each level of output, given that input price is now $10 instead of $15 but the level of productivity stays as it was originally shown in column 1. What will happen to the aggregate supply curve if this situation occurs?

_____.

4. Columns 1 and 2 in the table that follows are the aggregate supply schedule of an economy.

(1) Price level	(2) Real GDP	(3) AD₁	(4) AD₂	(5) AD₃	(6) AD₄	(7) AD₅	(8) AD₆
260	2540	940	1140	1900	2000	2090	2390
240	2490	1040	1240	2000	2100	2190	2490
220	2430	1140	1340	2100	2200	2290	2590
200	2390	1240	1440	2200	2300	2390	2690
190	2350	1390	1590	2250	2350	2540	2740
180	2300	1440	1640	2300	2400	2590	2890
160	2200	1540	1740	2400	2500	2690	2990
140	2090	1640	1840	2500	2600	2790	3090
120	1940	1740	1940	2600	2700	2890	3190
100	1840	1840	2040	2700	2800	2990	3290

a. If the aggregate demand in the economy were columns 1 and 3, the equilibrium real GDP would be

_____ and the equilibrium price level would

be _____, and if aggregate demand should increase to that shown in columns 1 and 4, the equilibrium

real GDP would increase to _____ and the

price level would _____.
b. Should aggregate demand be that shown in columns 1 and 5, the equilibrium real GDP would be

_____ and the equilibrium price would be

_____, and if aggregate demand should increase by 100 units to that shown in columns 1 and 6, the equilibrium real GDP would increase to

_____ and the price level would rise to

_____.

c. And if aggregate demand were that shown in columns 1 and 7, the equilibrium real GDP would

be _____ and the equilibrium price

level would be _____, but if aggregate

demand increased to that shown in columns 1 and 8, the equilibrium real GDP would _____ and the price level would rise to _____.

■ **SHORT ANSWER AND ESSAY QUESTIONS**

1. What is the aggregate demand curve? Draw a graph and explain its features.

2. Use the interest-rate effect, the real-balances effect, and the foreign purchases effect to explain the relationship between the price level and the real domestic output demanded.

3. Explain the wealth effect and its impact on purchasing power. Give an example.

4. What roles do the expectations of consumers and businesses play in influencing aggregate demand?

5. How is aggregate demand changed by changes in net export spending? What factors cause changes in net export spending?

6. Explain the shape of the immediate-short-run aggregate supply curve. How do time and prices affect its shape?

7. Why does the short-run aggregate supply curve slope upward? Why is it relatively flat at outputs below the full-employment output level and relatively steep at outputs above it?

8. Why is the aggregate supply curve in the long run a vertical curve? Why is output not affected by the price level in the long run?

9. Describe how changes in the international economy influence aggregate demand or aggregate supply.

10. How does an increase or decrease in per-unit production costs change aggregate supply? Give examples.

11. How does the legal and institutional environment affect aggregate supply? Give examples.

12. Explain how a change in business taxes affects aggregate demand and aggregate supply.

13. What real domestic output is the equilibrium real domestic output? What will happen to real output if the price level is below equilibrium?

14. What are the effects on the real domestic output and the price level when aggregate demand increases along the short-run aggregate supply curve?

15. What is the relationship between the effect of an increase in aggregate demand on real GDP and the rise in the price level that accompanies it? Discuss it in terms of the multiplier effect.

16. If prices were as flexible downward as they are upward, what would be the effects on real domestic output and the price level of a decrease in aggregate demand?

17. Give reasons why prices in the economy tend to be inflexible in a downward direction.

18. What are the effects on the real domestic output and the price level of a decrease in aggregate supply?

19. Describe and graph an increase in aggregate supply and its effects on the price level and real output.

20. How did the economy simultaneously achieve full employment, economic growth, and price stability between 1996 and 2000?

ANSWERS

Chapter 29 Aggregate Demand and Aggregate Supply

FILL-IN QUESTIONS

1. output, price
2. demanded, negative
3. downward, real-balances, interest, foreign
4. decreases, increases
5. movement along, aggregate demand
6. *a.* consumer wealth; *b.* consumer expectations; *c.* household borrowing; *d.* personal taxes (any order for *a–d*)
7. *a.* interest rates; *b.* expected returns on investment (either order for *a–b*)
8. increase, decrease
9. increase, increase, increase
10. supplied, horizontal, upsloping, vertical
11. increases, decreases, positive
12. *a.* (1) domestic resource availability, (2) prices of imported resources (any order for *1–2*); *b.* productivity; *c.* (1) business taxes and subsidies, (2) government regulation (any order for *1–2*)
13. intersection, equal to, accept, pay
14. less than, shortage
15. greater than, surplus
16. increase, increase, demand-pull
17. decrease, recession, rises
18. downward, contracts, efficiency, minimum, costs, price
19. decrease, increase, cost-push
20. increase, decrease, increase, offsets

TRUE–FALSE QUESTIONS

1. F, p. 584
2. F, p. 584
3. T, pp. 584–585
4. F, p. 585
5. F, p. 585
6. F, p. 585
7. T, p. 585
8. F, p. 585
9. F, p. 586
10. F, pp. 585–586
11. T, p. 587
12. F, pp. 587–588
13. T, pp. 588–589
14. T, pp. 590–591
15. T, p. 591
16. T, p. 593
17. T, p. 593
18. T, p. 594
19. T, pp. 594–596
20. F, pp. 594–596
21. F, p. 596
22. T, pp. 596–597
23. F, p. 597
24. T, pp. 597–598
25. T, pp. 598, 600

MULTIPLE-CHOICE QUESTIONS

1. b, p. 584
2. a, p. 585
3. d, p. 585
4. d, p. 586
5. c, pp. 586–587
6. b, p. 588
7. b, p. 589
8. c, p. 590
9. a, p. 592
10. a, p. 593
11. a, p. 593
12. c, p. 593
13. d, p. 593

14. b, pp. 593–594
15. c, p. 593
16. c, pp. 594–595
17. b, pp. 594–595
18. b, pp. 595–596
19. c, p. 598
20. d, pp. 594–596
21. c, p. 596
22. d, p. 597
23. b, p. 597
24. c, pp. 597–598
25. c, pp. 598, 600

SHORT ANSWER AND ESSAY QUESTIONS

1. p. 584
2. pp. 584–585
3. p. 586
4. pp. 586–587
5. p. 587
6. pp. 588–589
7. pp. 589–590

8. pp. 591–592
9. p. 587, 592
10. pp. 591–593
11. p. 593
12. pp. 593–594
13. pp. 594–595
14. pp. 594–595

15. pp. 595–596
16. pp. 596–597
17. p. 597
18. pp. 597–598
19. pp. 598, 600
20. pp. 598, 600

PROBLEMS

1. *b.* (1) 1700, 175, (2) 2000, 225, (3) 1000, 125
2. *a.* S, D, I, D; *b.* I, S, I, I; *c.* D, S, D, D; *d.* I, I, U, I; *e.* D, I, D, U
3. *a.* 5, 5, 5; *b.* 2.5, 2.5, 2.5; *c.* $3, $3, $3; *d.* $6, $6, $6, decrease; *e.* $2, $2, $2, it will increase
4. *a.* 1840, 100, 1940, 120; *b.* 2300, 180, 2350, 190; *c.* 2390, 200, 2490, 240

The Relationship of the Aggregate Demand Curve to the Aggregate Expenditure Model

This appendix explains how the aggregate expenditures (AE) model that you learned about in Chapter 28 is related to the aggregate demand (AD) curve that was presented in Chapter 29. There are two short sections to this appendix. The first one focuses on the derivation of the aggregate demand curve from the AE model. The second one explains how shifts in aggregate demand are related to shifts in aggregate expenditures.

Although the aggregate expenditures model is a fixed-price-level model and the aggregate demand–aggregate supply model is a variable-price-level model, there is a close relationship between the two models. The important thing to understand is that prices can be fixed or constant at different levels. The AD curve can be derived from the aggregate expenditures model by letting the price level be constant at different levels. For example, the lower (the higher) the level at which prices are constant in the aggregate expenditures model, the larger (the smaller) will be the equilibrium real GDP in that model of the economy. Various output-price-level combinations can be traced to derive an AD curve that slopes downward, as shown in Figure 1 in the text.

The aggregate demand curve can shift (increase or decrease) because of a change in the nonprice level *determinants of aggregate demand*. The determinants include changes in factors affecting consumer, investment, government, and net export spending. These determinants are similar to the components of the aggregate expenditures model. It is easy to show the relationship between the shifts in the two models. A change in spending will cause a shift (upward or downward) in the aggregate expenditures schedule as shown in Figure 2 in the text. The initial change in spending when multiplied by the multiplier would be equal to the size of the horizontal shift in AD, assuming a constant price level.

■ CHECKLIST

When you have studied this appendix you should be able to

☐ Contrast the aggregate expenditures and the aggregate demand–aggregate supply models by comparing the variability of the price level and real GDP.
☐ Use a graph to derive the aggregate demand curve from the aggregate expenditures model.
☐ Explain the effect of a change in a determinant of aggregate demand on aggregate expenditures.
☐ Use a graph to show the relationship between a shift in aggregate expenditures and a shift in aggregate demand.
☐ Discuss how the initial change in spending and the multiplier effect influence the size of the shift in aggregate demand.

■ APPENDIX OUTLINE

1. This appendix introduces the *aggregate demand–aggregate supply model* of the economy to explain why real domestic output *and* the price level fluctuate. This model has an advantage over the aggregate expenditures model because it allows the price level to vary (rise and fall) rather than be constant or fixed as in the aggregate expenditures model.

2. The aggregate demand curve can be derived from the intersections of the aggregate expenditures curves and the 45-degree curve. As the price level falls, the aggregate expenditures curve shifts upward and the equilibrium real GDP increases, but as the price level rises, the aggregate expenditures curve shifts downward and the equilibrium real GDP decreases. The inverse relationship between the price level and equilibrium real GDP is the aggregate demand curve. Note that for the aggregate expenditures model,

    a. changes in real balances (wealth) increase or decrease the consumption schedule;
    b. changes in the interest rate increase or decrease the investment schedule; and
    c. changes in imports or exports affect net exports, which can increase or decrease the net export schedule.

3. If the price level is constant, any change in nonprice-level determinants of consumption and planned investment that shifts the aggregate expenditures curve upward will increase the equilibrium real GDP and shift the AD curve to the right by an amount equal to the initial increase in aggregate expenditures times the multiplier. Conversely, any change in nonprice-level determinants of consumption and planned investment that shifts the aggregate expenditures curve downward will decrease the equilibrium real GDP and shift the AD curve to the left by an amount equal to the initial decrease in aggregate expenditures times the multiplier.

■ HINTS AND TIPS

1. Figure 1 is worth extra study to see the relationship between the quantity (real domestic output) and the price level in both models. The upper panel shows the aggregate expenditures model with aggregate expenditures on the vertical axis and quantity on the horizontal axis. The lower panel shows the aggregate demand model with the price level on the vertical axis and quantity on the horizontal axis. Thus the horizontal axes in both graphs are the same and directly related. The connection between the price levels in each graph is more indirect but they are related nevertheless as shown in Figure 1.

2. Figure 2 shows how shifts are accounted for in each model. A shift upward in aggregate expenditures is the same as a shift outward in aggregate demand. The magnitude of the change in quantity will depend on the multiplier effect, but in both models quantity increases by the same amount.

■ IMPORTANT TERMS

aggregate demand
determinants of
  aggregate demand

aggregate
  expenditures
  schedule
multiplier

SELF-TEST

■ FILL-IN QUESTIONS

1. In the aggregate demand–aggregate supply model, the price level is (fixed, variable) _____, but in the aggregate expenditures model, the price level is _____.

2. In the aggregate expenditures model, a lower price level would (raise, lower) _____ the consumption, investment, and aggregate expenditures curves, and the equilibrium level of real GDP would (rise, fall) _____.

3. In the aggregate expenditures model, a higher price level would (raise, lower) _____ the consumption, investment, and aggregate expenditures curves, and the equilibrium level of real GDP would (rise, fall) _____.

4. This relationship between the price level and equilibrium real GDP in the aggregate expenditures model is (direct, inverse) _____ and can be used to derive the aggregate (demand, supply) _____ curve.

5. If the price level were constant, an increase in the aggregate expenditures curve would shift the aggregate demand curve to the (right, left) _____ by an amount equal to the upward shift in aggregate expenditures times the (interest rate, multiplier) _____. A decrease in the aggregate expenditures curve would shift the aggregate demand curve to the (right, left) _____ by an amount equal to the (upward, downward) _____ shift in aggregate expenditures times the (interest rate, multiplier) _____.

■ TRUE–FALSE QUESTIONS

Circle T if the statement is true, F if it is false.

1. Both the graph of the aggregate demand curve and the aggregate expenditures model show the price level on the vertical axis.   **T F**

2. The higher the price level, the smaller the real balances of consumers and the lower the aggregate expenditures schedule.   **T F**

3. An increase in the price level will shift the aggregate expenditures schedule upward.   **T F**

4. An increase in investment spending will shift the aggregate expenditures curve upward and the aggregate demand curve leftward.   **T F**

5. A shift in the aggregate demand curve is equal to the initial change in spending times the multiplier.   **T F**

■ MULTIPLE-CHOICE QUESTIONS

Circle the letter that corresponds to the best answer.

1. If the price level in the aggregate expenditures model were lower, the consumption and aggregate expenditures curves would be
  (a) lower, and the equilibrium real GDP would be smaller
  (b) lower, and the equilibrium real GDP would be larger
  (c) higher, and the equilibrium real GDP would be larger
  (d) higher, and the equilibrium real GDP would be smaller

2. In the aggregate expenditures model, a decrease in the price level, other things held constant, will shift the
  (a) consumption, investment, and net exports curves downward
  (b) consumption, investment, and net exports curves upward
  (c) consumption and investment curves upward, but the net exports curve downward
  (d) consumption and net export curves upward, but the investment curve downward

3. An increase in investment spending will
  (a) increase aggregate expenditures and increase aggregate demand
  (b) decrease aggregate expenditures and decrease aggregate demand
  (c) increase aggregate expenditures and decrease aggregate demand
  (d) decrease aggregate expenditures and increase aggregate demand

4. A decrease in net export spending will shift the
(a) aggregate expenditures schedule upward and the aggregate demand curve rightward
(b) aggregate expenditures schedule upward and the aggregate demand curve leftward
(c) aggregate expenditures schedule downward and the aggregate demand curve rightward
(d) aggregate expenditures schedule downward and the aggregate demand curve leftward

5. An increase in aggregate expenditures shifts the aggregate demand curve to the
(a) right by the amount of the increase in aggregate expenditures
(b) right by the amount of the increase in aggregate expenditures times the multiplier
(c) left by the amount of the increase in aggregate expenditures
(d) left by the amount of the increase in aggregate expenditures times the multiplier

■ **PROBLEMS**

1. Column 1 of the following table shows the real GDP an economy might produce.

(1) Real GDP	(2) $AE_{1.20}$	(3) $AE_{1.00}$	(4) $AE_{0.80}$
$2100	$2110	$2130	$2150
2200	2200	2220	2240
2300	2290	2310	2330
2400	2380	2400	2420
2500	2470	2490	2510
2600	2560	2580	2600

a. If the price level in this economy were $1.20, the aggregate expenditures (AE) at each real GDP would be those shown in column 2 and the equilibrium real GDP would be $ _____.
b. If the price level were $1.00, the aggregate expenditures at each real GDP would be those shown in column 3 and the equilibrium real GDP would be $ _____.
c. If the price level were $0.80, the aggregate expenditures at each real GDP would be those shown in column 4 and the equilibrium real GDP would be $ _____.
d. Show in the following schedule the equilibrium real GDP at each of the three price levels.

Price level	Equilibrium real GDP
$1.20	$ _____
1.00	_____
0.80	_____

(1) This schedule is the aggregate (demand, supply) _____. schedule.

(2) The equilibrium real GDP is (directly, inversely) _____ related to the price level.

■ **SHORT ANSWER AND ESSAY QUESTIONS**

1. What do the horizontal axes measure in a graph of the aggregate expenditures model and the aggregate demand curve?

2. Why is there an inverse relationship between aggregate expenditures and the price level? Explain, using real balance, the interest rate, and foreign purchases.

3. Describe how the aggregate demand curve can be derived from the aggregate expenditures model.

4. What is the effect of an increase in aggregate expenditures on the aggregate demand curve? Explain in words and with a graph.

5. What role does the multiplier play in shifting aggregate expenditures and aggregate demand?

ANSWERS

Appendix to Chapter 29 The Relationship of the Aggregate Demand Curve to the Aggregate Expenditures Model

FILL-IN QUESTIONS

1. variable, fixed
2. raise, rise
3. lower, fall
4. inverse, demand
5. right, multiplier, left, downward, multiplier

TRUE–FALSE QUESTIONS

1. F, p. 604   **3.** F, p. 605   **5.** T, p. 605
2. T, p. 604   **4.** F, p. 605

MULTIPLE-CHOICE QUESTIONS

1. c, p. 604   **3.** a, pp. 605–605   **5.** b, p. 605
2. b, p. 604   **4.** d, p. 605

PROBLEMS

1. *a.* 2200; *b.* 2400; *c.* 2600; *d.* 2200, 2400, 2600, (1) aggregate demand, (2) inversely

SHORT ANSWER AND ESSAY QUESTIONS

1. p. 604   **3.** pp. 604–605   **5.** p. 605
2. p. 604   **4.** p. 605

CHAPTER 30

Fiscal Policy, Deficits, and Debt

Over the years, the most serious macroeconomic problems have been those resulting from the swings of the business cycle. Learning what determines the equilibrium level of real output and prices in an economy and what causes them to fluctuate makes it possible to find ways to achieve maximum output, full employment, and stable prices. In short, macroeconomic principles can suggest policies to control both recession and inflation in an economy.

As you will discover in Chapter 30, the Federal government may use **fiscal policy,** changes in government spending or taxation, to influence the economy's output, employment, and price level. The chapter first discusses discretionary fiscal policy to show how it affects aggregate demand. **Expansionary fiscal policy** is used to stimulate the economy and pull it out of a slump or recession by increasing government spending, decreasing taxes, or some combination of the two. **Contractionary fiscal policy** is enacted to counter inflationary pressure in the economy by cutting government spending, raising taxes, or a combination of the two.

Discretionary fiscal policy requires that Congress take action to change tax rates, transfer payment programs, or purchase goods and services. **Nondiscretionary fiscal policy** does not require Congress to take any action and is a **built-in stabilizer** for the economy. The economy has a progressive tax system that provides such automatic or built-in stability. When GDP increases, net tax revenues will increase to reduce inflationary pressure and when GDP declines, net tax revenues will fall to stimulate the economy.

To evaluate the direction of fiscal policy requires understanding of the **standardized budget** and the distinction between a **cyclical deficit** and a **standardized deficit.** This budget analysis enables economists to determine whether Federal fiscal policy is expansionary, contractionary, or neutral, and to determine what policy should be enacted to improve the economy's economic performance. From this budget analysis you will gain insights into the course of U.S. fiscal policy in recent years.

Fiscal policy is not without its problems, criticisms, or complications. There are timing problems in getting it implemented. There are political considerations in getting it accepted by politicians and voters. If the fiscal policy is temporary rather than permanent it is thought to be less effective. Some economists criticize the borrowing of money by the Federal government for expansionary fiscal policy because they think it will raise interest rates and crowd out investment spending, thus reducing the policy

effects. The debate over the value of fiscal policy is an ongoing one as you will learn from the chapter.

Any budget surplus or deficit from a change in fiscal policy affects the size of the **public debt** (often called the national debt). Over the years the United States accumulated a public debt that now totals slightly more than $9 trillion. This debt increased because budget deficits accumulate over time and are not offset by budget surpluses. The size of the public debt is placed into perspective by: (1) describing who owns the debt; (2) comparing it (and interest payments on the debt) to the size of the economy (GDP); and (3) looking at the sizes of the public debt in other industrial nations.

The last sections of the chapter examine the economic implications or **consequences of the public debt.** These economic problems do not include bankrupting the Federal government because the government can meet its obligations by refinancing and taxation. Nor does the public debt simply shift the economic burden to future generations because the public debt is a public credit for the many people who hold that debt in the form of U.S. securities. Rather, the public debt and payment of interest on the debt contribute to important problems: increased inequality in income, reduced incentives for work and production, decreased standard of living when part of the debt is paid to foreigners, and the possible crowding out of private investment.

■ **CHECKLIST**

When you have studied this chapter you should be able to

☐ Distinguish between discretionary and nondiscretionary fiscal policy.
☐ Explain expansionary fiscal policy on aggregate demand when the price level is inflexible downward.
☐ Compare and contrast an expansionary fiscal policy through increased government spending or decreased taxation.
☐ Describe contractionary fiscal policy on aggregate demand when the price level is inflexible downward.
☐ Compare and contrast a contractionary fiscal policy through decreased government spending or increased taxation.
☐ Assess whether it is preferable to use government spending or taxes to counter recession and reduce inflation.
☐ Explain the relationship between net tax revenues and GDP.

369

☐ Describe automatic or built-in stabilizers and their economic importance.

☐ Indicate how the built-in stabilizers help to counter recession and inflation.

☐ Describe how automatic stabilizers are affected by different tax systems (progressive, proportional, and regressive).

☐ Distinguish between the actual budget and the standardized budget for evaluating discretionary fiscal policy.

☐ Describe recent U.S. fiscal policy using the standardized budget.

☐ Describe projections for U.S. budget deficits and surpluses.

☐ Use the standardized budget to evaluate discretionary fiscal policy.

☐ Explain how Social Security affects the size of the federal budget.

☐ Outline three timing problems that may arise with fiscal policy.

☐ Discuss the political considerations affecting fiscal policy.

☐ Explain how expectations of policy reversals in the future change the effectiveness of fiscal policy.

☐ Describe how changes in state and local finances may offset fiscal policy at the federal level.

☐ Explain the crowding-out effect of fiscal policy.

☐ Identify when the crowding-out effect is or is not likely to be a problem.

☐ Discuss current thinking on fiscal policy.

☐ Explain the relationship of budget deficits and surpluses to the public debt.

☐ List the major types of owners of the public debt.

☐ Compare the size of the public debt to GDP.

☐ Compare interest payments on the public debt to GDP.

☐ Compare the U.S. public debt with those of other industrial nations.

☐ State two reasons why a large public debt will not bankrupt the federal government.

☐ Discuss whether the public debt imposes a burden on future generations.

☐ State the effect of the public debt on income distribution.

☐ Explain how the public debt affects incentives.

☐ Evaluate the differences between foreign and domestic ownership of the public debt.

☐ Describe the crowding-out effect from a public debt.

☐ State two factors that offset the crowding-out effect of a public debt.

☐ List the 10 items in the index of leading economic indicators (Last Word).

■ **CHAPTER OUTLINE**

1. Fiscal policy consists of the changes made by the Federal government in its budget expenditures and tax revenues to expand or contract the economy. In making these changes, the Federal government may seek to increase the economy's real output and employment, or control its rate of inflation.

2. Fiscal policy is *discretionary* when changes in government spending or taxation are designed to change the level of real GDP, employment, incomes, or the price level. The **Council of Economic Advisers (CEA)** advises the U.S. president on such policies. Specific action then needs to be taken by Congress to initiate this discretionary policy, in contrast to *nondiscretionary* fiscal policy that occurs automatically (see item 3).

   a. Expansionary fiscal policy is generally used to counteract the negative economic effects of a recession or cyclical downturn in the economy (a decline in real GDP and rising unemployment). The purpose of the policy is to stimulate the economy by increasing aggregate demand. The policy will create a **budget deficit** (government spending greater than tax revenues) if the budget was in balance before the policy was enacted. Assume the price level is fixed. There are three options for increasing aggregate demand:

   (1) The government can increase its discretionary spending. The initial increase from this spending will be increased by the multiplier effect. Since the price level is fixed, real output will rise by the full extent of the multiplier effect.

   (2) Another option would be for the government to reduce taxes. Some of the tax cut would be saved, but some of it would be spent. The spent portion would provide an initial stimulus to the economy that would be magnified by the full extent of the multiplier effect since the price level is fixed.

   (3) The government may decide to use some combination of increased government spending and tax reductions to increase aggregate demand.

   b. Contractionary fiscal policy is a restrictive form of fiscal policy generally used to correct an inflation gap. Assume that the economy is at a full-employment level of output. If aggregate demand increases (shifts rightward), it will increase output and at the same time pull up output prices creating demand-pull inflation. If government does nothing, input prices will rise in the long run to match the increase in output prices, creating more inflation. The purpose of contractionary fiscal policy is to reduce aggregate demand pressures that increase the price level. If the government budget is balanced before the policy is enacted, it will create a **budget surplus** (tax revenues are greater than government spending). The contractionary effect on the economy from the initial reduction in spending from the policy will be reinforced by the multiplier effect. Three policy options are used, but account should be taken of the ratchet effect (the price level is inflexible downward).

   (1) The government can decrease spending. If the price level is fixed because of the ratchet effect, the multiplier will have a full effect in decreasing output, but there will be no change in the price level. Government policy will have to take into account this ratchet effect to calibrate the decline in aggregate demand so it does not cause a recession.

   (2) The government can increase taxes. The amount of the tax increase will need to be greater than a decrease in government spending because some of the tax increase will reduce saving, and not just consumption.

(3) The government can use some combination of decreased government spending and increased taxes to reduce aggregate demand.

c. Whether government purchases or taxes should be altered to reduce recession and control inflation depends on whether an expansion or a contraction of the public sector is desired.

3. In the U.S. economy there are automatic or **built-in stabilizers** that serve as nondiscretionary or passive fiscal policy. Such stabilizers work through net tax revenues (tax revenues minus government transfer payments and subsidies). These net tax revenues automatically or passively increase as the GDP rises and automatically or passively decrease as the GDP falls.

a. The economic importance of this net tax system is that it serves as a built-in stabilizer of the economy. On the one hand, it reduces purchasing power during periods of prosperity to counteract increases in aggregate demand that can contribute to demand-pull inflation. On the other hand it expands purchasing power (after tax income) during periods of declining output and high employment.

b. The degree of built-in stability in the economy depends on the responsiveness of net tax revenues to changes in GDP. As GDP increases, the average tax rates will increase in a **progressive tax system,** remain constant in a **proportional tax system,** and decrease in a **regressive tax system.** Thus, there is more built-in stability or net tax responsiveness for the economy in progressive tax systems. Built-in stabilizers, however, can only reduce and cannot eliminate economic fluctuations, so discretionary fiscal policy or monetary policy may be needed to moderate large fluctuations in the business cycle.

4. To evaluate the direction of discretionary fiscal policy, adjustments need to be made to the actual budget deficits or surpluses.

a. The **standardized budget** is a better index than the actual budget of the direction of government fiscal policy because it indicates what the Federal budget deficit or surplus would be if the economy were to operate at full employment. In the case of a budget deficit, the standardized budget

(1) removes the **cyclical deficit** that is produced by a decline in real GDP because of a downturn in the business cycle, and

(2) reveals the size of the **standardized deficit,** indicating how expansionary the fiscal policy was that year if the economy had achieved its potential level of GDP.

b. Recent data on *standardized budget deficits or surpluses* show the years that fiscal policy was expansionary or contractionary. From 1993–1998 deficits declined and from 1999–2000 surpluses increased, so fiscal policy was contractionary. From 2000–2003 surpluses decreased and deficits increased, so fiscal policy was expansionary. From 2003–2007 deficits declined, so fiscal policy was contractionary.

c. Figure 30.5 in the text shows past changes in U.S. budget deficits and surpluses. It also shows projec-

tions, but these can change with changes in fiscal policy and economic growth.

d. The *Social Security* trust fund is a "pay-as-you-go" system that taxes payroll income and uses the money to pay for mandated benefits to retirees and others. The trust fund currently generates more tax revenue than expenditures for the federal government. This surplus in the Social Security trust fund decreases Federal budget deficits and increases Federal budget surpluses.

5. Certain **problems, criticisms, and complications** arise in enacting and applying fiscal policy.

a. There will be problems of *timing*. First, it takes time to recognize the need for fiscal policy because it takes time for data to be collected that provide strong evidence of downturns or upturns in the business cycles. Second, it takes time for the U.S. president and U.S. Congress to take the appropriate administrative and legislative actions to respond to a recognized problem. Third, there is the need for time for the policy to become operational and take the desired effect on output or inflation.

b. There may be *political considerations* with fiscal policy that counter the economic effects. Elected officials may cause a **political business cycle** if they lower taxes and increase spending before an election to stimulate the economy and then do the opposite after an election.

c. Fiscal policy may be less effective if people expect it to be reversed in the future, thus making the policy temporary rather than permanent.

d. The fiscal policies of state and local governments can run counter to Federal fiscal policy and offset it (for example, state and local fiscal policy can be contractionary while Federal fiscal policy is expansionary).

e. An expansionary fiscal policy may, by raising the level of interest rates in the economy, reduce investment spending and weaken the effect of the policy on real GDP. The extent of this **crowding-out effect** depends on the condition of the economy. The crowding-out effect is likely to be relatively small when the economy is in a recession and experiences slack investment demand. It is likely to be more serious when the economy is near full employment because the public demand for money to finance government competes with the private demand for money to fund economic investments.

f. Current thinking about discretionary fiscal policy shows differing perspectives. Some economists think that fiscal policy is ineffective because of all the potential problems and complications. They recommend the use of monetary policy to guide the economy. Other economists think that fiscal policy can be useful for directing the economy and that it can reinforce or support monetary policy. There is general agreement, however, that fiscal policy should be designed so that its incentives and investments strengthen long-term productivity and economic growth.

6. The **public debt** at any time is the sum of the Federal government's previous annual deficits, minus any annual surpluses. In 2007 the total public debt was slightly more than $9 trillion.

a. The public debt is owned by various holders of **U.S. securities** (financial instruments issued by the U.S. government to borrow money, such as U.S. Treasury bills, notes, and bonds). About half (53%) of the public debt is held by Federal government agencies (44%) and the Federal Reserve (9%). The other half (47%) is owned by a "public" that includes U.S. individuals (7%), U.S. banks and financial institutions (8%), foreigners (25%), and others such as state and local governments (7%).

b. It is better to consider the size of the debt as a percentage of the economy's GDP than the absolute amount because the percentage shows the capacity of the economy to handle the debt. The percentage in 2007 (30.6%) was well below that of the 1990s.

c. Many industrial nations have public debts as a percentage of GDP that are greater than that of the United States.

d. Interest payments as a percentage of the economy's GDP reflect the level of taxation (average tax rate) required to pay interest on the public debt. The percentage in 2007 (1.7%) was down from previous years.

7. The **false contentions** about a large debt are that it will eventually bankrupt the government and that borrowing to finance expenditures passes the cost on to future generations.

a. The debt *cannot bankrupt* the government because the government can refinance it by selling new bonds and using the proceeds to pay existing bondholders. It also has the constitutional authority to levy taxes to pay the debt.

b. The burden of the debt *cannot be shifted to future generations* because U.S. citizens and institutions hold most of the debt. Repayment of any portion of the principal and the payment of interest on it do not reduce the wealth or purchasing power in the United States because it would be paid to U.S. citizens and institutions. The only exception is the payment of the part of debt that would go to foreign owners of the debt.

8. The public debt does create **real and potential problems** in the economy.

a. The payment of interest on the debt probably increases *income inequality* because this payment typically goes to wealthier individuals.

b. The payment of taxes to finance these interest payments may *reduce incentives* to bear risks, to innovate, to invest, and to save, and therefore slow economic growth in the economy.

c. The portion of the debt held by foreign citizens and institutions (the **external public debt**) requires the repayment of principal and the payment of interest to foreign citizens and institutions. This repayment would *transfer to foreigners* a part of the real output of the U.S. economy.

d. An increase in government spending may impose a burden on future generations by *crowding out* private investment spending, and thus reducing the future stock of capital goods.

(1) If government spending is financed by increased public debt, the increased borrowing of the Federal government will raise interest rates and reduce private investment spending. Future generations will inherit a smaller stock of capital goods.

(2) The burden imposed on future generations is lessened if the increase in government expenditures is for worthwhile **public investments** that increase the productive capacity of the economy. This public investment also can complement and stimulate private investment spending that increases the future capital stock.

9. (Last Word). The index of leading economic indicators consists of 10 economic variables: the average length of the work week; initial claims for unemployment insurance, new orders for consumer goods, on-time performance of vendors, new orders for capital goods, building permits for houses, stock prices, the money supply, spread in interest rates, and consumer expectations. The index is used to provide clues or indications about the future direction of the economy, but it is not a precise measure and can be misleading at times.

■ **HINTS AND TIPS**

1. Fiscal policy is a broad concept that covers several kinds of policies. The main difference is between discretionary and nondiscretionary fiscal policies. Discretionary fiscal policy is active and means that Congress has taken specific actions to change taxes or government spending to influence the economy. It can be expansionary or contractionary. Nondiscretionary fiscal policy is passive, or automatic, because changes in net tax revenues will occur without specific actions by Congress.

2. An increase in government spending that is equal to a cut in taxes will not have an equal effect on real GDP. To understand this point, assume that the MPC is .75, the increase in government spending is $8 billion, and the decrease in taxes is $8 billion. The multiplier would be 4 because it equals 1/(1 − .75). The increase in government spending will increase real GDP by $32 billion ($8 billion × 4). Of the $8 billion decrease in taxes, however, one-quarter of it will be saved ($8 billion × .25 = $2 billion) and just three-quarters will be spent ($8 billion × .75 = $6 billion). Thus, the tax cut results in an increase in *initial* spending in the economy of $6 billion, not $8 billion as was the case with the increase in government spending. The tax cut effect on real GDP is $24 billion ($6 billion × 4), not $32 billion.

3. Make sure you know the difference between a **budget deficit** (government spending greater than tax revenue for a year) and the **public debt** (the accumulation over time of budget deficits that are offset by any budget surpluses). These two terms are often confused.

4. The best way to gauge the size of budget deficits, the public debt, or interest on the public debt is to calculate each one as a *percentage of real GDP*. The absolute size of these three items is *not* a good indicator of whether it causes problems for the economy.

5. Try to understand the real rather than the imagined problems caused by the public debt. The debt will not cause the country to go bankrupt, nor will it be a burden on future generations.

■ **IMPORTANT TERMS**

fiscal policy

Council of Economic Advisers (CEA)

expansionary fiscal policy

budget deficit

contractionary fiscal policy

budget surplus

built-in stabilizer

standardized budget

cyclical deficit

political business cycle

crowding-out effect

public debt

U.S. securities

external public debt

public investments

SELF-TEST

■ **FILL-IN QUESTIONS**

1. Policy actions taken by Congress designed to change government spending or taxation are (discretionary, non-discretionary) _____ fiscal policy, but when the policy takes effect automatically or independently of Congress, then it is _____ fiscal policy.

2. Expansionary fiscal policy is generally designed to (increase, decrease) _____ aggregate demand and thus _____ real GDP and employment in the economy. Contractionary fiscal policy is generally used to (increase, decrease) _____ aggregate demand and _____ thus real GDP to halt demand-pull inflation.

3. Expansionary fiscal policy can be achieved with an increase in (government spending, taxes) _____, a decrease in _____, or a combination of the two; contractionary fiscal policy can be achieved by a decrease in (government spending, taxes) _____, an increase in _____, or a combination of the two.

4. An increase of government spending of $5 billion from an expansionary fiscal policy for an economy might ultimately produce an increase in real GDP of $20 billion. This magnified effect occurs because of the (multiplier, crowding-out) _____ effect.

5. Net taxes equal taxes (plus, minus) _____ transfer payments and subsidies. (They are called "taxes" in this chapter.) In the United States, as GDP increases, tax revenues will (increase, decrease) _____, and as the GDP decreases, tax revenues will _____.

6. Because tax revenues are (directly, indirectly) _____ related to the GDP, the economy has some (artificial, built-in) _____ stability. If the GDP increases, then tax revenue will increase, and the budget surplus will (increase, decrease) _____, thus (stimulating, restraining) _____ the economy when it is needed. When GDP decreases, tax revenues decrease, and the budget deficit (increases, decreases) _____, thus (stimulating, restraining) _____ the economy when it is needed.

7. As GDP increases, the average tax rates will increase with a (progressive, proportional, regressive) _____ tax system, remain constant with a _____ tax system, and decrease with a _____ tax system. With a progressive tax system, there is (more, less) _____ built-in stability for the economy.

8. If there are growing deficits in the standardized budget, then the direction of fiscal policy is (contractionary, expansionary) _____ and if there are growing surpluses in the standardized budget, then fiscal policy is _____. A deficit produced by swings in the business cycle is (actual, cyclical) _____. When there is a cyclical deficit, the standardized budget deficit will be (greater, less) _____ than the actual budget deficit.

9. Current contributions for the Social Security system mean that tax revenues are (greater, less) _____ than benefit payouts to retirees. Contributions for Social Security, therefore, create a (deficit, surplus) _____ that (adds to, subtracts from) _____ the size of a Federal budget surplus.

10. There is a problem of timing in the use of discretionary fiscal policy because of the time between the beginning of a recession or inflation and awareness of it, or (an administrative, an operational, a recognition) _____ lag; the time needed for Congress to adjust fiscal policy, or _____ lag; and the time needed for fiscal policy to take effect, or _____ lag.

11. Political problems arise in the application of discretionary fiscal policy to stabilize the economy because government has (one, several) _____ economic goals, state and local fiscal policies may (reinforce, counter) _____ Federal fiscal policy, and politicians may use fiscal policies in a way that creates (an international, a political) _____ business cycle.

12. Expectations among households and businesses that fiscal policy will be reversed in the future make fiscal policy (more, less) _____ effective. For example, if taxpayers expect a tax cut to be temporary, they may save (more, less) _____ now to pay for a future increase in the tax rate and spend _____ now. As a result, consumption and aggregate demand (increase, decrease) _____.

13. When the Federal government employs an expansionary fiscal policy to increase real GDP and employment in the economy, it usually has a budget (surplus, deficit) _____ and (lends, borrows) _____ in the money market. These actions may (raise, lower) _____ interest rates in the economy and (stimulate, crowd out) _____ private investment spending.

14. Current thinking on the advisability and effectiveness of discretionary fiscal policy shows general (agreement, disagreement) _____ about the value of fiscal policy in the short run, and general _____ about evaluating fiscal policy for its contribution to long-run productivity growth.

15. The public debt is equal to the sum of the Federal government's past budget (deficits, surpluses) _____ minus its budget _____.

   a. Of the public debt, Federal government agencies and the Federal Reserve hold about (47, 53) _____%, and commercial banks, financial institutions, state and local governments, and individuals and institutions here and abroad hold about _____%.

   b. Most of the public debt is (internal, external) _____ because foreigners hold only about (10, 25) _____% of it.

   c. The most meaningful way to measure the public debt is relative to (interest rates, GDP) _____.

   d. Compared with the United States, the public debt as a percentage of GDP in Italy was (higher, lower) _____ and the public debt as a percentage of GDP in Poland was _____.

16. The possibility that the Federal government will go bankrupt is a false issue. It does not need to reduce its debt; it can retire maturing U.S. securities by (taxing, refinancing) _____ them. The government can also pay its debts by increasing (interest, tax) _____ rates.

17. If the public debt is held domestically, then for U.S. taxpayers it is (a liability, an asset) _____ and for U.S. citizens and institutions owning the U.S. debt securities, it is _____.

18. The public debt and the payment of interest on it may (increase, decrease) _____ income inequality in the economy and _____ the incentives to work, take risks, save, and invest in the economy. The public debt is a burden on an economy if it is held by (foreigners, U.S. citizens) _____.

19. A public debt imposes a burden on future generations if the borrowing done to finance an increase in government expenditures results in (an increase, a decrease) _____ in interest rates, _____ in investment spending, and _____ in the stock of capital good's for future generations.

20. The size of the burden from the crowding out of private investment is lessened if government expenditures are used to finance worthwhile (increases, decreases) _____ in physical and human capital that contribute to the productive capacity of the economy, or if they (encourage, discourage) _____ more private investment that complements the public investment.

■ TRUE–FALSE QUESTIONS

Circle T if the statement is true, F if it is false.

  1. Discretionary fiscal policy is independent of Congress and left to the discretion of state and local governments. **T F**

  2. Expansionary fiscal policy during a recession or depression will create a budget deficit or add to an existing budget deficit. **T F**

  3. A decrease in taxes is one of the options that can be used to pursue a contractionary fiscal policy. **T F**

  4. To increase initial consumption by a specific amount, government must reduce taxes by more than that amount because some of the tax cut will be saved by households. **T F**

  5. A reduction in taxes and an increase in government spending would be characteristic of a contractionary fiscal policy. **T F**

  6. Built-in stabilizers are not sufficiently strong to prevent recession or inflation, but they can reduce the severity of a recession or inflation. **T F**

  7. The less progressive the tax system, the greater the economy's built-in stability. **T F**

  8. The standardized budget indicates how much government must spend and tax if there is to be full employment in the economy. **T F**

  9. The key to assessing discretionary fiscal policy is to observe the change in the standardized budget. **T F**

10. In the Federal budget, surpluses obtained from Social Security are treated as an offset to current government spending. **T F**

11. Recognition, administrative, and operational lags in the timing of Federal fiscal policy make fiscal policies more effective in reducing the rate of inflation and decreasing unemployment in the economy. **T   F**

12. Economists who see evidence of a political business cycle argue that members of Congress tend to increase taxes and reduce expenditures before elections and to reduce taxes and increase expenditures after elections. **T   F**

13. If households expect that a tax cut will be temporary, they are likely to spend more and save less, thus reinforcing the intended effect of the tax cut on aggregate demand. **T   F**

14. State and local governments' fiscal policies have tended to assist and reinforce the efforts of the Federal government to counter recession and inflation. **T   F**

15. The crowding-out effect occurs when an expansionary fiscal policy decreases the interest rate, increases investment spending, and strengthens fiscal policy. **T   F**

16. The public debt is the total accumulation of the deficits, minus any surpluses, that the Federal government has incurred over time. **T   F**

17. The public debt as a percentage of GDP is higher in the United States than in most other industrial nations. **T   F**

18. Interest payments as a percentage of GDP reflect the level of taxation (average tax rate) required to service the public debt. **T   F**

19. A large public debt will bankrupt the Federal government because it cannot refinance the debt or increase taxes to pay it. **T   F**

20. The public debt is also a public credit. **T   F**

21. The payment of interest on the public debt probably increases income inequality. **T   F**

22. The additional taxes needed to pay the interest on the public debt increase incentives to work, save, invest, and bear risks. **T   F**

23. Selling U.S. securities to foreigners to finance increased expenditures by the Federal government imposes a burden on future generations. **T   F**

24. The crowding-out effect increases the investment-demand curve and investment in private capital goods. **T   F**

25. If government spending is for public investments that increase the capital stock, then this spending can increase the future production capacity of the economy. **T   F**

■ MULTIPLE-CHOICE QUESTIONS

Circle the letter that corresponds to the best answer.

1. Which combination of policies would be the most expansionary?
  (a) an increase in government spending and taxes
  (b) a decrease in government spending and taxes

  (c) an increase in government spending and a decrease in taxes
  (d) a decrease in government spending and an increase in taxes

2. An economy is in a recession and the government decides to increase spending by $4 billion. The MPC is .8. What would be the full increase in real GDP from the change in government spending?
  (a) $3.2 billion
  (b) $4 billion
  (c) $16 billion
  (d) $20 billion

3. Which combination of fiscal policies would be the most contractionary?
  (a) an increase in government spending and taxes
  (b) a decrease in government spending and taxes
  (c) an increase in government spending and a decrease in taxes
  (d) a decrease in government spending and an increase in taxes

4. When government tax revenues change automatically and in a countercyclical direction over the course of the business cycle, this is an example of
  (a) the political business cycle
  (b) nondiscretionary fiscal policy
  (c) the standardized budget
  (d) crowding out

5. If the economy is to have built-in stability, when real GDP falls,
  (a) tax revenues and government transfer payments both should fall
  (b) tax revenues and government transfer payments both should rise
  (c) tax revenues should fall and government transfer payments should rise
  (d) tax revenues should rise and government transfer payments should fall

Answer Questions 6, 7, and 8 on the basis of the following diagram.

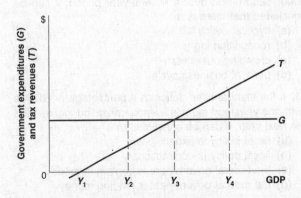

6. If the slope 'of the line *T* were steeper, there would be
  (a) more built-in stability for the economy
  (b) less built-in stability for the economy
  (c) no change in the built-in stability for the economy
  (d) the need for more emphasis on discretionary fiscal policy

7. If the slope of the line *T* were flatter, there would be
  (a) larger cyclical deficits produced as GDP moved from Y_3 to Y_2
  (b) smaller cyclical deficits produced as GDP moved from Y_3 to Y_2
  (c) larger standardized deficits produced as GDP moved from Y_3 to Y_2
  (d) smaller standardized deficits produced as GDP moved from Y_3 to Y_2

8. Actions by the Federal government to increase the progressivity of the tax system
  (a) flatten the slope of line *T* and increase built-in stability
  (b) flatten the slope of line *T* and decrease built-in stability
  (c) steepen the slope of line *T* and increase built-in stability
  (d) steepen the slope of line *T* and decrease built-in stability

Use the following table to answer question 9. The table shows the standardized budget deficit or surplus as a percentage of GDP over a five-year period.

Year	Deficit (−) Surplus (+)
1	−2.1%
2	−3.0
3	−1.5
4	+0.5
5	+1.0

9. In which year was fiscal policy expansionary?
  (a) Year 2
  (b) Year 3
  (c) Year 4
  (d) Year 5

10. If the standardized budget shows a deficit of about $200 billion and the actual budget shows a deficit of about $250 billion over a several-year period, it can be concluded that there is a
  (a) cyclical deficit
  (b) recognition lag
  (c) crowding-out effect
  (d) political business cycle

11. If the standardized deficit as a percentage of GDP is zero one year, and there is a standardized budget surplus the next year, it can be concluded that
  (a) fiscal policy is expansionary
  (b) fiscal policy is contractionary
  (c) the federal government is borrowing money
  (d) the federal government is lending money

12. If there is a surplus for the Social Security program in a given year, then this Social Security surplus will increase
  (a) a Federal budget deficit that year
  (b) a Federal budget surplus that year
  (c) interest payments on the public debt
  (d) holdings of U.S. securities by foreigners

13. The length of time involved for the fiscal action taken by Congress to affect output, employment, or the price level is referred to as the
  (a) administrative lag
  (b) operational lag
  (c) recognition lag
  (d) fiscal lag

14. The crowding-out effect of an expansionary (deficit) fiscal policy is the result of government borrowing in the money market which
  (a) increases interest rates and net investment spending in the economy
  (b) increases interest rates and decreases net investment spending
  (c) decreases interest rates and increases net investment spending
  (d) decreases interest rates and net investment spending

15. Current thinking about discretionary fiscal policy among mainstream economists is that it should be designed to
  (a) counteract the effects of monetary policy
  (b) contribute to long-run economic growth
  (c) "fine-tune" the economy in the short run, but not in the long run
  (d) control inflationary pressure, but not be used to fight recession

16. The public debt is the sum of all previous
  (a) expenditures of the Federal government
  (b) budget deficits of the Federal government
  (c) budget deficits minus any budget surpluses of the Federal government
  (d) budget surpluses less the current budget deficit of the Federal government

17. To place the public debt in perspective based on the wealth and productive capacity of the economy, it is more meaningful to
  (a) examine its absolute size
  (b) calculate the interest payments on the debt
  (c) measure it relative to the gross domestic product
  (d) compare it to imports, exports, and the trade deficit

18. According to many economists, the primary burden of the debt is the
  (a) absolute size of the debt for the economy
  (b) annual interest charges from bonds sold to finance the public debt
  (c) deficit arising from a decline in exports and increase in imports
  (d) government spending that the public debt finances for the economy

19. A major reason that a public debt cannot bankrupt the Federal government is because the Federal government has
(a) an annually balanced budget
(b) the Social Security trust fund
(c) the power to levy taxes
(d) a strong military defense

20. Incurring an internal debt to finance a war does not pass the cost of the war on to future generations because
(a) the opportunity cost of the war was borne by the generation that fought it
(b) the government need not pay interest on internally held debts
(c) there is never a need for government to refinance the debt
(d) wartime inflation reduces the relative size of the debt

21. Which would be a consequence of the retirement of the internally held (U.S.-owned) portion of the public debt?
(a) a reduction in the nation's productive capacity
(b) a reduction in the nation's standard of living
(c) a redistribution of the nation's wealth among its citizens
(d) a decrease in aggregate demand in the economy

22. Which is an important consequence of the public debt of the United States?
(a) It decreases the need for U.S. securities.
(b) It transfers a portion of the U.S. output to foreign nations.
(c) It reduces the income inequality in the United States.
(d) It leads to greater saving at every level of disposable income.

23. Greater interest charges on the public debt can lead to
(a) fewer purchases of U.S. securities by foreigners
(b) more private investment spending in the economy
(c) lower taxes, and thus greater incentives to work and invest
(d) higher taxes, and thus reduced incentives to work and invest

24. The crowding-out effect of borrowing to finance an increase in government expenditures
(a) reduces current spending for private investment
(b) increases the privately owned stock of real capital
(c) reduces the economic burden on future generations
(d) increases incentives to innovate

25. The crowding-out effect from government borrowing is reduced when
(a) interest rates are rising
(b) the economy is operating at full employment
(c) government spending improves human capital in the economy
(d) private investment spending can substitute for government spending

■ PROBLEMS

1. Columns 1 and 2 in the following table are an aggregate supply schedule. Columns 1 and 3 are aggregate demand schedules.

(1) Price level	(2) Real GDP$_1$	(3) AD$_1$	(4) AD$_2$
220	$2390	$2100	$2200
200	2390	2200	2340
190	2350	2250	2350
180	2300	2300	2400
160	2200	2400	2500

a. The equilibrium real GDP is $_____and the price level is _____.

b. Suppose that an expansionary fiscal policy increases aggregate demand from that shown in columns 1 and 3 to that shown in columns 1 and 4. The price level will increase to _____, and this rise in the price level will result in real GDP increasing to $_____.

2. The following table shows seven real GDPs and the net tax revenues of government at each real GDP.

Real GDP	Net tax revenues	Government purchases	Government deficit/surplus
$ 850	$170	$_____	$_____
900	180	_____	_____
950	190	_____	_____
1000	200	_____	_____
1050	210	_____	_____
1100	220	_____	_____
1150	230	_____	_____

a. Looking at the two columns on the left side of the table, it can be seen that
(1) when real GDP increases by $50, net tax revenues (increase, decrease) _____ by $_____.
(2) when real GDP decreases by $100, net tax revenues (increase, decrease) _____ by $_____.
(3) the relationship between real GDP and net tax revenues is (direct, inverse) _____.

b. Assume the simple multiplier has a value of 10 and that investment spending in the economy decreases by $10.
(1) If net tax revenues remained constant, the equilibrium real GDP would decrease by $_____.
(2) But when real GDP decreases, net tax revenues also decrease; and this decrease in net tax revenues will tend to (increase, decrease) _____ the equilibrium real GDP.

(1) Real GDP	(2) Net tax revenue	(3) Average tax rate	(4) Net tax revenue	(5) Average tax rate	(6) Net tax revenue	(7) Average tax rate	(8) Government spending
$1000	$100	____%	$100	____%	$100	____%	$120
1100	120	____	110	____	108	____	120
1200	145	____	120	____	115	____	120
1300	175	____	130	____	120	____	120
1400	210	____	140	____	123	____	120

(3) And, therefore, the decrease in real GDP brought about by the $10 decrease in investment spending will be (more, less) _____ than $100.

(4) The direct relationship between net tax revenues and real GDP has (lessened, expanded) _____ the impact of the $10 decrease in investment spending on real GDP.

c. Suppose the simple multiplier is also 10 and government wishes to increase the equilibrium real GDP by $50.

(1) If net tax revenues remained constant, government would have to increase its purchases of goods and services by $_____.

(2) But when real GDP rises, net tax revenues also rise, and this rise in net tax revenues will tend to (increase, decrease) _____ the equilibrium real GDP.

(3) The effect, therefore, of the $5 increase in government purchases will also be to increase the equilibrium real GDP by (more, less) _____ than $50.

(4) The direct relationship between net tax revenues and real GDP has (lessened, expanded) _____ the effect of the $5 increase in government purchases, and to raise the equilibrium real GDP by $50, the government will have to increase its purchases by (more, less) _____ than $5.

d. Imagine that the full-employment real GDP of the economy is $1150 and that government purchases of goods and services are $200.

(1) Complete the previous table by entering the government purchases and computing the budget deficit or surplus at each of the real GDPs. (Show a government deficit by placing a minus sign in front of the amount by which expenditures exceed net tax revenues.)

(2) The standardized surplus equals $_____.

(3) If the economy were in a recession and producing a real GDP of $900, the budget would show a (surplus, deficit) _____ of $_____.

(4) This budget deficit or surplus makes it appear that government is pursuing (an expansionary, a contractionary) _____ fiscal policy, but this deficit or surplus is not the result of a countercyclical fiscal policy but the result of the _____.

(5) If government did not change its net tax *rates*, it could increase the equilibrium real GDP from $900 to the full-employment real GDP of $1150 by

increasing its purchases by (approximately) $70. At the full-employment real GDP the budget would show a (surplus, deficit) _____ of $_____.

(6) If government did not change its purchases, it would increase the equilibrium real GDP from $900 to the full-employment real GDP of $1150 by decreasing net tax revenues at all real GDPs by a lump sum of (approximately) $80. The standardized budget would have a (surplus, deficit) _____ of $_____.

3. a. Complete the table at the top of the page by computing the average tax rates, given the net tax revenue data in columns 2, 4, and 6. Calculate the average tax rates in percentages to one decimal place (for example, 5.4%).

b. As real GDP increases in column 1, the average tax rate (increases, decreases, remains the same) _____ in column 3, _____ in column 5, and _____ in column 7. The tax system is (progressive, proportional, regressive) _____ in column 2, _____ in column 4, and _____ in column 6.

c. On the graph at the top of the next page, plot the real GDP, net tax revenue, and government spending data given in columns 1, 2, 4, 6, and 8. The tax revenue system with the steepest slope is found in column ____, and it is (progressive, proportional, regressive) _____ while the one with the flattest slope is found in column ____, and it is _____.

4. a. Complete the table below by stating whether the direction of discretionary fiscal policy was contractionary (C), expansionary (E), or neither (N), given the hypothetical budget data for an economy.

(1) Year	(2) Actual budget deficit (−) or surplus (+)	(3) Standardized budget deficit (−) or surplus (+)	(4) Direction of fiscal policy
1	− $170 billion	− $130 billion	
2	− 120 billion	− 90 billion	____
3	+ 40 billion	+ 20 billion	____
4	− 60 billion	− 50 billion	____
5	− 120 billion	− 100 billion	____

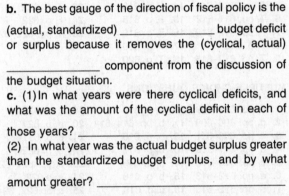

b. The best gauge of the direction of fiscal policy is the (actual, standardized) _____ budget deficit or surplus because it removes the (cyclical, actual) _____ component from the discussion of the budget situation.

c. (1) In what years were there cyclical deficits, and what was the amount of the cyclical deficit in each of those years? _____

(2) In what year was the actual budget surplus greater than the standardized budget surplus, and by what amount greater? _____

5. The following table gives data on interest rates and investment demand (in billions of dollars) in a hypothetical economy.

Interest rate	I_{d1}	I_{d2}
10%	$250	$300
8	300	350
6	350	400
4	400	450
2	450	500

a. Use the I_{d1} schedule. Assume that the government needs to finance a budget deficit and this public borrowing increases the interest rate from 4% to 6%. How much crowding out of private investment will occur?

_____

b. Now assume that the deficit is used to improve the capital stock of the economy and that, as a consequence, the investment-demand schedule changes from I_{d1} to I_{d2}. At the same time, the interest rate rises from 4% to 6% as the government borrows money to finance the deficit. How much crowding out of private investment will occur in this case?

_____

c. Graph the two investment-demand schedules on the next graph and show the difference between the two events. Put the interest rate on the vertical axis and the quantity of investment demanded on the horizontal axis.

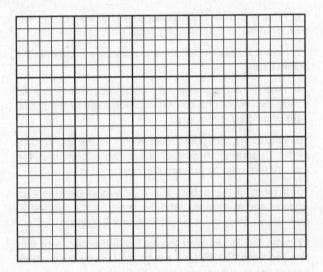

■ **SHORT ANSWER AND ESSAY QUESTIONS**

1. What are the Federal government's three options for conducting either an expansionary fiscal policy or a contractionary fiscal policy?

2. Compare and contrast the effect of expansionary fiscal policy and of contractionary fiscal policy on aggregate demand, output, and the price level. Draw a graph to illustrate the likely effects of each. Assume that there is a ratchet effect.

3. What is the effect of the multiplier on the initial change in spending from fiscal policy? When the government wants to increase initial consumption by a specific amount, why must the government reduce taxes by more than that amount?

4. Explain the fiscal policies that would be advocated during a recession and during a period of inflation by those who (a) wish to expand the public sector and (b) wish to contract the size of government.

5. What is a built-in stabilizer? How do the built-in stabilizers work to reduce rises and falls in the level of nominal GDP?

6. Supply definitions of progressive, proportional, and regressive tax systems. What are the implications of each type of tax system for the built-in stability of the economy?

7. Explain the distinction between a cyclical deficit and a standardized deficit. Which type of deficit provides the best indication of the direction of fiscal policy? Why?

8. Discuss the history of recent U.S. fiscal policy based on changes in the standardized budget.

9. Explain the three kinds of time lags that make it difficult to use fiscal policy to stabilize the economy.

10. How might the direction of fiscal policy at the Federal level be countered by the actions of state and local governments?

11. Evaluate the strength of a crowding-out effect when the economy is in recession or experiencing a period of strong economic growth.

12. What is the current thinking about the advisability and effectiveness of discretionary fiscal policy?

13. How are budget deficits and surpluses related to the public debt?

14. Who owns the public debt? What percentage is held by the two major groups? What percentage of the public debt is held by foreigners?

15. Why can't the public debt result in the bankruptcy of the Federal government? What two actions can the government take to prevent bankruptcy?

16. If most of the public debt was owned by American citizens and institutions, and the government decided to pay off the debt, what would happen? Explain.

17. Was the increase in the cost of the public debt that resulted from World War II a burden borne by the wartime generation or future generations? Explain.

18. How does the public debt affect the distribution of income and incentives to work, to save, or to assume risk in the economy?

19. What are the economic implications of the portion of the public debt held by foreigners?

20. How does the public debt crowd out private investment and impose a burden on future generations? What two qualifications might lessen the crowding-out effect on the size of the economic burden that has shifted to future generations?

ANSWERS

Chapter 30 Fiscal Policy, Deficits, and Debt

FILL-IN QUESTIONS

1. discretionary, nondiscretionary
2. increase, increase, decrease, decrease
3. government spending, taxes, government spending, taxes
4. multiplier
5. minus, increase, decrease
6. directly, built-in, increase, restraining, increases, stimulating
7. progressive, proportional, regressive, more
8. expansionary, contractionary, cyclical, less
9. greater, surplus, adds to
10. a recognition, an administrative, an operational
11. several, counter, a political
12. less, more, less, decrease
13. deficit, borrows, raise, crowd out
14. disagreement, agreement
15. deficits, surpluses; *a.* 53, 47; *b.* internal, 25; *c.* GDP; *d.* higher, lower
16. refinancing, tax
17. a liability, an asset
18. increase, decrease, foreigners
19. an increase, a decrease, a decrease
20. increases, encourage

TRUE–FALSE QUESTIONS

1. F, p. 608	**10.** T, p. 616	**19.** F, p. 620
2. T, p. 608	**11.** F, p. 617	**20.** T, p. 621
3. F, pp. 609, 611	**12.** F, p. 617	**21.** T, p. 621
4. T, p. 609	**13.** F, p. 617	**22.** F, pp. 621–622
5. F, pp. 609–611	**14.** F, p. 618	**23.** T, p. 622
6. T, pp. 611–612	**15.** F, p. 618	**24.** F, p. 622
7. F, pp. 612–613	**16.** T, p. 619	**25.** T, pp. 622, 624
8. F, p. 613	**17.** F, p. 620	
9. T, pp. 613–615	**18.** T, p. 620	

MULTIPLE-CHOICE QUESTIONS

1. c, pp. 608–609	**10.** a, p. 613	**19.** c, p. 621
2. d, pp. 608–609	**11.** b, pp. 614–614	**20.** a, p. 621
3. d, pp. 609–611	**12.** b, p. 616	**21.** c, p. 621
4. b, pp. 611–612	**13.** b, p. 617	**22.** b, p. 622
5. c, pp. 612–613	**14.** b, p.618	**23.** d, pp. 621–622
6. a, pp. 612–613	**15.** b, p. 618	**24.** a, p.622
7. b, pp. 612–613	**16.** c, p. 619	**25.** c, pp.622, 624
8. c, pp. 612–613	**17.** c, p. 620	
9. a, pp. 613–615	**18.** b, p. 620	

PROBLEMS

1. *a.* 2,300, 180; *b.* 190, 2,350
2. *a.* increase, $10, (2) decrease, $20, (3) direct; *b.* (1) $100, (2) increase, (3) less, (4) lessened; *c.* (1) $5, (2) decrease, (3) less, (4) lessened, more; *d.* (1) government purchases are $200 at all GDPs, government surplus or deficit: −30, −20, −10, 0, 10, 20, 30, (2) $30, (3) deficit, $20, (4) an expansionary, recession, (5) deficit, $40, (6) deficit, $50
3. *a.* column 3: 10.0, 10.9, 12.1, 13.5, 15.0; column 5: 10.0 at each GDP level; column 7: 10.0, 9.8, 9.6, 9.2, 8.8; *b.* increases, remains the same, decreases; progressive, proportional, regressive; *c.* 2, progressive, 6, regressive
4. *a.* (Year 1–2) contractionary, (Year 2–3) contractionary, (Year 3–4) expansionary, (Year 4–5) expansionary; *b.* standardized, cyclical; *c.* (1) year 1 ($40 billion), year 2 ($30 billion), year 4 ($10 billion), year 5 ($20 billion), (2) year 3 ($20 billion)
5. *a.* $50 billion; *b.* none; *c.* graph

SHORT ANSWER AND ESSAY QUESTIONS

1. pp. 608–611	**8.** pp. 614–615	**15.** p. 621
2. pp. 608–611	**9.** p. 617	**16.** p. 621
3. pp. 608–611	**10.** p. 618	**17.** p. 621
4. p. 611	**11.** p. 618	**18.** pp. 621–622
5. pp. 611–612	**12.** pp. 618–619	**19.** p. 622
6. pp. 612–613	**13.** p. 619	**20.** pp. 622, 624
7. pp. 613–614	**14.** pp. 619–620	

CHAPTER 31

Money and Banking

Chapter 31 explains how the financial system affects the operation of the economy. The chapter is largely descriptive and factual. Pay particular attention to the following: (1) what the money supply is and the function money performs; (2) what gives value to or "backs" money in the United States; and (3) the principal institutions of the U.S. financial system and their functions.

Several points are worth repeating. First, money is whatever performs the three functions of money **(medium of exchange, unit of account, store of value)**. People are willing to accept and trust the use of money for transactions because people are willing to exchange goods and services for it. So money is backed by trust or acceptability *and not by gold*. Money also helps people measure the value of goods and services they want to buy or sell. In addition, money stores value for people so they can use it in the future to make purchases.

Second, the central bank in the United States consists of the 12 **Federal Reserve Banks** and the **Board of Governors** of the **Federal Reserve System** which oversees their operation. These banks, while privately owned by the commercial banks, are operated more or less as public agencies of the Federal government. They operate on a not-for-profit basis but are used primarily to regulate the nation's money supply in the best interests of the economy as a whole, and secondarily, to perform other services for the banks, the government, and the economy. They are able to perform their primary function because they are bankers' banks in which depository institutions (commercial banks and the thrifts) can deposit and borrow money. They do not deal directly with the public.

Third, these depository institutions accept deposits and make loans, but they also are able to create money by lending checkable deposits. Because they are able to do this, they have a strong influence on the size of the money supply and the purchasing power of money. The Federal Reserve Banks exist primarily to regulate the money supply and its value by influencing and controlling the amount of money depository institutions create.

The final section of Chapter 31 discusses recent developments in money and banking. First, there has been a significant shift in financial assets from banks and thrifts to other types of financial services institutions. Second, many banks and thrifts have merged over the years to better compete with other regional or national firms. Third, there has been a convergence in the services provided by the different types of financial institutions. Fourth, financial markets are now global and more highly integrated than in previous decades. Fifth, technological advances have introduced electronic payments and changed the character of money.

■ CHECKLIST

When you have studied this chapter you should be able to

☐ List and explain the three functions of money.
☐ Describe the liquidity of an asset and give examples of it.
☐ Give an **M1** definition of money.
☐ Describe the characteristics of the currency component of **M1**.
☐ Explain the role of checkable deposits as a component of **M1**.
☐ Describe the two major types of institutions offering checkable deposits.
☐ Offer two qualifications about what is excluded from the money supply.
☐ Give an **M2** definition of money and describe its components.
☐ Distinguish between credit cards and money.
☐ Explain why money is debt in the U.S. economy and who holds that debt.
☐ State three reasons that currency and checkable deposits are money and have value.
☐ Use an equation to explain the relationship between the purchasing power of money and the price level.
☐ Discuss how inflation affects the acceptability of money.
☐ Explain what role government plays in maintaining or stabilizing the purchasing power of money.
☐ Describe the framework of the Federal Reserve.
☐ Explain the historical background of the Federal Reserve.
☐ Describe the purposes of the Board of Governors of the Federal Reserve.
☐ Explain why the Federal Reserve Banks are central, quasi-public, and bankers' banks.
☐ Discuss the functions of the FOMC of the Federal Reserve.
☐ Discuss the relationship between the Federal Reserve and commercial banks and thrifts.
☐ List and explain the seven major functions of the Federal Reserve System and indicate which one is most important.
☐ Discuss the reason for the independence of the Federal Reserve.

☐ Describe the relative decline of banks and thrifts.

☐ Explain the effects of consolidation on banks and thrifts.

☐ Discuss how globalization has changed financial markets.

☐ Explain how electronic payments have transformed banking.

☐ Discuss the reasons that U.S. currency is widely used in other nations (Last Word).

■ **CHAPTER OUTLINE**

1. Money is whatever performs the three **basic functions of money:** It is a **medium of exchange** for buying and selling goods and services. It serves as a **unit of account** for measuring the monetary cost of goods and services. It is a **store of value** so people can transfer purchasing power from the present to the future. A key advantage of money, especially in its cash form, is that it is widely accepted and easy to use for transactions. Other assets, such as real estate, stocks, or bonds, must first be converted to money before they can be use to make purchases. Ease with which such assets can be converted to money without losing purchasing power is a measure of the **liquidity** of an asset.

2. Money is a stock of items rather than a flow such as income. Any item that is widely accepted as a medium of exchange can serve as money, and many types of such items have done so throughout history.

a. The narrowly defined money supply is called **M1** and has two principal components.

(1) One component is *currency:* It consists of coins that are **token money,** which means the value of the metal in the coin is less than the face value of the coin. It also consists of paper money in the form of **Federal Reserve Notes.**

(2) The second component is **checkable deposits.** They allow a person to transfer ownership of deposits to others by the writing of checks; these checks are generally accepted as a medium of exchange.

(3) The two major types of financial institutions offering checkable deposits are **commercial banks** and **thrift institutions.**

(4) There also is currency and checkable deposits owned by the Federal government, commercial banks and thrift institutions, and the Federal Reserve Banks. They are excluded from the calculation of **M1** or in the other definitions of the money supply.

b. **M2** is a broader definition of money and includes not only the currency and checkable deposits in **M1** but also **near-monies** that do not function directly or fully as a medium of exchange, but which can be easily converted to currency or checkable deposits. **M2** includes

(1) **M1** (currency and checkable deposits); plus

(2) savings deposits, which include money in **savings accounts** and also **money market deposit accounts (MMDAs),** interest-bearing accounts with short-term securities; plus

(3) *small* **time deposits** of less than $100,000, such as "certificates of deposit" (CDs); plus

(4) **money market mutual funds (MMMFs)** held by individuals.

3. The **money supply gets it "backing"** from the ability of the government to keep the purchasing power of money stable.

a. Money is debt or the promise of a commercial bank, a thrift institution, or a Federal Reserve Bank to pay, but these debts cannot be redeemed for anything tangible.

b. Money has value only because:

(1) It is acceptable for the exchange of desirable goods and services.

(2) It is **legal tender** (legally acceptable for payment of debts).

(3) It is relatively scarce because its value depends on supply and demand conditions.

c. The purchasing power of money is the amount of goods and services a unit of money will buy.

(1) The purchasing power of the U.S. dollar is inversely related to the price level: Value of the dollar (V) = 1 divided by price level (P) expressed as an index number (in hundredths), or $V = 1/P$.

(2) Rapid inflation can erode the purchasing power of money and public confidence in it. Such situations limit the functions of money as a medium of exchange, measure of value, or store of value.

d. Money is backed by the confidence the public has that the purchasing power of money will remain stable. U.S. monetary authorities (the Federal Reserve) are responsible for using monetary policy to maintain price-level stability and the purchasing power of money. The actions of the U.S. government are also important because sound fiscal policy supports price-level stability.

4. The monetary and financial sector of the economy is significantly influenced by the **Federal Reserve System (the Fed)** and the nation's banks and thrift institutions.

a. The banking system remains centralized and regulated by government because historical problems in the U.S. economy led to different kinds of money and the mismanagement of the money supply. The U.S. Congress passed the Federal Reserve Act of 1913 to establish the Fed as the nation's central bank to be responsible for issuing currency and controlling the nation's money supply.

b. The **Board of Governors** of the Fed exercises control over the supply of money and the banking system. The U.S. president appoints the seven members of the Board of Governors, who serve for 14 years. The president also selects the board chair and vice chair, who serve 4-year terms.

c. The 12 **Federal Reserve Banks** of the Fed have three main functions.

(1) They serve as the nation's *central bank* to implement the policies set by the Board of Governors.

(2) They are *quasi-public banks* that blend private ownership of each Federal Reserve Bank with public control of each bank through the Board of Governors.

(3) They are *"bankers' banks"* that perform banking services for the member banks in their regions.

d. The **Federal Open Market Committee (FOMC)** is responsible for acting on the monetary policy set by the Board of Governors. The FOMC includes the seven members of the Board of Governors, the president of the New York Federal Reserve Bank, plus 4 other presidents of Federal Reserve banks (who serve on a rotating basis). The FOMC conducts open market operations to buy and sell government securities to control the nation's money supply and influence interest rates.

e. The U.S. banking system contains about 7,300 commercial banks. About three-fourths of these are banks charted by states and about one-fourth of these are banks chartered by the Federal government. The banking system also includes about 11,000 thrift institutions, such as savings and loans and credit unions. Both banks and thrifts are directly affected by the Fed's decisions concerning the money supply and interest rates.

f. The Fed performs seven functions: issuing currency, setting reserve requirements and holding reserves, lending money to banks and thrifts, collecting and processing checks, serving as the fiscal agent for the Federal government, supervising banks, and controlling the money supply. The last function is the most important.

g. The Federal Reserve is an independent agency of government with control of the money supply and influence over interest rates. This independence helps insulate it from political pressure from the U.S. Congress or the U.S. president when the Fed decides to adopt a necessary, but possibly unpopular, monetary policy such as raising interest rates to combat inflation.

5. Recent developments have affected money and banking in the U.S. economy.

a. The U.S. **financial services industry** consists not only of banks and thrifts, but also of insurance companies, mutual fund companies, pension funds, and securities firms. Over the past 25 years, the amount of financial assets managed by banks and thrifts fell from nearly 60 percent to about 24 percent as households shifted financial assets to these other types of financial services firms.

b. The number of banks and thrift institutions has declined, partly as a result of bank and thrift mergers. These mergers enable banks and thrifts to compete more effectively within the financial services industry on a national or regional basis.

c. There has also been a convergence and growing similarity in the types of financial services offered by different financial institutions such as banks, thrifts, insurance companies, mutual funds, pension funds, and securities firms.

d. Financial markets are now more integrated and operate worldwide because of advances in communications technologies and greater competition for financial capital assets around the globe.

e. The character of money has changed with the shift to the widespread use of **electronic payments** to make purchases and settle debts and greater use of electronic forms of money.

6. A large amount of U.S. currency is circulating abroad for use by residents of other nations. The "global greenback" is demanded because the dollar does a better job of holding its purchasing power relative to domestic currencies, especially in those nations that have experienced high inflation, wars, and political turmoil. The dollar in these nations serves an effective and reliable medium of exchange, store of value, and unit of account compared with domestic currencies.

■ HINTS AND TIPS

1. The value of money is largely based on trust or acceptability. You are willing to accept money in exchange for a good or service because you are confident you will be able to use that money to purchase other goods and services or store its value for later use. If you lose trust in money, then it no longer functions as a medium of exchange, store of value, or measure of value for you and probably many other people.

2. Most students typically think of money as only currency: coins and paper money in circulation. A key component of the money supply, however, is the checkable deposits held at banks and thrift institutions on which checks can be drawn.

3. There are two definitions of the **money supply** that you must know about, from the narrow **M1** to the broader **M2.** The essential relationship among them is that currency and checkable deposits are the main parts of each one.

4. A good portion of the chapter explains the framework of the Federal Reserve. The institutional features are important for understanding how the nation's central bank works, and the Fed will be a major focus of later chapters.

■ IMPORTANT TERMS

liquidity

medium of exchange

unit of account

store of value

M1

token money

Federal Reserve
  Notes

checkable deposits

commercial banks

thrift institutions

near-monies

M2

savings account

money market
  deposit account
  (MMDA)

time deposits

money market mutual
  fund (MMMF)

legal tender

Federal Reserve
  System

Board of Governors

Federal Reserve
  Banks

Federal Open Market
  Committee (FOMC)

financial services
  industry

electronic payments

SELF-TEST

■ FILL-IN QUESTIONS

1. When money is usable for buying and selling goods and services, it functions as (a unit of account, a store of value, a medium of exchange) _____, but when money serves as a measure of relative worth, it functions as _____, and when money serves as a liquid asset it functions as _____.

2. The ease with which an asset can be converted into money such as cash with little or no loss in purchasing power is its (credit, liquidity) _____. Assets that can be converted into cash more easily than other assets are (more, less) _____ liquid assets.

3. All coins in circulation in the United States are (paper, token) _____ money, which means that their intrinsic value is (less, greater) _____ than the face value of the coin.

4. Paper money and coins are considered (currency, checkable deposits) _____ and are one major component of **M1**; the other major component is (currency, checkable deposits) _____.

5. **M2** is equal to **M1** plus (checking, savings) _____ deposits that include money market (deposit accounts, mutual funds) _____, plus (small, large) _____ time deposits, and plus money market (deposit accounts, mutual funds) _____.

6. Credit cards (are, are not) _____ considered money but rather a form of (paper money, loan) _____ from the institution that issued the card.

7. Paper money is the circulating debt of (banks and thrifts, the Federal Reserve Banks) _____, while checkable deposits are the debts of _____. In the United States, currency and checkable deposits (are, are not) _____ backed by gold and silver.

8. Money has value because it is (unacceptable, acceptable) _____ in exchange for products and resources, because it is (legal, illegal) _____ tender, and because it is relatively (abundant, scarce) _____.

9. The purchasing power of money varies (directly, inversely) _____ with the price level. To find the value of $1 (multiply, divide) _____ 1 by the price level.

10. Runaway inflation may significantly (increase, decrease) _____ the purchasing power of money and _____ its acceptance as a medium of exchange.

11. Government's responsibility in stabilizing the purchasing power of money calls for effective control over the (demand for, supply of) _____ money and the application by the president and Congress of appropriate (monetary, fiscal) _____ policies.

12. The Federal Reserve System is composed of the Board of (Banks, Governors) _____ and the 12 Federal Reserve _____. These policies of the Federal Reserve are often carried out by the (Federal Deposit Insurance Corporation, Federal Open Market Committee) _____.

13. The Federal Reserve Banks are (private, quasi-public) _____ banks, serve as (consumers', bankers') _____ banks, and are (local, central) _____ banks whose policies are coordinated by the Board of Governors.

14. The Federal Open Market Committee meets regularly to buy and sell government (currency, securities) _____ to control the nation's money supply and influence (productivity, interest rates) _____.

15. The U.S. banking system is composed of about 7300 (thrifts, commercial banks) _____ and about 11,000 _____.

16. The seven major functions of the Fed are
a. _____
b. _____
c. _____
d. _____
e. _____
f. _____
g. _____
Of these, the most important function is _____.
_____

17. The Congress established the Fed as a(n) (dependent, independent) _____ agency of government. The objective was to protect it from political pressure so it could control (taxes, inflation) _____.

18. In the past decade, the number of banks and thrifts (increased, decreased) _____ because competition from other financial institutions has

_____ and also mainly because of (mergers, bankruptcies) _____ among banks and thrift institutions.

19. Two other recent developments in money and banking are the (convergence, globalization) _____ of services provided by U.S. financial institutions and the _____ of financial markets.

20. Households and businesses are also increasingly using (paper, electronic) _____ payments for transactions such as credit cards, debit cards, Fedwire transfers, and automated clearinghouse transactions (ACH). New forms of electronic money may include (credit, smart) _____ cards and (stored-value, transfer-value) _____ cards.

■ TRUE–FALSE QUESTIONS

Circle T if the statement is true, F if it is false.

1. When the price of a product is stated in terms of dollars and cents, then money is functioning as a unit of account. **T F**

2. Real estate would be an example of a highly liquid asset. **T F**

3. The money supply designated **M1** is the sum of currency and savings deposits. **T F**

4. The currency component of **M1** includes both coins and paper money. **T F**

5. If a coin is token money, its face value is less than its intrinsic value. **T F**

6. Both commercial banks and thrift institutions accept checkable deposits. **T F**

7. The checkable deposits of the Federal government at the Federal Reserve Banks are a component of **M1**. **T F**

8. M2 exceeds M1 by the amount of savings deposits (including money market deposit accounts), small time deposits, and the money market mutual funds of individuals. **T F**

9. A *small* time deposit is one that is less than $100,000. **T F**

10. The money supply in the United States essentially is "backed" by the government's ability to keep the value of money relatively stable. **T F**

11. The major components of the money supply are debts, or promises to pay. **T F**

12. Currency and checkable deposits are money because they are acceptable to sellers in exchange for goods and services. **T F**

13. If money is to have a fairly stable value, its supply must be limited relative to the demand for it. **T F**

14. The amount a dollar will buy varies directly with the price level. **T F**

15. Price-level stability requires effective management and regulation of the nation's money supply. **T F**

16. Members of the Board of Governors of the Federal Reserve System are appointed by the president of the United States and confirmed by the Senate. **T F**

17. The Federal Reserve Banks are owned and operated by the U.S. government. **T F**

18. Federal Reserve Banks are bankers' banks because they make loans to and accept deposits from depository institutions. **T F**

19. The Federal Open Market Committee (FOMC) is responsible for keeping the stock market open and regulated. **T F**

20. The Federal Reserve Banks are responsible for issuing currency. **T F**

21. At times, the Fed lends money to banks and thrifts, charging them an interest rate called the *bank and thrift rate*. **T F**

22. The Federal Reserve acts as the fiscal agent for the Federal government. **T F**

23. Congress established the Fed as an independent agency to protect it from political pressure so that it can effectively control the money supply and maintain price stability. **T F**

24. In recent years, banks and thrifts have increased their share of the financial services industry and control of financial assets. **T F**

25. Households and businesses are increasingly using electronic payments to buy and sell goods and services. **T F**

■ MULTIPLE-CHOICE QUESTIONS

Circle the letter that corresponds to the best answer.

1. Which one is an economic function of money?
 (a) a store of gold
 (b) a unit of account
 (c) a factor of production
 (d) a medium of communications

2. Each month Marti puts a certain percentage of her income in a bank account that she plans to use in the future to purchase a car. For Marti, the money saved in the bank account is primarily functioning as
 (a) legal tender
 (b) token money
 (c) store of value
 (d) medium of exchange

3. Which one of the following items would be considered to be perfectly liquid from an economic perspective?
 (a) cash
 (b) stocks

(c) real estate
(d) certificate of deposits

4. Which one of the following is included in *currency* component of **M1**?
(a) gold certificates
(b) silver certificates
(c) checkable deposits
(d) Federal Reserve Notes

5. Checkable deposits are money because they are
(a) legal tender
(b) fiat money
(c) token money
(d) a medium of exchange

6. What type of financial institution accepts deposits from and lends to "members," who are usually a group of people who work for the same company?
(a) credit unions
(b) commercial banks
(c) mutual savings banks
(d) savings and loan associations

7. Which of the following would be excluded from **M1** and other measures of the money supply?
(a) coins held by the public
(b) currency held by banks
(c) Federal Reserve Notes held by the public
(d) checkable deposits of individuals at commercial banks

8. Which constitutes the largest element in the **M2** money supply?
(a) savings deposits
(b) small time deposits
(c) checkable deposits
(d) money market mutual funds held by individuals

Use the following table to answer Questions 9 and 10 about the money supply, given the following hypothetical data for the economy.

Item	Billions of dollars
Savings deposits, including MMDAs	$3452
Small time deposits	997
Currency	721
Checkable deposits	604
Money market mutual funds of individuals	703
Money market mutual funds of businesses	1153

9. The size of the **M1** money supply is
(a) $1307
(b) $1325
(c) $1719
(d) $1856

10. The size of the **M2** money supply is
(a) $4777
(b) $5774
(c) $6477
(d) $7630

11. Are credit cards considered to be money?
(a) Yes, because their value is included in the calculation of **M1**.
(b) Yes, because their value is included in the calculation of **M2**.
(c) No, because they provide a short-term loan to cardholders from a financial institution that issued the card.
(d) No, because the card transactions are not insured either by the Federal Reserve banks or the U.S. Treasury.

12. The major components of the money supply—paper money and checkable deposits—are
(a) legal tender
(b) token money
(c) debts, or promises to pay
(d) assets of the Federal Reserve Banks

13. Which *best* describes the backing of money in the United States?
(a) the gold bullion that is stored in Fort Knox, Kentucky
(b) the belief of holders of money that it can be exchanged for desirable goods and services
(c) the willingness of banks and the government to surrender something of value in exchange for money
(d) the confidence of the public in the ability of government to pay off the national debt

14. If the price level increases 20%, the purchasing power of money decreases
(a) 14.14%
(b) 16.67%
(c) 20%
(d) 25%

15. High rates of inflation in an economy will
(a) increase the purchasing power of money
(b) decrease the conversion of money to gold
(c) increase the use of money as a measure of value
(d) decrease the use of money as a medium of exchange

16. To keep the purchasing power of money fairly stable, the Federal Reserve
(a) buys corporate stock
(b) employs fiscal policy
(c) controls the money supply
(d) uses price and wage controls

17. The members of the Board of Governors of the Federal Reserve System are appointed by
(a) member banks of the Federal Reserve System
(b) members of the Federal Open Market Committee
(c) the U.S. president and confirmed by the Senate
(d) the presidents of the 12 Federal Reserve Banks

18. The Board of Governors and 12 Federal Reserve Banks as a system serve as
(a) a central bank
(b) a regulator of the stock market

(c) the printer of U.S. paper money

(d) the issuer of the nation's gold certificates

19. The 12 Federal Reserve Banks are

(a) publicly owned and controlled

(b) privately owned and controlled

(c) privately owned, but publicly controlled

(d) publicly owned, but privately controlled

20. The Federal Reserve Banks perform essentially the same functions for

(a) the public as do commercial banks and thrifts

(b) Federal government as does the U.S. Treasury

(c) commercial banks and thrifts as those institutions do for the public

(d) commercial banks and thrifts as does the Federal Deposit Insurance Corporation

21. The Federal Open Market Committee (FOMC) of the Federal Reserve System is primarily responsible for

(a) supervising the operation of banks to make sure they follow regulations and monitoring banks so they do not engage in fraud

(b) handling the Fed's collection of checks and adjusting legal reserves among banks

(c) setting the Fed's monetary policy and directing the buying and selling of government securities

(d) acting as the fiscal agent for the Federal government and issuing currency

22. The Federal Reserve is responsible for

(a) supervising all banks and thrifts

(b) printing currency for banks and thrifts

(c) collecting Federal taxes from banks and thrifts

(d) holding the required reserves of banks and thrifts

23. The most important function of the Federal Reserve is

(a) issuing currency

(b) controlling the money supply

(c) supervising banks and thrifts

(d) lending money to banks and thrifts

24. Which one of the following is a recent development in the financial services industry?

(a) an increase in the number of banks and thrifts

(b) increased integration of world financial markets

(c) increased use of coins and currency as a medium of exchange

(d) an increase in the separation of services offered by financial institutions

25. Which one of the following would be a recent development in money and banking?

(a) less reliance on global markets by financial institutions

(b) less convergence in the types of services offered by financial institutions

(c) greater use of electronic payments by financial institutions

(d) a larger percentage of financial assets held by banks and thrifts compared to other financial institutions

■ **PROBLEMS**

1. From the figures in the following table it can be concluded that

Item	Billions of dollars
Small time deposits	$1014
MMMFs held by individuals	743
Checkable deposits	622
Savings deposits, including MMDAs	3649
Currency	730
MMMFs held by businesses	1190

a. M1 is equal to the sum of $ _____ and $ _____, so it totals $ _____ billion.

b. M2 is equal to **M1** plus $ _____ and $ _____ and $ _____ and $ _____, so it totals $ _____ billion.

2. Complete the following table that shows the relationship between a percentage change in the price level and the percentage change in the purchasing power of money. Calculate the percentage change in the purchasing power of money to one decimal place.

Change in price level	Change in purchasing power of money
a. *rises* by:	
5%	− ____.____%
10%	− ____.____
15%	− ____.____
20%	− ____.____
25%	− ____.____
b. *falls* by:	
5%	+ ____.____
10%	+ ____.____
15%	+ ____.____

■ **SHORT ANSWER AND ESSAY QUESTIONS**

1. How would you define money based on its three functions?

2. What is the definition of liquidity as it relates to money? Give examples of liquid and illiquid assets.

3. What are the two components of the **M1** supply of money in the United States?

4. Why are coins token money?

5. What are checkable deposits?

6. Describe the different types of institutions that offer checkable deposits.

7. Are the checkable deposits of government, the Fed, commercial banks, and other financial institutions included in **M1**? Explain.

8. Define **M2** and explain why it is used.

9. What is the purpose of having two definitions of the money supply? What is the relationship between the two definitions?

10. What backs the money used in the United States? What determines the purchasing power of money?

11. Explain the relationship between the purchasing power of money and the price level.

12. What must government do if it is to stabilize the purchasing power of money?

13. Describe the purpose and membership of the Board of Governors of the Federal Reserve System.

14. Explain the three major characteristics of the Federal Reserve Banks.

15. What is the Federal Open Market Committee and how does it operate?

16. Describe the differences in commercial banks and thrifts in terms of numbers, purpose, and regulation agencies.

17. What are the seven major functions of the Fed and which function is most important?

18. What are the basic reasons for the independence of the Federal Reserve System?

19. Describe the decline of and consolidation among banks and thrifts in recent years.

20. Discuss the meaning and effects of increased integration of world financial markets.

ANSWERS

Chapter 31 Money and Banking

FILL-IN QUESTIONS

1. a medium of exchange, a unit of account, a store of value
2. liquidity, more
3. token, less
4. currency, checkable deposits
5. savings, deposit account, small, mutual funds
6. are not, loan
7. the Federal Reserve Banks, banks and thrifts, are not
8. acceptable, legal, scarce
9. inversely, divide
10. decrease, decrease
11. supply of, fiscal
12. Governors, Banks, Federal Open Market Committee

13. quasi-public, bankers', central
14. securities, interest rates
15. commercial banks, thrifts
16. *a.* issuing currency; *b.* setting reserve requirements and holding reserves; *c.* lending money to banks and thrifts; *d.* collecting and processing checks; *e.* serving as fiscal agent for the Federal government; *f.* bank supervision; *g.* controlling the money supply; controlling the money supply
17. independent, inflation
18. decreased, increased, mergers
19. convergence, globalization
20. electronic, smart, and stored-value

TRUE–FALSE QUESTIONS

1. T, p. 630	**10.** T, p. 634	**19.** F, p. 638
2. F, p. 630	**11.** T, p. 634	**20.** T, p. 638
3. F, p. 631	**12.** T, p. 634	**21.** F, p. 638
4. T, p. 631	**13.** T, p. 634	**22.** T, p. 639
5. F, p. 631	**14.** F, pp. 634–635	**23.** T, p. 639
6. T, p. 632	**15.** T, p. 635	**24.** F, p. 639
7. F, p. 632	**16.** T, p. 636	**25.** T, p. 641
8. T, pp. 633–634	**17.** F, pp. 636–637	
9. T, pp. 633–634	**18.** T; p. 637	

MULTIPLE-CHOICE QUESTIONS

1. b, p. 630	**10.** c, pp. 632–633	**19.** c, p. 637
2. c, p. 630	**11.** c, p. 633	**20.** c, p. 637
3. a, p. 630	**12.** c, pp. 633–634	**21.** c, p. 638
4. d, p. 631	**13.** b, p. 634	**22.** d, p. 638
5. d, pp. 631–632	**14.** b, pp. 634–635	**23.** b, p. 639
6. a, p. 632	**15.** d, p. 635	**24.** b, pp. 640–641
7. b, p. 632	**16.** c, p. 635	**25.** c, p. 641
8. a, pp. 632–633	**17.** c, p. 636	
9. b, p. 632	**18.** a, p. 636	

PROBLEMS

1. *a.* 730, 622 (either order), 1,352; *b.* 3649, 1014, 743 (any order), 6758
2. *a.* 4.8, 9.1, 13, 16.7, 20; *b.* 5.3, 11.1, 17.6

SHORT ANSWER AND ESSAY QUESTIONS

1. p. 630	**8.** pp. 632–633	**15.** p. 638
2. p. 630	**9.** pp. 632–633	**16.** p. 638
3. p. 631	**10.** pp. 633–634	**17.** pp. 638–639
4. p. 631	**11.** pp. 634–635	**18.** p. 639
5. pp. 631–632	**12.** p. 635	**19.** pp. 639–640
6. p. 632	**13.** p. 636	**20.** pp. 640–641
7. p. 632	**14.** pp. 636–637	

Money Creation

Chapter 31 explained the institutional structure of banking in the United States today, the functions which banks and the other depository institutions and money perform, and the composition of the money supply. Chapter 32 explains how banks create money—**checkable-deposits**—and the factors that determine and limit the money-creating ability of commercial banks. The other depository institutions, such as thrift institutions, also create checkable deposits, but this chapter focuses on the commercial banks to simplify the discussion.

The convenient and simple device used to explain commercial banking operations and money creation is the **balance sheet.** Shown within it are the **assets, liabilities,** and **net worth** of commercial banks. All banking transactions affect this balance sheet. The first step to understanding how money is created is to understand how various simple and typical transactions affect the commercial bank balance sheet.

In reading this chapter you must analyze for yourself the effect of each and every banking transaction discussed on the balance sheet. The important items in the balance sheet are checkable deposits and reserves because **checkable deposits are money.** The ability of a bank to create new checkable deposits is determined by the amount of reserves the bank has. Expansion of the money supply depends on the possession by commercial banks of excess reserves. They do not appear explicitly in the balance sheet but do appear there implicitly because **excess reserves** are the difference between the **actual reserves** and the **required reserves** of commercial banks.

Two cases—the single commercial bank and the banking system—are presented to help you build an understanding of banking and money creation. It is important to understand that the money-creating potential of a single commercial bank differs from the money-creating potential of the entire banking system. It is equally important to understand how the money-creating ability of many single commercial banks is **multiplied** and influences the **money-creating ability** of the banking system as a whole.

■ CHECKLIST

When you have studied this chapter you should be able to

☐ Recount the story of how goldsmiths came to issue paper money and became bankers who created money and held fractional reserves.

☐ Cite two significant characteristics of the fractional reserve banking system today.

☐ Define the basic items in a bank's balance sheet.

☐ Describe what happens to a bank's balance sheet when the bank is created, it buys property and equipment, and it accepts deposits.

☐ Explain the effects of the deposit of currency in a checking account on the composition and size of the money supply.

☐ Define the reserve ratio.

☐ Compute a bank's required and excess reserves when you are given the needed balance-sheet figures.

☐ Explain why a commercial bank is required to maintain a reserve and why a required reserve is not sufficient to protect the depositors from losses.

☐ Indicate whether required reserves are assets or liabilities for commercial banks and the Federal Reserve.

☐ Describe how the deposit of a check drawn on one commercial bank and deposited into another will affect the reserves and excess reserves of the two banks.

☐ Show what happens to the money supply when a commercial bank makes a loan.

☐ Show what happens to the money supply when a commercial bank buys government securities.

☐ Describe what would happen to a commercial bank's reserves if it made loans (or bought government securities) in an amount greater than its excess reserves.

☐ State the money-creating potential of a commercial bank (the amount of money a commercial bank can safely create by lending or buying securities).

☐ Explain how a commercial bank's balance sheet reflects the banker's pursuit of the two conflicting goals of profit and liquidity.

☐ Explain how the Federal funds market helps reconcile the goals of profits and liquidity for commercial banks.

☐ State the money-creating potential of the banking system.

☐ Explain how it is possible for the banking system to create an amount of money that is a multiple of its excess reserves when no individual commercial bank ever creates money in an amount greater than its excess reserve.

☐ Define the monetary multiplier.

☐ Use the monetary multiplier and the amount of excess reserves to compute the money-creating potential of the banking system.

☐ Illustrate with an example using the monetary multiplier how money can be destroyed in the banking system.

☐ Discuss how bank panics during the early 1930s led to a contraction of the nation's money supply and worsened economic conditions (Last Word).

■ **CHAPTER OUTLINE**

1. The United States has a *fractional reserve banking system.* This term means that banks only keep a part or a fraction of their checkable deposits backed by cash reserves.

   a. The history of the early goldsmiths illustrates how paper money came into use in the economy and how banks create money. The goldsmiths accepted gold as deposits and began making loans and issuing money in excess of their gold holdings.

   b. The goldsmiths' fractional reserve system is similar to today's fractional reserve banking system, which has two significant characteristics: banks can create money in such a system and banks are subject to "panics" or "runs," and thus need government regulation.

2. The *balance sheet* of a single commercial bank is a statement of the *assets, liabilities,* and *net worth* (stock shares) of the bank at a specific time; and in the balance sheet, the bank's assets equal its liabilities plus its net worth. This balance sheet changes with various transactions.

   a. *Transaction 1: Creating a bank.* A commercial bank is founded by selling shares of stock and obtaining cash in return. Stock is a liability and cash is an asset.

   b. *Transaction 2: Acquiring property and equipment.* A commercial bank needs property and equipment to carry on the banking business. They are assets of the bank.

   c. *Transaction 3: Accepting deposits.* When a bank accepts deposits of cash, the cash becomes an asset to the bank, and checkable deposit accounts that are created are a liability. The deposit of cash in the bank does not affect the total money supply. It only changes its composition by substituting checkable deposits for currency (cash) in circulation.

   d. *Transaction 4: Depositing reserves in the Federal Reserve Bank.*

   (1) Three reserve concepts are vital to an understanding of the money-creating potential of a commercial bank.

   (a) The *required reserves,* which a bank *must* maintain at its Federal Reserve Bank (or as *vault cash* at the bank—which can be ignored in this textbook example), equal the reserve ratio multiplied by the checkable deposit liabilities of the commercial bank.

   (b) The *actual reserves* of a commercial bank are its deposits at the Federal Reserve Bank (plus the vault cash which is ignored in this textbook example).

   (c) The *excess reserves* are equal to the actual reserves less the required reserves.

   (2) The *reserve ratio* is the ratio of required reserves to a bank's own checkable deposit liabilities. The Fed has the authority to establish and change the ratio within limits set by Congress.

   e. *Transaction 5: Clearing a check drawn against the bank.* The writing of a check on the bank and its deposit in a second bank results in a loss of reserves (assets) and checkable deposits (liabilities) for the first bank and a gain in reserves and deposits for the second bank.

3. A **single commercial bank** in a multibank system can create money as the following two additional transactions show.

   a. *Transaction 6: Granting a loan.* When a single commercial bank grants a loan to a borrower, its balance sheet changes. Checkable deposit liabilities are increased by the amount of the loan and the loan value is entered as an asset. In essence, the borrower gives an IOU (a promise to repay the loan) to the bank, and in return the bank creates money by giving the borrower checkable deposits. The bank has "monetized" the IOU and created money. When the borrower writes a check for the amount of the loan to pay for something and that check clears, then the checkable deposits are reduced by the amount of that check. A bank lends its funds only in an amount equal to its preloan excess reserves because it fears the loss of reserves to other commercial banks in the economy.

   b. *Transaction 7. Buying government securities.* When a bank buys government securities, it increases its own checkable deposit liabilities and therefore the supply of money by the amount of the securities purchase. The bank assets increase by the amount of the securities it now holds. The bank buys securities only in an amount equal to its excess reserves because it fears the loss of reserves to other commercial banks in the economy.

   c. An individual commercial bank balances its desire for profits (which result from the making of loans and the purchase of securities) with its desire for liquidity or safety (which it achieves by having excess reserves or vault cash). The Federal funds market allows banks with excess reserves to lend funds overnight to banks that are short of required reserves. The interest rate paid on the overnight loans is the *Federal funds rate.*

4. The ability of a **banking system** composed of many individual commercial banks to lend and create money is a multiple (greater than 1) of its excess reserves and is equal to the excess reserves of the banking system multiplied by the checkable-deposit (or monetary) multiplier.

   a. The banking system as a whole can do this even though no single commercial bank ever lends an amount greater than its excess reserves because the banking system, unlike a single commercial bank, does not lose reserves. If a bank receives a deposit of currency, it increases its checkable deposits. This change increases the amount of excess reserves the bank has available for loan. If a loan is made on these excess reserves, then it creates additional checkable deposits that, when spent, may be deposited in another bank. That other bank now has additional excess reserves and can increase its lending, and so the process continues.

   b. The *monetary multiplier* is equal to the reciprocal of the required reserve ratio for checkable deposits. The maximum expansion of checkable deposits is equal to the initial excess reserves in the banking system times the monetary multiplier. To illustrate, if the required reserve ratio was 20 percent, then the monetary multiplier would be 5 (or 1 divided by .20). If excess reserves in the banking system were $80 million, then a maximum of $400 million in money could be created (or, 5 times $80 million).

c. The money-creating process of the banking system can also be reversed. When loans are paid off, money is destroyed.

5. (Last Word). During the early 1930s, more than 6,000 banks failed within three years. This resulted in a multiple contraction of the nation's money supply that totaled about 25 percent. The decline in the money supply contributed to the Great Depression. In 1933, banks were shut for a week for a bank holiday and a deposit insurance program was established to give confidence to bank depositors and to reduce the potential for panics, bank runs, and large withdrawals of deposits.

■ HINTS AND TIPS

1. Note that several terms are used interchangeably in this chapter: "commercial bank" (or "bank") is sometimes called "thrift institution" or "depository institution."

2. A bank's balance sheet must balance. The bank's assets are either claimed by owners (net worth) or by nonowners (liabilities). *Assets = liabilities + net worth.*

3. Make a running balance sheet in writing for yourself as you read about each of the eight transactions in the text for the Wahoo Bank. Then determine if you understand the material by telling yourself (or a friend) the story for each transaction without using the text.

4. The **maximum amount of checkable-deposit expansion** is determined by multiplying two factors: the excess reserves by the monetary multiplier. Each factor, however, is affected by the required reserve ratio. The monetary multiplier is calculated by dividing 1 by the required reserve ratio. Excess reserves are determined by multiplying the required reserve ratio by the amount of new deposits. Thus, a change in the required reserve ratio will change the monetary multiplier and the amount of excess reserves. For example, a required reserve ratio of 25% gives a monetary multiplier of 4. For $100 in new money deposited, required reserves are $25 and excess reserves are $75. The maximum checkable-deposit expansion is $300 (4 × $75). If the reserve ratio drops to 20%, the monetary multiplier is 5 and excess reserves are $80, so the maximum checkable-deposit expansion is $400. Both factors have changed.

5. Be aware that the monetary multiplier can result in *money destruction* as well as money creation in the banking system. You should know how the monetary multiplier reinforces effects in one direction or the other.

■ IMPORTANT TERMS

fractional reserve banking
  system
balance sheet
vault cash
required reserves
reserve ratio

excess reserves
actual reserves
Federal funds rate
monetary multiplier

SELF-TEST

■ FILL-IN QUESTIONS

1. The banking system used today is a (total, fractional) _____ reserve system, which means that (100%, less than 100%) _____ of the money deposited in a bank is kept on reserve.

2. There are two significant characteristics to the banking system of today. Banks can create (reserves, money) _____ depending on the amount of _____ they hold. Banks are susceptible to (panics, regulation) _____ or "runs," and to prevent this situation from happening, banks are subject to government _____.

3. The balance sheet of a commercial bank is a statement of the bank's (gold account, assets) _____, the claims of the owners of the bank, called (net worth, liabilities) _____, and claims of the nonowners, called _____. This relationship would be written in equation form as: _____.

4. The coins and paper money that a bank has in its possession are (petty, vault) _____ cash or (till, capital) _____ money.

5. When a person deposits cash in a commercial bank and receives a checkable deposit in return, the size of the money supply has (increased, decreased, not changed) _____.

6. The legal reserve of a commercial bank (ignoring vault cash) must be kept on deposit at (a branch of the U.S. Treasury, its district Federal Reserve Bank) _____.

7. The reserve ratio is equal to the commercial bank's (required, gold) _____ reserves divided by its checkable-deposit (assets, liabilities) _____.

8. The authority to establish and vary the reserve ratio within limits legislated by Congress is given to the (U.S. Treasury, Fed) _____.

9. If commercial banks are allowed to accept (or create) deposits in excess of their reserves, the banking system is operating under a system of (fractional, currency) _____ reserves.

10. The excess reserves of a commercial bank equal its (actual, required) _____ reserves minus its _____ reserves.

11. The basic purpose for having member banks deposit a legal reserve in the Federal Reserve Bank in their district is to provide (liquidity for, control of) _____ the banking system by the Fed.

12. When a commercial bank deposits a legal reserve in its district Federal Reserve Bank, the reserve is (a liability, an asset) _____ to the commercial bank and _____ to the Federal Reserve Bank.

13. When a check is drawn on Bank X, deposited in Bank Y, and cleared, the reserves of Bank X are (increased, decreased, not changed) _____ and the reserves of Bank Y are _____; deposits in Bank X are (increased, decreased, not changed) _____ and deposits in Bank Y are _____.

14. A single commercial bank in a multibank system can safely make loans or buy government securities equal in amount to the (required, excess) _____ reserves of that commercial bank.

15. When a commercial bank makes a new loan of $10,000, the supply of money (increases, decreases) _____ by $ _____. When a commercial bank buys a $10,000 government bond from a securities dealer, the supply of money (increases, decreases) _____ by $ _____.

16. A bank ordinarily pursues two conflicting goals; one goal is the desire to make money, or (profits, liquidity) _____, and the other goal is the need for safety, or _____.

17. When a bank lends temporary excess reserves held at its Federal Reserve Bank to other commercial banks that are temporarily short of legal reserves, it is participating in the (government securities, Federal funds) _____ market. The interest rate paid on these overnight loans is called the (government securities, Federal funds) _____ rate.

18. The monetary multiplier is equal to 1 divided by the (excess, required) _____ reserve ratio. The greater the reserve ratio, the (larger, smaller) _____ the monetary multiplier.

19. The banking system can make loans (or buy government securities) and create money in an amount equal to its (required, excess) _____ reserves multiplied by the (required reserve ratio, monetary multiplier) _____.

20. Assume that the required reserve ratio is 16.67% and the banking system is $6 million short of required reserves. If the banking system is unable to increase its reserves, the banking system must (increase, decrease) _____ the money supply by ($6, $36) _____ million.

■ **TRUE–FALSE QUESTIONS**

Circle T if the statement is true, F if it is false.

1. Goldsmiths increased the money supply when they accepted deposits of gold and issued paper receipts to the depositors.　**T　F**

2. Modern banking systems use gold as the basis for the fractional reserve system.　**T　F**

3. The balance sheet of a commercial bank shows the transactions in which the bank has engaged during a given period of time.　**T　F**

4. A commercial bank's assets plus its net worth equal the bank's liabilities.　**T　F**

5. Cash held by a bank is sometimes called vault cash.　**T　F**

6. When a bank accepts deposits of cash and puts them into a checking account, there has been a change in the composition of the money supply.　**T　F**

7. A commercial bank may maintain its legal reserve either as a deposit in its Federal Reserve Bank or as government bonds in its own vault.　**T　F**

8. The required reserves that a commercial bank maintains must equal its own checkable-deposit liabilities multiplied by the required reserve ratio.　**T　F**

9. The actual reserves of a commercial bank equal excess reserves plus required reserves.　**T　F**

10. Required reserves are sufficient to meet demands for the return of all funds that are held as checkable deposits at commercial banks.　**T　F**

11. Required reserves help the Fed control the lending ability of commercial banks.　**T　F**

12. The reserve of a commercial bank in the Federal Reserve Bank is an asset of the Federal Reserve Bank.　**T　F**

13. A check for $1000 drawn on Bank X by a depositor and deposited in bank Y will increase the excess reserves in Bank Y by $1000.　**T　F**

14. A bank that has a check drawn and collected against it will lose to the recipient both reserves and deposits equal to the value of the check.　**T　F**

15. When Manfred Iron and Coal Company borrows $30,000 from a bank, the money supply has increased by $30,000.　**T　F**

16. A single commercial bank can safely lend an amount equal to its excess reserves multiplied by the monetary multiplier ratio.　**T　F**

17. The granting of a $5000 loan and the purchase of a $5000 government bond from a securities dealer by a commercial bank have the same effect on the money supply.　**T　F**

18. The selling of a government bond by a commercial bank will increase the money supply.　**T　F**

19. A commercial bank seeks both profits and liquidity, but these are conflicting goals.　　　**T　F**

20. The Federal funds rate is the interest rate at which the Federal government lends funds to commercial banks.　　　**T　F**

21. The reason that the banking system can lend by a multiple of its excess reserves, but each individual bank can only lend "dollar for dollar" with its excess reserves, is that reserves lost by a single bank are not lost to the banking system as a whole.　　　**T　F**

22. The monetary multiplier is excess reserves divided by required reserves.　　　**T　F**

23. The maximum checkable-deposit expansion is equal to excess reserves divided by the monetary multiplier.　**T　F**

24. If the banking system has $10 million in excess reserves and if the reserve ratio is 25%, the system can increase its loans by $40 million.　　　**T　F**

25. When a borrower repays a loan of $500, either in cash or by check, the supply of money is reduced by $500.　　　**T　F**

■ **MULTIPLE-CHOICE QUESTIONS**

Circle the letter that corresponds to the best answer.

1. The fractional reserve system of banking started when goldsmiths began
(a) accepting deposits of gold for safe storage
(b) issuing receipts for the gold stored with them
(c) using deposited gold to produce products for sale to others
(d) issuing paper money in excess of the amount of gold stored with them

2. The claims of the owners of the bank against the bank's assets is the bank's
(a) net worth
(b) liabilities
(c) balance sheet
(d) fractional reserves

3. When cash is deposited in a checkable-deposit account in a commercial bank, there is
(a) a decrease in the money supply
(b) an increase in the money supply
(c) no change in the composition of the money supply
(d) a change in the composition of the money supply

4. A commercial bank has actual reserves of $9000 and liabilities of $30,000, and the required reserve ratio is 20%. The excess reserves of the bank are
(a) $3000
(b) $6000
(c) $7500
(d) $9000

5. The primary reason commercial banks must keep required reserves on deposit at Federal Reserve Banks is to
(a) protect the deposits in the commercial bank against losses
(b) provide the means by which checks drawn on the commercial bank and deposited in other commercial banks can be collected
(c) add to the liquidity of the commercial bank and protect it against a "run" on the bank
(d) provide the Fed with a means of controlling the lending ability of the commercial bank

6. Reserves that a commercial bank deposits at a Federal Reserve Bank are
(a) an asset to the Federal Reserve Bank and a liability of the commercial bank
(b) an asset of the commercial bank and a liability of the Federal Reserve Bank
(c) used as insurance funds for the Federal Deposit Insurance Corporation
(d) used as insurance for the National Credit Union Administration

7. A depositor places $750 in cash in a commercial bank, and the reserve ratio is 33.33%; the bank sends the $750 to the Federal Reserve Bank. As a result, the *actual reserves* and the *excess reserves* of the bank have been increased, respectively, by
(a) $750 and $250
(b) $750 and $500
(c) $750 and $750
(d) $500 and $500

8. A bank that has a check drawn and collected against it will
(a) lose to the recipient bank both reserves and deposits
(b) gain from the recipient bank both reserves and deposits
(c) lose to the recipient bank reserves, but gain deposits
(d) gain from the recipient bank reserves, but lose deposits

9. A commercial bank has no excess reserves until a depositor places $600 in cash in the bank. The bank then adds the $600 to its reserves by sending it to the Federal Reserve Bank. The commercial bank then lends $300 to a borrower. As a consequence of these transactions, the size of the money supply has
(a) not been affected
(b) increased by $300
(c) increased by $600
(d) increased by $900

10. A commercial bank has excess reserves of $500 and a required reserve ratio of 20%; it grants a loan of $1000 to a borrower. If the borrower writes a check for $1000 that is deposited in another commercial bank, the first bank will be short of reserves, after the check has been cleared, in the amount of
(a) $200
(b) $500
(c) $700
(d) $1000

11. The buying of government securities by commercial banks is most similar to the
(a) making of loans by banks because both actions increase the money supply
(b) making of loans by banks because both actions decrease the money supply
(c) repayment of loans to banks because both actions decrease the money supply
(d) repayment of loans to banks because both actions increase the money supply

12. A commercial bank sells a $1000 government security to a securities dealer. The dealer pays for the bond in cash, which the bank adds to its vault cash. The money supply has
(a) not been affected
(b) decreased by $1000
(c) increased by $1000
(d) increased by $1000 multiplied by the reciprocal of the required reserve ratio

13. A commercial bank has deposit liabilities of $100,000, reserves of $37,000, and a required reserve ratio of 25%. The amount by which a *single commercial bank* and the amount by which the *banking system* can increase loans are, respectively
(a) $12,000 and $48,000
(b) $17,000 and $68,000
(c) $12,000 and $60,000
(d) $17,000 and $85,000

14. If the required reserve ratio were 12.5%, the value of the monetary multiplier would be
(a) 5
(b) 6
(c) 7
(d) 8

15. The commercial banking system has excess reserves of $700, makes new loans of $2100, and is just meeting its reserve requirements. The required reserve ratio is
(a) 20%
(b) 25%
(c) 30%
(d) 33.33%

16. The commercial banking system, because of a recent change in the required reserve ratio from 20% to 30%, finds that it is $60 million short of reserves. If it is unable to obtain any additional reserves it must decrease the money supply by
(a) $60 million
(b) $180 million
(c) $200 million
(d) $300 million

17. Only one commercial bank in the banking system has an excess reserve, and its excess reserve is $100,000. This bank makes a new loan of $80,000 and keeps an excess reserve of $20,000. If the required reserve ratio for all banks is 20%, the potential expansion of the money supply from this $80,000 loan is
(a) $80,000
(b) $100,000

(c) $400,000
(d) $500,000

Use the following balance sheet for the First National Bank to answer Questions 18, 19, 20, 21, and 22. Assume the required reserve ratio is 20%.

Assets		Liabilities and Net Worth	
Reserves	$ 50,000	Checkable deposits	$150,000
Loans	70,000	Stock shares	100,000
Securities	30,000		
Property	100,000		

18. This commercial bank has excess reserves of
(a) $10,000
(b) $20,000
(c) $30,000
(d) $40,000

19. This bank can safely expand its loans by a maximum of
(a) $50,000
(b) $40,000
(c) $30,000
(d) $20,000

20. Using the original bank balance sheet, assume that the bank makes a loan of $10,000 and has a check cleared against it for the amount of the loan; its reserves and checkable deposits will now be
(a) $40,000 and $140,000
(b) $40,000 and $150,000
(c) $30,000 and $150,000
(d) $60,000 and $140,000

21. Using the original bank balance sheet, assume that the bank makes a loan of $15,000 and has a check cleared against it for the amount of the loan; it will then have excess reserves of
(a) $5,000
(b) $10,000
(c) $15,000
(d) $20,000

22. If the original bank balance sheet was for the commercial banking *system*, rather than a single bank, loans and deposits could have been expanded by a maximum of
(a) $50,000
(b) $100,000
(c) $150,000
(d) $200,000

Answer Questions 23 and 24 on the basis of the following consolidated balance sheet for the commercial banking system. All figures are in billions. Assume that the required reserve ratio is 12.5%.

Assets		Liabilities and Net Worth	
Reserves	$ 40	Checkable deposits	$200
Loans	80	Stock shares	120
Securities	100		
Property	200		

23. The maximum amount by which this commercial banking system can expand the supply of money by lending is
- **(a)** $120 billion
- **(b)** $240 billion
- **(c)** $350 billion
- **(d)** $440 billion

24. If there is a deposit of $20 billion of new currency into checking accounts in the banking system, excess reserves will increase by
- **(a)** $16.5 billion
- **(b)** $17.0 billion
- **(c)** $17.5 billion
- **(d)** $18.5 billion

25. If the dollar amount of loans made in some period is less than the dollar amount of loans paid off, checkable deposits will
- **(a)** expand and the money supply will increase
- **(b)** expand and the money supply will decrease
- **(c)** contract and the money supply will decrease
- **(d)** contract and the money supply will increase

■ PROBLEMS

1. The following table shows the simplified balance sheet of a commercial bank. Assume that the figures given show the bank's assets and checkable-deposit liabilities *prior to each of the following four transactions.* Draw up the balance sheet as it would appear after each of these transactions is completed and place the balance-sheet figures in the appropriate column. Do *not* use the figures you place in columns **a**, **b**, and **c** when you work the next part of the problem; start all parts of the problem with the printed figures.

		(a)	(b)	(c)	(d)
Assets:					
Cash	$100	$____	$____	$____	$____
Reserves	200	____	____	____	____
Loans	500	____	____	____	____
Securities	200	____	____	____	____
Liabilities and net worth:					
Checkable deposits	900	____	____	____	____
Stock shares	100	100	100	100	100

a. A check for $50 is drawn by one of the depositors of the bank, given to a person who deposits it in another bank, and cleared (column a).
b. A depositor withdraws $50 in cash from the bank, and the bank restores its vault cash by obtaining $50 in additional cash from its Federal Reserve Bank (column b).
c. A check for $60 drawn on another bank is deposited in this bank and cleared (column c).
d. The bank sells $100 in government bonds to the Federal Reserve Bank in its district (column d).

2. Following are five balance sheets for a single commercial bank (columns 1a–5a). The required reserve ratio is 20%.

a. Compute the required reserves (A), ignoring vault cash, the excess reserves (B) of the bank (if the bank is short of reserves and must reduce its loans or obtain additional reserves, show this by placing a minus sign in front of the amounts by which it is short of reserves), and the amount of new loans it can extend (C).

	(1a)	(2a)	(3a)	(4a)	(5a)
Assets:					
Cash	$ 10	$ 20	$ 20	$ 20	$ 15
Reserves	40	40	25	40	45
Loans	100	100	100	100	150
Securities	50	60	30	70	60
Liabilities and net worth:					
Checkable deposits	175	200	150	180	220
Stock shares	25	20	25	50	50
A. Required reserves	$____	$____	$____	$____	$____
B. Excess reserves	____	____	____	____	____
C. New loans	____	____	____	____	____

b. In the following table, draw up for the individual bank the five balance sheets as they appear after the bank has made the new loans that it is capable of making.

	(1b)	(2b)	(3b)	(4b)	(5b)
Assets:					
Cash	$____	$____	$____	$____	$____
Reserves	____	____	____	____	____
Loans	____	____	____	____	____
Securities	____	____	____	____	____
Liabilities and net worth:					
Checkable deposits	____	____	____	____	____
Stock shares	____	____	____	____	____

3. The following table shows several reserve ratios. Compute the monetary multiplier for each reserve ratio and enter the figures in column 2. In column 3 show the maximum amount by which a single commercial bank can increase its loans for each dollar's worth of excess reserves it possesses. In column 4 indicate the maximum amount by which the banking system can increase its loans for each dollar's worth of excess reserves in the system.

(1)	(2)	(3)	(4)
12.50%	$____	$____	$____
16.67	____	____	____
20	____	____	____
25	____	____	____
30	____	____	____
33.33	____	____	____

4. The table in the next column is the simplified consolidated balance sheet for all commercial banks in the economy. Assume that the figures given show the banks' assets and liabilities *prior to each of the following three transactions* and that the reserve ratio is 20%. Do *not* use the figures you placed in columns 2 and 4 when you begin parts **b** and **c** of the problem; start parts **a**, **b**, and **c** of the problem with the printed figures.

		(1)	(2)	(3)	(4)	(5)	(6)
Assets:							
Cash	$ 50	$___	$___	$___	$___	$___	$___
Reserves	100	___	___	___	___	___	___
Loans	200	___	___	___	___	___	___
Securities	200	___	___	___	___	___	___
Liabilities and net worth:							
Checkable deposits	500	___	___	___	___	___	___
Stock shares	50	50	50	50	50	50	50
Loans for Federal Reserve	0	___	___	___	___	___	___
Excess reserves		___	___	___	___	___	___
Maximum possible expansion of the money supply		___	___	___	___	___	___

a. The public deposits $5 in cash in the banks and the banks send the $5 to the Federal Reserve, where it is added to their reserves. Fill in column 1. If the banking system extends the maximum amount of new loans that it is capable of extending, show in column 2 the balance sheet as it would then appear.

b. The banking system sells $8 worth of securities to the Federal Reserve. Complete column 3. Assuming the system extends the maximum amount of credit of which it is capable, fill in column 4.

c. The Federal Reserve lends $10 to the commercial banks; complete column 5. Complete column 6 showing the condition of the banks after the maximum amount of new loans that the banks are capable of making is granted.

■ **SHORT ANSWER AND ESSAY QUESTIONS**

1. How did the early goldsmiths come to issue paper money and then become bankers?

2. Explain the difference between a 100% and fractional reserve system of banking.

3. What are two significant characteristics of a fractional reserve system of banking?

4. Why does a bank's balance sheet balance?

5. Explain what happens to the money supply when a bank accepts deposits of cash.

6. What are legal reserves? How are they determined? How are legal reserves related to the reserve ratio?

7. Define the meaning of excess reserves. How are they calculated?

8. Explain why bank reserves can be an asset to the depositing commercial bank but a liability to the Federal Reserve Bank receiving them.

9. Do the reserves held by commercial banks satisfactorily protect the bank's depositors? Are the reserves of commercial banks needed? Explain your answers.

10. The owner of a sporting goods store writes a check on her account in a Kent, Ohio, bank and sends it to one of her suppliers who deposits it in his bank in Cleveland, Ohio. How does the Cleveland bank obtain payment from the Kent bank? If the two banks were in Kent and New York City, how would one bank pay the other? How are the excess reserves of the two banks affected?

11. Explain why the granting of a loan by a commercial bank increases the supply of money.

12. Why is a single commercial bank able to lend safely only an amount equal to its excess reserves?

13. How does the buying or selling of government securities by commercial banks influence the money supply?

14. Commercial banks seek both profits and safety. Explain how the balance sheet of the commercial banks reflects the desires of bankers for profits and for liquidity.

15. What is the Federal funds rate?

16. Discuss how the Federal funds market helps banks reconcile the two goals of profits and liquidity.

17. No one commercial bank ever lends an amount greater than its excess reserves, but the banking system as a whole is able to extend loans and expand the money supply by an amount equal to the system's excess reserves multiplied by the reciprocal of the reserve ratio. Explain why this is possible and how the multiple expansion of deposits and money takes place.

18. What is the monetary multiplier? How does it work?

19. What would happen to maximum checkable-deposit creation if the reserve ratio increased or if the reserve ratio decreased? Explain using numerical examples.

20. Why does the repayment of a loan decrease the supply of money?

ANSWERS

Chapter 32 Money Creation

FILL-IN QUESTIONS

1. fractional, less than 100%
2. money, reserves, panics, regulation
3. assets, net worth, liabilities, assets = liabilities + net worth
4. vault, till
5. not changed
6. its district Federal Reserve Bank
7. required, liabilities
8. Fed
9. fractional
10. actual, required
11. control of
12. an asset, a liability
13. decreased, increased, decreased, increased
14. excess
15. increases, 10,000, increases, 10,000
16. profits, liquidity
17. Federal funds, Federal funds
18. required, smaller
19. excess, monetary multiplier
20. decrease, $36

TRUE–FALSE QUESTIONS

1. F, p. 646	**14.** T, pp. 649–650
2. F, p. 646	**15.** T, pp. 650–651
3. F, p. 647	**16.** F, pp. 650–651
4. F, p. 647	**17.** T, p. 652
5. T, p. 647	**18.** F, p. 652
6. F, p. 648	**19.** T, p. 652
7. F, pp. 648–649	**20.** F, p. 652
8. T, p. 648	**21.** T, p. 653
9. T, p. 649	**22.** F, p. 655
10. F, p. 649	**23.** F, p. 655
11. T, p. 649	**24.** T, p. 655
12. F, p. 649	**25.** T, p. 657
13. F, pp. 649–650	

MULTIPLE-CHOICE QUESTIONS

1. d, p. 646	**14.** d, p. 655
2. a, p. 647	**15.** d, p. 655
3. d, p. 648	**16.** c, p. 655
4. a, p. 649	**17.** c, p. 655
5. d, p. 649	**18.** b, p. 649
6. b, p. 649	**19.** d, p. 649
7. b, p. 649	**20.** b, pp. 649–651
8. a, pp.649–650	**21.** a, pp. 649–651
9. b, pp. 650–651	**22.** b, pp. 653–655
10. b, pp. 650–651	**23.** a, p. 655
11. a, p. 652	**24.** c, pp. 653–655
12. b, p. 652	**25.** c, p. 657
13. a, pp. 653–654	

PROBLEMS

1. Table

	(a)	(b)	(c)	(d)
Assets:				
Cash	$100	$100	$100	$100
Reserves	150	150	260	300
Loans	500	500	500	500
Securities	200	200	200	100
Liabilities and net worth:				
Checkable deposits	850	850	960	900
Stock shares	100	100	100	100

2. *a.* Table (and * below)

	(1a)	(2a)	(3a)	(4a)	(5a)
A. Required reserves	$35	$40	$30	$36	$44
B. Excess reserves	5	0	−5	4	1
C. New loans	5	0	*	4	1

b. Table (and * below)

	(1b)	(2b)	(3b)	(4b)	(5b)
Assets:					
Cash	$ 10	$ 20	$ 20	$ 20	$ 15
Reserves	40	40	25	40	45
Loans	105	100	*	104	151
Securities	50	60	30	70	60
Liabilities and net worth:					
Checkable deposits	180	200	*	184	221
Stock shares	25	20	25	50	50

*If an individual bank is $5 short of reserves it must either obtain additional reserves of $5 by selling loans, securities, or its own IOUs to the reserve bank or contract its loans by $25.

3. Table

(1)	(2)	(3)	(4)
12.50%	$8	$1	$8
16.67	$6	1	$6
20	$5	1	$5
25	$4	1	$4
30	$3.33	1	$3.33
33.33	$3	1	$3

4. Table

	(1)	(2)	(3)	(4)	(5)	(6)
Assets:						
Cash	$ 50	$ 50	$ 50	$ 50	$ 50	$ 50
Reserves	105	105	110	110	110	110
Loans	200	220	200	250	200	250
Securities	200	200	200	200	200	200
Liabilities and net worth:						
Checkable deposits	505	525	500	550	500	550
Stock shares	50	50	50	50	50	50
Loans from Federal Reserve	0	0	10	10	10	10
Excess reserves	4	0	10	0	10	0
Maximum possible expansion of the money supply	20	0	50	0	50	0

SHORT ANSWER AND ESSAY QUESTIONS

1. p. 646
2. p. 646
3. p. 646
4. p. 649
5. pp. 647–648
6. p. 648
7. p. 649
8. p. 649
9. p. 649
10. pp. 649–650

11. pp. 650–651
12. p. 651
13. p. 652
14. p. 653
15. p. 653
16. p. 653
17. pp. 653–655
18. p. 655
19. p. 655
20. p. 657

Interest Rates and Monetary Policy

Chapter 33 is the third chapter dealing with money and banking. It explains how the Federal Reserve affects output, income, employment, and the price level of the economy. Central bank policy designed to affect these variables is called **monetary policy,** the goal of which is price-level stability, full employment, and economic growth.

The work of the Fed focuses on the interest rate and supply and demand in the market for money. The total **demand for money** is made up of a **transactions demand** and an **asset demand** for money. Because money is used as a medium of exchange, consumers and business firms wish to hold money for transaction purposes. The quantity of money they demand for this purpose is directly related to the size of the economy's nominal GDP.

Money also is used as a store of value that creates an asset demand. Consumers and businesses who own assets may choose to have some of their assets in the form of money (rather than in stocks, bonds, goods, or property). Holding money, however, imposes a cost on those who hold it. This cost is the interest they lose when they own money rather than an interest-earning asset such as a bond. Consumers and businesses will demand less money for asset purposes when the rate of interest (the cost of holding money) is high and demand more money when the rate of interest is low; the quantity of money demanded as an asset is inversely related to the interest rate.

The total demand for money is the sum of the transactions demand and the asset demand. It is affected by both nominal GDP and the rate of interest. The total demand and the supply of money determine interest rates in the market for money. The inverse relationship between bond prices and interest rates helps this market adjust to shortages or surpluses of money.

The chapter explains how the Federal Reserve achieves its basic goal. In this discussion, attention should be paid to the following: (1) the important items on the balance sheet of the Federal Reserve Banks; and (2) the four major controls available to the Federal Reserve, and how the employment of these controls can affect the reserves, excess reserves, actual money supply, and money-creating potential of the banking system. The most important control is the buying and selling of government securities in the open market.

The Federal Reserve targets the Federal funds rate because it is the interest rate it can best control. This rate is the interest rate that banks charge each other on overnight loans of temporary excess reserves. The Federal Reserve uses open-market operations to sell government securities and this increases the excess reserves of banks, thus lowering the Federal funds rate. In this case, the Federal Reserve is pursuing an expansionary monetary policy that increases the money supply and decreases interest rates. Conversely, the Federal Reserve can buy government securities and decrease excess reserves, and thus raise the Federal funds rate. In this case, the Federal Reserve is pursuing a restrictive monetary policy that decreases the money supply and increases interest rates.

Professors McConnell and Brue follow the discussion of the Federal funds rate with an explanation of how changes in the money supply ultimately affect the economy. They achieve this objective by describing how the demand for money and the supply of money determine the interest rate (in the market for money), and how the interest rate and the investment demand schedule determine the level of equilibrium GDP. The effects of an expansionary monetary policy or a restrictive monetary policy in this cause-effect chain are illustrated with examples and summarized in Table 33.3. Changes in monetary policy shift aggregate demand across the aggregate supply curve, thus changing real output and the price level.

One of the concluding sections of the chapter evaluates monetary policy. The major strengths are related to its speed and flexibility and isolation from political pressures. The Federal Reserve has had many successes since the 1990s in countering recession by lowering the interest rate and in controlling inflation by raising the interest rate.

Monetary policy, however, is not without its problems or complications. There can be lags between the time actions are taken and the time the monetary policy influences economic activity. Monetary policy also can suffer from cyclical asymmetry by being more influential in controlling inflation than in preventing recession. There have been debates about whether there should be more or less discretion in the conduct of monetary policy and the adoption of inflation targeting.

The final section on the "Big Picture" is short but important. Figure 33.6 gives you an overview of the economic factors and government policies that affect aggregate demand and aggregate supply. It summarizes much of the economic theory and policy that have been discussed in this chapter and the eight chapters that preceded it.

■ CHECKLIST

When you have studied this chapter you should be able to

☐ Explain what interest is and why it is important.
☐ Give a definition of the transactions demand for money.

☐ Give a definition of the asset demand for money.

☐ Illustrate graphically how the transactions and asset demands for money combine to form the total demand for money.

☐ Describe the market for money and what determines the equilibrium rate of interest.

☐ Explain how changes in nominal GDP and in the money supply affect the interest rate.

☐ Illustrate with an example how disequilibrium in the market for money is corrected through changes in bond prices.

☐ List the important assets and liabilities of the Federal Reserve Banks.

☐ Identify the four tools of monetary policy.

☐ Explain how the Federal Reserve can expand the money supply by buying government securities from commercial banks and from the public.

☐ Explain how the Federal Reserve can contract the money supply by selling government securities to commercial banks and to the public.

☐ Describe how raising or lowering the reserve ratio can increase or decrease the money supply.

☐ Illustrate how raising or lowering the discount rate can increase or decrease the money supply.

☐ Explain how the Federal Reserve uses the term auction facility to alter bank reserves and bank lending.

☐ Discuss the relative importance of monetary policy tools.

☐ Explain how the Federal Reserve uses monetary policy to target the Federal funds rate.

☐ Describe the actions the Fed can take to pursue an expansionary monetary policy.

☐ Describe the relationship between the Federal funds rate and the prime interest rate.

☐ Describe the actions the Fed can take to pursue a restrictive monetary policy.

☐ Explain the Taylor rule and its implications for monetary policy.

☐ Draw the demand-for-money and the supply-of-money curves and use them to show how a change in the supply of money will affect the interest rate in the market for money.

☐ Draw an investment demand curve to explain the effects of changes in the interest rate on investment spending.

☐ Construct an aggregate supply and aggregate demand graph to show how aggregate demand and the equilibrium level of GDP are affected by changes in interest rates and investment spending.

☐ Use a cause-effect chain to explain the links between a change in the money supply and a change in the equilibrium level of GDP when there is an expansionary monetary policy and a restrictive monetary policy.

☐ List several advantages of monetary policy over fiscal policy.

☐ Evaluate recent monetary policy in the United States.

☐ Describe two problems or complications of monetary policy.

☐ Summarize the key factors and policies affecting aggregate supply and demand, and the level of output, employment, income, and prices in an economy using Figure 33.6.

☐ Explain the impact of the mortgage debt crisis (Last Word).

■ **CHAPTER OUTLINE**

1. The fundamental **goal of *monetary policy*** is to achieve and maintain price stability, full employment, and economic growth. The Federal Reserve can accomplish this goal by exercising control over the amount of excess reserves held by commercial banks, and thereby influencing the size of the money supply and the total level of spending in the economy.

2. Interest is the price paid for the use of money. Although there are many interest rates, the text uses the generic term "interest rate" for the purposes of this chapter. This interest rate is determined by demand and supply in the market for money.

a. Business firms and households wish to hold and, therefore, demand money for two reasons.

(1) Because they use money as a medium of exchange, they have a ***transactions demand*** for money that is directly related to the nominal gross domestic product (GDP) of the economy.

(2) Because they also use money as a store of value, they have an ***asset demand*** for money that is inversely related to the rate of interest.

(3) Their ***total demand for money*** is the sum of the transactions demand and asset demand for money.

b. In the **market for money,** the demand for money and the supply of money determine the equilibrium interest rate. Graphically, the demand for money is a downsloping line and the supply of money is a vertical line, and their intersection determines the equilibrium interest rate.

c. Disequilibrium in this market is corrected by changes in **bond prices** and their inverse relationship with interest rates.

(1) If there is a decrease in the money supply, there will be a shortage of money, so bonds will be sold to obtain money. The increase in supply of bonds will drive down bond prices, causing interest rates to rise until the shortage of money is eliminated.

(2) If there is an increase in the money supply, there will be a surplus of money, so bonds will be bought. The increased demand for bonds will drive up bond prices, causing interest rates to fall until the surplus of money is eliminated.

3. By examining the consolidated **balance sheet** and the principal assets and liabilities of the Federal Reserve Banks, an understanding of the ways the Federal Reserve can control and influence the reserves of commercial banks and the money supply can be obtained.

a. The principal **assets** of the Federal Reserve Banks are U.S. government securities and loans to commercial banks.

b. The principal **liabilities** are Federal Reserve Notes (outstanding), the reserve deposits of commercial banks, and U.S. Treasury deposits.

4. The Federal Reserve Banks use four principal tools (techniques or instruments) to control the reserves of banks and the size of the money supply.

a. The Federal Reserve can *buy or sell government securities* through its **open-market operations** to change the excess reserves of banks and thus the lending ability of the banking system.

(1) Buying government securities in the open market from either banks or the public increases the excess reserves of banks.

(2) Selling government securities in the open market to either banks or the public decreases the excess reserves of banks.

b. The Federal Reserve can *raise or lower* the **reserve ratio.**

(1) Raising the reserve ratio decreases the excess reserves of banks and the size of the monetary (checkable-deposit) multiplier.

(2) Lowering the reserve ratio increases the excess reserves of banks and the size of the monetary multiplier.

c. The Federal Reserve can *raise or lower* the **discount rate.** Raising the discount rate discourages banks from borrowing reserves from the Fed. Lowering the discount rate encourages banks to borrow from the Fed.

d. The Federal Reserve can auction off to banks the right to borrow reserves for a set period of time (usually 28 days) through its **term auction facility.** Banks submit bids for the amount of desired reserves and the interest rate they would pay for them. The equilibrium interest rate is the lowest rate that brings the quantity demanded and quantity supplied of reserves into balance. The use of such auctions by the Federal Reserve increases the excess reserves of banks.

e. Of the four main monetary tools, open-market operations is the most important because it is the most flexible and direct.

5. The **Federal funds rate,** the interest rate that banks charge each other for overnight loans of excess reserves, is a focus of monetary policy. The Federal Reserve can influence the Federal funds rate by buying or selling government securities. When the Federal Reserve buys bonds, banks have more excess reserves to lend overnight so the Federal funds rate falls. Conversely, when the Federal Reserve sells bonds, banks have fewer excess reserves to lend overnight so the Federal funds rate rises. A graph of the market for Federal funds has the interest rate on the vertical axis and the quantity of reserves on the horizontal axis. The demand for reserves is a downsloping demand curve. The supply of reserves is a horizontal line at the desired rate because the supply of reserves is set by the Federal Reserve.

a. An **expansionary monetary policy** can be implemented by actions of the Federal Reserve to buy government securities in open-market operations to lower the Federal funds rate. This policy expands the money supply, putting downward pressure on other interest rates, and helps to stimulate aggregate demand. The **prime interest rate** is the benchmark rate that banks use to decide on the interest rate for loans to businesses and individuals; it rises and falls with the Federal funds rate.

b. A **restrictive monetary policy** can be implemented by actions of the Federal Reserve to sell government securities in open-market operations that raises the Federal funds rate. This policy contracts the money supply, putting upward pressure on other interest rates, and helps to reduce aggregate demand to maintain a stable price level.

c. The Federal Reserve does not target inflation or follow a monetary rule, but it does appear to be guided by a rule of thumb called the **Taylor rule,** which specifies conditions for raising and lowering the Federal funds rate based on the current rate of inflation and the relationship between potential and real GDP. For example, when real GDP equals potential GDP and the inflation rate is at its Fed target rate of 2 percent, then the Federal funds rate should be 4 percent (or a 2 percent real rate). If real GDP should rise by 1 percent above potential GDP, the *real* Federal funds rate should increase by half a percentage point. Conversely, if real GDP should fall by 1 percent below potential GDP, the real Federal funds rate should decrease by half a percentage point.

6. Monetary policy affects the **equilibrium GDP** in many ways.

a. The cause-effect chain goes from the money market to investment spending to equilibrium GDP (see text Figure 33.5).

(1) In the market for money, the demand curve for money and the supply curve of money determine the real interest rate.

(2) This rate of interest in turn determines investment spending.

(3) Investment spending then affects aggregate demand and the equilibrium levels of real output and prices.

b. If recession or slow economic growth is a major problem, the Federal Reserve can institute an expansionary monetary policy that increases the money supply, causing the interest rate to fall and investment spending to increase, thereby increasing aggregate demand and increasing real GDP by a multiple of the increase in investment.

c. If inflation is the problem, the Federal Reserve can adopt a restrictive monetary policy that decreases the money supply, causing the interest rate to rise and investment spending to decrease, thereby reducing aggregate demand and controlling inflation.

7. Monetary policy is considered more important and valuable for stabilizing the national economy because of its several advantages over fiscal policy: it is quicker and more flexible; and it is more protected from political pressure.

a. Recent U.S. monetary policy has been expansionary and restrictive in response to concerns about recession and inflation (see Figure 33.4 in the textbook).

(1) In late 2000 to late 2002, the Federal Reserve reduced the Federal funds rate to counter an economic

slowdown and recession during that period. The rate was cut again in 2007 in response to the **mortgage debt crisis** and a term auction facility was initiated in December 2007 to increase the reserves of commercial banks.

(2) To curtail inflation, the Federal funds rate was raised from 1999 to late 2000. The rate was also raised from mid-2004 through mid-2006 to contain expected inflation.

b. There are limitations and real-world complications with monetary policy in spite of its successes over the years.

(1) It is subject to a recognition lag between the time the need for the policy is recognized and also an operations lag that occurs between the time the policy is implemented and it begins to influence economic activity.

(2) There is a **cyclical asymmetry** with monetary policy: A restrictive monetary policy works better than an expansionary monetary policy. A restrictive policy seems to work better because the Federal Reserve can easily withdraw and absorb excess reserves from banks and curtail economic activity. An expansionary policy may not work because even when the Federal Reserve makes more reserves available to banks, the economic conditions of recession or slow growth may make businesses hesitant to increase their borrowing and increase their investment spending.

8. The **"big picture" of macroeconomics** shows that the equilibrium levels of output, employment, income, and prices are determined by the interaction of aggregate supply and aggregate demand.

a. There are four expenditure components of aggregate demand: consumption, investment, government spending, and net export spending.

b. There are three major components of aggregate supply: the prices of inputs or resources, factors affecting the productivity with which resources are used, and the legal and institutional environment.

c. Fiscal, monetary, or other government policies may have an effect on the components of aggregate demand or supply, which in turn will affect the level of output, employment, income, and prices.

9. (Last Word). The **mortgage debt crisis** that began in 2007 required the Federal Reserve to take major actions to increase bank reserves to contain the financial disarray and stabilize the economy. The crisis started from defaults on subprime mortgages that had been packaged as bonds and sold as investments to banks and other financial institutions as creditworthy debt. The defaults produced losses that reduced bank reserves. The Federal Reserve responded to the financial crisis by serving as the lender of last resort for banks and lowering the discount rate, by introducing a term auction facility to auction off more reserves for banks, and by reducing the Federal funds rate. Such actions were designed to increase aggregate demand and help the economy counter an economic slowdown and possible recession.

■ HINTS AND TIPS

1. Spend extra time learning how the **total demand for money** is determined (see Figure 33.1 in the text). The total demand for money is composed of the transactions and the asset demands for money. The **transactions demand** for money is influenced by the level of nominal GDP and is not affected by the interest rate, so it *is graphed as a vertical line*. The **asset demand** for money is affected by the interest rate, so it *is graphed as a downsloping curve*. The total demand for money is also graphed as a *downsloping curve* because of the influence of the asset demand, but the curve is shifted farther to the right than the asset demand curve because of the influence of the transactions demand.

2. One of the most difficult concepts to understand is the *inverse* relationship between bond prices and interest rates. The simple explanation is that interest yield from a bond is the ratio of the *fixed* annual interest payment to the bond price. The numerator is fixed, but the denominator (bond price) is variable. If the bond price falls, the interest yield on the bond rises because the fixed annual interest payment is being divided by a smaller denominator.

3. To acquire a thorough knowledge of how the Federal Reserve transactions affect required reserves, excess reserves, the actual money supply, and the potential money supply, carefully study the **balance sheets** that are used to explain these transactions. The items to watch are the reserves and checkable deposits. Be sure that you know why a change is made in each balance sheet, and be able to make the appropriate balance-sheet entries as you trace through the effects of each transaction. Problem 2 in this chapter provides additional practice.

4. You must understand and remember the **cause-effect chain of monetary policy**. The best way to learn it is to draw your own chain (graphs) that shows the links for an expansionary monetary policy and for a restrictive monetary policy as in Figure 33.5. Then check each step for how monetary policy can be used to counter recession or limit inflation using Table 33.3 in the text.

5. The single most important figure for a "big picture" of the macroeconomics part of the textbook is Figure 33.6. It reviews and summarizes the determinants of aggregate supply and demand and identifies the key policy variables that have been discussed in this chapter and previous chapters.

■ IMPORTANT TERMS

monetary policy	expansionary monetary policy
transactions demand	
asset demand	prime interest rate
total demand for money	restrictive monetary policy
reserve ratio	Taylor rule
discount rate	cyclical asymmetry
term auction facility	mortgage debt crisis
Federal funds rate	

SELF-TEST

■ FILL-IN QUESTIONS

1. The goal of monetary policy in the United States is to achieve and maintain stability in the (price level, tax level) _____, a rate of (full, partial) _____ employment in the economy, and economic growth.

2. The transactions demand varies (directly, inversely) _____ with (the rate of interest, nominal GDP) _____, and the asset demand varies (directly, inversely) _____ with (the rate of interest, nominal GDP) _____.

3. The sum of the transactions and asset demands for money is the total (demand, supply) _____ of money, and the intersection of it with the _____ of money determines the equilibrium (interest rate, price level) _____.

4. When the quantity of money demanded exceeds the quantity of money supplied, bond prices (increase, decrease) _____ and interest rates _____. When the quantity of money demanded is less than the quantity of money supplied, bond prices (increase, decrease) _____ and interest rates _____.

5. The two important assets of the Federal Reserve Banks are (Treasury deposits, government securities) _____ and (reserves of, loans to) _____ commercial banks. The three major liabilities are (Treasury deposits, government securities) _____, (reserves of, loans to) _____ commercial banks, and (government securities, Federal Reserve Notes) _____.

6. The four tools the monetary authority uses to control the money supply are (open, closed) _____-market operations, changing the (loan, reserve) _____ ratio, changing the (prime interest, discount) _____ rate, and using a term (action, auction) _____ facility to lend reserves to banks for a set term. The most effective and most often used tool of monetary policy is a change in (the reserve ratio, open-market operations) _____.

7. When the Federal Reserve Banks buy government securities in the open market, the reserves of commercial banks will (increase, decrease) _____ and when they sell government securities in the open market, the reserves of commercial banks will _____.

8. If the Federal Reserve Banks were to sell $10 million in government bonds to the *public* and the reserve ratio were 25%, the supply of money would immediately be reduced by $_____, the reserves of commercial banks would be reduced by $_____, and the excess reserves of the banks would be reduced by $_____. But if these bonds were sold to the commercial banks, the supply of money would immediately be reduced by $_____, the reserves of the banks would be reduced by $_____, and the excess reserves of the banks would be reduced by $_____.

9. An increase in the reserve ratio will (increase, decrease) _____ the size of the monetary multiplier and _____ the excess reserves held by commercial banks, thus causing the money supply to (increase, decrease) _____. A decrease in the reserve ratio will (increase, decrease) _____ the size of the monetary multiplier and _____ the excess reserves held by commercial banks, thus causing the money supply to (increase, decrease) _____.

10. If the Federal Reserve Banks were to lower the discount rate, commercial banks would tend to borrow (more, less) _____ from them, and this would (increase, decrease) _____ their excess reserves.

11. A fourth tool the Federal Reserve can use for altering the excess reserves of banks is the (Taylor rule, term auction facility) _____. With this tool, the Federal Reserve specifies the amount of reserves banks can (lend, borrow) _____ for a specific period of time, and then banks submit bids stating the amount of reserves they want and the (exchange, interest) _____ rate they will pay. The rate for all reserves is set at the (lowest, highest) _____ rate bid by a bank that also ensures all available reserves will be taken by the banks.

12. The interest rate that banks charge one another for overnight loans is the (prime interest, Federal funds) _____ rate, but the rate banks use as a benchmark for setting interest rates on loans is the _____ rate. The (prime interest, Federal funds) _____ rate is the focus of the monetary policy of the Federal Reserve.

13. An expansionary monetary policy would be characterized by actions of the Federal Reserve to (increase, decrease) _____ the discount rate, _____ reserve ratios, and (buy, sell) _____ government bonds, whereas a restrictive monetary policy would include actions taken to (increase, decrease) _____ the discount rate, _____ reserve ratios, and (buy, sell) _____ government bonds.

14. There is a cause-effect chain of monetary policy.

a. In the market for money, the demand for and the supply of money determine the equilibrium rate of (discount, interest) _____.

b. This rate in turn determines the level of (government, investment) _____ spending based on the _____ demand curve.

c. This spending in turn affects aggregate (demand, supply) _____, and the intersection of aggregate supply and demand determines the equilibrium level of real (interest, GDP) _____ and the (discount, price) _____ level.

15. This cause-effect chain can be illustrated with examples.

a. When there is an *increase* in the money supply curve, the real interest rate will (increase, decrease) _____, investment spending will _____, aggregate demand will (increase, decrease) _____, and real GDP will _____.

b. When there is a *decrease* in the money supply curve, the real interest rate will (increase, decrease) _____, investment spending will _____, aggregate demand will (increase, decrease) _____, and real GDP will _____.

16. To eliminate inflationary pressures in the economy, the traditional view holds that the monetary authority should seek to (increase, decrease) _____ the reserves of commercial banks; this would tend to _____ the money supply and to (increase, decrease) _____ the rate of interest, and this in turn would cause investment spending, aggregate demand, and GDP to _____. This action by monetary authorities would be considered (an easy, a tight) _____ money policy.

17. If there were a serious problem with economic growth and unemployment in the economy, the Federal Reserve would typically pursue (an expansionary, a restrictive) _____ monetary policy, in which case the Federal Reserve would (buy, sell) _____ government bonds as a way of (increasing, decreasing)

_____ the money supply, and thereby _____ interest rates; these events would have the effect of (increasing, decreasing) _____ investment spending and thus _____ real GDP.

18. An increase in the money supply will shift the aggregate (supply, demand) _____ curve to the (right, left) _____. A decrease in the money supply will shift the aggregate (supply, demand) _____ curve to the (right, left) _____. If the marginal propensity to consume is .75, then the multiplier will be (3, 4) _____, an initial increase in investment of $10 billion will (increase, decrease) _____ aggregate demand by ($30, $40) _____ billion.

19. Monetary policy has strengths. Compared to fiscal policy, monetary policy is speedier and (more, less) _____ flexible, and _____ isolated from political pressure. Since 1990, the Federal Reserve has been successful in countering recession by (raising, lowering) _____ the Federal funds rate, and it has been successful in limiting inflation by _____ the Federal funds rate.

20. Monetary policy has shortcomings and problems, too. It may be subject to timing (limits, lags) _____ that occur between the time a need is recognized and the policy takes effect. It may be more effective in counteracting (recession, inflation) _____ than _____.

■ **TRUE–FALSE QUESTIONS**

Circle T if the statement is true, F if it is false.

1. The goal of monetary policy is to lower interest rates. **T F**

2. There is a transactions demand for money because households and business firms use money as a store of value. **T F**

3. An increase in the price level would increase the transactions demand for money. **T F**

4. An increase in the nominal GDP, other things remaining the same, will increase both the total demand for money and the equilibrium rate of interest in the economy. **T F**

5. Bond prices and interest rates are inversely related. **T F**

6. The securities owned by the Federal Reserve Banks are almost entirely U.S. government bonds. **T F**

7. If the Federal Reserve Banks buy $15 in government securities from the public in the open market, the effect will be to increase the excess reserves of commercial banks by $15. **T F**

8. When the Federal Reserve sells securities in the open market, the price of these securities falls. **T F**

9. A change in the reserve ratio will affect the multiple by which the banking system can create money, but it will not affect the actual or excess reserves of member banks. **T F**

10. An increase in the required reserve ratio will increase the lending capacity of banks. **T F**

11. If the reserve ratio is lowered, some required reserves are turned into excess reserves. **T F**

12. When commercial banks borrow from the Federal Reserve Banks at the discount rate, they increase their excess reserves and their money-creating potential. **T F**

13. The Federal Reserve uses the term auction facility to increase the money supply by auctioning off a specific amount of reserves that banks can borrow for a short time period. **T F**

14. The least effective and least used tool of monetary policy is the open-market operations, in which government securities are bought and sold. **T F**

15. The Federal Reserve announces its changes in monetary policy by changing its targets for the Federal funds rate. **T F**

16. To increase the Federal funds rate, the Federal Reserve buys bonds in the open market to increase the excess reserves of banks. **T F**

17. The prime interest rate is the rate that banks charge other banks for overnight loans of excess reserves at Federal Reserve banks. **T F**

18. If the monetary authority wished to follow a restrictive monetary policy, it would sell government securities in the open market. **T F**

19. The Taylor rule provides a rule of thumb that is used for calculating the target that the Federal Reserve is likely to set for the Federal funds rate. **T F**

20. In the cause-effect chain, an expansionary monetary policy increases the money supply, decreases the interest rate, increases investment spending, and increases aggregate demand. **T F**

21. A restrictive monetary policy is designed to correct a problem of high unemployment and sluggish economic growth. **T F**

22. It is generally agreed that fiscal policy is more effective than monetary policy in controlling the business cycle because fiscal policy is more flexible. **T F**

23. Monetary policy is subject to more political pressure than fiscal policy. **T F**

24. Monetary policy is limited by a time lag that occurs from when the problem is recognized to when the policy becomes operational. **T F**

25. An expansionary monetary policy suffers from a "You can lead a horse to water, but you can't make the horse drink" problem. **T F**

■ **MULTIPLE-CHOICE QUESTIONS**

Circle the letter that corresponds to the best answer.

1. The organization directly responsible for monetary policy in the United States is the
(a) U.S. Treasury
(b) Federal Reserve
(c) Internal Revenue Service
(d) Congress of the United States

2. If the dollars held for transactions purposes are, on the average, spent five times a year for final goods and services, then the quantity of money people will wish to hold for transactions is equal to
(a) five times the nominal GDP
(b) 20% of the nominal GDP
(c) five divided by the nominal GDP
(d) 20% divided by the nominal GDP

3. There is an asset demand for money because money is
(a) a store of value
(b) a measure of value
(c) a medium of exchange
(d) a standard of deferred payment

4. An increase in the rate of interest would increase
(a) the opportunity cost of holding money
(b) the transactions demand for money
(c) the asset demand for money
(d) the prices of bonds

Use the following information and table below to answer Questions 5 and 6. Suppose the transactions demand for money is equal to 10% of the nominal GDP, the supply of money is $450 billion, and the asset demand for money is that shown in the table.

Interest Rate	Asset demand (billions)
14%	$100
13	150
12	200
11	250

5. If the nominal GDP is $3000 billion, the equilibrium interest rate is
(a) 14%
(b) 13%
(c) 12%
(d) 11%

6. If the nominal GDP remains constant at $3000 billion an increase in the money supply from $450 billion to $500

billion would cause the equilibrium interest rate to
(a) rise to 14%
(b) fall to 11%
(c) fall to 12%
(d) remain unchanged

7. The total quantity of money demanded is
(a) directly related to nominal GDP and the rate of interest
(b) directly related to nominal GDP and inversely related to the rate of interest
(c) inversely related to nominal GDP and directly related to the rate of interest
(d) inversely related to nominal GDP and the rate of interest

8. The stock of money is determined by the Federal Reserve System and does not change when the interest rate changes; therefore the
(a) supply of money curve is downward sloping
(b) demand for money curve is downward sloping
(c) supply of money curve is upward sloping
(d) supply of money curve is vertical

9. Which one of the following points would be true?
(a) Bond prices and the interest rate are directly related.
(b) A lower interest rate raises the opportunity cost of holding money.
(c) The supply of money is directly related to the interest rate.
(d) The total demand for money is inversely related to the interest rate.

Answer Questions 10 and 11 on the basis of the following information: Bond price = $10,000; bond fixed annual interest payment = $1000; bond annual rate of interest = 10%.

10. If the price of this bond decreases by $2500, the interest rate in effect will
(a) decrease by 1.1 percentage points
(b) decrease by 1.9 percentage points
(c) increase by 2.6 percentage points
(d) increase by 3.3 percentage points

11. If the price of this bond increases by $2000, the interest rate in effect will
(a) decrease by 1.7 percentage points
(b) decrease by 2.4 percentage points
(c) increase by 1.1 percentage points
(d) increase by 2.9 percentage points

12. The largest single asset in the Federal Reserve Banks' consolidated balance sheet is
(a) securities
(b) the reserves of commercial banks
(c) Federal Reserve Notes
(d) loans to commercial banks

13. The largest single liability of the Federal Reserve Banks is
(a) securities
(b) the reserves of commercial banks
(c) Federal Reserve Notes
(d) loans to commercial banks

14. Assume that there is a 20% reserve ratio and that the Federal Reserve buys $100 million worth of government securities. If the securities are purchased from the public, this action has the potential to increase bank lending by a maximum of
(a) $500 million, but only by $400 million if the securities are purchased directly from commercial banks
(b) $400 million, but by $500 million if the securities are purchased directly from commercial banks
(c) $500 million, and also by $500 million if the securities are purchased directly from commercial banks
(d) $400 million, and also by $400 million if the securities are purchased directly from commercial banks

15. Assuming that the Federal Reserve Banks sell $20 million in government securities to commercial banks and the reserve ratio is 20%, then the effect will be
(a) to reduce the actual supply of money by $20 million
(b) to reduce the actual supply of money by $4 million
(c) to reduce the potential money supply by $20 million
(d) to reduce the potential money supply by $100 million

16. Lowering the reserve ratio
(a) changes required reserves to excess reserves
(b) increases the amount of excess reserves banks must keep
(c) increases the discount rate
(d) decreases the discount rate

17. Commercial bank borrowing from the Federal Reserve
(a) is not permitted because of the Federal Reserve Act
(b) is permitted but only for banks that are bankrupt
(c) decreases the excess reserves of commercial banks and their ability to offer credit
(d) increases the excess reserves of commercial banks and their ability to offer credit

18. Which is the most important control used by the Federal Reserve to regulate the money supply?
(a) the reserve ratio
(b) open-market operations
(c) the discount rate
(d) term auction facility

19. The Federal funds rate is the rate that
(a) banks charge for overnight use of excess reserves held at the Federal Reserve banks
(b) banks charge for loans to the most creditworthy customers
(c) the Federal Reserve charges for short-term loans to commercial banks
(d) is charged for government bonds sold in the open-market operations of the Federal Reserve

20. When the Federal Reserve Banks decide to buy government bonds from banks and the public, the supply of reserves in the Federal funds market
  (a) increases and the Federal funds rate decreases
  (b) decreases and the Federal funds rate decreases
  (c) increases and the Federal funds rate increases
  (d) decreases and the Federal funds rate increases

21. When the Federal Reserve uses open-market operations to reduce the Federal funds rate several times over a year it is pursuing
  (a) an expansionary monetary policy
  (b) a restrictive monetary policy
  (c) a prime interest rate policy
  (d) a discretionary fiscal policy

22. The economy is experiencing high unemployment and a low rate of economic growth and the Fed decides to pursue an expansionary monetary policy. Which set of actions by the Fed would be most consistent with this policy?
  (a) buying government securities and raising the reserve ratio
  (b) selling government securities and raising the discount rate
  (c) buying government securities and lowering the reserve ratio
  (d) selling government securities and lowering the discount rate

23. The economy is experiencing inflation and the Federal Reserve decides to pursue a restrictive monetary policy. Which set of actions by the Fed would be most consistent with this policy?
  (a) buying government securities and lowering the discount rate
  (b) buying government securities and lowering the reserve ratio
  (c) selling government securities and raising the discount rate
  (d) selling government securities and lowering the discount rate

24. In the chain of cause and effect between changes in the excess reserves of commercial banks and the resulting changes in output and employment in the economy,
  (a) an increase in excess reserves will decrease the money supply
  (b) a decrease in the money supply will increase the rate of interest
  (c) an increase in the rate of interest will increase aggregate demand
  (d) an increase in aggregate demand will decrease output and employment

25. Which is most likely to be affected by changes in the rate of interest?
  (a) tax rates
  (b) investment spending
  (c) government spending
  (d) the imports of the economy

Use the following graph to answer Questions 26 and 27.

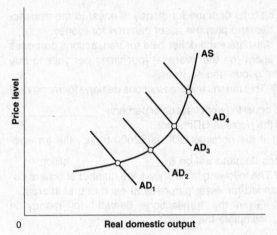

26. A shift from **AD₁** to **AD₂** would be most consistent with
  (a) an increase in the reserve ratio by the Federal Reserve
  (b) an increase in the discount rate by the Federal Reserve
  (c) the buying of securities by the Federal Reserve
  (d) the selling of securities by the Federal Reserve

27. Assume that the Federal Reserve lowers interest rates to increase investment spending. This monetary policy is most likely to shift
  (a) AD_3 to AD_2
  (b) AD_3 to AD_4
  (c) AD_4 to AD_3
  (d) AD_2 to AD_1

28. A restrictive monetary policy would be most consistent with
  (a) a decrease in the Federal funds rate and a decrease in the money supply
  (b) a decrease in the Federal funds rate and an increase in the money supply
  (c) an increase in the Federal funds rate and a decrease in the money supply
  (d) an increase in the Federal funds rate and an increase in the money supply

29. Assume that monetary policy increases interest rates and results in a decrease in investment spending of $5 billion. If the marginal propensity to consume is .80, then aggregate demand is most likely to
  (a) increase by $5 billion
  (b) decrease by $5 billion
  (c) increase by $25 billion
  (d) decrease by $25 billion

30. Assume the Fed creates excess reserves, but the policy does not encourage banks to make loans and thus increase the money supply. This situation is a problem of
  (a) a restrictive monetary policy
  (b) cyclical asymmetry
  (c) using a Taylor rule
  (d) targeting the Federal funds rate

■ PROBLEMS

1. The total demand for money is equal to the transactions demand plus the asset demand for money.

a. Assume each dollar held for transactions purposes is spent (on the average) four times per year to buy final goods and services.

(1) This means that transactions demand for money will be equal to (what fraction or percent) _____ of the nominal GDP, and,

(2) if the nominal GDP is $2000 billion, the transactions demand will be $_____ billion.

b. The following table shows the number of dollars demanded for asset purposes at each rate of interest.

(1) Given the transactions demand for money in (*a*), complete the table.

Interest rate	Amount of money demanded (billions)	
	For asset purposes	Total
16%	$ 20	$_____
14	40	_____
12	60	_____
10	80	_____
8	100	_____
6	120	_____
4	140	_____

(2) On the following graph, plot the total demand for money (D_m) at each rate of interest.

c. Assume the money supply (S_m) is $580 billion.

(1) Plot this money supply on the graph.

(2) Using either the graph or the table, the equilibrium rate of interest is _____%.

d. Should the money supply

(1) increase to $600 billion, the equilibrium interest rate would (rise, fall) _____ to _____%.

(2) decrease to $540 billion, the equilibrium interest rate would _____ to _____%.

e. If the nominal GDP

(1) increased by $80 billion, the total demand for money would (increase, decrease) _____ by $_____ billion at each rate of interest and the equilibrium rate of interest would (rise, fall) _____ by _____%.

(2) decreased by $120 billion, the total demand for money would _____ by $_____ billion at each rate of interest and the equilibrium interest rate would _____ by _____%.

2. Suppose a bond with no expiration date pays a fixed $500 annually and sells for its face value of $5000.

a. Complete the table at the top of the next column and calculate the interest rate (to one decimal place) that would be obtained from the bond when the bond price is given or calculate the bond price when the interest rate is given.

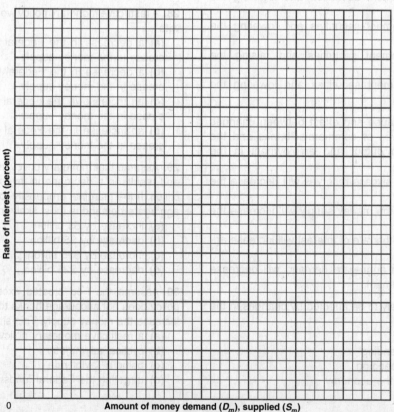

Rate of interest (percent)

0

Amount of money demand (D_m), supplied (S_m)
(billions of dollars)

Bond price	Interest rate
$4000	_____._____ %
$_____	11.0
$5000	_____._____
$5500	_____._____
$_____	8.0

b. Based on the results of the table, as the price increases on a bond with a fixed annual payment, the interest yield on the bond (decreases, increases) _____, but when the price of a bond decreases, the interest yield _____. Given this situation in an economy, you can conclude that a higher price for bonds (increases, decreases) _____ interest rates and that a lower price for bonds _____ interest rates.

3. Assume that the following consolidated balance sheet is for all commercial banks. Assume also that the required reserve ratio is 25% and that cash is *not* a part of the commercial banks' legal reserve.

Assets		Liabilities	
Cash	$ 50	Checkable deposits	$400
Reserves	100	Loans from Federal	
Loans	150	Reserve	25
Securities	200	Net worth	75
	$ 500		$500

a. To *increase* the supply of money by $100, the Fed could (buy, sell) _____ securities worth $_____ in the open market.

b. To *decrease* the supply of money by $50, the Fed could (buy, sell) _____ securities worth $_____ in the open market.

4. At the bottom of the page are the consolidated balance sheets of the Federal Reserve and of the commercial banks. Assume that the reserve ratio for commercial banks is 25%, that cash is *not* a part of a bank's legal reserve, and that the figures in column 1 show the balance sheets of the Federal Reserve and the commercial banks *prior to each of the following five transactions.* Place the new balance sheet figures in the appropriate columns and complete A, B, C, D, and E in these columns. Do *not* use the figures you place in columns 2 through 5 when you work the next part of the problem; start all parts of the problem with the printed figures in column 1.

a. The Federal Reserve Banks sell $3 in securities to the public, which pays by check (column 2).

b. The Federal Reserve Banks buy $4 in securities from the commercial banks (column 3).

c. The Federal Reserve Banks lower the required reserve ratio for commercial banks to 20% (column 4).

d. The U.S. Treasury buys $5 worth of goods from U.S. manufacturers and pays the manufacturers by checks drawn on its accounts at the Federal Reserve Banks (column 5).

	(1)	(2)	(3)	(4)	(5)	(6)
Federal Reserve Banks						
Assets:						
Gold certificates	$ 25	$____	$____	$____	$____	$____
Securities	30	____	____	____	____	____
Loans to commercial banks	10	____	____	____	____	____
Liabilities:						
Reserves of commercial banks	200	____	____	____	____	____
Treasury deposits	5	____	____	____	____	____
Federal Reserve Notes	10	____	____	____	____	____
Commercial Banks						
Assets:						
Reserves	$ 50	$____	$____	$____	$____	$____
Securities	70	____	____	____	____	____
Loans	90	____	____	____	____	____
Liabilities:						
Checkable deposits	200	____	____	____	____	____
Loans from Federal Reserve	10	____	____	____	____	____
A. Required reserves		____	____	____	____	____
B. Excess reserves		____	____	____	____	____
C. How much has the money supply changed?		____	____	____	____	____
D. How much more can the money supply change?		____	____	____	____	____
E. What is the total of C and D?		____	____	____	____	____

e. Because the Federal Reserve Banks have raised the discount rate, commercial banks repay $6 which they owe to the Federal Reserve (column 6).

5. On the following graph is the demand-for-money curve that shows the amounts of money consumers and firms wish to hold at various rates of interest (when the nominal GDP in the economy is given).

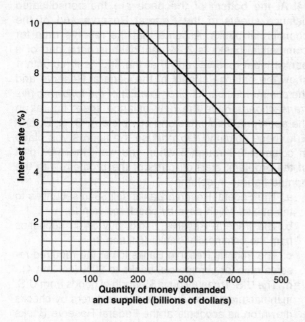

a. Suppose the supply of money is equal to $300 billion.
(1) Draw the supply-of-money curve on the above graph.
(2) The equilibrium rate of interest in the economy

is_____%.

b. Below is a graph of an investment demand curve which shows the amounts of planned investment at various rates of interest.

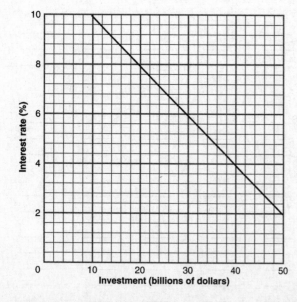

Given your answer to (2) above, how much will investors plan to spend for capital goods?
$_____ billion.

c. The following figure shows the aggregate supply (**AS**) curve in this economy. On the graph, draw an aggregate demand curve (**AD₁**) so that it crosses the **AS** in the middle of the curve. Label the price level (**P₁**) and output level (**Q₁**) associated with the intersection of **AD₁** and **AS**.

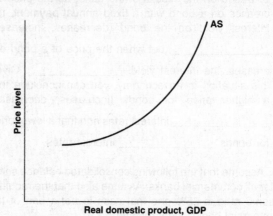

d. Now assume that monetary authorities increase the money supply to $400.
(1) On the market for money graph, plot the new money supply curve. The new equilibrium interest rate

is_____%.
(2) On the investment graph, determine the level of investment spending that is associated with this new

interest rate: $_____ billion. By how much has investment spending increased as a result of

the change in the interest rate? $_____ billion.
(3) Assume that the marginal propensity to consume

is .75. What is the multiplier? _____ By how much will the new investment spending increase

aggregate demand? $_____ billion.
(4) On the previous figure, indicate how the change in investment spending affects aggregate demand. Draw a new aggregate demand curve (**AD₂**) so that it crosses the **AS** curve. Also label the new price level (**P₂**) and output level (**Q₂**) associated with the intersection of **AD₂** and **AS**.

6. Columns 1 and 2 of the following table show the aggregate supply schedule. (The price level is a price index, and real domestic output is measured in billions of dollars.)

(1) Price level	(2) Real output	(3) AD₁	(4) AD₂
110	1600	1800	_____
120	1700	1700	_____
130	1790	1600	_____
140	1800	1500	_____
150	1940	1400	_____
160	2000	1300	

a. If the aggregate demand schedule were that shown in columns 1 and 3, the equilibrium real domestic output would be $_____ billion and the price level would be _____.

b. Now assume that the Federal Reserve took actions to lower the Federal funds rate, and these actions increased investment spending in this economy by $60 billion. Also assume that the marginal propensity to consume in the economy was .8. How much would aggregate demand increase? $_____ billion

c. In column 4, enter this amount of increase in real domestic output at each price level to define the new **AD** schedule (**AD₂**).

d. What is the new equilibrium real domestic output? $_____ billion. And the new price level? _____.

■ **SHORT ANSWER AND ESSAY QUESTIONS**

1. What is the basic goal of monetary policy?

2. What are the two reasons people wish to hold money? How are these two reasons related to the functions of money?

3. Explain the determinant of each of the two demands for money and how a change in the size of these determinants will affect the amount of money people wish to hold.

4. The rate of interest is a price. Of what good or service is it the price? Explain how demand and supply determine this price.

5. Describe how changes in bond prices correct disequilibrium in the market for money. What is the relationship between bond prices and interest rates?

6. What are the important assets and liabilities of the Federal Reserve Banks?

7. Explain how the four monetary policy tools of the Federal Reserve Banks would be used to contract the supply of money. How would they be used to expand the supply of money?

8. What is the difference between the effects of the Federal Reserve's buying (selling) government securities in the open market from (to) commercial banks and from (to) the public?

9. Which of the monetary policy tools available to the Federal Reserve is most effective? Why is it more important than other tools?

10. What happens to the Federal funds rate when the Federal Reserve expands or contracts the money supply through open-market operations?

11. What are the characteristics of an expansionary monetary policy? How does the Federal Reserve implement such policies?

12. What are the characteristics of a restrictive monetary policy? How does the Federal Reserve implement such policies?

13. What is the Taylor rule and how is it used?

14. Using four graphs, explain what determines (a) the equilibrium interest rate, (b) investment spending, and (c) the equilibrium GDP. Now use these four graphs to show the effects of a decrease in the money supply upon the equilibrium GDP.

15. Why are changes in the rate of interest more likely to affect investment spending than consumption and saving?

16. What policies will the Federal Reserve use to counter inflation, or unemployment and recession? Describe the effects on bank reserves, the money supply, interest rates, investment spending, aggregate demand, and real GDP from each policy.

17. What are the major strengths of monetary policy?

18. Discuss how monetary policy has been used to counter recession and limit inflation since the 1990s.

19. How do lags affect monetary policy?

20. What is meant by cyclical asymmetry and how does it apply to monetary policy?

ANSWERS

Chapter 33 Interest Rates and Monetary Policy

FILL-IN QUESTIONS

1. price level, full
2. directly, nominal GDP, inversely, the rate of interest
3. demand, supply, interest rate
4. decrease, increase, increase, decrease
5. government securities, loans to, Treasury deposits, reserves of, Federal Reserve Notes
6. open, reserve, discount, auction, open-market operations
7. increase, decrease
8. 10 million, 10 million, 7.5 million, 0, 10 million, 10 million
9. decrease, decrease, decrease, increase, increase, increase
10. more, increase
11. term auction facility, borrow, interest, lowest
12. Federal funds, prime interest, Federal funds
13. decrease, decrease, buy, increase, increase, sell
14. a. interest; b. investment, investment; c. demand, GDP, price
15. a. decrease, increase, increase, increase; b. increase, decrease, decrease, decrease
16. decrease, decrease, increase, decrease, a tight
17. an expansionary, buy, increasing, decreasing, increasing, increasing
18. demand, right, demand, left, 4, increase, $40
19. more, more, lowering, raising
20. lags, inflation, recession

TRUE–FALSE QUESTIONS

1. F, p. 660
2. F, p. 661
3. T, p. 661
4. T, pp. 661–663
5. T, p. 663
6. T, p. 664
7. F, p. 665
8. T, p. 667
9. F, pp. 667–668
10. F, pp. 667–668
11. T, p. 667
12. T, pp. 668–669
13. T, p. 669

14. F, pp. 669–670
15. T, p. 670
16. F, pp. 670–671
17. F, pp. 671–672
18. T, p. 672
19. T, pp. 672–673
20. T, pp. 674–676
21. F, pp. 676–678
22. F, p. 678
23. F, p. 678
24. T, p. 679
25. T, pp. 679, 682

MULTIPLE-CHOICE QUESTIONS

1. b, p. 660
2. b, p. 661
3. a, p. 661
4. a, p. 661
5. b, pp. 661–663
6. c, pp. 661–663
7. b, pp. 661–663
8. d, pp. 663, 674
9. d, p. 663
10. d, p. 663
11. a, p. 663
12. a, p. 664
13. c, p. 664
14. b, pp. 665–666
15. d, pp. 666–667

16. a, p. 667
17. d, p. 668
18. b, pp. 669–670
19. a, p.670
20. a, p. 671
21. a, pp. 671–672
22. c, pp. 671, 676–677
23. c, pp. 672, 677–678
24. b, pp. 674–675
25. b, pp. 675–676
26. c, pp. 676–677
27. b, pp. 676–677
28. c, p. 677
29. d, p. 677
30. b, p. 679

PROBLEMS

1. *a.* (1) 1/4 (25%), (2) 500; *b.* (1) 520, 540, 560, 580, 600, 620, 640; (2) see Figure 33.1 in the text for an example *c.* (1) see Figure 33.1 in the text for an example (2) 10; *d.* (1) fall, 8, (2) rise, 14; *e.* (1) increase, 20, rise, 2, (2) decrease, 30, fall, 3
2. *a.* 12.5%, $4,545, 10.0%, 9.1%, $6,250; *b.* decreases, increases, decreases, increases
3. *a.* buy, 25; *b.* sell, 12 1/2
4. See below
5. *a.* (2) 8; *b.* 20; *c.* see Figure 33.5 in text; *d.* (1) 6, (2) 30, 10, (3) 4, 40, (4) see Figure 33.5 in text
6. *a.* 1700, 120; *b.* 300 (multiplier of 5 × $60 billion = $300 billion); *c.* 2100, 2000, 1900, 1800, 1700, 1600; *d.* 1800, 140

SHORT ANSWER AND ESSAY QUESTIONS

1. p. 660
2. p. 661
3. p. 661
4. pp. 662–663
5. p. 663
6. p. 664
7. pp. 666–669
8. pp. 665–667
9. pp. 669–670
10. pp. 670–671

11. pp. 671–672
12. p. 672
13. p. 673
14. pp. 674—677
15. pp. 675–676
16. pp. 676–678
17. p. 678
18. pp. 678–679
19. pp. 679
20. pp. 679, 682

	(2)	(3)	(4)	(5)	(6)
Federal Reserve Banks					
Assets:					
Gold certificates	$ 25	$ 25	$ 25	$ 25	$ 25
Securities	27	34	30	30	30
Loans to commercial banks	10	10	10	10	4
Liabilities:					
Reserves of commercial banks	47	54	50	55	44
Treasury deposits	5	5	5	0	5
Federal Reserve Notes	10	10	10	10	10
Commercial Banks					
Assets:					
Reserves	$ 47	$ 54	$ 50	$ 55	$ 44
Securities	70	66	70	70	70
Loans	90	90	90	90	90
Liabilities:					
Checkable deposits	197	200	200	205	200
Loans from Federal Reserve	10	10	10	10	4
A. Required reserves	49.25	50	40	51.25	50
B. Excess reserves	−2.25	4	10	3.75	−6
C. How much has the money supply changed?	−3	0	0	+5	0
D. How much more can the money supply change?	−9	+16	+50	+15	−24
E. What is the total of C and D?	−12	+16	+50	+20	−24

Financial Economics

This chapter introduces you to financial economics—the study of investor preferences and how they affect the pricing and trading of financial assets such as stocks, bonds, and mutual funds. The chapter begins with a distinction between **financial investment,** which involves purchases of new or used assets for which there is an expected monetary return, and **economic investment,** which is spending for the production and accumulation of capital goods.

A central idea in financial economics is the concept of **present value.** This concept is important because it gives investors the ability to calculate the price to pay now for assets that will generate expected future payments. This concept is explained with the use of compound interest formula, which shows how a given amount of money will grow over time if interest is paid on both the amount initially invested and on any interest payments. The compound interest formula is then rearranged to determine the present value that a person would have to invest in today's dollars to receive a certain dollar payment in the future. The present value formula has applications to decisions involving payouts from lotteries to how to structure deferred compensation or salary packages.

The chapter also discusses three popular financial assets—**stocks, bonds, and mutual funds.** It explains the key differences among these three assets in terms of ownership, risk, and return. A fundamental concept presented in this section is that the rate of return for an investment is inversely related to its price. As the price for a financial asset increases, its rate of return decreases, and vice versa.

One of the peculiar results of financial investments is that the rates of return for assets that are essentially identical will also be equal. The process that produces this result is **arbitrage.** If there are two identical assets and one has a higher rate of return than the other, then investors will purchase more of the asset with the higher rate of return, thus driving up its price and driving down its rate of return. Investors will sell the asset with the lower rate of return, thus driving down its price and increasing its rate of return. This process will continue until rates of return for the two assets are equal.

Risk is a major factor affecting financial assets. Some risk can be diversified by purchasing different types of assets with different returns that offset each other. Other risk is nondiversifiable and is measured with the use of beta as you will learn in the chapter. A general relationship found with all types of financial assets is that the riskier the investment, the greater the compensation for bearing the risk that is demanded by investors, and thus the higher

average return that is expected for such risky investments. One investment, however, that is essentially risk free is short-term U.S. government bonds. Such an investment is used to measure time preferences for consuming now or consuming in the future.

The last few sections of the chapter pull together all the previous material to present the **Security Market Line (SML)** and use it to discuss Federal Reserve policy. The SML shows that the average expected return for any investment is composed of two parts—one that compensates for time preference (as measured by a risk-free investment) and one that compensates for nondiversifiable risk (as measure by beta). It can be used to determine an investment's average expected rate of return based on its risk level—the higher the risk level, the higher the average rate of return. The Federal Reserve can shift the SML by changing the short-term interest rate. This action has the effect of changing the average expected return on all assets and changing the asset prices, thus influencing the direction of economic activity in the overall economy.

■ **CHECKLIST**

When you have studied this chapter you should be able to

☐ Distinguish between economic investment and financial investment.

☐ State the compound interest formula.

☐ Calculate the compound interest when you are given the interest rate, amount invested, and years of compounding.

☐ State the formula for calculating the present value of a future amount of money.

☐ Apply the present value formula to lottery and salary decisions.

☐ Describe the characteristics of stocks.

☐ Describe bonds and explain how they differ from stocks.

☐ Describe mutual funds and explain how they differ from stocks and bonds.

☐ Define the percentage rate of return for calculating investment returns.

☐ Explain why an investment's rate of return is inversely related to its price.

☐ Describe how the arbitrage process equalizes rates of return for investments with similar characteristics.

☐ Define diversification and its relationship to risk.

☐ Calculate the average expected rate of return when you are given investment data.

☐ Define beta as a measure of risk.

☐ Explain the relationship of risk and average expected returns.

☐ Describe what determines the risk-free rate of return.

☐ Define the two parts of the equation for the average expected rate of return.

☐ Use a graph to illustrate the features of the Security Market Line model.

☐ Explain how arbitrage affects average expected rates of return in the Security Market Line (SML).

☐ Describe the effect of an increase in risk-free interest rates on the SML.

☐ Explain how a change in Federal Reserve policy will affect financial assets and the economy.

☐ Explain why the rates of return on index mutual funds beat the rates of return on actively managed funds over time (Last Word).

■ **CHAPTER OUTLINE**

1. There is a difference between *economic investment* and *financial investment*. Economic investment refers to new additions to the nation's capital stock from building roads, factories, and houses. Financial investment refers to the purchase of an asset (new or used) with the expectation it will generate a monetary return. In this chapter, the general term "investment" will mean financial investment.

2. *Present value* states the current value or worth of returns or costs that are expected in the future. An investment's current price is equal to the present value of the investment's future returns.

    a. The *compound interest* formula indicates how a given amount of money will increase if interest is paid on both the amount initially invested and also on any interest payments previously paid. The equation states that if X dollars are invested today at interest rate i and allowed to grow for t years, those dollars will become $(1 + i)^t X$ dollars in t years.

    b. The present value model uses the compound interest formula to calculate the present value that would have to be invested today to receive X dollars in t years. The equation states that an investment of $X/(1 + i)^t$ dollars today at interest rate i would increase to X dollars in t years.

    c. Present value has applications to everyday experiences such as lottery payouts and deferred compensation. For example, the present value formula can be used to calculate how much a person who won the lottery would receive if that person took the winnings as a lump-sum payout instead of receiving equal payments spread over many years.

3. Many financial investments are available to people. Whatever the type, they share three characteristics. They require that investors pay a market price to obtain them; they give the asset owner the right to receive future payments; and the future payments are typically risky. The three most common and popular investments are stocks, bonds, and mutual funds.

    a. *Stocks* are shares of ownership in corporations. Stocks have value because they give shareholders the right to receive any future profits produced by the corporations. Because of the *limited liability rule,* the risk of loss for investors is limited to the number of shares they own. Investors can gain from investing in profitable corporations because they can capture the *capital gains* (sell their shares at higher prices than they bought them) and they can often receive *dividends,* which are payouts of equal shares of the corporate profits. Stocks are risky because the future profits are unknown and it is possible for corporations to go *bankrupt.*

    b. *Bonds* are a type of debt or loan contract. Bonds give the holders the right to a fixed stream of future payments that serve to repay the loan or pay off the debt, so they are a more predictable investment than stocks. The risks from bonds involve possible *default,* or failure to make the promised payment by the corporations or government agencies that issued the bonds.

    c. *Mutual funds* are a type of financial investment offered by companies that combine the money invested by many investors to buy a *portfolio,* which typically consists of a large number of stocks and/or bonds. The returns that are generated from these portfolios are owned by the individual investors and are paid to them. The risks from mutual funds are related to the risks of the stocks and bonds that they hold in their portfolios. Some funds are *actively managed funds,* with portfolio managers constantly trying to buy and sell stocks to maximize returns while others are *index funds* that are *passively managed funds* that buy or sell assets to closely match a financial index.

    d. The *percentage rate of return* for a financial asset is calculated by determining the change in value of the asset (gain or loss) and dividing it by the purchase price for the asset, and expressing the result as a percentage.

    e. The rate of return for an investment is inversely related to its price. This means that the higher the price, the lower the rate of return.

4. *Arbitrage* is the process that, through the actions of investors, results in equalizing the *average expected rates of return* from assets that are very similar or identical. For example, if two identical assets have different rates of return, investors will buy the asset with the higher rate of return and sell the asset with the lower rate of return. As investors buy the asset with the higher rate of return, its price will increase and its average expected rate of return will decrease. As investors sell the asset with the lower rate of return, its price will decrease and its average expected rate of return will increase. The process continues until the average expected rates of return of the two assets converge and become equal.

5. *Risk* in financial investing means that future payments are uncertain. Many factors affect the degree of risk.

    a. *Diversification* is a strategy designed to decrease investment risk in a portfolio by selecting a group of assets that have risks or returns that compensate each other, so that when returns on one investment are lower, they are offset by higher returns from another investment. Risks that can be eliminated by asset diversification are called *diversifiable risks.* Risks that cannot be eliminated by asset diversification are called *nondiversifiable risks.* An example of a nondiversifiable risk would be a general downturn in the economy that can simultaneously affect the returns of all investments in a similar way so that different assets do not have offsetting returns.

b. Investment decisions often involve comparing return and risk, especially nondiversifiable risk.

(1) Investors compare investments using *average expected rates of return.* This return is a *probability weighted average* that gives higher weight to outcomes that are more likely to happen.

(2) *Beta* is a statistic measuring the nondiversifiable risk of an asset relative to the amount of nondiversifiable risk facing the *market portfolio.* This portfolio contains every asset trading in the financial markets, so it is diversified and consequently has eliminated all of its diversifiable risk and has only nondiversifiable risk.

c. There is a relationship between risk and average expected returns. Investors demand compensation for bearing risk. The riskier the asset, the higher its average expected rate of return will be. This relationship applies to all assets.

d. Rates of return compensate both for risk and time preference. Average expected rates of return must compensate for *time preference* because most people prefer to consume sooner rather than later. The rate of return that compensates *only* for time preference is assumed to be equal to the rate of interest from short-term U.S. government bonds. The return on these bonds is viewed as the *risk-free interest rate* because the U.S. government is almost 100% guaranteed to make its payments on time. The Federal Reserve has the power to set this interest rate and thereby influence the compensation for time preference across the economy.

6. An asset's average expected rate of return has two components. First there is the compensation for time preference which is the risk-free interest rate. Second, there is the compensation for nondiversifiable risk as measured by beta. This risk factor is often referred to by economists as the *risk premium.* The *Security Market Line (SML)* is a straight line that plots how the average expected rates of return on assets and portfolios in the economy must vary with their respective levels of nondiversifiable risk as measured by beta. The slope of the SML indicates how much investors dislike risk—a steeper slope shows that investors demand higher average expected rates of return for bearing increasingly large amounts of nondiversifiable risk and a flatter slope shows that investors require lower average expected rates of return to compensate them for risk bearing. Because of arbitrage, every asset in the economy should plot onto the SML.

7. The vertical intercept of the SML is determined by the risk-free interest rate and its slope is determined by amount of compensation investors need for assuming nondiversifiable risk. The risk-free interest rate is controlled by the **Federal Reserve** through its control over the rate for short-term U.S. government bonds. The Federal Reserve can shift the SML by changing this interest rate and thus the compensation for time preference that must be paid to investors of all assets regardless of risk. The Federal Reserve's power to shift short-run interest rates also gives

it the ability to change asset prices and influence economic conditions. For example, when the SML shifts upward, the average expected rate of return on all assets increases and asset prices decline, thus reducing investment, consumption, and eventually aggregate demand.

8. (Last Word). *Actively managed mutual funds* do much worse than *passively managed index funds* for several reasons. First, *actively managed funds* cannot select portfolios that do better than *passively managed funds* with similar levels of risk because of *arbitrage.* Second, *actively managed funds* charge higher fees than *passively managed funds,* thus increasing their cost and lowering their return.

■ HINTS AND TIPS

1. There are many new terms and concepts presented in this chapter, so take time to master each one in order to have the necessary knowledge to comprehend the chapter content. This content is not difficult once you master the basic terms and concepts.

2. The **Security Market Line** may seem more difficult than it is. It is simply a graph of the relationship between risk level (measured on the horizontal axis) and the average expected return (measured on the vertical axis). The line is upsloping, reflecting the fact that a greater risk level is associated with a higher average expected return. The average expected return, however, is divided into two parts. One part is compensation for time preference and it is measured by the risk-free interest rate (the vertical intercept). The other part is a risk premium for a risk level associated with an asset's beta.

3. One purpose of the chapter is to show how the **Federal Reserve** can change the short-term interest rate and influence financial investments and thus the economy. The last section of the chapter makes that important connection.

■ IMPORTANT TERMS

economic investment	percentage rate of return
financial investment	
compound interest	arbitrage
present value	risk
stocks	portfolios
bankrupt	diversification
limited liability rule	diversifiable risk
capital gains	nondiversifiable risk
dividends	average expected rate of return
bonds	beta
default	market portfolio
mutual funds	time preference
index funds	risk-free interest rate
actively managed funds	risk premium
passively managed funds	Security Market Line (SML)

SELF-TEST

■ FILL-IN QUESTIONS

1. Paying for new additions to the nation's capital stock would be (financial, economic) _____ investment whereas buying an asset in the expectation that it will generate a monetary gain would be _____ investment.

2. The compound interest formula defines the rate at which (present, future) _____ amounts of money can be converted to _____ amounts of money, and also the rate at which (present, future) _____ amounts of money can be converted into _____ amounts of money.

3. All financial investments share three features: They require that investors pay a (dividend, price) _____ to acquire them; they give the owners the chance to receive (present, future) _____ payments, and such payments are typically (riskless, risky) _____.

4. An investment's proper current price is equal to the sum of the (present, future) _____ values of each of the investment's expected _____ payments.

5. Ownership shares in a corporation are (stocks, bonds) _____ whereas debt contracts issued by corporations are _____.

6. The primary risk for stocks is that future profits are (predictable, unpredictable) _____ and the company may go bankrupt, whereas bonds are risky because of the possibility that the corporate or government issuers (may, may not) _____ make the promised payments.

7. A mutual fund is a company that maintains a portfolio of (stocks or bonds, artworks or antiques) _____. Portfolio managers who constantly buy and sell assets to generate high returns run (passively managed, actively managed) _____ funds and portfolio managers who buy and sell assets to match whatever assets are contained in an underlying index run _____ funds.

8. Average expected rates of return are (directly, inversely) _____ related to an asset's current price, so when an asset's price rises, the average expected rate of return (rises, fall) _____.

9. Assume that two assets are nearly identical, but one pays a higher rate of return than the other. As investors buy the asset with the higher rate of return, its price will (fall, rise) _____ causing its average expected rate of return to _____. At the same time, as investors sell the asset with the lower rate of return, its price will (fall, rise) _____, causing its average expected rate of return to _____. The process will continue until the two assets have (equal, unequal) _____ average expected rates of return.

10. Risk means that investors are (certain, uncertain) _____ what future payments from assets will be. Risks that can be canceled out by diversification are (diversifiable, nondiversifiable) _____ risks, and risks that cannot be canceled out by diversification are _____ risks.

11. Each investment's average expected rate of return is the probability (weighted, unweighted) _____ average of the investment's possible future return. This probability weighting means that each of the possible future rates of return is (multiplied, divided) _____ by its probability expressed as a decimal before being added together to obtain the average.

12. Beta is a relative measure of (diversifiable, nondiversifiable) _____ risk and shows how the _____ risk of a given asset or portfolio compares with that of the market portfolio.

13. Since the market portfolio contains every asset trading in the financial markets, it has eliminated all of its (diversifiable, nondiversifiable) _____ risk and only has _____ risk. The market portfolio is the perfect standard against which to measure levels of (diversifiable, nondiversifiable) _____ risk.

14. Investors' dislike of risk and uncertainty cause them to pay higher prices for (more, less) _____ risky assets and lower prices for _____ assets. This outcome means that asset prices and expected rates of return are (directly, inversely) _____ related.

15. The compensation for time preference is the risk-free interest rate on (short-term, long-term) _____ U.S. government bonds and the power to change this interest rate is held by the (U.S. Treasury, Federal Reserve) _____.

16. The Security Market Line shows the relationship between average expected rates of (return, risk) _____ and levels of _____ that hold for every asset or portfolio trading in financial markets. The line's upward slope shows that investors must be compensated for higher levels of risk with (lower, higher) _____ average expected rates of return.

17. If investors dislike risk, then the Security Market Line will be (flatter, steeper) _____, but if investors are more comfortable with risk, then the line will be (flatter, steeper) _____. When the line is steeper, it indicates that investors demand (more, less) _____ compensation in terms of higher average expected rates of return for bearing increasingly large amounts of nondiversifiable risk, but when the line is flatter it indicates that investors demand _____ compensation in terms of higher average expected rates of return for bearing higher levels of nondiversifiable risk.

18. Arbitrage will ensure that all investments having an identical level of risk will eventually also have an (equal, unequal) _____ rate of return—the return given by the Security Market Line. If such an investment has a return that is greater than the average for a level of risk, investors will (sell, buy) _____ it, thus (increasing, decreasing) _____ the price and _____ the average expected return. If such an investment has a return that is lower than the average for a level of risk, investors will (sell, buy) _____ it, thus (increasing, decreasing) _____ the price and _____ the average expected return.

19. The Security Market Line's vertical intercept is the (prime, risk-free) _____ interest rate set by the Federal Reserve, and the slope is determined by the amount of compensation investors demand for bearing (diversifiable, nondiversifiable) _____ risk. An increase in the interest rate by the Federal Reserve will shift the line (upward, downward) _____ and a decrease in the interest rate by the Federal Reserve will shift the line (upward, downward) _____.

20. An increase in the risk-free interest rate by the Federal Reserve will (increase, decrease) _____ asset prices and can eventually _____ aggregate demand, whereas a decrease in the risk-free interest rate by the Federal Reserve will (increase, decrease) _____ asset prices and can eventually _____ aggregate demand.

■ **TRUE–FALSE QUESTIONS**

Circle T if the statement is true, F if it is false.

1. The purchase of a share of corporate stock would be an example of a financial investment. **T F**

2. The compound interest formula states that if X dollars are invested today at interest rate i and allowed to grow for t years, they will become $(1 + i)^t X$ dollars in t years. **T F**

3. The present value formula states that a person would have to invest $X/(1 + i)^t$ dollars today at interest rate i for them to become X dollars in t years. **T F**

4. The current price of a financial investment should equal the total present value of all the asset's future payments. **T F**

5. Stocks are ownership shares in corporations and have value because they give shareholders the right to share in any future profits that the corporations may generate. **T F**

6. Bonds are risky because of the possibility that the corporations or government bodies that issued them may default on them, or not make the promised payments. **T F**

7. Mutual funds are investment companies that pool the money of many investors in order to buy a portfolio of assets. **T F**

8. Some mutual funds are actively managed while other mutual funds are passively managed index funds. **T F**

9. A financial investment's percentage rate of return is directly related to its price. **T F**

10. Arbitrage is the process whereby investors equalize the average expected rates of return generated by identical or nearly identical assets. **T F**

11. In finance, an asset is risky if its future payments are certain. **T F**

12. Diversification is an investment strategy that seeks to reduce the overall risk facing an investment portfolio by selecting a group of assets whose risks offset each other. **T F**

13. Nondiversifiable risks simultaneously affect all investments in the same direction so that it is not possible to select asset returns that offset each other. **T F**

14. Investors evaluate the possible future returns to risky projects using average expected rates of return, which give lower weight to outcomes that are more likely to happen. **T F**

15. Beta measures the nondiversifiable risk of an asset or portfolio relative to the amount of nondiversifiable risk facing the market portfolio. **T F**

16. By definition, the market portfolio has a beta of 1.0, so that if an asset has a beta of 0.67, it has a third more nondiversifiable risk as the market portfolio. **T F**

17. The riskier the asset, the higher its average expected rate of return will be. **T F**

18. The rate of return that compensates for time preference is assumed to be equal to the rate of interest generated by long-term U.S. government bonds. **T F**

19. The Federal Reserve has the power to set the short-term risk-free interest rate and thereby set the economy-wide compensation for time preference. **T F**

20. An asset's average expected rate of return will be the sum of the rate of return that compensates for time preference plus the rate of return that compensates for the asset's level of nondiversifiable risk as measured by beta. **T F**

21. The Security Market Line (SML) is a straight line that plots how the average expected rates of return on assets and portfolios in the economy must vary with their respective levels of nondiversifiable risk as measured by beta. **T F**

22. The slope of the Security Market Line indicates how much investors dislike risk. **T F**

23. Arbitrage ensures that every asset in the economy should plot onto the Security Market Line. **T F**

24. The Federal Reserve can shift the entire SML by changing risk-free interest rates and the compensation for time preference that must be paid to investors in all assets regardless of their risk level. **T F**

25. The power of the Federal Reserve to shift short-run interest rates also gives it the ability to shift asset prices throughout the economy. **T F**

■ **MULTIPLE-CHOICE QUESTIONS**

Circle the letter that corresponds to the best answer.

1. Which would be an example of an economic investment?
  (a) the sale of a stock
  (b) the building a new factory
  (c) the buying of a mutual fund
  (d) the purchase of a corporate bond

2. A $100 deposit is placed in a savings account that pays an annual interest rate of 8 percent. What will be its value after two years?
  (a) $116.64
  (b) $125.97
  (c) $136.05
  (d) $146.93

3. The compound interest rate formula defines the rate at which
  (a) a future amount of money can be converted to a present amount of money
  (b) a present amount of money can be converted into present interest rates
  (c) a present amount of money can be divided by the interest rate
  (d) a present amount of money can be multiplied by the interest rate

4. Cecilia has the chance to buy an asset that is guaranteed to return a single payment of exactly $370 in 17 years. Assuming that the interest rate is 8 percent, then the present value of that future payment is equal to:
  (a) ($370 − $70) = $300
  (b) ($370 − $29.6) = $340.4

  (c) $370/(1.08)^{17} = $100
  (d) ($370 × 1.08) + 17 = $416.60

5. Assume that Ricardo wins a $100 million lottery. Ricardo can be paid the $100 million in 20 payments of $5 million each over 20 years, or Ricardo can be paid a lump sum of the present values of each of the future payments. Assume that the interest rate is 5 percent a year. What is the lump sum?
  (a) $43.2 million
  (b) $50.4 million
  (c) $62.3 million
  (d) $110.5 million

6. Which of the following is NOT one of the common features of all investments?
  (a) The rate of return on the investments will be positive.
  (b) Investors are given the chance to receive future payments.
  (c) Investors are required to pay a market price to purchase them.
  (d) The future payments from the investments are typically risky.

7. Shares of ownership in a corporation are
  (a) bonds
  (b) stocks
  (c) dividends
  (d) mutual funds

8. Jamie buys 100 shares of General Electric stock for $35 a share one year and then sells the 100 shares for $40 a share the next year. After selling the shares, Jamie will realize a(n)
  (a) depreciation of $500
  (b) capital gain of $500
  (c) dividend increase of $500
  (d) interest payment of $500

9. Which type of investment is a loan contract?
  (a) bonds
  (b) stocks
  (c) actively managed mutual funds
  (d) passively managed mutual funds

10. Sang buys a house for $500,000 and rents it out for a monthly payment of $3,500. What is the percentage rate of return on this investment for the year?
  (a) 7.2 percent
  (b) 8.4 percent
  (c) 9.1 percent
  (d) 10.6 percent

11. Susie wants to buy a $10,000 bond that pays a fixed annual payment of $550. Before she is able to buy the bond, its price rises to $11,000. What happens to the rate of return on the bond because of the change in price?
  (a) It increased from 4.5% to 5.5%.
  (b) It decreased from 5.0% to 4.5%.
  (c) It increased from 5.0% to 5.5%.
  (d) It decreased from 5.5% to 5.0%.

12. The process whereby investors equalize the average expected rates of return generated by identical or nearly identical assets is
(a) beta
(b) arbitrage
(c) diversifiable risk
(d) nondiversifiable risk

13. In finance, an asset is risky if
(a) it does not pay dividends
(b) it does not have capital gains
(c) its present value is positive
(d) its future payments are uncertain

14. An investment strategy that seeks to reduce the overall risk facing an investment portfolio by selecting a group of assets whose risks offset each other is called
(a) indexing
(b) arbitrage
(c) diversification
(d) time preference

15. An investor wants to invest in the beverage industry, but does not know which of two major companies, Coca-Cola and Pepsi, will produce the greatest return, so the investor buys shares in both companies to lower the risk. In this case the investor is seeking to lower
(a) systemic risk
(b) diversifiable risk
(c) nondiversifiable risk
(d) the risk premium

16. The type of risk that pushes the returns from all investments in the same direction at the same time so there is no possibility of using good effects to offset bad effects is
(a) constant
(b) idiosyncratic
(c) nondiversifiable
(d) probability weighted

17. If an investment is 80 percent likely to return 10 percent per year and 20 percent likely to return 12 percent a year, then its probability weighted average is
(a) 8.0%
(b) 10.4%
(c) 11.0%
(d) 12.2%

18. Beta measures how the
(a) risk premium compares with the time preference
(b) risk-free interest rate compares with the diversifiable risk of a given asset
(c) nondiversifiable risk of a given asset compares with that of a market portfolio
(d) average expected rate of return compares with the probability weighted average

19. An asset with a beta of 2.0 has
(a) 2% more risk than the risk-free interest rate
(b) 100% more risk than the risk-free interest rate
(c) half the nondiversifiable risk of that in a market portfolio of assets
(d) twice the nondiversifiable risk of that in a market portfolio of assets

20. Asset prices and average expected returns are inversely related, so
(a) more risky assets will have average expected rates of return similar to less risky assets
(b) less risky assets will have higher average expected rates of return than more risky assets
(c) more risky assets will have lower average expected rates of return than less risky assets
(d) less risky assets will have lower average expected rates of return than more risky assets

21. The observation that people tend to be impatient and typically prefer to consume things in the present rather than the future is captured in the concept of
(a) beta
(b) risk premium
(c) time preference
(d) market portfolio

22. The best measure of the risk-free interest rate is the rate of return from
(a) a portfolio of company stocks
(b) bonds issued by U.S. corporations
(c) a passively managed mutual fund
(d) short-term U.S. government bonds

23. Each investment's average expected rate of return is
(a) the sum of the risk-free interest rate and the risk premium
(b) the risk-free interest rate multiplied times the risk premium
(c) the risk premium divided by the risk-free interest rate
(d) the risk premium minus the risk-free interest rate

24. The Security Market Line (SML) is a straight line that shows how the average expected rates of return on assets and portfolios in the economy must vary with their respective levels of
(a) diversifiable risk as measured by beta
(b) nondiversifiable risk as measured by beta
(c) the risk premium as measured by the risk-free interest rate
(d) time preference as measured by the risk-free interest rate

25. If the Federal Reserve decides to raise the interest rates on short-term U.S. government bonds, then the vertical intercept for the Security Market Line will shift
(a) upward and asset prices will fall
(b) upward and asset prices will rise
(c) downward and asset prices will fall
(d) downward and asset prices will rise

■ **PROBLEMS**

1. In the table below, enter the value at year's end of $100 compounded at 5 percent interest.

Years of compounding	Value at year's end
1	$_____
2	_____
3	_____
4	_____
5	_____

2. In the table below, enter the *present value* of $10,000 dollars that would be paid at the end of different years. Assume the interest rate is 5 percent. Round the answer to the nearest dollar.

Year period	Value at year's end
1	$_____
2	_____
3	_____
4	_____
5	_____

3. Assume that the investment pays a monthly amount of $2000, but has a different price.

a. Calculate the percentage rate of return for an investment that a person might buy at different prices and enter it into the table.

b. Describe the relationship between the percentage rate of return and the asset price.

Purchase price	Percentage rate of return
$ 50,000	_____
100,000	_____
150,000	_____
200,000	_____

4. The table below shows different probabilities for the rate of return on an investment that might pay 10 percent a year or 12 percent a year. Calculate the probability-weighted average for the return for this investment.

	10 percent return	12 percent return	Probability-weighted average
a.	50%	50%	_____%
b.	60	40	_____
c.	70	30	_____
d.	80	20	_____

■ SHORT ANSWER AND ESSAY QUESTIONS

1. Explain the difference between financial investment and economic investment and give examples.

2. Explain why the formula for compound interest defines not only the rate at which present amounts of money can be converted to future amounts of money, but also the rate at which future amounts of money can be converted to present amounts of money.

3. Assume you are given the choice between being paid $100 million in installments of $5 million per year over 20 years or having it all paid today. Assume the applicable interest rate for the installment payments is 5 percent. What would the present value be today and how did you calculate it?

4. Describe how present value can be used to analyze salary caps and deferred compensation issued.

5. What are the three common features of all financial investments?

6. Compare and contrast stocks, bonds, and mutual funds in terms of ownership, risk, and return.

7. What is the relationship between asset prices and rates of return? What is the cause of this relationship?

8. How does the arbitrage process work? Give an example.

9. Identify the two basic types of risk and explain the difference between them.

10. What is meant by the term *probability weighted average* as it applies to the average expected rate of return for investments? Give an example to illustrate the term.

11. Define beta and use it to explain risk. What is the beta for a market portfolio and why does it have this value?

12. Explain the relationship between risk and average expected return.

13. What is time preference? Give an example to illustrate its meaning.

14. Why are short-term U.S. government bonds considered to be risk-free investments?

15. How can the Federal Reserve influence the risk-free rate of return?

16. Define the components of the average expected rate of return.

17. What is the relationship between beta and the risk premium?

18. Describe the major graphical features (slope, intercept, boxes) of the Security Market Line.

19. Use the Security Market Line to explain how arbitrage will ensure that all investments having an identical level of risk will also have an identical rate of return.

20. Explain what happens to the Security Market Line and the economy when the Federal Reserve changes policy and uses open market operations to raise the interest rates of short-term U.S. government bonds.

ANSWERS

Chapter 34 Financial Economics

FILL-IN QUESTIONS

1. economic, financial
2. present, future, future, present
3. price, future, risky
4. present, future
5. stocks, bonds
6. unpredictable, may not
7. stocks or bonds, actively managed, passively managed
8. inversely, falls
9. rise, fall, fall, rise, equal
10. uncertain, diversifiable, nondiversifiable
11. weighted, multiplied
12. nondiversifiable, nondiversifiable
13. diversifiable, nondiversifiable, nondiversifiable
14. more, less, inversely
15. short-term, Federal Reserve
16. return, risk, higher
17. steeper, flatter, more, less
18. equal, buy, increasing, decreasing, sell, decreasing, increasing
19. risk-free, nondiversifiable, upward, downward
20. decrease, decrease, increase, increase

TRUE–FALSE QUESTIONS

1. T, p. 688		14. F, p. 695
2. T, p. 688		15. T, p. 695
3. T, p. 689		16. F, pp. 695–696
4. T, p. 689		17. T, p. 696
5. T, p. 691		18. F, p. 697
6. T, pp. 691–692		19. T, p. 697
7. T, p. 692		20. T, p. 697
8. T, p. 692		21. T, pp. 697–698
9. F, p. 693		22. T, p. 698
10. T, p. 693		23. T, p. 699
11. F, p. 694		24. T, pp. 698–699
12. T, p. 694		25. T, pp. 700, 702
13. T, p. 695		

MULTIPLE-CHOICE QUESTIONS

1. b, p. 688		14. c, p. 694
2. a, p. 688		15. b, p. 694
3. a, p. 688		16. c, p. 695
4. c, p. 689		17. b, p. 695
5. c, p. 689		18. c, p. 695
6. a, p. 691		19. d, p. 695
7. b, p. 691		20. d, p. 696
8. b, pp. 691–692		21. c, p. 697
9. a, pp. 691–692		22. d, p. 697
10. b, p. 693		23. a, pp. 697–698
11. d, p. 693		24. b, pp. 697–698
12. b, p. 693		25. a, pp. 700, 702
13. d, p. 694		

PROBLEMS

1. See table

Years of compounding	Value at year's end
1	$105.00
2	110.25
3	115.76
4	121.55
5	127.63

2. See table

Year period	Value at year's end
1	$9524
2	9070
3	8638
4	8227
5	7835

3. *a.* See table; *b.* As the asset or purchase price increases, the percentage rate of return decreases

Purchase price	Percentage rate of return
$ 50,000	48
100,000	24
150,000	16
200,000	12

4. See table

	10 percent return	12 percent return	Probability-weighted average
a.	50%	50%	11.0%
b.	60	40	10.8
c.	70	30	10.6
d.	80	20	10.4

SHORT ANSWER AND ESSAY QUESTIONS

1. p. 688		11. p. 696
2. pp. 688–689		12. p. 697
3. p. 689		13. p. 697
4. pp. 690–691		14. p. 697
5. p. 691		15. p. 697
6. pp. 691–692		16. p. 697
7. p. 693		17. p. 697
8. pp. 693–694		18. pp. 697–698
9. pp. 694–695		19. pp. 698–699
10. p. 695		20. pp. 700, 702

Extending the Analysis of Aggregate Supply

Chapter 35 adds to the aggregate demand–aggregate supply (AD–AS) model first introduced in Chapter 29. This addition will give you the analytical tools to improve your understanding of the short-run and long-run relationships between unemployment and inflation.

The major extension to the AD–AS model is the explanation for the **short-run aggregate supply curve** and the **long-run aggregate supply curve.** In the **short run,** nominal wages and other input prices do not adjust fully as the price level changes, so an increase in the price level increases business profits and real output. In the **long run,** nominal wages and other input prices are fully responsive to previous changes in the price level, so business profits and employment return to their original levels. Thus, the long-run aggregate supply curve is vertical at the full-employment level of output.

The distinction between the short-run and long-run aggregate supply curves requires a reinterpretation of demand-pull inflation and cost-push inflation. Although **demand-pull inflation** will increase the price level and real output in the short run, once nominal wages increase, the temporary increase in output is gone, but the price level will be higher at the full-employment level of output. **Cost-push inflation** will increase the price level and decrease real output in the short run, but again, once nominal wages fall, output and the price level will return to their original positions. If government policymakers try to counter cost-push inflation by increasing aggregate demand, they may make matters worse by increasing the price level and causing the short-run aggregate supply curve to decrease, thereby setting off an inflationary spiral.

The extended AD–AS model also is useful for understanding recession and ongoing inflation in an economy. As for recession, it is the result of a decrease in aggregate demand. This decline eventually lowers nominal wages and other input prices. When this happens, aggregate supply increases to restore the previous equilibrium. As for ongoing inflation, it is the result of increases in aggregate demand over time that raise the price level and counter the downward pressure on the price level from economic growth and a long-run increase in aggregate supply.

The relationship between inflation and unemployment has been studied for many years. One influential observation, supported by data from the 1950s and 1960s, was embodied in the **Phillips Curve,** which suggested that there was a stable and predictable trade-off between the rate of inflation and the unemployment rate. During the 1960s, it

was thought that this trade-off could be used for formulating sound monetary and fiscal policy to manage the economy.

The events of the 1970s and early 1980s, however, called into question the shape and stability of the Phillips Curve because the economy was experiencing both higher rates of inflation and unemployment—**stagflation.** The **aggregate supply shocks** of this period shifted the Phillips Curve rightward. When these shocks dissipated in the 1980s, the Phillips Curve began to shift back to its original position. From 1997 to 2005, points on the Phillips Curve were similar to those of the 1960s.

The conclusion to be drawn from studies of the Phillips Curve is that there is no long-run trade-off between inflation and unemployment. In the long run, the downsloping Phillips Curve is actually a vertical line at the natural rate of unemployment. In the short run, if aggregate demand increases and reduces the unemployment rate below its natural rate, the result is only temporary. Eventually, the unemployment rate will return to its natural rate, but at a higher rate of inflation.

Aggregate supply can also be affected by taxation. **Supply-side economics** contends that aggregate supply is important for determining levels of inflation, unemployment, and economic growth. Tax cuts are proposed by supply-siders as a way to create more incentives to work, save, and invest, thus increasing productivity and aggregate supply. The relationship between marginal tax rates and tax revenues is expressed in the **Laffer Curve,** which suggests that cuts in tax rates can increase tax revenues if tax rates are too high for the economy. Critics contend, however, that the incentive effects are small, potentially inflationary, and can have positive or negative effects on tax revenues.

■ CHECKLIST

When you have studied this chapter you should be able to

☐ Give a definition of the short run and long run in macroeconomics based on the flexibility of input prices.

☐ Draw the short-run aggregate supply curve and describe its characteristics.

☐ Explain how the long-run aggregate supply curve is determined.

☐ Draw a graph that illustrates long-run equilibrium in the extended AD–AS model.

☐ Explain demand-pull inflation using the extended AD–AS model and identify its short-run and long-run outcomes.

☐ Describe cost-push inflation using the extended AD–AS model.

☐ Give two generalizations about the policy dilemma for government in dealing with cost-push inflation.

☐ Explain recession and the process of adjustment using the extended AD–AS model.

☐ Discuss the reasons for ongoing inflation in the extended AD–AS model.

☐ Show that a shift outward in the production possibilities curve is equivalent to a rightward shift in the economy's long-run aggregate supply curve.

☐ Illustrate graphically in the extended AD–AS model how economic growth shifts the short-run and long-run aggregate supply curves and what happens to aggregate demand over time.

☐ Explain how the deflationary effects of increases in aggregate supply from economic growth are typically offset by increases in aggregate demand from monetary policy, thus producing ongoing inflation.

☐ Make three significant generalizations about the inflation and unemployment relationship based on the extended AD–AS model.

☐ Draw a Phillips Curve and explain the basic trade-off it presents.

☐ Define stagflation.

☐ Explain why adverse aggregate supply shocks shifted the Phillips Curve over time.

☐ List events that contributed to the demise of stagflation.

☐ Use short-run and long-run Phillips Curves to explain inflation.

☐ Use short-run and long-run Phillips Curves to explain disinflation.

☐ Describe supply-siders' views of the effects of taxation on incentives to work, save, and invest.

☐ Use the Laffer Curve to explain the hypothesized relationship between marginal tax rates and tax revenues.

☐ State three criticisms of the Laffer Curve.

☐ Offer a rebuttal of the criticisms and an evaluation of supply-side economics.

☐ Discuss findings from recent research on whether tax increases reduce real GDP (Last Word).

■ **CHAPTER OUTLINE**

1. The aggregate supply curve has short-run and long-run characteristics. The **short run** is a period of time in which input prices are inflexible or fixed. In the short run, nominal wages (and other input prices) are unresponsive to changes in the price level. The **long run** is a period of time in which input prices are flexible. In the long run, nominal wages and other input prices are fully responsive to changes in the price level. The short-run and long-run characteristics of aggregate supply in combination with aggregate demand create the extended AD–AS model.

   a. The **short-run aggregate supply curve** is upward sloping: An increase in the price level increases real output and also business revenues and profits because nominal wages and other input prices do not change; in contrast, when the price level decreases,

business revenue and profits decline, and so does real output, but nominal wages and other input prices do not change.

   b. The **long-run aggregate supply curve** is vertical at the potential level of output. Increases in the price level will increase nominal wages and other input prices and cause a decrease (shift left) in the short-run aggregate supply curve. Conversely, declines in the price level will reduce nominal wages and other input prices and cause an increase (shift right) in the short-run aggregate supply curve. In either case, although the price level changes, output returns to its potential level, and the long-run aggregate supply curve is vertical at the full-employment level of output.

   c. Equilibrium in the extended AD–AS model occurs at the price level and output where the aggregate demand crosses the long-run aggregate supply curve and also crosses the short-run aggregate supply curve.

2. The extended AD–AS model can be applied to explain conditions of inflation and recession in an economy.

   a. Demand-pull inflation will increase (shift right) the aggregate demand curve, which increases the price level and causes a temporary increase in real output above the potential output of the economy. The greater demand for inputs will eventually lead to an increase in nominal wages and other input prices. The short-run aggregate supply curve, which was based on fixed nominal wages and other input prices, now decreases (shifts left), resulting in an even higher price level with real output returning to its prior level.

   b. Cost-push inflation will decrease (shift left) the short-run aggregate supply curve. This situation will increase the price level and temporarily decrease real output, causing a recession. It creates a policy dilemma for government.

   (1) If government takes actions to counter the cost-push inflation and recession by increasing aggregate demand, the price level will move to an even higher level, and the actions may set off an inflationary spiral.

   (2) If government takes no action, the recession will eventually reduce nominal wages and other input prices, and eventually the short-run aggregate supply curve will shift back to its original position.

   c. If aggregate demand decreases, it will result in a **recession** that decreases real output and increases unemployment. If an assumption is made that prices and wages are flexible downward, then the decline in aggregate demand pushes down nominal wages and other input prices. This decline in input prices will eventually increase short-run aggregate supply, thus increasing real output and restoring full employment to end the recession, but the process does not occur without a long period of high unemployment and lost output.

   d. The AD–AS model also explains ongoing inflation in the economy. In the previous analysis inflation was finite, but the shifts in AD or AS were limited. But over time there are continuous shifts in AS and AD that give rise to ongoing inflation. Increases in AS because of economic growth would cause ongoing deflation. But such deflationary shifts from AS are more than offset by increases in AD thus creating ongoing inflation.

(1) A shift outward in the production possibilities curve is equivalent to a shift rightward in the long-run aggregate supply curve for the economy.

(2) In either model, changes in the price level are not important because it does not shift either curve.

e. The extended AD–AS model takes into account economic growth with a rightward shift in the vertical long-run aggregate supply curve that increases an economy's potential output over time. But this shift is also accompanied by increases in aggregate demand over time. These increases in aggregate demand occur because central banks permit a certain amount of inflation in the economy to offset some of the deflationary effects of the increase in aggregate supply.

3. The short- and long-run relationships between inflation and unemployment are important and lead to three generalizations. First, in the short run there is a trade-off between the rate of inflation and the rate of unemployment. Second, shocks from aggregate supply can cause both higher rates of inflation and higher rates of unemployment. Third, in the long run there is no significant trade-off between inflation and unemployment.

a. If aggregate supply is constant and the economy is operating in the upsloping range of aggregate supply, then the greater the rate of increase in aggregate demand, the higher the rate of inflation (and output) and the lower the rate of unemployment. This inverse relationship between the rate of inflation and unemployment is known as the *Phillips Curve.* In the 1960s, economists thought there was a predictable trade-off between unemployment and inflation. All society had to do was to choose the combination of inflation and unemployment on the Phillips Curve.

b. The *aggregate supply shocks* of the 1970s and early 1980s called into question the validity of the Phillips Curve. In that period, the economy experienced *stagflation*—both higher rates of inflation and unemployment. The aggregate supply shocks came from an increase in resource prices (oil), shortages in agricultural production, higher wage demands, and declining productivity. These shocks decreased the short-run aggregate supply curve, which increased the price level and decreased output (and unemployment). These shocks shifted the Phillips Curve to the right or showed there was no dependable trade-off between inflation and unemployment.

c. The **demise of stagflation** came in the 1982–1989 period because of such factors as a severe recession in 1981–1982 that reduced wage demands, increased foreign competition that restrained price increases, and a decline in OPEC's monopoly power. The short-run aggregate supply curve increased, and the price level and unemployment rate fell. This meant that the Phillips Curve may have shifted back (left). Recent unemployment–inflation data are now similar to the Phillips Curve of the 1960s.

4. In the long run, there is no apparent trade-off between inflation and unemployment. Any rate of inflation is consistent with the natural rate of unemployment at that time. The *long-run Phillips Curve* is vertical at the natural rate of unemployment. In the short run, there can be a trade-off between inflation and unemployment.

a. An increase in aggregate demand may temporarily reduce unemployment as the price level increases and profits expand, but the actions also set other events into motion.

(1) The increase in the price level reduces the real wages of workers who demand and obtain higher nominal wages; these actions return unemployment to its original level.

(2) Back at the original level, there are now higher actual and expected rates of inflation for the economy, so the short-run Phillips Curve has shifted upward.

(3) The process is repeated if aggregate demand continues to increase. The price level rises as the short-run Phillips Curve shifts upward.

b. In the long run, the Phillips Curve is stable only as a vertical line at the natural rate of unemployment. After all adjustments in nominal wages to increases and decreases in the rate of inflation, the economy returns to its full-employment level of output and its natural rate of unemployment. There is no trade-off between unemployment and inflation in the long run.

c. *Disinflation*—reductions in the inflation rate from year to year—is also explained by the distinction between the short-run and long-run Phillips Curves.

5. *Supply-side economics* views aggregate supply as active rather than passive in explaining changes in the price level and unemployment.

a. It argues that higher marginal tax rates reduce incentives to work and high taxes also reduce incentives to save and invest. These policies lead to a misallocation of resources, less productivity, and a decrease in aggregate supply. To counter these effects, supply-side economists call for a cut in marginal tax rates.

b. The *Laffer Curve* suggests that it is possible to lower tax rates and increase tax revenues, thus avoiding a budget deficit because the policies will result in less tax evasion and avoidance.

c. Critics of supply-side economics and the Laffer Curve suggest that the policy of cutting tax rates will not work because:

(1) It has only a small and uncertain effect on incentives to work (or on aggregate supply).

(2) It would increase aggregate demand relative to aggregate supply and thus reinforce inflation when there is full employment.

(3) The expected tax revenues from tax rate cuts depend on assumptions about the economy's position on the Laffer Curve. If tax cuts reduce tax revenues, it will create budget deficits.

d. Supply-siders argue that the tax cuts under the Reagan administration in the 1980s worked as would be expected: The cut in tax rates increased tax revenue. Critics contend that the reason was that aggregate demand increased as the economy came out of recession and not that aggregate supply increased. There is now general recognition that changes in marginal tax rates change people's behavior, although there is continuing debate about the size of the effect.

6. (Last Word). Economists Cristina Romer and David Romer developed a novel way to study the question of whether tax increases reduce real GDP. They identified four motivations for tax changes: to counteract other influences in the economy; to pay for more government spending; to correct budget deficits; and to promote long-term growth. The most reliable way to test for the effects of tax changes was to focus on one used to promote long-term growth or to correct budget deficits because they were uncomplicated by other factors. The results showed that tax changes affect output: a tax increase of 1 percent of GDP lowers real GDP by about 2 to 3 percent.

■ HINTS AND TIPS

1. Chapter 35 is a more difficult chapter because the AD–AS model is extended to include both short-run and long-run effects. Spend extra time mastering this material, but do not try to read everything at once. Break the chapter into its logical sections and practice drawing each graph.

2. Be sure you understand the distinction between the **short-run** and **long-run aggregate supply curves.** Then use these ideas to explain demand-pull inflation, cost-push inflation, and recession. Doing Problem 2 will be especially helpful.

3. Use Figure 35.9 in the text to help you understand why there is a difference in the short-run and long-run relationships between unemployment and inflation. Problem 4 will help your understanding of this complicated graph.

4. The rationales for tax cuts and tax increases have been at the forefront of fiscal policy since the 1980s. This chapter offers a detailed explanation of supply-side economics that has been used to justify the tax cut policies. The last section of the chapter will help you understand the arguments for and against such tax policies that have real-world applications.

■ IMPORTANT TERMS

short run	long-run Phillips Curve
long run	
Phillips Curve	disinflation
stagflation	supply-side economics
aggregate supply shocks	Laffer Curve

SELF-TEST

■ FILL-IN QUESTIONS

1. In an AD–AS model with a stable aggregate supply curve, when the economy is producing in the upsloping portion of the aggregate supply curve, an increase in aggregate demand will (increase, decrease) _____ real output and employment, but a decrease in aggregate supply will _____ real output and employment.

2. In the short run, when the price level changes, nominal wages and other input prices are (responsive, unresponsive) _____, but in the long run nominal wages and other input prices are _____. In the short run, the aggregate supply curve is (upsloping, vertical) _____, but in the long run the curve is _____.

3. Demand-pull inflation occurs with a shift in the aggregate demand curve to the (right, left) _____, which will (decrease, increase) _____ the price level and temporarily _____ real output. As a consequence, the (short-run, long-run) _____ aggregate supply curve will shift left because of a rise in (real, nominal) _____ wages, producing a (lower, higher) _____ price level at the original level of real output.

4. Cost-push inflation occurs with a shift in the short-run aggregate supply curve to the (right, left) _____; thus the price level will (increase, decrease) _____ and real output will temporarily _____.

5. If government takes no actions to counter cost-push inflation, the resulting recession will (increase, decrease) _____ nominal wages and shift the short-run aggregate supply curve back to its original position, yet if the government tries to counter the recession with a(n) _____ in aggregate demand, the price level will move even higher.

6. A recession will occur when there is (an increase, a decrease) _____ in aggregate demand. If the controversial assumption is made that prices and wages are flexible downward, then the price level (rises, falls) _____. Real wages will then (increase, decrease) _____, but eventually nominal wages will _____ and the aggregate supply curve will (increase, decrease) _____ and end the recession.

7. In the extended aggregate demand–aggregate supply model, economic growth is illustrated by an (increase, decrease) _____ in the long-run aggregate supply curve, which is (vertical, horizontal) _____. When the price level also increases over time, it indicates that the aggregate demand curve has increased (more, less) _____ rapidly than the long-run aggregate supply, and this results in ongoing inflation in an economy.

8. Along the upsloping portion of the short-run aggregate supply curve, the greater the increase in aggregate demand, the (greater, smaller) _____ the increase in the rate of inflation, the _____ the increase in real output, and the (greater, smaller) _____ the unemployment rate.

9. The original Phillips Curve indicates that there will be (a direct, an inverse) _____ relationship between the rate of inflation and the unemployment rate. This means that high rates of inflation will be associated with a (high, low) _____ unemployment rate, or that low rates of inflation will be associated with a _____ unemployment rate.

10. The policy trade-off based on a stable Phillips Curve was that for the economy to reduce the unemployment rate, the rate of inflation must (increase, decrease) _____, and to reduce the rate of inflation, the unemployment rate must _____.

11. During the 1970s and early 1980s, aggregate (demand, supply) _____ shocks made the Phillips Curve (stable, unstable) _____. These shocks produced (demand-pull, cost-push) _____ inflation that resulted in a simultaneous increase in the inflation rate and the unemployment rate, called (disinflation, stagflation) _____.

12. The standard explanation for the Phillips Curve is that during the stagflation of the 1970s, the Phillips Curve shifted (right, left) _____, and during the demise of stagflation from 1982–1989, the Phillips Curve shifted _____. In this view, there is a trade-off between the unemployment rate and the rate of inflation, but changes in (short-run, long-run) _____ aggregate supply can shift the Phillips Curve.

13. In the long run, the trade-off between the rate of inflation and the rate of unemployment (does, does not) _____ exist, and the economy is stable at its natural rate of (unemployment, inflation) _____.

14. The Phillips Curve may be downsloping in the (short run, long run) _____, but it is vertical in the _____ at the natural rate of unemployment. A shift in aggregate demand that reduces the unemployment rate in the short run, results in the long run in (an increase, a decrease) _____ in the rate of inflation and a return to the natural rate of unemployment.

15. When the actual rate of inflation is higher than the expected rate, profits temporarily (fall, rise) _____ and the unemployment rate temporarily (rises, falls) _____. This case would occur during a period of (inflation, disinflation) _____.

16. When the actual rate of inflation is lower than the expected rate, profits temporarily (fall, rise) _____ and the unemployment rate temporarily (rises, falls) _____. This case would occur during a period of (inflation, disinflation) _____.

17. It is the view of supply-side economists that high marginal tax rates (increase, decrease) _____ incentives to work, save, invest, and take risks. According to supply-side economists, a stimulus for the economy would be a substantial (increase, decrease) _____ in marginal tax rates that would _____ economic growth through (an increase, a decrease) _____ in aggregate supply.

18. The Laffer Curve depicts the relationship between tax rates and (inflation, tax revenues) _____. It is useful for showing how a (cut, rise) _____ in marginal tax rates will increase aggregate supply.

19. In theory, the Laffer Curve shows that as the tax rates increase from 0%, tax revenues will (increase, decrease) _____ to some maximum level, after which tax revenues will _____ as the tax rates increase; or as tax rates are reduced from 100%, tax revenues will (increase, decrease) _____ to some maximum level, after which tax revenues will _____ as tax rates decrease.

20. Criticisms of the Laffer Curve are that the effects of a cut in tax rates on incentives to work, save, and invest are (large, small) _____; that the tax cuts generate an increase in aggregate (demand, supply) _____ that outweigh any increase in aggregate _____ and may lead to inflation when at full employment; and that tax cuts can produce a (gain, loss) _____ in tax revenues that will only add to a budget deficit.

■ TRUE–FALSE QUESTIONS

Circle T if the statement is true, F if it is false.

1. The short run in macroeconomics is a period in which nominal wages are fully responsive to changes in the price level.   **T F**

2. The short-run aggregate supply curve has a negative slope.   **T F**

3. The long-run aggregate supply curve is vertical because nominal wages and other input prices eventually change by the same amount as changes in the price level.   **T F**

4. Demand-pull inflation will increase the price level and real output in the short run, but in the long run, only the price level will increase.   **T F**

5. Cost-push inflation results in a simultaneous increase in the price level and real output.   **T F**

6. When the economy is experiencing cost-push inflation, an inflationary spiral is likely to result when the government enacts policies to maintain full employment.   **T F**

7. A recession is the result of an increase in the short-run aggregate supply curve.   **T F**

8. If the economy is in a recession, prices and nominal wages and other input prices will presumably fall, and the short-run aggregate supply curve will increase, so that real output returns to its full-employment level.   **T F**

9. Supply factors that shift the economy's production possibilities curve outward also cause a leftward shift in its long-run aggregate supply curve.   **T F**

10. An increase in economic growth will increase the long-run aggregate supply curve and the short-run aggregate supply curve, but will decrease the aggregate demand curve.   **T F**

11. The Phillips Curve shows an inverse relationship between the rate of inflation and the unemployment rate.   **T F**

12. Stagflation refers to a situation in which both the price level and the unemployment rate are rising.   **T F**

13. Aggregate supply shocks can cause both higher rates of inflation and higher rates of unemployment.   **T F**

14. One explanation for the stagflation of the 1970s and early 1980s was an increase in aggregate demand.   **T F**

15. Among the factors that contributed to the demise of stagflation during the 1980s was a recession in 1981 and 1982.   **T F**

16. There is no apparent long-run trade-off between inflation and unemployment.   **T F**

17. When the actual rate of inflation is higher than the expected rate, profits temporarily fall and the unemployment rate temporarily rises.   **T F**

18. The long-run Phillips Curve is essentially a vertical line at the economy's natural rate of unemployment.   **T F**

19. Disinflation is the same as mismeasurement of the inflation rate.   **T F**

20. When the actual rate of inflation is lower than the expected rate of inflation, profits temporarily fall and the unemployment rate temporarily rises.   **T F**

21. Most economists reject the idea of a short-run trade-off between the unemployment and inflation rates but accept the long-run trade-off.   **T F**

22. Supply-side economists contend that aggregate demand is the only active factor in determining the price level and real output in an economy.   **T F**

23. One proposition of supply-side economics is that the marginal tax rates on earned income should be reduced to increase the incentives to work.   **T F**

24. Supply-side economists recommend a higher marginal tax rate on interest from saving because no productive work was performed to earn the interest.   **T F**

25. The Laffer Curve suggests that lower tax rates will increase the rate of inflation.   **T F**

■ MULTIPLE-CHOICE QUESTIONS

Circle the letter that corresponds to the best answer.

1. For macroeconomics, the short run is a period in which nominal wages and other input prices
   (a) do not fully adjust as the price level stays constant
   (b) change as the price level stays constant
   (c) do not fully adjust as the price level changes
   (d) change as the price level changes

2. Once sufficient time has elapsed for wage contracts to expire and nominal wage adjustments to occur, the economy enters
   (a) the short run
   (b) the long run
   (c) a period of inflation
   (d) a period of unemployment

3. A graph of the short-run aggregate supply curve is
   (a) downsloping, and a graph of the long-run aggregate supply curve is upsloping
   (b) upsloping, and a graph of the long-run aggregate supply curve is vertical
   (c) upsloping, and a graph of the long-run aggregate supply curve is downsloping

(d) vertical, and a graph of the long-run aggregate supply curve is upsloping

4. In the extended AD–AS model, demand-pull inflation occurs because of an increase in aggregate demand that will eventually produce
(a) an increase in real wages, thus a decrease in the short-run aggregate supply curve
(b) an increase in nominal wages, thus an increase in the short-run aggregate supply curve
(c) a decrease in nominal wages, thus a decrease in the short-run aggregate supply curve
(d) an increase in nominal wages, thus a decrease in the short-run aggregate supply curve

5. In the short run, demand-pull inflation increases real
(a) output and decreases the price level
(b) wages and increases nominal wages
(c) output and increases the price level
(d) wages and decreases nominal wages

6. In the long run, demand-pull inflation
(a) decreases real wages
(b) increases the price level
(c) increases the unemployment rate
(d) decreases real output

7. A likely result of the government trying to reduce the unemployment associated with cost-push inflation through stimulative fiscal policy or monetary policy is
(a) an inflationary spiral
(b) stagflation
(c) a recession
(d) disinflation

8. What will occur in the short run if there is cost-push inflation and if the government adopts a hands-off approach to it?
(a) an increase in real output
(b) a fall in unemployment
(c) demand-pull inflation
(d) a recession

9. If prices and wages are flexible, a recession will increase real wages as the price level falls. Eventually, nominal wages will
(a) fall, and the short-run aggregate supply will increase
(b) rise, and the short-run aggregate supply will increase
(c) fall, and the short-run aggregate supply will decrease
(d) rise, and the short-run aggregate supply will decrease

10. A shift outward of the production possibilities curve would be equivalent to a shift
(a) upward in aggregate demand
(b) downward in aggregate demand
(c) rightward in long-run aggregate supply
(d) leftward in long-run aggregate supply

Use the following graph to answer Questions 11 and 12.

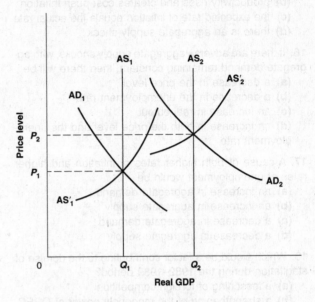

11. A shift from Q_1 to Q_2 is caused by a shift in the
(a) level of prices
(b) aggregate demand curve
(c) short-run aggregate supply curve
(d) long-run aggregate supply curve

12. Which combination would best explain a shift in the price level from P_1 to P_2 and an increase in real domestic output from Q_1 to Q_2?
(a) an increase in the long-run aggregate supply (AS_1 to AS_2) and in short-run aggregate supply (AS'_1 to AS'_2).
(b) an increase in aggregate demand (AD_1 to AD_2) and a decrease in long-run aggregate supply (AS_2 to AS_1).
(c) an increase in the long-run aggregate supply (AS_1 to AS_2), an increase in aggregate demand (AD_1 to AD_2), and an increase in short-run aggregate supply (AS'_1 to AS'_2).
(d) a decrease in the long-run aggregate supply (AS_2 to AS_1), a decrease in aggregate demand (AD_2 to AD_1), and a decrease in short-run aggregate supply (AS'_2 to AS'_1).

13. The traditional Phillips Curve is based on the idea that with a constant short-run aggregate supply curve, the greater the increase in aggregate demand
(a) the greater the unemployment rate
(b) the greater the rate of inflation
(c) the greater the increase in real output
(d) the smaller the increase in nominal wages

14. The traditional Phillips Curve shows the
(a) inverse relationship between the rate of inflation and the unemployment rate
(b) inverse relationship between the nominal wage and the real wage
(c) direct relationship between unemployment and demand-pull inflation
(d) trade-off between the short run and the long run

15. As the unemployment rate falls below its natural rate,
(a) excessive spending produces demand-pull inflation
(b) productivity rises and creates cost-push inflation
(c) the expected rate of inflation equals the actual rate
(d) there is an aggregate supply shock

16. If there are adverse aggregate supply shocks, with aggregate demand remaining constant, then there will be
(a) a decrease in the price level
(b) a decrease in the unemployment rate
(c) an increase in real output
(d) an increase in both the price level and the unemployment rate

17. A cause of both higher rates of inflation and higher rates of unemployment would be
(a) an increase in aggregate demand
(b) an increase in aggregate supply
(c) a decrease in aggregate demand
(d) a decrease in aggregate supply

18. Which would be a factor contributing to the demise of stagflation during the 1982–1989 period?
(a) a lessening of foreign competition
(b) a strengthening of the monopoly power of OPEC
(c) a recession brought on largely by a tight monetary policy
(d) an increase in regulation of airline and trucking industries

19. The economy is stable only in the
(a) short run at a high rate of profit
(b) short run at the natural rate of inflation
(c) long run at the natural rate of unemployment
(d) long run at the natural rate of inflation

20. When the actual inflation rate is higher than expected, profits temporarily
(a) fall and the unemployment rate temporarily falls
(b) rise and the unemployment rate temporarily falls
(c) rise and the unemployment rate temporarily rises
(d) fall and the unemployment rate temporarily rises

21. When the actual rate of inflation is lower than the expected rate, profits temporarily
(a) fall and the unemployment rate temporarily rises
(b) rise and the unemployment rate temporarily falls
(c) rise and the unemployment rate temporarily rises
(d) fall and the unemployment rate temporarily falls

22. In a disinflation situation, the
(a) actual rate of inflation is lower than the expected rate, so the unemployment rate will rise to bring the expected and actual rates into balance
(b) expected rate of inflation is lower than the actual rate, so the unemployment rate will rise to bring the expected and actual rates into balance
(c) actual rate of inflation is higher than the expected rate, so the unemployment rate will fall to bring the expected and actual rates into balance
(d) expected rate of inflation is higher than the actual rate, so the unemployment rate will fall to bring the expected and actual rates into balance

23. The long-run Phillips Curve is essentially
(a) horizontal at the natural rate of unemployment
(b) vertical at the natural rate of unemployment
(c) vertical at the natural rate of inflation
(d) horizontal at the natural rate of inflation

24. Supply-side economists contend that the U.S. system of taxation reduces
(a) unemployment but causes inflation
(b) incentives to work, save, and invest
(c) transfer payments to the poor
(d) the effects of cost-push inflation

25. Based on the Laffer Curve, a cut in the tax rate from 100% to a point before the maximum level of tax revenue will
(a) increase the price level
(b) increase tax revenues
(c) decrease real output
(d) decrease real wages

■ **PROBLEMS**

1. In columns 1 and 2 of the table at the bottom of the page is a portion of a short-run aggregate supply schedule. Column 3 shows the number of full-time workers (in millions) that would have to be employed to produce each of the seven real domestic outputs (in billions) in the short-run aggregate supply schedule. The labor force is 80 million workers and the full-employment output of the economy is $_____.

(1) Price level	(2) Real output supplied	(3) Employment (in millions)	(4) Real output demanded	(5) Real output demanded	(6) Real output demanded
130	$ 800	69	$2300	$2600	$1900
140	1300	70	2200	2500	1800
150	1700	72	2100	2400	1700
160	2000	75	2000	2300	1600
170	2200	78	1900	2200	1500
180	2300	80	1800	2100	1400
190	2300	80	1700	2000	1300

a. If the aggregate demand schedule were that shown in columns 1 and 4,

(1) the price level would be _____ and the real output would be $_____.

(2) the number of workers employed would be _____, the number of workers unemployed would be _____ million, and the unemployment rate would be _____%.

b. If aggregate demand were to increase to that shown in columns 1 and 5 and short-run aggregate supply remained constant,

(1) the price level would rise to _____ and the real output would rise to $_____.

(2) employment would increase by _____ million workers and the unemployment rate would fall to _____%.

(3) the price level would increase by _____ and the rate of inflation would be _____%.

c. If aggregate demand were to decrease to that shown in columns 1 and 6 and short-run aggregate supply remained constant,

(1) the price level would fall to _____ and the real output would fall to $_____.

(2) employment would decrease by _____ compared with situation **a,** and workers and the unemployment rate would rise to _____%.

(3) the price level would decrease and the rate of inflation would be (positive, negative) _____.

2. The following is an aggregate demand and aggregate supply model. Assume that the economy is initially in equilibrium at AD_1 and AS_1. The price level will be _____ and the real domestic output will be _____.

Real domestic output

a. If there is demand-pull inflation, then

(1) in the short run, the new equilibrium is at point _____, with the price level at _____ and real output at _____;

(2) in the long run, nominal wages will rise so the aggregate supply curve will shift from _____ to _____. The equilibrium will be at point _____ with the price level at _____ and real output at _____, so the increase in aggregate demand has only moved the economy along its _____ curve.

b. Now assume that the economy is initially in equilibrium at point **W,** where AD_1 and AS_1 intersect. If there is cost-push inflation, then

(1) in the short run, the new equilibrium is at point _____, with the price level at _____ and real output at _____.

(2) if the government tries to counter the cost-push inflation with expansionary monetary and fiscal policy, then aggregate demand will shift from _____ to _____, with the price level becoming _____ and real output _____, but this policy has a trap because the price level has shifted from _____ to _____ and the new level of inflation might shift _____ leftward.

(3) if government does not counter the cost-push inflation, the price level will eventually move to _____ and real output to _____ as the recession reduces nominal wages and shifts the aggregate supply curve from _____ to _____.

c. Now assume that the economy is initially in equilibrium at point **Y,** where AD_2 and AS_2 intersect. If there is a recession that reduces investment spending, then

(1) aggregate demand decreases and real output shifts from _____ to _____, and, assuming that prices and wages are flexible downward, the price level shifts from _____ to _____.

(2) The recession causes nominal wages and other input prices to (rise, fall) _____ and when this happens, the short-run aggregate supply curve shifts from _____ to _____ to its new equilibrium at point _____. The equilibrium price level is _____ and the equilibrium level of output is _____ at the long-run aggregate supply curve _____.

3. The following is a traditional Phillips Curve.

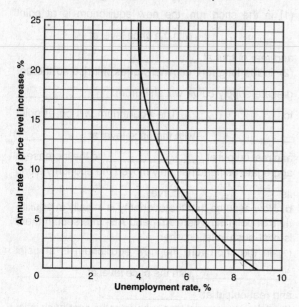

a. At full employment (a 4% unemployment rate) the price level would rise by _____% each year.

b. If the price level were stable (increasing by 0% a year), the unemployment rate would be _____%.

c. Which of the combinations along the Phillips Curve would you choose for the economy? _____

Why would you select this combination? _____

_____

4. Following is a model of short- and long-run Phillips Curves.

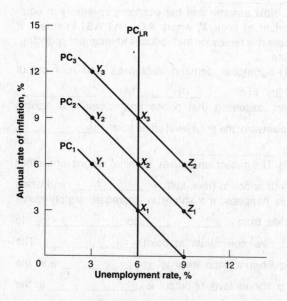

a. Suppose you begin at point **X₁** and an assumption is made that nominal wages are set on the original expectation that a 3% rate of inflation will continue in the economy.

(1) If an increase in aggregate demand reduces the unemployment rate from 6% to 3%, then the actual rate of inflation will move to _____%. The higher product prices will lift profits of firms and they will hire more workers; thus in the short run the economy will temporarily move to point _____.

(2) If workers demand and receive higher wages to compensate for the loss of purchasing power from higher than expected inflation, then business profits will fall from previous levels and firms will reduce employment; therefore, the unemployment rate will move from point _____ to point _____ on the graph. The short-run Phillips Curve has shifted from _____ to _____ on the graph.

(3) If aggregate demand continues to increase so that the unemployment rate drops from 6% to 3%, then prices will rise before nominal wages, and output and employment will increase, so that there will be a move from point _____ to point _____ on the graph.

(4) But when workers get nominal wage increases, profits fall, and the unemployment rate moves from point _____ at _____% to point _____ at _____%. The short-run Phillips Curve has now shifted from _____ to _____ on the graph.

(5) The long-run Phillips Curve is the line _____.

b. Suppose you begin at point **X₃**, where the expected and actual rate of inflation is 9% and the unemployment rate is 6%.

(1) If there should be a decline in aggregate demand because of a recession and if the actual rate of inflation should fall to 6%, well below the expected rate of 9%, then business profits will fall and the unemployment rate will decrease to 9% as shown by the movement from point **X₃** to point _____.

(2) If firms and workers adjust their expectation to the 6% rate of inflation, the nominal wages will fall, profits will rise, and the economy will move from point _____ to point _____. The short-run Phillips Curve has shifted from _____ to _____.

(3) If this process is repeated, the long-run Phillips Curve will be traced as line _____.

5. The following is a Laffer Curve.

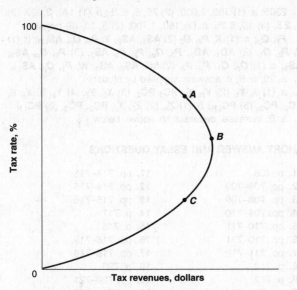

a. The point of maximum tax revenue is _____. As tax rates decrease from 100% to point **B,** tax revenues will (increase, decrease) _____. As tax rates increase from 0% to point **B,** tax revenues will _____.

b. Supply-side economists would contend that it would be beneficial for government to cut tax rates if they are (below, above) _____ point **B,** whereas critics of supply-side economics contend that it would be harmful for government to cut tax rates if they are _____ point **B.**

■ **SHORT ANSWER AND ESSAY QUESTIONS**

1. What distinguishes the short run from the long run in macroeconomics?

2. Identify the basic difference between a short-run and a long-run aggregate supply curve.

3. Explain what happens to aggregate supply when an increase in the price level results in an increase in nominal wages and other input prices.

4. Explain how to find equilibrium in the extended AD–AS model.

5. Describe the process of demand-pull inflation in the short run and in the long run.

6. How does demand-pull inflation influence the aggregate supply curve?

7. Describe cost-push inflation in the extended AD–AS model.

8. What two generalizations emerge from the analysis of cost-push inflation? Describe the two scenarios that provide the basis for the generalizations.

9. Describe recession in the extended AD–AS model.

10. Why do modern economies tend to experience positive rates of inflation? Explain using the extend AD–AS model.

11. What is a Phillips Curve? What two rates are related?

12. Explain how a Phillips Curve with a negative slope may be derived by holding aggregate supply constant and mentally increasing aggregate demand.

13. Were the rates of inflation and of unemployment consistent with the Phillips Curve in the 1960s? What do data on these two rates suggest about the curve since then?

14. What were the aggregate supply shocks to the U.S. economy during the 1970s and early 1980s? How did these shocks affect interpretation of the Phillips Curve?

15. How can there be a short-run trade-off between inflation and unemployment, but no long-run trade-off? Explain.

16. How can the Phillips Curve be used to explain both inflation and disinflation in the economy?

17. What are the characteristics of the long-run Phillips Curve? How is it related to the natural rate of unemployment?

18. Discuss why supply-side economists contend there are tax disincentives in the economy.

19. Draw and explain a Laffer Curve showing the relationship between tax rates and tax revenues.

20. Outline the three criticisms of the ideas expressed in the depiction of the Laffer Curve.

ANSWERS

Chapter 35 Extending the Analysis of Aggregate Supply

FILL-IN QUESTIONS

1. increase, decrease
2. unresponsive, responsive, upsloping, vertical
3. right, increase, increase, short-run, nominal, higher
4. left, increase, decrease
5. decrease, increase
6. a decrease, falls, increase, decrease, increase
7. increase, vertical, more
8. greater, greater, smaller
9. an inverse, low, high
10. increase, increase
11. supply, unstable, cost-push, stagflation
12. right, left, short-run
13. does not, unemployment
14. short run, long run, an increase
15. rise, falls, inflation
16. fall, rises, disinflation
17. decrease, decrease, increase, an increase
18. tax revenues, cut
19. increase, decrease, increase, decrease
20. small, demand, supply, loss

TRUE–FALSE QUESTIONS

1. F, p. 708
2. F, pp. 708–709
3. T, pp. 708–709
4. T, pp. 710–711
5. F, pp. 711–712
6. T, pp. 711–712
7. F, p. 712
8. T, p. 712
9. F, p. 713
10. F, pp. 713–714
11. T, pp. 714–715
12. T, p. 717
13. T, p. 717

14. F, p. 717
15. T, p. 718
16. T, p. 718
17. F, pp. 718–719
18. T, p. 719
19. F, p. 719
20. T, p. 719
21. F, pp. 718–719
22. F, p. 720
23. T, p. 720
24. F, p. 720
25. F, pp. 720–721

MULTIPLE-CHOICE QUESTIONS

1. c, p. 708
2. b, p. 708
3. b, pp. 708–709
4. d, pp. 710–711
5. c, pp. 710–711
6. b, pp. 710–711
7. a, pp. 711–712
8. d, pp. 711–712
9. a, p. 712
10. c, p. 713
11. d, pp. 713–714
12. c, pp. 713–714
13. b, pp. 714–715

14. a, pp. 714–715
15. a, p. 715
16. d, p. 717
17. d, p. 717
18. c, p. 717
19. c, p. 718
20. b, p. 718
21. a, p. 719
22. a, p. 719
23. b, p. 719
24. b, p. 720
25. b, pp. 720–721

PROBLEMS

1. 2300; *a.* (1) 160, 2,000, (2) 75, 5, 6.25; *b.* (1) 170, 2,200, (2) 3, 2.5, (3) 10, 6.25; *c.* (1) 150, 1,700, (2) 3, 10, (3) negative
2. P_1, Q_p; *a.* (1) X, P_2, Q_2 (2) AS_1, AS_2, Y, P_3, Q_p, AS_{LR}; *b.* (1) Z, P_2, Q_1, (2) AD_1, AD_2, P_3, Q_p, P_2, P_3, AS_2, (3) P_1, Q_p, AS_2, AS_1; *c.* (1) Q_p, Q_1, P_3, P_2, (2) fall, AS_2, AS_1, W, P_1, Q_p, AS_{LR}
3. *a.* 20; *b.* 9; *c.* answers supplied by student
4. *a.* (1) 6, Y_1, (2) Y_1, X_2, PC_1 PC_2, (3) X_2, Y_2, (4) Y_2, 3, X_3, 6, PC_2, PC_3, (5) PC_{LR}; *b.* (1) Z_2, (2) Z_2, X_2, PC_3, PC_2, (3) PC_{LR}
5. *a.* B, increase, decrease; *b.* above, below

SHORT ANSWER AND ESSAY QUESTIONS

1. p. 708
2. pp. 708–709
3. pp. 708–709
4. pp. 709–710
5. pp. 710–711
6. pp. 710–711
7. pp. 711–712
8. p. 712
9. p. 712
10. pp. 712–714

11. pp. 714–715
12. pp. 714–715
13. pp. 715–716
14. p. 717
15. p. 718
16. pp. 718–719
17. pp. 718–719
18. p. 720
19. pp. 720–721
20. pp. 721, 723

Current Issues in Macro Theory and Policy

Now that you understand the basic theory and models of the macro economy, you are ready to learn about different perspectives on how the economy functions and the current issues in macro theory and policy. The chapter achieves those purposes by breaking the discussion into three parts to address three important macro questions.

The first question is: **What causes macro instability in the economy?** Four different perspectives on the issues are given. First, from the *mainstream* view, this instability arises primarily from price stickiness that makes it difficult for the economy to adjust and achieve its potential output when there are aggregate demand or aggregate supply shocks to the economy. Second, *monetarists* focus on the money supply and assume that the competitive market economy has a high degree of stability, except when there is inappropriate monetary policy. The monetarist analysis is based on the equation of exchange and the assumption that the velocity of money is stable. Changes in the money supply, therefore, directly affect the level of nominal GDP. Third, *real-business-cycle* theorists see instability as coming from the aggregate supply side of the economy and from real factors that affect the long-term growth rather than monetary factors that affect aggregate demand. Fourth, some economists think that macroeconomic instability is the result of *coordination failures* that do not permit people to act jointly to determine the optimal level of output, and that the equilibrium in the economy changes as expectations change.

The next question the chapter discusses is: **Does the economy self-correct its macro instability?** The view of new classical economics is that internal mechanisms in the economy allow it to self-correct. The two variants of this new classical perspective are based on *monetarism* and the *rational expectations theory (RET)*. Monetarists think the economy will self-correct to its long-run level of output, although there can be short-run changes in the price level and real output. The rational expectations theory suggests that the self-correction process is quick and does not change the price level or real output, except when there are price-level surprises.

By contrast, mainstream economists contend that the downward inflexibility of wages limits the self-correction mechanisms in the economy. Several explanations are offered for this inflexibility. There can be long-term wage contracts that support wages. Firms also may pay an efficiency wage to encourage work effort, reduce turnover, and prevent shirking. Firms may also be concerned about maintaining the support and teamwork of key workers (insiders), so they do not cut wages even when other workers (outsiders) might be willing to accept a lower wage.

The different perspectives on macro instability and self-correction set the stage for discussion of the third and final question: **Should the macro economy be guided by policy rules or discretion?** To restrict monetary policy, monetarists and rational expectations economists call for a monetary rule that would have monetary authorities allow the money supply to grow in proportion to the long-term growth in the productive capacity of the economy. Both monetarists and rational expectations economists also oppose the use of fiscal policy, and a few call for a balanced budget requirement to limit the use of discretionary fiscal policy.

Mainstream economists see value in discretionary monetary and fiscal policies. They suggest that a monetary rule would be ineffective in achieving growth and would destabilize the economy. A balanced-budget requirement would also have a pro-cyclical effect that would reinforce recessionary or inflationary tendencies in the economy. And since government has taken a more active role in the economy, the historical record shows that discretionary monetary and fiscal actions have reduced macro instability.

As was the case in the past, macroeconomic theory and policy have changed because of the debates among economists. The disputes among mainstream economists, monetarists, rational expectationists, and real business cycle theorists have produced new insights about how the macro economy operates. In particular, it is now recognized that "money matters" and that the money supply has a significant effect on the economy. More attention is also being given to the influence of people's expectations on policy and coordination failures in explaining macroeconomic events. The disputes in macroeconomics in the past half-century forced economists to reconsider previous conclusions and led to the incorporation of new ideas about macro theory and policy into mainstream thinking.

■ **CHECKLIST**

When you have studied this chapter you should be able to

☐ Describe the mainstream view of stability in the macro economy and the two potential sources of instability.

☐ Explain the monetarist view of stability in the macro economy.

☐ Write the equation of exchange and define each of the four terms in the equation.

☐ Explain why monetarists think the velocity of money is relatively stable.

☐ Write a brief scenario that explains what monetarists believe will happen to change the nominal GDP and will happen to *V* (velocity of money) when *M* (money supply) is increased.

☐ Discuss the monetary causes of instability in the macro economy.

☐ Describe the real-business-cycle view of stability in the macro economy.

☐ Give noneconomic and macroeconomic examples of the coordination failures view of stability in the macro economy.

☐ Use a graph to explain the new classical view of self-correction in the macro economy.

☐ Discuss the differences between the monetarist and rational expectations views on the speed of adjustment for self-correction in the macro economy.

☐ State the two basic assumptions of the rational expectations theory (RET).

☐ Use a graph to explain how RET views unanticipated and fully anticipated changes in the price level.

☐ Describe the mainstream view of self-correction in the macro economy.

☐ Give two reasons why there may be downward wage inflexibility.

☐ State three reasons why a higher wage might result in greater efficiency.

☐ Use ideas from the insider–outsider theory to explain the downward inflexibility of wages.

☐ State why monetarists think there should be a monetary rule, and illustrate the rationale using aggregate demand and aggregate supply models.

☐ Explain why some economists have advocated inflation targeting.

☐ Describe how monetarists and new classical economists view the effectiveness of fiscal policy.

☐ Offer a mainstream defense of a discretionary stabilization policy and a critique of a monetary rule and balanced-budget requirement.

☐ Describe the possible reasons for increased stability in the macro economy in the past half-century.

☐ Summarize the three alternative views on issues affecting the macro economy.

☐ Explain the purpose and components of the Taylor rule (Last Word).

■ CHAPTER OUTLINE

1. There are four different views among economists on **instability** in the macro economy.

a. The **mainstream view** holds that instability in the economy arises from price stickiness and from unexpected shocks to either aggregate demand or aggregate supply. Sticky prices make it difficult for the economy to quickly and fully adjust to economic shocks from either unexpected changes in aggregate demand or aggregate supply.

(1) Changes in aggregate demand can arise from a change in any one of the components of aggregate demand (consumption, investment, government, and net export spending). Investment spending is a particularly volatile component of aggregate demand instability.

(2) Adverse aggregate supply shocks which cause cost-push inflation and recession.

b. **Monetarism** focuses on the money supply. Monetarists think markets are highly competitive and that government intervention destabilizes the economy.

(1) In monetarism, the **equation of exchange** is *MV* = *PQ*, where *M* is the money supply, *V* the **velocity** of money, *P* the price level, and *Q* the quantity of goods and services produced.

(2) Monetarists think that velocity is relatively stable or that the quantity of money demanded is a stable percentage of GDP (GDP/*M* is constant). If velocity is stable, there is a predictable relationship between *M* and nominal GDP (= *PQ*). An increase in *M* will leave firms and households with more money than they wish to have, so they will increase spending and boost aggregate demand. This causes nominal GDP and the amount of money they wish to hold to rise until the demand for money is equal to *M* and nominal GDP/*M* = *V*.

(3) Monetarists view macroeconomic instability as a result of inappropriate monetary policy. An increase in the money supply will increase aggregate demand, output, and the price level; it will also reduce unemployment. Eventually, nominal wages rise to restore real wages and real output, and the unemployment rate falls back to its natural level at long-run aggregate supply.

c. **Real-business-cycle theory** sees macroeconomic instability as being caused by real factors influencing aggregate supply instead of monetary factors causing shifts in aggregate demand. Changes in technology and resources will affect productivity and thus the long-run growth rate of aggregate supply.

d. A fourth view of instability in the macro economy attributes the reasons to **coordination failures.** These failures occur when people are not able to coordinate their actions to achieve an optimal equilibrium. A self-fulfilling prophecy can lead to a recession because if households and firms expect it, they individually cut back on spending and employment. If, however, they were to act jointly, they could take actions to counter the recession expectations to achieve an optimal equilibrium.

2. Economists also debate the issue of whether the macro economy self-corrects.

a. **New classical economics,** based on monetarism and rational expectations theory, says the economy may deviate from full-employment output, but it eventually returns to this output level because there are self-corrective mechanisms in the economy.

(1) Graphically, if aggregate demand increases, it temporarily raises real output and the price level. Nominal wages rise and productivity falls, so short-run aggregate supply decreases, thus bringing the economy back to its long-run output level.

(2) There is disagreement about the speed of adjustment. The monetarists adopt the adaptive expectations view that there will be a slower, temporary change in output but that in the long run it will return to its natural level. Other new classical economists adopt the **rational expectations theory (RET)** view that there will be a rapid adjustment with little or no change in

output. RET is based on two assumptions: People understand how the economy works so that they quickly anticipate the effect on the economy of an economic event; and all markets in the economy are so competitive that equilibrium prices and quantities quickly adjust to changes in policy.

(3) In RET, unanticipated price-level changes, called *price-level surprises,* cause short-run changes in real output because they cause misperceptions about the economy among workers and firms.

(4) In RET, fully anticipated price-level changes do not change real output even in the short run because workers and firms anticipate and counteract the effects of the changes.

b. The **mainstream view** of self-correction suggests that price and wages may be inflexible downward in the economy.

(1) Graphically, a decrease in aggregate demand will decrease real output but not the price level because nominal wages will not decline and cause the short-run aggregate supply curve to shift right.

(2) Downward wage inflexibility primarily arises because of wage contracts and the legal minimum wage, but they may also occur from efficiency wages and insider–outsider relationships.

(3) An *efficiency wage* minimizes the firm's labor cost per unit of output but may be higher than the market wage. This higher wage may result in greater efficiency because it stimulates greater work effort, requires less supervision costs, and reduces job turnover.

(4) *Insider–outsider theory* suggests that relationships may also produce downward wage inflexibility. During a recession, outsiders (who are less essential to the firm) may try to bid down wages to try to keep their jobs, but the firm may not lower wages because it does not want to alienate insiders (who are more essential to the firm) and disrupt the cooperative environment in the firm needed for production.

3. The debates over macro policy also focus on the need for **policy rules or discretion.**

a. Monetarists and new classical economists argue for policy rules to reduce government intervention in the economy. They believe this intervention causes macroeconomic instability.

(1) In regard to monetary policy, monetarists such as Milton Friedman have proposed a *monetary rule* that the money supply be increased at the same annual rate as the potential annual rate of increase in the real GDP. A monetary rule would shift aggregate demand rightward to match a shift in the long-run aggregate supply curve that occurs because of economic growth, thus keeping the price level stable over time. More recently, economists have advocated **inflation targeting** as an alternative to a Friedman-type monetary rule. Such targeting would involve the Fed specifying a target range for inflation and then using monetary policy tools to help the economy achieve its target.

(2) Monetarists and new classical economists question the value of fiscal policy, and some would like to see a balanced Federal budget over time. An expansionist fiscal policy will tend to crowd out investment and cause only a temporary increase in output. RET economists also think that fiscal policy is ineffective and that people will anticipate it and their acts will counteract its intended effects.

b. Mainstream economists think that discretionary fiscal and monetary policy can be effective and are opposed to a monetary rule and a balanced-budget requirement.

(1) They see the velocity of money as relatively unstable and a loose link between changes in the money supply and aggregate demand. This means that a monetary rule might produce too great a shift in aggregate demand (and demand-pull inflation) or too small a shift (and deflation) to match the shift in aggregate supply. Such a rule would contribute to price instability, not price stability.

(2) They support the use of fiscal policy during a recession or to counter growing inflation. Fiscal policy, however, should be reserved for those situations where monetary policy is relatively ineffective. They also oppose a balanced-budget amendment because its effects would be pro-cyclical rather than countercyclical and would reinforce recessionary or inflationary tendencies.

c. Mainstream economists also note that there has been greater stability in the macro economy since 1946, when discretionary monetary and fiscal policies were more actively used to moderate the effects of the business cycle.

4. The **disputes in macroeconomics** have led to the incorporation of several ideas from monetarism and rational expectations theories into the mainstream thinking about macroeconomics. First, monetarists have gotten mainstream economists to recognize that changes in the money supply are important in explaining long-lasting and rapid inflation. Second, mainstream economists now recognize that expectations matter because of arguments from the rational expectations theory and theories about coordination failures in the economy. There will be more price stability, full employment, and economic growth if government can create reliable expectations of those outcomes for households and businesses. In short, macroeconomics continues to develop. Table 36.1 summarizes the three alternative views of macroeconomics.

5. (Last Word). The *Taylor rule* specifies what actions the Fed should take in changing the Federal funds rate given changes in real GDP and inflation. This monetary rule has three parts: (a) when real GDP equals potential GDP, and inflation is equal to the Fed's 2% target for the inflation rate, the Federal funds rate should stay at 4 percent, to give a real interest rate of 2 percent; (b) if real GDP rises 1 percent above potential GDP, then the Fed should raise the real Federal funds rate .5 percentage points; and (c) if inflation rises by 1 percentage point above its target of 2%, then the Fed should raise the real Federal funds rate by .5 percentage point.

■ HINTS AND TIPS

1. The chapter may appear complex because many alternative viewpoints are presented. To simplify matters, first focus on the three questions that the chapter addresses: What causes macro instability in the economy? Does the economy self-correct? Should policymakers use rules or discretion? For each question, identify how different types of economists answer each question.

2. Review the discussions of aggregate demand and aggregate supply in Chapters 29 and 35 as preparation for the comparison of alternative views of the macro economy presented in this chapter.

3. Monetarist and mainstream views of the macro economy are two approaches of looking at the same thing. The similarities can best be seen in equations in nominal form. The monetarist equation of exchange is $MV = PQ$. The mainstream equation is $C_a + I_g + X_n + G = GDP$. The MV term is the monetarist expression for the mainstream equilibrium $C_a + I_g + X_n + G$. The PQ term is the monetarist expression for GDP. Monetarists give more emphasis to the role of money and assume that velocity is relatively stable. Mainstream economists give more emphasis to the instability caused by investment spending and to influences on GDP from consumption, net exports, and government spending.

■ IMPORTANT TERMS

monetarism

equation of exchange

velocity

real-business-cycle theory

coordination failures

rational expectations theory

new classical economics

price-level surprises

efficiency wage

insider–outsider theory

monetary rule

Inflation targeting

Taylor rule

SELF-TEST

■ FILL-IN QUESTIONS

1. The mainstream view is that instability in the economy arises from price (flexibility, stickiness) _____ and from shocks to aggregate demand or aggregate supply that are (expected, unexpected) _____.

2. One of the most volatile components of aggregate demand is (net export, investment) _____ spending. If it increases too rapidly, then (inflation, recession) _____ can occur, but if it decreases, then the economy can experience _____.

3. The economy also is subject to instability from wars or resource shortages that (raise, lower) _____ per-unit production costs. Such adverse aggregate (demand,

supply) _____ shocks can lead to cost-push inflation and recession.

4. Monetarists argue that capitalism is inherently (stable, unstable) _____ because most of its markets are (competitive, noncompetitive) _____. They believe that government intervention in the economy has contributed to macroeconomic (stability, instability) _____ and has promoted (flexibility, inflexibility) _____ in wages.

5. The basic equation of the monetarists is _____ = _____. Indicate what each of the following four letters in the equation represents:

    a. *M*: _____

    b. *V*: _____

    c. *P*: _____

    d. *Q*: _____

6. Monetarists believe that *V* is relatively (stable, unstable) _____ because people have a _____ desire to hold money relative to holding other financial and real assets or for making purchases. The amount of money people will want to hold will depend on the level of (real, nominal) _____ GDP.

7. An increase in *M*, to the monetarist's way of thinking, will leave the public with (more, less) _____ money than it wishes to have, induce the public to (increase, decrease) _____ its spending for consumer and capital goods, which will result in a(n) _____ in aggregate demand and nominal GDP until nominal GDP equals *MV*.

8. Monetarists believe that the most significant cause of macroeconomic instability has been inappropriate (fiscal, monetary) _____ policy. Too rapid increases in *M* cause (recession, inflation) _____; insufficient growth of *M* causes _____.

9. The theory that changes in resource availability and technology (real factors), which alter productivity, are the main causes of instability in the macro economy is held by (real-business-cycle, rational expectations) _____ economists. In this theory, shifts in the economy's long-run aggregate (demand, supply) _____ curve change real output. As a consequence, money demand and money supply change, shifting the aggregate demand curve in the (opposite, same) _____ direction as the initial change in long-run aggregate supply. Real output thus can change (with, without) _____ a change in the price level.

10. A coordination failure is said to occur when people (do, do not) _____ reach a mutually beneficial equilibrium because they lack some way to jointly coordinate their actions. In this view, there is(are) (one, a number of) _____ equilibrium position(s) in the economy. Macroeconomic instability is the result of changing (the money supply, expectations) _____ that result in changing the equilibrium position(s).

11. Monetarists and rational expectations economists view the economy as (capable, incapable) _____ of self-correction when it deviates from the full-employment level of real output. Monetarists suggest that this adjustment occurs (gradually, rapidly) _____, while rational expectations economists argue that it occurs _____.

12. Rational expectations theory assumes that with sufficient information, people's beliefs about future economic outcomes (are, are not) _____ accurate reflections of the likelihood of the outcomes occurring. It also assumes that markets are highly competitive, meaning that prices and wages are (flexible, inflexible) _____.

13. In the rational expectations theory, changes in aggregate demand that change the price level and real output are (anticipated, unanticipated) _____, while changes in aggregate demand that only change the price level and not real output are _____.

14. The view of mainstream economists is that many prices and wages are (flexible, inflexible) _____ downward for (short, long) _____ periods of time. This situation (increases, decreases) _____ the ability of the economy to automatically self-correct for deviations from full-employment output.

15. A higher wage can result in more efficiency because it results in (greater, less) _____ work effort, supervision costs that are (lower, higher) _____, and (more, less) _____ turnover in jobs. Efficiency wages (increase, decrease) _____ the downward inflexibility of wages because they make firms more reluctant to cut wages when aggregate demand declines.

16. Monetarists and rational expectations economists support a monetary rule because they believe that discretionary monetary policy tends to (stabilize, destabilize) _____ the economy. With this rule the money supply would be increased at a rate (greater than, less than, equal to) _____ the long-run growth of potential GDP; graphically, this can be shown by a shift in aggregate demand that would be _____ the shift in long-run aggregate supply resulting from economic growth.

17. In recent decades, the call for a monetary rule has faded and has been replaced with a call for (efficiency wages, inflation targeting) _____. In such an approach, the Federal Reserve would specify an acceptable range for (unemployment, inflation) _____ and use its monetary tools to achieve that objective.

18. Proponents of the rational expectations theory contend that discretionary monetary policy is (effective, ineffective) _____ and like the monetarists favor (rules, discretion) _____. When considering discretionary fiscal policy, most monetarists and RET economists (do, do not) _____ advocate its use.

19. Mainstream economists (support, oppose) _____ a monetary rule and a balanced-budget requirement. They view discretionary monetary policy as (effective, ineffective) _____, and think discretionary fiscal policy is _____ but should be held in reserve when monetary policy works too slowly. They say the use of discretionary monetary and fiscal policies since 1950 has produced (more, less) _____ stability in the macro economy.

20. Many ideas from alternative views of the macro economy have been absorbed into mainstream thinking about macroeconomics. There is more recognition that excessive growth of the money supply is a major cause of (recession, inflation) _____, and that expectations and coordination failures are (important, unimportant) _____ in the formulation of government policies for price stability, unemployment, and economic growth.

■ **TRUE–FALSE QUESTIONS**

Circle T if the statement is true, F if it is false.

1. The mainstream view is that macro instability arises from price stickiness and unexpected shocks to either aggregate demand or aggregate supply.　　**T　F**

2. Among the components of aggregate expenditures the most volatile is investment spending, which can cause unexpected shifts in the aggregate demand curve.　　**T　F**

3. Monetarists argue that the market system would provide for macroeconomic stability were it not for government interference in the economy.　　**T　F**

4. In the equation of exchange, the left side, *MV,* represents the total amount received by sellers of output, while the right side, *PQ*, represents the total amount spent by purchasers of that output.　　**T　F**

5. Monetarists argue that *V* in the equation of exchange is relatively stable and that a change in *M* will bring about a direct and proportional change in *PQ*.　　**T　F**

6. Most monetarists believe that an increase in the money supply has no effect on real output and employment in the short run.   **T   F**

7. In the monetarist view, the only cause of the Great Depression was the decline in investment spending.   **T   F**

8. Real-business-cycle theory views changes in resource availability and technology, which alter productivity, as the main cause of macroeconomic instability.   **T   F**

9. In the real-business-cycle theory, real output changes only with a change in the price level.   **T   F**

10. In real-business-cycle theory, macro instability arises on the aggregate demand side of the economy.   **T   F**

11. A coordination failure is said to occur when people do not reach a mutually beneficial equilibrium because they lack some way to jointly coordinate their actions to achieve it.   **T   F**

12. People's expectations have no effect on coordination failures.   **T   F**

13. New classical economists see the economy as automatically correcting itself when disturbed from its full-employment level of real output.   **T   F**

14. The rational expectations theory assumes that both product and resource markets are uncompetitive and wages and prices are inflexible.   **T   F**

15. In rational expectations an assumption is made that people adjust their expectations quickly as new developments occur that affect future economic outcomes.   **T   F**

16. In the rational expectations theory, a fully anticipated price-level change results in a change in real output.   **T   F**

17. Mainstream economists contend that many wages and prices are inflexible downward.   **T   F**

18. An efficiency wage is a below-market wage that spurs greater work effort and gives the firm more profits because of lower wage costs.   **T   F**

19. One reason a higher wage can result in greater economic efficiency is that it lowers supervision costs.   **T   F**

20. Insider–outsider theory offers one explanation for the downward inflexibility of wages in the economy.   **T   F**

21. Monetarists believe that a monetary rule would reduce instability in the macro economy.   **T   F**

22. Rational expectations economists argue that monetary policy should be left to the discretion of government.   **T   F**

23. Monetarists support the use of fiscal policy, especially as a means of controlling inflation.   **T   F**

24. Mainstream economists believe that discretionary monetary policy is an effective tool for stabilizing the economy.   **T   F**

25. The mainstream view of the economy since 1950 believes that the economy has become inherently less stable because of the use of fiscal policy.   **T   F**

■ **MULTIPLE-CHOICE QUESTIONS**

Circle the letter that corresponds to the best answer.

1. One of the sources of macro instability in the view of mainstream economists is that
  (a) output is fixed in the long run
  (b) output is fixed in the short run
  (c) prices are sticky in the short run
  (d) prices are flexible in the long run

2. From the perspective of mainstream economists, another source of macroeconomic instability is
  (a) a velocity of money that is stable
  (b) a velocity of money that is unstable
  (c) expected shocks to aggregate demand or aggregate supply
  (d) unexpected shocks to aggregate demand or aggregate supply

3. The mainstream view of the economy holds that
  (a) government intervention in the economy is not desirable
  (b) product and labor markets are highly competitive and flexible
  (c) changes in investment spending lead to changes in aggregate demand
  (d) economic growth is best achieved through implementation of a monetary rule

4. In the monetarist perspective
  (a) discretionary monetary policy is the most effective way to moderate swings in the business cycle
  (b) government policies have reduced macroeconomic stability
  (c) macroeconomic stability results from adverse aggregate supply shocks
  (d) markets in a capitalistic economy are largely noncompetitive

5. Which is the equation of exchange?
  (a) $PQ/M + V = GDP$
  (b) $V = M + PQ$
  (c) $MV = PQ$
  (d) $V + I_g + M = GDP$

6. In the equation of exchange, if V is stable, an increase in M will necessarily increase
  (a) the demand for money
  (b) government spending
  (c) nominal GDP
  (d) velocity

7. When nominal gross domestic product (GDP) is divided by the money supply (M), you will obtain the
  (a) velocity of money
  (b) monetary multiplier
  (c) equation of exchange
  (d) monetary rule

8. Monetarists argue that the amount of money the public will want to hold depends primarily on the level of
  (a) nominal GDP
  (b) investment
  (c) taxes
  (d) prices

9. Based on the equation of exchange, if nominal GDP is $550 billion and the velocity of money is 5, then the money supply is
(a) $55 billion
(b) $110 billion
(c) $550 billion
(d) $2,750 billion

10. Real-business-cycle theory suggests that
(a) velocity changes gradually and predictably; thus it is able to accommodate the long-run changes in nominal GDP
(b) the volatility of investment is the main cause of the economy's instability
(c) inappropriate monetary policy is the single most important cause of macroeconomic instability
(d) changes in technology and resources affect productivity, and thus the long-run growth of aggregate supply

11. In the real-business-cycle theory, if the long-run aggregate supply increased, then aggregate demand would increase by
(a) an equal amount, so real output and the price level would increase
(b) less than an equal amount, so real output would increase and the price level would decrease
(c) greater than an equal amount, so real output and the price level would increase
(d) an equal amount, so real output would increase and the price level would be unchanged

12. If aggregate demand declined and the economy experienced a recession due to a self-fulfilling prophecy, this would be an example of
(a) real-business-cycle theory
(b) insider–outsider theory
(c) a coordination failure
(d) a change in velocity

13. Which macroeconomic theory would be most closely associated with the concept that the economy can get stuck in less than optimal equilibrium positions because of a lack of consistency in the expectations of businesses and households?
(a) rational expectations
(b) real-business-cycle
(c) coordination failures
(d) monetarism

14. In the new classical view, when the economy diverges from its full-employment output,
(a) internal mechanisms within the economy would automatically return it to its full-employment output
(b) discretionary monetary policy is needed to return it to its full-employment output
(c) discretionary fiscal policy is needed to return it to its full-employment output
(d) the adoption of an efficiency wage in the economy would return it to its full-employment output

15. The views about the speed of adjustment for self-correction in the economy suggest that
(a) monetarists think it would be gradual, and rational expectations economists think it would be quick
(b) monetarists think it would be quick, and rational

expectations economists think it would be gradual
(c) monetarists and mainstream economists think it would be quick
(d) real-business-cycle theorists and rational expectations economists think it would be gradual

16. Proponents of the rational expectations theory argue that people
(a) are not as rational as monetarists assume them to be
(b) make forecasts that are based on poor information, causing economic policy to be driven by self-fulfilling prophecy
(c) form beliefs about future economic outcomes that accurately reflect the likelihood that those outcomes will occur
(d) do not respond quickly to changes in wages and prices, causing a misallocation of economic resources in the economy

17. In the rational expectations theory, a temporary change in real output would occur from a
(a) fully anticipated price-level change
(b) downward wage inflexibility
(c) coordination failure
(d) price-level surprise

18. The conclusion mainstream economists draw about the downward price and wage inflexibility is that
(a) the effects can be reversed relatively quickly
(b) efficiency wages do not contribute to the problem
(c) the economy can be mired in recession for long periods
(d) wage and price controls are needed to counteract the situation

19. Which one of the following would be a reason that a higher wage would result in greater efficiency?
(a) lower productivity
(b) reduced job turnover
(c) higher supervision costs
(d) less work effort by employees

20. According to mainstream economists, which of the following contribute to the downward inflexibility of wages?
(a) price-level surprises
(b) insider–outsider relationships
(c) adverse aggregate supply shocks
(d) inadequate investment spending

21. The rule suggested by the monetarists is that the money supply should be increased at the same rate as the
(a) price level
(b) interest rate
(c) velocity of money
(d) potential growth in real GDP

22. To stabilize the economy, monetarist and rational expectations economists advocate
(a) the use of price-level surprises and adoption of an efficiency wage
(b) a monetary rule and a balanced-budget requirement
(c) the use of discretionary fiscal policy instead of discretionary monetary policy
(d) the use of discretionary monetary policy instead of discretionary fiscal policy

23. Proponents of inflation targeting argue that such a policy would

(a) improve productivity and thus increase aggregate supply

(b) make the Fed more accountable by giving it a specific goal

(c) increase the coordination of fiscal and monetary policy to control inflation

(d) give more discretion to monetary policymakers in responding to economic crises

24. Mainstream economists support

(a) increasing the money supply at a constant rate

(b) eliminating insider–outsider relationships in business

(c) the use of discretionary monetary and fiscal policies

(d) a balanced-budget requirement and a monetary rule

25. Which of the following would be an idea from monetarism that has been absorbed into mainstream macroeconomics?

(a) how changes in investment spending change aggregate demand

(b) the importance of money and the money supply in the economy

(c) using discretion rather than rules for guiding economic policy

(d) building the macro foundations for microeconomics

■ **PROBLEMS**

1. Assume that you are a monetarist in this problem and that **V** is stable and equal to 4. In the following table is the aggregate supply schedule: the real output **Q** which producers will offer for sale at seven different price levels **P**.

P	Q	PQ	MV
$1.00	100	$_____	$_____
2.00	110	_____	_____
3.00	120	_____	_____
4.00	130	_____	_____
5.00	140	_____	_____
6.00	150	_____	_____
7.00	160	_____	_____

a. Compute and enter in the table the seven values of **PQ**.

b. Assume **M** is $90. Enter the values of **MV** on each of the seven lines in the table. The equilibrium

(1) nominal domestic output (**PQ** or **MV**) is

$ _____.

(2) price level is $_____.

(3) real domestic output (**Q**) is $_____.

c. When **M** increases to $175, **MV** at each price level

is $_____ and the equilibrium

(1) nominal domestic output is $_____.

(2) price level is $_____.

(3) real domestic output is $_____.

2. Indicate what perspective(s) of economics would be most closely associated with each position. Use the following abbreviations: **MAI** (mainstream economics), **MON** (monetarism), **RET** (rational expectations theory), and **RBC** (real-business-cycle theory).

a. macro instability from investment spending

_____

b. macro instability from inappropriate monetary policy _____

c. macro instability from changes in resource availability and technology _____

d. equation of exchange _____

e. fiscal policy can be effective _____

f. unanticipated price-level changes _____

g. downward inflexibility of wages and prices _____

h. monetary rule _____

i. neutral fiscal policy _____

j. economy automatically self-corrects _____

k. monetary policy is effective _____

3. Following are price-level (**PL**) and output (**Q**) combinations to describe aggregate demand and aggregate supply curves: (1) **PL** and Q_1 is AD_1; (2) **PL** and Q_2 is AD_2; (3) **PL** and Q_3 is AS_{LR1}; (4) **PL** and Q_4 is AS_{LR2}.

PL	Q_1	Q_2	Q_3	Q_4
250	0	200	400	600
200	200	400	400	600
150	400	600	400	600
100	600	800	400	600
50	800	1000	400	600

a. Use the following to graph AD_1, AD_2, AS_{LR1}, and AS_{LR2}. Label the vertical axis as the price level and the horizontal axis as real output (**Q**).

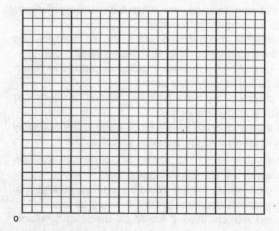

b. If the economy is initially in equilibrium where AD_1 and AS_{LR1} intersect, the price level will be

_____ and real output will be _____.

c. If, over time, the economy grows from AS_{LR1} to

AS_{LR2}, the equilibrium price level will be _____

and real output will be _____.

d. Assume a monetary rule is adopted that increases the money supply proportionate to the increase in aggregate supply. Aggregate demand will increase from

AD_1 to AD_2, making the price level _____ and

real output _____.

e. Mainstream economists would argue that velocity is unstable, so a constant increase in the money supply might not shift AD_1 all the way to AD_2. In this case, the price level would fall below the target of

_____. It might also be the case that the constant increase in the money supply might shift AD_1 beyond AD_2, so the price level would rise above the

target of _____.

■ **SHORT ANSWER AND ESSAY QUESTIONS**

1. Explain the two sources of macroeconomic instability in the view of mainstream economists.

2. Explain how changes in aggregate demand can produce economic instability.

3. Discuss the role that adverse aggregate supply shocks play in contributing to economic instability.

4. What do monetarists see as the cause of economic instability in the economy? Explain, using the equation of exchange, how a change in the money supply will affect nominal GDP.

5. Why do monetarists argue that the velocity of money is stable? If the money supply increases, how will people respond from a monetarist perspective?

6. Compare and contrast the monetarist and mainstream views on the causes of macroeconomic instability. How do monetarists explain the Great Depression?

7. Explain the real-business-cycle view of macroeconomic instability using an aggregate demand and supply graph.

8. Give a macroeconomic example of how coordination failures cause macroeconomic instability.

9. Explain the new classical view of self-correction in the macro economy. Contrast the monetarist perspective with that of rational expectations in terms of the real output, the price level, and the speed of adjustment.

10. Describe the two assumptions on which rational expectations are based. How realistic is it to expect that people will be able to accurately forecast economic outcomes?

11. Use a graph to illustrate and explain the mainstream view of self-correction in the macro economy.

12. Why would an efficiency wage lead to downward inflexibility in prices?

13. Give an example of insider–outsider relationships and explain how it affects wage flexibility.

14. What is the monetary rule? Why do monetarists suggest this rule to replace discretionary monetary policy?

15. What is the perspective of rational expectations economists on a monetary rule and the conduct of monetary policy?

16. What is the position of some monetarist and rational expectations economists on a requirement for a balanced budget? Why do they adopt such a position?

17. How do mainstream economists defend the use of discretionary monetary policy?

18. What arguments are made by mainstream economists to justify the use of discretionary fiscal policy?

19. What interpretation do mainstream economists make of the historical evidence over the past half century or so on the relationship between macroeconomic policy and stability in the economy?

20. What influences have monetarism and the rational expectations theory had on mainstream macroeconomic theory and policy? Give several examples of ideas that have changed mainstream thinking.

ANSWERS

Chapter 36 Current Issues in Macro Theory and Policy

FILL-IN QUESTIONS

1. stickiness, unexpected
2. investment, inflation, recession
3. raise, supply
4. stable, competitive, instability, inflexibility
5. *MV = PQ*; *a.* the money supply; *b.* the velocity of money; *c.* the average price of each unit of physical output; *d.* the physical volume of goods and services produced
6. stable, stable, nominal
7. more, increase, increase
8. monetary, inflation, recession
9. real-business-cycle, supply, same, without
10. do not, a number of, expectations
11. capable, gradually, rapidly
12. are, flexible
13. unanticipated, anticipated
14. inflexible, long, decreases
15. greater, lower, less, increase
16. destabilize, equal to, equal to
17. inflation targeting, inflation
18. ineffective, rules, do not
19. oppose, effective, effective, more
20. inflation, important

TRUE–FALSE QUESTIONS

1. T, p. 727	**14.** F, p. 732
2. T, p. 727	**15.** T, p. 731
3. T, pp. 727–728	**16.** F, p. 732
4. F, pp. 727–728	**17.** T, pp. 732–733
5. T, pp. 727–728	**18.** F, p. 733
6. F, pp. 728–729	**19.** T, p. 733
7. T, p. 729	**20.** T, pp. 733–734
8. T, p. 729	**21.** T, pp. 734–735
9. F, p. 729	**22.** F, p. 735
10. F, p. 729	**23.** F, p. 736
11. T, p. 729	**24.** T, p. 736
12. F, p. 730	**25.** F, p. 737
13. T, pp. 730–731	

MULTIPLE-CHOICE QUESTIONS

1. c, p. 727	**14.** a, pp. 730–731
2. d, p. 727	**15.** a, pp. 731–732
3. c, p. 727	**16.** c, pp. 731–732
4. b, p. 727	**17.** d, p.732
5. c, p. 727	**18.** c, p. 733
6. c, pp. 727–728	**19.** b, p. 733
7. a, pp. 727–728	**20.** b, pp. 733–734
8. a, p. 728	**21.** d, pp. 734–735
9. b, pp. 727–728	**22.** b, p.735
10. d, p. 729	**23.** b, p. 735
11. d, p. 729	**24.** c, p. 736
12. c, pp. 729–730	**25.** b, p.739
13. c, p. 730	

PROBLEMS

1. *a.* 100, 220, 360, 520, 700, 900, 1120; *b.* 360, 360, 360, 360, 360, 360, 360, (1) 360, (2) 3.00, (3) 120; *c.* 700, (1) 700, (2) 5.00, (3) 140

2. *a.* MAI; *b.* MON, RET; *c.* RBC; *d.* MON; *e.* MAI; *f.* RET; *g.* MAI; *h.* MON, RET; *i.* MON, RET; *j.* MON, RET; *k.* MAI

3. *a.* graph similar to Figure 36.3 in the text; *b.* 150, 400; *c.* 100, 600; *d.* 150, 600; *e.* 150, 150

SHORT ANSWER AND ESSAY QUESTIONS

1. p. 727	**8.** pp. 729–730	**15.** p. 735
2. p. 727	**9.** pp. 730–732	**16.** p. 736
3. pp. 727–728	**10.** pp. 731–732	**17.** p. 736
4. pp. 727–728	**11.** pp. 732–733	**18.** pp. 736–737
5. pp. 727–728	**12.** p. 733	**19.** p. 737
6. pp. 728–729	**13.** pp. 733–734	**20.** pp. 737, 739
7. p. 729	**14.** pp. 734–735	

CHAPTER 37

International Trade

In Chapter 5 you learned about the role of the United States in the global economy and the basic principles of international trade. Chapter 37 extends that analysis by giving you a more advanced understanding of comparative advantage. It also uses the tools of supply and demand to explain the equilibrium prices and quantities of imports and exports and the economic effects of tariffs and quotas. It examines the fallacious arguments for trade protectionism and the global efforts to liberalize trade.

After a brief review of the facts of international trade presented in Chapter 5, the text uses graphical analysis to explain why nations trade: to take advantage of the benefits of specialization. Nations specialize in and export those goods and services in the production of which they have a **comparative advantage.** A comparative advantage means that the opportunity cost of producing a particular good or service is lower in one nation than in another nation. Nations will avoid producing and will import the goods and services that other nations have a comparative advantage in producing. In this way, all nations are able to obtain products that are produced as inexpensively as possible. Put another way, when nations specialize in those products in which they have a comparative advantage, the world as a whole can obtain more goods and services from its resources; each nation of the world can enjoy a standard of living higher than it would have if it did not specialize and export and import.

The principle of comparative advantage tells us why nations trade, but what determines the equilibrium prices and quantities of the imports and exports resulting from trade? To answer this question, the text uses the **supply and demand analysis** originally presented in Chapter 3 to explain equilibrium in the world market for a product. A simplified two-nation and one-product model of trade is used to construct export supply curves and import demand curves for each nation. Equilibrium occurs where one nation's export supply curve intersects another nation's import demand curve.

Regardless of the advantages of specialization and trade among nations, people in the United States and throughout the world for well over 200 years have debated whether **free trade or protection** was the better policy for their nation. Economists took part in this debate and, with few exceptions, argued for free trade and against protection. Those who favor free trade contend that free trade benefits both the nation and the world as a whole. "Free traders" argue that tariffs, import quotas, and other barriers to international trade prevent or reduce specialization and decrease both a nation's and the world's production and standard of living.

Despite the case for trade, nations have erected and continue to erect **trade barriers** against other nations. The latter part of this chapter focuses attention on (1) what motivates nations to impose tariffs and to limit the quantities of goods imported from abroad; (2) the economic effects of protection on a nation's own prosperity and on the prosperity of the world economy; (3) the kinds of arguments those who favor protection use to support their position (on what grounds do they base their contention that their nation will benefit from the erection of barriers that reduce imports from foreign nations?); and (4) how the nations of the world have responded to trade liberalization through the **World Trade Organization (WTO).**

Whether the direction of the international trade policy in the United States will be toward freer trade or more protectionism is a question that gets debated as each new trade issue is presented to the U.S. public. The decision on each issue may well depend on your understanding of the advantages of free trade and the problems with trade protection for the nation and the world economy.

■ CHECKLIST

When you have studied this chapter you should be able to

☐ Cite some key facts about international trade.

☐ State the three economic circumstances that make it desirable for nations to specialize and trade.

☐ Compute the costs of producing two commodities when given the data in a two-nation example.

☐ Determine which nation has the comparative advantage in the production of each commodity using the cost data you computed for the two-nation example.

☐ Calculate the range in which the terms of trade will occur in the two-nation example.

☐ Explain how nations gain from trade and specialization based on the two-nation example.

☐ Discuss how increasing costs affect specialization in the two-nation example.

☐ Restate the case for free trade.

☐ Construct domestic supply and demand curves for two nations that trade a product.

☐ Construct export supply and import demand curves for two nations that trade a product.

☐ Use supply and demand analysis to explain how the equilibrium prices and quantities of exports and imports are determined for two nations that trade a product.

☐ Identify the four principal types of artificial barriers to international trade and the motives for erecting these barriers.

☐ Explain the economic effects of a protective tariff on resource allocation, the price of the commodity, the total production of the commodity, and the outputs of foreign and domestic producers of the commodity.

☐ Analyze the economic effects of an import quota and compare them with the economic effects of a tariff.

☐ Enumerate six arguments used to support the case for protection and find the problems with each argument.

☐ Describe the formation and purpose of the World Trade Organization (WTO).

☐ Describe how Frédéric Bastiat satirized the proponents of protectionism (Last Word).

■ **CHAPTER OUTLINE**

1. Some facts on international trade from Chapter 5 are worth reviewing.

   a. About 11% of the total output (GDP) of the United States is accounted for by exports of goods and services. While exports and imports account for a larger share of GDP in other nations, the size of the U.S. economy means that it has the largest combined volume of imports and exports in the world.

   b. The United States has a trade deficit in goods, a trade surplus in services, and a trade deficit in goods and services.

   c. The major exports of the United States are chemicals, consumer durables, agricultural products, semiconductors, and computers. The major imports are petroleum, automobiles, household appliances, computers, and metals. Most of the U.S. trade occurs with other industrially advanced nations and members of OPEC. Canada is the largest trading partner for the United States.

   d. The major participants in international trade are the United States, Japan, and the nations of Western Europe, and now China. Other key participants include the Asian economies of South Korea, Singapore, and Taiwan. Russia and the nations of Eastern Europe have expanded their international trade.

   e. International trade and finance link nations and are the focus of economic policy and debate in the United States and other nations.

2. The **economic basis for trade** is based on several circumstances. Specialization and trade among nations is advantageous because the world's resources are not evenly distributed and efficient production of different commodities requires different technologies and combinations of resources. Also, products differ in quality and other attributes, so people might prefer imported to domestic goods in some cases. Some nations have cost advantages in producing **labor-intensive goods** such as complex electronics that require much skilled work time. Other nations have cost advantages in producing **land-intensive goods** such as agricultural products that require abundant natural resources. Still other nations have cost advantages in producing **capital-intensive goods** such as chemicals or machinery because they have large amounts of physical capital available.

3. The **principle of comparative advantage**, first presented in Chapter 5 to explain the **gains from trade,** can now be reexamined with the aid of graphical analysis.

   a. Suppose the world is composed of only two nations, each of which is capable of producing two different commodities and in which the production possibilities curves are different straight lines (the nations' **opportunity-cost ratios** are constant but different).

   b. With different domestic **opportunity-cost ratios,** each nation will have a comparative (cost) advantage in the production of one of the two commodities, and if the world is to use its resources economically, each nation must specialize in the commodity in the production of which it has a comparative advantage.

   c. The ratio at which one product is traded for another—the **terms of trade**—lies between the **opportunity-cost ratios** of the two nations.

   d. Each nation **gains from this trade** because specialization permits a greater total output from the same resources and a better allocation of the world's resources.

   e. If **opportunity-cost ratios** in the two nations are not constant (if there is increasing cost), specialization may not be complete.

   f. The basic argument for free trade among nations is that it leads to a better allocation of resources and a higher standard of living in the world. Several side benefits from trade are that it increases competition and deters monopoly, and offers consumers a wider array of choices. It also links the interests of nations and can reduce the threat of hostilities or war.

4. **Supply and demand analysis of exports and imports** can be used to explain how the equilibrium price and quantity for a product (e.g., aluminum) are determined when there is trade between two nations (e.g., the United States and Canada).

   a. For the United States, there will be *domestic* supply and demand as well as *export* supply and import demand for aluminum.

   (1) The price and quantity of aluminum are determined by the intersection of the domestic demand and supply curves in a world without trade.

   (2) In a world with trade, the **export supply curve** for the United States shows the amount of aluminum that U.S. producers will export at each **world price** above the domestic equilibrium price. U.S. exports will increase when the world price rises relative to the **domestic price.**

   (3) The **import demand curve** for the United States shows the amount of aluminum that U.S. citizens will import at each world price below the domestic equilibrium price. U.S. imports will increase when world prices fall relative to the domestic price.

   b. For Canada, there will be domestic supply and demand as well as export supply and import demand for aluminum. The description of these supply and demand curves is similar to the account of those of the United States previously described in point **a.**

   c. The **equilibrium world price** and equilibrium world levels of exports and imports can be determined with further supply and demand analysis. The **export supply curves** of the two nations can be plotted on one graph. The **import demand curves** of both nations can be plotted on the same graph. In this two-nation model, equilibrium will be achieved when one nation's import demand curve intersects another nation's export supply curve.

5. Nations limit international trade by erecting **trade barriers.** Tariffs, import quotas, a variety of nontariff barriers, and voluntary export restrictions are the principal barriers to trade. A *revenue tariff* is an excise tax on an imported product not produced domestically that raises revenue for the government. A *protective tariff* is an excise tax on an imported product that is design to defend domestic producers from foreign competition. An *import quota* specifies the maximum amount of a commodity that can be imported in any time period. A *nontariff barrier* is an unreasonable requirement for licensing or standards for imported products. A *voluntary export restriction* is an agreement to limit the amount of exports to another nation.

   a. The imposition of a *tariff* on a good imported from abroad has both direct and indirect effects on an economy.

   (1) The tariff increases the domestic price of the good, reduces its domestic consumption, expands its domestic production, decreases its foreign production, and transfers income from domestic consumers to government.

   (2) It also reduces the income of foreign producers and the ability of foreign nations to purchase goods and services in the nation imposing the tariff, causes the contraction of relatively efficient industries in that nation, decreases world trade, and lowers the real output of goods and services.

   b. The imposition of a **quota** on an imported product has the same direct and indirect effects as a tariff has on that product, with the exception that a tariff generates revenue for government use whereas an *import quota* transfers that revenue to foreign producers.

   c. Special-interest groups benefit from protection and persuade their nations to erect trade barriers, but the costs to consumers of this protection exceed the benefits to the economy.

6. The arguments for **protectionism** are many, but often of questionable validity.

   a. The military self-sufficiency argument can be challenged because it is difficult to determine which industry is "vital" to national defense and must be protected; it would be more efficient economically to provide a direct subsidy to military producers rather than impose a tariff.

   b. Using tariff barriers to permit diversification for stability in the economy is not necessary for advanced economies such as the United States, and there may be great economic costs to diversification in developing nations.

   c. It is alleged that infant industries need protection until they are sufficiently large to compete, but the argument may not apply in developed economies: It is difficult to select which industries will prosper; protectionism tends to persist long after it is needed; and direct subsidies may be more economically efficient. For advanced nations, a variant of this argument is *strategic trade policy.* It justifies barriers that protect the investment in high risk, growth industries for a nation, but the policies often lead to retaliation and similar policies from other trading nations.

   d. Sometimes protection is sought against the *dumping* of foreign goods on U.S. markets at prices either below the cost of production or below the prices commonly charged in the home nation. Dumping is a legitimate concern and is restricted under U.S. trade law, but to use dumping as an excuse for widespread tariff protection is unjustified, and the number of documented cases is few. If foreign companies are more efficient (low-cost) producers, what may appear to be dumping may actually be comparative advantage at work.

   e. Trade barriers do not necessarily increase domestic employment because:

   (1) Imports may eliminate some jobs, but create others, so imports may change only the composition of employment, not the overall level of employment.

   (2) The exports of one nation become the imports of another, so tariff barriers can be viewed as "beggar thy neighbor" policies.

   (3) Other nations are likely to retaliate against the imposition of trade barriers, and as a result it will reduce domestic output and employment (that is what happened to the United States when it passed the *Smoot-Hawley Tariff Act* of 1930 that raised tariffs to a very high level); and

   (4) In the long run, barriers create a less efficient allocation of resources by shielding protected domestic industries from the rigors of competition.

   f. Protection is sometimes sought because of the cheap foreign labor argument that low-cost labor in other nations will undercut the wages of workers in the United States. There are several counterpoints to this argument. First, there are mutual *gains from trade* between rich and poor nations and they lower the cost of production for products. Second, it should be realized that nations gain from trade based on comparative advantage, and by specializing at what each nation does best, the productivity of workers and thus their wages and living standards rise. Third, there is an incorrect focus on labor costs per hour rather than labor cost per unit of production. Labor costs or wages per hour can be higher in one nation than in another because of the higher productivity of workers (and it results in lower labor cost per unit of production).

7. The *World Trade Organization (WTO)* is an international agency with about 153 participating nations that is responsible for overseeing trade agreements among nations that were established as part of the 1993 Uruguay Round of trade negotiations. The WTO also provides a forum for more trade liberalization negotiations under the *Doha Round* that was begun in Doha, Qatar, in 2001. These negotiations focus on additional reductions in tariffs and quotas and cutbacks in domestic subsidies for agricultural products.

8. (Last Word). Frédéric Bastiat (1801–1850) was a French economist who wrote a satirical letter to counter the proponents of protectionism. His "petition" to the French government called for blocking out the sun because it was providing too much competition for domestic candlestick makers, thus illustrating the logical absurdity of protectionist arguments.

■ **HINTS AND TIPS**

1. In the discussion of **comparative advantage,** the assumption of a constant-cost ratio means the production possibilities "curves" for each nation can be drawn as straight lines. The slope of the line in each nation is the opportunity cost of one product (wheat) in terms of the other product (coffee). The reciprocal of the slope of each line is the opportunity cost of the other product (coffee) in terms of the first product (wheat).

2. The **export supply and import demand curves** in Figures 37.3 and 37.4 in the text look different from the typical supply and demand curves that you have seen so far, so you should understand how they are constructed. The export supply and import demand curves for a nation do not intersect. Each curve meets at the price point on the *Y* axis showing the equilibrium price for domestic supply and demand. At this point there are no exports or imports.

    a. The export supply curve is upsloping from that point because as world prices rise above the domestic equilibrium price, there will be increasing domestic surpluses produced by a nation that can be exported. The export supply curve reflects the positive relationship between rising world prices (above the domestic equilibrium price) and the increasing quantity of exports.

    b. The import demand curve is downsloping from the domestic equilibrium price because as world prices fall below the domestic equilibrium price, there will be increasing domestic shortages that need to be covered by increasing imports. The import demand curve reflects the inverse relationship between falling world prices (below the domestic price) and the increasing quantity of imports.

3. One of the most interesting sections of the chapter discusses the arguments for and against trade protection. You have probably heard people give one or more of the arguments for trade protection, but now you have a chance to use your economic reasoning to expose the weaknesses in these arguments. Most are half-truths and special pleadings.

■ **IMPORTANT TERMS**

labor-intensive goods	equilibrium world price
land-intensive goods	tariff
capital-intensive goods	revenue tariff
opportunity-cost ratio	protective tariff
principle of comparative advantage	import quota
	nontariff barrier (NTB)
terms of trade	voluntary export restriction (VER)
trading possibilities line	strategic trade policy
gains from trade	dumping
world price	Smoot-Hawley Tariff Act
domestic price	World Trade Organization (WTO)
export supply curve	Doha Round
import demand curve	

■ **FILL-IN QUESTIONS**

1. The United States has a trade deficit in (goods, services) _____ and a trade surplus in _____.

2. In the United States, exports of goods and services make up about (12, 25) _____ percent of total U.S. output. Its volume of exports and imports in dollar terms makes it the world's (largest, smallest) _____ trading nation.

3. Nations tend to trade among themselves because the distribution of economic resources among them is (even, uneven) _____, the efficient production of various goods and services necessitates (the same, different) _____ technologies or combinations of resources, and people prefer (more, less) _____ choices in products.

4. The principle of comparative advantage means total world output will be greatest when each good is produced by that nation having the (highest, lowest) _____ opportunity cost. The nations of the world tend to specialize in the production of those goods in which they (have, do not have) _____ a comparative advantage and then export them, and they import those goods in which they _____ a comparative advantage in production.

5. If the cost ratio in country X is 4 Panama hats equal 1 pound of bananas, while in country Y 3 Panama hats equal 1 pound of bananas, then

    a. in country X hats are relatively (expensive, inexpensive) _____ and bananas relatively _____,

    b. in country Y hats are relatively (expensive, inexpensive) _____ and bananas relatively _____,

    c. X has a comparative advantage and should specialize in the production of (bananas, hats) _____, and Y has a comparative advantage and should specialize in the production of _____.

    d. When X and Y specialize and trade, the terms of trade will be somewhere between (1, 2, 3, 4) _____ and _____ hats for each pound of bananas and will depend on world demand and supply for hats and bananas.

    e. When the actual terms of trade turn out to be 3 1/2 hats for 1 pound of bananas, the cost of obtaining (1) 1 Panama hat has been decreased from (2/7, 1/3) _____ to _____ pounds of bananas in Y.

(2) 1 pound of bananas has been decreased from

(3 1/2, 4) _____ to _____ Panama hats in X.

f. International specialization will not be complete if the opportunity cost of producing either good (rises, falls)

_____ as a nation produces more of it.

6. The basic argument for free trade based on the principle of (bilateral negotiations, comparative advantage) _____ is that it results in a (more, less)

_____ efficient allocation of resources and a

(lower, higher) _____ standard of living.

7. The world equilibrium price is determined by the interaction of (domestic, world) _____ supply and demand, while the domestic equilibrium price is

determined by _____ supply and demand.

8. When the world price of a good falls relative to the domestic price in a nation, the nation will (increase,

decrease) _____ its imports, and when the world price rises relative to the domestic price, the nation

will _____ its exports.

9. In a two-nation model for a product, the equilibrium price and quantity of imports and exports occur where one nation's import demand intersects another nation's

export (supply, demand) _____ curve. In a highly competitive world market, there can be (multiple,

only one) _____ price(s) for a standardized product.

10. Excise taxes on imported products are (quotas,

tariffs) _____, whereas limits on the maximum amount of a product that can be imported are

import _____. Tariffs applied to a product not produced domestically are (protective, revenue)

_____ tariffs, but tariffs designed to shield domestic producers from foreign competition are

_____ tariffs.

11. There are other types of trade barriers. Imports that are restricted through the use of a licensing requirement or

bureaucratic red tape are (tariff, nontariff) _____ barriers. When foreign firms voluntarily limit their exports to another country, it would represent a voluntary (import,

export) _____ restraint.

12. Nations erect barriers to international trade to benefit the economic positions of (consumers, domestic producers)

_____ even though these barriers (increase,

decrease) _____ economic efficiency and trade among nations and the benefits to that nation are

(greater, less) _____ than the costs to it.

13. When the United States imposes a tariff on a good that is imported from abroad, the price of that good in the

United States will (increase, decrease) _____, the total purchases of the good in the United States will

_____, the output of U.S. producers of the

good will (increase, decrease) _____, and the

output of foreign producers will _____. The ability of foreigners to buy goods and services in the United

States will (increase, decrease) _____ and, as a result, output and employment in U.S. industries that sell

goods and services abroad will _____.

14. When comparing the effects of a tariff with the effects of a quota to restrict the U.S. imports of a product, the basic difference is that with a (tariff, quota)

_____ the U.S. government will receive revenue, but with a _____ foreign producers will receive the revenue.

15. List the six arguments that protectionists use to justify trade barriers.

a. _____

b. _____

c. _____

d. _____

e. _____

f. _____

16. The military self-sufficiency argument can be challenged because it is difficult to determine which industry

is (essential, unessential) _____ for national defense and must be protected. Rather than impose a tariff, a direct subsidy to producers would be (more, less)

_____ efficient in this case.

17. Using trade barriers to permit diversification for stability in an economy is not necessary for (advanced,

developing) _____ economies such as in the United States, and there may be great economic costs to

forcing diversification in _____ nations.

18. It alleged that (infant, mature) _____ industries need protection until they are sufficiently large to establish themselves, but a problem with such an argument

is that it is difficult to determine when a(n) _____

industry became a(n) _____ industry.

19. Trade barriers do not necessarily increase domestic employment because: imports may change only the (level,

composition) _____ of employment; trade barriers can be viewed as "beggar thy (customer, neighbor)

_____" policies; other nations can (protest,

retaliate) _____ against the trade barriers; and

in the long run, the barriers create an allocation of resources that is (more, less) _____ efficient by shielding protected domestic industries from competition.

20. Proponents of the cheap foreign labor argument tend to focus exclusively on large international differences that exist in labor costs (per unit, per hour) _____ and fail to mention that these differences are mostly the results of large national differences in productivity that serve to equalize labor costs _____.

■ TRUE–FALSE QUESTIONS

Circle T if the statement is true, F if it is false.

1. A trade deficit occurs when imports are greater than exports. **T F**

2. A factor that serves as the economic basis for world trade is the even distribution of resources among nations. **T F**

3. People trade because they seek products of different quality and other nonprice attributes. **T F**

4. Examples of capital-intensive goods would be automobiles, machinery, and chemicals. **T F**

5. The relative efficiency with which a nation can produce specific goods is fixed over time. **T F**

6. Mutually advantageous specialization and trade are possible between any two nations if they have the same domestic opportunity-cost ratios for any two products. **T F**

7. The principle of comparative advantage is that total output will be greatest when each good is produced by that nation which has the higher domestic opportunity cost. **T F**

8. By specializing based on comparative advantage, nations can obtain larger outputs with fixed amounts of resources. **T F**

9. The terms of trade determine how the increase in world output resulting from comparative advantage is shared by trading nations. **T F**

10. Increasing opportunity costs tend to prevent specialization among trading nations from being complete. **T F**

11. Trade among nations tends to bring about a more efficient use of the world's resources and a higher level of material well-being. **T F**

12. Free trade among nations tends to increase monopoly and lessen competition in these nations. **T F**

13. A nation will export a particular product if the world price is less than the domestic price. **T F**

14. In a two-country model, equilibrium in world prices and quantities of exports and imports will occur where one nation's export supply curve intersects the other nation's import demand curve. **T F**

15. A tariff on coffee in the United States is an example of a protective tariff. **T F**

16. The imposition of a tariff on a good imported from abroad will reduce the amount of the imported good that is bought. **T F**

17. A cost of tariffs and quotas imposed by the United States is higher prices that U.S. consumers must pay for the protected product. **T F**

18. The major difference between a tariff and a quota on an imported product is that a quota produces revenue for the government. **T F**

19. To advocate tariffs that would protect domestic producers of goods and materials essential to national defense is to substitute a political-military objective for the economic objectives of efficiently allocating resources. **T F**

20. One-crop economies may be able to make themselves more stable and diversified by imposing tariffs on goods imported from abroad, but these tariffs are also apt to lower the standard of living in these economies. **T F**

21. Protection against the "dumping" of foreign goods at low prices on the U.S. market is one good justification for widespread, permanent tariffs. **T F**

22. Tariffs and import quotas meant to increase domestic full employment achieve short-run domestic goals by making trading partners poorer. **T F**

23. The cheap foreign labor argument for protection fails because it focuses on labor costs per hour rather than on what really matters, which is labor cost per unit of output. **T F**

24. Most arguments for protection are special interest appeals that, if followed, would provide gains for consumers at the expense of protected industries and their workers. **T F**

25. The World Trade Organization was established by the United Nations to encourage purchases of products from developing nations. **T F**

■ MULTIPLE-CHOICE QUESTIONS

Circle the letter that corresponds to the best answer.

1. Which nation leads the world in the combined volume of exports and imports?
   (a) Japan
   (b) Germany
   (c) United States
   (d) United Kingdom

2. Which nation is the most important trading partner for the United States in terms of the percentage of imports and exports?
   (a) India
   (b) Russia
   (c) Canada
   (d) Germany

3. Nations engage in trade because
  (a) world resources are evenly distributed among nations
  (b) world resources are unevenly distributed among nations
  (c) all products are produced from the same technology
  (d) all products are produced from the same combinations of resources

Use the following tables to answer Questions 4, 5, 6, and 7.

NEPAL PRODUCTION POSSIBILITIES TABLE

Product	Production alternatives					
	A	B	C	D	E	F
Yak fat	0	4	8	12	16	20
Camel hides	40	32	24	16	7	0

KASHMIR PRODUCTION POSSIBILITIES TABLE

Product	Production alternatives					
	A	B	C	D	E	F
Yak fat	0	3	6	9	12	15
Camel hides	60	48	36	24	12	0

4. The data in the tables show that production in
  (a) both Nepal and Kashmir are subject to increasing opportunity costs
  (b) both Nepal and Kashmir are subject to constant opportunity costs
  (c) Nepal is subject to increasing opportunity costs and Kashmir to constant opportunity costs
  (d) Kashmir is subject to increasing opportunity costs and Nepal to constant opportunity costs

5. If Nepal and Kashmir engage in trade, the terms of trade will be
  (a) between 2 and 4 camel hides for 1 unit of yak fat
  (b) between 1/3 and 1/2 units of yak fat for 1 camel hide
  (c) between 3 and 4 units of yak fat for 1 camel hide
  (d) between 2 and 4 units of yak fat for 1 camel hide

6. Assume that prior to specialization and trade Nepal and Kashmir both choose production possibility C. Now if each specializes according to its comparative advantage, the resulting gains from specialization and trade will be
  (a) 6 units of yak fat
  (b) 8 units of yak fat
  (c) 6 units of yak fat and 8 camel hides
  (d) 8 units of yak fat and 6 camel hides

7. Each nation produced only one product in accordance with its comparative advantage, and the terms of trade were set at 3 camel hides for 1 unit of yak fat. In this case, Nepal could obtain a maximum combination of 8 units of yak fat and
  (a) 12 camel hides
  (b) 24 camel hides
  (c) 36 camel hides
  (d) 48 camel hides

8. What happens to a nation's imports or exports of a product when the world price of the product rises above the domestic price?
  (a) Imports of the product increase.
  (b) Imports of the product stay the same.
  (c) Exports of the product increase.
  (d) Exports of the product decrease.

9. What happens to a nation's imports or exports of a product when the world price of the product falls below the domestic price?
  (a) Imports of the product increase.
  (b) Imports of the product decrease.
  (c) Exports of the product increase.
  (d) Exports of the product stay the same.

10. Which one of the following is characteristic of tariffs?
  (a) They prevent the importation of goods from abroad.
  (b) They specify the maximum amounts of specific commodities that may be imported during a given period of time.
  (c) They often protect domestic producers from foreign competition.
  (d) They enable nations to reduce their exports and increase their imports during periods of recession.

11. The motive for barriers to the importation of goods and services from abroad is to
  (a) improve economic efficiency in that nation
  (b) protect and benefit domestic producers of those goods and services
  (c) reduce the prices of the goods and services produced in that nation
  (d) expand the export of goods and services to foreign nations

12. When a tariff is imposed on a good imported from abroad,
  (a) the demand for the good increases
  (b) the demand for the good decreases
  (c) the supply of the good increases
  (d) the supply of the good decreases

Answer Questions 13, 14, 15, 16, and 17 on the basis of the following diagram, where S_d and D_d are the domestic supply and demand for a product and P_w is the world price of that product.

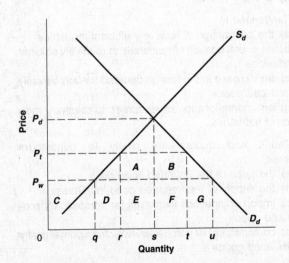

13. In a closed economy (without international trade), the equilibrium price would be
  (a) P_d, but in an open economy, the equilibrium price would be P_t
  (b) P_d, but in an open economy, the equilibrium price would be P_w
  (c) P_w, but in an open economy, the equilibrium price would be P_d
  (d) P_w, but in an open economy, the equilibrium price would be P_t

14. If there is free trade in this economy and no tariffs, the total revenue going to the foreign producers is represented by
  (a) area C
  (b) areas A and B combined
  (c) areas A, B, E, and F combined
  (d) areas D, E, F, and G combined

15. If a per-unit tariff was imposed in the amount of P_wP_t then domestic producers would supply
  (a) q units and foreign producers would supply qu units
  (b) s units and foreign producers would supply su units
  (c) r units and foreign producers would supply rt units
  (d) t units and foreign producers would supply tu units

16. Given a per-unit tariff in the amount of P_wP_t, the amount of the tariff revenue paid by consumers of this product is represented by
  (a) area A
  (b) area B
  (c) areas A and B combined
  (d) areas D, E, F, and G combined

17. Assume that an import quota of rt units is imposed on the foreign nation producing this product. The amount of *total* revenue going to foreign producers is represented by areas
  (a) $A + B$
  (b) $E + F$
  (c) $A + B + E + F$
  (d) $D + E + F + G$

18. Tariffs lead to
  (a) the contraction of relatively efficient industries
  (b) an overallocation of resources to relatively efficient industries
  (c) an increase in the foreign demand for domestically produced goods
  (d) an underallocation of resources to relatively inefficient industries

19. Tariffs and quotas are costly to consumers because
  (a) the price of the imported good rises
  (b) the supply of the imported good increases
  (c) import competition increases for domestically produced goods
  (d) consumers shift purchases away from domestically produced goods

20. The infant industry argument for tariffs
  (a) is especially pertinent for the European Union
  (b) generally results in tariffs that are removed after the infant industry has matured
  (c) makes it rather easy to determine which infant industries will become mature industries with comparative advantages in producing their goods
  (d) might better be replaced by an argument for outright subsidies for infant industries

21. Strategic trade policy is a modified form for advanced economies of which protectionist argument?
  (a) the increase-domestic-employment argument
  (b) the military self-sufficiency argument
  (c) the cheap foreign labor argument
  (d) the infant industry argument

22. "The nation needs to protect itself from foreign countries that sell their products in our domestic markets at less than the cost of production." This quotation would be most closely associated with which protectionist argument?
  (a) diversification for stability
  (b) increased domestic employment
  (c) protection against dumping
  (d) cheap foreign labor

23. Which is a likely result of imposing tariffs to increase domestic employment?
  (a) a short-run increase in domestic employment in import industries
  (b) a decrease in the tariff rates of foreign nations
  (c) a long-run reallocation of workers from export industries to protected domestic industries
  (d) a decrease in consumer prices

24. Which is the likely result of the United States using tariffs to protect its high wages and standard of living from cheap foreign labor?
  (a) an increase in U.S. exports
  (b) a rise in the U.S. real GDP
  (c) a decrease in the average productivity of U.S. workers
  (d) a decrease in the quantity of labor employed by industries producing the goods on which tariffs have been levied

25. What international agency is charged with overseeing trade liberalization and with resolving disputes among nations?
  (a) World Bank
  (b) United Nations
  (c) World Trade Organization
  (d) International Monetary Fund

■ **PROBLEMS**

1. Shown in the next column are the production possibilities curves for two nations: the United States and Chile. Suppose these two nations do not currently engage in international trade or specialization, and suppose that points **A** and **a** show the combinations of wheat and copper they now produce and consume.

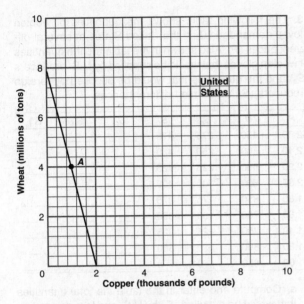

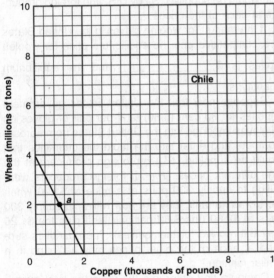

a. The straightness of the two curves indicates that the cost ratios in the two nations are (changing, constant) _____.

b. Examination of the two curves reveals that the cost ratio in

(1) the United States is _____ million tons of wheat for _____ thousand pounds of copper.

(2) Chile is _____ million tons of wheat for _____ thousand pounds of copper.

c. If these two nations were to specialize and trade wheat for copper,

(1) The United States would specialize in the production of wheat because _____

_____.

(2) Chile would specialize in the production of copper because _____

_____.

d. The terms of trade, if specialization and trade occur, will be greater than 2 and less than 4 million tons of wheat for 1000 pounds of copper because _____

_____.

e. Assume the terms of trade turn out to be 3 million tons of wheat for 1000 pounds of copper. Draw in the trading possibilities curve for the United States and Chile.

f. With these trading possibilities curves, suppose the United States decides to consume 5 million tons of wheat and 1000 pounds of copper while Chile decides to consume 3 million tons of wheat and 1000 pounds of copper. The gains from trade to

(1) the United States are _____ million tons of wheat and _____ thousand pounds of copper.

(2) Chile are _____ million tons of wheat and _____ thousand pounds of copper.

2. Following are tables showing the domestic supply and demand schedules and the export supply and import demand schedules for two nations (**A** and **B**). (Table **B** is on the next page.)

NATION A

Price	Q_{dd}	Q_{sd}	Q_{di}	Q_{se}
$3.00	100	300	0	200
2.50	150	250	0	100
2.00	200	200	0	0
1.50	250	150	100	0
1.00	300	100	200	0

a. For nation **A**, the first column of the table is the price of a product. The second column is the quantity demanded domestically (Q_{dd}). The third column is the quantity supplied domestically (Q_{sd}). The fourth column is the quantity demanded for imports (Q_{di}). The fifth column is the quantity of exports supplied (Q_{se}).

(1) At a price of $2.00, there (will, will not) _____ be a surplus or shortage and there _____ be exports or imports.

(2) At a price of $3.00, there will be a domestic (shortage, surplus) _____ of _____ units. This domestic _____ will be eliminated by (exports, imports) _____ of _____ units.

(3) At a price of $1.00, there will be a domestic (shortage, surplus) _____ of _____ units. This domestic _____ will be eliminated by (exports, imports) _____ of _____ units.

NATION B

Price	Q_{dd}	Q_{sd}	Q_{di}	Q_{se}
$2.50	100	300	0	200
2.00	150	250	0	100
1.50	200	200	100	0
1.00	250	150	100	0

b. For nation **B**, the first column is the price of a product. The second column is the quantity demanded domestically (Q_{dd}). The third column is the quantity supplied domestically (Q_{sd}). The fourth column is the quantity demanded for imports (Q_{di}). The fifth column is the quantity of exports supplied (Q_{se}).

(1) At a price of $1.50, there (will, will not) _____ be a surplus or shortage and there _____ be exports or imports.

(2) At a price of $2.50, there will be a domestic (shortage, surplus) _____ of _____ units. This domestic _____ will be eliminated by (exports, imports) _____ of _____ units.

(3) At a price of $1.00, there will be a domestic (shortage, surplus) _____ of _____ units. This domestic _____ will be eliminated by (exports, imports) _____ of _____ units.

c. The following table shows a schedule of the import demand in Nation **A** and the export supply in Nation **B** at various prices. The first column is the price of the product. The second column is the quantity demanded for imports (Q_{diA}) in Nation **A**. The third column is the quantity of exports supplied (Q_{seB}) in Nation **B**.

Price	Q_{diA}	Q_{seB}
$2.00	0	100
1.75	50	50
1.50	100	0

(1) If the world price is $2.00, then Nation (**A**, **B**) _____ will want to import _____ units and Nation _____ will want to export _____ units of the product.

(2) If the world price is $1.75, then Nation (**A**, **B**) _____ will want to import _____ units and Nation _____ will want to export _____ units of the product.

(3) If the world price is $1.50, then Nation (**A**, **B**) _____ will want to import _____ units and Nation _____ will want to export _____ units of the product.

3. The following table shows the quantities of woolen gloves demanded (**D**) in the United States at several different prices (**P**). Also shown in the table are the quantities of woolen gloves that would be supplied by U.S. producers (S_a) and the quantities that would be supplied by foreign producers (S_f) at the nine different prices.

P	D	S_a	S_f	S_t	S'_f	S'_t
$2.60	450	275	475	___	___	___
2.40	500	250	450	___	___	___
2.20	550	225	425	___	___	___
2.00	600	200	400	___	___	___
1.80	650	175	375	___	___	___
1.60	700	150	350	___	___	___
1.40	750	125	325	___	___	___
1.20	800	0	300	___	___	___
1.00	850	0	0	___	___	___

a. Compute and enter in the table the total quantities that would be supplied (S_t) by U.S. and foreign producers at each of the prices.

b. If the market for woolen gloves in the United States is a competitive one the equilibrium price for woolen gloves is $_____ and the equilibrium quantity is _____.

c. Suppose now that the United States government imposes an 80 cent ($.80) tariff per pair of gloves on all gloves imported into the United States from abroad. Compute and enter into the table the quantities that would be supplied (S'_t) by foreign producers at the nine different prices. [*Hint:* If foreign producers were willing to supply 300 pairs at a price of $1.20 when there was no tariff, they are now willing to supply 300 pairs at $2.00 (the $.80 per pair tariff plus the $1.20 they will receive for themselves). The quantities supplied at each of the other prices may be found in a similar fashion.]

d. Compute and enter into the table the total quantities that would be supplied (S'_t) by U.S. and foreign producers at each of the nine prices.

e. As a result of the imposition of the tariff the equilibrium price has risen to $_____ and the equilibrium quantity has fallen to _____.

f. The number of pairs sold by

(1) U.S. producers has (increased, decreased) _____ by _____.

(2) foreign producers has (increased, decreased) _____ by _____.

g. The total revenues (after the payment of the tariff) of

(1) U.S. producers—who do not pay the tariff— have (increased, decreased) _____ by $_____.

(2) foreign producers—who do pay the tariff—have (increased, decreased) _____ by $_____.

h. The total amount spent by U.S. buyers of woolen gloves has _____ by $_____.

i. The total number of dollars earned by foreigners has _____ by $_____, and, as a result, the total foreign demand for goods and services produced in the United States has _____ by $_____.

j. The tariff revenue of the United States government has _____ by $_____.

k. If an import quota were imposed that had the same effect as the tariff on price and output, the amount of the tariff revenue, $_____, would now be received as revenue by _____ producers.

■ SHORT ANSWER AND ESSAY QUESTIONS

1. Describe the quantity of imports and exports for the United States in absolute and relative terms. How has the quantity of imports and exports changed over time?

2. What are the major imports and exports of the United States? With which nations does the United States trade?

3. What role does the United States play in international trade? Who are the other major players in international trade?

4. What three factors—one dealing with the resource distribution, the second with production, and the third with the variety of product—are the basis for trade among nations?

5. Explain
(a) the theory or principle of comparative advantage;
(b) what is meant by and what determines the terms of trade; and
(c) the gains from trade.

6. What is the case for free trade?

7. Explain how the equilibrium prices and quantities of exports and imports are determined.

8. Why will exports in a nation increase when world prices rise relative to domestic prices?

9. What motivates nations to erect barriers to the importation of goods from abroad, and what types of barriers do they erect?

10. Suppose the United States increases the tariff on automobiles imported from Germany (and other foreign countries). What is the effect of this tariff-rate increase on
(a) the price of automobiles in the United States;
(b) the total number of cars sold in the United States during a year;
(c) the number of cars produced by and employment in the German automobile industry;
(d) production by and employment in the U.S. automobile industry;

(e) German income obtained by selling cars in the United States;
(f) the German demand for goods produced in the United States;
(g) the production of and employment in those U.S. industries that now export goods to Germany;
(h) the standards of living in the United States and in Germany;
(i) the allocation of resources in the U.S. economy; and
(j) the allocation of the world's resources?

11. Explain the economic effects of a tariff and show them in a supply and demand graph.

12. Compare and contrast the economic effects of a tariff with the economic effects of an import quota on a product.

13. What are the net costs of tariffs and quotas.

14. Critically evaluate the military self-sufficiency argument for protectionism. What industries should be protected?

15. What is the basis for the diversification-for-stability argument for protectionism? How can it be countered?

16. Explain the arguments and counterargument for protecting infant industries.

17. What is strategic trade policy and problems with such a policy?

18. Can a strong case for protectionism be made on the basis of defending against the "dumping" of products? How do you determine if a nation is dumping a product? What are the economic effects of dumping on consumers?

19. What are the problems with using trade barriers as a means of increasing domestic employment?

20. Does the economy need to shield domestic workers from competition from "cheap" foreign labor? Explain using the ideas of comparative advantage, standards of living, productivity, and labor cost per unit of output.

ANSWERS

Chapter 37 International Trade

FILL-IN QUESTIONS

1. goods, services
2. 12, largest
3. uneven, different, more
4. lowest, have, do not have
5. *a.* inexpensive, expensive; *b.* expensive, inexpensive; *c.* hats, bananas; *d.* 3, 4; *e.* (1) 1/3, 2/7, (2) 4, 3 1/2; *f.* rises
6. comparative advantage, more, higher
7. world, domestic
8. increase, increase
9. supply, only one
10. tariffs, quotas, revenue, protective
11. nontariff, export
12. domestic producers, decrease, less
13. increase, decrease, increase, decrease, decrease, decrease

14. tariff, quota
15. *a.* military self-sufficiency; *b.* support of infant industry; *c.* increase domestic employment; *d.* diversification for stability; *e.* protection against dumping; *f.* cheap foreign labor (any order for *a–f*)
16. essential, more
17. advanced, developing
18. infant, infant, mature
19. composition, neighbor, retaliate, less
20. per hour, per unit

TRUE–FALSE QUESTIONS

1. T, p. 744
2. F, pp. 744–745
3. T, p. 745
4. T, p. 745
5. F, p. 745
6. F, p. 745
7. F, p. 747
8. T, pp. 747–748
9. T, p. 747
10. T, p. 749
11. T, p. 750
12. F, p. 750
13. F, p. 750
14. T, pp. 751–752
15. F, p. 754
16. T, p. 754
17. T, pp. 755–756
18. F, p. 755
19. T, p. 756
20. T, pp. 756—57
21. F, pp. 757–758
22. T, p. 758
23. T, p. 759
24. F, p. 759
25. F, p. 759

MULTIPLE-CHOICE QUESTIONS

1. c, p. 744
2. c, p. 744
3. b, pp. 744–745
4. b, pp. 745–746
5. a, pp. 746–747
6. a, pp.746–748
7. c, pp. 746–748
8. c, pp. 750–753
9. a, pp. 750–753
10. c, p. 754
11. b, pp.754–755
12. d, p. 754
13. b, pp.754–755
14. d, pp. 754–755
15. c, pp. 754–755
16. c, pp. 754–755
17. c, p. 755
18. a, pp. 755–756
19. a, pp. 755–756
20. d, p. 757
21. d, p. 757
22. c, pp. 757–758
23. c, p. 758
24. c, pp. 758–759
25. c, p. 759

PROBLEMS

1. *a.* constant; *b.* (1) 8, 2, (2) 4, 2; *c.* (1) it has a comparative advantage in producing wheat (its cost of producing wheat is less than Chile's), (2) it has a comparative advantage in producing copper (its cost of producing copper is less than the United States'); *d.* one of the two nations would be unwilling to trade if the terms of trade are outside this range; *f.* (1) 1, 0, (2) 1, 0
2. *a.* (1) will not, will not, (2) surplus, 200, surplus, exports, 200, (3) shortage, 200, shortage, imports, 200; *b.* (1) will not, will not, (2) surplus, 200, surplus, exports, 200, (3) shortage, 100, shortage, imports, 100; *c.*(1) A, 0, B, 100, (2) A, 50, B, 50, (3) A, 100, B, 0
3. *a.* 750, 700, 650, 600, 550, 500, 450, 300, 0; *b.* $2.00, 600; *c.* 375, 350, 325, 300, 0, 0, 0, 0, 0; *d.* 650, 600, 550, 500, 175, 150, 125, 0, 0; *e.*$2.20, 550; *f.* (1) increased, 25, (2) decreased, 75; *g.* (1) increased, $95, (2) decreased, $345; *h.* increased, $10; *i.* decreased, $345, decreased, $345; *j.* increased, $260; *k.* $260, foreign

SHORT ANSWER AND ESSAY QUESTIONS

1. p. 744
2. p. 744
3. p. 744
4. pp. 744–745
5. pp. 745–749
6. p. 750
7. pp. 750–753
8. pp. 750–753
9. pp. 754–755
10. pp. 754–755
11. pp. 754–755
12. pp. 754–755
13. pp. 755–756
14. p. 756
15. pp. 756–757
16. p. 757
17. p. 757
18. pp. 757–758
19. p. 758
20. pp. 758–759

The Balance of Payments, Exchange Rates, and Trade Deficits

In the last chapter you learned *why* nations engage in international trade and *why* they erect barriers to trade with other nations. In Chapter 38 you will learn *how* nations using different currencies are able to trade goods and services or to buy and sell real and financial assets.

The means nations use to overcome the difficulties that result from the use of different currencies are fairly simple. When the residents of a nation (its consumers, business firms, or governments) wish to buy goods or services or real or financial assets from, make loans or gifts to, or pay interest and dividends to the residents of other nations, they *buy* some of the currency used in that nation. They pay for the foreign money with some of their own currency. In other words, they exchange their own currency for foreign currency.

When the residents of a nation sell goods or services or real or financial assets to, receive loans or gifts from, or are paid dividends or interest by the residents of foreign nations and obtain foreign currencies, they *sell* this foreign currency—often called foreign exchange—in return for some of their own currency. That is, they *exchange* foreign currency for their own currency.

The market in which one currency is sold and is paid for with another currency is called the **foreign exchange market.** The price that is paid (in one currency) for a unit of another currency is called the foreign exchange rate. And like most prices, the **foreign exchange rate** for any foreign currency is determined by the demand for and the supply of that foreign currency.

As you know from Chapter 37, nations buy and sell large quantities of goods and services across national boundaries. But the residents of these nations also buy and sell such financial assets as stocks and bonds and such real assets as land and capital goods in other nations, and the governments and individuals in one nation make gifts (remittances) to other nations. At the end of a year, nations summarize their foreign transactions with the rest of the world. This summary is called the nation's **balance of payments:** a record of how it obtained foreign currency during the year and what it did with this foreign currency.

Of course, all foreign currency obtained was used for some purpose—it did not evaporate—consequently the balance of payments *always* balances. The balance of payments is an extremely important and useful device for understanding the amounts and kinds of international transactions in which the residents of a nation engage. It also allows us to understand the meaning of a balance-of-payments deficit or surplus, the causes of these imbalances, and how to deal with them.

A balance-of-payments deficit occurs when the foreign currency receipts are less than foreign currency payments and the nation must reduce its **official reserves** of its central bank to balance its payments. Conversely, a balance-of-payments surplus occurs when foreign currency receipts are greater than foreign currency payments, and the nation must expand its official reserves to balance its payments.

How nations correct balance-of-payments deficits or surpluses or adjust to trade imbalances often depends on the **exchange-rate systems** used. There are two basic types of such systems—flexible and fixed. In a flexible or floating system, exchange rates are set by the forces of the demand for and supply of a nation currency relative to the currency of other nations. If the demand for a nation's currency increases, there will be an *appreciation* in its value relative to another currency, and if the demand of a nation's currency declines, there will be a *depreciation* in its value relative to another currency. Fixed-exchange-rate systems have been used by nations to peg or fix a specific amount of one nation's currency that must be exchanged for another nation's currency. Both types of systems have their advantages and disadvantages. Currently, the major trading nations of the world use a **managed float exchange-rate system** that corrects balance-of-payments deficits and surpluses.

The final section of the chapter examines the U.S. **trade deficits.** As you will learn, these deficits were the result of several factors—differences in national growth rates and a declining saving rate—that contributed to imports rising faster than exports. They also have several implications—increased current consumption at the expense of future consumption and increased U.S. indebtedness to foreigners.

■ CHECKLIST

When you have studied this chapter you should be able to

☐ Describe examples of transactions in international trade and the role that money plays in them.

☐ Explain how money is used for the international buying and selling of real and financial assets.

☐ Describe how U.S. imports create a domestic demand for foreign currencies that in turn generates a supply of dollars.

☐ Give a definition of a nation's balance of payments.

☐ Use the items in the current account to calculate the balance on goods and services and the balance on the current account when given the data.

☐ Describe how balance is achieved in the capital and financial account.

☐ Explain the relationship between the current account and the capital and financial account.

☐ Use a supply and demand graph to illustrate how a flexible-exchange-rate system works to establish the price and quantity of a currency.

☐ Discuss the role of official reserves when there is a balance-of-payments deficit or balance-of-payments surplus.

☐ Describe the depreciation and appreciation of a nation's currency under a flexible-exchange-rate system.

☐ Identify the six principal determinants of the demand for and supply of a particular foreign currency and explain how they alter exchange rates.

☐ Explain how flexible exchange rates eventually eliminate balance-of-payments deficits or surpluses.

☐ Describe three disadvantages of flexible exchange rates.

☐ Use a supply and demand graph to illustrate how a fixed exchange-rate system functions.

☐ Explain how nations use official reserves to maintain a fixed exchange rate.

☐ Describe how trade policies can be used to maintain a fixed exchange rate.

☐ Discuss advantages and disadvantages with using exchange controls to maintain a fixed exchange rate.

☐ Explain what domestic macroeconomic adjustments are needed to maintain a fixed exchange rate.

☐ Identify three different exchange-rate systems used by the world's nations in recent years.

☐ Discuss the pros and cons of the system of managed floating exchange rates.

☐ Describe the causes of recent trade deficits in the United States.

☐ Explain the economic implications of recent trade deficits in the United States.

☐ Assess the role that speculators play in currency markets (Last Word).

■ CHAPTER OUTLINE

1. International financial transactions are used for two purposes. First, there is the international trade of goods and services, such as food or insurance that people buy or sell for money. Second, there is the international exchange of financial assets, such as real estate, stocks, or bonds, that people also buy or sell with money. International trade between nations or the international exchange of assets differs from domestic trade or asset exchanges because the nations use different currencies. This problem is resolved by the existence of foreign exchange markets, in which the currency used by one nation can be purchased and paid for with the currency of the other nation.

2. The **balance of payments** for a nation is a summary of all the financial transactions with foreign nations; it records all the money payments received from and made to foreign nations. Most of the payments in the balance of payments accounts are for exports or imports of goods

and services or for the purchase or sale of real and financial assets. The accounts show the inflows of money to the United States and the outflows of money from the United States. For convenience, both the inflows and outflows are stated in terms of U.S. dollars so they can be easily and consistently measured.

a. The **current account** section of a nation's balance of payments records the imports and exports of goods and services. Within this section

(1) the *balance on goods* of the nation is equal to its exports of goods minus its imports of goods;

(2) the *balance on services* of the nation is equal to its exports of services minus its imports of services;

(3) the **balance on goods and services** is equal to its exports of goods and services minus its imports of goods and services (if the balance is positive there is a **trade surplus** and if it is negative there is a **trade deficit**); and

(4) the **balance on the current account** is equal to its balance on goods and services and two other "net" items (which can be positive or negative). First there is net investment income (such as dividends and interest) which is the difference in investment income received from other nations minus any investment income paid to foreigners. Second, there are net private and public transfers, which is the difference between such transfers to other nations minus any transfers from other nations. This balance on the current account may be positive, zero, or negative. In 2007, it was a negative $739 billion.

b. International asset transactions are shown in the **capital and financial account** of a nation's balance of payments.

(1) The *capital account* primarily measures debt forgiveness and is a "net" account. If Americans forgave more debt owed to them by foreigners than foreigners forgave debt owed to them by Americans, then the capital account would be entered as a negative (−).

(2) The financial account shows foreign purchases of real and financial assets in the United States. This item brings a flow of money into the United States, so it is entered as a plus (+) in the capital account. U.S. purchases of real and financial assets abroad result in a flow of money from the United States to other nations, so this item is entered as a minus (−) in the capital account. The nation has a surplus in its financial account if foreign purchases of U.S. assets (and its inflow of money) are greater than U.S. purchases of assets abroad (and its outflow of money). The nation has a deficit in its financial account if foreign purchases of U.S. assets are less than U.S. purchases of assets abroad. The **balance on the capital and financial account** is the difference between the value of the capital account and the value of the financial account.

c. The balance of payments must always sum to zero. For example, any deficit in the current account would be offset by a surplus in the capital and financial account. The reason that the accounts balance is that people trade currently produced goods and services or preexisting assets. If a nation imports more goods and services than it exports, then the deficit in the current account (and outflow of money) must be offset by sales of real and financial assets to foreigners (and inflow of money).

d. Sometimes economists and government officials refer to balance-of-payments deficits or surpluses. Whether a nation has a balance-of-payments deficit or surplus depends on what happens to its *official reserves.* These reserves are central bank holdings of foreign currencies, reserves at the International Monetary Fund, and stocks of gold.

(1) A nation has a *balance-of-payments deficit* when an imbalance in the combined current account and capital and financial account leads to a decrease in official reserves. These official reserves are an in-payment to the capital and financial account.

(2) A *balance-of-payments surplus* arises when an imbalance in the combined current account and capital and financial account results in an increase in official reserves. These official reserves become an out-payment from the capital and financial account.

(3) Deficits in the balance-of-payments will happen over time and they are not necessarily bad. What is of concern, however, for any nation is whether the deficits are persistent over time because in that case they require that a nation continually draw down its official reserves. Such official reserves are limited and if they are depleted, a nation will have to adopt tough macroeconomic policies (discussed later in the chapter). In the case of the United States, there are ample official reserves and their depletion is not a major concern.

3. There are two basic types of exchange-rate systems that nations use to correct imbalances in the balance of payments. The first is a *flexible- or floating-exchange-rate system* that will be described in this section of the chapter outline. The second is a *fixed-exchange-rate system* that will be described in the next section of the chapter outline. If nations use a flexible- or floating-exchange-rate system, the demand for and the supply of foreign currencies determine foreign exchange rates. The exchange rate for any foreign currency is the rate at which the quantity of that currency demanded is equal to the quantity of it supplied.

a. A change in the demand for or the supply of a foreign currency will cause a change in the exchange rate for that currency. When there is an increase in the price paid in dollars for a foreign currency, the dollar has *depreciated* and the foreign currency has *appreciated* in value. Conversely, when there is a decrease in the price paid in dollars for a foreign currency, the dollar has *appreciated* and the foreign currency has *depreciated* in value.

b. Changes in the demand for or supply of a foreign currency are largely the result of changes in the **determinants of exchange rates** such as tastes, relative incomes, relative price levels, relative interest rates, expected returns, and speculation.

(1) A change in tastes for foreign goods that leads to an increase in demand for those goods will increase the value of the foreign currency and decrease the value of the U.S. currency.

(2) If the growth of U.S. national income is more rapid than other nations', then the value of U.S. currency will depreciate because it will expand its imports over its exports.

(3) *Purchasing-power-parity theory* is the idea that exchange rates equate the purchasing power of various currencies. Exchange rates, however, often deviate from this parity. If the domestic price level rises sharply in the United States and it remains constant in another nation, then foreign currency of the other nation will appreciate in value and the U.S. currency will depreciate in value.

(4) Changes in the relative interest rate in two nations may change their exchange rate. If real interest rates rise in the United States relative to another major trading partner, the U.S. dollar will appreciate in value because people will want to invest more money in the United States and the value of the other nation's currency will depreciate.

(5) Changes in the expected returns on stocks, real estate, and production facilities may change the exchange rate. If corporate tax rates are cut in the United States, then such a change would make investing in U.S. stock or production facilities more attractive relative to other nations, so foreigners may demand more U.S. dollars and the dollar will appreciate in value and the value of the foreigner's currency may depreciate.

(6) If speculators think the U.S. currency will depreciate, they can sell that currency and that act will help depreciate its value.

c. Flexible exchange rates can be used to eliminate a balance-of-payments deficit or surplus.

(1) When a nation has a payment deficit, foreign exchange rates will increase, thus making foreign goods and services more expensive and decreasing imports. These events will make a nation's goods and services less expensive for foreigners to buy, thus increasing exports.

(2) With a payment surplus, the exchange rates will increase, thus making foreign goods and services less expensive and increasing imports. This situation makes a nation's goods and services more expensive for foreigners to buy, thus decreasing exports.

d. Flexible exchange rates have three disadvantages.

(1) Flexible rates can change often so they increase the uncertainties exporters, importers, and investors face when exchanging one nation's currency for another, thus reducing international trade and international purchase and sale of real and financial assets.

(2) This system also changes the terms of trade. A depreciation of the U.S. dollar means than the United States must supply more dollars to the foreign exchange market to obtain the same amount of goods and services it previously obtained. Other nations will be able to purchase more U.S. goods or services because their currencies have appreciated relative to the dollar.

(3) The changes in the value of imports and exports can change the demand for goods and services in export and import industries, thus creating more instability in industrial production and in implementing macroeconomic policy.

4. If nations use a *fixed-exchange-rate system,* the nations fix (or peg) a specific exchange rate (for example

$2 will buy one British pound). To maintain this fixed exchange rate, the governments of these nations must intervene in the foreign exchange markets to prevent shortages and surpluses of currencies caused by shifts in demand and supply.

a. One way a nation can stabilize foreign exchange rates is through **currency interventions.** In this case, its government sells its reserves of a foreign currency in exchange for its own currency (or gold) when there is a shortage of the foreign currency. Conversely, a government would buy a foreign currency in exchange for its own currency (or gold) when there is a surplus of the foreign currency. The problem with this policy is that it only works when the currency needs are relatively minor and the intervention is of short duration. If there are persistent deficits, currency reserves may be inadequate for sustaining an intervention, so nations may need to use other means to maintain fixed exchange rates.

b. A nation might adopt trade policies that discourage imports and encourage exports. The problem with such policies is that they decrease the volume of international trade and make it less efficient, so that the economic benefits of free trade are diminished.

c. A nation might impose **exchange controls** so that all foreign currency is controlled by the government, and then rationed to individuals or businesses in the domestic economy who say they need it for international trade purposes. This policy too has several problems because it distorts trade, leads to government favoritism of specific individuals or businesses, restricts consumer choice of goods and services they can buy, and creates a black market in foreign currencies.

d. Another way a nation can stabilize foreign exchange rates is to use monetary and fiscal policy to reduce its national output and price level and raise its interest rates relative to those in other nations. These events would lead to a decrease in demand for and increase in the supply of different foreign currencies. But such macroeconomic policies would be harsh because they could lead to recession and deflation, and cause civil unrest.

5. In the past, some type of fixed-exchange-rate system was used such as the gold standard or the Bretton Woods system. The exchange-rate system used today is a more flexible one. Under the system of **managed floating exchange rates,** exchange rates are allowed to float in the long term to correct balance-of-payments deficits and surpluses, but if necessary there can be short-term interventions by governments to stabilize and manage currencies so they do not cause severe disruptions in international trade and finance. For example, the G8 nations (United States, United Kingdom, Canada, Germany, France, Japan, Russia, and Italy) regularly discuss economic issues and evaluate exchange rates, and at times have coordinated currency interventions to strengthen a nation's currency. This "almost" flexible system is favored by some and criticized by others.

a. Its proponents contend that this system has *not* led to any decrease in world trade, and has enabled the world to adjust to severe economic shocks throughout its history.

b. Its critics argue that it has resulted in volatile exchange rates that can hurt those developing nations that are dependent on exports, has *not* reduced balance-of-payments deficits and surpluses, and is a "nonsystem" that a nation may use to achieve its own domestic economic goals.

6. The United States had large and persistent **trade deficits** in the past decade and they are likely to continue.

a. These trade deficits were the result of several factors:

(1) More rapid growth in the domestic economy than in the economies of several major trading partners, which caused imports to rise more than exports

(2) The emergence of large trade deficits with China and the use of a relatively fixed exchange rate by the Chinese

(3) A rapid rise in the price of oil that must be imported from oil-producing nations

(4) A decline in the rate of saving and a capital account surplus, which allowed U.S. citizens to consume more imported goods.

b. The trade deficits of the United States have had two principal effects.

(1) They increased current domestic consumption beyond what is being produced domestically, which allows the nation to operate outside its production possibilities frontier. This increased current consumption, however, may come at the expense of future consumption.

(2) They increased the indebtedness of U.S. citizens to foreigners. A negative implication of these persistent trade deficits is that they will lead to permanent debt and more foreign ownership of domestic assets, or lead to large sacrifices of future domestic consumption. But if the foreign lending increases the U.S. capital stock, then it can contribute to long-term U.S. economic growth. Thus, trade deficits may be a mixed blessing.

7. (Last Word). Speculators buy foreign currency in hopes of reselling it later at a profit. They also sell foreign currency in hopes of rebuying it later when it is cheaper. Although speculators are often accused of creating severe fluctuations in currency markets, that criticism is overstated because economic conditions rather than speculation are typically the chief source of the problem. One positive function of speculators is that they smooth out temporary fluctuations in the value of foreign currencies. Another positive role speculators play in currency markets is that they bear risks that others do not want by delivering the specified amount of foreign exchange at the contract price on the date of delivery.

■ HINTS AND TIPS

1. The chapter is filled with many new terms, some of which are just special words used in international economics to mean things with which you are already familiar. Other terms are entirely new to you, so you must spend time learning them if you are to understand the chapter.

2. The terms **depreciation** and **appreciation** can be confusing when applied to foreign exchange markets.

a. First, know the related terms. "Depreciate" means decrease or fall, whereas "appreciate" means increase or rise.

b. Second, think of depreciation or appreciation in terms of quantities:

(1) what *decreases* when the currency of Country A *depreciates* is the *quantity* of Country B's currency that can be purchased for *1 unit* of Country A's currency;

(2) what *increases* when the currency of Country A *appreciates* is the *quantity* of Country B's currency that can be purchased for *1 unit* of Country A's currency.

c. Third, consider the effect of changes in **exchange rates:**

(1) when the exchange rate for Country B's currency *rises*, this means that Country A's currency has *depreciated* in value because 1 unit of Country A's currency will now purchase a smaller quantity of Country B's currency;

(2) when the exchange rate for Country B's currency *falls*, this means that Country A's currency has *appreciated* in value because 1 unit of Country A's currency will now purchase a larger quantity of Country B's currency.

3. The meaning of the balance of payments can also be confusing because of the number of accounts in the balance sheet. Remember that the balance of payments must always balance and sum to zero because the current account in the balance of payments can be in deficit, but it will be exactly offset by a surplus in the capital and financial account. When economists speak of a balance-of-payments deficit or surplus, however, they are referring to adding *official reserves* or subtracting *official reserves* from the capital and financial account so that it just equals the current account.

■ IMPORTANT TERMS

balance of payments

current account

balance on goods and services

trade deficit

trade surplus

balance on current account

capital and financial account

balance on the capital and financial account

balance-of-payments deficit

balance-of-payments surplus

official reserves

flexible- or floating-exchange-rate system

fixed-exchange-rate system

purchasing-power-parity theory

currency interventions

exchange controls

managed floating exchange rate

■ SELF-TEST

■ FILL-IN QUESTIONS

1. The rate of exchange for the European euro is the amount in (euros, dollars) _____ that a U.S. citizen must pay to obtain 1 (euro, dollar) _____. The rate of exchange for the U.S. dollar is the amount in (euros, dollars) _____ that a citizen in the euro zone must pay to obtain 1 (euro, dollar) _____. If the rate of exchange for the euro is (1.05 euros, $0.95) _____, the rate of exchange for the U.S. dollar is _____.

2. The balance of payments of a nation records all payments (domestic, foreign) _____ residents make to and receive from _____ residents. Any transaction that *earns* foreign exchange for that nation is a (debit, credit) _____, and any transaction that *uses up* foreign exchange is a _____. A debit is shown with a $(+, -)$ _____ sign, and a credit is shown with a _____ sign.

3. If a nation has a deficit in its balance of goods, its exports of goods are (greater, less) _____ than its imports of goods. If a nation has a surplus in its balance of services, its exports of services are (greater, less) _____ than its imports of services. If a nation has a deficit in its balance on goods and services, its exports of these items are (greater, less) _____ than its imports of them.

4. The current account is equal to the balance on goods and services (plus, minus) _____ net investment income and net transfers. When investment income received by U.S. individuals and businesses from foreigners is greater than investment income Americans pay to foreigners, then net investment income is a (negative, positive) _____ number; when transfer payments from the United States to other nations are greater than transfer payments from other nations to the United States, then net transfers are a _____ number.

5. The capital account is a net measure of (investment, debt forgiveness) _____. When Americans forgive more debt owed to them by foreigners than foreigners forgive debt owed to them by Americans, the capital account has a (debit, credit) _____ that reflects an outpayment of funds.

6. The financial account measures the flow of monetary payments from the sale or purchase of real or financial assets. Foreign purchases of real and financial assets in the United States earn foreign currencies, so they are entered as a (plus, minus) _____ in the financial account, but U.S. purchases of real and financial assets abroad draw down U.S. holding of foreign currencies, so this item is entered as a _____.

7. If foreign purchases of U.S. assets are greater than U.S. purchases of assets abroad, the nation has a (surplus, deficit) _____ in its financial account, but if foreign purchases of U.S. assets are less than U.S. purchases of assets abroad, it has a _____.

8. A nation may finance a current account deficit by (buying, selling) _____ real or financial assets and may use a current account surplus to (buy, sell) _____ real or financial assets.

9. The sum of the current account and the capital and financial accounts must equal (0, 1) _____ so the balance of payments always balances. When economists or government officials speak of a balance-of-payments deficit or surplus, however, they are referring to the use of official reserves, which are the quantities of (foreign currencies, its own money) _____ owned by its central bank.

10. If a nation has a balance-of-payments deficit, then its official reserves (increase, decrease) _____ in the capital and financial account, but with a balance-of-payments surplus its official reserves _____ in the capital and financial account.

11. If foreign exchange rates float freely and a nation has a balance-of-payments *deficit*, that nation's currency in the foreign exchange markets will (appreciate, depreciate) _____ and foreign currencies will _____ compared to it. As a result of these changes in foreign exchange rates, the nation's imports will (increase, decrease) _____, its exports will _____, and the size of its deficit will (increase, decrease) _____.

12. What effect would each of the following have—either the appreciation (**A**) or depreciation (**D**) of the euro compared to the U.S. dollar in the foreign exchange market, *ceteris paribus*?

 a. The increased preference in the United States for domestic wines over wines produced in Europe: ____

 b. A rise in the U.S. national income: ____

 c. An increase in the price level in Europe: ____
 d. A rise in real interest rates in the United States: ____

 e. A large cut in corporate tax rates in Europe: ____
 f. The belief of speculators in Europe that the dollar will appreciate in the foreign exchange market: ____

13. There are three disadvantages of freely floating foreign exchange rates: the risks and uncertainties associated with flexible rates tend to (expand, diminish) _____ trade between nations; when a nation's currency depreciates, its terms of trade with other nations are (worsened, improved) _____; and fluctuating exports and imports can (stabilize, destabilize) _____ an economy.

14. To fix or peg the rate of exchange for the Mexican peso when the exchange rate for the peso is rising, the United States would (buy, sell) _____ pesos in exchange for dollars, and when the exchange rate for the peso is falling, the United States would _____ pesos in exchange for dollars.

15. Under a fixed-exchange-rate system, a nation with a balance-of-payments deficit might attempt to eliminate the deficit by (taxing, subsidizing) _____ imports or by _____ exports. The nation might use exchange controls and ration foreign exchange among those who wish to (export, import) _____ goods and services and require all those who _____ goods and services to sell the foreign exchange they earn to the (businesses, government) _____.

16. If the United States has a payments deficit with Japan and the exchange rate for the Japanese yen is rising, under a fixed-exchange-rate system the United States might adopt (expansionary, contractionary) _____ fiscal and monetary policies to reduce the demand for the yen, but this would bring about (inflation, recession) _____ in the United States.

17. The international monetary system has moved to a system of managed (fixed, floating) _____ exchange rates. This means that exchange rates of nations are (restricted from, free to) _____ find their equilibrium market levels, but nations may occasionally (leave, intervene in) _____ the foreign exchange markets to stabilize or alter market exchange rates.

18. The advantages of the current system are that the growth of trade (was, was not) _____ accommodated and that it has survived much economic (stability, turbulence) _____. Its disadvantages are its (equilibrium, volatility) _____ and the lack of guidelines for nations that make it a (bureaucracy, nonsystem) _____.

19. In recent years, the United States had large trade and current account (surpluses, deficits) _____. One cause of these deficits was

(stronger, weaker) _____ economic growth in the United States relative to Europe and Japan. Other contributing factors were a (rise, fall) _____ in trade deficits with China, a _____ in the price of oil, and a _____ in the saving rate.

20. One effect of the recent trade deficits of the United States has been a(n) (decrease, increase) _____ in current domestic consumption that allows the nation to operate outside its production possibility frontier, but may lead to a(n) _____ in future consumption. Another effect was a (rise, fall) _____ in the indebtedness of U.S. citizens to foreigners.

■ **TRUE–FALSE QUESTIONS**

Circle T if the statement is true, F if it is false.

1. The two basic categories of international financial transactions are international trade and international assets. **T F**

2. The balance of payments of the United States records all the payments its residents receive from and make to the residents of foreign nations. **T F**

3. Exports are a debit item and are shown with a minus sign (−), and imports are a credit item and are shown with a plus sign (+) in the balance of payments of a nation. **T F**

4. The current account balance is a nation's export of goods and services minus its imports of goods and services. **T F**

5. The capital account will be a negative number when Americans forgive more debt owed to them by foreigners than the debt foreigners forgive that was owed to them by Americans. **T F**

6. The nation's current account balance and the capital and financial account in any year are always equal to zero. **T F**

7. When a nation must make an in-payment of official reserves to its capital and financial account to balance it with the current account, a balance-of-payments deficit has occurred. **T F**

8. The two "pure" types of exchange-rate systems are flexible (or floating) and fixed. **T F**

9. When the U.S. dollar price of a British pound rises, the dollar has depreciated relative to the pound. **T F**

10. If the supply of a nation's currency increases, that currency will appreciate in value. **T F**

11. The purchasing-power-parity theory basically explains why there is an inverse relationship between the price of dollars and the quantity demanded. **T F**

12. If income growth is robust in Europe, but sluggish in the United States, then the U.S. dollar will appreciate. **T F**

13. If the expected returns on stocks, real estate, or production facilities increased in the United States relative to Japan, the U.S. dollar would depreciate in value relative to the Japanese yen. **T F**

14. The expectations of speculators in the United States that the exchange rate for Japanese yen will fall in the future will increase the supply of yen in the foreign exchange market and decrease the exchange rate for the yen. **T F**

15. If a nation has a balance-of-payments deficit and exchange rates are flexible, the price of that nation's currency in the foreign exchange markets will fall; this will reduce its imports and increase its exports. **T F**

16. Were the United States' terms of trade with Nigeria to worsen, Nigeria would obtain a greater quantity of U.S. goods and services for every barrel of oil it exported to the United States. **T F**

17. If a nation wishes to fix (or peg) the foreign exchange rate for the Swiss franc, it must buy Swiss francs with its own currency when the rate of exchange for the Swiss franc rises. **T F**

18. If exchange rates are stable or fixed and a nation has a balance-of-payments surplus, prices and currency incomes in that nation will tend to rise. **T F**

19. A nation using exchange controls to eliminate a balance-of-payments surplus might depreciate its currency. **T F**

20. Using the managed floating system of exchange rates, a nation with a persistent balance-of-payments surplus should allow the value of its currency in foreign exchange markets to decrease. **T F**

21. Two criticisms of the current managed floating-exchange-rate system are its potential for volatility and its lack of clear policy rules or guidelines for nations to manage exchange rates. **T F**

22. The trade deficits of the United States in recent years were caused by sharp increases in U.S. exports and slight increases in U.S. imports. **T F**

23. Improved economic growth in the economies of the major trading partners of the United States would tend to worsen the trade deficit. **T F**

24. The decline in the saving rate in the United States contributed to the persistent trade deficit of the past decade. **T F**

25. The negative net exports of the United States have increased the indebtedness of U.S. citizens to foreigners. **T F**

■ MULTIPLE-CHOICE QUESTIONS

Circle the letter that corresponds to the best answer.

1. If a U.S. citizen could buy £25,000 for $100,000, the rate of exchange for the pound would be
(a) $40
(b) $25
(c) $4
(d) $.25

2. U.S. residents demand foreign currencies to
(a) produce goods and services exported to foreign countries
(b) pay for goods and services imported from foreign countries
(c) receive interest payments on investments in the United States
(d) have foreigners make real and financial investments in the United States

3. Which of the following would be a credit in the current account?
(a) U.S. imports of goods
(b) U.S. exports of services
(c) U.S. purchases of assets abroad
(d) U.S. interest payments for foreign capital invested in the United States

4. A nation's balance on the current account is equal to its exports less its imports of
(a) goods and services
(b) goods and services, plus U.S. purchases of assets abroad
(c) goods and services, plus net investment income and net transfers
(d) goods and services, minus foreign purchases of assets in the United States

5. The net investment income of the United States in its international balance of payments is the
(a) interest income it receives from foreign residents
(b) value of dividends it receives from foreign residents
(c) excess of interest and dividends it receives from foreign residents over what it paid to them
(d) excess of public and private transfer payments it receives from foreign residents over what it paid to them

Answer Questions 6, 7, and 8 using data in the following table that contains data for the United States' balance of payments in a prior year. All figures are in billions of dollars.

(1)	U.S. goods exports	$+1149
(2)	U.S. goods imports	−1965
(3)	U.S. service exports	+479
(4)	U.S. service imports	−372
(5)	Net investment income	+74
(6)	Net transfers	−104
(7)	Balance on capital account	−2
(8)	Foreign purchases of U.S. assets	+1905
(9)	U.S. purchases of foreign assets	−1164

6. The balance on goods and services was a deficit of
(a) $107 billion
(b) $709 billion
(c) $816 billion
(d) $935 billion

7. The balance on the capital account was a
(a) surplus of $739 billion
(b) deficit of $739 billion
(c) surplus of $816 billion
(d) deficit of $816 billion

8. The balance on the financial account was a
(a) deficit of $372 billion
(b) surplus of $479 billion
(c) deficit of $739 billion
(d) surplus of $741 billion

9. In a flexible- or floating-exchange-rate system, when the U.S. dollar price of a British pound rises, this means that the dollar has
(a) appreciated relative to the pound and the pound has appreciated relative to the dollar
(b) appreciated relative to the pound and the pound has depreciated relative to the dollar
(c) depreciated relative to the pound and the pound has appreciated relative to the dollar
(d) depreciated relative to the pound and the pound has depreciated relative to the dollar

10. Which statement is correct about a factor that causes a nation's currency to appreciate or depreciate in value?
(a) if the supply of a nation's currency decreases, all else equal, that currency will depreciate
(b) if the supply of a nation's currency increases, all else equal, that currency will depreciate
(c) if the demand for a nation's currency increases, all else equal, that currency will depreciate
(d) if the demand for a nation's currency decreases, all else equal, that currency will appreciate

11. Assuming exchange rates are flexible, which of the following should increase the dollar price of the Swedish krona?
(a) a rate of inflation greater in Sweden than in the United States
(b) real interest rate increases greater in Sweden than in the United States
(c) national income increases greater in Sweden than in the United States
(d) the increased preference of Swedish citizens for U.S. automobiles over Swedish automobiles

12. Under a flexible-exchange-rate system, a nation may be able to correct or eliminate a persistent (long-term) balance-of-payments deficit by
(a) lowering the barriers on imported goods
(b) reducing the international value of its currency
(c) expanding its national income
(d) reducing its official reserves

13. If a nation had a balance-of-payments surplus and exchange rates floated freely, the foreign exchange rate for its currency would

(a) rise, its exports would increase, and its imports would decrease

(b) rise, its exports would decrease, and its imports would increase

(c) fall, its exports would increase, and its imports would decrease

(d) fall, its exports would decrease, and its imports would increase

Answer Questions 14, 15, and 16 using the graph below.

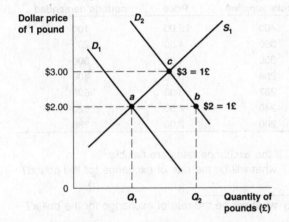

14. If D_1 moves to D_2, the U.S. dollar has
(a) appreciated, and the British pound has depreciated
(b) appreciated, and the British pound has appreciated
(c) depreciated, and the British pound has depreciated
(d) depreciated, and the British pound has appreciated

15. If D_1 moves to D_2, there will be a balance-of-payments
(a) deficit of Q_1
(b) surplus of Q_2
(c) deficit of Q_2 minus Q_1
(d) surplus of Q_2 minus Q_1

16. If D_1 moves to D_2, but the British government seeks to keep the exchange rate at $2 = 1£, then it can do so through policies that
(a) increase the supply of pounds and decrease the demand for pounds
(b) decrease the supply of pounds and increase the demand for pounds
(c) increase the supply of pounds and increase the demand for pounds
(d) decrease the supply of pounds and decrease the demand for pounds

17. Which would be a result associated with the use of freely floating foreign exchange rates to correct a nation's balance-of-payments surplus?
(a) The nation's terms of trade with other nations would be worsened.
(b) Importers in the nation who had made contracts for the future delivery of goods would find that they had to pay a higher price than expected for the goods.

(c) If the nation were at full employment, the decrease in exports and the increase in imports would be inflationary.
(d) Exporters in the nation would find their sales abroad had decreased.

18. The use of exchange controls to eliminate a nation's balance-of-payments deficit results in decreasing the nation's
(a) imports
(b) exports
(c) price level
(d) income

19. Assume a nation has a balance-of-payments deficit and it seeks to maintain a fixed exchange rate. To eliminate the shortage of foreign currency, it may have to adopt monetary policies that
(a) lower the interest rate
(b) raise the interest rate
(c) reduce the tax rate
(d) increase the tax rate

20. A system of managed floating exchange rates
(a) allows nations to stabilize exchange rates in the short term
(b) requires nations to stabilize exchange rates in the long term
(c) entails stable exchange rates in both the short and long term
(d) fixes exchange rates at market levels

21. Floating exchange rates
(a) tend to correct balance-of-payments imbalances
(b) reduce the uncertainties and risks associated with international trade
(c) increase the world's need for international monetary reserves
(d) tend to have no effect on the volume of trade

22. The trade problem that faced the United States in recent years was a
(a) deficit in its capital account
(b) surplus in its balance on goods
(c) deficit in its current account
(d) surplus in its current account

23. Which was a cause of the growth of U.S. trade deficits in recent years?
(a) protective tariffs imposed by the United States
(b) slower economic growth in the United States
(c) direct foreign investment in the United States
(d) a declining saving rate in the United States

24. What would be the effect on U.S. imports and exports when the United States experiences strong economic growth but its major trading partners experience sluggish economic growth?
(a) U.S. imports will increase more than U.S. exports
(b) U.S. exports will increase more than U.S. imports
(c) U.S. imports will decrease but U.S. exports will increase
(d) there will be no effect on U.S. imports and exports

25. Two major outcomes from the trade deficits of recent years were
  (a) decreased domestic consumption and U.S. indebtedness
  (b) increased domestic consumption and U.S. indebtedness
  (c) increased domestic consumption but decreased U.S. indebtedness
  (d) decreased domestic consumption but increased U.S. indebtedness

■ PROBLEMS

1. Assume a U.S. exporter sells $3 million worth of wheat to an importer in Colombia. If the rate of exchange for the Colombian peso is $.02 (2 cents), the wheat has a total value of 150 million pesos.
There are two ways the importer in Colombia may pay for the wheat.
  a. It might write a check for 150 million pesos drawn on its bank in Bogotá and send it to the U.S. exporter. The U.S. exporter would then sell the check to its bank in New Orleans and its checking account there would increase

by $ _____ million. The New Orleans bank would then arrange to have the check converted to U.S. dollars through a correspondent bank (a U.S. commercial bank that keeps an account in the Bogotá bank).
  b. The second way for the importer to pay for the wheat is to buy from its bank in Bogotá a draft on a U.S. bank for $3 million, pay for this draft by writing a check for 150 million pesos drawn on the Bogotá bank, and send the draft to the U.S. exporter. The U.S. exporter would then deposit the draft in its account in the New Orleans bank and its checking account there would

increase by $ _____ million. The New Orleans bank would then collect the amount of the draft from the U.S. bank on which it is drawn through the Federal Reserve Banks.

2. The following table contains hypothetical balance-of-payments data for the United States. All figures are in billions. Compute with the appropriate sign (+ or −) and enter in the table the six missing items.

Current account

(1)	U.S. goods exports	$+150
(2)	U.S. goods imports	−200
(3)	*Balance on goods*	____
(4)	U.S. exports of services	+75
(5)	U.S. imports of services	−60
(6)	*Balance on services*	____
(7)	*Balance on goods and services*	____
(8)	Net investment income	+12
(9)	Net transfers	−7
(10)	**Balance on current account**	____

Capital Account and Financial Account

(11)	Capital Account	−5

Financial Account:

(12)	Foreign purchases of assets in the U.S.	+90
(13)	U.S. purchases of assets abroad	−55
(14)	*Balance on financial account*	____
(15)	**Balance on capital and financial account**	____
		$ 0

3. The following table shows supply and demand schedules for the British pound.

Quantity of pounds supplied	Price	Quantity of pounds demanded
400	$5.00	100
360	4.50	200
300	4.00	300
286	3.50	400
267	3.00	500
240	2.50	620
200	2.00	788

  a. If the exchange rates are flexible
  (1) what will be the rate of exchange for the pound?
  $_____
  (2) what will be the rate of exchange for the dollar?
  £ _____
  (3) how many pounds will be purchased in the market?
  _____
  (4) how many dollars will be purchased in the market?
  _____

  b. If the U.S. government wished to fix or peg the price of the pound at $5.00, it would have to (buy, sell) _____ (how many) _____ pounds for $ _____.

  c. And if the British government wished to fix the price of the dollar at £ 2/5, it would have to (buy, sell) _____ (how many) _____ pounds for $ _____.

■ SHORT ANSWER AND ESSAY QUESTIONS

1. Explain the two basic types of international transactions and give an example of each one.

2. What is meant when it is said that "A nation's exports pay for its imports"? Do nations pay for all their imports with exports? Explain.

3. What is a balance of payments? What are the principal sections in a nation's balance-of-payments, and what are the principal "balances" to be found in it?

4. How can a nation finance a current account deficit? Explain the relationship between the current account and the capital and financial account.

5. Why do the balance-of-payments balance? Explain.

6. What is a balance-of-payments deficit, and what is a balance-of-payments surplus? What role do official reserves play in the matter?

7. Is a balance-of-payments deficit bad or a balance-of-payments surplus good? Explain.

8. Use a supply and demand graph to help describe how exchange rates for a currency appreciate and depreciate.

9. What types of events cause the exchange rate for a foreign currency to appreciate or to depreciate? How will each event affect the exchange rate for a foreign currency and for a nation's own currency?

10. How can flexible foreign exchange rates eliminate balance-of-payments deficits and surpluses?

11. What are the problems associated with flexible-exchange-rate systems for correcting payments imbalances?

12. How may a nation use its international monetary reserves to fix or peg foreign exchange rates? Be precise. How does a nation obtain or acquire these monetary reserves?

13. What kinds of trade policies may nations with payments deficits use to eliminate their deficits?

14. How can foreign exchange controls be used to restore international equilibrium? Why do such exchange controls necessarily involve the rationing of foreign exchange? What effect do these controls have on prices, output, and employment in nations that use them?

15. If foreign exchange rates are fixed, what kind of domestic macroeconomic adjustments are required to eliminate a payments deficit? To eliminate a payments surplus?

16. Explain what is meant by a managed floating system of foreign exchange rates.

17. When are exchange rates managed and when are they allowed to float? What organization is often responsible for currency interventions?

18. Explain the arguments of the proponents and the critics of the managed floating system.

19. What were the causes of the trade deficits of the United States in recent years?

20. What were the effects of the trade deficits of recent years on the U.S. economy?

ANSWERS

Chapter 38 The Balance of Payments, Exchange Rates, and Trade Deficits

FILL-IN QUESTIONS

1. dollars, euro, euros, dollar, $0.95, 1.05 euros
2. domestic, foreign, credit, debit, − +
3. less, greater, less
4. plus, positive, negative
5. debt forgiveness; debit
6. plus, minus
7. surplus, deficit
8. selling, buy
9. 0, foreign currencies
10. decrease, increase
11. depreciate, appreciate, decrease, increase, decrease
12. *a.* D; *b.* A; *c.* D; *d.* D; *e.* A; *f.* D
13. diminish, worsened, destabilize
14. sell, buy
15. taxing, subsidizing, import, export, government
16. contractionary, recession
17. floating, free to, intervene in
18. was, turbulence, volatility, nonsystem
19. deficits, stronger, rise, rise, fall
20. increase, decrease, rise

TRUE–FALSE QUESTIONS

1. T, p. 765	**10.** F, p. 771	**19.** F, p. 776
2. T, p. 765	**11.** F, p. 771	**20.** F, p. 777
3. F, p. 766	**12.** T, p. 771	**21.** T, p. 778
4. F, pp. 766–767	**13.** F, p. 771	**22.** F, p. 778
5. T, p. 767	**14.** T, p. 772	**23.** F, p. 779
6. T, p. 768	**15.** T, p. 773	**24.** T, p. 779
7. T, p. 769	**16.** T, p. 775	**25.** T, p. 780
8. T, p. 769	**17.** F, p. 775	
9. T, p. 770	**18.** T, p. 775	

MULTIPLE-CHOICE QUESTIONS

1. c, p. 765	**10.** b, p. 771	**19.** b, pp. 776–777
2. b, p. 765	**11.** b, pp. 771–773	**20.** a, p. 777
3. b, p. 766	**12.** b, pp. 773–774	**21.** a, pp. 777–778
4. c, p. 766	**13.** b, pp. 773–774	**22.** c, pp. 778–779
5. c, p. 767	**14.** d, pp. 773–774	**23.** d, p. 779
6. b, pp. 766–767	**15.** c, pp. 773–774	**24.** a, p.779
7. b, pp. 766–767	**16.** a, pp. 775–776	**25.** b, p. 780
8. d, pp. 766–767	**17.** d, p. 775	
9. c, pp. 769–771	**18.** a, p. 776	

PROBLEMS

1. *a.* 3; *b.* 3
2. −50, +15, −35, −30, +35, +30
3. *a.* (1) 4.00, (2) 1/4, (3) 300, (4) 1200; *b.* buy, 300, 1500; *c.* sell, 380, 950

SHORT ANSWER AND ESSAY QUESTIONS

1. p. 765	**8.** pp. 769–771	**15.** pp. 776–777
2. p. 765	**9.** pp. 771–773	**16.** p. 777
3. p. 765	**10.** pp. 773–774	**17.** p. 777
4. pp. 766–767	**11.** pp. 774–775	**18.** p. 778
5. p. 768	**12.** pp. 775–776	**19.** p. 779
6. pp. 768–769	**13.** p. 776	**20.** pp. 779–781
7. p. 769	**14.** p. 776	

Previous International Exchange-Rate Systems

Note: The Web supplement is available at: **www. mcconnell18e.com.**

The current exchange-rate system is a managed floating-exchange-rate system which is almost a flexible-exchange-rate system. Before this system started in 1971, two other exchange-rate systems were used that essentially were fixed-exchange-rate systems. The first one was the **gold standard** and it was used from 1879 to 1934. The second was called the **Bretton Woods system** based on the location of the New Hampshire conference where it was devised. It operated from 1944 until 1971. The purpose of this short chapter is to explain the characteristics and features of each of these previous international exchange-rate systems to illustrate how such fixed-exchange-rate systems worked.

■ CHECKLIST

When you have studied this chapter you should be able to

☐ Identify two previous exchange-rate systems used by the world's nations in recent years.
☐ List three conditions a nation had to fulfill if it were to be on the gold standard.
☐ Explain how the gold standard worked to maintain fixed exchange rates.
☐ Give reasons for the collapse of the gold standard.
☐ Explain how the Bretton Woods system attempted to peg exchange rates.
☐ Describe how the Bretton Woods system adjusted the peg for exchange rates.
☐ Discuss the role the International Monetary Fund (IMF) played in pegging or adjusting exchange rates.
☐ State reasons for the demise of the Bretton Woods system.

■ CHAPTER OUTLINE

1. The **gold standard** was used as the exchange-rate system from 1879 to 1934. Under this fixed-exchange-rate system, each nation had to define its currency in terms of a quantity of gold, maintain a fixed relationship between its gold and its money supply, and allow gold to be imported or exported without restrictions.

    a. The potential gold flows between nations would ensure that exchange rates remained fixed because people always knew the value of a national currency in terms of gold.

    b. Payment deficits and surpluses would be eliminated through domestic macroeconomic adjustments. For example, if a nation had a balance-of-payments deficit and gold flowing out of the country to another country, its money supply would decrease. This event would increase interest rates, and thus decrease total spending, output, employment, and the price level. The opposite would happen in the other country because it would have a payments surplus. The changes in both nations would eliminate any payments deficit or surplus. These domestic macroeconomic adjustments, however, were harsh because they could lead to more unemployment, falling incomes, and declining output as the adjustment process took place.

    c. During the worldwide depression of the 1930s, nations felt that remaining on the gold standard threatened the economic recovery of their economies. The nations often used a strategy of **devaluation** of their currencies to boost exports. This devaluation violated the basic tenant of the gold standard that currencies were set at a fixed rate in relation to gold. The devaluation of national currencies led to the breakdown and abandonment of the gold standard.

2. From the end of World War II until 1971, under the **Bretton Woods system,** nations were committed to the adjustable-peg system of exchange rates. It sought to maintain the advantages of fixed exchange rates established with a gold standard, but allowed for some adjustment that would not create the painful macroeconomic adjustments of the stricter gold standard. The **International Monetary Fund (IMF)** was created to keep this exchange-rate system feasible and flexible.

    a. This adjustable-peg system required each IMF member nation to define its currency in terms of gold (or dollars), which established fixed exchange rates among the currencies of all member nations. It also required IMF member nations to keep the exchange rates for their currencies stable. If a nation had a balance-of-payments deficit, it could eliminate it by supplying official reserves from its central bank, selling gold to buy its currency, or borrowing currency from the IMF.

    b. The system also provided for orderly changes in exchange rates to correct fundamental imbalances such as persistent and sizable balance-of-payments deficits. It did so by allowing a nation to devalue its currency within a 10-percent range, with any large devaluation subject to the approval of the IMF's board of directors.

Thus the system provided for orderly rather than competitive devaluations of a nation's currency.

c. The other nations of the world used gold and dollars as their international monetary reserves in the Bretton Woods system because the dollar was thought to be as sound as gold. For these reserves to grow, the United States had to continue to have balance-of-payments deficits; but to continue the convertibility of dollars into gold and keep the dollar sound, it had to reduce the deficits. Faced with this dilemma and the dwindling supply of gold, in 1971 the United States suspended the convertibility of the dollar. This change brought an end to the Bretton Woods system and allowed the exchange rates for the dollar and the other currencies to float.

■ **HINTS AND TIPS**

1. This chapter provides an explanation of how two different types of fixed-exchange rates systems worked. Make sure you understand the distinction between a fixed-exchange-rate system and a flexible-exchange-rate system as described in Chapter 38.

2. Notice the reasons for the collapse of both fixed-exchange-rate systems. The gold standard collapsed because it required harsh domestic macroeconomic adjustments in tough economic times when nations preferred to use currency devaluations. The Bretton Woods system collapsed in large part because persistent U.S. balance-of-payments deficits undermined the value of the dollar.

■ **IMPORTANT TERMS**

gold standard	**International**
devaluation	**Monetary Fund (IMF)**
Bretton Woods	
system	

_____

_____

SELF-TEST

■ **FILL-IN QUESTIONS**

1. Under the gold standard, each nation must define its currency in terms of a quantity of (dollars, gold) _____ , maintain a fixed relationship between its stock of _____ and the money supply, and allow _____ to be freely exported and imported.

2. Under the gold standard, when a nation had a payments deficit, gold flowed (into, out of) _____ the nation, its money supply (increased, decreased) _____, thus (raising, lowering) _____ output, employment, income, and perhaps prices; and thus its payments deficit decreased.

3. The collapse of the gold standard occurred in the early 1930s because nations sought to use currency devaluation to help (increase, decrease) _____ exports and _____ imports. Such currency valuations meant that exchange rates were no longer (flexible, fixed) _____ which was a basic tenant of the gold standard.

4. Under the Bretton Woods system, a member nation defined its monetary unit in terms of (oil, gold) _____ or dollars. Each member nation stabilized the exchange rate for its currency and prevented it from depreciating by (supplying, saving) _____ its official reserves of foreign currency, by (buying, selling) _____ gold, or by (borrowing from, lending to) _____ the International Monetary Fund.

5. Under the Bretton Woods system, a nation with a persistent balance-of-payments deficit could (devalue, revalue) _____ its currency. The system was designed so that in the short run exchange rates would be (stable, flexible) _____ enough to promote international trade and in the long run they would be _____ enough to correct balance-of-payments imbalances.

6. The role of the U.S. dollar as a component of international monetary reserves under Bretton Woods produced a dilemma. For the dollar to remain an acceptable international monetary reserve, the U.S. payments deficits had to be (continued, eliminated) _____, but for international monetary reserves to grow to accommodate world trade, the U.S payments deficits had to be _____. These persistent deficits caused an acceptability problem because they resulted in (a decrease, an increase) _____ in the foreign holding of U.S. dollars and (a decrease, an increase) _____ in the U.S. reserves of gold, which reduced the ability of the United States to convert dollars into gold and the willingness of foreigners to hold dollars as if they were as good as gold.

■ **TRUE–FALSE QUESTIONS**

Circle T if the statement is true, F if it is false.

1. Under the gold standard, the potential free flow of gold among nations would result in exchange rates that are fixed.　**T　F**

2. If country A defined its currency as worth 100 grains of gold and country B defined its currency as worth 20 grains of gold, then, ignoring packing, insuring, and shipping charges, 5 units of country A's currency would be worth 1 unit of country B's currency.　**T　F**

3. Currency devaluations during the 1930s contributed to the collapse of the gold standard.　**T　F**

4. To accommodate expanding world trade in the Bretton Woods system, the U.S. dollar served as a reserve currency and the United States ran persistent balance-of-payments deficits. **T F**

5. In the Bretton Woods system, a nation could not devalue its currency. **T F**

6. A basic shortcoming of the Bretton Woods system was its inability to bring about the changes in exchange rates needed to correct persistent payments deficits and surpluses. **T F**

■ MULTIPLE-CHOICE QUESTIONS

Circle the letter that corresponds to the best answer.

1. Which of these conditions did a nation have to fulfill if it were to be under the gold standard?
   (a) use only gold as a medium of exchange
   (b) maintain a flexible relationship between its gold stock and its currency supply
   (c) allow gold to be freely exported from and imported into the nation
   (d) define its monetary unit in terms of a fixed quantity of dollars

2. If the nations of the world were on the gold standard and one nation had a balance-of-payments surplus,
   (a) foreign exchange rates in that nation would rise
   (b) gold would tend to be imported into that country
   (c) the level of prices in that country would fall
   (d) employment and output in that country would fall

3. Which was the principal disadvantage of the gold standard?
   (a) unstable foreign exchange rates
   (b) persistent payments imbalances
   (c) the uncertainties and decreased trade that resulted from the depreciation of gold
   (d) the domestic macroeconomic adjustments experienced by a nation with a payments deficit or surplus

4. The objective of the adjustable-peg or Bretton Woods system was exchange rates that were
   (a) adjustable in the short run and fixed in the long run
   (b) adjustable in both the short and the long run
   (c) fixed in both the short and the long run
   (d) fixed in the short run and adjustable in the long run

5. Which is the best definition of international monetary reserves in the Bretton Woods system?
   (a) gold
   (b) dollars
   (c) gold and dollars
   (d) gold, dollars, and British pounds

6. The major dilemma created by the persistent U.S. payments deficits under the Bretton Woods system was that in order to maintain the status of the dollar as an acceptable international monetary reserve, the deficits had to
   (a) decrease, but to expand reserves to accommodate world trade, the deficits had to continue
   (b) continue, but to expand reserves to accommodate world trade, the deficits had to be eliminated
   (c) increase, but to expand reserves to accommodate world trade, the deficits had to be reduced
   (d) decrease, but to expand reserves to accommodate world trade, the deficits had to be eliminated

■ PROBLEMS

1. Assume that both the United States and the United Kingdom are on the gold standard. Assume that there are no costs of packing, shipping, or insuring an ounce of gold between the United States and the United Kingdom.
   a. If the United States defines the U.S. dollar as being worth 1/20 of an ounce of gold and the United Kingdom defines the British pound as being worth 1/10 of an ounce of gold, one British pound is worth _____ U.S. dollars and one U.S. dollar is worth _____ British pounds.
   b. If the United States defines the U.S. dollar as being worth 1/30 of an ounce of gold and the United Kingdom defines the British pound as being worth 1/10 of an ounce of gold, one British pound is worth _____ U.S. dollars and one U.S. dollar is worth _____ British pounds.

■ SHORT ANSWER AND ESSAY QUESTIONS

1. What is the gold standard? How did the international gold standard correct payments imbalances?

2. What were the disadvantages of the gold standard for eliminating payments deficits and surpluses?

3. Why did the gold standard collapse during the 1930s?

4. What did nations use as international monetary reserves under the Bretton Woods system? Why was the dollar used by nations as international money, and how could they acquire additional dollars?

5. Explain the dilemma created by the need for expanding international monetary reserves and for maintaining the status of the dollar under the Bretton Woods system.

6. Why and how did the United States shatter the Bretton Woods system in 1971?

ANSWERS

Web Supplement to Chapter 38 Previous International Exchange-Rate Systems

FILL-IN QUESTIONS

1. gold, gold, gold
2. out of, decreased, lowering
3. increase, decrease, fixed
4. gold, supplying, selling, borrowing from

5. devalue, stable, flexible
6. eliminated, continued, an increase, a decrease

Note: Page numbers for True–False, Multiple Choice, and Short Answer and Essay Questions refer to Web Supplement to Chapter 38.

TRUE–FALSE QUESTIONS

1. T, p. 2
2. F, p. 2
3. T, pp. 2–3
4. T, p. 3
5. F, p. 3
6. T, p. 4

MULTIPLE-CHOICE QUESTIONS

1. c, p. 2
2. b, p. 2
3. d, pp. 2–3
4. d, p. 3
5. c, p. 3
6. a, p. 4

PROBLEMS

1. *a.* 2,.5; *b.* 3,.33

SHORT ANSWER AND ESSAY QUESTIONS

1. p. 2
2. p. 2
3. p. 3
4. p. 3
5. pp. 3–4
6. p. 4

The Economics of Developing Countries

Note: The bonus Web chapter is available at: **www. mcconnell18e.com.**

This chapter looks at the critical problem of raising the standards of living in **developing countries** (DVCs) of the world. The development problems in these nations, especially the poorest ones, are extensive: low literacy rates, low levels of industrialization, high dependence on agriculture, rapid rates of population growth, and widespread poverty.

There is also a growing income gap between DVCs and **industrially advanced nations** (IACs). To close this gap, there needs to be more economic growth in the DVCs. Achieving that growth requires expansion of economic resources and the efficient use of these resources. As you will discover from the chapter, DVCs trying to apply these principles face **obstacles** quite different from those that limit growth in the United States and other IACs. DVCs have many problems with natural, human, and capital resources and with technology, all of which combine to hinder economic growth. Certain social, cultural, and institutional factors also create a poor environment for economic development.

These obstacles do not mean that it is impossible to increase the living standards of these DVCs. What they do indicate is that to encourage growth, the DVCs must do things that do not need to be done in the United States or other IACs. Population pressures need to be managed and there needs to be better use of labor resources. Steps must be taken to encourage capital investment. Governments must take an active role in promoting economic growth and limiting the public sector problems for economic development. Dramatic changes in social practices and institutions are required. Without taking these actions, it may not be possible to reduce the major obstacles to growth and break the **vicious circle of poverty** in the DVCs.

No matter how successful the DVCs are in overcoming these obstacles, they still will not be able to grow rapidly without more aid from IACs. This assistance can come in the form of lower trade barriers in IACs that would increase sales of products from DVCs to IACs. There can be more foreign aid in the form of government grants and loans to IACs. The banks, corporations, and other businesses in IACs can provide private capital in the form of loans or direct foreign investment in the building of new factories and businesses.

The final section of the chapter is a fitting ending to the discussion of economic problems in developing nations. It focuses on specific policies to promote economic growth in the DVCs and examines the issue from two sides. One side offers a set of policies from the perspective of DVCs, and the other side lists things IACs can do to foster economic growth in developing nations. You will have to decide after reading the chapter if any of these actions would be worthwhile.

■ CHECKLIST

When you have studied this chapter you should be able to

☐ Describe the extent of income inequality among nations.

☐ Give examples of industrially advanced nations (IACs) and developing countries (DVCs)

☐ Classify nations based on three levels of income.

☐ Compare the effects of differences in economic growth in IACs and DVCs.

☐ Discuss the human realities of poverty in DVCs.

☐ Identify two basic paths for economic growth in DVCs.

☐ Describe natural resource problems in DVCs.

☐ Identify the three problems related to human resources that plague the poorest DVCs.

☐ Explain the difficulties for economic growth that are created by population growth in DVCs.

☐ Compare the traditional and demographic transition views of population and economic growth in DVCs.

☐ Describe the conditions of unemployment and underemployment in DVCs.

☐ State reasons for low labor productivity in DVCs.

☐ Give three reasons for the emphasis on capital formation in the DVCs.

☐ Identify obstacles to domestic capital formation through saving.

☐ List obstacles to domestic capital formation through investment.

☐ Explain why it is difficult to transfer technologies from IACs to DVCs.

☐ Identify three socio-cultural factors that can potentially inhibit economic growth.

☐ Describe the institutional obstacles to growth.

☐ Explain why poverty in the poor nations is a vicious circle.

☐ List five ways governments in the DVCs can play a positive role in breaking the vicious circle of poverty.

☐ Describe the problems with the public sector in fostering economic development.

☐ Identify the three ways IACs can help the DVCs foster economic growth.

☐ Explain how reducing international trade barriers in IACs would help DVCs.
☐ Describe the two sources of foreign aid for DVCs.
☐ Give three criticisms of foreign aid to DVCs.
☐ Explain why foreign aid to DVCs has declined.
☐ Describe what groups in IACs provide private capital to DVCs.
☐ Discuss nine DVC policies for promoting economic growth.
☐ Explain five actions that IACs can take to encourage growth in DVCs.
☐ Discuss the natural and human causes of persistent famines in some African nations (Last Word).

■ **CHAPTER OUTLINE**

1. There is considerable **income inequality among nations.** The richest 20% of the world's population receives more than 80% of the world's income; the poorest 20% receives less than 2%.

   a. The World Bank classifies countries into two main groups.

   (1) *Industrially advanced countries (IACs)* are characterized by well-developed market economies based on large stocks of capital goods, advanced technology for production, and well-educated workers. Among the **high-income** nations are the United States, Japan, Canada, Australia, New Zealand, and most of the nations of Western Europe. These countries averaged $36,608 per capita income in 2006.

   (2) *Developing countries (DVCs)* are a diverse group of middle-income and low-income nations. **Middle-income** nations (e.g., Brazil, Iran, Poland, Russia, South Africa, and Thailand) have per capita incomes that range from $906 to $11,115, and average incomes of about $3,056 in 2006. There are also **low-income** nations with per capita incomes of $905 or less, and average incomes of $649 in 2006. This latter group is dominated by India and most of the sub-Saharan nations of Africa. These nations are not highly industrialized, are dependent on agriculture, and often have high rates of population growth and low rates of literacy. The low-income nations comprise about 37% of the world's population.

   b. There are major differences between the United States and DVCs. The GDP in the United States is greater than the combined GDPs of all DVCs; it produces 27% of the world's output, but has only 5% of the world's population; per capita GDP in the United States is 186 times greater than per capita GDP in Sierra Leone (one of the poorest nations).

   c. There are disparities in the growth rates of nations, resulting in large income gaps. Some DVC nations have been able to improve their economic conditions over time and become IACs. Other DVCs are now showing high rates of economic growth, but still other DVCs have experienced a decline in economic growth and standards of living. If growth rates were the same for high- and low-income nations, the gap in per capita income would widen because the income base is higher in high-income nations.

   d. The human realities of extreme poverty are important. Compared with IACs, persons in DVCs have not only lower per capita incomes but also lower life expectancies, and DVCs have higher infant mortality, lower literacy rates, more of the labor force in agriculture, and fewer nonhuman sources of energy.

2. The paths to economic development for DVCs require that: (1) they use their existing resources more efficiently, and (2) they expand their available supplies of resources. The physical, human, and socioeconomic conditions in these nations are the reasons why DVCs experience different rates of economic growth.

   a. Many DVCs possess inadequate **natural resources.** This limited resource base is an obstacle to growth. The agricultural products that DVCs typically export are also subject to significant price variations on the world market, creating variations in national income.

   b. There are problems with **human resources** in DVCs.

   (1) DVCs tend to be overpopulated and have high rates of population growth.

   (a) These growing populations reduce the DVCs' capacity to save, invest, and increase productivity. They also overuse land and natural resources, and the migration of rural workers to cities creates urban problems.

   (b) There is a qualification to the view that a high rate of population growth or population density is a major cause of low incomes in DVCs. The *demographic transition view* holds that rising incomes will reduce birthrates and that large populations are a result of poverty, not a cause of it.

   (2) DVCs often experience both unemployment and *underemployment,* which wastes labor resources.

   (3) DVCs have low levels of labor productivity because of insufficient physical capital and lack of investment in human capital. There is also a *brain drain* of the more talented and skilled workers from DVCs going to IACs to seek better employment opportunities.

   c. DVCs have inadequate amounts of **capital goods,** and so find it difficult to accumulate capital.

   (1) Domestic capital formation occurs through saving and investing. The potential for saving is low in many DVCs because the nations are too poor to save.

   (2) There is also *capital flight* of saving from DVCs to more stable IACs.

   (3) The investment obstacles include a lack of investors and entrepreneurs and a lack of incentives to invest in DVC economies.

   (4) The *infrastructure* (stock of public capital goods) is also poor in many DVCs.

   d. Technological advance is slow in DVCs. Although these nations might adopt the technologies of industrial nations, these technologies are not always appropriate for the resource endowments of the DVCs, so they must learn to develop and use their own technologies. Some advances can be achieved with *capital-saving technology* (ones that require less use of other capital goods or resources) than *capital-using technology* (ones that require more use of capital goods).

e. The **social, cultural, and institutional** factors in DVCs can be impediments to economic development, and there can be an intangible lack of *will to develop* among individuals and leaders.

(1) The socio-cultural obstacles to growth include such factors as tribal or ethnic allegiances that reduce national unity, a caste or class system, and a *capricious universe view* that sees little correlation between individual actions and outcomes or results.

(2) The institutional obstacles include problems with school systems and public services, weak tax systems, a lack of control over spending by governments, and the need for *land reform* to reduce the concentration of land holdings among a few wealthy families.

3. In summary, DVCs face a *vicious circle of poverty.* They save little because they are poor, and therefore invest little in real and human capital. And because they do not invest, their outputs per capita remain low and they remain poor. Even if the vicious circle were to be broken, a rapid increase in population would leave the standard of living unchanged.

4. There are differing views about the **role of government** in fostering economic growth in the DVCs.

a. The *positive* view holds that in the initial stages of economic development, government action is needed to help overcome major obstacles to growth by:

(1) Providing law and order to give political stability,

(2) Stimulating entrepreneurship to encourage business formation,

(3) Improving the *infrastructure* through the provision of public goods that also make the private sector more productive,

(4) Using policies to force more saving and investment,

(5) Changing the socio-institutional climate through land reform and efforts to shift public attitudes.

b. The *negative* view holds that there are problems and difficulties with using the public sector to promoting growth. They include bureaucratic impediments, *corruption*, maladministration, and the importance of political objectives over economic goals. Central planning does not work because it restricts competition and individual incentives, which are important ingredients in the growth process.

5. There are several **ways IACs can help DVCs.**

a. They can expand trade by **lowering the trade barriers** that prevent the DVCs from selling their products in the developed countries.

b. They can provide **foreign aid** in the form of public loans and grants to help improve infrastructure or public goods.

(1) This foreign aid can come directly from IAC governments; or

(2) The foreign aid can also come from international organizations such as the **World Bank,** which makes grants and loans for basic development projects, offers technical assistance, and serves as a lender of last resort to DVCs.

(3) This foreign aid has been criticized because it increases dependency on IACs, expands bureaucracy in DVCs, and encourages **corruption.** For these reasons, and because of the end of the cold war, foreign aid to DVCs has declined during the 1990s, but it has rebounded in recent years because of greater interest in reducing global poverty and the spending on the war on terrorism.

c. DVCs can also receive flows of private capital from IACs. *Direct foreign investment* in new factories and businesses can come from banks, corporations, and financial investment companies, but such investment tends to be highly selective among nations.

6. There are several **policies for promoting growth** that DVCs and IACs might undertake. Both DVC and IAC perspectives are offered.

a. **DVC policies** for promoting growth include establishing the rule of law, opening economies to international trade, controlling population growth, encouraging direct foreign investment, building human capital, making peace with neighbors, establishing independent central banks, making realistic exchange-rate policies, and privatizing state industries.

b. **IAC policies** for encouraging economic growth in DVCs are directing foreign aid to the poorest of the DVCs, reducing tariffs and import quotas, providing debt relief to DVCs, allowing more low-skilled immigration and discouraging brain drains, and limiting arms sales to DVCs.

7. (Last Word). Famines in Africa are caused by natural and human forces. The immediate cause of famine is drought. Other causes are more complex. Civil strife has torn many nations for decades. Population growth outstripped food production in many nations. Ecological degradation has occurred in nations that use marginal land for crop production. There are also poor public policies such as overspending on armaments, underspending on agriculture, and price controls on agricultural commodities that reduce economic incentives. Some nations also have large external debts to service that require cuts in spending for health care, education, and infrastructure.

■ HINTS AND TIPS

1. This chapter offers a comprehensive look at the various factors affecting growth and economic development. Keep in mind that *no one factor* explains why some nations prosper and others remain poor. The chapter should give you insights into how natural, human, and capital resources together with government policies may influence a nation's economic development.

2. Several economic and demographic statistics for comparing rich and poor nations appear in the chapter's tables. You need not memorize the numbers, but you should try to get a sense of the magnitude of the differences between IACs and DVCs on several key indicators. To do this, ask yourself questions calling for *relative comparisons.* For example, how many times larger is average per capita income in IACs than in low-income DVCs? Answer: 63 times greater ($32,040/$510 = 63).

3. The chapter ends with *policies* for increasing economic growth in DVCs. Be sure to look at these policies from the perspective of both DVCs and IACs. Identify those that you think are most important and explain your reasoning.

■ **IMPORTANT TERMS**

industrially advanced countries (IACs)	capital-using technology
developing countries (DVCs)	the will to develop
demographic transition view	capricious universe view
underemployment	land reform
brain drain	vicious circle of poverty
capital flight	corruption
infrastructure	World Bank
capital-saving technology	direct foreign investment

SELF-TEST

■ **FILL-IN QUESTIONS**

1. There is considerable income inequality among nations. The richest 20% of the world's population receives more than (40, 80) _____% of the world's income, while the poorest 20% of the world's population receives less than (2, 10) _____% of the world's income. The poorest 60% of nations receives less than (6, 30) _____% of the world's income.

2. High-income nations can be classified as (industrially advanced, developing) _____ countries, or (IACs, DVCs) _____, and the middle- or low-income nations as (industrially advanced, developing) _____ countries, or (DVCs, IACs) _____.

3. IACs have a (higher, lower) _____ starting base for per capita income than DVCs, so the same percentage growth rate for both IACs and DVCs means (an increase, a decrease) _____ in the absolute income gap.

4. Low per capita income in DVCs means that there are (lower, higher) _____ life expectancies, _____ adult literacy, (lower, higher) _____ daily calorie supply, _____ energy consumption, and (lower, higher) _____ infant mortality.

5. The process for economic growth is the same for IACs and DVCs. It involves (less, more) _____ efficient use of existing resources and obtaining _____ productive resources.

6. The distribution of natural resources among DVCs is (even, uneven) _____; many DVCs lack vital natural resources. Although oil resources have been used for economic growth in (OPEC nations, DVCs) _____, IACs own or control much of the natural resources in _____. Also, exports of products from DVCs are subject to (small, large) _____ price fluctuations in the world market, and that tends to make DVC incomes (more, less) _____ stable.

7. In terms of human resources,

a. many DVCs are (under, over) _____ populated and have (higher, lower) _____ population growth rates than IACs. Rapid population growth can cause per capita income to (increase, decrease) _____.

b. In DVCs, many people are unable to find jobs, so there is (underemployment, unemployment) _____, and many people are employed for fewer hours than they desire or work at odd jobs, so there is _____.

c. In DVCs, labor productivity is very (high, low) _____, partly because these countries have not been able to invest in (stocks and bonds, human capital) _____; when the best-trained workers leave DVCs to work in IACs, there is a (demographic transition, brain drain) _____ that contributes to the decline in skill level and productivity.

8. Capital accumulation is critical to the development of DVCs. If there were more capital goods, this would improve (natural resources, labor productivity) _____ and help boost per capita output. An increase in capital goods is necessary because the (demand for, supply of) _____ arable land is limited. The process of capital formation is cumulative, investment increases the (output, natural resources) _____ of the economy, and this in turn makes it possible for the economy to save more and invest more in capital goods.

9. The formation of domestic capital requires that a nation save and invest.

a. Saving is difficult in DVCs because of (high, low) _____ per capita income, and investment is difficult because of (many, few) _____ investors or entrepreneurs, and (strong, weak) _____ incentives to invest. There is also the problem of private savings being transferred to IACs; this transfer is called (brain drain, capital flight)

_____.

b. Many DVCs do not have the infrastructure or (private, public) _____ capital goods that are necessary for productive _____ investment by businesses.

c. Nonfinancial (or in-kind) investment involves the transfer of surplus labor from (agriculture, industry) _____ to the improvement of agricultural facilities or the infrastructure.

10. The technologies used in the advanced industrial countries might be borrowed by and used in the DVCs, but

a. the technologies used in the advanced countries are based on a labor force that is (skilled, unskilled) _____, labor that is relatively (abundant, scarce) _____, and capital that is relatively _____, and their technologies tend to be (labor, capital) _____-using, while

b. the technologies required in developing countries must be based on a labor force that is (skilled, unskilled) _____, labor that is relatively (abundant, scarce) _____, and capital that is relatively _____, and their technologies tend to be (labor, capital) _____-using.

c. If technological advances make it possible to replace a worn-out plow, costing $10 when new, with a new $5 plow, the technological advance is capital (-saving, -using) _____.

11. Other obstacles to economic growth in DVCs include those dealing with problems of national unity, religion, and customs, or (institutional, socio-cultural) _____ problems, and those dealing with such issues as political corruption, poor school systems, and land reform, or _____ problems.

12. In most DVCs, there is a vicious circle of poverty. Saving is low because the income per capita is (high, low) _____ and because saving is low, investment in real and human capital is _____. For this reason the productivity of labor and output (income) per capita remain (high, low) _____.

13. List five ways that government can serve a positive role in fostering economic growth in DVCs, especially during the early phases of growth:

a. _____
b. _____
c. _____
d. _____
e. _____

14. Government involvement in the economy of DVCs can create public sector problems because government bureaucracy can (foster, impede) _____ social and economic change, government planners can give too much emphasis to (political, economic) _____ objectives, and there can be (good, poor) _____ administration and corruption.

15. Three major ways that IACs can assist in the economic development in DVCs is by (increasing, decreasing) _____ international trade barriers, _____ foreign aid, and _____ the flow of private capital investment.

16. Direct foreign aid for DVCs generally comes from individual nations in the form of (private, public) _____ loans, grants, and programs. It can also come from the (Bank of America, World Bank), _____ which is supported by member nations. This organization is a (first, last) _____ resort lending agency for DVCs and provides (military, technical) _____ assistance for DVCs.

17. Foreign aid has been criticized in recent years because it may (increase, decrease) _____ dependency in a nation instead of creating self-sustained growth, may _____ government bureaucracy and control over a nation's economy, and may _____ the misuse of funds or corruption. These criticisms and the end of the cold war have led to a(n) _____ in the amount of foreign aid to DVCs.

18. There can also be private capital flows to DVCs in the form of direct foreign (aid, investment) _____ from IAC firms, individuals and commercial banks, and it has increased in recent years. The reason for this change is that many DVCs have reformed their economies and adopted policies that (limit, encourage) _____ economic growth and _____ direct foreign investment. Nevertheless, the flow of private capital to DVCs is (selective, widespread) _____ among nations.

19. DVCs can adopt policies to encourage economic growth. They can (open, close) _____ economies to international trade, (encourage, discourage) _____ direct foreign investment and the development of human capital, and (expand, control) _____ population growth.

20. IACs can also adopt policies to help DVCs. They can (raise, lower) _____ trade barriers, (encourage, discourage) _____ immigration of the brightest and best-educated, and direct foreign aid to the (middle-income, low-income) _____ DVCs.

■ TRUE–FALSE QUESTIONS

Circle T if the statement is true, F if it is false.

1. The richest 20% of the world's population receives about 50% of the world's income while the poorest 20% receives only about 20% of the world's income. **T　F**

2. Low-income developing countries typically have high unemployment, low literacy rates, rapid population growth, and a labor force committed to agricultural production. **T　F**

3. The United States has about 5% of the world's population and produces about 27% of the world's output. **T　F**

4. The absolute income gap between DVCs and industrially advanced countries has been declining. **T　F**

5. Economic growth in both IACs and DVCs requires using economic resources more efficiently and increasing the supplies of some of these resources. **T　F**

6. It is impossible to achieve a high standard of living with a small supply of natural resources. **T　F**

7. DVCs have low population densities and low population growth relative to IACs. **T　F**

8. The demographic transition view of population growth is that rising incomes must first be achieved, and only then will slower population growth follow. **T　F**

9. A major factor contributing to the high unemployment rates in urban areas of DVCs is the fact that the migration from rural areas to cities has greatly exceeded the growth of urban job opportunities. **T　F**

10. Saving in DVCs is a smaller percentage of domestic output than in IACs, and this is the chief reason total saving in DVCs is small. **T　F**

11. Before private investment can be increased in DVCs, it is necessary to reduce the amount of investment in infrastructure. **T　F**

12. Technological advances in DVCs will be made rapidly because the advances do not require pushing forward the frontiers of technological knowledge, and the technologies used in IACs can be easily transferred to all DVCs. **T　F**

13. When technological advances are capital-saving, it is possible for an economy to increase its productivity without any *net* investment in capital goods. **T　F**

14. A critical, but intangible, ingredient in economic development is the "will to develop." **T　F**

15. The capricious universe view is that there is a strong correlation between individual effort and results. **T　F**

16. Land reform is one of the institutional obstacles to economic growth in many developing countries. **T　F**

17. The situation in which poor nations stay poor because they are poor is a description of the vicious circle of poverty. **T　F**

18. The creation of an adequate infrastructure in a nation is primarily the responsibility of the private sector. **T　F**

19. Governments always play a positive role in fostering the economic growth of DVCs. **T　F**

20. One effective way that IACs can help DVCs is to raise trade barriers so that DVCs become more self-sufficient. **T　F**

21. The World Bank provides loans for basic development projects in DVCs. **T　F**

22. Two reasons why foreign aid is viewed as harmful are that it tends to promote dependency and generate government bureaucracy. **T　F**

23. An example of direct foreign investment would be the building of an automobile parts factory by General Motors in Brazil. **T　F**

24. In recent years, the flow of direct foreign investment to DVCs has significantly decreased. **T　F**

25. One policy suggested for promoting economic growth in DVCs is the establishment of independent central banks (where they do not already exist) to keep inflation in check and control the money supply. **T　F**

■ MULTIPLE-CHOICE QUESTIONS

Circle the letter that corresponds to the best answer.

1. Data on per capita income from the nations of the world indicate that there is considerable
  (a) income equality
  (b) income inequality
  (c) stability in the income growth
  (d) deterioration in incomes for most developing nations

2. Which nation would be considered a developing nation?
  (a) India
  (b) Italy
  (c) Japan
  (d) New Zealand

3. If the per capita income is $600 a year in a DVC and $12,000 in an IAC, then a 2% growth rate in each nation will increase the absolute income gap by
  (a) $120
  (b) $228
  (c) $240
  (d) $252

4. The poorest DVCs would probably exhibit high levels of
  (a) literacy
  (b) life expectancy
  (c) infant mortality
  (d) per capita energy consumption

5. The essential paths for economic growth in any nation are expanding the
  (a) size of the population and improving agriculture
  (b) role of government and providing jobs for the unemployed

(c) supplies of resources and using existing resources more efficiently

(d) amount of tax subsidies to businesses and tax credits for business investment

6. Based on the rule of 70, if the United States has an annual rate of population increase of 1% and a DVC has one of 2%, how many years will it take for the population to double in each nation?

(a) 140 years for the United States and 70 years for the DVC

(b) 35 years for the United States and 70 years for the DVC

(c) 70 years for the United States and 35 years for the DVC

(d) 70 years for the United States and 140 years for the DVC

7. Assume the total real output of a developing country increases from $100 billion to $115.5 billion while its population expands from 200 to 210 million people. Real per capita income has increased by

(a) $50

(b) $100

(c) $150

(d) $200

8. An increase in the total output of consumer goods in a DVC may not increase the average standard of living because it may increase

(a) capital flight

(b) population growth

(c) disguised unemployment

(d) the quality of the labor force

9. Which best describes the unemployment found in DVCs?

(a) the cyclical fluctuations in the nation's economy

(b) the migration of agricultural workers from rural areas to seek jobs in urban areas

(c) workers being laid off by large domestic or multinational corporations during periods of economic instability

(d) the education and training of workers in the wrong types of jobs and for which there is little demand

10. Which is an obstacle to economic growth in DVCs?

(a) the low demand for natural resources

(b) the low supply of capital goods

(c) the decline in demographic transition

(d) a fall in population growth

11. Which is a reason for placing special emphasis on capital accumulation in DVCs?

(a) the flexible supply of arable land in DVCs

(b) the high productivity of workers in DVCs

(c) the high marginal benefits of capital goods

(d) the greater opportunities for capital flight

12. Which is a factor limiting saving in DVCs?

(a) The output of the economy is too low to permit a large volume of saving.

(b) Those who do save make their savings available only to their families.

(c) Governments control the banking system and set low interest rates.

(d) There is an equal distribution of income in most nations.

13. When citizens of developing countries transfer savings to or invest savings in industrially advanced countries, this is referred to as

(a) brain drain

(b) capital flight

(c) savings potential

(d) in-kind investment

14. Which is a major obstacle to capital formation in DVCs?

(a) lack of oil resources

(b) lack of entrepreneurs

(c) lack of government price supports for products

(d) an excess of opportunities for financial investments

15. If it is cheaper to use a new fertilizer that is better adapted to a nation's topography, this is an example of

(a) a capital-using technology

(b) a capital-saving technology

(c) capital consumption

(d) private capital flows

16. Which is an example of infrastructure?

(a) a farm

(b) a steel plant

(c) an electric power plant

(d) a deposit in a financial institution

17. Which seems to be the most acute *institutional* problem that needs to be resolved by many DVCs?

(a) development of strong labor unions

(b) an increase in natural resources

(c) the adoption of birth control

(d) land reform

18. Which is a major positive role for government in the early stage of economic development?

(a) providing an adequate infrastructure

(b) conducting central economic planning

(c) improving the efficiency of tax collection

(d) creating marketing boards for export products

19. In recent years, many DVCs have come to realize that

(a) there are few disadvantages from government involvement in economic development

(b) entrepreneurship and economic incentives for individuals are necessary for economic development

(c) the World Bank is an institutional barrier to economic growth

(d) private capital is not essential for economic growth

20. Industrially advanced countries can best help DVCs by

(a) letting them raise tariffs and quotas to protect domestic markets

(b) reducing foreign grant aid but increasing loan aid

(c) increasing the flows of private capital

(d) increasing control over their capital markets

21. The major objective of the World Bank is to
(a) maximize its profits for its worldwide shareholders
(b) assist developing countries in achieving economic growth
(c) provide financial backing for the operation of the United Nations
(d) maintain stable exchange rates in the currencies of developing countries

22. A major criticism of foreign aid to developing nations is that it
(a) provides incentives for capital flight
(b) is capital-using rather than capital-saving
(c) encourages growth in government bureaucracy
(d) gives too much power and control to the World Bank

23. Which would be an example of direct foreign investment in DVCs?
(a) a low-interest loan from the U.S. government to Nigeria
(b) a grant from the World Bank to build a dam in Thailand
(c) the purchase of a computer business in Honduras by a U.S. firm
(d) a payment from a worker in the U.S. to a family in Iran

24. A suggested policy for DVCs to implement that promotes economic growth is
(a) reducing the control of monetary policy by central banks
(b) obtaining more low-interest loans from the World Bank
(c) encouraging more direct foreign investment
(d) expanding state industries

25. Which is a suggested policy for industrially advanced countries to adopt to foster economic growth in DVCs?
(a) increased appreciation of currencies in DVCs
(b) increased debt relief in DVCs
(c) elimination of the International Monetary Fund
(d) elimination of the OPEC oil cartel

■ **PROBLEMS**

1. Suppose that the real per capita income in the average industrially advanced country is $8000 per year and in the average DVC $500 per year.
a. The gap between their standards of living is $_____ per year.
b. If GDP per capita were to grow at a rate of 5% during a year in both the industrially advanced country and the DVC,
(1) the standard of living in the IAC would rise to $_____ in a year;
(2) the standard of living in the DVC would rise to $_____ in a year; and
(3) the gap between their standards of living would (narrow, widen) _____ to $_____ in a year.

2. While economic conditions are not identical in all DVCs, certain conditions are common to or typical of most of them. In the space after each of the following characteristics, indicate briefly the nature of this characteristic in many low-income DVCs.
a. Standard of living (per capita income): _____
b. Average life expectancy: _____
c. Extent of unemployment: _____
d. Literacy: _____
e. Technology: _____
f. Percentage of the population engaged in agriculture: _____
g. Size of the population relative to the land and capital available: _____
h. The birthrates and death rates: _____
i. Quality of the labor force: _____
j. Amount of capital equipment relative to the labor force: _____
k. Level of saving: _____
l. Incentive to invest: _____
m. Amount of infrastructure: _____
n. Extent of industrialization: _____
o. Size and quality of the entrepreneurial class and the supervisory class: _____
p. Per capita public expenditures for education and per capita energy consumption: _____
q. Per capita consumption of food: _____
r. Disease and malnutrition: _____

3. Suppose it takes a minimum of 5 units of food to keep a person alive for a year, the population can double itself every 10 years, and the food supply can increase every 10 years by an amount equal to what it was in the beginning (year 0).
a. Assume that both the population and the food supply grow at these rates. Complete the following table by computing the size of the population and the food supply in years 10 through 60.

Year	Food supply	Population
0	200	20
10		
20		
30		
40		
50		
60		

b. What happens to the relationship between the food supply and the population in the 30th year? _____
_____

c. What would actually prevent the population from growing at this rate following the 30th year? _____

_____

d. Assuming that the actual population growth in the years following the 30th does not outrun the food supply, what would be the size of the population in

(1) Year 40: _____

(2) Year 50: _____

(3) Year 60: _____

e. Explain why the standard of living failed to increase in the years following the 30th even though the food supply increased by 75% between years 30 and 60.

_____

_____

■ SHORT ANSWER AND ESSAY QUESTIONS

1. What is the degree of income inequality among nations of the world?

2. How do the overall levels of economic growth per capita and the rates of economic growth compare among rich nations and poor countries? Why does the income gap widen?

3. What are the human realities of poverty found in DVCs? (Use the socio-economic indicators in Table 39W.1 of the text to contrast the quality of life in IACs and DVCs.)

4. Describe the basic paths of economic growth. Do these avenues differ for IACs and DVCs?

5. How would you describe the natural resource situation for DVCs? In what ways do price fluctuations affect DVC exports? Is a weak natural resource base an obstacle to economic growth?

6. Describe the implications of the high rate of growth in populations and its effects on the standard of living. Can the standard of living be raised merely by increasing the output of consumer goods in DVCs? What is the meaning of the cliché "the rich get richer and the poor get children," and how does it apply to DVCs?

7. Compare and contrast the traditional view of population and economic growth with the demographic transition view.

8. What is the distinction between unemployment and underemployment? How do these concepts apply to DVCs?

9. What are the reasons for the low level of labor productivity in DVCs?

10. How does the brain drain affect DVCs?

11. What are the reasons for placing special emphasis on capital accumulation as a means of promoting economic growth in DVCs?

12. Why is domestic capital accumulation difficult in DVCs? Answer in terms of both the saving side and the investment side of capital accumulation. Is there capital flight from DVCs?

13. In addition to the obstacles that limit domestic investment, what other obstacles tend to limit the flow of foreign capital into DVCs? What role does infrastructure play in capital formation?

14. How might the DVCs improve their technology without engaging in slow and expensive research? Why might this be an inappropriate method of improving the technology used in the DVCs?

15. What is meant by the "will to develop"? How is it related to social and institutional change in DVCs?

16. Explain the vicious circle of poverty in the DVCs. How does population growth make an escape from this vicious circle difficult?

17. Why is the role of government expected to be a positive one in the early phases of development in DVCs? What have been the problems with the involvement of government in economic development?

18. What are three ways that IACs help DVCs?

19. How is it possible for the United States to assist DVCs without spending a penny on foreign aid? Is this type of aid sufficient to ensure rapid and substantial development in DVCs?

20. Discuss the World Bank in terms of its purposes, characteristics, sources of funds, promotion of private capital flows, and success. What are its affiliates and their purposes?

21. Discuss three criticisms of foreign aid to DVCs.

22. Describe the types of private capital flows to encourage economic growth in DVCs.

23. How have DVCs changed to encourage direct foreign investment? What is the problem with the selectivity of this type of investment?

24. Describe the variety of suggested policies that DVCs can adopt to promote economic growth.

25. Explain what IACs can do to assist DVCs in fostering economic growth.

ANSWERS

Chapter 39 Web The Economics of Developing Countries

FILL-IN QUESTIONS

1. 80, 2, 6

2. industrially advanced, IACs, developing, DVCs

3. higher, an increase

4. lower, lower, lower, lower, higher

5. more, more

6. uneven, OPEC nations, DVCs, large, less

7. *a.* over, higher, decrease; *b.* unemployment, underemployment; *c.* low, human capital, brain drain

8. labor productivity, supply of, output

9. *a.* low, few, weak, capital flight; *b.* public, private; *c.* agriculture

10. *a.* skilled, scarce, abundant, capital; *b.* unskilled, abundant, scarce, labor; *c.* saving
11. socio-cultural, institutional
12. low, low, low
13. *a.* establishing effective law and order; *b.* encouraging entrepreneurship; *c.* improving the infrastructure; *d.* promoting saving and investment; *e.* dealing with the social-institutional obstacles (any order for *a–e*)
14. impede, political, poor
15. decreasing, increasing, increasing
16. public, World Bank, last, technical
17. increase, increase, increase, decrease
18. investment, encourage, encourage, selective
19. open, encourage, control
20. lower, discourage, low-income

Note: Page numbers for True–False, Multiple Choice, and Short Answer and Essay Questions refer to Bonus Web Chapter 39.

TRUE–FALSE QUESTIONS

1. F, p. 2
2. T, p. 2
3. T, p. 2
4. F, p. 2
5. T, p. 4
6. F, pp. 4–5
7. F, pp. 5–6
8. T, pp. 6–7
9. T, p. 7
10. F, p. 8
11. F, pp. 8–9
12. F, p. 9
13. T, p. 9
14. T, p. 10
15. F, p. 10
16. T, p. 10
17. T, pp. 10–11
18. F, p. 12
19. F, p. 12
20. F, p. 13
21. T, p. 14
22. T, p. 14
23. T, p. 15
24. F, p. 15
25. T, p. 17

MULTIPLE-CHOICE QUESTIONS

1. b, pp. 1–2
2. a, p. 2
3. b, p. 2
4. c, p. 4
5. c, p. 4
6. c, p. 5
7. a, pp. 5–6
8. b, pp. 5–6
9. b, p. 7
10. b, pp. 7–8
11. c, p. 8
12. a, p. 8
13. b, p. 8
14. b, p. 8
15. b, p. 9
16. c, pp. 8–9
17. d, p. 10
18. a, p. 12
19. b, p. 12
20. c, p. 13
21. b, p. 14
22. c, p. 14
23. c, p. 15
24. c, pp. 15–17
25. b, p. 18

PROBLEMS

1. *a.* 7500; *b.* (1) 8400, (2) 525, (3) widen, 7875
2. *a.* low; *b.* short; *c.* widespread; *d.* low; *e.* primitive; *f.* large; *g.* large; *h.* high; *i.* poor; *j.* small; *k.* low; *l.* absent; *m.* small; *n.* small; *o.* small and poor; *p.* small; *q.* low; *r.* common
3. *a.* Food supply: 400, 600, 800, 1000, 1200, 1400; Population: 40, 80, 160, 320, 640, 1280; *b.* the food supply is just able to support the population; *c.* the inability of the food supply to support a population growing at this rate; *d.* (1) 200, (2) 240, (3) 280; *e.* the population increased as rapidly as the food supply

SHORT ANSWER AND ESSAY QUESTIONS

1. pp. 1–2
2. p. 2
3. pp. 2, 4
4. p. 4
5. pp. 4–5
6. pp. 5–6
7. pp. 6–7
8. p. 7
9. p. 7
10. p. 7
11. pp. 7–8
12. pp. 8–9
13. pp. 8–9
14. p. 9
15. p. 10
16. pp. 10–11
17. pp. 11–12
18. pp. 12–15
19. p. 13
20. p. 14
21. p. 14
22. p. 15
23. p. 15
24. pp. 15–17
25. p. 18

Glossary

Note: Terms set in *italic* type are defined separately in this glossary.

ability-to-pay principle The idea that those who have greater *income* (or *wealth*) should pay a greater proportion of it as taxes than those who have less income (or wealth).

acreage allotments A pre-1996 government program that determined the total number of acres to be used in producing (reduced amounts of) various food and fiber products and allocated these acres among individual farmers. These farmers had to limit their plantings to the allotted number of acres to obtain *price supports* for their crops.

actively managed funds *Mutual funds* that have portfolio managers who constantly buy and sell *assets* in an attempt to generate higher returns than some benchmark rate of return for similar *portfolios*.

actual investment The amount that *firms* invest; equal to *planned investment* plus *unplanned investment*.

actual reserves The funds that a bank has on deposit at the *Federal Reserve Bank* of its district (plus its *vault cash*).

adverse selection problem A problem arising when information known to one party to a contract or agreement is not known to the other party, causing the latter to incur major costs. Example: Individuals who have the poorest health are most likely to buy health insurance.

advertising A seller's activities in communicating its message about its product to potential buyers.

AFL-CIO An acronym for the American Federation of Labor–Congress of Industrial Organizations; the largest federation of *labor unions* in the United States.

agency shop A place of employment where the employer may hire either *labor union* members or nonmembers but where those who do not join the union must either pay union dues or donate an equivalent amount of money to a charity.

aggregate A collection of specific economic units treated as if they were one. For example, all prices of individual goods and services are combined into a *price level,* or all units of output are aggregated into *gross domestic product.*

aggregate demand A schedule or curve that shows the total quantity of goods and services demanded (purchased) at different *price levels.*

aggregate demand–aggregate supply (AD-AS) model The macroeconomic model that uses *aggregate demand* and *aggregate supply* to determine and explain the *price level* and the real *domestic output.*

aggregate expenditures The total amount spent for final goods and services in an economy.

aggregate expenditures–domestic output approach - Determination of the equilibrium *gross domestic product* by finding the real GDP at which *aggregate expenditures* equal *domestic output.*

aggregate expenditures schedule A schedule or curve showing the total amount spent for final goods and services at different levels of *real GDP.*

aggregate supply A schedule or curve showing the total quantity of goods and services supplied (produced) at different *price levels.*

aggregate supply shocks Sudden, large changes in resource costs that shift an economy's aggregate supply curve.

agribusiness The portion of the agricultural and food product industries that is dominated by large corporations.

Alcoa case A 1945 case in which the courts ruled that the possession of monopoly power, no matter how reasonably that power had been used, was a violation of the antitrust laws; temporarily overturned the *rule of reason* applied in the *U.S. Steel case.*

allocative efficiency The apportionment of resources among firms and industries to obtain the production of the products most wanted by society (consumers); the output of each product at which its *marginal cost* and *price* or *marginal benefit* are equal, and at which the sum of consumer surplus and *producer surplus* is maximized.

anticipated inflation Increases in the price level *(inflation)* that occur at the expected rate.

antitrust laws Legislation (including the *Sherman Act* and *Clayton Act*) that prohibits anticompetitive business activities such as *price fixing*, bid rigging, monopolization, and *tying contracts*.

antitrust policy The use of the *antitrust laws* to promote *competition* and economic efficiency.

appreciation (of the dollar) An increase in the value of the dollar relative to the currency of another nation, so a dollar buys a larger amount of the foreign currency and thus of foreign goods.

arbitrage The activity of selling one *asset* and buying an identical or nearly identical asset to benefit from temporary differences in prices or rates of return; the practice that equalizes prices or returns on similar financial instruments and thus eliminates further opportunities for riskless financial gains.

asset Anything of monetary value owned by a firm or individual.

asset demand for money The amount of *money* people want to hold as a *store of value;* this amount varies inversely with the *interest rate.*

asymmetric information A situation where one party to a market transaction has much more information about a product or service than the other. The result may be an under- or overallocation of resources.

average expected rate of return The *probability weighted average* of an investment's possible future returns.

average fixed cost (AFC) A firm's total *fixed cost* divided by output (the quantity of product produced).

average product (AP) The total output produced per unit of a *resource* employed (*total product* divided by the quantity of that employed resource).

average propensity to consume Fraction (or percentage) of *disposable income* that households plan to spend for consumer goods and services; consumption divided by *disposable income.*

average propensity to save (APS) Fraction (or percentage) of *disposable income* that households save; *saving* divided by *disposable income.*

average revenue Total revenue from the sale of a product divided by the quantity of the product sold (demanded); equal to the price at which the product is sold when all units of the product are sold at the same price.

average tax rate Total tax paid divided by total (taxable) income, as a percentage.

average total cost (ATC) A firm's *total cost* divided by output (the quantity of product produced); equal to *average fixed cost* plus *average variable cost.*

average variable cost (AVC) A firm's total *variable cost* divided by output (the quantity of product produced).

backflows The return of workers to the countries from which they originally migrated.

balance of payments (See *international balance of payments.*)

balance-of-payments deficit The amount by which *inpayments* from a nation's stock of *official reserves* are required to balance that nation's *capital and financial account* with its *current account* (in its *balance of payments*).

balance-of-payments surplus The amount by which *outpayments* to a nation's stock of *official reserves* are required to balance that nation's *capital and financial account* with its *current account* (in its *international balance of payments*).

balance on capital and financial account The sum of the *capital account balance* and the *financial account balance.*

balance on current account The exports of goods and services of a nation less its imports of goods and services plus its *net investment income* and *net transfers* in a year.

balance on goods and services The exports of goods and services of a nation less its imports of goods and services in a year.

balance sheet A statement of the *assets, liabilities,* and *net worth* of a firm or individual at some given time.

bank deposits The deposits that individuals or firms have at banks (or thrifts) or that banks have at the *Federal Reserve Banks.*

bankers' bank A bank that accepts the deposits of and makes loans to *depository institutions;* in the United States, a *Federal Reserve Bank.*

bank reserves The deposits of commercial banks and thrifts at *Federal Reserve Banks* plus bank and thrift *vault cash.*

bankrupt A legal situation in which an individual or *firm* finds that it cannot make timely interest payments on money it has borrowed. In such cases, a bankruptcy judge can order the individual or firm to liquidate (turn into cash) its assets in order to pay lenders at least some portion of the amount they are owed.

barrier to entry Anything that artificially prevents the entry of firms into an industry.

barter The exchange of one good or service for another good or service.

base year The year with which other years are compared when an index is constructed; for example, the base year for a *price index.*

beaten paths Migration routes taken previously by family, relatives, friends, and other migrants.

benefits-received principle The idea that those who receive the benefits of goods and services provided by government should pay the taxes required to finance them.

beta A relative measure of *nondiversifiable risk* that measures how the nondiversifiable risk of a given *asset* or *portfolio* compares with that of the *market portfolio* (the portfolio that contains every asset available in the financial markets).

bilateral monopoly A market in which there is a single seller (*monopoly*) and a single buyer (*monopsony*).

Board of Governors The seven-member group that supervises and controls the money and banking system of the United States; the Board of Governors of the Federal Reserve System; the Federal Reserve Board.

bond A financial device through which a borrower (a firm or government) is obligated to pay the principal and interest on a loan at a specific date in the future.

brain drains The exit or *emigration* of highly educated, highly skilled workers from a country.

break-even income The level of *disposable income* at which *households* plan to consume (spend) all their income and to save none of it.

break-even output Any output at which a (competitive) firm's *total cost* and *total revenue* are equal; an output at which a firm has neither an *economic profit* nor a loss, at which it earns only a *normal profit.*

break-even point An output at which a firm makes a *normal profit* (*total revenue = total cost*) but not an *economic profit.*

British thermal unit (BTU) The amount of energy required to raise the temperature of 1 pound of water by 1 degree Fahrenheit.

budget constraint The limit that the size of a consumer's income (and the prices that must be paid for goods and services) imposes on the ability of that consumer to obtain goods and services.

budget deficit The amount by which the expenditures of the Federal government exceed its revenues in any year.

budget line A line that shows the different combinations of two products a consumer can purchase with a specific money income, given the products' prices.

budget surplus The amount by which the revenues of the Federal government exceed its expenditures in any year.

built-in stabilizer A mechanism that increases government's budget deficit (or reduces its surplus) during a recession and increases government's budget surplus (or reduces its deficit) during an expansion without any action by policymakers. The tax system is one such mechanism.

Bureau of Economic Analysis (BEA) An agency of the U.S. Department of Commerce that compiles the national income and product accounts.

business cycle Recurring increases and decreases in the level of economic activity over periods of years; consists of peak, recession, trough, and expansion phases.

business firm (See *firm.*)

cap-and-trade program A government strategy for reducing harmful emissions or discharges by placing a limit on their total amounts and then allowing firms to buy and sell the rights to emit or discharge specific amounts within the total limits.

capital Human-made resources (buildings, machinery, and equipment) used to produce goods and services; goods that do not directly satisfy human wants; also called capital goods.

capital and financial account The section of a nation's *international balance of payments* that records (1) debt forgiveness by and to foreigners and (2) foreign purchases of assets in the United States and U.S. purchases of assets abroad.

capital and financial account deficit A negative balance on its *capital and financial account* in a country's *international balance of payments.*

capital and financial account surplus A positive balance on its *capital and financial account* in a country's *international balance of payments.*

capital flight (Web chapter) The transfer of savings from *developing countries* to *industrially advanced countries* to avoid government expropriation, taxation, higher

rates of inflation, or simply to realize greater returns on *financial investments.*

capital gain The gain realized when securities or properties are sold for a price greater than the price paid for them.

capital goods (See *capital.*)

capital-intensive goods Products that require relatively large amounts of *capital* to produce.

capitalism An economic system in which property resources are privately owned and markets and prices are used to direct and coordinate economic activities.

capital-saving technology (Web chapter) An improvement in *technology* that permits a greater quantity of a product to be produced with a specific amount of *capital* (or permits the same amount of the product to be produced with a smaller amount of capital).

capital stock The total available *capital* in a nation.

capital-using technology (Web chapter) An improvement in *technology* that requires the use of a greater amount of *capital* to produce a specific quantity of a product.

capricious-universe view (Web chapter) The view held by some people that fate and outside events, rather than hard work and enterprise, will determine their economic destinies.

cardinal utility Satisfaction (*utility*) that can be measured via cardinal numbers (1, 2, 3…), with all the mathematical properties of those numbers such as addition, subtraction, multiplication, and division being applicable.

cartel A formal agreement among firms (or countries) in an industry to set the price of a product and establish the outputs of the individual firms (or countries) or to divide the market for the product geographically.

causation A relationship in which the occurrence of one or more events brings about another event.

CEA (See *Council of Economic Advisers.*)

cease-and-desist order An order from a court or government agency to a corporation or individual to stop engaging in a specified practice.

ceiling price (See *price ceiling.*)

Celler-Kefauver Act The Federal act of 1950 that amended the *Clayton Act* by prohibiting the acquisition of the assets of one firm by another firm when the effect would be less competition.

central bank A bank whose chief function is the control of the nation's *money supply;* in the United States, the Federal Reserve System.

central economic planning Government determination of the objectives of the economy and how resources will be directed to attain those goals.

***ceteris paribus* assumption** (See *other-things-equal assumption.*)

change in demand A change in the *quantity demanded* of a good or service at every price; a shift of the *demand curve* to the left or right.

change in quantity demanded A change in the amount of a product that consumers are willing and able to purchase because of a change in the product's price.

change in quantity supplied A change in the amount of a product that producers offer for sale because of a change in the product's price.

change in supply A change in the *quantity supplied* of a good or service at every price; a shift of the *supply curve* to the left or right.

Change to Win A loose federation of American unions that includes the Service Workers and Teamsters and has a total membership of 6 million workers.

checkable deposit Any deposit in a *commercial bank* or *thrift institution* against which a check may be written.

checkable-deposit multiplier (See *monetary multiplier*.)

check clearing The process by which funds are transferred from the checking accounts of the writers of checks to the checking accounts of the recipients of the checks.

checking account A *checkable deposit* in a *commercial bank* or *thrift institution*.

circular flow diagram An illustration showing the flow of resources from *households* to *firms* and of products from firms to households. These flows are accompanied by reverse flows of money from firms to households and from households to firms.

Clayton Act The Federal antitrust act of 1914 that strengthened the *Sherman Act* by making it illegal for firms to engage in certain specified practices.

climate-change problem The problem of rising world temperatures that most climate experts believe are caused at least in part by increased carbon dioxide and other greenhouse gases generated as by-products of human economic activities.

closed economy An economy that neither exports nor imports goods and services.

closed shop A place of employment where only workers who are already members of a labor union may be hired.

Coase theorem The idea, first stated by economist Ronald Coase, that some *externalities* can be resolved through private negotiations of the affected parties.

coincidence of wants A situation in which the good or service that one trader desires to obtain is the same as that which another trader desires to give up and an item that the second trader wishes to acquire is the same as that which the first trader desires to surrender.

COLA (See *cost-of-living adjustment*.)

collective bargaining The negotiation of labor contracts between *labor unions* and *firms* or government entities.

collective voice The function a *labor union* performs for its members as a group when it communicates their problems and grievances to management and presses management for a satisfactory resolution.

collusion A situation in which firms act together and in agreement (collude) to fix prices, divide a market, or otherwise restrict competition.

command system A method of organizing an economy in which property resources are publicly owned and government uses *central economic planning* to direct and coordinate economic activities; command economy; communism.

commercial bank A firm that engages in the business of banking (accepts deposits, offers checking accounts, and makes loans).

commercial banking system All *commercial banks* and *thrift institutions* as a group.

communism (See *command system*.)

comparative advantage A situation in which a person or country can produce a specific product at a lower opportunity cost than some other person or country; the basis for specialization and trade.

compensating differences Differences in the *wages* received by workers in different jobs to compensate for nonmonetary differences in the jobs.

compensating wage differential (See *compensating differences*.)

compensation to employees *Wages* and salaries plus wage and salary supplements paid by employers to workers.

competition The presence in a market of independent buyers and sellers competing with one another along with the freedom of buyers and sellers to enter and leave the market.

competitive industry's short-run supply curve The horizontal summation of the short-run supply curves of the *firms* in a purely competitive industry (see *pure competition*); a curve that shows the total quantities offered for sale at various prices by the firms in an industry in the short run.

competitive labor market A resource market in which a large number of (noncolluding) employers demand a particular type of labor supplied by a large number of nonunion workers.

complementary goods Products and services that are used together. When the price of one falls, the demand for the other increases (and conversely).

complementary resources Productive inputs that are used jointly with other inputs in the production process; resources for which a decrease in the price of one leads to an increase in the demand for the other.

compound interest The accumulation of money that builds over time in an investment or interest-bearing account as new interest is earned on previous interest that is not withdrawn.

concentration ratio The percentage of the total sales of an industry made by the four (or some other number) largest sellers in the industry.

conflict diamonds Diamonds that are mined and sold by combatants in war zones in Africa as a way to provide the currency needed to finance their military activities.

conglomerate merger The merger of a *firm* in one *industry* with a firm in another industry (with a firm that is not a supplier, customer, or competitor).

conglomerates Firms that produce goods and services in two or more separate industries.

constant-cost industry An industry in which expansion by the entry of new firms has no effect on the prices firms in the industry must pay for resources and thus no effect on production costs.

constant opportunity cost   An *opportunity cost* that remains the same for each additional unit as a consumer (or society) shifts purchases (production) from one product to another along a straight-line *budget line* (*production possibilities curve*).

constant returns to scale   Unchanging *average total cost* of producing a product as the firm expands the size of its plant (its output) in the *long run*.

consumer equilibrium   In marginal utility theory, the combination of goods purchased based on *marginal utility* (MU) and *price* (P) that maximizes *total utility*; the combination for goods *X* and *Y* at which $MU_x/P_x = MU_y/P_y$. In indifference curve analysis, the combination of goods purchased that maximize *total utility* by enabling the consumer to reach the highest *indifference curve*, given the consumer's *budget line* (or *budget constraint*).

consumer goods   Products and services that satisfy human wants directly.

Consumer Price Index (CPI)   An index that measures the prices of a fixed "market basket" of some 300 goods and services bought by a "typical" consumer.

consumer sovereignty   Determination by consumers of the types and quantities of goods and services that will be produced with the scarce resources of the economy; consumers' direction of production through their *dollar votes*.

consumer surplus   The difference between the maximum price a consumer is (or consumers are) willing to pay for an additional unit of a product and its market price; the triangular area below the demand curve and above the market price.

consumption of fixed capital   An estimate of the amount of *capital* worn out or used up (consumed) in producing the *gross domestic product*; also called depreciation.

consumption schedule   A schedule showing the amounts *households* plan to spend for *consumer goods* at different levels of *disposable income*.

contractionary fiscal policy   A decrease in *government purchases* for goods and services, an increase in *net taxes*, or some combination of the two, for the purpose of decreasing *aggregate demand* and thus controlling inflation.

coordination failure   A situation in which people do not reach a mutually beneficial outcome because they lack some way to jointly coordinate their actions; a possible cause of macroeconomic instability.

copayment   The percentage of (say, health care) costs that an insured individual pays while the insurer pays the remainder.

copyright   A legal protection provided to developers and publishers of books, computer software, videos, and musical compositions against the copying of their works by others.

corporate income tax   A tax levied on the net income (accounting profit) of corporations.

corporation   A legal entity ("person") chartered by a state or the Federal government that is distinct and separate from the individuals who own it.

correlation   A systematic and dependable association between two sets of data (two kinds of events); does not necessarily indicate causation.

corruption   (Web chapter) The misuse of government power, with which one has been entrusted or assigned, to obtain private gain; includes payments from individuals or companies to secure advantages in obtaining government contracts, avoiding government regulations, or obtaining inside knowledge about forthcoming policy changes.

cost-benefit analysis   A comparison of the *marginal costs* of a government project or program with the *marginal benefits* to decide whether or not to employ resources in that project or program and to what extent.

cost-of-living adjustment (COLA)   An automatic increase in the incomes (wages) of workers when inflation occurs; guaranteed by a collective bargaining contract between firms and workers.

cost-push inflation   Increases in the price level (inflation) resulting from an increase in resource costs (for example, raw-material prices) and hence in *per-unit production costs*; inflation caused by reductions in *aggregate supply*.

Council of Economic Advisers (CEA)   A group of three persons that advises and assists the president of the United States on economic matters (including the preparation of the annual *Economic Report of the President*).

countercyclical payments (CCPs)   Cash *subsidies* paid to farmers when market prices for certain crops drop below targeted prices. Payments are based on previous production and are received regardless of the current crop grown.

craft union   A labor union that limits its membership to workers with a particular skill (craft).

creative destruction   The hypothesis that the creation of new products and production methods simultaneously destroys the market power of existing monopolies.

credible threat   In *game theory*, a statement of harmful intent by one party that the other party views as believable; often issued in conditional terms of "if you do this; we will do that."

credit   An accounting item that increases the value of an asset (such as the foreign money owned by the residents of a nation).

credit union   An association of persons who have a common tie (such as being employees of the same firm or members of the same labor union) that sells shares to (accepts deposits from) its members and makes loans to them.

cross elasticity of demand   The ratio of the percentage change in *quantity demanded* of one good to the percentage change in the price of some other good. A positive coefficient indicates the two products are *substitute goods;* a negative coefficient indicates they are *complementary goods.*

crowding model of occupational discrimination   A model of labor markets suggesting that *occupational discrimination* has kept many women and minorities out of high-paying occupations and forced them into a limited number of low-paying occupations.

crowding-out effect A rise in interest rates and a resulting decrease in *planned investment* caused by the Federal government's increased borrowing to finance budget deficits and refinance debt.

currency Coins and paper money.

currency appreciation (See *exchange-rate appreciation.*)

currency depreciation (See *exchange-rate depreciation.*)

currency intervention A government's buying and selling of its own currency or foreign currencies to alter international exchange rates.

current account The section in a nation's *international balance of payments* that records its exports and imports of goods and services, its net *investment income,* and its *net transfers.*

cyclical asymmetry The idea that *monetary policy* may be more successful in slowing expansions and controlling *inflation* than in extracting the economy from severe recession.

cyclical deficit A Federal *budget deficit* that is caused by a recession and the consequent decline in tax revenues.

cyclical unemployment A type of *unemployment* caused by insufficient total spending (or by insufficient *aggregate demand*).

deadweight loss (See *efficiency loss.*)

debit An accounting item that decreases the value of an asset (such as the foreign money owned by the residents of a nation).

declining industry An industry in which *economic profits* are negative (losses are incurred) and that will, therefore, decrease its output as firms leave it.

decreasing-cost industry An industry in which expansion through the entry of firms lowers the prices that firms in the industry must pay for resources and therefore decreases their production costs.

deductible The dollar sum of (for example, health care) costs that an insured individual must pay before the insurer begins to pay.

defaults Situations in which borrowers stop making loan payments or do not pay back loans that they took out and are now due.

defensive medicine The recommendation by physicians of more tests and procedures than are warranted medically or economically as a way of protecting themselves against later malpractice suits.

deflating Finding the *real gross domestic product* by decreasing the dollar value of the GDP for a year in which prices were higher than in the *base year.*

deflation A decline in the economy's *price level.*

demand A schedule showing the amounts of a good or service that buyers (or a buyer) wish to purchase at various prices during some time period.

demand curve A curve illustrating *demand.*

demand factor (in growth) The increase in the level of *aggregate demand* that brings about the *economic growth* made possible by an increase in the production potential of the economy.

demand management The use of *fiscal policy* and *monetary policy* to increase or decrease *aggregate demand.*

demand-pull inflation Increases in the price level (inflation) resulting from an excess of demand over output at the existing price level, caused by an increase in *aggregate demand.*

demand schedule (See *demand.*)

demographers Scientists who study the characteristics of human populations.

demographic transition (Web chapter) The idea that population growth slows once a developing country achieves higher standards of living because the perceived marginal cost of additional children begins to exceed the perceived marginal benefit.

demand shocks Sudden, unexpected changes in demand.

dependent variable A variable that changes as a consequence of a change in some other (independent) variable; the "effect" or outcome.

depository institutions Firms that accept deposits of *money* from the public (businesses and persons); *commercial banks, savings and loan associations, mutual savings banks,* and *credit unions.*

depreciation (See *consumption of fixed capital.*)

depreciation (of the dollar) A decrease in the value of the dollar relative to another currency, so a dollar buys a smaller amount of the foreign currency and therefore of foreign goods.

derived demand The demand for a resource that depends on the demand for the products it helps to produce.

determinants of aggregate demand Factors such as consumption spending, *investment,* government spending, and *net exports* that, if they change, shift the aggregate demand curve.

determinants of aggregate supply Factors such as input prices, *productivity,* and the legal-institutional environment that, if they change, shift the aggregate supply curve.

determinants of demand Factors other than price that determine the quantities demanded of a good or service.

determinants of supply Factors other than price that determine the quantities supplied of a good or service.

developing countries Many countries of Africa, Asia, and Latin America that are characterized by lack of capital goods, use of nonadvanced technologies, low literacy rates, high unemployment, rapid population growth, and labor forces heavily committed to agriculture.

diagnosis-related group (DRG) system Payments to doctors and hospitals under *Medicare* based on which of hundreds of carefully detailed diagnostic categories best characterize the patient's condition and needs.

differentiated oligopoly An *oligopoly* in which the firms produce a *differentiated product.*

differentiated product A product that differs physically or in some other way from the similar products produced by other firms; a product such that buyers are not indifferent to the seller when the price charged by all sellers is the same.

diffusion (Web chapter) The spread of an *innovation* through its widespread imitation.

dilemma of regulation The tradeoff faced by a *regulatory agency* in setting the maximum legal price a monopolist may charge: The *socially optimal price* is below *average total cost* (and either bankrupts the *firm* or requires that it be subsidized), while the higher, *fair-return price* does not produce *allocative efficiency*.

diminishing marginal returns (See *law of diminishing returns*.)

diminishing marginal utility (See *law of diminishing marginal utility*.)

direct foreign investment (See *foreign direct investment*.)

direct payments Cash subsidies paid to farmers based on past production levels; unaffected by current crop prices and current production.

direct relationship The relationship between two variables that change in the same direction, for example, product price and quantity supplied; positive relationship.

discount rate The interest rate that the *Federal Reserve Banks* charge on the loans they make to *commercial banks* and *thrift institutions*.

discouraged workers Employees who have left the *labor force* because they have not been able to find employment.

discretionary fiscal policy Deliberate changes in taxes (tax rates) and government spending by Congress to promote full employment, price stability, and economic growth.

discrimination The practice of according individuals or groups inferior treatment in hiring, occupational access, education and training, promotion, wage rates, or working conditions even though they have the same abilities, education, skills, and work experience as other workers.

discrimination coefficient A measure of the cost or disutility of prejudice; the monetary amount an employer is willing to pay to hire a preferred worker rather than a nonpreferred worker.

diseconomies of scale Increases in the *average total cost* of producing a product as the *firm* expands the size of its *plant* (its output) in the *long run*.

disinflation A reduction in the rate of *inflation*.

disposable income (DI) *Personal income* less personal taxes; income available for *personal consumption expenditures* and *personal saving*.

dissaving Spending for consumer goods and services in excess of *disposable income;* the amount by which *personal consumption expenditures* exceed disposable income.

diversifiable risk Investment *risk* that investors can reduce via *diversification;* also called idiosyncratic risk.

diversification The strategy of investing in a large number of investments in order to reduce the overall risk to an entire investment *portfolio*.

dividends Payments by a corporation of all or part of its profit to its stockholders (the corporate owners).

division of labor The separation of the work required to produce a product into a number of different tasks that are performed by different workers; *specialization* of workers.

Doha Round The latest, uncompleted (as of fall 2008) sequence of trade negotiations by members of the *World Trade Organization;* named after Doha, Qatar, where the set of negotiations began.

dollar votes The "votes" that consumers and entrepreneurs cast for the production of consumer and capital goods, respectively, when they purchase those goods in product and resource markets.

domestic capital formation The process of adding to a nation's stock of *capital* by saving and investing part of its own domestic output.

domestic output *Gross* (or net) *domestic product;* the total output of final goods and services produced in the economy.

domestic price The price of a good or service within a country, determined by domestic demand and supply.

dominant strategy In *game theory,* an option that is better than any other alternative option regardless of what the other firm does.

dumping The sale of a product in a foreign country at prices either below cost or below the prices commonly charged at home.

DuPont cellophane case The antitrust case brought against DuPont in which the U.S. Supreme Court ruled (in 1956) that while DuPont had a monopoly in the narrowly defined market for cellophane, it did not monopolize the more broadly defined market for flexible packaging materials. It was thus not guilty of violating the *Sherman Act*.

durable good A consumer good with an expected life (use) of 3 or more years.

earmarks Narrow, specially designated spending authorizations placed in broad legislation by Senators and representatives for the purpose of providing benefits to firms and organizations within their constituencies without undergoing the usual evaluation process or competitive bidding.

earned-income tax credit (EITC) A refundable Federal tax credit for low-income working people designed to reduce poverty and encourage labor-force participation.

earnings The money income received by a worker; equal to the *wage* (rate) multiplied by the amount of time worked.

economic concentration A description or measure of the degree to which an industry is dominated by one or a handful of firms or is characterized by many firms. (See *concentration ratio*.)

economic cost A payment that must be made to obtain and retain the services of a *resource;* the income a firm must provide to a resource supplier to attract the resource away from an alternative use; equal to the quantity of other products that cannot be produced when resources are instead used to make a particular product.

economic efficiency The use of the minimum necessary resources to obtain the socially optimal amounts of goods and services; entails both *productive efficiency* and *allocative efficiency.*

economic growth (1) An outward shift in the *production possibilities curve* that results from an increase in resource supplies or quality or an improvement in *technology;* (2) an increase of real output *(gross domestic product)* or real output per capita.

economic immigrants International migrants who have moved to a country from another to obtain economic gains such as better employment opportunities.

economic investment (See *investment.*)

economic law An *economic principle* that has been tested and retested and has stood the test of time.

economic model A simplified picture of economic reality; an abstract generalization.

economic perspective A viewpoint that envisions individuals and institutions making rational decisions by comparing the marginal benefits and marginal costs associated with their actions.

economic policy A course of action intended to correct or avoid a problem.

economic principle A widely accepted generalization about the economic behavior of individuals or institutions.

economic profit The *total revenue* of a firm less its *economic costs* (which include both *explicit costs* and *implicit costs*); also called "pure profit" and "above-normal profit."

economic regulation (See *industrial regulation* and *social regulation.*)

economic rent The price paid for the use of land and other natural resources, the supply of which is fixed *(perfectly inelastic).*

economic resources The *land, labor, capital,* and *entrepreneurial ability* that are used in the production of goods and services; productive agents; factors of production.

economics The social science concerned with how individuals, institutions, and society make optimal (best) choices under conditions of scarcity.

economic system A particular set of institutional arrangements and a coordinating mechanism for solving the economizing problem; a method of organizing an economy, of which the *market system* and the *command system* are the two general types.

economic theory A statement of a cause-effect relationship; when accepted by all or nearly all economists, an *economic principle.*

economies of scale Reductions in the *average total cost* of producing a product as the firm expands the size of plant (its output) in the *long run;* the economies of mass production.

economizing problem The choices necessitated because society's economic wants for goods and services are unlimited but the resources available to satisfy these wants are limited (scarce).

efficiency factors (in growth) The capacity of an economy to combine resources effectively to achieve growth of real output that the *supply factors* (of growth) make possible.

efficiency gains from migration Additions to output from *immigration* in the destination nation that exceeds the loss of output from *emigration* from the origin nation.

efficiency loss Reductions in combined consumer and producer surplus caused by an underallocation or overallocation of resources to the production of a good or service. Also called deadweight loss.

efficiency loss of a tax The loss of net benefits to society because a tax reduces the production and consumption of a taxed good below the level of *allocative efficiency.* Also called the deadweight loss of the tax.

efficiency wage A wage that minimizes wage costs per unit of output by encouraging greater effort or reducing turnover.

efficient allocation of resources That allocation of an economy's resources among the production of different products that leads to the maximum satisfaction of consumers' wants, thus producing the socially optimal mix of output with society's scarce resources.

elastic demand Product or resource demand whose *price elasticity* is greater than 1. This means the resulting change in *quantity demanded* is greater than the percentage change in *price.*

elasticity coefficient The number obtained when the percentage change in *quantity demanded* (or supplied) is divided by the percentage change in the *price* of the commodity.

elasticity formula (See *price elasticity of demand.*)

elasticity of resource demand A measure of the responsiveness of firms to a change in the price of a particular *resource* they employ or use; the percentage change in the quantity of the resource demanded divided by the percentage change in its price.

elastic supply Product or resource supply whose price elasticity is greater than 1. This means the resulting change in quantity supplied is greater than the percentage change in price.

electronic payments Purchases made by transferring funds electronically. Examples: Fedwire transfers, automated clearinghouse transactions (ACHs), payments via the PayPal system, and payments made through stored-value cards.

emigration The exit (outflow) of residents from a country to reside in foreign countries.

employment rate The percentage of the *labor force* employed at any time.

empty threat In *game theory,* a statement of harmful intent that is easily dismissed by the second party because the threat is not viewed as being believable; compare to *credible threat.*

entitlement programs Government programs such as *social insurance, food stamps, Medicare,* and *Medicaid* that guarantee particular levels of transfer payments or noncash benefits to all who fit the programs' criteria.

entrepreneurial ability The human resource that combines the other resources to produce a product, makes nonroutine decisions, innovates, and bears risks.

equality-efficiency trade-off The decrease in *economic efficiency* that may accompany a decrease in *income inequality;* the presumption that some income inequality is required to achieve economic efficiency.

equation of exchange $MV = PQ$, in which M is the supply of money, V is the *velocity* of money, P is the *price level,* and Q is the physical volume of *final goods and services* produced.

equilibrium GDP (See *equilibrium real domestic output.*)

equilibrium position In the indifference curve model, the combination of two goods at which a consumer maximizes his or her *utility* (reaches the highest attainable *indifference curve*), given a limited amount to spend (a *budget constraint*).

equilibrium price The *price* in a competitive market at which the *quantity demanded* and the *quantity supplied* are equal, there is neither a shortage nor a surplus, and there is no tendency for price to rise or fall.

equilibrium price level The price level at which the aggregate demand curve intersects the aggregate supply curve.

equilibrium quantity (1) The quantity demanded and supplied at the equilibrium price in a competitive market; (2) the profit-maximizing output of a firm.

equilibrium real domestic output The *gross domestic product* at which the total quantity of final goods and services purchased *(aggregate expenditures)* is equal to the total quantity of final goods and services produced (the real domestic output); the real domestic output at which the aggregate demand curve intersects the aggregate supply curve.

equilibrium real output (See *equilibrium real domestic output*)

equilibrium world price The price of an internationally traded product that equates the quantity of the product demanded by importers with the quantity of the product supplied by exporters; the price determined at the intersection of the export supply curve and the import demand curve.

euro The common currency unit used by 15 European nations (as of 2008) in the Euro zone, which consists of Austria, Belgium, Cyprus, Finland, France, Germany, Greece, Ireland, Italy, Luxembourg, Malta, the Netherlands, Portugal, Slovenia, and Spain.

European Union (EU) An association of 27 European nations (as of 2008) that has eliminated tariffs and quotas among them, established common tariffs for imported goods from outside the member nations, eliminated barriers to the free movement of capital, and created other common economic policies.

excess capacity Plant resources that are underused when imperfectly competitive firms produce less output than that associated with achieving minimum average total cost.

excess reserves The amount by which a bank's or thrift's *actual reserves* exceed its *required reserves;* actual reserves minus required reserves.

exchange controls (See *foreign exchange controls.*)

exchange rate The *rate of exchange* of one nation's currency for another nation's currency.

exchange-rate appreciation An increase in the value of a nation's currency in foreign exchange markets; an increase in the *rate of exchange* for foreign currencies.

exchange-rate depreciation A decrease in the value of a nation's currency in foreign exchange markets; a decrease in the *rate of exchange* for foreign currencies.

exchange-rate determinant Any factor other than the *rate of exchange* that determines a currency's demand and supply in the *foreign exchange market.*

excise tax A tax levied on the production of a specific product or on the quantity of the product purchased.

exclusive unionism The practice of a *labor union* of restricting the supply of skilled union labor to increase the wages received by union members; the policies typically employed by a *craft union.*

exhaustive expenditure An expenditure by government resulting directly in the employment of *economic resources* and in the absorption by government of the goods and services those resources produce; a *government purchase.*

exit mechanism The process of leaving a job and searching for another one as a means of improving one's working conditions.

expanding industry An industry whose firms earn *economic profits* and for which an increase in output occurs as new firms enter the industry.

expansion A phase of the *business cycle* in which *real GDP, income,* and employment rise.

expansionary fiscal policy An increase in *government purchases* of goods and services, a decrease in *net taxes,* or some combination of the two for the purpose of increasing *aggregate demand* and expanding real output.

expansionary monetary policy Federal Reserve system actions to increase the *money supply,* lower *interest rates,* and expand *real GDP*; an easy money policy.

expectations The anticipations of consumers, firms, and others about future economic conditions.

expected rate of return The increase in profit a firm anticipates it will obtain by purchasing capital (or engaging in research and development); expressed as a percentage of the total cost of the investment (or R&D) activity.

expected-rate-of return curve (Web chapter) As it relates to research and development *(R&D)*, a curve showing the anticipated gain in *profit,* as a percentage of R&D expenditure, from an additional dollar spent on R&D.

expenditures approach The method that adds all expenditures made for *final goods and services* to measure the *gross domestic product.*

expenditures-output approach (See *aggregate expenditures–domestic output approach.*)

explicit cost The monetary payment a *firm* must make to an outsider to obtain a *resource.*

exports Goods and services produced in a nation and sold to buyers in other nations.

export subsidies Government payments to domestic producers to enable them to reduce the *price* of a good or service to foreign buyers.

export supply curve An upward-sloping curve that shows the amount of a product that domestic firms will export at each *world price* that is above the *domestic price*.

export transaction A sale of a good or service that increases the amount of foreign currency flowing to a nation's citizens, firms, and government.

external benefit (See *positive externality*.)

external cost (See *negative externality*.)

external debt Private or public debt owed to foreign citizens, firms, and institutions.

externality A cost or benefit from production or consumption, accruing without compensation to someone other than the buyers and sellers of the product (see *negative externality* and *positive externality*) .

external public debt The portion of the public debt owed to foreign citizens, firms, and institutions.

extraction cost All costs associated with extracting a natural resource and readying it for sale.

face value The dollar or cents value placed on a U.S. coin or piece of paper money.

factors of production *Economic resources: land, capital, labor,* and *entrepreneurial ability.*

fair-trade movement The efforts by groups in high-income nations to get growers of agricultural crops in low-income nations to adhere to certain wage and workplace standards in exchange for their goods being promoted as "fair-trade goods" to consumers in the high-income nations, and the efforts by the groups to convince those consumers to buy these goods instead of otherwise close substitutes.

fair-return price The price of a product that enables its producer to obtain a *normal profit* and that is equal to the *average total cost* of producing it.

fallacy of composition The false notion that what is true for the individual (or part) is necessarily true for the group (or whole).

farm commodities Agricultural products such as grains, milk, cattle, fruits, and vegetables that are usually sold to processors, who use the products as inputs in creating *food products.*

fast-second strategy (Web chapter) An approach by a dominant firm in which it allows other firms in its industry to bear the risk of innovation and then quickly becomes the second firm to offer any successful new product or adopt any improved production process.

FDIC (See *Federal Deposit Insurance Corporation*.)

Federal Deposit Insurance Corporation (FDIC) The federally chartered corporation that insures deposit liabilities (up to $100,000 per account) of *commercial banks* and *thrift institutions* (excluding *credit unions*, whose deposits are insured by the *National Credit Union Administration*).

Federal funds rate The interest rate banks and other depository institutions charge one another on overnight loans made out of their *excess reserves.*

Federal government The government of the United States, as distinct from the state and local governments.

Federal Open Market Committee (FOMC) The 12-member group that determines the purchase and sale policies of the *Federal Reserve Banks* in the market for U.S. government securities.

Federal Reserve Banks The 12 banks chartered by the U.S. government to control the *money supply* and perform other functions. (See *central bank, quasi-public bank,* and *bankers' bank.*)

Federal Reserve Note Paper money issued by the *Federal Reserve Banks.*

Federal Reserve System The U.S. central bank, consisting of the *Board of Governors* of the Federal Reserve and the 12 *Federal Reserve Banks*, which controls the lending activity of the nation's banks and thrifts and thus the *money supply;* commonly referred to as the "Fed."

Federal Trade Commission (FTC) The commission of five members established by the *Federal Trade Commission Act* of 1914 to investigate unfair competitive practices of firms, to hold hearings on the complaints of such practices, and to issue *cease-and-desist orders* when firms were found to engage in such practices.

Federal Trade Commission Act The Federal act of 1914 that established the *Federal Trade Commission.*

fee for service In the health care industry, payment to physicians for each visit made or procedure performed rather than payment as an annual salary.

fiat money Anything that is *money* because government has decreed it to be money.

final goods and services Goods and services that have been purchased for final use and not for resale or further processing or manufacturing.

financial capital (See *money capital*.)

financial investment The purchase of a financial asset (such as a *stock, bond,* or *mutual fund*) or real asset (such as a house, land, or factories) or the building of such assets in the expectation of financial gain.

financial services industry The broad category of firms that provide financial products and services to help households and businesses earn *interest,* receive *dividends,* obtain *capital gains,* insure against losses, and plan for retirement. Includes *commercial banks, thrifts,* insurance companies, mutual fund companies, pension funds, investment banks, and securities firms.

firm An organization that employs resources to produce a good or service for profit and owns and operates one or more *plants.*

first-mover advantage In *game theory*, the benefit obtained by the party that moves first in a *sequential game.*

fiscal policy Changes in government spending and tax collections designed to achieve a full-employment and noninflationary domestic output; also called *discretionary fiscal policy.*

fishery A stock of fish or other marine animal that is composed of a distinct group, for example New England cod, Pacific tuna, or Alaskan crab.

fishery collapse A rapid decline in a fishery's population because the fish are being harvested faster than they can reproduce.

fixed cost Any cost that in total does not change when the *firm* changes its output; the cost of *fixed resources.*

fixed exchange rate A *rate of exchange* that is set in some way and therefore prevented from rising or falling with changes in currency supply and demand.

fixed resource Any resource whose quantity cannot be changed by a firm in the *short run.*

flexible exchange rate A *rate of exchange* determined by the international demand for and supply of a nation's money; a rate free to rise or fall (to float).

flexible prices Product prices that freely move upward or downward when product demand or supply changes.

floating exchange rate (See *flexible exchange rate.*)

follower countries As it relates to *economic growth,* countries that adopt advanced technologies that previously were developed and used by *leader countries.*

Food, Conservation, and Energy Act of 2008 Farm legislation that continued and extended previous agricultural subsides of three basic kinds: *direct payments, countercyclical payments,* and *marketing loans.*

food products Processed agricultural commodities sold through grocery stores and restaurants. Examples: bread, meat, fish, chicken, pork, lettuce, peanut butter, and breakfast cereal.

food-stamp program A program permitting low-income persons to purchase for less than their retail value, or to obtain without cost, coupons that can be exchanged for food items at retail stores.

foreign competition (See *import competition.*)

foreign direct investment Financial investments made to obtain a lasting ownership interest in firms operating outside the economy of the investor; may involve purchasing existing assets or building new production facilities.

foreign exchange control The control a government may exercise over the quantity of foreign currency demanded by its citizens and firms and over the *rates of exchange* in order to limit its *outpayments* to its *inpayments* (to eliminate a *payments deficit*).

foreign exchange market A market in which the money (currency) of one nation can be used to purchase (can be exchanged for) the money of another nation; currency market.

foreign exchange rate (See *rate of exchange.*)

foreign purchase effect The inverse relationship between the *net exports* of an economy and its price level relative to foreign price levels.

45° line A line along which the value of *GDP* (measured horizontally) is equal to the value of *aggregate expenditures* (measured vertically).

four-firm concentration ratio The percentage of total industry sales accounted for by the top four firms in the industry.

fractional reserve banking system A *reserve requirement* that is less than 100 percent of the checkable-deposit liabilities of a *commercial bank* or *thrift institution.*

freedom of choice The freedom of owners of property resources to employ or dispose of them as they see fit, of workers to enter any line of work for which they are qualified, and of consumers to spend their incomes in a manner that they think is appropriate.

freedom of enterprise The freedom of *firms* to obtain economic resources, to use those resources to produce products of the firm's own choosing, and to sell their products in markets of their choice.

Freedom to Farm Act A law passed in 1996 that revamped 60 years of U.S. farm policy by ending *price supports* and *acreage allotments* for wheat, corn, barley, oats, sorghum, rye, cotton, and rice.

free-rider problem The inability of potential providers of an economically desirable good or service to obtain payment from those who benefit, because of *nonexcludability.*

free trade The absence of artificial (government-imposed) barriers to trade among individuals and firms in different nations.

frictional unemployment A type of unemployment caused by workers voluntarily changing jobs and by temporary layoffs; unemployed workers between jobs.

fringe benefits The rewards other than *wages* that employees receive from their employers and that include pensions, medical and dental insurance, paid vacations, and sick leaves.

full employment (1) The use of all available resources to produce want-satisfying goods and services; (2) the situation in which the *unemployment rate* is equal to the *full-employment unemployment* rate and where *frictional* and *structural* unemployment occur but not *cyclical unemployment* (and the *real GDP* of the economy equals *potential output*).

full-employment unemployment rate The *unemployment rate* at which there is no *cyclical unemployment* of the *labor force;* equal to between 4 and 5 percent in the United States because some *frictional* and *structural unemployment* is unavoidable.

functional distribution of income The manner in which *national income* is divided among the functions performed to earn it (or the kinds of resources provided to earn it); the division of national income into wages and salaries, proprietors' income, corporate profits, interest, and rent.

future value The amount to which some current amount of money will grow if the interest earned on the amount is left to compound over time. (*See compound interest.*)

gains from trade The extra output that trading partners obtain through specialization of production and exchange of goods and services.

game theory A means of analyzing the business behavior of oligopolists that uses the theory of strategy associated with games such as chess and bridge.

GDP (See *gross domestic product.*)

GDP gap Actual *gross domestic product* minus potential output; may be either a positive amount (a *positive GDP gap*) or a negative amount (a *negative GDP gap*).

GDP price index A *price index* for all the goods and services that make up the *gross domestic product;* the price index used to adjust *nominal gross domestic product* to *real gross domestic product*.

G8 nations A group of eight major nations (Canada, France, Germany, Italy, Japan, Russia, United Kingdom, and United States) whose leaders meet regularly to discuss common economic problems and try to coordinate economic policies.

General Agreement on Tariffs and Trade (GATT) The international agreement reached in 1947 in which 23 nations agreed to give equal and nondiscriminatory treatment to one another, to reduce tariff rates by multinational negotiations, and to eliminate *import quotas*. It now includes most nations and has become the *World Trade Organization*.

generalization Statement of the nature of the relationship between two or more sets of facts.

Gini ratio A numerical measure of the overall dispersion of income among households, families, or individuals; found graphically by dividing the area between the diagonal line and the *Lorenz curve* by the entire area below the diagonal line.

gold standard A historical system of fixed exchange rates in which nations defined their currencies in terms of gold, maintained a fixed relationship between their stocks of gold and their money supplies, and allowed gold to be freely exported and imported.

government failure Inefficiencies in resource allocation caused by problems in the operation of the public sector (government), specifically, rent-seeking pressure by special-interest groups, shortsighted political behavior, limited and bundled choices, and bureaucratic inefficiencies.

government purchases (*G*) Expenditures by government for goods and services that government consumes in providing public goods and for public capital that has a long lifetime; the expenditures of all governments in the economy for those *final goods and services*.

government transfer payment The disbursement of money (or goods and services) by government for which government receives no currently produced good or service in return.

grievance procedure The method used by a *labor union* and a *firm* to settle disputes that arise during the life of the collective bargaining agreement between them.

gross domestic product (GDP) The total market value of all *final goods and services* produced annually within the boundaries of the United States, whether by U.S.- or foreign-supplied resources.

gross private domestic investment (*I_g*) Expenditures for newly produced *capital goods* (such as machinery, equipment, tools, and buildings) and for additions to inventories.

growth accounting The bookkeeping of the supply-side elements such as productivity and labor inputs that contribute to changes in *real GDP* over some specific time period.

guiding function of prices The ability of price changes to bring about changes in the quantities of products and resources demanded and supplied.

H1-B provision A provision of the U.S. immigration law that allows the annual entry of 65,000 high-skilled workers in "specialty occupations" such as science, R&D, and computer programming to work legally and continuously in the United States for six years.

health maintenance organizations (HMOs) Health care providers that contract with employers, insurance companies, labor unions, or government units to provide health care for their workers or others who are insured.

health savings accounts (HSAs) Accounts into which people with high-deductible health insurance plans can place tax-free funds each year and then draw on these funds to pay out-of-pocket medical expenses such as *deductibles* and *copayments*. Unused funds accumulate from year to year and later can be used to supplement *Medicare*.

Herfindahl index A measure of the concentration and competitiveness of an industry; calculated as the sum of the squared percentage market shares of the individual firms in the industry.

homogeneous oligopoly An *oligopoly* in which the firms produce a *standardized product*.

horizontal axis The "left-right" or "west-east" measurement line on graph or grid.

horizontal merger The merger into a single *firm* of two firms producing the same product and selling it in the same geographic market.

household An economic unit (of one or more persons) that provides the economy with resources and uses the income received to purchase goods and services that satisfy economic wants.

human capital The knowledge and skills that make a person productive.

human capital investment Any expenditure undertaken to improve the education, skills, health, or mobility of workers, with an expectation of greater productivity and thus a positive return on the investment.

hyperinflation A very rapid rise in the price level; an extremely high rate of inflation.

hypothesis A tentative explanation of cause and effect that requires testing.

illegal immigrants People who have entered a country unlawfully to reside there; also called unauthorized immigrants.

IMF (See *International Monetary Fund*.)

imitation problem (Web chapter) The potential for a firm's rivals to produce a close variation of (imitate) a firm's new product or process, greatly reducing the originator's profit from *R&D* and *innovation*.

immediate short-run aggregate supply curve An aggregate supply curve for which real output, but not the price level, changes when the aggregate demand curves shifts; a horizontal aggregate supply curve that implies an inflexible price level.

immigration The inflow of people into a country from another country. The immigrants may be either *legal immigrants* or *illegal immigrants*.

immobility The inability or unwillingness of a worker to move from one geographic area or occupation to another or from a lower-paying job to a higher-paying job.

imperfect competition All market structures except *pure competition;* includes *monopoly, monopolistic competition,* and *oligopoly.*

implicit cost The monetary income a *firm* sacrifices when it uses a resource it owns rather than supplying the resource in the market; equal to what the resource could have earned in the best-paying alternative employment; includes a *normal profit.*

import competition The competition that domestic firms encounter from the products and services of foreign producers.

import demand curve A downsloping curve showing the amount of a product that an economy will import at each *world price* below the *domestic price.*

import quota A limit imposed by a nation on the quantity (or total value) of a good that may be imported during some period of time.

imports Spending by individuals, *firms,* and governments for goods and services produced in foreign nations.

import transaction The purchase of a good or service that decreases the amount of foreign money held by citizens, firms, and governments of a nation.

incentive function of price The inducement that an increase in the price of a commodity gives to sellers to make more of it available (and conversely for a decrease in price), and the inducement that an increase in price offers to buyers to purchase smaller quantities (and conversely for a decrease in price).

incentive pay plan A compensation structure that ties worker pay directly to performance. Such plans include piece rates, bonuses, *stock options,* commissions, and *profit sharing.*

inclusive unionism The practice of a labor union of including as members all workers employed in an industry.

income A flow of dollars (or purchasing power) per unit of time derived from the use of human or property resources.

income approach The method that adds all the income generated by the production of *final goods and services* to measure the *gross domestic product.*

income effect A change in the quantity demanded of a product that results from the change in *real income (purchasing power)* caused by a change in the product's price.

income elasticity of demand The ratio of the percentage change in the *quantity demanded* of a good to a percentage change in consumer income; measures the responsiveness of consumer purchases to income changes.

income inequality The unequal distribution of an economy's total income among households or families.

income-maintenance system A group of government programs designed to eliminate poverty and reduce inequality in the distribution of income.

income mobility The extent to which income receivers move from one part of the income distribution to another over some period of time.

increase in demand An increase in the *quantity demanded* of a good or service at every price; a shift of the *demand curve* to the right.

increase in supply An increase in the *quantity supplied* of a good or service at every price; a shift of the *supply curve* to the right.

increasing-cost industry An *industry* in which expansion through the entry of new firms raises the prices *firms* in the industry must pay for resources and therefore increases their production costs.

increasing marginal returns An increase in the *marginal product* of a resource as successive units of the resource are employed.

increasing returns An increase in a firm's output by a larger percentage than the percentage increase in its inputs.

independent goods Products or services for which there is little or no relationship between the price of one and the demand for the other. When the price of one rises or falls, the demand for the other tends to remain constant.

independent unions U.S. unions that are not affiliated with the *AFL-CIO.*

independent variable The variable causing a change in some other (dependent) variable.

index funds *Mutual funds* that select stock or bond *portfolios* to exactly match a stock or bond index (a collection of stocks or bonds meant to capture the overall behavior of a particular category of investments) such as the Standard & Poor's 500 Index or the Russell 3000 Index.

indifference curve A curve showing the different combinations of two products that yield the same satisfaction or *utility* to a consumer.

indifference map A set of *indifference curves,* each representing a different level of *utility,* that together show the preferences of a consumer.

individual demand The demand schedule or *demand curve* of a single buyer.

individual supply The supply schedule or *supply curve* of a single seller.

individual transferable quotas A limit by a government or a fisheries commission on the total number or total weight of a species that an individual fisher can harvest during some particular time period; fishers holding the quota right can sell all or part of it to other fishers.

industrially advanced countries High-income countries such as the United States, Canada, Japan, and the nations of western Europe that have highly developed *market economies* based on large stocks of technologically advanced capital goods and skilled labor forces.

industrial regulation The older and more traditional type of regulation in which government is concerned with the prices charged and the services provided to the public in specific industries, in contrast to *social regulation.*

industrial union A *labor union* that accepts as members all workers employed in a particular industry (or by a particular firm).

industry A group of (one or more) *firms* that produce identical or similar products.

inelastic demand Product or resource demand for which the *elasticity coefficient* for price is less than 1.

This means the resulting percentage change in *quantity demanded* is less than the percentage change in *price*.

inelastic supply Product or resource supply for which the price elasticity coefficient is less than 1. The percentage change in *quantity supplied* is less than the percentage change in *price*.

inferior good A good or service whose consumption declines as income rises, prices held constant.

inflating Determining *real gross domestic product* by increasing the dollar value of the *nominal gross domestic product* produced in a year in which prices are lower than those in a *base year*.

inflation A rise in the general level of prices in an economy.

inflationary expectations The belief of workers, firms, and consumers about future rates of inflation.

inflationary expenditure gap The amount by which the *aggregate expenditures schedule* must shift downward to decrease the *nominal GDP* to its full-employment noninflationary level.

inflation premium The component of the *nominal interest rate* that reflects anticipated inflation.

inflation targeting The annual statement by a *central bank* of a goal for a specific range of inflation in a future year, coupled with monetary policy designed to achieve the goal.

inflexible prices Product prices that remain in place (at least for a while) even though supply or demand has changed; stuck prices or sticky prices.

information technology New and more efficient methods of delivering and receiving information through use of computers, fax machines, wireless phones, and the Internet.

infrastructure The capital goods usually provided by the *public sector* for the use of its citizens and firms (for example, highways, bridges, transit systems, wastewater treatment facilities, municipal water systems, and airports).

injection An addition of spending to the income-expenditure stream: *investment, government purchases,* and *net exports*.

injunction A court order directing a person or organization not to perform a certain act because the act would do irreparable damage to some other person or persons; a restraining order.

in-kind transfer The distribution by government of goods and services to individuals for which the government receives no currently produced good or service in return; a *government transfer payment* made in goods or services rather than in money; also called a noncash transfer.

innovation The first commercially successful introduction of a new product, the use of a new method of production, or the creation of a new form of business organization.

inpayments The receipts of domestic or foreign money that individuals, firms, and governments of one nation obtain from the sale of goods and services abroad, as

investment income and remittances, and from foreign purchases of domestic assets.

insider-outsider theory The hypothesis that nominal wages are inflexible downward because firms are aware that workers ("insiders") who retain employment during recession may refuse to work cooperatively with previously unemployed workers ("outsiders") who offer to work for less than the current wage.

insurable risk An event that would result in a loss but whose frequency of occurrence can be estimated with considerable accuracy. Insurance companies are willing to sell insurance against such losses.

interest The payment made for the use of money (of borrowed funds).

interest income Payments of income to those who supply the economy with *capital*.

interest rate The annual rate at which interest is paid; a percentage of the borrowed amount.

interest-rate-cost-of-funds curve (Web chapter) As it relates to research and development (*R&D*), a curve showing the *interest rate* the firm must pay to obtain any particular amount of funds to finance R&D.

interest-rate effect The tendency for increases in the *price level* to increase the demand for money, raise interest rates, and, as a result, reduce total spending and real output in the economy (and the reverse for price-level decreases).

interindustry competition The competition for sales between the products of one industry and the products of another industry.

interlocking directorate A situation where one or more members of the board of directors of a *corporation* are also on the board of directors of a competing corporation; illegal under the *Clayton Act*.

intermediate goods Products that are purchased for resale or further processing or manufacturing.

internally held public debt *Public debt* owed to citizens, firms, and institutions of the same nation that issued the debt.

international balance of payments A summary of all the transactions that took place between the individuals, firms, and government units of one nation and those of all other nations during a year.

international balance-of-payments deficit (See *balance-of-payments deficit*.)

international balance-of-payments surplus (See *balance-of-payments surplus*.)

international gold standard (See *gold standard*.)

International Monetary Fund (IMF) The international association of nations that was formed after the Second World War to make loans of foreign monies to nations with temporary *payments deficits* and, until the early 1970s, to administer the *adjustable pegs*. It now mainly makes loans to nations facing possible defaults on private and government loans.

international monetary reserves The foreign currencies and other assets such as gold that a nation can use to settle a *balance-of-payments deficit*.

international value of the dollar The price that must be paid in foreign currency (money) to obtain one U.S. dollar.

intertemporal choice Choices between benefits obtainable in one time period and benefits achievable in a later time period; comparisons that individuals and society must make between the reductions in current consumption that are necessary to fund current investments and the higher levels of future consumption that those current investments can produce.

intrinsic value The market value of the metal within a coin.

invention (Web chapter) The first discovery of a product or process through the use of imagination, ingenious thinking, and experimentation and the first proof that it will work.

inventories Goods that have been produced but remain unsold.

inverse relationship The relationship between two variables that change in opposite directions, for example, product price and quantity demanded; negative relationship.

inverted-U theory (Web chapter) The idea that, other things equal, *R&D* expenditures as a percentage of sales rise with industry concentration, reach a peak at a four-firm *concentration ratio* of about 50 percent, and then fall as the ratio further increases.

investment In economics, spending for the production and accumulation of *capital* and additions to inventories. (For contrast, see *financial investment*.)

investment banks Firms that help corporations and government raise money by selling stocks and bonds; they also offer advisory services for corporate mergers and acquisitions in addition to providing brokerage services and advice.

investment demand curve A curve that shows the amounts of *investment* demanded by an economy at a series of *real interest rates*.

investment goods Same as *capital* or capital goods.

investment in human capital (See *human capital investment*.)

investment schedule A curve or schedule that shows the amounts firms plan to invest at various possible values of *real gross domestic product*.

"invisible hand" The tendency of firms and resource suppliers that seek to further their own self-interests in competitive markets to also promote the interests of society.

Joint Economic Committee (JEC) Committee of senators and representatives that investigates economic problems of national interest.

Keynesianism The philosophical, ideological, and analytical views pertaining to *Keynesian economics*.

kinked-demand curve The demand curve for a noncollusive oligopolist, which is based on the assumption that rivals will match a price decrease and will ignore a price increase.

labor People's physical and mental talents and efforts that are used to help produce goods and services.

labor force Persons 16 years of age and older who are not in institutions and who are employed or are unemployed and seeking work.

labor-force participation rate The percentage of the working-age population that is actually in the *labor force*.

labor-intensive goods Products requiring relatively large amounts of *labor* to produce.

labor productivity Total output divided by the quantity of labor employed to produce it; the *average product* of labor or output per hour of work.

labor union A group of workers organized to advance the interests of the group (to increase wages, shorten the hours worked, improve working conditions, and so on).

Laffer Curve A curve relating government tax rates and tax revenues and on which a particular tax rate (between zero and 100 percent) maximizes tax revenues.

laissez-faire capitalism (See *capitalism*.)

land Natural resources ("free gifts of nature") used to produce goods and services.

land-intensive goods Products requiring relatively large amounts of *land* to produce.

land reform (Web chapter) A set of policies designed to create more efficient distribution of land ownership in developing countries; policies vary country to country and can involve everything from government purchasing large land estates and dividing the land into smaller farms to consolidating tiny plots of land into larger, more efficient private farms.

law of demand The principle that, other things equal, an increase in a product's price will reduce the quantity of it demanded, and conversely for a decrease in price.

law of diminishing marginal utility The principle that as a consumer increases the consumption of a good or service, the *marginal utility* obtained from each additional unit of the good or service decreases.

law of diminishing returns The principle that as successive increments of a variable resource are added to a fixed resource, the *marginal product* of the variable resource will eventually decrease.

law of increasing opportunity costs The principle that as the production of a good increases, the *opportunity cost* of producing an additional unit rises.

law of supply The principle that, other things equal, an increase in the price of a product will increase the quantity of it supplied, and conversely for a price decrease.

leader countries As it relates to *economic growth*, countries that develop and use advanced technologies, which then become available to *follower countries*.

leakage (1) A withdrawal of potential spending from the income-expenditures stream via *saving*, tax payments, or *imports*; (2) a withdrawal that reduces the lending potential of the banking system.

learning by doing Achieving greater *productivity* and lower *average total cost* through gains in knowledge and skill that accompany repetition of a task; a source of *economies of scale*.

least-cost combination of resources The quantity of each resource a firm must employ in order to produce a particular output at the lowest total cost; the combination at which the ratio of the *marginal product* of a resource to its *marginal resource cost* (to its *price* if the resource is employed in a competitive market) is the same for the last dollar spent on each of the resources employed.

legal cartel theory of regulation The hypothesis that some industries seek regulation or want to maintain regulation so that they may form or maintain a legal *cartel*.

legal immigrant A person who lawfully enters a country for the purpose of residing there.

legal tender A legal designation of a nation's official currency (bills and coins). Payment of debts must be accepted in this monetary unit, but creditors can specify the form of payment, for example, "cash only" or "check or credit card only."

lending potential of an individual commercial bank The amount by which a single bank can safely increase the *money supply* by making new loans to (or buying securities from) the public; equal to the bank's excess reserves.

lending potential of the banking system The amount by which the banking system can increase the *money supply* by making new loans to (or buying securities from) the public; equal to the *excess reserves* of the banking system multiplied by the *monetary multiplier*.

liability A debt with a monetary value; an amount owed by a firm or an individual.

limited liability Restriction of the maximum loss to a predetermined amount for the owners (stockholders) of a *corporation*. The maximum loss is the amount they paid for their shares of stock.

liquidity The ease with which an asset can be converted quickly into cash with little or no loss of purchasing power. Money is said to be perfectly liquid, whereas other assets have a lesser degree of liquidity.

loanable funds *Money* available for lending and borrowing.

loanable funds theory of interest The concept that the supply of and demand for *loanable funds* determine the equilibrium rate of interest.

lockout An action by a firm that forbids workers to return to work until a new collective bargaining contract is signed; a means of imposing costs (lost wages) on union workers in a collective bargaining dispute.

logrolling The trading of votes by legislators to secure favorable outcomes on decisions concerning the provision of *public goods* and *quasi-public goods*.

long run (1) In *microeconomics,* a period of time long enough to enable producers of a product to change the quantities of all the resources they employ; period in which all resources and costs are variable and no resources or costs are fixed. (2) In *macroeconomics,* a period sufficiently long for *nominal wages* and other sxinput prices to change in response to a change in the nation's *price level*.

long-run aggregate supply curve The aggregate supply curve associated with a time period in which input prices (especially *nominal wages*) are fully responsive to changes in the *price level*.

long-run competitive equilibrium The price at which firms in *pure competition* neither obtain *economic profit* nor suffer losses in the *long run* and the total quantity demanded and supplied are equal; a price equal to the marginal cost and the minimum long-run *average total cost* of producing the product.

long-run supply curve As it applies to macroeconomics, a supply curve for which price, but not real output, changes when the demand curves shifts; a vertical supply curve that implies fully flexible prices.

long-run supply In *microeconomics,* a shedule or curve showing the prices at which a purely competitive industry will make various quantities of the product available in the *long run*.

long-run vertical Phillips Curve The *Phillips Curve* after all nominal wages have adjusted to changes in the rate of inflation; a line emanating straight upward at the economy's *natural rate of unemployment*.

Lorenz curve A curve showing the distribution of income in an economy. The cumulated percentage of families (income receivers) is measured along the horizontal axis and cumulated percentage of income is measured along the vertical axis.

lump-sum tax A tax that is a constant amount (the tax revenue of government is the same) at all levels of GDP.

M1 The most narrowly defined *money supply,* equal to *currency* in the hands of the public and the *checkable deposits* of commercial banks and thrift institutions.

M2 A more broadly defined *money supply,* equal to *M1* plus *noncheckable savings accounts* (including *money market deposit accounts*), small *time deposits* (deposits of less than $100,000), and individual *money market mutual fund* balances.

macroeconomics The part of economics concerned with the economy as a whole; with such major aggregates as the household, business, and government sectors; and with measures of the total economy.

managed floating exchange rate An *exchange rate* that is allowed to change (float) as a result of changes in currency supply and demand but at times is altered (managed) by governments via their buying and selling of particular currencies.

managerial prerogatives The decisions that a firm's management has the sole right to make; often enumerated in the labor contract (work agreement) between a *labor union* and a *firm*.

marginal analysis The comparison of marginal ("extra" or "additional") benefits and marginal costs, usually for decision making.

marginal benefit The extra (additional) benefit of consuming 1 more unit of some good or service; the change in total benefit when 1 more unit is consumed.

marginal cost (MC) The extra (additional) cost of producing 1 more unit of output; equal to the change in *total cost* divided by the change in output (and, in the short run, to the change in total *variable cost* divided by the change in output).

marginal cost-marginal benefit rule   As it applies to *cost-benefit analysis*, the tenet that a government project or program should be expanded to the point where the *marginal cost* and *marginal benefit* of additional expenditures are equal.

marginal product (MP)   The additional output produced when 1 additional unit of a resource is employed (the quantity of all other resources employed remaining constant); equal to the change in *total product* divided by the change in the quantity of a resource employed.

marginal productivity theory of income distribution   The contention that the distribution of income is equitable when each unit of each resource receives a money payment equal to its marginal contribution to the firm's revenue (its *marginal revenue product*).

marginal propensity to consume (MPC)   The fraction of any change in *disposable income* spent for *consumer goods;* equal to the change in consumption divided by the change in disposable income.

marginal propensity to save (MPS)   The fraction of any change in *disposable income* that households save; equal to the change in *saving* divided by the change in disposable income.

marginal rate of substitution (MRS)   The rate at which a consumer is willing to substitute one good for another (from a given combination of goods) and remain equally satisfied (have the same *total utility*); equal to the slope of a consumer's *indifference curve* at each point on the curve.

marginal resource cost (MRC)   The amount the total cost of employing a *resource* increases when a firm employs 1 additional unit of the resource (the quantity of all other resources employed remaining constant); equal to the change in the *total cost* of the resource divided by the change in the quantity of the resource employed.

marginal revenue   The change in *total revenue* that results from the sale of 1 additional unit of a firm's product; equal to the change in total revenue divided by the change in the quantity of the product sold.

marginal-revenue–marginal-cost approach   A method of determining the total output where *economic profit* is a maximum (or losses are a minimum) by comparing the *marginal revenue* and the *marginal cost* of each additional unit of output.

marginal revenue product (MRP)   The change in a firm's *total revenue* when it employs 1 additional unit of a resource (the quantity of all other resources employed remaining constant); equal to the change in total revenue divided by the change in the quantity of the resource employed.

marginal revenue productivity   (See *marginal revenue product.*)

marginal tax rate   The tax rate paid on an additional dollar of income.

marginal utility   The extra *utility* a consumer obtains from the consumption of 1 additional unit of a good or service; equal to the change in total utility divided by the change in the quantity consumed.

market   Any institution or mechanism that brings together buyers (demanders) and sellers (suppliers) of a particular good or service.

market demand   (See *total demand.*)

market economy   An economy in which the private decisions of consumers, resource suppliers, and firms determine how resources are allocated; the *market system.*

market failure   The inability of a market to bring about the allocation of resources that best satisfies the wants of society; in particular, the overallocation or underallocation of resources to the production of a particular good or service because of *externalities* or informational problems or because markets do not provide desired *public goods.*

market for externality rights   A market in which firms can buy rights to discharge pollutants. The price of such rights is determined by the demand for the right to discharge pollutants and a *perfectly inelastic supply* of such rights (the latter determined by the quantity of discharges that the environment can assimilate).

market period   A period in which producers of a product are unable to change the quantity produced in response to a change in its price and in which there is a *perfectly inelastic supply.*

market portfolio   The portfolio consisting of every financial asset (including every *stock* and *bond*) traded in the financial markets. The market portfolio is used to calculate *beta* (a measure of the degree of riskiness) for specific stocks, bonds, and mutual funds.

market system   All the product and resource markets of a *market economy* and the relationships among them; a method that allows the prices determined in those markets to allocate the economy's scarce resources and to communicate and coordinate the decisions made by consumers, firms, and resource suppliers.

marketing loan program   A Federal farm subsidy under which certain farmers can receive a loan (on a per-unit-of-output basis) from a government lender and then, depending on the price of the crop, either pay back the loan with interest or keep the loan proceeds while forfeiting their harvested crop to the lender.

median-voter model   The theory that under majority rule the median (middle) voter will be in the dominant position to determine the outcome of an election.

Medicaid   A Federal program that helps finance the medical expenses of individuals covered by the *Supplemental Security Income (SSI)* and *Temporary Assistance for Needy Families (TANF)* programs.

Medicare   A Federal program that is financed by *payroll taxes* and provides for (1) compulsory hospital insurance for senior citizens, (2) low-cost voluntary insurance to help older Americans pay physicians' fees, and (3) subsidized insurance to buy prescription drugs.

Medicare Part D   The portion of Medicare that enables enrollees to shop among private health insurance companies to buy highly subsidized insurance to help reduce the out-of-pocket expense of prescription drugs.

medium of exchange   Any item sellers generally accept and buyers generally use to pay for a good or service;

money; a convenient means of exchanging goods and services without engaging in *barter.*

menu costs   The reluctance of firms to cut prices during recessions (that they think will be short lived) because of the costs of altering and communicating their price reductions; named after the cost associated with printing new menus at restaurants.

merger   The combination of two (or more) firms into a single firm.

microeconomics   The part of economics concerned with decision making by individual units such as a *household,* a *firm,* or an *industry* and with individual markets, specific goods and services, and product and resource prices.

Microsoft case   A 2002 antitrust case in which Microsoft was found guilty of violating the *Sherman Act* by engaging in a series of unlawful activities designed to maintain its monopoly in operating systems for personal computers; as a remedy the company was prohibited from engaging in a set of specific anticompetitive business practices.

midpoint formula   A method for calculating *price elasticity of demand* or *price elasticity of supply* that averages the two prices and two quantities as the reference points for computing percentages.

minimum efficient scale (MES)   The lowest level of output at which a firm can minimize long-run *average total cost.*

minimum wage   The lowest *wage* that employers may legally pay for an hour of work.

modern economic growth   The historically recent phenomenon in which nations for the first time have experienced sustained increases in *real GDP per capita.*

monetarism   The macroeconomic view that the main cause of changes in aggregate output and *price level* is fluctuations in the *money supply;* espoused by advocates of a *monetary rule.*

monetary multiplier   The multiple of its *excess reserves* by which the banking system can expand *checkable deposits* and thus the *money supply* by making new loans (or buying securities); equal to 1 divided by the *reserve requirement.*

monetary policy   A central bank's changing of the *money supply* to influence interest rates and assist the economy in achieving price stability, full employment, and economic growth.

monetary rule   The rule suggested by *monetarism.* As traditionally formulated, the rule says that the *money supply* should be expanded each year at the same annual rate as the potential rate of growth of the *real gross domestic product;* the supply of money should be increased steadily between 3 and 5 percent per year. (Also see *Taylor rule.*)

money   Any item that is generally acceptable to sellers in exchange for goods and services.

money capital   Money available to purchase *capital;* simply *money,* as defined by economists.

money income   (See *nominal income.*)

money market   The market in which the demand for and the supply of money determine the *interest rate* (or the level of *interest rates*) in the economy.

money market deposit accounts (MMDAs)   Bank- and thrift-provided interest-bearing accounts that contain a variety of short-term securities; such accounts have minimum balance requirements and limits on the frequency of withdrawals.

money market mutual funds (MMMFs)   Interest-bearing accounts offered by investment companies, which pool depositors' funds for the purchase of short-term securities. Depositors can write checks in minimum amounts or more against their accounts.

money supply   Narrowly defined, *M*1; more broadly defined, *M*2. (See *M1* and *M2*)

monopolistic competition   A market structure in which many firms sell a *differentiated product,* into which entry is relatively easy, in which the firm has some control over its product price, and in which there is considerable *nonprice competition.*

monopoly   A market structure in which the number of sellers is so small that each seller is able to influence the total supply and the price of the good or service. (Also see *pure monopoly.*)

monopsony   A market structure in which there is only a single buyer of a good, service, or resource.

moral hazard problem   The possibility that individuals or institutions will change their behavior as the result of a contract or agreement. Example: A bank whose deposits are insured against losses may make riskier loans and investments.

mortgage debt crisis   The period beginning in late 2007 when thousands of homeowners defaulted on mortgage loans when they experienced a combination of higher mortgage interest rates and falling home prices.

most-favored-nation (MFN) status   An agreement by the United States to allow some other nation's *exports* into the United States at the lowest tariff level levied by the United States. Now referred to as *normal-trade-relations status.*

MR = MC rule   The principle that a firm will maximize its profit (or minimize its losses) by producing the output at which *marginal revenue* and *marginal cost* are equal, provided product price is equal to or greater than *average variable cost.*

MRP = MRC rule   The principle that to maximize profit (or minimize losses), a firm should employ the quantity of a resource at which its *marginal revenue product* (MRP) is equal to its *marginal resource cost* (MRC), the latter being the wage rate in a purely competitive labor market.

multinational corporations   Firms that own production facilities in two or more countries and produce and sell their products globally.

multiple counting   Wrongly including the value of *intermediate goods* in the *gross domestic product;* counting the same good or service more than once.

multiplier   The ratio of a change in the equilibrium GDP to the change in *investment* or in any other component of *aggregate expenditures* or *aggregate demand;* the number by which a change in any such component must be multiplied to find the resulting change in the equilibrium GDP.

multiplier effect The effect on equilibrium GDP of a change in *aggregate expenditures* or *aggregate demand* (caused by a change in the *consumption schedule, investment,* government expenditures, or *net exports*).

mutual funds *Portfolios* of *stocks* and *bonds* selected and purchased by mutual fund companies, which finance the purchases by pooling money from thousands of individual fund investors; includes both *index funds* as well as *actively managed funds.* Fund returns (profits or losses) pass through to the individual fund investors who invest in the funds.

mutual interdependence A situation in which a change in price strategy (or in some other strategy) by one firm will affect the sales and profits of another firm (or other firms). Any firm that makes such a change can expect the other rivals to react to the change.

Nash equilibrium In *game theory,* an outcome from which neither firm wants to deviate; the outcome that once achieved is stable and therefore lasting.

national bank A *commercial bank* authorized to operate by the U.S. government.

National Credit Union Administration (NCUA) The federally chartered agency that insures deposit liabilities (up to $100,000 per account) in *credit unions.*

national health insurance (NHI) A proposed program in which the Federal government would provide a basic package of health care to all citizens at no direct charge or at a low cost-sharing level. Financing would be out of general tax revenues.

national income Total income earned by resource suppliers for their contributions to *gross domestic product* plus *taxes on production and imports*; the sum of wages and salaries, *rent, interest, profit, proprietors' income,* and such taxes.

national income accounting The techniques used to measure the overall production of the economy and other related variables for the nation as a whole.

National Labor Relations Act (Wagner Act of 1935) As amended, the basic labor-relations law in the United States; defines the legal rights of unions and management and identifies unfair union and management labor practices; established the *National Labor Relations Board.*

National Labor Relations Board (NLRB) The board established by the *National Labor Relations Act* of 1935 to investigate unfair labor practices, issue *cease-and-desist orders,* and conduct elections among employees to determine if they wish to be represented by a *labor union.*

natural monopoly An industry in which *economies of scale* are so great that a single firm can produce the product at a lower average total cost than would be possible if more than one firm produced the product.

natural rate of unemployment (NRU) The *full-employment unemployment rate;* the unemployment rate occurring when there is no cyclical unemployment and the economy is achieving its potential output; the

unemployment rate at which actual inflation equals expected inflation.

near-money Financial assets, the most important of which are *noncheckable savings accounts, time deposits,* and U.S. short-term securities and savings bonds, which are not a medium of exchange but can be readily converted into money.

negative externality A cost imposed without compensation on third parties by the production or consumption of sellers or buyers. Example: A manufacturer dumps toxic chemicals into a river, killing the fish sought by sports fishers; an external cost or a spillover cost.

negative GDP gap A situation in which actual *gross domestic product* is less than *potential output.* Also known as a recessionary output gap.

negative relationship (See *inverse relationship.*)

negative self-selection As it relates to international *migration,* the idea that those who choose to move to another country have poorer wage opportunities in the origin country than those with similar skills who choose not to *emigrate.*

negative-sum game In *game theory,* a game in which the gains ($+$) and losses ($-$) add up to some amount less than zero; one party's losses exceed the other party's gains.

net benefits The total benefits of some activity or policy less the total costs of that activity or policy.

net domestic product *Gross domestic product* less the part of the year's output that is needed to replace the *capital goods* worn out in producing the output; the nation's total output available for consumption or additions to the *capital stock.*

net exports (X_n) *Exports* minus *imports.*

net foreign factor income Receipts of resource income from the rest of the world minus payments of resource income to the rest of the world.

net investment income The interest and dividend income received by the residents of a nation from residents of other nations less the interest and dividend payments made by the residents of that nation to the residents of other nations.

net private domestic investment *Gross private domestic investment* less *consumption of fixed capital;* the addition to the nation's stock of *capital* during a year.

net taxes The taxes collected by government less *government transfer payments.*

net transfers The personal and government transfer payments made by one nation to residents of foreign nations less the personal and government transfer payments received from residents of foreign nations.

network effects Increases in the value of a product to each user, including existing users, as the total number of users rises.

net worth The total *assets* less the total *liabilities* of a firm or an individual; for a firm, the claims of the owners against the firm's total assets; for an individual, his or her wealth.

new classical economics The theory that, although unanticipated price-level changes may create macroeconomic instability in the short run, the economy is stable at the full-employment level of domestic output in the long run because prices and wages adjust automatically to correct movements away from the full-employment, noninflationary output.

NLRB (See *National Labor Relations Board.*)

nominal gross domestic product (GDP) The *GDP* measured in terms of the price level at the time of measurement (unadjusted for *inflation*).

nominal income The number of dollars received by an individual or group for its resources during some period of time.

nominal interest rate The interest rate expressed in terms of annual amounts currently charged for interest and not adjusted for inflation.

nominal wage The amount of money received by a worker per unit of time (hour, day, etc.); money wage.

noncash transfer A *government transfer payment* in the form of goods and services rather than money, for example, food stamps, housing assistance, and job training; also called in-kind transfers.

noncollusive oligopoly An *oligopoly* in which the firms do not act together and in agreement to determine the price of the product and the output that each firm will produce.

noncompeting groups Collections of workers in the economy who do not compete with each other for employment because the skill and training of the workers in one group are substantially different from those of the workers in other groups.

nondiscretionary fiscal policy (See *built-in stabilizer.*)

nondiversifiable risk Investment *risk* that investors are unable to reduce via *diversification;* also called systemic risk.

nondurable good A *consumer good* with an expected life (use) of less than 3 years.

nonexcludability The inability to keep nonpayers (free riders) from obtaining benefits from a certain good; a *public good* characteristic.

nonexhaustive expenditure An expenditure by government that does not result directly in the employment of economic resources or the production of goods and services; see *government transfer payment.*

nonincome determinants of consumption and saving All influences on consumption and saving other than the level of *GDP.*

noninterest determinants of investment All influences on the level of investment spending other than the *interest rate.*

noninvestment transaction An expenditure for stocks, bonds, or secondhand *capital goods.*

nonmarket transactions The value of the goods and services that are not included in the *gross domestic product* because they are not bought and sold.

nonprice competition Competition based on distinguishing one's product by means of *product differentiation* and then *advertising* the distinguished product to consumers.

nonproduction transaction The purchase and sale of any item that is not a currently produced good or service.

nonrenewable natural resource Things such as oil, natural gas, and metals, which are either in actual fixed supply or which renew so slowly as to be in virtual fixed supply when viewed from a human time perspective.

nonrivalry The idea that one person's benefit from a certain good does not reduce the benefit available to others; a *public good* characteristic.

nontariff barriers (NTBs) All barriers other than *protective tariffs* that nations erect to impede international trade, including *import quotas,* licensing requirements, unreasonable product-quality standards, unnecessary bureaucratic detail in customs procedures, and so on.

normal good A good or service whose consumption increases when income increases and falls when income decreases, price remaining constant.

normal profit The payment made by a firm to obtain and retain *entrepreneurial ability;* the minimum income entrepreneurial ability must receive to induce it to perform entrepreneurial functions for a firm.

normal-trade-relation (NTR) status A designation for countries that are allowed to export goods and services into the United States at the lowest tariff rates available to any other country allowed to export those goods to the United States; until recently called *most-favored-nation status.*

normative economics The part of economics involving value judgments about what the economy should be like; focused on which economic goals and policies should be implemented; policy economics.

North American Free Trade Agreement (NAFTA) A 1993 agreement establishing, over a 15-year period, a free-trade zone composed of Canada, Mexico, and the United States.

occupation A category of activities or tasks performed by a set of workers for pay, independent of employer or industry. Examples are managers, nurses, farmers, and cooks.

occupational licensure The laws of state or local governments that require that a worker satisfy certain specified requirements and obtain a license from a licensing board before engaging in a particular occupation.

occupational segregation The crowding of women or minorities into less desirable, lower-paying occupations.

official reserves Foreign currencies owned by the central bank of a nation.

offshoring The practice of shifting work previously done by American workers to workers located abroad.

Okun's law The generalization that any 1-percentage-point rise in the *unemployment rate* above the *full-employment unemployment rate* is associated with a rise in the negative *GDP gap* by 2 percent of *potential output* (potential GDP).

oligopoly A market structure in which a few firms sell either a *standardized* or *differentiated product,* into which entry is difficult, in which the firm has limited control over product price because of *mutual interdependence* (except when there is collusion among firms), and in which there is typically *nonprice competition.*

one-time game In *game theory,* a game in which the parties select their optimal strategies in a single time period without regard to possible interaction in subsequent time periods.

OPEC (See *Organization of Petroleum Exporting Countries.*)

open economy An economy that exports and imports goods and services.

open-market operations The buying and selling of U.S. government securities by the *Federal Reserve Banks* for purposes of carrying out *monetary policy.*

open shop A place of employment in which the employer may hire nonunion workers and the workers need not become members of a *labor union.*

opportunity cost The amount of other products that must be forgone or sacrificed to produce a unit of a product.

opportunity-cost ratio An equivalency showing the number of units of two products that can be produced with the same resources; the cost 1 corn $\equiv$ 3 olives shows that the resources required to produce 3 units of olives must be shifted to corn production to produce 1 unit of corn.

optimal amount of R&D (Web chapter) The level of R&D at which the *marginal benefit* and *marginal cost* of R&D expenditures are equal.

optimal reduction of an externality The reduction of a *negative externality* such as pollution to the level at which the *marginal benefit* and *marginal cost* of reduction are equal.

ordinal utility Satisfaction that is measured by having consumers compare and rank products (or combinations of products) as to preference, without asking them to specify the absolute amount of satisfaction provided by the product.

Organization of Petroleum Exporting Countries (OPEC) A cartel of 13 oil-producing countries (Algeria, Angola, Ecuador, Indonesia, Iran, Iraq, Kuwait, Libya, Nigeria, Qatar, Saudi Arabia, Venezuela, and the UAE) that attempts to control the quantity and price of crude oil exported by its members and that accounts for a large percentage of the world's export of oil.

other-things-equal assumption The assumption that factors other than those being considered are held constant; *ceteris paribus* assumption.

outpayments The expenditures of domestic or foreign currency that the individuals, firms, and governments of one nation make to purchase goods and services, for remittances, to pay investment income, and for purchases of foreign assets.

output effect The situation in which an increase in the price of one input will increase a firm's production costs and reduce its level of output, thus reducing the demand for other inputs; conversely for a decrease in the price of the input.

paper money Pieces of paper used as a *medium of exchange;* in the United States, *Federal Reserve Notes.*

paradox of voting A situation where paired-choice voting by majority rule fails to provide a consistent ranking of society's preferences for *public goods* or services.

parity concept The idea that year after year a specific output of a farm product should enable a farmer to acquire a constant amount of nonagricultural goods and services.

parity ratio The ratio of the price received by farmers from the sale of an agricultural commodity to the prices of other goods paid by them; usually expressed as a percentage; used as a rationale for *price supports.*

partnership An unincorporated firm owned and operated by two or more persons.

passively managed funds *Mutual funds* whose *portfolios* are not regularly updated by a fund manager attempting to generate high returns. Rather, once an initial portfolio is selected, it is left unchanged so that investors receive whatever return that unchanging portfolio subsequently generates. *Index funds* are a type of passively managed fund.

patent An exclusive right given to inventors to produce and sell a new product or machine for 20 years from the time of patent application.

payments deficit (See *balance-of-payments deficit.*)

payments surplus (See *balance-of-payments surplus.*)

payroll tax A tax levied on employers of labor equal to a percentage of all or part of the wages and salaries paid by them and on employees equal to a percentage of all or part of the wages and salaries received by them.

P = MC rule The principle that a purely competitive firm will maximize its profit or minimize its loss by producing that output at which the *price* of the product is equal to *marginal cost,* provided that price is equal to or greater than *average variable cost* in the short run and equal to or greater than *average total cost* in the long run.

peak The point in a business cycle at which business activity has reached a temporary maximum; the economy is near or at full employment and the level of real output is at or very close to the economy's capacity.

per capita GDP *Gross domestic product* (GDP) per person; the average GDP of a population.

per capita income A nation's total income per person; the average income of a population.

percentage rate of return The percentage gain or loss, relative to the buying price, of an *economic investment* or *financial investment* over some period of time.

perfectly elastic demand Product or resource demand in which *quantity demanded* can be of any amount at a particular product *price;* graphs as a horizontal *demand curve.*

perfectly elastic supply Product or resource supply in which *quantity supplied* can be of any amount at a particular product or resource *price;* graphs as a horizontal *supply curve.*

perfectly inelastic demand Product or resource demand in which *price* can be of any amount at a particular quantity of the product or resource demanded; *quantity demanded* does not respond to a change in price; graphs as a vertical *demand curve*.

perfectly inelastic supply Product or resource supply in which *price* can be of any amount at a particular quantity of the product or resource demanded; *quantity supplied* does not respond to a change in price; graphs as a vertical *supply curve*.

per se violations Collusive actions, such as attempts by firms to fix prices or divide a market, that are violations of the *antitrust laws,* even if the actions themselves are unsuccessful.

personal consumption expenditures The expenditures of *households* for *durable* and *nondurable consumer goods* and *services*.

personal distribution of income The manner in which the economy's *personal* or *disposable income* is divided among different income classes or different households or families.

personal income (PI) The earned and unearned income available to resource suppliers and others before the payment of personal taxes.

personal income tax A tax levied on the taxable income of individuals, households, and unincorporated firms.

personal saving The *personal income* of households less personal taxes and *personal consumption expenditures; disposable income* not spent for *consumer goods*.

per-unit production cost The average production cost of a particular level of output; total input cost divided by units of output.

Phillips Curve A curve showing the relationship between the *unemployment rate* (on the horizontal axis) and the annual rate of increase in the *price level* (on the vertical axis).

planned investment The amount that *firms* plan or intend to invest.

plant A physical establishment that performs one or more functions in the production, fabrication, and distribution of goods and services.

"play or pay" A means of expanding health insurance coverage by requiring that employers either provide insurance for their workers or pay a special *payroll tax* to finance insurance for noncovered workers.

policy economics The formulation of courses of action to bring about desired economic outcomes or to prevent undesired occurrences.

political business cycle The alleged tendency of Congress to destabilize the economy by reducing taxes and increasing government expenditures before elections and to raise taxes and lower expenditures after elections.

portfolio A specific collection of *stocks, bonds,* or other *financial investments* held by an individual or a *mutual fund.*

positive economics The analysis of facts or data to establish scientific generalizations about economic behavior.

positive externality A benefit obtained without compensation by third parties from the production or consumption of sellers or buyers. Example: A beekeeper benefits when

a neighboring farmer plants clover. An *external benefit* or a spillover benefit.

positive GDP gap A situation in which actual *gross domestic product* exceeds *potential output*. Also known as an inflationary output gap.

positive relationship (See *direct relationship*.)

positive sum game In *game theory*, a game in which the gains (+) and losses (−) add up to more than zero; one party's gains exceeds the other party's losses.

***post hoc, ergo propter hoc* fallacy** The false belief that when one event precedes another, the first event must have caused the second event.

potential competition The new competitors that may be induced to enter an industry if firms now in that industry are receiving large *economic profits*.

potential output The real output *(GDP)* an economy can produce when it fully employs its available resources.

poverty A situation in which the basic needs of an individual or family exceed the means to satisfy them.

poverty rate The percentage of the population with incomes below the official poverty income levels that are established by the Federal government.

preferred provider organization (PPO) An arrangement in which doctors and hospitals agree to provide health care to insured individuals at rates negotiated with an insurer.

present value Today's value of some amount of money that is to be received sometime in the future.

price The amount of money needed to buy a particular good, service, or resource.

price ceiling A legally established maximum price for a good or service.

price discrimination The selling of a product to different buyers at different prices when the price differences are not justified by differences in cost.

price elasticity of demand The ratio of the percentage change in *quantity demanded* of a product or resource to the percentage change in its *price;* a measure of the responsiveness of buyers to a change in the price of a product or resource.

price elasticity of supply The ratio of the percentage change in *quantity supplied* of a product or resource to the percentage change in its *price;* a measure of the responsiveness of producers to a change in the price of a product or resource.

price fixing The conspiring by two or more firms to set the price of their products; an illegal practice under the *Sherman Act*.

price floor A legally determined minimum price above the *equilibrium price.*

price index An index number that shows how the weighted-average price of a "market basket" of goods changes over time.

price leadership An informal method that firms in an *oligopoly* may employ to set the price of their product: One firm (the leader) is the first to announce a change in price, and the other firms (the followers) soon announce identical or similar changes.

price level The weighted average of the prices of all the final goods and services produced in an economy.

price-level stability A steadiness of the price level from one period to the next; zero or low annual inflation; also called "price stability."

price-level surprises Unanticipated changes in the price level.

price maker A seller (or buyer) that is able to affect the product or resource price by changing the amount it sells (or buys).

price support A minimum price that government allows sellers to receive for a good or service; a legally established or maintained minimum price.

price taker A seller (or buyer) that is unable to affect the price at which a product or resource sells by changing the amount it sells (or buys).

price war Successive and continued decreases in the prices charged by firms in an oligopolistic industry. Each firm lowers its price below rivals' prices, hoping to increase its sales and revenues at its rivals' expense.

prime interest rate The benchmark *interest rate* that banks use as a reference point for a wide range of loans to businesses and individuals.

principal-agent problem A conflict of interest that occurs when agents (workers or managers) pursue their own objectives to the detriment of the principals' (stockholders') goals.

principle of comparative advantage The proposition that an individual, region, or nation will benefit if it specializes in producing goods for which its own *opportunity costs* are lower than the opportunity costs of a trading partner, and then exchanging some of the products in which it specializes for other desired products produced by others.

private good A good or service that is individually consumed and that can be profitably provided by privately owned firms because they can exclude nonpayers from receiving the benefits.

private property The right of private persons and firms to obtain, own, control, employ, dispose of, and bequeath *land, capital,* and other property.

private sector The *households* and business *firms* of the economy.

probability weighted average Each of the possible future rates of return from an investment multiplied by its respective probability (expressed as a decimal) of happening.

process innovation (Web chapter) The development and use of new or improved production or distribution methods.

producer surplus The difference between the actual price a producer receives (or producers receive) and the minimum acceptable price; the triangular area above the supply curve and below the market price.

product differentiation A strategy in which one firm's product is distinguished from competing products by means of its design, related services, quality, location, or other attributes (except price).

product innovation (Web chapter) The development and sale of a new or improved product (or service).

production possibilities curve A curve showing the different combinations of two goods or services that can be produced in a *full-employment, full-production* economy where the available supplies of resources and technology are fixed.

productive efficiency The production of a good in the least costly way; occurs when production takes place at the output at which *average total cost* is a minimum and *marginal product* per dollar's worth of input is the same for all inputs.

productivity A measure of average output or real output per unit of input. For example, the productivity of labor is determined by dividing real output by hours of work.

productivity growth The increase in *productivity* from one period to another.

product market A market in which products are sold by *firms* and bought by *households*.

profit The return to the resource *entrepreneurial ability* (see *normal profit*); *total revenue* minus *total cost* (see *economic profit*).

profit-maximizing combination of resources The quantity of each resource a firm must employ to maximize its profit or minimize its loss; the combination in which the *marginal revenue product* of each resource is equal to its *marginal resource cost* (to its *price* if the resource is employed in a competitive market).

profit-sharing plan A compensation device through which workers receive part of their pay in the form of a share of their employer's profit (if any).

progressive tax A tax whose *average tax rate* increases as the taxpayer's income increases and decreases as the taxpayer's income decreases.

property tax A tax on the value of property (*capital, land, stocks* and *bonds,* and other *assets*) owned by *firms* and *households*.

proportional tax A tax whose *average tax rate* remains constant as the taxpayer's income increases or decreases.

proprietor's income The net income of the owners of unincorporated firms (proprietorships and partnerships).

protective tariff A *tariff* designed to shield domestic producers of a good or service from the competition of foreign producers.

public assistance programs Government programs that pay benefits to those who are unable to earn income (because of permanent disabilities or because they have very low income and dependent children); financed by general tax revenues and viewed as public charity (rather than earned rights).

public choice theory The economic analysis of government decision making, politics, and elections.

public debt The total amount owed by the Federal government to the owners of government securities; equal to the sum of past government *budget deficits* less government *budget surpluses.*

public good A good or service that is characterized by *nonrivalry* and *nonexcludability;* a good or service with these characteristics provided by government.

public interest theory of regulation The presumption that the purpose of the regulation of an *industry* is to protect the public (consumers) from abuse of the power possessed by *natural monopolies.*

public investments Government expenditures on public capital (such as roads, highways, bridges, mass-transit systems, and electric power facilities) and on *human capital* (such as education, training, and health).

public sector The part of the economy that contains all government entities; government.

public utility A firm that produces an essential good or service, has obtained from a government the right to be the sole supplier of the good or service in the area, and is regulated by that government to prevent the abuse of its monopoly power.

purchasing power The amount of goods and services that a monetary unit of income can buy.

purchasing power parity The idea that exchange rates between nations equate the purchasing power of various currencies. Exchange rates between any two nations adjust to reflect the price-level differences between the countries.

pure competition A market structure in which a very large number of firms sells a *standardized product,* into which entry is very easy, in which the individual seller has no control over the product price, and in which there is no nonprice competition; a market characterized by a very large number of buyers and sellers.

purely competitive labor market A *resource market* in which many firms compete with one another in hiring a specific kind of labor, numerous equally qualified workers supply that labor, and no one controls the market wage rate.

pure monopoly A market structure in which one firm sells a unique product, into which entry is blocked, in which the single firm has considerable control over product price, and in which *nonprice competition* may or may not be found.

pure profit (See *economic profit.*)

pure rate of interest An essentially risk-free, long-term interest rate that is free of the influence of market imperfections.

quantity demanded The amount of a good or service that buyers (or a buyer) desire to purchase at a particular price during some period.

quantity supplied The amount of a good or service that producers (or a producer) offer to sell at a particular price during some period.

quasi-public bank A bank that is privately owned but governmentally (publicly) controlled; each of the U.S. *Federal Reserve Banks.*

quasi-public good A good or service to which excludability could apply but that has such a large *positive externality* that government sponsors its production to prevent an underallocation of resources.

R&D Research and development activities undertaken to bring about *technological advance.*

rate of exchange The price paid in one's own money to acquire 1 unit of a foreign currency; the rate at which the money of one nation is exchanged for the money of another nation.

rate of return The gain in net revenue divided by the cost of an investment or an *R&D* expenditure; expressed as a percentage.

rational behavior Human behavior based on comparison of marginal costs and marginal benefits; behavior designed to maximize total utility.

rational expectations theory The hypothesis that firms and households expect monetary and fiscal policies to have certain effects on the economy and (in pursuit of their own self-interests) take actions that make these policies ineffective.

rationing function of prices The ability of market forces in competitive markets to equalize *quantity demanded* and *quantity supplied* and to eliminate shortages and surpluses via changes in prices.

real-balances effect The tendency for increases in the *price level* to lower the real value (or purchasing power) of financial assets with fixed money value and, as a result, to reduce total spending and real output, and conversely for decreases in the price level.

real-business-cycle theory A theory that *business cycles* result from changes in technology and resource availability, which affect *productivity* and thus increase or decrease long-run aggregate supply.

real capital (See *capital.*)

real GDP (See *real gross domestic product.*)

real GDP per capita *Inflation*-adjusted output per person; *real GDP*/population.

real gross domestic product (GDP) *Gross domestic product* adjusted for inflation; gross domestic product in a year divided by the GDP *price index* for that year, the index expressed as a decimal.

real income The amount of goods and services that can be purchased with *nominal income* during some period of time; nominal income adjusted for inflation.

real interest rate The interest rate expressed in dollars of constant value (adjusted for *inflation*) and equal to the *nominal interest rate* less the expected rate of inflation.

real wage The amount of goods and services a worker can purchase with his or her *nominal wage;* the purchasing power of the nominal wage.

recession A period of declining real GDP, accompanied by lower real income and higher unemployment.

recessionary expenditure gap The amount by which the *aggregate expenditures schedule* must shift upward to increase the real *GDP* to its full-employment, noninflationary level.

Reciprocal Trade Agreements Act A 1934 Federal law that authorized the president to negotiate up to 50 percent lower tariffs with foreign nations that agreed to reduce their tariffs on U.S. goods. (Such agreements incorporated the *most-favored-nation* clause.)

refinancing the public debt Selling new government securities to owners of expiring securities or paying them money gained from the sale of new securities to others.

regressive tax A tax whose *average tax rate* decreases as the taxpayer's income increases and increases as the taxpayer's income decreases.

regulatory agency An agency, commission, or board established by the Federal government or a state government to control the prices charged and the services offered by a *natural monopoly*.

remittances Payments by *immigrants* to family members and others located in the origin countries of the immigrants.

rental income The payments (income) received by those who supply *land* to the economy.

renewable natural resources Things such as forests, water in reservoirs, and wildlife that are capable of growing back or building back up (renewing themselves) if they are harvested at moderate rates.

rent-seeking behavior The actions by persons, firms, or unions to gain special benefits from government at the taxpayers' or someone else's expense.

repeated game In *game theory*, a game that is played again sometime after the previous game ends.

replacement rate The birthrate necessary to offset deaths in a country and therefore to keep the size of its population constant (without relying on immigration). For most countries, the replacement rate is about 2.1 births per woman per lifetime.

required reserves The funds that banks and thrifts must deposit with the *Federal Reserve Bank* (or hold as *vault cash*) to meet the legal *reserve requirement;* a fixed percentage of the bank's or thrift's checkable deposits.

reserve ratio The fraction of *checkable deposits* that a bank must hold as reserves in a *Federal Reserve Bank* or in its own bank vault; also called the *reserve requirement*.

reserve requirement The specified minimum percentage of its checkable deposits that a bank or thrift must keep on deposit at the Federal Reserve Bank in its district or hold as *vault cash*.

resource A natural, human, or manufactured item that helps produce goods and services; a productive agent or factor of production.

resource market A market in which *households* sell and *firms* buy resources or the services of resources.

restrictive monetary policy Federal Reserve system actions to reduce the *money supply*, increase *interest rates,* and reduce *inflation*; a tight money policy.

revenue tariff A *tariff* designed to produce income for the Federal government.

right-to-work law A state law (in about 22 states) that makes it illegal to require that a worker join a *labor union* in order to retain his or her job; laws that make *union shops* and *agency shops* illegal.

risk The uncertainty as to the actual future returns of a particular *financial investment* or *economic investment*.

risk-free interest rate The *interest rate* earned on short-term U.S. government bonds.

risk premium The *interest rate* above the *risk-free* interest rate that must be paid and received to compensate the lender or investor for *risk*.

rule of reason The rule stated and applied in the *U.S. Steel case* that only combinations and contracts unreasonably restraining trade are subject to actions under the antitrust laws and that size and possession of monopoly power are not illegal.

rule of 70 A method for determining the number of years it will take for some measure to double, given its annual percentage increase. Example: To determine the number of years it will take for the *price level* to double, divide 70 by the annual rate of *inflation*.

sales and excise taxes (See *sales tax; see excise tax*.)

sales tax A tax levied on the cost (at retail) of a broad group of products.

saving Disposable income not spent for consumer goods; equal to *disposable income* minus *personal consumption expenditures*.

savings The accumulation of funds that results when people in an economy spend less (consume less) than their incomes during a given time period.

savings account A deposit in a *commercial bank* or *thrift institution* on which interest payments are received; generally used for saving rather than daily transactions; a component of the *M2* money supply.

savings and loan association (S&L) A firm that accepts deposits primarily from small individual savers and lends primarily to individuals to finance purchases such as autos and homes; now nearly indistinguishable from a *commercial bank*.

saving schedule A schedule that shows the amounts *households* plan to save (plan not to spend for *consumer goods*), at different levels of *disposable income*.

savings deposit A deposit that is interest-bearing and that the depositor can normally withdraw at any time.

savings institution (See *thrift institution*.)

Say's law The largely discredited macroeconomic generalization that the production of goods and services (supply) creates an equal *demand* for those goods and services.

scarce resources The limited quantities of *land, capital, labor,* and *entrepreneurial ability* that are never sufficient to satisfy people's virtually unlimited economic wants.

scientific method The procedure for the systematic pursuit of knowledge involving the observation of facts and the formulation and testing of hypotheses to obtain theories, principles, and laws.

secular trend A long-term tendency; a change in some variable over a very long period of years.

Security Market Line (SML) A line that shows the average expected rate of return of all financial investments at each level of *nondiversifiable risk*, the latter measured by *beta*.

self-interest That which each firm, property owner, worker, and consumer believes is best for itself and seeks to obtain.

seniority The length of time a worker has been employed absolutely or relative to other workers; may be used to determine which workers will be laid off when there is insufficient work for them all and who will be rehired when more work becomes available.

self-selection As it relates to international migration, the idea that those who choose to move tend to have greater motivation for economic gain or greater willingness to sacrifice current consumption for future consumption than those with similar skills who choose to remain at home.

separation of ownership and control The fact that different groups of people own a *corporation* (the stockholders) and manage it (the directors and officers).

sequential game In *game theory,* a game in which the parties make their moves in turn, with one party making the first move, followed by the other party making the next move, and so on.

service An (intangible) act or use for which a consumer, firm, or government is willing to pay.

Sherman Act The Federal antitrust act of 1890 that makes monopoly and conspiracies to restrain trade criminal offenses.

shirking Workers' neglecting or evading work to increase their *utility* or well-being.

shocks Sudden, unexpected changes in *demand* (or *aggregate demand*) or supply (or *aggregate supply*).

shortage The amount by which the *quantity demanded* of a product exceeds the *quantity supplied* at a particular (below-equilibrium) price.

short run (1) In microeconomics, a period of time in which producers are able to change the quantities of some but not all of the resources they employ; a period in which some resources (usually plant) are fixed and some are variable. (2) In macroeconomics, a period in which nominal wages and other input prices do not change in response to a change in the price level.

short-run aggregate supply curve An aggregate supply curve relevant to a time period in which input prices (particularly *nominal wages*) do not change in response to changes in the *price level.*

short-run competitive equilibrium The price at which the total quantity of a product supplied in the *short run* in a purely competitive industry equals the total quantity of the product demanded and that is equal to or greater than *average variable cost.*

short-run supply curve A supply curve that shows the quantity of a product a firm in a purely competitive industry will offer to sell at various prices in the *short run;* the portion of the firm's short-run marginal cost curve that lies above its *average-variable-cost* curve.

shutdown case The circumstance in which a firm would experience a loss greater than its total *fixed cost* if it were to produce any output greater than zero; alternatively, a situation in which a firm would cease to operate when the *price* at which it can sell its product is less than its *average variable cost.*

simple multiplier The *multiplier* in any economy in which government collects no *net taxes,* there are no *imports,* and *investment* is independent of the level of income; equal to 1 divided by the *marginal propensity to save.*

simultaneous consumption The same-time derivation of *utility* from some product by a large number of consumers.

simultaneous game In *game theory,* a game in which both parties choose their strategies and execute them at the same time.

single-tax movement The political efforts by followers of Henry George (1839-1897) to impose a single tax on the value of land and eliminate all other taxes.

skill transferability The ease to which people can shift their work talents from one job, region, or country to another job, region, or country.

slope of a straight line The ratio of the vertical change (the rise or fall) to the horizontal change (the run) between any two points on a line. The slope of an upward-sloping line is positive, reflecting a direct relationship between two variables; the slope of a downward-sloping line is negative, reflecting an inverse relationship between two variables.

Smoot-Hawley Tariff Act Legislation passed in 1930 that established very high tariffs. Its objective was to reduce imports and stimulate the domestic economy, but it resulted only in retaliatory tariffs by other nations.

social insurance programs Programs that replace the earnings lost when people retire or are temporarily unemployed, that are financed by payroll taxes, and that are viewed as earned rights (rather than charity).

socially optimal price The price of a product that results in the most efficient allocation of an economy's resources and that is equal to the *marginal cost* of the product.

social regulation Regulation in which government is concerned with the conditions under which goods and services are produced, their physical characteristics, and the impact of their production on society; in contrast to *industrial regulation.*

Social Security The social insurance program in the United States financed by Federal payroll taxes on employers and employees and designed to replace a portion of the earnings lost when workers become disabled, retire, or die.

Social Security trust fund A Federal fund that saves excessive Social Security tax revenues received in one year to meet Social Security benefit obligations that exceed Social Security tax revenues in some subsequent year.

sole proprietorship An unincorporated *firm* owned and operated by one person.

special-interest effect Any result of government promotion of the interests (goals) of a small group at the expense of a much larger group.

specialization The use of the resources of an individual, a firm, a region, or a nation to concentrate production on one or a small number of goods and services.

speculation The activity of buying or selling with the motive of later reselling or rebuying for profit.

SSI (See *Supplemental Security Income.*)

stagflation Inflation accompanied by stagnation in the rate of growth of output and an increase in unemployment in the economy; simultaneous increases in the *inflation* rate and the *unemployment rate*.

standardized budget A comparison of the government expenditures and tax collections that would occur if the economy operated at *full employment* throughout the year; the full-employment budget.

standardized product A product whose buyers are indifferent to the seller from whom they purchase it as long as the price charged by all sellers is the same; a product all units of which are identical and thus are perfect substitutes for each other.

Standard Oil case A 1911 antitrust case in which Standard Oil was found guilty of violating the *Sherman Act* by illegally monopolizing the petroleum industry. As a remedy the company was divided into several competing firms.

start-up (firm) A new firm focused on creating and introducing a particular new product or employing a specific new production or distribution method.

state bank A *commercial bank* authorized by a state government to engage in the business of banking.

static economy A hypothetical economy in which the basic forces such as resource supplies, technological knowledge, and consumer tastes are constant and unchanging.

statistical discrimination The practice of judging an individual on the basis of the average characteristic of the group to which he or she belongs rather than on his or her own personal characteristics.

sticky prices (See *inflexible prices*.)

stock (corporate) An ownership share in a corporation.

stock options Contracts that enable executives or other key employees to buy shares of their employers' stock at fixed, lower prices even when the market price subsequently rises.

store of value An *asset* set aside for future use; one of the three functions of *money*.

strategic behavior Self-interested economic actions that take into account the expected reactions of others.

strategic trade policy The use of trade barriers to reduce the risk inherent in product development by domestic firms, particularly that involving advanced technology.

strike The withholding of labor services by an organized group of workers (a *labor union*).

structural unemployment Unemployment of workers whose skills are not demanded by employers, who lack sufficient skill to obtain employment, or who cannot easily move to locations where jobs are available.

subprime mortgage loans High-interest rate loans to home buyers with above-average credit risk.

subsidy A payment of funds (or goods and services) by a government, firm, or household for which it receives no good or service in return. When made by a government, it is a *government transfer payment*.

substitute goods Products or services that can be used in place of each other. When the price of one falls, the demand for the other product falls; conversely, when the price of one product rises, the demand for the other product rises.

substitute resources Productive inputs that can be used instead of other inputs in the production process; resources for which an increase in the price of one leads to an increase in the demand for the other.

substitution effect (1) A change in the quantity demanded of a *consumer good* that results from a change in its relative expensiveness caused by a change in the product's price; (2) the effect of a change in the price of a *resource* on the quantity of the resource employed by a firm, assuming no change in its output.

sunk cost A cost that has been incurred and cannot be recovered.

Supplemental Security Income (SSI) A federally financed and administered program that provides a uniform nationwide minimum income for the aged, blind, and disabled who do not qualify for benefits under *Social Security* in the United States.

supply A schedule showing the amounts of a good or service that sellers (or a seller) will offer at various prices during some period.

supply curve A curve illustrating *supply*.

supply factor (in growth) An increase in the availability of a resource, an improvement in its quality, or an expansion of technological knowledge that makes it possible for an economy to produce a greater output of goods and services.

supply schedule (See *supply*.)

supply shocks Sudden, unexpected changes in *aggregate supply*.

supply-side economics A view of macroeconomics that emphasizes the role of costs and *aggregate supply* in explaining *inflation, unemployment,* and *economic growth*.

surplus The amount by which the *quantity supplied* of a product exceeds the *quantity demanded* at a specific (above-equilibrium) price.

surplus payment A payment to a resource that is not required to ensure its availability in the production process; for example, land rent.

tacit understanding An unspoken, unwritten agreement by an oligopolist to set prices and outputs that does not involve outright (or overt) *collusion. Price leadership* is a frequent example.

TANF (See *Temporary Assistance for Needy Families*.)

tariff A tax imposed by a nation on an imported good.

taste-for-discrimination model A theory that views discrimination as a preference for which an employer is willing to pay.

tax An involuntary payment of money (or goods and services) to a government by a *household* or *firm* for which the household or firm receives no good or service directly in return.

taxes on production and imports A *national income accounting* category that includes such taxes as *sales, excise*, business property taxes, and *tariffs* which firms treat as costs of producing a product and pass on (in whole or in part) to buyers by charging a higher price.

tax incidence The person or group that ends up paying a tax.

tax subsidy A grant in the form of reduced taxes through favorable tax treatment. For example, employer-paid health insurance is exempt from Federal income and payroll taxes.

tax-transfer disincentives Decreases in the incentives to work, save, invest, innovate, and take risks that result from high *marginal tax rates* and *transfer payments*.

Taylor rule A modern monetary rule proposed by economist John Taylor that would stipulate exactly how much the Federal Reserve should change real interest rates in response to divergences of real GDP from potential GDP and divergences of actual rates of inflation from a target rate of inflation.

technological advance New and better goods and services and new and better ways of producing or distributing them.

technology The body of knowledge and techniques that can be used to combine *economic resources* to produce goods and services.

Temporary Assistance for Needy Families (TANF) A state-administered and partly federally funded program in the United States that provides financial aid to poor families; the basic welfare program for low-income families in the United States; contains time limits and work requirements.

term auction facility The *monetary policy* procedure used by the Federal Reserve, in which commercial banks anonymously bid to obtain loans being made available by the Fed as a way to expand reserves in the banking system.

terms of trade The rate at which units of one product can be exchanged for units of another product; the price of a good or service; the amount of one good or service that must be given up to obtain 1 unit of another good or service.

theoretical economics The process of deriving and applying economic theories and principles.

theory of human capital The generalization that *wage differentials* are the result of differences in the amount of *human capital investment* and that the incomes of lower-paid workers are raised by increasing the amount of such investment.

thrift institution A *savings and loan association, mutual savings bank,* or *credit union*.

till money (See *vault cash*.)

time deposit An interest-earning deposit in a *commercial bank* or *thrift institution* that the depositor can withdraw without penalty after the end of a specified period.

time preference The human tendency for people, because of impatience, to prefer to spend and consume in the present rather than save and wait to spend and consume in the future; this inclination varies in strength among individuals.

time-value of money The idea that a specific amount of money is more valuable to a person the sooner it is received because the money can be placed in a financial

account or investment and earn *compound interest* over time; the *opportunity cost* of receiving a sum of money later rather than earlier.

token money Bills or coins for which the amount printed on the *currency* bears no relationship to the value of the paper or metal embodied within it; for currency still circulating, money for which the face value exceeds the commodity value.

total allowable catch A limit set by government or a fisheries commission on the total number of fish or tonnage of fish that fishers collectively can harvest during some particular time period.

total cost The sum of *fixed cost* and *variable cost*.

total demand The demand schedule or the *demand curve* of all buyers of a good or service; also called market demand.

total demand for money The sum of the *transactions demand for money* and the *asset demand for money*.

total fertility rate The average total number of children that a woman is expected to have during her lifetime.

total product (TP) The total output of a particular good or service produced by a firm (or a group of firms or the entire economy).

total revenue (TR) The total number of dollars received by a firm (or firms) from the sale of a product; equal to the total expenditures for the product produced by the firm (or firms); equal to the quantity sold (demanded) multiplied by the price at which it is sold.

total-revenue test A test to determine elasticity of *demand* between any two prices: Demand is elastic if *total revenue* moves in the opposite direction from price; it is inelastic when it moves in the same direction as price; and it is of unitary elasticity when it does not change when price changes.

total spending The total amount that buyers of goods and services spend or plan to spend; also called *aggregate expenditures*.

total supply The supply schedule or the *supply curve* of all sellers of a good or service; also called market supply.

total utility The total amount of satisfaction derived from the consumption of a single product or a combination of products.

Trade Adjustment Assistance Act A U.S. law passed in 2002 that provides cash assistance, education and training benefits, health care subsidies, and wage subsidies (for persons age 50 or older) to workers displaced by imports or relocations of U.S. plants to other countries.

trade balance The export of goods (or goods and services) of a nation less its imports of goods (or goods and services).

trade bloc A group of nations that lower or abolish trade barriers among members. Examples include the *European Union* and the nations of the *North American Free Trade Agreement*.

trade controls *Tariffs, export subsidies, import quotas,* and other means a nation may employ to reduce *imports* and expand *exports*.

trade deficit The amount by which a nation's *imports* of goods (or goods and services) exceed its *exports* of goods (or goods and services).

trademark A legal protection that gives the originators of a product an exclusive right to use the brand name.

trade-off The sacrifice of some or all of one economic goal, good, or service to achieve some other goal, good, or service.

trade surplus The amount by which a nation's *exports* of goods (or goods and services) exceed its *imports* of goods (or goods and services).

trading possibilities line A line that shows the different combinations of two products that an economy is able to obtain (consume) when it specializes in the production of one product and trades (exports) it to obtain the other product.

tragedy of the commons The tendency for commonly owned *natural resources* to be overused, neglected, or degraded because their common ownership gives nobody an incentive to maintain or improve them.

transactions demand for money The amount of money people want to hold for use as a *medium of exchange* (to make payments); varies directly with *nominal GDP*.

transfer payment A payment of *money* (or goods and services) by a government to a *household* or *firm* for which the payer receives no good or service directly in return.

trough The point in a *business cycle* at which business activity has reached a temporary minimum; the point at which a *recession* has ended and an expansion (recovery) begins.

tying contract A requirement imposed by a seller that a buyer purchase another (or other) of its products as a condition for buying a desired product; a practice forbidden by the *Clayton Act*.

unanticipated inflation Increases in the price level (*inflation*) at a rate greater than expected.

underemployment A situation in which workers are employed in positions requiring less education and skill than they have.

undistributed corporate profits After-tax corporate profits not distributed as dividends to stockholders; corporate or business saving; also called retained earnings.

unemployment The failure to use all available *economic resources* to produce desired goods and services; the failure of the economy to fully employ its *labor force*.

unemployment compensation (See *unemployment insurance*).

unemployment insurance The social insurance program that in the United States is financed by state *payroll taxes* on employers and makes income available to workers who become unemployed and are unable to find jobs.

unemployment rate The percentage of the *labor force* unemployed at any time.

unfulfilled expectations Situations in which households and businesses were expecting one thing to happen but instead find that something else has happened;

unrealized anticipations or plans relating to future economic conditions and outcomes.

uninsurable risk An event that would result in a loss and whose occurrence is uncontrollable and unpredictable. Insurance companies are not willing to sell insurance against such a loss.

union (See *labor union*.)

unionization rate The percentage of a particular population of workers that belongs to *labor unions;* alternatively, the percentage of the population of workers whom unions represent in *collective bargaining*.

union shop A place of employment where the employer may hire either *labor union* members or nonmembers but where nonmembers must become members within a specified period of time or lose their jobs.

unit elasticity Demand or supply for which the *elasticity coefficient* is equal to 1; means that the percentage change in the quantity demanded or supplied is equal to the percentage change in price.

unit labor cost Labor cost per unit of output; total labor cost divided by total output; also equal to the *nominal wage* rate divided by the *average product* of labor.

unit of account A standard unit in which prices can be stated and the value of goods and services can be compared; one of the three functions of *money*.

unlimited liability Absence of any limits on the maximum amount that an individual (usually a business owner) may become legally required to pay.

unlimited wants The insatiable desire of consumers for goods and services that will give them satisfaction or *utility*.

unplanned changes in inventories Changes in inventories that firms did not anticipate; changes in inventories that occur because of unexpected increases or decreases of aggregate spending (or of *aggregate expenditures*).

unplanned investment Actual investment less *planned investment;* increases or decreases in the *inventories* of firms resulting from production greater than sales.

Uruguay Round A 1995 trade agreement (fully implemented in 2005) that established the *World Trade Organization (WTO),* liberalized trade in goods and services, provided added protection to intellectual property (for example, *patents* and *copyrights*), and reduced farm subsidies.

user cost The *opportunity* cost of extracting and selling a nonrenewable resource today rather than waiting to extract and sell the resource in the future; the *present value* of the decline in future revenue that will occur because a nonrenewable resource is extracted and sold today rather than being extracted and sold in the future.

U.S. securities U.S. Treasury bills, notes, and bonds used to finance *budget deficits*; the components of the *public debt*.

U.S. Steel case The antitrust action brought by the Federal government against the U.S. Steel Corporation in which the courts ruled (in 1920) that only unreasonable restraints of trade were illegal and that size and the possession of monopoly power were not violations of the antitrust laws.

usury laws State laws that specify the maximum legal interest rate at which loans can be made.

utility The want-satisfying power of a good or service; the satisfaction or pleasure a consumer obtains from the consumption of a good or service (or from the consumption of a collection of goods and services).

utility-maximizing rule The principle that to obtain the greatest *utility*, the consumer should allocate *money income* so that the last dollar spent on each good or service yields the same marginal utility.

value added The value of the product sold by a *firm* less the value of the products (materials) purchased and used by the firm to produce the product.

value-added tax A tax imposed on the difference between the value of the product sold by a firm and the value of the goods purchased from other firms to produce the product; used in several European countries.

value judgment Opinion of what is desirable or undesirable; belief regarding what ought or ought not to be (regarding what is right (or just) or wrong (or unjust)).

value of money The quantity of goods and services for which a unit of money (a dollar) can be exchanged; the purchasing power of a unit of money; the reciprocal of the *price index*.

variable cost A cost that in total increases when the firm increases its output and decreases when the firm reduces its output.

VAT (See *value-added tax*.)

vault cash The *currency* a bank has in its vault and cash drawers.

velocity The number of times per year that the average dollar in the *money supply* is spent for *final goods and services;* nominal GDP divided by the money supply.

venture capital (Web chapter) That part of household saving used to finance high-risk business enterprises in exchange for shares of the profit if the enterprise succeeds.

vertical axis The "up-down" or "north-south" measurement line on a graph or grid.

vertical integration A group of *plants* engaged in different stages of the production of a final product and owned by a single *firm*.

vertical intercept The point at which a line meets the vertical axis of a graph.

vertical merger The merger of one or more *firms* engaged in different stages of the production of a final product.

very long run A period in which *technology* can change and in which *firms* can introduce new products.

vicious circle of poverty (Web chapter) A problem common in some *developing countries* in which their low *per capita incomes* are an obstacle to realizing the levels of saving and investment needed to achieve rates of growth of output that exceed their rates of population growth.

voice mechanism Communication by workers through their union to resolve grievances with an employer.

voluntary export restrictions (VER) Voluntary limitations by countries or firms of their exports to a particular foreign nation to avoid enactment of formal trade barriers by that nation.

wage The price paid for the use or services of *labor* per unit of time (per hour, per day, and so on).

wage differential The difference between the *wage* received by one worker or group of workers and that received by another worker or group of workers.

wage rate (See *wage*.)

wages The income of those who supply the economy with *labor*.

wealth Anything that has value because it produces income or could produce income. Wealth is a stock; *income* is a flow. Assets less liabilities; net worth.

wealth effect The tendency for people to increase their consumption spending when the value of their financial and real assets rises and to decrease their consumption spending when the value of those assets falls.

welfare programs (See *public assistance programs*.)

Wheeler-Lea Act The Federal act of 1938 that amended the *Federal Trade Commission Act* by prohibiting and giving the commission power to investigate unfair and deceptive acts or practices of commerce (such as false and misleading advertising and the misrepresentation of products).

"will to develop" (Web chapter) The state of wanting *economic growth* strongly enough to change from old to new ways of doing things.

World Bank A bank that lends (and guarantees loans) to developing nations to assist them in increasing their *capital stock* and thus in achieving *economic growth*.

world price The international market price of a good or service, determined by world demand and supply.

World Trade Organization (WTO) An organization of 153 nations (as of fall 2008) that oversees the provisions of the current world trade agreement, resolves trade disputes stemming from it, and holds forums for further rounds of trade negotiations.

WTO (See *World Trade Organization*.)

X-inefficiency The production of output, whatever its level, at a higher average (and total) cost than is necessary for producing that level of output.

zero-sum game In *game theory*, a game in which the gains (+) and losses (−) add up to zero; one party's gain equals the other party's loss.